Communications
in Computer and Information Science 190

Ajith Abraham Jaime Lloret Mauri
John F. Buford Junichi Suzuki
Sabu M. Thampi (Eds.)

Advances in Computing and Communications

First International Conference, ACC 2011
Kochi, India, July 22-24, 2011
Proceedings, Part I

Springer

Volume Editors

Ajith Abraham
Machine Intelligence Research Labs (MIR Labs)
Auburn, WA, USA
E-mail: ajith.abraham@ieee.org

Jaime Lloret Mauri
Polytechnic University of Valencia
Valencia, Spain
E-mail: jlloret@dcom.upv.es

John F. Buford
Avaya Labs Research
Basking Ridge, NJ, USA
E-mail: john.buford@gmail.com

Junichi Suzuki
University of Massachusetts
Boston, MA, USA
E-mail: jxs@acm.org

Sabu M. Thampi
Rajagiri School of Engineering and Technology
Kochi, India
E-mail: smthampi@acm.org

ISSN 1865-0929 e-ISSN 1865-0937
ISBN 978-3-642-22708-0 ISBN 978-3-642-22709-7 (eBook)
DOI 10.1007/978-3-642-22709-7
Springer Heidelberg Dordrecht London New York

Library of Congress Control Number: Applied for

CR Subject Classification (1998): C.2, H.4, I.2, H.3, D.2, H.5

Typesetting: Camera-ready by author, data conversion by Scientific Publishing Services, Chennai, India

Printed on acid-free paper

Springer is part of Springer Science+Business Media (www.springer.com)

Preface

The First International Conference on Advances in Computing and Communications (ACC 2011) was held in Kochi during July 22–24, 2011. ACC 2011 was organized by Rajagiri School of Engineering & Technology (RSET) in association with the Association of Computing Machinery (ACM)- SIGWEB, Machine Intelligence Research Labs (MIR Labs), International Society for Computers and Their Applications, Inc. (ISCA), All India Council for Technical Education (AICTE), Indira Gandhi National Open University (IGNOU), Kerala State Council for Science, Technology and Environment (KSCSTE), Computer Society of India (CSI)- Div IV and Cochin Chapter, The Institution of Electronics and Telecommunication Engineers (IETE), The Institution of Engineers (India) and Project Management Institute (PMI),Trivandrum, Kerala Chapter. Established in 2001, RSET is a premier professional institution striving for holistic excellence in education to mould young, vibrant engineers.

ACC 2011 was a three-day conference which provided an opportunity to bring together students, researchers and practitioners from both academia and industry. ACC 2011 was focused on advances in computing and communications and it attracted many local and international delegates, presenting a balanced mixture of intellects from the East and from the West. ACC 2011 received 592 research papers from 38 countries including Albania, Algeria, Bangladesh, Brazil, Canada, Colombia, Cyprus, Czech Republic, Denmark, Ecuador, Egypt, France, Germany, India, Indonesia, Iran, Ireland, Italy, Korea, Kuwait, Malaysia, Morocco, New Zealand, P.R. China, Pakistan, Rwanda, Saudi Arabia, Singapore, South Africa, Spain, Sri Lanka, Sweden, Taiwan, The Netherlands, Tunisia, UK, and USA. This clearly reflects the truly international stature of ACC 2011. All papers were rigorously reviewed internationally by an expert technical review committee comprising more than 300 members. The conference had a peer-reviewed program of technical sessions, workshops, tutorials, and demonstration sessions.

There were several people that deserve appreciation and gratitude for helping in the realization of this conference. We would like to thank the Program Committee members and additional reviewers for their hard work in reviewing papers carefully and rigorously. After careful discussions, the Program Committee selected 234 papers (acceptance rate: 39.53%) for presentation at the conference. We would also like to thank the authors for having revised their papers to address the comments and suggestions by the referees.

The conference program was enriched by the outstanding invited talks by Ajith Abraham, Subir Saha, Narayan C. Debnath, Abhijit Mitra, K. Chandra Sekaran, K. Subramanian, Sudip Misra, K.R. Srivathsan, Jaydip Sen, Joyati Debnath and Junichi Suzuki. We believe that ACC 2011 delivered a high-quality, stimulating and enlightening technical program. The tutorials covered topics of great interest to the cyber forensics and cloud computing communities. The tutorial by Avinash Srinivasan provided an overview of the forensically important artifacts left behind on a MAC computer. In his tutorial on "Network Forensics," Bhadran provided an introduction to network forensics, packet capture and analysis techniques, and a discussion on various RNA tools. The tutorial on Next-Generation Cloud Computing by Pethuru Raj focused on enabling technologies in cloud computing.

The ACC 2011 conference program also included five workshops: International Workshop on Multimedia Streaming (MultiStreams 2011), Second International Workshop on Trust Management in P2P Systems (IWTMP2PS 2011), International Workshop on Cloud Computing: Architecture, Algorithms and Applications (CloudComp 2011), International Workshop on Identity: Security, Management and Applications (ID2011) and International Workshop on Applications of Signal Processing (I-WASP 2011). We thank all the workshop organizers as well as the Workshop Chair, El-Sayed El-Alfy, for their accomplishment to bring out prosperous workshops. We would like to express our gratitude to the Tutorial Chairs Patrick Seeling, Jaydeep Sen, K.S. Mathew, and Roksana Boreli and Demo Chairs Amitava Mukherjee, Bhadran V.K., and Janardhanan P.S. for their timely expertise in reviewing the proposals. Moreover, we thank Publication Chairs Pruet Boonma, Sajid Hussain and Hiroshi Wada for their kind help in editing the proceedings. The large participation in ACC2011 would not have been possible without the Publicity Co-chairs Victor Govindaswamy, Arun Saha and Biju Paul.

The proceedings of ACC 2011 are organized into four volumes. We hope that you will find these proceedings to be a valuable resource in your professional, research, and educational activities whether you are a student, academic, researcher, or a practicing professional.

July 2011

Ajith Abraham
Jaime Lloret Mauri
John F. Buford
Junichi Suzuki
Sabu M. Thampi

Organization

ACC 2011 was jointly organized by the Department of Computer Science and Engineering and Department of Information Technology, Rajagiri School of Engineering and Technology (RSET), Kochi, India, in cooperation with ACM/SIGWEB.

Organizing Committee

Chief Patrons

Fr. Jose Alex CMI	Manager, RSET
Fr. Antony Kariyil CMI	Director, RSET

Patron

J. Isaac, Principal	RSET

Advisory Committee

A. Krishna Menon	RSET
A.C. Mathai	RSET
Fr. Varghese Panthalookaran	RSET
Karthikeyan Chittayil	RSET
Vinod Kumar, P.B.	RSET
Biju Abraham Narayamparambil	RSET
Kuttyamma A.J.	RSET
Asha Panicker	RSET
K. Rajendra Varmah	RSET
P.R. Madhava Panicker	RSET
Liza Annie Joseph	RSET
Varkey Philip	RSET
Fr. Joel George Pullolil	RSET
R. Ajayakumar Varma	KSCSTE
K. Poulose Jacob	Cochin University of Science & Technology
H.R. Mohan, Chairman	Div IV, Computer Society of India (CSI)
Soman S.P., Chairman	Computer Society of India (CSI), Cochin Chapter
S. Radhakrishnan, Chairman	Kerala State Centre, The Institution of Engineers (India)

Steering Committee

John F. Buford	Avaya Labs Research, USA
Rajkumar Buyya	University of Melbourne, Australia
Mukesh Singhai	University of Kentucky, USA
John Strassner	Pohang University of Science and Technology, Republic of Korea
Junichi Suzuki	University of Massachusetts, Boston, USA
Ramakrishna Kappagantu	IEEE India Council
Achuthsankar S. Nair	Centre for Bioinformatics, Trivandrum, India

Conference Chair

Sabu M. Thampi	Rajagiri School of Engineering and Technology, India

ACC 2011 Program Committee Chairs

General Co-chairs

Ajith Abraham	Machine Intelligence Research Labs, Europe
Chandra Sekaran K.	National Institute of Technology Karnataka, India
Waleed W. Smari	University of Dayton, Ohio, USA

Program Co-chairs

Jaime Lloret Mauri	Polytechnic University of Valencia, Spain
Thorsten Strufe	Darmstadt University of Technology, Germany
Gregorio Martinez	University of Murcia, Spain

Special Sessions and Workshops Co-chairs

El-Sayed El-Alfy	King Fahd University of Petroleum and Minerals, Saudi Arabia
Silvio Bortoleto	Positivo University, Brazil

Tutorial Co-chairs

Patrick Seeling	University of Wisconsin - Stevens Point, USA
Jaydeep Sen	Tata Consultancy Services, Calcutta, India
K.S. Mathew	Rajagiri School of Engineering and Technology, India
Roksana Boreli	National ICT Australia Ltd., Australia

Demo Co-chairs

Amitava Mukherjee	IBM Global Business Services, India
Bhadran V.K.	Centre for Development of Advanced Computing, Trivandrum, India
Janardhanan P.S.	Rajagiri School of Engineering and Technology, India

Publicity Co-chairs

Victor Govindaswamy	Texas A&M University, USA
Arun Saha	Fujitsu Network Communications, USA
Biju Paul	Rajagiri School of Engineering and Technology, India

Publication Co-chairs

Pruet Boonma	Chiang Mai University, Thailand
Sajid Hussain	Fisk University, USA
Hiroshi Wada	University of New South Wales, Australia

ACC 2011 Technical Program Committee

A. Hafid	Network Research Lab, University of Montreal, Canada
Abdallah Shami	The University of Western Ontario, Canada
Abdelhafid Abouaissa	University of Haute Alsace, France
Abdelmalik Bachir	Imperial College London, UK
Abdelouahid Derhab	CERIST, Algeria
Abhijit Mitra	Indian Institute of Technology Guwahati, India
Adão Silva	University of Aveiro, Portugal
Adel Ali	University Technology Malaysia
Ahmed Mehaoua	University of Paris Descartes, France
Ai-Chun Pang	National Taiwan University, Taiwan
Ajay Gupta	Western Michigan University, USA
Alberto Dainotti	University of Naples "Federico II", Italy
Alessandro Leonardi	University of Catania, Italy
Alex Galis	University College London, UK
Alexey Vinel	Saint Petersburg Institute, Russia
Ali Abedi	University of Maine, USA
Alicia Triviño Cabrera	Universidad de Málaga, Spain
Alireza Behbahani	University of California, Irvine, USA
Alois Ferscha	University of Linz, Austria
Al-Sakib Khan Pathan	International Islamic University, Malaysia
Amar Prakash Azad	INRIA, France
Amirhossein Alimohammad	University of Alberta, Canada
Amit Agarwal	Indian Institute of Technology, Roorkee, India

Amitava Mukherjee	IBM Global Business Services, India
Anand Prasad	NEC Corporation, Japan
Andreas Maeder	NEC Laboratories Europe, Germany
Ankur Gupta	Model Institute of Engineering and Technology, India
Antonio Coronato	ICAR-CNR, Naples, Italy
Antonio Pescapé	University of Naples Federico II, Italy
António Rodrigues	IT / Instituto Superior Técnico, Portugal
Anura P. Jayasumana	Colorado State University, USA
Arnab Bhattacharya	Indian Institute of Technology, Kanpur, India
Arun Saha	Fujitsu Network Communications, USA
Arvind Swaminathan	Qualcomm, USA
Ashley Thomas	Secureworks Inc., USA
Ashraf Elnagar	Sharjah University, UAE
Ashraf Mahmoud	KFUPM, Saudi Arabia
Ashwani Singh	Navtel Systems, France
Athanasios Vasilakos	University of Western Macedonia, Greece
Atilio Gameiro	Telecommunications Institute/Aveiro University, Portugal
Aydin Sezgin	Ulm University, Germany
Ayman Assra	McGill University, Canada
Aytac Azgin	Georgia Institute of Technology, USA
B. Sundar Rajan	Indian Institute of Science, India
Babu A.V.	National Institute of Technology, Calicut, India
Babu B.V.	BITS-Pilani, Rajasthan, India
Babu Raj E.	Sun College of Engineering and Technology, India
Balagangadhar G. Bathula	Columbia University, USA
Borhanuddin Mohd. Ali	Universiti Putra Malaysia
Brijendra Kumar Joshi	Military College, Indore, India
Bruno Crispo	Università di Trento, Italy
C.-F. Cheng	National Chiao Tung University, Taiwan
Chang Wu Yu	Chung Hua University, Taiwan
Charalampos Tsimenidis	Newcastle University, UK
Chih-Cheng Tseng	National Ilan University, Taiwan
Chi-Hsiang Yeh	Queen's University, Canada
Chitra Babu	SSN College of Engineering, Chennai, India
Chittaranjan Hota	BITS Hyderabad Campus, India
Chonho Lee	Nanyang Technological University, Singapore
Christian Callegari	University of Pisa, Italy
Christos Chrysoulas	Technological Educational Institute, Greece
Chuan-Ching Sue	National Cheng Kung University, Taiwan
Chung Shue Chen	TREC, INRIA, France

Chun-I. Fan	National Sun Yat-sen University, Taiwan
Chutima Prommak	Suranaree University of Technology, Thailand
Dali Wei	Jiangsu Tianze Infoindustry Company Ltd, P.R. China
Danda B. Rawat	Old Dominion University, USA
Daniele Tarchi	University of Bologna, Italy
Davide Adami	CNIT Pisa Research Unit, University of Pisa, Italy
Deepak Garg	Thapar University, India
Demin Wang	Microsoft Inc., USA
Dennis Pfisterer	University of Lübeck, Germany
Deyun Gao	Beijing Jiaotong University, P.R. China
Dharma Agrawal	University of Cincinnati, USA
Dhiman Barman	Juniper Networks, USA
Di Jin	General Motors, USA
Dimitrios Katsaros	University of Thessaly, Greece
Dimitrios Vergados	National Technical University of Athens, Greece
Dirk Pesch	Cork Institute of Technology, Ireland
Djamel Sadok	Federal University of Pernambuco, Brazil
Eduardo Cerqueira	Federal University of Para (UFPA), Brazil
Eduardo Souto	Federal University of Amazonas, Brazil
Edward Au	Huawei Technologies, P.R. China
Egemen Cetinkaya	University of Kansas, USA
Elizabeth Sherly	IIITM-Kerala, India
El-Sayed El-Alfy	King Fahd University, Saudi Arabia
Emad A. Felemban	Umm Al Qura University, Saudi Arabia
Eric Renault	TELECOM & Management SudParis, France
Errol Lloyd	University of Delaware, USA
Ertan Onur	Delft University of Technology, The Netherlands
Faouzi Bader	CTTC, Spain
Faouzi Kamoun	WTS, UAE
Fernando Velez	University of Beira Interior, Portugal
Filipe Cardoso	ESTSetubal/Polytechnic Institute of Setubal, Portugal
Florian Doetzer	ASKON ConsultingGroup, Germany
Francesco Quaglia	Sapienza Università di Roma, Italy
Francine Krief	University of Bordeaux, France
Frank Yeong-Sung Lin	National Taiwan University, Taiwan
Gianluigi Ferrari	University of Parma, Italy
Giuseppe Ruggeri	University “Mediterranea” of Reggio Calabria, Italy
Grzegorz Danilewicz	Poznan University of Technology, Poland
Guang-Hua Yang	The University of Hong Kong, Hong Kong
Guo Bin	Institut Telecom SudParis, France

Hadi Otrok	Khalifa University, UAE
Hamid Mcheick	Université du Québec à Chicoutimi, Canada
Harry Skianis	University of the Aegean, Greece
Hicham Khalife	ENSEIRB-LaBRI, France
Himal Suraweera	Singapore University of Technology and Design, Singapore
Hiroshi Wada	University of New South Wales, Australia
Hong-Hsu Yen	Shih-Hsin University, Taiwan
Hongli Xu	University of Science and Technology of China, P.R. China
Houcine Hassan	Technical University of Valencia, Spain
Hsuan-Jung Su	National Taiwan University, Taiwan
Huaiyu Dai	NC State University, USA
Huey-Ing Liu	Fu-Jen Catholic University, Taiwan
Hung-Keng Pung	National University of Singapore
Hung-Yu Wei	NTU, Taiwan
Ian Glover	University of Strathclyde, UK
Ian Wells	Swansea Metropolitan University, UK
Ibrahim Develi	Erciyes University, Turkey
Ibrahim El rube	AAST, Egypt
Ibrahim Habib	City University of New York, USA
Ibrahim Korpeoglu	Bilkent University, Turkey
Ilja Radusch	Technische Universität Berlin, Germany
Ilka Miloucheva	Media Technology Research, Germany
Imad Elhajj	American University of Beirut, Lebanon
Ivan Ganchev	University of Limerick, Ireland
Iwan Adhicandra	The University of Pisa, Italy
Jalel Ben-othman	University of Versailles, France
Jane-Hwa Huang	National Chi Nan University, Taiwan
Jaydeep Sen	Tata Consultancy Services, Calcutta, India
Jiankun Hu	RMIT University, Australia
Jie Yang	Cisco Systems, USA
Jiping Xiong	Zhejiang Normal University of China
José de Souza	Federal University of Ceará, Brazil
Jose Moreira	IBM T.J. Watson Research Center, USA
Ju Wang	Virginia State University, USA
Juan-Carlos Cano	Technical University of Valencia, Spain
Judith Kelner	Federal University of Pernambuco, Brazil
Julien Laganier	Juniper Networks Inc., USA
Jussi Haapola	University of Oulu, Finland
K. Komathy	Easwari Engineering College, Chennai, India
Ka Lok Hung	The Hong Kong University, Hong Kong
Ka Lok Man	Xi'an Jiaotong-Liverpool University, China
Kaddar Lamia	University of Versailles Saint Quentin, France
Kainam Thomas	Hong Kong Polytechnic University

Kais Mnif	High Institute of Electronics and Communications of Sfax, Tunisia
Kang Yong Lee	ETRI, Korea
Katia Bortoleto	Positivo University, Brazil
Kejie Lu	University of Puerto Rico at Mayaguez, USA
Kemal Tepe	University of Windsor, Canada
Khalifa Hettak	Communications Research Centre (CRC), Canada
Khushboo Shah	Altusystems Corp, USA
Kotecha K.	Institute of Technology, Nirma University, India
Kpatcha Bayarou	Fraunhofer Institute, Germany
Kumar Padmanabh	General Motors, India
Kyriakos Manousakis	Telcordia Technologies, USA
Kyung Sup Kwak	Inha University, Korea
Li Zhao	Microsoft Corporation, USA
Li-Chun Wang	National Chiao Tung University, Taiwan
Lin Du	Technicolor Research and Innovation Beijing, P.R. China
Liza A. Latiff	University Technology Malaysia
Luca Scalia	University of Palermo, Italy
M Ayoub Khan	C-DAC, Noida, India
Maaruf Ali	Oxford Brookes University, UK
Madhu Kumar S.D.	National Institute of Technology, Calicut, India
Madhu Nair	University of Kerala, India
Madhumita Chatterjee	Indian Institute of Technology Bombay, India
Mahamod Ismail	Universiti Kebangsaan Malaysia
Mahmoud Al-Qutayri	Khalifa University, UAE
Manimaran Govindarasu	Iowa State University, USA
Marcelo Segatto	Federal University of Espírito Santo, France
Maria Ganzha	University of Gdansk, Poland
Marilia Curado	University of Coimbra, Portugal
Mario Fanelli	DEIS, University of Bologna,Italy
Mariofanna Milanova	University of Arkansas at Little Rock, USA
Mariusz Glabowski	Poznan University of Technology, Poland
Mariusz Zal	Poznan University of Technology, Poland
Masato Saito	University of the Ryukyus, Japan
Massimiliano Comisso	University of Trieste, Italy
Massimiliano Laddomada	Texas A&M University-Texarkana, USA
Matthias R. Brust	University of Central Florida, USA
Mehrzad Biguesh	Queen's University, Canada
Michael Alexander	Scaledinfra Technologies GmbH, Austria
Michael Hempel	University of Nebraska - Lincoln, USA
Michael Lauer	Vanille-Media, Germany
Ming Xia	NICT, Japan
Ming Xiao	Royal Institute of Technology, Sweden
Mohamed Ali Kaafar	INRIA, France

Ronny Yongho Kim	Kyungil University, Korea
Ruay-Shiung Chang	National Dong Hwa University, Taiwan
Ruidong Li	NICT, Japan
S. Ali Ghorashi	Shahid Beheshti University, Iran
Sahar Ghazal	University of Versailles, France
Said Soulhi	Ericsson, Swedan
Sajid Hussain	Fisk University, USA
Salah Bourennane	Ecole Centrale Marseille, France
Salman Abdul Moiz	CDAC, Bangalore, India
Sameh Elnikety	Microsoft Research, USA
Sanjay H.A.	Nitte Meenakshi Institute, Bangalore, India
Sathish Rajasekhar	RMIT University, Australia
Sergey Andreev	Tampere University of Technology, Finland
Seshan Srirangarajan	Nanyang Technological University, Singapore
Seyed (Reza) Zekavat	Michigan Technological University, USA
Sghaier Guizani	UAE University, UAE
Shancang Li	School of Engineering, Swansea University, UK
Shi Xiao	Nanyang Technological University, Singapore
Siby Abraham	University of Mumbai, India
Silvio Bortoleto	Positivo University, Brazil
Simon Pietro Romano	University of Naples Federico II, Italy
Somayajulu D. V. L. N.	National Institute of Technology Warangal, India
Song Guo	The University of British Columbia, Canada
Song Lin	University of California, Riverside, USA
Soumya Sen	University of Pennsylvania, USA
Stefano Ferretti	University of Bologna, Italy
Stefano Giordano	University of Pisa, Italy
Stefano Pesic	Cisco Systems, Italy
Stefano Tomasin	University of Padova, Italy
Stefanos Gritzalis	University of the Aegean, Greece
Steven Gordon	Thammasat University, Thailand
Suat Ozdemir	Gazi University, Turkey
Subir Saha	Nokia Siemens Networks, India
Subramanian K.	Advanced Center for Informatics and Innovative Learning, IGNOU, India
Sudarshan T.S.B.	Amrita Vishwa Vidyapeetham, Bangalore, India
Sugam Sharma	Iowa State University, USA
Surekha Mariam Varghese	M.A. College of Engineering, India
T. Aaron Gulliver	University of Victoria, Canada
Tao Jiang	Huazhong University of Science and Technology, P.R. China
Tarek Bejaoui	Mediatron Lab., Carthage University, Tunisia
Tarun Joshi	University of Cincinnati, USA
Theodore Stergiou	Intracom Telecom, UK

Yu-Kai Huang	Quanta Research Institute, Taiwan
Yusuf Ozturk	San Diego State University, USA
Zaher Aghbari	University of Sharjah, UAE
Zbigniew Dziong	University of Quebec, Canada
Zhang Jin	Beijing Normal University, P.R. China
Zhenghao Zhang	Florida State University, USA
Zhenzhen Ye	iBasis, Inc., USA
Zhihua Cui	Taiyuan University of Science and Technology, China
Zhili Sun	University of Surrey, UK
Zhong Zhou	University of Connecticut, USA
Zia Saquib	C-DAC, Mumbai, India

ACC 2011 Additional Reviewers

Akshay Vashist	Telcordia Telchnologies, USA
Alessandro Testa	University of Naples Federico II, Italy
Amitava	Academy of Technology, India
Ammar Rashid	Auckland University of Technology, New Zealand
Anand	MITS, India
Bjoern W. Schuller	Technical University, Germany
Chi-Ming Wong	Jinwen University of Science and Technology, Taiwan
Danish Faizan	NIC-INDIA, India
Fatos Xhafa	UPC, Barcelona Tech, Spain
Hooman Tahayori	Ryerson University, Canada
John Jose	IIT Madras, India
Jyoti Singh	Academy of Technology, India
Koushik	West Bengal University of Technology, India
Long Zheng	University of Aizu, Japan
Manpreet Singh	M.M. Engineering College, India
Maria Striki	Telcordia Technologies, Piscataway, USA
Mohamad Zoinol Abidin	Universiti Teknikal Malaysia Melaka, Malaysia
Mohamed Dahmane	University of Montreal,Canada
Mohd Helmy Abd Wahab	Universiti Tun Hussein Onn Malaysia, Malaysia
Mohd Riduan Bin Ahmad	Universiti Teknikal Malaysia Melaka, Malaysia
Mohd Sadiq	Jamia Millia Islamia, India
Mudhakar Srivatsa	IBM T.J. Watson Research Center, USA
Nan Yang	CSIRO, Australia
Nurulnadwan Aziz Aziz	Universiti Teknologi MARA, Malaysia

Pooya Taheri	University of Alberta, Canada
R.C. Wang	NTTU, Taiwan
Roman Yampolskiy	University of Louisville, USA
Shuang Tian	The University of Sydney, Australia
Syed Abbas Ali	Ajman University of Science & Technology, UAE
Velayutham	Adhiparasakthi Engineering College, Melmaruvathur, India
Yeong-Luh Ueng	National Tsing Hua University, Taiwan

International Workshop on Identity: Security, Management and Applications (ID 2011)

General Chairs

Program Chairs

Organizing Chair

Organizing Co-chairs

Technical Program Committee

C. Sunil Kumar	Jawaharlal Nehru Technological University, India
Chandrabali Karmakar	Infosys Technologies Limited, India
Farooq Anjum	On-Ramp Wireless, USA
Gudipati Kalyan Kumar	Excellence India, India
Hamid Sharif	University of Nebraska-Lincoln, USA
Hui Chen	Virginia State University, USA
Jie Li	University of Tsukuba, Japan
Kalaiselvam	Infineon Technologies, Germany
Lau Lung	UFSC, Brazil
Lukas Ruf	Consecom AG, Switzerland
Manik Lal Das	Dhirubhai Ambani Institute of Information and Communication Technology (DA-IICT), India
Manimaran Govindarasu	Iowa State University, USA
Narendra Ahuja	University of Illinois, USA
Omar	University of Jordan, Jordan
Pradeep Kumar T.S.	Infosys Technologies Limited, India
Pradeepa	Wipro Technologies, India
Rajiv Tripathi	NIT, Allahabad, India
Rakesh Chithuluri	Oracle, India
Sanjay Chaudhary	Dhirubhai Ambani Institute of Information and Communication Technology (DA-IICT), India
Santosh Pasuladi	Jawaharlal Nehru Technological University, India
Satheesh Kumar Varma	IIIT, Pune, India
Saurabh Barjatiya	IIIT, Hyderabad, India
Sreekumar Vobugari	Education & Research, Infosys Technologies Limited, India
Suthershan Vairavel	CTS, India
Tarun Rao	Infosys Technologies Limited, India
Thomas Little	Boston University, USA
Tim Strayer	BBN Technologies, USA
V. Balamurugan	IBM, India
Vasudeva Varma	IIIT, Hyderabad, India
Vinod Babu	Giesecke & Devrient, Germany
Yonghe Liu	UT Arlington, USA

International Workshop on Applications of Signal Processing
(I-WASP 2011)

Workshop Organizers

Jaison Jacob	Rajagiri School of Engineering and Technology, India
Sreeraj K.P.	Rajagiri School of Engineering and Technology, India
Rithu James	Rajagiri School of Engineering and Technology, India

Technical Program Committee

A. Vinod	NTU, Singapore
Aggelos Katsaggelos	Northwestern University, USA
Bing Li	University of Virginia, USA
Carlos Gonzalez	University of Castilla-La Mancha, Spain
Damon Chandler	Oklahoma State University, USA
Egon L. van den Broek	University of Twente, The Netherlands
Feng Wu	Microsoft Research Asia, P.R. China
Hakan Johansson	University of Linkoping, Sweden
Joaquim Filipe	EST-Setubal, Portugal
Lotfi Senahdji	Université de Rennes 1, France
Reyer Zwiggelkaar	Aberystwyth University, UK
Xianghua Xie	Swansea University, UK
Yoshikazu Miyanaga	Hokkaido University, Japan

International Workshop on Cloud Computing: Architecture, Algorithms and Applications (CloudComp 2011)

Workshop Organizers

Binu A.	Cochin University of Science and Technology, India
Biju Paul	Rajagiri School of Engineering and Technology, India
Sabu M. Thampi	Rajagiri School of Engineering and Technology, India

Technical Program Committee

Antonio Puliafito	University of Messina, Italy
Bob Callaway	IBM, USA
Chee Shin Yeo	Institute of High-Performance Computing, Singapore
Chin-Sean Sum	National Institute of Information and Communications Technology, Japan
Ching-Hsien Hsu	Chung Hua University, Taiwan
Drissa Houatra	Orange Labs, France
Deepak Unnikrishnan	University of Massachusetts, USA
Jie Song	Northeastern University, P.R. China
Salah Sharieh	McMaster University, Canada
Francesco Longo	Universitá di Messina, Italy
Fabienne Anhalt	Ecole Normale Supérieure de Lyon–INRIA, France
Gaurav Somani	LNMIIT, Jaipur, India
Haibing Guan	Shanghai Jiao Tong University, P.R. China
Hongbo Jiang	Huazhong University of Science and Technology, P.R. China
Hongkai Xiong	Shanghai Jiao Tong University, P.R China
Hui Zhang	Nec Laboratories America, USA
Itai Zilbershtein	Avaya, Israel
Jens Nimis	University of Applied Sciences, Germany
Jie Song	Software College, Northeastern University, China

Jorge Carapinha	PT Inovaçao S.A. Telecom Group, Portugal
Junyi Wang	National Institute of Information and Communications Technology, Japan
K. Chandra Sekaran	NITK, India
Kai Zheng	IBM China Research Lab, P.R. China
Krishna Sankar	Cisco Systems, USA
Laurent Amanton	Havre University, France
Luca Caviglione	National Research Council (CNR), Italy
Lukas Ruf	Consecom AG, Switzerland
Massimiliano Rak	Second University of Naples, Italy
Pallab Datta	IBM Almaden Research Center, USA
Pascale Vicat-Blanc Primet	INRIA, France
Prabu Dorairaj	NetApp Inc, India
Shivani Sud	Intel Labs, USA
Shuicheng Yan	National University of Singapore, Singapore
Siani Pearson	HP Labs, UK
Simon Koo	University of San Diego, USA
Srikumar Venugopal	UNSW, Australia
Stephan Kopf	University of Mannheim, Germany
Thomas Sandholm	Hewlett-Packard Laboratories, USA
Umberto Villano	University of Sannio, Italy
Vipin Chaudhary	University at Buffalo, USA
Yaozu Dong	Intel Corporation, P.R. China
Zhou Lan	National Institute of Information and Communications Technology, Japan

International Workshop on Multimedia Streaming (MultiStreams 2011)

Program Chairs

Pascal Lorenz	University of Haute Alsace, France
Fan Ye	IBM T.J. Watson Research Center, USA
Trung Q. Duong	Blekinge Institute of Technology, Sweden

Technical Program Committee

Guangjie Han	Hohai University, P.R. China
Alex Canovas	Polytechnic University of Valencia, Spain
Brent Lagesse	Oak Ridge National Laboratory, USA
Chung Shue Chen	INRIA-ENS, France
Debasis Giri	Haldia Institute of Technology, India
Mario Montagud	Universidad Politécnica de Valencia, Spain
Doreen Miriam	Anna University, India
Duduku V. Viswacheda	University Malaysia Sabah, Malaysia
Elsa Macías López	University of Las Palmas de Gran Canaria, Spain
Eugénia Bernardino	Polytechnic Institute of Leiria, Portugal
Fernando Boronat	Instituto de Investigación para la Gestión Integrada de Zonas Costeras, Spain
Jen-Wen Ding	National Kaohsiung University of Applied Sciences, Taiwan
Joel Rodrigues IT	University of Beira Interior, Portugal
Jo-Yew Tham	A*STAR Institute for Infocomm Research, Singapore
Marcelo Atenas	Universidad Politecnica de Valencia, Spain
Jorge Bernabé	University of Murcia, Poland
Bao Vo Nguyen	Posts and Telecommunications Institute of Technology, Vietnam
Hans-Juergen Zepernick	Blekinge Institute of Technology, Sweden
Jose Maria Alcaraz Calero	University of Murcia, Spain
Juan Marin Perez	University of Murcia, Spain
Lei Shu	Osaka University, Japan
Lexing Xie	The Australian National University, Australia
Marc Gilg	University of Haute-Alsace, France
Miguel Garcia	Polytechnic University of Valencia, Spain
Mohd Riduan Bin Ahmad	Universiti Teknikal Malaysia, Malaysia

Phan Cong-Vinh	London South Bank University, UK
Alvaro Suárez-Sarmiento	University of Las Palmas de Gran Canaria, Spain
Song Guo	University of British Columbia, Canada
Tin-Yu Wu	Tamkang University, Taiwan
Zhangbing Zhou	Institut Telecom & Management SudParis, France
Zuqing Zhu	Cisco System, USA
Juan M. Sánchez	University of Extremadura, Spain
Choong Seon Hong	Kyung Hee University, Korea

Second International Workshop on Trust Management in P2P Systems (IWTMP2PS 2011)

Program Chairs

Visvasuresh Victor Govindaswamy	Texas A&M University-Texarkana, USA
Jack Hu	Microsoft, USA
Sabu M. Thampi	Rajagiri School of Engineering and Technology, India

Technical Program Committee

Haiguang	Fudan University, P.R. China
Ioannis Anagnostopoulos	University of the Aegean, Greece
Farag Azzedin	King Fahd University of Petroleum & Minerals, Saudi Arabia
Roksana Boreli	National ICT Australia, Australia
Yann Busnel	University of Nantes, France
Juan-Carlos Cano	Universidad Politecnica de Valencia, Spain
Phan Cong-Vinh	London South Bank University, UK
Jianguo Ding	University of Luxembourg, Luxemburg
Markus Fiedler	Blekinge Institute of Technology, Sweden
Deepak Garg	Thapar University, Patiala, India
Felix Gomez Marmol	University of Murcia, Spain
Paulo Gondim	Universidade de Brasilia, Brazil
Steven Gordon	Thammasat University, Thailand
Ankur Gupta	Model Institute of Engineering and Technology, India
Houcine Hassan	Universidad Politecnica de Valencia, Spain
Yifeng He	Ryerson University, Canada
Michael Hempel	University of Nebraska-Lincoln, USA
Salman Abdul Moiz	CDAC, India
Guimin Huang	Guilin University of Electronic Technology, P.R. China
Renjie Huang	Washington State University, USA
Benoit Hudzia	SAP Research, UK
Helge Janicke	De Montfort University, UK

Mohamed Ali Kaafar	INRIA, France
Eleni Koutrouli	National University of Athens, Greece
Stefan Kraxberger	Graz University of Technology, Austria
Jonathan Loo	Middlesex University, UK
Marjan Naderan	Amirkabir University of Technology, Iran
Lourdes Penalver	Valencia Polytechnic University, Spain
Elvira Popescu	UCV, Romania
Guangzhi Qu	Oakland University, USA
Aneel Rahim	COMSATS Institute of Information Technology, Pakistan
Yonglin Ren	SITE, University of Ottawa, Canada
Andreas Riener	University of Linz, Austria
Samir Saklikar	RSA, Security Division of EMC, India
Thomas Schmidt	HAW Hamburg (DE), Germany
Fangyang Shen	Northern New Mexico College, USA
Thorsten Strufe	TU Darmstadt, Germany
Sudarshan Tsb	Amrita School of Engineering, India
Demin Wang	Microsoft, USA
Fatos Xhafa	UPC, Barcelona, Spain
Jiping Xiong	Zhejiang Normal University, P.R. China
Chang Wu Yu	Chung Hua University, Taiwan

Table of Contents – Part I

Adhoc Networks

An Enhanced Port Hiding Design to Handle DoS Attacks in an Ad-Hoc Environment 1
Jayashree Padmanabhan, Abhinaya Sukumar, Ezhilarasi Elumalai, and Sunanda Ramesh

An Efficient Routing Protocol for Ad Hoc Networks 11
Chiranjeev Kumar, Neeraj Tyagi, Rajeev Tripathi, M. Lakshmi Prasanth Kumar, Dhirendra Kumar Sharma, and Sanjay Kumar Biswash

3-Disjoint Paths Fault-Tolerant Multi-stage Interconnection Networks .. 21
Ravi Rastogi, Rohit Verma, Nitin, and Durg Singh Chauhan

Reduction of Inter Carrier Interference by Pilot Aided Self Cancellation Compared to Self Cancellation Method 34
Anitha Sheela Kankacharla, Tarun Kumar Juluru, and Saritha Dedavath

A Novel Attack Model Simulation in OLSR 44
Manish Kumar, Rajbir Kaur, Vijay Laxmi, and Manoj Singh Gaur

Performance Investigations of Routing Protocols in MANETs........ 54
Surendra Singh Choudhary, Vijander Singh, and Reena Dadhich

Mobile Query Processing-Taxonomy, Issues and Challenges 64
Diya Thomas and Sabu M. Thampi

A Compact Low-Cost Phase Shifter for Wireless Applications 78
Ch. Rajasekhar, D. Srinivasa rao, M. Vanaja, and K. Vijay

A Study on the Effect of Traffic Patterns in Mobile Ad Hoc Network ... 83
Arindarjit Pal, Jyoti Prakash Singh, and Paramartha Dutta

I-SAODV: Improving SAODV to Mitigate Hop-Count Attack in Mobile Adhoc Network 91
Sanjeev Rana and Manpreet Singh

Social Network Aware Routing for Delay Tolerant Networks 101
Rajiv Misra and Shailendra Shukla

Sybil Secure Architecture for Multicast Routing Protocols for MANETs 111
E.A. Mary Anita

Fault Diagnosis in MANET 119
Madhu Chouhan, Manmath Narayan Sahoo, and P.M. Khilar

Mobile Agent Security Based on Trust Model in MANET 129
Chandreyee Chowdhury and Sarmistha Neogy

An Efficient Protocol to Study the Effect of Flooding on Energy Consumption in MANETS 141
Anita Kanavalli, N. Chandra Kiran, P. Deepa Shenoy, K.R. Venugopal, and L.M. Patnaik

An Approach to Suppress Selfish Behavior of a Node in MANET by Hiding Destination Identity in Routing Path 153
Rahul Raghuvanshi, Mukesh Kumar Giluka, and Vasudev Dehalwar

Broken Link Fraud in DSDV Routing - Detection and Countermeasure . 162
H. Meena Sharma, Rajbir Kaur, Manoj Singh Gaur, and Vijay Laxmi

Advanced Micro Architecture Techniques

Research on Power Optimization Techniques for Multi Core Architectures 172
A.S. Radhamani and E. Baburaj

Optimization Techniques and Performance Evaluation of a Multithreaded Multi-core Architecture Using OpenMP 182
M. Rajasekhara Babu, P. Venkata Krishna, and M. Khalid

Review on VLSI Architectures for Optical OFDM Receivers 192
Magesh Kannan Parthasarathy, Karthik Govindarajan, G. Gunaraj, and S. Lakshmi Prabha

A Pre-fetch Enabled Cache-Core Architecture for Multi-cores 204
B. Parvathy

Performance Analysis of Adaptive Scan Compression Methodology and Calculations of Compression Ratio 213
Avani Rao, Mahesh Devani, Mitesh Limachia, and Nikhil Kothari

Autonomic and Context-Aware Computing

Better Debugging of Logical Errors Using Optimized Call Stack Restricted Slicing 223
L.D. Dhinesh Babu, M. Nirmala, S. Santhoshkumar, and S. Panneerselvam

Towards Incremental Reasoning for Context Aware Systems 232
Mohammad Oliya and Hung Keng Pung

On the Potential of Using Conventional Mobile Communication Technology for Human Context Awareness in Ubiquitous Computing ... 242
Abhijan Bhattacharyya

A Novel Adaptive Monitoring Compliance Design Pattern for Autonomic Computing Systems ... 250
Vishnuvardhan Mannava and T. Ramesh

Bioinformatics and Bio-computing

Predictive Analysis of Lung Cancer Recurrence ... 260
Shweta Srivastava, Manisha Rathi, and J.P. Gupta

Development and Validation of Matlab Models for Nanowire Sensors ... 270
P. Vipeesh and N.J.R. Muniraj

Application of Recurrence Quantification Analysis (RQA) in Biosequence Pattern Recognition ... 284
Saritha Namboodiri, Chandra Verma, Pawan K. Dhar, Alessandro Giuliani, and Achuthsankar S. Nair

New Feature Vector for Apoptosis Protein Subcellular Localization Prediction ... 294
Geetha Govindan and Achuthsankar S. Nair

Hurst CGR (HCGR) – A Novel Feature Extraction Method from Chaos Game Representation of Genomes ... 302
Vrinda V. Nair, Anita Mallya, Bhavya Sebastian, Indu Elizabeth, and Achuthsankar S. Nair

Hub Characterization of Tumor Protein P53 Using Artificial Neural Networks ... 310
J. Sajeev and T. Mahalakshmi

Lacunarity Analysis of Protein Sequences Reveal Fractal Like Behavior of Amino Acid Distributions ... 320
G. Gopakumar and Achuthsankar S. Nair

Classification and Rule-Based Approach to Diagnose Pulmonary Tuberculosis ... 328
Jyotshna Dongardive, Agnes Xavier, Kavita Jain, and Siby Abraham

Identification and Analysis of Cell Cycle Phase Genes by Clustering in Correspondence Subspaces ... 340
Ai Sasho, Shenhaochen Zhu, and Rahul Singh

Reliability Assessment of Microarray Data Using Fuzzy Classification Methods: A Comparative Study ... 351
Ajay K. Mandava, Latifi Shahram, and Emma E. Regentova

Association Rule Mining for the Identification of Activators from Gene Regulatory Network 361
Seema More, M. Vidya, N. Sujana, and H.D. Soumya

Cloud, Cluster, Grid and P2P Computing

MPI Performance Analysis of Amazon EC2 Cloud Services for High Performance Computing 371
Florian Schatz, Sven Koschnicke, Niklas Paulsen, Christoph Starke, and Manfred Schimmler

Algorithmic Approach to Calculating Minimal Resource Allocation Recommender for Grid Using Reliability and Trust Computations 382
Gutha Jaya Krishna and Rajeev Wankar

Virtualization Techniques: A Methodical Review of XEN and KVM 399
A. Binu and G. Santhosh Kumar

An Optimal Workflow Based Scheduling and Resource Allocation in Cloud 411
P. Varalakshmi, Aravindh Ramaswamy, Aswath Balasubramanian, and Palaniappan Vijaykumar

Energy Efficient Time Synchronization Protocol for Wireless Sensor Networks 421
Gopal Chand Gautam and T.P. Sharma

Elastic VM for Cloud Resources Provisioning Optimization 431
Wesam Dawoud, Ibrahim Takouna, and Christoph Meinel

Employing Bloom Filters for Enforcing Integrity of Outsourced Databases in Cloud Environments 446
T. Aditya, P.K. Baruah, and R. Mukkamala

Parallel Implementation of Part of Speech Tagging for Text Mining Using Grid Computing 461
Naveen Kumar, Saumesh Kumar, and Padam Kumar

SLA with Dual Party Beneficiality in Distributed Cloud 471
P. Varalakshmi, K.H. Priya, J. Pradeepa, and V. Perumal

Privacy Preserving Keyword Search over Encrypted Cloud Data 480
S. Ananthi, M. Sadish Sendil, and S. Karthik

Preventing Insider Attacks in the Cloud 488
Sudharsan Sundararajan, Hari Narayanan, Vipin Pavithran, Kaladhar Vorungati, and Krishnashree Achuthan

C2C (Cloud-to-Cloud): An Ecosystem of Cloud Service Providers for Dynamic Resource Provisioning 501
Ankur Gupta, Lohit Kapoor, and Manisha Wattal

Modeling Cloud SaaS with SOA and MDA 511
Ritu Sharma, Manu Sood, and Divya Sharma

Cognitive Radio and Cognitive Networks

Optimized Subcarrier Power Allocation in OFDM Underlay Cognitive Radio System 519
Dibyajnan Basak, Seba Maity, and Santi P. Maity

Multimedia Traffic Transmission over Cognitive Radio Networks Using Multiple Description Coding 529
Abdelaali Chaoub, Elhassane Ibn Elhaj, and Jamal El Abbadi

Cyber Forensics

Digital Image Evidence Detection Based on Skin Tone Filtering Technique 544
Digambar Povar, Divya S. Vidyadharan, and K.L. Thomas

BlackBerry Forensics: An Agent Based Approach for Database Acquisition 552
Satheesh Kumar Sasidharan and K.L. Thomas

Scattered Feature Space for Malware Analysis 562
P. Vinod, V. Laxmi, and M.S. Gaur

Database and Information Systems

Multilevel Policy Based Security in Distributed Database 572
Neera Batra and Manpreet Singh

Mining Indirect Positive and Negative Association Rules 581
B. Ramasubbareddy, A. Govardhan, and A. Ramamohanreddy

Application of FOP and AOP Methodologies in Concert for Developing Insurance Software Using Eclipse-Based Open Source Environment 592
Amita Sharma and S.S. Sarangdevot

Revisiting B-Trees 607
Kushal Gore, Pankaj Doke, and Sanjay Kimbahune

Multi-density Clustering Algorithm for Anomaly Detection Using KDD'99 Dataset 619
Santosh Kumar, Sumit Kumar, and Sukumar Nandi

LLAC: Lazy Learning in Associative Classification 631
S.P. Syed Ibrahim, K.R. Chandran, and R.V. Nataraj

Association Rule Mining Using Genetic Algorithm: The Role of Estimation Parameters 639
K. Indira and S. Kanmani

UDSCA: Uniform Distribution Based Spatial Clustering Algorithm 649
Animesh Tripathy, Sumit Kumar Maji, and Prashanta Kumar Patra

A Classification Model for Customer Segmentation 661
Chithra Ramaraju and Nickolas Savarimuthu

A Rough Set Based Approach for Ranking Decision Rules 671
M.K. Sabu and G. Raju

A Kernel Based Feature Selection Method Used in the Diagnosis of Wisconsin Breast Cancer Dataset 683
P. Jaganathan, N. Rajkumar, and R. Nagalakshmi

Comparative Study on Data Warehouse Evolution Techniques 691
Garima Thakur and Anjana Gosain

An Adaptive Framework for Clustering Data Streams 704
Chandrika and K.R. Ananda Kumar

Author Index 713

Table of Contents – Part II

Database and Information Systems

Balancing between Utility and Privacy for k-Anonymity 1
Korra Sathya Babu and Sanjay Kumar Jena

Evaluation of Approaches for Modeling of Security in Data Warehouses 9
Krishna Khajaria and Manoj Kumar

Content Based Compression for Quicx System 19
Radha Senthilkumar, C. Lingeshwaraa, and A. Kannan

Distributed Software Development

NL-Based Automated Software Requirements Elicitation and Specification 30
Ashfa Umber, Imran Sarwar Bajwa, and M. Asif Naeem

Automatic Interface Generation between Incompatible Intellectual Properties (IPs) from UML Models 40
Fateh Boutekkouk, Zakaria Tolba, and Mustapha Okab

Deadlock Prevention in Distributed Object Oriented Systems 48
V. Geetha and N. Sreenath

Identification of Error Prone Classes for Fault Prediction Using Object Oriented Metrics 58
Puneet Mittal, Satwinder Singh, and K.S. Kahlon

An Automated Tool for Computing Object Oriented Metrics Using XML 69
N. Kayarvizhy and S. Kanmani

Traceability Matrix for Regression Testing in Distributed Software Development 80
B. Athira and Philip Samuel

Testing Agent-Oriented Software by Measuring Agent's Property Attributes 88
N. Sivakumar, K. Vivekanandan, and S. Sandhya

Human Computer Interaction and Interface

Classifier Feature Extraction Techniques for Face Recognition System under Variable Illumination Conditions 99
Sneha G. Gondane, M. Dhivya, and D. Shyam

Bispectrum Analysis of EEG in Estimation of Hand Movement 109
Adity Saikia and Shyamanta M. Hazarika

Wavelet Selection for EMG Based Grasp Recognition through CWT 119
Adity Saikia, Nayan M. Kakoty, and Shyamanta M. Hazarika

Information Visualization for Tourist and Travelling in Indonesia 130
Adityo Ashari Wirjono, Ricky Lincoln Z.S., William, and Dewi Agushinta R.

The Smart Goal Monitoring System 138
Dewi Agushinta R., Bima Shakti Ramadhan Utomo, Denny Satria, Jennifer Sabrina Karla Karamoy, and Nuniek Nur Sahaya

Web Based Virtual Agent for Tourism Guide in Indonesia 146
Kezia Velda Roberta, Lulu Mawaddah Wisudawati, Muhammad Razi, and Dewi Agushinta R.

Local Feature or Mel Frequency Cepstral Coefficients - Which One is Better for MLN-Based Bangla Speech Recognition? 154
Foyzul Hassan, Mohammed Rokibul Alam Kotwal, Md. Mostafizur Rahman, Mohammad Nasiruddin, Md. Abdul Latif, and Mohammad Nurul Huda

Power Optimization Techniques for Segmented Digital Displays 162
Rohit Agrawal, C. Sasi Kumar, and Darshan Moodgal

Language Independent Icon-Based Interface for Accessing Internet 172
Santa Maiti, Debasis Samanta, Satya Ranjan Das, and Monalisa Sarma

Contribution of Oral Periphery on Visual Speech Intelligibility 183
Preety Singh, Deepika Gupta, V. Laxmi, and M.S. Gaur

ICT

Geo-Spatial Pattern Determination for SNAP Eligibility in Iowa Using GIS 191
Sugam Sharma, U.S. Tim, Shashi Gadia, and Patrick Smith

Project Management Model for e-Governance in the Context of Kerala State 201
Anu Paul and Varghese Paul

ICT Its Role in e-Governance and Rural Development 210
Deka Ganesh Chandra and Dutta Borah Malaya

Enhancing Sustainability of Software: A Case-Study with Monitoring Software for MGNREGS in India 223
C.K. Raju and Ashok Mishra

Internet and Web Computing

Proficient Discovery of Service in Event Driven Service Oriented Architecture 234
P. Dharanyadevi, P. Dhavachelvan, S.K.V. Jayakumar, R. Baskaran, and V.S.K. Venkatachalapathy

Web User Session Clustering Using Modified K-Means Algorithm 243
G. Poornalatha and Prakash S. Raghavendra

FOL-Mine – A More Efficient Method for Mining Web Access Pattern 253
A. Rajimol and G. Raju

Semantic Association Mining on Spatial Patterns in Medical Images 263
S. Saritha and G. SanthoshKumar

FCHC: A Social Semantic Focused Crawler 273
Anjali Thukral, Varun Mendiratta, Abhishek Behl, Hema Banati, and Punam Bedi

A Dynamic Seller Selection Model for an Agent Mediated e-Market 284
Vibha Gaur and Neeraj Kumar Sharma

A Modified Ontology Based Personalized Search Engine Using Bond Energy Algorithm 296
Bhaskara Rao Boddu and Valli Kumari Vatsavayi

A Client Perceived Performance Evaluation of Web Servers 307
Ash Mohammad Abbas and Ravindra Kumar

Enhanced Quality of Experience through IVR Mashup to Access Same Service Multiple Operator Services 317
Imran Ahmed and Sunil Kumar Kopparapu

Information Content Based Semantic Similarity Approaches for Multiple Biomedical Ontologies 327
K. Saruladha, G. Aghila, and A. Bhuvaneswary

Taking Project Tiger to the Classroom: A Virtual Lab Case Study 337
Harilal Parasuram, Bipin Nair, Krishnashree Achuthan, and Shyam Diwakar

Green Communications through Network Redesign 349
Sami J. Habib, Paulvanna N. Marimuthu, and Naser Zaeri

Unsupervised Modified Adaptive Floating Search Feature Selection 358
D. Devakumari and K. Thangavel

Fast and Efficient Mining of Web Access Sequences Using Prefix Based Minimized Trees 366
M. Thilagu and R. Nadarajan

Mobile Computing

Scalable, High Throughput LDPC Decoder for WiMAX (802.16e) Applications 374
Muhammad Awais, Ashwani Singh, and Guido Masera

Unique Mechanism of Selection of Traffic Flow Templates for Mobility IP Protocols Using Multihoming and IP Flow Mobility on the NGMN 386
Gustavo Jiménez and Yezid Donoso

Elliptic Curve Cryptography for Smart Phone OS 397
Sharmishta Desai, R.K. Bedi, B.N. Jagdale, and V.M. Wadhai

An Improved Secure Authentication Protocol for WiMAX with Formal Verification 407
Anjani Kumar Rai, Shivendu Mishra, and Pramod Narayan Tripathi

Secured Fault Tolerant Mobile Computing 417
Suparna Biswas and Sarmistha Neogy

A Survey of Virtualization on Mobiles 430
Suneeta Chawla, Apurv Nigam, Pankaj Doke, and Sanjay Kimbahune

Mobile Peer to Peer Spontaneous and Real-Time Social Networking 442
Abhishek Varshney and Mohammed Abdul Qadeer

Analysis of a Traffic Classification Scheme for QoS Provisioning over MANETs 452
Chhagan Lal, V. Laxmi, and M.S. Gaur

Multi Agent Systems

Modeling and Verification of Chess Game Using NuSMV 460
Vikram Saralaya, J.K. Kishore, Sateesh Reddy, Radhika M. Pai, and Sanjay Singh

SMMAG: SNMP-Based MPLS-TE Management Using Mobile Agents 471
Muhammad Tahir, Dominique Gaiti, and Majid Iqbal Khan

Multimedia and Video Systems

Face Detection and Eye Localization in Video by 3D Unconstrained Filter and Neural Network 480
Pradipta K. Banerjee, Jayanta K. Chandra, and Asit K. Datta

Secret Image Sharing Using Steganography with Different Cover Images 490
Noopa Jagadeesh, Aishwarya Nandakumar, P. Harmya, and S.S. Anju

A Secure Data Hiding Scheme Based on Combined Steganography and Visual Cryptography Methods 498
Aishwarya Nandakumar, P. Harmya, Noopa Jagadeesh, and S.S. Anju

Cognitive Environment for Pervasive Learners 506
Sattvik Sharma, R. Sreevathsan, M.V.V.N.S. Srikanth, C. Harshith, and T. Gireesh Kumar

A Robust Background Subtraction Approach Based on Daubechies Complex Wavelet Transform 516
Anand Singh Jalal and Vrijendra Singh

File System Level Circularity Requirement 525
Mukhtar Azeem, Majid Iqbal Khan, and Arfan Nazir

An Adaptive Steganographic Method for Color Images Based on LSB Substitution and Pixel Value Differencing 535
Azzat A. Al-Sadi and El-Sayed M. El-Alfy

Parallel and Distributed Algorithms

Communication Aware Co-scheduling for Parallel Job Scheduling in Cluster Computing 545
A. Neela Madheswari and R.S.D. Wahida Banu

Shared Resource Allocation Using Token Based Control Strategy in Augmented Ring Networks 555
Rajendra Prasath

An Algorithmic Approach to Minimize the Conflicts in an Optical Multistage Interconnection Network 568
Ved Prakash Bhardwaj, Nitin, and Vipin Tyagi

An Efficent Methodology for Realization of Parallel FFT for Large Data Set 577
Peter Joseph Basil Morris, Saikat Roy Chowdhury, and Debasish Deb

A Novel Approach for Adaptive Data Gathering in Sensor Networks by Dynamic Spanning Tree Switching 585
Suchetana Chakraborty and Sushanta Karmakar

Hardware Efficient Root-Raised-Cosine Pulse Shaping Filter for DVB-S2 Receivers 595
Vikas Agarwal, Pansoo Kim, Deock-Gil Oh, and Do-Seob Ahn

Security, Trust and Privacy

Security Analysis of Multimodal Biometric Systems against Spoof Attacks 604
Zahid Akhtar and Sandeep Kale

A Novel Copyright Protection Scheme Using Visual Cryptography 612
Amitava Nag, Jyoti Prakash Singh, Sushanta Biswas, D. Sarkar, and Partha Pratim Sarkar

A Weighted Location Based LSB Image Steganography Technique 620
Amitava Nag, Jyoti Prakash Singh, Srabani Khan, Saswati Ghosh, Sushanta Biswas, D. Sarkar, and Partha Pratim Sarkar

Comments on ID-Based Client Authentication with Key Agreement Protocol on ECC for Mobile Client-Server Environment 628
SK Hafizul Islam and G.P. Biswas

Covariance Based Steganography Using DCT 636
N. Sathisha, K. Suresh Babu, K.B. Raja, K.R. Venugopal, and L.M. Patnaik

An Efficient Algorithm to Enable Login into Secure Systems Using Mouse Gestures 648
Usha Banerjee and A. Swaminathan

Intrusion Detection by Pipelined Approach Using Conditional Random Fields and Optimization Using SVM 656
R. Jayaprakash and V. Uma

A Flow-Level Taxonomy and Prevalence of Brute Force Attacks 666
Jan Vykopal

Multi Application User Profiling for Masquerade Attack Detection 676
Hamed Saljooghinejad and Wilson Naik Rathore

A Novel Technique for Defeating Virtual Keyboards - Exploiting Insecure Features of Modern Browsers 685
Tanusha S. Nadkarni, Radhesh Mohandas, and Alwyn R. Pais

SQL Injection Disclosure Using BLAH Algorithm 693
Justy Jameson and K.K. Sherly

Author Index 703

Table of Contents – Part III

Security, Trust and Privacy

Chaotic Integrity Check Value 1
Prathuri Jhansi Rani and S. Durga Bhavani

An In-Depth Analysis of the Epitome of Online Stealth: Keyloggers; and Their Countermeasures 10
Kalpa Vishnani, Alwyn Roshan Pais, and Radhesh Mohandas

Cancelable Biometrics for Better Security and Privacy in Biometric Systems 20
Sanjay Ganesh Kanade, Dijana Petrovska-Delacrétaz, and Bernadette Dorizzi

Advanced Clustering Based Intrusion Detection (ACID) Algorithm 35
Samarjeet Borah, Debaditya Chakravorty, Chandan Chawhan, and Aritra Saha

Measuring the Deployment Hiccups of DNSSEC 44
Vasilis Pappas and Angelos D. Keromytis

Sensor Networks

Self-organizing MAC Protocol Switching for Performance Adaptation in Wireless Sensor Networks 54
Fan Yu and Subir Biswas

DFDNM: A Distributed Fault Detection and Node Management Scheme for Wireless Sensor Network 68
Indrajit Banerjee, Prasenjit Chanak, Biplab Kumar Sikdar, and Hafizur Rahaman

An Optimized Reduced Energy Consumption (OREC) Algorithm for Routing in Wireless Sensor Networks 82
Joydeep Banerjee, Swarup Kumar Mitra, Pradipta Ghosh, and Mrinal Kanti Naskar

Improving Energy Efficiency of Underwater Acoustic Sensor Networks Using Transmission Power Control: A Cross-Layer Approach 93
Sumi A. Samad, S.K. Shenoy, and G. Santhosh Kumar

A Collaborative, Secure and Energy Efficient Intrusion Detection Method for Homogeneous WSN 102
T. Mohamed Mubarak, Syed Abdul Sattar, Appa Rao, and M. Sajitha

An Efficient and Hybrid Key Management Scheme for Three Tier Wireless Sensor Networks Using LU Matrix 111
Manivannan Doraipandian, Ezhilarasie Rajapackiyam, P. Neelamegam, and Anuj Kumar Rai

Grey System Theory-Based Energy Map Construction for Wireless Sensor Networks 122
Vivek Katiyar, Narottam Chand, and Surender Soni

An Entropic Approach to Data Aggregation with Divergence Measure Based Clustering in Sensor Network 132
Adwitiya Sinha and D.K. Lobiyal

Energy Efficient Routing Protocols for Wireless Sensor Networks Using Spatial Correlation Based Collaborative Medium Access Control 143
A. Rajeswari and P.T. Kalaivaani

Signal and Image Processing

Palmprint Authentication by Phase Congruency Features 157
Jyoti Malik, G. Sainarayanan, and Ratna Dahiya

Design and Implementation of 3D DWT for 4D Image Based Noninvasive Surgery 168
P.X. Shajan, N.J.R. Muniraj, and John T. Abraham

Stratified SIFT Matching for Human Iris Recognition 178
Sambit Bakshi, Hunny Mehrotra, and Banshidhar Majhi

Quality Index Based Face Recognition under Varying Illumination Conditions 185
K.T. Dilna and T.D. Senthilkumar

Noise Adaptive Weighted Switching Median Filter for Removing High Density Impulse Noise 193
Madhu S. Nair and P.M. Ameera Mol

SMT-8036 Based Implementation of Secured Software Defined Radio System for Adaptive Modulation Technique 205
Sudhanshu Menta, Surbhi Sharma, and Rajesh Khanna

Abstraction of Exudates in Color Fundus Images 213
Richu Paul and S. Vasanthi

A Histogram Adaptation for Contrast Enhancement 221
Lisha Thomas and K. Santhi

Evaluating the Performance of a Speech Recognition Based System 230
Vinod Kumar Pandey and Sunil Kumar Kopparapu

Unified Approach in Food Quality Evaluation Using Machine Vision 239
Rohit R. Parmar, Kavindra R. Jain, and Chintan K. Modi

Mach-Zehnder Interferometer Based All-Optical Peres Gate 249
G.K. Maity, J.N. Roy, and S.P. Maity

Using PSO in Image Hiding Scheme Based on LSB Substitution 259
Punam Bedi, Roli Bansal, and Priti Sehgal

Matrix Embedding Using Random Linear Codes and Its Steganalysis ... 269
P. Harmya, S.S. Anju, Noopa Jagadeesh, and Aishwarya Nandakumar

An Efficient Directional Weighted Median Switching Filter for Impulse Noise Removal in Medical Images 276
Madhu S. Nair and J. Reji

An Improved Handwritten Text Line Segmentation Technique 289
M. Mohammadi, S.S. Mozaffari Chanijani, V.N. Manjunath Aradhya, and G.H. Kumar

Skew Estimation for Unconstrained Handwritten Documents 297
V.N. Manjunath Aradhya, C. Naveena, and S.K. Niranjan

Recognition of Simple and Conjunct Handwritten Malayalam Characters Using LCPA Algorithm 304
M. Abdul Rahiman and M.S. Rajasree

A Fuzzy Genetic Approach to Impulse Noise Removal 315
K.K. Anisha and M. Wilscy

Chain Code Histogram Based Facial Image Feature Extraction under Degraded Conditions 326
Soyuj Kumar Sahoo, Jitendra Jain, and S.R. Mahadeva Prasanna

Object Recognition Based on Fuzzy Morphological Polynomial Signal Representation 334
Chin-Pan Huang, Ping S. Huang, Chaur-Heh Hsieh, and Tsorng-Lin Chia

Face Detection for Skin-Toned Images Using Signature Functions 342
H.C. VijayLakshmi and Sudarshan PatilKulkarni

Recurrent Neural Network Based Phoneme Recognition Incorporating Articulatory Dynamic Parameters 349
Mohammed Rokibul Alam Kotwal, Foyzul Hassan, Md. Mahabubul Alam, Abdur Rahman Khan Jehad, Md. Arifuzzaman, and Mohammad Nurul Huda

Gaussian Noise and Haar Wavelet Transform Image Compression on Transmission of Dermatological Images 357
Kamil Dimililer and Cemal Kavalcioğlu

Image Processing Techniques for Glaucoma Detection 365
Mishra Madhusudhan, Nath Malay, S.R. Nirmala, and Dandapat Samerendra

Transmitter Preprocessing Assisted MIMO SDMA Systems over Frequency-Selective Channels 374
Shriram Swaminathan, Suraj Krishnan, and Prabagarane Nagaradjane

A Fuzzy Neuro Clustering Based Vector Quantization for Face Recognition 383
Elizabeth B. Varghese and M. Wilscy

3D Face Recognition Using Orientation Maps 396
B.H. Shekar, N. Harivinod, and M. Sharmila Kumari

The Optimal Wavelet for Speech Compression 406
Shijo M. Joseph and P. Babu Anto

Skew Angle Estimation and Correction for Noisy Document Images 415
M. Manomathi and S. Chitrakala

Face Recognition Using ATP Feature Set under Difficult Lighting Conditions 425
Lincy Thomas and Komathy Karuppanan

Classification of Mammogram Images Using Discrete Wavelet Transformations 435
K.K. Rajkumar and G. Raju

Optimized Trace Transform Based Feature Extraction Architecture for CBIR 444
Meena S. Maralappanavar, K. Pramod, and K. Linganagouda

Multi-algorithm Fusion for Speech Emotion Recognition 452
Gyanendra K. Verma, U.S. Tiwary, and Shaishav Agrawal

Combining Chain-Code and Fourier Descriptors for Fingerprint Matching 460
C.Z. Geevar and P. Sojan Lal

Facial Emotion Recognition Using Different Multi-resolution Transforms 469
Gyanendra K. Verma, U.S. Tiwary, and Mahendra K. Rai

Robust Watermarking through Spatially Disjoint Transformations 478
Reena Gunjan, Saurabh Maheshwari, Vijay Laxmi, and M.S. Gaur

Soft Computing Techniques

An ANN Based Approach to Calculate Robotic Fingers Positions 488
Ankit Chaudhary, J.L. Raheja, Kunal Singal, and Shekhar Raheja

Word Classification Using Neural Network 497
A. Muthamizh Selvan and R. Rajesh

Very Short Term Wind Power Forecasting Using PSO-Neural Network Hybrid System 503
E. Pratheepraj, Anuj Abraham, S.N. Deepa, and V. Yuvaraj

A Class of Recurrent Neural Network (RNN) Architectures with SOM for Estimating MIMO Channels 512
Kandarpa Kumar Sarma and Abhijit Mitra

An Efficient Framework for Prediction in Healthcare Data Using Soft Computing Techniques 522
Veena H. Bhat, Prasanth G. Rao, S. Krishna, P. Deepa Shenoy, K.R. Venugopal, and L.M. Patnaik

Process Oriented Guided Inquiry Learning for Soft Computing......... 533
Clifton Kussmaul

A Modified and Efficient Shuffled Frog Leaping Algorithm (MSFLA) for Unsupervised Data Clustering 543
Suresh Chittineni, Dinesh Godavarthi, A.N.S. Pradeep, Suresh Chandra Satapathy, and P.V.G.D. Prasad Reddy

Neighborhood Search Assisted Particle Swarm Optimization (NPSO) Algorithm for Partitional Data Clustering Problems 552
R. Karthi, C. Rajendran, and K. Rameshkumar

System Software

Portability in Incremental Compilers 562
P.R. Mahalingam and C. Unnikrishnan

Test Case Optimization Using Artificial Bee Colony Algorithm 570
Adi Srikanth, Nandakishore J. Kulkarni, K. Venkat Naveen, Puneet Singh, and Praveen Ranjan Srivastava

Vehicular Communications Networks

Adaptive Power Allocation in CI/MC-CDMA System Using Genetic Algorithms 580
Santi P. Maity and Sumanta Hati

PHY Abstraction for MIMO Based OFDM Systems 590
Tarun kumar Juluru and Anitha Sheela Kankacharla

Level Crossing Rate in Land Mobile Satellite Channel with a Modified Nakagami-Lognormal Distribution 601
Sayantan Hazra and Abhijit Mitra

Cache Invalidation for Location Dependent and Independent Data in IVANETS 609
Anurag Singh, Narottam Chand, and Lalit Kr Awasthi

VCAR: Scalable and Adaptive Data Dissemination for VANET 615
K. Naveen and Komathy Karuppanan

Efficient Distributed Group Authentication Protocol for Vehicular Ad Hoc Network 624
Priya Karunanithi and Komathy Karuppanan

Opportunistic Dissemination for Accident Management Using Vehicular Networks 634
R. Namritha and Komathy Karuppanan

Machine Learning Approach for Multiple Misbehavior Detection in VANET 644
Jyoti Grover, Nitesh Kumar Prajapati, Vijay Laxmi, and Manoj Singh Gaur

Improved Position-Based Routing in Vehicular Ad Hoc Networks Using P-DIR Method 654
Ram Shringar Raw and D.K. Lobiyal

IMS and Presence Service Integration on Intelligent Transportation Systems for Future Services 664
Andrés Garcia, José Santa, Antonio Moragón, and Antonio Fernando Gómez-Skarmeta

Author Index 677

Table of Contents – Part IV

Position Papers

Impact of Node Density on Node Connectivity in MANET Routing Protocols 1
G. Jisha and Philip Samuel

Survey and Comparison of Frameworks in Software Architecture 9
S. Roselin Mary and Paul Rodrigues

Two Layered Hierarchical Model for Cognitive Wireless Sensor Networks 19
K. Vinod Kumar, G. Lakshmi Phani, K. Venkat Sayeesh, Aparna Chaganty, and G. Rama Murthy

3D-CGIN: A 3 Disjoint Paths CGIN with Alternate Source 25
Meenal A. Borkar and Nitin

Architecture for Running Multiple Applications on a Single Wireless Sensor Network: A Proposal 37
Sonam Tobgay, Rasmus L. Olsen, and Ramjee Prasad

Feature Based Image Retrieval Algorithm 46
P.U. Nimi and C. Tripti

Exploiting ILP in a SIMD Type Vector Processor 56
Abel Palaty, Mohammad Suaib, and Kumar Sambhav Pandey

An Extension to Global Value Numbering 63
Saranya D. Krishnan and Shimmi Asokan

Data Privacy for Grid Systems 70
N. Sandeep Chaitanya, S. Ramachandram, B. Padmavathi, S. Shiva Skandha, and G. Ravi Kumar

Towards Multimodal Capture, Annotation and Semantic Retrieval from Performing Arts 79
Rajkumar Kannan, Frederic Andres, Fernando Ferri, and Patrizia Grifoni

A New Indian Model for Human Intelligence 89
Jai Prakash Singh

Stepping Up Internet Banking Security Using Dynamic Pattern Based Image Steganography 98
P. Thiyagarajan, G. Aghila, and V. Prasanna Venkatesan

A Combinatorial Multi-objective Particle Swarm Optimization Based Algorithm for Task Allocation in Distributed Computing Systems 113
Rahul Roy, Madhabananda Das, and Satchidananda Dehuri

Enhancement of BARTERCAST Using Reinforcement Learning to Effectively Manage Freeriders 126
G. Sreenu, P.M. Dhanya, and Sabu M. Thampi

A Novel Approach to Represent Detected Point Mutation 137
Dhanya Sudarsan, P.R. Mahalingam, and G. Jisha

Anonymous and Secured Communication Using OLSR in MANET 145
A.A. Arifa Azeez, Elizabeth Isaac, and Sabu M. Thampi

Bilingual Translation System for Weather Report (For English and Tamil) 155
S. Saraswathi, M. Anusiya, P. Kanivadhana, and S. Sathiya

Design of QRS Detection and Heart Rate Estimation System on FPGA 165
Sudheer Kurakula, A.S.D.P. Sudhansh, Roy Paily, and S. Dandapat

Multi-document Text Summarization in E-Learning System for Operating System Domain 175
S. Saraswathi, M. Hemamalini, S. Janani, and V. Priyadharshini

Improving Hadoop Performance in Handling Small Files 187
Neethu Mohandas and Sabu M. Thampi

Studies of Management for Dynamic Circuit Networks 195
Ana Elisa Ferreira, Anilton Salles Garcia, and Carlos Alberto Malcher Bastos

International Workshop on Identity: Security, Management and Applications (ID 2011)

Game Theoretic Approach to Resolve Energy Conflicts in Ad-Hoc Networks 205
Juhi Gupta, Ishan Kumar, and Anil Kacholiya

Software Secureness for Users: Significance in Public ICT Applications 211
C.K. Raju and P.B.S. Bhadoria

Vector Space Access Structure and ID Based Distributed DRM Key Management 223
Ratna Dutta, Dheerendra Mishra, and Sourav Mukhopadhyay

Multiple Secrets Sharing with Meaningful Shares 233
Jaya and Anjali Sardana

On Estimating Strength of a DDoS Attack Using Polynomial Regression Model 244
B.B. Gupta, P.K. Agrawal, A. Mishra, and M.K. Pattanshetti

Finding New Solutions for Services in Federated Open Systems Interconnection 250
Zubair Ahmad Khattak, Jamalul-lail Ab Manan, and Suziah Sulaiman

Duplicate File Names-A Novel Steganographic Data Hiding Technique 260
Avinash Srinivasan and Jie Wu

A Framework for Securing Web Services by Formulating an Collaborative Security Standard among Prevailing WS-* Security Standards 269
M. Priyadharshini, R. Baskaran, Madhan Kumar Srinivasan, and Paul Rodrigues

Improved Web Search Engine by New Similarity Measures 284
Vijayalaxmi Kakulapati, Ramakrishna Kolikipogu, P. Revathy, and D. Karunanithi

International Workshop on Applications of Signal Processing (I-WASP 2011)

Recognition of Subsampled Speech Using a Modified Mel Filter Bank ... 293
Kiran Kumar Bhuvanagiri and Sunil Kumar Kopparapu

Tumor Detection in Brain Magnetic Resonance Images Using Modified Thresholding Techniques 300
C.L. Biji, D. Selvathi, and Asha Panicker

Generate Vision in Blind People Using Suitable Neuroprosthesis Implant of BIOMEMS in Brain 309
B. Vivekavardhana Reddy, Y.S. Kumara Swamy, and N. Usha

Undecimated Wavelet Packet for Blind Speech Separation Using Independent Component Analysis 318
Ibrahim Missaoui and Zied Lachiri

A Robust Framework for Multi-object Tracking 329
Anand Singh Jalal and Vrijendra Singh

SVM Based Classification of Traffic Signs for Realtime Embedded Platform 339
Rajeev Kumaraswamy, Lekhesh V. Prabhu, K. Suchithra, and P.S. Sreejith Pai

A Real Time Video Stabilization Algorithm 349
Tarun Kancharla and Sanjyot Gindi

Object Classification Using Encoded Edge Based Structural Information 358
Aditya R. Kanitkar, Brijendra K. Bharti, and Umesh N. Hivarkar

Real Time Vehicle Detection for Rear and Forward Collision Warning Systems 368
Gaurav Kumar Yadav, Tarun Kancharla, and Smita Nair

PIN Generation Using Single Channel EEG Biometric 378
Ramaswamy Palaniappan, Jenish Gosalia, Kenneth Revett, and Andrews Samraj

International Workshop on Cloud Computing: Architecture, Algorithms and Applications (CloudComp 2011)

A Framework for Intrusion Tolerance in Cloud Computing 386
Vishal M. Karande and Alwyn R. Pais

Application of Parallel K-Means Clustering Algorithm for Prediction of Optimal Path in Self Aware Mobile Ad-Hoc Networks with *Link Stability* 396
Likewin Thomas and B. Annappa

Clouds' Infrastructure Taxonomy, Properties, and Management Services 406
Imad M. Abbadi

A Deduced SaaS Lifecycle Model Based on Roles and Activities 421
Jie Song, Tiantian Li, Lulu Jia, and Zhiliang Zhu

Towards Achieving Accountability, Auditability and Trust in Cloud Computing 432
Ryan K.L. Ko, Bu Sung Lee, and Siani Pearson

Cloud Computing Security Issues and Challenges: A Survey 445
Amandeep Verma and Sakshi Kaushal

A Deadline and Budget Constrained Cost and Time Optimization Algorithm for Cloud Computing 455
Venkatarami Reddy Chintapalli

International Workshop on Multimedia Streaming (MultiStreams 2011)

A Bit Modification Technique for Watermarking Images and Streaming Video 463
Kaliappan Gopalan

Efficient Video Copy Detection Using Simple and Effective Extraction of Color Features 473
R. Roopalakshmi and G. Ram Mohana Reddy

Mobile Video Service Disruptions Control in Android Using JADE 481
Tatiana Gualotuña, Diego Marcillo, Elsa Macías López, and Alvaro Suárez-Sarmiento

Performance Analysis of Video Protocols over IP Transition Mechanisms 491
Hira Sathu and Mohib A. Shah

Performance Comparison of Video Protocols Using Dual-Stack and Tunnelling Mechanisms 501
Hira Sathu, Mohib A. Shah, and Kathiravelu Ganeshan

IPTV End-to-End Performance Monitoring 512
Priya Gupta, Priyadarshini Londhe, and Arvind Bhosale

A Color Image Encryption Technique Based on a Substitution-Permutation Network 524
J. Mohamedmoideen Kader Mastan, G.A. Sathishkumar, and K. Bhoopathy Bagan

Second International Workshop on Trust Management in P2P Systems (IWTMP2PS 2011)

Comment on the Improvement of an Efficient ID-Based RSA Mutlisignature 534
Chenglian Liu, Marjan Kuchaki Rafsanjani, and Liyun Zheng

A Secure Routing Protocol to Combat Byzantine and Black Hole Attacks for MANETs 541
Jayashree Padmanabhan, Tamil Selvan Raman Subramaniam, Kumaresh Prakasam, and Vigneswaran Ponpandiyan

A Convertible Designated Verifible Blind Multi-signcryption Scheme 549
Subhalaxmi Das, Sujata Mohanty, and Bansidhar Majhi

Middleware Services at Cloud Application Layer 557
Imad M. Abbadi

Attribute Based Anonymity for Preserving Privacy 572
Sri Krishna Adusumalli and V. Valli Kumari

An Anonymous Authentication and Communication Protocol for Wireless Mesh Networks 580
Jaydip Sen

Data Dissemination and Power Management in Wireless Sensor Networks 593
M. Guerroumi, N. Badache, and S. Moussaoui

Performance Evaluation of ID Assignment Schemes for Wireless Sensor Networks 608
Rama Krishna Challa and Rakesh Sambyal

Author Index 617

An Enhanced Port Hiding Design to Handle DoS Attacks in an Ad-Hoc Environment

Jayashree Padmanabhan, Abhinaya Sukumar, Ezhilarasi Elumalai, and Sunanda Ramesh

Department of Computer Technology
Madras Institute of Technology, Anna University, India
pjshree@annauniv.edu

Abstract. In environments like virtual classrooms and defence areas, an ad-hoc cloud is increasingly being deployed. Ad-hoc cloud is prone to Denial of Service (DoS) attacks caused by addition of illegitimate clients to the cloud and busty requests from a single or multi-client. In this paper a client transparent approach is proposed using enhanced port hiding technique to mitigate these attacks and attain high performance in the ad-hoc cloud. Admission control is performed to bring control on the number of clients joining the ad-hoc cloud. A fair service to all requests of clients is achieved by a combined scheduling and congestion control mechanism for which wireless Greedy Primal Dual Algorithm (wGPD) is deployed and the algorithm achieves a greater hit ratio of 85 percent. A modified RTS/CTS technique suiting ad-hoc environment is also discussed to handle the hidden and exposed terminal problems.

Keywords: ad-hoc cloud, Port key, challenge server, trust token, Hide-port, DoS, Cluster head, scheduling, congestion, RTS/CTS.

1 Introduction

A decentralised wireless network without an infrastructure where the mobile stations form a network by directly communicating and coordinating with each other is called an ad-hoc network. The topology of an ad-hoc network changes dynamically and this lack of a concrete infrastructure makes it easy for intruders to conjoin the network making dependability a critical issue. Over the years many secure protocols to address various security issues have been deployed with a continuous effort to develop a hack proof network. In this paper an enhanced port hiding technique for admission control of clients along with a combined scheduling and congestion control technique to secure an ad-hoc cloud against DoS attacks is proposed.

2 Dependability

Dependability can be defined as a property that addresses the attributes confidentiality, availability, integrity, reliability and maintainability. The confidential data for a

A. Abraham et al. (Eds.): ACC 2011, Part I, CCIS 190, pp. 1–10, 2011.

client must only be accessible by the destined user. Data Integrity ensures that the message is not tampered in the network. Availability ensures that the system functions even in the presence of malicious nodes. Consistent network performance with minimal degradation ensures reliability. How fast a network restores from failure shows its maintainability. The major threat to availability is Denial of Service (DoS) attack.

3 Denial of Service Attacks

Ad-hoc networks due to their dynamic configuration of topology are more prone to intruders conjoining the network. These illegitimate nodes can target bottleneck network resources and bandwidth causing Denial of Service to legitimate nodes. Ad-hoc networks are less secure as each of the end nodes also acts as routers and there are no predetermined central controls. This can lead to poisoning of routing information and massive flooding of request resulting in complete breakdown of the response rate of requests. Hence bringing lightweight control on the number of nodes entering the network and proper congestion control techniques is important to prevent Denial of Service (DoS) attacks.

4 Proposed Architectural Design

The architectural design is given in fig 1. In the proposed system, resilience to DoS attacks is achieved by using an enhanced port hiding design along with a combined scheduling and congestion control technique. The very first request from a client side browser is directed to a challenge server which presents an image challenge to the client. On solving the image challenge, the client receives a trust token embedded

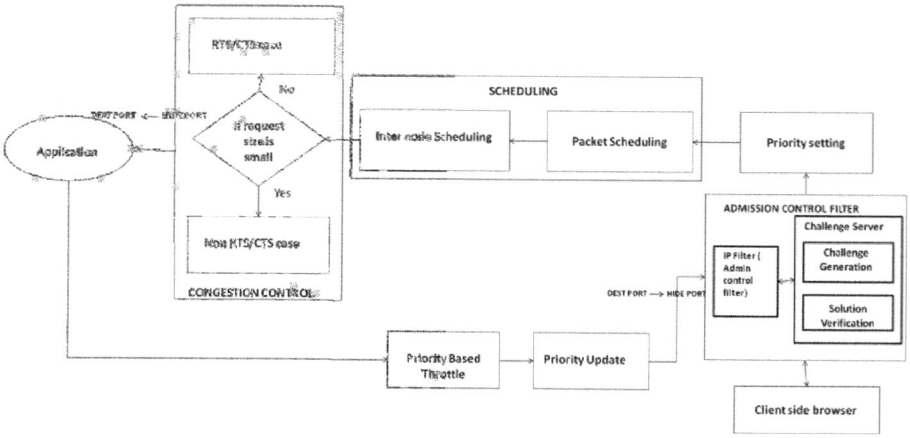

Fig. 1. Architectural Design

cookie. This trust token is used in all further requests from the client and the trust token is valid only for a stipulated period of time after which the trust token needs to be renewed. The IP filter uses the trust token along with the client IP , server IP, destination port number and time of request to generate a *hide port number* which is embedded into the destination port number field of the request. So any client can now access the application only by knowing the hide port number. The requests are forwarded to the priority setting phase where each request is assigned priority based on the priority of the corresponding client, nature of the request and the validity of the trust token. This is termed as the initial level priority.

After priority setting, the requests need to be scheduled for determining the order in which they can be serviced. This occurs in two phases namely, packet scheduling and inter node scheduling. Packet scheduling involves determining which packet among those queued at a particular node is to be serviced next and inter node scheduling determines which node among all competing nodes can be allowed to access the wireless medium.

A wireless medium is prone to hidden and exposed terminal problems. Hence to address this in the ad-hoc cloud, a modified RTS/CTS based congestion avoidance is used. Also if the request size is very small, a non RTS/CTS based scheme using broadcasted requests and piggy backed acknowledgements is used.

5 Admission Control

5.1 Challenge Server

Selecting a node from the ad-hoc cloud to act as the challenge server is important. . A distributed score based clustering algorithm for mobile ad-hoc networks (DSBCA) is used [2] .The node is selected depending on factors like the Battery Remaining, Number of Neighbours, Number of Members, and Stability. The score of node *N* is defined as Equation [2]

$$\text{Score} = ((Br\times C1) + (Nn\times C2) + (S\times C3) + (Nm\times C4)) \tag{1}$$

Where C1, C2, C3, C4 are the score factors ,B_r is the Battery Remaining ,N_n is the Number of Neighbours, N_m is the Number of Members (N_m), S is the Stability that determines how long a node stays in its transmission range .S is defined as

Equation

$$S = \sum_{i=1}^{n} T \qquad \text{where,} T = T_{RF} - T_{RL}$$

Where n is the number of node's neighbours, T_{RF} is the time of the first packet reception and T_{RL} is the time of the last packet reception.

Distributed Score Based Clustering Algorithm for cluster head selection:

```
Step 1:(Updating Neighbourhood table)
 Flag=0
 While(Timer not expired)
{If (Score received)
  {Insert node_score_value pair into
  Neighbourhood table
    Flag=1}
}
If (Flag==0)
{ Drop node from the Neighbourhood table }

Step 2: (Calculating Score value)
Calculate score for every node i
Broadcast message (node_id,Score)

Step 3: (Selecting cluster head)
choose node with highest score as cluster head from
Neighbourhood table
Broadcast message (node_id,Clusterhead_id, init time)

Step 4. (Broadcasting messages)
Broadcast type_of_node message (node_id, is-border, is-
Clusterhead)

Step 5: Calculating new timer value
If (node_type==CH)
{ Local_density=Nm +1
  Timer_value = ((step duration × b ×
  local_density )+ i)}
If(node_type==border node)
  Timer_value = Random (1600, current_time of  cluster
head's timer)
If(node_type==ordinary node)
  Timer_value = Random (200, initial time of cluster
head's timer)
```

5.2 IP Filter

In the proposed architecture, IP Filter performs two operations. The operations include filtering packets based on (i) the destination port number and (ii) the node's priority level. Hence, most of the packets from nodes that do not know their port key would be dropped at the IP filter (firewall). Filtering packets at the firewall greatly reduces the memory utilization, CPU power and network resources. As the request packet is checked at IP layer, traversal through the entire networking stack is preserved thereby saving the processing power.

5.3 Challenge Phase

Here user authentication is done using PHP scripting. The user id and password are encrypted and stored in database. The password checking is followed by presentation of an image challenge to the user. The Challenge presented for every user is to select a series of images in a certain order. Based on order of clicking images a unique value is computed for every client and this remains to be the identifier for the client. Thus unmanned attacks targeting the database cannot easily guess the challenge as the order of choosing and the image chosen are hidden and only known to the conscious legitimate client. On solving the image challenge the client is authenticated and request is forwarded to the IP filter. This proposed technique is more secure than capcha scheme for authentication, as the captcha are can be easily solved by image recognition software and are proven prone to unmanned attacks.

5.4 Hide Port Generation

The hide port number is constructed using a pseudo random function (PRF) *H* of the client IP address (*cip*), server IP address (*sip*), and current time of request (*t*) and the actual destination port [1] :

$$\text{hide port} = \text{dest port} \oplus H_k\,(\text{cip, sip, } t_{nb}). \tag{2}$$

The hide port number changes every t_{nb} seconds. So even if the code is guessed right by the user once, that information will not be valid for the next time period. Hence, one can filter out illegitimate packets based on the reconstructed destination port number *dest port*.

5.5 Trust Token

A trust token (*tt*) is constructed as follows [1]

$$\text{tt} = \text{cip, sip, tv, priority, } H_{MK}(\text{cip, sip, tv, priority}) \tag{3}$$

Here *tv* denotes the time at which the trust token was issued, *MK* is a confidential cryptographic key. The priority-level is taken to be combination of throughput priority level priority_{thru} and response time priority level.

A client gets an initial trust token (tt) by solving a challenge, and the token is then embedded into a HTTP cookie in the client-side browser. The client uses this token (tt) in all the HTTP requests to the server. Next check for valid trust token is done. A trust token is valid if tt.tv is less than the current time. Also the tt.cip and tt.sip must match with the client's IP and server IP addresses respectively. Otherwise the request packet is served at the lowest priority level.

6 Congestion Control

A joint congestion control and scheduling technique is proposed for bringing a fair channel access. An inter node scheduling mechanism is used to determine the node which can gain access to the channel. If a node gains access to channel, packet scheduling is done to determine which packet among those queued at the particular node has to be sent next. Finally, the congestion control mechanism determines how much data can be injected into the network at the particular instant. This joint scheduling and congestion control is based on the adaptive wireless Greedy primal Dual Algorithm proposed based on the greedy primal algorithm for for dynamic resource allocation in complex networks.

6.1 Adaptive Wireless Greedy Primal Dual Algorithm

The scheduling algorithm involves two phases (i) Intra node and (ii) packet scheduling. Each node maintains a per destination queue (PDQ). The per-destination queue at node i, denoted Q^{i}_{d}, stores all the packets at node i that have address d as their destination. Let q^{i}_{d} be the amount of data in the queue. Let $n(i,d)$ be the next hop for destination-d bound traffic after it leaves node i. Each PDQ has an associated concept of urgency weight. The urgency weight for queue Q^{i}_{d} is denoted by w^{i}_{d} and is defined by [4]

$$w^{i}_{d} = [\, q^{i}_{d} - q^{n(i,d)}_{d} \,]\, r_{i,n(i,d)} \quad (4)$$

Thus the urgency weight is taken to be the difference of the PDQ size at the current node and the associated PDQ size at the downstream node, multiplied by the channel rate between the two nodes. In the adaptive algorithm urgency weight is used to greedily select an optimal node based on the PDQ size for effectively selecting the next node for handover of challenge server properties and to determine the next scheduled node.

Inter Node Scheduling

This used to determine which node can gain access to channel next if multiple nodes have data to transmit. The node with maximum urgency weight among all competing transmissions is chosen.

Packet Scheduling

The intra node scheduling is used to determine which data packet among those queued at a particular node is to be sent next. The packet with maximum positive w^{i}_{d} chosen here.

RTS/CTS Based Congestion Control

To tackle the problems of hidden and exposed terminal problems in the ad-hoc cloud control and data phases for data transfer are used. The nodes send their requests in a contention period and send data packets in a contention-free period and a state transition mechanism supports a change between contention and contention-free phases.

Control phase (Contention period)
The node continuously senses the medium. If it overhears RTS from other nodes it adds its priority class to a data structure called priority information table and waits to hear RACK (RTS Acknowledgement). If its own packet's priority class is higher than that packet's priority class and the medium is idle, it sends its RTS. Otherwise, it initiates a DIFS timer. If a node does not receive a RACK it implies collision and the back-off timer is initiated. If the medium is idle on expiry of timer, RTS is resent. After receiving a RACK, the node waits for two consecutive DIFS time periods and the data phase then starts. If the medium is sensed idle for two consecutive DIFS periods it means there are no packets with higher priority or lower priority classes and all packets have exchanged their priority information.

Data phase (Contention free period)
Using the priority information from PIT, the sender sends packet and receives the DACK from the receiver. After data phase, next turn control phase begins and the cycle goes on.

Non RTS/CTS case
If the request size is small RTS/CTS is not used and data packets themselves are broadcast along with back pressure mechanism and the ACK packets are piggy backed with the data packets itself .

6.2 Priority Update

Once the request is serviced by the application, the server sends a response to a client with updated priority level. The cost function used is, [1]

$$C(rq) = ut - \gamma * nrt \tag{5}$$

Where *nrt* denotes the normalized response time and γ is a tune-able parameter. The new priority level is computed as *priority* = *g(priority, C)*, where priority is the current effective priority level of the client. When the client behaves properly, the priority increases in an additive fashion. Otherwise the priority is multiplicatively decreased.

$$\text{If } C(rq) \geq 0, \text{ priority} = \text{priority} + \alpha * C(rq)$$
$$\text{Else priority} = \text{priority} / \beta * (1 - C(rq))$$

7 Results

The graph in fig 4 gives the throughput response comparison while using TCP 802.11 standard for wireless networks and the proposed adaptive wGPD algorithm. While using adaptive wireless Greedy Primal Dual algorithm (wGPD), the throughput is found to remain constant after a certain threshold and does not drop off, proving lesser number of collisions. This stabilization of throughput even with increased number of nodes is accounted due to the greedy scheduling of nodes based on local optimal values thereby giving early stabilization in the cloud despite the dynamically changing topology. As the priority update is done after every response to request, misbehaving clients get into a low priority state very soon. The request hit to miss ratio of legitimate clients is found to be more than 80 percent as in fig 3 for scenarios scalable up to 100 nodes in the ad-hoc cloud. But the memory utilization in using PIT in challenge server selection phase proves to be an overhead refining which will be the future work in this project. Also modification of the basic RTS/CTS and the standard TCP protocols and its implementation in real time scenario is being worked upon. Fig 2 shows that the number of packets transmitted increases upon application of congestion control. It also describes the reduction in packet transfer during hand over (hand over between challenge servers due to mobility) and during the time interval when hide port gets regenerated. The packet transmission time and time for hand over process are decreased, when the number of nodes in ad-hoc cloud is increased.

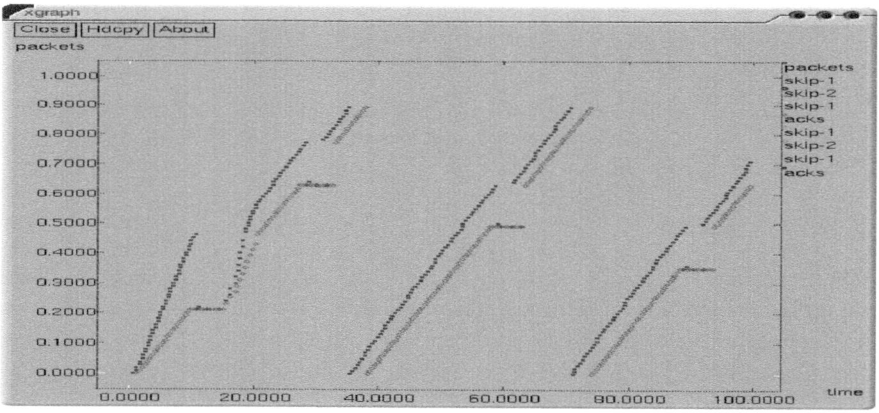

Fig. 2. Packet transmission with hide port design and congestion control

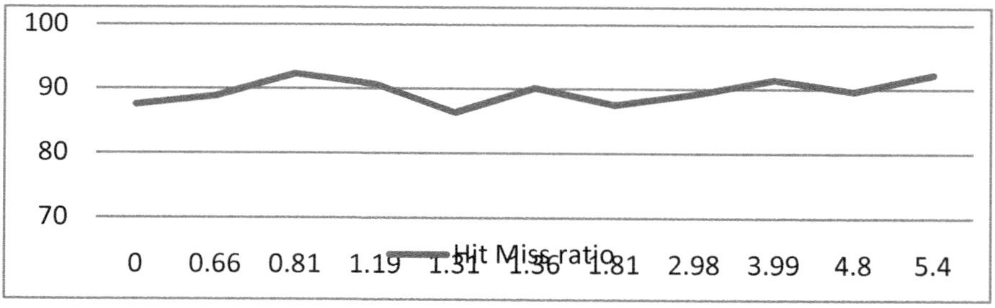

Fig. 3. Hit miss ratio in packet transmission

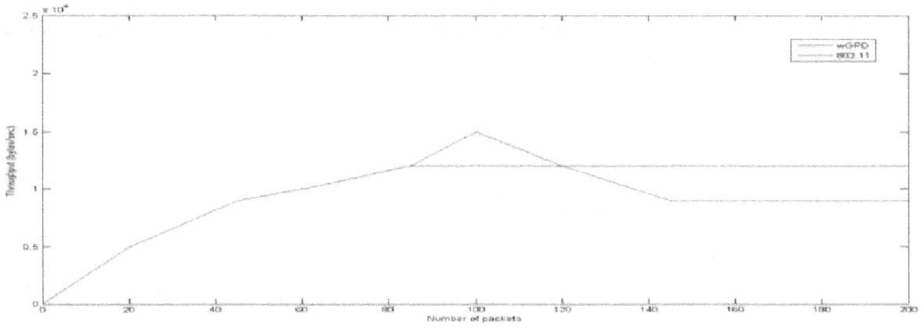

Fig. 4. Throughput versus number of packets in using standard TCP and adaptive wGPD algorithm

8 Conclusion

The proposed scheme affectively handles DoS attacks by initially authenticating the nodes into the ad-hoc cloud using admission control and further bringing control on request they send by using an effective scheduling and congestion control mechanism. This technique is found to give effective throughput in terms of number of packets serviced even with a highly populated cloud and is shown to stabilize with time. As the congestion control is a greedy approach, convergence to optimal state occurs sooner. Also as the hide port is regenerated after regular intervals of time, the use of old trust tokens by any malicious node are prevented and also priority of such clients is multiplicatively decreased leading to effective congestion control. Hence a fair service is ensured to all legitimate users preventing DoS attacks efficiently with a high hit ratio for legitimate requests.

Also the image challenge proposed in this paper prevents any possible unmanned attacks which are a main means of DoS attack emerging in the internet world today.

The future work is based on two dimensions, first to improve the scalability to greater than 100 nodes by refining the data structure used for PIT and PDQ. Second is to modify the RTS/CTS scheme more suitable for an ad-hoc environment by reducing the number of control packets.

References

1. Srivatsa, M., Iyengar, A., Yin, J.: Mtigating Appilcation-Level Denial of Service Attacks on Web Servers: A Client-Transparent Approach. ACM Transaction on the Web 2(3), Article 15 (2008)
2. Adabi, S., Jabbehdari, S., Rahmani, A., Adabi, S.: A Novel Distributed Clustering Algorithm for Mobile Ad-hoc Networks. Journal of Computer Science 4(2), 161–166 (2008)
3. Yin, J., Zeng, Q.-A., Agrawal, D.P.: A Novel Priority based Scheduling Scheme for Ad Hoc Networks. In: Cincinnati, OBR Center for Distributed and Mobile Computing. IEEE, Los Alamitos (2003)

4. Akyol, U., Andrews, M., Gupta, P., Hobby, J., Saniee, I., Stolyar, A.: Joint Scheduling and Congestion Control in Mobile Ad-Hoc Networks. In: 27th Conference on Computer Communications, IEEE, INFOCOM (2008)
5. Elizabeth, Y.S., Belding-Royer, M., Perkins, C.E.: Internet Connectivity for Ad hoc Mobile Networks. International Journal of Wireless Information Networks 9(2) (2002)
6. Stolyar, A.L.: Maximizing Queueing Network Utility Subject to Stabality: Greedy Primal-Dual Algorithm. Queueing Systems 50, 401–457 (2005)

An Efficient Routing Protocol for Ad-Hoc Networks

Chiranjeev Kumar[1], Neeraj Tyagi[2], Rajeev Tripathi[2], M. Lakshmi Prasanth Kumar[2], Dhirendra Kumar Sharma[1], and Sanjay Kumar Biswash[1]

[1] Indian School of Mines (ISM), Dhanbad – 826 004, Jharkhand (India)
[2] Motilal Nehru National Institute of Technology (MNNIT), Allahabad – 211 004, UP (India)
k_chiranjeev@yahoo.co.uk

Abstract. A mobile ad-hoc network is infrastructure less, self organizable, multi hop packet switched network. In ad-hoc network, node movements results in dynamic topology and frequent link failures. Studies shows that on demand protocols perform better compared to table driven protocols. Ad-hoc On Demand Routing (AODV) is one of the popular on demand routing protocol. In this paper, we have proposed an innovative method by considering the MAC layer feed back to reduce the route discovery latency and routing overhead of AODV protocol. Also proposed a new approach of preemptive route maintenance to mitigate the delays and overhead incurred during the original AODV. We implemented and simulated the proposed scheme in NS2. Simulation results show that the proposed scheme performs better than AODV.

Keywords. Ad-Hoc networks, TTL, route discovery, route maintenance, ring search technique.

1 Introduction

Wireless networks have become popular in recent years due to advances in portable computing and wireless technology. But the presence of a fixed supporting structure limits the adaptability of wireless systems. Ad-hoc network can be considered as a special type of wireless mesh networks which is a collection of mobile wireless nodes formed without any infrastructure or any standard services.

Mobile Ad-hoc Networks (MANETs) are decentralized and mobile node (MN) act as router and also as host. The MNs can transmit the packets to the nodes which are in its proximity. If a MN has to send the packet to other MNs which are out of its range then the nodes within its range forwards packets to the next hop until packets reaches intended destination. Thus MANET are also called mobile multi-hop wireless networks [1]. The MANET can be setup between few nodes or can be extended by connecting to fixed network. Ad-hoc networks can be set up any where, any time. In MANET networks the topology of network changes dynamically as nodes move in and out of each others range. As Ad-hoc networks does not rely on pre-established infrastructure so MANET can be deployed in places without any infrastructure. Ad-hoc networks can set up on fly and they are perfectly suited for disaster scenarios, search and rescue operations.

A. Abraham et al. (Eds.): ACC 2011, Part I, CCIS 190, pp. 11–20, 2011.

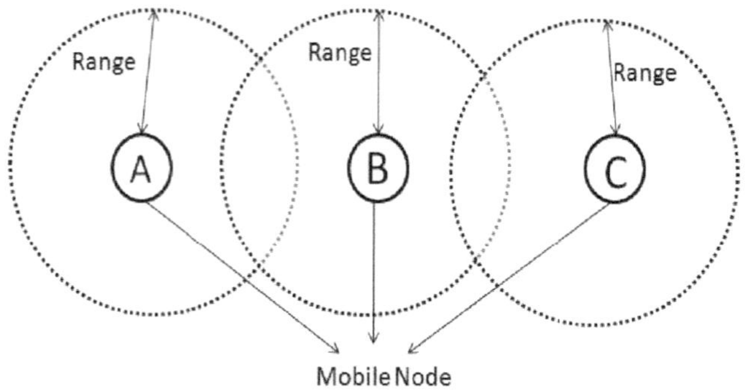

Fig. 1. A Mobile Ad-hoc network

A MANET is illustrated in Figure 1 consists of three wireless MNs A, B and C. Transmission range of a node represented by dotted circle. MN A is not with in the transmission range of C and vice versa. If A wants to establish communication with C. Node B which in the transmission range of A and C forwards the packets so that A and C are able to communicate each other successfully. The fundamental difference between fixed networks and MANET is that, in MANET nodes and dynamic. Due to the mobility of these nodes, there are some characteristics that are only applicable to MANET: Dynamic Network Topologies, Bandwidth constrained links, Energy constrained operation [8], Limited physical security, Decentralized.

A multi hop routing protocol is required to establish the communication between two mobile hosts which are out of range. MANETnetwork requires a dynamic routing protocol to find efficient routes between MNs [4]. Routing protocol for MANET must be able to keep up with high degree of mobility that often changes randomly [2].

The link state and distance vector algorithms used in fixed networks do not scale in large MANETs. This is because periodic or frequent route updates in large networks may consume significant part of the available bandwidth and may require each node to frequently recharge their power supply. Depending on routing behavior routing protocols in Ad-hoc networks are classified into proactive, reactive and hybrid.

In proactive routing protocol, each MN contains routes to all destinations [10]. All MNs broadcast their routing tables periodically so that all nodes maintain up-to-date network topology information. Main advantage of proactive routing are: no need for route discovery before transmitting a packet. Proactive protocols are also called table driven protocols. These protocols are not suitable for larger networks. The Proactive routing is implemented on: Destination Sequenced Distance Vector routing (DSDV), Wireless Routing Protocol (WRP) and Cluster head Gateway Switch Routing (CGSR). In reactive routing protocols routes are determined only when they are required by sources using route discovery process. Reactive protocols are also called as on demand protocols as they reduce over head of periodic broadcast in proactive routing by maintaining information for active routes only. In these protocols routes are determined and maintained only when a node requires a route to send data to a particular destination. Reactive routing protocols can be classified into source routing and hop by hop routing [5-6]. In source routing, a data packet carry the whole path from source to destination address. Example for source routed on demand protocol is

Dynamic Source Routing (DSR) [12]. Source routing protocols not scale well for larger networks because of two reasons. As the number of intermediate nodes increases, the probability of the route failure also increases. Other reason is packet header overhead as each data packet contains the whole path. In hop by hop routing, each data packet carries only destination address and next hop address. Example for hop by hop routing is Ad-hoc on demand Distance Vector routing protocol (AODV) [3]. These routing protocols are adaptable to dynamically changing environment. The shortcoming of this type of protocol is that each intermediate node must store and maintain for each active route [11]. The Hybrid routing protocols are combination of both proactive and reactive routing behavior. Proactive routing is used to maintain routing information of all the near by nodes and Reactive routing is used for all other nodes. Example for hybrid routing protocol is Zone Routing Protocol (ZRP).

In this paper, we have considered AODV routing protocol. Our main focus is on improving the performance of AODV by reducing overhead in route discovery and route maintenance phases. During route discovery route request (RREQ) messages are broadcast by source to establish the path. The AODV uses expanding ring search method to discover the route to the intended destination. Broadcasting of RREQ messages constitute more overhead and it is unacceptable as MNs are energy and bandwidth constrained. To address this problem we have used medium access control mechanisms. In AODV Route Maintenance phase, when a node on the path moves out of range, upstream node detects link failure and reports to the source about the link error so that it will do route discovery for destination again. Performance of AODV can be greatly affected by delay in identifying link failure and rebuilding the path again for same destination if required. We used preemptive route maintenance scheme to reduce delay and routing overhead.

Rest of the paper organized as follows, section 2 for the proposed enhancement of AODV protocol. In section 3, we are discussing about the simulation and its results. The overall conclusion is summarized in section 4 and followed by the references.

2 Proposed Scheme

In this section, we have discussed about the improvements that can be made to the original AODV protocol [7]. First, we will discuss about MAC layer feedback mechanism that reduces route discovery latency and routing overhead. Further, we will discuss about the new scheme of route maintenance process.

2.1 Route Discovery

The AODV routing protocol initiates route discovery process by using expanding ring search (ERS) technique. It uses three constants TTL START, TTL INCREMENT and TTL THRESHOLD and its corresponding values are 1, 2 and 7 respectively. Source node S starts the route discovery process by broadcasting the route request RREQ with TTL value TTL START. Then, S waits for route reply, RREP with RING TRAVERSAL TIME.

RING TRAVERSAL TIME = 2 × NODE TRAVERSAL TIME × TTL VALUE

Here, NODE TRAVERSAL TIME is the time required by the node to process and transmits the packet. And NODE TRAVERSAL TIME = 40ms.

If S is not able to receive RREP within the RING TRAVERSAL TIME, S reinitiates the route discovery by increased TTL VALUE (by its TTL INCREMENT value). The S repeats this process until it receives the RREP or TTL VALUE reaches TTL THRESHOLD. If S is not able to receive RREP with the TTL value less than TTL THRESHOLD, the value of the TTL is set to NET DIAMETER which is equal to 35. Source node rebroadcast the same RREQ with increased TTL VALUE if it fails to receive RREP with previous one. Again source node has to wait for RING TRAVERSAL TIME.

This route discovery latency can be reduced by making intelligent use of IEEE 802.11 MAC layer mechanisms [9]. The basic access method in IEEE 802.11 is DCF (Distributed Coordinated Function). The proposed scheme is based on the underlying use of RTS (Request-to-send) and CTS (Clear-to-send).

We can describe the scheme as follows: The source node (S) starts the route discovery by broadcasting RREQ to all of its neighbors. If a neighbor has a route to the desired destination in its routing table, it would reserve the channel to send RREP to S. This node would send RTS to S and, S would respond with a CTS frame, which can be heard by all neighbors of S in promiscuous mode. If those neighbors who do not have route to the destination, after receiving the CTS from S (this is the indication that one of neighbor has a route to the destination), they will drop the RREQ without propagating further. Otherwise, they will propagate further by re-broadcasting to their neighbors. Initiator of the route discovery i.e. S waits for RREP after broadcasting the RREQ. If the initiator receives neither a RREP nor a broadcast from any of its neighbors, it means there is no route discovery in progress and it is isolated node (a node which is not able to communicate with its neighbors).

In our proposed model, neighbors do not broadcast RREQs immediately after receiving the RREQ. Rather they will wait for some time. The wait time can be calculated as follows. The time T, neighbors spend listening channel for CTS from S can be decided based on the underlying physical layer. This T equals to the sum of the time spent during DIFS interval, back-off time, time required to send RTS, SIFS interval and finally time needed to send CTS.

T = (TDIFS + TBO + TRTS + TSIFS + TCTS)
Where,
TDIFS = DIFS time interval
TBO = Back off time
This time selected randomly following a uniform distribution from (0, CW) where CW is current window size.
TRTS = Time spent in transmitting RTS
TCTS = Time spent in transmitting CTS
TSIFS = SIFS interval

For DSSS (Direct Sequence Spread spectrum) assuming no collision on broadcast from S, this time value is 1ms [9]. Assuming, TBO on average aCWmin/2 (15 time slots, where each time slot is equal to 20 microseconds). In worst case back-off time can be taken as aCWmax/2 (512 time slots), giving T equals to 11 ms approximately. The value of T can be assigned between these two.

Above approach surely reduces the latency in route discovery process as source node will not rebroadcast RREQ. We can clearly visualize that the above mechanism reduces the latency involved in the route discovery process. If after broadcasting the RREQ source node detects collision or no subsequent RREP or broadcast from its neighbors, source node reinitiates the route discovery process. This mechanism not only reduces the route discovery latency but also the routing overhead as source node does not rebroadcast RREQ. In this approach, source node initiate route discovery by setting larger TTL values so that there is no need of initiating the RREQ from source. This process greatly reduces the routing packets in the network, there by it reduces the routing overhead. The shortcoming of this approach is the waiting time that occurs when a node waits to hear CTS packets from other nodes in promiscuous mode.

2.2 Route Maintenance

We propose a new scheme of route maintenance in which source nodes will switch to alternate route before the link on the route is broken. The route established by the source after receiving the warning message may be less reliable than the existing route. This problem is also addressed in our scheme. First we will discuss about the modifications required to the existing AODV and later the proposed approach in detail.

1. A counter field CNT is added to the routing table.
2. A list called SRCLIST is added to each routing table entry contains the list of nodes for which the MN sent the warning message.
3. A new message header called Route Warning message (RWRN) is created. RWRN message contains addresses of source node which is IP destination and destination node.

Extended routing table is as shown in Figure 2. The newly added routing table entries are shown in bold italic font. At the time of resolving the route to a data packet, MN calculates the received power of the packet. If the power of the received packet is less than the threshold value, the counter value CNT is incremented. If CNT value equals two and SRCLIST not contain the address of source node of the data packet then warning message is created. This is to avoid the unnecessary warning messages that may occur due to channel fading effect. Warning message generated by the node contains the addresses of the source node of the data packet (destination of warning message) and the destination which is soon become unreachable. Send the created warning message to the source and address of the source node is added to SRCLIST.

DEST	NXT HOP	....	***CNT***	***SRCLIST***
		⋮		

Fig. 2. Extended Routing Table

The Algorithm shown below is showing all the steps of resolving the route to a data packet:

```
1) Data Packet is received
2) If Received Signal Strength < Preemptive Signal Threshold
      then { Increment CNT Value.
      If CNT = = 2 AND SRCLIST not contain the source
      node then
      { Create and Send RWRN message to the source.
      Add source node address to SRCLIST of the routing  table
      entry.}}
3)  If RWRN message is received
     then if RWRN message is arrived at the source node then
     {Generate Route request.
     Drop the RWRN message.}
     else
     if SRCLIST not contain the source node
     then
    { Add source node address to SRCLIST of the routing table entry.
    Send warning message. }
4) If Route request is received
    then
    If Received signal strength > Preemptive Signal Threshold
                then
                Discard the Route Request packet.
                If current node contains route AND SRCLIST is not
                empty
                then
                Broadcast the Route Request packet.
5) If Route reply is received
    then
    Empty the SRCLIST of destination routing table entry
```

If a MN receives the RWRN message destined for itself then it broadcast route request to determine the route to the destination in the RWRN message. MN checks SRCLIST for source node in the routing table entry of the destination after receiving the warning message at intermediate node. If SRCLIST contain the source node then MN discards the warning message. Otherwise, source node is added to the SRCLIST and warning message is forwarded towards the source.

Consider a network as shown in Figure 3. Source S is routing packets to destination D via the link C. As S moves away from C, the received power of the packet falls below the threshold value and generate the warning message to S. Source node S broadcast route request for D. This route request is received by all the nodes A, B and C which are in the maximum transmission range of S. B broadcast the route request and is discarded by the nodes A and C as they already heard the route request. Source node S may establish the route SAD or SBD which is undesirable as both B and C nodes are in preemptive region. This problem can be solved by discarding all the

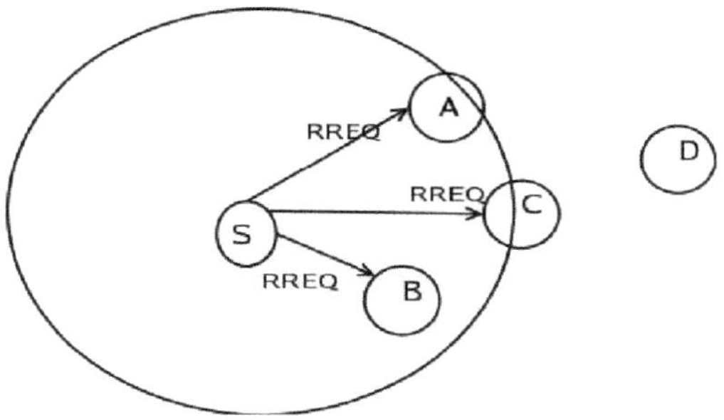

Fig. 3. Ad-hoc Network

requests which are received from long distance. So the route requests received by nodes B and C will be discarded.

A MN cannot generate route reply message if it has route to the destination and SRCLIST is not empty. SRCLIST not empty indicates that a link on the route to the destination is weak. When a node receives a route reply message, SRCLIST of destination routing table entry is emptied. If a node unable to determine the route before it is broken, then original AODV route maintenance is followed.

By the above method of route maintenance it is clear that the source node will switch to alternate route before a link on the route will be broken. Time between detection of broken link on the route and restoring the route is saved. The overhead of generation of RERR message is reduced.

3 Simulation Results

In this section we will discuss simulation topology and environment and we will compare results of proposed scheme with original AODV. The three important metrics to evaluate the performance of a routing protocol are defined as follows:

1. Packet Delivery Ratio: It is the ratio of total number of packets received at the destination to those of generated at the source.
2. Average End to End delay: Delays during route discovery, queuing at interface queue, retransmission delay at MAC, propagation and transfer times.
3. Normalize Routing Load: This metric can be defined as number control packets transmitted for each data packet. Each hop-wise transmission of a routing packet is counted as one transmission.

Packet delivery ratio and average end to end delay are the best effort metrics and normalized routing load determines the efficiency of a routing protocol.

3.1 Simulation Topology and Environment

The proposed method is simulated on ns-2 simulator and the changes have been made to base AODV code. We set the following simulation parameter, traffic is CBR, numbers of node is 50, maximum connections are 20, packet rate is 4 packets/ second, maximum speed: 20m/s, simulation time = 100 sec., simulation grid size: 500x500, packet size =512bytes.

3.2 Results

Route Discovery

The graph shows that our approach performs efficiently than the original AODV. Network topology is more dynamic if pause time is less and it affects the packet delivery ratio. In the graph shown in Figure 4(a) & Figure 4 (b), packet delivery ratio drops at pause time 10, this is because of congestion in the network or due to mobility of the nodes. If a link breaks MN cannot transmit data packets until the link is restored.

Figure 4(c), Figure 4(b) shows average end-to-end delay comparison of our enhanced AODV with original AODV. Packet delay may occur due to the retransmissions, congestion in network and multiple access interferences. As shown in Figure 4(c), our approach performs better than original AODV in dynamic conditions. As you observe, there is increase in average end to end delay at pause time 20 of modified AODV with ERS because of route construction delay. By analyzing the trace files we found that there are more number of route requests than original AODV.

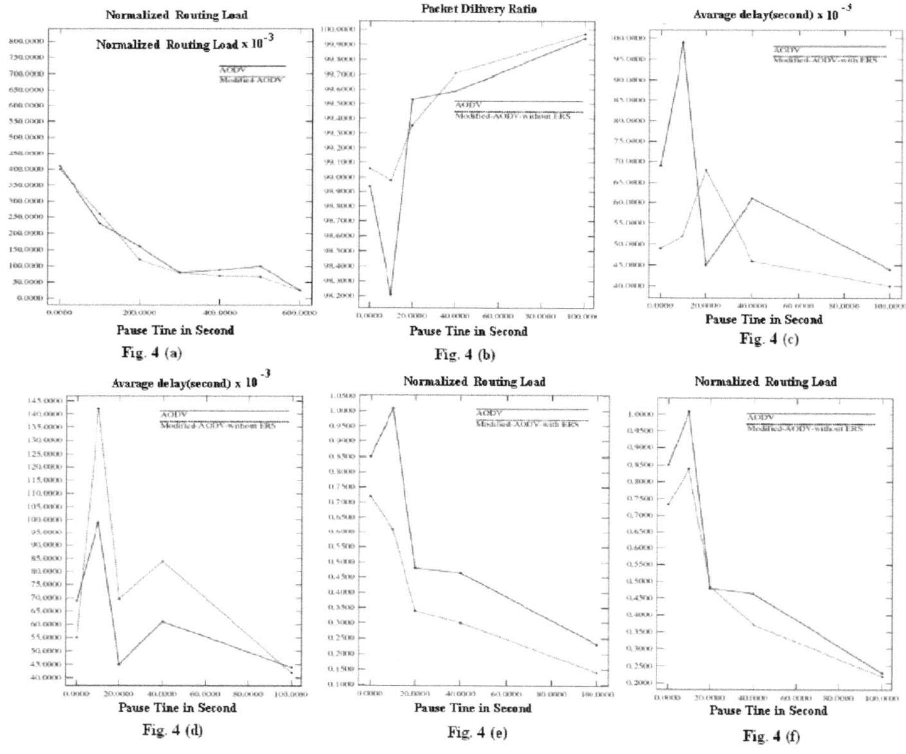

Fig. 4. (a) & (b) shows the packet delivery ratio of both original AODV and modified AODV with expanding ring search (ERS) and without ERS, (c) & (d) shows average end-to-end delay comparison of our enhanced AODV with original AODV, (e) & (f) shows the comparison of normalized routing load.

Figure 4(e), Figure 4(f) shows the comparison of normalized routing load. Our proposed approach of using MAC layer acknowledgements significantly performs better than original AODV in both dynamic and stable conditions of the network. As route requests are dropped by the MNs by using MAC layer acknowledgements, the routing packets routed through the network are reduced.

Route Maintenance

In this section we will discuss about the results obtained for original AODV and Modified AODV with new approach of route maintenance. Same simulation parameters are considered except simulation time 600 seconds. Results are plotted by varying pause time.

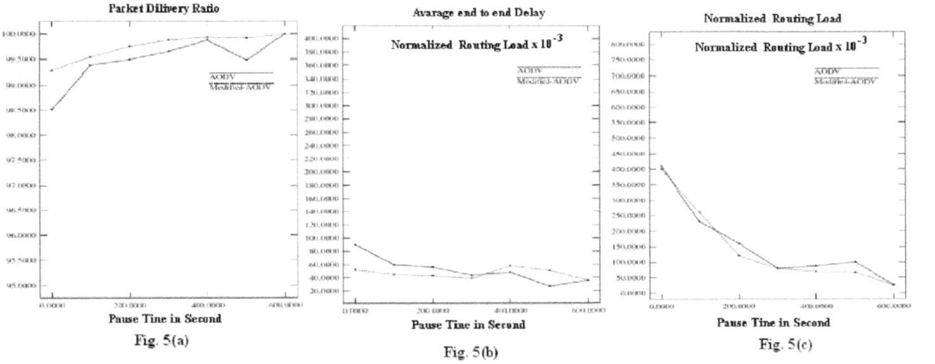

Fig. 5. (a)Packet delivery ratio (b)Average end-to-end delay (c)normalized routing load comparisons of both original AODV and modified AODV

The graph shows that our approach outperforms original AODV. As stable links are established and the availability of the route before a link broken makes more packets to be transmitted over a network. Our approach performs better in dynamic conditions. As the pause time increases, mobility of the nodes decreases and packet delivery ratio increases. The modified AODV performs equally with original AODV in less dynamic conditions.

During pause times 400 and 500, modified AODV is having high average end to end delay than the original AODV because the route established between the source and destination may be long. In many cases modified AODV is having less average end to end delay than original AODV. We established stable links by dropping the requests received from large distance. Route construction delay and transfer times of the packet increases as the route requests are dropped. For the above reasons average end to end delay of modified AODV is more than original AODV in some cases. Figure 5 (a), Figure 5 (b) and Figure 5 (c) shows the packet delivery ratio and average end to end delay comparisons and normalized routing load of modified with original AODV.

Our approach of preemptive route maintenance in AODV performs better than original AODV in both dynamic and stable conditions of the network. As we observed, in some cases the routing load of modified one in more than original one. This is due to warning message propagation. If alternate route is not established before the link break then warning messages create extra overhead.

4 Conclusions

In this paper, we enhanced the performance of AODV protocol by reducing the routing overhead during route discovery and route maintenance process. The MAC layer feedback mechanism is used instead of expanding ring search method to avoid the rebroadcast of RREQ from source. Also, a new preemptive route maintenance approach is proposed to reduce the delay and overhead which occur at the time of link breaks. We used ns-2 simulator to implement and validate our approach.

References

[1] Xue, Q., Ganz, A.: QoS Routing for Mesh-Based Wireless LANs. International Journal of Wireless Information Networks 9(3), 179–190 (2002)

[2] Jayakumar, G., Gopinath, G.: Ad-hoc Mobile Wireless Networks Routing Protocols – A Review. Journal of Computer Science 3(8), 574–582 (2007)

[3] Perkins, C., Royer, E.M.: Ad-hoc On Demand Distance Vector (AODV) Routing. In: IEEE Workshop Mobile Computing Systems and Applications, pp. 1–11 (1999)

[4] Royer, E.M., Toh, C.K.: A Review of Current Routing Protocols for Ad-hoc Mobile Wireless Networks. IEEE Personal Communications 6(2), 46–55 (1999)

[5] Abolhasan, M., Wysocki, T., Dutkiewicz, E.: A review of Routing Protocols for Mobile Ad-hoc Networks. Ad-hoc Networks Journal 2(1), 1–22 (2004)

[6] Belding-Royer, E.M., Perkins, C.E.: Evolution and Future Directions of the Ad-hoc On Demand Distance Vector Routing Protocol. Ad-hoc Networks Journal 1(1), 125–150 (2003)

[7] Perkins, C., Belding-Royer, E.M., Das, S.: Ad-hoc On Demand Distance Vector (AODV) Routing, RFC 3561 (July 2003)

[8] Park, J.K.I., Pu, I.: Blocking Expanding Ring Search Algorithm for Efficient Energy Consumption in Mobile Ad-hoc Networks. In: IFIP WONS Third Annual Conference on Wireless On demand Network Systems and Services (January 2006)

[9] Wireless, L.A.N.: Medium Access Control (MAC) and Physical Layer (PHY) Specifications, ANSI/IEEE Std 802.11, Edition (1999)

[10] Goff, T., Abu Ghazaleh, N.B., Phatak, D.S., Kahvecioglu, R.: Preemptive Routing in Ad-hoc Networks. In: Proc. of ACM MobiCom, pp. 43–52 (2001)

[11] Srinath, P., Abhilash, P., Sridhar, I.: Router Handoff: A Preemptive Route Repair Strategy for AODV. In: IEEE International Conference Personal Wireless Communications, pp. 168–171 (December 2002)

[12] Das, S.R., Perkins, C.E., Royer, E.M.: Performance Comparison of two On Demand Routing Protocols for Ad-hoc Networks. In: Proceedings of INFOCOM 2000, pp. 1–11 (March 2000)

3-Disjoint Paths Fault-Tolerant Multi-stage Interconnection Networks

Ravi Rastogi[1], Rohit Verma[1], Nitin[2], and Durg Singh Chauhan[3]

[1] Department of Computer Science & Engineering and Information Technology,
Jaypee University of Information Technology, Waknaghat, Solan-173234,
Himachal Pradesh, India
ravi.rastogi@juit.ac.in
[2] College of Information Science and Technology, The Peter Kiewit Institute,
University of Nebraska at Omaha, Omaha-68182-0116,
Nebraksa, United States of America
fnunitin@mail.unomaha.edu
[3] Uttarakhand Technical Univesity, Post Office Chandanwadi,
Prem Nagar, Sudohwala, Dehradun-248007, Uttarakhand, India
pdschauhan@gmail.com

Abstract. In this paper, we have compared the existing 3-Disjoint Paths Fault-tolerant Omega Multi-stage Interconnection Network (3-DON) with newly proposed 3-Disjoint Fault-tolerant Gamma Interconnection Network (3-DGMIN) using the concept of reachable sets and coloring scheme. A 3-Disjoint network can concurrently send packets from the source node to increase the arrival ratio or tolerate a maximum of 2 faults in the network by re-routing the packet through another path. We have used red blue, green and yellow color for the coloring the nodes. The 3-DON is better than existing Omega Multi-stage Interconnection Network (OMIN) for every performance parameter except the cost. Moreover, the new 3-DGMIN is also better than existing Gamma Multi-stage Interconnection Network (GIN) for every performance parameter. Further, the experimental results show that the 3-DGMIN outperforms 3-DON when compared for the throughput.

Keywords: Multi-stage Interconnection Network, Fault-tolerance, 3-Disjoint Paths, Omega Network, Gamma Network, Reachable Sets, Coloring Schemes.

1 Introduction and Motivation

Multi-stage Interconnection Networks (MINs) [1-10] are used to design a network in which there are several independent paths between two modules being connected which increases the available bandwidth. With the performance requirement of the switches exceeding several terabits/sec and teraflops/sec, it becomes imperative to make them dynamic and fault-tolerant. For high reliability and performance, several methods have been suggested that provide fault-tolerance to MINs [11-23]. The basic idea for fault-tolerance is to provide multiple paths for a source–destination pair, so that alternate paths can be used in case of a fault in a path. However, to guarantee

A. Abraham et al. (Eds.): ACC 2011, Part I, CCIS 190, pp. 21–33, 2011.

1–fault tolerance, a network should have a pair of alternate paths for every source-destination pair, which are Disjoint in nature [24-32]. Now-a-days applications of MINs are widely used for on-Chip communication. In past number of techniques has been used to increase the reliability and fault-tolerance of MINs, a survey of the fault-tolerance attributes of these networks is found in [1-6]. The modest cost of unique paths MINs makes them attractive for large multiprocessors systems, but their lack of fault-tolerance, is a major drawback. To mitigate this problem, three hardware options are available:

1. Replicate the entire network,
2. Add extra stages,
3. And /or Add chaining links.
4. Rearranging of the connection patterns with the addition or deletion of hardware links.

In addition to this, MINs can be designed to achieve fault tolerance and collision solving by providing a set of disjoint paths. Many researchers have done sufficient work on providing 1-fault tolerance to the MINs however; little attention has been paid to design the 3-Disjoint Paths Fault-tolerant MINs.

We have been inspired by the work presented by the authors in [31]. Therefore, in this paper, we study the fault-tolerance of multiprocessor systems with 3-Disjoint multistage interconnection networks. The characterization of 3-Disjoint paths with respect to reachable sets and coloring scheme is introduced and is used to discuss fault-tolerance of the network under a given set of fault conditions. A 3-Disjoint network can concurrently send packets from the source node to increase the arrival ratio or tolerate a maximum of two faults in the network by re-routing the packet through another path [31]. This paper presents

1. Design of reachable sets and coloring scheme to analyze the fault-tolerance capability of any network,
2. Design scheme that enables the GIN to be 3-Disjoint with minimal hardware cost involved,
3. Comparison of the proposed 3-DGMIN with other existing 3-DON proposed in [32] with respect to network parameters,
4. Simulation results of the designed networks to realize the proposed fault tolerant capability.

As per our proposed method, design schemes and simulation results, a designer can analyze and develop cost-efficient 3-Disjoint paths networks. We have taken Omega and Gamma Multi-stage Interconnection Network as running example throughout this paper.

The rest of the paper is organized as follows, Section II, describes the theory regarding the application of Reachable Sets and Coloring Schemes to the MIN and more specifically converting them into the 3-Disjoint Paths MIN. The techniques are well supported by the theorem and definitions. Section III, provides the techniques of using Reachable Sets and Coloring Scheme to convert the existing Omega Network into 3-Disjoint Paths Fault-tolerant Omega MIN and to convert the existing Gamma Network into 3-Disjoint Paths Fault-tolerant Gamma MIN. Further, it shows various examples of parallel communication between different source and destinations supported by pseudocode and followed by the conclusion and the references.

2 Concept of Coloring Schemes and Reachable Sets for Disjoint MINs

In this section, the application of Reachable Sets and Coloring Schemes to the MIN and to convert them into the 3-Disjoint Paths MIN have been discussed. The techniques are well supported by the theorem and definitions.

We can compute the reachable sets for some specific destination nodes as according to their routing behavior for the given network. According to definitions, we have defined the reachable set at different stages to include switches that can deliver packets to particular destination nodes.

Definition 2.1: A reachable set $S(i,j)$ for $(i,j)^{th}$ switch at the ith stage is defined as a set of j_n switches at the $(i-1)^{th}$ stage that can deliver packets to the $(i,j)^{th}$ switch.

Definition 2.2: Reachable set $S^m(i,j)$ for j^{th} switch at the ith stage is defined as a set of j_n switches at the $(i-m)^{th}$ stage that can deliver packets to $(i,j)^{th}$ switch.

For a typical Interconnection Network, atleast one path between each source and destination pair nodes, the reachable set $S^m(i,j)$ contains all the source nodes where,

m→ the number of stages in the network,
i → the final stage,
j → any destination node in the current network.

2.1 Three Theorems for Supporting the Application of Coloring Schemes and Reachable Sets to the Disjoint MINs

For a network to be 3-Disjoint, there must exits atleast, 3-Disjoint paths between each source-destination pair. We considered the 3-Disjoint paths to be labeled with three colors-Red, Green and Blue. We start coloring by calculating the first (reachable set for a destination node. We then backtrack to calculate the reachable set in order to reach the source nodes, where is the number of stages in a network.

Theorem 2.1.1: The final destination node(s) must obtain packets from at least three nodes from the prefinal stage, which are subsequently labeled as red, green and blue.

$S(i,j)$, where
i→ the final stage,
j→ any destination node.

Must contain at least three nodes and these are colored as red, green and blue.

1. All the nodes in the reachable set of Red, Green and Blue nodes in the prefinal stage are colored as Red, Green and Blue respectively.
2. If a node delivers packets to other nodes of varying color, then such a node remains in the reachable set of both the colors.
3. A node can be labeled with one or more colors.
4. A multicolored node can be considered as node of one color only.

Proof: We assume that packets are delivered to the final node by two nodes in the prefinal stage. The network, fails if the two nodes are faulty and therefore, the network is not 2 fault-tolerant. If the packets are delivered to the final node by three

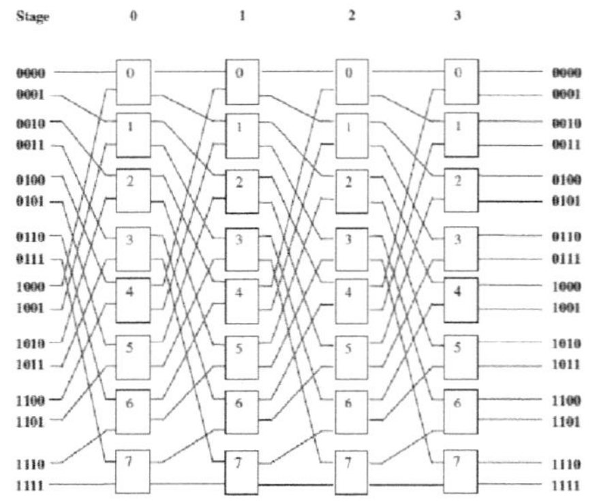

Fig. 1. Topology of 16 x 16 Omega Multi-stage Interconnection Network

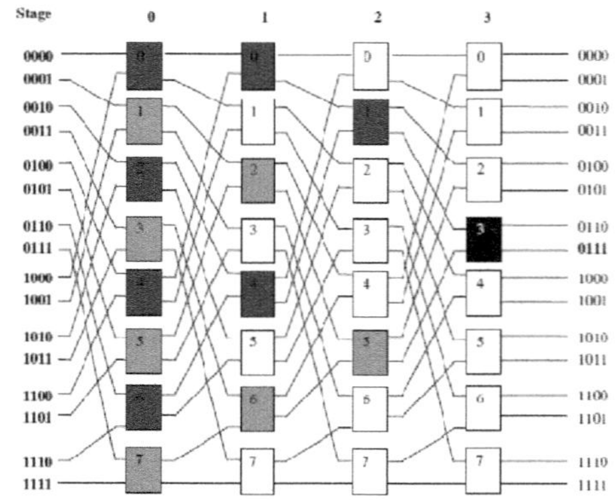

Fig. 2. Coloring Scheme of 16 x 16 Omega Multi-stage Interconnection Network

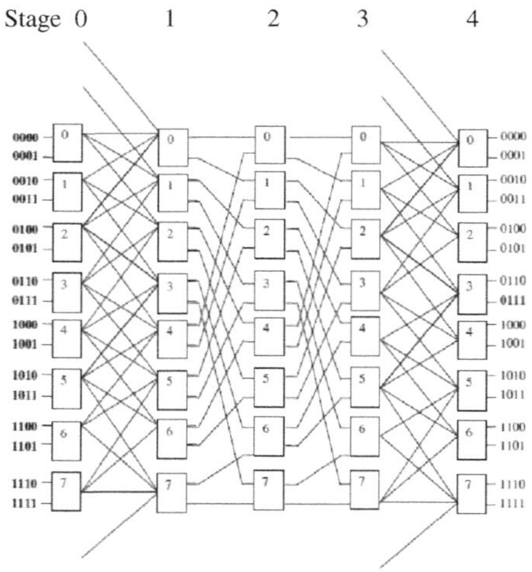

Fig. 3. 16 x 16 3-Disjoint Paths Fault-tolerant Omega Multi-stage Interconnection Network

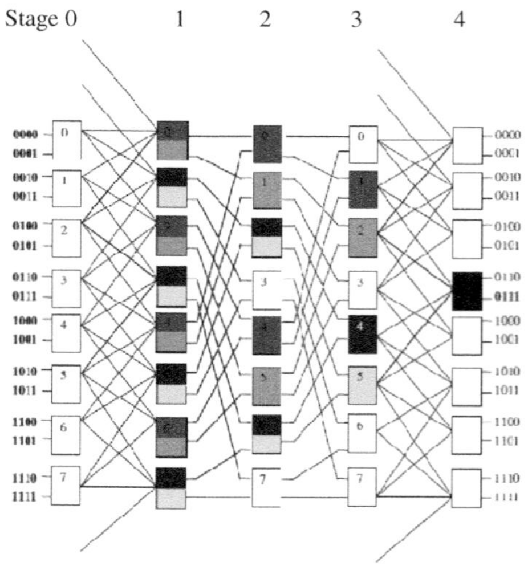

Fig. 4. Coloring Scheme of 16 x 16 3-Disjoint Paths Fault-tolerant Omega Multi-stage Interconnection Network with 0111 as the Destination Node

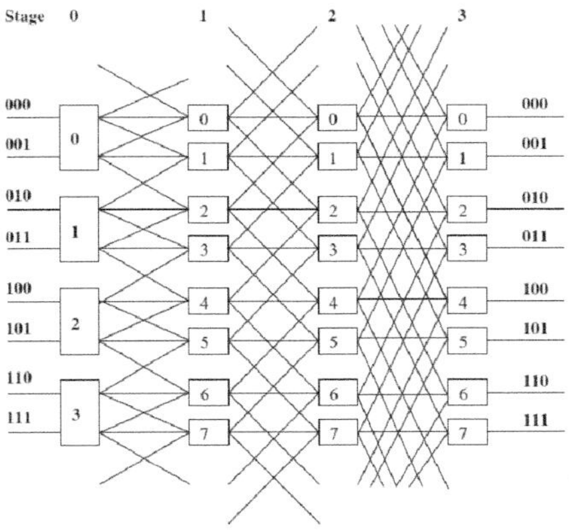

Fig. 5. Topology of 8 x 8 Gamma Multi-stage Interconnection Network

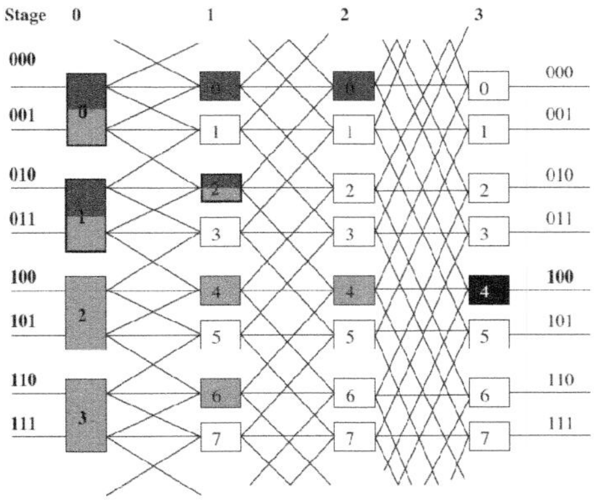

Fig. 6. Coloring Scheme of 8 x 8 Gamma Multi-stage Interconnection Network

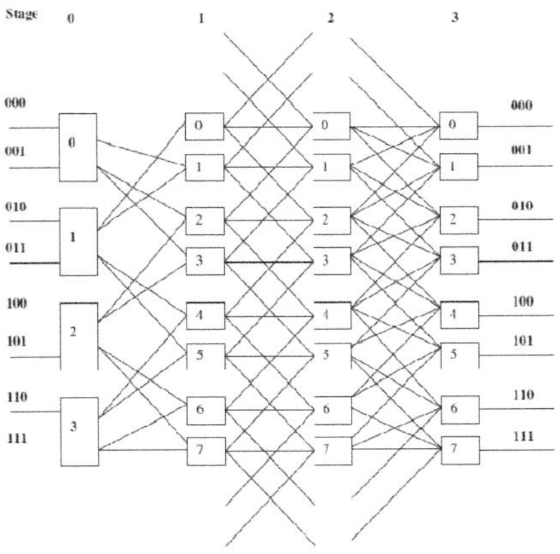

Fig. 7. 8 x 8 3-Disjoint Paths Fault-tolerant Gamma Multi-stage Interconnection Network

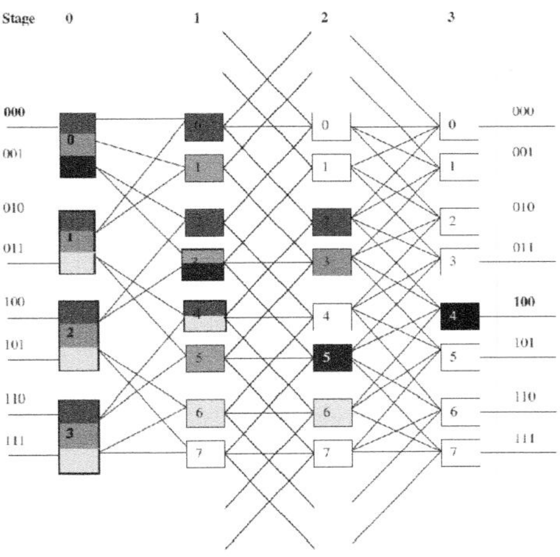

Fig. 8. Coloring Scheme of 8 x 8 3-Disjoint Paths Fault-tolerant Gamma Multi-stage Interconnection Network with 0111 as the Destination Node

nodes in the prefinal stage and the two nodes are simultaneously faulty, then the network does not fail (assuming that there are no other faults in the network) as there is a third path available.

Theorem 2.1.2: Each source node must deliver packets to atleast three nodes of different color. In other words, all the source nodes must be labeled with all the three colors.

Proof: We assume that the source node delivers packets to two nodes in the first stage. The entire network fails, if the two nodes are simultaneously faulty and therefore, the network is not 2 fault-tolerant. If the source node delivers packets to three nodes in the first stage and the two nodes are simultaneously faulty, then the network does not fail (assuming that there are no other faults in the network) as a third path is available.

Theorem 2.1.3: For a network to be 3-Disjoint their must exist at least one node of each color (including multicolored nodes) at each stage in the network.

Proof: The 3-Disjoint paths are labeled as Red, Green and Blue. Each of the three paths delivers packets from source to destination and pass through all the intermediate stages in the network. If there exists at least one path between each source-destination node pairs then all the source nodes have all the colors i.e. Red, Green and Blue.

3 Comparison of Disjoint Paths Fault-Tolerant Multi-stage Interconnection Networks on the Basis of Architecture, Coloring Schemes and Reachable Sets

3.1 Disjoint Paths 16 x 16 Omega Fault-Tolerant Multi-stage Interconnection Network

Analysis of Existing Omega Multi-stage Interconnection Network. An OMIN (see figure 1) is described by the perfect k-shuffle permutation σ^k for $0 \leq I \leq n-1$. Connection pattern C_n is selected to be β_0^k. MINs interconnect N input/output ports using k x k switches, $log_k N$ switch stages, each with N/K switches and $N/(k * (log_k N))$ total number of switches [1-5]. As the MINs size increases the cost also increases and the reduction in MINs, switch cost comes at the price of performance. The Network has the property of being blocking and the contention is more likely to occur on network links moreover the paths from different sources to different destinations share one or more links.

Analysis by Coloring Scheme and Reachable Sets. As shown in the figure 2,

1. Every destination node obtains packets from two nodes in the previous stage,
2. Every source node delivers packets to only one node at stage 0. The packet follows either the red or the green path to reach the destination node.

As shown in the figure 2, the reachable set for the destination node are as follows:

1. $S^1(3,3)$ = 1(Red), 5(Green),
2. $S^2(3,3)$ = 0(Red), 4(Red), 2(Green), 6(Green),
3. $S^3(3,3)$ = 0(Red), 1(Green), 2(Red), 3(Green), 4(Red), 5(Green), 6(Red), 7(Green).

Description of 16 x 16 3-Disjoint Paths Fault-tolerant Omega Multi-stage Interconnection Network. Out of four hardware options as listed these options as listed in Secion 1, we have choose "to add an extra stages to the network" in order to improve to convert the omega network into fault-tolerant network called as 3-DON. A 3-DON (see figure 3) of size $N = 2^n$ is similar to Omega Network, except the source nodes $2i$ and $2i + 1$ are combined into one 2 x 4 switch and with an extra stage. The 2 x 4 switches at the $2i$ stage deliver packets to

1. $i-2, i-1, i+1$ *and* $i+2$ (where i is not equal to 0 or $N-1$),
2. $i, i+1$ *and* $i+2$ (where i is equal to 0),
3. $i, i-1$ *and* $i-2$ (where i is equal to $N-1$).

Similarly, the destination nodes $2i$ and $2i+1$ are also combined into a 2 x 4 switch. These 2 x 4 switches recieve packets from

1. $i-2, i-1, i+1$ *and* $i+2$ (where i is not equal to 0 or $N-1$),
2. $i, i+1,$ *and* $i+2$ (where i is equal to 0),
3. $i, i-1,$ *and* $i-2$ (where i is equal to $N-1$).

Analysis by Coloring Scheme and Reachable Sets. As shown in figure 4,

1. Every destination node obtains packets from four nodes in the previous stage,
2. Every source node delivers packets to three node of different color including the source node 0 and 7, therefore, there exists only 3-Disjoint paths between the source 0 (0000) and destination 4 (0100). Hence, the network is perfectly 3-Disjoint,
3. There is a node of every color at each stage of the network; hence, there exists 3-Disjoint paths from each of the source nodes.

As shown in figure 4, the reachable set for the destination node are as follows:

1. $S^1(3,4)$ = 1(Red), 2(Green), 4(Blue), 5(Yellow),
2. $S^2(3,4)$ = 0(Red), 1(Green), 2(Blue, Yellow), 4(Red), 5(Green), 6(Blue, Yellow),
3. $S^3(3,4)$ = 0(Red, Green), 1(Blue, Yellow), 2(Red, Green), 3(Blue, Yellow), 4(Red, Green), 5(Blue, Yellow), 6(Red, Green), 7(Blue, Yellow).

3.2 Disjoint Paths 8 x 8 Gamma Fault-Tolerant Multi-stage Interconnection Network

Analysis of Existing Gamma Multi-stage Interconnection Network. A GIN (see figure 5) of size $N = 2^n$ has $n+1$ stages labeled from 0 to n and each stage involves N switches. Switches of sizes 1 x 3 and 3 x 1 are coupled with the first and the last stage respectively. Each switch at intermediate stages is a 3 x 3 crossbar. Each switch j at stage I has three output link connections to switches at stage $(i+1)$ according to the plus-minus-2^i function. The jth switch at stage I has three output links to switches $[(j - 2^i)\ mod\ N], j$ and $[(j+2^i)\ mod\ N]$ at each consecutive stage [1-5], [28-31].

Analysis by Coloring Scheme and Reachable Sets. As shown in the figure 6,

1. Every destination node obtains packets from two nodes (in the previous stage) only,
2. Every source node delivers packets to three nodes. These three nodes are not of different colors,
3. There exist only two disjoint paths from source nodes 000, 001, 010, 011 to the destination node. There exists only one disjoint path from source nodes 100, 101, 110, 111 to the destination node 100,
4. Therefore, the network is neither 2-Disjoint nor 3-Disjoint.

As shown in the figure 6, the reachable set for the destination node are as follows:

1. $S^1(3,4)$ = 0(Red), 4(Green),
2. $S^2(3,4)$ = 0(Red), 2(Red, Green), 4(Green), 6(Green),
3. $S^3(3,4)$ = 0(Red, Green), 1(Red, Green), 2(Green), 3(Green).

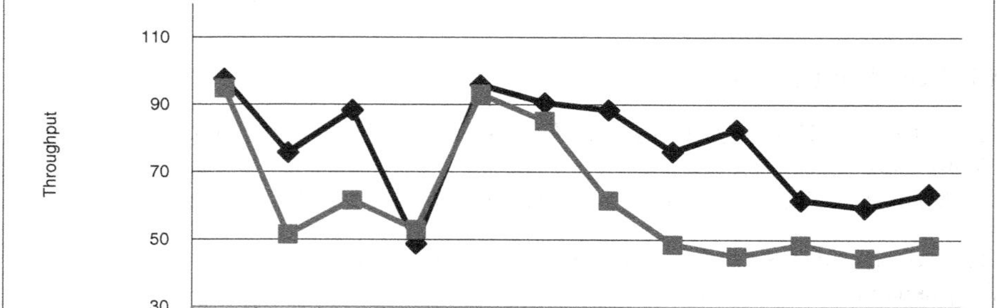

	One to One	One to All	All to One	All to All	Two to One	Two to Two	One to Half Network	Upper Half To Lower Half of Network	Alternate Half to Half(0, 2,4)to(1,3,5)	Upper Half to Upper Half	Half to All	All To Half
Gamma	97.6	75.7	88.3	48.74	95.8	90.55	88.4	76	82.56	61.6	59.3	63.5
Omega	94.75	51.45	61.5	52.85	93.1	85.13	61.56	48.59	45.1	48.5	44.6	48.4

Fig. 9. Comparison of 3-Disjoint Paths 16 x 16 Omega and 8 x 8 Gamma Fault-tolerant Multistage Interconnection Networks based on the parameters suggested on the y-axis against the throughput values given on the x-axis.

Description of Proposed 8 x 8 3-Disjoint Paths Fault-tolerant Gamma Multistage Interconnection Network. Out of four hardware options as listed in Secion 1, we have used "to rearrange the connection patterns with the addition or deletion of the hardware links" in order to convert the existing gamma network into fault-tolerant network called as 3-DGMIN. A 3-DGMIN (see figure 7) of size $\boldsymbol{N} = \boldsymbol{2^n}$ is similar to gamma network, except the source nodes $\boldsymbol{2i}$ and $\boldsymbol{2i+1}$ are combined into one 2 x 4 switch. These 2 x 4 switches deliver packets to

1. $i-2, i-1, i+1$ *and* $i+2$ (where i is not equal to 0 or $N-1$),
2. $i, i+1,\ i+2$ *and* $i+3$ (where i is equal to 0),
3. $i, i-1,\ i-2$ *and* $i-3$ (where i is equal to $N-1$).

Similarly, the destination nodes $2i$ and $2i+1$ are also combined into a 2 x 4 switch. These 2 X 4 switches recieve packets from

1. $i-2, i-1, i+1$ *and* $i+2$ (where i is not equal to 0 or $N-1$),
2. $i, i+1,\ i+2$ *and* $i+3$ (where i is equal to 0),
3. $i, i-1,\ i-2$ *and* $i-3$ (where i is equal to $N-1$).

Analysis by Coloring Scheme and Reachable Sets. As shown in figure 8,

1. Every destination node obtains packets from three nodes in the previous stage,
2. There exist three disjoint paths from source nodes 000, 001, 010, 011 to the destination node and from source nodes 100, 101, 110, 111 to the destination node 100,
3. There is a node of every color at each stage of the network; hence, there exists 3-Disjoint paths from each of the source nodes.

As shown in figure 8, the reachable set for the destination node are as follows:

1. $S^1(3,4) =$ 2(Red), 3(Green), 5(Blue), 6(Yellow),
2. $S^2(3,4) =$ 0(Red), 1(Green), 2(Red), 3(Green, Blue), 4(Red, Yellow), 5(Green), 6(Yellow),
3. $S^3(3,4) =$ 0(Red, Green, Blue), 1(Red, Green, Yellow), 2(Red, Green, Yellow), 3(Red, Green, Yellow).

Pseudocode. In this section, we present the Pseudocode for sending the data from source to destination

```
Input: Source node(s), Destination node(d), N = 2^n - 1
Output: List of all available paths between the source and
destination node pair

        stage_s(s/2,d,0,str);

1.  stage_s(int s,int d,int n,String str)
            int a[]={-1,-1,-1,-1};
            if(s==0)
                a[0]=s;
                  a[1]=s+1;
                  a[2]=s+2;
                  a[3]=s+3;

          else if(s==N)
                a[0]=s-3;
                a[1]=s-2;
                a[2]=s-1;
                a[3]=s;

          else if((s>-1)&&(s<=N))
                a[0]=2*s-2;
                a[1]=2*s-1;
                a[2]=2*s+2;
                a[3]=2*s+3;

    for(int i=0;i<4;i++)
            stage12(a[i],d,n+1,str+"-"+a[i]);

    2.  stage12(int s,int d,int n,String str)
              int a[]={-1,-1,-1};

            a[0]=s-2;
            a[1]=s;
            a[2]=s+2;
              for(int i=0;i<3;i++)
                if((a[i]>-1)&&(a[i]<=N))
                    stage_f(a[i],d,n+1,str+"-"+a[i]);

   3.  stage_f(int s,int d,int n,String str)
              int a[]={-1,-1,-1,-1};

              if(s==0)
                a[0]=s;
                a[1]=s+1;
                  a[2]=s+2;
```

```
          else if(s==N)
             a[0]=s-2;
             a[1]=s-1;
             a[2]=s;

           else if((s>-1)&&(s<=N))
             a[0]=s-2;
             a[1]=s-1;
             a[2]=s+1;
             a[3]=s+2;

   for(int i=0;i<4;i++)
     if(a[i]==d)
       print(str+"-"+d);
```

3.3 Comparison of 3-Disjoint Paths 16 x 16 Omega and 8 x 8 Gamma Fault-Tolerant Multi-stage Interconnection Networks

Testbed, Experimental Setup and Simulation Outputs. We have designed both the networks using the Fast Interconnections tool and the architectural design of the software is already published in [33-34]. We have build this tool using Java Technology (i.e. JDK 1.6) and this version is running on top of the IBM System x, running with Novell's SUSE Linux Enterprise Server 11. We have used advanced java features to build our system. The most important part of the tool is designing of the components, which are used to design disjoint paths MINs. We have design them in paint and stored them in component library. We have provided the access of this component within the tool using ComponentChooser class.

3-DON. In this section, we are showing the output of the simulation program designed for the 3-Disjoint Omega Multi-stage Interconnection Networks.

Node 0 to Node 4. The set of all available paths between node0 and node4 are:-

0-0-0-0-0-2-4...100%
0-0-0-0-1-2-4...97%
0-0-0-1-3-2-4...96%
0-0-1-2-4-2-4...97%
0-0-2-4-0-2-4...95%
0-0-2-4-1-2-4...92%
0-0-2-5-3-2-4...91%
==
Number Of paths=7
Average Value=95.42857

Node 0 to Node 4 and Node 5. The set of all available paths between node0 and node4 are:-

0-0-0-0-0-2-4...100%
0-0-0-0-1-2-4...97%
0-0-0-1-3-2-4...96%
0-0-1-2-4-2-4...97%
0-0-2-4-0-2-4...95%
0-0-2-4-1-2-4...92%
0-0-2-5-3-2-4...91%
==
Number Of paths=7

The set of all available paths between node0 and node5 are :-

0-0-0-0-0-2-5..86%
0-0-0-0-1-2-5..83%
0-0-0-1-3-2-5..83%
0-0-1-2-4-2-5..87%
0-0-2-4-0-2-5..81%
0-0-2-4-1-2-5..78%
0-0-2-5-3-2-5..78%

===

Number Of paths=7
Average Value=88.85714

3-DGMIN. In this section, we are showing the output of the simulation program designed for the 3-Disjoint Gamma Multi-stage Interconnection Networks.

Node 0 to Node 4. The set of all available paths between node0 and node4 are:-

0-0-0-2-4..100%
0-0-1-3-4..99%
0-0-2-2-4..97%
0-0-3-3-4..96%
0-0-3-5-4..95%

===

Number of Paths=5
Average Value=97.4

Node 0 to Node 4 and Node 5. The set of all available paths between node0 and node4 are:-

0-0-0-2-4..100%
0-0-1-3-4..99%
0-0-2-2-4..97%
0-0-3-3-4..96%
0-0-3-5-4..95%

===

Number of Paths=5
The set of all available paths between node0 and node5 are:-

0-0-1-3-5..92%
0-0-2-4-5..93%
0-0-3-3-5..88%

===

Number of Paths=3
Average Value=95.0

From the subsection 3.3 (see figure 9) and the values of throughput generated by the software [33-34] shows that, it is depicted that the 8 x 8 3-DGMIN outperforms the 16 x 16 3-DON for most of the fault-tolerant communication patterns setup between source and the destination nodes and hence the 3-DGMIN is better than 3-DON.

4 Conclusion

This paper, presents a novel method to study the fault tolerance capability of MINs under multiple faults. The characterization of 3-Disjoint paths with respect to reachable sets and coloring scheme is introduce to discuss the fault-tolerance of the network under a given set of fault conditions. Further, we have designed a 16 x 16 3-Disjoint Paths Fault-tolerant Omega Multi-stage Interconnection Network. This Disjoint network is modified version of existing Omega Multi-stage Interconnection Network and provides 3-Disjoint paths to tolerate two switches or link faults between any source-destination pair (s). Furthermore, we have designed a 8 x 8 3-Disjoint Paths Fault-tolerant Gamma Multi-stage Interconnection Network. This Disjoint network is modified version of existing Gamma Multi-stage Interconnection Network and provides 3-Disjoint paths to tolerate two switches or link faults between any source-destination pair (s).

References

1. Feng, T.Y.: A survey of interconnection networks. IEEE Computer 14, 12–27 (1981)
2. Adams III, G.B., Agrawal, D.P., Siegel, H.J.: A survey and comparison of fault-tolerant multi-stage interconnection networks. IEEE Computer 20, 14–27 (1987)
3. Dally, W.J.: Scalable Switching Fabrics for Internet Routers, White paper, Avici Systems Incorporation (2001)
4. Bhuyan, L.N.: Special issue of interconnection networks. IEEE Computer 20(6) (June 1987)
5. Siegel, H.J.: Interconnection Network for Large Scale Parallel Processing: Theory and Case Studies. McGraw-Hill, New York (1990) ISBN 0-07-057561-4
6. Hwang, K.: Advanced Computer Architecture: Parallelism, Scalability, Programmability. Tata McGraw-Hill, India (2000) ISBN 0-07-053070-X
7. Duato, J., Yalamanchili, S., Ni, L.M.: Interconnection Networks: An Engineering Approach. Morgan Kaufmann, San Francisco (2003) ISBN 1-55860-852-4
8. Dally, W., Towles, B.: Principles and Practices of Interconnection Networks. Morgan Kaufmann, San Francisco (2004) ISBN 978-0-12-200751-4
9. Arabnia, H.R., Oliver, M.A.: Arbitrary Rotation of Raster Images with SIMD Machine Architectures. International Journal of Eurographics Association (Computer Graphics Forum) 6(1), 3–12 (1987)
10. Bhandarkar, S.M., Arabnia, H.R., Smith, J.W.: A Reconfigurable Architecture For Image Processing And Computer Vision. International Journal of Pattern Recognition And Artificial Intelligence 9(2), 201–229 (1995)
11. Bhandarkar, S.M., Arabnia, H.R.: The Hough Transform on a Reconfigurable Multi-Ring Network. Journal of Parallel and Distributed Computing 24(1), 107–114 (1995)
12. Wani, M.A., Arabnia, H.R.: Parallel Edge-Region-Based Segmentation Algorithm Targeted at Reconfigurable Multi-Ring Network. The Journal of Supercomputing 25(1), 43–63 (2003)
13. Duato, J.: A New Theory of Deadlock-free Adaptive Routing in Wormhole Networks. IEEE Transactions on Parallel and Distributed Systems 4(12), 1320–1331 (1993)
14. Duato, J.: A Necessary and Sufficient Condition for Dead lock-free Adaptive Routing in Wormhole Networks. IEEE Transactions on Parallel and Distributed Systems 6(10), 1055–1067 (1995)
15. Dally, W.J., Seitz, C.L.: Deadlock-Free Message Routing in Multiprocessor Interconnection Networks. IEEE Transactions on Computers C-36(5), 547–553 (1987)
16. Dally, W.J., Aoki, H.: Deadlock-Free Adaptive Routing in Multi computer Networks Using Virtual Channels. IEEE Transactions on Parallel Distributed Systems 4(4) (1993)
17. Duato, J.: Deadlock-Free Adaptive Routing Algorithms for the 3DTorus: Limitations and Solutions. In: Proceedings of Parallel Architectures and Languages Europe 1993 (1993)

18. Nitin, C., Subramanian, A.: Efficient Algorithms to Solve Dynamic MINs Stability Problems using Stable Matching with Complete TIES. Journal of Discrete Algorithms 6(3), 353–380 (2008)
19. Singh, A., Dally, W.J., Gupta, A.K., Towels, B.: Adaptive Channel Queue Routing on k-ary n-cubes. In: Proceedings of the Sixteenth Annual ACM Symposium on Parallelism in Algorithms and Architectures (2004)
20. Nitin, C., Garhwal, S., Srivastava, N.: Designing a Fault-tolerant Fully-chained Combining Switches Multi-stage Interconnection Network with Disjoint Paths. The Journal of Supercomputing 55(3), 400–431 (2009), doi:10.1007/s11227-009-0336-z
21. Nitin, C., Chauhan, D.S.: Comparative Analysis of Traffic Patterns on *k-ary n-tree* using Adaptive Algorithms based on Burton Normal Form. Journal of Supercomputing, 1–20 (2010), doi:10.1007/s11227-010-0454-7
22. Nitin, C., Sehgal, V.K., Bansal, P.K.: On MTTF analysis of a Fault-tolerant Hybrid MINs. WSEAS Transactions on Computer Research 2(2), 130–138 (2007) ISSN 1991-8755
23. Nitin, C.: Component Level Reliability analysis of Fault-tolerant Hybrid MINs. WSEAS Transactions on Computers 5(9), 1851–1859 (2006) ISSN 1109-2750
24. Chen, C.W., Chung, C.P.: Designing a Disjoint path interconnection network with collision solving and fault tolerance. The Journal of Supercomputing 34(1), 63–80 (2005)
25. Chen, C.W.: Design schemes of dynamic rerouting networks with destination tag routing for tolerating faults and preventing collisions. The Journal of Supercomputing 38(3), 307–326 (2006)
26. Siegal, H.J., Jose, D.R., Fortes, A.B.: Destination tag routing techniques based on a state model for the IADM network. IEEE Transaction on Computers 41(3), 274–285 (1992)
27. Smith, B.: Design of dynamic rerouting networks with destination tag routing for tolerating faults and preventing collisions. Springer Science, Heidelberg (2006)
28. Parker, D.S., Raghavendra, C.S.: The gamma network. IEEE Transactions on Computers 33, 367–373 (1984)
29. Chuang, P.J.: CGIN: A fault tolerant modified gamma interconnection network. IEEE Transactions on Parallel and Distributed Systems 7(12), 1301–1306 (1996)
30. Chen, C.W., Lu, N.P., Chen, T.F., Chung, C.P.: Fault-tolerant gamma interconnection networks by chaining. IEE Proceedings on Computers and Digital Techniques 147(2), 75–80 (2000)
31. Chen, C.W., Lu, N.P., Chung, C.P.: 3-Disjoint gamma interconnection networks. The Journal of Systems and Software 66, 129–134 (2003)
32. Rastogi, R., Nitin, C., Chauhan, D.S.: 3-Disjoint Paths Fault-tolerant Omega Multi-stage Interconnection Network with Reachable Sets and Coloring Scheme. In: Proceedings of the 13th IEEE International conference on Computer Modeling and Simulation (IEEE UKSim), Emmanuel College, Cambridge (2011)
33. Rastogi, R., Nitin, C.: Fast Interconnections: A Case Tool for Developing Fault-tolerant Multi-stage Interconnection Networks. International Journal of Advancements in Computing Technology 2(5), 13–24 (2010) ISSN: 2005-8039
34. Rastogi, R., Nitin, C.: On a Fast Interconnections. International Journal of Computer Science and Network Security 10(8), 74–79 (2010) ISSN: 1738-7906

Reduction of Inter Carrier Interference by Pilot Aided Self Cancellation Compared to Self Cancellation Method

Anitha Sheela Kankacharla[1], Tarun Kumar Juluru[2], and Saritha Dedavath[2]

[1] Department of ECE, JNTU College of Engineering, Hyderabad, Andhra Pradesh, India
kanithasheela@gmail.com
[2] Department of ECE, Ramappa Engineering college, Warangal, Andhra Pradesh, India
tarunjuluru@yahoo.com, schandrabhanu2@gmail.com

Abstract. Orthogonal frequency division multiplexing is a digital modulation technique in which the available spectrum is split into numerous narrow band channels of dissimilar frequencies to achieve high data rate in a multi path fading environment. In OFDM number of sub carriers is considered which are orthogonal to each other. As the number of sub carriers is increased there is no indemnity of sustaining orthogonality. At some point the carriers are not independent to each other, where the orthogonality can be loosed and which might escort to interference and also owing to the lack of synchronization among transmitter and receiver local oscillator, leads to interference known as inter carrier interference (ICI). The ICI cause power leakage amid sub carriers consequently degrading the system performance. In order to enhance the system performance and to diminish the inter carrier interference a novel scheme is proposed in this paper. In this scheme at the transmitter side the modulated data and a few predefined pilot symbols are mapped onto the non neighboring sub carriers with weighting coefficients of +1 and -1. With the aid of pilot symbols the frequency offset is exactly estimated by using maximum likelihood estimation and can be minimized. At demodulation stage the received signals are linearly combined along with their weighted coefficients and pilot symbols, called as pilot aided self cancellation method. By this the CIR can be improved ~10 dB. In this paper the effectiveness of pilot aided self cancellation scheme is compared with the self cancellation method. It provides accurate estimation of frequency offset and when residual CFO is less significant the ICI can be diminished successfully.

Keywords: CFO, Fading, ICI, OFDM, Pilot aided.

1 Introduction

In order to attain the requirements of modern Transreceivers a system has to provide high capacity and variable bit rate information transmission with high bandwidth efficiency. But in the wireless environment signals are usually impaired by fading and multipath delay spread phenomenon and the traditional single carrier mobile communication systems do not perform well.

A. Abraham et al. (Eds.): ACC 2011, Part I, CCIS 190, pp. 34–43, 2011.

These channels suffer from extreme fading of the signal amplitude and Inter symbol Interference due to frequency selectivity of the channel which appears at receiver side. Many techniques like channel coding and adaptive equalization have been widely used as solution to these problems, but due to their inherent delay in the coding and equalization process and high cost of the hardware, it is quite difficult to use these techniques in the systems operating at high bit at high bit rates. An alternative solution is to use a multi carrier system; [1] one of its examples is Orthogonal Frequency Division Multiplexing System. OFDM is a broad band multi carrier modulation method that offers efficient performance and many advantages over the older methods. [2][3].

Where as OFDM is not a new technique. The technology was first conceived in 1960s and 1970s during research into minimizing interference among channels near each other in frequency.[4] Priority is given to minimizing the interference, or crosstalk among the channels & symbols comprising the data stream. At that time OFDM was extremely difficult to implement with the electronic hardware present at that time. Today for all the wireless technique OFDM is the method of choice.

2 OFDM Architecture

OFDM is a combination of modulation and multiplexing. Multiplexing generally refers to independent signals, those produced by different sources. In OFDM the signal itself is first split into independent channels, modulated by data and then re multiplexed to create the OFDM carrier. Fig.1 shows the transmission and reception of OFDM.

The transmitter section converts digital data to be transmitted, into mapping of sub carrier amplitude and phase. The input data stream is converted into N parallel data streams each with symbol Period Ts through a serial-to-parallel Port. When the parallel Symbol streams are generated, each stream would be modulated and carried over at different center frequencies.

The sub-carriers are spaced by 1/NTs in frequency, thus they are orthogonal over the interval (0, Ts). Then, the N symbols are mapped to bins of an inverse fast Fourier transform (IFFT). These FFT bins correspond to the orthogonal sub carriers in the OFDM symbol. Therefore, the OFDM symbol can be expressed as

$$x(n)=\frac{1}{\sqrt{N}}\sum_{k=1}^{N-1} X_m(K)e^{-j2\pi Kn/N} \tag{1}$$

Xm's are the base band symbols on each sub-carrier. The digital-to-analog (D/A) converter then creates an analog time-domain signal which is transmitted through the channel.

At the receiver, the signal is converted back to a discrete N point sequence y(n), corresponding to each sub carrier. This discrete signal is demodulated using an N-point Fast Fourier Transform (FFT) operation at the receiver.

The demodulated symbol stream is given by

$$Y(m)=\sum_{n=0}^{N-1} y(n)e^{i2\pi nm} + W(m) \tag{2}$$

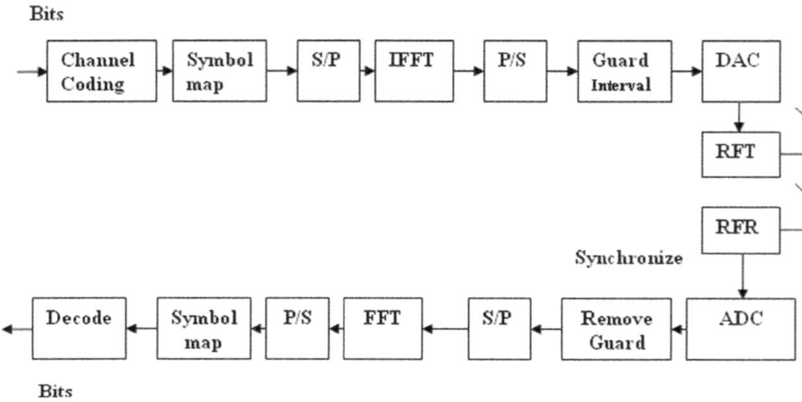

Fig. 1. Block diagram of standard OFDM system

Where W (m) corresponds to the Additive White Gaussian Noise (AWGN) introduced in the channel.

Out of all the benefits and efficient performance OFDM suffers with a drawback of synchronization error, such as frequency or phase offsets. The frequency offset can result from a Doppler shift due to a mobile environment, as well as from a carrier frequency synchronization error. Such frequency offset cause a loss of the carrier's orthogonality, which causes ICI. Researchers proposed many techniques to mitigate the ICI of OFDM. They can be listed as Frequency Domain Equalization[5],[6], Time Domain Windowing[7],[8], ICI self cancellation scheme[9],Maximum likelihood method[10], Kalman filter method[11], and Polynomial cancellation coding and finite differences[12].

All the above schemes will estimate CFO as well as eliminate ICI but these schemes degrades the system performance in Peak to average power ratio (PAPR) [13].

A new approach is proposed to control both ICI and PAPR at the same time is conjugate data self cancellation. The PAPR problem can be copped with new technique called pilot aided self cancellation.

3 Self Cancellation Method

ICI self cancellation is a hopeful technique introduced by Zhao and Gustav to combat and restrain ICI in OFDM .The scheme works in two steps at the transmitter side, one data symbol is modulated onto a cluster of adjacent sub carriers with a group of weighting coefficients. The weighting coefficients are intended so that the ICI caused by the channel frequency errors can be minimized. At the receiver side by linearly combining the received signals on these sub carriers with projected coefficients, the outstanding ICI contained in the received signals can then be further condensed.

However this system degrades the performance in peak-to-average power ratio (PAPR). Besides it is not bandwidth efficient.

4 Pilot Aided Self Cancellation Technique

A pilot is a signal usually a single frequency, transmitted over a communication system for supervisory, control, equalization, continuity, synchronization or reference purpose. Each pilot sub carrier signal is placed at different sub carrier location for each successive signal of OFDM signal to form a sliding pilot sub carrier signal.
The block diagram of the proposed pilot-aided ICI Self-cancellation scheme is shown in Fig.2.In pilot aided self cancellation scheme the modulated data symbols are mapped along with some pilot symbols onto the un adjacent sub carriers with weighting coefficients. In OFDM at the transmitter after the FFT the nth sub carrier of the ith symbol is given by

$$r_{i,n} = \frac{1}{\sqrt{N}} \sum_{k=1}^{N} X_{i,K} e^{\frac{j2\pi Kn}{N}}, n = 1, 2.....N. \tag{3}$$

Where $X_{i,k}$ given as

$$X_{i,k} = \begin{cases} P_{i,k} & k\varepsilon\beta \\ S_{i,k} & k\varepsilon\alpha \end{cases}. \tag{4}$$

Where $r_{i,n}$ is the nth sub carrier of the ith OFDM symbol.

Where $P_{i,k}$ and $S_{i,k}$ stands for the pilot symbols and the complex data symbols which are transmitted. N is the size of IFFT. The non neighboring sub carriers k and (N-k+1) with weighting coefficients of +1 and -1 are mapped by pilot symbols set to one at the ICI self cancellation stage. The sub carriers are transmitted as

$X_{i,N}=-X_{i,1}$......... , $X_{i,N-1}= -X_{i,2}$.... etc.

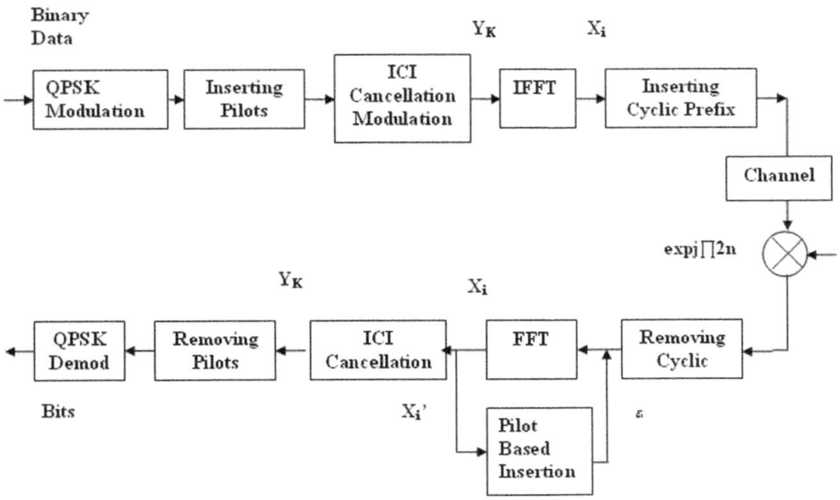

Fig. 2. Block diagram of Pilot Aided ICI Self Cancellation

The ICI weighted coefficients can be derived between the ith and the lth sub carrier can be expressed as

$$W_{i,(k-l)} = \frac{Sin(\pi(l+\varepsilon-K))}{N\sin\frac{\pi}{N}((l+\varepsilon-K))} exp(j\pi\frac{1}{N})(l+\varepsilon-K)). \quad (5)$$

The first term in the right hand side of eqn.(5) is the desired signal. When the frequency offset ε is null then the ICI coefficient is maximum $W_{i,(k-0)}$ =1. The second term is the ICI weighted coefficients components. The desired received signal power on the kth sub carrier can be given as

$$P[|C(K)|^2] = \mathrm{E}[|\mathrm{X(k)W}_{i,0}|^2]. \quad (6)$$

And the ICI power is given as

$$P[|I(K)|^2] = E[|\sum_{l=0 l\neq K}^{N-1} X(l)\mathrm{W}_{i,(l-k)}|^2]. \quad (7)$$

4.1 Pilot Modulation

The data symbols and the pilot symbols are mapped onto the non neighboring sub carrier's k and (N-k+1) along with their weighting coefficients +1 and -1 i.e.

$X_{i,N}$= -X $_{i,1}$ ……, X $_{i,n-1}$=-X $_{i,2}$.etc modulated sthe transmitted symbols can be depicted as

$$X_{i,l} = \sum_{K=1}^{N} X_{i,k} W_{i,(k-l)} = \sum_{K=1}^{(N-Np)/2} X_{i,k}(W_{i,k-l} - W_{i,N-l-K+1}) + \sum_{j=(N-N_{P+2})/2}^{N/2} X_{i,j}(W_{i,j-l} - W_{i,N-j-l+1}) \quad (8)$$

Where the second term in eqn.(8) is the ICI weighted coefficient at the non neighboring sub carriers and n_k is the noise. N_p is the number of pilot carriers inserted.

At the stage of ICI self cancellation demodulation block the sub carriers are received with normalized frequency offset ε which is expressed as

$$Y_{i,l} = X_{i,l'} - X_{i,N-l+1}$$

$$= 2X_{i,k}W_{i,0} + \sum_{K=1,k\neq l}^{(N-N_p)/2} X_{i,k}(W_{i,(k-l)} - W_{i,N-k-l+1} - W_{i,k-N+l-1}) + . \quad (9)$$

$$\sum_{j=(N-N_p+2)/2}^{N/2} X_{i,j}(W_{i,l-1} + W_{i,l-j} - W_{i,N-j-l+1} - W_{i,j-N+l-1})$$

The first term in (8) is the desired signal destroyed by the frequency offset, the second term is the ICI component caused by the data symbols and the last term is another ICI element resulting from the pilot symbols. It can be further simplified as

$$Y_{i,l} = 2X_{i,k}W_{i,0} + A + B \cdot \tag{10}$$

Evaluation of CIR. The system ICI power can be evaluated by using the CIR. When the data is of zero mean and is statistically independent, the CIR expression for a traditional self cancellation sub carrier $0 \leq K \leq N-1$ can be derived as

$$CIR = \frac{|W_i(k)|^2}{\sum_{l=0,l\neq K}^{N-1} |W_{i(k-l)}|^2} = \frac{|W_{i,0}|^2}{\sum_{l=1}^{N-1} |W_{i,l}|^2} . \tag{11}$$

Efficiently the CIR can be evaluated for the proposed scheme by adding 4 pilot carriers. Nevertheless, since pilot symbols can be adopted to estimate the CFO, the residual frequency offset becomes small enough so that ICI self cancellation demodulation can be operated properly.

$$CIR_{pilotaided} = \frac{4|W_{i,0}|^2}{|A+B|^2} . \tag{12}$$

Comparing (11) and (12) we can rationalize that the improvement in the CIR level is about 10 dB. The performance can be improved .the pilot symbols can be adopted to estimate CFO.

5 Algorithm in Support of Estimation of CFO

The carrier frequency offset can be estimated by applying the MLE to two successive OFDM symbols.

1. When the synchronization is perfect the cyclic prefix can be removed. After the FFT operation the pth demodulated pilot symbol of the ith OFDM symbol is given by

$$X_{i,p'} = \frac{1}{\sqrt{N}} \sum_{n=1}^{N} Y_{i,n} e^{\frac{-j2\pi p'n}{N}} \quad p' \in \beta .$$

$$= \frac{1}{N} \sum_{n=1}^{N} \sum_{k=1}^{N} X_{i,k} e^{\frac{j2\pi kn}{N} + \frac{2j\pi \varepsilon n}{N} - \frac{j2\pi p'n}{N}} . \tag{13}$$

2. In addition to the pth demodulated pilot symbol of (i+1)^th^ OFDM symbol is given by

$$X_{i+1,p'} = \frac{1}{\sqrt{N}} \sum_{n=1}^{N} r_{i+1,n} e \frac{-j2\pi p'n}{N} \quad p' \in \beta .$$

$$= \frac{1}{N} \sum_{n=1}^{N} \sum_{k=1}^{N} X_{i,k} e \frac{j2\pi kn}{N} + \frac{j2\pi e(n+N)}{N} - \frac{j2\pi p'n}{N} .$$

$$= \frac{1}{N} e^{\frac{j2\pi \varepsilon N}{N}} \sum_{n=1}^{N} \sum_{k=1}^{N} X_{i,k} e \frac{j2\pi kn}{N} + \frac{j2\pi \varepsilon n}{N^{e}} - \frac{j2\pi p'n}{N} . \qquad (14)$$

3. When eqn.(12) and eqn.(13) are shared, the estimated partial CFO is given by

$$\hat{\varepsilon} = \frac{1}{2\pi} \tan^{-1} \left[\sum_{P^1 \in \beta} X_{i,p}^{*} X_{i+1,P^1} \right] . \qquad (15)$$

More accurate partial CFO estimation can be obtained if more pilot symbols are inserted. In addition, the pilot symbols can be adopted for channel estimation, and the over all system performance can be further improved .Besides the efficient performance the pilot symbols decrease the band width utilization. Therefore the proposed scheme can tolerate larger CFO then the traditional ICI self cancellation scheme.

6 Simulations

The proposed method is compared with ICI self cancellation method. The simulations were performed in AWGN channel by taking 64 point FFT operation. The CFO is estimated as 0.5.The modulation is BPSK with a data sub carriers of 52, number of bits per symbol are 52 for the E_b/No from 0 to 10 dB

PARAMETERS	VALUES
Number of carriers	104
Modulation	BPSK
Frequency offset	0. 5
No. of OFDM symbols	10^2
No. of pilot symbols added	4
Bits per OFDM symbols	52
E_b-No	0:10
FFT size	64

The CIR for the self cancellation method is shown in figure 3. The frequency offset is taken above 0.5.In order to get better performance 4 pilot carriers are supplemented and the CIR is predicted for the same frequency offset in figure 4.

However the anticipated scheme can be justified in terms of BER. In figure 5 and 6 the bit error rates simulated by means of both the methods.

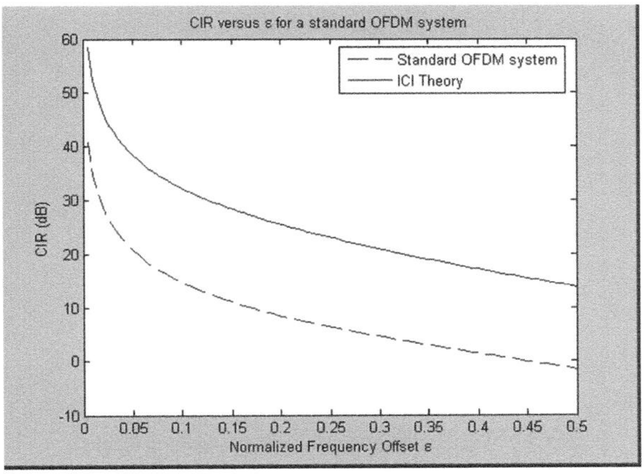

Fig. 3. CIR versus normalized frequency offset of a ICI self cancellation technique

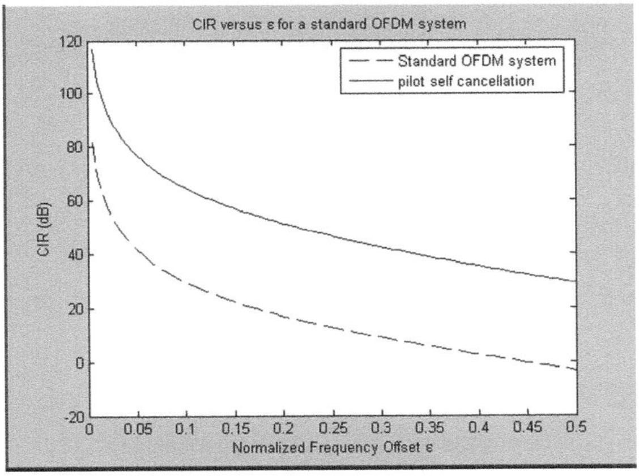

Fig. 4. CIR versus normalized frequency offset of a pilot aided ICI self cancellation technique

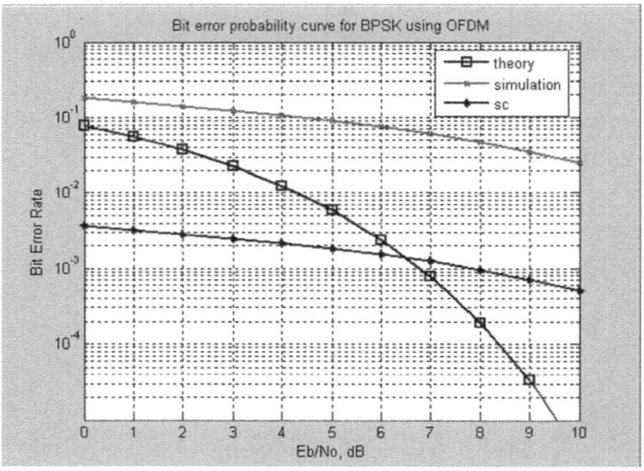

Fig. 5. BER performance of OFDM with ICI self cancellation

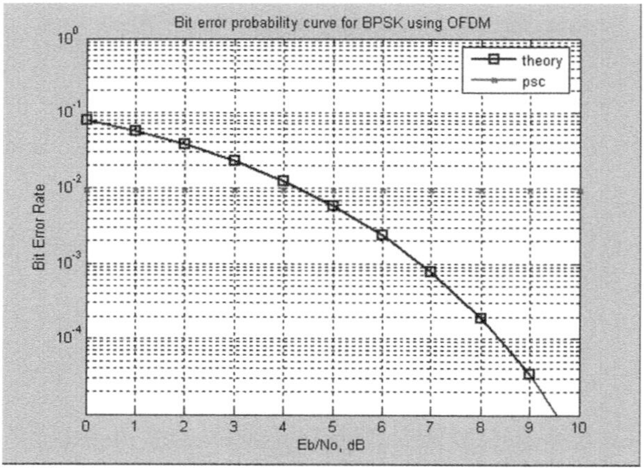

Fig. 6. BER performance of OFDM using pilot aided self cancellation

7 Conclusions

Pilot aided self cancellation is simpler in edifice. It improves the system performance better as compared to self cancellation scheme. The proposed scheme estimates the precise CFO by using maximum likelihood estimation and compensates better. When compared to the ICI self cancellation Technique it works superior for upper CFO which has been studied theoretically and by simulations. The proposed scheme improves the BER significantly by adding only few pilot symbols and best performance can be extracted by adding more number of carriers.

Future scope

Further work can be done by growing the numeral of pilot carriers and within rural area channel models as well as explore the performance in multi path fading channels.

References

1. Zhang, H., Yuan, D., Wang, C.-X.: A study on the PAPRS in multi carrier modulation system with different orthogonal base. Wireless Communication and Mobile Computing 7, 311–318 (2007)
2. Prasad, R.: OFDM for wireless communication system. Artech House, Boston (2004)
3. Weinstein, S., Ebert, P.: Data transmission by Frequency-division multiplexing using the discrete Fourier transform. IEEE Trans. Communication 19, 628–634 (1971)
4. Ahn, J., Lee, H.S.: Frequency domain equalization of OFDM signal over frequency Non selective Rayleigh fading channels. Electron. Lett 29(16), 1476–1477 (1993)
5. Witrisal, K., Kim, Y.H., Prasad, R.: A novel approach for performance evaluation of OFDM with error correction coding & interleaving. In: IEEE VTS 50th Vehicular Technology Conference 1999 (1999)
6. Dhahi, N.A.: Optimum finite-length equalization for multicarrier transceivers. IEEE Trans. Commun. 44, 56–64 (1996)
7. Li, R., Stette, G.: Time-limited orthogonal multicarrier modulation scheme. IEEE Trans. Commun. 43, 1269–1272 (1995)
8. Muschallik, C.: Improving an OFDM reception using an adaptive Nyquist windowing. IEEE Trans. Communication 42(10), 2908–2914 (1994)
9. Zhao, Y., Haggman, S.G.: Inter carrier interference self-cancellation scheme for OFDM Mobile communication systems. IEEE Trans. Communication 49(7), 1185–1191 (2001)
10. Moose, P.H.: A technique for orthogonal frequency division multiplexing frequency offset correction. IEEE Trans. Communication 42(10), 2908–2914 (1994)
11. Kumar, R., Malarvizhi, S.: Reduction of inter carrier interference in OFDM systems.Dept. Of Electronics and Communication. Engg., SRM University, Chennai, India-603203
12. Seston, K.A., Armstrong, J.: Polynomial cancellation coding and finite differences. IEEE Transactions on Information Theory 46(1) (January 2000)
13. Fu, Y., Kang, S.G., Ko, C.C.: A New Scheme for PAPR Reduction in OFDM Systems with ICI Self Cancellation. Dept of electrical and computer engineering Natinal University of Singapore (2002)

A Novel Attack Model Simulation in OLSR

Manish Kumar, Rajbir Kaur, Vijay Laxmi, and Manoj Singh Gaur

Department of Computer Engineering,
Malaviya National Institute of Technology, Jaipur, India
manukumar200629@gmail.com, {rajbir,vlaxmi,gaurms}@mnit.ac.in

Abstract. The Optimized Link State Routing (OLSR) protocol [4] is a route management protocol for mobile ad hoc networks (MANET)s. Such networks have dynamic, rapidly-changing, multi-hop topologies composed of relatively bandwidth-constrained wireless links. OLSR is responsible for maintaining routing tables used for routing packets. Multi Point Relay (MPR) is the key optimization used in OLSR. In absence of any security mechanism, OLSR is prone to routing disorder or resource consumption attacks caused by malicious nodes. In this paper, we propose a novel routing disorder attack against OLSR. In this attack, a malicious node updates its repositories with fake neighborhood information resulting in generation of incorrect control messages. Neighboring nodes choose the malicious node as their MPR node. Data packets passing through malicious node may be diverted to improper routes and packets may never reach their destination. A large amount of packets sent from source to destination get dropped. Simulations on *ns-3* confirm validity of our approach.

1 Introduction

In order to enable communication between any two nodes in a MANET, a routing protocol is employed, which keeps track of all the nodes present in the network at any point of time. There are two basic type of routing protocols for Ad-hoc networks – (1) reactive and (2) proactive. Proactive routing protocols maintain routing information periodically. Fresh lists of destinations and their routes are maintained by periodically distributing routing tables throughout the network. Whenever there is any change in network topology, routing tables are updated. Reactive routing protocols are demand driven. Routes are calculated as and when requirement arises.

In conventional wired networks, security systems are already implemented at different layers such as IP, application, or transport layer. In ad-hoc networks each node works as a router, necessitating security mechanisms at routing layer or protocol. Each node is capable of deleting, modifying and adding routes in routing tables. This is the main cause of the vulnerabilities of routing protocols in ad-hoc networks. Detecting a malicious node is difficult as ad-hoc networks are decentralized, distributed and dynamic in nature. This routing insecurity makes ad-hoc networks vulnerable to attackers for attacks.

In this paper we propose a novel attack model on OLSR based ad-hoc networks. In this attack methodology the attacking node sends false topology control messages resulting in huge packet drop. The rest of the paper is organised as follows: Section 2

A. Abraham et al. (Eds.): ACC 2011, Part I, CCIS 190, pp. 44–53, 2011.

introduces OLSR protocol. In Section 3 related work is discussed. Section 4 describes the cause of vulnerabilities in OLSR. Section 5 describes our proposed attack model. In Section 6 the simulation details and results are discussed. Section 7 gives a brief detail about our proposed detection methodology. Section 8 concludes our work.

2 OLSR Protocol

OLSR is table-driven and pro-active and utilizes an optimization called Multi point Relaying for control traffic flooding. OLSR maintains state by keeping a variety of information repositories. Information repositories are updated by processing received control messages. Information stored is used to further generate control messages. Different information repositories of relevance are as follows: Link Set, Neighbor Set, 2-hop Neighbor Set, MPR Set, MPR Selector Set, Topology Information Base. In this section we explain how control messages are processed to populate different information repositories and for route calculation.

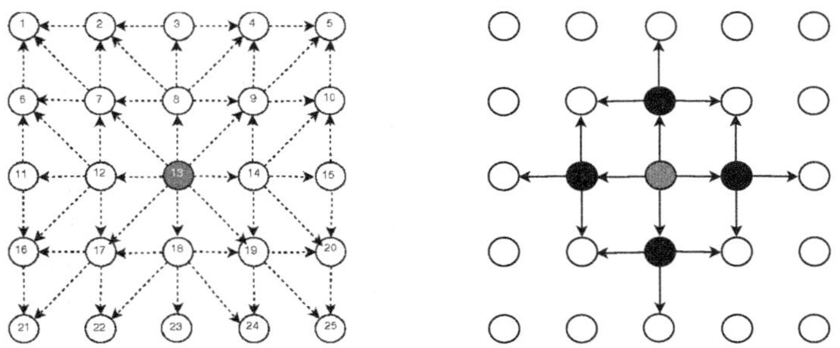

(a) Normal Broadcast

(b) Broadcast by MPR Flooding

Fig. 1. There are redundant transmissions in normal broadcast as shown by dashed lines

An MPR set for a node is the minimal set of its one hop neighbors, which covers all 2-hop neighbors of that node. In OLSR, flooding of control messages is minimized using MPRs. In a **normal broadcast** scenario, a node forwards a packet (data or control) to all its 1-hop neighbors. 1-hop neighbors in turn forward the received packet to all their 1-hop neighbors and so on until the packet inundates the entire network. The drawback of this approach is that a lot of duplicate traffic is created in the network. In **MPR flooding** [4] used in OLSR, a node selects some of its 1-hop neighbor as its MPR (Multi-Point Relay) node such that all its 2-hop neighbors can be reached through this MPR node. Whenever a node has a packet to broadcast into the network, it forwards the packet to its MPR nodes only. The MPR nodes in turn forward the packet to their MPRs. Packets are broadcast with minimal redundancy. Considerably less duplicate packets are forwarded to nodes by the use of MPRs. Difference between normal broadcast and broadcast by MPR flooding mechanism in OLSR can be understood from Figure 1.

2.1 HELLO Messages

HELLO messages are broadcast at regular intervals to detect neighbors and the state of the communication lines to them. In HELLO messages, nodes transmit information about all known links and neighbors. These messages populate 1-hop neighbor set, 2-hop neighbor set and link set. Link set is maintained to keep current information of the status of the link between a node and its neighbor. A change in link status may update neighbor set repository.[1] HELLO messages also populate the MPR and MPR selector set. All MPRs of a node are maintained in MPR set. Nodes selecting a particular node as their MPR are maintained in MPR selector set. Let us consider a topology in Figure 2.

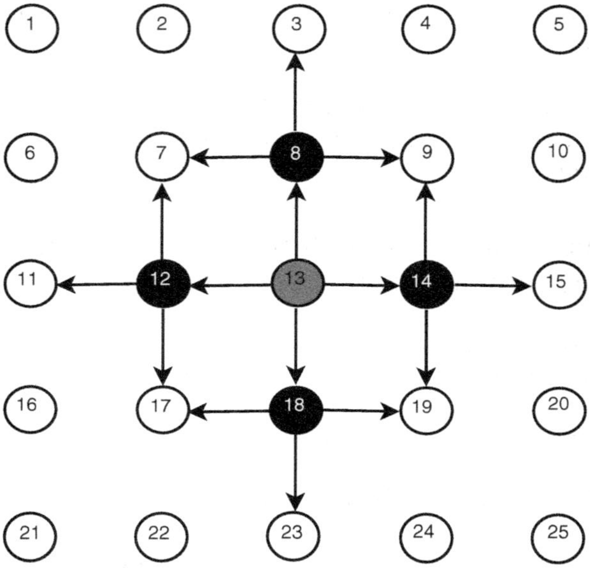

Fig. 2. An Example Topology

Let us consider node N_{18} for topology shown in Figure 2. It transmits information about known 1-hop neighbors in HELLO message – (N_{17}, N_{19}, N_{23}, N_{13}). N_{18} also receives HELLO messages from its 1-hop neighbors who transmit information about their 1-hop neighbors. For example,

Information transmitted by N_{17} in its HELLO message: ($N_{12}, N_{16}, N_{18}, N_{22}$)
Information transmitted by N_{19} in its HELLO message: ($N_{14}, N_{18}, N_{20}, N_{24}$)

In the same way, information about their 1-hop neighbors will be transmitted by N_{23} and N_{13}. N_{18} processes received HELLO messages and update its various repositories.

1-hop neighbor set of N_{18}: ($N_{17}, N_{19}, N_{23}, N_{13}$).
2-hop neighbor set of N_{18} (calculated as 1-hop neighbors of its 1-hop neighbors): (N_{12}, $N_{16}, N_{22}, N_{14}, N_{20}, N_{24}, N_{8}$).

[1] We assume symmetric (bidirectional) links between neighbors.

To calculate MPR set

2-hop neighbors that can be reached through 1-hop neighbor N_{17}: (N_{12}, N_{16}, N_{22})
2-hop neighbors that can be reached through 1-hop neighbor N_{19}: (N_{14}, N_{20}, N_{24})
2-hop neighbors that can be reached through 1-hop neighbor N_{23}: (N_{22}, N_{24})
2-hop neighbors that can be reached through 1-hop neighbor N_{13}: (N_{12}, N_{8}, N_{14})

Therefore, MPR set of N_{18} (1-hop neighbor of N_{18}, through which all its 2-hop neighbors can be reached): (N_{17}, N_{19}, N_{13}), N_{23} is excluded as N_{22} and N_{24} can also be reached through N_{17} and N_{19} respectively.

Therefore, MPR selector set of nodes N_{17}, N_{19} and N_{13}: (N_{18}).
Link set has following fields among others (Local node address, neighbor node address, link status). There will be one tuple for each 1-hop neighbor of N_{18}. Link status is symmetric. From the above example we see how HELLO messages are used to populate different repositories associated with a node.

2.2 TC Messages

Topology control messages are diffused in the network using MPR optimization with the purpose of providing each node with sufficient link state information to allow route calculation.

In OLSR, TC messages describe links between a nodes and the nodes in its MPR selector set. TC messages are generated immediately when changes are /detected in the MPR selector set. TC messages are used to populate the topology set.

Considering the example given in 2.1, N_{18} generates a TC message advertising its MPR set: (N_{17}, N_{19}, N_{13}). This is forwarded N_{13} as $N_{13} \in (N_{17}, N_{19}, N_{13})$. This will be forwarded by MPR of N_{13} and so on. Given TC information, each node forms a topology table. Topology table has the format (destination, Next Hop, Number of Hops). One sample tuple in the table of N_{18} is $(N_{14}, N_{13}, 1)$.

2.3 Route Calculation

Routing tables based on local link table and topology table are maintained at each node in the network. Routes are calculated based on the shortest path algorithm [4].

3 Related Work

Adjih *et al* [2] and Clausen *et al* [6] emphasize vulnerabilities specific to OLSR. They mention that attacks can be due to

1. incorrect traffic generation and
2. incorrect traffic relaying

They specify that a misbehaving node can become an MPR by performing link spoofing in HELLO messages. In contrast our proposed work performs link spoofing by updating link repository. HELLO messages are automatically generated when there is change in link set. Changes are not made in control messages.

4 Vulnerabilities in OLSR

In this section we discuss various security vulnerabilities in OLSR. In OLSR, each node has two different responsibilities – (1) to generate correct routing protocol control traffic according to protocol specification, (2) to forward routing control traffic on behalf of other nodes present in the network. Malicious behavior of a node can result in generation of incorrect control messages or incorrect relay of control messages.

There is no mechanism in OLSR to validate correctness of information sent by a node to its neighbors. Neighbor nodes process and forward all information even if it is generated by a malicious node. This may cause various problems in the network. In the following section we propose a novel attack model where a malicious node exploits the vulnerabilities inherent in OLSR to cause routing misbehavior.

5 Proposed Attack Model

In this section we propose an attack model that exploits flaws in OLSR. In our proposed attack model, a misbehaving node updates its link table with incorrect neighborhood information. Erroneous neighborhood information disseminates in the network. Inaccurate routing tables are generated. Packets intended for destination do not reach it, resulting in packets being dropped. The attack is performed in three steps as discussed in following subsections.

5.1 Collecting Network Information

In OLSR, several repositories are maintained at each node. These repositories present a view of the network topology. A node can have an idea about total number of nodes in network at a particular instance of time from the topology set. Routing table contains information about routes to all destinations. A malicious node collects following information about the network.

1. Its 1- hop neighbor from the 1-hop neighbor repository.
2. Its 2-hop neighbors from its 2-hop neighbor repository.
3. State of link between a node and its neighbor from link set.
4. All nodes in the network from topology set and routing table.

5.2 Updating Own Topology Information

A malicious node has sufficient information about the network and its proximity. It updates its link repository with false information by including network nodes that are not its 1-hop or 2-hop neighbors. These are the nodes having k-hop (k¿2) distance. Malicious node fills the link table with entries depicting all these nodes, actually at a distance greater than 2 hops from it as its 1-hop neighbors. Thus a malicious node includes almost every network node as 1 or 2-hop neighbors.
And, *nodes beyond 2-hop distance = nodes in routing table - (nodes in 1-hop neighbor repository + nodes in 2-hop repository)* are included as 1-hop neighbors.

5.3 Broadcast Fake Information

HELLO messages are generated when any change in link set is detected. Malicious HELLO messages containing incorrect neighbor information is broadcast to 1-hop neighbors of the malicious node. 1-hop neighbors of malicious node update their repositories with fresh (fake) received information. Honest nodes are forced into believing that malicious node is a good candidate for MPR node as its provides connectivity to many of their 2-hop neighbors. Malicious node is advertising itself as 1-hop distant to many nodes which are at a distance of 2-hops from its 1-hop neighbors. This ensures that malicious node is selected as the MPR node and most of the traffic is forwarded through this node. Consider the topology in Figure 2. Let N_{13} be the attacker.

1-hop neighbor set of N_{13}: $(N_8, N_{12}, N_{14}, N_{18})$.
2-hop neighbor set of N_{13}: $(N_7, N_9, N_{16}, N_{15}, N_{17}, N_{19}, N_{23})$.

Remaining nodes in the network are broadcast as its 1-hop neighbors by N_{13}. Let us consider a node, say, N_8. When N_8 receives an update from N_{13} that it provides reachability to most of its 2-hop neighbors N_2, N_4, N_6, N_{10}, N_{12}, N_{14}, N_{18}. N_8 selects N_{13} as its MPR.

5.4 Packets Do Not Reach Intended Recipient

Once malicious node has updated its link tuples with false information and is successfully selected as MPR of other nodes, the actual attack is launched. The main objective is to attract the traffic and drop the packets. This shall result in drop of network performance. When a data packet arrives at this malicious node for forwarding, link set is referred to fetch route information. If there is a direct route to the destination, the hop count of the packet is decremented by one and forwarded. If no direct route to the destination exists, the packet may loop due to combination of incorrect routing tables and eventually get dropped. A malicious node can advertise as many nodes as its 1-hop neighbor as it wants. There are increased chances that a lot of traffic is sent through it and is, in turn, gets dropped due to absence of proper link.

6 Simulation Results

The attack was simulated on *ns-3* [3] simulator [Developer Version]. We modified OLSR routing protocol module in ns-3 to simulate the attack. We have assumed that,

1. There is only one attacker
2. Initially all nodes are placed in a grid
3. Attacker has complete information of network topology after a period known as *convergence time*

6.1 Experimental Setup

We consider grid topology of size 5×5, 6×6, 7×7 and 8×8 respectively to observe the effect of the attack on different network sizes. Distance between two nodes is kept at

Table 1. Simulation Parameters

Simulator	NS3(Developer Version)
Topology	Grid (n X n by default)
Number of Nodes	Variable (25 to 64)
Protocol Used	OLSR
Size of Data Packet	500 Bytes
Packet Generation Rate	1 packet per second
Medium	Wireless
Distance between 2 Nodes	500 meter
Convergence Time	30 Seconds
Simulation Time	Variable with different number of nodes
Channel Capacity	1 Mbps

Table 2. Parameter Values

Network Size	Source	Sink	Attacker
5×5	N_0	N_{24}	N_{12}
6×6	N_0	N_{35}	N_{21}
7×7	N_0	N_{48}	N_{24}
8×8	N_0	N_{63}	N_{24}

500 meters. Size of data packets considered is 500 bytes. Two values of simulation time were considered. Packets are generated at a rate of one packet/sec. Table 6.1 lists the simulation parameters used. For our simulations, the values of source, sink and attacker for each network size is listed in Table 2. In *ns-3*, first node has an index 0, second node has index 1 and so on.

In our simulation, the malicious node updates its routing table with fake information after a period of 5 seconds. It waits for its different information repositories to be populated to get an idea of network topology. Once its information repositories are populated, it updates its table with fake information about its 2-hop neighborhood. Incorrect control messages are generated and malicious node is selected as MPR. We have kept the time for convergence of the protocol to be 30 seconds. Data packets are sent from the 30th second onwards. The attacker has already taken control by then. The packets automatically drop due to incorrect routing tables.

6.2 Results

Figures 3, 4, 5 show the effect of the attack on the network. From the graph we observe that in no attack situation, all packets are received by the sink. In situation of an attack, the number of packets reaching the sink are only a small percentage of packets sent by the source. Incorrect routes caused by malicious node results in huge packets drops. We experiment with two cases:

case 1: 100 packets are sent from source to the destination, and
case 2: 200 packets are sent from source to the destination.

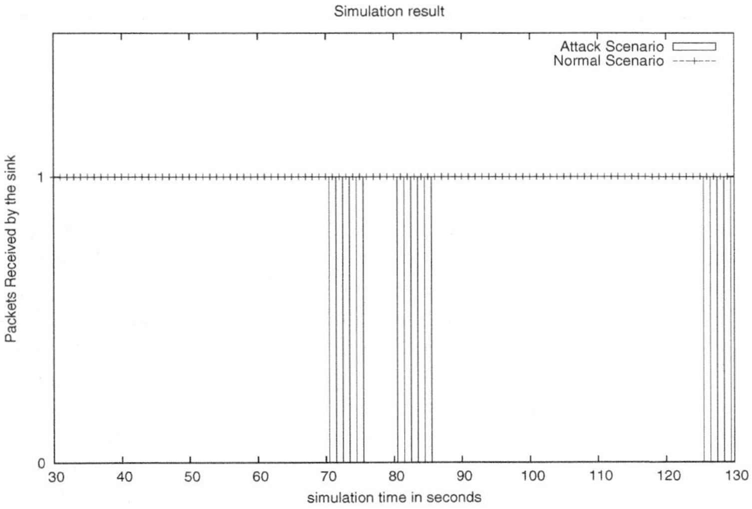

Fig. 3. Simulation results with 100 data packets

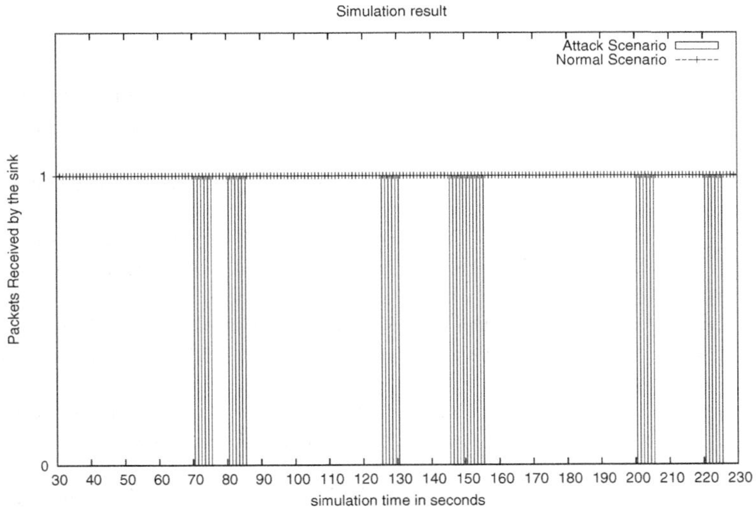

Fig. 4. Simulation results with 200 data packets

Figure 3 shows the packets delivered to sink for *case 1* in normal condition as well as in attack condition. The occurrence of a packet received by sink in normal condition (without attack) is shown by dotted line with vertical linespot, while that of under attack condition is denoted by a vertical bar (continuous line). On X-axis we have time in seconds. On Y-axis 0 means a packet drop and 1 means packet received. It is clear from the graph that in normal condition all the packets are delivered to the sink. In an

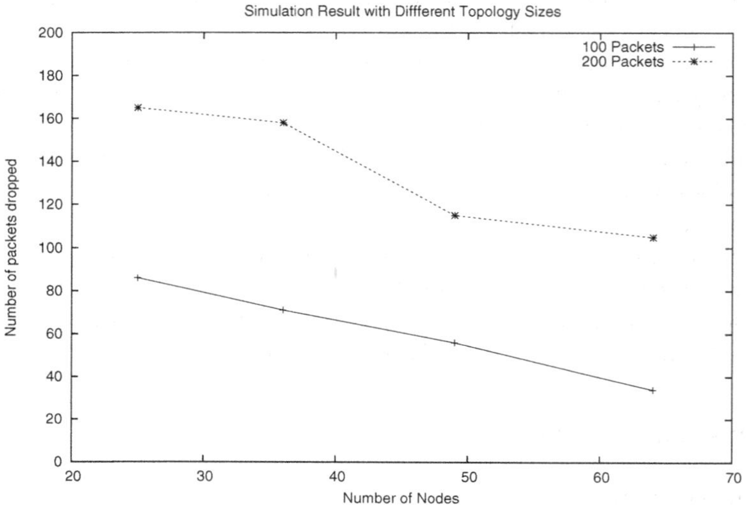

Fig. 5. Simulation results with different topology sizes

attack situation only a few packets reach the sink. Other packets are dropped due to the generation of incorrect routing tables.

Figure 4 shows number of packets received by the sink for *case 2*. Here also we observe that a large number of packets get dropped when the experiment is carried under attack conditions. In normal condition all the 200 packets reach the sink.

Figure 5 shows the effect of the attack on different network sizes. We observe from the graph that there is a gradual decrease in the effect of attack with increase in network size. The number of packet drops decrease with increase in number of nodes. Number of available routes from source to destination increase with increase in network size. It is possible that data packets reach the sink through an alternate path not going through malicious node. In the graph shown in the figure, (+) represents the number of packet drops when 100 packets are sent by the source. (*) shows number of packet drops when 200 packets are sent from source to sink. X-axis represents the total number of nodes in the simulation and Y-axis represents total number of packets dropped. It is clear from the graph that the number of packet drops decrease with increase in topology size. We observe from the graph that in *case 1* number of packet drop is 85 for network size 25 which gets reduces to 34 when the network size increases to 64 nodes. So it is very clear that increasing the size of network results in a decrease of effect of the proposed attack as more routs are available with larger topology size.

7 Proposed Detection Methodology

TC messages broadcast every 5 seconds forces each node to recompute its MPR sets. Dynamic topology ensures that nodes in MPR set change with time. If a node occurs repeatedly in the MPR set, it may indicate malicious activity. Detection may incorporate each node keeping track of nodes in MPR set for an observed period. If an MPR node occurs repeatedly, the observing node blacklists the node for certain duration.

8 Conclusion

In this paper we have proposed a new routing disorder attack model. We have shown by simulation that the attack results in huge packet drops. We have also conducted our experiments on network of different sizes. We conclude that effect of the attack decreases with increase in network size. Number of available routes from source to destination increase with increase in network size. An alternate path sans malicious node is possible. In future, we will analyze the effect of the attack on neighboring nodes. We will also work with co-operative attackers to see if the impact of the attack can be sustained with increase in network size.

References

1. Kannhavong, B., Nakayama, H., Kato, N., Nemoto, Y., Jamalipour, A.: Analysis of the Node Isolation Attack Against OLSR-based Mobile Ad Hoc Networks. In: Proceedings ISCN 2006. IEEE, Los Alamitos (2006) 1-4244-0491-6/06
2. Adjih, C., Clausen, T., Laouiti, A., Mühlethaler, P., Raffo, D.: Securing the OLSR routing protocol with or without compromised nodes in the network. Technical Report INRIA RR-5494, HIPERCOM Project, INRIA Rocquencourt (February 2005)
3. Network simulator 3, http://www.nsnam.org
4. Jacquet, P., Mijhlethaler, P., Clausen, T., Laouiti, A., Qayyum, A., Viennot, L.: Optimized Link State Routing Protocol for Ad Hoc Networks, pp. 62–68 (2001)
5. Corson, S., Macker, J.: Mobile Ad hoc Networking (MANET): Routing Protocol Performance Issues and Evaluation Considerations. IETF RFC 2501 (January 1999)
6. Clausen, T., Baccelli, E.: Securing OLSR problem statement, February 14 (2005), Internet-Draft, draft-clausen-manet-solsr-ps-00.txt

Performance Investigations of Routing Protocols in Manets

Surendra Singh Choudhary[1], Vijander Singh[2], and Reena Dadhich[3]

[1] Research Scholler, Banasthali University, Tonk, India
Affiliated to UGC
ssc_jaipur@yahoo.com
[2] MCA DEPTT., Sri Balaji College of Engg. & Tech., Jaipur
Affiliated to RTU, Kota
vijan2005@yahoo.com
[3] MCA DEPTT., Govt. Engg. College, Ajmer, India
Affiliated to RTU, Kota
reena.dadhich@gmail.com

Abstract. In MANETs each node acts both as a host and a router and therefore forwards packets for other nodes using different routing protocols. The primary objective of this paper is to compare the performance of different routing protocols for wireless ad hoc networks in a simulated environment against varying network parameters and traffic (UDP, different number of connections/streams) to provide a qualitative assessment of applicability of protocols in different scenarios. The performance differentials are analyzed using varying node mobility, network size, maximum speed, traffic load and data rate on NS-2.34[1]. We will also simulate and analyze the wireless ad-hoc network routing protocols considering TCP as transport protocol and FTP as traffic generator against different network parameters.

Keywords: Ad-hoc Network, Routing, Performance, Protocols.

1 Introduction

Routing protocols in traditional wired networks were developed keeping in view that they will select the path from source to the destination and maintain the flow of packets through the best routes available. These protocols were based on link-state or distance vector algorithms those find an optimal path. But in wireless ad-hoc networks [3],[4] topology change frequently and determination of path is too expensive because each host is in direct communication only with the nodes those are within its transmission range. Moreover the bandwidth available with such networks are very less as compared to the wired networks, hence the periodic updates might consume a large amount of bandwidth and cannot promptly reflect the frequent topology changes in ad-hoc networks. Therefore, routing is one of the most important issues for an ad-hoc network to make their existence in the present world and prove to be divine for generations to come.

A. Abraham et al. (Eds.): ACC 2011, Part I, CCIS 190, pp. 54–63, 2011.

A lot of research has been done on the title of the paper. We have studied the work held during different years starting from 1994. Since 1994 to 2007 many researchers had proposed different routing protocols [5],[6],[11],[12] using various parameters for ad-hoc networking environment. During this period a lot of comparative studies [7-10] has also been done and published time to time, but no detailed performance comparison between the protocols has previously been done. This paper makes contributions in this area. In this paper, we compared ad-hoc network routing protocols DSR, AODV and DSDV based on their throughput (Kbytes/second), packet delivery fraction (%), average end-to-end delay (seconds), routing overhead (packets) and packets lost (packets) under a wide range of simulated network conditions considering UDP as transport protocol and CBR as traffic generator. We have experimented by changing the pause time, maximum speed, node density, traffic generators and data rate.

2 Performance Investigations on Ad-Hoc Network Routing Rotocols with CBR Traffic

2.1 Varying Mobility

Mobility refers to how much time a node is in motion. Node having pause time 200 means the node did not move throughout the simulation time (200 seconds). It is observed that DSR outperforms other protocols by delivering maximum throughput of 125 Kbytes/s. Source routing protocols AODV and DSR maintain constant throughput regardless of the mobility rate. DSDV on the other hand has difficulties in finding routes when mobility increases. DSDV initially shows throughput of 86.36 Kbytes/s at pause time of 0 second, but increases to 123.66 Kbytes/s as the pause time increased to 200 seconds. All the three protocols DSDV, DSR and AODV deliver a greater percentage of the originated data packets at low node mobility (i.e. at large pause time), converging to 100% delivery of packets when there is no node motion. DSR and AODV perform particularly well, delivering over 98% of the data packets regardless of mobility rate. At higher rates of mobility (lower pause times), DSDV does poorly, dropping to a 68% packet delivery ratio. DSDV shows shortest end-to-end delay of the order of 0.02 seconds when the nodes are in motion because only packets belonging to valid routes at the sending instant get through. The source routing protocols have a longer delay because their route discovery takes more time as every intermediate node tries to extract information before forwarding the reply. It is observed that routing overhead for source routing protocols decreases as the mobility decreases. Among source routing protocols, AODV shows greater overheads than DSR, transmitting 6086 packets whereas DSR is able to transmit 6019 packets at pause time of 0 second because AODV broadcasts periodic HELLO messages to its neighbors and needs to send control messages more frequently to find and repair routes. DSDV imposes a constant overhead transmitting near about 6025 packets in the network at all pause times because of the periodic nature of the routing updates. The number of packets lost is quite high initially for DSDV, dropping 1929 packets at pause time of 0 second because of high movement of nodes. As pause time of nodes increases, the number of packets loss fall drastically, drops 142 packets at pause time of 200 seconds and it directly affects the number of packets that reach destination. It is clear from here that the performance of DSDV mainly depends upon pause time. For source routing protocols, DSR and AODV, packets lost are quite low and shows zero packet loss at lowest mobility.

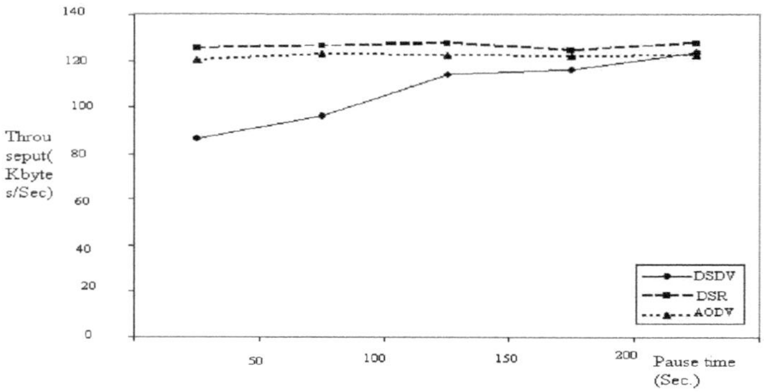

Fig. 1. Throughput vs Pause time

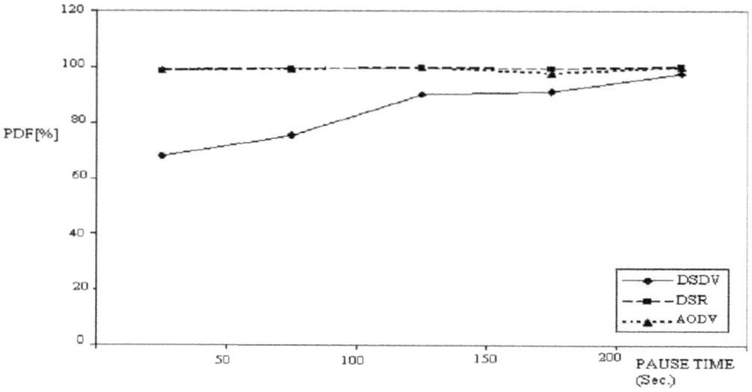

Fig. 2. Packet Delivery Fraction vs Pause time

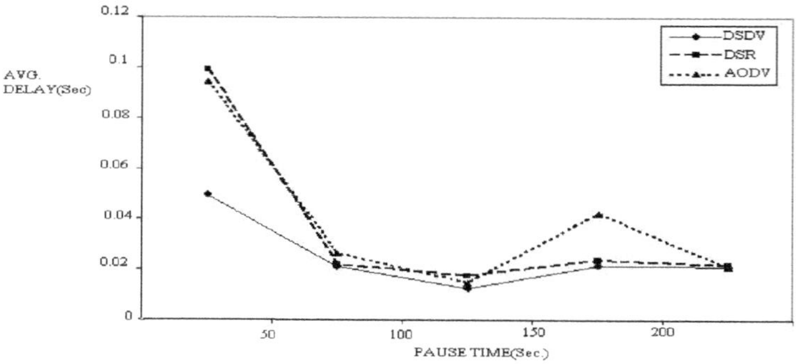

Fig. 3. Average Delay vs Pause time

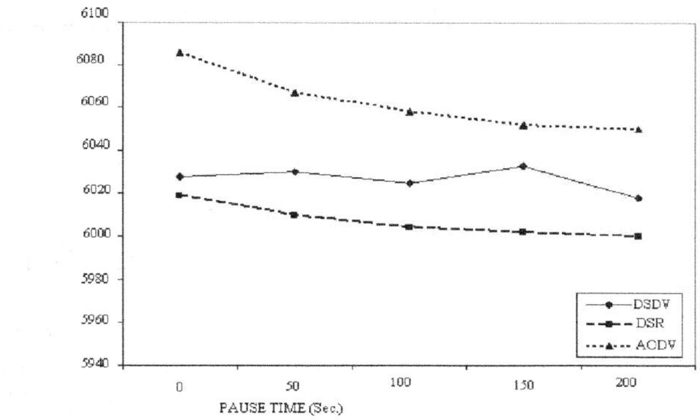

Fig. 4. Overhead vs Pause time

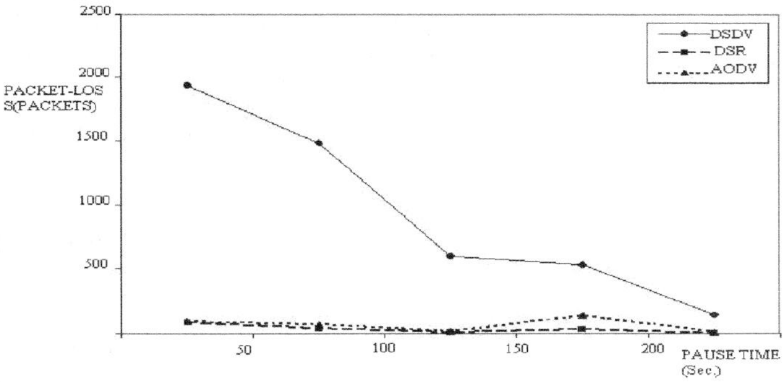

Fig. 5. Packet lost vs Pause time

2.2 Varying Scalability

Simulation are conducted for three different size networks of 25, 50 and 100 wireless nodes, generated for a pause time of 0 seconds. It is observed that none of the three protocols shows significant change on the throughput (Kilobytes/second) with the change in node density. DSDV shows slight variation in the throughput with the change in node density which is negligible. It is also observed that none of the three protocols shows any significant effect on the packet delivery fraction with the change in network size. DSR and AODV shows constant packet delivery ratio above 99% for any node density due to its source routing nature. Whereas DSDV shows minor change in the packet delivery ratio with the change in scalability which is not much significant. As we study, it is observed that DSR shows the maximum delay of 0.17 seconds in the network of 25 nodes but delay falls drastically to 0.05 seconds when the node density increases to 100 nodes. When density of the nodes increases, route acquisition time also increases considerably. Route Acquisition time is the time required to establish routes when required. Route acquisition time has increased considerably but delay is still decreasing because there are more number of routes available from source to the destination and there are very less route make/break in such situations. Whereas AODV and DSDV do not show much change in delay with the change in node density as compared to DSR protocol. DSR shows minimum overheads transmitting 6009 packets in the network of 25 nodes but introduces drastic increase in overheads transmitting 6081 packets in the network of 100 nodes and this in turn reduces the efficiency of DSR protocol. Data packet header of DSR carries complete hop-by-hop source route to destination, thereby increases overhead with the increase in network size. Another reason for DSR is variable header size due to inclusion of address of intermediate nodes present on route from source to destination. AODV and DSDV show slight decrease in the overheads with the increase in node density because of availability of more number of routes in dense network. DSDV shows considerable packet loss whereas the source routing protocols AODV and DSR shows negligible packet loss. None of the protocols show significant change in packet loss with the increase in number of nodes.

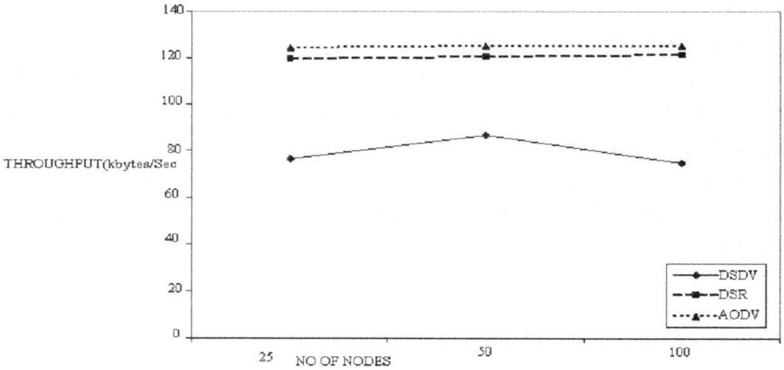

Fig. 6. Throughput vs No. of nodes

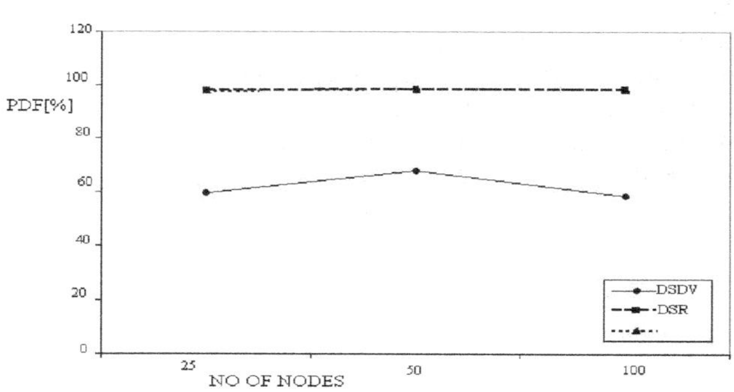

Fig. 7. PDF vs No. of nodes

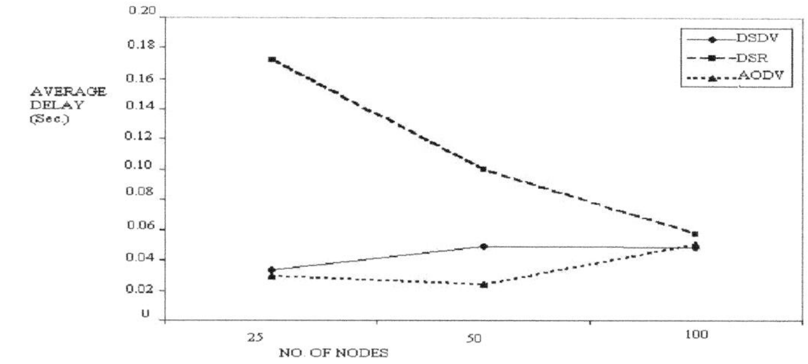

Fig. 8. Avg delay vs No of nodes

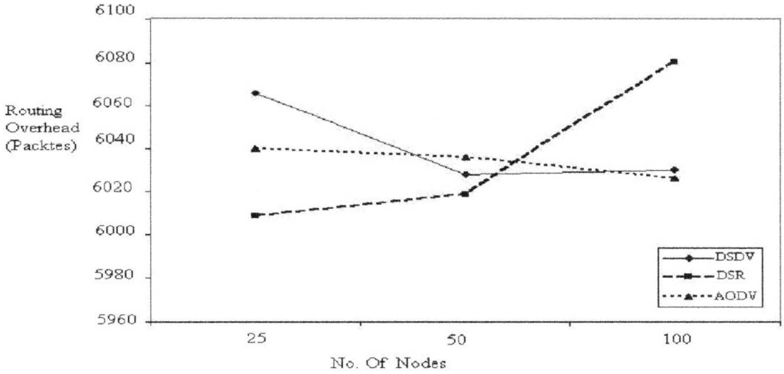

Fig. 9. Overhead vs No. of nodes

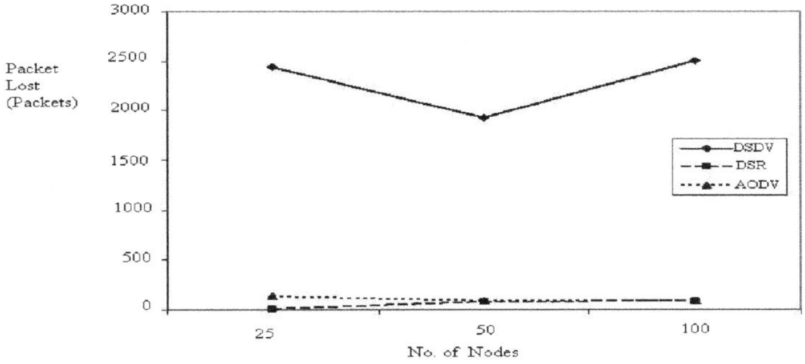

Fig. 10. Packet lost vs No of nodes

2.3 Varying Maximum Speed

Mobility of the nodes basically shows how fast the nodes are moving. In this scenario, simulations are conducted with movement patterns generated for 5 different maximum speeds: 1, 2, 5, 10, 20, and 50 m/s, which correspond to 3.6, 7.2, 18, 36, 72 and 180 km/hour, respectively. We have considered a wide range of speeds for our mobile nodes from 1 m/s (3.6 km/hour) that corresponds to walking at a slow pace, to 50 m /s

(180 km/hour), the speed of a very fast car. For source routing protocols DSR and AODV, throughput is independent of change in maximum speed of nodes. Whereas DSDV suffers decrease in the throughput to 70 Kbytes/s at highest speed of 50 m/s because of frequent link changes and connection failures. It is observed that AODV and DSR perform particularly well delivering 100% of the packets irrespective of their node speeds. DSDV delivers 97% of the packets at low speed but indicates drop in packet delivery ratio up to 55% at higher speeds.

Simulation study indicates that increase in node speeds results in significant increase in the average end-to-end delay of all protocols. Delay introduced in DSDV is least of the order of 0.01141 seconds but shows considerable increase up to 0.06296 seconds as the speed approaches 50 m/s. The source routing protocols have a longer delay because their route discovery takes more time as every intermediate node tries to extract information before forwarding the reply. DSR and AODV shows delay of 0.01112 seconds, 0.0146 seconds, respectively at lowest speed of 1m/s and delay increases up to 0.13183 seconds, 0.10512 seconds respectively as the speed approaches 50 m/s. DSDV presents constant routing overhead regardless of the change in the speed. However, for DSR and AODV the routing overhead increases with the increase in speed. AODV experiences maximum overheads, transmitting 6068 packets as the speed approaches 50 m/s. Source routing protocols DSR and AODV shows zero packets lost at lowest speed of 1 m/s but shows increase of approximately 150 packets in the number of packets lost with the increase in speed. DSDV shows drastic increase in the packets lost of the order of 2661 packets as the speed approaches 50 m/s. We observed that even with increased node movement the performance of DSR and AODV protocol is quite high and is better as comparison with DSDV.

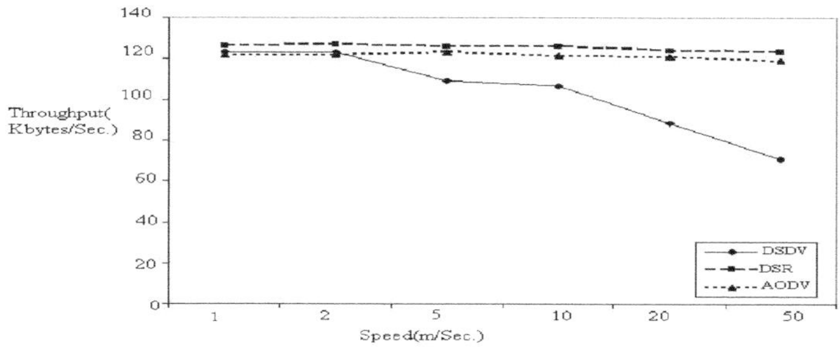

Fig. 11. Throughput vs Speed

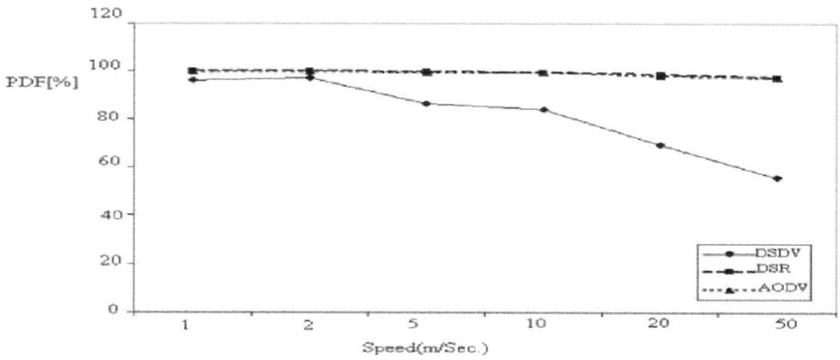

Fig. 12. PDF vs Speed

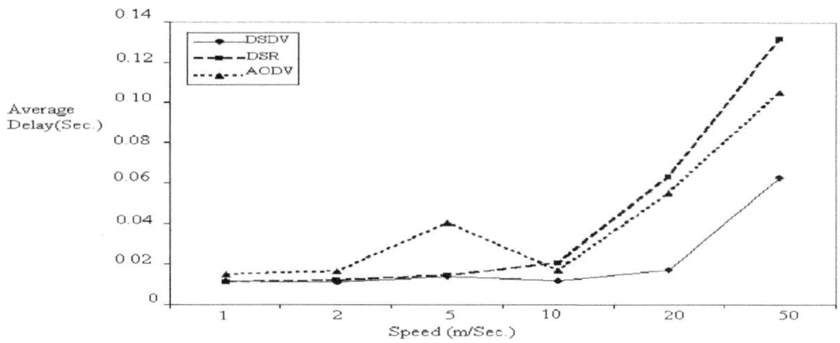

Fig. 13. Avg. Delay vs Speed

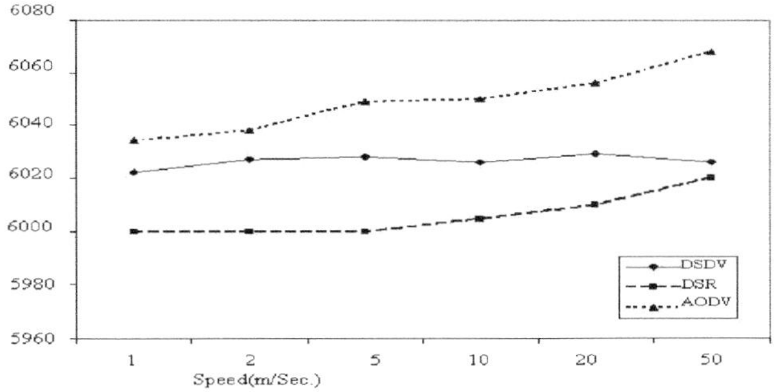

Fig. 14. Overhead vs Speed

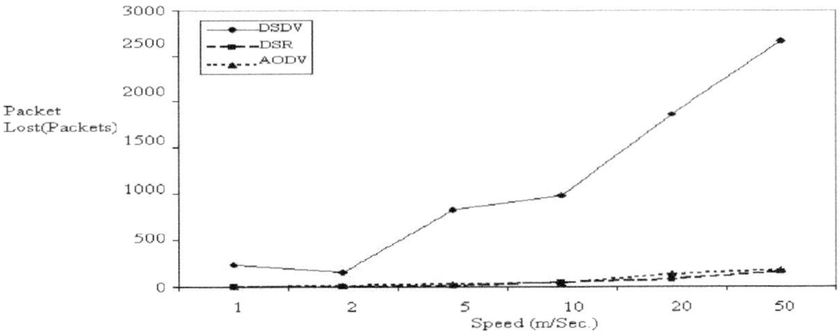

Fig. 15. Packet lost vs Speed

3 Conclusions

This paper presents simulations results of the comparative investigation of the performance of routing protocols DSDV, DSR and AODV for wireless ad hoc networks in a simulated environment against different parameters considering UDP as the transport protocol and CBR as traffic generator. It is evident from the discussions that each of the protocols studied performs well in some cases yet has certain drawbacks in others. Proactive routing protocol DSDV performs well, delivering virtually all data packets when node mobility rate and movement speed are low, and failing to converge as node mobility and speed of node increases. Hence, performance of DSDV depends on the node mobility rate and speed and is suitable for the low mobility and low speed scenarios. Results indicate that although reactive protocols AODV and DSR performed significantly better than DSDV regardless of the mobility rates and movement speeds still have certain drawbacks. The performance of DSR is effected with the change in scalability. DSR introduces higher routing overheads with the increase in network size which shows poor scalability of DSR which is attributed to the source routing nature of DSR. If we compare among source routing protocols DSR and AODV, it is observed that DSR performs better than AODV for low traffic loads, since it discovers routes more efficiently. At higher traffic loads, however, AODV performs better than DSR due to less additional load being imposed by source routes in data packets. Hence, although AODV is suitable for high mobility scenarios, but fails to performs under low traffic loads.

References

1. Network Simulator - NS-2, `http://www.isi.edu/nsnam/ns/`
2. Corson, S., Macker, J.: Mobile Ad-hoc Networking (MANET): Routing protocol Performance Issues and Evaluation Considerations. IETF RFC 2501 (January 1999)
3. Sarkar, S.K., Basawaraju, T.G., Puttamadappa, C.: Ad-hoc Mobile Wireless Networks: Principles, Protocols and Applications, p. 1. Auerbach Publications (2008)
4. Frodigh, M., Johansson, P., Larsson, P.: Wireless Ad-hoc networking: The Art of networking without a network. Ericsson Review (4), 248–263 (2000)
5. Perkins, C.E., Bhagwat, P.: Highly dynamic Destination Sequenced Distance-Vector routing (DSDV) for mobile computers. In: Proc. of SIGCOMM 1994 Conference on Communications Architectures, Protocols and Applications, pp. 234–244 (August 1994)
6. Johnson, D.B., Maltz, D.A.: Dynamic Source Routing in Ad-Hoc Wireless Networks. In: Imielinski, T., Korth, H. (eds.) Proc. of Mobile Computing, ch. 5, Kluwer Academic Publishers, Dordrecht (1996)
7. Johansson, P., Larsson, T., Hedman, N., Mielczarek, B., Degermark, M.: Scenario- based performance Analysis of Routing Protocols for Mobile Ad-Hoc Networks. In: Proc. of IEEE/ACM Mobicom 1999, Seattle, WA, pp. 195–206 (August 1999)
8. Ari, I., Jethani, N., Rangnekar, A., Natarajan, S.: Performance Analysis and Comparison of Ad-Hoc Routing Protocols, CMSC 691t, Mobile Computing, Project Report, May 22 (2000)
9. Das, S.R., Perkins, C., Royer, E.: Performance Comparison of Two On- demand Routing Protocols for Ad-Hoc Networks. In: Proc. of IEEE INFOCOM 2000, vol. 1, pp. 3–12 (March 2000)

10. Jayakumar, G., Ganapathy, G.: Performance Comparison of Mobile Ad-hoc Network Routing Protocol. Proc. of IJCSNS International Journal of Computer Science and Network Security 7(11) (November 2007)
11. Larsson, T., Hedman, N.: Routing Protocols in wireless ad-hoc networks –A simulation study, Masters thesis in computer science and engineering, p. 9 (1998)
12. Perkins, C., Belding-Royer, E., Das, S.: Ad-hoc on demand distance vector (AODV) routing, IETF RFC3561 - Experimental Standard (July 2003)

Mobile Query Processing-Taxonomy, Issues and Challenges

Diya Thomas and Sabu M. Thampi

Department of Computer Science
Rajagiri School of Engineering and Technology, Kerala, India
diyaabs13@gmail.com,
sabum@rajagiritech.ac.in

Abstract. With advancement in wireless technologies like development of Wireless Application Protocol and third generation mobile system that has many powerful capabilities like storage of small database, query processing in mobile environment has become a hottest topic of research. Lot of research work is done on how to do efficient query processing in mobile environment taking into consideration the asymmetric features of mobile environment like low battery power, reduced communication bandwidth, frequent network disconnection. The query processing in a mobile environment involves join processing among different sites which include servers and mobile computers. Because of the presence of asymmetric features in a mobile computing environment and also the need for energy saving, the conventional distributed query processing cannot be directly applied to a mobile computing system. Now with advent of location based services and GPS enabled mobile devices different types of queries to obtain location based information has evolved in mobile environment like location dependent queries, location aware queries etc. Processing of such queries is another area of research. This paper deals with the mobile query processing with special focus on classification of mobile queries and issues in mobile query processing.

Keywords: Location based service, Query processing, Mobile database.

1 Introduction

Improvements in hardware technology and wireless communication networks have lead to the emergence of mobile database systems [1]. With emergence of these mobile database that can store mobile data, researchers are paying more attention towards mobile query processing as means of accessing these mobile data. The mobile data can be information about mobile users or it can be information about the location of mobile users thus we can classify the query basically into two categories: *Data query* and *Location related query*. Data queries are issued to retrieve information about mobile object. Query like *"Retrieve car id of car A that is chasing a car B"* is an example for data query. That is in data query the location information is not retrieved in implicit or explicit manner. In location related query, the location information is specified or retrieved in implicit

A. Abraham et al. (Eds.): ACC 2011, Part I, CCIS 190, pp. 64–77, 2011.

or explicit manner. The query like *"Retrieve closest hotel near to my location"* is an implicit location query and one like *"Retrieve closest hotel near to Cochin City"* is explicit location query. In both these queries the mobile issuer may be static or mobile and the query may be targeted to a static or mobile object. Location dependent data access is an important feature of mobile computing application. This feature has opened new areas of research like context aware query processing in location dependent environment. The context aware query or location based queries support location based services. These queries are the backbone of location based services like Emergency services, Billing services, Navigation services, tracking services etc. Most of the queries in mobile environment are continuous queries[2]. Continuous queries are those queries whose results need to be refreshed continuously. Mobile devices are in motion most of the time and the result of the query depends upon the location of mobile devices. As each time location of mobile user changes results retrieved by the query also changes accordingly. Thus, there is a need for continuous refreshment of result. Several update policies have been addressed to solve this problem. To develop efficient query processing strategies that can resolve several limitation of mobile environment like limited battery power, frequent disconnection, less bandwidth is an important area of research in query processing. Several query processing strategies have been discussed in paper[3,4,5]. Several other issues also need to be addressed while doing query processing in mobile environment like handoff management, uncertainty management, location management. In this paper we discuss different types of mobile queries with a main focus on location dependent query. Issues and challenges in query processing are also discussed.

The rest of this paper is organized as follows: In section 2, we describe context for query processing. In section 3, we present a classification of mobile queries. Section 4 deals with location dependent query processing. In section 5,some issues and challenges in query processing are discussed. Finally section 6 concludes the paper.

2 Context

Mobile computing environment is divided into cells. The components of a mobile environment are mobile devices (laptop, cell phone PDA, etc.), base stations and location server[6]. Mobile devices are those devices that have inherent mobility feature. Each cell consist of a base station. Base station controls and coordinates mobile devices under its domain. Base station itself is controlled by mobile switching office which is also called location server. Base stations are connected each other using wired network and the base station and mobile devices have a wireless connection. Base station and location server are connected via a standard network. The main functionality of location server is to store location of mobile users under its domain. The location information is usually stored as cell ID. A database which is distributed among different location server is used to store the location of mobile devices. This location information needs to be frequently updated because of mobility feature inherent in mobile devices. The

Mobile device or mobile host have a home network and is permanently registered under a location server in this home network. Location server in its home network is called home agent. The mobile host may also move to a foreign network and register to the location server of that network. The location server in foreign network is called foreign agent. When mobile host is in its home network it is called resident and when it is moved to foreign network it is called visitor to location server. Each agent has four databases, two are mobile host databases and other two are location databases. Mobile host databases are home database and visitor database. Home database store data of residents like name, age, salary and visitor database store data of visitors. The location databases are home location database and visitor location database that store the location information of mobile host. These databases help in efficient querying in mobile environment.

3 Classification of Mobile Queries

In a mobile environment there are two general categories of queries. They are mobile data query or non location related query and location related query. The mobile data query helps in retrieving data about mobile user excluding location information. Example of mobile data query is *"Give the list of medicine that a person A have"*. Location related information of mobile users is usually retrieved using location related query where location related information is specified or retrieved in implicit or explicit manner. Example of location related query is *"Give me list of hospital closest to Cochin city"*.

We can again classify these queries based on two constraints like mobility constraint and location constraint. Based on mobility constraint there are other two categories of queries [7]: (i) Queries issued by mobile devices and querying data related to fixed objects (e.g. hospital). (ii) Queries issued by mobile or

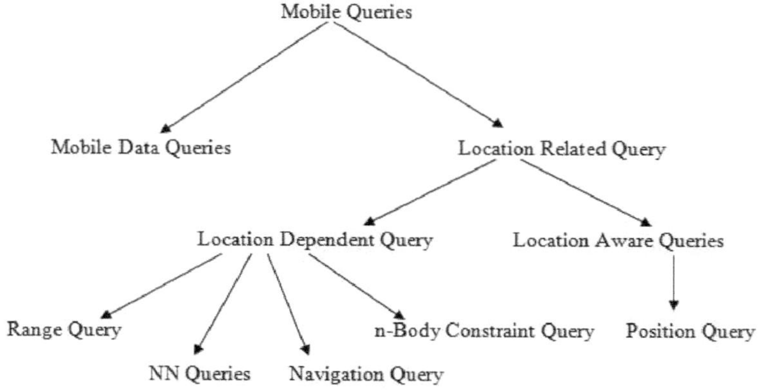

Fig. 1. Classification of Mobile Queries

static devices and querying data related to moving objects (e.g. taxi). Based on location constraint we can classify the queries into location aware queries and location dependent queries. Both are moving object database queries.

In location aware query, the location information is specified explicitly. It retrieves the result based on explicitly specified location. In another words location aware queries are those queries that has atleast one location related attribute or predicate [8]. Consider a query like *'Retrieve hospital names in cochin"*. In this query the city Cochin is explicitly specified location that is it is a location related attribute so the above example query is a location aware query. Position query or location query is one type of location aware query. In position query the location information of the mobile host is retrieved. As an example consider the query *"Where is car A"*, in this we retrieve the location information of car A so it is a position query or location query.

In location dependent query, the query response depends on the location of query issuer. Query like *"Find me closest hospital within 2 miles from my current location"* is an example for location dependent query. In this example it is clear that result retrieved by the query depends on the query issuer. Mobile data keeps on changing time to time especially location information thus the query that refers to such dynamic information are called continuous query. Location dependent queries can be considered as continuous query [8,9]. As the results retrieved by such query depend on mobility of issuer there is a need for continuous refreshment of result to keep the result valid. How to set an appropriate refreshment frequency and how to design an efficient update policy is an issue while dealing with the processing of such queries.

3.1 Moving Object Database Queries

Tradition databases are not capable of storing continuously changing data. Hence, they are not suitable for storing information about moving object and their location. In such databases, data remains constant unless it is explicitly modified. For example, if the name field is 20K, then this name field is assumed to hold (i.e. 20K is returned in response to queries) until explicitly updated. To process queries in mobile environment, we need a database that is capable of storing dynamic information thus arose the need for moving object database[8]. They are those databases that can efficiently store information about moving objects and their locations and thus enable efficient processing of mobile queries.

Moving Object database queries are queries that are issued by mobile or fixed object and that retrieve data from moving object database. Shape and size of moving object are not much important in such queries and they include spatial objects and temporal constraints. Consider for example the query *"Retrieve the mobile objects within circular range R within the next 2 minutes"*. This is a spatial and temporal range query. The spatial range is the circular range R and the temporal range is the time interval between now and 2 minutes from now. Traditional query languages like SQL are suitable for expressing such queries. Usually an integration of temporal and spatial languages is used to express such queries (e.g. SQL extension language STQL). For performance reason while answering Moving Object Database query, indexing location attribute approach is usually followed rather than examining location of each mobile object. Issues like modeling and querying mobile object, uncertainty management, tracking mobile object, location management etc need to be tackled while processing such queries.

3.2 Classification of Moving Object Database Queries

Moving object database queries can be categorized into location query, range query and within-distance query [7,9].

Location query: This query retrieves moving object whereabouts and time. It is of two types like where-at(t,obid) query and when-at(x,y,obid) query. Where-at(t,obid) query returns the expected location coordinate of an object with object id obid at time t and When-at(x,y,obid) query returns the time when the object with object id obid will be at location (x,y).

Range query: They are used to retrieve an object within a particular range for a given time interval. Example *"Retrieve mobile objects inside a circular range R within 2 minutes from now"*. Operators like inside(R, t1, t2) are used in such queries.

Within-Distance query: Retrieve objects within a particular distance from the query issuer. Query issuer and query target object can be static or mobile. Based on that, we have four variants of queries such as Dynamic issuer and Dynamic target object query(DD query),Dynamic issuer and Static target object query(DS query),Static issuer and Static target object query(SS query),Static issuer and Dynamic target object query(SD query).

4 Location Dependent Query Processing

At the beginning, the main aim of wireless network was to enable mobile communication but nowadays with the technological evolution and continuous development of positioning systems like GPS devices have contributed to the emergence of location based services and applications in mobile environment. This location based service (LBS) is called mobile location services. LBS provides value added information based on the location of user. The technologies that provide contextual environment for implementing LBS are WAP, GPRS (General Packet Radio Service), UMTS (Universal Mobile Telecommunication System),GIS (Geographic Information System). Example of location based services are Navigation and information service, Advertising service, Billing service, Emergency service etc.

Location dependent query is one of the direct consequence of location based services and applications in database field. Such queries are the basic building blocks of LBS. Location dependent query is a query whose query response depends on the location of the query issuer. Example *"Finds me a hotel within 10 miles"*.

5 Classification of Mobile Queries

5.1 Clasification of Location Dependent Query

Location dependent query is generally classified into temporal queries and spatial queries which is further refined into continuous queries and non-continuous queries [10].Location dependent query is a type of moving object database query. It is further classified based on their purpose as Range queries, nearest neighbor queries, Navigation queries, n-body constraint queries etc [11].

Range query: This query is used to retrieve mobile objects within a particular range. Range can be circular range, rectangular range etc. within-distance query and window query are two type of range query based on the type of range. If the range is circular we have within-distance range query and if range is rectangular window we have window range query.

Nearest-neighbor (NN) queries: These queries retrieve objects closet to a particular object or location specified in the query. As an example, consider the query *"retrieve police cars close to robbed car"* where we retrieve nearest neighbor police cars closed to robbed car is an example for nearest neighbor query. If are specifying that we need to retrieve only k nearest neighbor then the query we choose to specify is KNN queries. If we want to specify a range constraint while retrieving nearest neighbor then we choose a constrained NN query to specify such constraint. We can classify NN queries into two categories; they are static NN queries and dynamic NN queries [11]. In static NN queries target object is static as it cannot move whereas in dynamic NN queries target object will be in motion.

n-Body constraints query: In this type of queries we can specify location constraints like should be greater than or less than a particular distance and the query retrieves a set of n objects satisfying the location constraint. Varying the values of n we have 2-Body constraint query if value of n=2, 3-Body constraint query if n=3.example *"Retrieve police cars within a circular range with r=2 from the police station"*.

Navigation Queries: These queries help the mobile users to fetch best path to the destination by taking into consideration of network traffic. Some of the location dependent queries are also classified into snapshot queries, continuous

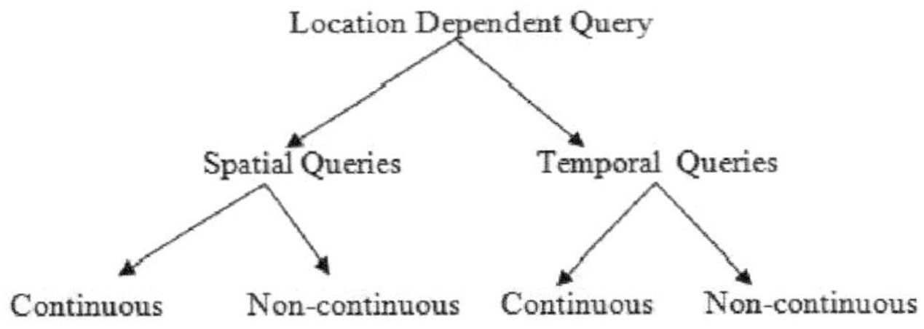

Fig. 2. General Classification of Location Dependent Queries

queries and persistent queries. If the query result is computed only once then that query is snapshot query or instantaneous query. If query result is computed continuously until terminated by user then that query is continuous query and if this query considers both past state and current state of moving object while evaluating the result then that query is Persistent query. The above classification is based on history of movement and evaluation time. Further classification of location dependent query is discussed in [11].

5.2 Query Execution and Optimization

In centralized static system execution, site for processing queries are determined in advance, that is which steps are performed on the server and which on the client are obtained in advance. In mobile environment it is very difficult to determine in advance which execution site is most suitable for processing each phase of the query. Thus, depending on current situations like current location of mobile unit in mobile environment, the mobile database system should be capable of choosing exact sites to process each phase of the query and revise the plan with changes in environment like change in position of mobile units.

In centralized environment, query execution plan aims to minimize CPU cost, input/output cost etc where as in mobile environment the main objective of query execution plans is to minimize the communication cost. Communication cost is very difficult to measure as the mobile host is located in different locations. A dynamic optimization method is needed in mobile environment because of mobility feature inherent in mobile environment.

6 Issues and Challenges in Query Processing in Mobile Environment

Several issues need to be addressed while doing query processing in mobile environment. The main issues are limited bandwidth for data transfer, frequent handoff, frequent disconnection, limited battery power. These issues reduce the efficiency of query processing. Efficient query processing strategies that consider some of these issues is discussed in [3,4,5]. Mobility is an important feature of mobile computing environment. Location is a piece of information that relates to mobility. Location information is specified in implicit or explicit manner in certain types of queries and result of such queries depends on the current location of mobile units. In such a case, efficient methods to locate these mobile units and efficient way to represent this location information need to be designed. Thus localization of mobile units and location management is an issue that needs special focus. Certain queries may be continuous queries whose results changes continuously. Certain operators like *close to*, *straight ahead*, *within* are used while specifying the Location query, an efficient processing method to process this operators and need for suitable query language to express this queries is another challenge that need special mention. Location binding is performed when location information is specified in the query. Location information to do

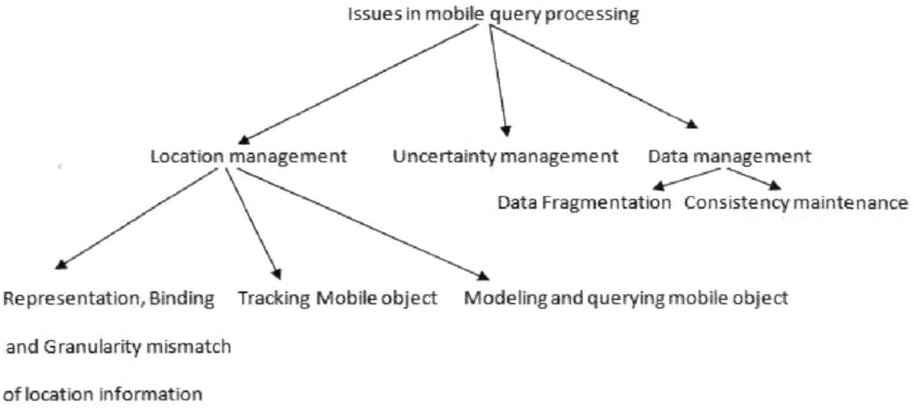

Fig. 3. Main Issues in Mobile query Processing

the binding can be obtained from network operator databases or from positioning system like GPS system. Another solution to obtain location information is discussed in [12] where actual location of mobile user is retrieved by sending client identifier to location based services. But how to obtain valid location information in a time bound and cost effective manner is still a challenge that needs consideration. Difference in the location model used by the application and location services can cause problems like location granularity mismatch. Due to unpredictable behavior and continuous movement, imprecision of positioning system and delays in network there is a limited accuracy in current and future position of moving object. This uncertainty issues need to be managed for valid result retrieval. How to model and query moving object in an efficient way is another issue that needs to be taken care of during query processing. We can have an efficient query processing in mobile environment if all these challenges and issued are addressed in an appropriate manner. Most important issues that is to be solved is discussed briefly in the subsequent sections.

6.1 Location Management

Location management involves modeling and querying location information, tracking moving object [12]. Two basic operations in location management are look ups and update. Look ups are done to retrieve location of mobile host and update operations are needed when there is a change in the position of mobile host. Storing the location information is done in two ways either every site in mobile network stores up to date data or only one site stores the up to date and all other site have to query this site to retrieve up to date data. When up to date data is stored in multiple sites update cost will be greater than look up cost. Update cost will be smaller than look up cost when the information is stored at only one site. Usually higher update cost is compromised for getting accurate location information. Methods like Point location management method is discussed in [12]. In this method, location coordinate of object location along with time at which object reach that location is stored in the database. The stored location is retrieved using SQL. One of the drawbacks of this method is the need for frequent location update as object location goes on changing time to time. A trajectory location management method is also proposed in [12]. In this method the trajectory of moving object is stored in the database of server and the location information is updated only if there is a change in the predicted data. Moreover an uncertainty threshold is attached to the location information in the database and this uncertainty threshold is used to decide whether location information is exact or not.

Modeling, Binding and Granularity Mismatch of Location Information

Location information is specified in implicit or explicit manner in location related queries. When such queries are issued, there should be some mechanism to bind the location specified in the query with the query itself. Location information is usually obtained from GPS or from other location server database. But this is not an appropriate solution. Another efficient solution is discussed in [9] where author has discussed about location based services which provide necessary location information and bind the location information with the query. When a client identifier of a client who issued the query is given to location based service, it bind location of client specified in query with the query. As an example suppose the client issued a query like *Select closest cinema theater to my current position*. Here we want the location of query issuer only then cinema theater near to issuer location can be identified. For that, query is first sent to location based service which do the work of identifying location information and binding it with the query. After binding location information with query it is then easy to retrieve closest cinema theater just by simple look up in the database. The problem with this approach is that location model used by query and location model used by location based service may differ. Location model used to represent location is of two types namely Geometric model and Symbolic model. In symbolic model, location is represented by real world entities like pin code, cities, streets etc. In geometric model location is represented by two dimensional or three dimensional coordinates like latitude and longitude. Thus, if geometric model is used by the query and symbolic model is used by Location based service or vice versa then there is a location granularity mismatch which need to be addressed for efficient query processing.

Modeling and Querying of Moving Objects

Mobile objects are those objects that can move or whose position changes with time. Modeling a mobile object implies modeling their movement in the database. To model their movement in the database, we need their location information to be tracked in a continuous manner. Existing databases are not efficient in storing continuously changing information like location information. Thus, there is a greater need to solve the issue of modeling mobile objects. One solution to efficiently model a mobile object is discussed in [9] where author proposed a data model called MOST (Moving Object Spatial Temporal) data model. The MOST model introduces the concept of dynamic attribute whose value changes with time. Such an attribute can efficiently represent motion of a mobile object. The MOST model also enhances the capability of DBMS to predict the future position of a moving object. Author also discussed about a spatial temporal query language called FTL. This query language uses both spatial operator like *INSIDE, WITHIN* and temporal operators like *UNTIL, EVENTUALLY* to operate with the dynamic attribute. Abstract data type model and constraint data type model are two other models used to model mobile objects [8,9,10]. These two models focus on history of movement and trajectory of moving object whereas MOST model is interested only in the present and future position of object. Abstract model uses base type (Int, Real, String etc), spatial type (Point, line etc) and temporal type (intime). One of the most important type constructor used in the model is *moving. moving* type constructor is used to construct type whose value changes dynamically. We can represent movement of object as well as moving region using this constructor. For example *moving(point), moving (region)*. In constraint database model, spatial object is considered as infinite set of point satisfying first order logic formulae. Simple standard language like SQL is used in this model.

Tracking of Mobile Objects

Several location management techniques are also discussed in [12]. Short battery life, frequent disconnections are some of the issues in mobile environment that prevent the efficient retrieval of location information. An efficient technique to retrieve locations of moving objects is needed in such cases. Object tracking architecture like two tier, tree structured and non-hierarchy approaches are discussed in [12]. In two tier architecture, two network sites are used to store location information. In tree structured architecture, location information is stored in network sites arranged hierarchically. Non hierarchy approach uses centralized database to store location information. Partitioning, caching and replication techniques are used with these architectures to track the object efficiently.

6.2 Uncertainty Management

Location information of mobile devices stored in the database and actual location of mobile device may differ. There is a certain level of uncertainty associated with the location of moving object. This uncertainty may be due to unpredictable movement behaviors of mobile objects, frequent disconnection,delays etc. In [13] a method that quantifies the uncertainty in location information is discussed. The proposed method reduces the uncertainty in past location data but keeps the uncertainty associated with current location of object little bit higher. Another method that considers the uncertainty on the trajectory of moving object is discussed in [14]. New operators like *possibly*, *always* etc are used to represent uncertainty in this method. Processing algorithm to process these operators is also discussed in [14].

6.3 Data Management

In this section we focus on data management issues in query processing [10] and discuss the methods like caching and broadcasting data to solve those issues. In conventional distributed databases the continuously changing data like location information are not stored. Even if the user is mobile the data was static or constant unless explicitly modified and hence data management issues were not much complex in such databases. However, in mobile databases data stored especially the location information changes continuously with movement of mobile host and hence there is a great need to manage mobile data in an efficient way. Data management issues like data fragmentation, replication, among mobile units, consistency maintenance etc are little bit complex issues in mobile environment. Managing data in mobile computing environment because of asymmetric features like frequent disconnection, frequent handoff of mobile environment, communication constraint, spatial data, user movement etc is a challenge.

Caching and Prefetching mobile data

Caching is an efficient method to solve data management issues[10]. In data caching method, mobile users keeps a copy of data. Prefetching, cache replacement, cache invalidation are three important issues related to caching method. Cache invalidation can be implemented by giving a valid scope to location data so that if there is a greater difference in location data valid scope and users current location data then we can conclude that there is a less chance of reusability. Invalid data can be removed using various replacement techniques. Manhattan distance and Furthest away replace are replacement technique mentioned in [15]. Prefetching is a method wherein which the mobile data are stored beforehand in users cache for use in near future. The data is fetched before it is actually needed. Cooperative caching is a caching technique where query results are shared with database server. This technique utilizes communication bandwidth efficiently. Another caching technique used is semantic caching[16]. This scheme is mainly used for location dependent queries. Semantic caching makes use of Voronoi diagram for nearest neighbor queries. Processing location dependent query using this caching technique is a challenge as only similar queries can reuse the cache. Semantic caching cannot support complex queries rather it supports different variants of location dependent queries like NN queries, range queries etc. There is a lot difficulty in managing cached data while using this technique. Semantic caching is used to process location dependent queries as it improves availability of data and efficiency of data access. One of the benefits of semantic caching technique is that it stores results of already issued queries so that this result data can be used to answer queries in future. Thus, this caching technique support fast query result retrieval. Because of some drawbacks of semantic caching scheme we propose a shared incremental update caching mechanism which can overcome many disadvantages of semantic caching. It is similar to cooperative caching mechanism. In shared incremental update mechanism, results of already evaluated queries are cached and redundant results are eliminated. This enables minimizing data transfer. The cached data are shared among different queries eliminating the drawback that we faced in semantic caching mechanism. Shared incremental update mechanism is not semantically dependent on the query type unlike previous caching mechanism.

Broadcasting mobile data

Mobile data are distributed to large number of users in a mobile environment using broadcasting technique. A push based data delivery technique can be used for data distribution[17]. Validated cached copies of modified data items are broadcasted periodically or on demand by the server and the entire mobile host get the broadcasted cached copies while listening to the broadcast channels. This technique eliminates the need for querying the server to get the validated cached copy to validate their cache. In another technique[18], the cached data in the server are broadcasted whenever a change is made to cached data items. This technique has drawbacks like high data transfer cost. As an improvement to this technique another method was proposed in [19] where broadcasting of modified data items takes place only when user demands. This technique makes use of mobile service station on behalf of data server for communicating with mobile unit thereby reducing traffic between mobile unit and data server.

7 Conclusion

With the emergence of mobile databases, location based services and with the development of wireless communication, query processing in mobile environment is an important area of research. In this paper, we focused on query processing in mobile environment. We first described the mobile computing context where the query processing is done. Then we focused on the classifications of mobile queries where we described different categories of queries. We have dedicated a section for describing more on moving object database queries and location dependent queries. Features of query processing and optimization are also discussed with special focus on location dependent query processing. Finally we discuss the issues and challenges in mobile environment. Some of the issues in mobile query processing are location management, uncertainty management, data management, handoff management, frequent disconnection etc. We also proposed a shared incremental update mechanism as solution to data management issues. Shared incremental update mechanism is a better caching mechanism than semantic caching mechanism. We will be focusing more on location dependent query processing that make use of shared incremental update mechanism in our furthur studies.

References

1. Sharma, S.D., Kasana, R.S.: Mobile Database System: Role of Mobility on the Query Processing. Journal of Computer science and Information Security 7, 211–216 (2010)
2. Illari, S., Mena, E., Illarramendi, A.: Location Dependent Queries in Mobile Context: Distributed Processing Using Mobile Agents. IEEE Transaction on Mobile Computing 5, 1029–1043 (2006)
3. Lee, C.H., Chen, M.S.: Using Remote Joins for Processing of Distributed Mobile Queries. In: 7th International Conference on Database Systems for Advanced Applications, USA, pp. 226–233 (2001)
4. Chen, M.s., Yu, P.S.: Interleaving a Join Sequence With Semijoins in Distributed Query Processing. IEEE Transaction on Parallel and Distributed Systems 3, 611–621 (1992)
5. Peng, W.C., Chen, M.S.: Query Processing in a Mobile Computing Environment: Exploiting the Features of Asymmetry. IEEE Transaction on Knowledge and Data Engineering 17, 982–996 (2005)
6. Imielinski, T., Badrinath, B.R.: Querying in Highly Mobile and Distributed Environment. In: 18th International Conference on Very Large Databases, China, pp. 41–52 (1992)
7. Marsit, N., Hameurlain, A., Mammeri, Z., Morvan, F.: Query Processing in Mobile Environments: a Survey and Open Problems. In: 1st International Conference on Distributed Frame Works for Multimedia Applications, France, pp. 150–157 (2005)
8. Wolfson, O., Jiang, L., Chamberlain, S.: Moving Objects Databases: Issues and Solutions. In: 10th International Conference on Scientific and Statistical Database Management, Italy, pp. 111–122 (1998)
9. Seydim, A.Y., Dunham, M.H., Kumar, V.: Location Dependent Query Processing. In: 2nd ACM International Workshop Data Engineering For Wireless and Mobile Access, USA, pp. 47–54 (2001)
10. Tabassum, K., Hijab, M., Damodaram, A.: Location Dependent Query Processing - Issues, Challenges and Applications. In: 2nd International Conference on Computer and Network Technology, India, pp. 239–243 (2010)
11. Ilarri, S., Mena, E., Illarramendi, A.: Location Dependent Query Processing: Where We are and Where We are Heading. ACM Computing Survey, 1–73 (2010)
12. Fengli, Z., Xinggao, H., Mingtian, Z.: Location Management in Mobile Environment. In: 1st International Conference on Communication, Circuit and System, China, pp. 1491–1496 (2004)
13. Pfoser, D., Jensen, C.S.: Capturing the Uncertainty of Moving-Object Representations. In: 6th International Symposium on Advances in Spatial Databases, China, pp. 111–132 (1991)
14. Trajcevski, G.: The Geometry of Uncertainty in Moving Objects Databases. In: 8th International Conference on Extending Database Technology, Berlin, pp. 233–250 (2002)
15. Zheng, B., Xu, J., Lee, D.L.: Cache Invalidation and Replacement Strategies for Location-Dependent data in Mobile Environment. IEEE Transaction on Computers 51, 1141–1153 (2002)
16. Zheng, B., Lee, D.L.: Semantic Caching in Location Dependent Query Processing. In: 7th International Symposium on Advances in Spatial and Temporal Database, Berlin, pp. 97–116 (2001)

17. Barbara, D., Lmielinski, T.: Sleepers and Workaholics: Caching Strategies in Mobile Environment. In: Proceedings of the ACM SIGMOD conference on Management of Data, China, pp. 1–24 (1994)
18. Kian-Lee, T., Cai, J., Beng, C.O.: An Evaluation of Cache Invalidation Strategies in Wireless Environment. IEEE Transaction on Parallel and Distributed System 12, 789–807 (2001)
19. Jing, J., Elmagarmid, A., Helal, A., Alonso, R.: Bit Sequence: An Adaptive Cache Invalidation Method in Mobile Client -Server Environment. ACM-Baltzer Journal on Special Topics in Mobile Network and Application 2, 115–127 (1997)

A Compact Low-Cost Phase Shifter for Wireless Applications

Ch. Rajasekhar[1], D. Srinivasa rao[2], M. Vanaja[3], and K. Vijay[3]

[1] ECE, GITAM University, India
[2] GMR-IT, India
[3] GITAM University, India
{chukkarajasekhar,srinivasa.dasari}@gmail.com

Abstract. A low cost phase shifter is presented in this paper. It contains microstrip lines on one side of PCB backed with slot array on the ground plane. In addition, the moveable PCB having five metal strips serves as a phase shifter. By dynamically moving movable PCB, we can adjust the Number and shielding area of the slot array and then alter the distribution of phase angle at each port of the feeding network accordingly. The progressive phase between array elements is achieved by adjusting the line lengths of movable PCB. Simulations were conducted using ads software. Ease in fabrication, tilting mechanism, and low cost are the main reasons for choosing this type of phase shifting mechanism.

Keywords: Base-station antenna, perturbation, phases shifter.

1 Introduction

The design of a phase shifter has attracted much interest now days because of its importance in numerous applications. Reviewing earlier literature concerning this topic, we found that various methods were developed to tilt the beam pattern of array antennas, such as mechanical [1], electrical [2]–[18]. Phase shifters are a critical element for electronically scanned phased array antennas, and typically account for a significant amount of the cost of producing an antenna array. The conventional phased-array system can scan at a fast rate but requires a complex integration of many circuits, including many expensive ferrite or solid-state phase shifters and beam forming networks. Since the technique is expensive, the use of phased arrays is limited to a few sophisticated military and space systems. It is difficult to implement for base-station antennas. This paper describes phase shifter with low cost and easy fabrication which is most suitable for base-station antenna design. Many low-cost beam steering antennas have been developed recently. For example, a metal plate mounted on a piezoelectric actuator was employed to perturb the propagation constant of microstrip dominant mode and then to change its phase angle [10]–[12]. A dielectric image line equipped with a moveable metal ground plate was used to serve as a phase shifter [13] - [16].Are configurable photonic band gap (PBG) structure operated near the Bragg reflection regime was also studied for this application [17].

A. Abraham et al. (Eds.): ACC 2011, Part I, CCIS 190, pp. 78–82, 2011.

Basic mechanism based on the waveguide theory, we know that for a fixed length transmission line, a perturbation imposed on it will lead to the variation in its propagation constant. This will cause a phase change when compared with that of the uniform transmission line without any perturbations. In addition, the position of the perturbation is also an important issue that affects the level of phase angle change. In order to obtain a considerable phase change, we have to perturb the structure at the position possessing the maximum electric- or magnetic-field distribution. Since the maximum field distribution is located within the substrate exactly under the strip line, the slot on the ground plane will interrupt the electric field line and cause a considerable variation on its propagation constant of the microstrip dominant mode, and what follows would be the phase angle. The change in phase angle can be achieved by moving the metal strip directly above the slots. According to our experimental studies, for a 12^0 beam-tilting angle, just a light metal strip is needed and the moving distance is equal to 7 mm, which can be carried out in practical applications. On the operating frequency, thus, it can be employed for broad-band array systems.

2 Splitter and Phase Shifter Design

We have implemented the one- to -five splitter in frequency range of 824MHz to 960MHz, using the rogers substrate with relative dielectric constant of 3.3 and 0.8mm thickness. The movable PCB is printed with metallic strips, using the Rogers substrate with relative dielectric constant of 3.3 and 1.54mm thickness. The slot is 12 mm in width and 1 mm in length; the period of the slot array is 2 mm. To have a progressive phase difference between the elements, the difference in the lengths between adjacent metal strips must be equal, and then a basic progressive phase difference angle is determined. After dynamically moving the perturbed lower PCB, it follows the same fashion for each metal strip directly above the slot array. We can alter the progressive phase difference angle for the splitter accordingly.

3 Progressive Phase Delay Numerical Results for an Array Antenna

Radiation main beam towards certain direction. If sequentially change the phase difference, we continuously steer the main beam within a certain range of spatial direction. We consider. Here a five element antenna array having unequal amplitudes and a progressive phase difference. The relationship between the progressive phase differences Angle Ψ and the main beam angle is θ is $\Psi=\beta d\cos(\theta)/\lambda$, and is the operating wavelength λ.

For example, if a main beam is tilting from 0 to 12, with a 1 step, the progressive phase-delay angles are given as 0.00^0,4.71^0,9.42^0,14.14^0,18.84^0,23.54^0,28.24^0, 32.92^0,37.6^0,42.26^0,46.91^0 and 56.16^0 respectively.

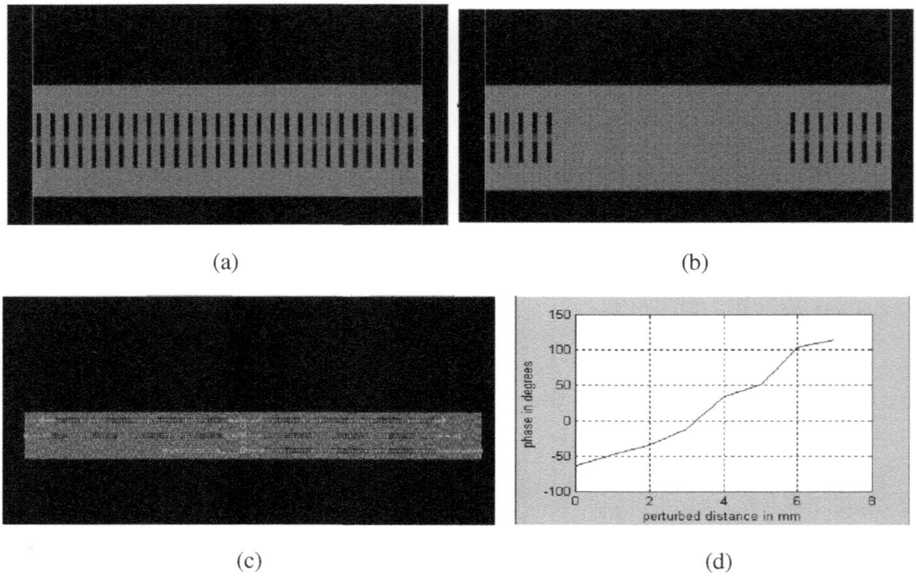

Fig. 1. Simulation models (a) microstrip line minimum tilt condition (b) microstrip line maximum tilt condition (c) full design (d) Phase plot

4 Simulation Results

The simulation is done for single micro-strip line as shown Fig.1 (a). The length of the line is 205mm is taken to get the desired phase of 204^0 .For the maximum tilt of 12^0. The simulated result plot is shown in Fig.1 (d) between the perturbed distance and phase angle. The plot obtained shows that linearity between the perturbed distance and phase angle. Linearity shows as perturbed distance increases the phase achieved is more. The same length of 206mm is used for the splitter's 50 ohm lines to achieve the desired phase. The total design is shown in Fig.1(c) simulations are done using ADS software.

Table 1. Measured data For Perturbed Distance (mm) and Phases (degrees) for all ports

	0	1	2	3	4	5	6	7
PORT1	-115	-88	-65	-25	15	22	86	88.2
PORT2	-76.2	-61	-44	-12	40	60	96	109.7
PORT3	-64	-47	-34	-12	34.7	52	103	113
PORT4	-73	-43	-33	-2	42.4	68	107	115.2
PORT5	-115	-84	-64	-29	9	37	82	88

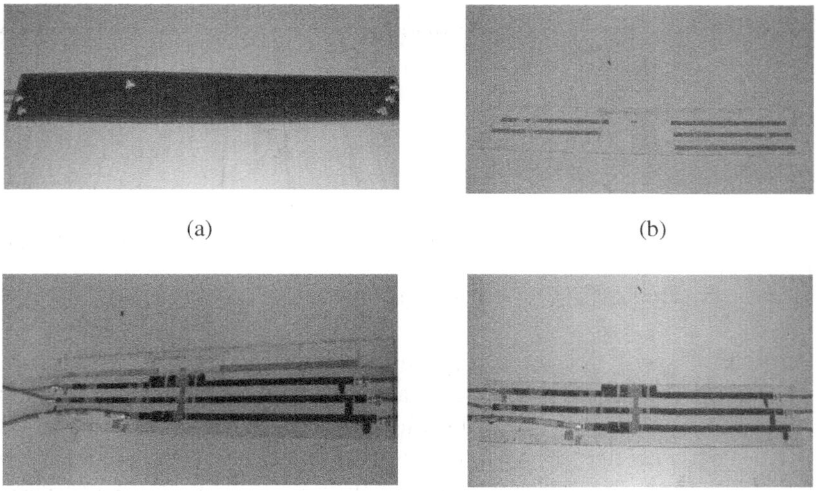

(a) (b) (c) (d)

Fig. 2. Different views of phase shifter. (a) Overall phase shifter (b) splitter (c) spots on the ground plane (d) Movable PCB

5 Measured Result

The fabricated phase shifter is shown in Fig.2. The measurement is carried by moving the movable PCB from the 0mm perturbed distance to 7mm perturbed distance. Measured results are represented in Table.1. It shows that as the perturbed distance increases the phase is obtained in linear manner. The practical results are agreed with the simulation results.

6 Conclusion

In this paper, the microstrip line backed with slotted ground plane is employed as a basic transmission line in the feeding network design. . By means Of dynamical perturbation performed of the slots on the ground plane by the microstrip line, a reconfigurable feeding network of progressive phase difference between each port can be achieved. The distributions of phase angles at each port in various perturbed distances are verified in both simulated and experimental studies.

References

[1] Kuramoto, A., Yamane, T., Endo, N.: Mechanically steered tracking antenna for land mobile satellite communications. In: Proc. EEE Int. Symp. Antennas Propagation Society, pp. 1314–1317 (1988)

[2] Manasson, V.A., Sadovnik, L.S.: Monolithic electronically controlled millimeter-wave beam-steering antenna. In: Proc. Silicon Monolithic Integrated Circuits in RF Systems Topical Meet, pp. 215–217 (1998)

[3] Brown, A.D., Kempel, L.C., Volakis, J.L.: Design method for antenna arrays employing ferrite printed transmissionline phase shifters. In: Proc. Inst. Elect. Eng. Microwaves, Antennas Propagat., vol. 149, pp. 33–40 (February 2002)
[4] Iskander, M.F., Zhang, Z., Yun, Z., Isom, R., Hawkins, M., Emrick, R., Bosco, B., Synowczynski, J., Gersten, B.: New phase shifters and phased antenna array designs based on ferroelectric materials and CTS technologies. In: Proc. IEEE MTT-S Int. Microwave Symp. Dig., vol. 1, pp. 259–262 (2001)
[5] Teo, P.T., Jose, K.A., Gan, Y.B., Varadan, V.K.: Beam scanning of array using ferroelectric phase shifters. Electron. Lett. 36, 1624–1626 (2000)
[6] Romanofsky, R.R., Qureshi, A.H.: A model for ferroelectric phase shifters. IEEE Trans. Magn. 36, 3491–3494 (2000)
[7] Iskander, M.F., Yun, Z., Zhang, Z., Jensen, R., Redd, S.: Design of a low-cost 2-D beam-steering antenna using ferroelectric material and CTS technology. IEEE Trans. Microwave Theory Tech. 49, 1000–1003 (2001)
[8] Barker, N.S., Rebeiz, G.M.: Optimization of distributed MEMS transmission-line phase shifters-U-band and W-band designs. IEEE Trans. Microwave Theory Tech. 48, 1957–1966 (2000)
[9] Back, C.-W., Song, S., Cheon, C., Kim, Y.-K., Kwon, Y.: 2-D mechanical beam steering antenna fabricated using MEMS technology. In: IEEE MTT-S Int. Microwave Symp. Dig., vol. 1, pp. 211–214 (2001)
[10] Yun, T.-Y., Chang, K.: A low-loss time-delay phase shifter controlled by piezoelectric transducer to perturb microstrip line. IEEE Microwave and Guided Wave Lett. 10, 96–98 (2000), Hwang, et al.: Beam Tilting Base Station Antennas 121
[11] Analysis and optimization of a phase shifter controlled by a piezoelectric transducer. IEEE Trans. Microwave Theory Tech. 50, 105–111 (2002)
[12] Alow-cost 8 to 26.5 GHz phased array antenna using a piezoelectric transducer controlled phase shifter. IEEE Trans. Antennas Propagat. 49, 1290–1298 (2001)
[13] Rodenbeck, C.T., Li, M.-Y., Chang, K.: A novel millimeter-wave beam-steering technique using a dielectric imageline- fed grating film. In: IEEE MTT-S Int. Microwave Symp. Dig., vol. 1, pp. 267–270 (2001)
[14] Li, M.-Y., Chang, K.: Novel low-cost beam-steering techniques using microstrip patch antenna arrays fed by dielectric image lines. IEEE Trans. Antennas Propagat. 47, 453–457 (1999)
[15] Novel beam-control techniques using dielectric image-line-fed microstrip patch-antenna arrays for millimeter-wave applications. IEEE Trans. Microwave Theory Tech. 46, 1930–1935 (1998)
[16] New tunable phase shifters using perturbed dielectric image lines. IEEE Trans. Microwave Theory Tech. 46, 1520–1523 (1998)
[17] Elamaran, B., Chio, I.-M., Chen, L.-Y., Chiao, J.-C.: A beam-steerer using reconfigurable PBG ground plane. In: IEEE MTT-S Int. Microwave Symp. Dig, pp. 835–838 (2000)
[18] Rodenbeck, C.T., Li, M.-Y., Chang, K.: A novel millimeter-wave beam-steering technique using a dielectric-imageline-fed grating film. In: IEEE MTT-S Int. Microwave Symp. Dig., vol. 1, pp. 267–270 (2001)

A Study on the Effect of Traffic Patterns in Mobile Ad Hoc Network

Arindarjit Pal[1], Jyoti Prakash Singh[2], and Paramartha Dutta[3]

[1] Dept. of Computer Science and Engineering,
Academy of Technology,
West Bengal, India
arindrajit@gmail.com

[2] Dept. of Information Technology,
Academy of Technology,
West Bengal, India
jyotip.singh@gmail.com

[3] Department of Computer and System Sciences,
Visva-Bharati University,
West Bengal, India
paramartha.dutta@gmail.com

Abstract. The multimedia application through mobile Ad-hoc network is gradually becoming very popular. The traffic patterns of multimedia applications are quite different from the traditional data applications. The constant bit rate (CBR) traffic does not accommodate the specific features of multimedia applications. To characterize, the multimedia application, Exponential or Pareto traffic sources have been explored. The popular routing protocols for mobile ad hoc network were developed considering the Constant Bit Rate (CBR) traffic only. In case of multimedia traffic they do not work as expected. In this article, we have tried to study the behavior of mobile ad hoc network routing protocols considering Exponential and Pareto traffic. To the best of our knowledge, this is the first attempt to analyze the effect of traffic patterns on mobile ad hoc network routing. We have chosen the Normalized routing load and Packet Delivery Fraction as our figure of merit to compare various protocols. The Normalized Routing Load is high for both Exponential and Pareto traffic in Dynamic Source Routing (DSR) protocol. The Packet Delivery Fraction is very high for Ad hoc On Demand Distance Vector (AODV) routing protocol in all types of traffic patterns whereas it is less in Dynamic Source Routing (DSR) for both Exponential and Pareto traffic.

Keywords: network traffic, routing, mobility pattern, ad hoc network, Exponential traffic, Pareto traffic.

1 Introduction

Ad hoc network is a wireless network technology where there is no wired or cellular infrastructure. Nodes in an ad-hoc network can communicate with each

A. Abraham et al. (Eds.): ACC 2011, Part I, CCIS 190, pp. 83–90, 2011.

other at any time, subject to connectivity limitations. This is one type of wireless network which use multi-hop radio relay transmission and there are no fixed base station for this type of networks. In Ad-hoc network the routing and the resource management are realized through different nodes in distributed manner and several nodes are connected to each other for communication. In ad hoc wireless networks each mobile node acts as a router as well as a host. Most ad hoc networks do not have any provisions for restricting or regulating the traffic that flows through a node, i.e., they do not implement any network access control. The mobility patterns of mobile nodes can be captured by different mobility models such as Random Way Point (RWP) [2,10,15,14], Manhattan Grid (MGM)[6], Reference Point Group Mobility Model (RPGM) [7] etc.. A survey of the most frequently used mobility models is presented in [4]. A number of routing protocols have been proposed for ad hoc network considering the constant bit rate traffic source. These routing protocols can be classified into two main categories based on the way they maintain their routes. They are (i) Proactive routing protocol and (ii) Reactive routing protocol. Proactive protocols maintain unicast routes between all pairs of nodes regardless of whether all routes are actually used. Therefore, when a traffic source begins a session with a remote destination, it has a route readily available and does not have to incur any delay for route discovery. These protocols also can find optimal routes (shortest paths) for given a model of link costs. Destination-Sequenced Distance-Vector (DSDV) [12] was one of the early proactive routing protocols developed for ad hoc networks. However, this protocol is not directly suitable for resource-poor and mobile ad hoc networks because of its high overheads and somewhat poor convergence behavior. On the contrary the main idea in reactive or on-demand routing is to find and maintain only needed routes. The Ad hoc On-demand Distance Vector (AODV) [13] is a nice example of on-demand approach for finding routes. In AODV, a route is established only when it is required by a source node for transmitting data packets. AODV uses traditional routing tables, one entry per destination. Dynamic Source Routing (DSR) [9] is another example of reactive routing which stores the complete hop-by-hop route to the destination. These routes are stored in a route cache. The data packets carry the source route in the packet header. The major difference between AODV and DSR is that DSR uses source routing in which a data packet carries the complete path to be traversed. On the contrary in AODV, the source node and the intermediate nodes store the next-hop information corresponding to each flow for data packet transmission. The traffic patterns play an important role in any routing protocol. Different applications generate different types of traffic. Traditional data applications generate constant bit rate traffic which is the traffic model of choice of most of the researchers for a long time in the area of mobile ad hoc network. Recently a lot of people have taken interest in multimedia applications in mobile ad hoc network. These multimedia applications have a radically different traffic patterns. The data rate in voice application increases till it reaches a maximum point. It is followed over an ideal period. This pattern of traffic can be captured by Exponential or Pareto traffic. The rest of this paper is organized as follows. Section 2 contains a brief introduction on different traffic patterns. In section 3, we describe two popular reactive routing protocols. Section 4 contains the simulation settings and results. We conclude the article in section 5 with some suggestions regarding future directions.

2 Traffic Models in MANET

2.1 Constant Bit Rate (CBR)

Constant Bit Rate (CBR) traffic model is widely used traffic model in network simulation. This generates traffic at a deterministic constant rate with some randomizing vacillate enabled on the inter packet departure interval. The CBR class is commonly used for data services. In this traffic, the data rate and the delay remain constant during the packet transmission. However, the CBR traffic class is not applicable in real time multimedia traffic generated on demand and video-conferencing services [5][1].

2.2 Exponential Traffic

The exponential traffic model is an ON/OFF model with an exponential distribution. There are three parameters in this traffic generator. The first parameters denotes the rate at which the traffic can be generated during ON period. The second and third parameter denotes the ON and OFF periods respectively. The Exponential Traffic class is adapted for real time multimedia, video and voice traffic.

2.3 Pareto Traffic

The Pareto traffic model is an ON/OFF model with an Pareto distribution. There are three parameters in this traffic generator. The first parameter denotes the rate at which the traffic can be generated during ON period. The second and third parameter denotes the ON and OFF periods respectively. The multimedia, video and voice transmission can be generated through Pareto traffic generator.

3 Routing Models in MANET

3.1 Ad Hoc On-Demand Distance Vector (AODV)

Ad hoc On-Demand Distance Vector (AODV) is an effective example of reactive on-demand routing protocol. It uses on-demand approach for finding routes i.e. a route is established only when it is requested by a source node for transmitting data packets to the receivers and these routes are maintained until they are in need by the source. In AODV, each node maintains at most one route per destination and as a result, the destination replies only once to the first arriving request during a route discovery. Being a single path protocol, it has to invoke a new route discovery whenever the only path from the source to the destination fails. When topology changes frequently, route discovery needs to be initiated time and again which can be very inefficient since route discovery flood is associated with significant latency and overhead. AODV maintains a destination sequence number generated by the receivers and determines an up-to-date path to the destination. A node updates its route information only if the destination sequence number of the current by received packet is greater than the destination sequence number stored at the node. It indicates the freshness of the route accepted by the source. To prevent multiple broadcast of the same packet, AODV uses broadcast identifier number that ensures loop freedom. This is because the intermediate nodes only forward the first copy of the same packet and discard the duplicate copies. When a route to a new destination is needed, the node uses a broadcast RREQ to find a route to the destination. Nodes that receive the RREQ find out whether they are the destination or whether they have a fresh route to the destination. Then they respond to the RREQ by unicasting a route reply (RREP) back to the source node [8]. A route can be determined when the request reaches either the destination itself, or an intermediate node with a fresh enough route to the destination. Since each node receiving the request keeps track of a route back to the source of the request, the RREP Reply can be unicast back from the destination to the source, or from any intermediate node that is able to satisfy the request back to the source.

3.2 Dynamic Source Routing (DSR)

Dynamic source routing (DSR) is another example of reactive routing protocol. It generates the proper route only when packet needs to be forwarded from source to destination. Within the limit of the transmission range, the process of finding a path is only executed when a path is needed by a node. DSR makes aggressive use of source routing and route caching. With source routing, complete path information is available and routing loops can be easily detected and eliminated without requiring any special mechanism. Because route requests and replies are both source routed, the source and destination, in addition to learning routes to each other, can also learn and cache routes to all intermediate nodes. The intermediate nodes addresses of the route are kept within the delivered packets. The route discovery process broadcasts a ROUTE REQUEST packet that is flooded across the network in a controlled manner. ROUTE REQUEST packets use sequence numbers to prevent duplication. The request is answered by a ROUTE REPLY packet either from the destination node or an intermediate node that has a cached route to the destination[6]. To take full advantage of route caching, DSR replies to all requests reaching a destination from a single request cycle. Thus the source learns many alternate routes to the destination, which will be useful in case the primary route fails.

4 Simulation Results and Analysis

Our target in the experiment is to study the behavior of routing protocol with different types of traffic sources under a specific mobility scenario. We use

Bonn-Motion [3] for generating mobility scenarios. We generate four mobility patterns with 30, 40 and 50 nodes moving in an area of 1000m X 1000m for a period of 1000 s with the first 3600 sec of each mobility pattern ignored. It has been observed that with the Random Way Point model, nodes have a higher probability of being near the center of the simulation area, while they are initially uniformly distributed over the simulation area initially. So, we skip 3600 s at the beginning to mitigate the boundary effects of node movement simulation. The maximum speed V_{max} of a node is set to 10m/s. The minimum speed v_{min} of a node is always set to 0.5m/s. The v_{min} is set to a positive value because Yoon and Liu [16] proved mathematically that the average speed of the nodes using Random way point mobility model decreases constantly and would eventually reach zero. One of their suggestion for getting rid of this problem is to use non zero minimum speed. This is what has been followed here. The cbrgen tool which is a part of ns-2 [11] distribution is used to generate Constant Bit Rate traffic(CBR) for 1000s with 1 packet/sec per source. The number of sources and destinations were chosen randomly by cbrgen tool. Similar to cbrgen tool we developed our own tool to generate Exponential and Pareto traffic. The Exponential traffic source generates traffic at 2 kb/s during ON period. The average ON and OFF periods are 315 ms and 325 ms respectively. The Pareto traffic source generates traffic at 2 kb/s during ON period. The average ON and OFF periods are 315 ms and 325 ms respectively. The source and destinations are chosen randomly in each traffic generator. We have used ns-2 [11] for network simulation and traces are generated in new trace format. To compare the performance of different routing protocols under various traffic, we have chosen Normalized Routing Load and Packet Delivery Fraction as out metric.

4.1 Packet Delivery Fraction

Packet Delivery Fraction (PDF) is an important figure of merit for Ad-hoc network routing protocols. Packet Delivery Fraction is the ratio of the number of data packets successfully delivered to the destinations to those generated by traffic sources.

$$pdf = \frac{data\_pkt\_rec}{data\_pkt\_sent} * 100; \qquad (1)$$

where *data_pkt_rec* and *data_pkt_send* are the number of data packets received and data packet sent respectively by the application. The packet delivery fraction(PDF) for CBR, Exponential and Pareto traffic sources with AODV and DSR routing protocol is shown graphically in Fig 1. From the Fig 1, we observe that the packet delivery fraction is very high for AODV and DSR routing protocol in CBR traffic. For node 30, the Packet delivery fraction is slightly low due to few number of nodes. In Exponential and Pareto traffic environment in AODV routing protocol, the Packet Delivery Fraction is very high for various number of nodes. The Packet Delivery Fraction in DSR routing for Exponential and Pareto traffic is average. We also observed that if the number of nodes increases then the Packet Delivery Fraction(PDF) is also high. From the following Fig.1, the Packet Delivery Fraction increases for large number of mobile nodes.

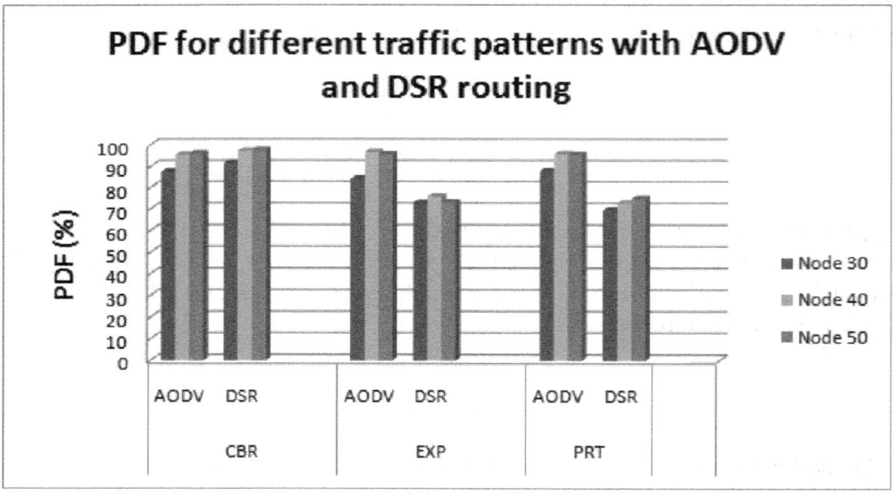

Fig. 1. Packet Delivery Fraction (%) in AODV and DSR for different traffic models in RWP

4.2 Normalized Routing Load

The Normalized Routing Load (NRL) denotes the measure of control packets sent and forwarded by router to transmit for every byte of data packet. the Normalized Routing Load is given by

$$nrl = \frac{cp\_sent + cp\_forw}{data\_pkt\_rec} * 100 \tag{2}$$

where cp_sent and cp_forw are the control packets sent and forwarded by the router and $data\_pkt\_rec$ is the data packet received by the application. Fig. 2 shows the routing overhead in Normalized Routing Load. Normalized routing load is the ratio of the number of control packets propagated by every node in the network and the number of data packets received by the destination nodes. In case of DSR each intermediate node records the number of packets queued in control packet. The destination node uses this information when selecting the route. Route breaks occur more frequently in DSR because it often uses old routes. Hence, more ROUTE ERROR packets are transmitted, and consequently, more ROUTE REQUESTS are sent to reconstruct routes. This causes the Normalized Routing Load to increase in DSR which is supported by our experimental results as shown in Fig.2. The Normalized Routing Load is maximum for DSR routing in Exponential and Pareto traffic. In case of Constant Bit Rate(CBR) traffic, the packets are generated at a constant rate. So, the Normalized Routing Load is very less for both AODV and DSR routing.

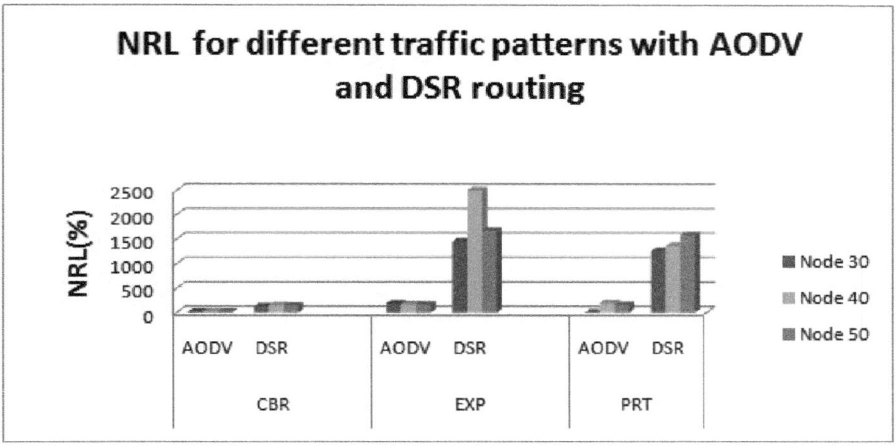

Fig. 2. Normalized Routing Load(%) in AODV and DSR for different traffic models in RWP

5 Conclusion

In this article, we conducted detailed study of several Traffic models and mobility models in MANET research. We have shown the relation between different traffic and routing protocols for different parameters. Through simulations, we found significant effect on Normalized routing load(NRL)and Packet Delivery Fraction(PDF) in routing performance of multimedia. Because, both AODV and DSR are based on Constant Bit Rate(CBR) traffic. But in multimedia data transmission we have used Exponential and Pareto traffic. All the earlier works are based on Constant Bit Rate(CBR) traffic. Constant Bit Rate(CBR) traffic is good for data application but not well suited for multimedia application. On the other hand Exponential and Pareto traffic can module the characteristics of multimedia traffic because they possesses variation in rate of data packet generation followed by an OFF period. The authors are currently engaged in supplementing the current routing protocols for multimedia application using Exponential and Pareto traffic sources.

References

1. Al-Maashri, A., Ould-Khaoua, M.: Performance analysis of manet routing protocols in the presence of self-similar traffic. In: 31st IEEE Conference on Local Computer Networks, Tampa, Florida, USA, pp. 811–818 (November 2006)
2. Bettstetter, C.: Topology properties of ad hoc networks with random waypoint mobility. ACM SIGMOBILE Mobile Computing and Communication Review 7(3), 50–52 (2003)
3. University of Bonn: Bonnmotion - a mobility scenario generation and analysis tool, `http://www.cs.uni-bonn.de/IV/bomonet/BonnMotion.htm`

4. Camp, T., Boleng, J., Davies, V.: A survey of mobility models for ad hoc network research. Wireless Communications and Mobile Computing (WCMC): Special issue on Mobile Ad Hoc Networking: Research, Trends and Applications 2(5), 483–502 (2002)
5. Chowdhury, M.U., Perera, D., Pham, T.: A performance comparison of three wireless multi-hop ad-hoc network routing protocols when streaming mpeg-4 traffic. In: 8th International Multitopic Conference, pp. 516–521 (December 2004)
6. Pucha, H., Das, S.M., Hu, Y.C.: The performance impact of traffic patterns on routing protocols in mobile ad hoc networks. Computer Networks 51, 3595–3616 (2007)
7. Hong, X., Gerla, M., Pei, G., Chiang, C.C.: A Group Mobility Model for Ad Hoc Wireless Networks. In: Workshop on Modelling and Simulation of Wireless and Mobile Systems (MSWiM), pp. 53–60 (1999)
8. Jayakumar, G., Ganapathi, G.: Reference point group mobility and random way point models in performance evaluation of manet routing protocols. Journal of Computer Systems, Networks, and Communications 2008 (December2008)
9. Johnson, D.B., Maltz, D.A., Broch, J.: Dsr: The dynamic source routing protocol for multi-hop wireless ad hoc networks. In: Perkins, C.E. (ed.) Ad Hoc Networking, ch. 5, pp. 139–172. Addison-Wesley, Reading (2001)
10. Lassila, P., Hyyti, E., Koskinen, H.: Connectivity properties of random waypoint mobility model for ad hoc networks. In: MedHoc-Net, le de Porquerolles, pp. 159–168 (2005)
11. McCanne, S., Floyd, S.: NS-2 Network Simulator, http://www.isi.edu/nsnam/ns/
12. Perkins, C.E., Bhagwat, P.: Highly dynamic destination-sequenced distance-vector routing (dsdv) for mobile computers. ACM SIGCOMM Computer Communication Review 24, 234–244 (1994)
13. Perkins, C.E., Royer, E.M.: Ad-hoc on-demand distance vector routing. In: Proceedings of the 2nd IEEE Workshop on Mobile Computing Systems and Applications, pp. 90–100 (1997)
14. Singh, J.P., Dutta, P.: Temporal behavior analysis of mobile ad hoc network with different mobility patterns, pp. 696–702. ACM, New York (2009)
15. Singh, J.P., Dutta, P.: Temporal modeling of node mobility in mobile ad hoc network. Journal of Computing and Information Technology 18(1), 19–29 (2010)
16. Yoon, J., Liu, M., Noble, B.: Random waypoint considered harmful. In: INFOCOM 2003, pp. 1312–1321 (2003)

I-SAODV: Improving SAODV to Mitigate Hop-Count Attack in Mobile Adhoc Network

Sanjeev Rana[1] and Manpreet Singh[2]

[1] Assoc. Professor, Computer Science & Engineering Department,
M. M. Engineering College, M. M. University, Ambala, India
sanjeevrana@rediffmail.com
[2] Professor, Computer Science & Engineering Department,
M. M. Engineering College, M. M. University, Ambala, India
dr.manpreet.singh.in@gmail.com

Abstract. A mobile adhoc network (MANET) is a collection of wireless nodes, communicating among themselves over possibly multi hop paths, without the help of any central infrastructure such as base stations. Ad hoc On Demand Vector Routing (AODV) is perhaps the most well known routing protocol for MANET. A variety of attacks can be launched against AODV [1] protocol. One of major attack is modification of hop count in route request and route reply control messages. This attack propagates distorted view of hop counts between two legitimate nodes in the network Secure AODV (SAODV) is a secure extension of the AODV routing protocol. SAODV [2] only prevents from decrease of the hop count attack, while attackers can still forward routing messages with the same hop count or increase in hop count on the network. In this paper, we have proposed a security scheme to improve SAODV (I-SAODV) which uses hash chain and markle hash tree for authentication to protect not only from same hop count fraud but also prevent from maliciously increase in hop count in the message. The effectiveness of I-SAODV is analyzed using network simulator NS2.

Keywords: Hop count, Authentication, SAODV, Hash Chain.

1 Introduction

MANET is a network wherein a number of mobile nodes communicate with each other without any predefined infrastructure or centralized administration. The mobile nodes set up temporary paths among themselves to transmit packets. Thus, a pair of nodes can communicate directly or over a sequence of wireless links including one or more intermediate nodes [3]. Many routing protocols [4], [5], [6], [7] have been proposed for MANET as communication between mobile nodes has to rely on intermediate nodes. AODV is perhaps the most well-known routing protocol for a MANET. AODV routing was created without taking security into major concern. Each node, which acts like a mobile router, has full control over the data that pass through it. Some of these are malicious nodes, which enter the network during establishment phase while others may originate indigenously by compromising an existing benevolent node. These malicious nodes can carry out both passive and active attacks against

A. Abraham et al. (Eds.): ACC 2011, Part I, CCIS 190, pp. 91–100, 2011.

the network. In passive attacks, a malicious node only eavesdrops upon packet contents without disrupting the network operation, while active attacks can fabricate, modify or drop a packets [8] [9]. A variety of attacks [10, 11] can be launched against AODV protocol. One of major attack is modification of hop count in route request and route reply control messages. This attack propagates distorted view of hop counts between two legitimate nodes in the network. A malicious node can decrease the hop count to attract traffic towards itself. A node refuses to forward packets either intensely or maliciously by increasing hop count a high value.

SAODV is an extension of the AODV routing protocol providing security features like integrity, authentication and non-repudiation. SAODV uses two mechanisms to secure the AODV messages: Digital signatures to authenticate the non-mutable fields i.e. source address, destination address and hash chains to secure mutable fields i.e. hop count information in the control messages. In order to protect the mutable hop count field of the AODV packet, SAODV uses a one-way hash chain. An initial *seed* value is generated. This value is then repeatedly hashed *max_hop_count* times to arrive at the value stored in the *Top_Hash* field. The seed value is used as the initial value of the Hash field. Formally this means

$$Top\_Hash = h^{\max\_hop\_count}(seed)$$

Where, h is a one-way hash function and $h^i(x)$ is the iterative hashing of x, i times. Upon receiving an SAODV message, the receiving node has to confirm that

$$Top\_Hash = h^{\max\_hop\_count - hop\_count}(Hash)$$

It must then increment the Hop Count field and set *Hash =h(Hash)*. Since a one-way hash function is used, it should be computationally infeasible for a node to determine a value in the hash chain it has not seen, which would correspond to a hop count lower than that specified in the routing message it received. But intermediate nodes can forward the same hop count or can increase the hop count maliciously and the next node cannot detect this change in SAODV. In this paper, we present the improvement in SAODV (I-SAODV) routing protocol which prevent from the distance frauds of SAODV routing protocol. In section II, we present the overview of I-SAODV). Section III describes the implementation of I-SAODV. We present security analysis of I-SAODV for different hop count attack scenario in section IV. Section V describes the effectiveness of the proposed scheme over SAODV using NS2.34 simulator. In section VI, we conclude our work with future scope.

2 Overview of I-SAODV

In this section, we propose a security enhancement scheme I-SAODV to improve SAODV to prevent from increase or same hop-count fraud attack. There are no changes to the AODV protocol operation itself but each node now performs additional, security related functions. Security services are implemented by extending existing control messages of the SAODV protocol. The attributes added in the control message of SAODV are the node list. The purpose of node list is limited for node authentication and it will not be included in the cache of nodes routing table for later route selection. Nodes will store only next hop address in the routing table for a destination as in AODV.

I-SAODV uses hash chain and authenticated hash tree. Hash chain uses this node list to encode the address of node sending the route advertisement for authentication only. Since the authenticator has the address of the node so a node cannot tell lie about distance with a valid authenticator. This authentication will take place during route discovery or route maintenance phase. Authenticated hash tree is used to prevent any modification in the route list i.e. change in the position of node list node (from S-A-B-C-D to S-A-C-B-D). The attribute node list is included only in the control messages not in the data messages. The proposed security scheme takes following assumptions:

- The scheme uses public key cryptography for the integrity of non-mutable fields as in SAODV.
- There is a secret number between source and destination node.
- Each node is capable of storing its own certificate and, as required of other nodes.

2.1 One-Way Hash Chain

A one way hash chain [12] is built on a one way hash function. A one way hash function H, maps an input of any length to a fixed length bit string. Thus, H: $\{0,1\}^* \rightarrow \{0,1\}^\rho$, Where ρ is the length in bits of the output of the hash function. The function H should be simple to compute yet must be computationally infeasible in general to invert. To create a one way hash chain, a node chooses a random initial value $x \in \{0,1\}^\rho$ and computes the list of values $h_0; h_1; h_2; h_3; \ldots ; h_n$ Where $h_0=x$, and $h_i=H(h_{i-1})\ for\ 0 < i \leq n$, for some n.

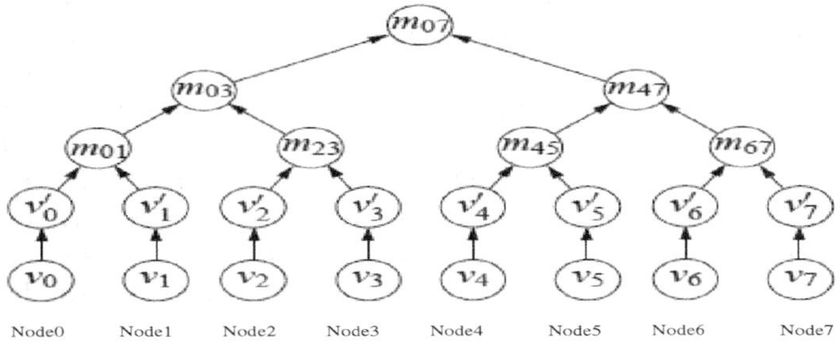

Fig. 1. Hash Tree Authenticated values

2.2 Tree Authenticated Values

The mechanism of tree authenticated values [12] is an efficient hash tree authentication mechanism; first presented by Merkle and also known as Merkle hash trees. To authenticate values $v_0; v_1; \ldots; v_{w-1}$, we place these values at the leaf nodes of a binary tree (For simplicity we assume a balanced binary tree). We first blind all the v_i values with a one way hash function H, so v_i'= H[v_i]. We then use the Merkle hash tree construction to commit to the values v_0'; ... ; v_{w-1}'. Each internal node of the binary tree is derived from its two child nodes. Consider the derivation of some parent node m_p from its left and right child nodes m_l and m_r : $m_p=H[m_l||m_r]$, where || denotes concatenation. We compute the levels of the tree recursively from the leaf nodes to the root node. Figure1 shows this construction over the eight values v_0; v_1; ... ; v_7, e.g., $m_{01}=H(v_0'||v_1'),m_{03}=H[m_{01}||m_{23}]$. The root value of the tree is used to commit to the entire tree and is used to authenticate the leaf values.

3 Implementation of I-SAODV

During route discovery phase, the control messages route request (RREQ) and route reply (RREP) have two types of attributes. Non-Mutable fields which does not change from hop to hop i.e. source address, destination address. Mutable fields which change from hop to hop i.e. hop count, time to live. Source node and destination node use digital signature to secure non-mutable fields for RREP and RREQ respectively as in SAODV. I-SAODV uses hash chain and merkle hash tree for authentication of mutable fields. This authentication is achieved by encoding the address of node sending or forwarding in the route advertisement. I-SAODV uses additional fields in the route request secure extension RREQ-SE control message packet as shown in Table1.

When any intermediate node, say A, receives a RREQ, the node check its local table of (source, RREQ_id) values from recent RREQ it has received, to determine if it has already seen a RREQ. If it has, the node discards the packet. Otherwise, the node modifies the RREQ by appending its own address to the *node list* in the RREQ, and replacing the *hash* field with H [A, hash chain'], finally, the node rebroadcasts the modified RREQ. When the target node receives the RREQ message, it performs two actions. First it calculates the *hash* using node list and secret number as shown below: $H[node_n,H[node_{n-1},H[node_{n-2},H[......,H[node_1,H[secret\ number]]]]]]$.

Where, $node_i$, is the node address at position i of the node list from source node and n represents the number of nodes in the node list in the RREQ. If the calculated hash value is equal to the received hash in the RREQ, it means RREQ message is valid control message. Destination node calculates the hop count either using the length of node list or the number of times hash is performed for verification.

Table 1. RREQ Signature Extension Fields

Field	Value
Type	64 in RREQ-SE
Hash Function	The hash function used to compute the Hash chain field.
Signature	The signature of all the non-mutable fields in the AODV packet.
Hash	Hash chain=H[node address, previous hash chain element]. The node address is the address of node handling the RREQ message and the previous hash chain element is the hash chain element which the node got in the RREQ message from previous node.
Node list	Node list is the node addresses which are in the path from source node to destination node.

Table 2. RREP Signature Extension Fields

Field	Value
Type	65 in RREP -SE
Hash Function	The hash function used to compute the Hash field.
Actual Hop Count	The Actual Hop Count is the number of times the hash is performed by the destination for verifying the RREQ message (except hash with secret number).
Hash_root	This is the root value (commitment value) in the merkle hash tree
Signature	The signature of all the non-mutable fields in the AODV packet.
Node list	Reverse of node list got in the RREQ message. (This indicates the path followed by the RREP message)

Second, destination node verifies non-mutable fields using digital signature. If both steps successful, destination node prepare route reply control message towards source node containing additional fields in the route reply control message {type, hash function, actual hop count, hash_root, signature, node list} as shown in Table2. Destination node calculates the hash_root using of merkle hash tree with node list as leaf node. Leaf nodes must uniquely identify any node in the network. So, we can also use node public key for hash_root calculation because it can foil identity spoofing attack. hash_root is the commitment of these leaf node addresses.

As shown in the figure2 the v_0, v_1, v_2....v_7 are the node addresses (or their public key) in the node list sent by the destination. This hash_root field and the actual hop count field of our approach are included in the digital signature. So, they will not change during transmission. The source node after getting the RREP message verifies the message. The source node got the hash-root field and the actual hop count field from the RREP message. If actual hop count is not equal to the number of nodes in the node list then it means RREP message is not valid and some malicious activity is performed. But it does not protect about change in the position of node in the node list.

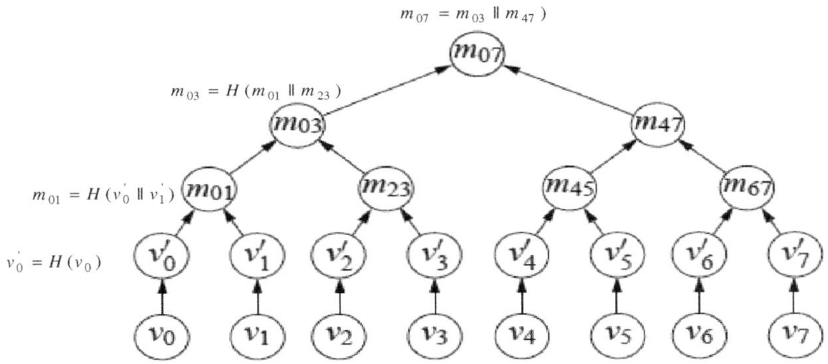

Fig. 2. Calculation of Hash_root using node list as leaf nodes

Now, the source node calculates the merkle hash tree in the same way as by the destination node. If this calculated value of hash root using node list is equal to the value got in the RREP message (hash_root field) then the source node verified that the RREP message is valid and no malicious activity is performed i.e. modification in node list. Node list indicates the route path but in reverse order. Otherwise the RREP message is not valid so source node rejects the RREP message. The role of node list is only for authentication to protect malicious activity. Node list is used only for control messages not for data messages. It will not be used by node for their routing table for route discovery of other nodes.

4 Security Analysis of I-SAODV

In this section, we evaluate security aspects of our proposed security scheme I-SAODV using JDK1.5.0. In I-SAODV, the hash chain elements include the address of nodes processing the request thus preventing an attacker from playing an authenticator maliciously. For example the source node is S, the destination node is D, the *hash function* is H, the *secret number x* between the source and the destination. In starting the *node list* is blank since *node list* represent the nodes in the path from source to destination. The node S floods the RREQ message in the network.

S: h_0= H[x]; S → *: {64, H, signature, h_0, ()}
A: h_1=H[A, h_0]; A → * : {64, H, signature, h_1, (A)}
B: h_2=H[B, h_1]; B → * : {64, H, signature, h_2,(A, B)}
C: h_3=H[C, h_2]; C → *: {64, H, signature, h_3,(A, B, C)}

The destination node D got the RREQ message. The hop count attacks are verified by the hash chain calculation.

Hashchainverifier=H[C, H[B, H[A, H[x]]]].

If received *hash* is equal to the calculated *Hashchainverifier* then it means the RREQ message is valid. No malicious activity is performed. So no hop count fraud occurred. Now the destination node D can send the RREP. The *hash_root* field is calculated using merkle hash tree construction by destination node as shown in figure3 (For simplicity we add extra value w which has no effect since both source and destination node uses this w value at the same place).

D → C: {65, H, 3, m_{cw}, signature, (C, B, A)};
C → B: {65, H, 3, m_{cw}, signature, (C, B, A)};
B → A: {65, H, 3, m_{cw}, signature, (C, B, A)};
A → S: {65, H, 3, m_{cw}, signature, (C, B, A)};

As intermediate nodes are simply forwarding the route reply messages toward source and does not perform any additional security related job, the performance of I-SAODV improved compare to SAODV where intermediates nodes are involved. Thus The RREP message reaches to source node by following the path indicated by the node list (C, B, A). The actual hop count, i.e. 3, is equal to the no of nodes in the node list then the source node again reconstruct the markle hash tree using received node list as leaf nodes as shown in figure4. This root is now *hash_root_verifier*. So if the *hash_root_verifier* is equal to the received *hash_root* field of RREP then this means that the RREP message is valid. The value 64 and 65 represents route request and route reply messages.

4.1 Attacks on RREQ Message

Preventing Decrease in Hop count: The property of hash chain is that it is infeasible to find a hash previous in the list. So a node got the hash chain element cannot generate the previous hash chain element thus it cannot decrease the hop count.

Preventing Same hop count: In same hop count fraud the node send the same hash value to the next node as received from the previous node in the RREQ message. Suppose the B node send the same hash value that is h_1 to the C node.

B→ *: {64, H, signature, h_1, (A, B)}; C: h_2=H[C, h_1];
C→ *: {64, H, signature, h_2, (A, B, C)}

As the node D got the RREQ message and calculates:

Hashchainverifier=H[C, H[B, H[A, H[x]]]].

This *hashchainverifier* is not equal to the *hash* field because the *hash* field received in RREQ message is H[C, H[A, H[x]]]] (because node B send the same hash chain value (h_1) received from previous node) then it means the RREQ message is not valid.

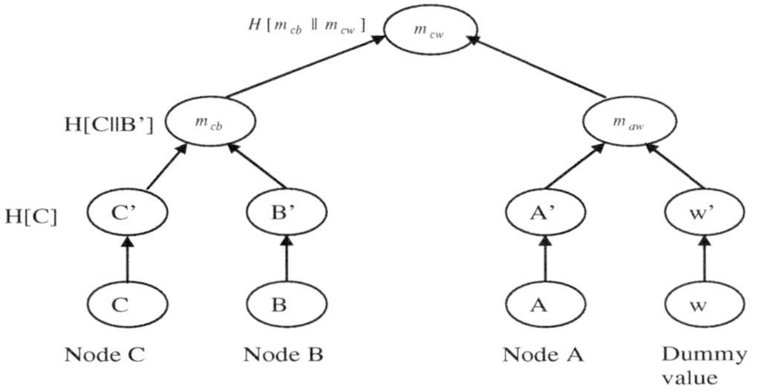

Fig. 3. Construction of hast tree root value to foil modification in node list

Preventing Increase in Hop count: To increase hop count the malicious node increase the nodes in the path maliciously. Suppose node B do this.

B: h_2= H[B, h_1] , h_3= H[F, h_2]

(Node B increases the hop count corresponding to node F)

B→ *: {64, H, signature, h_3, (A, B)}

(Node F will not be in *node list* since it is malicious increase)

C: h_4=H[C, h_3]; C→ *: {64, H, signature, h_4, (A, B, C)}

As the node D got the RREQ message. D calculates:

Hashchainverifier=H[C, H[B, H[A, H[x]]]].

This *Hashchainverifier* is not equal to the received *hash* field because the hash field received in RREQ message is H[C, H[F, H[B, H[A, H[x]]]]] (because node B send the extra increase in hash chain corresponding to node F without being node F in the path) then it means the RREQ message is not valid.

4.2 Attacks on RREP Messages

Change the position of nodes in the node list (change the route): Suppose the node A change the position as:

A→S: {65, H, 3, m_{cw}, signature, (B, C, A)}

(The position of B and C is changed)

This RREP message reaches to source node. Since the actual hop count, i,e 3, is equal to the number of nodes in the node list. The source node compares *hash_root_verifier* to the *hash_root* field as shown in figure4 (for simplicity we add extra value w which has no effect since both trees uses w at same place). This *hash_root_verifier* is not equal to the *hash_root* field. So it means that RREP message is not valid.

Preventing Increase the Hop count: Some malicious node can add extra node in the node list so increase the hop count. Suppose the node A do this attack.

A→S: {65, H, 3, m_{cw}, signature, (C, B, F, A)}

(The node A add node F in *node list* maliciously)

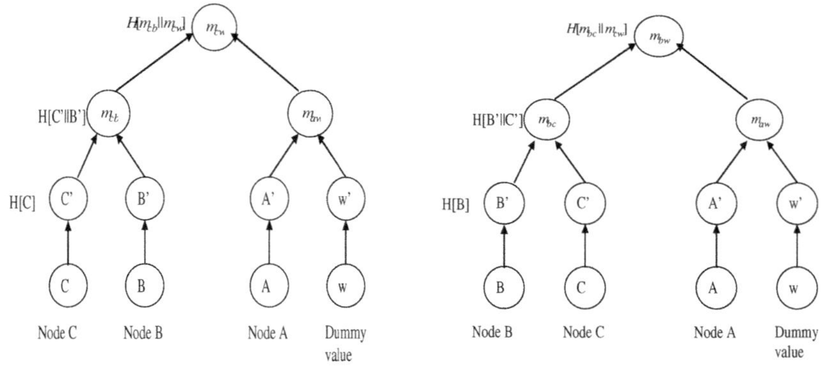

Fig. 4. Markle Hash tree showing the verification of hash field (m_{cw}) and hashverifier (m_{bw})

This RREP message reaches to source node. Since actual hop count, i.e. 3, is not equal to the number of nodes in the node list, i.e. 4. So it means RREP message is not valid so no need for calculation of *hashverifier* (if any node remove the node from node list means decrease the hop count it also gives the unequal actual hop count and number of nodes in the node list with same discussion). So it means that some malicious activity is performed and the source node rejects this RREP message. So in this way hop count fraud is identified. Table3 also describes the effectiveness of our proposed scheme over AODV and SAODV.

Table 3. Effectiveness of I-SAODV over AODV and SAODV

Description	AODV	SAODV	I-SAODV
Security mechanism for Non-Mutable attributes	No	Digital signature	Digital Signature
Security mechanism for Mutable attributes	No	Hash Chain with TTL and Hop count field	Hash Chain and Authenticated Hash Tree with node identity
Intermediate nodes verify control messages for hop count attacks	No	Yes	No
Prevent from Decrease in Hop Count Attack	No	Yes	Yes
Prevent from Same in Hop Count Attack	No	No	Yes
Prevent from Increase in Hop Count Attack	No	No	Yes
Prevent from Route Modification Attack	No	No	Yes

Table 4. Simulation parameter of NS2 for Experiment

Simulation Parameters	Values
Number of Nodes	50
Maximum Connections	40 traffic sources
Mobility Model	Random Waypoint
Mobility Speed	40 m/s
Data Rate	8kbps
Topology Size	500m X 500m
Total Time	100seconds
Pause Time	10 seconds

5 Performance Analysis of I-SAODV

In this research paper, the comparisons of three routing protocols between AODV, SAODV and I-SAODV have been measured using network simulator NS2.34. NS2.34 is a open source code. We used average end to end delay as performance metric to study each routing protocols in a free-attack simulation environment. The scenario is defined with a set of parameters as in Table 4.

Average End-to-End Delay: The delay experienced by packet from the time it was sent by a source till the time it reached the destination. This includes all possible delays caused by buffering during route discovery latency, queuing at the interface queue, retransmission delays at the MAC and propagation and transfer times. Average end to end delay can be calculated by averaging the send time and receive time for each packet sent. As the results shown in Figure 5, since the usage of signatures and verifications method in the SAODV and I-SAODV routing protocols, higher delays produced in SAODV and I-SAODV as compared to AODV. From the result, we can see that I-SAODV had lower delay and giving much better performance as compared to SAODV because intermediate nodes are not involved in the verification of control messages.

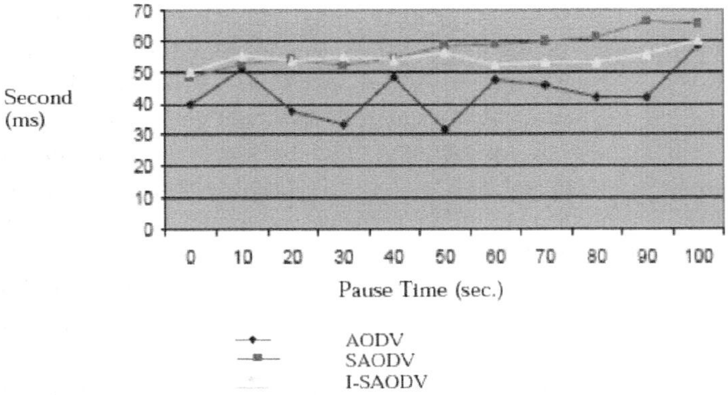

Fig. 5. Average End to End Delay Vs. Pause Time

This simulation shows that in the secure routing protocols, the usage of security techniques like digital signatures, authentications and hash chains have major impacts on the performance since it will use more processing power and time.

6 Conclusion and Future Scope

In this paper, we proposed a security scheme, which improves existing SAODV, that is I-SAODV which prevents an attacker not to advertise a route shorter or longer than the one it heard by changing the hop-count attribute of RREQ and RREP control messages. When a node received the hash from previous node, it unable to generate the previous hash chain element thus it cannot decrease the hop count. Even attacker cannot create a valid advertisement with a larger or smaller route by altering hop count. We prevent the distance fraud by tying the authenticator to the address of the node sending a route advertisement, thus an attacker cannot produce the distance metric maliciously. The intermediate node does not verify the RREQ and RREP messages, so little computation time is required as compared to SAODV for mutable attributes. I-SAODV not only prevents from hop count attack but also prevent from modification in node list using authenticated markle hash tree.

This paper is focus only for hop count attack issue of SAODV not for digital signed non mutable information which also has major impacts on the performance because of asymmetric cryptography. In future, further optimizations of non-mutable attributes in secure routing protocols are required to minimize the processing overhead, delays and to maximize the routing throughputs.

References

[1] Royer, E.M., Perkins, C.E.: Ad-hoc on-demand distance vector routing. In: Proceedings of the 2nd IEEE Workshop on Mobile Computing Systems and Applications, p. 90 (1999)

[2] Zapata, M.G., Asokan, N.: Securing ad hoc routing protocols. In: Proceedings of ACM Workshop on Wireless Security (WiSe), pp. 1–10 (2002)

[3] Perkins, C.E., Belding-Royer, E.M., Das, S.R.: Ad hoc on-demand distance vector (AODV) routing, RFC 3561, The Internet Engineering Task Force, Network Working Group (July 2003)

[4] Johnson, D.B., Maltz, D.A.: Dynamic source routing in ad hoc wireless networks. In: Imielinski, Korth (eds.) Mobile Computing, vol. 353, pp. 153–181. Kluwer Academic Publishers, Dordrecht (1996)

[5] Maltz, D.A., Johnson, D.B., Hu, Y.: The dynamic source routing protocol (DSR) for mobile ad hoc networks for IPv4, RFC 4728, The Internet Engineering Task Force, Network Working Group (February 2007)

[6] Perkins, C.E., Bhagwat, P.: Highly dynamic destination-sequenced distance-vector routing (DSDV) for mobile computers. In: Proc. Conf. Commun. Architect. Protocols, Appl., pp. 234–244 (August 1994)

[7] Hu, Y., Perrig, A., Johnson, D.B.: Wormhole attacks in wireless networks. IEEE Journal on Selected Areas in Communication 24(2) (February 2006)

[8] Wu, B., Chen, J., Wu, J., Cardei, M.: A survey of attacks and countermeasures in mobile ad hoc networks. Wireless Network Security 30(3), 103–135 (2007)

[9] Win, K.S.: Analysis of detecting wormhole attack in wireless networks. World Academy of Science, Engineering and Technology 36 (December 2008)

[10] Juwad, M.F., Al-Raweshidy, H.S.: Experimental Performance Comparisons between SAODV & AODV. In: IEEE Second Asia International Conference on Modeling & Simulation (2008)

[11] Arshad, J., Azad, M.A.: Performance Evaluation of Secure on-Demand Routing Protocols for Mobile Ad-hoc Networks, 1-4244-0626-9/06 © 2006 IEEE

[12] Hu, Y., Johnson, D., Perrig, A.: SEAD: Secure efficient distance vector routing for mobile wireless ad hoc networks. Ad Hoc Networks I, 175–192 (2003)

Social Network Aware Routing for Delay Tolerant Networks

Rajiv Misra and Shailendra Shukla

Dept. of Computer Science and Engineering
Indian Institute of Technology, Patna
Patliputra Colony Patna 800 013
{rajivm,s.shukla}@iitp.ac.in

Abstract. In delay tolerant network, the intermittent connectivity makes it difficult to guarantee end to end connectivity and due to long delays makes impossible to provide timely data transfers. The challenges in DTN for providing routing services using store and forward approach over intermittent network connectivity opportunistically using limited buffering capacity of nodes. In this paper, we proposed a routing approach for delay tolerant networks where nodes move in community. Our approach beats the use of buffering on comparing with some of prominent DTN routing algorithms such as Maxprop,Epidemic,Prophet, Spray and wait.The simulation results show the reduction in the use of buffer capacity compared to Epidemic routing in community based social network model while keeping message delivery at desired level.

Keywords: Social network analysis, Delay tolerant networks, Community and Storage (buffer optimization).

1 Introduction

The primary challenge for routing in delay tolerant network is its intermittent connectivity and node availability. Nodes are mobile and connection happens when they are in wireless range of other node. Delay tolerant network experiences frequent partitions which result in large end to end delay. In such network there is no guarantee of full end to end connectivity. In such scenario traditional adhoc routing protocols fails to send packet due to unavailability of path or carrier deny to accept new message due to full buffer space. If nodes have sufficient mobility, the messages will be forwarded to intermediate nodes, which further buffer these packets for some period of time and forward it on contact with other nodes. Eventually, few of the stored message reaches to destination. Flooding is one such approach of buffering and replication of messages. DTN routing and application protocols have shown that their performance is highly dependent on the underlying mobility and node characteristics.

In this paper we have introduced social network aware routing for disconnected network where nodes are socially connected and move in community. Community is naturally formed in networks such as crowd, groups according to

A. Abraham et al. (Eds.): ACC 2011, Part I, CCIS 190, pp. 101–110, 2011.

human social relationship, etc. Social network community is derived from the small world phenomenon [2] which was first proved by Milgram [1]. Community is define as group of node interacting each other for certain percentage of time together. Generally nodes move around in their own community, and sometimes relocate to other community. Nodes are wirelessly connected so communities could be in or out of range. In range communities forms overlapping community [1]. When two or more node lies between two different community then it forms overlapping community. Communities have the ability to move about in the network, frequently mixing and merging with other communities and splitting into smaller community in a networks. Some past work has shown that DTN routing performance are highly dependent on the underlying mobility and node characteristics[8].

Traditional DTN routing protocols like epidemic routing[4] use replica of messages to improve message delivery in different delay tolerant scenario. The basic idea behind replication schemes is to inject identical copies of data into the network. Relay node carry copy of data towards destination. A message delivered is successful if at least one of the multiple copies is received by the destination. When network resources (e.g., buffer space and network bandwidth) are limited, then replication based schemes tend to degrade the delivery ratio (percentage of packets delivered to their destinations). Flooding scheme degrade the network and increase overhead when network resources are limited.Flooding of control messages result in increment of redundant broadcasts which cause serious contention and collision problems in wireless network. Limited replica can be used for wireless mobile node to achieve scalability. Specific movement and location patterns of node can provide an efficient way of buffer optimization.we can achieve significant resource utilization if node mobility and buffer relays are chosen effectively.

Section 2 discusses the related works reported. The section 3 discuss the framework of the proposed work, section 4 is about the proposed routing and buffering scheme of this work, section 5 brings out the performance comparison based on simulations. Section 6 concludes the paper.

2 Related Works

Many reported works of routing algorithms in DTNs [3,4,5,6,7,8,9] discusses sending messages opportunistically in wake of disconnected end to end networks using forwarding and buffering. In Epidemic routing, Vahdat and Becker[4] in his paper proposed routing protocol for intermittently connected networks.Epedermic routing delivers message where no assumption is make regarding node mobility and global topology knowledge. Epidermic routing relies on basic principle of flooding, when message carrying node reaches in contact of other node it eventually copy message till it delivered to destination. Node buffer messages if it there is no path to the destination available. Every node contains an index of these messages called a summary vector, and when nodes meet they exchange summary vectors. Once node exchanges their summary vector, each node gets information that other node has some message that was previously unseen.The process replication continues till the buffer space available.

Prophet, Lindgren, Doria and Olov[5] in their paper proposed routing protocol for DTN. They claim that Prophet delivers more message than Epidemic Routing. Prophet routing uses history of encounters and transitivity of node.Prophet protocol first estimates a probabilistic metric called delivery predictability $P(i, j)$, at every node I to all known node j. This value indicates that how likely it will going to deliver message to destination. The operation of Prophet is same as that of Epidemic routing, when two nodes meet they exchange summary vector and predictability vector which contains delivery predictability for destination known.

Spray and Wait Routing, Spyropoulos, Psounis, S. Raghavendra [7] in his paper proposed randomized flood based routing for DTN. Spray and Wait protocol works in two phase spray phase and wait phase. In spray phase initially source create L copies of message and forwarded it to L relays.Spray and Wait bounds the number of replications of a packets to L, where L is computed on the basis of total number of node in network. In wait phase if destination in not found,than each of the L node will carry a message copy and perform direct delivery to destination.Spray and Wait routing reduce data delay, but it does not consider bandwidth or storage constraints.

MAXprop[6],is another protocol which usage previous encounter knowledge for minimizations of data delay. John Burgess[6] in his paper proposed an effective routing protocol for DTN.The algorithm is based on likelihood of meeting next node. MaxProp is controlled flooding based in nature.If a contact is discovered in MAXprop, then the messages which is not exchange while contact is replicated and transferred.Each node has a vector $Fi{=}(f_{i0}...f_{j-1})$,normalized so the sum is equal to 1.When one node encounter other node than their corresponding vector is incremented by 1, and than all vector elements are divided by 2.

MAXProp prioritize both the schedule of packet transmitted to other peers and the schedule of packets dropped. Maxprop Routing operation proceeds in three stages. Neighbor discovery,peer discovers each other before transfer begin. Data transfer when peer comes in contact with others they do not know the duration of each other. Storage management, as node receive packet from neighbor each node manage their finite buffer space by deleting some of the buffered packet according to ranking algorithm.

3 Frame Work

In this paper we are assuming that nodes are mobile and sparsely connected. Whenever set of node interact for sufficiently large period of time they form community. The proposed protocol attempts to exploit such community structure and node characteristic in order to provide better data delivery with limited replication. The main design goals of proposed work can be classified as follows.

1. Community detection and maintenance.
2. Reduce pathfinding complexity of DTN networks using Social network centrality.
3. Using controlled replication to increase packet delivery and resource utilization.

3.1 Community Formation

Application of social network analysis using graph theoretic representation is emerging topic in delay tolerant networks. Many few researchers has used the concept of social network analysis in DTN. Mobile node on contact with other form a connected graph. In Social network analysis node of graph is represented

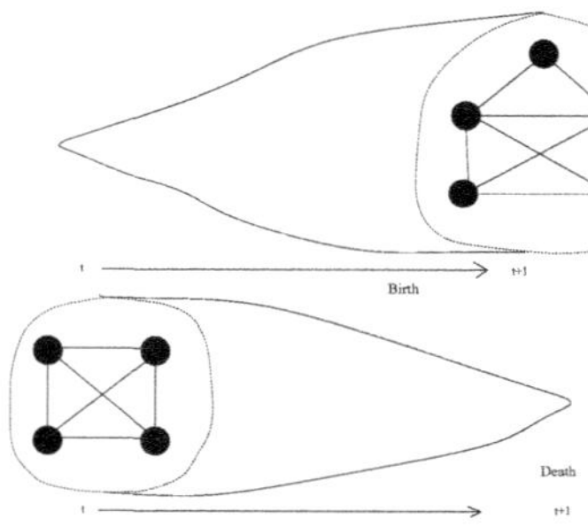

Fig. 1. Birth and death of community

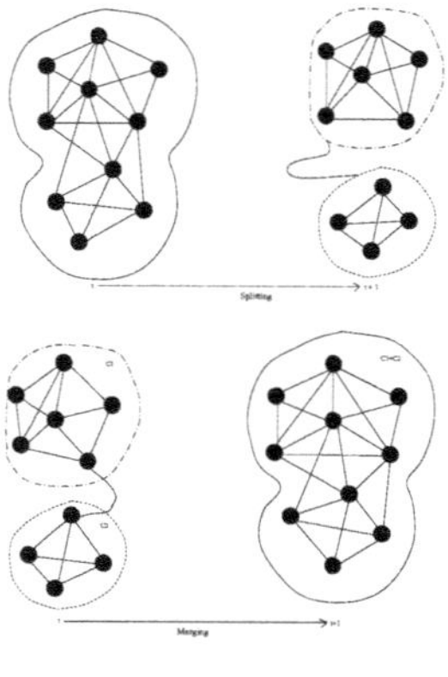

Fig. 2. Split and merger of community

as entity of the real world and link between node is represented as relationship between them. Community is a form of social network, which is represented as group of familiar node. In delay torrent networks, communities formation happens when they are densely connected similarly community split into smaller isolated communities when sparsely connected. Hence the generic operation on intermittently connected social mobile nodes can be define as (birth and death) and (splitting and merge) of community.

Birth and Death of Community happens, when nodes comes in contact of other node and start making their small group of familiar set.Familiar set [9] is set of node formed on past contact experience. Similarly community dies when node start scatting with time,as illustrated in fig1.

Split and merger of community happens when node or component of community at time t splits due to high mobility or change in node direction. Merge of community happens when communities come closure to other and merge to form one large community i.e union of communities. Mostly peripheral node of community which are loosely coupled and away from central node plays important role in merger, as illustrated in fig2.

3.2 Overlapping Community

Nodes linking different community forms overlapping community [1]. Most real networks exhibits well defined behavior of overlapping and nesting of community in social networks. The overlapping community [1] are community structure which makes different community to overlap so that node may become part of more than one community.Overlapping community forms when mobility of node (or community) exceeds the mobility of other community in network, illustrated in fig3.

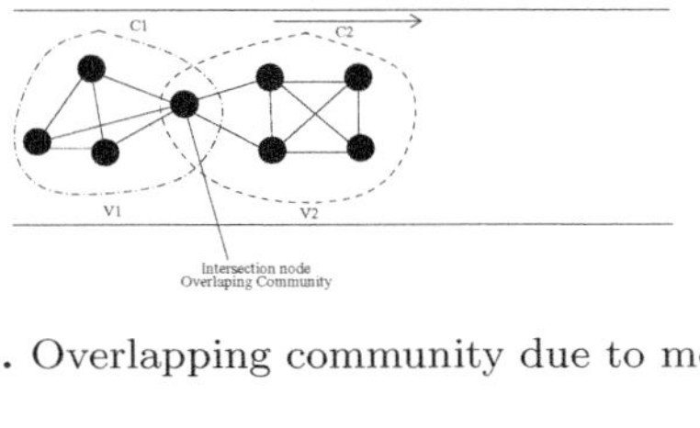

Fig. 3. Overlapping community due to mobility

4 Proposed Routing and Buffer Management Scheme

Assume that the underlying network is represented as forest of mobile nodes. Moving node keeps track of nodes which they encounter. Each node locally maintains commutative contact duration of encounter node t_{cn}). When node's commutative contact duration t_{cn} exceeds the contact threshold value t_{th} ($t_{cn} \geq t_{th}$) then node is included in familiar set, as P.Hui's has mentioned in his paper [9]. t_{th} is maximum contact hour depends on node availability in network. Each node has its local community set which contains all the nodes which satisfies $t_{cn} \geq t_{th}$ in familiar sets and direct neighbor. When node encounter other node than they exchange local knowledge of network. On the basis of exchange data node decides, whether to put neighbor in familiar set or in local community.We divide the operations into:

Make-Set(x), *Find-Set*(x), *Union*$(C1, C2)$, *Split*$(C1)$, *In-PathBuffer*(x, y).

Make-Set(x) forms a community with set of nodes call it local community set C_o as illustrated in fig5.We have used ego betweeness centrality for path finding and route discovery, Marsden[10,8]. Ego betweeness measure the extent to which a given node linking other node.Ego network do not required global knowledge of networks or topology of network so can be easily deployed in wireless mobile

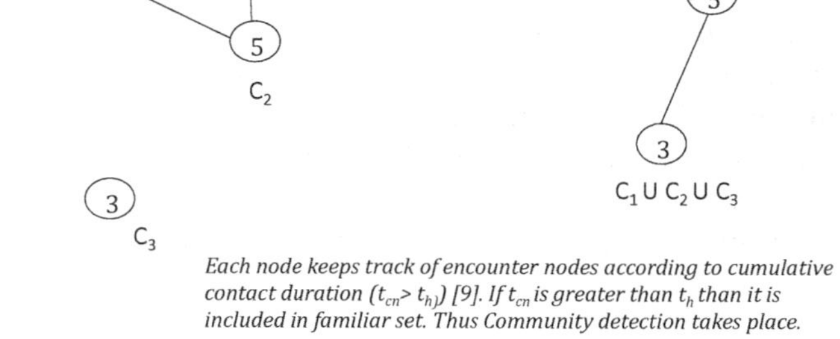

Fig. 4. Community evolution or Birth of community

networks. When node encounter other node they exchange list of contact to update their ego betweeness value.Call the most egocentric betweeness node as r_o .

Find-Set(x) is set of representative element or component of community containing biconnected nodes identified by our modified dfs as illustrated in fig.5. *Find-Set*(x) periodically search for the destination node y. If destination node y is in *Find-Set*(x) then transmit message otherwise node x will buffer to all the cut-vertex till message reaches to destination.To avoid multiple replication and flooding, messages are buffered at the cut-vertex for the $TTL{=}finishtime(v.f)$ - $starttime(v.d)$. Whenever buffered node or cut-vertex of one community merge with another community, it compute path to find the destination of the buffered message. Eventually the message is delivered and all the buffered messages are purged according to TTL.

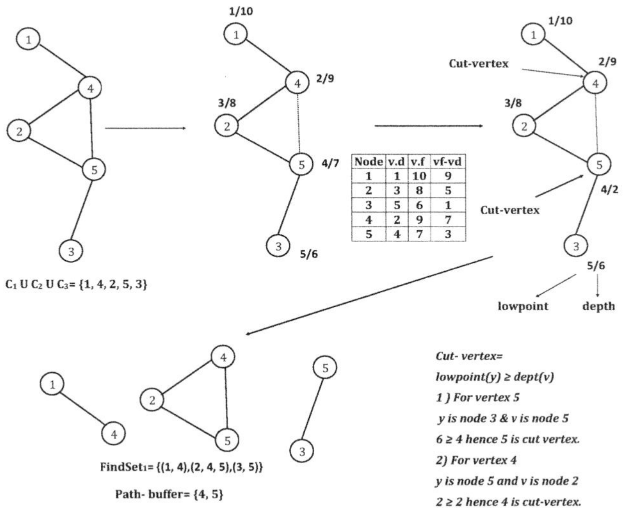

Node	v.d	v.f	vf-vd
1	1	10	9
2	3	8	5
3	5	6	1
4	2	9	7
5	4	7	3

Fig. 5. Detection of cut-vertex and Bi-connected component

Union$(C1, C2)$ will merge two communities $C1$ and $C2$ by rank into new community. *Split*$(C1)$ will form new communities with the representative elements. *In-PathBuffer*(x, y) will find out in path buffering for the message originated from node x which is destined to node y. Summarized algorithm is given below.

Algorithm 1. Social Network Aware Routing in DTN

1: **Input :** Familiar set $F_i = t_{cn} \geq t_{th}$, Local community set C_o and adjacent nodes. Each node V_i and V_o on encounter exchange their familiar set F_i, Local community set C_o and adjacent nodes.
if $|F_i \cap C_o|/F_i| > \lambda$ **then**
  Node V_i is included in node V_o community.
end if
λ is threshold value lies between (.5 to .9) [9].
2: Compute ego betweeness centrality for route discovery. Call it centric node r_o
3: Run $dfs(v)$ to compute the depth of each vertex,
for each vertex v **do**
  the lowest depth of neighbors of all descendants of v in the depth-first-search tree, called the *lowpoint*, and $finishtimes\ v.f.$.
end for
4: Identify *Cut-vertex* (v), and biconnected component *Find-Set*(v) if there is a child y of v such that *lowpoint*$(y) >$ *depth*(v)).
(*Cut-vertex*$(v) \cup$ *Find-Set*$(v)) \in C_o$.
5: ***Phase:I*** Communication within community
Send-msg(x, y):
Case-I:
if $y \in$ *Find-Set*(x) **then**
  trivial in same component.
  send message
end if
Case-II:
if $y \notin$ *Find-Set*(x) **then**
  find *In-Pathbuffer*(x) is all *cut-vertex*(v).Send message to all *cut-vertex*(x) via centric node r_o and purge buffer exceeding $TTL = (v.f - v.d)$
end if
6: ***Phase:II*** Communication in different community
Union$(C1, C2)$:
buffer (v) is destined for y. Node y is in different community.
if *Find-Set*$(v) \in$ *Union*$(C1, C2)$ **then**
  deliver
else
  buffer in *cut-vertex* v via centric node r_o and purge buffer exceeding $TTL = (v.f - v.d)$.
end if
7: Split $(C1)$:Run *step* 2-4.

5 Simulation and Results

We have performed simulation to study the number of packet delivered to destination with respect to the increase in relay's buffer size. We have compared performance of our approach with Maxprop,Epidemic,Spray and wait and Prophet routing protocols. We have considered the following two scenarios (i) when the node moving in six groups different velocity and (ii) when the number of nodes are increased by half. The simulation parameters are summarized in the table.

Simulation parameters	
Area	5km x 5 km
Simulation time	12 hours
Interface transmission speed	10Mbps
Interface transmission range	140 m
Number of groups	6
Total number of nodes	40
Speed of groups	1= 2.7 -13.9 m/s 2 - 3 = .5-1.5 m/s 4 - 6 = 7-10m/s
Buffer size of nodes	(0 to 35)Mb
Message size	500kb - 1Mb
Message generation time	12 hours
Total packet Created	1461

The graph in fig.6 shows that buffer requirement in above scenario is maximum in case of Maxprop compared to Spray and wait,Epidermic,Prophet and our proposed approach. Thus the buffer requirement of our proposed approach is comparable to Epidemic with considerable good amount of packet delivery.

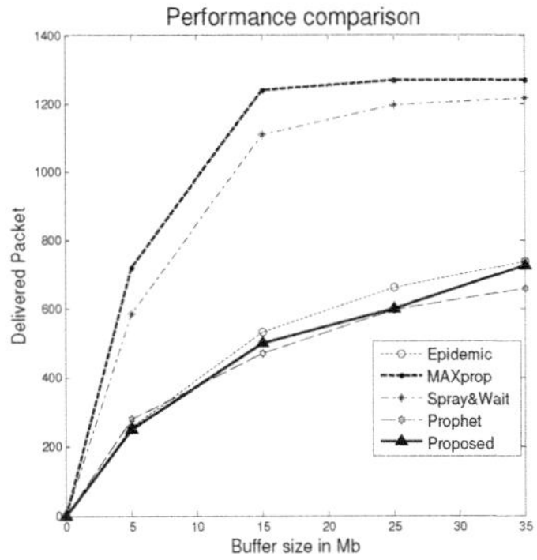

Fig. 6. Performance Comparison

6 Conclusions

A DTN routing is an emerging area of networks that provides ample challenges to researchers.The routing protocols have common objective of trying to increase delivery ratio while decreasing latency and resource consumption.In this paper we have presented a approach for routing in disconnected delay tolerant networks.In this paper, we are assuming that nodes are socially aware of their surrounding and moves in community for sufficient time.In this paper we exploited community structure and used our modified *dfs* for buffering. The future scope of the work includes study of network in complex and highly mobile environment where node mobility is high and intermittent time is quite less. Our future work is to design a robust DTN protocol which can provide high packet delivery ratio for harsh operational environment with limited resource usage.

References

1. Palla, G., Derenyi, I., Farkas, I., Vicsek, T.: Uncovering the overlapping community structure of complex networks in nature and society. Nature 435, 814–818 (2005)
2. Milgram, S.: The Small World Problem. Psychology Today, 60–67 (May 1967)
3. Mundur, P., Lee, S., Seligman, M.: Routing for Data Delivery in Dynamic Networks. In: Proc. of IEEE MILCOM, Washington DC, October 23-25 (2006)
4. Vahdat, A., Becker, D.: Epidemic Routing for Partially Connected Ad Hoc Networks. Technical Report CS-200006, Duke University (2000)
5. Lindgren, D., et al.: Probabilistic routing in intermittently connected networks (2004)
6. Burgess, J., Gallagher, B., Jensen, D., Levine, B.N.: MaxProp: Routing for Vehicle-Based Disruption-Tolerant Networks (2006)
7. Spyropoulos, T., Psounis, K., Raghavendra, C.S.: Spray and wait: an efficient routing scheme for intermittently connected mobile networks (2005)
8. Daly, E., Haahr, M.: Social Network Analysis for Information Flow in Disconnected Delay-Tolerant MANET. IEEE Transactions on Mobile Computing 8(5), 606–621 (2009)
9. Hui, P., Yoneki, E., et al.: Distributed community detection in delay tolerant networks. In: Sigcomm Workshop MobiArch 2007 (August 2007)
10. Marsden, P.V.: Egocentric and sociocentric measures of network centrality. Social Networks 24, 407–422 (2002)

Sybil Secure Architecture for Multicast Routing Protocols for MANETs

E.A. Mary Anita

Anna University, Chennai
anitareginald@yahoo.co.in

Abstract. The Sybil attack is a particularly harmful threat to mobile ad hoc networks where a single node illegitimately claims multiple identities. A malicious node may generate an arbitrary number of additional node identities using only one physical device thereby disrupting the normal functioning of the network. In this paper, a certificate based localized authentication scheme is proposed to prevent Sybil attack. Simulation results show that the proposed method can sustain the Sybil attack and protect the system throughput and hence the performance of the network to a considerable extent.

Keywords: Sybil, MAODV, Certificate, Throughput.

1 Introduction

Sybil attack is an attack against identity in which an individual entity masquerades as multiple simultaneous identities. Many distributed applications and everyday services assume each participating entity controls exactly one identity. When this assumption is unverifiable, the service is subject to attack and the results of the application are questionable if not incorrect [1].

A typical example of this would be an online voting system where one person can vote using many online identities. It is a severe and pervasive problem in many areas. For example, it is possible to rig Internet polls by using multiple IP addresses to submit votes to gain advantage in any results. A Sybil attack is also used by companies that increase the Google Page Rank rating of the pages of their customers, and has been used to link particular search terms to unexpected results for political commentary [1]. Reputation systems are a common target for Sybil attacks including real-world systems like eBay. Spammers can use this attack to gain access to multiple accounts on free email systems. Peer-to-peer computing systems which use voting to verify correct answers are also susceptible to accepting false solutions from a Sybil attacker [8]. Ad hoc mobile network routing can be manipulated when a Sybil attacker appears to be many different mobile nodes. Most designs against such malicious behavior rely on the assumption that a certain fraction of the nodes in the system are honest. This makes routing protocols vulnerable to sybil attacks. With sybil nodes comprising a large fraction of the nodes in the system, the malicious user is able to out vote the honest users, effectively breaking previous defenses against malicious behaviors.

A. Abraham et al. (Eds.): ACC 2011, Part I, CCIS 190, pp. 111–118, 2011.

2 Sybil Attack in MANETs

Sybil attack is a harmful threat to mobile ad hoc networks, in which a malicious node illegally forges an unbounded number of identities by impersonating other nodes or simply claiming multiple forged IDs and/or locations to defeat redundancy mechanisms. Such attacks pose a serious threat to the security of self- organized networks like mobile ad-hoc networks that require unique and unchangeable identity per node for detecting routing misbehavior and reliable computation of node's reputation.

In such an attack, the attacker may use multiple identities simultaneously or one by one, to play with the trust computation system. He may alter trust values of nodes arbitrarily to out-vote honest nodes, thereby disrupting the entire routing structure which depends on these values for selection of appropriate nodes for route setup and maintenance. Absence of any central authority and the pure peer to peer nature of an open MANET make the unique identification of nodes a challenging task [4].

Sybil nodes also can launch selective forwarding attack, in which many pieces of packets will not be transmitted to other forwarding nodes. If the number of dropped pieces reaches to a threshold, the effectiveness of some secure data scheme will be significantly degraded. If each physical node's unique identity can be verified, Sybil attack will be disabled [9].

2.1 Problems with Centralized Authority

A trusted central authority that issues and verifies credentials unique to an actual human being can control sybil attacks easily. But the central authority can easily be a single point of failure, a single target for denial-of-service attacks, and also a bottleneck for performance, unless its functionality is widely distributed. Unfortunately, such a scenario is not possible in a decentralized, network like mobile ad hoc network. Also this destroys the self organizing nature of ad hoc networks. Given the physical vulnerability of mobile nodes in ad hoc networks, it is not effective to burden a single node with the responsibility of providing a security service [7]. A natural way to address this problem is to distribute the security service to multiple nodes.

3 Sybil Secure Routing in MANETs

In MANETs redundant algorithms are used by many systems to ensure data flow from one node to another [2]. This makes the attackers difficult to destroy the integrity of the message. If the same packet is sent over different paths, any modification to the packet can be easily detected and the malicious node may be isolated. In case of fragments of data transmitted over distinct routes, the adversary may find it difficult to put together all the fragments. In the case of a single node taking multiple identities, the attacker gains access to all fragments and hence may alter all packets towards the same destination [3]. This can be prevented only if nodes are authenticated.

Sybil attacker presents multiple identities simultaneously at application layer and exclusively at network layer [6]. From the network layer point of view, IP address may be considered as an identifier for the nodes. Since IP address of each node is unique through the entire network at a time, Sybil attack presenting multiple identities may be prevented.

Given the restrictive fundamental constraints for a Sybil-proof system, we propose a localized certification mechanism for a relaxed set of constraints to defend against Sybil attacks.

3.1 Algorithm for Sybil Secure Architecture

Notations:

```
SN    :   Source Node
IN    :   Intermediate Node
DN    :   Destination Node
NHN   :   Next Hop Node
```

a) Initial Certification Phase

```
Nodes register id with neighboring nodes on joining
the network,
NHN generates public key based on id
Nodes create private key locally
NHN checks repository to check for similar identity
NHN issues certificates encrypted with private key
Store certificates in repository
Exchange Certificates with neighbor nodes
```

If verification fails:

```
Incoming node is prevented from joining network
Certificate issued to existing node with similar id
is revoked
```

b) Route Discovery process

```
SN broadcasts RREQ appended with certificate
IF (IN is NOT DN) THEN
Rebroadcast RREQ after inserting its certificate
All INs append their certificates and forward the
RREQ
ELSE return RREP DN unicast RREP
All INs forward the RREP RREP reaches SN
Sybil Secure route is established between SN and DN
```

Our approach works as follows

As nodes enter the network, they register their identity with their neighboring nodes. The IP address of the node may be taken as an identity. On registering the identity, the neighboring node applies a one way hash function H to the identity and calculates the public key. The corresponding private key is created locally. Since the same hash function is used by all nodes to generate the public key, the public key of a node generated by different next hop nodes are the same. The neighboring nodes issue certificates to the incoming node by verifying the repository to check if a similar identity exists. If the verification succeeds, a certificate is issued to the incoming node. The issued certificates are stored in the repository of the issuer as well as the subject node. The certificates are exchanged with the neighboring nodes. Only after this successful registration nodes are allowed to join the network.

For example if node A is within the radio range of incoming node B, node A issues a certificate to B.

$$\text{Cert}\ (A \rightarrow B) = [ID_{B,}\ K_{B,}\ t,\ e]\ K_a \tag{1}$$

The certificate contains the identity of node B, the public key of B, the time of issue of the certificate and the time of its expiry signed by the private key of A. This certificate is stored in the repositories of node A and node B [5].

If the verification fails, that is, if the identity posed by the incoming node is already present in the issuing node's repository, then the incoming node is prevented from joining the network. Also the certificate issued to the already existing node is revoked. If a malicious node has issued false certificate, the certificate issued to the existing legitimate node with the similar id is revoked. Only nodes with authenticated certificates are thus allowed to take part in the route discovery process.

During the route discovery process of MAODV, every node participating in the routing process appends its certificate. The destination node replies to a route request only if certified nodes form the path to the source. Thus a Sybil secure route is established between the source and destination.

4 Results and Discussions

Simulation results comparing the protocols MAODV, and Sybil Secure MAODV are presented in this section. The simulations are carried out in NS2 using a MANET environment consisting of wireless mobile node count from 100 to 500 roaming over a simulation area of 1000 meters x 1000 meters flat space operating for 900 seconds of simulation time. The radio and IEEE 802.11 MAC layer models were used. Nodes in our simulation move according to Random Waypoint mobility model, which is in random direction with speed ranges from 0 m/s to 50 m/s. A free space propagation channel is assumed. Group scenario files determine which nodes are receivers or sources and when they join or leave a group.

MAODV is used as the routing protocol. A multicast member node joins the multicast group at the beginning of the simulation and remains as a member throughout the whole simulation. Multicast sources start and stop sending packets; each packet has a constant size of 512 bytes, with a transmission range of 250m and uses CBR traffic model. Each data point represents an average of at least three runs for each scenario. Only one multicast group was used for all the experiments. The malicious nodes are chosen in random among the number of nodes and the behavior is also chosen in random.

4.1 Throughput

Throughput is the percentage of the data packets sent that are successfully delivered over a communication channel or through a certain network node.

For the given size of the network varying from 100 to 500 nodes, the throughput of the network is measured in the presence of sybil nodes. For each experiment, the following metrics are derived; the average total throughput with Sybil node but without secure mechanism and the average total throughput with Sybil node and the secure routing mechanism. Each sybil node is set to claim 5 to 10 different identities. For each identity, the route discovery process is performed as MAODV specifies. The sybil nodes drop the data packets they receive with a probability of 0.9.

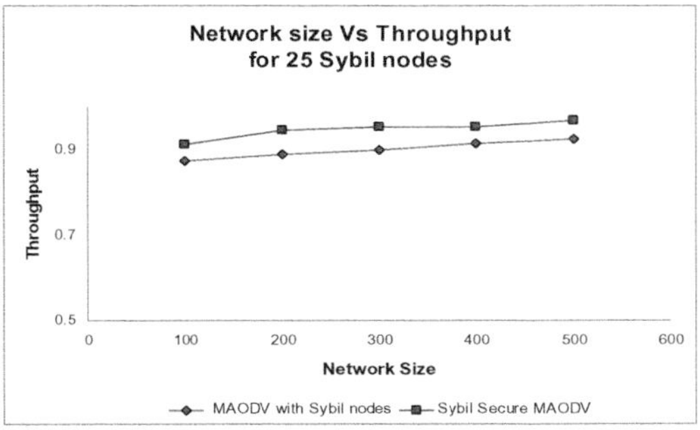

Fig. 1. Variation of throughput with network size

Figure 1 shows the variation of throughput with network size in the presence of 25 Sybil nodes in the network. With increase in the size of the network, the impact of the sybil nodes is lesser. Our proposed Sybil Secure algorithm improves the network performance by preventing sybil nodes from joining the network.

Figure 2 shows the variation of throughput when there are 50 numbers of claimed Sybil identities. As we can see, with the increase of Sybil identity, the impact of Sybil attack becomes severe and the system throughput decreases rapidly when compared to figure 1.Given the number of Sybil identities, the impact of sybil attack is less severe n larger scale network. Even in a network of 500 nodes, however, significant loss is still observed when there are 50 or more Sybil identities. Sybil Secure MAODV is effective in protecting the system from Sybil attack, implying that it can recognize the Sybil identities and thus avoid the use of them.

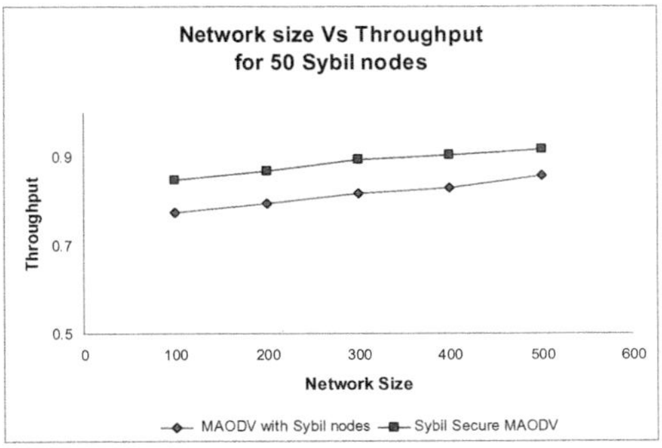

Fig. 2. Variation of throughput with network size

This proposed method provides a way for building initial trust between nodes. The localized certificate chaining allows a node's identity to be proved to other nodes that it needs to communicate with.

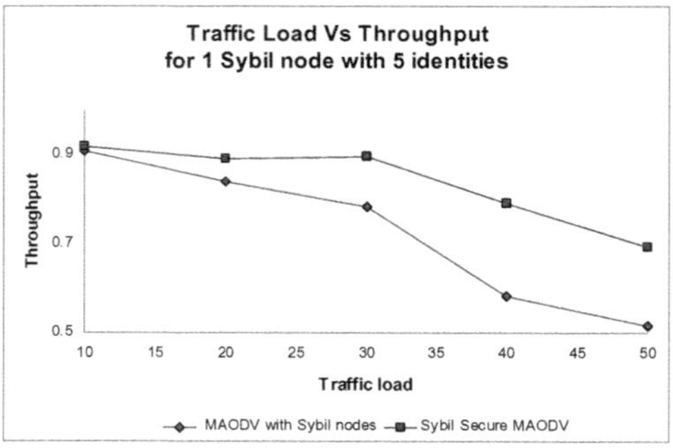

Fig. 3. Variation of throughput with traffic load

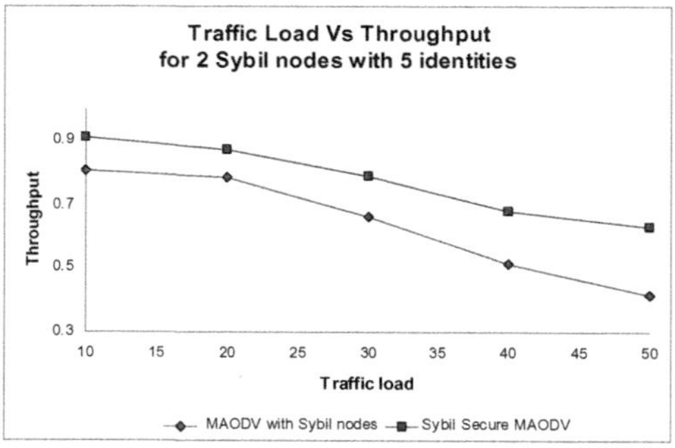

Fig. 4. Variation of throughput with traffic load

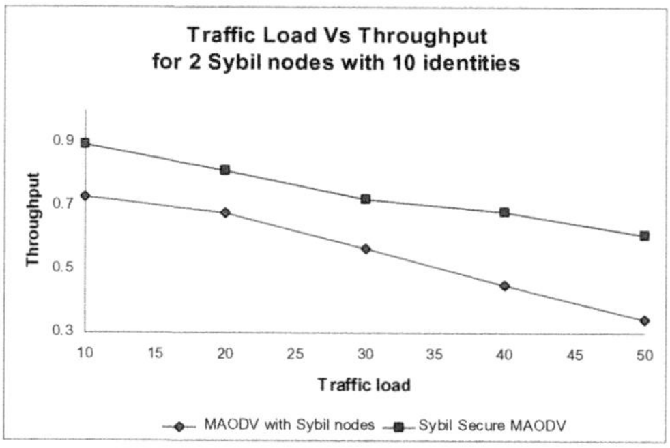

Fig. 5. Variation of throughput with traffic load

Figure 3, 4 and 5 show the performance under different traffic load with different amount of Sybil nodes in a 50 node network where each Sybil node creates 5 or 10 Sybil identities. We see that the impact of Sybil attack is very severe. Furthermore, the heavier the traffic load, the larger loss the entire performance has. This is because that the probability to choose Sybil identity in data forwarding increases with more data flows given no detection mechanism is deployed.

5 Conclusion

Security is one of the major issues in MANETs. In this article, a solution is proposed for Sybil attack by authenticating nodes using localized certificates. Our simulations show that Sybil Secure MAODV is as effective as MAODV in discovering and maintaining routes in addition to providing required security. It can sustain the Sybil attack thereby protecting the system throughput and hence the performance of the network.

When the number of Sybil nodes increase, the impact is more severe. For example, the impact of 2 Sybil nodes that create 5 Sybil identities in total is far larger than of single node claiming 5 identities. The impact is still more severe in the case of 2 sybil nodes with 10 sybil identities. The degradation in the throughput is improved by our proposed method by around 40% to 50%.

This authentication mechanism eliminates the need for a centralized trusted authority, which is not practical in MANETs. The additional certificate publishing happens only during the initial phase. After a period of time each node has a directory of certificates, making the overhead incurred in this process reasonable with a good network performance in terms of security.

References

[1] Levine, B.N., Shields, C., Boris Margolin, N.: A Survey of Solutions to the Sybil Attack, Tech report 2006-052, University of Massachusetts Amherst, Amherst, MA (2006)

[2] Dinger, J., Hartenstein, H.: Defending the Sybil Attack in P2P Networks: Taxonomy, Challenges, and a Proposal for Self-Registration. In: Proceedings of the First International Conference on Availability, Reliability and Security (ARES), Vienna, Austria, pp. 756–763 (2006)

[3] Douceur, J.: The Sybil Attack. In: Proceedings of the 1st International Workshop on Peer-to-Peer Systems (IPTPS), pp. 251–260 (2002)

[4] Hashmi, S., Brooke, J.: Authentication Mechanisms for mobile ad hoc networks and resistance to Sybil attack. Secureware, 120–126 (2008)

[5] Mary Anita, E.A., Vasudevan, V.: Prevention of Black Hole Attack in Multicast Routing Protocols for Mobile Ad-Hoc Networks Using a Self-Organized Public Key Infrastructure. Information Security Journal: A Global Perspective 18(5), 248–256 (2009)

[6] Pal, S., Mukhopadhyay, A.K., Bhattacharya, P.P.: Defending Mechanisms against Sybil attack in Next Generation Mobile Ad Hoc Networks. IETE Technical Review 25(4), 209–215 (2008)

[7] Yi, S., Kravets, R.: Composite Key Management for ad Hoc Networks. In: Proc. of the first annual International Conference on Mobile and Ubiquitous Systems (MobiQuitous 2004), pp. 52–61 (2004)
[8] Yu, H., Kaminsky, M., Gibbons, P.H., Flaxman, A.: SybilGuard: Defending Against Sybil Attacks via Social Networks. In: Proceedings of ACM SIGCOMM Computer Communication Review, pp. 267–278. ACM Press, New York (2006)
[9] Su, Z., Lin, C., Ren, F., Zhan, X.: Security mechanisms Analysis of Wireless Sensor Networks specific Routing Attacks. In: First International Symposium on Pervasive Computing and Applications, pp. 579–584 (2006)

Fault Diagnosis in MANET

M. Chouhan, Manmath Narayan Sahoo, and P.M. Khilar

Department of Computer Science and Engineering
National Intitute of Technology Rourkela, Odisha, India
{209cs1067,sahoom,pmkhilar}@nitrkl.ac.in

Abstract. Fault diagnosis in Mobile Ad-hoc Network is very challenging task. Diagnosis algorithm should be efficient enough to find the status (either *faulty* or *fault-free*) of each mobile in the network. The models in the literature are either for static fault or dynamic fault. Dynamic fault identification is more complex and difficult than static fault. In this paper, we proposed a Dynamic Distributed Diagnosis Model to identify dynamic faults arising in the testing phase of the diagnosis session.In order to concretize it, our model works on a network with n number of nodes, which is σ-diagnosable. We have given the proof of correctness and completeness of our model and found the time complexity.

Keywords: fault diagnosis, MANET: Mobile Ad-hoc Network, dynamic fault, static fault.

1 Introduction

An Ad-hoc wireless network consists of a set of mobile nodes (hosts) that are connected through the wireless links. The varied characteristics of wireless networks as compared to their wired counterparts, address various issues such as mobility of nodes, limited bandwidth, error prone broadcast channels, hidden and exposed terminal problems and power constraints.

An important problem in designing MANET is handling failure of nodes. Each node in the system can be in one of two states *faulty* or *fault-free*. The nodes may fail because of battery discharge, crash, or limitation in age. In this paper we consider the faults to be permanent, i.e., a faulty mobile remains faulty until it is repaired or replaced. However we consider both hard and soft faults, soft faulted units can communicate with its neighbors but with altered behaviors, hard faulted units can not communicate with its neighbors. Again we consider both static and dynamic faults. Static faults can not arise during diagnosis session but dynamic faults can.

The first diagnosis model for wired network was proposed by Preparata, Metze and Chien in 1967 [11]. In PMC model only *fault-free* nodes execute tests and examine test results reliably. Later Hakimi and Amin in 1974 [8] characterized the PMC model. Each node is tested by at least t nodes, and $N \geq 2t+1$. In BGM model [1]: each test is executed by a single unit; each unit has the capability of testing any other unit; no unit tests itself.

A. Abraham et al. (Eds.): ACC 2011, Part I, CCIS 190, pp. 119–128, 2011.

Similar models are proposed by Malek in 1980 [10], and by Chwa and Hakimi in 1981 [4]. These models assume a central observer which collects and examines the result about diagnosis. The MM model [10] assumes that comparisons are executed by the units themselves, and only results are sent to the central observer if both the units are fault free. The MM* model [9] a node performs comparisons for its neighbors. Later on many variants of these models are proposed and discussed in [12,5,2]. Chessa and Santi in [3] and M. Elhadef et.al in [7] discussed a diagnosis approach for static topology in MANETs. In 2004, Sibbiah and Blough [13], introduced a dynamic failure problem, where bounded correctness is made up of three properties: bounded diagnostic latency, bounded start-up time and accuracy. A node sends heartbeat message to other nodes and then rely those messages. In this paper heartbeats mechanism has been used for a node to notify other nodes that, it is working.

2 Proposed Model

2.1 System and Fault Model

A system is composed by N number of nodes called mobiles; they communicate with each other via a packet radio network. Every node has M number of task with the task id. The topology of the network at time t illustrated as a directed graph $G(t) = (V, L(t))$, where V is the set of nodes, and $L(t)$ is the set of communication links at time t. Given that $x, y \in V$, edge $(x, y) \in L(t)$ if and only if y is in the communicating range of x at time t or neighbor of x. The communication protocol supports a one-hop reliable broadcast.

Maximum number of faulty nodes could be σ such that $\sigma \leq k - 1$ for a connected network, where the k is minimum number of nodes, removal of which results in a disconnected graph.

2.2 Dynamic Distributed Diagnosis Model

In this paper we discuss a Dynamic Distributed Diagnosis model, which is based on heartbeat dynamic fault identification model [13]. Heartbeat model identify the hard faulty nodes for the fully connected and partially connected networks. In the proposed model we find the *soft* as well as *hard* faults in mobile ad Hoc network. The diagnosis session is divided into three main phases: Testing Phase, Building phase and dissemination phase.

Testing Phase: The main part of the fault diagnosis model is Testing Phase, which conclude for a mobile node that which of its neighbor is *faulty* and which is *fault-free*. At the end of this phase every node possesses list of faulty and fault free neighbors. The algorithm for Testing Phase is shown in Algorithm-1. First the data structure of mobile node x is listed. Node x receives following packet from the mobile node y during the Testing Phase:

`INIT_DIAGNOSTIC`: We consider a fault free node as initiator, which will generate the `INIT_DIAGNOSTIC` packet to intimate the mobile nodes of the network

Algorithm 1. **Testing Phase**

Data Structure for any mobile node x :
$N'_t(x)$: neighbors set of mobile node x at the time diagnosis i.e. $t \leq t' \leq t + T_{out}$.
$F(x)$: set of mobile nodes diagnosed as faulty, initialized to ϕ.
$FF(x)$: set of mobile nodes diagnosed as faulty-free, initialized to ϕ.
t_x : current time (associated with mobile node x).

```
mobile node x will recieve following packets from mobile node y ∈ N(x):

INIT_DIAGNOSIS : < INIT_DIAGNOSIS, θ, T_out >
if ((not)INIT_DIAGNOSIS_x) then
   INIT_DIAGNOSIS_x ← true;
   TIMEOUT_x ← t_x + T_out;
   rebroadcast the INIT_DIAGNOSIS packet;
   SENDLIFE_RESPONSE(θ);
else
   Drop the packet;
end if
LIFE_RESPONSE : < LIFE_RESPONSE, id_y, id_task, R_y, seq_no_y >
if ((not)TIMEOUT) then
   if ((< id_y, seq_no_y > ≠ < id_y, seq_no_last_seq_no >)and(id_y ∉ F_x)) then
      node[y].last_seq_no ← seq_no_y;
      generate the response R for task having task id i.e. id_task and compare with R_y;
      if (R_y == R) then
         FF_x ← FF_x ∪ {y};
      else
         F_x ← F_x ∪ {y};
         FF_x ← FF_x − {y};
      end if
   else
      Drop the packet;
   end if
else
   Drop the packet;
end if
TIMEOUT : when timeout occur to the mobile node x i.e. the Testing Phase of diagnosis session is
over.
TIMEOUT ← true;
F_x ← F_x ∪ {N_x(t') − (FF_x ∪ F_x)};
for all l ∈ FF_x do
   if (node[l].last_seq_no < node[x].last_seq_no) then
      F_x ← F_x ∪ {l};
      FF_x ← FF_x − {l};
   end if
end for
```

about the starting of Diagnosis session and flood it to the network. The format of the packet is as follows: $<$ INIT_DIAGNOSTIC, $\theta, T_{out} >$ Where θ is the time interval for generating the LIFE_RESPONSE packet and T_{out} is the time duration of the testing phase. Each node after receiving receives the INIT_DIAGNOSTIC packet first time, performs following things:

- Set $INIT\_DIAGNOSTIC_x$ as true.
- Call the procedure $SENDLIFE\_RESPONSE$ with θ i.e. the time interval as the parameter.
- Set $Timeout_x$ as current time t_x plus T_{out} and rebroadcast the INIT_DIAGNOSTIC packet.

The procedure $SENDLIFE\_RESPONSE$ is used to generate the LIFE_RESPONSE packet at every θ intervel till the timeout occurs. The procedure is defined more precisely in Algorithm-2.

Algorithm 2. SENDLIFE_RESPONSE

```
procedure SENDLIFE_RESPONSE(θ)                         ▷ where θ is the time intervel
    if (t_x == θ  and  t_x ≠ Timeout_x) then
        randomly pick the task from the memory and generate the response R_x for lask i;
        seq_no_x ← lastseq_no_x + 1;
        l_rb(LIFE_RESPONSE, id_x, id_task, R_x, seq_no_x);
        SENDLIFE_RESPONSE(t_x + θ);
    end if
end procedure
```

LIFE_RESPONSE: After getting the intimation of the initialization of the diagnosis session the mobile node sends the LIFE_RESPONSE packet with the interval θ till timeout occurs. The format of the packet is $<$ LIFE_RESPONSE, id_y, id_{task}, R_y, $seq\_no_y >$ Where id_y is the sender *id*, id_{task} is the task *id*, R_y is the response generated by node y with task id_{task} and sequence number of the response. The mobile node who receives the LIFE_RESPONSE packet does the following things:

- Check if TIMEOUT occurs, the receiver node does not process the LIFE_RESPONSE packet, otherwise it process the packet and check further.
- If mobile node previously received the LIFE_RESPONSE with same sequence number or the sender node is in the faulty set, then drop the packet, otherwise do further processing.
- After receiving the fresh response packet by the node it updates the last sequence number received and generate the response of the task for given task *id*.
- Compare the generated response R with the received response R_y.
- If both responses are same, add the sender node *id* to the fault-free node set; otherwise add the sender node *id* to the faulty node set and remove the sender *id* from the *fault-free* node set.

In this way, the hard faults can be found after the timeout occur to the mobile node.

TIMEOUT: When timeout occurs to the mobile node i.e. the time delay expires for the Testing Phase then variable TIMEOUT become true and calculate the hard fault with the given conditions in the algorithm. The neighbor nodes which doesn't respond till the timeout were considered as hard fault nodes and the nodes, stop sending the response after some time were also considered as hard faulty nodes and add those fault node *ids* to the faulty set.

After the testing phase we do not allow any new faults into the network. Just after the timeout the initiator node starts sending the ST_MSG to construct the spanning tree in the Building Phase.

Building Phase: For disseminating the diagnosis information in the network we used existing approach, i.e., spanning tree [7]. There are two popular methods; flooding based and spanning tree based. Flooding based method is very easy but consume more energy because of redundancy and complexity. Flooding doesn't require building phase to disseminate the information at all. Whereas spanning tree method consumes less energy and consumes less message

Algorithm 3. Building Phase

Data Structure for any mobile node x :
$ParentSelected$: set to **true** once the mobile x sends its `ST_MSG` message, initialized to **false**.
$Children_x$: the set of mobile nodes that are considered as children of node x in the Spanning Tree.
FF_y : fault free set of node y.
F_y : faulty set of node y.

```
mobile node x will recieve following packets from mobile node y ∈ N(x):
ST_MSG : < ST_MSG, y, z >
if (y ∈ FF_x) then
    if (x == z) then
        Children_x ← Children_x ∪ {y};
    else if (ParentSelected == false) then
        Parent_x ← y;
        ParentSelected ← true;
        l_rb(ST_MSG, x, y);
        SetTimer(Tout);
    end if
else
    Drop the packet;
end if
TIMEOUT : when the delay Tout has expired.
if (Children_x == φ) then
    l_rb(LOCAL_DIAGNOSTIC, F_x, FF_x);
end if
```

complexity. Therefore, in the proposed model we use spanning tree based approach to disseminate the local as well as global diagnosis information to the network. In Building Phase we construct the spanning tree, as explain in [6, 7]. Construction of ST (spanning tree) is done by the set of *fault-free* nodes. In the algorithm described in Algorithm-3 `ST_MSG` packet is used to construct the ST. The initiator node initiate the building phase by broadcasting the `ST_MSG` packet with two information; *sender id* and the *parent id* of the sender with the format as follows: $<$ ST_MSG, $y, z >$

If a mobile node does not have parent, the sender node becomes its parent, if the sender is not faulty. After finding the parent, mobile node set the variable *ParentSelected* as true, so that it can ignore further `ST_MSG` message it receives from the fault free nodes. After that it broadcasts the `ST_MSG` as sender itself and with the determined parent node id, for making the children and intimating the parent node. After a mobile sends the `ST_MSG` message, another timer is set to the time bound T_{out}. If the parent node of the sender is itself then add the sender node id to the set of children. If timeout occurs, the node which does not have any children starts sending the local diagnosis information to its parents and initiates the dissemination phase.

Dissemination Phase: After the spanning tree has been constructed, all the leave nodes of the spanning tree start sending their local diagnostic information to their parents. After receiving the local diagnostic information of all its children, a parent will forward the aggregated local diagnostic information to its parent, by adding its own local diagnostic information. This process continues until the all local diagnostic information has reached the initiator node which is the root of the ST. Now Initiator node has the global diagnostic information of the fault status of the network and will forward it down the ST, which result in all *fault-free* mobile nodes having a global view of the network [7].

Algorithm 4. **Dissemination Phase**
Data Structure for any mobile node x :
$SystemDiagnosed$: set to **true** once the states of all mobiles are identified, initialized to **false**.
$children$: initialized to ϕ.

```
mobile node x will recieve following packets from mobile node y ∈ N(x):

repeat
    LOCAL_DIAGNOSTIC : < LOCAL_DIAGNOSTIC, F_y, FF_y >
    if (y ∈ Children_x) then
        FF_x ← FF_x ∪ FF_y;
        F_x ← F_x ∪ F_y;
        children ← children ∪ {y};
        if (Children_x == children) then    ▷ mobile x waits for all its children's diagnosis views.
            l_rb(LOCAL_DIAGNOSTIC, F_x, FF_x);
        end if
    end if
    GLOBAL_DIAGNOSTIC : < GLOBAL_DIAGNOSTIC, F, FF >
    if (x == initiator) then
        l_rb(GLOBAL_DIAGNOSTIC, F_x, FF_x);
        SystemDiagnosed ← true;
    end if
    if (y == Parent_x) then
        FF_x ← FF;
        F_x ← F;
        if (Children_x ≠ φ) then
            l_rb(GLOBAL_DIAGNOSTIC, F, FF);
        end if
        SystemDiagnosed ← true;
    end if
until (SyetemDiagnosed == true)
```

3 Proposed Model Analysis

In this section we analysis the proposed model in terms of completeness, correctness and complexity.

3.1 Correctness Proof

Fault-free mobiles diagnosis and disseminate information correctly. If the status of any node is correctly identify by atleast one *fault-free* neighbor node at the end of testing phase then, it is called correct partial local diagnosis and it is completely diagnosed at end of dissemination phase if every *fault-free* node has the correct status of all mobiles in the system, then correct dissemination is achieved.

Lemma 1. ***(Partial Diagnosis)****The σ-diagnosable MANET is modeled as the connected graph $G = (V, L)$, let $x \in V$ and $N(x)$ indicates x's neighbors. If node x is fault-free, then node is correctly identify by atleast one fault-free neighbor node. Every node x has at least one fault free neighbor.*

Proof. Let assume that $| N(x) | \leq \sigma$, all are faulty. If we discard all neighbor of x, will generate the disconnected graph, and hence $| N(x) | \geq k$. According to this it will be $\sigma \geq k$. The assumption of our model is the total number of faulty nodes σ, should not exceed k, that means σ should less or equal to the number of neighbors i.e. $\sigma \leq k - 1$.

Spanning tree is constructed through all *fault-free* mobiles. Only *fault-free* node can correctly diagnose the status of its neighbors. In this way we can achieve complete diagnosis.

Lemma 2. ***(Fault-Free Spanning Tree)*** *Let $G = (V, L)$ be the connected graph which is σ-diagnosable and every node contains two set FF and F' where F' denote the set of faulty mobiles such that $\mid F' \mid \leq \sigma$. In tree all fault-free node disseminates information not only to its neighbours also to all nodes in the network.*

Proof. Given that the graph G is connected and the number of *faulty* nodes $\mid F' \mid \leq \sigma < k$, by removing *faulty* nodes we get another connected graph G' by node set $V - F'$. Since $\mid F' \mid < k$ then every *fault-free* node must be connected by altleast one *fault-free* neighbor. In this way tree propagates correct information to all *fault-free* nodes.

Lemma 3. ***(Correct Dissemination)*** *Let $G = (V, L)$ be graph which represents a σ-diagnosable MANET, and F' be the set of fault nodes in the network which is $\mid F' \mid \leq \sigma$. ST is constructed by the fault-free nodes and is used to disseminate all global information in the network by the root node in a finite time.*

Proof. Firstly we have to prove that status of each node is correctly diagnosed by at least one *fault-free* neighbor, then after we have to prove that spanning tree is constructed by *fault-free* nodes only. These two are already proved in Lemma 1 and Lemma 2 respectively. Each *fault-free* node participats to disseminate the correct information. In this way, correct dissemination phase acheived by *fault-free* nodes.

3.2 Completeness Proof

Theorem 1. *Let $G = (V, L)$ be graph which represents a σ-diagnosable MANET. At the end of the dissemination phase each fault-free node x knows the faulty node set F_x which is same as total faulty nodes in the network $F_x = F'$ and fault-free nodes FF_x which is $FF_x = V - F'$.*

Proof. To prove this theorem, firstly we have to prove that every *fault-free* node have correctly diagnosed the state of all its neighbors at the end of the diagnosis session and we have to prove that all leaf node have transmitted its own neighbor information to its parent and parent combines all its children information and disseminates in the spanning tree. These are already proved in Lemma 3. After receiving local information, the root node combines all local information and generates the global information, which is disseminated to each node in the spanning tree in finite time. Hence each *fault-free* mobile knows the correct status of every node in the network.

3.3 Communication Complexity

Let n is total number of mobiles in the σ-diagnosable MANET. Different type of messages transmitted in diagnosis session is presented in the Table 1 with the message complexity.

Table 1. The message complexity of proposed model

Message Type	Number of messages	Description of the message
INIT_DIAGNOSIS	n	All nodes generate at most one message. One initiator node generates this packet and sends to the neighbor then neighbor broadcast this packet to its own neighbor.
LIFE_RESPONSE	$\beta * n$, where β is (T_{out}/θ)	Each mobile generates LIFE_RESPONSE message. It depends on the no. of interval during testing phase.
ST_MSG	n	In worst case all mobile are fault free and all mobile send ST_MSG including initiator mobile.
LOCAL_DIAGNOSTIC	$n-1$	Each mobile sends one LOCAL_DIAGNOSTIC to its parent except the initiator, .
GLOBAL_DIAGNOSTIC	$n-1$	In the worst case all node are fault-free so the depth of the tree is $n-1$. Hence, $n-1$ GLOBAL_DIAGNOSTIC messages broadcast in spanning tree.

Theorem 2. *The message complexity of proposed model is* $(4n - 2 + \beta * n)$.

Proof. The total number of messages transmit during the diagnosis session in the proposed model is $(4n - 2 + \beta * n)$.

3.4 Time Complexity

The time complexity is expressed in terms of the following bounds:

- D_G : diameter of graph $G(V, L)$ that represents the MANET.
- D_{ST} : depth of the spanning tree.
- T_{GEN} : maximum time elapsed between the reception of the LIFE_RESPONSE message and computing the own task to evaluate the received response.
- T_{PROP} : maximum time to propagate a message in the network.
- T_{INIT} : maximum time elapsed between sending the INIT_DIAGNOSIS packet to the neighbor and receiving the first LIFE_RESPONSE packet from the neighbor.
- T_{OUT} : time delay of diagnosis session.

Lemma 4. *The time complexity of the init diagnosis session is* $D_G * T_{PROP} + T_{INIT}$.

Proof. The initiator node starts sending INIT_DIAGNOSIS message to its neighbors. A neighbor node receives the packet and broadcasts to its neighbors. So the last fault free node to receive INIT_DIAGNOSIS message and send the INIT_DIAGNOSIS will do so in at most $D_G * T_{PROP} + T_{INIT}$ time bound .

Lemma 5. *The time complexity of the testing phase is $D_G * T_{GEN} * \beta + T_{OUT}$.*

Proof. The last *fault-free* node to receive a `LIFE_RESPONSE` message and compute the own task will take at most $D_G * T_{GEN}$. Every fault free node should send the number of `LIFE_RESPONSE` message equal to the number of interval β, hence the time complexity will be $D_G * T_{GEN} * \beta$. Any *fault-free* node takes at most T_{out} time to diagnose at least one *fault-free* neighbor. Hence the time complexity of testing phase is at most $D_G * T_{GEN} * \beta + T_{OUT}$.

Lemma 6. *The time complexity of spanning tree construction is $D_{ST} * T_{PROP} + T_{OUT}$.*

Proof. We adapt the building phase discussed in [7], and this lemma follows directly from that.

Lemma 7. *The time complexity of the disseminating phase is $2D_{ST} * T_{PROP}$.*

Proof. The proof of this lemma is similar to that of given by M. Elhadef et.al in [7].

Theorem 3. *The time complexity of our proposed model is $3D_{ST} * T_{PROP} + D_G * T_{PROP} + \beta * D_G * T_{GEN} + T_{INIT} + 2T_{OUT}$.*

Proof. The proof of this theorem is trivial. Lemma 4-7 describe the time complexites of each of the phase of the proposed model and collectively the model takes at most $3D_{ST} * T_{PROP} + D_G * T_{PROP} + \beta * D_G * T_{GEN} + T_{INIT} + 2T_{OUT}$.

4 Conclusion

Proposed model makes the *fault-free* nodes to correctly identify the status, not only its neighbor, but also every nodes of the network. Our model is based on the heart beat message and comparison approach in order to achieve a correct and complete diagnosis. It diagnoses both hard and soft fault. In our model, once all nodes have diagnosed the fault status of their neighbors, dissemination phase starts to spread the global information of all nodes to complete the diagnosis in network. Dissemination approach is based on the spanning tree that reduces the message complexity. Our model is based on dynamic diagnosis, in this approach node can be faulty any time during the diagnosis session. A mobile tests many time during the diagnosis session, hence the number of message will increase and communication complexity is higher as compare to static diagnosis. The time complexity is also higher as compare to static diagnosis. The proposed model can reduce the communication and message complexity if value of θ will increase.

References

1. Barsi, F., Grandoni, F., Maestrini, P.: A theory of diagnosability of digital systems. IEEE Transactions On Computers 25(6), 585–593 (1976)
2. Blough, D.M., Brown, H.W.: The broadcast comparison model for on-line fault diagnosis in multicomputer systems: Theory and implementation. IEEE Transactions on Computers, 470–493 (1999)
3. Chessa, S., Santi, P.: Comparison-based system-level fault diagnosis in ad hoc networks. In: Proc. of the 20th Symp. On Reliable Distributed Systems, pp. 257–266 (2001)
4. Chwa, K.Y., Hakimi, S.L.: Schemes for fault-tolerant computing: A comparison of modularly redundant and t-diagnosable systems. Information and Control 49, 212–238 (1981)
5. Dahbura, A.T., Sabnani, K.K., King, L.L.: The comparison approach to multiprocessor fault diagnosis. IEEE Transactions on Computers 36(3), 373–378 (1987)
6. Elhadef, M., Boukerche, A., Elkadiki, H.: Performance analysis of a distributed comparison based self-diagnosis protocol for wireless ad-hoc networks. In: Proc. of 9th ACM Int. Symp. On Modeling, Analysis and Simulation of Wireless and Mobile Systems, pp. 165–172. ACM, New York (2006)
7. Elhadef, M., Boukerche, A., Elkadiki, H.: A distributed fault identication protocol for wireless and mobile ad hoc networks. Journal of Parallel and Distributed Computing 68, 321–335 (2008)
8. Hakimi, S.L., Amin, A.T.: Characterization of connection assignment of diagnosable systems. IEEE Transactions on Computers 23(1), 86–88 (1974)
9. Maeng, J., Malek, M.: A comparison connection assignment for self-diagnosis of multiprocessor systems. In: Proc. of the 11th IEEE Fault-Tolerant Computing Symp., 1981, pp. 173–175 (1981)
10. Malek, M.: A comparison connection assignment for diagnosis of multiprocessor systems. In: Proc. of the 7th Annual Intl. Symp. on Computer Architecture, pp. 31–36. ACM, New York (1980)
11. Preparata, F., Metze, G., Chien, R.T.: On the connection assignment problem of diagnosable systems. IEEE Transactions on Computers EC-16, 848–854 (1967)
12. Sengupta, A., Dahbura, A.T.: On self-diagnosable multiprocessor systems: Diagnosis by comparison approach. IEEE Transactions on Computers, 1386–1396 (1992)
13. Subbiah, A., Blough, D.M.: Distributed diagnosis in dynamic fault environments. IEEE Transactions on Computers, 453–467 (2004)

Mobile Agent Security Based on Trust Model in MANET

Chandreyee Chowdhury and Sarmistha Neogy

Dept. of Computer Science and Engineering
Jadavpur University
sarmisthaneogy@gmail.com

Abstract. There is an emerging trend of using mobile agents for wireless network applications. For instance mobile agents can be used to protect the mobile ad hoc network (MANET) itself by using agent based IDS or IPS.In this paper we consider security issues that need to be addressed before multi-agent systems in general, and mobile agents in particular, can be used for a broad range of commercial applications for MANET. Here we propose a distributed scheme to protect both the agents and the host platforms (running at the nodes) from possible threats. This paper seeks to form a distributed trust model of the network. Here the agents and the host platforms work together to so that each trusted node may form a consistent trust view of the network. Each agent is given with a list of nodes (host platforms) to visit by their owner (a node). The agents, while migrating share their view of the trusted hosts to the platform they currently reside. The agents use combination of encryption and digital signature (to create hash code) to provide privacy and authentication services.Here smooth random mobility model is used to generate node mobility. The connectivity between the nodes is decided by the Two-Ray model of radio propagation in order to consider multipath propagation effect. The effect of environmental noise is also studied. Our proposed algorithm is simulated using java and the results show the robustness of our proposed scheme.

Keywords: Mobile Agent, Security, Digital Signature, Trust, Mobility Model.

1 Introduction

A mobile agent is a combination of software program and data which migrates from a site to another site to perform tasks assigned by a user according to a static or dynamic route [1]. It can be viewed as a distributed abstraction layer that provides the concepts and mechanisms for mobility and communication [2]. An agent consists of three components: the program which implements it, the execution state of the program and the data. A mobile node (MN) may migrate in two ways namely weak migration and strong migration [3]. Weak migration occurs when only the code of the agent migrates to its destination, a strong migration occurs when the mobile agent carries out its migrations between different hosts while conserving its data, state and code. The platform is the environment of execution. The platform makes it possible to create mobile agents; it offers the necessary elements required by them to perform their tasks such as execution, migration towards other platforms and so on.Typical

A. Abraham et al. (Eds.): ACC 2011, Part I, CCIS 190, pp. 129–140, 2011.

benefits of using mobile agents include bandwidth conservation, reduced latency, load balancing etc.

The route of the mobile agent can be decided by its owner or it can decide its next hop destination on the fly.

Here, we assume the underlying network to be a Mobile Ad Hoc Network (MANET) that typically undergoes constant topology changes, which disrupt the flow of information over the existing paths. Mobile agents are nowadays used in MANETs for various purposes like service discovery [4], network discovery, automatic network reconfiguration etc. In fact there are many situations where every MN (needed by the application) may not be connected to each other at the same time, so the user can submit tasks for processing to the mobile agent. The agent can return the results of the calculation thereby greatly reducing the amount of network data transmission.

But before mobile agent based applications become commercially available, securing them from possible threats is very essential. Besides, security of agent platform is also important. So, we try to propose a trust model for the nodes. Based on this trust, an agent will be asked to visit different nodes (trusted) in order to accomplish a task. In the following section we will first discuss about the possible threats to mobile agents in MANET. Then in section 3, the state of art regarding this area of research is elaborated. In the subsequent section (4) our model is introduced that is designed to detect a malicious agent as well as a malicious platform (depending on trust level defined later) in a distributed way. Section 5 gives the experimental results followed by concluding remarks in section 6.

2 Security Issues

Before discussing about countermeasures, let us discuss about who we are securing our agents from and why. Threats in a Mobile Agent system can be categorized as [5]:

- Threats from mobile agent to host platform- A malicious agent may attempt denial of service (DoS), damage the software and data, penetrate virus/worms and finally action repudiation [5]. It may also steal some secret information of the hosts.
- Threats from host platform to mobile agent- A host platform may also attack an agent in several ways, like, reveal private or sensitive action performed by mobile agent, execute agents code incorrectly, sending agent to unintended destination, cheat agent with false information and information or action repudiation [6]. Behavior of the agent can also be altered sometimes by code manipulation. It can be stopped if one can cryptographically sign the code of the agent. But it (signature) is only feasible when the code is not changed frequently. But, the control flow of agent execution cannot be fully protected; hence the host can easily deduce information about the state of the agent.
- Threats from mobile agent to mobile agent-Finally, an agent could face threats from other agents in the system like stealing agent information, convey false information, render extra messages, DoS and unauthorized access [5, 6].

3 Related Work

Many researches have been conducted regarding the security issues of Mobile Agent based system (MAS). Some are to protectonly the code and some are to protect the host platforms. But very few works address all the security aspectsof mobile agent system in an ad hoc network. Interestingly most of them do not consider the effect of mobility and/or the underlying environment into the security services provided. Some of the existing works are discussed below.

1. In [6] Threshold Cryptography is used to protect the agents and their host platforms against possible threats. There is a master public/private key pair to sign a certificate (for a service or server). The master public key is known to all hosts and any certificate signed by the master private key (k_{pr}) is considered to be trusted.It is divided into a no. of shares and is stored in a group of nodes. Thus, to decrypt an agent, the shares should be collected to form the private key. But due to reasons like, node mobility, transient failure of the links and limited battery backup, a node of that group (having one share) may not be available and hence the entire system performance would degrade.
2. In [7] concept of a Secure Image Controller (SIC) is introduced that works like a trusted third party. SIC generates an image (a version) of the agent and sends the image to the compromised host. After completion of execution the agent image is compared with the original agent by the SIC. But SIC may become a bottleneck especially in a resource constrained network like MANET.
3. The method[8] of signing the code allows authenticating and authorizing a mobile agent. Digital signature can be used for this purpose. The signature may be provided by either the creator of the agent or the owner or some third party. The security policy of the platform decides whether to trust those signed codes and how much. But such methods need a central certificate authority-not suitable for a distributed system like MANET.In [8] a blackbox security approach, obfuscated code, is mentioned thatscrambles an agent's code to make it unreadable. But it is difficult to quantify the protection time provided by the obfuscation algorithm. Also no black-box algorithms exist that work for arbitrary data.
4. Symmetric Key Cryptography can be usedto protect the intermediate state of partial result of an agent[9] after being executed on a host platform. Strong migration [3] is assumed here. But to enforce this, a large no. of symmetric keys should be generated and maintained – a bottleneck in mobile ad hoc network.
5. In this scheme[10] three agents are used. A dummy agent moves first to a host, returns results of its calculation back to the original agent. If that indicates a safe host then the agent records the path with the cooperator agent and encrypts its data to finally move to the host platform. As is evident this system suffers from poor performance and utilizes bandwidth (expensive in MANET) inefficiently.

Only a few works is done on trust management system for MAS and we found none of them to focus specifically on MANET. However,managing trust in MANET is thoroughly dealt with in literature. The framework of a typical Trust Management System(TMS) contains a Watchdogand a Reputation System (RS) [11]. In [12] such a reputation-based trust model for MAS is presented where the agents and the nodes they visit are asked to provide feedback about their interaction in a timely manner (to a feedback storage server). This paper also presents an algorithm that inspires each participant in each transaction to faithfully provide its truthful feedback. However the work focuses on Bayesian networks and thus constraints like node mobility, limited bandwidth or absence of a coordinator (always available) are not considered. Thus assuming the availability of feedback server is unrealistic in MANET.

4 Our Work

In this paper, we define our mobile agent-based system (S) to be consisting of M independent agents deployed by k owners that may move in the underlying MANET. To describe our model we will take help of the following abstraction of MANET.Here we try to protect mobile agents from visiting malicious hosts (nodes) and to prevent trusted nodes from sending agents to malicious ones. We assume compromised nodes can send malicious agents to mislead a node or it can send a no. of agents to a trusted node in order to block its traffic and hence launch DoS attack.

4.1 Modeling MANET

We model the underlying network as an undirected graph G= (V,E) where V is the set of MNs and E is the set of edges among them. Let the network consist of N nodes, thus |V|=N that may or may not be connected via bidirectional links (e).

Initial locations of the nodes (v_is) are assumed to be provided. The mobility of nodes in MANET can be simulated using SRMM [13]. This model is like Random Waypoint Mobility Model [13] but more realistic as it prevents the mobile nodes (MNs) from taking sharp turns or making sudden stops.

To incorporate SRMM [13] a Poisson event determines the time instant of change in speed. A new speed is chosen from the interval $[0,V_{max}]$ where 0 and V_{max} are given higher preference and rest of the values are uniformly distributed. Once a target speed is chosen the current speed is changed according to the acceleration a(t), which is once again uniformly distributed in $[0, a_{max}]$. The values of V_{max} and a_{max} may be different for different users. For example for vehicular traffic these will have higher values than pedestrians. Thus as in [13],

$$v_i(t) := v_i(t-\Delta t)+a_i(t)*\Delta t \tag{1}$$

A new target direction is chosen only when $v_i(t)=0$ (*stop turn and go[13]*). At every time instant direction ($\Delta\varphi_i(t)$) changes incrementally to attain the target direction as [13],

$$\varphi_i(t)= \varphi_i(t-\Delta t) + \Delta\varphi_i(t) \tag{2}$$

Now, using $v_i(t)$, $a_i(t)$ and $\varphi_i(t)$, we can estimate the node position (x_i,y_i) at $(t+\Delta t)$ as

$$x_i(t+\Delta t)=x_i(t)+\Delta t*v_i(t)*\cos\varphi_i(t)+0.5*a_i(t)*\cos\varphi_i(t)* \tag{3}$$

$$y_i(t+\Delta t)=y_i(t)+\Delta t*v_i(t)*\sin\varphi_i(t)+0.5*a_i(t)*\sin\varphi_i(t)*\Delta t^2 \tag{4}$$

The distance between a pair of nodes (d_{ij}) can be calculated as follows

$$d_{ij}(t) = \sqrt{(x_i - x_j)^2 + (y_i - y_j)^2} \quad (5)$$

The probability of link existence (P_{link}) not only depends on the distance between the nodes but also on environmental factors.So, even when two nodes remain within the transmission range of each other, quality of transmission can degrade appreciably[14]due to multipath propagation. The average received power (p_r) is a function of the distance between the transmitter and the receiver. Here we take the two-ray model for radio propagation in order to show how the transmitted signal power (p_t) incurs loss while reaching the receiving end. Thus $p_r(d)$ can be stated as follows [14]:

$$p_r(d) = p_t G_t G_r \frac{h_t^2 h_r^2}{d^4} \quad (6)$$

In free space, the received power varies inversely to the square of the distance but here we have assumed the exponent to be 4 to indicate the presence of a medium.

Thus at a certain time instant we get a view of the MANET as G(V,E') where E' is a subset of E. (E-E') denote the edges deleted due to environmental factors.

As we know that in an ad hoc network it is not possible touse a central server or a single point of trust, so trust should bedistributed here among the connected nodes. We define our MAS on MANET as follows.

4.2 ModelingMobile Agents Based System

In this scenario we can think of a mobile agent as a token visiting one node to another in the network (if the nodes are connected) based on some strategy as needed by the underlying applications to accomplish its task.

An important use of Mobile Agent may be to collect data from a network like in service discovery [4] or clustering in MANET. In ecommerce applications also the agents are expected to visit all the nodes in the network [7].We take an example where people may want to share real time data among them in a meeting. Here we consider that, the people in the meeting have established an ad hoc network to get and stay connected with each other. We also consider that communicating devices (i.e. Laptop/PDA) used by them have the ability to process an Agent code, that means all the nodes can act as potential hosts for the agents. Now, assume that person 1 (MN_A) wants to gather some data from other members and has launched a mobile agent for that purpose. That agent will move from one node to another, collect data and at last return with the collected data to its owner, that is, the node that launched it. Thus an agent starts its journey from a given owner and moves from one node to another at its will. The owner provides a *Priority List(PL)* to the agent which contains a list of node ids that are most beneficial migration sites (for the application that deployed that particular agent). So, an agent will always try to visit those nodes from the priority list as its first preference. But this movement is successful if the two nodes are connected and there is no simultaneous transmission in the neighborhood of the intended destination (taken care of by the MAC protocol). So, we associate a probability with the movement to indicate transient characteristics of the environment, since, for example, the routing table may not be updated properly or the link quality may have degraded so much (due to increased noise level) that the agents are unable to migrate. Thus, if an agent residing at node MN_A decides to move to node MN_B (connected to MN_A) then the agent successfully moves to MN_B with probability p_t. Here p_t denotes the problem of unpredictable background noise level mentioned above. For example, noise level may increase due to heavy rainfall.

4.3 Our Model

The following data structures are needed

Priority_list of agent j:	PL:-it has two fields- node_id and trust_level (unvisited 0; suspected -1; trusted +1)
Trust_threshold:	k (a positive integer)
Default trust level:	TS (> k)

Trust level view of the MANET by node i: (Trust $level_1$, Trust $level_2$, Trust $level_3$,.....................$)_i$where trust $level_1$ represents the trust value assigned to node id=1 by the current node

Initially the priority lists (PL) of all agents have 0 trust level corresponding to every node id in their PL. So also then any node I's view of the network will be $(TS,TS,......)_{i.}$

The workflow can be divided into two parts: (i) Algorithm I gives the function of the agents that helps to collect first hand information about an agent's trust; (ii) Algorithm II running at the nodes takes its input from algorithm I and any broadcast message received by the node (second hand information) to update the distributed trust model and hence the node's trust level view of the network. This in turn affects the route taken by newer agents.Steps followed by each agent

Algorithm – I: *Agent_code()*

1. While task given to the agent is not completed
   1.1. Move to an agent site (MN) (unvisited) according to the PL provided.
   1.2. If that destination falls in the same cluster as it is now residing, the agent moves to the new destination with probability p
   1.3. Before processing, take hashcode of the agent's own code and data.
   1.4. If the hashcode matches with the one stored in a *secured way* in the agent's data, then
      1.4.1. Share information regarding the visited nodes with the host platform.
      1.4.2. Set the trust value of this node to +1 in the PL.
      1.4.3. Gather information needed by the application that deployed this agent.
      1.4.4. Update the computed results.
      1.4.5. Compute hashcode of the new updated code and data and store it in a secured way.
   1.5. Otherwise put the trust level of this node to -1 in its PL and go to step 2.//inference: most likely- agent data has been changed
2. Move back to the owner.
3. Stop.

Steps followed by every MN (host platform)
Algorithm – II: *MN_code()*

1. Input network configurations.
2. For t=t_0 to T repeat the following.
   2.1. Some nodes may also fail because of software/hardware failure according to Weibull distribution. Node failure can be simulated by deleting the edges e from E' further that are incident on the failed node $v \in V$.
   2.2. If a node fails then go to step 3.
   2.3. Movement of nodes according to the SRMM is updated as follows
      2.3.1. Update the speed and direction according to equations 1 and 2.
      2.3.2. With the new velocity update the node locations according to equations 3 and 4.
      2.3.3. Distance between each pair of nodes is calculated using equation (5) and E' is populated according to equation (6).
   2.4. If an agent comes to this site/node (MN_j)
      2.4.1. If the visit frequency of agent from a particular node (MN_k) reaches threshold then
         2.4.1.1. The agent is killed (since it can be an indication of DoS attack.)
         2.4.1.2. A message will be broadcast stating MN_k to be compromised.
         2.4.1.3. Delete the current trust level view stored at MN_j.
      2.4.2. Otherwise
         2.4.2.1. Update the trust level of the nodes as follows.
            2.4.2.1.1. If the agent is found to trust a node (MN_k) (has a positive trust level in its PL) then increment the trust value of (MN_k) in the trust level view of MN_j by 0.5.
            2.4.2.1.2. If the agent is found to suspect a node (MN_k) (has a negative trust level in its PL) then
               2.4.2.1.2.1. Kill that agent.
               2.4.2.1.2.2. Decrease the trust level of its owner and *learn* not to migrate an agent via this node.
   2.5. If an agent owned by this node comes back containing at most one suspected node in its PL then
      2.5.1. Update the results.
      2.5.2. Update the trust level view of the network according to the agent's PL (increase by 0.5 or decrease by +1)
      2.5.3. If a node is found to be suspected then *learn* to avoid the existing route followed by the agents
      2.5.4. Kill the agent (Algorithm – I, steps 1.4 and 1.5).
   2.6. If the resulting trust level of any node falls below Trust_threshold value then advertise the node id to be a suspected one to the rest of the nodes.

2.7. Whenever a message regarding suspected node id is received from a trusted node, then depending on its trust level, the relevant information would be updated.
2.8. The PL for each agent containing trusted node ids is also formed and kept with the owners.
2.9. Deploy the agents.
3. Stop.

In step 1.3 of Agent_code(), the secured way of storing means that we assume the hashcode is stored in a way that is not easily understandable/modifiable by a host platform. For example it can be encrypted by the owner and the hashcode calculation may include the encryption key along with the agent's code. Moreover we assume that the hashcode calculation and matching part (step 1.4 of algorithm I) is stored in such a (secured) manner that it cannot be changed in transit. Further, in the next step (1.4) if the current host platform (where the agent currently resides) is found to be malicious, then most likely the data part of the agent is changed, not the code. So to save network bandwidth and improve performance of MAS, killing of the agent cannot be suggested rather the agent can be asked to move back to its owner (so that the owner may update its trust level accordingly). Because the PL (kept as part of agent's data) could also be corrupted. Individual node failures are considered in step 2.1 of MN_code(). But we did not consider the fault tolerance of the nodes. In step 2.4.2.1 and 2.5.2 of MN_code(), the trust value is incremented slowly but decremented rapidly from agent's feedback. This is done to avoid agent migration to compromised sites under all circumstances. A node learns about a suspected area in the network in steps 2.4.2.1.4 and step 2.5.3.

As can be seen, agents in our system migrate and collect feedback about the trustworthiness of the nodes they visit. So, they work like watchdogs [11]. Their feedbacks (stored in the status of the PL) work like firsthand information [11] for the reputation system working at the nodes (step 2.4.2.1.1 of algorithm II). The broadcast messages from a trusted node (step 2.7 of algorithm II) to others act as second hand information [11] for the recipients. The reputation system at the nodes based on the first hand and second hand information updates its view of the network and accordingly guides (providing PL) the agents it deploys.

5 Experimental Results

The simulation is carried out in java and can run in any platform. For simplicity, in our simulation the PL tells the agents which nodes to visit. After visiting all the nodes from the PL successfully, the agent moves back to its owner. We have taken an instance where there are six nodes in the network. Two mobile agents are deployed by four different owners. Agents 0 and 1 start their journey from nodes MN_0 and MN_1 respectively and roam around the network to accomplish its task. Thus an application (for example service discovery) running on MN_1 deploys agent 1. Our job is to protect the agents from malicious hosts and to kill a compromised agent as soon as possible. Initially all nodes are initialized with a default trust level. The agents are provided with a given PL by their respective owners (agent 0 needs to visit MN_1 and MN_2 whereas agent 1 needs to visit MN_2 and MN_3). For example, visiting nodes MN_1 andMN_2 will be most beneficial for agent 0 and so on.

The nodes are taken close enough so that they form a connected network initially as shown in figure 1(a). Every 3 seconds the positions of the nodes are updated according to SRMM. The simulation is carried out for 120 seconds. SRMM generates realistic and smooth movement of the nodes.Connectivity of the nodes is calculated according to the Two-ray model. The network topology at 4 successive time instants is shown in figure 1(a, b and c). Agents are also shown in figure 1 by callouts along with a numeral to indicate agent ids. The dotted ones (callouts) represent the starting position and the bold ones (callouts) represent end point of their journey at that time instant. The status of their PL is also shown in the figure. MN_3 is assumed to be malicious in a sense that it tries to change the data carried by an agent.

Table 1. Trust Level view of MN_1

MN_0	MN_2	MN_3	MN_4	MN_5
5	6	4	5	5

Table 2. Default values of our configuration

Parameter	Default Values
M	20
N	25
Trust View default	5
Trust_threshold	3
Minimum required signal power	18 dBm
Length of priority list	0.5N

In time instant t (say) both agent 0 and agent 1migrate to MN_2 (figure 1(b)), do necessary calculations, compare hash code, update results, take new hash code (algorithm-I in section 4.4) and then move towards the next node in its PL.Consequently agent 0 migrates to MN_1, computes and compares hash code and shares its belief of MN_2. Thus trust level for MN_2 at MN_1 gets increased by 0.5. In the mean time agent 1 suspects $MN_3$and decides to move back without computing results at MN_3. Thus in the next time instant MN_1 finds agent 1 back and decreases the trust

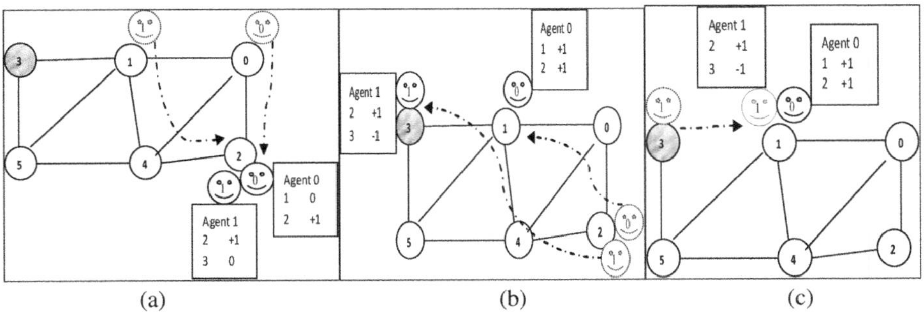

Fig. 1. (a) Initial configuration of MANET having 6 nodes
(b) MANET configuration and corresponding agent locations after 3 seconds
(c) MANET configuration in next 3 seconds indicating end of agent 1's journey

level of MN_3 before creating a new agent (figure 1(c)). Due to transient faults agent 1 could not make a successful migration this time and stays back at MN_1. After this time, the trust view of MN_1 is shown in table-2. The trust value for MN_2 is increased twice by 0.5 (by visiting agent 0 and then by agent 1) thus making it 6. The trust value for MN_3 is decreased by 1 as is indicated by the PL of agent 1. The process goes on and as the trust value of MN3 reaches below 4 at MN_1, it broadcasts a message which in turn updates the trust view about MN_3 at MN_0. This process goes on and eventually all the nodes get a consistent view of the network only if they create or are visited by the agents.

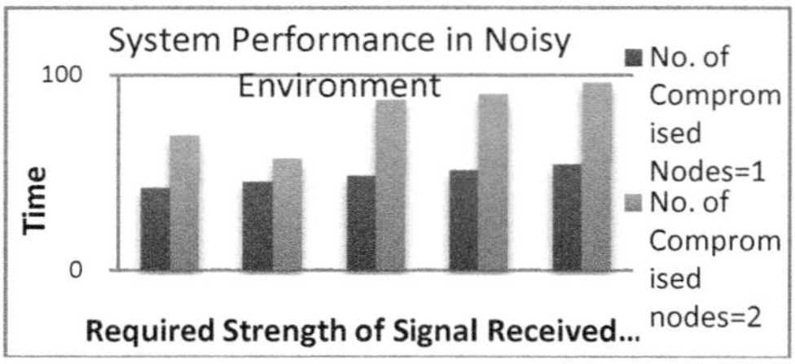

Fig. 2. System performance in noisy environments

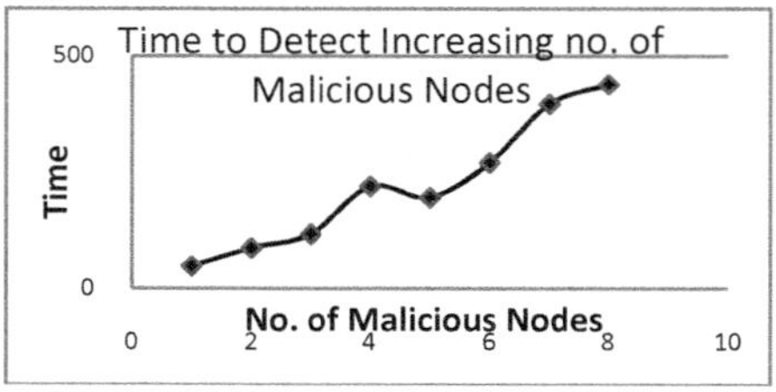

Fig. 3. System performance as threat to the agents increases

We have done a series of experiments to show the robustness of our proposed algorithm. The default values for the experiments are shown in table-3. We will explicitly mention any change in these values for individual experiments.

First the effect of theinherent background noise is shown in figure 2. As background noise increases, stronger signal becomes necessary for successful transmission. This increases the minimum required $p_r$thereby decreasing coverage area of a node. Thus it takes longer times to detect compromised nodes in the network.As more nodes in the network become compromised, more time is needed to detect them. This difference in time increases further with increase in background noise. Thus for a highly noisy environment, longer time is needed before the trust views of the nodes in MANET reach a steady state.

If we fix the background noise level to a particular value and hence the minimum required p_r and vary the no. of malicious nodes in the network, the time to detect all of them increases even further. By step 1.5 of algorithm I, whenever an agent finds a suspected node, it comes back to its owner without discovering the MANET any further. As the result carried by this agent is meaningless for its owner- roaming in the MANET any further would not serve the purpose for which this agent was deployed.This strategy saves bandwidth but makes detection of other malicious nodes in the network a time consuming task. Hence figure 3shows that as no. of compromised nodes increases, the time to detect all of them increases even further.

But if we increase the size of MANET keeping other parameters fixed, then the result is shown in figure 4. Here we have kept the percentage of trusted nodes almost fixed to 84%.Correspondingly the PL of the agents also becomes larger (table-3). Thus with larger networks, because of inherent mobility, the network becomes partitioned into a no. of components making the movement of the agents in some parts of the network impossible. As agent migration gets delayed, the process of trust calculation and sharing is also hampered. Thus for larger MANETs longer time is necessary to find all suspicious nodes.

We introduce a new metric called the ratio of agents passed that is defined as follows

$$RatioofAgentsPassed(t) = \frac{No.ofagentsgoingthroughmaliciousnodestilltimet}{Totalno.ofagentsdeployedtilltimet} \quad (7)$$

We assume MN_2 and/or MN_3 to be compromised where MN_2 behaved maliciously from the beginning but MN_3 was compromised during simulation (see figure 5). It is observed that after a certain time (513 units) the ratio of agents passed becomes independent of the reference point when a node becomes compromised. This explains the robustness of our protocol as all malicious nodes can eventually be detected by the trusted ones.

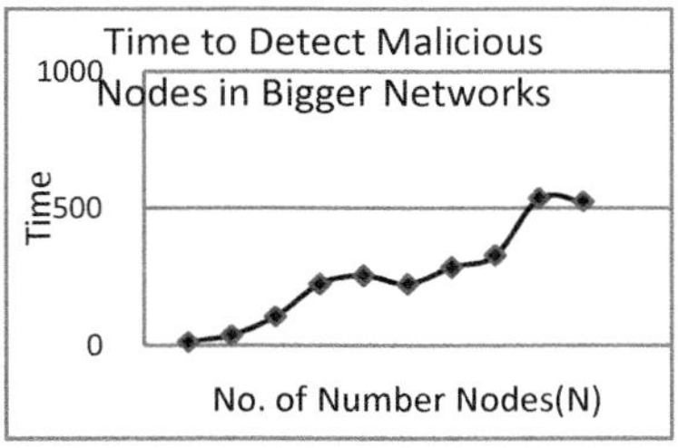

Fig. 4. System performance for bigger networks

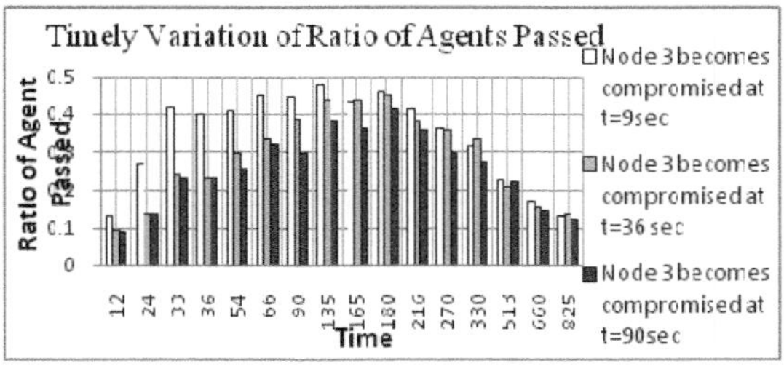

Fig. 5. Ratio of agents passed where MN_3 becomes compromised in run time

6 Conclusions

This paper provides a solution for securing mobile agents in MANET against possible threats of modification of agent data and/or code by compromised nodes.It attempts to find distributed trust model for the network so that each trusted node may eventually get a consistent trust level view of the network and hence prevent agents deployed by them from visiting compromised nodes any further. Herewe take hash code of an agent's data and code in order to detect possible modification. Our model provides methodology to secure not only the agents, but also the agent owners(nodes). It provides prime security services like integrity, authenticity.The agent owners are given the responsibility of killing malicious agents and creating new ones. If any node is found to be malicious, its entry is removed from the PL of new agents.The scheme enables an agent to share information about MANET with the nodes it trusts, helping MNs update their trust levels.Modification of agent's code and/or data in transit is also detected eventually and is broadcast.To protect from malicious broadcasts, the nodes only listen to (and update trust level) broadcastmessages from the senders they trust.The protocol is validated and results are shown in section 5. It can be observed that for a larger MANET longer time is necessary to detect all compromised nodes.

References

[1] Chowdhury, C., Neogy, S.: Estimating Reliability of Mobile Agent System for Mobile Ad hoc Networks. In: IEEE Proc. 3rd International Conference on Dependability, pp. 45–50 (2010)

[2] Cao, J., Feng, X., Lu, J., Das, S.K.: Mailbox-Based Scheme for Designing Mobile Agent Communications. Computer 35(9), 54–60 (2002)

[3] Migas, N., Buchanan, W.J., McArtney, K.: Migration of mobile agents in ad-hoc, Wireless Networks. In: Proc.11th IEEE International Conference and Workshop on the Engineering of Computer-Based Systems, pp. 530–535 (2004)

[4] Meier, R.T., Dunkel, J., Kakuda, Y., Ohta, T.: Mobile agents for service discovery in ad hoc networks. In: Proc. 22nd International Conference on Advanced Information Networking and Applications, pp. 114–121 (2008)

[5] Jansen, W., Karygiannis, T.: Mobile Agent Security, NIST Special Publication, http://csrc.nist.gov/publications/nistpubs/800-19/sp800-19.pdf

[6] Rizvi, S.M.S.I., Sultana, Z., Bo, S., Islam, M.W.: Security of Mobile Agent in Ad hoc Network using Threshold Cryptography. In: The Proc. of the International Conference on Cryptography, Coding and Information Security (2010)

[7] Tarig, M.A.: Using secure-image mechanism to protect mobile agent against malicious host. In: Proc. of World Academy and Science, Engineering and Technology, pp. 439–444 (2009)

[8] Borselius, N.: Mobile agent security. The Electronics & Communication Engineering Journal 14(5), 211–218 (2002)

[9] Yee, B.S.: A Sanctuary for Mobile Agents. In: Ryan, M. (ed.) Secure Internet Programming. LNCS, vol. 1603, pp. 261–273. Springer, Heidelberg (1999)

[10] Haghighat, R., Yarahmadi, H.: A New Approach for Mobile Agent Security. In: The Proc. of the World Acadamy of Science, Engineeringand Technology, vol. 32 (2008)

[11] Li, N., Das, S.K.: A trust-based framework for data forwarding in opportunistic networks. Ad Hoc Networks (in press)

[12] Songsiri, S.: MTrust: A Reputation-Based Trust Model for a Mobile Agent System. In: Yang, L.T., Jin, H., Ma, J., Ungerer, T. (eds.) ATC 2006. LNCS, vol. 4158, pp. 374–385. Springer, Heidelberg (2006)

[13] Bettstetter, C.: Smooth is better than sharp: a random mobility model for simulation of wireless networks. In: The Proc. of the Fourth ACM International Workshop on Modeling, Analysis and Simulation of Wireless and Mobile Systems, pp. 19–25 (2001)

[14] Rooryck, M.: Modelling multiple path propagation- Application to a two ray model. The Journal of L'Onde Electrique 63, 30–34 (1983) ISSN 0030-2430

An Efficient Protocol to Study the Effect of Flooding on Energy Consumption in MANETS

Anita Kanavalli[1], N. Chandra Kiran[1], P. Deepa Shenoy[1], K.R. Venugopal[1], and L.M. Patnaik[2]

Department of Computer Science and Engineering
[1] University Visvesvaraya College of Engineering, Bangalore, India
[2] Vice Chancellor, Defence Institute of Advanced Technology (Deemed University) Pune, India
anita.kanavalli@gmail.com

Abstract. Mobile Ad-hoc network (MANET) comprises of mobile nodes which can communicate with each other through wireless channel. MANET is different from fixed wired networks, as the nodes are mobile, and they have a limited transmission range. A major issue with ad-hoc networks is energy consumption since node mobility is dependent on battery-operation. The mobility of the nodes introduces a new challenge to find the location of the node. Most of the MANET routing protocols rely on flooding for finding the location of the node. In this paper an attempt is made to study the effects of flooding on the energy consumption of the nodes. The comparison is made on the protocols DSDV, AODV, DSR which rely on flooding, with the Ring routing protocol which does not use flooding for finding the location of the node. The ring protocol introduces a new conceptual design, which does not depend on flooding nor uses location dependent identifiers for locating the node. The ring protocol is well suited for studying the effect of flooding on the energy consumption as this protocol does not use flooding. This paper covers the introduction and working of the protocol, and the results of comparison. The simulation is carried out using ns-2 simulator.

Keywords: Ad-hoc routing, Energy consumption.

1 Introduction

A Mobile Ad-hoc Network is a collection of wireless mobile nodes without the need of any network infrastructure or a central administration they can form a network[1]. The Mobile Ad-hoc networks do not have any fixed routers; the nodes are capable of movement and can connect dynamically in arbitrary manner. The nodes are capable of computation and communication and hence act as routers. They can maintain routes to other nodes in the network. In order to facilitate the communication in the network, a routing protocol is used to establish the routes between nodes, which are different from routing protocols for wired-networks. The primary goal of the routing protocols in ad-hoc networks is to establish the routes correctly and efficiently between the pair of nodes and to ensure that the messages are delivered in a timely manner. The initial

A. Abraham et al. (Eds.): ACC 2011, Part I, CCIS 190, pp. 141–152, 2011.

Mobile Ad-Hoc Network routing protocols emerged by introducing some modifications to the existing wired routing protocols. The routing protocols can be classified into two types, namely Table-Driven routing protocols and Source-Initiated on demand routing protocols. In the case of table-driven routing protocols the nodes maintain routing information even before it is needed. Hence these protocols are also called as proactive routing protocols. Each and every node in the network knows the route to every other node in the network. Routing information is usually kept in routing tables and is periodically updated as the network topology changes. On the contrary, the source-initiated on demand routing protocols do not maintain routing information or routing connectivity if there is no communication. If a node wants to send a packet to another node then the protocol searches the route in an on-demand manner and establishes the connection in order to transmit and receive the packet. Hence this protocol is also called as reactive protocol. The Destination Sequenced Distance Vector (DSDV) [2] routing protocol is an example for Table-Driven proactive MANET routing protocol, Dynamic Source Routing (DSR) [3] and Ad-hoc On-demand Distance Vector (AODV) [4] routing protocols are examples of the source-initiated reactive MANET routing protocol. Both the proactive and the reactive classes of routing protocols rely on flooding for connection establishment and transfer of packets. The proactive routing protocols resort to flooding whenever network or topology changes, whereas the reactive class of routing protocols uses flooding for route discovery. The use of flooding increases the message overhead, which further increase the congestion in the network, where a network is flooded by the control packets there by blocking the data packets to reach to the node successfully. As the size of the network increases the amount of flooding also increases, there by drastically reducing the performance of the protocol. The energy of the node is decremented when it sends or receive the packets. Once the energy of the node reaches zero, the node is shut-down and is considered terminated by the system. If the network has a large number of control messages, most of the energy is exhausted on reading, analyzing and handling the control packets, there by will have adverse effects on the energy efficiency. Most of the research is done on how to conserve the energy of the ad-hoc networks[5], and many power aware[6] and energy aware[7] routing protocols are introduced. Proposals were made on how to reduce the flooding in the networks, so as to reduce the number of control message required. Advancements were also made in the area of basis ad-hoc routing protocols, a new family of protocols called as hybrid protocols were introduced which combined the advantages of both proactive and reactive protocols. These protocols mainly concentrated on increasing the scalability of the networks. In recent years alternative strategies, for locating the position of the node have been proposed. The Zone Routing Protocol (ZRP) [8] is an example of the hybrid routing protocol and the LANMAR is an example of the location-based routing protocol. Most of these protocols were compared with respect to the scalability and the performance of the network, no attempt was made to study how energy efficient are, these networks.

In the ring routing protocol the nodes are organized in the shape of a ring. The assignment of the nodes in this ring is done in the order of their location independent identifiers. Each node maintains a routing path to its neighbors in the ring. In addition the nodes along the path store the next hop towards each path end point in a routing table. The ring protocol performs well because it does not flood and it does not use location dependent addresses, which helps in minimizing the control overhead required, thereby increasing the performance of the protocol. This work mainly concentrates on the energy consumed by the protocol. The protocol is compared with the traditional routing protocols namely DSDV, AODV and DSR using the network simulator-2[9].

The paper is organized as follows, in section II an overview of traditional MANET routing protocols is presented. Section III describes the ring protocol in detail. Section IV covers the performance evaluation. Section V gives the conclusion.

2 Related Work

This section covers the existing ad-hoc routing protocols and gives a brief comparison of these protocols. The basic wired routing protocols were modified in order to adapt them to the Mobile Ad-Hoc networks.

2.1 Destination Sequenced Distance Vector (DSDV)

First, The Destination Sequenced Distance Vector protocol is one of the first protocols proposed for ad-hoc networks. It is an enhanced version of Bellman's Ford algorithm where each node maintains the table that contains the shortest distance and the first node of the shortest path to every other node in the network. It is a hop by hop proactive protocol In DSDV protocol the updates due to broken links lead to very heavy control overhead during high mobility, even a small network with high mobility or a large network with low mobility can choke up the bandwidth. Hence this protocol suffers from excessive control overhead that is directly proportional to the number of nodes in the network.

2.2 Dynamic Source Routing (DSR)

Dynamic Source routing (DSR) protocol is an on-demand routing protocol designed to restrict the bandwidth consumed by control packets. The major difference between this and the other on-demand routing protocols is that it is beacon less and hence does not require the periodic *HELLO* packets transmissions, which are used by a node to inform to its neighbor nodes of its presence. The bandwidth is restricted by finding the path only when required. The disadvantage of this protocol is that the broken link cannot be repaired by the route maintenance phase. Stale route cache information can also lead to inconsistencies during route reconstruction.

2.3 Ad-Hoc on Demand Distance Vector (AODV)

Ad-Hoc on-demand distance vector (AODV) routing protocol uses on-demand approach for finding the routes, that is a route is established only when it is required by a source node for transmitting packets. It belongs to the class of Reactive routing algorithms. It employs destination sequence numbers to identify the most recent path. AODV does not repair a broken path locally. When a link breaks, it is usually observed through the periodic beacons or through link-level acknowledgments, and are notified to the end nodes.

2.4 Other Routing Protocols

Distance Routing Effect Algorithm for Mobility (DREAM) [10] is an example of restricted directional flooding routing protocols. Cell Hash Routing (CHR), is designed to cope with problems like limited available energy, communication range or node mobility. CHR overcomes these problems by using the distributed hash table of clusters than individual nodes [11].

There are some new hybrid protocols which try to introduce the concept of hashing into the ad-hoc networks to increase the performance. Examples of these protocols are Dynamic Address RouTing (DART) [12] protocol, Virtual Ring Routing (VRR) [13] Protocol.

3 Ring Protocol

The main motivation of ring protocol is to reduce flooding of control messages in ad-hoc networks. The performance and efficiency of ad-hoc routing protocols depends on how efficiently the routing protocol finds the neighbors or the peers of the node, this is usually done by exchange of control packets between the nodes through flooding. The ring protocol does not flood the network and it also uses location independent identifiers for the nodes, which do not require any external or complex mechanism for finding the location of the node, there by reducing the complexity of the protocol and to attain high performance.

3.1 Node Identifier

Each node is assigned a unique global identifier generated through a 3-digit hexadecimal number generation algorithm; these identifiers are used to distinguish different nodes. The generated identifiers are random unsigned integers. The protocol works on the assumption that the node identifiers are fixed, unique and location independent. The protocol does not impose any structure on the node identifiers. It only requires that they are unique and totally ordered. Figure 1 shows an ad-hoc network with node identifiers assigned.

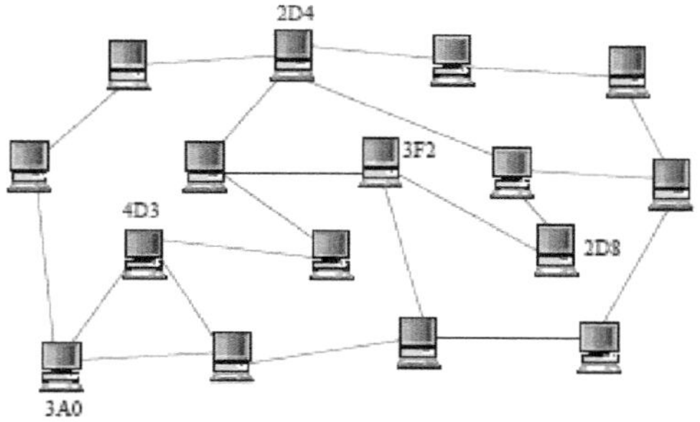

Fig. 1. Network with node identifiers

3.2 Ring Formation

After successfully assigning the identifiers to the nodes they are placed in a circular ring in the increasing order of their node identifiers. For any given node, the other nodes which are adjacent to the node in the ring are part of registered neighbors of the node. They are termed as registered neighbors as they get registered in the nodes' Neighbor_Registry table. The registered neighbors of a particular node can be of two types, the physical neighbors of the node in the network and the other type are the non-physical neighbors of the node which are nothing but the nodes which are lying beside the given node in the ring. Figure 2 shows the equivalent ring for the network topology in Figure 1 and also shows the non-physical neighbors of node *3A0* and also its routing-paths.

3.3 Neighbor_Registry Table

Each and every node in the network maintains a Neighbor_Registry table with information about the routing paths to all its registered neighbors, both physical and non physical. It also tries to maintain the neighboring nodes of the nodes, which may help in constructing the alternative routing paths in case of the failures in the network. Each entry in the Neighbor_Registry table denotes the two routing-path endpoints and the next hop towards each endpoint.

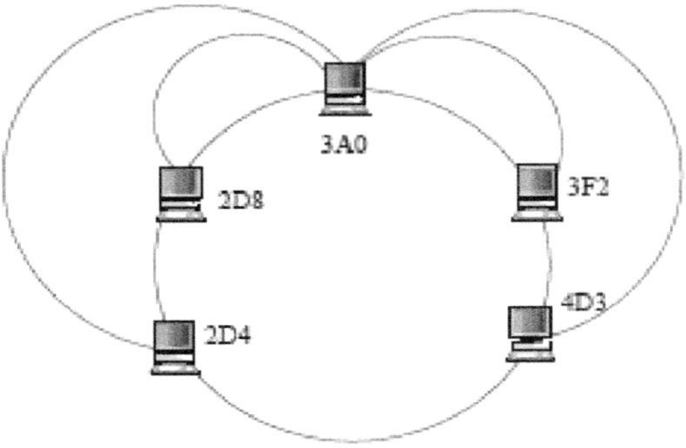

Fig. 2. The nodes in a ring

Table 1. Neighbor_Registry Table

EndPointA	NextHopA	EndPointB	NextHopB	Status
3A0	null	2D8	8D2	00
3A0	null	2D4	E57	00
3A0	null	3F2	E57	00
3A0	02A	4D3	8D2	10
A02	8D2	A92	E57	00
35F	12E	37A	6D3	00
3A0	null	8D2	8D2	01
3A0	null	E57	E57	01

The Neighbor_Registry table also stores the status flag which is used to indicate the type of the node(EndPointB). The status flag is actually a 2-bit flag. The meaning of each flag is given below.

00	-	Non Physical Neighbor
01	-	Physical Neighbor (1-hop)
10	-	Physical Neighbor(multi-hop)
11	-	Failed Nodes

Each routing path is attached with a timestamp which will help to uniquely identify the path. Each node originates at most one path to each of its two non-physical neighbors on the ring. Table I shows the Neighbor_Registry table for the node 3A0.

3.4 New Node Joining the Network

This section discusses about how to build the state as the new node joins the network. Initially the node transmits a RequestToJoin (RTJ) message in the form of a broadcast, and at the same time also listens to the broadcasts sent by the other nodes. When a new node joins the network, it initializes the non-physical neighbor set and physical neighbor set and it sets up routing-paths to its neighbors. The joining process of a node has three steps:

- The node discovers all its neighbors.
- The new node must build path-vectors to ensure it can directly reach each of its neighbors(both physical and non physical).
- The nodes must remove paths to nodes that are no longer their neighbors.

When this process completes, the new node will be just like any other node in the network, it can route to any other node by traversing its overlay neighbors. The ring protocol maintains routing state for virtual-paths which detects both node and path failures using only direct communication between the physical neighbors. The protocol also supports a feature repair the routes locally.

4 Performance Evaluation

The performance evaluation is done with network simulator ns-2. The performance of ring protocol is compared with existing traditional routing protocols namely DSDV, AODV and DSR. The simulation is done for *50* nodes over *670mx670m* area. The experiments were run for the duration of *500* sec. Here a random way point model[15] is used for the mobility, which has been generated using the Bonn Motion tool. For the mobility model the speed parameters used are (1, 5, 10) m/sec. The measurement is done for the fraction of packets delivered correctly and the energy consumed per packet by keeping the number of nodes to constant as *50* nodes and varied the number of connections. The following metrics were considered for measuring the performance of the protocol. For all the simulations the number of data packets sent are kept constant, so the number of packets successfully received at their destinations will give a comparison as to how efficient the underlying routing algorithm is under similar traffic load.

$$PDF = \frac{Number\ of\ packets\ received\ by\ destination}{Number\ of\ packets\ sent\ by\ source}$$

It is represented as shown above.

- Energy Consumption per Successful Data Delivery is the ratio of total network energy consumption to the number of data packets successfully delivered to the sink. The network energy consumption includes all the energy consumptions except MAC

layer controls. It is represented as shown below, where E_{ik} is the initial energy of the kth node E_{rk} is the remaining energy of the kth node after the simulation. Figure 3 shows the packet delivery fraction of AODV, DSR, DSDV and ring protocol at low speed of mobility. Figure 4, shows the energy consumption of AODV, DSR, DSDV and the ring protocol for low speed of mobility, DSDV and the ring protocol uses less energy per packet because the probability of the link breakage is less.

$$Energy\ Consumption = \frac{\Sigma_{k=1}^{N} E_{ik} - E_{rk}}{Number\ of\ Nodes}$$

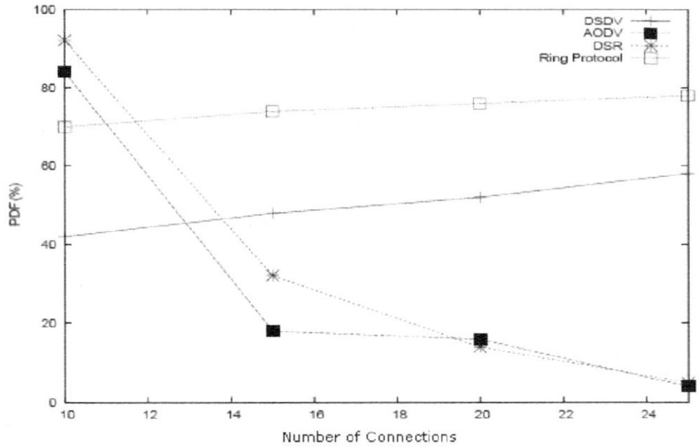

Fig. 3. Packet delivery at low mobility speed

The energy consumption per successful delivery of both DSDV and ring protocols is decremented when the numbers of connections become large. This is due to the fact that once the routes are established; large number of traffic uses the routes without the need of additional energy to construct new routes. This value is larger than the maximum energy consumption per successful delivery of ring protocol. Energy consumption of AODV and DSR increases when the number of connections increases. This is due to the fact that these routing protocols are on-demand. Hence, this feature increases energy consumption of routing overhead The graph shown here is for scenario with a faster mobility. The Figure 5. shows the comparison packet delivery factor of the routing protocols. The DSR and AODV show better performance than the other two protocols for *10* and *15* number of connections. This is due to the fact that DSR and AODV establish the routes on demand. This provides better chances to avoid usage of staled routes for DSR and AODV. When the number of connections is greater than *15*, the PDF of DSR and AODV degrades. This is due to the increase in the routing overhead. The ring protocol shows good results here even though the value of PDF is less for *10* and *15* nodes its value is constant. From the graph we can see that the ring protocol performed fairly well this is because of the local repairs which help to find the alternate routes quickly there by decreasing the number of staled routes. The packet delivery factor of DSR is greater than AODV's. This is due to two reasons, the first is that routing overhead of DSR is less than AODV. Secondly, AODV is aggressive to maintain broken links. AODV starts new route discovery for link breakage. Unlike AODV, DSR uses the cached route for route maintenance. Figure 6.demonstrates the energy consumption per successful delivery of three MANETS routing protocols with speed of *5m/sec*. The simulation result of this scenario shows that DSR consumes less energy per packet than all the three protocols initially, but as the number of connections increases the ring protocol performs better than the rest of the protocols tested. The probability of the link bre akage goes up when the speed of node mobility increases in case of DSDV. Because of staled routing table entries, packets are sent or forwarded over the broken links. This increases the retransmission attempts for successful transmission. It leads DSDV to consume large amount energy for unsuccessful communication. In addition, DSDV consumes significant amount of energy to construct unusable routes periodically. AODV and DSR start route discovery as soon as there is demand of routes. On demand route discovery avoid energy consumption to construct unusable routes. It also provides fresh route for data communication.

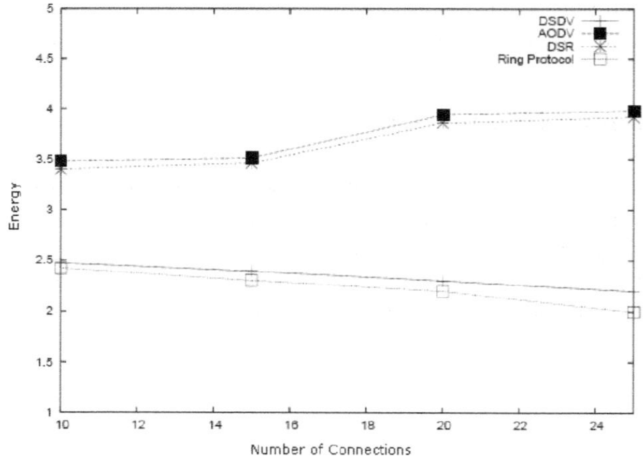

Fig. 4. Energy Consumption

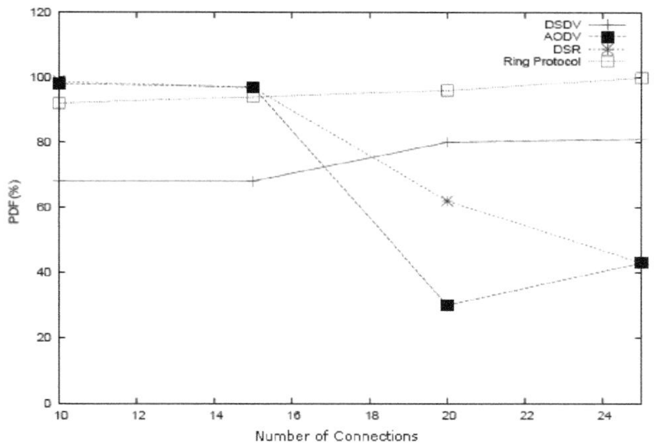

Fig. 5. Packet delivery factor

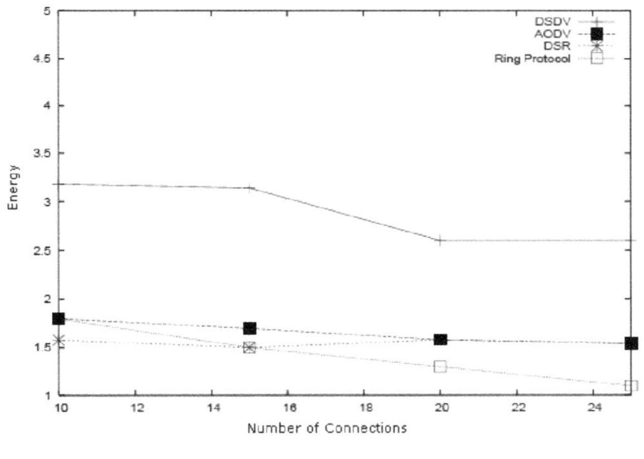

Fig. 6. Energy Consumption

Use of fresh route reduces the rate of retransmission that leads to consume significant amount of energy. Because of lower overhead and usage of route cached for route maintenance, DSR consumes smaller amount energy per packet than AODV. In case of the ring protocol the local repair mechanism helps in faster repair of the links, by using the existing alternate nodes there is no need of re-transmissions thereby energy is not wasted. The Figure 7, shows that DSR and AODV outperform DSDV in PDF, by high mobility, DSDV acts very poorly. Due to the stale routing table entries, packets are sent or forwarded over broken links and PDF fails at high speed. PDF of DSR is better than AODV because DSR has access to a significantly greater amount of routing information than AODV in single cycle of route discovery. By virtue of source routing in DSR, using a single request-reply cycle, the source can learn routes to each intermediate node on the route in addition to the intended destination. Both DSR and the AODV protocols give better results than the ring protocol initially but as the number of connection increases, the rate of decrease of PDF is less in the ring protocol when compared to both AODV and DSR protocols, the ring protocol gives better results. As shown in the Figure 8, both DSR and the ring protocol uses less energy consumed for successful packet delivery than the remaining two protocols. DSDV does not have upto date route entry to send the data packets in dynamic network. The node sends a packet on staled out routes. The packet is transmitted successfully after a number of attempts, this leads to more energy consumption. In addition, DSDV requires periodic transmission of reach ability information; this also leads to higher energy consumption of DSDV. High mobility increases incidence of link and connection failures. Since AODV does not cache multiple routes, the failure of a link requires all sessions currently using that path to issue new route requests. It causes high flooding, which drain the battery energy of the nodes.

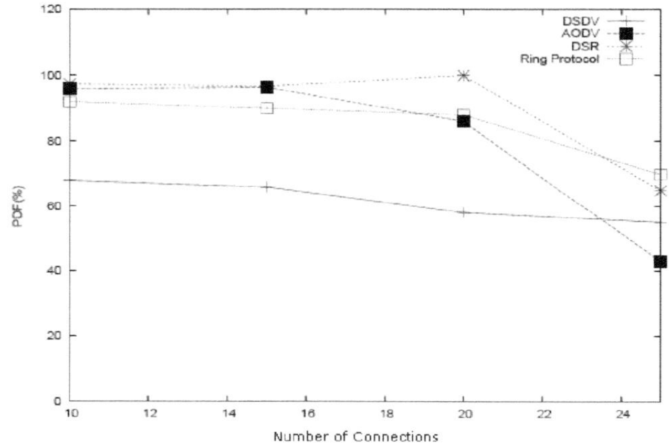

Fig. 7. Packet delivery at high mobility

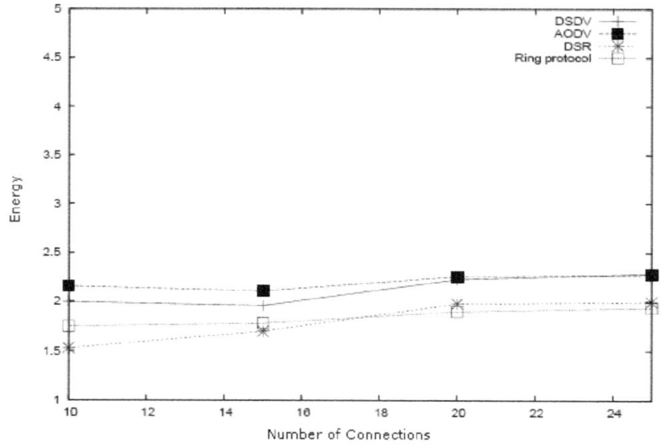

Fig. 8. Energy Consumption

The energy consumption of the three routing protocols increases as the numbers of connections increase, The energy consumption per successful delivery of DSR increases dramatically as the numbers of connections increases. This is due to the fact that DSR caches large number of routes large number of connections. But these routes are not valid longer due to high mobility. In case of the ring protocol the energy is dissipated due to the periodic exchange of the *Hello* packets, but when compared to other protocols the ring protocol consumes low energy.

5 Conclusion

Reducing power consumption in Ad-hoc networks has received increased attention among researchers in recent years. The design of energy efficient routing protocols must address reducing of power consumption from the viewpoint of the node and network. In this paper, the evaluation is done for the energy efficiency of the existing well known MANETs routing protocols and compare it with the ring protocol. The simulation results showed that the ring routing protocol outperforms all the remaining protocols. It is finally concluded that flooding not only reduces the performance of the protocol by increasing the congestion, but also leads to high energy consumption.

References

1. Ilyas, M.: The Handbook of Ad-hoc Wireless Networks. CRC Press, Boca Raton (2002)
2. Perkins, C.E., Bhagwat Clerk Maxwell, P.: Highly Dynamic Destination Sequenced Distance Vector Routing for Mobile Computers. In: ACM SIGCOMM Symposium on Communications, Architecture and Protocols, pp. 234–244 (September 1994)
3. Johnson, D., Hu, Y., Maltz, D.: The Dynamic Source Routing Protocol (DSR) for Mobile Ad-hoc Networks for IPv4. RFC 4728 (February 2007)
4. Perkins, C., Belding-Royer, E., Das, S., Elissa, R.: Ad-hoc On Demand Distance Vector Routing. RFC 3561 (February 2007)
5. Tennenhouse, D., Smith, J., Sincoskie, D., Wetherall, D., Minden, G.: A Survey of Active Network Research. IEEE Communications Magazine 35(1), 80–86 (1997)
6. Maleki, M., Dantu, K., Pedram, M.: Power -Aware Source Routing in Mobile Ad-hoc Networks. In: Proceedings of ISLPED, Monterey, CA, pp. 72–75 (2002)
7. Li, M., Zhang, L., Li, V.O.K., Shan, X., Ren, Y.: An Energy-Aware-Multipath Routing Protocol for Mobile Ad-hoc Networks. In: ACM Sigcomm Asia 2005, April 10-12, pp. 166–174 (2005)
8. Haas, Z.J., Pearlman, M.R.: The Zone Routing Protocol (ZRP) for Ad- hoc Networks. draft-ietf-manet-zone-zrp-04 (July 2002)
9. The Network Simulaotr ns-2, `http://www.isi.edu/nsnam/ns/ns-documentation.html`
10. Qabajeh, L.K., Kiah, L.M., Qabajeh, M.M.: A Qualitative Comparison of Position-Based Routing Protocols for Ad-hoc networks. IJCSNS International Journal of Computer Science and Network Security 9(2), 131–140 (2009)
11. Araujo, F., Rodrigues, L., Kaiser, J., Lu, C., Mithderi, C.: CHR: A Distributed Hash Table for Wireless Ad-hoc Networks. In: Proceedings of the Fourth International Workshop on Distributed Event-Based Systems (DEBS 2005), pp. 407–413 (2005)

12. Eriksson, J., Faloutus, M., Krishnamurthy, S.: Dynamic Address RouTing, University of California, Riverside
13. Caesar, M., Castro, M., Nightingale, E.B., Shea, G.O., Rowstrom, A.: Virtual Ring Routing: Network Routing Inspired by DHTs. In: ACM Sigcomm 2006 (September 2006)
14. Gao, L., Li, M.: Virtual Backbone Content Routing in Wireless Ad-hoc Network. International Journal of Wireless & Mobile Networks (IJWMN) 1(2), 30–47 (2009)
15. Ni, S., Tseng, Y., Chen, Y., Sheu, J.: The Broadcast Storm Problem in a Mobile Ad- hoc Network. In: MobiCom (1999)
16. Saltzer, J.: On the Naming and Binding of Network Destinations, RFC 1498 (August 1993)
17. Gowrishankar, S., Basavaraju, T.G., Sarkar, S.K.: Effect of Random Mobility Models Pattern in Mobile Ad–hoc Networks. IJCSNS International Journal of Computer Science and Network Security 7(6), 160–164 (2007)

An Approach to Suppress Selfish Behavior of a Node in MANET by Hiding Destination Identity in Routing Path

Rahul Raghuvanshi, Mukesh Kumar Giluka, and Vasudev Dehalwar

D-52 Nehru nager, Bhopal, 462003, Madhya Pradesh, India
{rahulraghuvanshi_mtech,mkgiluka_mtech,vasudev}@manit.ac.in

Abstract. In wireless ad hoc networks, each node cooperates with each other to forward the data packet. However, some of the nodes behave selfishly and disincline to share their resources with other nodes. This selfish behavior of nodes at network layer degrades the performance of the network significantly. In this paper, a novel approach is proposed, to suppress the selfish behavior of nodes and encourage each node to forward the data to its next node in the routing path. This work is inspired from the One More Hop (OMH) approach, in which each node in the network is believed to be rational i.e. each node want to send and receive its own packet in the network. In this paper, a source node always finds a longer path for destination. Here, the term longer path consists of actual routing path from source to destination and an extra path from destination to other disjoint nodes. This extra path may be either fake or real depending on availability of extra path at destination.

Keywords: Extra path, fake path, longer path, MANET, OMH, RREQ, RREP.

1 Introduction

Unlike wired network, mobile ad hoc network (MANET) does not have any fixed infrastructure and there is no central body to govern the network. In MANET, it is possible that nodes may not be within the communication range of each others. Such ad hoc networks extend the transmission range by multi hop packet forwarding. That is a reason for ad hoc network being well suited for scenarios in which pre deployed infrastructure support are not available e.g. emergency relief military operation and terrorism response. In ad hoc network nodes can be of four following types:

1. *Cooperative nodes*: Nodes which comply with the standard at all times.
2. *Inactive nodes*: Nodes which include lazy nodes and constrained nodes e.g. energy constrained or field strength constrained.
3. *Malicious nodes*: Nodes which drops packet with the intention to cause network attack.
4. *Selfish nodes*: Selfish nodes try to save their own resource since resources are very constrained in wireless network. Selfish nodes may decide to conserve their resources by not forwarding data packet for other nodes. This can be achieved in two ways:

A. Abraham et al. (Eds.): ACC 2011, Part I, CCIS 190, pp. 153–161, 2011.

a) *Selfish node type 1*: These nodes participate correctly in routing function but not forward data packets they receives for other nodes, so data packets may be dropped rather than forward to their destination.
b) *Selfish node type 2*: These nodes do not participate correctly in the routing function, by not advertisement available roots. In DSR, selfish nodes may drop all RREQ packet they receive or not forward RREP packet to some destination.

In these networks, energy conservation is the key, which not only extends the life of the nodes but also prevents a node to become selfish in the network. Conventional routing algorithms ignore residual battery power of nodes. Sooner or later, the node with depleted battery will be reluctant to participate or withdraw itself in the existing routing which leads to Denial of Service (DoS) attacks [1]. To save its battery a node might behave selfishly by not forwarding packets originated from other nodes, while using their resources to relay its own packets towards remote recipients. Therefore, countermeasures against node selfishness are mandatory requirements in mobile ad hoc network. Selfish nodes can intensively lower the efficiency of the network since they do not easily participate in the network operation. This paper deals with the first category of selfish node (type 1) misbehavior.

Our approach encourages a node to forward data packet to know whether the actual destination is itself or not. Our work is inspired from the One More Hop approach [2], where a source node finds a longer path for destination and sends the data packet through this longer path.

Section 2 gives previous research work on selfish node misbehavior. In section 3, we present the modified RREQ format of DSR protocol. Section 4, gives the basic assumption made in our approach. Proposed scheme and algorithm is presented in section 5. Finally, conclusion and future work is provided in section 6.provide the comparative study of these techniques in section IV and conclusion of this paper in section V.

2 Related Work

There are several techniques that have been proposed on selfish node detection, and mitigation of their selfish behavior and removal of them from the network. These techniques can be classified into two categories: reputation based and credit based.

Reputation based schemes uses the node's reputation or behavior to mitigate the selfish behavior. Node's reputation can be obtained using direct observation or from reputation messages from other nodes in the network. In this, each node monitor (overhear) its neighbor's transmission. Marti et al. [3] scheme consists of two components: *Watchdog and Pathrater*. The watchdog component detects misbehaving nodes, and the pathrater rates paths according to the knowledge it gains from the watchdog. Buchegger et al. [4] proposed the *CONFIDANT* scheme, utilizing the watchdog/pathrater model where detected misbehavior is broadcast using alarm messages and rogue nodes are punished. Michiardi et al. [5] proposed CORE scheme which is similar to CONFIDANT in the sense that both supports first hand reputation; and indirect, reported reputation and it is different from CONFIDANT by the fact that it doesn't allow negative rating. He. et. al. [6] proposed SORI, which propagate monitored behavior, thus relying on first and second-hand information. Since, the Reputation-based scheme is totally depended on the reputation of a node. Therefore, such system has to make sure the reputation information is highly secure, which causes high complexity of the system design. It also suffers from the problem that the detected selfish node will be isolated and will not be able to take part in data forwarding. So, overall network performance will be degraded.

Credit based schemes uses some incentive to motivate nodes to cooperate. That is, the node will get some incentive if it serves the network and pays back some price when it gains help from the network. In [7, 8, 9], author proposed a currency based scheme. It provides incentives for cooperation. Buttyan et al. [7] proposed a system where nodes receive credit (nuglets) for forwarding packets and need to spend credit to transmit their own packets. The problem with this scheme is that it needs a tamper-proof hardware to manage the increments and decrements in number of credits for each node.

Zhong et al. [8] proposed Sprite which uses a Credit Clearance Service (CCS) that manages the rewards and the credit payments for each node. Credit for forwarding a packet depends on fact that packet forwarding was successful or not. Forwarding is considered successful if and only if the next node on the path reports a valid receipt to the CCS. The problem with this scheme is that it requires a centralized server as CCS which does not meet many ad-hoc practical scenarios. In [9], a game-theoretic scheme for routing in MANETs, called Ad hoc Vickrey, Clarke, and Groves (Ad hoc-VCG) that consists of greedy and selfish agents was considered. Those agents accept payments for forwarding data for other agents if the payments cover their individual costs incurred by forwarding data. The problem with this scheme is that, it does not pay attention to the fairness issue in routing when some nodes do not get any reward due to some reasons, e.g., location.

3 Modified RREQ Packet in DSR Protocol

This approach is applicable to the DSR [11] protocol and it can also be applied to the AODV [12] routing protocol with some modification in RREQ packet. Dynamic Source Routing (DSR) provides a rapid, dynamic network connection, featuring low processing loads and low memory consumption. Messages in the network can be divided into routing messages and data messages, and routing messages can be further divided into path discovery and path maintenance messages. The former includes Route Request (RREQ) and Route Reply (RREP), while the latter includes Route Error (RERR). Each node maintains a cache and updates the content while receiving a routing message. The cache contains multiple paths to different destination from itself. When source node needs to send data to the destination, if in the source node's cache, the path towards the destination is out of date, or there is simply no path towards the destination, the source node would broadcast a RREQ packet to all nodes in the network. Each intermediate node receiving a RREQ packet would first judge whether it is the originator or if such a RREQ packet is repeated. If yes, this RREQ packet would be dropped. If not, the RREQ packet would be processed and broadcasted again. In processing the RREQ packet, an intermediate node first checks that a corresponding reverse route exists in its cache or not. If not, the node would create an entry for a reverse route. The purpose of a reverse route is to let the intermediate node send an RREP packet back to the originator. If there is already a reverse route, the intermediate node checks the content of this entry. If the identification field in the RREQ packet is same as the recently received RREQ packet then the intermediate node simply discard this RREQ packet because of duplicate RREQ packet. If intermediate node receives a RREQ packet with different identification number then it searches for the corresponding target address path in its cache. If it does not have a (forward) route to the destination, it will broadcast the RREQ packet to continue the searching of a route to the destination node.

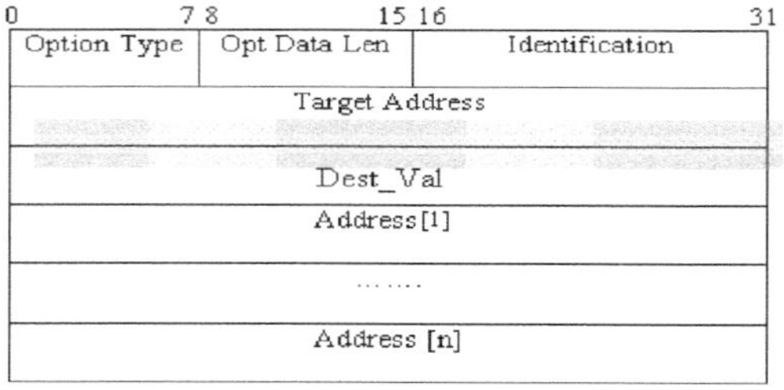

Fig. 1. Modified RREQ Packet format

In our protocol, in addition to target address field, source node also uses one more field in the RREQ packet which is encrypted by a symmetric encryption algorithm. Figure 1 shows the modified RREQ packet. A field (Desti_Val) represents the extra field of RREQ packet. Desti_Val represents a fake extra path from destination. On receiving the RREQ packet, destination node searches for an extra path in its cache. If it finds an actual extra path in its cache, then it append this extra path to the received path in RREQ packet and send this longer path to the source node, through a RREP packet. Otherwise, destination decrypts the Desti_Val field and finds a fake path and uses this fake path as an extra path

4 Basic Assumptions

In this paper, we make the following assumptions.

1) There is no centralized server or administrator present in the network to detect malicious behavior of a node.
2) Each source and destination node pair are trusted entities and all nodes know about their neighbors via MAC link layer acknowledgement or technique present in [10].
3) Each node in the network behaves rationally.
4) A selfish node can return a key to its previous nodes if it knows that the destination exists among previous node.
5) We also assumed that no malicious entity exist in the network. In DSR, we assumed that the links are bidirectional.

6) A packet can be received by all neighbors present in the transmission range of a transmitting node because of the broadcast nature of wireless medium.
7) There is no conspiracy among nodes.
8) Each node operates in promiscuous node [11].

5 Proposed Scheme

In our proposed solution, source node always finds a longer path from destination. A longer path is the routing path in which destination itself is an intermediate node. For example in Figure 2 (a) and (b), A and F are the source and destination respectively and B,D are the intermediate nodes between them, then routing path will be A→B→D→F but longer path would be A→B→D→F→I→J→K, where I→J→K is the extra path from destination F.

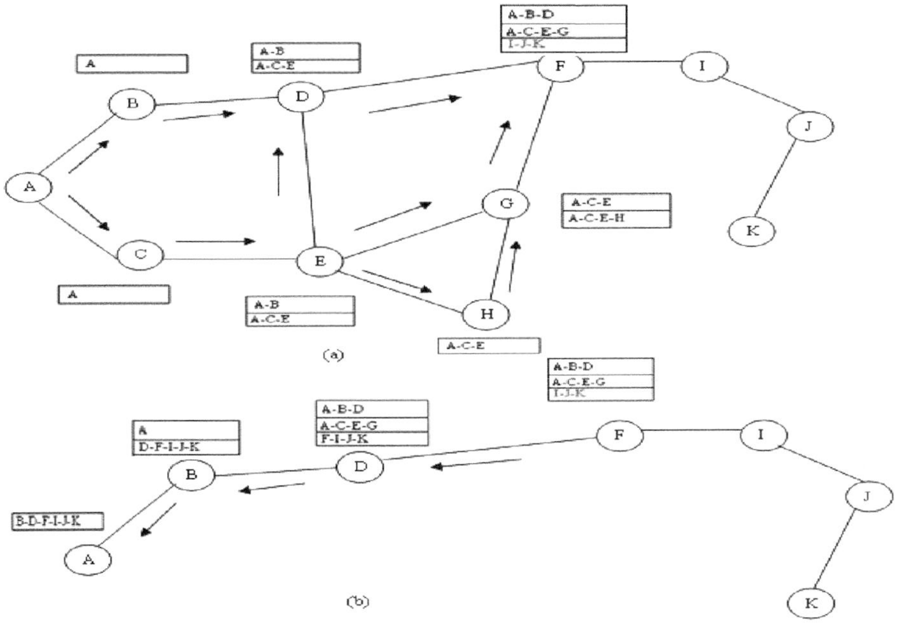

Fig. 2. (a) RREQ Packet, (b) RREP Packet

In OMH, source node adds special information for each node in the data packet header. This information includes: 1) whether the packet's real destination is its previous node and 2) if it is, then the key *K* to open the packet. In our approach, source node does not need to add this special information for each node. Instead, it adds this information for some of the selected nodes. Selection of these nodes is based on a temporary variable (*Temp*). Source node sets an appropriate value of this variable. Each node decrements this *Temp* value by one. When it reaches to zero, then only the corresponding node reads this information, otherwise sends packet to the next node in the path. This reduces the overall computation overhead of the routing path as compared to OMH.

In OMH, if a no longer path exists to the source node then source node sends different information in packet header. However, this different information in the packet header may be detected by a selfish node and packet may be discarded by this node. To solve this problem, in our approach, the source node finds the longer path in all the cases. When no longer path is found for destination then source uses a fake extra path in the longer path to send data packet but intermediate nodes always assume that the routing path is legitimate. Only source knows the truth.

Fig 2 shows the route discovery process of this approach. For this, it broadcasts a RREQ packet. When an intermediate node receives a RREQ packet, it saves the RREQ path, contained in the RREQ packet, in its cache. The node appends its identification (Node_id) in RREQ path. Now, it searches a longer path for destination in its cache. If it does not find a longer path then it broadcasts the RREQ packet. If it finds one, it sends it (lngr_path) to source node through reverse path by an RREP packet.When a destination node receives a RREQ packet, it also saves the received RREQ path in its cache and appends its *Node_id* in RREQ path. Now, it searches for an extra path in its cache. If it finds the extra path then it appends this extra path to the RREQ path; otherwise, it opens the encrypted field (*Desti_Val*) of the RREQ packet by using its own symmetric key and finds a fake extra path. This encryption is done by a symmetric key algorithm (e.g. DES algorithm). The destination node appends this fake extra path (*Fake_Path*) to RREQ path. In both the cases, the destination node will copy this appended RREQ path in an RREP packet and sends it to the source node through reverse path. When an intermediate node receives a RREP packet, it saves the reverse path in its cache and forwards the RREP packet to the next node in the reverse path.

Algorithm 1
/*When destination or intermediate node (N_K) receives the RREQ or RREP packets, does the following*/

1. **if** type=RREQ **then**
   /* when RREQ packet is received*/
2.   save (RREQ_path, cache);
   /* save received RREQ path in cache for future use */
3.   RREQ_path = RREQ_path + Node_id;
4.   total_path=search_path (cache);
   /*searches a path to the destination along with an extra path from the destination in its cache*/
5.   **if** total_path=true **then**
   /*if the total path is found in the cache */
6.   RREP_path = RREQ_path + total_path;
7.   send (RREP, S);
   /* send RREP packet containing longer path to the source node S through reverse path*/

```
8.    else
9.       if Node_id!= D then
  /* if it is the intermediate node then broadcast the RREQ packet */
10.            broadcast (RREQ);
11.      else
  /* if it is the destination (D) then opens the encrypted destination value(Desti_val),
  which contains a fake path, by using its own private key */
12.            open (D_K (E_K(Desti_Val)));
13.            RREP_path = RREQ_path + Fake_Path;
14.            send (RREP, S);
15.      endif /* line 9 */
16.   endif /* line 5 */
17.endif /* line 1 */
18.if type=RREP then
       /* when RREP packet is received */
19.   if Node_id!=D then
20.      if Node_id!= S then
   /* if it is the intermediate node then save the RREP_path in the cache and
   forward the RREQ packet */
21.            save (RREP_path, cache);
22.            send(RREP, S);
23.        else
24.            save(RREP_path, cache);
  /* if it is the source node then save the RREP_path in its cache. */
25.      endif /* line 20 */
26.   else
27.      discard_RREP_pkt;
  /* if it is the destination node then discard the packet */
28.   endif /* line 19 */
29.endif /* line 18 */
```

In this approach, encryption is used in a novel way. With this approach, only the upstream nodes (path after the receiving node of data packet) can find out whether a packet is destined to the node or not. Only destination and upstream nodes know the symmetric key. As a result intermediate nodes cannot drop packets because they cannot determine if the packet is destined for them or not. The transmission ends at the upstream node of destination node. Here, symmetric algorithm (e.g. DES) is used for data packet encryption and asymmetric algorithm (e.g. RSA) is used to encrypt the special information in the data packet header.

When a source node receives a RREP packet then it starts sending data packet to the destination node. In the data packet header, the source node sets a Temporary variable (*Temp*) whose value decreases with each node traversal of data packet. This variable is set in such a way that it always becomes zero at the destination node (it does not mean that Temp can not be zero at intermediate nodes). Source node sets *Temp*=δ, $1 \le \delta \le I$, where I is the length of the extra path. Figure 3 shows the data packet routing in our scheme, with δ=2.

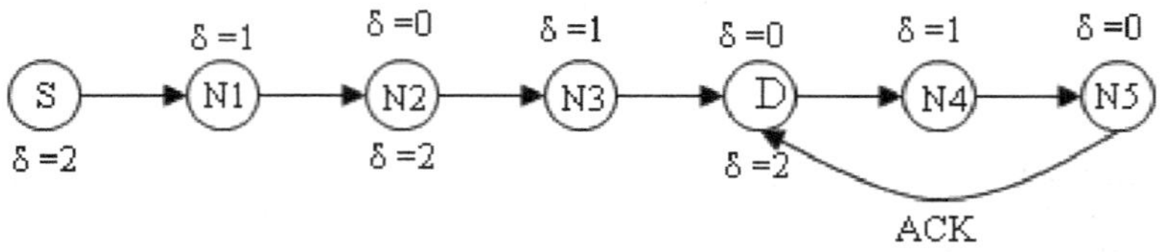

Fig. 3. Data packet forwarding

Main aim of using this *Temp* variable is to reduce computation overhead (checking special information) at each node. When source node sends the encrypted data packet ($E_K(M)$), with *Temp* variable, then each node uses following algorithm:

Algorithm 2

/* Let the packet transferred by source node is: (*Temp*, longer_path, E_K (M)) */

1. **if** *Temp*>0 **then**
2. *Temp*=*Temp*-1;
3. save a copy of data packet.
4. send (*Temp*, longer_path, E_K (M));

// send data packet to the next node if *Temp* is not equal to zero.

5. **else**
6. find destination node in δ limit

/* the node at which *Temp* becomes zero, checks that whether the packet is destined to any of the nodes having *Temp* value between 1 and δ. */

7. **if** destination node found **then**
8. Ack (K, node_id);

/* send an acknowledgement along with the symmetric key to the destination.*/

9. **else**
10. **if** Next_node=true **then**

/* if the destination node is not found then it checks for a valid next node(not a member of fake extra path) in the longer path */

11. *Temp*= δ;
12. send (*Temp*, longer_path, E_K (M));

/* if next node is a valid node then set the value of *Temp* to δ and forward the packet. */

13. **else**
14. Open ($D_K(E_K$ (M));

/* if next node is not a valid node, it means that it is itself the destination node. */

15. **endif** /* line 10 */
16. endif /* line 7 */
17. **endif** /* line 1 */

6 Conclusion and Future Work

MANET is highly dependent on the cooperation of nodes to perform networking functions. This makes it highly vulnerable to selfish node. This approach suppresses the selfish behavior of nodes by hiding destination identity in the routing path. The proposed approach is applicable to the DSR protocol and it can also be applied to the AODV routing protocol with some modification in RREQ packet. In this paper, we propose an enhanced version of One More Approach to encourage packet forwarding in a non cooperative ad hoc network. Unlike OMH, in our approach, only selected nodes needs to know whether the packet is destined to previous nodes or not, which reduces the unnecessary delay at each node. On the other hand, in OMH each node performs this operation. This scheme also solves the longer path problem of OMH. In this paper, a source node always finds a longer path, while in case of OMH a source node may fail to find a longer path.

We are working on the following aspects in the future:

- To build an elaborate simulation environment to experiment with and evaluate our proposed scheme in DSR and AODV protocol.
- To insert security mechanism to defend against misbehaving nodes.

References

1. Yang, H., Luo, H.Y., Ye, F., Lu, S.W., Zhang, L.: Security in Mobile Ad Hoc networks: challenges and solutions. IEEE Wireless Communications 11, 38–47 (2004)
2. Song, C., Zhang, Q.: OMH—Suppressing Selfish Behavior in Ad hoc Networks with One More Hop. In: Mobile Netw Appl., pp. 178–187 (2009)
3. Marti, S., Giuli, T., Lai, K., Baker, M.: Mitigating routing misbehavior in mobile ad hoc networks. In: MobiCom 2000, pp. 255–265 (2000)
4. Buchegger, S., Boudec, J.Y.L.: Self-policing mobile ad-hoc networks by reputation systems. IEEE Communications Magazine, 101–107 (2005)
5. Michiardi, P., Molva, R.: Core: A collaborative reputation mechanism to enforce node cooperation in mobile ad hoc networks. In: CMS 2002 (2002)
6. He, Q., Wu, D., Khosla, P.: Sori: A secure and objective reputation-based incentive scheme for ad hoc networks. In: WCNC 2004 (2004)
7. Buttyan, L., Hubaux, J.-P.: Stimulating cooperation in self-organizing mobile ad hoc networks. In: ACM/Kluwer Mobile Networks and Applications (2003)
8. Zhong, S., Chen, J., Yang, Y.R.: Sprite: A simple cheat-proof, credit-based system for mobile ad-hoc networks. In: INFOCOM 2003, pp. 1987–1997 (2003)
9. Anderegg, L., Eidenbenz, S.: Ad hoc-VCG: A truthful and cost-efficient routing protocol for mobile ad hoc networks with selfish agents. In: International Conference on Mobile Computing and Networking, pp. 245–259 (2003)
10. Nguyen, H.L., Nguyen, U.T.: A study of different types of attacks on multicast in mobile ad hoc networks. ELSEVIER Journal of Ad Hoc Network (2006)
11. Johnson, D., Maltz, D., Broch, J.: The dynamic source routing protocols for mobile ad hoc networks. Internet Draft, IETF Mobile Ad Hoc Network Working Group (1999)
12. Perkins, C.E., Royer, E.M., Das, S.R.: Ad hoc on demand distance vector (AODV) routing. In: Proceedings of IEEE WMCSA 1999, New Orleans, LA (1999)

Broken Link Fraud in DSDV Routing - Detection and Countermeasure

H. Meena Sharma, Rajbir Kaur, Manoj Singh Gaur, Vijay Laxmi

Department of Computer Engineering, Malaviya National Institute of Technology, Jaipur, India
sharma.meena.26@gmail.com, {rajbir,gaurms,vlaxmi}@mnit.ac.in

Abstract. Routing protocols employed in Mobile Ad Hoc Networks (MANET) lack security mechanisms. Vulnerabilities in protocols are exploited by malicious/compromised nodes to launch attacks.Consequently network performance is degraded. 'Broken Link Fraud'is a Denial of Service (DoS) attack launched against Destination Sequence Distance Vector (DSDV) Protocol. Malicious node announces a 'broken link'to victim node. Honest nodes in the network are fooled into believing that route to victim does not exist. Network performance in terms of Packet Delivery Ratio (PDR) is severely affected. In this paper, we propose a countermeasure for the attack. Our method has an advantage that it does not rely on cryptographic techniques. It is suitable for resource constrained MANETs. Simulation results confirm the effectiveness of our technique in improving PDR.

1 Introduction

In MANETs, routing protocols determine how a packet ultimately gets to its destination via a series of intermediate nodes. Design of routing protocols is challenging owing to constraints on MANET resources (bandwidth, memory). Routing protocols can be either proactive or reactive. Proactive protocols require more memory but take comparatively less time to deliver information. They are easy to implement and computationally more efficient than reactive protocols. With the continued increase in memory of hand held devices, proactive protocols can be easily deployed in MANETs. Destination Sequenced Distance Vector (DSDV) [6] is a proactive protocol used in MANET. It is simple and efficient and is based on distributed Bellman-Ford Algorithm [3].

Routing protocols in MANET assume trustworthiness of participating nodes. Malicious nodes frequently deviate from defined specifications. A single malicious node can severely disrupt network performance by exploiting vulnerabilities in routing algorithms to launch attacks. It is essential to study attacks in routing protocols and incorporate provisions for detection and response to minimize impacts of attacks. In this paper, we propose a method to detect and prevent Broken Link Fraud [7] in DSDV. Proposed method does not use public key infrastructure (PKI) or expensive cryptographic based methods [10]. To detect malicious node, each node observes the frequency with which a node occurs as next hop neighbor for the destination. A node is labelled suspicious, if the observed frequency for the node exceeds a specific threshold. Countermeasure entails blacklisting suspicious node. No messages are accepted from the blacklisted node.

A. Abraham et al. (Eds.): ACC 2011, Part I, CCIS 190, pp. 162–171, 2011.

Our simulation results show that the detection rate in most cases is 100%. Results indicate that there is a significant improvement in network performance once malicious node is detected and blacklisted.

The rest of the paper is organized as follows. Section 2 introduces DSDV. Section 3 highlights the need to study vulnerabilities of the protocol. This section introduces 'Broken Link Attack'in DSDV. Section 4 presents related work. Section 5 discusses the metric that can be a good candidate to detect the probability of an attack. It also describes our proposed detection method and countermeasure. Simulation of the method and its analysis are presented in Section 6. In Section 7, we describe our conclusions and future work. In the following discussion terms misbehaving node, malicious node and attacker node has been used interchangeably.

2 DSDV Protocol

In MANETs, information is exchanged between nodes through a process called routing. Routing protocols provide means of data transfer in MANETs by selecting the optimal path from available paths to destination. Routing protocols are classified as either *link state* or *distance vector* [15] based on metric used to select the best path. In distance vector routing, distance is calculated as total number of hops to destination and optimal path is the one with minimum hop count. In link state, status of each link determines the best path. Link state routing protocols require more processing power and memory than simple distance vector protocols. An earliest distance vector protocol is RIP [4]. It suffers from *count to infinity* problem [6]. DSDV avoids the problem by associating a sequence number with each route entry. The decision to update the routing table is based on sequence number.

DSDV is a proactive protocol. Every node maintains one or more routing tables that are updated regularly. Routes are always available on request. Routing table consists of following entries.

1. All known destinations (`dest`)
2. Next hop node to reach the destination (`nxtHop`)
3. Number of hops to reach the destination (`hopCnt`)
4. Sequence number originating from destination (`seqNum`)
5. Time when entry was made (`insTime`)
6. Owner of the entry (`owner`)

Owner nodes usually update the sequence number with even values. In case a broken link is detected on a route, non owner nodes update the sequence number of that route with odd values. A node periodically advertises its own routing information to each of its neighbor by communicating recent entries. Each entry contains following information.

1. `dest`
2. `hopCnt`
3. `seqNum`

On each advertisement, the node increments own destination sequence number. Neighbors compare received information with entries in own routing table. For a destination, entry in routing table is updated through application of following rules.

1. Route with higher `seqNum` is selected to ensure route with newest information,
2. When sequence numbers are equal, route with lower `hopCnt` is selected to ensure better path

As topological changes are detected, routing tables are either broadcast immediately or periodically. Information on new routes, broken links, hop count change is immediately propagated to neighbors as incremental updates. Figure 1 shows a typical MANET consisting of nine nodes. Let us consider that n_1 has packets to sent to n_6. Some of the possible routes available are:

- Route 1: $n_1 - n_3 - n_6$ with sequence number say $s1$ and hop count 2
- Route 2: $n_1 - n_5 - n_6$ with sequence number say $s2$ and hop count 2
- Route 3: $n_1 - n_2 - n_3 - n_6$ with sequence number say $s3$ and hop count 3.
- Route 4: $n_1 - n_2 - n_4 - n_3 - n_6$ with sequence number say $s4$ and hop count 4.

Given that $s3 \geq s2 > s1 > s4$. Route 3 is selected to forward packets even though routes with lower hop count exist. If $s3 = s2$, Route 2 is preferred as it has a lower hop count.

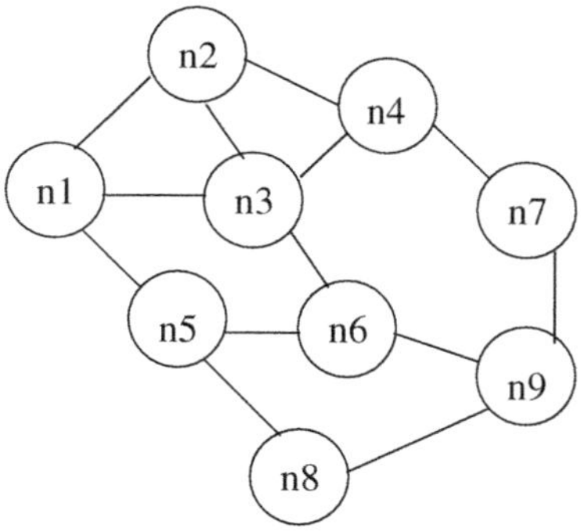

Fig. 1. An Ad Hoc Network

Another field of relevance to our discussion is `insTime`. It is used to determine when to delete stale routes. Stale routes expire when

$$insTime - currentTime > expiryTime$$

where *expiryTime* is the minimum time of considering a routing entry as fresh.

3 Attack Models in DSDV

Mobile devices employed in MANET have limited resources. They are heavily dependent on other nodes for data access and information processing. Reliable and cooperative network topology is assumed. Routing protocols lack security mechanisms. Several attacks can be performed on the routing protocols [13] in ad hoc networks. Without any secure mechanism, nodes can perform any actions in the packets they forward. A misbehaving node may change packet content, drop it, or even inject new packets leading to partial/complete disruption of packet transfer. In this section we discuss threats to DSDV by a misbehaving node. We introduce a new DoS attack 'Broken Link Fraud'on DSDV [7]. This attack is launched in two steps. In the first step the misbehaving node launches *byzantine* attack to become next hop neighbor for the target. In the second step, it announces a broken link to target by propagating infinite distance to the target.

3.1 Step 1: Byzantine Attack

A malicious node exhibits byzantine behaviour by sending false route information to misdirect traffic [2]. To improve the chances of false information being accepted, the malicious node falsely advertises favourable routing metrics (e.g. `seqNum`, `hopCnt`). Possible Byzantine behaviour in DSDV may include

1. Advertising smaller distance to destination (Small Distance Fraud)
2. Advertising route to destination with higher sequence number (Large Sequence Number Fraud)

If a malicious node advertises lower `hopCnt` to destination, it becomes part of the perceived shortest route. If it advertises a route with a high `seqNum`, neighboring nodes legitimately choose it to forward packets. Malicious node can drop all data packets passing through it (black hole attack) [14] or selectively drop packets (gray hole attack) [14]. It might also forge packets and carry out message forging attacks [2].

Consider the topology in Figure 1. If n_1 has packets to send to n_6, the evident shortest route is n_1-n_3-n_6 or n_1-n_5-n_6 . n_3 legitimately broadcasts that n_6 is one hop away from it. Let n_2 be the malicious node. It tries to include itself in the route to destination by either manipulating the `seqNum` or `hopCnt` or both. In DSDV, preference is given to the route with higher `seqNum`. In case the `seqNum` is same, the route with lowest hop count is selected. If n_2 broadcasts the route n_1-n_2-n_4-n_3-n_6 with higher sequence number, it will be treated as fresh route and given preference over other routes. Alternatively, if n_2 broadcasts a distance to n_6 that is less than that broadcast by n_3, there are increased chances of n_2 being included in path to destination n_6.

3.2 Step 2: Broken Link Fraud

Broken Link Fraud [7] uses long distance to launch an active attack. It is a DoS attack wherein, a malicious node targets an innocent node by propagating an infinite distance to it. Target node never features in the path to destination or as destination itself. Consider again the topology in Figure 1. After being included in path to destination (Step 1), malicious node n_2 advertises a fake table as shown in Table 1.

n_2 advertises a broken link to n_6. This creates a make-believe situation for other nodes that n_6 is unreachable.Node n_6 become unavailable for forwarding packets. Packets destined for n_6 cannot be sent.

Table 1. Advertised Fake Table

destination	next hop	hop count	seq num	owner	install time
n_1	n_1	1	4	n_1	t_{n+1}
n_2	n_2	0	6	n_2	t_{n+2}
n_3	n_3	1	2	n_3	t_{n+1}
n_4	n_4	1	4	n_4	t_{n+1}
n_5	n_1	2	4	n_5	t_{n+1}
n_6	n_3	∞	5	n_2	t_{n+1}
n_7	n_4	2	4	n_7	t_n
n_8	n_1	3	4	n_8	t_{n+1}
n_9	n_4	3	4	n_9	t_{n+1}

4 Related Work

Wang *et al* [12] have studied the security properties of DSDV by simulating false distance vector and false destination sequence attacks. They have not studied the impact of large distance fraud on DSDV.

In [8], Kumar discusses threats like modification and replay to distance vector routing protocols. He proposes using Message Authentication Codes to secure information exchanged between neighbors. Though these methods ensure integrity of communication between nodes, they do not withstand node compromise. In particular, metric in each routing table entry is not secured. A compromised router may claim routes of any length to any destination.

Smith *et al* [9] provides countermeasures for routing message and routing update protection. They propose using digital signatures for authentication and integrity of routing messages. Though this method may protect against sequence number frauds, they do not protect against short/long distance fraud. Their techniques also do not apply well in ad hoc network since they require knowledge of predecessors.

SEAD proposed by Hu *et al* [5] uses efficient cryptographic mechanisms like one way hash chains and authentication trees for authenticating sequence numbers and distances of advertised routes. However, SEAD does not prevent a misbehaving node from advertising a distance longer than the one it has received (e.g. broken link fraud).

Wan *et al* [11] propose S-DSDV. All messages are cryptographically protected. Cryptography-based methods are expensive in terms of resource consumption. They also require a *priori* trust. Wan *et al* state that longer distance frauds can only be used to launch passive attacks (e.g., selfishness). 'Broken Link Fraud'uses long distance fraud to launch active attacks that severely hampers network performance.

All of the above methods use either `seqNum` or `hopCnt` or both for detection purpose. Our proposed detection method and countermeasure use frequency of occurrence of node as `nxtHop` to detect attacker.

5 Methodology

In this section, we identify a metric that can be a good candidate to detect probability of an attack. We, then, present a frequency based method that uses the same metric to detect a malicious node. Further, we present a countermeasure so that impact of broken link fraud can be mitigated.

5.1 Metric

In MANETs, intermediate nodes cooperate to forward packets from source to destination. MANETs also have a dynamically varying topology due to mobility of nodes. Mobility prevents communication among nodes outside each others transmission range through same intermediate nodes. Mobility reduces chances of a node having same set of neighbors for a long duration. A nodes neighbor provides a good reference for detecting misbehavior. If a node has same neighbor for an observed duration, it may indicate the presence of a malicious node.

In DSDV, a routing table having same `nxtHop` neighbor for a `dest` for an observed duration may indicate improper behavior. The `nxtHop` neighbor is a good attribute for prevention of broken link attack.

We demonstrate by two sets of experiments that misbehaving node may be identified by an attribute `nxtHop`. The first experiment investigates for a `dest`, the number of times that a node occurs as `nxtHop`. This observation is done for a fixed duration. In the second experiment we assess the `nxtHop` for a destination in situation of an attack. We experimented with a topology of 16 nodes moving at a speed of 10m/sec according to random waypoint model. We monitor a destination's `nxtHop` for a period of 10 sec. The results of our observation is shown in Figure 2. The graph indicates that in case of *no attack*, any single node occurs as `nxtHop` with a frequency less that 50%. But in case of an *attack*, some node may occur as `nxtHop` with a frequency close to 80%. Based on this observation we design a method to deal with both byzantine and broken link fraud. This method consists of two parts: detection and countermeasure.

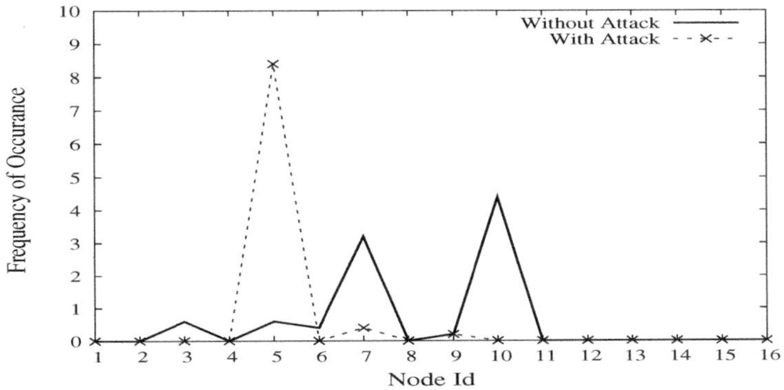

Fig. 2. Frequency of a node occurring as next hop for a destination

5.2 Detection

Each node in the network keeps track of the number of times that a node becomes next hop neighbor for each destination. In order to collect this information, we introduce a special variable `count` with each destination entry in the routing table. It is initially set to one. Each node broadcasts its routing table at regular intervals. Neighboring nodes update their tables based on routing information received. Value of `count` is also modified on each routing update as follows

- *count* = *count* + 1, if the received routing update has the same next hop neighbor as the one contained in own routing table.
- *count* = 1, if the next hop neighbor is different.

The `nxtHop` neighbor for a destination is designated as malicious if the value of `count` for that destination exceeds beyond a certain threshold value.

5.3 Response

Let us label the node that identifies a malicious node as *suspecting node*. Many *suspecting node*s may exist in the network at the same time. These nodes blacklist their identified malicious nodes. *Suspecting nodes* do not accept further messages from the blacklisted node for a period equal to *expiry time*. Routing tables are rebuilt at each node after this period. Value of *count* is again reset to one. This restarts the detection process. In DSDV,

expiry time = *periodic update interval* * *hold time*.

Hold time is the time for which the node waits since the last update before flushing the route from the routing table. *Periodic update interval* specifies the periodic time interval between which a node broadcasts its entire routing table.

6 Simulation

In this section we describe simulation environment used to implement our proposed countermeasure. We made the following assumptions:

- There is only one attacker.
- Attack starts from the beginning of simulation.
- Sink is the target node.

6.1 Simulation Setup

We use *ns-3* [1] for simulation. MANET characteristics for simulation are tabulated in Table 2. To incorporate our detection and countermeasure, we have made changes to DSDV module. We call it **modDSDV**.

Table 2. Simulation Parameters

Number of Nodes	16
Signal Range of each node	200 meters
Mobility Model	Random Waypoint Model
Traffic Type	UDP Traffic
Number of packets sent from source to destination	1 packet/sec
Simulation Time	60 - 100 seconds

Performance Metrics. To test and evaluate our proposed detection and countermeasure, we use Packet Delivery Ratio (PDR) to encapsulate network performance. This is defined as the ratio of number of packets received at destination to the number of packets sent by the source. In no attack scenario, only packets dropped are because of collision and PDR is very high. As an attack is launched and packets are dropped because of the absence of link to target, PDR falls down.

Movement and Communication Model. We use UDP traffic type. The UDP source sends packets at the rate of one packet/sec. The packets are sent from 5th sec onwards. We measure the performance of our proposed scheme for different simulation durations. We have randomly placed 16 nodes in a square area of 1000 $\times$ 1000. We vary the simulation time from 60 to 100 sec in steps of 10 sec.

Random waypoint model is used as the mobility model. The nodes move with a speed of 10 m/sec along pre generated random paths. Table 2 shows the simulation parameters used.

Experimental Setup. We assume that the malicious node exhibits malicious behavior from the start of simulation. We observe the frequency of next hop neighbor for each destination. `Count` is modified on each routing update. Nodes in the network identify a malicious node when the value of `count` exceeds a particular threshold. Messages from malicious node are not processed until `expiry time`. Routing tables are rebuilt and the value of `count` is again reset to 1. We experimented with different values of threshold. A value that gives practically no false positives was chosen as threshold value. We performed ten simulations for each simulation duration to get a single point. Threshold is not changed for the same topology. Detection procedure restarts on each rebuilt of routing tables. We have kept *periodic update interval* = 10 sec and *hold time* = 3 sec. Thus, `expiry time` = 30 sec.

6.2 Simulation Result and Discussion

Figure 3 shows the PDR for different simulation periods. In the graph we plot curves for three scenarios:

1. normal - countermeasure: PDR when the routing protocol functions normally. This depicts "no attack situation".

2. attack + countermeasure: PDR in presence of attack. Countermeasure is applied. This depicts scenario when suspected attacker is blacklisted and attack is contained.
3. attack - countermeasure : PDR in attack situation. No countermeasure is applied.

From the graphs it is clear that in situation of an attack, the PDR drops to a low level. When the countermeasure is applied, there is a huge improvement in PDR. PDR is in the range of 85 - 90%. There is a gap between the top two curves designated by *Normal - countermeasure* and *Attack + countermeasure*. We observed through simulations that it takes 2 - 3 seconds for the detection procedure to converge. During this period, the attacker claims itself as next hop for the destination. Routing tables at all nodes have misbehaving node as the next hop for the destination. This combination of incorrect routing tables causes a packet to loop endlessly. The packet is discarded when its time-to-live (TTL) is exhausted. Packets cannot be forwarded to the destination and PDR drops during this period. We have taken 10 readings by designating different nodes as attackers for each simulation. Average of these simulations have resulted in one point.

We observe through simulations that our proposed detection and countermeasure can effectively detect the malicious node without introducing too much control overhead into the network.

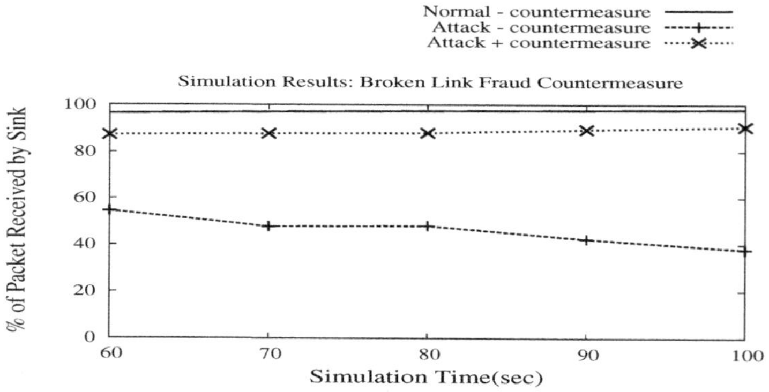

Fig. 3. PDR of the network under different scenarios

7 Conclusion and Future Work

Broken link fraud is a denial of service attack that severely affects the Packet Delivery Ratio of the network. In this paper we have proposed a detection and countermeasure for the attack. The results show that our proposed method detects the attacker. Our method does not use expensive computations as those required by cryptographic methods. It is suitable for MANET situations that are already resource constrained. In future, we will extend this work so as to detect attacks that may start at any time during simulation. We will also see the effect of the attacker on nodes other than the sink. In addition, we would like to experiment with cases where the misbehaving node assumes the identity of other nodes to avoid detection (Sybil Attack).

References

1. Network simulator 3, http://www.nsnam.org
2. Awerbuch, B., Curtmola, R., Holmer, D., Rotaru, C.N., Rubens, H.: Mitigating Byzantine Attacks in Ad Hoc Wireless Networks. Technical report, Department of Computer Science. Johns Hopkins University, Tech. (2004)
3. Bellman, R.: On a Routing Problem. Quarterly of Applied Mathematics 16(1), 87–90 (1958)
4. Hedrick, C.: Routing Information Protocol. RFC 1058. Technical report, IETF (June 1988)
5. Hu, Y.C., Johnson, D.B., Perrig, A.: SEAD:Secure Efficient Distance Vector Routing for Mobile Wireless Ad Hoc Networks. In: Fourth IEEE Workshop on Mobile Computing Systems and Applications, pp. 3–13 (2002)
6. Perkins, C.E., Bhagwat, P.: Highly Dynamic Destination-Sequenced Distance-Vector Routing (DSDV) for Mobile Computers. SIGCOMM Comput. Commun. Rev. 24(4), 234–244 (1994)
7. Kaur, R., Gaur, M.S., Laxmi, V.: A Novel Attack Model Simulation in DSDV Routing. In: Proceedings of the 4th IFIP International Conference on New Technologies, Mobility and Security, IEEE Xplore (2011)
8. Kumar, B.: Integration of Security in Network Routing Protocols. SIGSAC Rev. 11(2), 18–25 (1993)
9. Smith, B.R., Murthy, S., Garcia-Luna Aceves, J.J.: Securing Distance-Vector Routing Protocols. In: SNDSS 1997: Proceedings of the 1997 Symposium on Network and Distributed System Security, p. 85. IEEE Computer Society, Washington, DC, USA (1997)
10. Sun, B., Guan, Y., Chen, J., Pooch, U.W.: Detecting black-hole attack in mobile ad hoc networks. In: 5th European Personal Mobile Communications Conference (Conf. Publ. No. 492), pp. 490–495 (2003)
11. Wan, T., An, H.-C., van Oorschot, P.C.: Securing the destination-sequenced distance vector routing protocol (S-DSDV). In: López, J., Qing, S., Okamoto, E. (eds.) ICICS 2004. LNCS, vol. 3269, pp. 358–374. Springer, Heidelberg (2004)
12. Weichao, W., Lu, Y., Bhargava, B.: On Security Study of Two Distance Vector Routing Protocols for Mobile Ad Hoc Networks. In: Proceedings of the First IEEE International Conference on Pervasive Computing and Communications, pp. 179–186 (2003)
13. Wu, B., Chen, J., Wu, J., Cardei, M.: A Survey of Attacks and Countermeasures in Mobile Ad Hoc Networks. In: Wireless Network Security, Signals and Communication Technology, Part II. Springer, Heidelberg (2007)
14. Kaur, R., Gaur, M.S., Suresh, L., Laxmi, V.: DOS Attacks in MANETs. Cyber Security, Cyber Crime and Cyber Forensics: Applications and Perspectives, pp. 124–145 (2011), doi: 10.4018/978-1-60960-123-2
15. Gorantala, K.: Routing Protocols in Mobile Ad-hoc Networks. Master Thesis in Computer Science, Dept. of Comp.Sci., Umea Univ., Swedan (2006)

Research on Power Optimization Techniques for Multi Core Architectures

A.S. Radhamani[1] and E. Baburaj[2]

[1] Research Scholar/Department of Computer Science and Engineering, Manonmanium Sundaranar University, Tirunelveli, India
asradhamani@gmail.com
[2] Professor/Department of Computer Science and Engineering, Sun College of Engineering and Technology, Nagercoil, India
alanchybabu@gmail.com

Abstract. Continuous effort to achieve higher performance without driving up the power consumption and thermal effects has led the researchers to look for alternative architectures for microprocessors. Like the parallel processing which is extensively used in today's all microprocessors, multi-core architecture which combines several independent microprocessor cores in a single die has currently become very popular in most high performance integrated circuits. Although multi-core processor offers excellent instruction execution speed with reduced power consumption, optimizing performance of individual processors and then incorporating them by interconnection on a single chip is a non-trivial task. This paper investigates the leading challenges associated with current high performance multi-core processor in terms of different types of power optimization techniques.

1 Introduction

Multi-core processing is a growing industry trend as single core processors rapidly reach the physical limits of possible complexity and speed. The multi-core design puts several such processor "cores" and packages them as a single physical processor. The multi-core design enables two or more cores to run at somewhat slower speeds and at much lower temperatures. The combined throughputs of these cores deliver processing power greater than the maximum of today's available single-core processors and at a much lower level of power consumption. The demand for high performance processing has resulted in the introduction of chip multiprocessor architectures to enable continued performance scaling without having to increase the chip clock frequencies to make multi-core processing platforms power and energy efficient [20].

1.1 Multi Core Challenges

At present, it is the time for the turning point in the processor design. The many-core shift is gaining momentum within the processor design spectrum. This emerging

A. Abraham et al. (Eds.): ACC 2011, Part I, CCIS 190, pp. 172–181, 2011.

paradigm substitutes a few complex processors with larger number of simple cores. Chips with thousands of cores promise high computing power, and are ideal when multiple applications are running simultaneously, each with multiple tasks and threads [10] there are a number of design challenges for such architectures including power consumption, memory and cache coherence, routing network, and the impact of process, voltage, and temperature (PVT) variations, Software decomposition into instructions, communication between two or more tasks, controlling resource contention and determining an optimum or acceptable number of units that need to execute in parallel .Power consumption is the major concern in computing equipments need to be optimized to meet the all the challenges mentioned above. Thus, various techniques have been applied within these components to optimize the power consumption either by improving the design and construction of the hardware, optimizing the application software which controls the hardware behavior, to optimize or to minimize the power consumption of the overall system.

2 Related Work

There are a number of works for analyzing power reduction for multicore platforms. They attempted to reduce power consumption using various methods like voltage/delay dependence, task scheduling algorithms, dynamic task allocation techniques and dynamic power management techniques etc. In the following, a quick review of some of the works that are directly related to the power optimization is discussed.

2.1 Power Optimization Algorithm

In modern computing system, processor technology has evolved tremendously with ever increasing processor frequency and number of processors cores. With better performance, more power is utilized. This research focuses on manipulating processor frequency, taking advantage of frequency scaling feature and combining with processor affinity to optimize power consumption in processors, with the objective to propose a power optimization algorithm [1]. Various test scenarios and test cases are presented to confirm and support the power optimization algorithm using frequency scaling and processor affinity with the optimum configuration.

2.2 Simultaneous Optimization of Power and Energy Based on Game Theory

Game theory is conventional approaches that try to maximize the performance of both power and energy by using Dynamic Voltage Scaling (DVS) technique [2]. DVS is a power reduction technique where the voltage used in a component is increased or decreased, depending upon circumstances. Under volting is based on DVS, which is done in order to consume power, particularly in multicore systems.

2.3 Power Optimization Using Transcoding systems

To implement and evaluate a power-efficient and traffic-aware transcoding system on multicore servers that appropriately adjusts the processor operating level is proposed.

The system is capable of configuring the number of active cores and core "frequency on-the-fly" according to the varying traffic rate. As a result, transcoding has been adopted as an essential component in media servers to adapt to various platforms and fluctuating network conditions. Reducing power consumption for those systems is undoubtedly critical in achieving energy efficiency [3].

2.4 Power Optimization Based on DVFS-Enabled H.264 Decoder

To find how the number of cores and working frequency affect the power consumption and provide several power management strategies for the future multicore system designs and software applications by applying four experimental scenarios. To break down and analyze the power consumed by three main components, DSP logic, local memory, and the external DDR2, of a multi-core platform there are four configurations provided [4]. One DSP with full and half clock rates and two DSP's with full and half clock rates.

2.5 A Meta Heuristics Approach for Multi Objective Optimization

Parallel Metaheuristics Framework (PMF) aims to serve a different role. By focusing exclusively on multicore parallelism as opposed to distributed multiprocessing. This has led to an increase in interest in technologies and techniques that enable programmers and users to take fuller advantage of the parallel processing power on almost every desktop and laptop [5]. This work describes the design and implementation of a framework for constructing parallel metaheuristics called, appropriately, the Parallel Meta heuristics Framework (PMF)

2.6 Resource Constrained Optimization

In order to cope with the high complexity of performance simulation for multi-core architectures, asymptotic analytical performance models are derived for exploring a high-level design space of a multi-core architecture. A set of equations are derived based on Amdahl's law asymptotically capturing the performance benefits of a multicore processor [6]. The model guides the architectural decision and given research direction for optimizing the power performance of multi-core architectures.

2.7 Optimization in Volunteer Computing

Volunteer computing (VC), which selects more active nodes over idle nodes for scheduling foreign application tasks to achieve significant energy savings. The efficacy of volunteer computing model by evaluating the energy saves and performance impact of co-executing resource-intensive foreign workloads with native personal computing tasks were discussed by authors [7]. VC is motivated by two observations: (1) the incremental energy cost incurred by running an additional workload W on an active PC is smaller than that of running W alone on a separate machine, and (2) with the increasing hardware parallelism in multi-core computers, VC is feasible.

2.8 Optimized Cache Architecture

Energy consumption as well as performance should be considered when designing high-performance multicore processors. The significant part of total energy consumption is accounted by the instruction cache. Therefore, energy-aware instruction cache design techniques are essential for high-performance multicore processors. A new instruction cache architecture, which is based on the level-0 cache composed of filter cache and victim cache together, for multicore processors, is proposed [8]. The proposed architecture reduces the energy consumption in the instruction cache by reducing the number of accesses to the level-1 instruction cache.

2.9 Exploring Power Optimization

A performance and power analysis methodology based on a simulation model for multi-core systems with integrated power management is implemented in SLATE (System-Level Analysis Tool for Early Exploration). SLATE allows designers to assemble, configure and simulate multi-core systems with L1 and L2 caches and memory controllers interconnected by a coherent bus, and under the control of a global on-chip power manager [9]. For managing power, two algorithms namely, the MaxBIPS algorithm and Continuous Power Modes (CPM) algorithm have been implemented, based on non linear programming for discrete and continuous power modes.

2.10 Coordinated Power optimization

There is many multiple clock domain architectures have been implemented to improve the power problem by assigning different frequency/voltage values. A feedback control solution for accurate power management in multiprocessor systems is implemented [10]. It consist of two parts, a Global Power Manager (GPM) to correct the power of individual voltage/frequency islands at the first-level and Local Per-Island Controllers (LPIC) at the second-level, which normalize island power consumption using DVS in response to varying workload requirements.

2.11 Coordinating System Software for Power Savings

The motivation is to explore more opportunities for power optimization by coordinate components working at various levels to take full benefits provided by compiler and OS. The compiler and OS interact with an application at different stages, thus they have different knowledge about the application [11]. Taking the whole application as input, the classic compilers are highly informed with the structure of applications. It then evaluates the power consumption of applications and use power saving schedule algorithms for task scheduling.

2.12 On Line Optimization Based on Analog Computation

The solution to the problem of online optimization of the dissipated energy in multi-processing element systems with unified tasks under timing constraints using the basic principles of analog computation by converging on the global minima of the constrained optimization problem which are represented as stable operating points of a simple resistive network (RN). The input set of the circuit consists of individual workload estimates for each task and for each PE [12], while the output consists of assigned supply voltage/frequency values for each PE as well as the allocated time duration for each task.

2.13 Power Exploration for Parallel Applications

The impacts of the choice of several architectural parameters of CMPs on power/performance/ thermal metrics were discussed [13]. The experimental framework consists of a detailed micro architectural simulator, integrated with Watch and CACTI power models. This environment makes a fast and accurate exploration of the target design space possible. The main contribution is the analysis of several design energy/performance trade-offs when varying the core complexity, L2 cache size, and number of cores for parallel applications. In particular, the interdependence of energy/thermal efficiency, performance, and architectural-level chip floor plan is discussed.

2.14 Power Optimization/ Scheduling for Real Time Applications

The authors focus on design issues of a real-time power aware scheduler for a high-performance multicore processor [14] . This scheduler adapts the global frequency of the cores to the computation requirements of soft real-time tasks while improving power savings. The scheduler pursues to minimize the number of DVS transitions by increasing or decreasing the voltage and frequency of all the cores at the same time. The algorithm applies dynamic voltage and frequency scaling, and adjust the processor speed to the running soft real-time workload.

2.15 Power Optimization Scheduling

A fuzzy logic based approach to schedule the program to its optimum core by analyzing key program characteristics such as the instruction dependency distance, data reuse distance, and the branch transition rate with the built-in human intelligence in its rule system. The fuzzy logic method can measure the suitability of the hard-to-model program-core relationship and use that suitability to guide the program scheduling [15]. These characteristics determine the ILP, the data locality as well as the branch predictability of the applications, which largely define the applications overall resource demands.

2.16 Parallelization and Energy Consumption

An analytical framework to study the trade-offs between parallelization, program performance, and energy consumption was developed [16]. Although this framework is based on many simplifying assumptions, some of which are inherited from Amdahl's law and some of which are specific to variable-speed processors, it provides interesting insights on these trade-offs.

2.17 Removal-Cost Method: Voltage Selection Algorithm

A novel solution to the Voltage Selection Problem for large multi-core architectures is presented under the influence of within-die process, temperature, and voltage variations to show the superiority of the algorithm in speed as well as energy saving is considered[17]. Removal Cost method is an energy optimization technique that uses voltage island technique which is based on the variation in the voltage level is described. The algorithm maintains an ordered list of selected voltage levels and a voltage assignment procedure for each core

2.18 Energy Optimization Based on PVT Aware Voltage Island Formation

In a voltage-island-based design, an island is a contiguous physical part of the chip operating at the same voltage level and consists of one or more cores. Within-die (WID) process variation causes some of these cores to run slower than others within one island [18]. The purpose of voltage-islands is to supply different blocks of a design with a finite number of supply voltages to reduce the total consumed power.

2.19 Power Management Based on Supervised Learning

The motivation for utilizing supervised learning in the form of a Bayesian classifier is to reduce the overhead of the PM which has to repetitively determine and assign voltage-frequency settings for each processor core in the system [19]. This work describes a supervised learning based on DVFS for the multicore processor, which enables the PM to predict the performance state of the processor for each incoming task by inspecting some readily available input features, followed by a Bayesian classification technique.

2.20 Optimization Based on 3D Torus Network on Chip

3D IC technology drives Network-On-Chip (NoC) design on towards 3D trend and relevant multi-core system further development. However, most recent researches still focus on the fundamental 3D Mesh structure and have no convincible traffic pattern models in realistic applications. A complete design framework of a Distributed Shared Memory homogenous multi-core system based on 3D Torus interconnects is based on 3D Torus homogenous multi-core system [20]. The Gray code deadlock free routing mechanism and analyzes the effects of typical IP floor plan on NoC interconnected multi-core system.

3 Future Challenges

Modern hardware technologies increased the capability to reduce both dynamic and static power consumptions. However several mechanisms to save power at circuit level require an adequate software support to be effectively exploited. Indeed, to properly satisfy applications QoS demands is required to track system resources availability and usage which directly impact on energy consumptions. Moreover the need for support of heterogeneous usage scenarios makes the management of resources and power saving a challenging design goal. The CPM approach allows capturing energy savings while fulfilling Qos constraints. The same approach can be extended towards multi core architectures. As a next step it is planned to investigate the effect of system software such as task scheduling on the integrated power manager and interactions between them.

By manipulating several key parameters, an optimized power utilization algorithm can be produced by combining both frequency scaling in modem processors and processor affinity in current operating system process scheduler. Although processors technology has improved drastically with higher frequency and more cores in one processor package, the common workload does not really require such high performance. Most of the time, the processors are running at low load or idle. As such, power utilization can be minimized by lowering the processor frequency and distributing the load to all available processors. Most researchers have not considered performance factor, which is a very subjective and varies from individual to individual's experience. This could be considered in future works which may take into account of balancing between power utilization and performance.

Also increasing the memory power consumption is becoming a severe concern for modern high performance computing systems. In the available methods contemporary DRAM architectures and design choices with perspective of both power consumption and performance under multicore processor systems compared and evaluated. This can be extended for I/O power management to organize the memory subsystems and device configurations can have significant impact on power efficiency.

4 Summary of Power Optimization Techniques

This study mainly highlights the recent research work in the field of power optimization in multi core architectures. This paper primarily focuses about the proposed frame work for comparing various optimization techniques. The comparative study is based on the survey, which is made by analyzing the existing algorithms, considering the key characteristic factors as discussed below.

Sl. No	Detailed Work	System implementation/ Optimization technique/ Algorithm used	Parameters Involved	Optimization Rate	Disadvantages
1	Power Management Based on Supervised Learning	Power Management Framework	Bayesian Classifier	Better optimization	PM has to monitor the workload of a system and make decisions
2	Energy optimization for Many core Systems	RCM Algorithm	Process, Voltage and temperature variations	Better optimization	Splitting the voltage islands for different applications
3	On line Optimization based on Analog Computation	Analog Optimizer	Current based Approach (KCL)	Better online optimization	Settling time of the ghost circuit
4	Exploring Power Optimization	PM Algorithms (MAXBIPS and CPM algorithms)	Continuous Voltage and frequency ranges	Better optimization	Scheduling can be done to get a integrated power management
5	Parallelization and Energy Consumption	Frame work based on Machine models	Amdahl's Law	Greater optimization	Changing speed and turning off processors
6	Coordinated power optimization	Global Power Manger and Local per Island Controllers	Power control architecture using feedback control loop	Very high accuracy and max. overshoot in power consumption	Processor queue utilization
7	Optimized Cache Architecture	Filter Cache Architecture and Victim Architecture	Architecture based implementation	Reduces energy consumption	-
8	Coordinating System Software for Power Savings	DPM via Compiler Assisted I/O Prediction	OS based implementation	Significant power savings	-

5 Conclusion

Various techniques for ensuring power optimization in multicore architectures have been surveyed and investigated both at the higher level as well as the low levels. The literature shows the counter measures which have been proposed to overcome the hurdles in increasing the speed and efficiency of the core. Though some tangible results have been obtained in ensuring the performance enhancement in multicore, there is room for further improvement. Multicore processor architectures are built to adhere reasonable power consumption, heat dissipation, and cache coherence protocols. However, many issues remain unsolved. First, identification of an optimal trade-off between expected performances and reduced and reduced power consumptions. Secondly, to investigate the effect of system software such as task scheduling on integrated power manager and the interactions between them. There is a real need for active research and analysis on power optimization to keep the pace of tremendous changes in multicore architecture technology.

References

1. Wee, A.S.M., Tan, C.E., Lau, S.P.: Power optimization in multi-processor systems. In: International Symposium in Information Technology, ITSim, vol. 2, pp. 826–830 (2010)
2. Ahmad, I., Ranka, S., Khan, S.U.: Using Game Theory for Scheduling Tasks on Multi-Core Processors for Simultaneous Optimization of Performance and Energy. In: IEEE International Symposium Parallel and Distributed Processing, pp. 1–6 (2008)
3. Guo, D., Kuang, J., Bhuyan, L.: Power Optimization for Multimedia Transcoding on Multicore Servers. In: ACM/IEEE Symposium on Architectures for Networking and Communications Systems (ANCS), pp. 1–2 (2010)
4. King, C.-T., Lin, K.-H., Tseng, S.-Y., Wang, W.-S., Chang, S.-H.: Performance and Power Consumption Analysis of DVFS Enabled H264 Decoderon Heterogeneous Multi-Core Platform. In: International Conference on Computer and Information Technology (CIT), pp. 1758–1763 (2010)
5. Garrett, D.: A Multicore-Enabled Framework for the Construction of Metaheuristics for Single and Multiobjective Optimization, pp. 351–360. Springer, Heidelberg (2010)
6. Lee, D.-W., Jung, E., Lee, J.-G.: Asymptotic Performance Analysis and Optimization of Resource-Constrained Multi-Core Architectures. In: International Conference on Microelectronics, pp. 462–465 (2008)
7. Deshpande, J.L., Srinivasan, A., Ma, J.X.: Energy and Performance Impact of Aggressive Volunteer Computing with Multi-core Computers. In: IEEE International Symposium on Modeling, Analysis & Simulation of Computer and Telecommunication Systems, pp. 1–10 (2009)
8. Hong, C., Choi, H.J., Kim, J.-M., Park, Y.J.: Energy-aware Filter Cache Architecture for Multicore Processors. In: Fifth IEEE International Electronic Design, Test and Application, pp. 58–62 (2010)
9. Bergamaschi, R., Bose, P., Buyuktosunoglu, A., Dhanwada, N., Darringer, J., Dittmann, G., Han, G., IJanssen, G., Patel, H., Nair, Z.H.: Exploring Power Management in Multi-Core Systems. In: Asia and South Pacific Design Automation Conference, pp. 708–713 (2008)
10. Mishra, A.K., Das, C.R., Kandemir, M., Srikantaiah, S.: CPM in CMPs: Coordinated Power Management in Chip-Multiprocessors. In: International Conference for High Performance Computing, Networking, Storage and Analysis (SC), pp. 1–12 (2010)
11. Xiang, L., Huang, J., Chen, T.: Coordinating System Software for Power Savings. International Journal of Advanced Science and Technology 2, 222–225 (2008), International Conference on Future Generation Communication and Networking
12. Vittoz, E.A., IEEE, Leblebici, Y., IEEE, Deniz, Z.T., IEEE: On-Line Global Energy Optimization in Multi-Core Systems Using Principles of Analog Computation. IEEE Journal of Solid-State Circuits 42(7), 1593–1606 (2007)
13. Monchiero, M., Canal, R., González, A.: Power/Performance/Thermal Design-Space Exploration for Multicore Architectures. IEEE Transactions on Parallel and Distributed Systems 19(5) (2008)
14. Bautista, D., Duato, J., Sahuquillo, J., Hassan, H., Petit, S.: A Simple Power-Aware Scheduling for Multicore Systems when Running Real-Time Applications. In: IEEE International Symposium Parallel and Distributed Processing, pp. 1–7 (2008)
15. Chen, J., John, L.K.: Energy-Aware Application Scheduling on a Heterogeneous Multi-core System. In: IEEE International Symposium on Workload Characterization, pp. 5–13 (2008)

16. Cho, S., Melhem, R.G.: On the Interplay of Parallelization, Program Performance, and Energy Consumption. IEEE Transactions on Parallel and Distributed Systems 21(3), 342–353 (2010)
17. Majzoub, S., Saleh, R., Wilton, S.J.E., Ward, R.: Removal-Cost Method: An Efficient Voltage Selection Algorithm for Multi-Core Platforms under PVT. In: IEEE Conferences, pp. 357–360 (2009)
18. Majzoub, S.S., Saleh, R.A., Wilton, S.J.E., Ward, R.K.: Energy Optimization for Many-Core Platforms: Communication and PVT Aware Voltage-Island Formation and Voltage Selection Algorithm. IEEE Transactions on Computer-Aided Design of Integrated Circuits and Systems 29(5), 816–829 (2010)
19. Jung, H., Pedram, M.: Supervised Learning Based Power Management for Multicore Processors. IEEE Transactions on Computer-Aided Design of Integrated Circuits and Systems 29(9), 1395–1408 (2010)
20. Jiao, J., Wang, H., Liu, T., Han, X., Fu, Y.: Multi-core System based on 3D Torus Network on Chip. In: 8th IEEE International NEWCAS Conference (NEWCAS), pp. 313–316 (2010)
21. Blake, G., Dreslinski, R.G., Mudge, T.: A Survey of Multicore Processors. IEEE Signal Processing Magazine 26(6), 26–37 (2009)
22. Zheng, H., IEEE, Zhu, Z., IEEE: Power and Performance Trade-Offs in Contemporary DRAM System Designs for Multi core Processors. IEEE Transactions on Computers 59(8), 1033–1046 (2010), IEEE Journals

Optimization Techniques and Performance Evaluation of a Multithreaded Multi-core Architecture Using OpenMP

M. Rajasekhara Babu, P. Venkata Krishna, and M. Khalid

Intel Multi-Core Research Laboratory
School of Computing Science and Engineering,
VIT University, Vellore-14, TN, India
{mrajasekharababu,pvenkatakrishna,mkhalid}@vit.ac.in

Abstract. Optimization techniques are the crucial steps in parallelizing the programs for multi-core architectures. These Multi-Core architectures have become more popular due to improvement in performance, power concerns, thermal dissipations and more efficient simultaneous processing of multi tasks. There are wide variety of optimization techniques, but there is no history notify about the order in which these techniques to be applied for a program to obtain maximum performance. This paper mainly focuses on analysis of various program optimization techniques for multi-Core architectures. Finally this paper shows how the sequential code can be parallelized using OpenMP programming environment and will be explaining the interest findings with V-Tune analyzer.

Keywords: Multi-Core, Optimization Techniques, Compilers, Parallelism.

1 Introduction

Increasing number of cores on multi-core architectures provide a solution to increase the performance capability on a single chip without requiring a complex system and increasing the power requirements. As the momentum behind the chip multiprocessor (CMP) [5.7] architectures continues to grow, it is expected that future microprocessors will have several cores sharing the on-die and off-die resources. The success of CMP platforms depends not only on the number of cores but also heavily on the platform resources (cache [5], memory [2], etc) available and their efficient usage. Program optimization is an important feature in software development. This paper covers various issues such as optimization techniques which touches the program development at different stages. The program development includes the main algorithm definition, the general design of the program, and detailed design of each implemented function. These optimizations techniques can be implemented in parallel in several ways, one of that is OpenMP; it has established itself as an important method and language extension for programming shared memory [2] parallel computers. It contains the set of compiler directives, runtime library routines and environment variables, is the de-facto programming standard for parallel programming C/C++ on multi-core [6] architectures. Threads and processes are used to determine the performance efficiency of the model like OpenMP. V-Tune is the tool for this evaluation of performance.

A. Abraham et al. (Eds.): ACC 2011, Part I, CCIS 190, pp. 182–191, 2011.

1.1 Multi-core

Computer Architecture tells about the conceptual design and operation structure of the computer system. That means it refers to those attributes of a system that have direct impact on the logical execution of program. The processor industry has made giant strides in terms of speed and performance. The first microprocessor, Intel 4004, ran at 784 KHz while the microprocessors of today run easily in the GHz range due to significantly smaller and faster transistors. The increase in performance has been historically consistent with moore's law [7,8] that states that the number of transistors on the processor die keeps doubling every eighteen months due to the transistors getting smaller every successive process technology.

1.2 OPENMP

The OpenMP [3] (open multi-processing) is an application program interface that supports multi-platform shared memory multiprocessing [3] programming in C or C++ on much architecture, including UNIX and windows operating systems. It consists of set of compiler directives, library routines, and environment variables that influence run-time behavior. OpenMP is an implementation of multithreading [1,2], a method of parallelization whereby the master "thread" divided as specified number of slave "threads" and a task is divided among them. OpenMP uses the fork-join model [2] of parallel execution. This fork-join model used to solve the many problems. OpenMP is specified for support programs that will execute both as parallel programs and as sequential programs

2 Over View of The System

Functionality: Fig. 1. & Fig. 2. representing the functionality of the program optimization implementation. This paper focuses mainly on four modules: Code generation module, parallelization module, analysis module and statistical module.

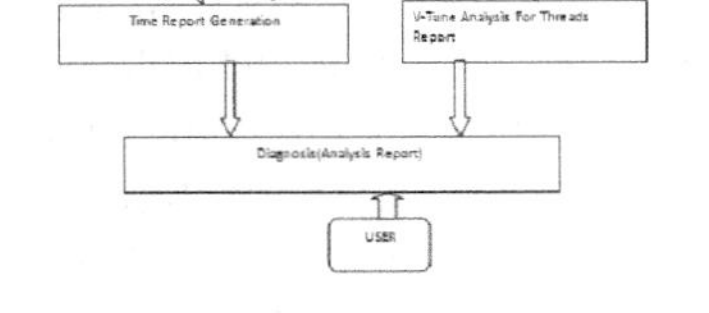

Fig. 1. Expanded System design forl parallel implementaion

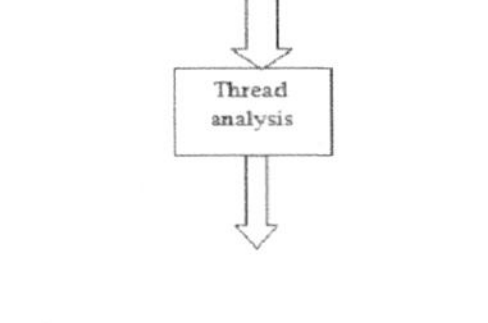

Fig. 2. Abstract view of parallel implementation design

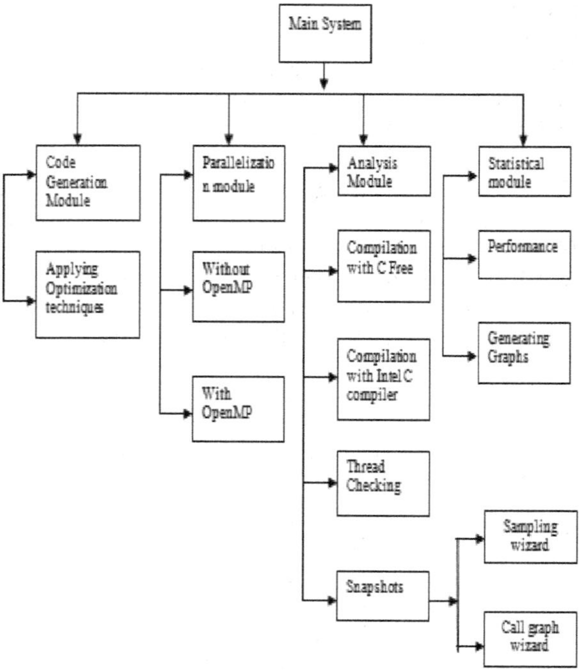

Fig. 3. Statistical module DFD diagram

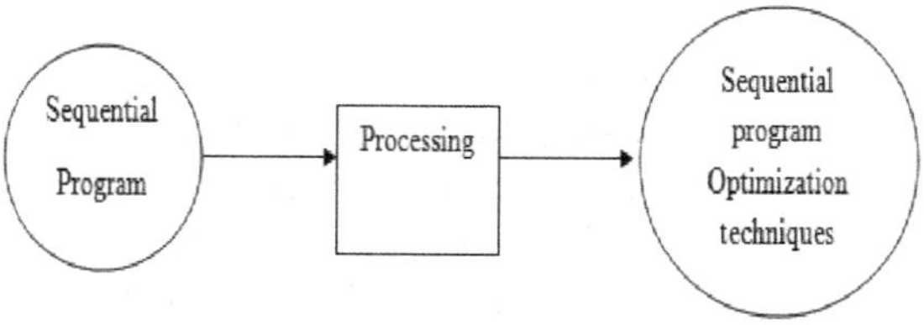

Fig. 4. DFD for Code generation

Code Generation Module: In fig 4., Application of optimization techniques is the prime function of this module. This module analyzes code and applies the various optimizations to reduce the execution time. Input is Sequential code, and Output is optimized sequential code The Fig. 6. is representing the parallelization module. The function of parallel module is to parallelize the code as per the analysis of optimization techniques output. This module parallelizes the code using OpenMP. OpenMP is an API (application program interface) used to explicitly direct multi-threaded, shared memory parallelism. With the advent of Multi-core processors, there has been renewed interest in parallelizing programs. After generating the code with optimization should parallelize the code. This parallelization can be done with using the OpenMP thread library. The OpenMP (open multi-processing) is an application program interface that supports multi-platform shared memory multiprocessing programming in C or C++ on much architecture. OpenMP consists of a set of compiler #pragmas that control how the program works. Input: Sequential Code with Optimization techniques, Output: Parallel code with set of pragmas The DFD of the Parallelization Module.

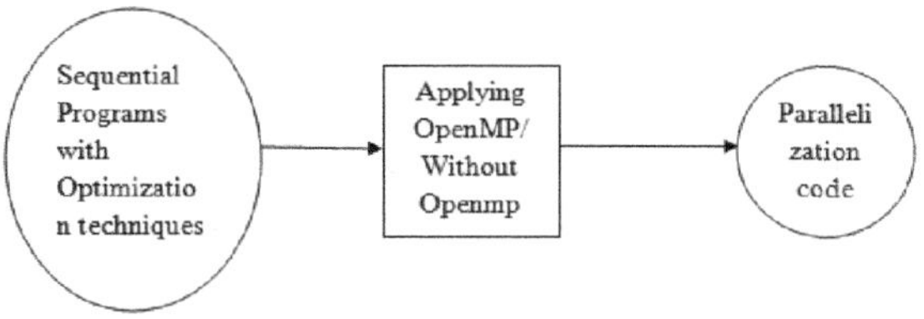

Fig. 5. DFD for Parallel Module

Analysis Module: The Intel V-Tune Performance Analyzer is a performance analysis tool that utilizes hardware interrupts to give the developer a true picture of how an application is performing. Available on Microsoft Windows* and various flavors of Linux*, this is a great tool for focusing in on the performance-intensive sections of an application. There are two technologies in this tool that are useful when analyzing code for threading opportunities: sampling and call graph. Input: OpenMP Program, Output: Call graphs and sampling graphs.

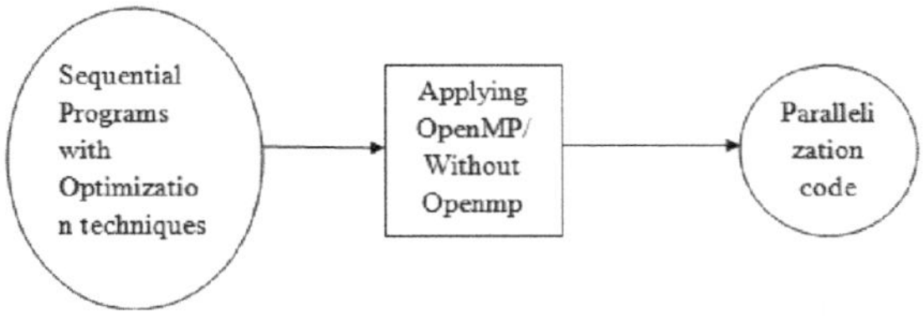

Fig. 6. DFD for Analysis Module

```
#pragma omp parallel
{
   for(i=0;i<=k;i++)
   {
      a[i]=1;
      a[i]+a[i]=a[k];
   }
} /* End of Parallel
region */
for(k=0;k<1000;k++)
{
    #pragma omp parallel
   {
       for(j=0;j<=k;j++)
       {
          b[j]=2;
       }
   }  /* End of  Parallel
region */
```

Statistical Module: In this module the outputs of the programs which run in the single-core and dual-core system as the execution time will taken as a input and generating the respective graphs for each optimization technique is done.

Analysis Module: The Intel V-Tune Performance Analyzer is a performance analysis tool that utilizes hardware interrupts to give the developer a true picture of how an application is performing. Available on Microsoft Windows* and various flavors of Linux*, this is a great tool for focusing in on the performance-intensive sections of an application. There are two technologies in this tool that are useful when analyzing code for threading opportunities: sampling and call graph. Input: OpenMP Program, Output: Call graphs and sampling graphs.

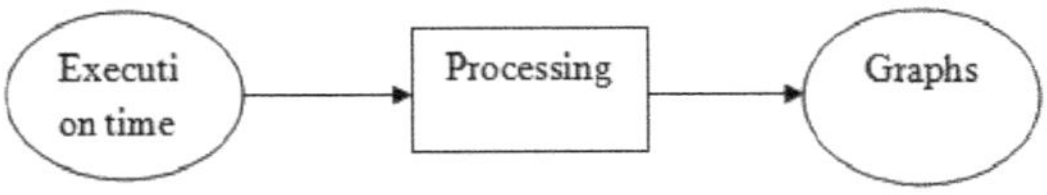

Fig. 7. DFD for Statistical Module

3 Implementation and Testing

Above said four modules implemented. In Code generation module, the code generated on basis of optimization techniques. That means the code consists the blocks like before applying the technique and after applying technique. Total twenty optimization techniques are used to develop code. Each one will give the output execution time before technique and time after technique. Execution of these programs is done in single-core and multi-core. Following pseudo code-1 is from the branch optimization technique. Algorithm starts with function call which is not in the pseudo code. After that it spawns a parallel region (line 1) then one of the threads takes a position for execution of remaining (line 3. 7) part. After completing the for loop execution parallel region will end (line 8). For loop will starts for thousand iterations for each iteration it spawns a parallel region (line 11). Next remaining execution will be done. 2. Parallelization module: OpenMP is an API (application program interface) used to explicitly direct multi-threaded, shared memory parallelism. With the advent of Multi-core processors, there has been renewed interest in parallelizing programs. OpenMP directives are used to extract the multi-level parallelism. Outer loop can be parallelized between processors and inner loop is parallelized for processing the elements inside each processor.

```
#pragma omp parallel
shared(a,b,c,nthreads,chunk)
private(tid,i,j,k)
{
tid = omp_get_thread_num();
if (tid == 0)
{
nthreads =
omp_get_num_threads();
printf("Starting matrix
multiple example with %d
threads\n",nthreads);
printf("Initializing
matrices...\n");
}
/*** Initialize matrices ***/
#pragma omp for schedule
(static, chunk)
for (i=0; i<NRA; i++)
for (j=0; j<NCA; j++)
a[i][j]= i+j;
#pragma omp for schedule
(static, chunk)
for (i=0; i<NCA; i++)
for (j=0; j<NCB; j++)
b[i][j]= i*j;
#pragma omp for schedule
(static, chunk)
for (i=0; i<NRA; i++)
for (j=0; j<NCB; j++)
c[i][j]= 0;
printf("Thread %d starting
matrix multiply...\n",tid);
#pragma omp for schedule
(static, chunk)
for (i=0; i<NRA; i++)
{
printf("Thread=%d did
```

The pseudo code is about matrix multiplication program with OpenMP pragmas. This will start with spawning a parallel region (line 1). Next the variable tid will has a thread number which is defined by the function omp_get_thread_num(), if the thread number is zero then number threads will be create. Matrix initialization can be done with maximum number of threads created in the parallel region. This can two for all matrices initialization. The Analysis module can be implemented in the Microsoft visual studio 2005 using Intel C++ compiler for OpenMP and V-Tune analyzer. This module takes OpenMP programs as input and gives the thread analysis as output. OpenMP programs have OpenMP directives. Number of threads created in the program and how the threads are worked in the execution of the program will generated by the V-Tune analyzer. The working this module can be showed by following snapshots. These can be helpful for working with visual studio. Statistical module: In this module taking execution time of optimization techniques without OpenMP and with OpenMP in dual-core plotting the graphs. In single core execution time is taken as before applying the optimization techniques and after applying the techniques.

4 Results and Discussion

The performance of each optimization technique has been observed by taking the execution time. In the later phase , Parallelize the program using OpenMP application program interface. Subsequently, creating the threads externally and analyzing the threads by using the V-Tune thread checker. Then Obtain the graph analysis of threads with call graph wizard in V-Tune thread analyzer, and finally Performance of the optimization technique with and without using the optimization technique observed and drawn conclusions.

The results and analysis can be shown in following manner. 1. Execution of Optimization techniques in single-core, 2.Execution of Optimization techniques with and without OpenMP in dual-core, 3. Generating graphs for execution time in single-core, 4. Generating graphs for execution time with and without OpenMP in dual-core. Few of optimization are disused in this section.

Loop fission optimization technique: Loop fission optimization technique tells about splitting the loop into two loops according to the induction variables. If the inner loop is depend on the outer loop induction variable then we cannot spit the loop. That means if there is no data dependency we can apply the technique. Execution time has taken before splitting the loops and after splitting the loops. Execution time takes for thousand iterations. Write the output into a file for plotting graphs.

Loop fusion optimization technique: This technique defines that merging the two loops into a single loop when one loop is not depend on the other. That means if there is no data dependency we can merge and split the loops. Execution time takes for thousand iterations.

Expression simplification optimization technique: This technique can used when some expression are there which are replaced with an equivalent expression that is more efficient. Execution of Optimization techniques with and without using OpenMP has been observed. 1. Expression simplification optimization technique: This technique can used when some expression are there which are replaced with an equivalent expression that is more efficient. Here execution time has taken for one lack iterations. 2. Function in lining optimization technique: The overhead associated with calling and returning from a function can be eliminated by expanding the body of the function inline, and additional opportunities for optimization may be exposed as well.

Instruction combining: This technique can be done at two levels. At source code level combining two statements into one statement. At Intermediate language level, combine two instructions into one instruction.

Graphs For Execution Time In Single-Core

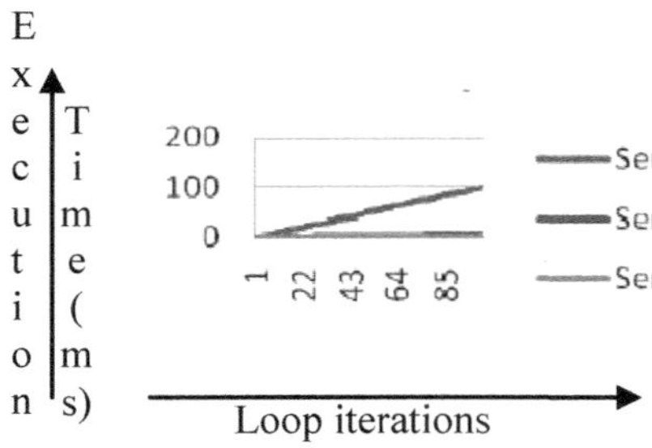

Fig. 8. Branch Optimizaton Technique

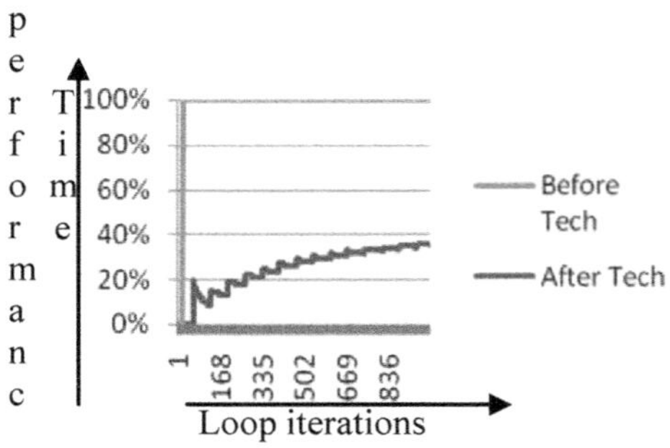

Fig. 9. Alias by type optimization technique

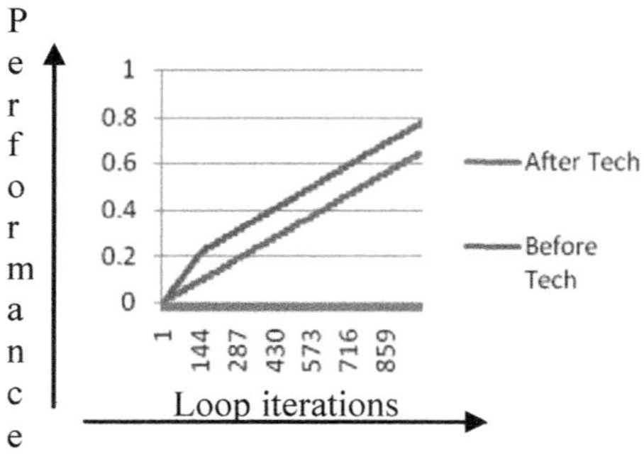

Fig. 10. Alias by address technique

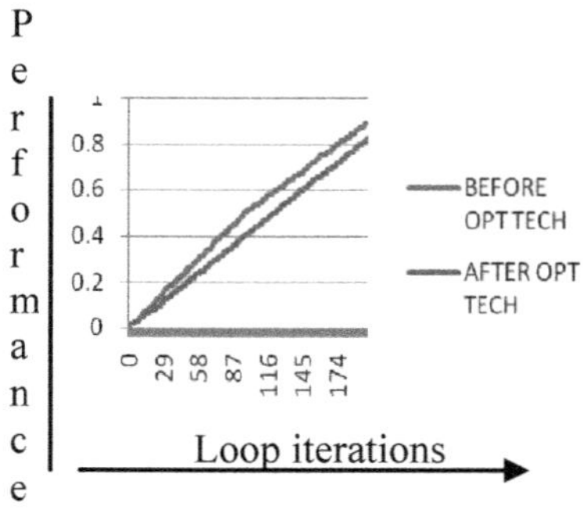

Fig. 11. Common sub expression elimination

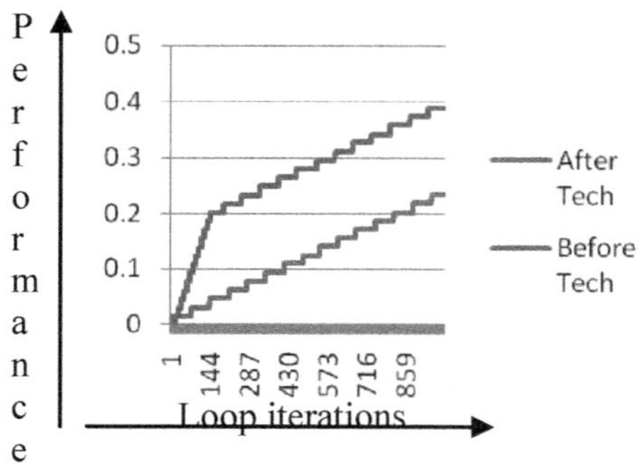

Fig. 12. Constant propagation technique

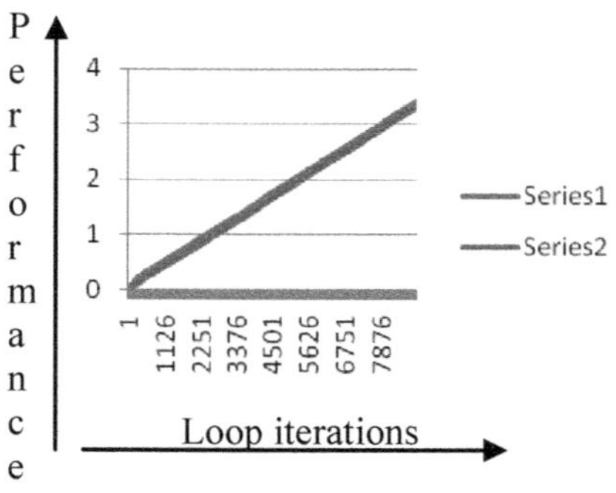

Fig. 13. Dead code elimination

Fig. 8. Presents the Execution time before applying technique it reaches 100% and it is constant. After applying it slightly changing. Fig. 9. explains Execution time of this technique is varying upto 144th iteration after that it is parallel changing. Fig. 10. Describing Execution time of this technique is continuously 0 after applying technique. Fig. 11. Dealing Execution time of this technique is varying upto 130th iteration after that it is parallel changing. Fig. 12. Tells Execution time of this technique is not varying upto 28th iteration after that varying is very low. Fig. 13. presents Execution time of this technique is varying upto 128th iteration after that parallel changing.

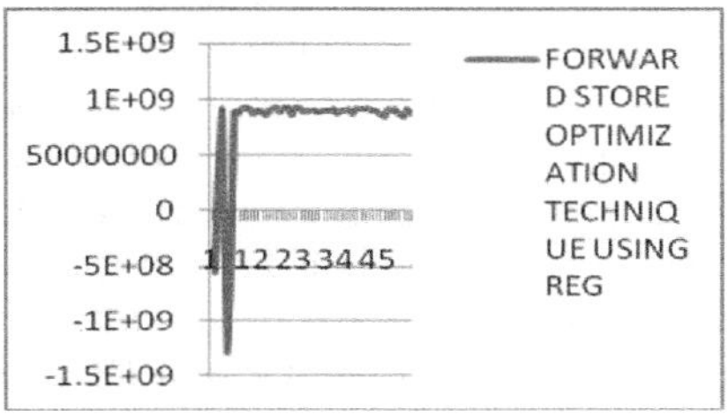

Fig. 14. Forward optimization technique

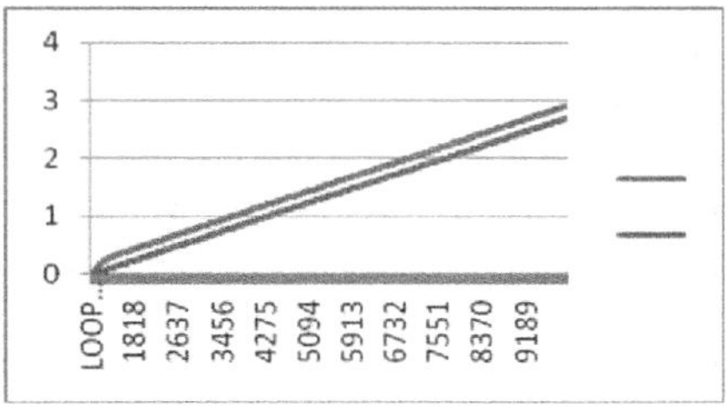

Fig. 15. Induction variable elimination

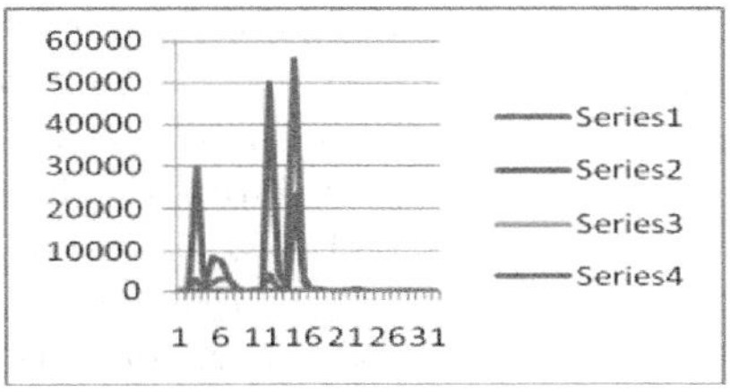

Fig. 16. Function in lining technique

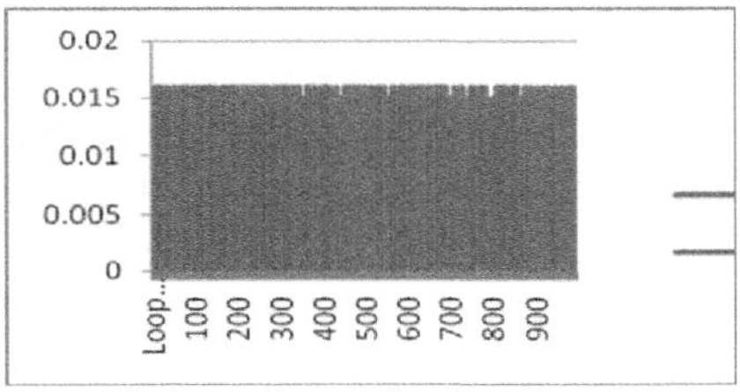

Fig. 17. Induction variable elimination

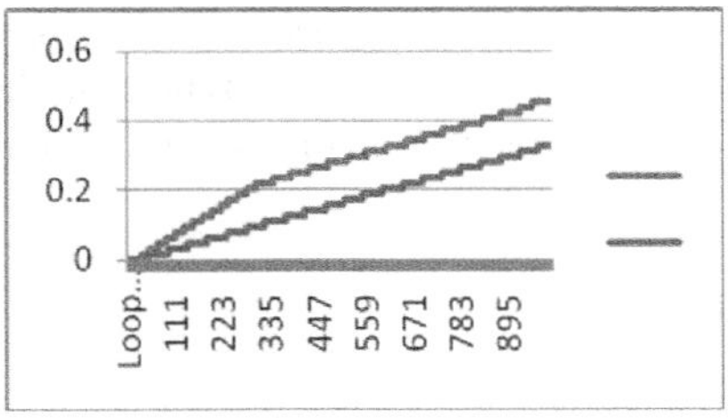

Fig. 18. Loop collapsing technique

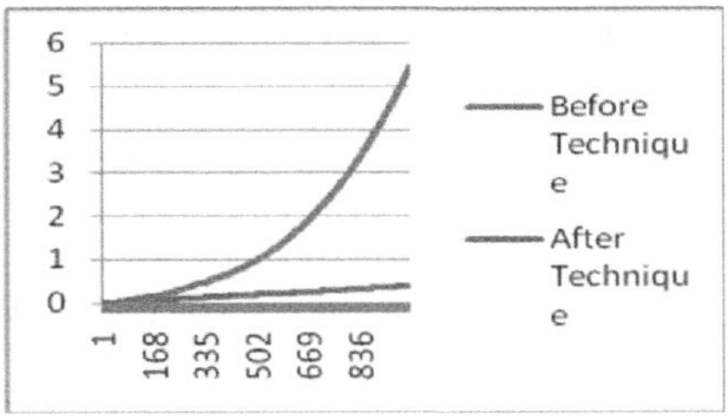

Fig. 19. Loop fission technique

Fig. 14. Presents the Execution time of this technique is slightly varying, Fig. 15. Shows the Execution time of this technique giving negatives upto 10 iterations after that positive values. Fig. 16. Shows Execution time of this technique changing disorderly, Fig. 17. Describes Execution time of this technique changing in parallel.

Fig. 18. Shows the difference between before and after applying technique for some values time is giving 0, but before applying it is reaching 100%, Fig. 19. Shows the before and after applying technique, it is increasing continuously, but before applying it is changes up 300th iteration is in not in continuously. Fig. 20. Before applying technique it is exponential changes, after applying it is slightly changing.

Graphs on Execution Time with and without Openmp in Dual-Core

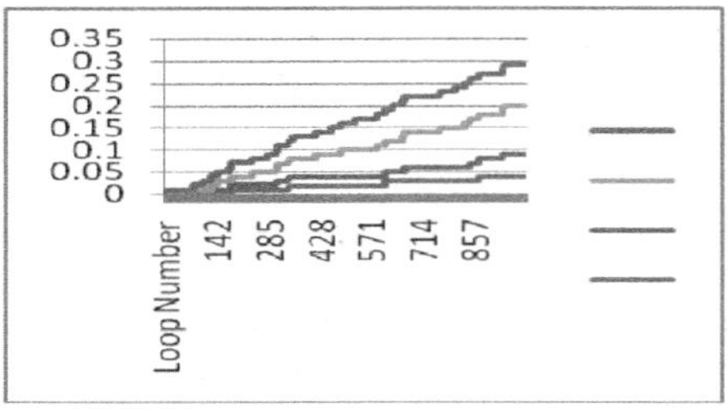

Fig. 20. Branch optimization technique

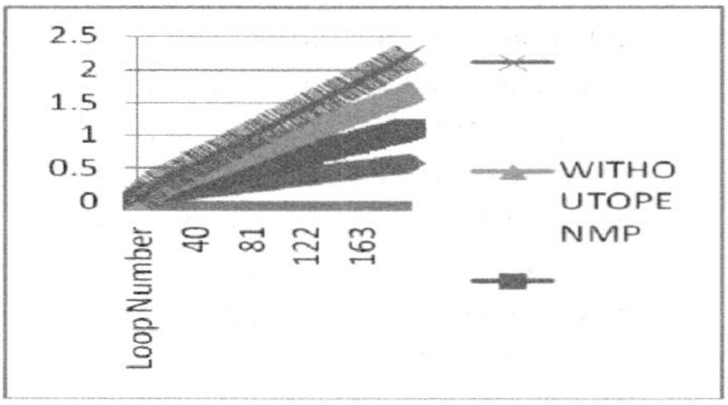

Fig. 21. Constant propagation technique

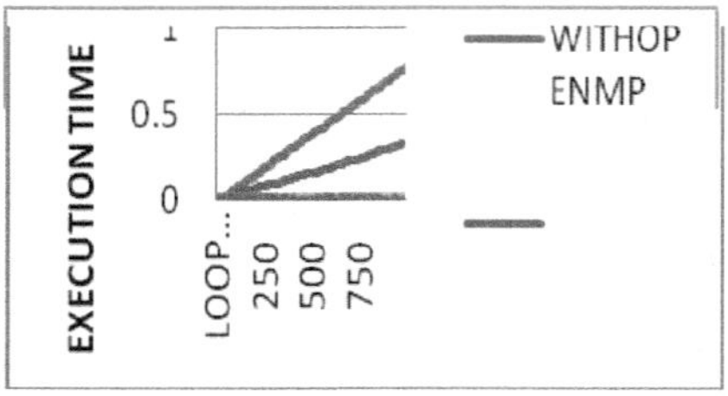

Fig. 22. Instruction combining

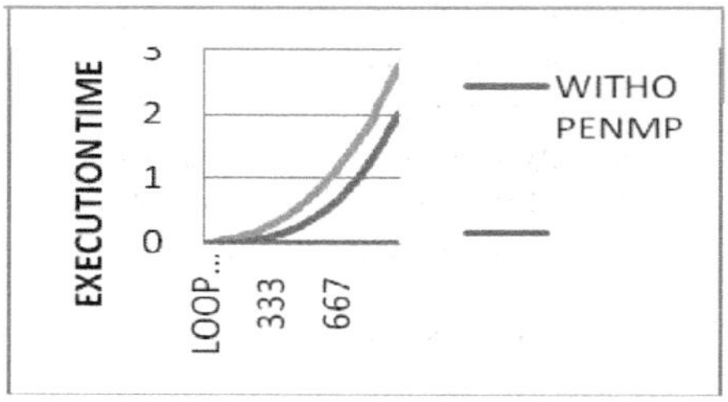

Fig. 23. Loop fission technique

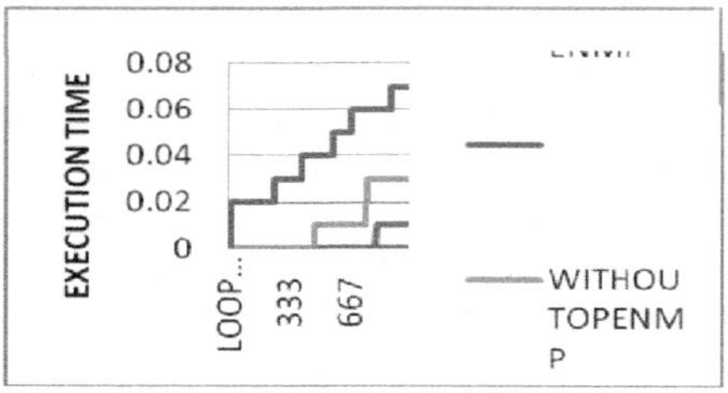

Fig. 24. Instruction combining

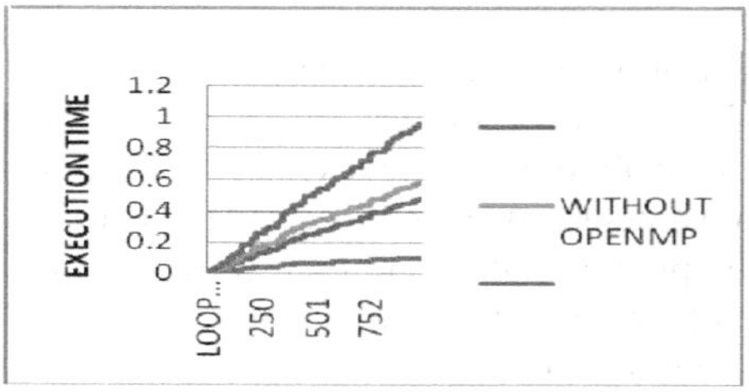

Fig. 25. Instruction combining

Fig. 21. Changing time at 250th iteration before applying technique. Fig. 22. Time changes disorderly before applying and after applying the OpenMP, Fig. 23.Time change is in order before applying and after applying g OpenMP, Fig. 24. Upto 863 iterations time is not changing, but after 863 before applying OpenMp is increased, Fig. 25. Before applying OpenMP time is changing, but after applying OpenMp time is 0, changing in the time is equal after applying and before applying OpenMP, after applying tech and OpenMP Execution time is 0.

These screen shots will represent the thread analysis in the V-Tune analyzer. These thread analysis are two types one is in sampling wizard and another in call graph wizard Expression simplification technique: Call graph wizard: Snapshot 15. Thread analysis report of Expression In the execution of this program in V-Tune it is creating two threads, and the two threads are running in parallel, further dividing into small threads for processing Function inlining optimization technique Call graph wizard:

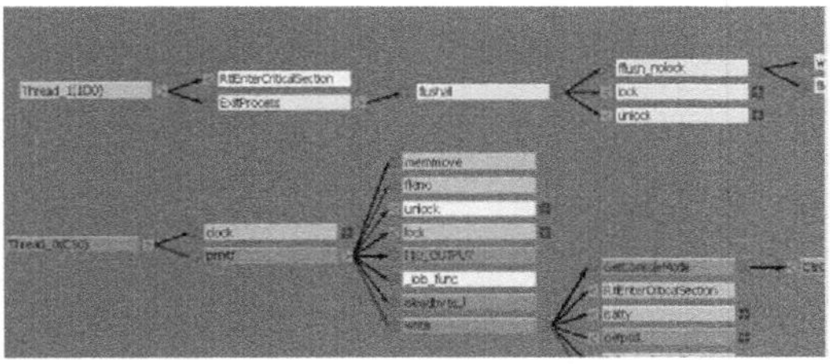

Fig. 26. Call graph for thread analysis

6 Conclusion and Future Work

Various program optimization techniques have been analyzed for the single core as well as multicore. The Applications of OpenMP for the Dual-core architectures has been studied. This report generated the graphical analysis outputs for execution time and Studied about how the optimization techniques can give the better performance than a sequential program without applying the techniques with techniques. Finally, the behavior and functionality of threads have been examined to achieve parallelism in Dual Core Environment. The performance of the each optimization technique has analyzed by drawing graphs.

References

[1] Adhianto, L., Chapman, B.: Performance modeling of communication and computation in hybrid MPI and OpenMP applications. In: Simulation Modeling Practice and Theory, pp. 481–491 (2007)

[2] Basumallik, A., Min, S.j., Eigenmann, R.: Programming Distributed Memory systems using OpenMP. IEEE Computer (2007)

[3] Brown, J.A., Kumar, R., Tullsan, D.: Proximity- Aware directory based coherence for Multi-core architectures. ACM Computer (2007)

[4] Schirrmeister, F.: Multi-core processors: Fundamentals, trends and challenges. In: Embedded System Conference (2007)

[5] Domeika, M.: Development and Optimization Techniques for Multi-core Processors, intel corp.Embedded.com (September 2006)

[6] Packirisamy, V., Barathvajasankar, H.: OpenMP in Multi-core Architectures (2005)

[7] Psarris, K.: Program analysis techniques for transforming programs for parallel execution (2002)

[8] Magee, G.I.: Code optimization techniques, Northwestern University (August 10, 2000)

[9] User manual of OpenMP API C and C++ interface specification version 2.5, `http://www.openmp.org/`

[10] Intel C++ compiler installation manual and user manuals, `http://www.intel.com/downloads/compilers/`

Review on VLSI Architectures for Optical OFDM Receivers

Magesh Kannan Parthasarathy[1], Karthik Govindarajan[2], G. Gunaraj[2], and S. Lakshmi Prabha[2]

[1] VLSI Division, School of Electronics Engineering (SENSE), VIT University, Vellore, Tamilnadu, India
mageshkannan.p@vit.ac.in

[2] Students, M.Tech VLSI Design, School of Electronics Engineering (SENSE), VIT University, Vellore, Tamilnadu, India
karthik4cynosure@yahoo.com

Abstract. Orthogonal Frequency Division Multiplexing (OFDM) is one of the most recent modulation techniques that enable us to reach higher data rates, both in wired and wireless communication systems. Recently, it has proved more efficient in optical networks. This paper gives a comparison review of existing OFDM receiver architectures and their modes of operation. Also, most of the OFDM systems used Fourier transform for modulation and demodulation. The performance of Fourier Transform algorithm with other algorithm (Hartley Transform) will be explored. This detailed review and performance analysis of various receiver architectures will provide guidelines for an individual to design an OFDM receiver and the important parameters to be considered.

Keywords: Modulation, Optical communication, Orthogonal Frequency Division Multiplexing (OFDM), Wireless Communication.

1 Introduction

Orthogonal frequency division multiplexing is one of the recent modulation technique used in broadband wired and wireless methods of data transmission which uses the principle of multi carrier technique. It enables better resistance to inter-symbol interference (ISI) and inter-carrier interference (ICI) caused by channel dispersion. One major advantage of OFDM is that it transits the analog domain of transmitters and receivers to digital domain [1]. The principle of OFDM is quite simple. Data is transmitted in parallel on a number of different frequencies, and as a result, the symbol period is much longer than for a serial system with the same total data rate. Because the symbol period is longer, ISI affects at most one symbol, and equalization is simplified. In most OFDM implementations any residual ISI is removed by using a form of guard interval called cyclic prefix.

OFDM does have certain disadvantages. High Peak-to-Average Power Ratio (PAPR) has been recognized as one of the major practical problem which results from the type of the modulation itself where multiple subcarriers/sinusoids are added

A. Abraham et al. (Eds.): ACC 2011, Part I, CCIS 190, pp. 192–203, 2011.

together to form the signal to be transmitted. High PAPR signals are usually undesirable for it usually strains the analog circuitry. It's been noticed that in OFDM systems, some input sequences would result in higher PAPR than other set of inputs. Another problem is the frequency offset which arises due to difference in synchronization of data. This leads to a problem when we receive data in receiver blocks. Phase noise, too is another problem. Since oscillators are used, these suffer from random perturbations of phase of the steady sine wave which arises to phase noise. Also OFDM does not map easily onto an optical carrier and directly modulating a laser with OFDM requires a large bias.

OFDM is in fact, very different from Frequency Division Multiplexing (FDM) or Wave Length Division Multiplexing (WDM) as shown in Fig. 1. In this OFDM, the subcarrier frequencies are chosen so that the signals are mathematically orthogonal over one symbol period. The process of modulation and multiplexing is achieved by using Inverse Fourier Transform (IFFT), thus generating orthogonal signals precisely and demodulation and demultiplexing is done by Fast Fourier Transform (FFT) at the receiver. The spectrum of an individual OFDM subcarrier is $|\sin x/x|^2$ where each OFDM subcarrier has significant side lobes over a frequency range which includes many other subcarriers [1] leading to high sensitivity to phase noise and frequency offset.

A wide variety of OFDM systems have been proposed for different applications. So, it is essential to know the fundamentals of each block of the OFDM system. This paper explores overall view of various blocks used in the receiver system and also the various receiver system architecture proposed. In this survey paper, the basics of OFDM are first explained and the comparison of typical OFDM and Optical OFDM is done and different types of it are explained in the first section. In the next section, the building blocks of the receiver system is explained. Also various receiver system architecture proposed are surveyed and a brief tutorial of these ideas are given. In the third section, the receiver architectures are compared based on their data rate speed. Also, comparison of FFT and Fast Hartley transform is also made. The last section concludes the paper, thus giving a raw idea of how to choose the Optical OFDM receiver architecture.

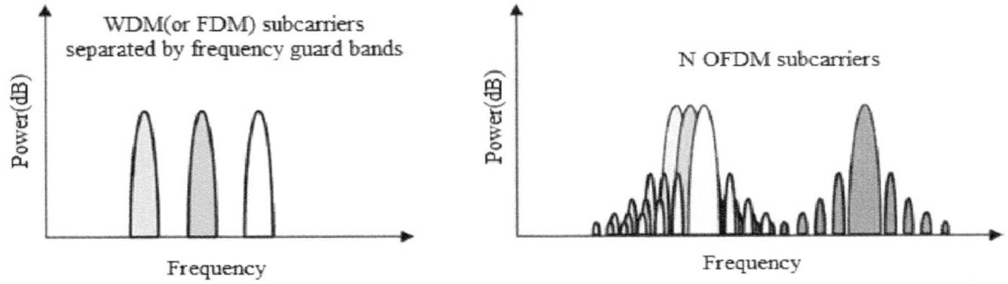

Fig. 1. Spectrum of 1) FDM or WDM signals and 2) OFDM signal

2 Optical OFDM versus Typical OFDM Systems

Despite the many advantages of OFDM, and its widespread use in wireless communications, OFDM has only recently been applied to optical communications

[1]. This is partly because of the recent demand for increased data rates across dispersive optical media and partly because developments in digital signal processing (DSP) technology make processing at optical data rates feasible. However another important obstacle has been the fundamental differences between conventional OFDM systems and conventional optical systems as shown in Table 1.

Table 1. Comparison between Typical and Optical OFDM systems

Typical OFDM System	Bipolar	Electrical domain	Local oscillator at receiver	Coherant detection
Optical OFDM system	Unipolar	Optical domain	No local oscillator at receiver	Direct detection

Optical OFDM solutions can be broadly divided into two groups [1]. The first group comprises techniques for systems where many different optical modes are received, for example, optical wireless, multimode fiber systems and plastic optical fiber systems. The second group includes techniques for single mode fiber, where only one mode of the signal is received and for these the OFDM signal should be represented by the optical field.

Optical OFDM modulation is done by two ways. One is done by intensity modulation and other by linear modulation. Two types of intensity modulations are dc-biased optical OFDM (DCO-OFDM) [3], [4] and asymmetrically clipped OFDM (ACO-OFDM) [5], [6]. In dc-biased OFDM, a DC bias is added to the signal, however because of the large peak-to-average power ratio of OFDM, even with a large bias some negative peaks of the signal will be clipped and the resulting distortion limits performance [6]. In ACO-OFDM the bipolar OFDM signal is clipped at the zero level and all negative going signals are removed. The use of DCO-OFDM has been demonstrated experimentally for optical wireless [8], multimode fiber [9] and plastic optical fiber [10].

Two types of linear modulations are direct-detection optical OFDM (DD-OOFDM) [11] or coherent detection can be used where the received signal is mixed with a locally generated carrier signal as in coherent optical OFDM (CO-OFDM) [12].Both techniques have advantages. DD-OOFDM has a simple receiver, but some optical frequencies must be unused if not to cause interference. DD-OOFDM also requires more transmitted optical power. CO-OFDM requires a laser at the receiver to generate the carrier locally, and is more sensitive to phase noise [13], [14].

Another approach for optical communication is by Multiple Input Multiple Output (MIMO) system. The term “MIMO” is used to describe a range of systems with multiple transmits and/or receives antennas [1]. The usage of MIMO system enhances the system information capacity and high data rate [15] [16] [17] [18].

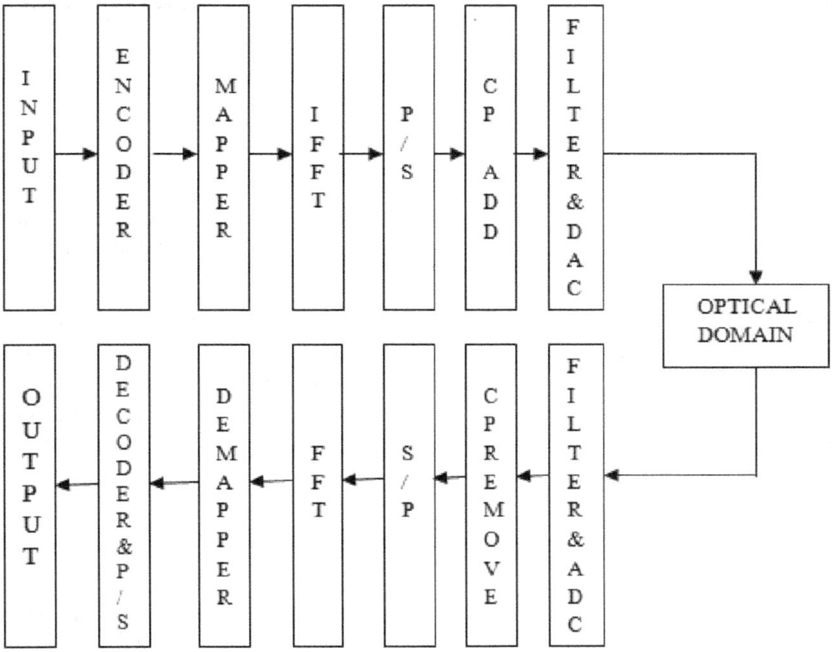

Fig. 2. Optical OFDM system

Now coming on to the working of OFDM system, it consists of transmitter and receiver. As this paper emphasizes mainly on receiver part, only the detailed description about the receiver is explained. One such Optical OFDM system is shown in Fig. 2. The working of the receiver system is explained as follows. The receiver performs the reverse operations of the transmitter, with additional training tasks. In the first step, the receiver has to estimate frequency offset and timing so that the transmitted and received data are synchronized. The cyclic prefix added in the transmitter, is removed, converted from serial to parallel and then applied to a Fast Fourier Transform to recover the modulated values of all subcarriers. The modulated values are then demapped into binary values, decoded to get the information bits and finally converted to serial data stream. The sub carriers used in OFDM are modulated individually by Phase Shift Keying (PSK) or Quadrature Amplitude Modulation (QAM). In order to know the functionality of the receiver, it is necessary to know more about the blocks of the receiver, explained in detail as follows.

2.1 FFT

FFT block is the heart of the OFDM receiver. Now the question arises that why Discrete Fourier Transform (DFT) is not being used. The FFT algorithm is much faster and efficient than DFT in many ways. Secondly, the DFT needs N^2 operations while FFT needs N log N operations. As data rates increases, DFT becomes slower as shown by Table 1. Also, the inputs and outputs of FFT have the same average power and total energy. The well known FFT formula according is given by

$$Y_k = {}^{1}/_{\sqrt{N}} \sum_{m=0}^{N-1} y_m \, exp\left(\frac{-j2\pi km}{N}\right) \; for\; 0 \le k \le N-1$$

Where, y= [$y_0 y_1$ y_2 y_3...] is the vector showing the sampled time domain signal, given as input to the FFT. Y= [$Y_0 Y_1 Y_2 Y_3$...] is the output of FFT block, in frequency domain. As the data transmission rate of OFDM systems increases, OFDM symbols are generated with high data rate which arises the need of very high speed FFT processor.

In general, there are two approaches in implementing the FFT for OFDM, including the pipelining and memory based recursive processing. Pipelining deals with the data throughput in real-time, while it consists of log r N stages (radix-r) and each stage has one butterfly computation unit, one commutator shift register and one complex twiddle multiplier. The pipelining leads to much more silicon area. The memory-based FFT can save much area than the pipelined FFT, but it needs higher clock rates for iteration on each butterfly calculation [2].

Table 2. Comparison of DFT and FFT

OPERATION	DFT	FFT
COMPLEX MULTIPLICATIONS	N^2	$N/2(\log_2 N-1)$
COMPLEX ADDITIONS	N(N-1)	$N(\log_2 N)$
REAL MULTIPLICATIONS	$4N^2$	$2N(\log_2 N-1)$
REAL ADDITIONS	N(4N-2)	$2N(\log_2 N)$

A number of ideas for FFT calculation have been proposed. One of the ideas given uses the pipelining concept [3]. It should be noted that only the FFT process is taken into account irrespective of whether the system is MIMO or not. The proposed highly pipelined double data rate FFT/IFFT processor is depicted in Fig. 3. It consists of butterfly unit, the control unit (CU), the complex multiplier and the First-In First-Out (FIFO) registers. The number of FIFO registers depends on the algorithm followed by the FFT process. For example of the radix-2 64-point FFT/IFFT, the first stage of the 64-point FFT/IFFT structure is constructed by 32 FIFO registers. The other five stages require 16, 8, 4, 2, and 1 registers, respectively. The inputs Xin and Pin follow a interlacing way of sharing the FIFO [19].

The Butterfly unit has two adders and two multipliers for complex multiplication. According to the radix-2 algorithm, the butterfly unit needs 2 input data in N/2 clock intervals, where N is the point number of the FFT/IFFT processor. This shows that the butterfly unit works at the second half input signals, so the butterfly unit can be shared by the two input sequences to enhance the hardware efficiency [19]. The control unit enables to switch to FFT and/or IFFT operation. This tells us that FFT can be performed to one input while IFFT can be performed to another input. The control unit is regulated by Ctrl-Reg, a 5 bit counter.

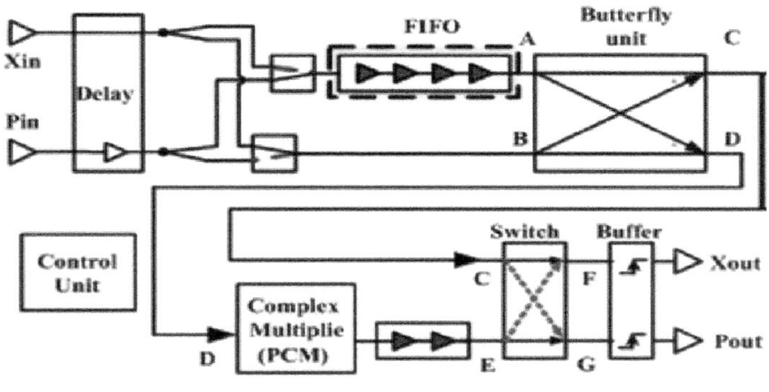

Fig. 3. Dual Input FFT/IFFT Processor

The Pipelined complex multiplication performs the multiplication process for FFT/IFFT. As said earlier, FFT is the heart of receiver. So, pipelined multiplication is done to raise the clock rate [19]. The processor has an area of $0.66mm^2$ and a power dissipation of 97mW at 200MHz. Also the dual FFT/IFFT reduces the hardware complexity.

When MIMO systems is used, pipelined FFT operations can be used [20]. The system consists of four modules as shown in Fig. 4.

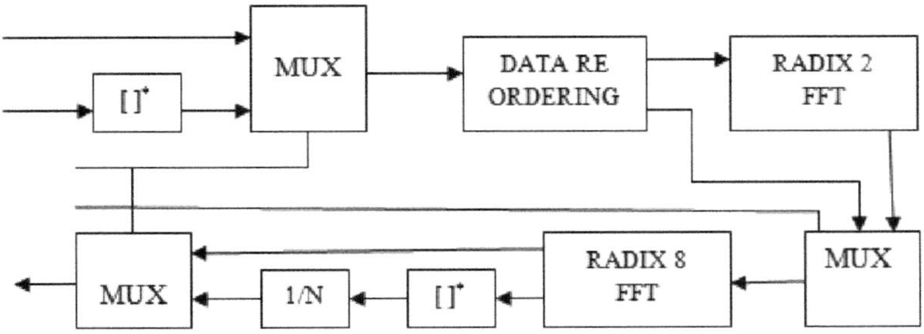

Fig. 4. Block Diagram of 128/64 FFT/IFFT processor

The first module does the operation of data reordering. One goal is to let Module 2, Module 3, and Module 4 implement the operation of FFT and IFFT with 1-4 simultaneous data sequences more efficiently. The second goal is to avoid the data sequences in Module 3 to be multiplied by the same twiddle factor in each data path simultaneously [20]. The second module consists of four complex multipliers which are needed in the parallel approach to implement a radix-2 FFT algorithm. Multiple data sequences and only two complex multipliers are used in this module. The second module consists of a memory, 4 butterfly units of radix-2 FFT algorithm, two complex multipliers, two ROMs, and some multiplexers [20]. The third and the fourth module perform the operation of Radix-8 FFT. The received outputs are multiplied by non trivial twiddle factors before they enter in to next stages. This design [20] consists of memory size is 514 words, 16 complex multipliers and 48 complex adders. The output is received at 6 ns and has a power consumption of 2.26 mw.

2.2 Fast Hartley Transform

All the receivers are based on the usage of FFT or IFFT for modulating or de modulating. Instead, Hartley transform can be used effectively for modulation and de modulation. The direct and inverse transforms are identical for Hartley transform, and the Hartley transform of a real signal is real. Fourier transform always implies a complex processing and the phase carries fundamental information, while Hartley transform is a real trigonometric transform. Furthermore, the real and imaginary parts of the Discrete Fourier Transform (DFT) coincide with the even and the negative odd parts of the DHT, respectively: the transform kernels only differ for the imaginary unit [24]. Unlike FFT, Hartley transform has less complexity. Hartley transform requires same number of multiplication but one extra addition than FFT. In the case of radix-2 algorithm, reported in [25], for both the decimation-in-time and decimation-in-frequency, the number of multiplications required by the DHT is $N\ log_2 - 3N+4$ and the number of additions is $(3N\ log_2N-3N+4)/2$, with the transform order. The FHT-based algorithm has the same number of multiplications and N-2 more additions than the corresponding FFT algorithm [24].

Table 3. Comparison of FFT and Hartley Transform

Type of Demodulation Algorithm	Fast Hartley Transform	FFT
Supported Constellation	Real	Imaginary
Complexity	$P=(Nlog_2N-3N+4)/2$ $A=(3Nlog_2-5N)/2+6$ Self inverse NO additional Resources	$P=(Nlog_2N-N+4)/2$ $A=(3Nlog_2-5N)/2+4$ NOT self inverse Resources for QAM

2.3 Cyclic Prefix Removal

The cyclic prefix is added in the transmitter side to counter the effect of inter carrier interference and inter symbol interference is removed in the receiver side. Cyclic prefix is nothing but a bit of data copied from the symbol data and appended at the beginning of the symbol as shown in Fig. 5. Care should be taken before the removal of cyclic prefix because in case of errors, the data too may be removed. So synchronization of the transmitted and received data is necessary. Proper delay should be added or removed for effective removal of cyclic prefix.

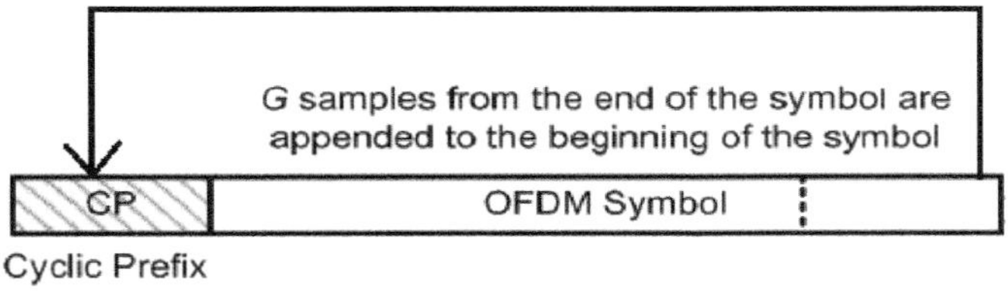

Fig. 5. Cyclic prefix

2.4 Decoder and Demapper

The data from the FFT module is demapped. The demapped data is decoded using any decoders like Viterbi or Reed Solomon Decoder. There are certain serial to parallel converters and parallel to serial converters. Serial data occupies most of the bandwidth, leads to distortions, overlapping of data and hence, causes most of the errors. So parallel data is used to counter the effects of serial data and most of all parallel data is resistive to frequency fading.

Coming to the design of the receiver, there are many ideas proposed to achieve high data rate and get higher efficiency. One of the proposed architecture gives us a double rate of data reception [21] as shown in Fig. 6. The idea proposed enables us for faster reception and faster processing of the transmitted to receive the real output data.

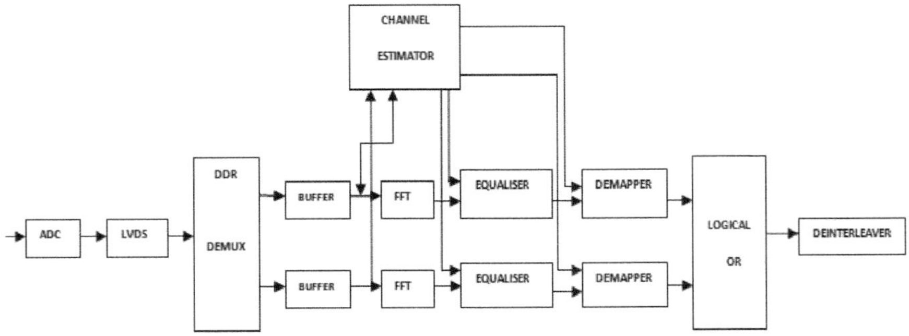

Fig. 6. Double rate receiver architecture

The working principle of a receiver is explained as follows, the received symbols from the ADC's are collected into blocks of the FFT and split into two paths. Each path starts with a Buffer to capture the odd and even signals and then to output a single stream of symbols for the following FFT. The FFT feeds the equalizer in the conventional way. Due to the two Equalizers being present, the channel estimates for both paths are required to be available at the same time, and in this CODEC system, this is achieved by having a Channel Estimator with two dedicated output ports (using two sets of dual-port RAM) to supply the channel estimate for each Equalizer. The signal from equalizer is given to demapper for demapping. Since the output signals from demapper arrive at different times, the signals are merged with a simple OR function. This architecture results in a maximum clock rate of 264 MHz instead of the expected 528 MHz clock rate existing anywhere on the baseband CODEC [21].

Another receiver designed has a speed of 120 Gb/s over 500 km based on the principle of Self Coherent Detection OFDM [22]. The first stage of the receiver (filter /demux) consists of optical filters to separate the carrier and sideband spectral components. The filter also provides Amplified Spontaneous Emission (ASE) bandwidth limiting to reduce shot noise. The separated carrier and sideband signals are then optically pre-amplified and drive the inputs of the polarization-diverse optical hybrid. The hybrid has an internal polarization beam splitter on the signal input and an internal linear polarizer on the LO input. The linear polarizer ensures equal carrier power for each polarization and the polarization controller maximizes carrier output. Outputs from the optical hybrid, $I_{x,}$ is mixed with the signals from the local oscillator, Q_x after passing through balanced photo detector [17]. I and Q outputs from the mixer is converted to digital and the digitized outputs are converted to complex parallel data blocks and the CP is removed. The IQ compensation, channel estimation, and polarization demultiplexing are performed in the DSP block, before the QAM symbols are demodulated into binary data as shown in Fig. 7.

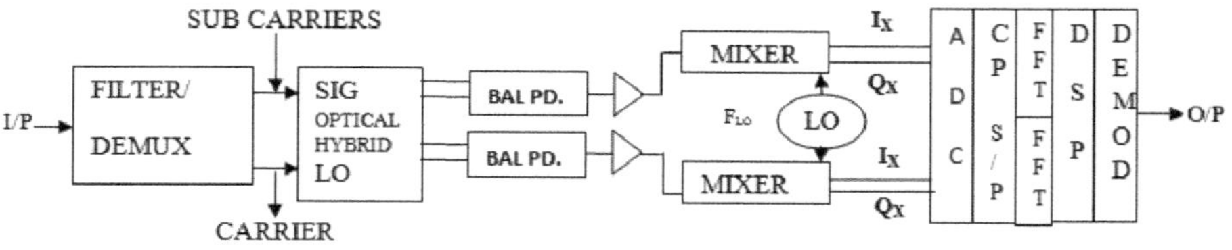

Fig. 7. Dual polarization optical OFDM Receiver

An architecture which achieves the data rate of 1Tb/s too has been proposed [23]. This architecture uses to Coherent detection OFDM (CO-OFDM). The basic principle of this receiver, OBM-OFDM (Orthogonal band multiplexed OFDM) is to partition the OFDM into multiple sub-bands, while maintaining their orthogonal property. The output signal after fiber transmission is detected using a polarization diversity coherent receiver comprising a receive local laser, a polarization beam splitter, two hybrids and four balanced receivers as shown in Fig. 8. The relative phase shift between subcarriers or channel estimation is calculated by using training sequences. The phase drift from the laser phase noise is also estimated and compensated using pilot subcarriers. Two ways of receiving the signals are considered. In first method, the receiver laser is tuned to the center of each band. Each band is detected separately by using an 'anti-alias filter' that low-passes only one-band RF signal. In second method, the local laser is tuned to the center of the guard band. Two bands are detected by using an 'anti-alias filter' that low-passes two-band RF signals simultaneously [23].

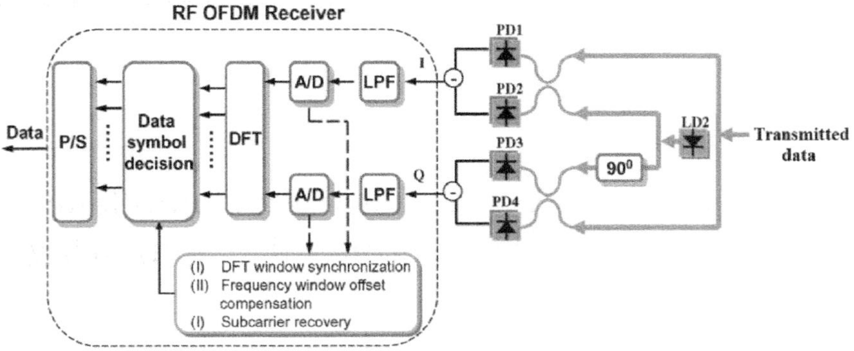

Fig. 8. OBM-OFDM Receiver

Passive Optical Network (PON) systems also guarantee a promising technique for faster transmission and reception of signals in optical domain. An PON architecture together with OFDM, polarization multiplexing (POLMUX), and direct detection proposed gives a data rate of 108 Gbps. The new technique of POLMUX helps us to simplify the receiver architecture compared to coherent receivers, also giving possibility of data rates higher than 40 Gbps. In both coherently and directly detected optical OFDM systems, the optical OFDM signal is generated through subcarrier multiplexing of a multi-Gigahertz electrical OFDM signal onto an optical carrier. Consequently, since the electrical OFDM signal can only be generated by high-speed DAC, current DAC technology with maximum sample rate of 10 Giga sample/s at 8-bit resolution, limits achievable OFDM bandwidth to 5 GHz. Thus, in order to generate a 40 Gb/s OFDM signal in a 5 GHz bandwidth, 256-QAM modulation would be required, which, currently, cannot be realized at 8-bit DAC resolution. A directly detected POLMUX solution, on the other hand, it would enable 40 Gb/s transmission in a 5 GHz bandwidth using 16 QAM, which can be readily achievable with currently available DAC technology.

3 Results

Different architecture of receivers having different configuration and using different detection techniques have been discussed. Every architecture has its own merits and demerits. The criterion of speed is taken for the comparison as shown in Table 4.

Table 4. Comparison of Proposed Architectures

Architecture	Double rate receiver	Dual polarization	CO OFDM With OBM-OFDM	OFDM WITH POLMUX
Speed	2X (X=speed)	120Gb/s	1Tb/s	108Gb/s

4 Conclusion

Thus, different receiver architectures are compared in this paper. Also, the heart of the receiver, the FFT module and certain ideas proposed for optimizing this module is also explained. It is been noted that Hartley transform is much more efficient than FFT for de modulation. Also, the double rate architecture can be implemented to get the faster processing of data to get the real transmitted data. In case of using FFT as demodulator, parallel processing can be used for this process, but at the cost of increased silicon area. Hence, it is possible to select better receiver architecture design for faster processing.

References

1. Armstrong, J., IEEE: OFDM for Optical Communication. Journal of Lightwave Technology 27(3) (February 1, 2009)
2. Wei, W., Wang, C., Yu, J., Cvijetic, N., Wang, T.: Optical Orthogonal Frequency Division Multiple Access Networking for the Future Internet. Journal of Optical. Communication Networks 1(2) (July 2009)
3. Carruthers, J.B., Kahn, J.M.: Multiple-subcarrier modulation for nondirected wireless infrared communication. IEEE J. Sel. Areas Commun. 14, 538–546 (1996)
4. Gonzalez, O., Perez-Jimenez, R., Rodriguez, S., Rabadan, J., Ayala, A.: OFDM over indoor wireless optical channel. In: IEE Proc.—Optoelectronics, vol. 152, pp. 199–204 (2005)
5. Armstrong, J., Lowery, A.J.: Power efficient optical OFDM. Electron.Lett. 42, 370–371 (2006)
6. Armstrong, J., Schmidt, B.J.C.: Comparison of asymmetrically clipped optical OFDM and DC-biased optical OFDM in AWGN. IEEE Commun. Lett. 12, 343–345 (2008)
7. Li, X., Mardling, R., Armstrong, J.: Channel capacity of IM/DD optical communication systems and of ACO-OFDM. In: Proc. ICC 2007, pp. 2128–2133 (2007)
8. Cvijetic, N., Qian, D., Wang, T.: 10 Gb/s free-space optical transmission using OFDM. Presented at the Proc. OFC/NFOEC 2008, San Diego, CA (2008), Paper, OTHD2
9. Lee, S.C.J., Breyer, F., Randel, S., Schuster, M., Zeng, J., Huiskens, F., van den Boom, H.P.A., Koonen, A.M.J., Hanik, N.: 24-Gb/s transmission over 730 m of multimode fiber by direct modulation of 850-nm VCSEL using discrete multi-tone modulation. Presented at the Proc. of C/NFOEC 2007, Anaheim, CA, March 25-29 (2007), Paper PDP6.
10. Lee, S.C.J., Breyer, F., Randel, S., Ziemann, O., van den Boom, H.P.A., Koonen, A.M.J.: Low-cost and robust 1-Gbit/s plastic optical fiber link based on light-emitting diode technology. Presented at the Proc. of C/NFOEC 2008, San Diego, CA (2008), Paper, OWB3
11. Lowery, A.J., Armstrong, J.: Orthogonal-frequency-division multiplexing for dispersion compensation of long-haul optical systems. Opt. Expr. 14, 2079–2084 (2006)
12. Shieh, W., Athaudage, C.: Coherent optical orthogonal frequency division multiplexing. Electron. Lett. 42, 587–588 (2006)
13. Jansen, S.L., Morita, I., Takeda, N., Tanaka, H.: 20-Gb/s OFDM transmission over 4,160-km SSMF enabled by RF-pilot tone phase noise compensation. Presented at the Proc. OFC/NFOEC 2007, Anaheim, CA, March 25-29 (2007), Paper PDP15

14. Jansen, S.L., Morita, I., Schenk, T.C.W., van den Borne, D., Tanaka, H.: Optical OFDM—A candidate for future long-haul optical transmission systems. Presented at the Proc. OFC/NFOEC 2008, San Diego, CA (2008), Paper, OMU3
15. Molisch, A.F., Win, M.Z.: MIMO systems with antenna selection. IEEE Microw. Mag. 5, 46–56 (2004)
16. Paulraj, A.J., Gore, D.A., Nabar, R.U., Bolcskei, H.: An overview of MIMO communications—A key to gigabit wireless. Proc. IEEE 92, 198–218 (2004)
17. Lau, A.P.T., Lei, X., Ting, W.: Performance of receivers and detection algorithms for modal multiplexing in multimode fiber systems. IEEE Photon. Technol. Lett. 19, 1087–1089 (2007)
18. Jansen, S.L., Morita, I., Tanaka, H.: 16 x 52.5-Gb/s, 50-GHz spaced, POLYMUX-CO-OFDM transmission over 4,160 km of SSMF enabled by MIMO processing. Presented at the Proc. ECOC 2007 (2007), Paper PD1.3
19. Lin, H.-L., Lin, H., Chang, R.C., Chen, S.-W., Liao, C.-Y., Wu, C.-H., National Chung Hsing University, Taiwan: A High-Speed Highly Pipelined 2^n-Point FFT Architecture for a Dual OFDM Processor. In: MIXDES 2006, Gdynia, Poland, June 22-24 (2006)
20. Chitra, M.P., Srivatsa, S.K.: Design of low power mixed radix FFT processor for MIMO OFDM systems. In: 2009 International Conference on Advances in Computing, Control, and Telecommunication Technologies (2009)
21. Simon Sherratt, R., IEEE, Cadenas, O.: A Double Data Rate Architecture for OFDM Based Wireless Consumer Devices. IEEE Transaction on Consumer Electronics 56, 23–26 (2010)
22. Schmidt, B.J.C., Zan, Z., Du, L.B., Lowery, A.J., IEEE: 120 Gbit/s Over 500-km Using Single-Band Polarization-Multiplexed Self- Coherent Optical OFDM. Journal of Lightwave Technology 28(4) (February 15, 2010)
23. Tang, Y., Shieh, W., IEEE: Coherent Optical OFDM Transmission Up to 1 Tb/s per Channel. Journal of Lightwave Technology 27(16) (August 15, 2009)
24. Moreolo, M.S., Munoz, R., Junyent, G.: Novel Power Efficient Optical OFDM Based on Hartley Transform for Intensity-Modulated Direct-Detection Systems. Journal of Lightwave Technology 28(5) (March 1, 2010)
25. Sorensen, H.V., Jones, D.L., Burrus, C.S., Heideman, M.T.: On computing the discrete Hartley transform. IEEE Trans. Acoust,Speech, Signal Process SP-33(5), 1231–1238 (1985)

A Pre-fetch Enabled Cache-Core Architecture for Multi-cores

B. Parvathy

Department of Computer Science & Engineering
Anna University, Chennai
parvathynath@gmail.com

Abstract. In this paper a new method is proposed to improve the memory performance of multi-core architectures, a pre-fetch enabled cache-core architecture. This technique can be implemented in multi-core processors which mainly have a local storage in their cores, apart from the main shared memory. It involves configuring the local storage of cores as a level two cache and pre-fetching the data into the L2 cache. The pre-fetch enabled cache-core mechanism on the Cell Broadband Engine processor has been simulated using the Cell BE simulator and its performance has been evaluated for various benchmark programs.

Keywords: Software cache, Cache-core, Pre-fetching.

1 Introduction

Multi-cores, which have been designed for speeding up processing through parallel executions has brought a new revolution in processor performance and speed. For the past few years processor performance have showed a much faster improvement when compared to memory performance. These wide differences have made the memory performance a bottle neck. The introduction of cache memories, which uses the principle of locality have helped to improve the performance to some extent. But the caches have to be fully utilized by reducing the miss rates to the maximum. Several memory optimization techniques have been adopted for multi-core processors. In heterogeneous multi-core processors like Cell Broadband Engine (Cell BE) and GPGPU's the cores have a local memory apart from the system memory. These cores bring instruction and data from main memory to local storage for execution. The local memory of these cores can be configured as a software managed cache. Cache-core architecture is the new usage of the local storage as a software managed level two cache. If data is being pre-fetched to the cache-core, then it will further help to reduce the cache misses.

The rest of the paper is organized as follows. Section 2 describes the related works. Section 3 describes the new architecture for a pre-fetch enabled cache core. Section 4 discusses on the implementation methodology and evaluation results. Section 5 concludes the paper.

A. Abraham et al. (Eds.): ACC 2011, Part I, CCIS 190, pp. 204–212, 2011.

2 Background and Related Work

There are many researches and implementations for software managed caches, data pre-fetching and optimization techniques for multi-cores with local memory. Jairo et.al [2] motivates the use of a novel software cache for managing asynchronous data transfers. For asynchronous data transfers, it is possible to overlap the memory access time with computation time by initiating the data transfer request in advance. The placement of such memory access calls will change the overlap between data communication and affects the overall application performance. A new method to pre-fetch irregular references accessed through the software cache that is built upon hardware such as cell has been proposed [3]. This method involves transformation of code in the compiler and a run time library support for the software cache and it simplifies the synchronization required when pre-fetching data into software cache.

A new software managed cache design Extended Set Index cache has also been proposed [4]. It has the benefits of both set associative and fully associative cache and based on 4-way set associative cache. Yosuke et.al [5] has proposed the cache core architecture to enhance the performance of multi-core processors. Nicola et.al [1] has proposed software pre-fetching for the cell Broadband engine processors. Their techniques involve automatic pre-fetching for regular memory references and modulo scheduling for irregular memory references.

The next two subsections gives a brief description on the target cell BE architecture used for the simulation and the cache-core architecture.

2.1 The Cell BE Architecture

The target architecture that is used for the simulation of pre-fetch enabled cache-core is the Cell Broad Band Engine (Cell BE) architecture [9] which is shown in Figure 1. The cell is basically a heterogeneous multi-core processor designed specifically for compute intensive applications [6] [7]. It comprises of a 64-bit Power Processing Element (PPE) which is multithreaded and eight Synergistic Processing Elements (SPEs). The PPE and SPEs communicate through a high speed element interconnect bus. PPE is the cell's main processor that runs the operating system. It has the Power PC architecture with 32KB L1 cache and 512KB L2 cache. The SPE consist of a Synergistic Processing Unit (SPU) and a Memory Flow Controller (MFC). The MFC includes a Memory Management Unit, a Direct Memory Access (DMA) controller, bus interface unit and atomic unit for synchronizing with other SPUs and PPE.

The cell has shared memory architecture. Apart from the main memory, each SPU's has a 256KB Local Storage (LS) to store instructions and data. SPUs cannot access the main memory directly. They can only issue DMA commands to the MFC which brings data and instructions from the main storage to the local storage and write back data to main memory. Each local storage can be managed using software. The DMA transfer can happen between the local storage and any other resource connected on chip, such as the main memory, another SPE's local storage or an I/O device.

The communication architecture of Cell BE describes that each SPU's can use either mail boxes or signals for signaling to the PPE or other SPU's. The signal notification facility has two channels Sig_Notify_1 and Sig_Notify_2. SPU's can read its own channels using the read blocking SPU channels SPU_RdSigNotify1 and SPU_RdSigNotify2. Each SPU has a mail box that act as a 32-bit communication channel to the PPE or another SPE.

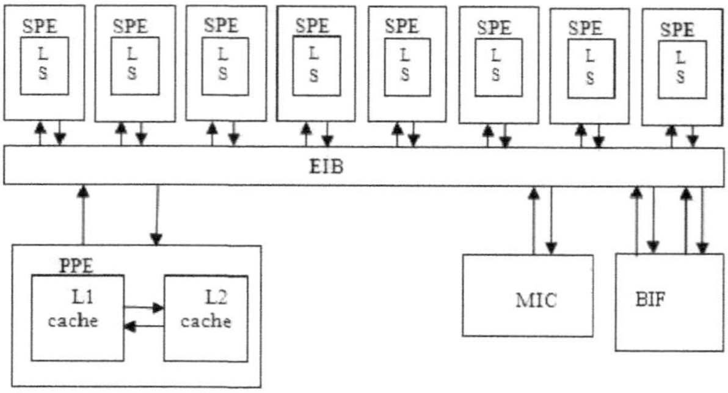

Fig. 1. The Cell Broadband Engine Architecture

The Element Interconnect Bus (EIB) is the main component which enables communication between among the PPE, the SPE's, the main memory and the external I/O. The EIB data network consists of four 16-byte data rings and each ring can allow up to three concurrent data transfers. The Memory Interface Controller (MIC) provides a peak bandwidth of 25.6 GB/s to main memory. A coherent protocol called Broadband Interface connects two cell processors in a single coherent network.

2.2 Cache-Core Architecture

The Cell BE architecture uses the local storage for caching instruction and data. Hence these local stores act as a level one cache. The Cache-core mechanism involves configuring the local storage of the Cell Broadband Engine as a level two cache. In the Cell BE processor the SPU's act as the cores used for computation. When such application programs are made to run on the processor all cores (SPU's) may not participate in computation. There will be many cores that are sitting idle. In cache-core architecture one of the idle cores' local storage can be configured as a level two cache.

When an application program runs in the computation core, it checks that data is also present in the L2 cache of the idle core, if a miss occurs in the L1 cache. As the result of the cache-core the cache miss ratio decreases in a very high rate, because most of the memory references when missed in L1 cache will hit in the cache-core rather than going for a memory access.

One of the advantage of using Cache-core for such multi-cores is that, the contention for the main memory decreases. In cell, the communication between two cores is much faster when compared to that between the core and the shared memory. The communication with shared memory requires a DMA transfer, whereas to communicate between two cores, either mail boxes or signaling can be used which is of much less overhead than a DMA operation.

3 Design of Pre-fetch Enabled Cache-Core Architecture

This section describes the design of the new approach. Data pre-fetching involves fetching the data far ahead before it is actually used in a computation. Data pre-fetching when combined with cache-core will reduce the miss rates further. The pre-fetch enabled cache-core architecture is shown in figure 2. The computation core contains the application program and the L1 cache. The cache-core has a level two cache. First a look up operation is performed in the L1 cache. If data is not present, then L2 cache is checked. If an L2 miss occurs then data is brought to L2 cache from memory during look up and also written to the L1 cache, since L2 is configured as an Inclusive cache here. After the look up operation, pre-fetching of data occurs. The data which is likely to be used in the next iteration of the loop and which in not guaranteed to be present in both the caches are being fetched into the level two cache.

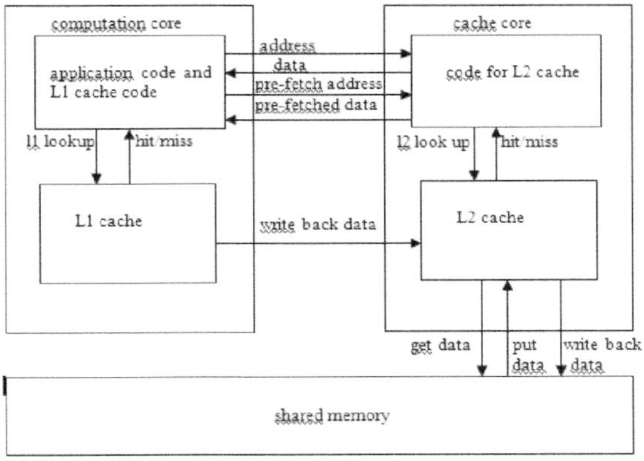

Fig. 2. Pre-fetch enabled cache-core architecture

In this paper a write back policy has been adopted for memory. During an L1 miss, if L1 line is found to be dirty, then it is written back to L2 cache. Similarly during an L2 miss, the dirty L2 line is written back to the main memory.

3.1 Methodology

For pre-fetching regular accesses we used the methodology similar to the one by Nicola et.al [1]. The programming model for a pre-fetch enabled cache core is as shown below.

Consider a for loop of the form

```
for(i=0;i<N;i++)
{
  temp=array[i];
}
```

This for loop can be transformed as follows

```
i=0;
while(i<N)
{
    n=N;
    s=stride(array,array[i]);
    mem_map(array[i],s);
    n=min(n,i+iter);
    prefetch(array[i+iter]);
    for(;i<=n;i++)
    {
        temp=mem_read(array[i]);
    }
}
```

stride(ref, address) : Predicts the stride of the memory access for the current iteration from the previous iteration for a particular memory reference.
mem_map (address, stride) : Performs the look up operation in the L1 cache and if a miss occurs, it checks in L2. If the required line is not present in L2 it will fetch the line from global memory.

iter : The variable which returns the number of iterations to iterate for the reference on the current cache line without producing a miss.

prefetch (address) : Performs pre-fetch operation into the level two cache.

For predicting the stride, a stride prediction table is used [8]. The address of the references is stored in the table along with the reference identifier during each iteration of the loop. For the current iteration, the predicted stride value will be the difference between the current address of the reference and the previous address. The mem_map function will perform a look up operation based on the address received. After checking the address in the L1 cache, the computational core will communicate the address to the cache-core for a look up operation in the L2 cache. If a miss occurs in L2, then a DMA operation will bring the required data from the memory. Data is also written into the L1 cache. The mem_map function will also set the iter variable which indicates the number of iterations for which the reference will be present in the cache block. So, by the end of look up operation data will be available in the L1 cache. The pre-fetch function will pre-fetch the next address which is not likely to be present in the L1 cache. The computation core will communicate the address to be pre-fetched to the cache core. Cache-core will bring the corresponding line from the memory to the cache.

The number of memory accesses will not be reduced by pre-fetching, but the cache miss rate definitely decreases. This is because the data is definitely going to hit in L2 cache in the next iteration due to pre-fetch. Another advantage is that we can overlap the computation time with the fetching time into the cache, since pre-fetch is occurring in parallel to computation in a different core.

4 Evaluation

This section briefly describes the system configuration and evaluation parameter used for the architecture. Table 1 shows required configuration for evaluating the new architecture. The Cell Broadband Engine simulator was used for simulations [9]. Four application programs Quick sort, Merge sort, Matrix multiplication and Dijikstras were used as benchmarks.

Table 1. System Configuration

Platform	Fedora 9
Simulator	Cell BE
Library	CellSDK3.1
IDE	Eclipse

The percentage of cache misses for these programs have been plotted against varying data sizes. The graphs show a comparison between cache-core architecture with pre-fetch and cache core architecture without pre-fetch. It has been observed that programs like quick sort and merge sort, which are highly dominated by regular references showed a much less reduction in cache miss rate compared to the other two programs.

The two caches are implemented as direct mapped caches. L1 cache in computation core has a size of 8KB and L2 cache (Cache-core) has capacity 128KB. The cache line size is taken as 128 bytes.

The matrix multiplication program is dominated by irregular references. Only the regular references were pre-fetched in this case. The size of integer numbers is taken as 4 bytes. If the column size of the matrix is very small, then majority of the references will become regular references when the matrices are stored in row major order. Figure 3 shows the miss rate of matrix multiplication with matrix size varied from 10 X 10 to 100 X 100.

Figure 4 shows the graph for Dijikstras, which has the least miss rate of 0.108% when the number of nodes is 300. From the graph it is clear that there is a wide reduction in miss rate for Dijikstras when the accesses are prefetched. This is because the inner loop of Dijikstras has more or less a regular access pattern which is being pre-fetched. The minimum miss rate for matrix multiplication is 0.042% when data size is 10K.

Figure 5 and 6 shows the cache miss rate in percentage for quick sort and merge sort. Integer numbers each of size 4 bytes with data size varying from 100 to 10K were considered. The quick sort and merge sort programs are dominated by regular references. Both the read and write memory accesses were pre-fetched for these programs. The miss rate tends to be very low, i.e. in the range of 0.005% for these benchmarks when data size is more than 1K.

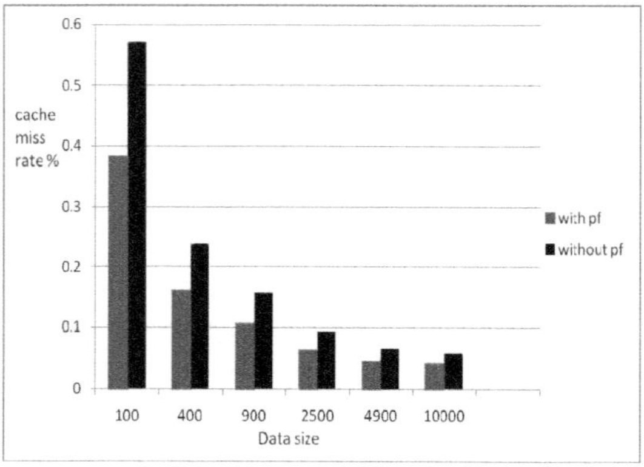

Fig. 3. Cache miss rate in percentage for varying data sizes for matrix multiplication

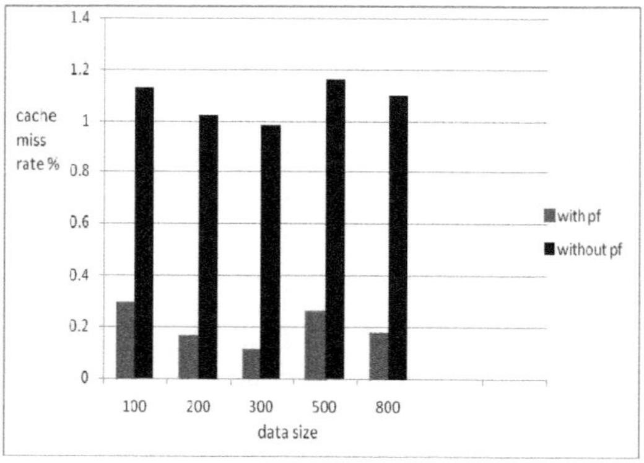

Fig. 4. Cache miss rate in percentage for Dijikstras

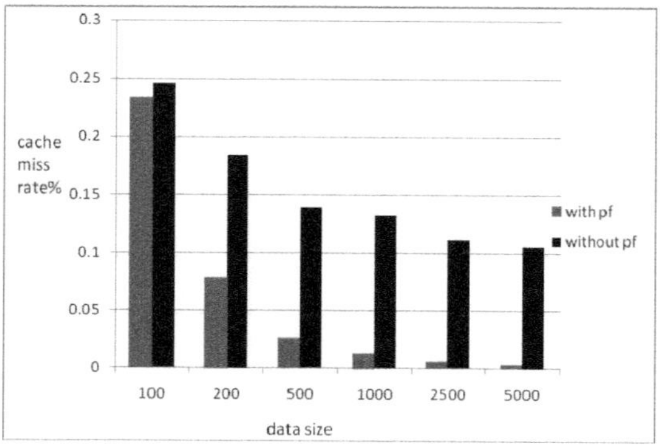

Fig. 5. Cache miss rate in percentage for varying data sizes for quick sort

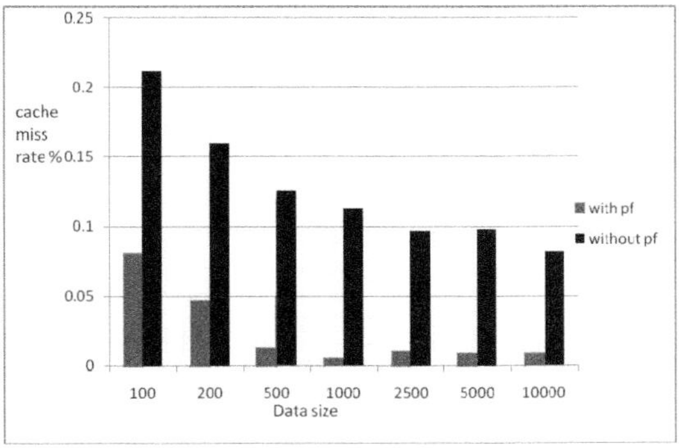

Fig. 6. Cache miss rate in percentage for merge sort

The decrease in miss rate is much more for merge sort, since it is more memory intensive than quick sort. For both the programs, as the data size increases, the miss rate will decrease for version without pre-fetch and also for the version with pre-fetch. With increase in data size more number of accesses are found to hit on the level two cache which is having a size of 128KB.

5 Conclusion

In this paper a pre-fetch enabled cache-core was simulated in a cell BE simulator and the cache miss ratios were evaluated for four benchmark programs. Only single cache and computation core were used for evaluation. The regular references of these benchmarks were pre-fetched into the level two cache or the cache-core. A considerable reduction in cache miss rate was obtained for cache core with pre-fetching when compared to cache core without pre-fetching. Future work involves considering the irregular references also and evaluating the execution time. Since data is pre-fetched to the level two cache, it is possible to overlap the computation time and the fetching time and execution time should reduce. Multiple cache and computational cores can also be considered if we go for parallelizing the benchmarks.

References

1. Vujic, N., González, M., Martorell, X., Ayguade, E.: Automatic Prefetch and Modulo Scheduling Transformations for the Cell BE Architecture. IEEE Transactions on parallel and Distributed Systems 21(4), 494–505 (2009)
2. Balart, J., Gonzalez, M., Martorell, X., Ayguade, E., Sura, Z., Chen, T., Zhang, T., O'Brien, K., O'Brien, K.: A Novel Asynchronous Software Cache Implementation for the Cell-BE Processor. In: Adve, V., Garzarán, M.J., Petersen, P. (eds.) LCPC 2007. LNCS, vol. 5234, pp. 125–140. Springer, Heidelberg (2008)
3. Chen, T., Zhang, T., Sura, Z., Tallada, M.G.: Prefetching irregular references for software cache on cell. In: Proceedings of the sixth annual IEEE/ACM International Symposium on Code Generation and Optimization, pp. 155–164. ACM, New York (2008)

4. Seoy, S., Lee, J., Sura, Z.: Design and Implementation of Software-Managed Caches for Multi-cores with Local Memory. In: Proceedings of the 15th IEEE International Symposium on High Performance Computer Architecture, pp. 55–66 (February 2009)
5. Mori, Y., Kise, K.: The Cache-Core Architecture to Enhance the memory Performance on Multi-Core Processors. In: Proceedings of 10th IEEE International Conference on Parallel and Distributed Computing, Applications and Technologies, pp. 445–450 (December 2009)
6. Phametal, D.: The Design and Implementation of a First- Generation Cell Processor. In: Proceedings of 2nd IEEE International Conference on Integrated Circuit Design and Technology, pp. 49–52 (May 2005)
7. Peter Hofstee, H., et al.: Power Efficient Processor Architecture and the Cell Processor. In: Proceedings of the 11th IEEE International on Symposium High-Performance Computer Architecture, pp. 258–262 (February 2005)
8. Fu, J.W.C., Patel, J.H., Janssens, B.L.: Stride Directed Prefetching in Scalar Processors. In: Proceedings of the 25th IEEE Annual Symposium on Micro Architecture, pp. 102–110 (December 1992)
9. Full-System Simulator, I.B.M.: for the Cell Broadband Engine Processor (June 1, 2009), `http://www.alphaworks.ibm.com/tech/cellsystemsim`

Performance Analysis of Adaptive Scan Compression Methodology and Calculations of Compression Ratio

Avani Rao[1], Mahesh Devani[2], Mitesh Limachia[1], and Nikhil Kothari[1]

[1] Dharmsinh Desai University, Nadiad, Gujarat
avani.rao@einfochips.com,
miteshjlimachia@rediffmail.com, nil_kothari@ddu.ac.in
[2] eInfochips Pvt. Ltd., Ahmedabad, Gujarat
mahesh.devani@einfochips.com

Abstract. During fabrication of chip, manufacturing defects like open or shot may occur which cause malfunctioning of the chip. Design-for-Test (DFT) is extensively used to identify such defects. On tester, test data is applied to the chip to identify the defects. For larger chip, the amount of test data volume and test application time is higher on tester. Adaptive scan compression method is used to reduce test application time and test data volume. This paper gives an overview of the technique and discusses the factors that influence test parameters: compression ratio, test data volume reduction (TDVR) and test application time reduction (TATR). We also present the relationship of TATR, TDVR and Total no of internal scan chain. Results of experiments conducted to validate the relationship are also reported.

Keywords: Tester cycle count, Test Application Time Reduction (TATR), Test Data Volume Reduction (TDVR), Compression Ratio.

1 Introduction

During manufacturing of a chip, there is a possibility of defects like open, short. To identify such defects, test data are applied to the chip on tester. It is desirable to apply smaller test data while attempting identification of all faults on the design during manufacturing test. This would also reduce cost of the test. Currently almost all of the design-for-test (DFT) techniques start with a baseline of scan technology. However, the chip complexity continuously increases, which results in excessive test data volume even for single-stuck-at fault with single-detection [1]. In conventional external testing, this huge amount of test data must be stored on the external automatic test equipment (ATE) and be transferred to and from the circuit-under-test (CUT) through the limited test channels [22]. This poses a serious problem on manufacturing test. As test data volume increases, it takes more tester buffer space to hold the complete test set and larger simulation time to deliver the test set through limited test channels, both leading to higher test cost. Therefore, reduction in tester storage and tester channel bandwidth for million-gate designs are recognized as extremely important requirements and have received a lot of attention in the recent years [21].

A. Abraham et al. (Eds.): ACC 2011, Part I, CCIS 190, pp. 213–222, 2011.

There are a few methods focused on reducing external test channels to achieve good compression for designs with multiple scan chains. A technique using a single input supporting multiple scan chains has been proposed in [2]. However, its application is limited to test multiple independent full scan circuits in parallel. Illinois scan architecture [3] overcomes this limitation by using two modes of scan operation, parallel scan and serial scan. Circular Scan [4] configures the scan chains in a circular form enabling the generation of the next pattern from the captured response. While it efficiently overcomes the tester channel bandwidth limitation; it introduces a new problem on the test diagnosis process due to the undeterministic property of the test response. Approaches proposed in [5] and [6] explores the logic dependencies of the internal scan chains to construct a simple logic gates based decompression network so that a great number of scan chains could be driven by a limited number of external scan channels and test cost is reduced.

In this paper, we discuss a DFT technique – Adaptive Scan Compression, which drastically reduces test cost for scan-based designs [23]. Main benefit of the technique is a small amount of on-chip circuitry that reduces both test storage and test time required for testing a core-based design [8]. Fully specified test vectors provided by the core vendor are stored in compressed form in the tester memory and transferred to the chip where they are decompressed and applied to the core. Instead of having transferred entire test vector from the tester to the core, a smaller amount of compressed data is transferred. This in turn reduces the amount of compressed data that must be stored on the tester and hence reduces the total amount of test time required for transferring the data with a given test data bandwidth[10][12].

This paper derives a new compression relationship to calculate Test Application Time Reduction (TATR), Test Data Volume Reduction (TDVR) and calculation of total number of internal scan chains. The paper is organized as follows. Hierarchical implementation of compression method and decompression architecture is discussed in Section 2. Section 3 presents the analysis of effect of compression on test coverage. Pattern inflation from compression method is described in Section 4. Section 5 & 6 discuss the experimental results and conclusion respectively.

2 Basics of Adaptive Scan Compression

Adaptive Scan technology inserts a combinational decompression structure between the chip scan pins and the numerous short internal scan chains. Compressed scan input values are loaded in the adaptive scan module that associates them internally to the internal scan chains [22]. To maximize test coverage, the association adapts to the needs of ATPG to supply the required values in the scan cells. Adaptive Scan optimizes traditional scan chains into smaller segments enabling savings in test time [7], while the adaptive scan module and the output compactor significantly reduce the amount of test data needed to comprehensively test the chip [1]. As shown in Fig. 1, the compressed patterns are inserted into decompressed block of the architecture. Internal scan chains are connected to this block and allow patterns to propagate through them. Furthermore, these decompressed patterns are compressed at compressor block.

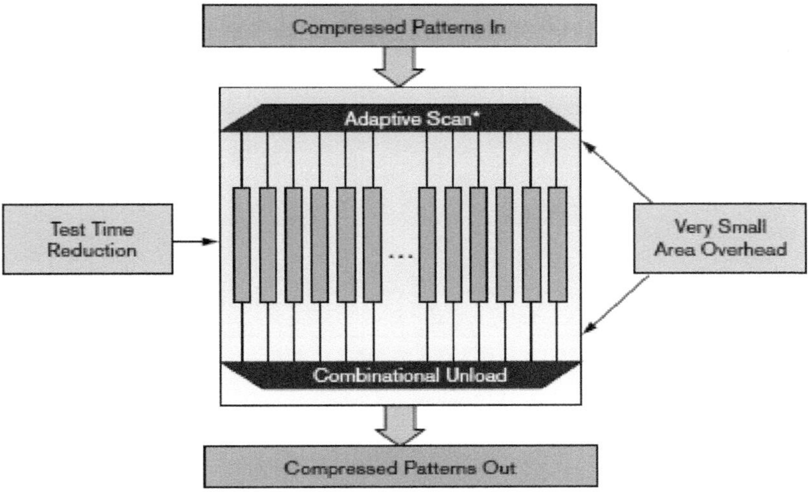

Fig. 1. Adaptive Scan Compressor Architecture

3 Fault Coverage Loss vs. Compression

Fault coverage loss measures a compression tool's ability to accommodate unknown logic states without exhibiting a significant loss in fault coverage. Even if the compression solution is fully *X-tolerant,* fault coverage can still decrease at high compression levels if design contains a very large number of unknowns [12]. Fig. 2 shows the result of the experiment conducted to validate effect of fault coverage on compression ratio. We begin the experiment with the execution of basic scan on the design without adding any compression[1] and testable fault coverage is measured. Fault coverage is defined as the ratio of detected faults to detectable faults in the uncollapsed fault list. The flat characteristic in Fig. 2 shows that there is negligible loss in coverage at the higher compression levels.

Based on this experiment, it is observed that the fault coverage does not change significantly with compression ratio. Note that fault coverage statistics can vary slightly from one tool to the next due to differences in fault accounting. Simply lowering a tool's maximum fault coverage target to compensate for these differences will always favor the tool with the highest reported fault coverage [16]. This is because the most difficult-to-detect faults are near the end of the ATPG run — in the tail of the fault coverage convergence curve — where many more patterns are required to detect relatively fewer faults [24]. Thus, lowering the coverage target significantly reduces the number of patterns needed. Since it is often difficult to determine exactly how the fault lists differ, it is advisable to create a single fault list with faults common to all ATPG tools while evaluating different compression solutions.

---

[1] Total no of scan flip-flops were 51560 and total number of scan chains were 8 in design under test (DUT).

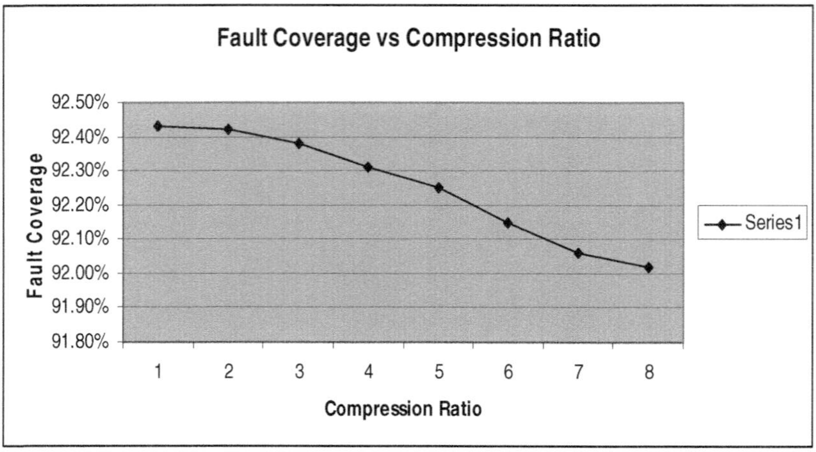

Fig. 2. Fault Coverage Vs Compression Ratio

4 Pattern Inflation from Compression

Although compression reduces the amount of data in each test pattern, more patterns are needed to achieve the same high testable fault coverage as the compression ratio is increased. The pattern count line should be fairly linear and have a relatively small slope. The pattern count without compression P and the pattern inflation rate ε both affect the tester cycle count, which is also a function of the number of scan flip-flops in the design F, the number of scan channels C, and the compression ratio x [12]. If we assume the internal scan chains are balanced, then as x increases the tester cycle count decreases according to equation (1).

This simple expression is accurate to within 1%. It may be noted that all compression solutions behave in this manner. Tester cycle count can be calculated as:

$$\text{Tester Cycle T} = (F\ x\ P)/(C\ x\ X) \qquad (1)$$

Although the ratio F/C is determined by design and I/O constraints, from a tool-comparison perspective more tester cycles will be required for each compression ratio if either the pattern count without compression P or the pattern inflation rate ε is relatively higher. We validate the equation (1) with the help of an experiment as shown in Fig. 3 which displays plot of Tester Cycle Count Vs Compression Ratio[§]. The experiment started with the different values of compression ratio. Based on compression ratio values, the scan chain length are different. With each values of compression ratio, values of F, P and C are different. Hence the value of tester cycle count vary with different values of compression ratio.

The plot indicates that compression ratio is inversely proportional to the Tester cycle count. As the compression ratio increases Tester cycle count reduces. Hence for larger designs with a high scan chain length, this method is useful. It also reduces pattern count and tester cycle count. Hence it reduces Test application time on tester.

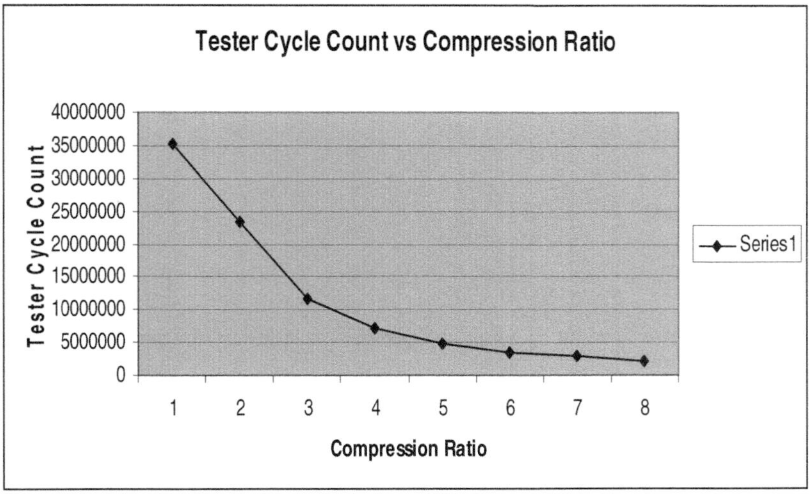

Fig. 3. Tester Cycle Count Vs Compression Ratio

Test application time is the ratio of tester cycle count without compression (x=1) (i.e. internal scan mode) to tester cycle count with compression (i.e. compression mode):

$$TATR = \frac{\text{Cycle Count (Basic Scan)}}{\text{Cycle Count (Compression Scan)}} \tag{2}$$

Above equation indicates test time reduction on increasing compression ratio. Test time reduction is equally proportional to Compression ratio as observed in Fig. 4. As

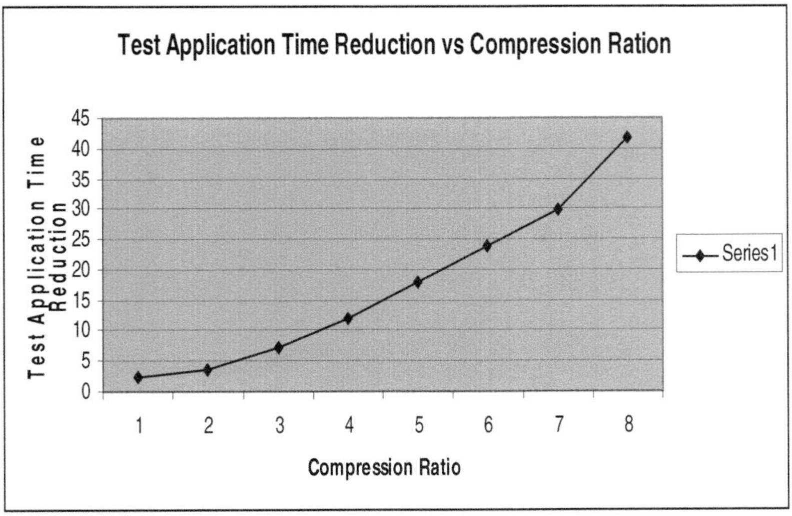

Fig. 4. Cycle Count (Basic Scan) Vs Cycle Count (Compression)

shown in Fig. 4, with increase in compression ratio test application time reduction also increases. As compression ratio increases the scan chain length reduces. This results in to reduction in required tester time. As compression ration increases further scan chain length reduces more. Hence, with increase in compression ratio, TATR ratio increases more.

5 Experimental Results

In this section, we present results of experiments conducted on 2 industrial designs (DUT). To compute the fault coverage and test application time reduction (TATR) numbers, we inserted the basic scan and compression scan with the use of given scan-in and scan-out. First experiment is conducted on design with 51560 shift registers, 8 scan-in and 8 scan-out pins. Second experiment is conducted on design having 30 shift registers, 5 scan-in and 5 scan-out pins.

The experiments were conducted on Synopsys Design Compiler tool [24] and TetraMax tool [25] over Linux platform with kernel version 2.6.18. To start compression method we replaced flip-flop with its scan equivalent model. We also checked the total number of external scan chains and total number of flip-flip-flops present in the design. Based on compression ratio, Adaptive Scan de-compressor splits down scan chain into smaller scan chains. Note that in adaptive scan compression, external pin count of scan-in and scan-out is same [22].

As shown in Table 1, there are two designs ckt1 and ckt2, which have 8 and 5 input and outputs respectively. Ckt1 has 51560 flip-flops and Ckt2 has 150 flip-flops. There are total 8 scan chains in Ckt1 and 5 scan chains in Ckt2. Pattern count of both designs is 10061 and 32.

Table 1. Pattern Count, Test Application Time Reduction (TATR), Test Data Volume Reduction (TDVR) for Basic Scan

Design	I/Ps	O/Ps	No of. Flip-flops/ chain	No of Scan Chains	Pattern count	TATR (s)	TDVR (bit)
ckt1	8	8	6445	8	10061	64859651	259855508
ckt2	5	5	30	5	32	1022	826304

Scan Test Time is calculated based on the relationship shown below:

Scan Test Time = F + (1+F) * V (3)

Scan Test Data Volume = (I + O + 2* F) * P (4)

In above equations, F indicates number of flip-flops, V is the test vector, I is Inputs, O is Outputs, and P is no. of Test Vectors. Subsequently, Compression method was implemented on the same designs and results were analyzed. Table 2 shows the calculations for all the outputs (Compressed test time reduction and test data volume reduction) of the experiment. It appears from the comparison of Table 1 and Table 2 that Test Application Time and Test Data Volume are reduced by applying Compression method. However, it also increases Pattern Count.

Table 2. Pattern Count, Test Application Time Reduction (TATR), Test Data Volume Reduction (TDVR) for Scan Compression

Design	I/Ps	O/Ps	Comp. Ratio	No of scan chain	No of flip-flops/chain	Pattern count	TATR (s)	TDVR (bit)
Ckt1	8	8	35	336	154	10981	1702209	3557844
Ckt2	5	5	7	40	4	54	274	972.00

From all the above results we have observed one relationship to find out total number of internal scan chains after compression by only known value of external scan chain count and compression ratio. Total number of Internal scan chains depends on multiplication of external scan chain count and compression ratio.

Internal Scan Chain Count = 1.2 * Scan Chain * Compression Ratio (5)

As shown in Table 3, number of internal compressed scan chains is approximately equal to the above equation (5). For compression ratio 3 and scan chain count 8, the internal scan chain count will be 1.2 * 8 * 3 = 29. Thus, Tester cycle count also reduces by the equation (2). This can be seen in Table 3 below.

Table 3. Compression Ratio, No of Scan Chain (compressed), Fault Coverage and Tester Cycle Count Calculations

Compression Ratio	No of Scan Chains	Fault Coverage	Tester Cycle Count
2	20	92.43%	34989905
3	29	92.42%	23379070
6	58	92.38%	11709945
10	96	92.31%	7044747.2
15	144	92.25%	4705197.6
20	192	92.15%	3536919.6
25	240	92.06%	2831808
35	336	92.02%	2029880.8

From Table 3, we can observe that as compression ratio increases, the tester cycle count decreases. It is also observed that the fault coverage does not change significantly with compression ratio increases.

6 Conclusion

In this paper, we discuss the adaptive scan compression technique which significantly reduces test data volume and test application time of the chip on tester. In order to validate the merits of adaptive scan compression methodology, we carried out experiments. Following observation can be made from the results of these experiments. (i) Based on the incremental value of compression ratio, tester cycle count and required test application time reduces. (ii) Test data volume required to test the chip reduces significantly. (iii) The relationship of internal scan chain count gives the total number of internal scan chain created with the applied compression ratio.

Results of experiments conducted on DUT indicated that Adaptive scan compression technique significantly reduced the tester cycle count from 34989905 to 2029880, test data volume from 259Mb to 3.5Mb and test application time from $64\text{x}10^6$ sec to $1.7\text{x}10^6$ sec. This in turn validated the relationship for test parameters: test application time, test data volume and internal scan chain count.

However, we noticed the major drawback of this method as significant increase in pattern count from 10061 to 10981. Moreover the technique does not change fault coverage considerably.

References

1. Furukawa, H., Hsu, F., Lin, S., Tsai, S., Abdel-hafez, K., Wang, L., Wen, X., Wu, S.: VirtualScan: A New Compressed Scan Technology for Test Cost Reduction. In: Proceedings IEEE International Test Conference (ITC), pp. 916–925 (October 2004)

2. Chen, J.-J., Lee, K.-J., Huang, C.-H.: Using a single input to support multiple scan chains. In: Proceedings International Conference on Computer-Aided Design (ICCAD), pp. 74–78 (November 1998)
3. Butler, K., Hsu, F., Patel, J.: A case study on the implementation of the Illinois scan architecture. In: Proceedings IEEE International Test Conference (ITC), pp. 538–547 (October 2001)
4. Arslan, B., Orailoglu, A.: CircularScan A Scan Architecture for Test Cost Reduction. In: Proceedings Design, Automation, and Test in Europe (DATE), pp. 1290–1295 (March 2004)
5. Orailoglu, A., Rao, W., Su, G.: Frugal: Linear Network-Based Test Decompression for Drastic Test Cost Reduction. In: Proceedings International Conference on Computer-Aided Design (ICCAD), pp. 721–725 (November 2004)
6. Kajihara, S., Li, L., Chakrabarty, K., Swaminathan, S.: Efficient Space/Time Compression to Reduce Test Data Volume and Testing Time for IP Cores. In: Proceedings IEEE VLSI Design (VLSID), pp. 53–58 (January 2005)
7. Kim, K.S., Zhang, M.: Hierarchical test compression for SOC designs. IEEE Design and Test of Computers, 142–148 (March/April 2008)
8. Iyengar, V., Chandra, A.: A unified SOC test approach based on test data compression and TAM design. In: Proc. of IEEE Int. Symp. on Defect and Fault Tolerance in VLSI Systems, pp. 511–518 (2003)
9. Gonciari, P.T., Rosinger, P., Al-Hashimi, B.M.: Compression considerations in test access mechanism design. In: IEEE Proc. of Computers and Digital Techniques, vol. 152, pp. 89–96 (2005)
10. Lingappan, L., et al.: Test-volume reduction in systems-ona-chip using heterogeneous and multilevel compression techniques. IEEE Trans. on Computer-Aided Design 25, 2193–2206 (2006)
11. Kaushik, S.: Complex SoC testing with a core-based DFT strategy. EE Times-India (February 2008), `http://eetindia.com`
12. Allsup, C.: Synopsys Inc.: Measuring Scan Compression Performance
13. Lin, C.-Y., Chen, H.-M.: A Selective Pattern-Compression Scheme for Power and Test-Data Reduction
14. Gonciari, P.T., Rosinger, P., Al-Hashimi, B.M.: Compression considerations in test access mechanism design. In: IEEE Proc. of Computers and Digital Techniques, vol. 152, pp. 89–96 (2005)
15. Bushnell, M.L.: Essentials_Of_Electronic_Testing for Digital, memory, mixed-signal and VLSI circuits
16. Wang, L.-T., Wu, C.-W., Wen, X.: Vlsi Test Principle and Architecture –Design For Testability
17. Abramouci, M., Breuer, M.A., Friedman, A.D.: Digital System Testing & Testable Design. Jaico Publication house
18. Jas, A., Touba, N.: Using an Embedded Processor for Efficient Deterministic Testing of Systems-on-a-Chip. In: Proceedings International Conference on Computer Design, pp. 418–423 (October 1999)
19. Hamzaoglu, I., Patel, J.H.: Reducing Test Application Time for Full Scan Embedded Cores. In: Proc. IEEE Int. Symp. on Fault Tolerant Computing, pp. 260–267 (1999)
20. Pandey, A., Patel, J.H.: Reconfiguration Technique for Reducing Test Time and Test Data Volume in Illinois Scan Architecture Based Designs. In: Proc. IEEE VLSI Test Symp., pp. 9–15 (2002)

21. Hamzaoglu, I., Patel, J.H.: Reducing Test Application Time for Built-in Self-Test Test Pattern Generators. In: Proc. IEEE VLSI Test Symp., pp. 369–375 (2000)
22. Nicolici, N., Gonciari, P.T., Al-Hashimi, B.M.: Improving Compression Ratio, Area Overhead, and Test Application Time for System-on-a-Chip Test Data Compression/Decompression
23. Synopsys : DFT MAX 1-pass Test Compression Synthesis
24. Synopsys: DFT Compiler User Guide: Scan. Version B-2008.09-SP2 (December 2008)
25. Synopsys: TetraMax ATPG User Guide. version 2002.05 (May 2002)

Better Debugging of Logical Errors Using Optimized Call Stack Restricted Slicing

L.D. Dhinesh Babu*, M. Nirmala, S. Santhoshkumar, S. Panneerselvam

School of Information Technology and Engineering, VIT University, Vellore 632014, Tamil Nadu, India
{lddhineshbabu,mnirmala,santhoshkumars2007, pannerselvams2007}@vit.ac.in

Abstract. Logical errors are the program bugs that are caused due to the programmer's faulty reasoning. Logical errors in a program are not easy to find since the point of failure is shown in a statement but actual bug may be in any other statement(s). Debugging of this kind of errors is tedious. To debug the logical errors backward slicing is very useful. But, in most cases, backward slices are as large as the original program itself. This again creates problem in finding the original bug. This paper presents Optimized Call-stack Restricted slicing which reduces the number of lines to be checked while debugging. In other words, this technique reduces the size of the slice and also ensures that Optimized Call-Stack Restricted slices are smaller than the slices produced by any other slicing techniques. Optimized Call-stack restricted slicing is very effective. The size of slice ranges from 3 to 80 percent of the original program. Under any circumstances, the size of slices produced by optimized call stack restricted slicer is not greater than that of other slicers.

Keywords: Logical error, Debugging, Slicing, Slice size, Faulty reasoning, Call-stack, Call site, Backward slicing.

1 Introduction

A program may fail in two ways at run time. First, the program may not be executed fully due to the production of uncaught exception. Next, the program works fine with bad output. i.e., the program executes fully but it produces wrong output. Both these failures are due to logical errors. For the second case, we can find the line which has the wrong output in two steps: 1. Trace the actual output with reference output to find point of failure and 2. Use call stack (procedures called at the time of failure) to find actual bug. But it is not easy to find the actual bug that produced the bad output. The wrong output is because of logical errors in the program. To solve this problem program slicing technique [1] is very useful. It reduces the number of statements to be checked for the error. Slicing is finding the statements that are dependent on the line of failure (the first instance of failure).

The first step is to find the intermediate representation of the program. Intermediate representation is a directed graph which represents various dependencies of the

* Corresponding author.

A. Abraham et al. (Eds.): ACC 2011, Part I, CCIS 190, pp. 223–231, 2011.

program. As discussed below graph will show different dependencies of the program. C programs [11] (GCC [12], [13]) that confirms to gcc coding standards are the inputs for this slicing.

Program Slicing extracts only relevant parts of the program at the chosen line with respect to the chosen set of variables (slicing criterion). Based on the direction of slicing, program slicing has two types [8]: Backward Slicing and Forward Slicing. The statements that affect the point of failure are called **backward slices**. In terms of System Dependence graph [2] (SDG), it is nothing but travelling backwards from the line of failure to the entry in SDG. The statements that are affected by the point of failure are called **forward slices**. In terms of SDG, it is nothing but travelling forward from the line of failure to the exit in SDG.

Call-Stack Restricted Slicing considers the call sites which are called at the time of failure. The called sites at the time of execution are stored in a stack called call-stack. While slicing, the slice follows the edge that is at the top of the stack [5]. Optimized call stack restricted slicing reduces the number of call sites in the stack i.e., the call stack is reduced to a set of minimum call sites.

The next Section will discuss about the System Dependence Graph. Section 3 describes about the related works. Section 4 will discuss about Optimized Call-Stack Restricted Slicing and its advantages over other slicing methods. Section 5 will describe experimental results of the proposed slicing and compares the results with context insensitive slicing method which is widely used and conclusions are presented in Section 6.

2 System Dependence Graph

System Dependence Graph (SDG) is intermediate graphical representation of the source program. This mainly represents flow and data dependence of the original program. SDG is a Directed Graph. In this graph, nodes represent the statements of the original program and edges represent the different dependencies between statements. SDG contains Program Dependence Graph [2] (PDG), summary nodes and edges. Summary edges represent transitive dependency of nodes which are due to procedure calls. Summary edges map the link between actual-out nodes from actual-in nodes by inter procedurally realizable path which travels on SDG through the called procedure. SDG is inter-procedural dependence graph i.e., all procedure dependence graphs in a program are connected through summary edges to get SDG.

PDG basically has control dependence and data dependence with formal-in and formal-out nodes for every formal parameters of the procedure. Control dependence Graph is a graphical representation of the program that shows the execution of a node controlled by other node. A Data Dependence Graph is a graphical representation that shows the flow of data (variables) between statements. Four types of nodes in PDG are Statement node, Predicate node, Entry node and Region Node. The edges in SDG are created using different dependencies of the program. Usually dependencies are of many types like Control Dependence, Data Dependence and Summary Dependence.

Control Dependence

Control Dependence represents Execution control of the program. Two nodes are connected through an edge if a node controls the execution of other node. Specific iteration statements and recursive functions are controls themselves. They are represented using self directed edges. Control statements have more than one control dependence. For Example, in a simple if-else control structure if part controls the execution of else part. A formal Definition [18] is as follows: Node B is Control Dependent on A if and only if, B is not post dominant of A and there exists sub path to B through every node other than A in path A to B.

Data Dependence

Data dependence shows the data flow between statements. Data flow starts from a variable declaration. Whenever the variable changes or used, the data dependency exists. In this case each variable and its dependencies are found first. Data Dependency of a program has 4 main types [19], [20]. They are Data-flow dependencies (Read After Write), Output Dependencies (Write After Write), Anti-Dependencies (Write After Read) and Def-order dependence. A data dependency may pass through many procedures via parameter passing edges. This is inter-procedural data dependence. The scope of the data differs through this kind of dependencies.

Summary Dependence

Summary dependence of the program is used to find the transitive dependence through procedure calls in the program. Summary dependence can be obtained from PDGs of the program by introducing some additional (summary) nodes and edges. Table 1 Shows the Summary nodes and respective edges.

Table 1. Summary nodes and edges

Node in calling Procedure	Node in called Procedure	Connecting Edge
Call node	Entry of Procedure	Call Edge
Actual-in	Formal-in	Parameter-in
Actual-out	Formal-out	Parameter-out

Consider an example SDG to find the factorial of a number:

```
E0 main(){
S1 int k;
S2 int f;
S3 printf("Enter the number:");
S4 scanf("%d",&k);
C1 f=fact(k);
S5 printf("The factorial is %d",f);
E1 int fact(int k)
    {
S6 int i
S7 int j=1;
S8 while(i<k)
   {
S9 j=j+j*I;
S10i++;}
S11 return j;
        }
```

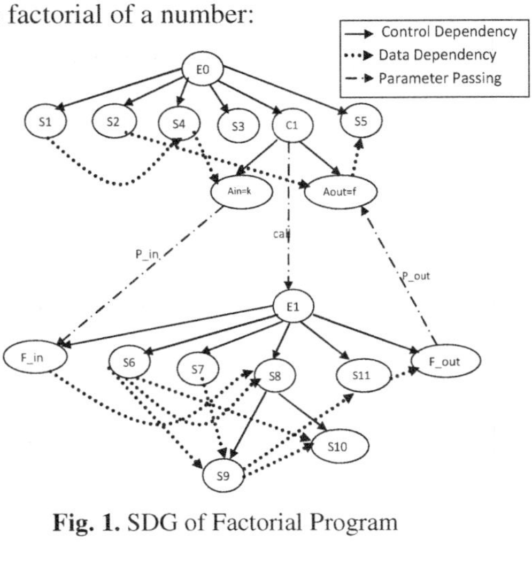

Fig. 1. SDG of Factorial Program

3 Related Works

Program slicing techniques are used in many fields. Some of these include debugging, testing, program integration, program understanding, reverse engineering, software maintenance and software quality assurance. Construction of a slice is removing irrelevant parts of the program with respect to a slicing criterion. A Slicing criterion is generally a tuple <*s*, *V*> Where, *s* is statement number, *V* is a subset of variable in program which is relevant to that statement *s*.

According to context of the program, slicing can be classified into two types: Context insensitive Slicing and Context Sensitive Slicing. Program Context implies the program feature which changes depending on the action that one does in the program. Context insensitive slicing [4] on SDG is reach-ability of nodes with respect to a slicing criterion i.e., slice is vertices of a realizable path.

3.1 Context Sensitive Slicing

Context Sensitive slicing [4], [10] is a program analysis technique which considers inter-procedural realization. This analysis will be based on calling context. Context sensitive analysis is explicit encoding of call string in a sequence of call sites. Call string is simulated as a call stack which is sequence of called procedures in a program. Context sensitive slicing is more precise than context insensitive slicing since it considers sequence of call sites of a program. This slicing technique has several variants [16]. They are Explicit context slicing, Folded context slicing, Limited context slicing. Chopping is another technique. Chopping is transitive dependence between two different statements in a program. It has two different criterions. One is source criterion and another one is target criterion.

Few tools are available for slicing. A popular slicing tool is Wisconsin Program Slicing tool [6]. This tool is called Code Surfer [14]. This slicing technique is static [7]. This tool supports backward and forward slicing. Since this is static slicing tool, it produces comparatively big size of slices. This tool is also useful in finding SDG.

4 Optimized Call Stack Restricted Slicing

Program slicing is decomposition of program based on dataflow and control flow analysis. A useful slice must provide pieces with predictable properties i.e., a slice is a subset of a program. Slicing basically reduces any program into a minimal form that still retains its behavior. During debugging a programmer is interested in a specific execution and not all possible executions. A particular bug might be due to that specific execution. A program might crash at a certain point in a different set of execution. For this reason dynamic slicers [17] are needed.

Call-Stack Restricted (Context Restricted [3]) Slicing considers called sites only at the time of failure with respect to point of failure. Hence this kind of slicing is dynamic slicing [9]. Dynamic slicing is more advantageous than static slicing.

Call-Stack Restricted slicing restricts the number of procedures for analysis to called procedures at the time of failure. Using a dynamic slicer like call-stack restricted slicer is efficient but it reduces the speed [15] of finding slice. We propose an optimized call-stack restricted slicing which will increase the speed by having few call sites only to find the slice. In best case, time required to find the slice will be very less compared to context-insensitive slicing. In worst case, this technique performs at the same speed of the context insensitive slicer. In majority of the cases this technique is better than its counterparts. Call sites are the statement number at the calling time. So the statement numbers are stored in the call stack.

Detailed algorithm of Call-Stack Restricted Slicing is provided by Krinke. This algorithm is formerly called as Context Restricted Slicing [3]. In this technique slicing back from a program line involves backward traversal of edges in the SDG of program. In this algorithm the call stack is used. But our algorithm reduces the number of call sites by removing the repeated call sites. $s=<c_1,\ldots,c_k>$ can be reduced to $s=<c_1,\ldots,c_q>$. $q<=k$. Removal of repeated call sites is possible as the extraction of lines is carried based on static SDG. The changing value of a variable will not affect the slicing process as it does not depend on dynamic SDG.

This algorithm has 2 phases. Phase 1 computes slices for every call site of the minimized call stack. During each iteration of phase 1, every node is reachable via edges of a particular procedure (intra procedure) calculated for slicing, which is stored in W. If parameter-in or call edge is traversed, and if reached node is part of the call site, it will be the initial node for next iteration (Stores in W^{up}) i.e., it finds the intra procedural realizable path from that node. If Parameter-out edge is traversed then the node is stored in W^{down}. These nodes will be processed at phase 2. At Phase 2 the edges are traversed from parameter-out edge to parameter-in edge i.e., the travel is between actual-out nodes to actual-in nodes. Second phase is to get the inter procedural realizable path through called procedure.

In context restricted slicing, the algorithm has to scan the SDG for each call site in the call stack. But a call site may be called more than once at the time of execution. Since it scans the static graph, scanning of SDG more than once for the same call site will produce the same answer. In this proposed algorithm the call stack is transferred to be an array call sites in which the repeated call sites are removed from the call stack and minimized call stack is created.

In context restricted slicing, for every call site in the stack the SDG is scanned. So the SDG as a whole has to be scanned for k (number of sites in call stack) times. At the time of parameter-in or call edge traversal the edge is checked whether it is at current call stack.

This is not required in the modified algorithm. The SDG is scanned with array of call sites. So we can check whether parameter-in or call edge is any one of the call sites. This will reduce that scanning of the SDG fully for each site. This technique checks for call sites while traversing the parameter-in or call edge itself. So this algorithm scans the SDG only once. It obviously reduces the running time of the algorithm.

This technique will produce the same number of lines which are produced by context restricted slicing by using less number of call sites and hence we call it as Optimized call stack restricted slicing.

Optimized Call Stack Restricted Slicing:

```
Input: G = (N, E) the given SDG
n ∈ N the given slicing criterion
s = <c1,...,ck> the given call stack
Output: S ⊆ N the slice for the criterion n
Procedure Call Stack minimization
      Input: s=<c1,...,ck>
      Output: s=< c1,...,cq >
      for i=1 to k do
        for j=1 to k do
                  if ci==cj
                    remove cj
                    for p=j+1 to k do
                    shift cp+1 to cp
                    k=k-1
q=k
return s=<c1,...cq> a set of minimized call stack
Procedure Optimized Slicing
W^up= {n}
W^down= Ø
S = {n}
first pass, descending slice
W = W^up
W^up= Ø
while W  = Ø worklist is not empty do
W = W / {n} remove one element from the worklist
 for each m → n ∈ E do
        if m ∉ S then
               if m → n is a parameter-out edge (m→ n )
            then
                   W^down= W^down ∪ {m}
                   S = S ∪ {m}
        elsif m → n is a parameter-in or call edge (m→ n)
        and for i = q . . . 1 do the call site of m is ci
        then
                   W^up=W^up ∪ {m}
                   S = S ∪ {m}
        else
                   W = W ∪ {m}
                   S = S ∪ {m}
second pass, ascending slice
 while W^down = Ø worklist is not empty do
        W^down = W^down /{ n} remove one element from the worklist
        for each m→ n ∈ E do
                   if m ∉ S then
```

if m→ n is not a parameter-in or call edge (m→ n) **then**

$W^{down} = W^{down} \cup \{m\}$

$S = S \cup \{m\}$

return S *the set of all visited nodes*

5 Experimental Results

We have considered all three types of programs as inputs for our optimized call stack restricted slicing technique. First type of input program has no call sites. 2nd one has call sites but flow of program is sequential i.e., each function is called exactly once in the program. 3rd one has call sites and different call stacks for the same point of failure. We have compared the output of this technique with context insensitive slicing technique for all three input categories. For the first category there is no difference between the proposed and existing technique. For second and third categories, we have shown the results in graphical format. 'x' axis of each graph represents different points of failure for various call stack combinations. In Fig 2(a), y axis shows the ratio between Context Insensitive (CIS) and Optimized Call stack Restricted Slicing (OCRS) techniques when the input program has call sites but with sequential program flow. In Fig 3(a), y axis shows the ratio between Context Insensitive (CIS) and Optimized Call stack Restricted Slicing (OCRS) techniques when the input program has call sites and different call stacks for the same point of failure. Fig 2(b) and 3(b) shows the slice size of both slicing techniques. Y axis represents size of the slice (number of lines).

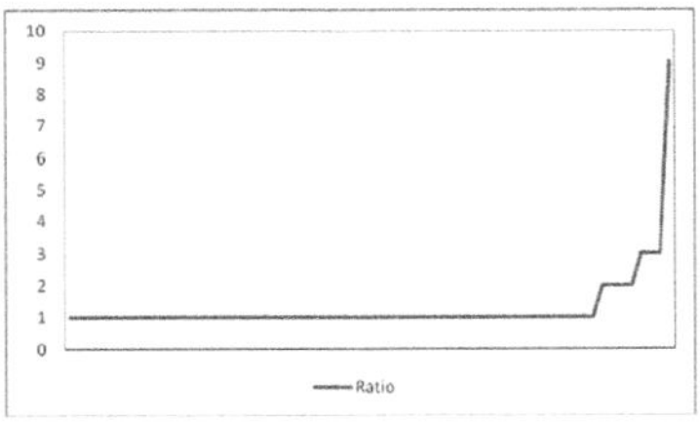

Fig. 2(a)

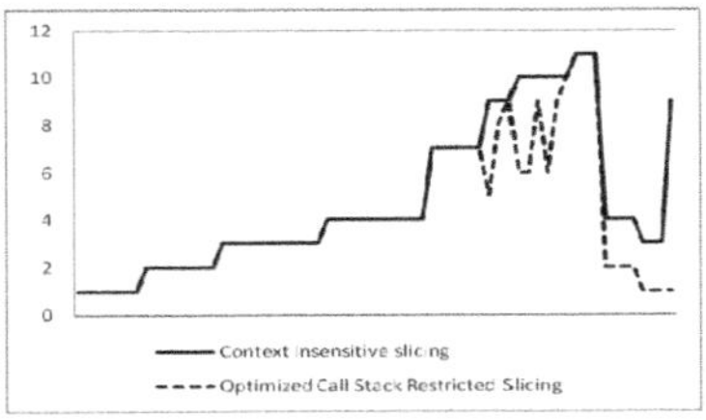

Fig. 2(b)

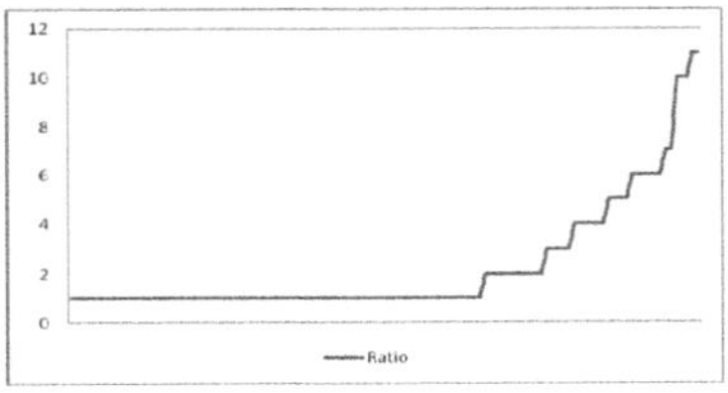

Fig. 3(a)

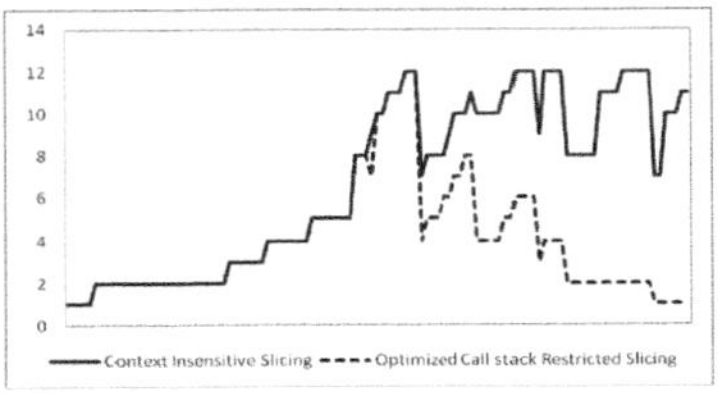

Fig. 3(b)

From above results we can conclude: Slices of the program which has no call sites have no reduction in size in optimized call-stack restricted slicing. Both methods produce same size of slices. For second category, results show the reduction in slice size in the proposed method. For the third category there is a drastic reduction in slice size in the proposed optimized technique. Optimized Call-stack restricted slicer produces comparatively very small size of slices for programs. This reduced slice statements are very much helpful in finding the actual bug from the point of failure. The bug could be in any or all of the slice statements and/or in point of failure.

6 Conclusions

For debugging of logical errors, Optimized Call-Stack Restricted Slicing proposed in this paper produces slices of smaller size compared with other slicing techniques. Logical errors can be easily found by tracing this small subset (slice) of the programs. Logical errors may reside in some or all statements within the slice. Our presented approach which generates slices using SDG, an intermediate graphical representation of the input program. Context restricted slicer and optimized call stack sensitive slicer produces same size of slices but our algorithm uses minimum set of call sites and minimum number of iterations to find those slices. Optimized Call-stack restricted slicing is compared with context-insensitive slicing. In future, this technique can be compared with other slicers to find the most efficient slicing technique.

References

1. Weiser, M.: Program Slicing. IEEE Trans. Software Eng. 10(4), 352–357 (1984)
2. Horwitz, S., Reps, T., Binkley, D.: Interprocedural Slicing Using Dependence Graphs. ACM Trans. Programming Languages and Systems 12(1), 26–60 (1990)
3. Krinke, J.: Context-Sensitivity Matters, but Context Does Not. In: Proc. Int'l Workshop Source Code Analysis and Manipulation, p. 2935 (2004)
4. Krinke, J.: Evaluating context-sensitive slicing and chopping. In: International Conference on Software Maintenance, pp. 22–31 (2002)
5. Horwitz, S., Liblit, B., Polishchuk, M.: Better Debugging via Output Tracing and Callstack-Sensitive Slicing. IEEE Trans. Soft. Eng. 36(1) (January/February 2010)
6. Wisconsin Program-Slicing Tool 1.1 Reference Manual, Wisconsin
7. Alumni Research Foundation (November 2000), `http://www.cs.wisc.edu/wpis/slicing-tool/slicing-manual.ps`
8. Binkley, D., Harman, M.: A Large-Scale Empirical Study of Forward and Backward Static Slice Size and Context Sensitivity. In: Proc. 2003 Int'l Conf. Software Maintenance (September 2003)
9. Korel, B., Laski, J.: Dynamic Program Slicing. Information Processing Letters 29(3), 155–163 (1988)
10. Krinke, J.: Effects of Context on Program Slicing. J. Systems and Software 79(9), 1249–1260 (2006)
11. The GNU C Library, 0th ed., The Free Software Foundation (July 2001)
12. GNU Binutils, binutils 2.17 ed., The Free Software Foundation (June 2006)
13. Stallman, R.M., and the GCC Developer Community: Using the GNU Compiler Collection (GCC), gcc 4.1.1 ed., The Free Software Foundation (May 2006)
14. GrammaTech, Codesurfer (September 2006), `http://www.codesurfer.com`
15. Reps, T., Horwitz, S., Rosay, G.: Speeding up Slicing. In: Proc. ACM SIGSOFT Int'l Symp. Foundations of Software Eng., pp. 11–20 (December 1994)

16. Agrawal, G., Guo, L.: Evaluating explicitly context sensitive program slicing. In: Workshop on Program Analysis for Software Tools and Engineering, pp. 6–12 (2001)
17. Mock, M., Atkinson, D.C., Chambers, C., Eggers, S.J.: Improving program slicing with dynamic points-to data. In: Proceedings of the 10th International Symposium on the Foundations of Software Engineering (2002)
18. Ferrante, J., Ottenstein, K.J., Warren, J.D.: The program dependence graph and its use in optimization. ACM Trans. Program. Lang. Syst. 9(3), 319–349 (1987)
19. http://everything2.com/title/data+dependency
20. http://hpc.serc.iisc.ernet.in/~govind/hpc/L10-Pipeline.txt

Towards Incremental Reasoning for Context Aware Systems

Mohammad Oliya and Hung Keng Pung

National University of Singapore, 13 Computing Drive, Singapore 117417
{oliya,dcsphk}@nus.edu.sg

Abstract. Context awareness is one of the key requirements for realizing the vision of ubiquitous computing. Formal representation of context information fosters interoperability, eases evolvability and maintainability of applications, and enables a number of reasoning services. The proposed formal models are mainly based on the emerging standards such as the Web Ontology Language (OWL). Reasoning with ontology based models of context, however, is inherently complex and is further complicated by the dynamism of the context data. In this paper, we advocate an incremental approach for reasoning about dynamic context data; so as to avoid redundant computations and alleviate the cost of reasoning from scratch. The continuity of contextual states and existence of long-lasting subscription queries further encourage this approach. We present the related work on reasoning with dynamic data and conclude that the efforts do not address the problem adequately and are not tailored for specific considerations of context aware systems.

Keywords: ubiquitous computing, context awareness, incremental reasoning, ontology, rule.

1 Introduction

"The most profound technologies are those that disappear. They weave themselves into the fabric of everyday life until they are indistinguishable from it." This is how Mark Weiser describes the vision of ubiquitous computing in his seminal paper [27]. Such a utopia is saturated with pervasive computing and communication technologies. Everyday objects and places are smart, sensors and actuators maintain rich connections between the physical and virtual worlds, and computing is spread throughout the environment [15]. A highly anticipated property of this new paradigm is its graceful integration with human lives. To be minimally intrusive, a ubiquitous computing environment must be context-aware. Context data can be used for adapting user interface, tailoring the set of application-relevant data, increasing the precision of information retrieval, discovering services, or making the user interaction implicit [6].

Despite the availability of constituent technologies, the vision of ubiquitous computing is still far from realization. Surprisingly, most of the constituent technologies are now available or even viable commercial products. Portable devices,

A. Abraham et al. (Eds.): ACC 2011, Part I, CCIS 190, pp. 232–241, 2011.

wireless technologies, and sensing devices are already widespread. The required software components such as location tracking, face and speech recognition, and online calendars have also reached a sophisticated level of maturity. The major challenge for developing ubiquitous context aware systems is seamless integration of the component technologies [21]. This is due to the sheer diversity of the context sources as well as different software which collect, process, and change the information.

The ubiquitous computing community increasingly understands benefits of formal context information modeling. Firstly, the formal expression of context data alleviates the heterogeneity by providing well-defined semantics. This in turn fosters reuse and sharing of context information which can be expensive to gather, evaluate and maintain. Secondly, a formal context model reduces the complexity of context-aware applications and improves their maintainability and evolvability [4]. Lastly, a number of reasoning services are enabled which can be used to derive implicit or abstract information, answer queries, and detect the inconsistencies peculiar to context data.

Proposed formal context models usually take advantage of emerging standards such as the Web Ontology Language (OWL) [18] proposed by W3C. This language is characterized by the formal semantics of Description Logics (DL) [3] and its RDF-based serializations [1]. Unfortunately, one major concern with the use of ontology based models is the inefficiency of the reasoning services. Moreover, unlike other application domains such as semantic web, the dynamism of the contextual information should be considered as the main concern. Traditional reasoning methods, however, assume that the knowledge base is static or seldom changes. In fact, research on reasoning over dynamic knowledge is quite limited [28][24][8][12].

One way to address the problem is to reuse the results of the previous computations in an incremental fashion. This, however, depends on the nature of the changes and on how a knowledge base is accessed. Firstly, incremental reasoning can have the same worst complexity as a normal reasoning task, if the changes to the knowledge base make the new knowledge base completely different. Secondly, exploiting previous computations makes sense, only if it can be used later. We highlight two observations made in the ubiquitous computing environments that satisfy these assumptions. Firstly, two subsequent contextual states usually do not differ completely, allowing the reuse of the common required computations. Secondly, a considerable portion of envisioned queries are long running subscriptions, making the reuse sensible as long as the queries are valid.

In this paper we elaborate on these observations and present the related work in reasoning with dynamic knowledge (albeit in different areas). We conclude that the existing work do not address the problem sufficiently and are not designed with specific considerations of context aware systems in mind; namely, the distribution and imperfection of context data.

2 Ontology-Based Modeling and Reasoning

Useful context information can be retrieved from physical or virtual sensors. Physical sensors refer to hardware sensing devices capturing a wide range of data types. These include location, motion and acceleration, audio, light, visual context (camera images), touch, temperature, ECG sensors and so on. These sources of information can be consumed directly or be used in deriving more abstract information such as the activity of the users. On the other hand, virtual sensors refer to information sources which are provided by various software applications and services through different APIs. Consider, for example, traffic and weather information, identity, profile, and calendar of users, and flight information.

Many context-aware systems based on various context models have been developed over the years. Models based on Key-value pairs use simple dictionary like structures for representation of context (e.g. ¡temperature, 25¿). Markup scheme models usually extend the XML based models such as Composite Capabilities/Preferences Profile (CC/PP)[2]. Object oriented methods introduce concepts such as encapsulation, inheritance, and reusability into the modeling process. The details of context processing are hidden within objects and access to the context data is provided through specified interfaces. Spatial models stress the significance of location information and provide constructs as well as data storage and retrieval mechanisms for location aware manipulation of the context. In a logic based model, context is defined as facts, expressions and rules which is added to, updated in, and deleted from a logic based system. The experiences with the proposed context models and the challenges faced in practice have influenced the set of the requirements defined for context modeling. In fact, many of these modeling approaches have been shown to be insufficient for (i) representing a variety of context types, (ii) capturing relationships, dependencies, timeliness, and quality of context information, (iii) allowing consistency checking, or (iv) supporting reasoning on context [6][4][23][13][5].

The ubiquitous computing community increasingly understands benefits of formal context information modeling [4]. In fact, in order to facilitate interoperability, powerful knowledge representation methods should be taken. Adhoc formalisms with insufficient expressiveness make this process difficult [14]. The Web Ontology Language (OWL) is a formal approach for modeling context which is widely used in the literature. OWL has several variants which differ in their expressiveness and the efficiency of the reasoning. *OWL-DL*, specifically, is based on a decidable fragment of description logics and is the fragment of choice in many application scenarios. In principle, an OWL knowledge base consists of two parts. The *TBox* is comparable to the schema in databases, the intentional knowledge, which defines knowledge structure in terms of concepts and their relationships. The *ABox* corresponds to database instances, the extensional knowledge, and describes the actual individuals and relationships.

Using the supported constructors in OWL, complex contextual situations can be described in terms of domain knowledge and existing definitions. Such descriptions are built by composing elementary definitions through specific operators provided by the language such as conjunction, existential quantification, and number restrictions. For instance, one can express the context of a business meeting as:

$$BusinessMeeting \equiv Meeting \sqcap \geq_5 hasParticipant.Employee \sqcap \exists hasVenue.ExecutiveRoom,$$

which defines a business meeting as a specific kind of meeting involving more than five people and happening in an executive room. In the above definition Meeting, Employee, and ExecutiveRoom are concepts, and, hasParticipant and hasVenue are relations (a.k.a. properties).

On top of a formal context representation model, appropriate reasoning mechanisms can exploit the available context information for a number of purposes. As the context data originates from various sources, the chances to encounter inconsistencies are not negligible. For instance, location information identified by a user's GPS receiver can be in contradiction with the one identified in his calendar. DL based reasoning techniques allow verification of the acquired context information for possible inconsistencies. Furthermore, TBox reasoning services allow for deriving implicit relationships in TBox, and ABox reasoning services help in answering instance retrieval queries. These reasoning services can be helpful in improving the quality of the existing data, inferring knew knowledge or answering queries.

Many of the existing DL based reasoners (e.g. Pellet [22]) are based on the tableau process for detecting inconsistencies. A tableau is a graph corresponding to the underlying model of the knowledge base. Several expansion rules are applied continually which correspond to the logical constructs of the language, such as disjunction, qualifiers, and number restrictions. The algorithm terminates either when no more rules can be applied, or when contradictions are detected. The tableau decision procedure determines the consistency of a set of arguments, and can be used for other reasoning tasks such as classification, instance retrieval, and realization [3]. Realization amounts to finding the most specific class in the knowledge base to which the individual representing the current context belongs to. In [14] and [17], contextual situations are defined as classes in OWL, and the set of sensor inputs are considered to be instances in the knowledge base. Determining the current context is then formulated as realization.

Formal representation of the context data also facilitates reasoning based on additional information in the form of rules. SOCAM [9] allows users to define rules for specific application domains to derive high level context information. The system supports forward chaining, backward chaining, and hybrid execution mode (thanks to the use of Jena rule engine). For instance, consider the following rule:

$$(?user\ \mathbf{situation}\ Sleeping) \leftarrow (?user\ \mathbf{locatedIn}\ ?bedroom) \wedge (?bedroom\ \mathbf{lightLevel}\ Low) \wedge (?user\ \mathbf{hasPosture}\ LieDown),$$

which decides if a user is sleeping based on his current location, his posture, and the lighting level. In Semantic Spaces project [26], users can submit the domain specific rules to the system to perform the forward chaining reasoning using the Jena rule engine. This is the only form of reasoning supported and the results of the reasoning are not stored.

For a more comprehensive study of semantic models and reasoning techniques in context aware systems, interested readers may refer to [4][5].

3 Incremental Reasoning

With regards to the streaming data, the focus of research has mainly been on the management, query evaluation, and optimization; nevertheless, research on deductive reasoning on streaming data is very limited [28][24][8][12]. A naive approach to handle reasoning on streaming data is to re-initiate the inference upon a change in the data, which is impractical for real world scenarios with large knowledge bases and frequent changes. The reasoning techniques need to be incremental so as to reuse the results of previous computations. In this section we review the DL/OWL reasoning methods which take the dynamism of the knowledge base into consideration.

In [16], the authors provide a formal analysis of the most basic ABox updates of the form: [¬]a:A and r(a,b). They show that in order to incorporate the new information resulting from an update, the language should support nominals; and further, the @ concept constructor from hybrid logic or Boolean ABoxes. As a result, both $\mathcal{SHIF}$ and $\mathcal{SHOIN}$ (corresponding to OWL Lite and OWL DL) can not represent the updates without the '@' operator. They also highlight that an important issue is the size of the updated ABox, which can be unavoidably exponential both in the size of the original ABox and the new information. In [7], the DL-Lite is proved to be closed with respect to instance level updates; that is to say, the result of an update is always expressible by a new DL Lite ABox. This is in contrary for updates in more expressive description logics (as stated before). We note that these studies are mainly from a theoretical point of view. Furthermore, the preliminary algorithms provided do not come with an implementation and hence we will not evaluate them here.

The work in [12], is motivated by the existence of various dynamic sources of data in the semantic web, including web portals, syndication frameworks (e.g. RSS feeds), and semantic services frameworks (e.g. OWL-S). They provide a syndication framework which matches conjunctive queries submitted by users against a set of dynamic publications which contain rich semantic content. Each publication is essentially a set of ABox assertions which is incorporated in the central knowledge base of the broker.

One of the main arguments is that the central knowledge base should be kept consistent, because otherwise, any information can be derived from it, which is undesirable. For this purpose they develop an incremental consistency checking algorithm. This is to address the main performance issue in traditional tableau-based OWL reasoners which re-build the entire completion graph from scratch in the event of an update to the KB. The overall goal is to incrementally update a completion graph from a previous consistency check.

Having secured the consistency of the central knowledge base of the broker, they consider incrementally resolving registered subscriptions in the syndication framework which are represented as DL conjunctive retrieval queries. Rather than considering the entire knowledge base after an update, they develop techniques which aim to reduce the portion of the KB that must be considered as candidate answers. That is to say, the query only needs to be re-evaluated over a subset of the KB over the updated broker's KB.

Nevertheless, we point that despite some good steps in addressing the problem, this work is limited to DL reasoning and the application of rules is not considered. Furthermore, the suitability of the method needs to be tested in pervasive computing environments with high change rates, imperfect data, and distributed sources of information.

Another line of research is towards incremental maintenance of materializations of ontological entailments. The classic reasoning tasks are usually triggered when the user queries the system, which is responded by deriving entailed information from asserted information. Under this setting, when the queries are frequent, or the reasoning process is time consuming or complex, the performance may not be acceptable. Materialization amounts to precomputing and storing a set of implicit entailments, so that frequent and/or crucial queries to the ontology can be answered efficiently [25]. It basically saves the reasoner from recomputing the entailed information for every single query. As re-calculating the materialization upon a change is not efficient, the proper solutions should be incremental; i.e. reuse the result of previous calculations.

In [25], one such approach for incremental maintenance of materialized ontological entailments is presented. It can only be applied to the ontologies which can be axiomatized as logic programs. A logic program LP is a set of rules of the form $H : -B_1, \ldots, B_m$; where H, B_i belong to the set of predicates P. Similar to the differentiation between the TBox and ABox in description logics, logic programs also distinguish between intensional and extensional predicates. Intensional predicates are materialized, if their derived extension is stored in the database. RDFS and Description Logic Programs (DLP) are among the ontologies which can be transformed into logic programs. One main advantage of this approach is the default support for rule-based reasoning.

The work takes a declarative variant of the delete and re-derive algorithm (DRed) [10] which consists of three steps:

1. Overestimate a deletion: compute all the direct consequences of a deletion
2. Re-derive: neglect those estimated deletions which could be still derived by other facts
3. Insert: insert the new derivations that are consequences of the added facts.

The maintenance process starts with a setup, where the maintenance program is created for a given source program and the initial materialization of the intentional predicates is computed. Afterwards, upon a change in the extensional knowledge (ABox), the actual maintenance is triggered. As shown in the experiments, after materialization the cost of accessing the materialized predicates is negligible.

Nevertheless, all maintenance operations (including setup, add, and removal of facts) are more expensive than the cost of evaluating a single query on the original program. Furthermore, if the original ontology is large or consists of complex rules, the time for evaluation of the maintenance rules can be significantly large (around 15 minutes [10]). As discussed by the authors, materialization is a good technique in application domains where queries are dominated by read operations. They exemplify the process as caching employed in web servers to enable fast access to dynamic data. Although many good applications for the technique can be thought of in the semantic web, the technique is far suitable for non-read-dominant context aware systems with severe real-time requirements.

LarkC [8] takes a similar approach while trying to couple traditional DL reasoners with powerful, reactive, and throughput-efficient Data Stream Management Systems (DSMS). The main advantage of this approach is that it uses available techniques for stream processing and DL reasoning. LarkC consists of five steps which are to be repeated continually until a good enough answer has been calculated. Data is first retrieved, and then abstracted by transforming to logics (e.g. using statistical methods). Relevant data is selected and reasoned about, and the cycle ends by deciding if the answer is appropriate enough. If that is not the case, a new cycle needs to be repeated. Nevertheless, we argued that this approach is good for read-dominant scenarios, to where reasoning on streaming data clearly does not belong. In fact, as shown in the experiments, the solution cannot cope well with the streaming data, despite some improvements over the original work.

At the end, we mention that there are specific formalisms which incorporate the notion of time, and consider reasoning to be an ongoing process. Representatives are temporal logic, dynamic logic, and active logics. Nevertheless, they have not been applied in context aware systems and their performance has been less studied.

4 Conclusion and Future Work

Ontology-based models of context information take a formal approach to foster interoperability, ease software development, and enable sound reasoning mechanisms. The existing reasoning services, however, can be of high worst case complexity. On the other hand, context data is potentially dynamic which poses severe requirements on the efficiency of the reasoning. We presented two observations made in the ubiquitous computing environments. Firstly, the relevant contextual information do not change completely between subsequent states. This allows for reusing the common computations that were made previously. Secondly, many of the queries concerning context aware systems are long-running, and are in the form of subscriptions. This makes reusing of the previous computations useful as long as the queries are present. In this regard, having efficient incremental reasoning mechanisms would alleviate the inefficiency of redoing reasoning for each change in context data.

The related work can be categorized into two groups; those based on incremental maintenance of tableau completion graph, and those incrementally maintaining materialized ontologies. Having discussed the related work, we conclude that, firstly, they can not handle high change rates. This issue may by alleviated by usage-driven identification and discarding of unnecessary updates. In fact, in many of envisioned pervasive computing scenarios, changes have patterns or at least do not happen randomly. For instance, the environmental factors, road traffic data, and the interactions within ambient intelligence environments have identifiable patterns. The question is, how the assumptions on the distribution of the incoming data may be exploited to improve the efficiency of the incremental reasoning.

Another way to better equip the reasoner in handling high change rates is trading soundness and/or completeness of the reasoning for *good enough* answers under time pressure. Approximation has been identified as a potential way to reduce the complexity of reasoning [19]. In ubiquitous computing scenarios, the reasoner can consider factors such as user, his current task and its priority, quality of service and SLA to provide approximations. In DL based reasoning, for instance, the sources of the complexity are non deterministic choices made during expansion of the tableau completion graph - corresponding to disjunction and value restrictions, among others. Approximations based on the mentioned factors can target these sources of complexity by selectively ignoring or estimating their results.

A major issue with the existing work in incremental reasoning is that they mainly take a central approach – where all the data necessary for the inference are gathered in a central processing node. This method suffers from a single processing bottleneck, single point of failure, and suboptimal utilization of network resources. Despite some recent efforts on distributed reasoning (e.g. [29]), the methods do not address the problem adequately and are not incremental. Moreover, in a distributed setting, different sources may have different update rates and quality of context (freshness,delay, and trust) which may lead to anomalies. For instance, in rule based reasoning, it can lead to concurrent firing of the rules and race conditions [20]. In fact, the traditional view of the existing methods which is concerned with ideal reasoning under ideal circumstances do not hold anymore.

A fundamental assumption in existing reasoning algorithms is that the knowledge base should be consistent, because otherwise any conclusions can be made from it. Nevertheless, this is quite restricting in practice where the distribution and heterogeneity of knowledge sources may result in frequent inconsistencies. The existing work mainly assumes that the incoming updates are consistent with the existing knowledge. Even if appropriate belief revision methods can be devised (e.g. [12]), incorporating them in the incremental solution can be inefficient. Therefore, there is the need for robust incremental solutions which tolerate some detected inconsistencies.

Our recent effort focuses on the development of a service-oriented middleware known as Coalition [30]. Ir provides a number of system-level services, such as context data acquisition, context storage, context reasoning, service organization and discovery, to facilitate the development and deployment of various ubiquitous computing applications. The middleware infrastructure separates context data and context-aware services in different layers that are accessible by the applications. Our infrastructure assumes autonomous sources of context data which are categorized and organized into different context domains. This allows for low-level processing of the data and associated reasoning operations to be distributed among individual domains. We are working on incremental reasoning solutions in the previously-mentioned directions to further make the middleware suitable for ubiquitous computing environments.

References

1. Resource description framework (rdf): Concepts and abstract syntax (2004), `http://www.w3.org/TR/2004/REC-rdf-concepts-20040210/`
2. CC/PP Information Page (2007), `http://www.w3.org/Mobile/CCPP/`
3. Baader, F.: The description logic handbook: theory, implementation, and applications. Cambridge University Press, Cambridge (2010)
4. Bettini, C., Brdiczka, O., Henricksen, K., Indulska, J., Nicklas, D., Ranganathan, A., Riboni, D.: A survey of context modelling and reasoning techniques. Pervasive and Mobile Computing 6(2), 161–180 (2010)
5. Bikakis, A., Patkos, T., Antoniou, G., Plexousakis, D.: A survey of semantics-based approaches for context reasoning in ambient intelligence. In: Muhlhauser, M., Ferscha, A., Aitenbichler, E. (eds.) Constructing Ambient Intelligence. Communications in Computer and Information Science, vol. 11, pp. 14–23. Springer, Heidelberg (2008)
6. Bolchini, C., Curino, C.A., Quintarelli, E., Schreiber, F.A., Tanca, L.: A data-oriented survey of context models. SIGMOD Rec. 36, 19–26 (2007)
7. De Giacomo, G., Lenzerini, M., Poggi, A., Rosati, R.: On the update of description logic ontologies at the instance level. In: Proceedings of the 21st National Conference on Artificial Intelligence, vol. 2, pp. 1271–1276. AAAI Press, Menlo Park (2006)
8. Della Valle, E., Ceri, S., Barbieri, D.F., Braga, D., Campi, A.: A first step towards stream reasoning. In: Domingue, J., Fensel, D., Traverso, P. (eds.) FIS 2008. LNCS, vol. 5468, pp. 72–81. Springer, Heidelberg (2009)
9. Gu, T., Pung, H.K., Zhang, D.Q.: Toward an osgi-based infrastructure for context-aware applications. IEEE Pervasive Computing 3, 66–74 (2004)
10. Gupta, A., Mumick, I.S., Subrahmanian, V.S.: Maintaining views incrementally. In: Proceedings of the 1993 ACM SIGMOD International Conference on Management of Data, pp. 157–166. ACM, New York (1993)
11. Haarslev, V., Möller, R.: RACER system description. In: Goré, R.P., Leitsch, A., Nipkow, T. (eds.) IJCAR 2001. LNCS (LNAI), vol. 2083, pp. 701–706. Springer, Heidelberg (2001)
12. Halaschek-Wiener, F.C.: Expressive syndication on the web using a description logic-based approach. Ph.D. thesis, University of Maryland, College Park, College Park, MD, USA, aAI3297367 (2007)
13. Hoareau, C., Satoh, I.: Modeling and processing information for context-aware computing: A survey. New Generation Computing 27, 177–196 (2009)
14. Lassila, O., Khushraj, D.: Contextualizing applications via semantic middleware. In: Proceedings of the The Second Annual International Conference on Mobile and Ubiquitous Systems: Networking and Services, pp. 183–191. IEEE Computer Society, Washington, DC, USA (2005)

15. Lei, H.: Context awareness: a practitioner's perspective. In: International Workshop on Ubiquitous Data Management, pp. 43–52 (2005)
16. Liu, H., Lutz, C., Milicic, M., Wolter, F.: Updating description logic aboxes. In: International Conference of Principles of Knowledge Representation and Reasoning. AAAI, Menlo Park (2006)
17. Luther, M., Fukazawa, Y., Wagner, M., Kurakake, S.: Situational reasoning for task-oriented mobile service recommendation. Knowl. Eng. Rev. 23, 7–19 (2008)
18. McGuinness, D., Harmelen, F.: Owl web ontology language overview 2003, `http://www.w3.org/TR/owl-features/`
19. Pan, J.Z., Thomas, E.: Approximating owl-dl ontologies. In: Proceedings of the National Conference on Artificial Intelligence (2007)
20. Sama, M., Elbaum, S., Raimondi, F., Rosenblum, D.S., Wang, Z.: Context-aware adaptive applications: Fault patterns and their automated identification. IEEE Transactions on Software Engineering 36, 644–661 (2010)
21. Satyanarayanan, M.: Pervasive computing: vision and challenges. IEEE Personal Communications 8(4), 10–17 (2001)
22. Sirin, E., Parsia, B., Grau, B.C., Kalyanpur, A., Katz, Y.: Pellet: A practical owl-dl reasoner. Web Semantics: Science, Services and Agents on the World Wide Web 5(2), 51–53 (2007)
23. Strang, T., Linnhoff-Popien, C.: A context modeling survey. In: 1st Int. Workshop on Advanced Context Modelling, Reasoning and Management (2004)
24. Unel, G., Roman, D.: Stream reasoning: A survey and further research directions. In: Andreasen, T., Yager, R.R., Bulskov, H., Christiansen, H., Larsen, H.L. (eds.) FQAS 2009. LNCS, vol. 5822, pp. 653–662. Springer, Heidelberg (2009)
25. Volz, R., Staab, S., Motik, B.: Incrementally maintaining materializations of ontologies stored in logic databases. In: Spaccapietra, S., Hwang, J., Jajodia, S., King, R., McLeod, D., Orlowska, M.E., Strous, L. (eds.) Journal on Data Semantics II. LNCS, vol. 3360, pp. 1–34. Springer, Heidelberg (2005)
26. Wang, X., Dong, J.S., Chin, C., Hettiarachchi, S., Zhang, D.: Semantic space: An infrastructure for smart spaces. IEEE Pervasive Computing 3, 32–39 (2004)
27. Weiser, M.: The computer for the 21st century. In: Baecker, R.M., Grudin, J., Buxton, W.A.S., Greenberg, S. (eds.) Human-Computer Interaction, pp. 933–940. Morgan Kaufmann Publishers Inc., San Francisco (1995)
28. Weithöner, T., Liebig, T., Luther, M., Böhm, S., von Henke, F.W., Noppens, O.: Real-world reasoning with OWL. In: Franconi, E., Kifer, M., May, W. (eds.) ESWC 2007. LNCS, vol. 4519, pp. 296–310. Springer, Heidelberg (2007)
29. Gu, T., Pung, H.K., Zhang, D.: Peer-to-peer context reasoning in pervasive computing environments. In: 6th Annual IEEE International Conference on Pervasive Computing and Communications, PerCom 2008, pp. 406–411 (2008)
30. Pung, H., Gu, T., Xue, W., Palmes, P., Zhu, J., Ng, W., Tang, C., Chung, N.: Context-aware middleware for pervasive elderly homecare. IEEE Journal on Selected Areas in Communications 27(4), 510–524 (2009)

On the Potential of Using Conventional Mobile Communication Technology for Human Context Awareness in Ubiquitous Computing

Abhijan Bhattacharyya

Innovation Lab,
Tata Consultancy Services Ltd., Kolkata, India
abhijan.bhattacharyya@tcs.com

Abstract. Human context acquisition is an important aspect of human computer interaction (HCI) for context aware ubiquitous computing. There are many state-of-art relatively obtrusive and unobtrusive approaches to accomplish the task of human context extraction. This paper surveys the state-of-the-art approaches and establishes the possibility of using the conventional mobile communication as an enabler for nearly unobtrusive human context acquisition in a smart ubiquitous environment. This paper studies the technical intricacies behind using the mobile communication technologies for such purposes and proposes how it can be used for such an 'augmented' utility in smart spaces.

Keywords: Bluetooth, Context Awareness, Face Recognition, HCI, Human Context, Mobile Communication, PDA, RFID, Ubiquitous Computing, WiFi.

1 Introduction

The aim of ubiquitous system is not just to support ubiquity in its literal meaning by interlinking all systems into an omnipresent domain, but to support 'context based ubiquity' as per the objectives set by Weiser in his seminal paper [1]. So, a system needs to be context aware such that it fits into a human-centric personalized environment, interacting less obtrusively with humans and become part of the physical environment by sensing more of it [1][2]. Ref. [3] provides a good exemplary vision on personalized smart environment services. Ref. [4] provides a good account of the different efforts to define 'context' and provides a broad definition of 'context' and 'context aware system'. In terms of practical usage this broad definition of 'context' can be classified into three categories [2]: 'physical environment context', 'human context' and 'virtual environment context'. 'Human context', the topic of this paper, helps to personalize a service based on user presence, user identification and task preferences set by prior user experience.

There are many proposed and in-use techniques for achieving the purpose of human context acquisition which is the key in terms of personalization of services. These techniques span a wide range of technologies. However, all these approaches have some advantages and some disadvantages when we try to evaluate them in terms of real life aspects which essentially involve human factors. What we find interesting

A. Abraham et al. (Eds.): ACC 2011, Part I, CCIS 190, pp. 242–249, 2011.

is that mobile phones can be a very good choice for such a purpose by virtue of its normal course of operation in the very basic form without relying on convergence with other associated technologies like Bluetooth, WiFi, etc. However, conventional mobile phone operation has not found much mention in the relevant researches in personalization of smart environment services compared to other approaches.

In this paper, we first perform a survey of the state-of-the approaches starting from computer vision to short range wireless communications and compare them against some real life issues around the human factor. Then we shall do a technical feasibility study for using mobile phones for the given purpose followed by the researches done in this area which can help as the launching pad. Next we shall evaluate the proposed approach against similar factors as we have done for other state-of-the-art technologies.

2 State-of-the-Art Approaches

The problem of mechanized presence detection and identification in a premise / system to perform some predefined task relevant to the identified person is not new. A very common example is the access control system in an office entrance where the user has to swipe an access card through an access controller for opening the door. Again, consider a software system which gets unlocked only when a user types the right user ID and password leading the system to activate with the settings specific to the current user profile. There can be many such examples. However, these conventional systems, though context aware in true sense, are not 'unobtrusive' so far as the HCI is considered as they require explicit human interaction to initiate the process. Following part concisely presents a survey of different dominant technologies proposed in different literatures.

Active Badge using modulated infrared beacon: One of the earliest approaches is to create an "active badge" which emits a periodic[1] unique code in the form of a beacon by way of pulse-width-modulation of infrared signals as described in [5]. The users wearing these badges can be picked up by a network of sensors placed around the host building.

RFID based detection: RFID has been proposed as a very popular technology for identification of objects for smart applications and future Internet of Things (IoT) [6][7][8]. It uses electromagnetic coupling in the radio frequency (RF) portion of the electro magnetic spectrum to uniquely identify an object or a person with an RFID tag. Ref. [7] discusses about several prototypes of smart identification based UbiCom applications which use RFID for identity acquisition. RFID tags are *passive* or *active*. Passive RFID tags receive their power to exchange from the signal sent by the RFID reader itself. Active RFID tags are battery powered.

Detection using short range wireless communication – Bluetooth and WiFi: Short range wireless communication like Bluetooth and WiFi have become a very popular choice for human presence detection [9][10][11][12][13] . This works on a simple idea. The Bluetooth and WiFi devices transmit there unique MAC addresses which the detectors detect. The devices are usually personalized and thus their addresses can

---

[1] Approximately a tenth of a second every 15 seconds.

be tagged with the users using them. One of the biggest reasons for these techniques to be popular is that they are usually integrated into PDAs and Handhelds which users carry around quite habitually.

Detection based on computer vision – Face Recognition: Face recognition using computer vision is a promising technology for presence detection in smart environment [14][15][16][17][18]. This technique uses artificial intelligence (AI) on captured camera images and the identification works using a classifier which has been trained with the end users (like members of a home, preferred customers of a superstore, etc.) in advance.

3 Analysis of the Surveyed Approaches

In line with Ref. [5] and [16] we can come up with several issues which can be treated as real life attributes for judging the effectiveness of different approaches as below.

- **Confidence** on the means of identification is important. Based on degree of confidence we can treat the identification as weak or strong [18]. For example, the biometric scheme like face-recognition is stronger than schemes like 'active-badge' and RFID tags (unless embedded into the body) which are more vulnerable to faking. Bluetooth and WiFi based approach can be treated with medium confidence if they come integrated with handhelds/PDAs as these devices are more or less personalized. But vulnerability to faking is always there.
- **Detection range** suggests proximity requirement of the identity advertiser to the identifier. Passive RFIDs suffer from low detection range and may not be good choice for larger areas like super stores [7]. Same applies for 'Active Badge' [5]. Bluetooth based schemes also have range problem as the transmitted signal is usually not very strong.
- **Technical issues** pose limitations leading to false alarm, missed detection opportunity, etc. 'Active Badge' and RFID has quite significant chance of false alarm[5][7]. Again, insufficient lighting and too much background noise can lead to error in face recognition scheme [15] apart from high algorithmic complexity.
- **Power requirement** especially at the user end is an important issue as it has a direct linear relation with the number of users in a premise. For example active RFID tags, though have a good range, does consume battery power and the same is applicable for active badge scheme. Bluetooth and WiFi also drain additional power even if they come integrated with handhelds. Of course, face recognition does not demand any user end power source being a totally passive technique.
- **Ease of use / unobtrusiveness** means how transparent is the HCI to the user and how easily can user adapt to the system. For example, face recognition should ideally be totally unobtrusive. But for schemes like RFID tags and actives badge the users have to be conscious about wearing the badge which may create discomfort to the user. Again, the Bluetooth and WiFi based schemes requires the user to remember to keep the Bluetooth / WiFi service

switched on so that the detection can happen even if they come integrated with handhelds.

- **Psychological factors** in using the system may impact the user. Although it relates to the fundamental issue of privacy in automatic identity disclosure, there may be differences in the degree of concern depending on what feature is being used as the 'identification mark'. For example, the face recognition scheme may be unwelcome for users as it captures the user's image, perhaps without his/her active consent. Again, wearing tags and badges just to get identified may not be a comfortable solution for some users, besides wearing active RFID badges which have large form factor [7]. Users may also dislike keeping the WiFi / Bluetooth on while they are actually not using those services for any content transfer and they can complain about draining of the battery power.
- **Cost effectiveness** of the system is also important. Schemes like RFID may not be very feasible detection mechanism for home like environment. Active RFID tags are quite costly as well [7]. Again the schemes requiring user end battery source add to the cost in terms of per user power usage.

4 Potential Use of Standard Mobile Communication Technique

Although not many references are found which explicitly use the standard mobile communication for presence detection and identification for personalization of services in smart environments, there is potential of using this conventional technology for such purpose and thereby opening up huge possibilities in context aware services through mobile HCI.

Mobile phones transmit the device identity as well as the subscriber identity in order to get identified and registered in a mobile network. For example, GSM (Global System for Mobile communication) uses IMSI (International Mobile Subscriber Identity) and IMEI (International Mobile Equipment Identity) numbers. Ref. [19] can be consulted for the different exchanges of these identifiers under different circumstances. It is because of these identities that we roam around across different geographical cells and the visiting locations identify the users and the users remain connected with the network. The total system is totally unobtrusive so far as human intervention in HCI is concerned. Intuitively, we can think of extending this property of mobile communication into smart spaces for personalization of services and extend the utility of mobile communication beyond what this was originally meant for.

However, the transmitter identity, for security reasons, is many a time encrypted such that only a legitimate base station can detect the mobile and the subscriber. Again, most of the time, the mobile phones remain idle when not in use. However, there is solution [21][22] to detect and identify idle mobile phones and we can see that such schemes can be extended to support human context acquisition for a wider range of applications.

Ref. [20] proposes a straight forward approach for presence service using femtocell by monitoring the attach request and detach request of subscribers.

Ref. [21] discloses a method for detecting the presence of a mobile phone in idle mode using a signal generating unit generating pseudo base station signal and a detecting unit that detects the response of the mobile phone against the pseudo base station signal. However, the intention of this invention is mainly to create an alarm for areas like a flying aircraft, theatre halls, etc. which should be devoid of any switched on mobile phone. It does not reveal the identity of the phone.

Ref. [22] takes this concept further to a more context aware application. Ref. [22] has proposed different approaches to detect presence of a user near a suitable IP (Internet Protocol) domain to control active hand-off between cellular and IP domain. In one of the schemes the inventors have used a pseudo base station which broadcasts the 'registration invitation' signal. A mobile phone in the range of pseudo base station would transmit back its 'registration information' containing the mobile identification number (MIN) and electronic serial number (ESN) (Fig. 1).

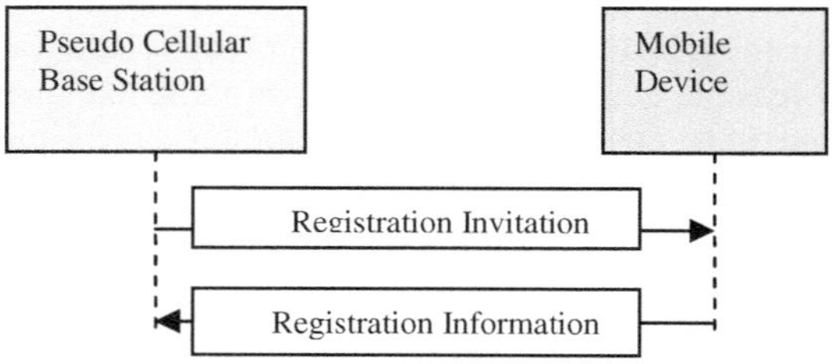

Fig. 1. Procedure to get mobile phone identity using pseudo base station [22]

These identifiers are used to route all calls to the MIN to the appropriate location and device. This approach can be generalized and explored for providing different personalized services in a smart space as conceptualized in Fig. 2.

The conceptual smart space is equipped with a gateway that senses the user presence through a virtual base station and controls the applications as per the personalized

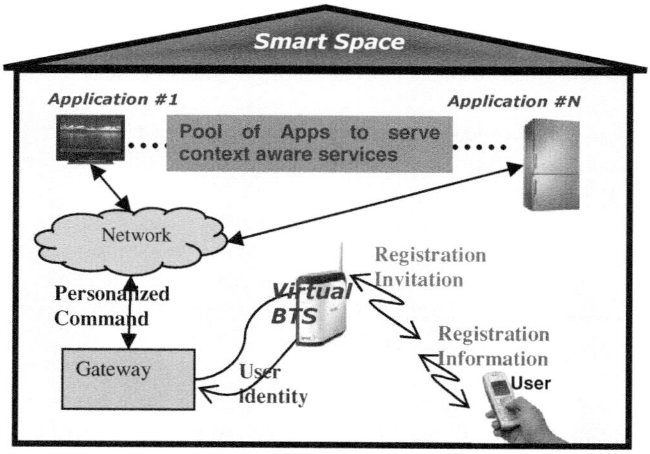

Fig. 2. Extracting human context using mobile phone identifiers in a smart space

requirements of the user. This shows the potential of unobtrusive use of conventional mobile communication for human context acquisition in a smart space in a very unobtrusive way.

5 Analysis of the Mobile Communication Based Scheme

Now let us compare the proposed scheme based on the same attributes as in section 3.

- In terms of confidence the mobile phones are 'moderately strong' as they are usually very much personalized.
- Detection range should not be a problem as they usually transmit at a power sufficient to reach a standard base station.
- This approach does not require any additional power just to perform the detection activity as the scheme relies on the normal communication standard unlike schemes like Bluetooth/ WiFi, etc.
- This scheme should be quite unobtrusive as the user just need to keep the mobile powered on which is quite habitual and does not need to switch on additional services like Bluetooth / WiFi for this purpose. Again, carrying around the mobile phone does not normally add any discomfort to the user as mobile phones have become a part of our living.
- This scheme does not add any psychological discomfort as discussed for other schemes in section 3.
- This scheme does not incur any additional cost other than that of the mobile phone which can of a very basic variety so far as human context acquisition is concerned.

The above points show the advantages of the proposed scheme over others. However, there are some technical and other issues which need to be addressed before arriving at an applicable solution. The major issues that this paper identifies are:

- Due to broadcast nature advertiser's radiation may overlap with neighbouring region causing false alarm.
- Artificially revealing subscriber identity may be a breach of the standard security feature and may need special permission from competent authority.
- The mobile communication operates in licensed band. Using the licensed band for detection should require spectrum usage permission. However, this does not apply for scenarios where the premises are equipped with legitimate femto-cells like [20].

6 Conclusion

In this paper we have surveyed different state-of-art approaches for human context acquisition in smart environments for personalization of services and compared them based on some real-life human centric attributes. Then we have explored the potential of using standard mobile communication method for human presence identification and proposed a possible scheme. We have also shown how this scheme can provide us with a very good unobtrusive HCI compared to other techniques. Also, we have discussed about the issues that need to be addressed for making the proposed scheme a usable choice. The discussion on this scheme can provide good motivation to come up with innovative solutions with mobile HCI for personalization of services in a ubiquitous environment.

Acknowledgments. I sincerely thank **Mr. Arpan Pal**, Research Group Manager, Innovation Lab, Kolkata, Tata Consultancy Services Ltd., for his guidance in nurturing the topic of human context extraction and context awareness at large. I thank my senior **Ms. Soma Bandyopadhyay** for her support and guidance by way of a thorough review of the present work. I thank my colleagues **Mr. Souvik Maiti** and **Ms. Munmun Sen Gupta** for helping me with important references.

References

1. Weiser, M.: The computer for the 21st century. Scientific American 265(3), 66–76 (1991)
2. Poslad, S.: Ubiquitous Computing: Smart Devices, Environment and Interactions. John Wiley & Sons Ltd., Chichester (2009)
3. Jason Weiss, R., Philip Craiger, J.: Ubiquitous computing. The Industrial-Organizational Psychologist 39(4)
4. Dey, A.K., Abowd, G.D.: Towards a Better Understanding of Context and Context-Awareness. In: Workshop on the What, Who, Where, When, and How of Context-Awareness (2000)
5. Want, R., Hopper, A., Falcão, V., Gibbons, J.: The Active Badge Location System. ACM Transactions on Information Systems (1992)
6. Marrocco, G.: Pevasive Electromagnetics: Sensing Paradigmes by Passive RFID Technology. IEEE Wireless Communications 17(6), 10–17 (2010)
7. Römer, K., Schoch, T., Mattern, F., Dübendorfer, T.: Smart Identification Frameworks for Ubiquitous Computing Applications. Wireless Networks-Special issue: Pervasive Computing and Communications 10(6) (November 2004)
8. US Patent : RFID Based Personnel Tracking, Inventor: Andrew Scott Braunstein, Aplication No.: 11/346,451, Filing date: 2nd February, 2006, Date of Patent: 13th January, 2009
9. Maestre, I.M., Machuca, M., Navarro, A., Velasco, J.R.: A practical aproach to user location awareness in smart home environments using Bluetooth home environments using Bluetooth. In: (Un enfoque práctico para la localización de usuarios mediante Bluetooth en entornos domóticos), 1st Iberoamerican Congress on Ubiquitous Computing, CICU 2005 (2005)
10. Velasco, J.R., Maestre, I.M., Navarro, A., López, M.A., Vicente, A.J., de la Hoz, E., Paricio, A., Machuca, M.: Location aware services and interfaces in smart homes using multi-agent systems. In: Juan, R. (ed.) Proceedings of Int. Conferecence on Pervasive Systems and Computing (PSC 2005), Las Vegas (2005)
11. Sharifi, M., Payne, T., David, E.: Public display advertising based on Bluetooth device presence. In: Proceedings of the Workshop Mobile Interaction with the Real World, MIRW 2006 (2006)
12. `http://www.automatedhome.co.uk/index2.php?option=com_content&do_pdf=1&id=9629`
13. `http://echodittolabs.org/blog/2008/01/presence-detection-iphone-and-wifi`

14. Pentland, A., Choudhury, T.: Personalizing Smart Environments: Face Recognition for Human Interaction. IEEE Computer, Special issue on Biometrics (2000)
15. Hämmerle, S., Wimmer, M., Radig, B., Beetz, M.: Sensor-based Situated, Individualized, and Personalized Interaction in Smart Environments. In: Workshop on Situierung, Individualisierung, and Personalisierung, Informatik 2005, Bonn, Germany (2005)
16. Ivanov, B., Ruser, H., Kellner, M.: Presence detection and person identification in Smart Homes. In: International Conference on Sensors and Systems. State Technical University, Saint-Petersburg (2002)
17. Raducanu, B., Subramanian, S., Markopoulos, P.: Human Presence Detection by Smart Devices. In: Proc. of 4th International ICSC Symposium on Engineering of Intelligent Systems, Island of Madeira, Portugal (2004)
18. Siegemund, F., Floerkemeier, C., Vogt, H.: The value of handhelds in smart environments. In: Personal and Ubiquitous Computing, vol. 9(2) (March 2005)
19. ETSI TS 100 929 V8.0.0(2000-10), `http://pda.etsi.org/exchangefolder/ts_100929v080000p.pdf`
20. US Patent : Method and System for SMS Based Ticket Numbering Service Over Femto Cell, Inventors: Mustafa Ergen, Tushar Shah, Rafi Assilian, Singaraselvan Singaraselvan, Oguz Oktay, Aplication No.: 12/814,934, Filing date: 14th June, 2010, Date of Patent: 16th December, 2010
21. US Patent : Apparatus and method for Detecting a mobile phone in Idle State, Inventors: Young-Soo park, Yun-Hee Lee, Sang-Hwan park, Aplication No.: 09/240,030, Filing date: 29th January, 1999, Date of Patent: 3rd December, 2002
22. US Patent : Presence Detection for Cellular and Internet Protocol Telephony, Inventors: Aborn, J.A., et al., Aplication No.: 11/183,379, Filing date: 18th July, 2005, Date of Patent: 5th October, 2010

A Novel Adaptive Monitoring Compliance Design Pattern for Autonomic Computing Systems

Vishnuvardhan Mannava[1] and T. Ramesh[2]

[1] Department of Computer Science and Engineering, KL University, Vaddeswaram, 522502, A.P, India
vishnu@klce.ac.in
[2] Department of Computer Science and Engineering, National Institute of Technology, Warangal, 506004, A.P, India
rmesht@nitw.ac.in

Abstract. The need for adaptability in software is growing, driven in part by the emergence of pervasive and autonomic computing. In many cases, it is desirable to enhance existing programs with adaptive behavior, enabling them to execute effectively in dynamic environments. Increasingly, software systems should self-adapt to satisfy new requirements and environmental conditions that may arise after deployment. Due to their high complexity, adaptive programs are difficult to specify, design, verify, and validate. Moreover, the current lack of reusable design expertise that can be leveraged from one adaptive system to another further exacerbates the problem. In this paper we proposed an adaptive design pattern called adaptive sensor factory to make the monitoring infrastructure of the adaptive system more dynamic by fusing the sensor factory pattern, observer and strategy patterns. This pattern will determine the type of sensor that suits best for monitoring the client. We have applied it to a sample application which is monitoring compliant and makes use of this monitoring infrastructure.

Keywords: Design patterns, Adaptive patterns, Autonomic computing.

1 Introduction

Advances in software technologies and practices have enabled developers to create larger, more complex applications to meet the ever increasing user demands. In today's computing environments, these applications are required to integrate seamlessly across heterogeneous platforms and to interact with other complex applications. The unpredictability of how the applications will behave and interact in a widespread, integrated environment poses great difficulties for system testers and managers. Autonomic computing proposes a solution to software management problems by shifting the responsibility for software management from the human administrator to the software system itself. It is expected that autonomic computing will result in significant improvements in terms of system

A. Abraham et al. (Eds.): ACC 2011, Part I, CCIS 190, pp. 250–259, 2011.

management, and many initiatives have begun to incorporate autonomic capabilities into software components.

On the other hand as applications grow in size, complexity, and heterogeneity in response to growing computational needs, it is increasingly difficult to build a system that satisfies all requirements. and design constraints that it will encounter during its lifetime. Furthermore, many of these systems are required to run continuously, disallowing downtimes while code is modified. As a result, it is important for an application to self-adapt in response to changing requirements and environmental conditions. Autonomic computing has been proposed to meet this need, where a system manages itself based on high-level objectives from a systems administrator. Due to their high complexity, adaptive and autonomic systems are difficult to specify, design, verify, and validate. In addition, the current lack of reusable design expertise that can be leveraged from one adaptive system to another further exacerbates the problem.

Adaptive and autonomic systems comprise a monitoring, decision-making, and reconfiguration infrastructure. Monitoring enables an adaptive system to be aware of its environment and detect conditions warranting reconfiguration. Decision-making processes monitoring information and determines which particular reconfiguration to apply in response. The reconfiguration infrastructure enables an application to change itself in order to fulfill its requirements. Developers must not only design and implement these elements correctly; they must also carefully determine their interactions. For instance, if the monitoring process fails to report an environmental change, then a decision-making process may incorrectly trigger an unnecessary and potentially detrimental reconfiguration. Until recently, however, most approaches have addressed adaptation through ad hoc techniques. To address these concerns, researchers have built adaptation-enabling frameworks [4,5], middleware [6,7], and language-based support [8]. These approaches, however, may be tightly coupled with specific domains or technologies, possibly limiting their applicability across different domains. In contrast, design patterns work at the modeling and design level of abstraction, thus facilitating design reuse. The pattern proposed is a generic solution that can be easily adapted to specific situations.

Our paper is organized as follows. Section 2 presents a survey of related work. In Section 3 we introduce the Adaptive Sensor Factory design pattern template. In section 4 we have discussed a case study of an adaptive Online Library Management System and described its fundamental entities. Lastly, in Section 5 we draw our conclusion sketching the path for future work.

2 Related Work

There are number of publications reporting the adaptive patterns to monitor, to make decisions and to reconfigure at run time. But they are limited to their applications only. In this paper we proposed a monitoring compliance autonomic design pattern that can be applied to applications/components that support push and pull actions on sensors and needs an external monitoring infrastructure this relieves the developers from implementing the monitoring infrastructure.

Gamma et al.[1] introduced a set of design patterns for dynamically reconfiguring specific types of software architectures. These design patterns leverage the concept of dynamic change management [3] by specifying the behavior required to dynamically reconfigure master/ slave, server/client, centralized, and decentralized architectures. Most importantly, Gamma et al.'s reconfiguration patterns identify when it is safe to perform a reconfiguration based on the application's architecture. To this end, they used hierarchical UML state diagram templates to depict, at a high level of abstraction, the behavior required to reconfigure these system architectures. While these reconfiguration design patterns provide a valuable reference for developers implementing dynamically adaptive systems, their contents are not organized in a template format, such as Gamma et al.'s design patterns [1]. Moreover, the set of reconfiguration design patterns are neither presented, nor integrated, within the context of an adaptive system comprising monitoring and decision-making processes. This paper presents an adaptive monitoring pattern to make the internal or external monitoring adaptive decoupling the selection of the sensor type to monitor a distributed component. This pattern is an extension to the sensor factory[2] by combining the observer pattern and strategy pattern by Gamma et al.[1].

3 Adaptive Sensor Factory Design Pattern Template

To facilitate the organization, understanding, and application of the adaptation design patterns, this paper uses a template similar in style to that used by Ramirez et al.[2]. Likewise, the Implementation and Sample Code fields are too application-specific for the design patterns presented in this paper.

3.1 Proposed Pattern

1. **Pattern Name:**
   Adaptive Sensor Factory
2. **Classification:**
   Stuctural-Monitoring
3. **Intent:**
   Systematically deploy software sensors across a network to probe distributed components decoupling the client from choosing the suitable sensor.
4. **Context:**
   The Adaptive Sensor-Factory Pattern may be used when:
   - the applications/components to be monitored are distributed.
   - each application/component provides an interface that can be probed for the required information
   - to decouple the clients from choosing the sensor type required to monitor the distributed application/component.

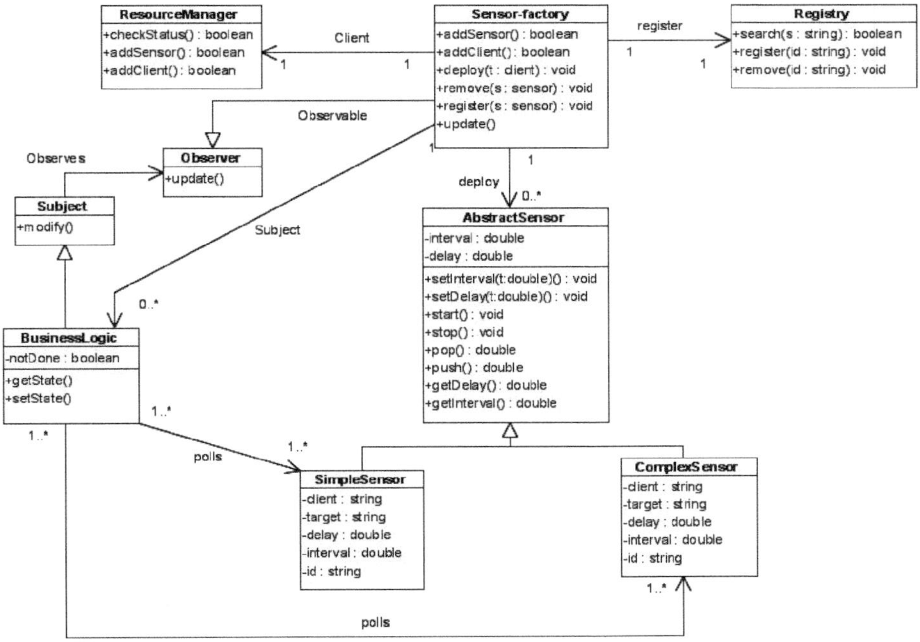

Fig. 1. UML class diagram for the Adaptive Sensor-Factory Pattern

5. **Proposed Pattern Structure:**
   A UML class diagram for the Adaptive Sensor-Factory Pattern can be found in Figure 1.

   There are two different types of sensors that can be found in this design pattern. Simple Sensors can handle booleans, integers, and real data types. Complex Sensors, on the other hand, are capable of either reporting more complex data types or of aggregating the outputs of a Simple Sensor. Regardless of their specific type, Simple Sensor and Complex Sensor both inherit the interface from the Abstract-Sensor abstract class. As a result, they should provide an interface with basic functionalities such as pushing and polling for data.
6. **Participants:**
   (a) **Abstract Sensor:**
      i. Declare a common interface to all sensors.
      ii. Simple Sensor and Complex Sensor both inherit from this abstract class. As a result, these sensors share an interface to common operations such as pushing and pulling data.
      iii. Sensor factory uses this interface to call the required sensor.

   (b) **Business Logic:**
   This class is used to represent any application/component that needs to perform either internal or external monitoring.

(c) **Complex-Sensor:**
This type of sensor contains greater computing resources onboard than a Simple Sensor does. As a result, a Complex Sensor is capable of reporting complex data types, aggregating various Simple Sensor data feeds, and performing on-board computations.

(d) **Simple Sensor:**
   i. This is the most basic sensor available
   ii. It is capable of reporting boolean, integer, and real data types. Additionally, it can be configured to poll a component at different intervals and periods.

(e) **Registry:**
   i. Responsible for tracking deployed sensors across the network.
   ii. Each entry should at least record the sensor name, the sensor type, the Client it is providing data to, and the component it is monitoring.
   iii. Provides a search functionality based on the available fields.

(f) **Resource Manager:**
   i. Determines if an existing sensor can be shared with one or more clients.
   ii. A sensor can be shared as long as it does not violate any existing constraint.
   iii. It determines if the system has enough resources to deploy a new sensor across the network.

(g) **Subject:**
   i. knows its observers. Any number of Observer objects may observe a subject.
   ii. provides an interface for attaching and detaching Observer objects.

(h) **Observer:**
Defines an updating interface for objects that should be notified of changes in a subject.

(i) **Sensor-Factory:**
   i. Clients must interact with this class in order to gain access to a sensor.
   ii. It regulates the dynamic access and management of sensors across a network.
   iii. Is configured with a simple and complex sensor.
   iv. Maintains a reference to abstract-sensor
   v. May define an interface that lets abstract-factory access its data.

7. **Consequences:**
(a) This design pattern eliminates the overhead of the client in determining the sensor type needed to monitor the distributed component.
(b) This design pattern reuses the provided functionality and interface of a distributed component to extract the desired attributes. However, if a component's interface is excessively polled, then it could interfere and alter the component's behavior.
(c) Different types of sensors can be systematically deployed at run time while providing a flexible monitoring infrastructure that is amenable to adaptation.

(d) This design pattern ensures system integrity by accessing a component's attributes through its interface.
(e) The Registry and Resource Manager share existing sensors whenever possible. This avoids wasting resources in the form of duplicate sensors.
(f) This design pattern introduces a management layer between a Client and a sensor. This additional overhead may degrade performance.
(g) Monitoring is only supported for those components with an interface to the required attributes.

8. **Related Design Patterns:**
   - **Strategy Design Pattern [1]:**
     This pattern can be used to make the sensors interchangeable. Strategy lets the sensor vary independently from clients that use it.
   - **Adapter Design Pattern [1]:**
     This pattern can enable the interaction between a Client and a sensor whenever their interfaces are incompatible.
   - **Reflective Monitoring Design Patterns [2]:**
     This pattern can be used whenever a component does not provide an interface to the required attributes. Such values may be accessible through Introspection.
   - **Adaptation Detector Design Pattern [2]:**
     This pattern is responsible for interpreting the results provided by a sensor and determining when an adaptation is required.

4 Experimental Setup

This section shows a proof of the concept study. We have developed an Online Library Management Application that makes use of this autonomic design pattern. This application is built based on EJB 3.0, JBoss application server and coding is done using Netbeans IDE.

4.1 Application Desciption

Online Library Management Application is a web site that helps user to search, place order and pay for the ordered books online. The system should avoid losing its customers due to high response times. So it needs to be monitored for performance like operational cost, latency. To make adaptations according to the environment the application is monitored by our adaptive pattern. Figure 2 describes the uml use case schema of this sample application. First the customer will log into the system then makes search for a particular book or books and then places an order for those books and makes payment. Upon successful transaction of the payment the user will be notified with a success message else a failure message along with the reason for failure.

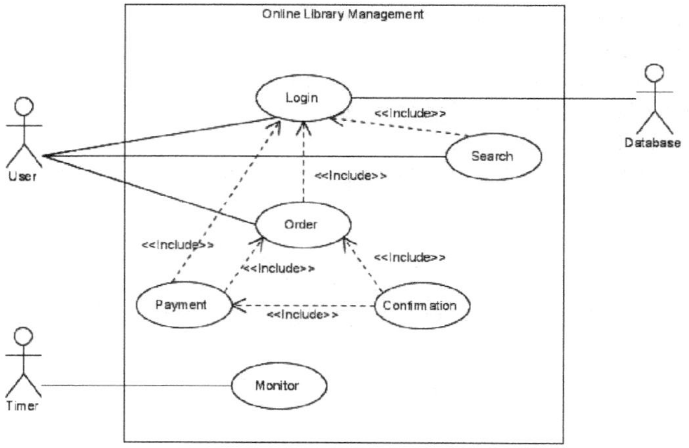

Fig. 2. UML UseCase view for Online Library Management Application

4.2 Making Application Monitoring Compliance

Our testing application have implemented the following

- **Database:** We have used MySql to form the database layer. It is responsible for storing all the application needed data.
- **BookBankBean:** We defined an entity class bean that has three properties title, author and price to model a Book product.
- **BookCatalogInterface:** This is a simple Java class that declares all the business methods.
- **BookCatalogBean:** This is the concrete implementation of the BookCatalogInterface and responsible for making objects persist.
- **MonitorBean:** This is the class that is responsible for making the application to be monitoring compliance. The observer part of the proposed pattern will able to update the SensorFactory class of the proposed pattern.
- **WebClient.jsp:** It is Jsp file that is accountable for collecting the data from user and to bind the BookcatalogBean.
- **Index.jsp:**This is the landing page of the application that provides interface to the user.

4.3 Proposed Pattern Approach

Our proposed pattern defines a framework that can monitor any application/ component that supports monitoring compliance requirements.Our case study application satisfies the requirements for making it monitoring compliance.Our proposed system approach will have an administrator who will set the operational environment base on which the monitoring is done.The client who is monitoring compliant can request to take care of monitoring it.The observer will make an update to the sensor factory about the client.In this context we used client to refer the application/component.Based on the update from the observer the sensor factory will determine the sensor type that best suits the client for monitoring it will create and deploy that type of sensor.Before deploying the sensor the sensorFactory will check whether the existing sensors can satify the client interms of monitoring or if it have to create a new sensor then the sensorFactory will register that sensor and then it deploys that sensor.We have discussed it further using java like syntax used to build this pattern.

```
public class Sensor_factory extends Observer {
    ResourceManager _check;
    Vector<Client> _requests = new Vector<Client>();
    Registry _register;
    Vector<AbstractSensor> _deploy = new Vector<AbstractSensor>();
    public boolean addSensor() {
    }
    public boolean addClient() {
    }
    public void deploy(client aT) {
    }
    }
    public void register(sensor aS) {
    }
    public void update() {
    }
```

Here the sensorFactory will behave like both a context when we consider the strategy pattern and also as a concrete observer with reference to observer pattern.

```
public class SimpleSensor extends AbstractSensor {
    private String _client;
    private String _target;
    private double _delay;
    private double _interval;
    private String _id;
    Vector<Client> _polls = new Vector<Client>();
}
```

Here abstract sensor class is an interface.This is similar to that of the strategy in the strategy pattern.

```
public class ResourceManager {
    public boolean checkStatus() {
    }
    public boolean addsensor() {
    }
    public boolean addClient() {
```

```
    }
}
public class SimpleSensor extends AbstractSensor {
    private String _client;
    private String _target;
    private double _delay;
    private double _interval;
    private String _id;
    Vector<Client> _polls = new Vector<Client>();
}
```

This class is the concrete implements of the abstractSensor class.Based on the context provided by sensorfactory the correct type of sensor is deployed to monitor client. To describe the efficiency of the pattern the profiling results is taken using the NetBeans IDE profilier tool for ten runs and graph is plotted as shown in Figure 3.

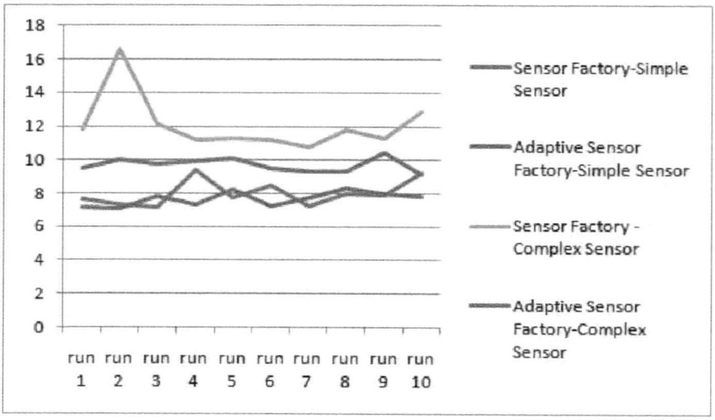

Fig. 3. Profiling Graph

5 Conclusion and Future Work

This paper introduced an autonomic design pattern to monitor the distributed component decoupling the higher level of abstraction in determining the sensor type needed by client to probe the distributed component and the burden of making the decision module. We extended the Ramirez et al. sensor factory [1] by amalgamating the Gamma et al strategy pattern [2].

Several directions for future work are possible. We are examining how these design patterns can be inserted into a non-adaptive application through the use of aspect-oriented techniques [12]. we are exploring the use of evolutionary computation techniques [11] to determine how adaptation design patterns can be automatically instantiated and integrated into legacy systems to meet adaptation needs. We are making a generic decision making and reconfiguration infrastructure so that any application that needs dynamic adaptability can make use of them.

References

1. Gamma, E., Helm, R., Johnson, R., Vlissides, J.: Design Patterns: Elements of Reusable Object-Oriented Software (1995)
2. Ramirez, A.J., Cheng, B.H.C.: Design Patterns for Developing Dynamically Adaptive Systems. ACM, New York (2010)
3. Kramer, J., Magee, J.: The evolving philosophers problem: Dynamic change management. IEEE Trans. on Soft. Eng. 16(11), 1293–1306 (1990)
4. Cámara, J., Canal, C., Cubo, J., Murillo, J.M.: An aspect-oriented adaptation framework for dynamic component evolution. Electron. Notes Theor. Comput. Sci. 189, 21–34 (2007)
5. Garlan, D., Cheng, S.-W., Huang, A.-C., Schmerl, B., Steenkiste, P.: Rainbow: Architecture-based self-adaptation with reusable infrastructure. Computer 37(10), 46–54 (2004)
6. Kon, F., Román, M., Liu, P., Mao, J., Yamane, T., Magalhães, L.C., Pasquale, F.: Monitoring, security, and dynamic configuration with the *dynamicTAO* reflective ORB. In: Coulson, G., Sventek, J. (eds.) Middleware 2000. LNCS, vol. 1795, pp. 121–143. Springer, Heidelberg (2000)
7. Mikalsen, M., Paspallis, N., Floch, J., Stav, E., Papadopoulos, G.A., Chimaris, A.: Distributed context management in a mobility and adaptation enabling middleware (MADAM). In: SAC 2006: Proc. of the 2006 ACM symposium on Applied Computing, pp. 733–734. ACM, New York (2006)
8. Sadjadi, S.M., McKinley, P.K.: ACT: An adaptive CORBA template to support unanticipated adaptation. In: Proceedings of the IEEE International Conference on Distributed Computing Systems, pp. 74–83 (2004)
9. Oreizy, P., Gorlick, M., Taylor, R.N., Heimbigner, D., Johnson, G., Medvidovic, N., Quilici, A., Rosenblum, D.S., Wolf, A.L.: An Architecture-Based Approach to Self-Adaptive Software. IEEE Intelligent Systems 14(3), 54–62 (1999)
10. Ramirez, A.J.: Betty H.C. Cheng. Design patterns for monitoring adaptive ULS systems. In: Proceedings of the 2nd International Workshop on Ultra-Large-Scale Software Systems-Intensive Systems, pp. 69–72. ACM, New York (2008)
11. McUmber, W.E., Cheng, B.H.C.: A general framework for formalizing uml with formal languages. In: ICSE 2001: Proc. of the 23rd Intl. Conf. on Soft. Eng., pp. 422–433. IEEE Computer Society Press, Washington, DC, USA (2001)
12. Sadjadi, S.M., McKinley, P.K., Cheng, B.H.C.: Transparent shaping of existing software to support pervasive and autonomic computing. In: DEAS 2005: Proc. Of the 2005 workshop on Design and Evolution of Autonomic Application Software. ACM, New York (2005)

Predictive Analysis of Lung Cancer Recurrence

Shweta Srivastava, Manisha Rathi, and J.P. Gupta

Computer Science Department, Jaypee Institute of Information Technology,
A-10, Noida, India
shwetasrivastava21@gmail.com,
{manisha.rathi,jp.gupta}@jiit.ac.in

Abstract. The paper is about the predictive analysis of lung cancer recurrence based on non-small cell lung cancer carcinoma gene expression data using data mining and machine learning techniques. Prediction is one of the most significant factors in statistical analysis. Predictive analysis is a term describing a variety of statistical and analytical techniques used to develop models that predict future events or behaviours. Prediction of cancer recurrence has been a challenging problem for many researchers. The proposed method involves four phases: data collection, gene selection, designing classifier model, statistical parameter calculation and finally the comparison with previous results. The major part of the method is the gene selection and classification. A hybrid method for gene selection and classification is used for statistical analysis of lung cancer recurrence. The most suitable techniques are used for this work on the basis of comparative analysis of different classification method and optimization techniques.

Keywords: Lung Cancer Recurrence, Data Mining, Statistical Analysis, Gene Expression Data.

1 Introduction

Prediction of cancer recurrence is concerned with predicting the likelihood of redeveloping the cancer after some treatment to disease. Data mining along with machine learning can be used for the prediction of the cancer recurrence. Through predictive analysis, the recurrence possibility may be known in advance. With the prediction in prior, the treatment can be started at initial stage. Thus the survivability can be improved. The biopsy like method is available for this but it is quite costly. With data mining and machine learning this work can be done with less cost, equivalent accuracy and easily.

The paper is organized as follows: Section 1 gives the introduction of the research work. Section 2 is the background study. Section 3 depicts about the proposed method in this paper and different parameters for analysis. Section 4 gives the description of results obtained. Section 5 is summary and section 6 discusses about the concluding points and future work.

A. Abraham et al. (Eds.): ACC 2011, Part I, CCIS 190, pp. 260–269, 2011.

2 Background Study

2.1 Gene Expression Data and Its Complexities

Gene expression refers to the level of production of protein molecules defined by a gene [11]. A typical microarray data is consist of a small number of samples and thousands numbers of genes [4].Although gene expression data are very useful for this study but there are some complexities associated with it like it has so many genes relative to only few samples gives a high possibility of getting "false positives" and the gene expression data is usually too large which may cause the problem of "over-fitting".

2.2 Feature Selection Methods for Gene Expression Data

There are basic three methods for gene selection such as: Filter Method, Wrapper Method and Embedded Method.

Filter methods evaluate the relevance of attributes by looking only at the inherent properties of data [8]. In filter method highest ranking features are selected and left over are eliminated [7]. The major drawback of filter method is that it ignores interaction with the classifier. Wrapper method implants the model hypothesis search within the feature subset search [8]. Once a number of subsets of feature are obtained, each subset is to be evaluated with the classifier [33]. It has more risk of overfitting and is more computationally exhaustive. Embedded method has feature selection method built into the classifier construction. It has better computational complexity than wrapper methods but it is classifier reliant selection.

2.3 Classification Techniques for Recurrence Prediction

There are various classification methods which have been applied for the cancer recurrence prediction. There are various classification techniques such as: Decision Tree Algorithm, K-Nearest Neighbor, Support Vector Machine, Artificial Neural Network, and Bayesian Classifier etc. Comparative study of different classifiers is discussed below:

Table 1. Comparative Analysis of Different Classification Techniques in Data Mining

Decision Tree Algorithm	**K-Nearest Neighbor**	**Support Vector Machine**	**Artificial Neural Network**	**Naive Bayes Classifier**
Trees created from numerical dataset are complex.	K-NN classifier needs all available data, which leads to an overhead if data set is very large.	Support vector machines are sensitive to noisy data.	Determining the network structure and parameters is difficult	Performs well for both categorical and continuous data.

Table 1. (*continued*)

Best Suited for categorical data. Not suited for missing and noisy data.	Deciding the value of k is a big problem.	It only considers 2 classes.	It is a black box model. It doesn't assume any relationship between the independent variables and let the data define the functional relationship.	Best suited for noisy data.
Output attribute should be categorical.	Prediction accuracy degrades when number of attributes increase.	Selection of kernel function is very difficult.	High speed prediction is a great challenge in NN.	A clear dependency is defined between attributes.
As the number of data increases, no of operations increase to build the tree model.	It is a distance based learning, and it is not clear which type of distance to be used.	It suffers from overfitting.	It also suffers from overfitting.	It handles overfitting.
They produce very complex production rules.	It is not known that which attributes will produce best results.	It takes long time to process.	It consumes lot of memory.	It consumes very less memory.

3 Proposed Method

For the predictive analysis of lung cancer recurrence following steps are used:

1. Data collection (to collect the data of the patient who have suffered from lung cancer once and their surgery is done)
2. Gene Selection using hybrid method (Correlation based feature subset evaluator and best first search technique).
3. Obtain the classifier model on the training data set using Naïve Bayes & Bagging/Boosting Ensemble method.
4. Find statistical parameters on test data set sample before and after optimizing.

For the implementation WEKA API version 3.4 with jdk 1.6 is used.

3.1 Data Collection

The data of lung cancer recurrence from the kent ridge biomedical data repository (http://leo.ugr.es/elvira/DBCRepository/LungCancer/LungCancer-Ontario.html) is taken for the experiment.

3.2 Hybrid Method for Gene Selection

The results of feature selection can be improved by combining filter method with wrapper method. The method used for feature selection is CFS [28] with best first search technique. The gene subset with highest Merits is returned as the result of gene selection.

3.3 Hybrid Method for Classification

Here, the hybrid method proposed for classification is the combination of base classifier with meta classifier. The optimized method consists of the base and meta classifier both. The most current meta classifiers are bagging (bootstrap aggregating)[35] and boosting [35]. Bagging reduces the variance and boosting reduces the bias. Bagging and boosting both builds a classifier from a training set of instances [34]. Boosting shows the greater performance enhancement. Boosting is likely to learn faster than bagging as it focuses more in the misclassified cases.

First of all, the 66% split is done on the dataset to divide the data in training and test dataset. Now the data of 25 patients is in training dataset and data of 14 patients in test dataset. Then following steps need to be followed:

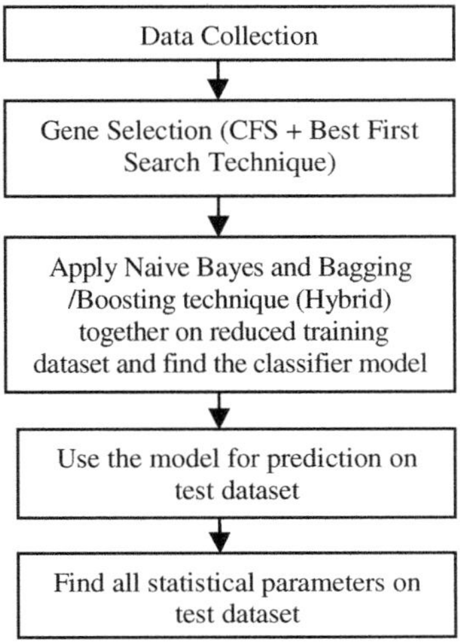

Fig. 1. Proposed solution approach

3.4 Calculation of Statistical Parameters

The result is obtained in the form of confusion matrix i.e.

	Relapse Predicted (t)	Relapse Free Predicted (f)
Patient with Relapse (t)	tt	tf
Relapse free patient (f)	ft	ff

Fig. 2. Confusion matrix structure

The following parameters are calculated as:

Accuracy= (tt+ff) / (tt+tf+ft+ff), Sensitivity= tt / (tt+ft), Specificity= ff / (tf+ff) In AUROC, the false positive rate is on the X-axis and the true positive rate is on the Y-axis. The AUROC curve of a model has the values in the interval 0.0<=AUROC<=1.0.

4 Results

About dataset: Total no of instances: 39, Number of instances in training dataset: 25, Number of instances in test dataset: 14

Last 3 rows of table 2 show the result calculated by proposed method.

Here are the steps to be followed to obtain the result:

4.1 Step I (Gene Selection)

The gene selection process is applied on the whole dataset of 39 patients. As the result of the gene selection we get least redundant and most relevant genes, other genes are removed. So each subset created by best first search technique is evaluated by CFS evaluation technique. The gene subset with highest merit 0.663 is selected.

Search Method: Best first.
Attribute Subset Evaluator (supervised, Class (nominal): 2881 Class): CFS Subset Eval.
Selected attributes: Gene Ids: 323796, 34954, 491026, 292938, 67043, 28243, 50416, 278729, 40935, 200101,151009

Fig. 3. Step I (Gene Selection)

4.2 Step II (Classification Accuracy, Prediction Accuracy and Other Statistical Parameters (Before and After Optimization))

The classifier model is obtained by applying base classifier (Naive Bayes) on training dataset for the selected genes of patients after gene selection. As a result of the model some statistical parameters such as mean, standard deviation, weight sum. Precision are calculated for all selected genes. The classification accuracy is 84%. Below is the fig. 4. showing the actual class and predicted class for the sample of 25 patients. Then the confusion matrix containing the numbers of correctly & incorrectly classified instances is formulated. 21 patients have correct predicted class and 4 patients have incorrect predicted class.

```
----actual and predicted class of training dataset---
For ID: 1,3,5,7,9,10,11,13,14,16,18,21,22,23,25:
actual: Relapse, predicted: Relapse
For ID: 2: actual: Relapse, predicted: Non-relapse
For ID: 4,6,12,15,17,19: actual: Non-relapse, predicted: Non-relapse
For ID: 8,20,24 actual: Non-relapse, predicted: Relapse
--------Confusion Matrix for training dataset-------
15.0  1.0
3.0   6.0
Total training instances are: 25.0, Correctly classified instances are: 21.0 or 84.0%,
Incorrectly classified instances are: 4.0 or 16.0%
```

Fig. 4. Classification accuracy of the classifier model

Next the obtained classifier model is applied on the test dataset. The actual and predicted class of the patient is compared to be same or not. Out of 14 patients, 11 are classified correctly and 3 incorrectly. The prediction accuracy, specificity, sensitivity and AUROC are 78.57%, 100%, 72.72% and 97.92% respectively. Refer fig.5.

```
---actual and predicted class of test dataset-----
For ID: 1,3,7,8,10,11,12,13: actual: Relapse, predicted: Relapse
For ID: 2,6,14: actual: Non-relapse, predicted: Relapse
For ID: 4,5,9: actual: Non-relapse, predicted: Non-relapse
-------Confusion Matrix for test dataset---------
8.0  0.0
3.0  3.0
Correctly classified instances are: 11.0 or 78.571%, Incorrectly classified instances are:
3.0 or 21.428%, Specificity of the classifier is: 100.0%, Sensitivity of the classifier is:
72.727%
```

Fig. 5. (Prediction accuracy, specificity, sensitivity) before optimization

With hybrid method of classification (NB+ Bagging), the improved prediction accuracy, sensitivity and AUROC is 85.71%, 80% and 100% respectively. Refer fig.6. With NB + Boosting, more improved prediction accuracy, sensitivity, specificity and AUROC is 92.86%, 88.89%, 100% and 97.92% respectively. Refer fig. 7.

------actual and predicted class of test dataset------
For ID: 1,3,7,8,10,11,12,13 actual: Relapse, predicted: Relapse
For ID: 2,4,5,9 actual: Non-relapse, predicted: Non-relapse
For ID: 6,14: actual: Non-relapse, predicted: Relapse
-------Confusion Matrix for test dataset------------
8.0 0.0
2.0 4.0
Correctly classified instances are: 12.0 or 85.714%, Incorrectly classified instances are: 2.0 or 14.285%, Specificity of the classifier is: 100.0%, Sensitivity of the classifier is: 80.0%, Area under ROC: 100%

Fig. 6. (Prediction accuracy, specificity, sensitivity) after optimization with Bagging

------actual and predicted class of test dataset--------
For ID: 1,3,7,8,10,11,12,13: actual: Relapse, predicted: Relapse
For ID: 2,4,5,6,9: actual: Non-relapse, predicted: Non-relapse
For ID: 14, actual: Non-relapse, predicted: Relapse
--------------Confusion Matrix for test dataset----------
8.0 0.0
1.0 5.0
Correctly classified instances are: 13.0 or 92.857%, Incorrectly classified instances are: 1.0 or 7.142%, Specificity of the classifier is: 100.0%, Sensitivity of the classifier is: 88.888%, Area under ROC: 97.92%

Fig. 7. (Prediction accuracy, specificity, sensitivity) after optimization with Boosting

4.3 Comparison with Previous Results

Below is the comparison between the performances of the naive bayes classifier applied on the gene expression data of lung cancer patients obtained in [31] and our result:

Table 2. Comparison with others results

Data Set	Techniques used	Prediction Accuracy	Sensitivity	Specificity
Genetic (after giving Carboplatin drug) [31]	Naive bayes	78%	76%	80%
Genetic(after giving Paclitaxel drug) [31]	Naive bayes	81%	72%	87%
Genetic(after giving Cisplatin drug) [31]	Naive bayes	80%	85%	74%
Genetic(after giving Etoplocide drug) [31]	Naive bayes	73%	80%	67%

Table 2. (*continued*)

Genetic(after giving Erlotinib drug) [31]	Naive bayes	79%	79%	80%
Genetic(after giving Gefitinib drug) [31]	Naive bayes	94%	92%	95%
Genetic (after surgery)	**Naive bayes**	**78.57%**	**72.72%**	**100%**
Genetic (after surgery)	**Naive bayes +Bagging**	**85.71%**	**80%**	**100%**
Genetic (after surgery)	**Naive bayes +Boosting**	**92.86%**	**88.89%**	**100%**

It is seen in the result that with naive bayes only, the results are not so good. But there is very good prediction accuracy (better than other 5 results) and sensitivity (better than 3 and same as another result) with bagging + NB technique. With NB + Boosting prediction accuracy and sensitivity is better than other 5 results. 100% specificity shows that the proposed classifier model is best for the prediction of those instances which have class as non-relapse.

5 Summary

The predictive analysis of the lung cancer recurrence is done on the dataset collected from kent ridge biomedical data repository. For this complete analysis best first search with correlation based feature selection for gene selection and naive bayes with bagging/boosting is used for classification and prediction. This paper contributes in knowing about the early prediction of recurrence chances after the surgical treatment of the lung cancer patient.

6 Conclusions and Future Work

In this paper it is discussed that the prediction accuracy can be improved by using different hybrid techniques of gene selection and classification. The method proposed is giving 100% accurate results for the patients where the recurrence will not happen. If the recurrence is known a prior, the suitable treatment can be given to the patient. Early prediction about recurrence can prolong the life of the patient. As per the future work, the result can be optimized using some other optimization techniques such as genetic algorithm etc.

References

1. Ali, A., Tufail, A., Khan, U., Kim, M.: A Survey of Prediction Models for Breast Cancer Survivability. In: Proceedings of the 2nd International Conference on Interaction Sciences: Information Technology (2009)
2. Zhang, Y., Ding, C., Li, T.: Gene selection algorithm by combining reliefF and mRMR. In: IEEE 7th International Conference on Bioinformatics and Bioengineering at Harvard Medical School (2007)
3. National Cancer Institute, USA, `http://www.cancer.gov`
4. Piatetsky-Shapiro, G., Tamayo, P.: Microarray data mining: facing the challenges. ACM SIGKDD Explorations Newsletter, Articles on microarray data mining 5(2) (2003)
5. Rangasamy, M., Venketraman, S.: An Efficient Statistical Model Based Classification Algorithm for Classifying Cancer Gene Expression Data With Minimal Gene Subsets. International Journal of Cyber Society and Education 2(2), 51–56 (2009)
6. Yu, L., Liu, H.: Redundancy based Feature Selection for Microarray Data. In: Proceedings of the 10th ACM SIGKDD International Conference on Knowledge Discovery and Data Mining (2004)
7. Kojadinovic, I., Wottka, T.: Comparasion between a filter and wrapper approach to variable subset selection in regression problems. ESIT (2000)
8. Yvan, S., Inza, I., Larranaga, P.: A review of feature selection techniques in bioinformatics. Bioinformatics 23(19) (2007)
9. Choi, J.P., Han, T.H., Park, R.W.: A Hybrid Bayesian Network Model for Predicting Breast Cancer Prognosis. Journal of Korean Society of Medical Informatics (2009)
10. Delen, D., Walker, G., Kadam, A.: Predicting breast cancer survivability: A comparasion of three data mining methods. Artificial Intelligence in Medicine 34(2), 113–127 (2005)
11. Li, T., Zhang, C., Ogihara, M.: A Comparative Study of Feature Selection and Multiclass Classification Methods for Tissue Classification Based on Gene Expression. Oxford Journals of Bioinformatics (2004)
12. Bellaachia, A., Guven, E.: Predicting Breast Cancer Survivability Using Data Mining Techniques, White Paper, George Washington University (2006)
13. Xiong, X., Kim, Y., Baek, Y., Rhee, D.W., Kim, S.-H.: Analysis of Breast Cancer Using Data Mining & Statistical Techniques. In: Proceedings of 6th International Conference on Software Engineering, Artificial Intelligence (2005)
14. Ahmad, F.K., Deris, S., Othman, N.H.: Toward Integrated Clinical and Gene-Expression Profiles for Breast Cancer Prognosis: A Review Paper. International Journal of Biometric and Bioinformatics 3(4), 31–66 (2009)
15. Sarhan, A.M.: Cancer Classification Based on Microarray Gene Expression Data Using DCT and ANN. Journal of Theoretical and Applied Information Technology 6(2) (2009)
16. Giarratana, G., Pizzera, M., Masseroli, M., Madico, E., Lanzi, P.L.: Data Mining Techniques for the Identification of Genes with Expression Levels Related to Breast Cancer Prognosis. In: IEEE 9th International Conference on Bioinformatics and Bioengineering (2009)
17. Abraham, R., Simha, J.B.: Iyengar S. S: Medical datamining with a new algorithm for Feature Selection and Naïve Bayesian classifier. In: 10th International Conference on Information Technology (2007)
18. Soria, D., Garibaldi, J.M., Biganzoli, E.: A Comparison of Three Different Methods for Classification of Breast Cancer Data. In: 7th International Conference on Machine Learning and Application (2008)

19. Guyon, I., Elisseeff, A.: An Introduction to Variable and Feature Selection. Journal of Machine Learning Research 3 (2003)
20. Ben-Dor, A., Bruhn, L., Friedman, N., Nachman, I., Schummer, M., Yakhini, Z.: Tissue Classification with Gene Expression Profiles. Journal of Computational Biology 7 (2000)
21. Ding, C., Peng, H.: Minimum Redundancy Feature Selection from Microarray Gene Expression Data. In: Proceedings of Computational Systems BioInformatics (2003)
22. Bontempi, G., Haibe-Kains, B.: Feature selection methods for mining bioinformatics data (2005), http://www.ulb.ac.be/di/mlg
23. Huang, Y., McCullagh, P.J., Black, N.D.: Feature Selection via Supervised Model Construction. In: Proceedings of the 4th IEEE International Conference on Data Mining (2004)
24. Wang, Y., Tetko, I.V., Hall, M.A., Frank, E., Facius, A., Mayer, K.F., Mewes, H.W.: Gene selection from microarray data for cancer classification–a machine learning approach. Computational Biology and Chemistry 29(1), 37–46 (2005)
25. Aouf, M., Liyanage, L., Hansen, S.: Critical Review of Data Mining Techniques for Gene Expression Analysis. In: 4th International Conference on Information and Automation for Sustainability (2008)
26. Fishel, I., Kaufman, A., Ruppin, E.: Meta-Analysis of Gene Expression Data: a Predictor-Based Approach. Oxford Journal of BioInformatics 23(13), 1599–1606 (2007)
27. Cruz, J.A., Wishart, D.S.: Applications of Machine Learning in Cancer Prediction and Prognosis. Cancer Informatics (2006)
28. Abraham, R., Simha, J.B., Sitharama Iyengar, S.: Effective Discretization and Hybrid feature selection using Naive Bayesian Classifier for Medical data mining. International Journal of Computational Intelligence Research 5, 116–129 (2009)
29. Ahmed, F.E.: Artificial neural networks for diagnosis and survival prediction in colon cancer. Molecular Cancer 4(29) (2005)
30. Hall, M., Smith, L.: Practical Feature Subset Selection for Machine Learning. In: Proceedings of 21st Australian Computer Science Conference, pp. 181–191. Springer, Heidelberg (1998)
31. Wan, Y.-W., Sabbagh, E., Raese, R., Qian, Y., Luo, D., Denvir, J., Vallyathan, V., Castranova, V., Guo, N.L.: Hybrid Models Identified a 12-Gene Signature for Lung Cancer Prognosis and Chemoresponse Prediction. Journal of PLoS ONE (2010)
32. Beane, J., Sebastiani, P., Whitfield, T.H., Steiling, K., Dumas, Y.-M., Lenburg, M.E., Spira, A.: A Prediction Model for Lung Cancer Diagnosis that Integrates Genomic and Clinical Features. Journal from AACR on Cancer Prevention Research (2008)
33. Karegowda, A.G., Jayaram, M.A., Manjunath, A.S.: Feature Subset Selection Problem using Wrapper Approach in Supervised Learning. International Journal of Computer Applications (0975 – 8887) 1(7) (2010)
34. Quinlan, J.R.: Bagging, Boosting, and C4.5. In: Proceedings of the Thirteenth National Conference on Artificial Intelligence (1996)
35. Oza, N.C.: Online Bagging and Boosting. In: IEEE International Conference on Systems, Man and cybernetics, vol. 3, pp. 2340–2345 (2006)

Development and Validation of Matlab Models for Nanowire Sensors

P. Vipeesh[1] and N.J.R. Muniraj[2]

[1] Research Scholars, Karpagam University, Coimbatore, India
vinuvipeesh@gmail.com
[2] Professor & Head, Department of ECE, Karpagam College of Engineering, Coimbatore, India
njrmuniraj@yahoo.com

Abstract. In this paper, mathematical models required to describe the functionality of nanodevices are reviewed, and based on the mathematical models sensor equivalent circuit is developed. An experimental setup is developed to analyze the characteristics of ISFET, nanowire and nanosphere devices. Impact of geometrical properties on device performance is estimated based on the experimental setup. Settling time and surface analyte concentration graphs obtained using the experimental setup is used in designing a nanobio sensor (DNA) for disease detection. Based on the test results a mathematical model is develop in Matlab to model nanodevices. The DNA sensors modeled can be used for automated drug detection and delivery unit.

Keywords: Nanodevices, DNA sensor, ISFET, matlab, nanotube, nanohub.

1 Introduction

Vast numbers of studies and developments in the nanotechnology area have been conducted and many nanomaterials have been utilized to detect cancers at early stages. Nanomaterials have unique physical, optical and electrical properties that have proven to be very useful in sensing. Quantum dots, gold nanoparticles, magnetic nanoparticles, carbon nanotubes, gold nanowires and many other materials have been developed over the years. Nanotechnology has been developing rapidly during the past few years and with this, properties of nanomaterials are being extensively studied and many attempts are made to fabricate appropriate nanomaterials. Due to their unique optical, magnetic, mechanical, chemical and physical properties that are not shown at the bulk scale, nanomaterials have been used for more sensitive and precise disease detection. For developing a system to detect disease, software modeling is one of the major requirements. Matlab environment is predominantly used for developing software reference models, thus various sensor models (electrical and mechanical) are already inbuilt in Matlab and are readily available for development of automotive and mechanical system. There is large number of nanobio sensors that are being used for medical applications such as disease detection. Developing a software reference model for disease detection using Matlab, there is a need for a mathematical model of nano-bio sensor. Thus in this work, we develop a mathematical model for nanowire, that

A. Abraham et al. (Eds.): ACC 2011, Part I, CCIS 190, pp. 270–283, 2011.

is used for cancer detection. Section II discusses the geometrical and mathematical models of nanowires. Section III discusses the diffusion capture model that is used for modeling nanosensors, section IV presents the experimental setup for simulation of nanowire sensors and design of biosensors. Section V presents the Matlab models developed based on the simulation results obtained.

2 DNA Sensors

Human genome have billions of DNA base spheres, to sense the DNA sequence an array of sensors are used for genome sensing. Nanobio sensor consists of X-Y array of elements consists of pixels called as electronic components, each component is a sensor that can be a nanowire transistor, carbon nanotube, planar transistor etc. Each element has a unique and known DNA sequence (genome) bound to the sensor. As in figure, Q1 is one such sequence consisting of ACGAT molecule arranged in an order. Each location in the X-Y array has a known sequence attached to it. Figure below shows the array of sensors, and the corresponding DAN sequence attached to the sensor.

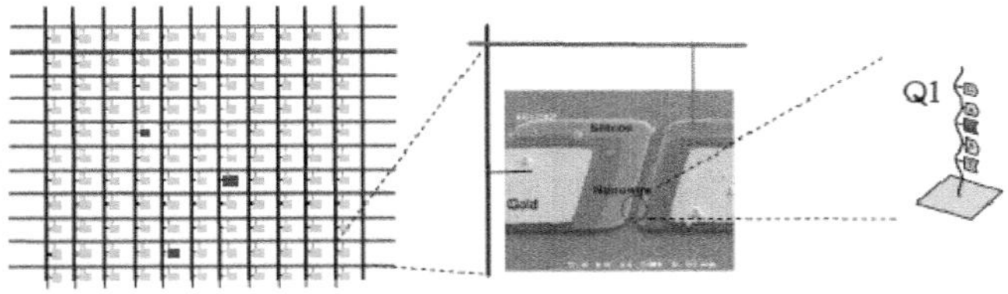

Fig. 1. Nanosensor array and DNA sensor

When an unknown DNA sequence is introduced into the XY array, the unknown sequence finds its conjugate in the XY array and binds with the DNA sequence present on the array. Since the DNA sequence at every location along the XY array is known, the binding of unknown sequence with known DNA sequence modulates the current in the corresponding element in the XY array. Thus by detecting the amount of current change, the corresponding concentration of unknown DNA sequence in a given electrolyte is detected. This is the basic principle of detection in nanobio sensor. Figure below shows the change in conduction of sensors due to detection of unknown sequence.

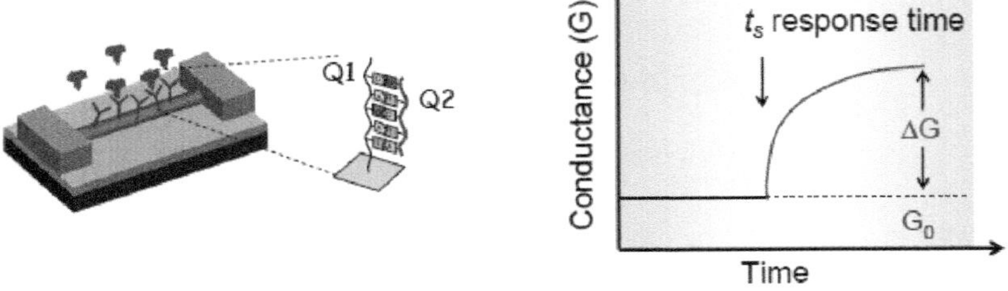

Fig. 2. DNA strand and sensor response time

There are different kinds of nanobio sensors such as Chem FET, IsFET, Nanowire, Nanosphere, Nanodots and CNT. Sensitivity is one of the major parameter that need to be considered to select a appropriate sensor for drug delivery.

Sensors consist of source and drain regions place above a gate. Gate consists of receptors that capture the unknown molecules that diffuse across the target molecules. Figure below shows the basic two kinds of sensor (ISFET and Nanosensor).

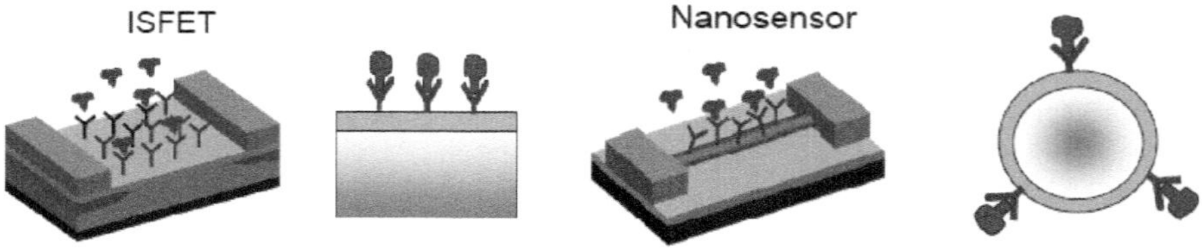

Fig. 3. ISFET and Nanosensor

Current flows between source and drain, and the molecules that are bound to the sensor determine the soruce-drain current. The sensitivity of such sensor is found to be between molar and few micro molar (10^{-6}M). This is a very small value, thus it requires that for disease detection sensors should have higher sensitivity. To improve sensitivity of a sensor for bio applications, CNT where introduced, and the sensitivity of CNT sensors compared with nanosensor were increased by several orders of magnitude (femto molar). In order to further improve sensitivity, nanodots can also be used. It is found in the literature that the cylindrical or nanowire sensors is much better than a planar sensor, is because of geometry of electrostatics. In a nanowire, the unknown molecules surrounds all around the gate consisting of receptor molecules compared to a planar transistor where the receptor molecules are on top of the plane, thus there is higher sensitivity in nanowire. The currents in nanowires are in tens of nanometer dimension, which is very large. The cross section of nanowire sensor is shown in figure below. The nanowire is immersed in water or pH containing material and the DNA molecules are swimming around in the electrolyte.

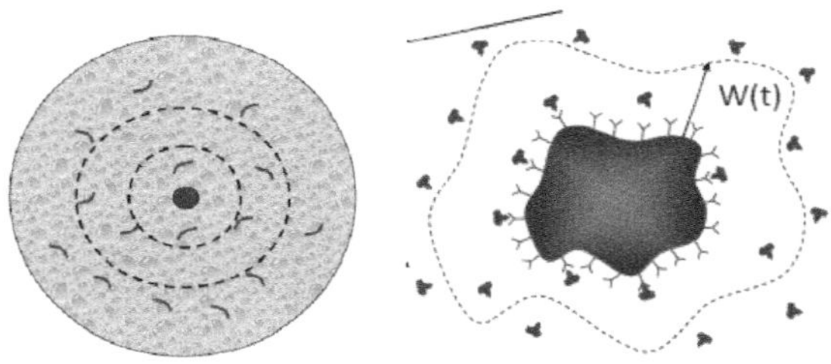

Fig. 4. Diffusion region and sensor detection boundary

In order to understand or model sensor for use in drug delivery applications, it is required to analyze the working principle of nanowire sensor and develop mathematical relationships that can be used for sensor design.

A sensor consisting of many receptors is shown in figure above. The unknown molecules (target) get captured by the receptors as they diffuse along the surface of receptors, only when the unknown molecule has s conjugate sequence compared to the receptor sequence. It is required to establish the relations ship between number of molecules detected, current, time involved in detection and concentration of molecules.

3 Diffusion-Capture Model

There are two equations that explain the diffusion-capture activity in a nanobio sensor. The capture equation is given below:

$$\frac{dN}{dt} = K_F(N_o - N)\rho_s - K_R N \tag{1}$$

N is the number of conjugated molecule, N_o is the initial number of molecules (receptors, blue y shaped). To know how many of conjugated, this is proportional to number of unconjugated molecules thus is determined by $(N_0\text{-}N)$, k_F is reaction constant. There are possibilities of molecules that are bound to deconjugate due to chemical reaction, thus the second term k_RN represents the number of deconjugated molecules (k_R is reverse reaction constant). Deconjugation is very weak in nanobio sensors, thus the diffusion equation can be approximated to equation below.

$$\frac{dN}{dt} \approx K_F N_o \rho_s \tag{2}$$

ρ_s is the surface concentration of the captured molecules.

As the molecules present in the electrolyte diffuse across the receptors, the diffusion equation is given by

$$\frac{d\rho}{dt} = D\nabla^2\rho \tag{3}$$

D is the diffusion coefficient; ρ is the concentration of molecules. This equation defines that the molecules have to diffuse around the sensor surface before they could be captured. It is required to find an analytical solution for the above two equations to understand the sensitivity of sensors. The diffusion-capture equation needs to be solved to understand the behaviour of the sensor.

Consider the figure given below, it consists of cylindrical sensor (red) at the centre, and the outermost red circle is the area of constant density. It is required to find how many molecules per unit time will be captured by the sensor, if uniform density is maintained within the outermost circle.

ρ_o is the concentration at the boundary at a distance of W from the sensor, and ρ_s is the concentration of molecules at the sensor surface. Howard burg in 1960 equated this problem with a coaxial capacitor problem as shown in figure below. Considering a capacitor with central field Φ_s and boundary potential of Φ_o at a distance W the electric filed and the potential is related using poisson equation. Diffusion constant D is equated with ϵ in a capacitor.

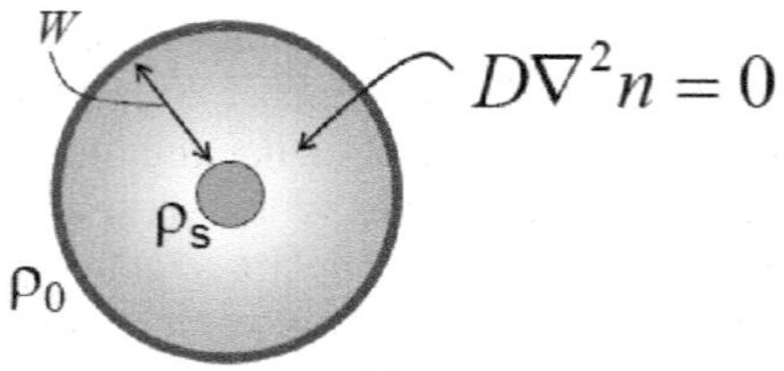

Fig. 5. Diffusion boundary

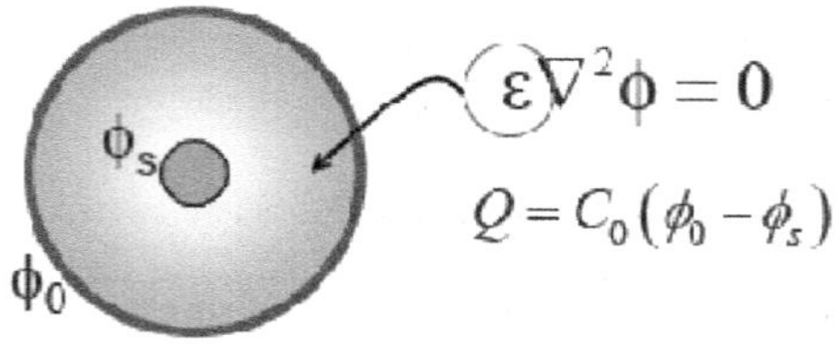

Fig. 6. Electric field boundary

As per poissons equation, the charge Q is related to capacitance and potential is given by

$$Q = C_o(\emptyset_o - \emptyset_s) \tag{4}$$

The capacitance Co is given by the equations below for various geometries of capacitors.

$$C_o = \frac{\varepsilon}{W}(Planar)$$
$$= \frac{2\pi\varepsilon}{\log\left(W + {}^{a_o}/_{a_0}\right)}(Cylinder)$$
$$= \frac{4\pi\varepsilon}{a_0^{-1} - (W - a_0)^{-1}}(sphere) \tag{5}$$

By using the above equations, the solution for a nanowire sensor is given below:

$$I = C_0(\rho_0 - \rho_s) \tag{6}$$

$$C_0 = \frac{D}{W}(Planar)$$
$$\frac{2\pi D}{\log\left(W + {}^{a_o}/_{a_0}\right)}(NW)$$
$$= \frac{4\pi D}{a_0^{-1} - (W - a_0)}(ND) \tag{7}$$

Electrostatic constant i.e. the dielectric constant ϵ is replaced by diffusion constant D.

Consider equation 6, solving for this equation, the rate of change of number of molecules captured changes the flux and is given by the equation below (substituting for dN/dt).

$$I = A\frac{dN}{dt} = AK_F N_0 \rho_s \tag{8}$$

Solving the above two equations, gives the solution for number of molecules captured and is given by

$$N(t) = \rho_0 t \left[\frac{A}{C_0} + \frac{1}{K_F N_0}\right]^{-1} \tag{9}$$

The above equation is used to compute the number of molecules that have been captured for a certain period of time. The capacitance Co is chosen based on different kind of sensor being used. Thus it can be seen that the dimensionality of sensor influences the number of molecules captured, thus affecting the sensitivity of the sensor. The above analysis is carried out assuming steady state analysis, i.e. the concentration of diffusion is constant within the outer boundary. In order to model the sensor behaviour in transient state, figure below shows a sensor at the centre, and the analyte with unknown molecules (blue). The sensor captures the molecules closer to it and thus as the distance increases the analyte concentration increases, as the molecules closer to the sensor are being captured (white).

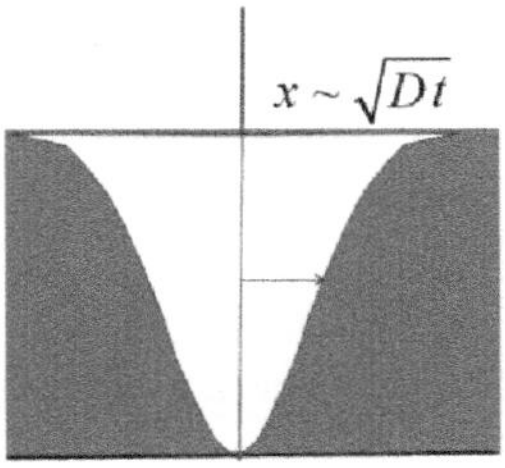

Fig. 7. Diffusion changes

As the boundary of diffusion changes and is time dependent, the factor W is time dependent. The boundary surface increases with time as in figure below.

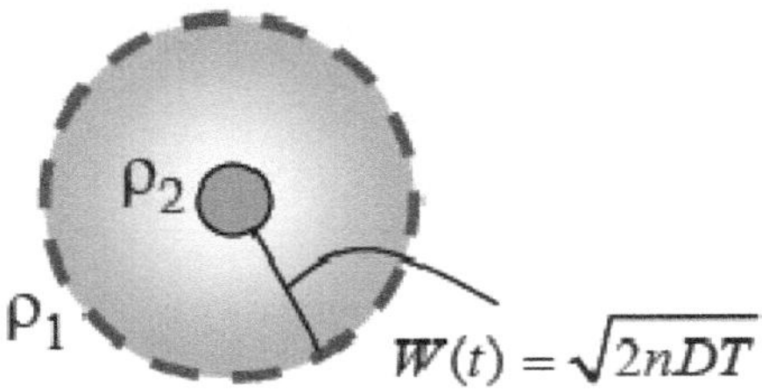

Fig. 8. Variable diffusion boundary

Thus the diffusion concentration is varying with time the modified equations for N(t) is given in equation below.

$$C_t = \frac{D}{\sqrt{D_t}} = \frac{2\pi D}{\log(\sqrt{D_t} + {}^{a_o}/_{a_0})} = \frac{4\pi D}{a_0^{-1}(\sqrt{6D_t}+a_o)^{-1}} \quad (10)$$

For different sensors as shown in figure below, the factor W changes with the geometry.

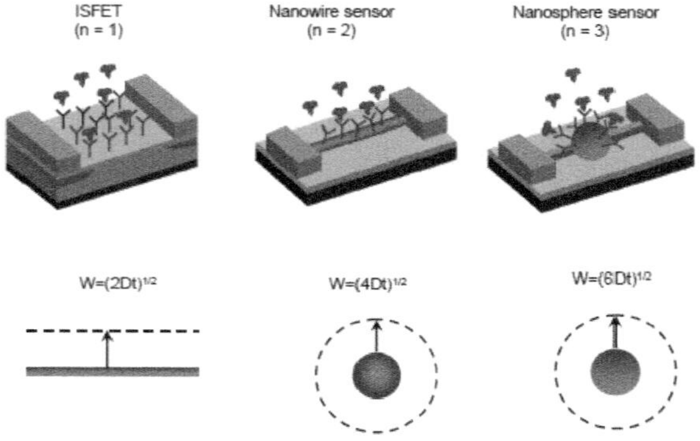

Fig. 9. Different types of sensors

Based on the mathematical models developed for different sensors, the mathematical models have been validated with numerical simulation results.

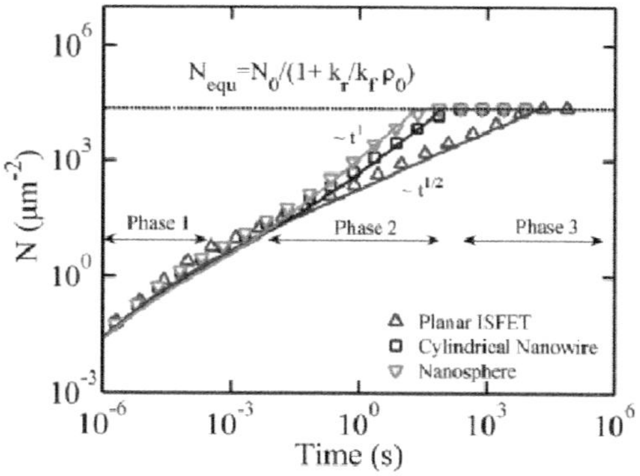

Fig. 10. Analyte concentration variations

From the results obtained and given in above figure it is found that the planar sensor is less sensitive compared to nanosphere sensor.

4 Experimental Setup for Nanosensor Simulation

Based on the mathematical models discussed, biosensor tool available in Nanohub.org is used for simulation of ISFET, nanowire and nanosphere. For a biosensor the most important parameters that are required for are:

- Size of micro channel: 5mm x 0.5mm x 50um
- Flow rate of fluid in the channel: 0.15ml/h
- Concentration of antigens in fluid: $2 \cdot 10^{-15} \cdot 6 \cdot 10^{23} \approx 10^{9}$
- Number of antigens through channel per hour: $1.5 \times 10^{-4} \times 10^{9} \sim 10^{5}$ (~ 42 per second)
- Total area occupied by Antibodies: 5mmx0.5mm ~ $25 \times 10^{-7} m^{2}$
- Area of one Si NW occupied by Antibodies (Assumption: r~10nm, l~2um): $2\pi rl \sim 1.26 \times 10^{-15}\ m^{2}$
- Target receptor conjugation
- Type of antigen: DNA
- Ratio between total occupied area and Si NW: 2×10^{9}
- Mean time between one antigen reacts with one antibody on the Si NW: <3 minutes

Based on the above parameters, the parameters in the biosensor lab is developed and the models available in the sensor lab are simulated. Figure below shows the experimental setup using the biosensors lab for simulating three different sensors.

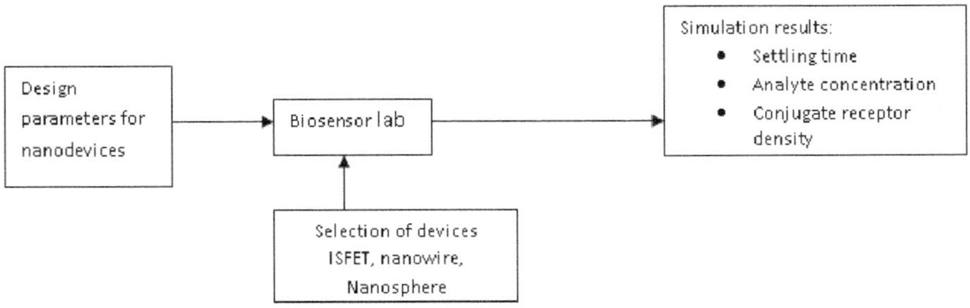

Fig. 11. Experimental setup for sensor characterization

Figures below show the simulation results for three different sensors, and their characteristics based on the design parameters given above.

From the results, it is found that the analyte concentration dips largely for nanosphere at 1E0 time, thus indicating the detection of targets by the receptors in a given analyte. Thus, nanosphere has good sensitivity compared with nanowire and ISFET.

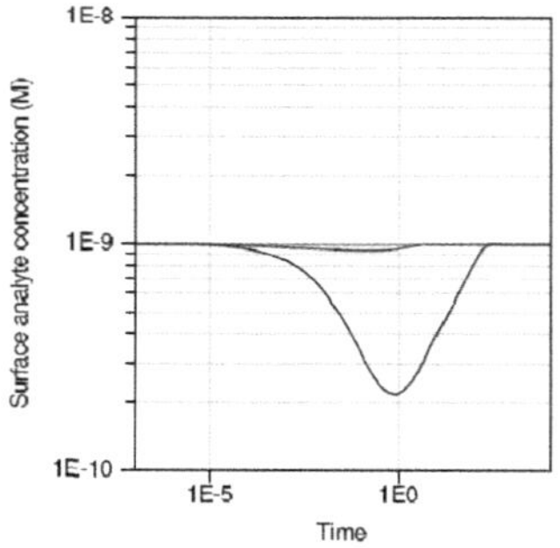

Fig. 12. The graph of surface analyte concentration variation with time (ISFET – green, Nanowire-Red, Nanosphere-Blue)

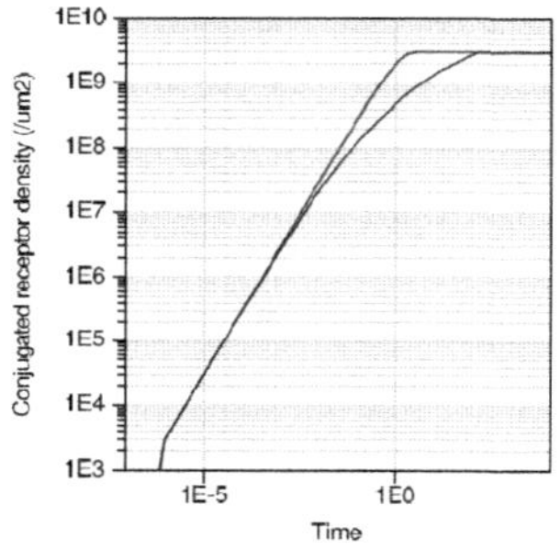

Fig. 13. The conjugated receptor density against time

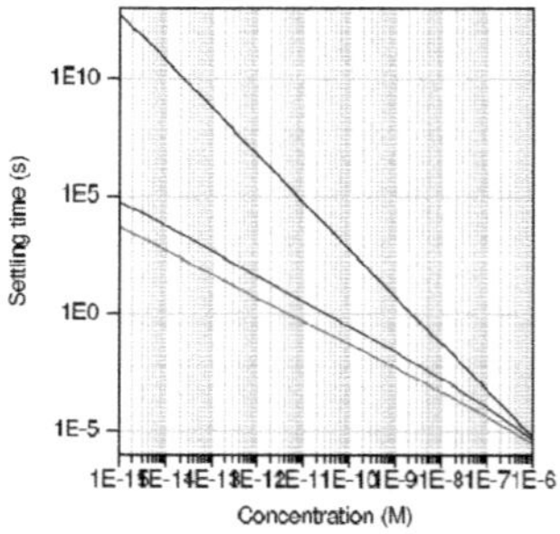

Fig. 14. The settling time for all three sensors

For the graph it is found that there exist linear relationships among all the three sensors. As the surface analyte concentration is reduced (previous figure), the conjugated receptor density also gets affected.

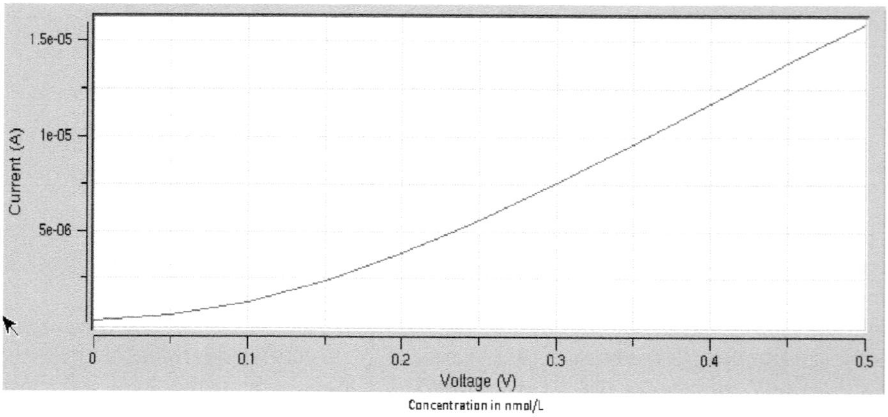

Fig. 15. The graph of concentration vs. device current characteristics for nanowire sensors

As the concentration increases, settling time has large variation for nanosphere compared to nanowire and ISFET, thus nanosphere is more sensitive to concentration of target ions.

From the results obtained, nanosphere has is found to have higher sensitive to analyte concentration, thus diseases are detected with higher accuracy, however, the construction of nanosphere is quite complex, thus in this work, nanowire is selected for sensor modeling.

4.1 VI Characteristics of Silicon Nanowire

A silicon nanowire is developed with the following parameters, the VI characteristics of the nanowire is simulated using the biosensor tool. Sensor parameters: Diameter of silicon nanowire: 10nm, Oxide thickness: 5nm, Gate length: 50nm, Channel doping: 1 e+21 /cm^3. Analyte concentration parameter is varied from 0.1 to 1 nmol/L, corresponding changes drain current in the nanowire sensor is determined.

Table 1. The equivalents in terms of voltage samples for various sets of iterations carried out. The results have been obtained using Matlab simulations.

Concentration in nmol/L	Sensor current equivalents	Concentration in nmol/L	Sensor current equivalents	Concentration in nmol/L	Sensor current equivalents
0.4629	0.8332	0.3646	0.6564	0.349	0.6283
0.3706	0.667	0.2211	0.398	0.3154	0.5676
0.4616	0.8308	0.2109	0.3796	0.5427	0.9769
0.3751	0.6753	0.4324	0.7783	0.4263	0.7673
0.1138	0.2049	0.3445	0.6201	0.7965	1.4338
0.2336	0.4205	0.3558	0.6404	0.6919	1.2454
0.5667	1.02	0.1213	0.2184	0.1302	0.2343
0.6277	1.1298	0.2161	0.3891	0.124	0.2232
0.3818	0.6873	0.1137	0.2046	0.7293	1.3128
0.4559	0.8207	0.1532	0.2758	0.5636	1.0145
0.34	0.6121	0.1406	0.253	1.4003	2.5205
0.3101	0.5582	0.2606	0.469	0.6937	1.2487
0.2772	0.4989	0.235	0.423	0.4923	0.8862
0.5925	1.0665	0.116	0.2088	0.1055	0.1899
0.4978	0.8961	0.1988	0.3578	0.1297	0.2335
0.4881	0.8786	0.2067	0.372	0.9062	1.6312

Table 1. (*continued*)

0.3285	0.5913	0.0604	0.1088	0.9573	1.7231
0.3457	0.6222	0.1742	0.3136	0.387	0.6966
0.2778	0.5001	0.1478	0.2661	0.5344	0.962
0.2002	0.3604	0.1288	0.2319	0.4633	0.834
0.5852	1.0534	0.139	0.2503	0.1911	0.344
0.3123	0.5622	0.166	0.2989	0.4768	0.8582
0.583	1.0494	0.2258	0.4064	0.2374	0.4272
0.3932	0.7077	0.2193	0.3948	0.3346	0.6023
0.4084	0.7351	0.1846	0.3323	0.2624	0.4723
0.3939	0.709	0.1292	0.2326	0.5181	0.9326
0.2934	0.5281	0.261	0.4698	0.262	0.4716
0.3818	0.6872	0.2218	0.3993	0.1192	0.2146
0.5059	0.9107	0.0826	0.1487	0.0907	0.1633
0.5227	0.9408	0.2237	0.4026	0.271	0.4878
0.445	0.8011	0.1165	0.2097	0.4029	0.7252
0.307	0.5526	0.1325	0.2385	0.644	1.1592
0.1723	0.3101	0.3161	0.569	0.4642	0.8355
0.4376	0.7876	0.2097	0.3775	0.1705	0.3069
0.3059	0.5506	0.2113	0.3803	0.228	0.4105
0.3914	0.7046	0.3077	0.5539	0.3317	0.597
0.4727	0.8508	0.1829	0.3293	0.6877	1.2378
0.3376	0.6076	0.2147	0.3865	0.6617	1.1911
0.2386	0.4295	0.274	0.4932	0.5943	1.0697
0.1768	0.3183	0.2581	0.4646	0.9265	1.6678
0.5035	0.9064	0.1799	0.3238	0.3296	0.5933
0.4297	0.7734	0.1099	0.1978	0.7458	1.3425
0.3029	0.5452	0.2529	0.4552	0.5271	0.9487
0.3945	0.7101	0.2432	0.4377	0.4593	0.8267
0.3986	0.7174	0.1736	0.3126	0.3569	0.6425

5 Mathematical Models for Nanowire Sensor

From the results obtained using biosensor lab, a Matlab model is developed for silicon nanowire. The Matlab model is based on the results obtained in table 1. The experimental setup developed using biosensors lab is used to identify the equivalent current values that flow in the drain of nanowire sensor with changes in analyte concentration. During the experimental setup, 135 different values of analyte concentration is set to identify the variations in drain current. The analyte concentration is varied from 0.1 to 0.5 mmol/L, corresponding drain currents are identified and is recorded. The Matlab model is a look up table of these values obtained in the biosensor lab. Figure below shows the top level diagram of Matlab model for nanowire sensor.

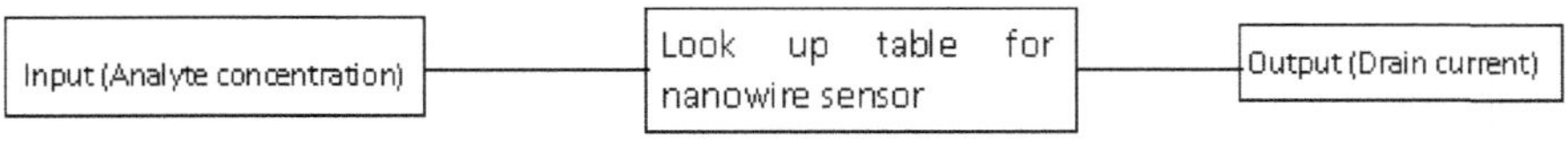

Fig. 16. Matlab model developed using look up table

The Matlab model developed is used in developing system level design of disease detection unit using nanowire sensors. In order to validate the developed Matlab model with biosensor model, an experimental setup is used to compare the performance of Matlab model with the biosensor model.

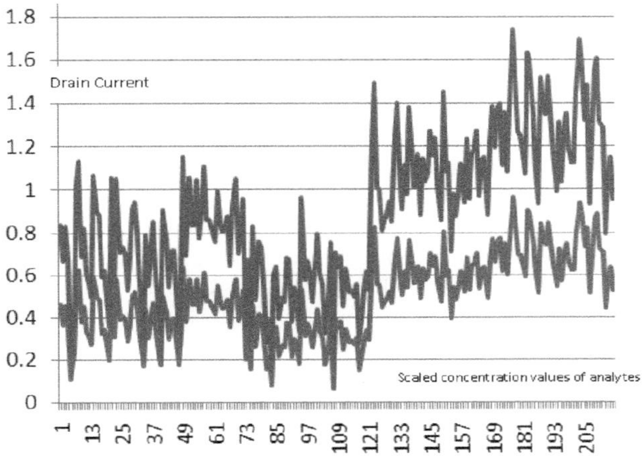

Fig. 17. The results of the two sensor models

From the results obtained it is found that the Matlab models (red), have the same variations as that of biosensor models (blue), but the numerical values of both the models have a maximum deviation of 1.2, thus the Matlab models developed follow the variations of biosensor models, but have an error of 1.2. Thus it is recommended that during system development it is required to address this error during signal processing.

6 Conclusion

In this paper, we have analyzed the mathematical models for nanowire sensors, variation in sensor properties with geometrical parameters have been analyzed. Experimental setup is developed to simulate three different nanosensor (ISFET, nanowire and nanosphere). Sensitivity of nanosphere is found to be better than nanowire and ISFET, however, it is practically difficult to realize nanosphere. Thus nanowire sensor is selected for system level design (disease detection), nanowire sensor is simulated and its response to variations in analyte concentration is identified. Based on the results obtained, Matlab model is developed. The developed mathematical model is validated against biosensor model, the results shows that both the models have linear variations for changes in analyte concentration, but there is an error of 1.2 (maximum), between the drain currents of biosensor model and Matlab model. This can be minimized by developing accurate results using the biosensor model for large number of analyte concentration.

Acknowledgement. The authors would like to acknowledge Nanohub.org for providing permission to access the biosensor labs simulation tools and to carry out the experiments.

References

1. Ludwig, J., Weinstein, J.: Biomarkers in cancer staging, prognosis and treatment selection. Nature Rev. Cancer 5, 845–856 (2005)
2. Catalona, W.: Clinical utility of measurements of free and total prostate-specific antigen (PSA): a review. Prostate 7, 64–69 (1996)
3. Beckett, M., Cazares, L., Vlahou, A., Schellhammer, P., Wright, G.: Prostate-specific membrane antigen levels in sera from healthy men and patients with benign prostate hyperplasia or prostate cancer. Clin. Cancer Res. 5, 4034–4040 (1995)
4. Henderson, C., Patek, A.: The relationship between prognostic and predictive factors in the management of breast cancer. Breast Cancer Res. Treat. 52, 261–288 (1998)
5. Dandachi, N., Dietze, O., Hauser-Kronberger, C.: Chromogenic in situ hybridization: a novel approach to a practical and sensitive method for the detection of HER2 oncogene in archival human breast carcinoma. Lab. Invest. 82, 1007–1014 (2002)
6. Molina, R., Auge, J., Escudero, J., Marrades, R., Vinolas, N., Carcereny, E., Ramirez, J., Filella, X.: Mucins CA 125, CA 19.9, CA 15.3 and TAG-72.3 as tumor markers in patients with lung cancer: comparison with CYFRA 21-1, CEA, SCC and NSE. Tumor Biol. 29, 371–380 (2008)
7. Landman, J., Chang, Y., Kavaler, E., Droller, M., Liu, B.: Sensitivity and specificity of NMP-22, telomerase, and BTA in the detection of human bladder cancer. Urology 52, 398–402 (1998)
8. Prow, T.W., Rose, W.A., Wang, N., Reece, L.M., Lvov, Y., Leary, J.F.: Biosensor-Controlled Gene Therapy/Drug Delivery with Nanoparticles for Nanomedicine. In: Proc. of SPIE, vol. 5692, pp. 199–208 (2005)

9. Prow, T.W., Smith, J.N., Grebe, R., Salazar, J.H., Wang, N., Kotov, N., Lutty, G., Leary, J.F.: Construction, Gene Delivery, and Expression of DNA Tethered Nanoparticles. Molecular Vision 12, 606–615 (2006)
10. Prow, T.W., Grebe, R., Merges, C., Smith, J.N., McLeod, D.S., Leary, J.F., Gerard, A., Lutty, G.A.: Novel therapeutic gene regulation by genetic biosensor tethered to magnetic nanoparticles for the detection and treatment of retinopathy of prematurity. Molecular Vision 12, 616–625 (2006)

Application of Recurrence Quantification Analysis (RQA) in Biosequence Pattern Recognition

Saritha Namboodiri[1], Chandra Verma[2], Pawan K. Dhar[3], Alessandro Giuliani[4], and Achuthsankar S. Nair[1,*]

[1] State Inter University Centre of Excellence in Bioinformatics, University of Kerala, Kariyavattom Campus, Thiruvananthapuram, Kerala, India
Tel.: +91 (0) 471 2308759
sankar.achuth@gmail.com
[2] Bioinformatics Institute (BII), Singapore
[3] Centre for Systems and Synthetic Biology, University of Kerala, Kariyavattom Campus, Thiruvananthapuram, Kerala, India
[4] Environment and Health Dept. Istituto Superiore di Sanità, Roma, Italy

Abstract. Recurrence Quantitative Analysis is a relatively new pattern recognition tool well suited for short, non-linear and non stationary systems. It is designed to detect recurrence patterns that are expressed as a set of Recurrence Quantification variables. In our work we made use of this tool on allosteric protein system to identify residues involved in the transmission of the structural rearrangements as an upshot of allostery. Allostery is the phenomenon of changes in the structure and activity of proteins that appear as a consequence of ligand binding at sites other than the active site. Here, we scrutinized the sequence landscape of 'ras' protein by partitioning its residues into windows of equal size. An 11 element characteristic vector, comprising of 10 features extracted from the Recurrence Quantification Analysis along with a feature relating to allosteric involvement, was defined for each windowed sequence set. By applying multivariate statistical analysis tools including Principal Component Analysis and Multiple Regression Analysis upon the characteristic feature vectors extracted from all the windowed sequence set, we could develop a significant linear model to identify the residues that are critical to allostery of 'ras' protein.

Keywords: Recurrence Quantitative Analysis, pattern recognition, allostery, hydrophobicity.

1 Introduction

Patterns are inherent in nature. Tools based on pattern recognition are aplenty. RQA, a relatively new entry in the field in pattern recognition has been extensively applied, since its induction days, in varying areas including physiology, economics, climate regime and biology [1, 2, 3, 4].

* Corresponding author.

A. Abraham et al. (Eds.): ACC 2011, Part I, CCIS 190, pp. 284–293, 2011.

Recurrence Quantification Analysis (RQA) is a pattern recognition tool based on Recurrence plot, a graphical tool, developed by Eckmann et al. [5] to study recurrence phenomena. It was later quantified by Webber and Zbilut [6] and popularised as Recurrence Quantification Analysis. RQA has been found to be suitable in finding patterns in short, non-stationary numerical sequences and has been successfully applied to the analysis of amino acid sequences of proteins [7, 8, 9, 10, 11]. We applied RQA in our study to identify the amino acids involved in allosteric transmission of 'ras' proteins, a well known allosteric protein. Allostery is a phenomenon initiated by binding of a ligand at particular sites of certain protein which produces unique structural changes in the protein. This accompanies conformational changes associated with altering interactions at the active sites (which may be far away from the causal binding site) [12]. The restructuring of allosteric proteins or allosteric transition involves long range communication among the residues well separated in sequence [13] Identifying residues involved in alloteric transmission is crucial to gain insight into the mechanisms controlling allosteric regulation and for building working proposition on signal processing by protein domains.

Different computational models to identify the major residues involved in mechanism of conformational switching based on sequence mechanical linkage, protein dynamics and thermodynamics, graphs and networks analysis and of late machine learning and data mining approaches have been developed. Using the sequence-based statistical approach, Ranganathan and co-workers [14] could model the signal transducing interaction network of the G-protein-coupled receptor family. Elastic network models introduced to study the protein dynamics has been used to predict critical residues in this transitions [15] Molecular dynamics simulations [16, 17, 18, 19] have been used to identify residues involved in conformational transitions that occur in the nanosecond timescale. The Rosetta high-resolution structure prediction methodology [20, 21] has been used to identify residues in various proteins including 'ras' proteins [22]. Daily et al. [23, 24] investigated coupling among residues by calculating networks of contact rearrangement.

Daily and coworkers [25] inferred that moving residues in allosteric proteins are structurally linked with other residues. We exploit this inference to develop a computational model using RQA, based on hydrophobicity ordering along the sequence of 'ras' protein, to identify the residues involved in its allosteric transition. RQA outperforms all other approaches by providing a structure oriented description of the system in hand.

2 Materials and Methods

2.1 Materials

The amino acid sequence of 'ras' protein obtained from Protein Data Bank (PDB) having the accession code, 4Q21, was looked into to identify the amino acids which are involved during allosteric transmission. The two different 3D structures of ras protein, corresponding to the 'active' and 'inactive' forms as a result of re-structuring due to allostery was also obtained from PDB. We also used the six different metrics which represented different aspects of conformational motions of 'ras' protein as computed by Daily and coworkers [25]. The adopted metrics had to do with both dihedral angles motions which involve changes in φ and ψ backbone torsion angles, side-chain torsion angles, and changes in between residues contact matrices. The transition between non-allosteric and allosteric behavior was determined over an average of 10-20 residues in sequence space and 10-20 Å in Cartesian space. All the six metrics of 'ras' protein was threshold by the comparative analysis of 'non-allosteric' motions to convert the basically continuous measure (allostery) into a 'yes/no' allosteric/non-allosteric property.

2.2 Method

2.2.1 Windowed Recurrence Quantification Analysis (RQA) as Applied to 'ras' Protein

We applied windowed RQA on the 'ras' sequence. For this, we partitioned the entire sequence of ras protein into window of 36 amino acid. The choice of 36 residues comes from the fact that 36 is approximately the length of the smallest 'proper' protein and allows a sufficient statistics for the computation of RQA descriptors [8]. The first 36 amino acids of the primary sequence of the protein formed the first window. Subsequent overlapping windows were formed by shifting amino acid one at a time. Thus the first window has amino acids starting from position 1 to 36 of the protein, the second window has amino acids from position 2 to 37 and so on. The entire 'ras' protein was thus partitioned into 154 windows. Each amino acid of windowed sequence set was substituted with Miyazawa Jernigham hydrophobicity index value [26]. Among several options available, we choose hydrophobicity as a key as it has a great role in folding and dynamics of the protein.

To obtain the recurrence plot for each of the hydrophobicity mapped windowed sequence set, we first produce an embedding matrix which projects the sequence into a higher dimensional space. A distance matrix is computed from this embedding matrix by finding the Euclidean distance among all the rows of the matrix. From the distance matrix, the values that fall below a predefined radius are considered as recurrences and set to 1 and the rest to 0 to form the recurrence matrix. Recurrence plot is a visualization of a recurrence matrix where all the 1's and 0's of the recurrence matrix are replaced by black and white dots respectively.

Our method is elaborated by considering the following windowed sample sequence:

SARMMMMMMSARRGSARGKLSARIMMMMMMVALSARCMMMMMMHSA
RETQSARITMMMMMMHAFFGDSARMMMMMMNSARETYVSARNMMMM
MMKLSARTRESAR

The amino acid sequence of 'ras' protein is coded in terms of relative hydrobhobicity according to the Miyazawa Jernigan hydrophobicity scale. The resulting numerical discrete series is transformed into a three dimensional embedding matrix. The embedding procedure results in a three column matrix of the original linear series by shifting the series at fixed time delay thereby obtaining the transformed multivariate embedding matrix. The number of elements considered in a row is the embedding dimension. A distance matrix is now worked out by computing the pairwise Euclidean norm of all the rows of the embedding matrix as follows:

$$D(P,Q) = \sqrt{(P_1 - Q_1)^2 + (P_2 - Q_2)^2 + \ldots (P_n - Q_n)^2} \quad (1)$$

where (P1, P2, P3…Pn) and (Q1, Q2, Q3…Qn) are the two rows in consideration.

The distance matrix is then filtered by a predefined radius to form a recurrence plot. In the recurrence plot, all the elements of the distance matrix which have distance less than or equal to the predefined radius are darkened leaving the rest as white.

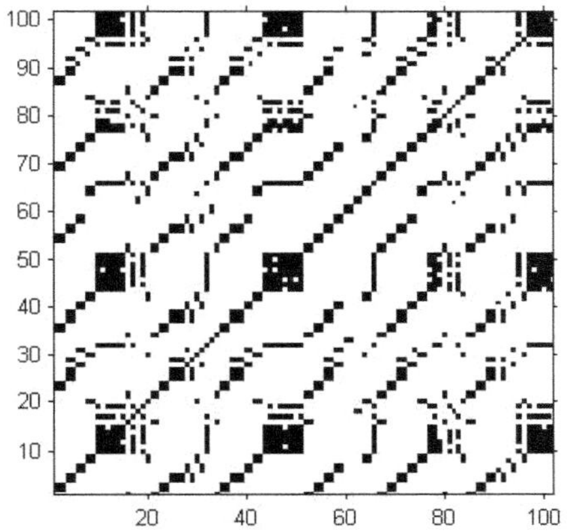

Fig. 1. Recurrence plot of the sample windowed sequence (Embedding dimension=3, radius =0.5 and time delay=2) 0 is in white and 1 is in black

For quantitative studies, from the patterns present in the recurrence plot as shown in Fig. 1, meaningful quantification indexes are derived. R1, the Recurrence measure, corresponds to the fraction of recurrence plot filled by darkened dots. R2, the Deterministic measure, represents the proportion of the recurrent points forming diagonal lines having a length of at least 2. Diagonal lines orthogonal to the main diagonal line are not considered. R2 is defined as the number of points in the diagonal lines divided by the total number of recurrence points excluding the elements of the main diagonal. R3: Lmax, is is the length of the longest diagonal line excluding the main diagonal line. R4 is an Information entropy measure. This is a measure of the Shannon information entropy computed over the frequency distribution of the lengths of the diagonal lines of recurrent points. R5, the Laminarity measure, is a measure of the proportion of recurrence points forming vertical/horizontal lines having at least a minimum length of 2. R6: Trap Time, measures the average length of vertical lines. This measures the mean time that the system will remain in a specific state. R6 is defined as the number of recurrence points forming vertical/horizontal lines divided by the length of the vertical/ horizontal structure. R7: T1 (Mean Recurrence Time - Type I) is the average time distance between a point and its recurrence in the embedding matrix. R8: T2 (Mean Recurrence Time -Type II) is the average time distance between a point and its recurrence in the embedding matrix excluding time distance of one unit. This removes all the points except for the first point forming the vertical lines. Therefore this is a measure of time distance with laminarity measure removed.

In addition to the above order-dependant quantifications, we also append two order independent quantifications for our analysis. These are R9, the hydrophobicity values of all amino acids in the given sequence and R10, the standard deviation of the hydrophobicity value of all the amino acids in the sequence. The 10 element RQA feature vector for the sample windowed example is as follows:

	R1	R2	R3	R4	R5	R6	R7	R8	R9	R10
R=	[0.15	0.43	2.5	0.69	0.43	2.86	2.69	4.23	5.48	1.67]

In our study, RQA was used to transform each windowed sequence set of 'ras' protein into a 10 characeristic feature vector. The allosteric involvement of each residue in the windowed sequence set was measured by computing the average over the six allosteric motions metrices [25] and thereafter the allosteric involvement of all the residues of each windowed sequence set was summed to obtain allosteric involvement measure, allostcount. This was repeated for all the 154 windowed sequence set. Thus an 11 element characteristic feature vector comprising of 10 features extracted from the Recurrence Quantification Analysis and a feature relating to allosteric involvement was defined for each windowed sequence set. A data matrix, A, of 154 rows representing the windowed sequence set and 11 columns representing the characteristic feature vector (10 RQA features and allostcount) was constructed.

2.2.2 Predictive Model Using Multivariate Statistical Analysis

Data matrix A was subjected to Principal Component Analysis to extract the most prominent features. We first processed the data matrix A by subtracting the mean value of each of the columns from each element of the column and from the standardized matrix B so obtained, a standardized correlation matrix C was determined using the formula:

$$C = \frac{1}{n-1} BB^T \tag{2}$$

The correlation matrix C, which represents the interrelationship between the standardized variables and how they co-vary, is used in the characteristic equation $|C - \lambda I| = 0$, where I is the identity matrix, λ represents the eigen-value. Solving this equation gives rise to eigen-values and eigenvectors. Each eigen-value is the amount of the variance and the corresponding eigenvector represents the direction of variance, each eigenvector is a factor. We found eleven factors that are orthogonal to each other and whose eigen-values are a linear combination of the variance of the eleven variables. Table I shows the factors, eigen-values, the proportion of variance accounted for by the factor in percentage and the cumulative variance in percentage. The eigen-values were arranged in descending order to highlight the important eigen-values (Table 1).

Initially factors 1 to 4 (shown in bold), which covered up to 97.7% of the total variance, were retained. From the factors retained, all factor loadings with values of ±4.0 or greater were considered significant and selected as key factors. The first component, factor 1, collects generically all the RQA descriptors and can be intended as a global measure of deterministic structuring of the sequence. Factor 2 has to do with recurrent times (T1 and T2) that correspond to the average distances between two consecutive recurrent points. Factor 3 is the average hydrophobicity, Factor 4 has to do with minor subtleties of recurrent times. The amount of variance of the original variables on each of these retained factors is represented in Table 2.

Table 1. Eigen-value distribution of the characteristic matrix A

Factors	Eigen values (or variance)	Proportion of variance	
		In %	In Cumulative %
1	**6.72**	**0.68**	**67.19**
2	**1.31**	**0.13**	**80.25**
3	**0.98**	**0.10**	**90.02**
4	**0.76**	**0.08**	**97.66**
5	0.13	0.01	98.93
6	0.08	0.01	99.75
7	0.01	0.00	99.89
8	0.00	0.00	99.97
9	0.00	0.00	99.98
10	0.00	0.00	99.99
11	0.00	0.00	100

Table 2. Eigen-value distribution of the characteristic matrix A

	Factor 1	Factor 2	Factor 3	Factor 4
R10	0.21	0.29	**0.92**	-0.13
R11	**0.98**	-0.04	0.11	-0.09
R1	**0.98**	**-0.09**	-0.10	-0.15
R2	**0.99**	**-0.08**	-0.07	-0.08
R3	**0.96**	-0.03	-0.01	0.01
R4	**0.98**	-0.02	-0.06	-0.02
R5	**0.98**	-0.16	-0.07	-0.01
R6	**0.87**	-0.16	0.13	0.40
R7	0.33	**0.78**	-0.25	**-0.46**
R8	.030	**0.75**	-0.10	**0.58**

The most significant factor loadings are shown in bold. Among the retained factors, factor 2 and factor 3 were found to correlate well with allostcount. A significant linear model using multiple linear analysis with allosteric involvement measure as dependent variable and factor 2 and factor 3 as independent variables was developed.

3 Results

Recurrence plots contain single black dots, diagonal lines and vertical / horizontal lines. Single dots occur when the states occur sporadically. Diagonal lines running parallel to the main diagonal indicate recurrences consecutively occurring in the sequence. The diagonal lines perpendicular to the main diagonal are formed when the same states are revisited but in the reverse temporal order. Vertical/horizontal lines are formed when states are not altered for a successive period of time, i.e. when the same value is repeated. Such patches are found repeating horizontally and vertically. Fig. 2 shows the recurrence plot of the first window (1-36 residues) of 'ras' protein having PDB accession code 42Q1.

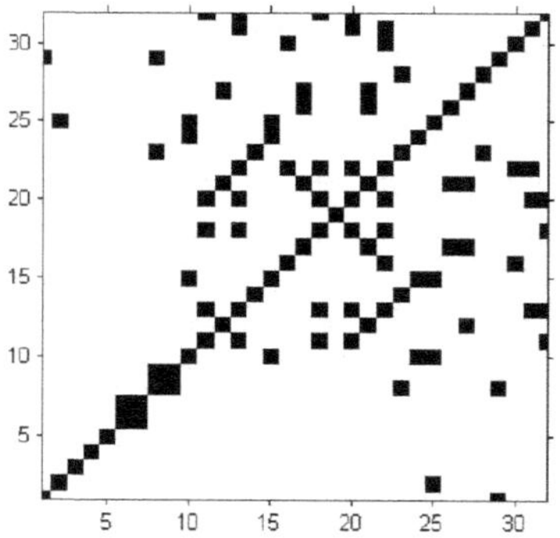

Fig. 2. Windowed recurrence plot (First window) of 'ras' protein

Principal Component Analysis on the feature vector extracted from all the windows of 'ras' protein gave rise to two significant factors namely factor 2 and factor 3. Factor 2, hydrophobicity-recurrence-decorrelation-time measure, corresponds to the average distance between two consecutive recurrence points. It represents the inter-space between consecutive recurrences. Factor 3, mean hydrophobicity measure, represents the average hydorphobicty. Factor 2 and factor 3 were found to correlate well with allosteric involvement measure, allostcount and could be considered crucial factors related to allosteric transmission in 'ras' protein. A multiple regression analysis with allostcount as dependant variable and factor 2 and 3 as independent variable produced a very significant linear model. Fig. 3 shows the observed and estimated allosteric involvement based on our proposed model. Our present model identifies two major flexible, allosteric zones of 'ras' proteins vey evident from Fig. 3. Fig. 4 shows the contribution of factor 2 and factor 3 in identifying the residues involved in allosteric transmission.

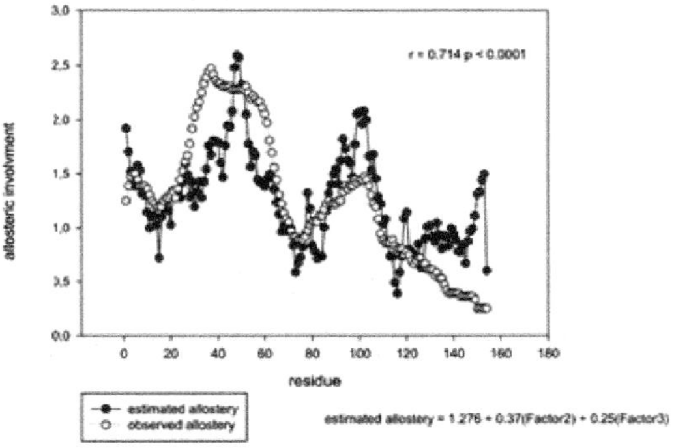

Fig. 3. Observed v/s Estimated allostery

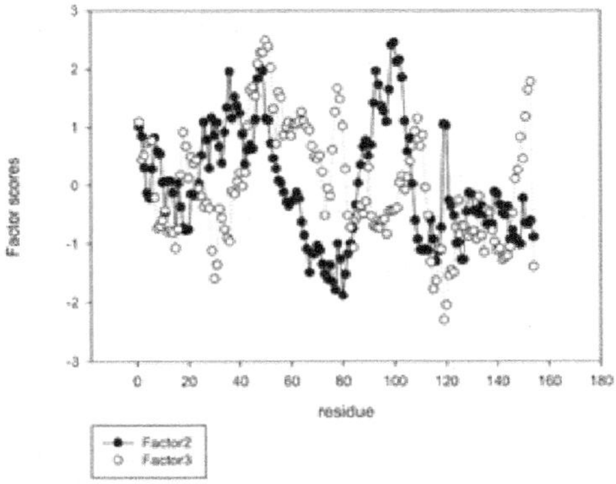

Fig. 4. Contribution of factor 2 and factor 3 in identifying residues involved in allosteric transmission of 'ras' protein

4 Discussion

Allostery is an important biological regulatory mechanism in organisms. Identifying residues involved in alloteric transmission is crucial to gain insight into the mechanisms controlling allosteric regulation Different computational models to identify the major residues involved in mechanism of conformational switching based on sequence mechanical linkage, protein dynamics and thermodynamics, graphs and networks analysis and of late machine learning and data mining approaches have been developed.

In this study, we used a reductionist approach whereby the primary sequence data of the protein was considered for Recurrence Quantitative Analysis, with hydrophobicity as the key driver of the conformational change exhibited by such proteins. The hydrophobicity index describing the various amino acids was quantified into variables using Recurrence Quantitative Analysis. Six different metrics which represented different aspects of conformational motions of 'ras' protein that had to do with both dihedral angles motions which involve changes in φ and ψ backbone torsion angles, side-chain torsion angles, and changes in between residues contact matrices were used to compute the allosteric involvement of each amino acid of 'ras' protein. The RQA features and allosteric involvement of all the windowed sequence set of 'ras' protein formed a characteristic feature vector. Multivariate statistical analysis on this feature vector, led to the developed a model which could significantly identify amino acids which play a major role in allostery of 'ras' protein. We are able to identify two major flexibility zones that are well approximated by the convolution of recurrence decorrelation time (factor 2) and mean hydrophobicity (factor 3). Daily et al. [25] had noted some characteristic spacing between 'allosteric' residues based on structure information. RQA proved very useful in providing a holistic representation of amino acid sequence in terms of the degree of structuring. Thus we could demonstrate, using this global, coarse-grained view of the primary structure of protein, that inter-space between consecutive patches of hydrophobic recurrences play a pivotal role in identifying residues involved in allosteric transistion thereby providing valuable pointers to allosteric mechanism.

References

1. Webber Jr., C.L., Zbilut, J.P.: Dynamical assessment of physiological systems and states using recurrence plot strategies. Journal of Applied Physiology 76, 965–973 (1994)
2. Kyrtsou, C., Vorlo, C.E.: Complex dynamics in macroeconomics: A novel approach in new trends in macroeconomics, pp. 223–238. Springer, Heidelberg (2005)
3. Marwan, N., Donges, J.F., Zou, Y., Donner, R.V., Kurths, J.: Complex network approach for recurrence analysis of time series. Phy. Letters A 373, 4246–4254 (2009)
4. Marwan, N., Wessel, N., Meyerfeldt, U., Schirdewan, A., Kurths, J.: Recurrence-plot-based measures of complexity and their application to heart-rate-variability data. Phys. Rev. E 66, 026702 (2002)
5. Eckmann, J.P., Oliffson, K.S., Ruelle, D.: Recurrence Plots of Dynamical Systems. Europhys Lett. 91, 973–977 (1987)
6. Zbilut, J.P., Webber, J.C.L.: Embeddings and delays as derived from quantification of recurrence plots. Physics Letters A 171, 199–203 (1992)
7. Porrello, A., Soddu, S., Zbilut, J.P., Crescenzi, M., Giuliani, A.: Discrimination of Single Amino Acid Mutations of the p53 Protein by Means of Deterministic Singularities of Recurrence Quantification Analysis. PROTEINS: Structure, Function and Bioinformatics 55, 743–755 (2004)
8. Zbilut, J.P., Giuliani, A., Colosimo, A., Mitchell, J.C., Colafrancesch, M., Marwan, N., Webber, C.L., Uversky, V.: Charge and Hydrophobicity Patterning Along the Sequence Predicts the Folding Mechanism and Aggregation of Proteins: A Computational Approach. Journal of Proteome Res. 3, 1243–1253 (2004)
9. Colafranceschi, M., Colosimo, A., Zbilut, J.P., Uversky, V.N., Giuliani, A.: Structure-Related Statistical Singularities along Protein Sequences: A Correlation Study. J. Chem. Inf. Model 45, 183–189 (2005)
10. Bruni, R., Costantino, A., Tritarelli, E., Marcantonio, C., Ciccozzi, R.M., El, S.G., Giuliani, A., Ciccaglione, A.R.: A computational approach identifies two regions of Hepatitis C Virus E1 protein as interacting domains involved in viral fusion process. BMC Struct. Biol. 9, 48 (2009)

11. Namboodiri, S., Verma, C., Dhar, P.K., Giuliani, A., Nair, A.S.: Sequence signatures of allosteric proteins towards rational design. Systems and Synthetic Biology (2011)
12. Monod, J., Changeux, J.P., Jacob, F.: Allosteric Proteins and Cellular Control Systems. J. Mol. Biol. 20, 306–329 (1963)
13. Dima, R.I., Thirumalai, D.: Determination of network of residues that regulate allostery in protein families using sequence analysis. Protein Science 15, 258–268 (2006)
14. Suel, G.M., Lockless, S.W., Wall, M.A., Ranganathan, R.: Evolutionarily conserved networks of residues mediate allosteric communication in proteins. Nat. Struct. Biol. 10, 59–69 (2003)
15. Williams, G.: Elastic network model of allosteric regulation in protein kinase PDK1. BMC structural Biology 10, 11 (2010)
16. Ota, N., Agard, D.A.: Intramolecular signaling pathways revealed by modeling anisotropic thermal diffusion. J. Mol. Biol. 351, 345–354 (2005)
17. Formaneck, M.S., Ma, L., Cui, Q.: Reconciling the "old" and "new" views of protein allostery: a molecular simulation study of chemotaxis Y protein (CheY). Proteins 63, 846–867 (2006)
18. Yu, H., Ma, L., Yang, Y., Cui, Q.: Mechanochemical coupling in the myosin motor domain. II. Analysis of critical residues. PLoS Comput. Biol. 3, e23 (2007)
19. Kong, Y., Karplus, M.: Signaling pathways of PDZ2 domain: a molecular dynamics interaction correlation analysis. Proteins 4, 145–154 (2009)
20. Rohl, C.A., Strauss, C.E.M., Misura, K.M.S., Baker, D.: Protein Structure Prediction Using Rosetta Methods in Enzymology. Numerical Computer Methods 383, 66–93 (2004)
21. Rousseau, F., Schymkowitz, J.: A systems biology perspective on protein structural dynamics and signal transduction. Current Opinion in Structural Biology 15, 23–30 (2005)
22. Kidd, B.A., Baker, D., Thomas, W.E.: Computation of Conformational Coupling in Allosteric Proteins. PLoS Computational Biology 5(8), e1000484 (2009)
23. Daily, M.D., Upadhyaya, T.J., Gray, J.J.: Contact rearrangements form coupled networks from local motions in allosteric proteins. Proteins-Structure Function and Bioinformatics 71, 455–466 (2008)
24. Daily, M.D., Gray, J.J.: Allosteric Communication Occurs via Networks of Tertiary and Quaternary Motions in Proteins. Plos Computational Biology 5 (2009)
25. Daily, M.D., Gray, J.J.: Local Motions in a Benchmark of Allosteric Proteins. Bioinformatics Proteins 67, 385–399 (2007)
26. Jernigan, M.R.: Estimation of Effective Interresidue Contact Energies from Protein Crystal Structures: Quasi-Chemical Approximation. Macromolecules 18, 534–552 (1985)

New Feature Vector for Apoptosis Protein Subcellular Localization Prediction

Geetha Govindan[1] and Achuthsankar S. Nair[2]

[1] Research Scholar, Centre for Bioinformatics, University of Kerala, Thiruvananthapuram
geetha_gn@yahoo.com
[2] Director, Interuniversity Centre for Excellence in Bioinformatics,
University of Kerala, Thiruvananthapuram
sankar.achuth@gmail.com

Abstract. It is widely recognized that the information for determining the final subcellular localization of proteins is found in their amino acid sequences. In this work we present new features extracted from the full length protein sequence to incorporate more biological information. Features are based on the occurrence frequency of di-peptides - traditional, higher order. Naïve Bayes classification along with correlation-based feature selection method is proposed to predict the subcellular location of apoptosis protein sequences. Our system makes predictions with an accuracy of 83% using Naïve Bayes classification alone and 86% using Naïve Bayes classification with correlation-based feature selection. This result shows that the new feature vector is promising, and helps in increasing the prediction accuracy.

Keywords: protein subcellular localization, naïve bayes classification, correlation-based feature selection, di-peptides.

1 Introduction

Apoptosis is the term given to programmed cell death that occurs in multi cellular organisms. This is a form of death the cell itself initiates, regulates, and executes using cellular and molecular machinery. Because of this Apopotosis is also called "programmed cell death". The word apoptosis has ancient Greek origins, referring to the falling of leaves,. Cell death may be initiated when a cell is no longer needed, when a cell becomes a threat to the organism's health, or for other reasons. Cells undergoing apoptosis have changes in the cell membrane such as loss of membrane asymmetry and attachment, cell shrinkage, nuclear fragmentation, chromatin condensation, and chromosomal DNA fragmentation etc. This disposal of cellular debris through this process does not damage the organism and it is for the good of the organism as a whole. Excessive apoptosis causes hypotrophy, such as in ischemic damage, whereas an insufficient amount results in uncontrolled cell proliferation, such as cancer[1].

Organs shape is developed through Apoptosis. A human fetus initially has webbed hands and feet and later apoptosis process removes few skin cells, forming individual fingers and toes. Another example is the eyelid formation in foetus.

A. Abraham et al. (Eds.): ACC 2011, Part I, CCIS 190, pp. 294–301, 2011.

To understand the apoptosis protein mechanism and functions fully, it is important to obtain the information about their subcellular location. This is because subcellular location is closely related to their function [2, 3, and 4]. It has been known that there are about 62503 proteins (Reviewed 5659) with name "apoptosis" in UniProtKB. With the increase in the number of known protein sequences, it is time consuming and expensive to determine the specific subcellular location a given protein belongs to. In spite of great technical advance in the past decades, it is still laborious to experimentally determine protein subcellular locations on a high throughput scale. Therefore, it is very essential to develop an accurate and reliable prediction method for apoptosis protein subcellular location. For this, a good feature representation of sequences is very essential.

Zhou and Doctor [5] attempted to identify four kinds of subcellular locations of 98 apoptosis proteins based on amino acid composition by means of the covariant discriminant function. Chou [6] proposed the concept "pseudo amino acid compositions". Chou and Cai [7, 8] proposed a method by integrating the pseudo amino acid compositions and the information of gene ontology. Feng [9] proposed a new representation of unified attribute vector; all of proteins have their representative points on the surface of the 20-D globe. Cherian and Nair [10] proposed prediction of subcellular location using global features and amino acid composition using SVM. Li Zhang [11] proposed Support Vector based method for prediction of subcellular localization in Apoptosis Proteins using distance frequencies. Kumar Kandaswamy [12] proposed a new Genetic Algorithm, SVM based feature vector formation. Chaohong Song, Feng Shi [16] proposed a method using K-nearest neighbor. These results indicated that the subcellular location of apoptosis proteins is predictable to a considerably extent if a good vector representation of protein can be established. It is expected that, with a continuous improvement of feature representation methods by incorporating amino acid properties, and by combining more powerful mathematics methods [13], better accuracy in prediction can be achieved.

In this work, the amino acid di-peptide composition of a protein sequence is used to construct the feature vector. This numerically transformed sequence is used as input feature vector for the Naïve Bayes classifier to predict the subcellular location of apoptosis proteins.

2 Materials and Methods

2.1 Data Sets

For this study, dataset compiled denoted as ASN_G 315 is used. This dataset is generated from SWISSPROT (release 2011-02) by selecting the sequences which has a decided single subcellular location for human apoptosis proteins. This dataset is classified into six subcellular location and details are described in Table 1. While compiling the data sets, it became clear that subcellular location is not annotated for all apoptosis proteins and hence the data set is relatively small.

To ensure that our results are not biased , we have used a 10 fold cross validation to measure the performance of the classifier with different feature vectors.

Table 1. Subcellular location distribution of the dataset of 315 chosen apoptosis proteins

Subcellular localization sites	Number of proteins
Cytoplasmic	111
Endoplasmic Reticulum	47
Membrane	54
Mitochondrial	34
Nucleus	52
Secreted	17
Total	315

2.2 Naive Bayes Classification

Bayesian classifiers are statistical classifiers that can predict class membership probabilities, such as the probability that a given sample belongs to a particular class. Bayesian classification is based on the Bayes' theorem (Feller, 1971). Bayes theorem relates the probability of the occurrence of an event to the occurrence or non occurrence of an associated event. In particular, Naive Bayes classifiers assume that the effect of a variable value on a given class is independent of the values of other variable. This assumption is called class conditional independence. It is made to simplify the computation and in this sense considered to be Naïve.

An advantage of the Naive Bayes classifier is that it requires a small amount of training data to estimate the parameters (means and variances of the variables) necessary for classification. Because independent variables are assumed, only the variances of the variables for each class need to be determined.

Algorithm first uses the Bayes rule to express P (class I features) in terms of P (class) and P (features I class)

$$P\frac{class}{features} = \frac{P(class)*P(\frac{features}{class})}{P(features)} \tag{1}$$

The algorithm then makes the 'naive' assumption that all features are independent of every other feature. This means that

$$P\frac{class}{features} = \frac{P(class)*P\left(\frac{f1}{class}\right)*P\left(\frac{f2}{class}\right)*\cdots\cdots*P\left(\frac{fn}{class}\right)}{P(features)} \tag{2}$$

The above equation can be written as

$$\text{posterior} = \frac{\text{prior} \times \text{likelihood}}{\text{evidence}}. \tag{3}$$

A simple Bayes Classifier system works as follows:-

Data sample is represented by n dimensional feature vector. Suppose there are m classes. Given an unknown data sample *X*, the classifier will predict that *X* belongs to the class having the highest posterior probability, conditional on X.

To classify an unknown sample X, $P(X|C_i)* P(C_i)$ is computed for each class C_i Sample X is assigned to the class C_i if and only if $P(X|C_i)* P(C_i) > P(X|C_j)* P(C_j)$ for $1 <= j <= m$, where j is different from i.

2.3 Correlation Based Feature Selection (CFS)

CFS is a simple attribute selection algorithm [14] that gives high scores to feature subsets according to a correlation based evaluation. Features that are highly correlated with class and uncorrelated to each other are assigned with high. Irrelevant features are ignored because they will have low correlation with the class. Redundant features are screened out as they will be highly correlated with one or more of the remaining features.

Merit of a given attribute is calculated taking into account the correlation of the attribute with the target class as well as the correlation of the attribute with other attributes in the dataset. Attributes with stronger correlation with the target class and weaker correlation with other attributes are ranked higher.

Since attribute selection is the process of identifying and removing as much of the irrelevant and redundant information from a dataset, the reduction of dimensionality in a dataset presents a number of benefits, such as enabling algorithms to operate faster and more effectively, improving classification accuracy, improving data visualization, and enhancing better understanding of the derived classification models.

2.4 Feature Vector

Machine learning techniques require fixed length patterns as input feature vector or classification. The aim of calculating the composition of proteins is to capture the meaningful biological information from the protein sequences of different length to fixed length information. This is an important and most crucial step in classification problems. In this paper, di-peptide occurrence frequency is used for forming the feature vector for classification.

Di-peptide is a molecule consisting of two amino acids joined by a single peptide bond and that gave a feature vector having dimension of 400 from the 20 amino acid combination. The advantage of di-peptide sequence composition over amino acid composition is that it encapsulates information about the fraction of amino acids as well as their local order.

Consider a sequence A A A P Y Q A A C A Q.

The di-peptide count with 0 skips d0 is calculated by counting all pairs of amino acid condition with no skips (ie the case were they occur adjacent to each other. In this figure below the count of $d0_{AA}$ is shown as 3.

A A A P Y Q A A C A Q -> $d0_{AA}=3$

Di-peptide counts with n skips, dn , counts pairs with n skips between them. For instance, $d1_{AA}$ is calculated as 2.

A A A P Y Q A A C A Q -> $d1_{AA}=2$

Since di-peptide comprises of two consecutive residues, the 400 possible types of di-peptides are formed from the grouping of all 20 amino acids by properties. This conversion of protein sequence to di-peptide frequency count with different orders will help to encapsulate the sequence order and properties of the protein numerically [11].

The simplest feature vector using the occurrence frequency of di-peptide amino acid composition to represent protein sequence is formulated as follows. Given a protein sequence P with l amino acid residues, P= [$R_1R_2R_3R_4R_5R_6R_7$......R_l], where R_1, R_2 ..... R_l are the residues, then we can map the sequence into a fixed length feature vector as P= $f_1\ f_2\ f_3$ ...... f_{400} where f_u (u = 1,2,...400) are the normalized occurrence frequencies of the 400 native di-peptides in P.

400 numbers of di-peptides from 20 amino acids A, C, D, E, F, G, H, I, K, L, M, N, P, Q, R, S, T, V, W, Y are:-

[AA,AC,AD,AE,AF,AG,AH,AI,AK,AL,AM,AN,AP,AQ,AR,AS,AT,AV,AW,AY,
CA,CC,CD,CE, CF,CG, CH,CI,CK,CL,CM,CN, CP,CQ,CR, CS,CT, CV,CW,CY,
....,
YA,YC,YD,YE,YF,YG,YH,YI,YK,YL,YM,YN,YP,YQ,YR,YS,YT,YV,YW,YY].

The feature vector of the sequence 'A A A P Y Q A A C A Q ' for di-peptide d0,d1,d2,d3 is as follows :-

Feature vector for occurrence frequency d0
= [3 1 0 0 0 0 0 0 0 0 0 0 0 1 1 0 0 0 0 0 0 0 1 0 0 0 0 ......0]
Feature vector for occurrence frequency d1
= [2 1 0 0 0 0 0 0 0 0 0 0 0 1 0 0 0 0 0 0 0 1 0 0 0 0 0 ......0]
Feature vector for occurrence frequency d2
= [1 0 0 0 0 0 0 0 0 0 0 0 0 1 2 0 0 0 0 0 0 1 0 0 0 0 0 ......0]

Each protein sequence is represented as four separate numeric sequence of its di-peptide d0, d1 and d2 count having 400 components and forms the feature vector for further the classifier. Feature vector for the combination of di-peptide d0, d1 and di-peptide d0, d1, d2 is obtained by adding the corresponding feature vectors.

3 Results and Discussion

In this trial, Naive Bayes classifier is tested to predict the subcellular location of apoptosis proteins. This classifier was adopted because it is most effective and efficient classification, it is simple to implement and gives a better accuracy. Also it exploits our method for parameter selection. Naive Bayes classifier available at Weka, version 3.6.4 was used.

Each protein sequence from the set of 315 is converted to three numeric sequence based on its di-peptide occurrence frequency count, forming the feature vector of 400 dimension using +1, +2 and +3 groups. Data is classified with 10 fold cross validation. In one fold of cross-validation, sample of data is divided into subsets, and analysis is performed on each subset (called the training set), and validated on the other

Table 2. Results of Naïve Bayes classification (Pr- Precision Re- Recall Fs – F- Score)

	Cytoplasm			Endoplasmic			Membrame			Mitochondr			Nucleus			Secreted			Accu-racy
Feature Vector	Pr	Re	Fs	Pr	Re	Fs	Pr	Re	Fs	Pr	Re	Fs	Pr	Re	Fs	Pr	Re	Fs	
D0	83	86	84	100	85	92	73	87	79	86	71	77	70	81	75	100	41	58	81
D1	81	75	78	100	85	92	67	86	75	80	71	75	70	85	77	90	53	67	78
D2	77	73	75	100	85	92	68	87	76	79	65	71	64	77	70	90	53	67	76
D0 + CFS (85 attributes)	86	85	86	100	85	92	80	89	85	79	77	78	74	83	78	67	59	63	83
D1 + CFS (93 attributes)	86	85	86	100	87	93	71	87	78	77	71	74	73	77	75	83	59	69	81
D2 + CFS (87 attributes)	85	80	82	100	85	92	77	89	82	79	79	79	71	77	74	67	71	69	81
D3 + CFS (85 attributes)	86	85	86	100	85	92	80	89	85	79	77	78	74	83	78	67	59	63	83
D0 + D1	85	88	88	100	85	92	73	95	83	89	68	77	80	87	83	100	47	64	84
D0 + D1 + D2	79	85	82	100	85	92	79	93	85	89	68	77	77	83	80	100	59	74	83
D0 + D1 + CFS (118 attributes)	85	86	85	98	89	93	82	87	84	90	77	83	73	89	80	100	59	74	85
D0 + D1 + D2 + CFS (150 attributes)	87	91	89	100	89	94	83	91	87	84	79	82	77	83	80	100	59	74	86

subset (called the validation set or testing set). Multiple rounds of cross-validations are performed using different partition. The validated results are averaged over the rounds to reduce the variability.

The prediction results using various protein features are shown in Table 2. All the results are estimated using 10 fold cross validation. The first column represents the features and the feature selection method used. The overall accuracy for the combination of di-peptide +1,+2+3 reached to 86% from 84% with the feature reduction method. Combination of di-peptide frequency count further enhanced prediction performance to some extent. These results shows that the selected feature vector is indeed capable of extracting more information from the protein sequence and has given a better prediction performance. Hence the current approach is effective.

For the subcellular location of a apoptosis protein, it is very important to select a set of reasonable biological information feature as different feature extraction can bring different accuracy. Our result shows that di-peptide compositions are very useful for apoptosis protein and Naïve Bayes classifier is much suitable for such predictions. This approach can be used for other protein subcellular location predictions.

4 Conclusion

The new feature vector based on the occurrence frequency of di-peptide along with Naïve Bayes classification can be effectively used for predicting subcellular locations of apoptosis proteins. However, in the future research; we would try to improve our method to increase the accuracy using other amino acid parameters and test in many different datasets, expecting our method will have general applicability. We do recognize the reductionist nature of our approach and its consequent limitations. Wider trials for more appropriate feature vector elements are to be carried out if the prediction accuracies are to be improved further. The analysis of organism-wise tuning of predictors also to be investigated in future works.

References

1. Potten, C., Apoptosis, J.W.: The Life and Death of Cells (Developmental & Cell Biology Series)
2. Emanuelsson, O., Nielsen, H., Brunak, S., Gunnar, H.: Predicting Subcellular Localization of Proteins Based on Their N-Terminal Amino Acid Sequence. J. Molecular Biology. 300, 1005–1006 (2000)
3. Chou, K.C.: A New Branch of Proteomics Prediction of Protein Cellular Attributes. Gene Cloning and Expression Technologies 4, 57–70 (2002)
4. Huang, J., Shi, F.: Support Vector Machines for Predicting Apoptosis Proteins Types. Acta Bioinformatics 53, 39–47 (2005)
5. Zhou, G.P., Doctor, K.: Subcelluar Location of Apoptosis Proteins. Proteins: Structure, Function, and Genetic 50, 44–48 (2003)
6. Chou, K.C.: Prediction of Protein Cellular Attributes using Pseudoamino Acid Composition. Proteins: Structure. Functions. Genetics. 43(3), 246–255 (2001)

7. Chou, K.C., Cai, Y.D.: Using Functional Domain Composition and Support Vector Machines for Prediction of Protein Subcellular Location. J. Bio. Chem 227(48), 45765–45769 (2002)
8. Chou, K.C., Cai, Y.D.: Predicting Subcellular Localization of Proteins by Hybridizing Functional Domain Composition and Pseudo-amino acid Composition. J. Cell Biochem. 91(3), 1197–1203 (2004)
9. Feng, Z.P.: Prediction of the Subcellular Location of Prokaryotic Proteins based on a New Representation of the Amino acid Composition. Biopolymers 58(4) (2001)
10. Cherian, B.S., Nair, A.S.: Protein Location Prediction using Atomic Composition of the Amino acid Sequence. Biochemical and Biophysical Research Communications 391, 1670–1674 (2010)
11. Zhang, L., Liao, B., Li, D., Zhu, W.: A Novel Representation for Apoptosis Protein Subcellular Localization Prediction Using Support Vector Machine. Journal of Theoretical Biology 259, 361–365 (2009)
12. Kumar Kandaswamy, K., Pugalenthi, G., Moller, S.: Prediction of Apoptosis Protein Locations with Genetic Algorithms and Support Vector Machines Through a New Mode of Pseudo Amino Acid Composition. Protein Peptide Letters 17(12) (2010)
13. Ding, Y.S., Zhang, T.L.: Using Chou's Pseudo Amino Acid Composition to Predict Subcellular Localization of Apoptosis Proteins: An Approach with Immune Genetic Algorithm Based Ensemble Classifier. Pattern Recognition Letters 29, 1887–1892 (2008)
14. Hall, M.A., Holmes, G.: Benchmarking Attribute Selection Techniques for Discrete Class Data Mining. IEEE Transactions on Knowledge and Data Engineering 15, 1–16 (2003)
15. Ding, Y., Cai, Y., Zhang, G., Xu, W.: The Influence of Dipeptide Composition on Protein Thermostability. FEBS Letters 569, 284–288 (2004)
16. Song, C., Shi, F.: Prediction of Subcellular Localization of Apoptosis Proteins by Dipeptide Composition. JDCTA: International Journal of Digital Content Technology and its Applications 4(1.4), 32–36 (2010), doi:10.4156/jdcta

Hurst CGR (HCGR) – A Novel Feature Extraction Method from Chaos Game Representation of Genomes

Vrinda V. Nair[1], Anita Mallya[1], Bhavya Sebastian[1], Indu Elizabeth[1], and Achuthsankar S. Nair[2]

[1] College of Engineering, Thiruvananthapuram, Kerala, India
[2] Centre for Bioinformatics, University of Kerala, Thiruvananthapuram, Kerala, India
nairvrinda@rediffmail.com,
{anita.mallya.9779,bhavyapsebastian,induelizabeth20,
sankar.achuth}@gmail.com

Abstract. The performance of a classifier depends on the exactness of the feature vectors extracted from the dataset. Here, a novel method for feature extraction from genome sequences is presented which combines Chaos Game Representation (CGR) and Hurst exponent. The former maps genome sequences into fractal images while the latter acts as a quantifier for such images. The suitability of the new feature vector is attested by classifying 8 categories of eukaryotic genomes accessed from NCBI. The classification results prove that application of Hurst exponent over Chaos Game Representation formats of genome sequences can extract signature features representative of the underlying sequences, thus presenting HCGR as a new feature for classification of genomes.

Keywords: genome sequence, feature extraction, chaos game representation, fractals, Hurst exponent, SVM classifiers.

1 Introduction

Any classification problem deals with proper selection of feature vectors as its major initial concern. In this work, a novel technique for feature extraction from genome sequences is presented. A combination of Chaos Game Representation (CGR) and Hurst exponent forms the foundation of this new technique. The appropriateness of the proposed feature vector is validated by classifying 8 categories of eukaryotic genomes using a Support Vector Machine (SVM) classifier. Genome classification in turn finds wide application in evolutionary studies of organisms as well as practical applications such as bio-diversity studies, forensic investigations and food and meat authentication, to name a few. Hence the need for efficient feature extraction techniques.

R. Sandberg et al. [1] classified archeal and bacterial genomes based on the dinucleotide composition of the sequences using a naïve Bayesian approach and an accuracy of 85% is seen reported. Principal Component Analysis was used to extract the feature descriptors from three tuple words from genome sequences by S.

A. Abraham et al. (Eds.): ACC 2011, Part I, CCIS 190, pp. 302–309, 2011.

Narasimhan et al. [2]. The descriptors were visually represented using polar coordinates. No quantitative measures of accuracy are seen reported. Frequency CGR (FCGR) [3] & [4] was used for genome classification in a previous investigation [5].

The focus of this paper is on investigating a novel method for feature extraction from the CGR format of the genome sequences using Hurst exponent. Hurst exponent which is conventionally used for quantifying a time series trend is used in this context. Hurst exponent, as is related to fractal dimension [6], could in turn be considered as a quantifying feature for a fractal image. CGR of genome sequences are indeed fractals [7] and hence the motivation behind this novel method. Hurst exponent has been previously used by Sk. Sarif Hassan et. al [8] for exploring genomic evolution through quantitative measures of fractals and morphology.

Support Vector Machine (SVM) was used for the classification. SVM is a supervised classification algorithm that learns by example to discriminate among two or more given classes of data [9]. In this work, classification was implemented using multi class SVM, since 8 categories of organisms are classified. A Radial Basis kernel function was used results of which are reported.

1.1 Chaos Game Representation and Hurst Exponent

The scope of CGRs as useful signature images of bio-sequences such as DNA has been investigated since early 1990s. CGR of genome sequences was first proposed by H. Joel Jeffrey [10]. To derive a chaos game representation of a genome, a square is first drawn to any desired scale and corners marked A, T, G and C. The first point is plotted halfway between the center of the square and the corner corresponding to the first nucleotide of the sequence, and successive points are plotted halfway between the previous point, and the corner corresponding to the base of each successive nucleotide. Mathematically, co-ordinates of the successive points in the chaos game representation of a DNA sequence is described by an iterated function system defined in Eq. (1) and Eq. (2).

$$X_i = 0.5(X_{i-1} + g_{ix}). \tag{1}$$

$$Y_i = 0.5(Y_{i-1} + g_{iy}). \tag{2}$$

g_{ix} and g_{iy} are the X and Y co-ordinates respectively of the corners corresponding to the nucleotide at position i in the sequence [11]. The CGR of a random sequence gives a uniformly filled square. The CGR of DNA sequences plotted for various species gives images illustrating the non-randomness of genome sequences, which indeed means that the sequence has a structure, indirectly captured by the signature image. Features of CGRs include marked double scoops, diagonals, varying vertical intensities, absence of diagonals etc. signifying corresponding sequence characteristics. The CGR is thus found to be unique for every species. Hence CGR of genomic sequences are expected to furnish features of discriminative nature which could subsequently be presented to classifiers. Fig. 1. shows the CGR for Musmusculus (house mouse), sequence of which is retrieved from NCBI.

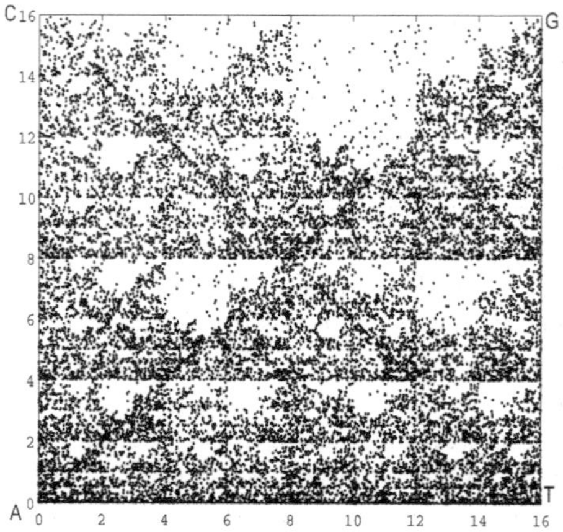

Fig. 1. CGR of Musmusculus (NC_005089, 16299nt)

CGRs exhibit the property of self-similarity which is the foundation for considering them as fractals [7]. Each fractal has a characteristic called fractal dimension, which is an indication of how completely a fractal fills space as one zooms down to finer and finer scales [12]. Fractal dimension is linearly related to Hurst exponent by the equation

$$H = 2 - D . \tag{3}$$

where D denotes Fractal dimension and H, Hurst exponent [6]. The fractal dimension also provides an indication of how rough a surface is [13]. As is evident from Eq. (3), a small Hurst exponent has a higher fractal dimension and a rougher surface and a larger Hurst exponent has a smaller fractional dimension and a smoother surface.

Hurst exponent is referred to as the "index of dependence," and is the relative tendency of a time series to either strongly regress to the mean or 'cluster' in a direction [6]. It is a numerical estimate of the predictability of a time series. The values of the Hurst exponent range between 0 and 1. A value between 0 and 0.5 indicates anti-persistency, value between 0.5 and 1 indicates persistency and a value of 0.5 indicates a random process. Hurst exponent occurs in several areas such as applied mathematics, including fractals and chaos theory, long memory processes, financial analysis, biophysics, computer networking etc.

This paper explores the possibility of using Hurst exponent as a fractal image quantifier and in turn as a feature vector for classifying genome sequences based on their chaos game representation images.

2 Materials and Methods

2.1 Dataset

A novel feature vector is derived by computing the Hurst exponent from the CGR format of a whole genomic sequence or a fragment. This is then used in identifying its origin. Mitochondrial genomes are considered here. They are the sites of aerobic respiration, and are the major energy production center in eukaryotes. The low mutation rate in metazoan mitochondrial genome sequence makes these genomes useful for scientists assessing genetic relationships of individuals or groups within a species and for the study of evolutionary relationships [14]. Mitochondrial genomes were downloaded from the NCBI Organelle database [14]. Table 1 shows the data used for classification. The number of organisms shown is as listed in NCBI on 01/01/2011.

Table 1. Dataset used for classification

Serial number	Name of category	Number of organisms
1	Acoelomata	33
2	Cnidaria	35
3	Fungi	76
4	Plant	42
5	Porifera	27
6	Protostomia	437
7	Pseudocoelomata	47
8	Vertebrata	1406
	Total	2103

2.2 Methodology

In this paper, a novel feature vector is extracted from fragments of genome sequences which are mapped into their CGR formats. The feature vector comprises of the Hurst exponent of sub-quadrants of CGR which is subsequently classified using SVM classifier. Training as well as test sequences limited to 20000 bases are first mapped into the corresponding Hurst exponent matrices. For this the CGR was divided into grids of 2^nx2^n cells where n is an integer and the Hurst exponent of each of these sub-regions were calculated using rescaled range method [17] with the x and y coordinates of the points in each of the cells. Hurst exponent was also calculated using the dispersional analysis method [15] adopted from [16] for comparison.

Rescaled range analysis (R/S analysis) [17]. A time series of full length N is divided into a number of shorter time series of length n. The average rescaled range is then calculated for each value of n. For a (partial) time series of length n, the rescaled range is calculated as follows:

1. Calculate the mean; $m = \frac{1}{n} \sum_{i=1}^{n} X_i$

2. Create a mean-adjusted series;

$$Y_t = X_t - m \text{ for t = 1, 2, 3...n.}$$

3. Calculate the cumulative deviate series Z;

$$Z_t = \sum_{i=1}^{t} Y_i \quad \text{for t =1, 2, ...n.}$$

4. Create a range series R;

$$R_t = \max\left(Z_1, Z_2, \ldots Z_t\right) - \min\left(Z_1, Z_2, \ldots Z_t\right) \quad \text{for t =1, 2, ...n.}$$

5. Create a standard deviation series S;

$$S_t = \sqrt{\left(\frac{1}{t}\sum_{i=1}^{t}\left(X_i - u_t\right)^2\right)} \quad \text{for t =1, 2, ...n.}$$

where u_t is the mean for the time series values.

6. Calculate the rescaled range series (R/S)

$$\left(R/S\right)_t = \frac{R_t}{S_t} \quad \text{for t =1, 2, ...n.}$$

$(R/S)_t$ is averaged over the regions $[X_1, X_t]$, $[X_{t+1}, X_{2t}]$ until $[X_{(m-1)t+1}, X_{mt}]$ where m=floor(n/t). In practice, to use all data for calculation, a value of t is chosen that is divisible by n. Hurst found that (R/S) scales by power-law as time increases, which indicates $(R/S)_t = c * t^H$. Here c is a constant and H is called the Hurst exponent. To estimate the Hurst exponent, plot (R/S) versus n in log-log axes. The slope of the regression line approximates the Hurst exponent.

Dispersional analysis [15]. Consider the set of n observations in a time series, X_1, $X_2, \ldots X_N$.

1. Calculate the standard deviation of the series.

$$SD(m) = \frac{1}{n}\sqrt{\left(n\sum X_i^2 - \left(\sum X_i\right)^2\right)} \quad \text{where m is the group size.}$$

For this first calculation, consider the data set of N points to be composed of n groups of points where in this case each group consists of one datum.

2. Next, aggregate adjacent samples into groups, each consisting of two adjacent data points, and define a group size m = 2. Calculate the mean for each pair, and calculate the SD of the means of the groups.

3. Repeat Step 2 with increasing group sizes of 4, 8, 16, 32, etc., until the number of groups, n, ≤ 4 (this is an arbitrary stopping point based on the idea that the SD would not be accurate if $n < 4$). For each grouping, m x n = N.

4. Plot log SD(m) versus log m, where m is the group size. For each m there are N/m = n values used in calculating the SD.

5. Determine the slope and intercept for the logarithmic relationship.

6. Calculate the fractal D from the power law slope: the estimate of D = 1 - slope, Equivalently, the estimate of H = slope + 1.

Support Vector Machine classifier. Support Vector Machine was introduced to solve dichotomic classification problems [18] & [19]. Given a training set in a vector space, SVMs find the best decision hyper plane that separates two classes. The quality of a decision hyper plane is determined by the distance between two hyper planes defined by support vectors. The best decision hyper plane is the one that maximizes this margin. SVM extends its applicability on the linearly non-separable data sets by either using soft margin hyper planes or by mapping the original data vectors into a higher dimensional space in which the data points are linearly separable. There are several typical kernel functions. In this work, Support Vector Machine with Radial Basis kernel function is used.

3 Results and Discussions

Using the methods outlined in the above section, feature vectors were computed as Hurst matrices, by dividing the CGR into 4 cells, 16 cells and 64 cells. These were then applied to an SVM classifier with Radial Basis Kernel. Out of the total number of sequences falling under the Eukaryotic category, all subcategories with sufficient number of organisms listed in NCBI are chosen for the experiment. Roughly 50% of the total number is taken for training and remaining for testing. A set of Hurst matrices obtained by dividing the CGRs into 16 cells for a sample from each category is shown in Fig. 2.

.90 .92 .94 .85	.57 .66 .60 .55	.76 .79 .79 .72	.88 .95 .96 .87
.56 .55 .54 .50	.59 .52 .61 .59	.75 .76 .70 .70	.54 .64 .62 .63
.52 .50 .55 .58	.52 .59 .65 .57	.61 .70 .67 .71	.69 .63 .66 .71
.55 .59 .58 .54	.58 .50 .61 .59	.80 .84 .74 .80	.67 .67 .63 .63
Acoelomata	Cnidaria	Fungi	Plant

.74 .81 .82 .73	.85 .92 .92 .83	.84 .61 .62 .76	.91 .94 .95 .89
.62 .64 .64 .74	.74 .56 .58 .65	.85 .87 .83 .84	.64 .59 .63 .59
.76 .66 .75 .76	.61 .63 .64 .72	.84 .81 .87 .81	.63 .67 .64 .63
.65 .64 .63 .68	.67 .58 .65 .66	.91 .86 .88 .93	.52 .65 .53 .69
Porifera	Protostomia	Pseudocoelomata	Vertebrata

Fig. 2. Sample Hurst matrices using x co-ordinates of points in CGR

The accuracy of classification is computed as follows: Sensitivity = TP/(TP + FN), Specificity = TN/(TN + FP), Accuracy = (TP + TN)/(TP + TN + FP + FN), where TP = True Positive, FP = False Positive, TN = True Negative and FN = False Negative. Since this is a multi class classification, true positive is taken as the queried category identified as itself, false negative denotes the queried category recognized as any one from the other 7 categories, true negative denotes all other 7 categories recognized not as the queried category and false positive denotes any member belonging to the other 7 categories being recognized as the queried category. The results are shown in Fig. 3 and Fig. 4 (Hurst matrices computed by dividing CGR into 64 cells is not shown since the accuracy declined due to lack of sufficient number of points in each cell). In Fig. 3 and Fig. 4, Method I & II denote methods using rescale range, dividing the CGR into 2x2 and 4x4 matrices, Method III & IV denote methods using dispersional analysis, dividing the CGR into 2x2 and 4x4 matrices respectively. AC in Fig. 3 denotes Acoelomata, CN – Cnidaria, FN- Fungi, PT- Plant, PO- Porifera, PR- Protostomia, PS – Pseudocoelomata, and VB – Vertebrata.

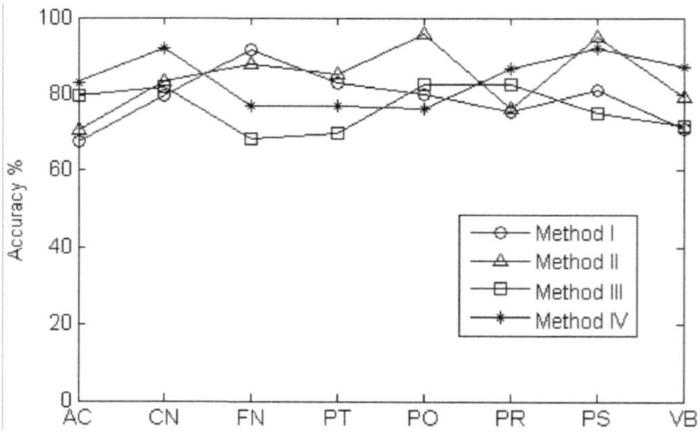

Fig. 3. Accuracy of classification of 8 categories of eukaryotic genomes taking the Hurst matrix as the feature vector for classification

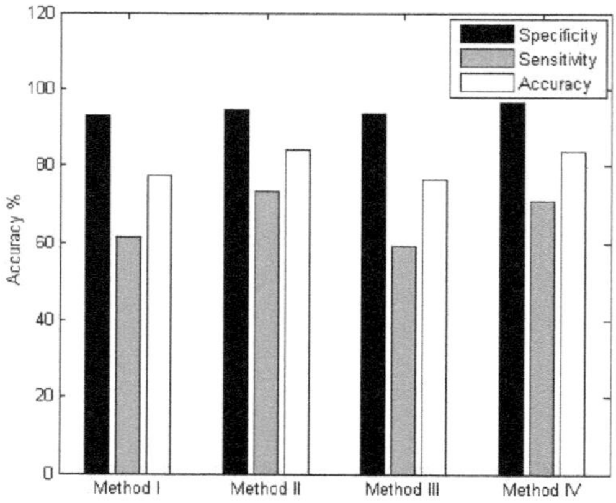

Fig. 4. Average Specificity, Sensitivity and Accuracy for the various methods

4 Conclusion

A novel combination of chaos game representation and Hurst exponent was used to extract features from genome sequences. The investigation is focused on whether Hurst exponent of CGR images provide features of discriminative nature. Classification of 8 categories of mitochondrial Eukaryotic genomes was attempted using the new feature vector. An average accuracy of 84% was obtained thus attesting to the suitability of this new signature matrix from CGR. It could also thus be concluded that Hurst CGR contain major phylogenetic information.

References

1. Sandberg, R., Winberg, G., Branden, C.I., Kaske, A., Ernberg, I., Coster, J.: Capturing Whole – Genome characteristics in short sequences using a naive Bayesian classifier. Genome Res. 11, 1404–1409 (2001)
2. Narasimhan, S., Sen, S., Konar, A.: Species identification based on mitochondrial genomes. In: Proceedings of the International Conference of Cognition and Recognition, Mysore, India, December 22-23 (2005)
3. Deschavanne, P.J., Giron, A., Vilain, J., Fagot, G., Fertil, B.: Genomic signature: characterization and classification of species assessed by chaos game representation of sequences. Mol. Biol. Evol. 16, 1391–1399 (1999)
4. Almeida, J.S., Carrico, J.A., Maretzek, A., Noble, P.A., Fletcher, M.: Analysis of genomic sequences by chaos game representation. Bioinformatics 17, 429–437 (2001)
5. Nair, V.V., Nair, A.S.: Combined classifier for unknown genome classification using chaos game representation features. In: Proceedings of the International Symposium of Bio Computing, NITC Calicut, India, February 15-17 (2009)
6. Peitgen, H.O., Jurgens, H., Saupe, D.: Chaos and Fractals New Frontiers of Science, 2nd edn. Springer, Heidelberg (2004)
7. Nair, A.S., Nair, V.V., Arun, K.S., Kant, K., Dey, A.: Bio-sequence Signatures Using Chaos Game Representation. In: Fulekar, M.H. (ed.) Bioinformatics: Applications in Life and Environmental Sciences, pp. 62–76. Springer, New York (2009)
8. Hassan, S., Choudhury, P. P., Daya Sagar, B. S., Chakraborty, S., Guha, R., Goswam, A.: Understanding Genomic Evolution of Olfactory Receptors through Fractal and Mathematical Morphology. In: Nature Proceedings: hdl:10101/npre.2011.5674.1 (February 14, 2011)
9. Noble, W.S.: Support vector machine applications in computational biology. In: Kernel Methods in Computational Biology, pp. 71–92. MIT Press, Cambridge (2004)
10. Jeffrey, H.J.: Chaos game representation of gene structure. Nucleic Acids Res. 18, 2163–2170 (1990)
11. Joseph, J., Sasikumar, R.: Chaos game representation for comparison of whole genomes. BMC Bioinformatics 7, 243 (2006)
12. Mandelbrot, B.: The fractal geometry of nature. W. H. Freeman, New York (1982)
13. http://www.bearcave.com/misl/misl_tech/wavelets/hurst/
14. http://www.ncbi.nlm.nih.gov/Genomes/ORGANELLES/ organelles.html
15. Bassingthwaighte, J.B., Raymond, G.M.: Evaluation of the dispersional analysis method for fractal time series. Annals Biomed. Engg. 23, 491–505 (1995)
16. http://www.mathworks.com/matlabcentral/fileexchange/9842
17. Qian, B., Rasheed, K.: Hurst exponent and financial market predictability. In: IASTED conference on Financial Engineering and Applications, pp. 203–209 (2004)
18. Cristianini, N., Taylor, J.S.: Support vector machines and other kernel-based learning methods. Cambridge University Press, Cambridge (2000)
19. Vapnik, V.N.: The Nature of Statistical Learning Theory. Springer, Berlin (1995)

Hub Characterization of Tumor Protein P53 Using Artificial Neural Networks

J. Sajeev and T. Mahalakshmi

Abstract. This paper presents a supervised Back Propagation Neural network (BPN) for the hub characterization of the tumor protein P53. This paper proposes a method to predict the P53 protein as Hub or Non-Hub from the sequence information of protein alone. The hubness characterization of this protein has been carried out using Hydrophobicity, one of the important physio-chemical properties of the amino acid. The proposed method has been tested on the P53 and its interacting proteins successfully. The same method on the whole set of Human proteins from the database HPRD and APID has shown around 90% of accuracy, sensitivity and specificity with the help of Artificial Neural Network (ANN).

Keywords: P53, Pathway, Hub protein, ANN, Hydrophobic, PIN, Degree of Connectivity.

1 Introduction

P53 (also known as tumor protein 53) is a protein in humans encoded by the TP53 gene which is a tumor suppressor gene[1], i.e., its activity stops the formation of tumors. Over the years P53 has been shown to interact with more than hundred proteins, which is evident from the pathway information [2]. This shows the importance of P53 as a Hub protein [3].

Among the different types of proteins, Hub proteins are that class of proteins having high degree of connectivity in its interaction network. They participate in significant number of protein interactions and play a very important role in the organization of cellular protein interaction pathways [3, 4, 5].

Most of the biological pathways and processes [6] are believed to be directed by complex protein interactions and are controlled by Hubs. If these proteins are disrupted it can lead to biological lethality [4]. So understanding the characteristic of Hub proteins may in turn increase the significance in understanding the causes of diseases.

Studies in this area have revealed existence of a few methods [5, 7, 3, 8, 9] with various percentages of accuracy measures ranging from 34% to 84% and majority of the approaches used in these methods are of statistical in nature. Application of Artificial Neural Networks (ANN) is an untouched one in this area.

The proposed method uses ANN to characterize the hubness of P53 protein. ANN have proved useful in solving various biological problems like microRNA target prediction [10], Coding region recognition and gene identification [11], Protein

A. Abraham et al. (Eds.): ACC 2011, Part I, CCIS 190, pp. 310–319, 2011.

structure prediction [12] etc. Amino acids which make protein have various physical and chemical properties. In one of the previous work in this area has made use of more than 1300 of such properties [3]. In the proposed method only the hydrophobicity property of the amino acid is used since it has already proved its role in the structure prediction and interaction of proteins [13] and is seen to have good output.

Three types of data sets are used in this paper for testing the proposed method. One is from the Human Protein Reference Database (HPRD)[14]. The whole set of human proteins were selected from this database to test the proposed method. The second data set is obtained from Agile Protein Interaction Database (APID) [15]. The third set of data is obtained from the P53 interaction data [2, 16] and the sequence information is obtained from the NCBI Database [17].

The proposed method on these three data sets has shown very promising output with 89% sensitivity, 91% specificity and 90% accuracy. This method will certainly prove to be useful in characterizing Hub proteins using sequence information.

2 Background

This session describes breifly the biological background pertinent to this paper and some of the tools used in the proposed method.

2.1 Hub Protein

Protein interactions are generally respresented in the form of a network known as Protein Interaction Network (PIN). These are visualized in the form of graphs with nodes representing proteins and edges representing interactions between them. One of the attributes associated with each protein in PIN is the connectivity measure. This is the count of number of interactions that a protein has with other members (proteins) of the network.

PIN belongs to the category of Scale Free Networks which has the property that only a few proteins have high connectiviy measure [6, 18]. This is because the connectivity measure in a Scale Free Network follows a power law distribution [7]. There is an ongoing debate on the threshold value of connectivity measure which is mainly used to classify a protein as Hub or non-Hub[3]. Different methods in this area proposes the threshold of connectivity based on various techniques. In the proposed method the statistical property of the connectivity measure is used to find the threshold value and is used to chacterize Hub proteins.

2.2 Artificial Nerual Network (ANN)

An ANN is a type of mathematical tool that employs non-linear mathematics and are used to model highly complex and non-linear systems. The design of an ANN is similar to the design and techniques of human brain. A three layer neural network is shown in the figure 1 which has three inputs i1, i2, i3 and one output y0.

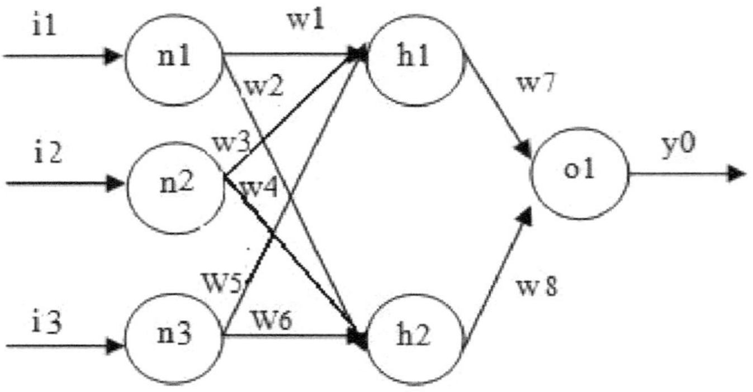

Fig. 1. Three layer neural network for protein sequence

There are three neurons, n1, n2 and n3, in the input layer. h1 and h2 are the two neurons in the hidden layer and o1 is the neuron in the output layer. The output is y0 which determines the class to which the data belongs to. w1, w2, w3, w4, w5 and w6 are the weights of the arms from the neuron in the input layer to the neuron in the hidden layer. w7 and w8 are the weights of the arms from the neurons in the hidden layer to the neurons in the output layer.

Training of the network consists of the iterative refinement of the associated 'weights' such that the specified error condition is minimized. The training patterns, which are composed of a group of matching input and output vectors, are used by the learning algorithm to train the network. It measures the difference between the desired output vectors and the resulting error back propagates to alter the connecting weights in the direction of reducing error [20].

This process runs several times until the error is within the desired level. Once this process is over the network holds the weights constantly and becomes a valid model for prediction. Here each neuron performs a very simple calculation. It performs a weighted sum of its inputs and then an activation function is applied to this value. The method uses sigmoid functions as activation functions for the hidden and output layers. A linear activation function is used for input layer.

In this paper a fully connected feed forward multilayer configuration using back propagation learning algorithm described has been employed to characterize Hub proteins.

2.3 Hydrophobicity

Relative hydrophobicity can be measured using the hydrophobicity index. It shows how soluble an amino acid is in water. In a protein, hydrophobic amino acids are likely to be found in the interior part. Hydrophobicity is a measure of affinity to aqueous environment. Researchers suggest that stability of co-existence of amino acids with similar hydrophobicity is better than those with dissimilar hydrophobicity.

The proposed method makes use of the hydrophobic measure [21] given in table 1 which are normalized so that the most hydrophobic residue is given a value of 100.

Table 1. Font sizes of headings. Table captions should always be positioned above the tables

Amino Acid	Hydrophobic Measure	Amino Acid	Hydrophobic Measure
A	13.134	M	1.940
C	10.597	N	53.134
D	80.597	P	24.328
E	74.328	Q	48.805
F	0	R	100
G	16.865	S	19.402
H	41.940	T	15.671
I	3.731	V	6.865
K	78.059	W	11.343
L	5.671	Y	27.462

3 Existing Methods

The existing methods in the area of PIN are generally classified as experimental and computational. The experimental (large-scale proteomic experiment) techniques, do not give much information about the interacting residues [6], though they have vast coverage and sensitivity. Computational analysis of PIN is based on various attributes like gene proximity, gene fusion events, phylogenic profiling, identification of interacting protein domains and text mining techniques [8]. Each of these approaches has its own strengths and weaknesses especially with regard to sensitivity and specificity. Some of the existing methods are given below.

3.1 Method 1

A method for the prediction of Hubs in Scale-free networks is seen in [3] which is based on List Dominating Set problem (LDS). This method gives due importance to identifying communities which are sub networks known as 'Quasi Cliques' of a given PIN with 'small' number of edges missing in contrast to cliques that are completely connected. If the network is very dense then the system will typically not give a solution in most of the cases. The characterization of community is identified through this method.

3.2 Method 2

A method has been developed based on one of the findings in [22] that Hub proteins with common interaction partners tend to interact with them through a common interacting motifs[9]. The input of this method is the binary protein interactions; neither sequence nor structure information is required here. By building an interaction network and applying clustering technique this method identifies interacting motifs. These interacting motifs are assigned to Hub proteins and then analyzed [9]. The number of interacting partners, connectivity, has been chosen as 20. The study also revealed that as connectivity decreases sensitivity of the method decreases.

3.3 Hub Classifier

Hub classifier method uses Gene Ontology terms with 84.96% accuracy, 34.41% sensitivity and 90.27% specificity [3]. Gene ontology annotation of the target protein is needed to predict whether a target protein is Hub or not. Michel Hsing et al [3] have stated that the performance of Hub classifier will primarily rely on the number of Gene Ontology annotations available for each species and according to them, the reason for the low sensitivity is "the lack of gene ontology annotations for certain proteins in the training sets" [3].

3.4 Other Methods

A notable approach used for the prediction of interaction between proteins is by using the amino acid sequence itself [23, 24, 25]. All these computational prediction techniques have focused on the identification of pair wise protein-protein interactions with varying degrees of accuracy [3, 26].

Here the proposed method states that, if it is possible to predict the interaction between proteins from the amino acid sequence alone, then there is a good chance of characterizing Hub proteins from sequence information.

4 Data Set

In this paper three sets of data have been used to test the proposed method. The first set is taken from HPRD [14]. From this database whole set of human protein ID's were obtained. In this database there were 27080 human proteins. Among them 9630 have interactions with others. From the binary interactions obtained from the database it was possible to find the count of number of interactions of each protein and it ranged from 0 to 267. The number of proteins having the degree of connectivity k is given in table 2.

Table 2. Degree of connectivity Vs Protein frequency in HPRD Database

Degree of Connectivity (k)	Number of proteins
1	2237
2	1424
3	1009
4	759
5	618
6	468
7	422
8	287
>> 8	2406
Total	27080

Mean of the degree of connectivity was calculated from this and was obtained as 8.0557. It is again evident from the table 2 that frequency count of the proteins with $k < 9$ is 7224. That is there are 2406 proteins with $k > 8$ which is around 25% of the total interacting proteins. In the proposed method the threshold for connectivity of hub proteins for this database is taken as 8 based on the above analysis.

The second set is taken from APID database. In this database there were 12057 human proteins having connectivity in the range of 1 to 414. But it was possible to get amino acid sequences for only 11813 proteins. Search of the remaining 244 did not yield any data. Table 3 gives the number of proteins having the degree of connectivity k.

Table 3. Degree of connectivity Vs Protein frequency in APID Database

Degree of Connectivity (k)	**Number of proteins**
1	2782
2	1668
3	1101
4	840
5	687
6	546
7	437
8	351
9	320
10	262
>>10	2819
Total	11813

From the table 3 it can be seen that as the value of k increases the frequency of the protein decreases same as in the previous case. Using this information as a frequency table, its mean was calculated and it was obtained as 9.84. The frequency count of the proteins with $k < 11$ is 8994. That is there are 2819 proteins with $k > 10$ which is around 25% of the total interacting proteins. In the proposed method the threshold for connectivity of Hub proteins is taken as 10 based on the above analysis for this data base.

The third set is taken from the interacting protein set of P53 protein[16]. In this database there were 99 proteins which have shown interaction with P53. The sequence information is obtained from the NCBI Database [17].

To test the system performance the positive data used are proteins which are known to have interactions with many other proteins, that is proteins with high degree of connectivity. The system is also trained using negative data which are proteins that are known to have low interactions with other proteins, that is proteins with low degree of connectivity. In the present situation positive data are Hub proteins and negative data are Non-Hub proteins. Based on the threshold value of connectivity, proteins from each database are categorized as Hub or Non-Hub which are positive and negative data respectively.

5 Proposed Method

In the proposed method three types of characteristics are obtained from each protein in the train set. These three attributes are used to train the ANN. This is the first stage of the ANN. In the second stage the trained network is used to test the validity of the system.

Hydrophobicity measure is used to derive out the three characteristics used to train the network such as HS (Hydrophobic Sum), Hydrophobic Count (HC) and Arginine Count (AC). The entire set of data belonging to HPRD and APID databases are divided into train set and test set for this purpose. Both positive and negative data are distributed equally across train and test set. For HPRD dataset proteins having degree of connectivity greater than 8 is selected as positive data. For APID database it is set as 10. So it makes four sets of data such as Hub train, Non Hub train, Hub test and Non Hub test.

After the data is split, using Hydrophobic measure the protein sequences are digitized to find the hidden attributes such as HS, HC and AC.

Sequence information is retrieved from the set of both Hub and Non Hub proteins one by one and available dense areas are fished out. A dense area in a protein sequence is the substring s whose sum of hydrophobic value is greater than the average of the hydrophobic value of all amino acids [13], which is calculated as 31.7 and set as the threshold. Here the window size, the length of the substring is set as 25.

The algorithm searches for the dense area right from the first character onwards. If the dense is found in the substring (i, i+25) then the search for the dense area is continued from i+26 onwards. Otherwise the search restarts from the i+1 position. HS of a sequence is the sum of the hydrophobic values of amino acids in each dense area in the sequence and HC is the number of dense area contained in a sequence. AC is the count of the highly hydrophobic amino acid residue Arginine in the protein sequence. As an example if a protein sequence has dense areas d1,d2,...,d10 with the sum of hydrophobic values as h1,h2,....,h10 in each dense area then HS, HC and AC can be derived out as

HS=h1+h2+. . . . +h10
HC=10
AC= Arginine Count

These are the three attributes associated with each protein. Thus each protein sequence can be associated with three numerical sequences. Using ANN tool these three numerical sequences are analyzed to find any hidden attributes in it.

The same process is repeated with all the members of the train data set which contains 3612 Non Hub and 1203 Hub proteins.

In order to train the Neural Network it is essential to feed both the input and output data. The input data are the three important characteristic set derived from the train data. For Hub set the output is set to 3 and for Non Hub the output is set as 0. This value was used after doing experiments with some trial values and was found that 0 and 3 yielded best result. Once the network training is over, the test characteristic data is fed. The same network is also tested with the P53 interaction data. The target protein is Hub if the following condition is satisfied:

$O>=1.8$ and $O<=3$, where O is the obtained output of Neural Network after the simulation with the test data. Here also the range is assigned after doing experiments with some trial values. By subjecting the test data to the designed neural network the accuracy, sensitivity and specificity obtained for both the data sets is given in the table 4.

Table 4. Results of proposed method on the data sets

Data Set	Accuracy	Sensitivity	Specificity
HPRD	90%	89%	91%
APID	91%	90%	92%
P53 Interaction Data	92%	91%	92%

6 Results and Discussions

In the proposed method the prediction system is made to learn with each Hub and Non-Hub protein from the training sets. The learning system keeps the knowledge of the HS, HC and AC values calculated to find the characteristics of the training data.

Since the average area of contact between two interacting proteins is around 2000 A^{-2} with each partner contributing 1000 A^{-2} where around 25 amino acids from each partner takes part in the interaction the length of the dense area used in the proposed method is 25.The hydrophobic force of the amino acids plays a major role in the dense area.

In the proposed method the hydrophobic measure of amino acids in the dense area is used to predict if a target protein is Hub or not. The dense area is a region of protein sequence in which a subsequence might be interacting with other subsequences or is more interactive in nature. This is possible because of the tertiary structure of the protein. A tertiary structure has interaction between alpha helixes and beta sheets whose respective structures are folded and curved [13]. This increases the chances of interaction in a protein among others as it provides more dense area for interaction.

The proposed method solely relies on the sequence information of the proteins whereas the method based on interacting motifs to analyze hub is solely relying on experimentally detected interactions which affects the accuracy of the method [9].

When the proposed method applied on the P53 interaction data it has shown very promising results. So the proposed method is able to characterize Hub protein better than other methods.

7 Conclusion

Protein interactions are ubiquitous and essential for cellular functions. The compendium of all the physical protein-protein interactions for a given cell or organism is complex bio-molecular network mapped as PIN. Predicting the Hub proteins of this network is a challenging computational problem.

The proposed method is a two stage process which uses hydrophobic measure of amino acids to obtain the Hubness characteristic of a protein. The application of this method on the tumor protein P53 has revealed a high accuracy, sensitivity and specificity.

As a continuation of this work, the application of this method may be applied on proteins to bring out its biological significance as that of the tumor proteins.

The proposed method may be applied with other organisms, but for this it is necessary to obtain the threshold value of the connectivity of PIN of these organisms.

References

[1] Vazquez, A., Bond, E.E., Levine, A.J., Bond, G.L.: The genetics of the p53 pathway, apoptosis and cancer therapy. Nature Reviews Drug Discovery 7(12), 979–987 (2008)
[2] Prives, C., Hall, P.A.: The p53 pathway. The Journal of Pathology. Special Issue: Molecular and Cellular Themes in Cancer Research 187(1), 112–126 (1999)
[3] Hsing, M., Byler, K.G., Cherkasov, A.: The use of Gene Ontology terms for predicting highly-connected 'hub' nodes in protein-protein interaction networks. BMC Systems Biology 2, 80 (2008)
[4] Barabasi, A.L., Oltvai, Z.N.: Network biology: understanding the cell's functional organization. Nat. Rev. Genet. 5(2), 101–113 (2004)
[5] Srihari, S., et al.: Detecting Hubs and Quasi Cliques in Scale-free Networks. IEEE, Los Alamitos (2008)
[6] Albert, R.: Scale-free networks in cell biology. J. Cell Sci. 118(Pt 21), 4947–4957 (2005)
[7] Bataba, N.N., Hurst, L.D., Tyers, M.: Evolutionary and Physiological Importance of Hub Proteins. PLOS Computational Biology 2(7), 748–756 (2006)
[8] Agarwal, S., et al.: Revisiting date and party hubs: Novel approaches to role assignment in protein interaction networks. PLOS Computational Biology 6(6) (June 2010)
[9] Aragues, R., et al.: Characterization of Protein Hubs by Inferring Interacting Motifs from Protein Interactions. PLOS Computational Biology 3(9) (September 2007)
[10] Vinod Chandra, S.S., Reshmi, G., Nair, A.S., S., S., Radhakrishna Pillai, M.: MTar: a computational microRNA target prediction architecture for human transcriptome. BMC Bioinformatics 11, S2, ISSN 1471-2105
[11] Ying, X., Mural, R.J., Einstein, J.R., Shah, M.B., Uberbacher, E.: GRAIL: a multi-agent neural network system for gene identification. Proceedings of the IEEE 84(10) (1996)
[12] Chae, M.H., Krull, F., Lorenzen, S., Knapp, E.: Predicting protein complex geometries with a neural network. Proteins 78(4), 1026–1039 (2010)
[13] Agrawal, R.K., et al.: A novel approach to predict protein-protein interaction using protein sequence data. Bioinformatics Trends 1(1) (2006)
[14] `http://www.hprd.org/` (release 9 dated May 24, 2010)
[15] Prieto, C., De Las Rivas, J.: APID: Agile Protein Interaction Data Analyzer. Nucl. Acids Res. 34, W228–W302 (2006)

[16] `http://en.wikipedia.org/wiki/P53` (dated 18/9/2011 at 9.00 a.m.)
[17] `http://www.ncbi.nlm.nih.gov/` (dated 18/9/2011 at 11.00 a.m.)
[18] Wutchy, S.: Scale-free behavior in protein domain networks. Mol. Bio. Evolution 18 (2001)
[19] Ashok, V.: Determination of blood glucose concentration by back propogation neural network
[20] Latha, A., Vijayakumar Reddy, K.: Performance Analysis on modeling of loop heat pipes using artificial neural network. Indian Journal of Science and Technology 3(4) (2010)
[21] `http://www.sigmaaldrich.com/life-science/metabolomics/learning-centre/amino-acid-reference-chart.html` (dated July 15, 2010)
[22] Kim, P.M., Lu, L.J., Xia, Y.: Gerstein MB Relating three-dimensional structures to protein networks provides evolutionary insights. Science 314, 1938–1941 (2006)
[23] Najafabadi, H.S., Salavati, R.: Sequence-based prediction of protein-protein interactions by means of codon usage. Genome Biology 9, R87 (2008)
[24] Bock, J.R., Gough, D.A.: Predicting protein-protein interaction from primary structure. Bioinformatics 17, 455–460 (2001)
[25] Shen, J., Zhang, J., Luo, X., Zhu, W., Yu, K., Chen, K., Li, Y., Jiang, H.: Predicting protein-protein interactions based only on sequence information. Proceedings of the National Academy of Sciences of the USA 104, 4337–4341 (2007)
[26] Qi, Y., Bar-Joseph, Z., Klein-Seetharaman, J.: Evaluation of different biological data and computational classification methods for use in protein interaction prediction. Proteins 63(3), 490–500 (2006)

Lacunarity Analysis of Protein Sequences Reveal Fractal Like Behavior of Amino Acid Distributions

G. Gopakumar and Achuthsankar S. Nair

Centre for Bioinformatics, North-Campus Kariyavattom,
University of Kerala, Thiruvananthapuram, 695581, Keralam, India
{gopu.kg,sankar.achuth}@gmail.com
http://www.cbi.keralauniversity.edu

Abstract. This paper reports the use of lacunarity analysis of protein sequences as a new method to analyze the distribution of amino acids in a protein sequence. One of the key results is that distribution of hydrophobic amino acids in a protein sequence exhibit fractal like behavior. It is found that lacunarity plots of distribution of hydrophobic amino acids follow similar patterns for a given protein sequence as well as for amino acid sequences that are extracted from the given protein sequence as prefixes with length reduced by half from the original sequence length. Another interesting result is that using the lacunarity values of chaos game representations of amino acid sequences, we can prove the non-random nature of protein sequences. Lacunarity values also help us to classify a set of true and random protein sequences. These two findings affirm lacunarity analysis as a novel and promising bio-sequence analysis method.

Keywords: Lacunarity analysis, Sequence analysis, Amino acid distribution, Chaos game representation, Fractal, Protein sequences.

1 Introduction

Amino acid composition and their distribution are two key elements in understanding the structure and function of various proteins in a living organism. In a latest study, simple amino acid composition alone is used in predicting protein-protein interactions [14]. The importance of amino acid composition in determining the tertiary structure of a protein is already proved [22]. Determination of protein secondary structure is another area where amino acid composition is successfully applied [20]. Amino acid composition is also a widely used parameter in many of the protein sub-cellular localization prediction approaches [23], [24]. Along with amino acid composition, the distribution of various amino acids or polypeptides in a protein sequence is proved to be useful in understanding protein structure and their interactions [25]. These studies clearly show the importance of amino acid composition and their distribution in better understanding the role of various proteins in our body.

A. Abraham et al. (Eds.): ACC 2011, Part I, CCIS 190, pp. 320–327, 2011.

Lacunarity is a concept introduced by Mandelbrot [1] as a measure to further classify fractals [1] that have same fractal dimensions and varying visual appearance or textures. It is a measure of the size distribution of holes in a fractal within a set of multiple scales. In the case of self similar fractals, lacunarity follows the scaling properties [6], [7]. Low lacunarity geometric objects are homogeneous because all gap sizes are the same, whereas high lacunarity objects are heterogeneous. Therefore, lacunarity can be considered as a scale dependent measure of heterogeneity [6], [11], [16]. Lacunarity analysis is generally applied on spatial pattern dispersion (habitat types or species locations) problem [6], [8], [9] and also to measure the textures associated with them [8]. One of the latest studies [12] prove that lacunarity analysis of dermoscopic images is a promising method for the automated assessment of skin diseases like Melanoma.

Lacunarity analysis of bio-sequences is not well explored as compared to the fractal analysis of bio-sequences which has produced many useful findings [2], [3], [4], [5], [10]. But as lacunarity analysis could able to produce useful findings [6], [8], [9] on the spatial distribution problems, there exists some scope in investigating the distribution of various amino acids and polypeptides in protein sequences. This motivated us to carry out the present investigations on lacunarity of protein sequences and the results obtained prove that it is a promising bio-sequence analysis method.

2 Methods

2.1 Lacunarity Measurement Using the Gliding Box Algorithm

A number of algorithms are proposed to measure the lacunarity [6] of fractal sets. Most of these methods are based on the distribution of holes in a given fractal or map. A general fruitful approach for reliably determining the lacunarity of a random or deterministic fractal consists of analyzing the fluctuations of the mass distribution function. One of the most commonly applied lacunarity measuring methods is the gliding box algorithm proposed by Allain and Cloitre [7] for fractal sets. Plotnick [6] extended this method to study the spatial datasets and came to the conclusion that this method can be applied to nonfractal set of data as well. In this work we also apply the same algorithm to measure the lacunarity of protein sequences and it is described below:

Consider an M x M binary map with a value of 1 at a position for the presence of an object and a 0 for the absence. Now an r x r box (r may vary from 1 to M) is placed over the upper left corner of the matrix. The number of occupied sites (a 1 is present) is taken as the box mass. The box is now moved one column to the right and the new box mass is calculated. This process is repeated over all columns and rows and from the values of these box masses a frequency distribution of the box masses can be generated.

The number of boxes of size r containing P occupied sites is taken as n (P, r) and the total number of boxes of size r by N (r). As the map size is M,

$$N(r) = (M - r + 1)^2. \quad (1)$$

This frequency distribution can be converted to a probability distribution Q (P, r) by dividing the total number of boxes:

$$Q(P,r) = n(P,r)/N(r). \tag{2}$$

Now the first and second moments of this frequency distribution are calculated as:

$$Z^{(1)} = \sum PQ(P,r). \tag{3}$$

$$Z^{(2)} = \sum P^2Q(P,r). \tag{4}$$

Lacunarity of the map for the box size r is defined as,

$$\lambda(r) = Z^{(2)}/(Z^{(1)})^2. \tag{5}$$

One approach that is commonly applied in lacunarity analysis is calculating the lacunarity for various box sizes, say r = 1 to size of map, and then plotting a graph between log ($\lambda(r)$) and log (r). For an exact fractal, the plot of log ($\lambda(r)$) vs. log (r) will be a straight line with similar appearances across scales [6], [7]. We have followed the above steps to carry out lacunarity analysis of protein sequences in the present work.

2.2 Lacunarity Analysis of the Distribution of Hydrophobic Amino Acids in a Protein Sequence

To carry out the lacunarity analysis of distribution of hydrophobic amino acids in a protein sequence, we have represented a protein sequence as a binary row matrix. The amino acids A, C, F, G, I, L, M, P, V, W and Y are taken as the hydrophobic and the remaining D, E, H, K, N, Q, R, S and T are taken as hydrophilic. We have created the binary row matrix corresponding to the protein sequence based on the presence or absence of a hydrophobic amino acid. A window of size equal to one is slid from the N terminus to C terminus of the given amino acid sequence, one position each time. A value of 1 is stored in the binary row matrix whenever a hydrophobic amino acid is present in the window. Otherwise a 0 is stored in the matrix.

Lacunarity analysis is then carried out using boxes of size 1 x r with r ranging from 1 to length of the protein sequence. In this experiment, for each protein sequence we have extracted two other sets (set1 and set2) of protein sequences which are prefixes of varying length of the given amino acid sequence. Sequences in the set1 are formed as described below. Let N be the length of given amino acid sequence and p_i be the length of ith prefix subsequence obtained from the given amino acid sequence. p_i is defined as:

$$p_i = \frac{N}{2^i}. \tag{6}$$

Using the above relation, set1 contains the given amino acid sequence and a fixed number of prefix subsequences extracted according to the above relation.

We have taken i=1 to 3 or 4 in the present study according to the length of the protein sequence. But set2 contains the given amino acid sequence and a fixed set of prefix subsequences whose length have no specific relation as in set1. We have extracted sequences of random length for this purpose.

2.3 Lacunarity Analysis of Chaos Game Representation of Protein Sequences

In the second experiment, we have considered the Chaos Game Representation (CGR)[15], [19] of protein sequences based on the detailed HP model [26]. According to the detailed HP model, the 20 amino acids are classified into 4 groups: non-polar (A, I, L, M, F, P, W, V), negative polar (D, E), uncharged polar (N, C, Q, G, S, T, Y) and positive polar (R, H, K). These four groups are assigned to the four corners of a unit square. To draw the CGR of a protein sequence, we start from the middle position of the unit square and a dot is put at the half way position between the current position and the corner corresponding to the first amino acid. This is repeated for each amino acid taken sequentially from the N-terminus of protein sequence. Corresponding to this final unit square, an equivalent binary matrix can be formed in such a way that a value of 1 represents the presence of a dot and a value of 0 representing its absence. We have taken 64 x 64 matrices for plotting the CGR images in the current study and the r x r box sizes for the lacunarity analysis are varied from 1 to 64, in multiples of 2.

2.4 Dataset

We have downloaded protein sequences of various organisms for the present study from Uniprot [18] and Genbank [17] databases. Length of protein sequences vary from 195 to 3135 amino acids.

3 Results

One of the major findings of this work is that lacunarity analysis of the distribution of hydrophobic amino acids can reveal self-similarity property of amino acid distributions in protein sequences. For each protein sequence we have plotted the lacunarity plots of each sequence in the two sets of sequences that are extracted as described in section 2.2 on page 323. For all protein sequences taken in this study, it is found that the lacunarity plots of individual sequences in the first set showed similar appearances. But in the second set of sequences this characteristic was not observed. This shows that the distribution of hydrophobic amino acids follow the same pattern along the whole length of a protein sequence and also along prefix subsequences that satisfies the relation mentioned in section 2.2 on page 322. In another way, we can say their distribution follow self-similarity property on multiple scales. Fig.1, Fig.2, Fig.3 and Fig.4 show sample lacunarity plots obtained for one Human and one Yeast protein sequences.

Investigations on the lacunarity analysis of CGR matrices of amino acid sequences show that the proposed method is a promising biosequence analysis tool

Table 1. Lacunarity values of the CGR matrices of protein sequences

Sequence ID/Type	**Sequence length**	**Lacunarity (r=1)**	**Slope of lacunarity plot**
FBgn0040371	195	1.045965	-0.008405
Random	195	1.043301	-0.008031
P04637	393	1.088204	-0.015864
Random	393	1.084746	-0.015441
P32569	687	1.163967	-0.028758
Random	687	1.148626	-0.027037
P06400	928	1.199414	-0.035315
Random	928	1.18897	-0.033444
Q17878	1424	1.295383	-0.051143
Random	1424	1.282003	-0.04939
P38398	1864	1.409498	-0.068757
Random	1864	1.352708	-0.061344
F64669	2890	1.601877	-0.096452
Random	2890	1.493256	-0.080903
P68874	3135	1.715961	-0.108696
Random	3135	1.566348	-0.091109

like that of fractal analysis. One useful finding based on the lacunarity analysis of CGR matrices of protein sequences can be used to distinguish true and random protein sequences. For the present study, we have taken eight amino acid sequences of varying length from different organisms and also eight random amino acid sequences. The random amino acid sequences were generated using the RandSeq tool from the ExPASy proteomics server [21]. Table 1 lists the details like: sequence ID/type, sequence length, lacunarity value for box size r=1 and slope of the lacunarity plot for the 16 amino acid sequences considered. From the table we can see that lacunarity values of true amino acid sequences

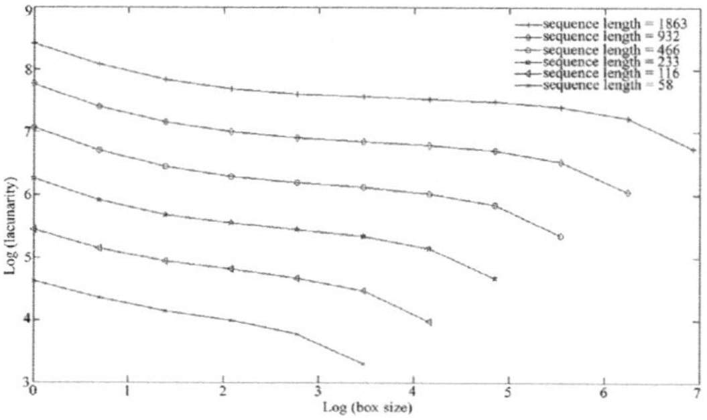

Fig. 1. Lacunarity plots of Human Breast cancer type 1 susceptibility protein and its prefix subsequences satisfying the relation mentioned in section 2.2 on page 322

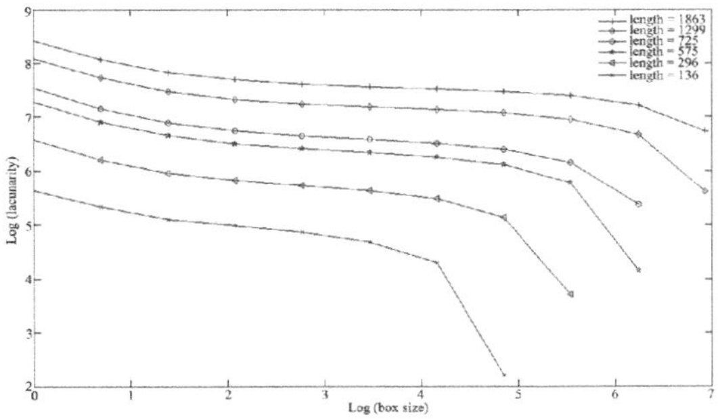

Fig. 2. Lacunarity plots of Human Breast cancer type 1 susceptibility protein and its prefix subsequences of randomly selected lengths

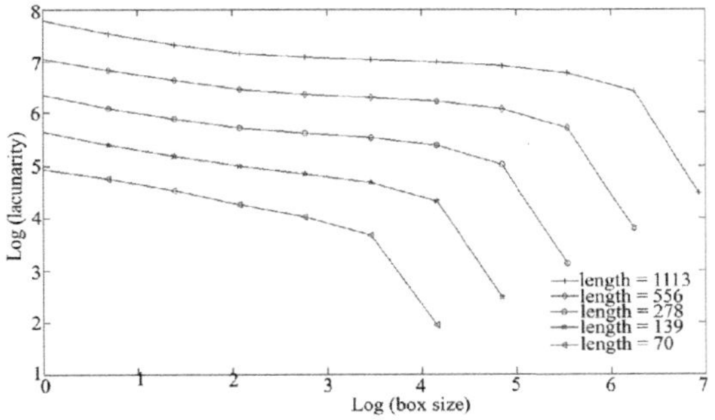

Fig. 3. Lacunarity plots of Yeast Nucleoporin NUP116/NSP116 and its prefix subsequences satisfying the relation mentioned in section 2.2 on page 322

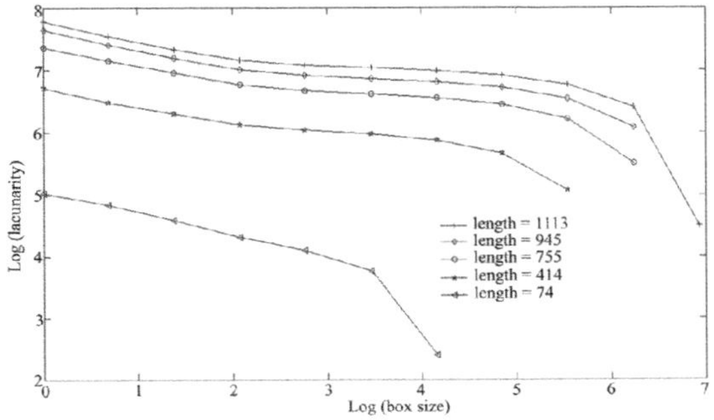

Fig. 4. Lacunarity plots of Yeast Nucleoporin NUP116/NSP116 and its prefix subsequences of randomly selected lengths

are always greater than that of random amino acid sequences of same length. This was observed for all box sizes. Also the slope of lacunarity plots in each case shows this property.

4 Conclusions

In this paper we have demonstrated the use of lacunarity analysis of amino acid sequences as a promising sequence analysis method. The method proved to be powerful in extracting the self-similarity property exhibited by the distribution of hydrophobic amino acids in a protein sequence and its prefixed subsequences. Fractal nature of an entire amino acid sequence is already reported in the literature [26]. But we are reporting for first time the fractal behavior of distribution of a subset of amino acids. This finding may have impact on other related experiments with amino acid sequences. The method could also may be used to demonstrate the non-random nature of protein sequences and the result can be used to classify true and random amino acid sequences in a sequence analysis experiment. This needs to be validated with larger number of sequences and we are planning to publish it in another work. We hope that the proposed lacunarity analysis of amino acid sequences may be used as a fruitful sequence analysis technique in the area of bioinformatics.

References

1. Mandelbrot, B.: The Fractal Geometry of Nature. Freeman, New York (1983)
2. Li-Qian, Z., Zu-Guo, Y., Ji-Qing, D., Vo, A., Sgun-Chao, L.: A Fractal Method to Distinguish Coding and Non-coding Sequences in a Complete Genome Based on a Number Sequence Representation. J. Theor. Biol. 232, 559–567 (2005)
3. Peng, C.K., Buldyrev, S.V., Goldberger, A.L., Havlin, S., Sciortino, F., Simons, M., Stanley, H.E.: Long-Range Correlations in Nucleotide Sequences. Nature 356, 168–170 (1992)
4. Garte, S.: Fractal Properties of Human Genome. J. Theor. Biol. 230, 251–260 (2004)
5. Zn-Guo, Y., Anh, V., Zhi-Min, G., Shun-Chao, L.: Fractals in DNA Sequence Analysis. Chinese Phys. 11, 1313 (2002)
6. Plotnick, R.E., Gardner, R.H., Hargrove, W.W., Prestegaard, K., Perlmutter, M.: Lacunarity Analysis: A General Technique for the Analysis of Spatial Patterns. Phys. Rev. E. 53, 5461–5468 (1996)
7. Allain, C., Cloitre, M.: Characterizing the Lacunarity of Random and Deterministic Fractal Sets. Phys. Rev. A. 44, 3552–3558 (1991)
8. Plotnick, R.E., Gardner, R.H., O'Neill, R.V.: Lacunarity Indices as Measures of Landscape Texture. Landscape Eco. 8, 201–211 (1993)
9. McIntyre, N.E., Wiens, J.A.: A Novel Use of the Lacunarity Index to Discern Landscape Function. Landscape Eco. 15, 313–321 (2000)
10. Gopakumar, G., Achuthsankar, N.S.: Fractality of Numeric and Symbolic Sequences. IEEE Potentials 29, 36–39 (2010)
11. Roya, A., Perfecta, E., Dunnea, W.M., Odlingb, N., Kim, J.: Lacunarity Analysis of Fracture Networks: Evidence for Scale-Dependent Clustering. J. Struct. Geol. 32, 1444–1449 (2010)
12. Gilmore, S., Hofmann-Wellenhof, R., Muir, J., Soyer, H.P.: Lacunarity Analysis: A Promising Method for the Automated Assessment of Melanocytic Naevi and Melanoma. PLoS One 4, e7449 (2009)

13. Katti, M.V., Sami-Subbu, R., Ranjekar, P.K., Gupta, V.S.: Amino Acid Repeat Patterns in Protein Sequences: Their Diversity and Structural-Functional Implications. Prot. Science. 9, 1203–1209 (2000)
14. Roy, S., Martinez, D., Platero, H., Lane, T., Werner-Washburne, M.: Exploiting Amino Acid Composition for Predicting Protein-Protein Interactions. PLoS ONE 4, e7813 (2009)
15. Jeffrey, H.J.: Chaos Game Representation of Gene Structure. Nucleic Acids Res. 18, 2163–2170 (1990)
16. Gilmore, S., Hofmann-Wellenhof, R., Muir, J., Soyer, H.P.: Lacunarity Analysis: A Promising Method for the Automated Assessment of Melanocytic Naevi and Melanoma. PLoS One 4, e7449 (2009)
17. Benson, D.A., Boguski, M.S., Lipman, D.J., Ostell, J., Francis Ouellette, B.F.: Lacunarity Analysis: A Promising Method for the Automated Assessment of Melanocytic Naevi and Melanoma. PLoS One 4, e7449 (2009)
18. The Universal Protein Resource, `http://www.uniprot.org/`
19. Nair, S.A., Nair, V.V.: K, S.A., Kant, K., Dey, A.: Bio-sequence Signatures using Chaos Game Representation. In: Bioinformatics: Applications in Life and Environmental Sciences, Capital Publishing Company, New Delhi (2008)
20. Otaki, J.M., Tsutsumi, M., Gotoh, T., Yamamoto, H.: Secondary Structure Characterization Based on Amino Acid Composition and Availability in Proteins. J. Chem. Inf. Model. 50, 690–700 (2010)
21. ExPASy Proteomics Server, `http://expasy.org/tools/randseq.html`
22. Ding, Y.S., Zhang, T.L., Chou, K.C.: Prediction of Protein Structure Classes with Pseudo Amino Acid Composition and Fuzzy Support Vector Machine Network. Protein Pept. Lett. 14, 811–815 (2007)
23. Lin, H., Wang, H., Ding, H., Chen, Y., Li, Q.: Prediction of Subcellular Localization of Apoptosis Protein Using Chous Pseudo Amino Acid Composition. Acta Biotheoritica 57, 321–330 (2009)
24. Wang, W., Geng, X.B., Dou, Y., Liu, T., Zheng, X.: Predicting Protein Subcellular Localization by Pseudo Amino Acid Composition with a Segment-Weighted and Features-Combined Approach. Protein Pept. Lett. (to be appeared, 2011)
25. Argos, P., Palau, J.: Amino Acid Distribution in Protein Secondary Structures. Int. Jour. Peptide and Prot. Research. 19, 380–393 (1982)
26. Yu, Z.G., Anh, V., Lau, K.S.: Chaos Game Representation of Protein Sequences Vased on the Detailed HP Model and Their Multifractal and Correlation Analyses. J. Theor. Biol. 226, 341–348 (2004)

Classification and Rule-Based Approach to Diagnose Pulmonary Tuberculosis

Jyotshna Dongardive[1], Agnes Xavier[1], Kavita Jain[1], and Siby Abraham[2,*]

[1] University Department of Computer Sciences, University of Mumbai
Vidyanagari, Santacruz (E), Mumbai 400098.
[2] G. N. Khalsa College, University of Mumbai, Mumbai – 400019
sibyam@gmail.com

Abstract. The pulmonary tuberculosis (TB) is diagnosed conventionally from the test results obtained from different medical examinations. The paper proposes a novel methodology using the classification technique called Identification tree (IDT) to diagnose TB computationally. The model reduces the number of parameters required for the diagnosis substantially. It also offers a list of rules for the speedy and easy diagnosis. The effectiveness of the method has been validated by comparing with existing techniques using standard detection measures.

Keywords: Pulmonary Tuberculosis, Diagnosis, Classification, Identification tree, Reduction of parameters.

1 Introduction

Tuberculosis (TB) is a disease caused by bacteria called Mycobacterium tuberculosis [1]. TB is one of the leading causes of infectious disease mortality in the world, with over two million deaths recorded annually, and it is estimated that one third of the world's population is latently infected [2]. Typical signs of TB are chronic or persistent cough and sputum production. If the disease is at an advanced stage, the sputum will contain blood. The other symptoms are fatigue, lack of appetite, weight loss, fever and night sweats.

Medically, TB is diagnosed using x-rays of chest, analysis of sputum or/and skin test [3].The results of these tests can be used as inputs to various computational models. The two major approaches to diagnose TB computationally are based on either images of sputum/x-ray or the results of various chemical/pathological tests which are collectively called as parameters.

The paper proposes a novel classification and rule based approach which uses exhaustive list of parameters. It employs an IDT as a classification technique and reduces the exhaustive list of parameters into an optimal set of parameters. This, in turn, deduces the rules required for diagnosis of TB.

* Corresponding author.

A. Abraham et al. (Eds.): ACC 2011, Part I, CCIS 190, pp. 328–339, 2011.

The paper is organized in six sections. Section 2 gives literature survey. Section 3 introduces the model proposed. Section 4 provides the experimental setup and results. Section 5 offers conclusion and future work.

2 Literature Survey

The literature discusses various computational models which use images as inputs. Sadaphal et al [4] recognizes Ziehl-Neelsen (ZN) stained acid-fast bacilli (AFB) in digital images where each pixel on the image is classified as a TB or non TB object based on shape and size. Makkapati et al [5] discussed diagnosis of TB from ZN-stained sputum smear images where the presence of TB is based on the beaded structure of the bacilli. K. Veropoulos et al [6] used image processing techniques and neural network classifiers for the automatic identification of TB bacilli on Auramine stained sputum specimens. Forero et al [7] used a classification tree to categorize whether a sample is positive or negative based on the heuristic knowledge extracted from the bacilli shape contour and color. Manuel et al [8] presented a new autofocus algorithm and a bacilli detection technique to reduce the time required to analyze sputum images. It used k-means clustering technique for diagnosing TB.

The other approach to diagnose TB is by analyzing various parameters which are collected from chemical/pathological tests such as preliminary reports, blood tests, urine tests etc. Nitaya et al [9] performed chemical detection of TB in sputum by using gas chromatographic analysis and pattern recognition. Fend et al [10] concluded that ZN staining for TB diagnosis is a time consuming approach and hence they proposed a gas sensor array for detecting different mycobacterium in the sputum samples. An artificial neural network (ANN) technique was further used to classify the patients into TB and non-TB group. Orhan et al [11] have taken patient's epicrisis reports and used a multilayer neural network (MLNN) model. Erhan et al [12] used a MLNN with two hidden layers and a genetic algorithm for training the network. Solh et al [13] developed ANN using clinical and radiographic information to predict active pulmonary TB and further showed that ANN can identify patients with active pulmonary TB more accurately than physicians' clinical assessment. Santos et al [14] used only symptoms and physical signs to construct an ANN model for diagnosis of smear negative pulmonary tuberculosis (SNPT). Fernanda et al [15] developed a prediction model using logistic regression and CART to estimate the risk of SNPT based on symptoms, physical signs and chest X-rays. Bakar et al [16] have used hybrid rough neural network (RNN), results of which indicated that RNN had better accuracy rate. Asha et al [17] used the association rule technique which offered a number of rules to describe the association between different symptoms.

3 Proposed Model

The computational diagnosis of TB in the proposed model has been realized in the following three steps:

Step 1: Collection of exhaustive list of parameters.
Step 2: Creation of an IDT
Step 3: Deduction of rules by traversing through IDT

3.1 Collection of Parameters

The parameters used in the model are collected from five different medical examinations which are preliminary, sputum, blood, urine and bio-chemistry. Table 1 shows the exhaustive list of 45 parameters used. Each of these parameters has a range of values, which are tabulated and used in the subsequent steps. Table 2 shows the snapshot of the tabulated data used in the training of the proposed system. Column 1 shows the patients ID. Columns 2, 3 and 4 show the three parameters amongst exhaustive list of 45 parameters. Column 5 gives the result of the sample used.

Table 1. List of Parameters used

Examinations	No of Parameters	Parameters
Preliminary examination	9	Cough, Fever , Loss of Appetite, Loss of Weight, Chest Pain, Sputum with Blood, Breathlessness, Smoking, Alcohol
Sputum Examinations	6	Mucopurulent , Blood , Saliva, Elastic Tissue, Epithelial Cells,Pus Cells
Blood Examinations	8	Haemoglobin, Total WBC, Polymorphs, Lymphocyte , Eosihophils , Monocytes, Basophils, Netrophils
Urine Examinations	11	Urine Color, Urine Appearance, Reaction, Albumin, Sugar, Bile Salt, Bile Pigment, Occult Blood, Epithelial Cells, Pus Cells, RBC
Bio-Chemistry	11	Blood Urea, Sr. Creatinine, Sr. Uric Acid, Total Bilirubin, Direct Bilirubin, Indirect Bilirubin, SGOT, SGPT, Total Protein,Sr.Albumin, Sr.Globulin

Table 2. Snapshot of some of the parameters with its values

ID	weight	fever	urine appearance	Result
1	light	Yes	s.turbid	TB
2	heavy	no	Clear	NO TB
3	light	Yes	s.turbid	TB
4	average	No	Cloudy	TB
5	heavy	No	s.turbid	NO TB
6	light	No	s.turbid	NO TB
7	light	No	Cloudy	NO TB
8	average	Yes	Cloudy	TB
9	average	Yes	s.turbid	NO TB
10	average	yes	s.turbid	NO TB

3.2 Creation of an IDT

A classification method known as IDT is used to find the most significant parameters in the diagnosis of TB. The tree uses an Average Disorder Score (ADS) given by the following formula, for each of the parameters listed in Table1.

$$ADS = \sum_{b} (nb/nt) * (\sum_{c} (-nbc/nb) * \log_2(nbc/nb))$$

where 'nb' is the number of samples in branch 'b'; 'nt' is the total number of samples in all branches and 'nbc' is the number of samples in branch 'b' of parameter 'c'.

The pseudo code used for the generation of IDT is shown in Figure 1

```
Step 1: For each parameter P, calculate ADS.
Step 2: Select a parameter P with least ADS.
            2.1 Make this P as the root of the tree.
            2.2 Place this P in Selected Parameter (SP).
            2.3 Calculate ADS for all the branches b of SP.
Step3: For each b of SP
          IF (ADS! = 0) for b,
                    Label it as Non-Homogenous (NH).
          Else
                    Label it as Homogenous (H).
          End if
      End for
Step 4: For each NH
          Do
                    Calculate ADS.
                    Select Parameter with least ADS from P for this NH.
                     Populate this P to SP.
           End do
Step 5: Return the tree with SP and H.
Step 6: Repeat Step 3 until ADS = 0.
           End For
Step 7: Stop.
```

Fig. 1. Pseudo code for IDT

The above pseudo code is illustrated as given below.

Step 1: Table 3 gives the list of 45 parameters and their ADS.

Table 3. ADS of each of the parameters

Parameter	**ADS**	**Para meter**	**ADS**	**Parameter**	**ADS**
Cough	0.9	HB	0.9	OB	0.7
Fever	0.7	Total WBC	0.9	Epi Cells	0.8
Sputum	0.7	Poly	0.8	Pus Cells	0.9
Loss of weight	***0.5***	Lym	0.9	RBC	0.7
Loss of Appetite	0.6	Eosi	0.9	BU	0.7
Breathl-essness	0.9	Mono	0.9	Create-nine	0.9

Table 3. (*continued*)

Smoking	0.9	Baso	0.9	Uric acid	0.9
Alcohol	0.8	Netr-ophils	0.9	T.Bili	0.9
Chest Pain	0.9	Urine Color	0.8	D. Bili	0.9
Mucopurulent	0.9	Urine Appear	0.537	In.Bili	0.9
Blood	0.7	React-ion	0.9	SGOT	0.9
Saliva	0.9	Alb	0.6	SGPT	0.6
Epithelial Cells	0.9	BS	0.9	T.Pro-tein	0.8
Pus Cells	0.9	BP	0.9	Sr.Al-bumin	0.9
Elastic Tissue	0.9	Sugar	0.9	Sr.Gl-obulin	0.6

Step 2: From Table 3, '*Loss of weight*' is the parameter with the least ADS, which is added to SP. Now,

SP = {'*Loss of weight*'}

This becomes the root of the tree which has three branches namely 'light', 'heavy' and 'average' as shown in

Figure 2. Calculate ADS of each of these branches.

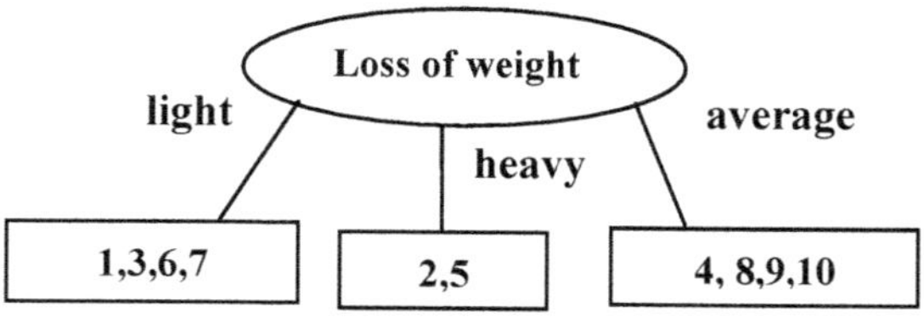

Fig. 2. Branches of '*Loss of weight*'

Step 3: We label the branches '*light*' and '*average*' as NH as their ADS are non-zero. The branch '*heavy*' is labelled as H as its ADS is zero.
Step 4: Calculate ADS of the NH branches '*light*' and '*average*'. Since the ADS of '*light*' is the least, its parameter '*fever*' has been appended to SP. Similarly the parameter '*urine appearance*' is also appended to SP. Now,

SP = { '*Loss of weight*', '*Fever*', '*Urine Appearnce*'}

Step 5: The tree returned in this step is shown in Figure 3.

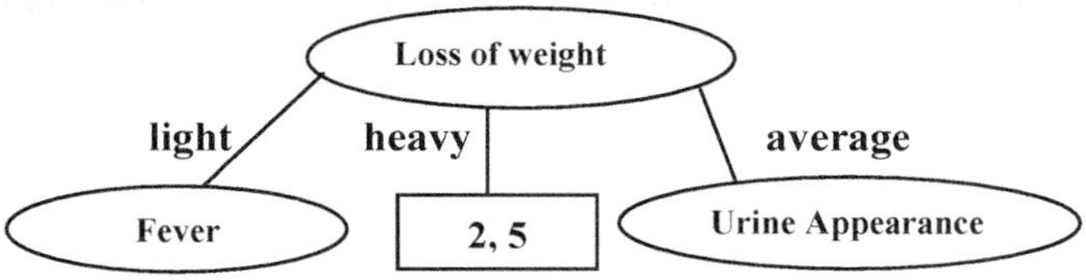

Fig. 3. Appended tree based on 'Loss of weight'

Step 6: The process is continued. Now, the parameter with the least ADS is '*fever*' which has two branches '*yes*' and '*no*'. These branches are Homogeneous as their ADS are zero. Similarly, the node '*urine appearance*' has two branches '*cloudy*' and '*s-turbid*', out of which '*cloudy*' is a Homogeneous branch and '*s-turbid*' is Non-Homogeneous'. Figure 4 shows branches of '*fever*' and '*urine appearance*'.

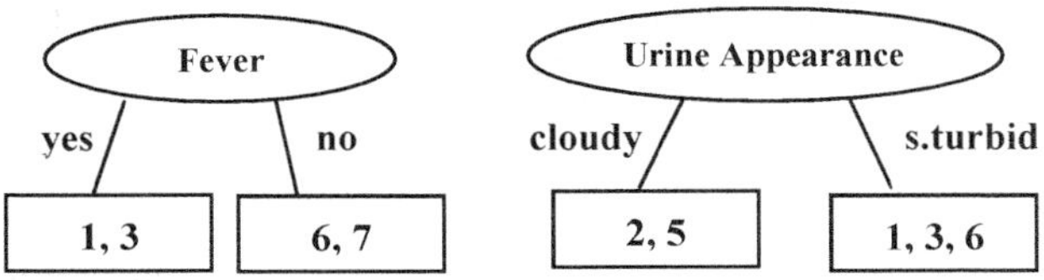

Fig. 4. Branches of '*Fever*' and '*Urine Appearance*'

The process is continued until all the Non-Homogeneous branches are converted to Homogeneous.

Step 7: Once all the nodes are made Homogeneous, we get a complete IDT. Figure 5 shows the snapshot of the IDT generated.

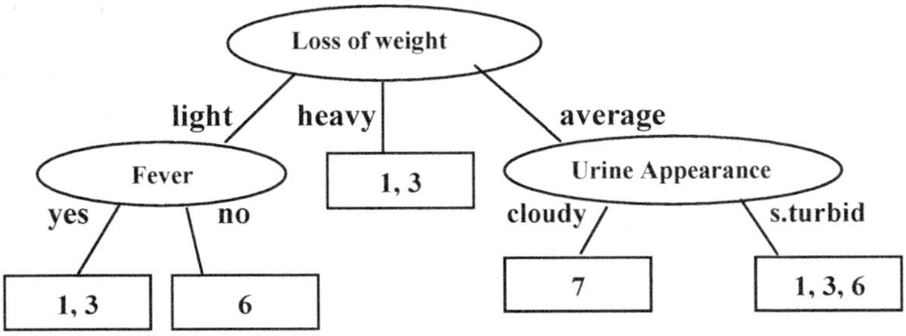

Fig. 5. Snapshot of IDT

3.3 Deduction of Rules by Traversing through IDT

We can deduce rules by traversing through the IDT from the root to each of its leaf nodes. The rules deduced from Figure 5 are listed below.

1. If a person's weight is *light* and has *fever*, then the person is infected from TB.

2. If a person's weight is *light* and does not have *fever*, then the person is not infected from TB.
3. If a person's weight is *heavy*, then the person is not infected from TB.
4. If a person's weight is *average* and *urine appearance* is *cloudy*, then the person is not infected from TB.

These rules can then be used for speedy and easy diagnosis of TB.

4 Experimental Setup and Results

The real time data was collected from Group of T.B Hospital, Mumbai. The dataset was prepared based on the clinical case history of patients, which contained 250 samples for two classes- class 1 contains 131 patients with TB and class 2 contains 119 patients without TB. The system was trained using 150 samples and the remaining was used for testing.

The model has been implemented using VBA 2007 and Java jdk1.5.0_07. The database used is Microsoft Excel 2007. The experiments were conducted on a workstation with an Intel Pentium(R) 4 CPU, 3.06GHz, 512MB of RAM, running on Microsoft Windows XP Home Edition, Version 2002, Service Pack 3.

4.1 Complete IDT

The IDT generated for diagnosis of TB is shown in Figure 6.

4.2 Rules for Diagnosis

The following are the 12 rules generated from the IDT.

1. If a person's weight is heavy, then the person is not infected from TB.
2. If a person's weight is light, do not have fever and urine appearance is clear, then the person is not infected from TB.
3. If a person's weight is light, do not have fever and urine appearance is s.turbid, then the person is not infected from TB.
4. If a person's weight is average and urine appearance is s.turbid, then the person is not infected from TB.
5. If a person's weight is average, urine appearance is clear and blood urea range is between 15 and 40, then the person is not infected from TB.
6. If a person's weight is average, urine appearance is clear and blood urea range is less than 15 and greater than 40 and pus cells are 1 to 2, then the person is not infected from TB.
7. If a person's weight is average, do not have chest pain, elastic tissue is absent, epithelial cells is nil, pus cells is nil, WBC range is between 4500 and 11000, lymphocytes range is between 20 and 40, monocytes range is between 2 and 8, urine color is pale yellow , urine appearance is clear, albumin is absent, pus cells is nil, RBC is absent, occult blood is absent, blood urea range is less than 15 and greater than 40, Sr,uric acid range is between 2 and 7, direct bilirubin is 0.2 and sr.albumin range is less than 3.6 and greater than 5.2, then the person is not infected from TB.

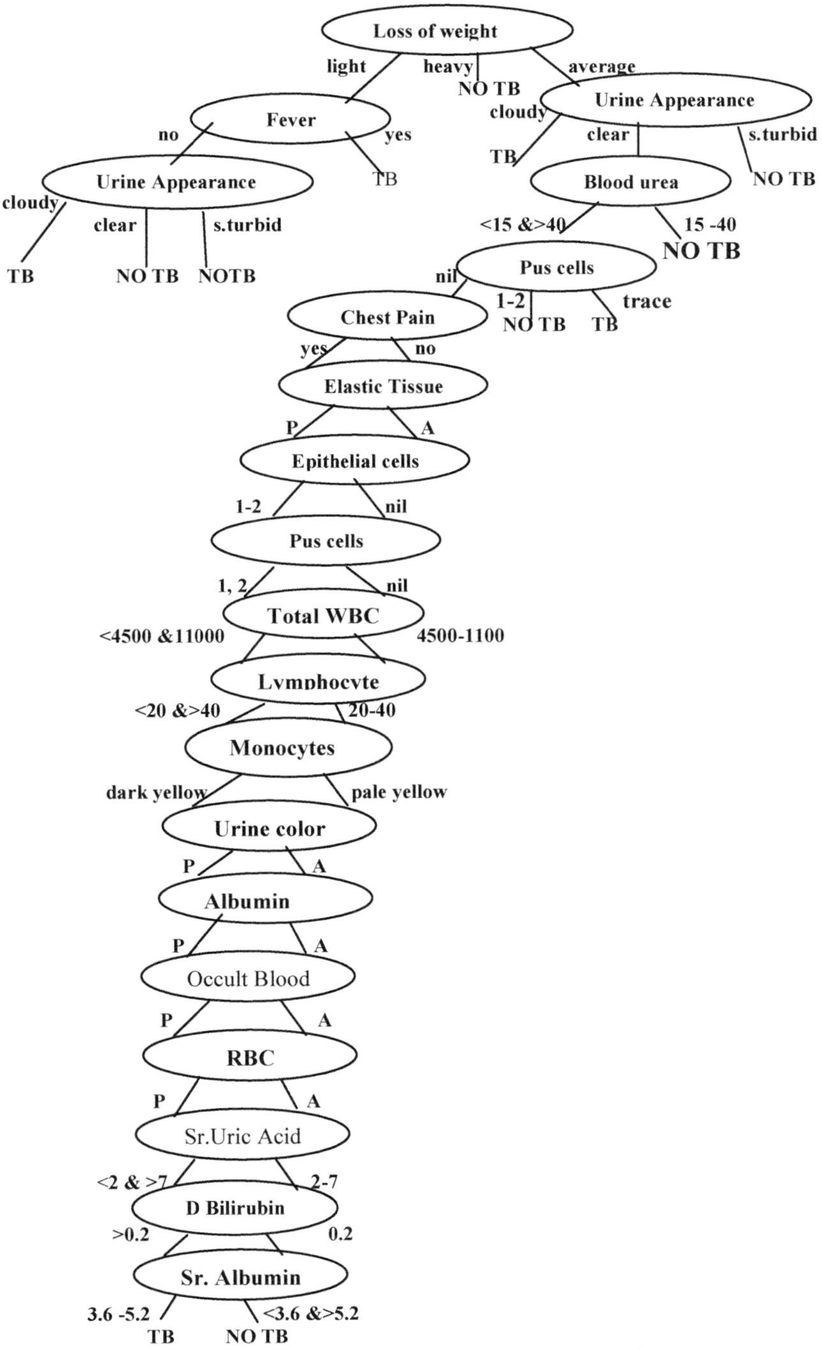

Fig. 6. Complete IDT

8. If a person's weight is light and has fever, then the person is infected from TB.
9. If a person's weight is light, do not have fever and urine appearance is cloudy, then the person is infected from TB.
10. If a person's weight is average and urine appearance is cloudy, then the person is infected from TB.
11. If a person's weight is average, urine appearance is clear, blood urea range is less than 15 and greater than 40 and trace of pus cells is present, then the person is infected from TB.
12. If a person's weight is average, have chest pain, elastic tissue is present, epithelial cells are 1 to 2, pus cells are 1 to 2, WBC range is less than 4500 and greater than 11000, lymphocytes range is less than 20 and greater than 40, monocytes range is less than 2 and greater than 8, urine color is dark yellow, urine appearance is clear, albumin is present, occult blood is present, pus cells is nil, RBS is present, blood urea range is less than 15 and greater than 40, Sr,uric acid range is less than 2 and greater than 7, direct bilirubin is greater than 0.2 and sr.albumin range is between 3.6 and 5.2, then the person is infected from TB.

4.3 Reduction of Parameters

In the process of traversing through the IDT, the total number of parameters appended to the tree was 19. Hence the exhaustive list of 45 parameters has been reduced to 19 parameters. The reduced list of parameters is shown in Table 4.

Table 4. Reduced list of parameters

No	Reduced List	No	Reduced List
1	Fever	11	Urine Color
2	Loss of Weight	12	Albumin
3	Chest pain	13	Occult Blood
4	Elastic Tissue	14	RBC
5	Epithelial Cells	15	Pus Cells
6	Pus Cells	16	Blood Urea
7	Total WBC	17	Sr. Uric acid
8	Lymphocytes	18	Direct Bilirubin
9	Monocytes	19	Sr.Albumin
10	Urine Appearance		

4.4 Effectiveness of the System

The proposed methodology was validated using the following standard detection measures.

- ***Accuracy**:* It is defined as the ratio of the number of correct classification of input-output data to the total number of testing data.
- ***Sensitivity**:* It is defined as the ratio of the correctly classified TB cases to the total number of TB cases.

- ***Specificity***: It is defined as the ratio of the correctly classified non-TB cases to the total number of non-TB cases

Table 5 shows the results obtained for these measures.

Table 5. Detection measures

Measures	Result in %
Accuracy	94.50
Sensitivity	98.00
Specificity	91.00

Figure 7 shows the relationship between the number of samples and its accuracy for five sets of samples. It is observed that as the number of samples increases the accuracy of the system also increase and then it tends to stabilize from the sample of size 80 onwards.

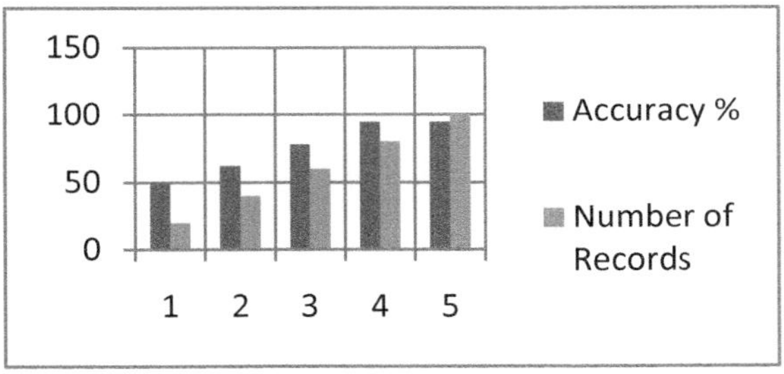

Fig. 7. System Accuracy

4.5 Comparative Study

Table 6 gives the comparative study of the accuracy of diagnosis of TB using different methodologies with different inputs such as images and parameters. It was observed that the proposed model gave competitive results as compared with other models.

Table 6. Comparative study with existing methodologies

Methodology	Accuracy in %
DIP	93.50
Gas chromatographic analysis and pattern recognition	75.00
MLNN with LM(two hidden layers)	95.08
MLNN with GA(two hidden layers)	94.88
The proposed model	**94.50**

Table 7 shows the comparative study of the accuracy of the proposed model with existing systems which also use the parameters as inputs. These systems use 38 parameters. In order to have a better comparison, the proposed model has been tested with the same number of parameters of which 17 were matched. Still, the proposed model could offer competitive result.

Table 7. Comparative results of systems which use parameters

Methods	Accuracy in %
MLNN with BPwM(one hidden layer)	93.04
MLNN with BPwM(two hidden layers)	93.93
MLNN with LM(one hidden layer)	93.42
MLNN with LM(two hidden layers)	95.08
MLNN with GA(two hidden layers)	94.88
The proposed model	**94.50**

5 Conclusion

The paper offers a novel methodology to diagnose pulmonary tuberculosis computationally. It uses identification tree which reduces an exhaustive list of forty-five parameters to an optimal set of nineteen parameters. It also offers a list of twelve rules. This composite approach of classification and generation of rules aids in speedy and easy diagnosis of tuberculosis.

In future, the proposed model is intended to be converted as a generic tool for diagnosing similar diseases. This can be done by testing the system with different data sets from diverse areas of medical field.

Acknowledgments

The authors acknowledge the contribution of staff of Group of TB hospital, Mumbai for providing the authentic data.

References

[1] Kumar, V., Abbas, A.K., Fausto, N., Mitchell, R.N.: Robbins Basic Pathology, 8th edn., pp. 516–522. Saunders Elsevier, Philadelphia (2007) ISBN 978-1-4160-2973-1

[2] Corbett, E.L., Watt, C.J., Walker, N., Maher, D., Williams, B.G., Raviglione, M.C., et al.: The growing burden of tuberculosis: global trends and interactions with the HIV epidemic. Arch. Intern. Med. 163, 1009–1021 (2003)

[3] Australian Prescriber 33 (1), 12–18, `http://www.australianprescriber.com/magazine/33/1/12/18/`

[4] Sadaphal, P., Rao, J., Comstock, G.W., Beg, M.F.: Image processing techniques for identifying Mycobacterium tuberculosis in Ziehl-Neelsen stains. Int. J. Tuberc. Lung., 579–582 (2008)

[5] Makkapati, Agrawal, V., Acharya, R., Philips, R.: Segmentation and classification of tuberculosis bacilli from ZN-stained sputum smear images. In: IEEE International Conference on Automation Science and Engineering, CASE 2009, pp. 217–220 (2009)
[6] Veropoulos, K., Campbell, C., Learmonth, G., Knigh, B., Simpson, J.: The Automated Identification of Tubercle Bacilli using Image Processing and Neural Computing. In: Proceedings of the 8th International Conference on Artificial Neural Networks, vol. 2, pp. 797–802
[7] Forero, M.G., Cristobal, G., Alvarez-Borrego, J.: Automatic identification techniques of tuberculosis bacteria. In: Applications of Digital Image Processing XXVI, San Diego, CA, USA. Proc. SPIE, vol. 5203, p. 71 (2003)
[8] Forero, M.G., Sroubek, F., Cristóbal, G.: Identification of tuberculosis bacteria based on shape and color. Imaging in Bioinformatics: Part III, ACM Digital library 10(4), 251–262 (2004)
[9] Maliwan, N., Reid, R.W., Pliska, S.R., Bird, T.J., Zvetina, J.R.: Direct diagnosis of tuberculosis by computer assisted pattern recognition gas chromatographic analysis of sputum. Biomedical Chromatography 5(4), 165–170 (1991)
[10] Fend, R., Kolk, A.H.J., Bessant, C., Buijtels, P., Klatser, P.R., Woodman, A.C.: Prospects for Clinical Application of Electronic-Nose Technology to Early Detection of Mycobacterium tuberculosis in Culture and Sputum. Journal of Clinical Microbiology 44(6), 2039–2045 (2006)
[11] Er, O., Temurtas, F., Çetin Tanrıkulu, A.: Tuberculosis Disease Diagnosis Using Artificial Neural Networks. Springer Science + Business Media, LLC, Heidelberg (2008)
[12] Elveren, E., Yumuşak, N.: Tuberculosis Disease Diagnosis Using Artificial Neural Network Trained with Genetic Algorithm. Springer Science + Business Media, LLC, Heidelberg (2009)
[13] El-Solh, A.A., Hsiao, C.B., Goodnough, S., Serghani, J., Grant, B.J.: Predicting active pulmonary tuberculosis using an artificial neural network. Chest 116(4), 968–973 (1999)
[14] Santos, A., Pereira, B., Six's, J., Mello, F., Kritski, A.: Neural Networks: An Application for Predicting Smear Negative Pulmonary Tuberculosis. In: Advances in Statistical Methods for the Health Sciences Statistics for Industry and Technology, Part V, pp. 275–287 (2007)
[15] de Queiroz Mello, F.C., do Valle Bastos, L.G., Soares, S.L.M., Rezende, V.M.C., Conde, M.B., Chaisson, R.E., Kritski, A.L., Ruffino-Netto, A., Werneck, G.L.: Predicting smear negative pulmonary Tuberculosis with classification trees and logistic regression: a cross-sectional study. BMC Public Health (2006)
[16] Bakar, A.A., Febriyani, F.: Rough Neural Network Model for Tuberculosis Patient Categorization. In: Proceedings of the International Conference on Electrical Engineering and Informatics, Institut Teknologi Bandung, Indonesia, June 17-19 (2007)
[17] Asha, T., Natarajan, S., Murthy, K.N.B.: Association-rule-based tuberculosis disease diagnosis. In: Jusoff, K., Xie, Y. (eds.) Second International Conference on Digital Image Processing, 75462Y Methods for the Health Sciences Statistics for Industry and Technology, Part V, pp. 275–287 (2007)

Identification and Analysis of Cell Cycle Phase Genes by Clustering in Correspondence Subspaces*

Ai Sasho[1], Shenhaochen Zhu[2], and Rahul Singh[2,**]

[1] Department of Chemistry and Biochemistry
[2] Department of Computer Science
San Francisco State University, San Francisco, CA
rahul@sfsu.edu

Abstract. Correspondence analysis (CA) is a statistical method that is widely used in multiple disciplines to reveal relationships amongst variables. Among others, CA has been successfully applied for microarray data analysis. One of CA's strengths is its ability to help visualize the complex relationships that may be present in the data. In this sense, CA is a powerful exploratory tool that takes advantage of human pattern analysis abilities. The power of CA can, however, be diluted, if the patterns are embedded in data clutter. This is because CA is a dimensionality reduction approach and not a data reduction method; thus, is powerless to remove clutter. Unfortunately, our visual analysis abilities can be overwhelmed in such conditions causing failures in identifying relationships. In this paper, we propose a solution to this problem by combining CA with one-way analysis of variance (ANOVA) and subsequently by clustering in the low-dimensional space obtained from CA. We investigate the proposed approach using microarray data from 6200 *S. cerevisiae* genes and demonstrate how visual analysis is facilitated by removal of unnecessary clutter as well as facilitating the discernment of complex relationships that may be missed through application of CA alone.

Keywords: Correspondence Analysis, UPGMA Clustering, One-way ANOVA, Microarray Time Course Data.

1 Introduction

Microarray technology enables the analysis of the mRNA levels of thousands of genes simultaneously providing a powerful tool for researchers. This technology has been widely used and became a standard tool for studying the fundamental aspects of growth and development of organisms as well as the genetic causes of many diseases. Microarrays provide an opportunity to study interactions not only among genes but also relationships between genes and experimental conditions. In microarray experiments, typically, gene expressions of thousands of genes are measured over a period of time, accumulating a large volume of data very quickly. Thus, such

* This research was funded in part by the NSF grant IIS-064418 (CAREER).
** Corresponding author.

A. Abraham et al. (Eds.): ACC 2011, Part I, CCIS 190, pp. 340–350, 2011.

experiments necessitate the development of efficient and automated way of analyzing the data. Furthermore, these analysis techniques must also ultimately help in data interpretation and data exploration; revealing the issues that need to be explored further. Consequently, solutions need not only to address issues of automation and algorithmic efficacy, but must also aid the human-algorithm interface.

In this paper, we propose a method to address the somewhat dichotomous requirements of the above design formulation. In doing so, we base ourselves on a dimensionality reduction technique called correspondence analysis (CA) which has also been shown to be of promise in microarray data analysis [2]. CA offers a way of revealing the relationship between and among variables in a data set by applying a specific form of dimensionality reduction and produces a graph including all the variables in a single low-dimensional subspace. For instance, using CA, one may simultaneously visualize relationships between genes and hybridizations as well as within genes and within hybridizations. However, the interpretation of the visual results generated by CA still requires human intervention. The human visual system, though extremely powerful in discerning patterns, is not very efficacious in environments containing a large amount of self-similar data (cluttered environments). To address this issue, we propose the use of ANOVA and clustering in the reduced-dimension space identified using CA. Our goal is to accentuate the meaningful data (signal) while minimizing the background data clutter and thus reduce the cognitive load during analysis. We begin this paper in the following with a review of related work and distinctions of the proposed approach from them. This is followed by a detailed description of the proposed method and experimental analysis of its performance.

1.1 Prior Research and Overview of Proposed Method

The microarray data analysis is one of the most heavily research areas in contemporary bioinformatics. However, most methods that have been proposed for this problem can be thought of as belonging to one of the following classes [2]: (1) clustering methods, (2) dimensionality reduction techniques, and (3) techniques that treat the problem as that within the classification/regression framework. Of these, the dimensionality reduction methods are of direct relevance for us. The commonly used methods in this class include principle component analysis (PCA) and Multi-dimensional scaling (MDS). PCA utilizes the properties of covariance matrix and transforms correlated variables into orthogonal (uncorrelated) variables while preserving as much information as possible present in the original data set. The use of PCA in microarray data analysis was demonstrated by Raychaudhuri *et al.* [5] who successfully applied PCA to a sporulation time series microarray data to find the temporal gene expression patterns. MDS is a set of statistical methods to reveal the underlying structure of the data set by using a dimensionality reduction technique. MDS has been used in many applications of data mining; however, the computational complexity of MDS makes it difficult to apply the method to a large set of data [8]. In this context, Tzeng *et al.* [8] has developed a modified MDS which reduces the computational complexity of MDS, and proved effectiveness of MDS to expose correlation of certain human genes.

Like these two methods, CA is also a technique that belongs to the class of dimensionality reduction approaches. However, unlike the above class of methods, CA has certain properties that make it more suitable for revealing association among variables. Specifically, CA can aid in investigating the association amongst variables (row and column variables) by projecting them in single joint space. Furthermore, CA has a low computational complexity. Thus, if our goal is to study the interdependencies between genes and hybridizations (experimental conditions), then correspondence analysis is arguably a very apt technique. This conclusion was demonstrated by Fellenberg *et al.* in their seminal paper [2]. Fellenberg *et al.* applied CA to the *Saccharomyces cerevisiae* gene expression microarray data produced by Spellman *et al.* [6], and successfully showed that CA can be used to visualize relationships between genes and experimental conditions. However, the method in [2] did not address the issue of data clutter. Furthermore, dimensionality reduction approaches (CA included) require a complete data matrix and cannot function in the presence of missing information. However, it is inevitable to avoid missing values when dealing with microarray data. Such questions were also not considered in [2]. Finally, at the current state-of-the-art, the question of algorithmic analysis beyond application of CA has not been considered. In our work, we address all these questions in context of the problem of relating the genes of *S. cerevisiae* to the specific cell-cycle phases in which they are expressed. For this purpose, the microarray data compiled by Spellman [6] is represented in a matrix containing genes in rows and cell cycle phase time points in columns.

In the proposed method, first, the missing data problem is addressed. To replace missing values, we investigate several missing value estimation techniques, including row average, cell cycle row average, and Bayesian Principle Component Analysis (BPCA) (http://hawaii.sys.i.kyoto-u.ac.jp/~oba/tools/BPCAFill.html). These methods are evaluated in terms of the percentage of correctly associated gene-cell cycle phase pairs after correspondence analysis. Thus, our assessment studies the impact of these techniques on the actual analysis. Our assessment criterion is different (and arguably richer) than the standard approach of synthetically removing data and using linear error measures (such as RMSD) to judge efficacy. We next address the issue of ameliorating data clutter in two steps; the first step occurs before application of CA. In this step, we apply ANOVA to the microarray data to identify the genes showing differential expression. The effectiveness of ANOVA in determining genes with differential expression was proved by Cui *et al.* [1]. By performing ANOVA, we reduce the data (by filtering out genes that are expressed in the constant levels) without negatively influencing subsequent analysis. Furthermore, removal of non-differentially expressed genes also reduces the computational requirements from subsequent analysis steps and simplifies visual analysis. Next, we perform the dimensionality reduction step by using CA. This specific step is similar to the work in [2]. Following CA, we perform clustering in the low dimensional space to further reduce data clutter and aid in interpretation. In this paper, we use UPGMA algorithm to further study relationships between genes. We note that other clustering algorithms are equally applicable. Our choice of the specific clustering method is motivated by two reasons: first, the UPGMA algorithm is well understood leading to easier analysis of the final outcomes, especially as the clustering is performed on a reduced dimensional yet information-rich subspace. Second, the input data for UPGMA is a distance matrix which can be easily constructed by calculating the distances between all data points in the correspondence subspace. The UPGMA produces an ultrametric tree, depicting the relationships among data elements. Analysis of the tree can provide additional information about the associations among variables which cannot be discerned easily from the output of correspondence analysis alone.

2 Proposed Approach

2.1 Data Set

To evaluate our implementation of computational methods, we use the microarray data of *Saccharomyces cerevisiae* collected by Spellman *et al.* [6] as an input data. The data set contains the color intensities of approximately 6200 *S. cerevisiae* genes whose gene expression was synchronized by four different synchronization methods: α-factor, *CDC15*, *CDC28* and elutriation. For each method, the gene expression was recorded every 10 minutes for up to 390 minutes. Each time point (10 minute interval) is mapped to the biological cell cycle phases, namely M/G1, G1, S, S/G2 and G2/M [6]. A CSV file containing the microarray data is created and used as an input file for the program developed in this paper.

2.2 Missing Value Estimation

Correspondence analysis requires a complete set of data. Unfortunately, gene expressions measured by microarrays often include missing values; thus, a missing value estimation step is necessary for further analysis. Three missing value estimation methods are evaluated as part of our investigations: (1) missing value estimation by row average, (2) by cell cycle row average, and (3) by the Bayesian Principle Component Analysis Missing Value Estimator [4]. The effectiveness of a missing value estimation method is evaluated by computing the percentage of correctly associated gene-cell cycle phase pairs based on the microarray data published by Spellman et al. [6]. For the missing value estimation by row average, the average gene expression value of each row is calculated and used to fill in the missing values. Similarly, missing value estimation by cell cycle row average imputes the missing values by calculating the average of the row by only using the columns that belong to the same phase as the missing value. The BPCA Missing Value Estimator is a publicly available program developed by Oda *et al.* [4].

2.3 Identification of Non-differential Genes Using ANOVA

Our interest is to identify genes showing different temporal profiles through cell cycle phases and associate these genes with a specific cell cycle phase. Therefore, genes that are constantly expressed at the same level throughout the cell cycle phases, such as house keeping genes, can be filtered out prior to correspondence analysis and UPGMA. After estimating missing values, the one-way ANOVA method is applied to the microarray data to identify the genes that are showing differential expression. The F value calculated by ANOVA is evaluated against the critical F value to determine if genes are expressed differently through cell cycle phases.

The microarray data contains genes in rows and cell cycle phase time points in columns. Since the columns represent cell cycle phase time points, they can be categorized by cell cycle phases, and the columns belonging to the same cell cycle phase can be considered as a group in the ANOVA process. To perform ANOVA, the total sum of square is calculated. The total sum of square is defined by the following equation:

$$SS_{total} = \sum X^2 - \frac{G^2}{N} \tag{1}$$

In the above equation, X represents the sum of squared data points in a group; G is the sum of all the data points; and N is the total number of data points. Next, the squared sum within a group is calculated in Eq. (2), where n is the number of data points in a group. Similarly, the squared sum between the groups is calculated in Eq. (3) below.

$$SS_{within} = \sum X^2 - \frac{(\sum X)^2}{n} \tag{2}$$

$$SS_{between} = \sum \frac{T^2}{n} - \frac{G^2}{N} \tag{3}$$

where T is the sum of data points for each group. After calculating the above values, SS_{total} should equal the sum of $SS_{between}$ and SS_{within}. The means of squares within and between are calculated by:

$$MS_{within} = SS_{within} / df_{within} \tag{4}$$

$$MS_{between} = SS_{between} / df_{between} \tag{5}$$

where df stands for the degree of freedom (which by $N - 1$). By using the means of squares within and between, F-statistics value is calculated as follows:

$$F = \frac{MS_{between}}{MS_{within}} \tag{6}$$

The F-statistics value indicates the variance among the groups. Therefore, genes with a higher F-statistics value than the critical F value show differential expression during the cell cycle and are subject to further analysis by correspondence analysis.

2.4 Correspondence Analysis

CA is applied to the genes that are identified by the ANOVA process as genes showing differential expression. Here, by using correspondence analysis, our aim is to associate a gene with a specific cell cycle phase by identifying a cell cycle phase in which the gene is up-regulated or down-regulated. The microarray data is represented as I x J matrix containing genes in rows and cell cycle phase time points in columns. The symbols I and J denote for the number of genes and the number of cell cycle phase data points respectively. A datum in a matrix at the ith row and the jth column is written as n_{ij}. After a series of matrix manipulations, correspondence analysis calculates coordinates of the row variables (genes) and the column variables (cell cycle phases), which are then used to plot a graph in the desired dimension [3]. The main steps of correspondence analysis are the followings [2, 3]:

Step 1: The mass of each column and row are calculated. The mass of a column is defined as the sum of the data elements in the column divided by the sum of all data elements.

$$c_j = n_{+j} / n_{++} \quad (7) \qquad r_i = n_{i+} / n_{++} \quad (8)$$

In Eq. (7), c_j is the mass of the jth column, n_{+j} is the sum of the data at the jth column, and n_{++} denotes the sum of all the elements in the matrix. Similarly, the mass of a row is calculated in Eq. (8), where r_i represents the mass of the ith row, and n_{i+} is the sum of the data in the ith row.

Step 2: A correspondence matrix P is calculated by dividing each datum by the sum of all the data elements as shown in Eq. (9).

$$p_{ij} = n_{ij} / n_{++} \quad (9) \qquad s_{ij} = (p_{ij} - r_i c_j)\sqrt{r_i c_j} \quad (10)$$

In Eq. (9), p_{ij} is a value in the correspondence matrix at the ith row and the jth column, and n_{ij} represents a data point at the ith row and the jth column in the original matrix.

Step 3: By using the values form the correspondence matrix, the singular matrix S is derived using Eq. (10), where s_{ij} represents a value in the singular matrix and r_i and c_j are the mass of the ith row and the jth column respectively.

Step 4: The matrix S is factored using singular value decomposition (SVD). We use the Java Matrix package (http://math.nist.gov/javanumerics) to compute the SVD. As a consequence of the SVD, the matrix S is decomposed into three matrices U, Λ, and V as shown in Eq. (11).

$$S = U \Lambda V^T \quad (11)$$

In Eq. (11), U denotes the matrix containing left singular vectors, Λ stands for a diagonal matrix containing diagonal elements in a sorted order, and V denotes the matrix containing the right singular vectors.

Step 5: The values from the U, Λ, and V matrices are used to determine a 2D mapping of the data where the row variables (genes) are mapped to the x-axis and the column variables (cell cycle phases) are mapped to the y-axis. The row variable (gene) coordinates are calculated as shown in Eq. (12).

$$f_{ik} = \lambda_k * \upsilon_{ik} * \sqrt{r_i} \quad (12) \qquad g_{jk} = \lambda_k * v_{jk} * \sqrt{c_j} \quad (13) \qquad Inertia = \sum_i \sum_j \frac{(p_{ij} - r_i c_j)^2}{r_i c_j} \quad (14)$$

In Eq. (12), f_{ik} is a gene coordinate at the ith row and the kth column where $k = 1,\ldots, J$. The λ_k denotes a diagonal element in the singular matrix Λ at the kth position. The υ_{ik} represents a value in the U matrix at the ith row and the kth column. Similarly, the coordinates of the column variables (cell cycle phases) are calculated using Eq. (13), where g_{jk} is a cell cycle phase coordinate at the jth row and the kth column with $k = 1,\ldots, I$, and v_{jk} stands for a value in the V matrix at the kth position. The gene coordinate and cell cycle phase coordinate matrices are multidimensional matrices, and each column represents a dimension. For instance, the first column contains the x-axis values (the 1st dimension), and similarly the second column contains the y-axis values (the 2nd dimension). Since a two-dimensional graph is plotted in this paper, the values from the first two columns are used for drawing a biplot. This constitutes a dimensionality reduction step. Although correspondence analysis retains information present in the original data as much as possible, some information is lost during the dimensionality reduction process. The information lost in the process is called inertia, and is calculated by Eq. (14).

2.5 UPGMA Clustering in the Correspondence Subspace

UPGMA is a hierarchical clustering algorithm for grouping data points based on distances between elements in a cluster. UPGMA takes a dissimilarity matrix as an input and joins the nearest clusters until only one cluster is left. First, the nearest clusters are identified by finding the pairwise minimum distance between elements. These clusters are removed from the dissimilarity matrix, and a new joint cluster is inserted. The new cluster contains the average distances between elements in two clusters that are merged. The procedure to join nearest clusters and compute distances for the new cluster is repeated until all the clusters are joined. The information about joined clusters and the minimum distances are saved through the iterations and used to construct an ultrametric tree to show the relationships between the elements.

3 Experimental Investigations and Results

The proposed method was applied to the yeast gene microarray data [6] to demonstrate the effectiveness of the combined methods. The data set contains 6179 genes in rows and 73 cell cycle phase time points in columns, and the columns are categorized into five different cell cycle phases. We evaluated our results by comparing our gene-cell cycle associations against the list of gene-cell cycle pairs created by Spellman *et al.* [6]. The percentage of correctly associated gene-cell cycle pairs was calculated using the metrics of *precision* and *recall*. Precision is the fraction of correctly associated gene-cell cycle pairs within the data set analyzed by the program. On the other hand, recall refers to the fraction of correctly associated gene-cell cycle pairs in the data set containing all the known gene-cell cycle pairs identified by Spellman *et al.* [6]. In this section, we present the results obtained from missing value estimation, ANOVA, correspondence analysis and UPGMA, following the order the procedures were applied.

3.1 Missing Value Estimation

Three missing value estimation techniques: estimation by row average, cell cycle row average and BPCA Missing Value Estimator [4], were evaluated in this project. Each technique was assessed by calculating the percentage of genes that were associated to a correct phase after the CA step. By doing so, our goal was to assess the impact of the missing value estimation method on the overall analysis. The results are shown in Fig. 1.

Missing value estimation by cell cycle row average produced approximately 77.50% and 69.84% of correct gene-cell cycle phase pairs in precision and recall respectively, producing the best results among the techniques evaluated in this paper. The row average method produced about 77.44% and 69.59% in terms of precision and recall, and BPCA Estimator resulted in the precision of 76.59% and the recall of 69.21%.

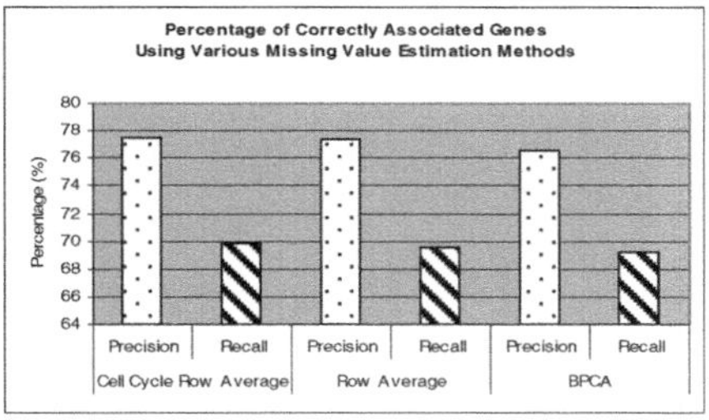

Fig. 1. The graph shows the precision and recall in percentage using different missing value estimation techniques after CA

3.2 Influence of ANOVA

In the ANOVA process, 3054 genes were identified as genes showing differential expression using the F critical value at $p = 0.3$. This included approximately 90.11% of the differentially expressed genes identified by Spellman *et al.* [6]. These genes constituted our "genes of interest" [7] and served as an input data set for correspondence analysis. To evaluate the effectiveness of ANOVA, the percentages of correctly associated gene-cell cycle phase pairs were compared with and without ANOVA. Without using ANOVA, the percentage of genes assigned to a correct phase after CA was approximately 28.79%, and the ratio was increased to 69.84% when ANOVA was incorporated.

3.3 Analyzing the Data Using Correspondence Analysis and Clustering

The biplot in Fig. 2 was produced by applying correspondence analysis on the genes of interest. In the graph, genes are represented by black dots, and the cell cycle phase data points are in various shapes according to the assigned phase. The cell cycle phase centroids were calculated by plotting the average x-coordinate and y-coordinate of the data points belonging to each cell cycle phase. The lines were extended from the origin of the graph to the centroids, so that the user can readily recognize the scattering pattern of cell cycle phase data points. For purposes of the comparison with Fellenberg *et al.* [2], we added the labels to the genes that are known to participate in histone production. Histones are used to coil strands of DNA; thus, histone related genes should be up-regulated during the DNA synthesis phase, as shown in Fig. 1. There is an empty spot surrounding the origin of the graph. In a correspondence analysis graph, data points closer to the origin of the graph do not show a strong association to any of the other data points. In the context of our problem, the genes near the center do not show differential expression. The ANOVA step removed such genes prior to the application of CA. It should be noted that from a visual analysis perspective, this reduces unnecessary clutters due to genes that are irrelevant (non-differentially expressed). Our CA biplot resembled the biplot produced by Fellenberg *et al.* [2]. A visual inspection of two biplots reveled that the locations of cell cycle phase data points, histone genes, and the order of cell cycle phase clusters show similarities between two graphs.

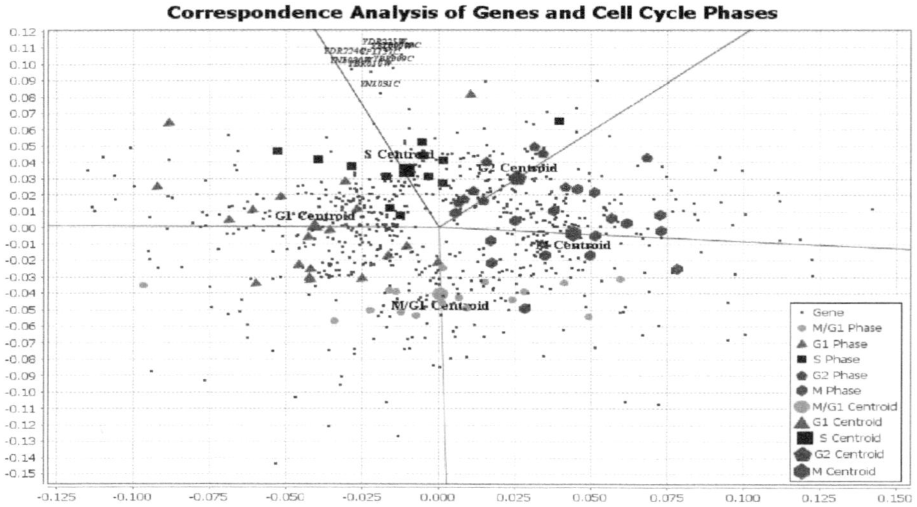

Fig. 2. Biplot produced by correspondence analysis. Black dots represent genes and the symbols represent cell cycle phase time points. Lines were extended to centroids. The histone genes cluster around the S cell cycle phase.

In CA, genes were associated to a cell cycle phase by identifying the closest phase centroid and the percentage of correct gene-phase associations was calculated in terms of precision and recall. The precision measures the accuracy of our analysis given our data set, and the recall measures the accuracy against the complete data set. After application of CA, the precision was calculated to be 77.50%, and the recall was found to be 69.84%. The reader may note that in the work by Fellenberg *et al.* [2], this type of assessment of accuracy was not performed.

In the final step of our method, the data in the correspondence subspace were clustered by using the UPGMA algorithm. The coordinates of data elements in the CA biplot were used to construct a distance matrix, containing the all-pair Euclidean distances (computed in the correspondence subspace). The UPGMA algorithm was applied using the distance matrix and the tree structure in Newick format was produced by UPGMA. Fig. 3 represents a dendrogram constructed based on the Newick string. By inspecting the dendrogram, it can be noticed that the genes assigned to the same cell cycle phase cluster together, and these clusters are placed in a pattern. The most noticeable cluster is the G1 cluster (in black) occupying the large part of the second row in Fig. 3. This observation consists with the correspondence biplot produced in the CA step, which also shows a large number of G1 genes crowded together in one area. In the Fig. 3 dendrogram, the clusters appear in the order of: M (blown) (mixed with some G2), G1 (black), S (blue), G2 (red), S, G1 (the long stretch), M/G1 (orange), and M. Barring a few exceptions, this order resembles the reverse order of the cell cycle phases: M, G2, S, G1, and M/G1. We can also notice large clusters of M genes present both at the beginning and the end of the dendrogram. This is due to the circular distribution of the data in the reduced dimensional correspondence subspace as can be seen in Fig. 2.

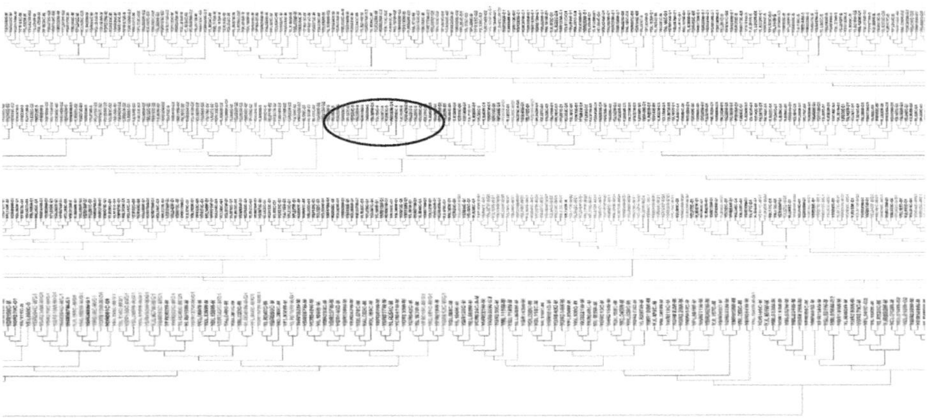

Fig. 3. The dendrogram constructed by UPGMA clustering. A leaf represents a gene. The genes are color coded according to the cell cycle phase assigned by Spellman *et al.* [6]. The color codes are: M/G1 genes in orange, G1 genes in black, S genes in blue, G2 genes in red, and M genes in brown. Histone genes are circled in blue. Note that the continuous dendrogram was divided in sections to fit in the paper.

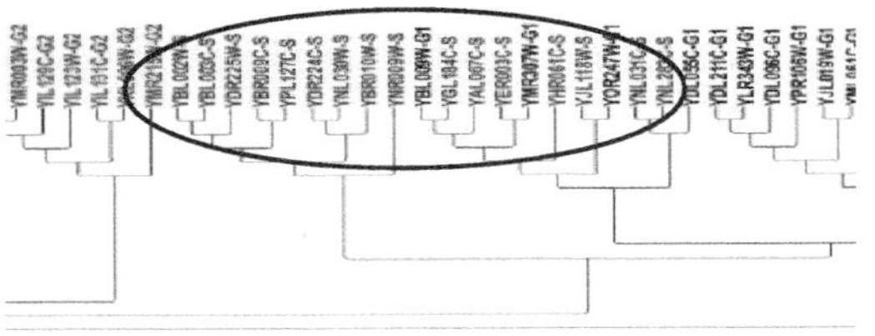

Fig. 4. The blue circle in Fig. 3 is magnified here to show a cluster containing histone genes

In the relation to the correspondence biplot, the clusters appearing in the correspondence subspace stay as clusters in the dendrogram. For example, the histone genes assigned to the S cell cycle phase formed a cluster in both CA biplot (Fig. 2) and in the dendrogram (Fig. 4). In addition, the genes surrounding the cluster centroids in the CA biplot tend to form large clusters in the dendrogram. There are some genes that are spread in a different phase cluster, e.g. a dozen G2 genes are interspersed among the M phase genes at the beginning of the dendrogram, and several M/G1 genes are spread among the long stretch of the G1 cluster. It is usually found that when random genes disturb a cluster, these random genes belong to a neighboring cluster.

4 Conclusions and Discussions

This paper demonstrates a novel approach to reveal hidden relationships among variables by combining CA with ANOVA and UPGMA-based clustering. The method provides a simple visual representation of the complex relationships in the data. Through the application of ANOVA, the accuracy of the analysis was increased by approximately 41.0% and the data set was reduced by 50.0%. In the process of applying ANOVA, about 9.0% of relevant genes were lost. CA associated approximately 77.5% of the genes to the correct cell cycle phase and produced a graph exposing associations among the data elements. The UPGMA algorithm, which was applied to the correspondence subspace, revealed additional associations not only between genes and cell cycle phases, but also within genes. UPGMA produced a hierarchical graph revealing the clusters of genes, while showing how strongly the clusters were related. One of the thrust areas of our further research is to reduce the percentage of relevant genes that were eliminated by ANOVA. The source code and input files for this project are publicly accessible at http://tintin.sfsu.edu/projects/mace.html.

Author Contributions

Research conceptualization and overall method design (RS). Correspondence analysis (AS) and ANOVA (SZ). The experiments were conducted by AS and SZ. The paper was written by RS and AS with contributions from SZ.

References

1. Cui, X.Q., Churchill, G.A.: Statistical tests for differential expression in cDNA microarray experiments. Genome Biol. 4, article 210 (2003)
2. Fellenberg, K., Hauser, N., Brors, B., Neutzner, A., Hoheisel, J., Vingron, M.: Correspondence Analysis Applied to Microarray Data. Proc. Nat. Acad. Sci. 98, 10781–10786 (2001)
3. Greenacre, M.: Correspondence Analysis in Practice. Chapman & Hall/CRC, Taylor & Francis Group, Boca Raton (2007)
4. Oba, S., Sato, M., Takemasa, I., Monden, M., Matsubara, K., Ishii, S.: A Bayesian Missing Value Estimation Method For Gene Expression Profile Data. Bioinformatics 19(16), 2088–2096 (2003)
5. Raychaudhuri, S., Stuart, J.M., Altman, R.B.: Principal Components Analysis to Summarize Microarray Experiments: Application to Sporulation Time Series. In: Pacific Symposium on Biocomputing, pp. 455–466 (2000)
6. Spellman, P., Sherlock, G., Zhang, M., Iyer, V., Anders, K., Eisen, M., Brown, P., Botstein, D., Futcher, B.: Comprehensive Identification of Cell Cycle–regulated Genes of the Yeast Saccharomyces cerevisiae by Microarray Hybridization. Molecular Biology of the Cell 9, 3273–3297 (1998)
7. Tai, C., Speed, C.: Statistical Analysis of Microarray Time Course Data, Walter and Eliza Hall Institute of Medical Research. In: DNA Microarrays, vol. ch. 20, Taylor and Francis, New York (2005)
8. Tzeng, J., Lu, H-S., Li, W-H.: Multidimensional Scaling For Large Genomic Data Sets. BMC Bioinformatics 9 (2008)

Reliability Assessment of Microarray Data Using Fuzzy Classification Methods: A Comparative Study

Ajay K. Mandava, Latifi Shahram, and Emma E. Regentova

Electrical and Computer Engineering
University of Nevada, Las Vegas
4505 Maryland Parkway, Box 454026
Las Vegas, NV 89154-4026
mandavaa@unlv.nevada.edu,
{shahram.latifi,emma.regentova}@unlv.edu

Abstract. Microarrays have become the tool of choice for the global analysis of gene expression. Powerful data acquisition systems are now available to produce massive amounts of genetic data. However, the resultant data consists of thousands of points that are error-prone, which in turn results in erroneous biological conclusions. In this paper, a comparative study of the performance of fuzzy clustering algorithms i.e. Fuzzy C-Means, Fuzzy C-medoid, Gustafson and Kessel, Gath Geva classification, Fuzzy Possibilistic C-Means and Kernel based Fuzzy C-Means is carried out to separate microarray data into reliable and unreliable signal intensity populations. The performance criteria used in the evaluation of the classification algorithm deal with reliability, complexity and agreement rate with that of Normal Mixture Modeling. It is shown that Kernel Fuzzy C-Means classification algorithms appear to be highly sensitive to the selection of the values of the kernel parameters.

Keywords: Clustering; Classification; Kernels; Reliable; Unreliable.

1 Introduction

Clustering plays a key role for statistical data analysis in many fields including data mining, image processing, pattern recognition and bioinformatics. Clustering algorithm usually partitions a dataset into different subsets, so that data in each subset share some similarities. Recently clustering has gained significant popularity in genetics and genomics research, especially in gene expression data analysis. Gene expression data, such as microarry data [1], measures the expression level of a large number of genes within a number of different experimental conditions (samples). Clustering analysis assigns genes into different groups based on their expression values under different experimental conditions. A classification method [2] based on univariate and bivariate Normal Mixture Modeling (NMM) [3] for the reliability analysis of microarray data is described by Asyali. Musa Alci [4] described a Fuzzy C-Means classification for the reliability analysis of microarray data. In this study we evaluate the use of different classification methods (i.e. Fuzzy C-Means [5,6], Kernel Fuzzy C-Means methods algorithms[7], Fuzzy C-medoid[8], Gustafson and Kessel

A. Abraham et al. (Eds.): ACC 2011, Part I, CCIS 190, pp. 351–360, 2011.

[9], Gath Geva [10] and Fuzzy Possibilistic C-Means [11,12]) and compare the results with that of NMM. The paper is organized as follows: Section 2 describes the different methods of classification. Experimental data and test results are presented in Section 3 and Section 4 concludes the paper.

2 Classification Methods

2.1 Classification Using Normal Mixture Modeling (NMM)

For probability density function estimation mixture modeling is a widely used technique and found significant applications in various biological problems. We modeled the probability density function (*pdf*) of the microarray data with two bivariate normal *pdf*s as follows:

$$f(x) = ð_1 N(x;\, ì_i, \Sigma_i) + (1 - ð_1) N(x;\, ì_i, \Sigma_i)$$

where, $N(x;\, ì_i, \Sigma_i) = (2ð)^{-1} \det(\Sigma_i)^{-1/2} \exp\{-(x - ì_i)^T \Sigma_i^{-1} (x - ì_i)/2\}$, for i = 1,2 is a bivariate normal *pdf* with mean $ì_i \in R^2$ and 2x2 covariance matrix Σ_i.The $ð_i(\geq 0)$denotes the weight of $N(x;\, ì_i, \Sigma_i)$. For each component, we have 2 parameters for the mean vector and 3 parameters for the covariance matrix (because of its symmetry) to estimate. In addition, we have only one weight to estimate, as $ð_1 + ð_2$ must be 1, for *f*(*x*) to be proper *pdf*. The weighted bivariate normal *pdf*s or components, i.e. $ð_1\, N(x;\, ì_i, \Sigma_i)and(1 - ð_1)\, N(x;\, ì_i, \Sigma_i)$, correspond to the class posterior probabilities. By equating the class posterior probabilities and solving for *x*, we obtain gives the decision boundary, which is a quadratic curve in our case. We used EM algorithm to estimate the mixture parameters.

2.2 Fuzzy C-Means Classification (FCM)

Fuzzy C-Means (FCM) developed by Dunn [5] and improved by Bezdek [6] is an unsupervised clustering algorithm that has been applied successfully to a number of problems involving feature analysis, clustering and classifier design. It is based on minimization of the following objective function:

$$J_m = \sum_{i=1}^{N} \sum_{j=1}^{C} u_{ij}^m \left\| x_i - c_j \right\|^2 \quad 1 \leq m < \infty$$

Algorithm:

Step 1: Fix c , t_{max} , $m > 1$ and $\varepsilon > 0$

Step 2: Initialize the memberships u_{ik}^0 ;

$$\sum_{i=1}^{c} u_{ki}^t = 1, \qquad \forall\, k$$

Step3: Compute the fuzzy centroids $v_i^{(t)}$ s as:

$$v_i^{(t)} = \sum_{k=1}^{n} \left(u_{ki}^{(t)}\right)^m x_k \Big/ \sum_{k=1}^{n} \left(u_{ki}^{(t)}\right)^m$$

Step 4: Update all memberships $u^{(t+1)}$, with Eqs:

$$u_{ik}^{(t+1)} = \left[\sum_{j=1}^{c}\left(\|x_k - v_i^{(t)}\| \Big/ \|x_k - v_j^{(t)}\| \right)^{2/(m-1)}\right]^{-1}$$

Step 5: Compute $E^t = \| u^{(t+1)} - u^{(t)} \| < \varepsilon$
stop; else $t=t+1$.

2.3 Kernel Fuzzy C-Means Classification (KFCM)

The KFCM algorithm proposed by Chen [7], and briefed here.

Algorithm:

Step 1: Fix c , t_{max} , $m > 1$ and $\varepsilon > 0$
Step 2: Initialize the memberships u_{ik}^{0} ;
Step 3: For $t = 1,2,\ldots, t_{max}$, do:

(a) Update all prototypes v_i^t with Eqs.

$$v_i = \frac{\sum_{k=1}^{n} u_{ik}^{m} K(x_k , v_i)\, x_k}{\sum_{k=1}^{n} u_{ik}^{m} K(x_k , v_i)} \quad \forall i = 1,2, \ldots \ldots c$$

where $K(x,v)$ is a kernel function

(b) Update all memberships $u_{ik}^{(t)}$ with Eqs.

$$u_{ik} = \frac{\left(\frac{1}{(1 - K(x_k, v_i))}\right)^{1/(m-1)}}{\sum \left(\frac{1}{(1 - K(x_k, v_i))}\right)^{1/(m-1)}}$$

$$\forall\, i = 1,2, \ldots \ldots c, \qquad k = 1,2 \ldots \ldots n$$

(c) Compute $E^t = max_{ik} |u_{ik}^{t} - u_{ik}^{t-1}|$, $E^t \leq \varepsilon$
stop; else t=t+1.

Three different kernels have been used in this algorithms for analysis, they are

1. Gaussian Radial Basis Function
$$k(x,y) = \exp\,(-\|x-y\|^2/\sigma^2)$$
where σ is the adjustable parameter for the above kernel function.
2. Laplacian Radial Basis Function
$$k(x,y) = \exp\,(-\frac{\|x-y\|}{ó})$$
where σ is the adjustable parameter for the above kernel function.
3. Radial Basis Function
$$k(x,y) = \exp\,(-\gamma\|x-y\|^2)$$
where $\gamma > 0$, is the adjustable parameter for the above kernel function.

2.4 Fuzzy C-Medoid Classification (FCMdd)

Fuzzy C-medoids [8] proposed by Krishnapuram is a modified version of FCM where the means are replaced with medoids.

Algorithm:

Step 1: Fix c , t_{max} , $m > 1$ and $\varepsilon > 0$
Step 2: Compute membership u_{ik}

$$u_{ik} = \frac{\left(\frac{1}{(1 - K(x_k, v_i))}\right)^{1/(m-1)}}{\Sigma\left(\frac{1}{(1 - K(x_k, v_i))}\right)^{1/(m-1)}}$$

Step 3: Save the current medoids
Step 4: Compute the new medoids v_i

$$x_i^* = argmin_i \, (d_{ik}^2 u_{ik}^m)$$
$$v_i = x_i^*$$

where

$$d_{ik}^2 = (x_k - v_i)\, A_i (x_k - v_i)^T$$

Until $\prod_{k=1}^{n} max|v^t - v^{(t-1)}| \neq 0$

2.5 Gustafson and Kessel Classification (GK)

Gustafson and Kessel [9] extended the standard FCM algorithm by employing an adaptive distance norm, in order to detect clusters of different geometrical shapes in one data set. The algorithm uses the Mahalanobis distance norm. The underlying objective function is

$$J = \sum_{i=1}^{c}\sum_{k=1}^{N} u_{ik}^m \, d_{ik}^2$$

Algorithm:

Step1: Computing of the cluster covariance matrices:

$$F_i = \frac{\sum_{k=1}^{N} u_{ik}^m \, (x_k - v_i)^T \, (x_k - v_i)}{\sum_{k=1}^{N} u_{ik}^m}$$

Where

$$V_i = \frac{\sum_{k=1}^{N} (u_{ik})^m x_k}{\sum_{k=1}^{N} (u_{ik})^m} \quad i = 1,2, \ldots . c \quad k = 1,2, \ldots . N$$

Step 2: Computing of the distances:

$$d_{ik}^2 = (x_k - v_i) A_i (x_k - v_i)^T$$

Where $A_i = [\tilde{n}_i \det(F_i)]^{1/n} F_i^{-1}$

Step 3: Updating of the partition matrix

$$u_{ik} = \frac{1}{\sum_{j=1}^{c} \left({d_{ik}}/{d_{jk}} \right)^{2/(m-1)}}$$

$$i = 1,2, \dots c, \qquad k = 1,2, \dots N$$

Until $E^t = max_{ik} |u_{ik}^t - u_{ik}^{t-1}|$, $E^t \leq \varepsilon$

2.6 Gath Geva Classification (GG)

The fuzzy maximum likelihood estimates (FMLE) clustering algorithm employs a distance norm based on the fuzzy maximum likelihood estimates, proposed by Bezdek and Dunn[10].

Algorithm:

Step 1: Calculate the cluster centers.

$$V_i = \frac{\sum_{k=1}^{N} (u_{ik})^m x_k}{\sum_{k=1}^{N} (u_{ik})^m} \quad i = 1,2, \dots .. c \quad k = 1,2, \dots . N$$

Step 2: Compute the distance measure d_{ik}^2.
The distance to the prototype is calculated based the fuzzy covariance matrices of the cluster

$$F_i = \frac{\sum_{k=1}^{N} u_{ik}^m \,(x_k - v_i)^T \,(x_k - v_i)}{\sum_{k=1}^{N} u_{ik}^m}$$

The distance function is chosen as

$$d_{ik}^2 = \frac{(2ð)^{\left(\frac{n+1}{2}\right)} \sqrt{\det (F_i)}}{á_i} \exp \left(\frac{1}{2} (x_k - v_i) F_i^{-1} (x_k - v_i)^T\right.$$

with the *a priori* probability $á_i$, the $á_i$ is the prior probability of selecting cluster *i*, given by:

$$á_i = \frac{1}{N} \sum_{k=1}^{N} u_{ik}$$

Step 3: Update the partition matrix

$$u_{ik} = \frac{1}{\sum_{j=1}^{c} \left({d_{ik}}/{d_{jk}} \right)^{2/(m-1)}}$$

$$i = 1,2, \dots c, \qquad k = 1,2, \dots N$$

Until $E^t = max_{ik} |u_{ik}^t - u_{ik}^{t-1}|$, $E^t \leq \varepsilon$

2.7 Fuzzy Possibilistic C-Means (FPCM)

The original FCM uses the probabilistic constraint that the memberships of a data point across classes sum to one. While this is useful in creating partitions, the memberships resulting from FCM and its derivatives, however, do not always correspond to the intuitive concept of degree of belonging or compatibility. Krishnapuram and Keller [11, 12] relax this constraint and propose a possibilistic approach to clustering (PCM) by minimizing the following object function.

$$J_m = \sum_{i=1}^{c}\sum_{k=1}^{n} u_{ik}^m \|x_k - v_i\|^2 + \sum_{i=1}^{c} ç_i \sum_{k=1}^{n}(1 - u_{ik})^m$$

where $ç_i$ are suitable positive numbers.
It is recommended to select $ç_i$ as

$$ç_i = K\frac{\sum_{k=1}^{n} u_{ik}^m \|x_k - v_i\|^2}{\sum_{k=1}^{n} u_{ik}^m}$$

Algorithm:

Step 1: Fix c , t_{max} , $m > 1$ and $\varepsilon > 0$
Step 2: Initialize the memberships u_{ik}^0 ;
Step 3: Estimate η_i
Step 3: For $t = 1,2,\ldots, t_{max}$, do:

(a) Update all prototypes v_i^t with Eqs.

$$V_i = \frac{\sum_{k=1}^{N}(u_{ik})^m x_k}{\sum_{k=1}^{N}(u_{ik})^m} \quad i = 1,2,\ldots..c \quad k = 1,2,\ldots.N$$

(b) Compute the distances

$$d_{ik}^2 = (x_k - v_i)A_i(x_k - v_i)^T.$$

(c) Update all memberships u_{ik}^l with Eqs.

$$u_{ik} = \frac{1}{1 + (\frac{\|x_k - v_i\|^2}{ç_i})^{1/(m-1)}}$$

Until $E^t = max_{ik}|u_{ik}^t - u_{ik}^{t-1}|$, $E^t \leq \varepsilon$ stop; else $t=t+1$.

3 Experimental Results

For experiments, we used biological data consisting of only true positives (i.e. reliable) and true negatives (i.e. unreliable) derived from three independent experiments of microarray gene expression from the same cell system [13] in order to test and compare different classification approaches. Information about microarray preparation, image acquisition and intensity extraction procedures are explained in Asyali [2]. Table 1 shows summary statistics, including mean, SD, and the correlation between the channels $(\rho Cy3, Cy5)$ and the number of samples (n), for the two channel data in the three datasets.

Table 1. Summary statistics for the three microarray expression datasets [4]

	Dataset 1		Dataset 2		Dataset 3	
	Cy3	Cy5	Cy3	Cy5	Cy3	Cy5
Mean±SD	6.28±1.08	6.16±1.16	6.21±1.05	6.08±1.15	6.24±1.15	5.90±1.56
ρCy3,Cy5	0.9255		0.9239		0.8672	
n	3027		3040		6455	

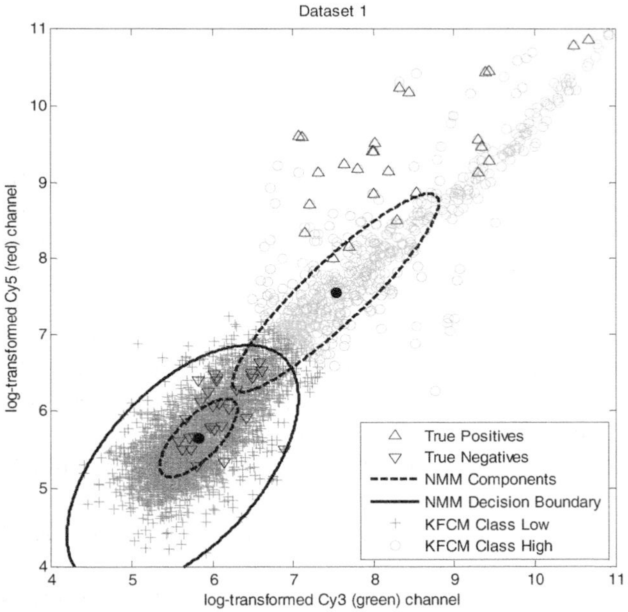

Fig. 1. Pictorial representation of classification

The above algorithms have been implemented using MATLAB R2007b on 2.0 GHz Intel core 2 processor with 2GB of memory. Fig. 1 shows a pictorial representation of classification result obtained using KFCM and NMM, for dataset. For all the methods, belonging to the low (or unreliable) class are marked with dark-gray plus marks, whereas the data points belonging the high (or reliable) class are marked with light gray circle marks. The decision boundary for all the methods can be visualized as curve passing through the points where circles and plus marks are intersecting and an ellipse whose major axis aligned with the cy3 = cy5 axis is the NMM decision boundary. The data points that fall outside this ellipsoid decision boundary are marked or identified as reliable data points. The classification performance, in terms of sensitivity (Sn) and specificity (Sp), of the both approaches against the reference sets for the three cases are reported in Table 2. Reliable (R) and unreliable (UR) refer to the results of classification done by the algorithms, whereas the true positive (TP) and true negatives (TN) refer to the true or actual class information available in the reference sets. The time (in seconds) spent by the central processing unit (CPU) to run the algorithms and the number of iterations is also shown in Table 2. For kernel FCM, we varied σ and γ from 5 to 50 with an increment of 5. For gaussian radial basis kernel function, it attains maximum agreement rate at σ = 5, 10, 35 for dataset 1, 2 and 3 respectively. For laplacian radial basis kernel function, it attains maximum agreement rate at σ = 50, 50, 50 for dataset 1, 2 and 3 respectively. For radial basis kernel function it attains maximum agreement rate at γ = 15, 30, 25 for dataset 1, 2 and 3 respectively. Fig.2. shows the comparison of overall agreement between the different classification methods with respect to NMM classification results. KFCM has better agreement rate with NMM for reference datasets 1 and 2 and FCMdd has better agreement rate for dataset3.

Table 2. Classification results using FCM, FPCM, FCMdd, GK, GG and NMM

		FCM		FPCM		FCMdd		GK		GG		NMM	
		R	UR	R	UR	R	UR	R	UR	R	UR	R	UR
	TP	26	0	26	0	26	0	21	5	26	0	26	0
	TN	0	27	0	27	0	27	4	23	0	27	0	27
	Sn (%)	100		100		100		80.76		100		100	
	Sp (%)	100		100		100		85.18		100		100	
	time (sec)	0.0625		0.3438		0.1238		0.146		0.1875		0.1563	
set 1	# of iter	25		52		26		22		32		40	
	TP	27	0	27	0	27	0	21	6	27	0	27	0
	TN	0	27	0	27	0	27	1	26	0	27	0	27
	Sn (%)	100		100		100		77.77		100		100	
	Sp (%)	100		100		100		96.29		100		100	
	time (sec)	0.0313		0.2813		0.0675		0.125		0.1094		0.1406	
set 2	# of iter	27		56		25		28		26		39	
	TP	27	2	27	2	27	2	6	23	6	23	29	0
	TN	0	14	0	14	0	14	2	12	2	12	1	13
	Sn (%)	93.1		93.1		93.1		20.68		20.68		100	
	Sp (%)	100		100		100		85.7		85.7		92.9	
	time (sec)	0.0469		0.4688		0.0921		0.2188		1.3594		0.5	
set 3	# of iter	22		88		27		28		205		70	

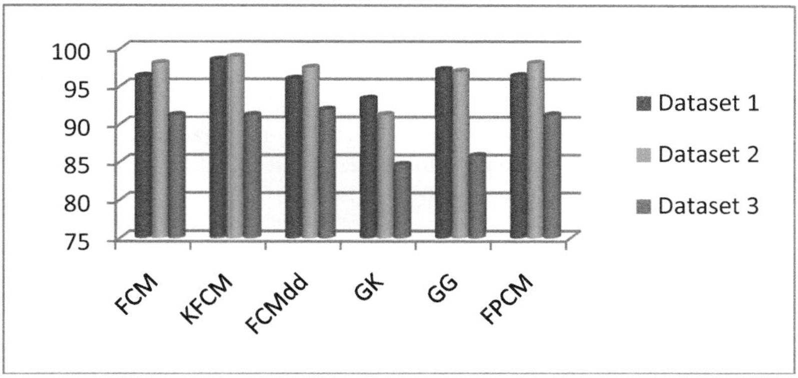

Fig. 2. Comparison of overall agreement between the FCM, KFCM, FCMdd, GK, GG and FPCM with respect to NMM classification results

4 Conclusion

Based on the performance comparison against the reference datasets, which indicates that FCM, KFCM, FCMdd, FPCM and NMM algorithms are performing equally well. However, overall performance of the kernel based methods is not very impressive due to similar (or) only slight increases in overall agreement rates compared to FCM. A major disadvantage of kernel-based algorithms is their sensitivity to the kernel parameters. In fact in some cases a change in the kernel parameters could reduce the overall agreement rate. Thus kernel-based fuzzy clustering requires tuning in order to achieve optimal performance.

References

1. Schena, M.: Quantitative monitoring of gene expression patterns with a complementary DNA microarray. Science 270, 467–470 (1995)
2. Asyali, M.H., Shoukri, M.M., Demirkaya, O., Khabar, K.S.A.: Estimation of Signal Thresholds for Microarray Data Using Mixture Modeling. Nucleic Acids Research 32(7), 1–13 (2004)
3. McLachlan, G.J., Basford, K.E.: Mixture Models, Inference and Applications to Clustering. Marcel Dekker, New York (1989)
4. Alci, M., Asyali, M.H.: Assessment of Reliability of Microarray Data Using Fuzzy C-Means Classification. In: Pal, N.R., Kasabov, N., Mudi, R.K., Pal, S., Parui, S.K. (eds.) ICONIP 2004. LNCS, vol. 3316, pp. 1322–1327. Springer, Heidelberg (2004)
5. Dunn, J.C.: A Fuzzy Relative of the ISODATA Process and Its Use in Detecting Compact Well-Separated Clusters. Journal of Cybernetics, 32–57 (1973)
6. Bezdek, J.C.: Pattern Recognition with Fuzzy Objective Function Algorithm. Plenum Press, New York (1981)
7. Chen, S.C., Zhang, D.Q.: Robust image segmentation using FCM with spatial constrains based on new kernel-induced distance measure. IEEE Trans. Systems Man Cybernet. Pt. B 34, 1907–1916 (2004)

8. Krishnapuram, R., Joshi, A., Yi, L.: A fuzzy relative of the k-medoids algorithm with application to web document and snippet clustering. In: IEEE International Fuzzy Systems Conference, Seoul, Korea, pp. 1281–1286 (1999)
9. Gustafson, E., Kessel, W.: Fuzzy clustering with a fuzzy covariance matrix. In: Proc. of IEEE CDC (1979)
10. Gath, I., Geva, A.B.: Unsupervised optimal fuzzy clustering. IEEE Transactions on Pattern Analysis and Machine Intelligence, 773–781 (1989)
11. Krishnapuram, R., Keller, J.M.: Fuzzy and Possibilistic Clustering Methods for Computer Vision. In: Mitra, S., Gupta, M., Kraske, W. (eds.) Neural and Fuzzy Systems, S. SPIE Institute Series, vol. IS 12, pp. 133–159 (1994)
12. Krishnapuram, R., Keller, J.M.: A possibilistic approach to clustering. IEEE Transactions on Fuzzy Systems 1(2), 98–110 (1993)
13. Murayama, T., Ohara, Y., Obuchi, M., Khabar, K.S., Higashi, H., Mukaida, N., Matsushima, K.: Human cytomegalovirus induces interleukin-8 production by a human monocytic cell line, THP-1, through acting concurrently on AP-1- and NF-kappa B-binding sites of the interleukin-8 gene. J. Virol. 71, 5692–5695 (1997)

Association Rule Mining for the Identification of Activators from Gene Regulatory Network

Seema More, M. Vidya, N. Sujana, and H.D. Soumya

Department of Computer Science & Engineering
M S Ramaiah Institute of Technology
Bangalore
seemashedole@yahoo.co.in

Abstract. Recent advances in Microarray technologies have encouraged to extract gene regulatory network from microarray data in order to understand the gene regulation (in terms of activators and inhibitors) from time-series gene expression patterns in a cell. The concept of positive and negative co-regulated gene clusters (pncgc)[1] Association Rule Mining is used to analyze the gene expression data that more accurately reflects the co-regulations of genes than the existing methods which are computationally expensive.

Experiments were performed with Saccharomyces cerevisiae and Homo Sapiens dataset through which semi co-regulated gene clusters and positive and negative co-regulated gene clusters were extracted. The resulting semi co-regulated gene clusters were used in inferring a gene regulatory network which was compared with large scale regulatory network inferred from modified association rule mining algorithm. The usage of positive and negative co-regulated gene cluster approach of identifying the network outperformed the modified association rule mining [2], especially when analyzing large numbers of genes.

Keywords: Association rule mining; Gene regulatory network; Precision threshold; Frequency threshold.

1 Introduction

A DNA microarray is a high-throughput technology used to represent hundreds of thousands of genes simultaneously. Such high-throughput experimental data have initiated research on large-scale gene expression data analysis. Recent research advances have encouraged to extract gene regulatory network from such time-series data in order to reveal the pattern of gene regulation (in terms of activation and inhibition) process by examining gene expression pattern. Various data mining techniques have been applied to identify the interactions between the genes.

Association rule mining has been applied to uncover gene networks in bioinformatics. An association rule is of the form LHS => RHS where LHS and RHS are sets of genes and conditions, and the RHS set is likely to occur whenever the LHS set occurs. Association rules can describe how the expression of one gene may be associated with the expression of a set of genes; given such a rule exists, we can easily infer that the genes involved participate in some kind of gene networks.

A. Abraham et al. (Eds.): ACC 2011, Part I, CCIS 190, pp. 361–370, 2011.

Association rules can be used to relate the expression of genes to their cellular environment.

For example, association rules can help to detect cancer genes, especially when the cancer is caused by a set of genes acting together instead of a single gene. While association rules provide insights into gene expression analysis, there are several limitations with the existing techniques.

First, existing techniques determine rules based on the magnitude of the expression data which may not adequately capture co-regulation.

Second, existing association rule mining algorithms employ the 'support–confidence' framework, i.e. an expression LHS → RHS is a rule if Probability(LHS U RHS) and Probability(RHS|LHS) are above certain user-specified support and confidence threshold values, respectively. As such, the algorithms are very sensitive to the values of support and confidence that are set—too small a support–confidence pair of values will lead to too many rules and too large a pair of values will lead to too few rules. More importantly, under the support–confidence framework, rules may be generated that involve uncorrelated genes that have high support. Moreover, the rules generated do not consider the negative implication.

For example, a rule 'when gene A is highly expressed, both genes B and C are highly expressed' may not be useful if genes B and C remained highly expressed even if gene A is highly repressed. In addition, interesting **rules** may be missed out because the support for the genes may be too low to be picked out.

Analysis of gene expression data can provide insights into the positive and negative co-regulation of genes. However, existing association rule mining methods are computationally expensive and the quality and quantities of the rules are sensitive to the support and confidence values which is one of its limitations when applied to analysis of gene expression data. Therefore we use the concept of positive and negative co-regulated gene cluster (PNCGC) that describes genes of the same or opposite changing tendency on expression values under a set of conditions/samples shifts. PNCGCs consider both the positive and negative implications of gene regulations under certain conditions which accurately reflect the co-regulation of genes. By considering the negative implications, PNCGCs greatly reduce the redundant rules generated by the 'support-confidence' framework, and hence deliver more valuable regulation information of gene network. The general purpose of gene regulatory network analysis is to extract pronounced gene regulatory features (e.g., activation and inhibition) by examining gene expression patterns. Many components in regulatory networks are involved in pathological processes such as diabetes and cancer. Thorough analysis of regulatory networks provide a better understanding of the mechanism of these diseases and will help in the development of diagnosis methods, selection of gene therapy candidates, and help is designing the appropriate drug.

In this paper concept of semi-cgcs and pncgs[1] is adopted. The results of semi-cgcs are used to infer a gene regulatory network for the Yeast and Homo Sapiens datasets. These gene regulatory networks (GRNs) are compared with that of the ones derived using modified association rule mining algorithm (MAR).

The remainder of the paper is organized as follows. Section 2 deals with the related work. Section 3 deals with the methodology used in analyzing the gene expression data. Section 4 deals with the understanding of gene regulatory networks. Section 5 presents the analysis of results. The paper is concluded in Section 6 by dealing with the conclusion and future enhancements.

2 Related Work

Analysis of gene expression data can provide insights into the positive and negative co-regulation of genes. Previous works on gene expression association rule mining are mostly based on the 'support–confidence' framework. The Apriori algorithm was adopted in [9] with some additional criteria, such as extracting frequent itemsets larger than size of seven, to narrow the search space of candidate itemsets. Even so, tens of thousands of frequent itemsets were extracted out, many of which were redundant, and it is still very time-and-memory consuming to generate rules from such large number of itemsets. A manual search was done with the itemsets that seemed to be closed (itemsets that were not subsets of some larger itemsets), based on which rules were finally extracted. [1] Adopted the Peano Count Tree (P-tree) to efficiently calculate the support and confidence by a high-order bit first and a single attribute first approach. Those methods of setting additional criteria to prune the itemsets before and after applying Apriori helps to narrow the vast majority of frequent itemsets to some extent; however, since the relations of gene expression data are very complicated and there is little Apriori knowledge about the gene network, it is a great challenge for researchers to set the proper criteria.

The temporal and spatial coordination of gene expression patterns is the complex integration of regulatory signals at the promoter of the target gene. Numerous techniques are proposed to infer gene regulatory networks, such as Boolean Networks [6][7], Bayesian networks [7][8], differential equations and evolutionary algorithms.

The earlier models proposed for learning gene regulatory networks from microarray data were discrete models. Several studies proposed to construct Boolean regulatory networks in which the gene expression levels were represented as 0 (not expressed) or 1 (expressed) [5]. These models are based on the assumption that biological networks can be represented by binary, synchronously updating switching networks. However, large amounts of information might be lost during binary discretization.

3 Mining Positive and Negative Co-related Gene Clusters

We discuss here the concept of semi-cgcs and pngs from [1] which is later used in the inference of gene regulatory network. Let E(G, A) denote the expression value of a gene G at condition A. A set of genes G = {G1,G2, . . . ,Gi } is said to behave in the same way under conditions A1 and A2 if

$\forall$ G $\in$ G, E(G,A1) > E(G,A2)
or $\forall$ G $\in$ G, E(G,A1) < E(G,A2)

Two genes G1 and G2 are considered to behave in the opposite manner under conditions A1 and A2 if

(E(G1,A1) > E(G1,A2) and E(G2,A1)<E(G2,A2)) (1)

Or

(E(G1,A1) < E(G1,A2) and E(G2,A1) > E(G2,A2))

A positive co-regulated gene cluster (PCGC) has the form
(G1,G2, . . . ,Gi)@(A1A2,A3A6, . . . ,AxAy)

which means that genes G1,G2, . . . ,Gi , have the same changing tendency [satisfies Equation (1)] under the conditions {(A1,A2), (A3,A6), . . . , (Ax ,Ay)}.

On the other hand, a negative co-regulated gene cluster (NCGC) has the form
(G1 : G2, . . . , Gi) @(A1A2,A3A6, . . . ,AxAy)

which means that for any gene G Є {G2, . . . , Gi }, G1 and G behave in an opposite manner [satisfies Equation (2)] under the conditions {(A1,A2), (A3,A6), . . . , (Ax , Ay)}.

The algorithm comprises three phases. In the first phase, the gene expression matrix is transformed into a larger matrix that captures the pair-wise conditions changing tendency. In the second phase, the semi-coregulated gene clusters (Semi-CGCs) are extracted. Finally, in phase three, PNCGCs are generated.

The algorithm proposed in this paper to extract PNCGC comprises 3 phases:

Phase1: Gene expression matrix is transformed.
Phase2: Semi co-regulated gene clusters are extracted.
Phase3: PNCGCs are generated.

- ***Phase 1: Matrix transformation***

The gene expression data can be represented as a O = n × m matrix, where entry Oi,j in this matrix corresponds to the value of gene I on attribute Aj

In this phase, matrix O is transformed and binned into O' = n × [m × (m − 1)]/2.
The matrix O' is obtained in two steps. In the first step, O is transformed into O″ = n×[m×(m−1)]/2 matrix by using the following conditions

$$O''_{i,kj} = \begin{cases} \frac{O_{i,j}-O_{i,k}}{|O_{i,k}|} & \text{if } O_{i,k} \neq 0, \\ 1 & \text{if } O_{i,k} = 0 \text{ and } O_{i,j} > 0, \\ -1 & \text{if } O_{i,k} = 0 \text{ and } O_{i,j} < 0, \\ 0 & \text{if } O_{i,k} = 0 \text{ and } O_{i,j} = 0. \end{cases}$$

In step2 we set a normalization threshold t(t > 0) to bin the O" matrix to get binned O' matrix as follows

$$O''_{i,kj} = \begin{cases} 1 & \text{if } O''_{i,kj} \geq t, \\ -1 & \text{if } O''_{i,kj} \leq -t, \\ 0 & \text{otherwise.} \end{cases}$$

Thus the matrix O' reflects the changing tendencies of gene expression values in different conditions or tissues.

- ***Phase 2: extraction of semi-co-regulated gene clusters Semi-CGCs***

It considers only half of the implication of gene regulations under certain situations delivering information such as 'when a certain gene increases or decreases, what changing tendency the other genes may display accordingly'. In order to extract these Semi-CGCs we set two thresholds:

Frequency threshold - The lowest permitted percentage of Gene i's increasing (or decreasing) status with respect to Gene i's whole status

Precision threshold - The lowest permitted percentage of status when Gene i increases (or decreases) that the corresponding GeneX also increases (or decreases), with respect to Gene i's whole increasing (or decreasing) status, which is the conditional probability. The extracted Semi-CGCs will be in four basic forms.

- ***Phase 3: Generation of the PNCGCs***

The forms (1) and (3) are combined and forms (2) and (4) are combined.

4 Gene Regulatory Networks

The purpose of gene regulatory network analysis is to extract gene regulatory features (e.g., activation and inhibition) by examining gene expression patterns. Changes of expression levels of genes across different samples provide information that allows reverse engineering techniques to construct the network of regulatory relations among those genes. Data-driven regulatory network analysis would eventually lead to better understanding of the complex genetic regulatory process, which has important implications in the pharmaceutical industry and many other biomedical fields.

Many components in regulatory networks are involved in pathological processes such as diabetes and cancer. Detail studies of regulatory networks provide a better understanding of the mechanism of these diseases and will help in the development of diagnosis methods, selection of gene therapy candidates, and innovating new drug therapy. For instance, the strategy for new cancer drug searching has shifted from finding chemicals that kill tumor cells towards identifying molecular targets that lie at the level of cell transformation. The latter approach relies on deeper understanding of the regulatory processes and involves promises to discover more effective and safer drugs. Gene regulatory network analysis, may not directly help researchers in identifying markers for disease diagnosis and providing drug target, but may provide new insights in basic genetic research to understand the mechanism of gene regulation pathways and ultimately achieve an understanding of the genetic regulatory process, which provides the foundation for applications in disease diagnosis and drug design.

5 Analysis of Results

The PNCGC algorithm gives us straight forward results by finding the activation and inhibition relationship types among the genes involved. i.e, these results in the form of semi-cgcs can be used to infer the gene regulatory networks.

The algorithm was run for different values of frequency threshold (Ft) and precision threshold (Pt) .The frequency threshold is always set to 0% in the algorithm to avoid missing the low–frequency clusters while precision threshold set as 40%,60% and 80% co-ordinates the precision degree and permit slight abnormal cases and PNCGs extracted are shown in tables 1 and 2.

Table 1. Threshold values for Saccharomyces cerevisiae dataset

Algorithm	Ft	Pt	Rules
PNCGC1	0%	40%	11
PNCGC2	0%	60%	7
PNCGC3	0%	80%	2

Table 2. Threshold values for Homo Sapiens dataset

Algorithm	Ft	Pt	Rules
PNCGC1	0%	40%	2
PNCGC2	0%	60%	2
PNCGC3	0%	80%	2

From this result we can see obviously that although the PNCGC lowers the frequency threshold to 0% and considers all the low-frequency clusters, the number of resulting clusters is still manageable and in cases of Homo Sapiens dataset number of cluster formed is constant as only 3 attributes/conditions are taken into consideration and there is no much difference in there expression values under those conditions hence the clusters formed is constant.

- ***Performance of PNCGCs Algorithm for Saccharomyces cerevisiae dataset***

Semi-CGCs were extracted using PNCGCs algorithm and were tested for different values of frequency threshold (Ft) and precision thresholds (Pt) (Table 3).

The value of Ft and Pt with which the best performance was achieved was selected.

Table 3. Evaluation results of PNCGCs Algorithm

Ft	Pt	Activation	Inhibition
0	0.5	24	0
0	0.6	25	1
0	0.7	26	2

With Ft=0.0 and Pt= 0.7, best performance was achieved.

- ***Performance of PNCGCs Algorithm forHomosapiens dataset***

Semi-CGCs were extracted using PNCGCs algorithm and were tested for different values of frequency threshold (Ft) and precision thresholds (Pt) (Table 4). The value of Ft and Pt with which the best performance was achieved was selected.

Table 4. Evaluation results of PNCGCs Algorithm

Ft	Pt	Activation	Inhibition
0	0.5	18	6
0	0.6	14	6
0	0.7	10	2

With Ft= 0.0and Pt=0.5, best performance was achieved.

- ***Comparison with MAR algorithm***

We took a subset of particular genes present in gene regulatory network inferred by modified association rule mining algorithm [2] as it is the only paper published till date to infer Gene regulatory network based on association rule and compared with the Gene regulatory network inferred from the semi-CGCs extracted from PNCGCs algorithm as shown by the figures 1, 2, 3 and 4. Table 5 shows the evaluation results.

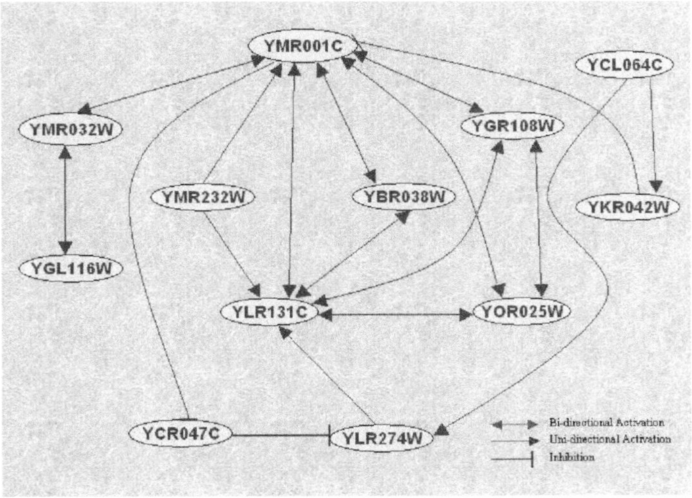

Fig. 1. Gene regulatory network from PNCGCs algorithm for Homosapiens dataset

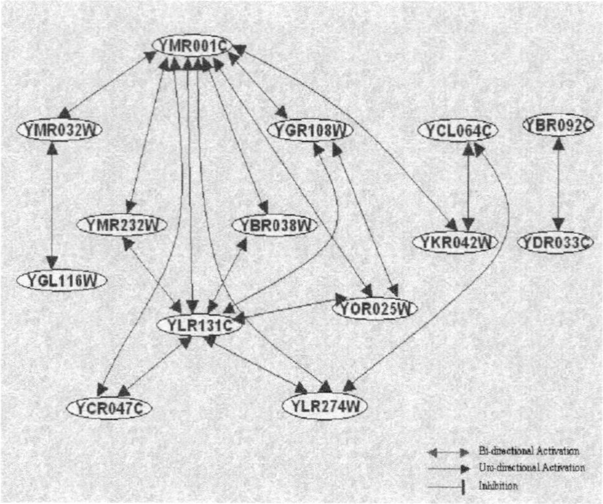

Fig. 2. Gene regulatory network from MAR algorithm for Homosapiens dataset

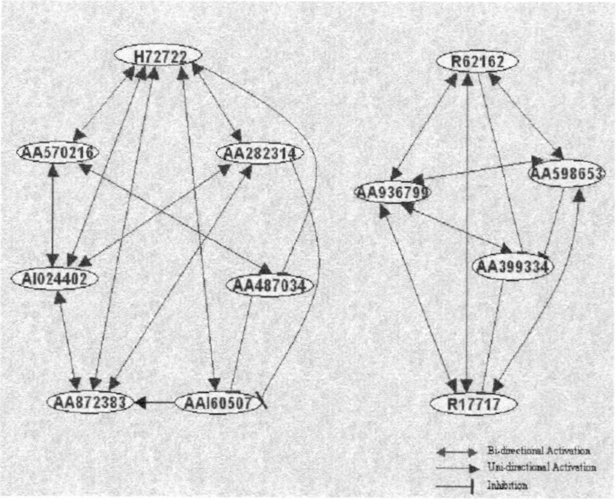

Fig. 3. Gene regulatory network from PNCGCs algorithm for Saccharomyces cerevisiae

Table 5. Evaluation results

Algorithm	Activation	Inhibition
MAR_human	17(85%)	3(15%)
MAR_yeast	20(100%)	0(0%)
PNCGCs_human	18(75%)	6(25%)

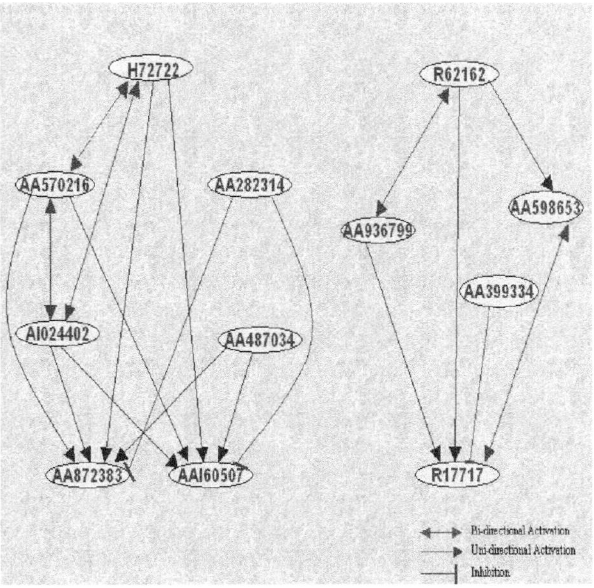

Fig. 4. Gene regulatory network from MAR algorithm for Saccharomyces cerevisiae dataset

6 Conclusion and Future Enhancements

PNCGC captures the pair-wise conditions' changing tendency. It considers both positive and negative implications and generates more number of activation and inhibition relationship types, greatly reducing the redundant rules generated by 'support –confidence' framework.

Compared with modified association rule mining algorithm (MAR), PNCGCs deliver more reliable, explicit and closer relations among genes along with their conditions. Our general conclusion is that regulatory network analysis on microarray data can capture large portions of underlying regulatory structures. A longer-term future direction of this work is to assess the real value of the large-scale rough genetic regulatory networks learned from small sample-size gene expression data by systematic long term user studies that involve researchers using such networks in their daily research activities. Another important practical extension of our research is to integrate the core algorithm development into an interactive gene regulatory network analysis and visualization system, which allows the users to input microarray datasets and manipulate the algorithms and results by interactively setting the domain-dependent algorithmic and visualization parameters.

Acknowledgments

We are thankful Soumya, Sujana and Vidya for their contribution towards the implementation. We would like to thank the authors of [1] and [2] for providing us with the datasets.

References

1. Ji, L., Tan, K.-L.: Mining gene expression data for positive and negative co-regulated gene clusters (May 14, 2004)
2. Huang, Z., Watts, G.S.: Large-scale regulatory network analysis from micro-array data: modified Bayesian network learning and association rule mining (April 2006)
3. Karel, F., Kléma, J.: Quantitative association rule mining in genomics using apriori knowledge, Department of cybernetics, Czech Technical University in Prague, Technická 2, Praha 6, 166 27 karelf1@fel.cvut.cz, klema@labe.felk.cvut.cz
4. Han, J., Kamber, M.: Data Mining Concepts and Techniques, 2nd edn. Morgan Kaufmann Publishers, San Francisco
5. Liang, S., Fuhrman, S., Somogyi, R.: REVEAL, a general reverse engineering algorithm for inference of genetic network architectures. In: Proceedings of the Pacific Symposium on Biocomputing, pp. 18–29 (1998)
6. Tang, B., Wu, X., Tan, G., Chen, S.-S., Jing, Q., Shen, B.: Computational inference and analysis of genetic regulatory networks via a supervised combinatorial-optimization pattern. In: Third Internation Symposium on Optimization and System Biology, Zhangjiajie, China, September 20-22 (2009)
7. Hickman, G.J., Charlie Hodgman, T.: Inference of gene regulatory networks using boolean-network inference methods. Journal of Bioinformatics and Computational Biology 7(6), 1013–1029 (2009)
8. Ko, Y., Zhai, C., Rodriguez-Zas, S.: Inference of gene pathways using mixture Bayesian networks. BMC Systems Biology (May 2009)
9. Creighton, C., Hanash, S.: Mining gene expression databases for association rules. Bioinformatics 19(1), 79–86 (2003)

MPI Performance Analysis of Amazon EC2 Cloud Services for High Performance Computing

Florian Schatz, Sven Koschnicke, Niklas Paulsen,
Christoph Starke, and Manfred Schimmler

Department of Computer Science, Christian-Albrechts-Universitaet zu Kiel,
Hermann-Rodewald-Strasse 3, Kiel, Germany
mail@florianschatz.de, svk@informatik.uni-kiel.de

Abstract. Cloud computing offers a highly scalable infrastructure for high performance computing. Using the Amazon EC2 Cloud service, it is possible to get a set of computing instances on demand without requiring a lot of maintenance and financial resources a common cluster would need. The drawback for communicational intensive algorithms is, that the distribution of the instances is arbitrary and the communication speed might vary a lot which might affect the overall speed of the algorithms significantly.

We present a benchmark for cloud computing on EC2 using the MPI to measure communication speeds of a set of cloud instances. This benchmark can visualize the actual network infrastructure. By adapting the measured data to the algorithms constraints it can help to manage the distribution of tasks to cloud instances to get an optimal distribution concerning network communication speeds.

Keywords: High Performance Computing; Cloud Computing; MPI; Communication Benchmark.

1 Background and Introduction

Scientific research projects and complex software solutions usually have algorithmic parts, where small sections of an algorithm consume the main fraction of all computational resources. To speed these routines up, high performance computing with clusters or special purpose hardware can be used. Unfortunately, these have the disadvantage of requiring a lot of maintenance and financial resources, while the tasks often do not occur continuously. For these applications, the integration of cloud computing is very reasonable, because a high number of computational resources can be obtained instantly while paying only for the time consumed. In addition to the saved resources, this approach supports the green IT paradigm.

There are already a lot of scientific applications designed to be run on cloud computing services, such as Amazon EC2 [2,4,6,8].

As cloud computing has only recently become concerned with algorithms, there is a huge number of possible optimizations, because this new technology

A. Abraham et al. (Eds.): ACC 2011, Part I, CCIS 190, pp. 371–381, 2011.

brings new challenges with it. Using cloud computing means working on an unknown physical network topology and different communication schemes can result in extremely different performances in communication speeds or latency, even when running the same computations a second time on new instances.

While an abstraction layer exists with MPI, this layer does not offer an automatic or semi-automatic optimization for communication schemes if deployed in a cloud environment. This is, however, very important, especially for working on a cloud.

Our examinations also showed a correlation between physical location and internal IP-address in the amazon cloud, which was assumed by others [7] and can lead to better network performance estimates in the future.

In this work, we propose a benchmark for cloud computing services and offer a freely available implementation of this benchmark. This benchmark can help manage the distribution of tasks to cloud instances to get an optimal distribution concerning network communication speeds. Our benchmark measures average communication speeds, the variance and min/max values. It also offers a graphical display of these, which helps the user to get a fast overview of whether the instances are usable for a particular computing task. The user may then react accordingly.

2 Methods

Working on an unknown network infrastructure can result in many complications. A set of EC2 spot instances, for example, can be located in different data centers so that the physical distance can result in different communication latencies. The location within a datacenter is arbitrary, while spot instances can be on the same machine as well. Furthermore, the problem of noisy neighbors can affect communication. These are instances within the same routing level, e.g., virtual machines on the same system or another system within the same physical location that are very communication intensive. As resources are shared, these neighbors can greatly affect the own communication pattern. Finally, the physical distance increases from a certain amount of instances as there are limits on physical space. This too affects latency.

To get an objective view of interconnections we created a tool that measures the maximum communication speeds as well as maximum throughput for larger data sets.

2.1 Testing Communication Speeds

The problem of measuring communication speed is complex due to the unknown and unpredictable communication behavior of the surrounding machines (neighbors) and the unknown physical distance between instances which result in varying communication speeds. Other factors are changing hardware on which an instance runs which may also impact communication speeds due to different processing speeds and I/O performance. We propose for practical application, a maximum duration of two minutes for the performance analysis as this is within the booting time instances need. This ensures that the analysis can be run before the actual computation task starts and adjustments to the communication schemes can be made based on the performance analysis. All presented tools can be modified to run for a longer time and get more constant results.

We use a $N \times N$ communication scheme where all instances apply speed tests individually to all other instances. This is done by randomly and equally choosing a neighbor and sending a message of a previously defined size s for r repeats. Furthermore, this procedure is run c times to get timely measurements with more distant and a better mean value over the measured time.

To counter routing maps we run the test for $r = 1$.

From the collected data, mean values $\mu_{i,j}$ and standard deviation $\sigma_{i,j}$ for all pairs of instances are calculated and output. If $\sigma_{i,j}$ exceeds a threshold σ_m, a warning is output as the measurement is not precise enough for the time frame of the measurement.

2.2 Implementation of Speed Tests

For running the tests on Amazon EC2 we chose a 32bit Fedora Linux image created by the author of the management scripts that we are using for deployment [9]. The installed MPI implementation is MPICH2, version 1.0.5 [3].

The deploy script (`ec2-mpi-config.py`) searches for all instances with the same AMI-ID and creates the needed MPI-configuration (a file mpd.hosts with the hostnames of all found instances) on the master node (the first instance found is chosen as the master node). SSH keys are also distributed to all client nodes. Then, the benchmark program is compiled and executed on the master node using `mpicc` and `mpirun`, which distributes the program to all client nodes and gathers execution results. The benchmark program is run multiple times with different parameters for message size, number of runs and number of repeats per run by the launch script.

Listing 1.1. Benchmark program

```
read own identity (zone and node name)
figure out nodetype (master or slave)
if nodetype is master
  generate pairings
  send pairings to slaves
  send parameters to slaves
    (message size, number of runs and repeats per run)
if nodetype is slave
  receive pairings
  receive parameters
for n runs do
  for m repeats do
    measure time to send message using MPI_Wtime()
if nodetype is slave
  send timing data to master
```

```
if nodetype is master
  receive timing data from all slaves
  generate reports from data
```

The actual benchmark program is written in C using MPI and performs the following steps (see also Listing 1.1): First, the own identity and given parameters are read. Then, the master node generates pairings for the runs (see 2.1 above) and sends them together with the parameters for message size, number of runs and number of repeats to the client nodes. All nodes now perform the message sending and receiving benchmarks for the determined number of runs and repeats per run, using `MPI_Wtime()` to measure the time a message takes to travel from the sending to the receiving node. After all tests are finished, the recorded benchmark data is sent back to the master node, which generates a report and sends it back to the user.

2.3 Analysis of Results

Results can be written to the users terminal in two modes. The standard mode gives only a table with average sending speeds between all nodes (see Figure 2), the verbose mode gives tables for average speeds, minimal speeds, maximum speeds and standard deviation. Because of the textual representation, these results can be both easily read by humans or processed further by other programs. Based on the processing, it can be decided if the given nodes are suitable for the task and how the task should be distributed for optimal performance.

2.4 Graphical Display

To make it easier for users to identify the quality of connectivity in the given set of nodes, the results can also be shown as a graph where communication speed is shown by the length of the edges connecting two nodes (see Figure 1). The graph is defined in textual Graphviz format [1] and rendered using Neato [5], which runs a heuristic algorithm to distribute the nodes of the graph based on the given edge lengths. This lets the user identify slow nodes and clusters of nodes with high communication speeds.

2.5 Appling Performance Tests

To run the actual benchmark, we created an Amazon Web Services account and registered for the EC2 service. The account data together with the ID of the virtual machine image to be used was written into a configuration file (`EC2config.py`). The source code of the benchmark program as described above was put into the `programs` directory. We configured the parameters to be used to execute the benchmark in the file `program.config`. The syntax of the configuration allows for specifying the combinations of parameters very easily, for example, the line

```
benchmark.c 3000 [1|2|5]
```

will compile the program which source code is found in `programs/benchmark.c` and execute the binary three times with the arguments `3000 1`, `3000 2` and `3000 5`. After this configuration is done, we started the benchmarking by calling the script `ec2-start-cluster.py` and entering the desired number of instances to use when prompted. When using this script, only normal instances are used. For using spot instances, these have to be requested before in the Amazon management console and instead of `ec2-start-cluster.py` we have to use

```
ec2-notifier -m <MIN> -c './ec2-mpi-config.py'
```

to start the benchmarking after `<MIN>` instances were found. When not using spot instances, a simple call of `ec2-mpi-config.py` suffices.

Results are written in the `logs` directory after completion of the benchmark. As long as the started instances are not stopped by calling `ec2-stop-cluster.py`, new versions of the program can be run by modifying the program source or the parameters and calling `runProgrs.py -n -g`.

3 Results and Discussion

We performed a series of different use cases for performance evaluations.

3.1 Instances from One Zone

The most common use case is probably requesting EC2 instances from one availability zone to perform a computational task. One would expect a set of instances with an almost equal interconnection speed. Our results show that instances from one zone can have significantly varying communication speeds.

As Figure 1 and 2 show, node 10 is further apart from other nodes than the remaining nodes. Having an algorithm that has to communicate a lot with node 10, and other nodes with a bad interconnection might significantly affect the total runtime.

3.2 Normal Instances from Different Zones

Requiring instances from EC2 one can select the zone of availability required. Amazon offers different availability zones, which can be used for instances that are independent from each other. If requiring instances from one zone, e.g., us-east-1a, instances from exactly this zone are created. One might request instances from different zones to increase reliability by using independent parts of a data center.

Our test confirms that interconnections between instances from one zone are significantly faster than to instances from other zones. Figures 3 and 4 illustrate this.

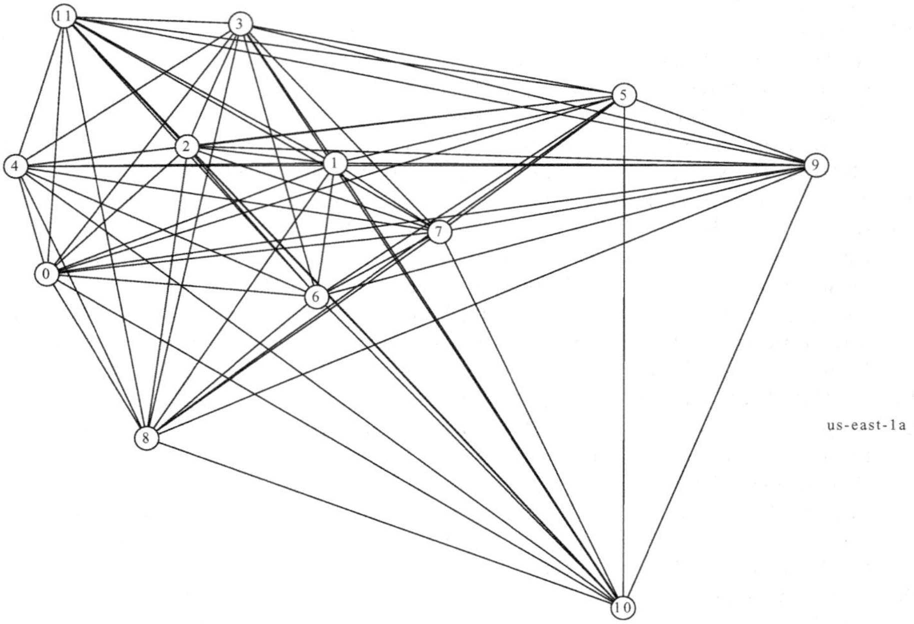

Fig. 1. Graphic display of 12 normal instances requested from EC2 from one availability zone. A node represents an instance, an edge between two nodes has a length which relates to the latency measured by the performance test. Clusters of instances with fast interconnection can be easily identified by the user.

Speed [s]:

	1	2	3	4	5	6	7	8	9	10	11
0	0.0209	0.0172	0.0323	0.0677	0.0243	0.0185	0.0149	0.0257	0.0364	0.0509	0.0325
1		0.0150	0.0319	0.0335	0.0205	0.0158	0.0153	0.0297	0.0242	0.0432	0.0312
2			0.0334	0.0244	0.0239	0.0197	0.0216	0.0218	0.0352	0.0405	0.0403
3				0.0344	0.0298	0.0283	0.0257	0.0309	0.0271	0.0566	0.0260
4					0.0296	0.0502	0.0273	0.0368	0.0317	0.0499	0.0350
5						0.0226	0.0266	0.0350	0.0339	0.0464	0.0347
6							0.0179	0.0294	0.0270	0.0390	0.0313
7								0.0231	0.0324	0.0494	0.0257
8									0.0388	0.0553	0.0366
9										0.0545	0.0323
10											0.0496
11											

Fig. 2. Speed table of 12 instances requested from EC2 within one zone. Every entry describes the median time in seconds it took for a message to travel from one instance to another. Message size was 102400 bytes, sending of a message between two instances where repeated five times and the whole test was repeated 25 times.

3.3 Spot Instances

Spot instances are EC2 instances that are requested without a timely constraint, but with a certain limit of cost per hour. These instances are then made available, as soon as the demand and bids compared to the request decrease. The requested instances might be in different zones.

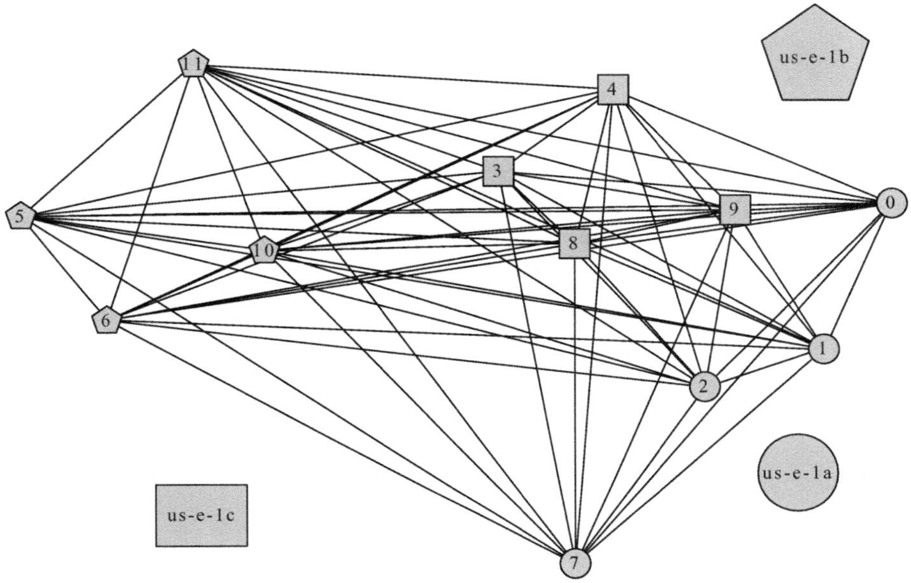

Fig. 3. Graphic display of 12 normal instances requested from EC2 from three different availability zones. The chosen zones where us-east-1a, us-east-1b and us-east-1c. The form of the node shows to which zone the represented instance belongs.

Speed [s]:

	1	2	3	4	5	6	7	8	9	10	11
0	0.0053	0.0068	0.0147	0.0146	0.0274	0.0267	0.0141	0.0153	0.0164	0.0287	0.0290
1		0.0034	0.0120	0.0134	0.0246	0.0248	0.0086	0.0160	0.0164	0.0259	0.0250
2			0.0126	0.0153	0.0293	0.0243	0.0096	0.0162	0.0138	0.0242	0.0277
3				0.0052	0.0137	0.0168	0.0197	0.0041	0.0059	0.0166	0.0134
4					0.0147	0.0150	0.0225	0.0053	0.0063	0.0151	0.0138
5						0.0073	0.0311	0.0190	0.0171	0.0074	0.0065
6							0.0311	0.0175	0.0178	0.0069	0.0071
7								0.0217	0.0210	0.0331	0.0357
8									0.0077	0.0141	0.0182
9										0.0186	0.0178
10											0.0059

Fig. 4. 12 instances requested from EC2 from three zones. Every entry describes the median time it took for a message to travel from one instance to another. Message size was 100 bytes, sending of a message between two instances where repeated 15 times and the whole test was repeated 100 times.

For this use case, we performed several tests. In our tests, spot instances were present in 65% of the time within one zone, while in the remaining cases, instances were in different zones.

As the results from spot instances within one zone do not differ significantly for the use case of normal instance within one zone (see below), we only show the results for spot instances from different zones.

As shown in Figure 5, the latencies differ significantly first between zones and then between nodes.

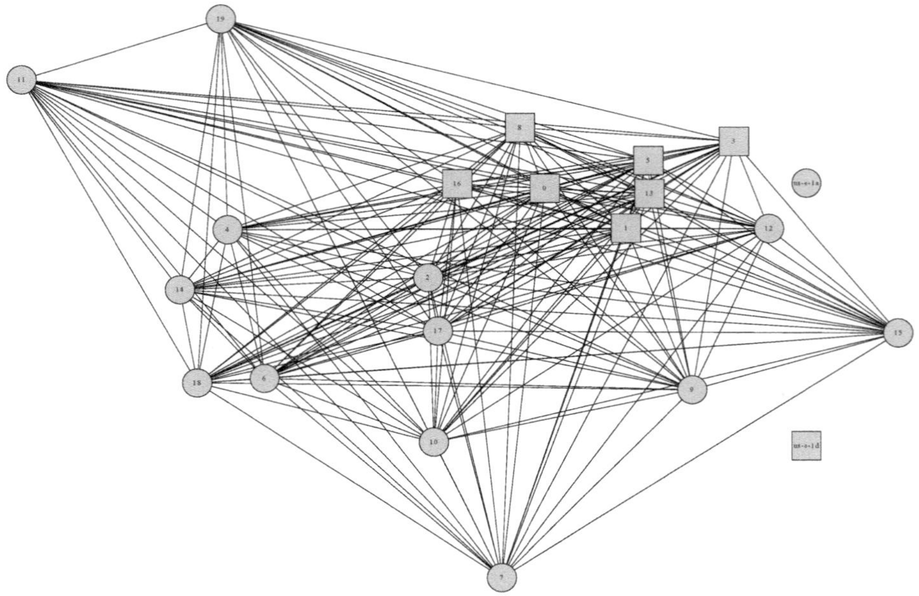

Fig. 5. Graphic display of 20 spot instances requested from EC2. In this test the instances where spread over two availability zones, us-east-1a und us-east-1d, indicated by the different form of the nodes.

These results are very important, as they show that using spot instances can result in large differences in communication speeds.

3.4 Variance of Performance Values

The average speed of an interconnection is not all that is important for high performance computing. Also important is variance (or standard deviation). An interconnection with a high variance might be as bad as an interconnection that is slow. From our test, we found that slow interconnections, as seen above, are correlated to high standard deviations, which means that there are interconnections that are not in general slow, but tend to be less reliable when fast. See Figure 6 for an example.

3.5 Consistency of Results

As our measurements reflect a short period of time only, one measurement might not be representative for a longer period of time. Circumstances like noisy neightbors might affect this.

To satisfactorily show that our statements can be applied for long term calculations, we ran our tests for a duration of 30 hours while running the described procedures every five minutes. From these measurements we took the speed matrices and calculated the average value and standard deviation for each of the $N \times N$ communications (see Figure 7).

Speed standard deviation [s]:

	1	2	3	4	5	6	7	8	9	10	11
0	0.0964	0.0452	0.0966	0.8457	0.0178	0.0415	0.0081	0.0675	0.2410	0.1289	0.0738
1		0.0355	0.0745	0.1080	0.0088	0.0159	0.0297	0.0929	0.0758	0.0760	0.0679
2			0.0969	0.0438	0.0324	0.0627	0.0826	0.0438	0.2060	0.0450	0.0977
3				0.0814	0.0528	0.0749	0.0548	0.0515	0.0556	0.0953	0.0595
4					0.0468	0.3716	0.0683	0.0789	0.0718	0.0679	0.0800
5						0.0111	0.0939	0.0636	0.0778	0.0201	0.0636
6							0.0549	0.0703	0.0528	0.0769	0.0715
7								0.0565	0.0985	0.1028	0.0607
8									0.0860	0.1449	0.0703
9										0.0888	0.0824
10											0.0669
11											

Fig. 6. Standard deviation for 12 instances requested from EC2. These values where computed from the results of the first performance test described in this paper, shown in Figure 1 and 2.

Standard deviation [s]:

	1	2	3	4	5	6	7	8	9	10	11
0	0.00101	0.00057	0.00064	0.00079	0.00055	0.00064	0.00059	0.00107	0.00131	0.00143	0.00135
1		0.00078	0.00082	0.00086	0.00129	0.00140	0.00099	0.00068	0.00132	0.00111	0.00109
2			0.00079	0.00070	0.00093	0.00115	0.00085	0.00079	0.00103	0.00108	0.00100
3				0.00077	0.00082	0.00098	0.00082	0.00077	0.00093	0.00085	0.00097
4					0.00076	0.00081	0.00065	0.00071	0.00064	0.00071	0.00055
5						0.00075	0.00075	0.00107	0.00088	0.00097	0.00089
6							0.00073	0.00069	0.00090	0.00169	0.00095
7								0.00059	0.00079	0.00079	0.00067
8									0.00104	0.00084	0.00077
9										0.00065	0.00060
10											0.00066
11											

Fig. 7. Standard deviation for 12 instances requested from EC2. The test was run over a period of 30 hours, executing a run every five minutes. Message size was 10 kilobytes, sending of a message between two instances where repeated 20 times and the whole test was repeated 150 times.

test 1	test 2	test 3	test 4
a: e j f k l h b g d i c	a: e g j f l k h d b i c	a: e f g j l k h b d i c	a: g j f e k l h b d i c
b: f e g j l d k c a i h	b: e g j l k f d c a h i	b: e f g j k l d c a i h	b: e f j l g k d a i c h
c: e g l f k h j b d i a	c: e g f k j h b l d i a	c: f e g j b h l k d i a	c: g f e l k h j d b a i
d: g f j e b k l a i h c	d: e h g k f a b j l i c	d: f e g b l j h i a k c	d: g f e j h k b l a i c
e: g j a f k b h l c d i	e: f b l j d g c k i a h	e: f b k g l h a j c i d	e: g f b j k l c h a d i
f: e b g j h k i d c l a	f: e h g j k b i c a l d	f: e g h b d j k c i l a	f: g e k b j h d c l a i
g: j e d k f h b i c l a	g: k e f j b l i d c a h	g: e f h j b l k c i a d	g: f i d e k a l c h j b
h: f g j e l k a c d i b	h: f k l j d e g a c i b	h: f g e j k l a d c i b	h: j k f g e l c a d i b
i: g f j e l k d b h c a	i: e j f g l k d h b c a	i: f j e g l k d h b c a	i: g k e f l h j b d a c
j: g e f h l b k d i a c	j: e g f b i h k l a c d	j: k g f h b i e a c d l	j: e a h b f g l k d c i
k: g e f j h l c b a i d	k: g e f b l h j a d c i	k: e j f l g h b a i d c	k: g f h e j c l i b a d
l: j e g h c b i k f a d	l: e b k h g j a f i d c	l: e g k f h b a d j i c	l: g b e j f c k h a i d

Fig. 8. Neighbors ordered by connection speed over multiple timely distant tests. For better visibility, groups of instances are colored differently. While there are differences in the ordering of instances, fast connections are relatively constant over time.

As these results show, our measurements can be applied for a long time computations.

Furthermore, we performed a timely stretched measurement of the same set of instances over an interval of one hour. In intervals of 15 minutes we performed the same benchmark and measured almost constant speeds. Only small variances where found which might be a result of noisy neighbors (see above). Anyhow, the variances were insignificant for the overall distribution. Figure 8 shows the order of fastest neighbors for each instance.

4 Discussion and Conclusions

We presented a tool to measure communication speeds between a set of instances requested from EC2. Our results show that actual instances set communication vary a lot in speed. Communication between zones is, as expected, generally slower than within one zone while on the other hand speed within one zone can be very slow in single cases, too. These tools can help adapt algorithms to the actual network communication structure before running them to increase speed. To improve the results, supplemental data like the internal IP-address of an instance can be used to get more information about the physical location of the instance [7].

5 Availability

The implementation is public available at http://www.informatik.uni-kiel.de/~fsch/cloud

6 Future Work

Further work will be an MPI and EC2 independent implementation as a C library. Furthermore, we plan to add functionalities to output a suggestion of distributing nodes to a given communication scheme. This could be used before running a program to adjust to the current network interconnection state.

References

1. Ellson, J., Gansner, E.R., Koutsofios, E., North, S.C., Woodhull, G.: Graphviz - Open Source Graph Drawing Tools. Graph Drawing, 483–484 (2001)
2. Evangelinos, C., Lermusiaux, P.F.J., Xu, J., Haley, P.J., Hill, C.N.: Many task computing for multidisciplinary ocean sciences: real-time uncertainty prediction and data assimilation. In: Proceedings of the 2nd Workshop on Many-Task Computing on Grids and Supercomputers, MTAGS 2009, pp. 14:1–14:10. ACM, New York (2009)
3. Gropp, W.D.: MPICH2: A new start for MPI implementations. In: Kranzlmüller, D., Kacsuk, P., Dongarra, J., Volkert, J. (eds.) PVM/MPI 2002. LNCS, vol. 2474, pp. 37–42. Springer, Heidelberg (2002)
4. Langmead, B.T.: Highly Scalable Short Read Alignment with the Burrows-Wheeler Transform and Cloud Computing. PhD thesis (2009)
5. North, S.C.: Drawing graphs with neato. NEATO User Manual (April 26, 2004)
6. Pallickara, S.L., Pierce, M., Dong, Q., Kong, C.: Enabling large scale scientific computations for expressed sequence tag sequencing over grid and cloud computing clusters. In: PPAM 2009 Eigth International Conference on Parallel Processing and Applied Mathematics, pp. 13–16 (2009)

7. Ristenpart, T., Tromer, E., Savage, S.: Hey, You, Get Off of My Cloud: Exploring Information Leakage in Third-Party Compute Clouds. In: Artificial Intelligence (2009)
8. Schatz, M.C.: CloudBurst: highly sensitive read mapping with MapReduce.. Bioinformatics 25(11), 1363–1369 (2009)
9. Skomoroch, P.: Mpi cluster with python and amazon ec2 (2009), `http://www.datawrangling.com/mpi-cluster-with-python-and-amazon-ec2-part-2-of-3`

Algorithmic Approach to Calculating Minimal Resource Allocation Recommender for Grid Using Reliability and Trust Computations

Gutha Jaya Krishna and Rajeev Wankar

University of Hyderabad, Gachibowli, Hyderabad, India
krishna.gutha@gmail.com,
wankarcs@uohyd.ernet.in

Abstract. In this paper we aim at minimally allocating resources on the grid by providing a recommender that gives us a recommendation of which allocation is a minimal resource allocation out of allocation matrices space. The recommender uses reliability, trust and search(2-way split backward search) algorithms. The resource allocation matrices are generated according to the search algorithm. The reliability and trust computations are used as factors to judge the minimal resource allocation from the resource allocation matrices generated by the 2-way split backward search algorithm[6]. Reliability is based on rate of failure of grid nodes, communication links and also on reliability of services on the grid. Trust is internally based on reputation which is overall grid service reliability and direct trust which is the availability of resources. In this work it is assumed that the arrival rate of failure of grid elements follows the Poisson process.

Keywords: Reliability, Trust, Grid Computing, Search.

1 Introduction

Grid computing system addresses the challenge of service execution on heterogeneous complex systems by resource sharing across the organizational boundaries in a cooperative way through the global communication channels like Internet[5]. The performance of computing system will be highly influenced by reliable resource allocation. In grid environment, there are multiple grid nodes, say n, called member nodes spatially distributed over large territorial area connected through global communication channel like Internet. Multiple programs/services and resources distributed over these n nodes. A node say G_i capable to execute a service say S_i that need a set of few resources say R_s. The node G_i may not hold all the resources in set R_s and deficient resources are to be fetched from other grid nodes by communication channels.[4]

When a service S_i is held by multiple nodes constituting a set say S_n and all such nodes are capable to invoke the execution of service S_i. A serious question arises that which node $G_k \in S_n$ should invoke the service S_i for possible minimal resource allocation? Similarly, when a needed resource say R_i is held by multiple

A. Abraham et al. (Eds.): ACC 2011, Part I, CCIS 190, pp. 382–398, 2011.

nodes constituting a set say R_n. A serious question arises that the executing node G_k which is deficient of resource R_i , from which node $G_l \in S_n$ the needed resource to be fetched and by using which communication channels when multiple paths available between executing node Gk and donating node G_l?

2 Resource Allocation Matrix

Service Matrix: A binary matrix representing the service capability of the nodes. For example Service Matrix 1100 means that node is capable to invoke service 1 and 2 only out of set of 4 services.

Resource Matrix: A binary matrix representing the resource possession of the nodes. For example Resource Matrix 1101 means that node possesses the resources 1, 2 & 4 only out of set of 4 resources.[1]

Generate the Resource Allocation Matrix with all possible free resources from Initial Allocation Matrix. Initial Allocation Matrix for a sample Grid Computing System is shown in Figure 1 which have four nodes capable to execute two services and having four resources. These services and resources held by different nodes are defined by service matrix and resource matrix.

Initially we take an assumption that resource allocation with all possible free resources allocated. This approach helps the search procedure to search backward.

An example is given in Figure 2 where all free resources are made available.

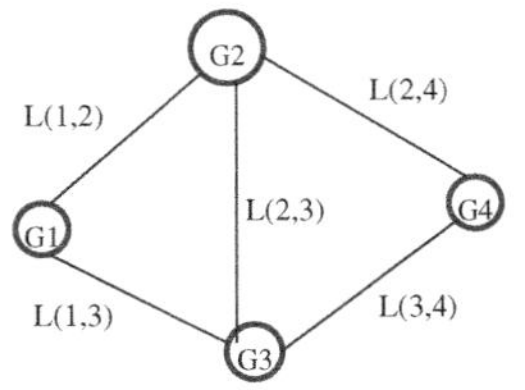

	R1	R2	R3	R4	S1	S2
G1	1	1	−1	0	1	0
G2	−1	−1	1	0	0	1
G3	−1	−1	−1	−1	0	0
G4	−1	1	−1	−1	1	0

−1 --> free(Available and Not Binded)

0 --> Not Available or Not Binded

1 --> Available and Binded

Fig. 1. Initial Allocation Matrix

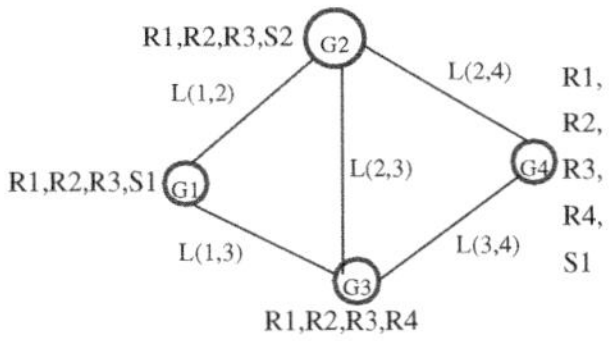

	R1	R2	R3	R4	S1	S2
G1	1	1	1	0	1	0
G2	1	1	1	0	0	1
G3	1	1	1	1	0	0
G4	1	1	1	1	1	0

Fig. 2. Initial Resource Allocation

Algorithm 1. Resource Allocation Matrix with all possible free resources

```
begin
    Initial Grid Resource Allocation GridRes
    m=0,GridResTmp=0
    for node g ∈ G(where G set of grid nodes) do
        for node r ∈ R(where R set of resources) do
            if GridRes[g][r]=-1 && m ≤ no. of free resources then
                GridResTmp[g][r]=1
                q[m]=1
                m++
            else GridResTmp[g][r]=GridRes[g][r]
```

3 Minimum Resource Spanning Tree, MRST

- **Resource Spanning Tree:** *"Resource Spanning Tree, RST, is defined as the spanning tree that connects the node that execute the given service to some other nodes such that its vertices hold all the required resources for exchanging information with the program."*

- **Minimal Resource Spanning Tree (MRST):** *"For a given program executed by given computing node an $MRST_i$ is a RST_i such that there exist no other resource spanning tree, say RST_j which is subset of RST_i ."* i.e.

$$\neg\exists : RST_j \subset RST_i$$

4 Reliability Computations[11]

The IEEE defines reliability as ". . . the ability of a system or component to perform its required functions under stated conditions for a specified period of time."[8].

4.1 Important Terms

- **L(i,j) :** Link between nodes Gi and Gj.
- **D(i,j) :** Total size of data exchanged through the link L(i,j).
- **S(i,j) :** Mean speed of data exchange through the link L(i,j).
- **T(i,j) :** D(i,j)/S(i,j), communication time between node Gi and Gj.
- λ : The rate of failure (links and nodes).

Algorithm 2. Generating possible MRST's(Minimum Resource Spanning Tree) of each service

```
begin
  for resource r ∈ R(where R set of resources) do
    if Particular Service need Resource r in R then
      for For all possible combination's k ∈ K(where K set of grid
      nodes) of g ∈ G (where G set of grid nodes) do
        SUMG[k][r]=SUMG[k][r] OR GridResTmp[g][r]
        where SUMG holds resources of particular combination k ∈
        K
  for all possible combination's k ∈ K(where K set of grid nodes) of r ∈
  R (where R set of resources) do
    SUMR[k]=SUMR[k] AND SUMG[k][r]
    where SUMK holds value resources of particular combination k ∈
    K satisfying need
    if SUMR[k]==1 then
      The possible grid node combination satisfy the need
      if g of selected combination ∈ G' (where G' set of grid nodes on
      which grid services are present) then
        Insert these combination's to a list L
  for all grid nodes g ∈ L do
    Generate Resource Spanning Tree using Link Matrix LMAT and
    insert into list L'
  for all RST's g ∈ L' do
    if RST_j ⊆ RST_i then
      Then remove RST_i from L'
  L' is the list of MRST's of service S_i
```

4.2 Reliability of Minimum Resource Spanning Tree, MRST[3]

Reliability of Root Node. The root node of the spanning tree is responsible to execute the given service as well as to perform communication with other donor nodes to fetch the needed resources.

$$R_{root} = e^{-\lambda[T_r + T_{c,d}]} \tag{1}$$

where T_r is the execution of root node, $T_{c,d}$ communication time of links 'c' and execution time of donor nodes 'd'.

Reliability of Communication Links. Let T(m,n) be the spanning tree rooted at node n and capable to execute service m and L(i,j) is one of the

Algorithm 3. Calculation of Working Time of MRST

begin
Procedure to calculate Working Time of MRST
for *all MRST's* $\in \mathcal{L}'$ *(where* $\mathcal{L}'$ *is the list of MRST's of service* S_i*)* **do**
COMPUTE
linkld(i,j)=D(i,j)/S(i,j)
where
linkld(i,j) the communication time of link L(i,j) and i,j $\in \mathcal{G}$(set of grid nodes)
D(i,j) is the total size of data exchanged through link L(i,j)
S(i,j) is the mean speed data exchange between link L(i,j)
COMPUTE
non-root communication load(execution time)=$\sum$linlld(i,j) where i,j $\in \mathcal{G}$(set of grid nodes)
COMPUTE
Root Node Execution Time = Execution Time of Service T_{S_i} + Load of link between root node and donor nodes $T_{r,D}$
where $S_i \in \mathcal{S}$ and r,D $\in \mathcal{G}$
Store the working times of MRST's in $\mathcal{P}$

links in T(m,n). This link expected to be live for the time when communication is being carried out via this link. The communication time for link L(i,j) is given as $\frac{D(i,j)}{S(i,j)}$.

The reliability of link L(i,j), R_{link} is

$$R_{link} = e^{-\lambda_{i,j}[T_c(i,j)]} \tag{2}$$

Reliability of Donor Nodes. Let k be one of the donor nodes of the spanning tree T(m,n) for service m rooted at node n. The donor node is expected to be live for the time of communication.

The reliability of donor node k, R_{donor} is

$$R_{donor} = e^{-\lambda \sum T_c(k,i)} \tag{3}$$

where $T_c(k,i) = \frac{D(k,i)}{S(k,i)}$

Overall Reliability of RST. The reliability of the entire RST, T(m,n) denoted by R(T(m,n)) [13] can be computed as the product of the reliability of its elements by using equation (1), (2) & (3),

$$R(T(m,n)) = \{R_{root}\} \times \{R_{link}\} \times \{R_{donor}\} \tag{4}$$

4.3 Grid Service Reliability

Given a service, its reliability can be described as the probability of having at least one of its MRST's reliable. E_i represents the event in which the $MRST_i$ is

Algorithm 4. Calculation of Reliability for the working time

begin
  Procedure to calculate Reliability of MRST
  for *all* $p \in \mathcal{P}$ *of* $MRST \in \mathcal{L}'$ *(where* $\mathcal{L}'$ *is the list of MRST's of service* S_i*)* **do**
    COMPUTE
    Reliability of Communication Links(α)=$e^{-\lambda linkld(i,j)}$
    where
    linkld(i,j) the communication time of link L(i,j) and i,j $\in \mathcal{G}$(set of grid nodes)
    λ is failure rate of links
    COMPUTE
    Reliability of Non-Root Node(β)=$e^{-\lambda \sum linlld(i,j)}$ where i,j $\in \mathcal{G}$(set of grid nodes)
    λ is failure rate of Non-Root Nodes
    COMPUTE
    Reliability of Root Node(γ) $= e^{-\lambda(T_{S_i}+T_{r,D})}$
    where $S_i \in \mathcal{S}$ and r,D $\in \mathcal{G}$
    λ is failure rate of Root Node
    Reliability of MRST=$\{\alpha\} \times \{\beta\} \times \{\gamma\}$
  Store the reliability of MRST's in list $\mathcal{Q}$

Algorithm 5. Calculation of Reliability for the services

begin
  $Reliability_{service}$=0.0
  if *number of* $MRST \in \mathcal{L}'$ $== 1$ **then**
    then $Reliability_{service} = Reliability_{MRST}$
  else for *each* $MRST \in \mathcal{L}'$ *and* $i \leq \mid \mathcal{L}' \mid$ **do**
    $Reliability_{service} = Reliability_{service} + Reliability_{MRST} \times$ relvec[i]
  return $Reliability_{service}$

reliable to successfully execute the given service. By using conditional probability[12], the events can be decomposed into mutually exclusive events as

$$GSR = Pr[E_1] + Pr[E_2]Pr[\overline{E_1}|E_2] + \cdots + Pr[E_{N_i}]Pr[\overline{E_1} \wedge \overline{E_2} \wedge \ldots \wedge \overline{E_{N_i-1}}|E_{N_i}] \quad (5)$$

4.4 Overall Grid Service Reliability

The grid service reliability measures the reliability of one service executed in the grid. However, for the grid computing system, it is important to obtain a global reliability measure that describes how reliable the overall grid is for a given distribution of services and resources. One way of measuring the reliability of the grid computing system is by determining overall grid service reliability which is defined as the probability that all the computing services are executed successfully[9]. Thus, the overall grid service reliability equation can be written as the probability of the intersection of the set of MRST's of each service.

E_i represents the event in which the intersected $MRST_i$ is reliable. By using conditional probability, the events can be decomposed into mutually exclusive events as

$$OGSR = Pr[E_1] + Pr[E_2]Pr[\overline{E_1}|E_2] + \cdots \\ + Pr[E_{N_i}]Pr[\overline{E_1} \wedge \overline{E_2} \wedge \ldots \wedge \overline{E_{N_i-1}}|E_{N_i}] \quad (6)$$

Algorithm 6. Calculation of Overall Grid Service Reliability(OGSR)

```
begin
    n=0
    fo=number of MRST's of L'_1
    for i ≤ number of services do
        for j ≤ fo do
            for k ≤ number of MRST's of each L'_k of each service do
                TotalService_WT = P_jWT + P_kWT
                n++;
        fo=n
        n=0
```

5 Trust Computations[14]

Trust is the firm belief in the entity to behave as expected and this firm belief is a dynamic value which may change with behavior and context of time[2].

Trust has the following properties[7]:

- Trust is a continuous and dynamic value in the range of [0,1].
- 1 means very trustworthy.
- 0 means very trust unworthy
- It is built on past experience.
- It is context based (under different context may have a different trust value or values)

5.1 Direct Trust Based on Availability

Direct Trust based on Availability($DTA(MFA_{i,k}, TF)$) is a ratio of minimum number of free resources available of a particular resource allocation i satisfying need $k(MFA_{i,k})$to the total number of free resources(TF).

$$DTA(MFA_{i,k}, TF) = \frac{MFA_{i,k}}{TF} \quad (7)$$

5.2 Reputation Based on Reliability Computation

The reputation($Rp(OGSR_i)$ for a particular allocation scheme i is computed based on reliability of Overall Grid Service Reliability computation($OGSR_i$)(See Section 2 for reliability computations).

5.3 Trust Evaluation Based on Reputation

Trust Value(TV) is computed based on Reputation($Rp(OGSR_i)$ and Direct Trust based on Availability($DTA(MFA_{i,k}, TF)$) by giving them weights δ_1 and δ_2 between 0 and 1 such that $\delta_1 + \delta_2 = 1$.

$$TV = \delta_1[TA(MFA_{i,k}, TF)] + \delta_2[Rp(OGSR_i)]$$
$$where \delta_1 + \delta_2 = 1, \delta_1 > 0, \delta_1 > 0 \tag{8}$$

where δ_1 and δ_2 are weights given to direct trust and reputation relationships respectively.

5.4 Trust Update

Trust Value(TV_k) of kth instance is updated based on past Trust Value(TV_{k-1}) of $k - 1^{th}$ instance by using weights.

$$TV_k = \alpha[TV_k] + (1 - \alpha)[TV_{k-1}] \quad 0 \le \alpha \le 1 \tag{9}$$

If $\alpha > 0.5$, more preference will be given to k^{th} instance of Trust Value(TV_k), else if $\alpha < 0.5$, more preference will be given to $k - 1^{th}$ instance of Trust Value(TV_{k-1}).

Algorithm 7. Using trust computations to find out the minimal allocation with maximal reliability

```
begin
  Minimal_Resource_Allocation
  {
  Direct Trust(X)= Minimum number of free resources available(MFA) / total number of free resources(TF)
  X=1-X
  TrustValue(TV) = δ1[Xi]+δ2[Rp(OGSRi)]   δ1+δ2 = 1, δ1 > 0, δ1 > 0
  TVk = α[TVk] + (1 − α)[TVk−1]   0 ≤ α ≤ 1
  if Tk > TK−1 then
      possible minimal allocation
      return 1
  else TK=TK−1 return 0
  }
```

6 Search

Search is the process of considering various possible sequences of operators applied to the initial state, and finding out a sequence which culminates in a goal state[10].

6.1 2-Way Split Backward Search

2-Way Split Backward Search is an algorithm proposed to improve the search process by dividing the search space into two parts one at the back and one in the middle. If the mid-way search yields better results than at the back then start from the middle and split the other half from middle to front and repeat the process. Else start from back ignore the search space from mid-way and split the half from backward point to mid-way into another half and repeat the process. The algorithm for this search process is given below.

Algorithm 8. Generating possible resource allocation matrices using 2-Way Split Backward Search algorithm

```
begin
    Initailly L plys
    M=L , L=L/2
    Initially allocation with all free resources is assumed to be maximal
    reliable
    TWO_WAY_SPLIT_BS(M,L)
    {
    X=MAX_OGSR(M^th Ply)
    Y=MAX_OGSR(L^th Ply)
    if !Minmal_Resource_Allocation() then
        if X > Y then
            TWO_WAY_SPLIT_BS(M-1,L+L/2)
        if X ≤ Y then
            TWO_WAY_SPLIT_BS(L-1,L/2)
        else break
    }
```

6.2 M-Way Split Backward Search

We can increase the number of splits(M=2,3,4,...,N/2) to speed up the search process where $M < N/2$(N is total number of plys in the search space) at the cost of increased computations. Generally 2,3 Way split are optimal in terms of computations and search speed when number of plys are less.

7 Example of Sample Grid Network

7.1 Grid Configuration Information

For reliability computations we need information about grid configuration that includes rate of failure of each node i.e λ_i , rate of failure of each link L(i,j) i.e $\lambda_{i,j}$ etc. The grid configuration information is needed about following grid elements.

Table 1. Configuration Information About Grid Nodes

Grid Node i	Rate of Failure, λ_i
1	0.001
2	0.002
3	0.003
4	0.004

Table 2. Configuration Information About Grid Communication Links

Link, L(i,j)	Mean Speed	Rate of Failure, $\lambda_{i,j}$
L(1,2)	30	0.001
L(1,3)	20	0.002
L(2,3)	40	0.003
L(2,4)	50	0.004
L(3,4)	45	0.005

Table 3. Configuration Information About Grid Services

Program	Execution Time	Resource need				Data Exchanged			
		R_1	R_2	R_3	R_4	R_1	R_2	R_3	R_4
S_1	30	1	1	1	0	500	400	300	0
S_2	50	0	0	1	1	0	0	200	600

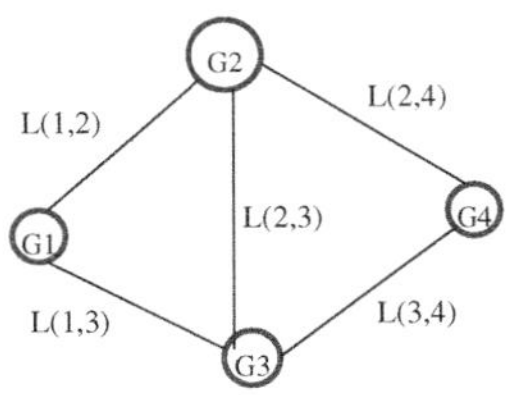

	R1	R2	R3	R4	S1	S2
G1	1	0	0	−1	1	0
G2	−1	0	−1	1	0	1
G3	−1	1	−1	1	0	0
G4	−1	0	−1	−1	1	0

−1 --> free(Available and Not Binded)

0 --> Not Available or Not Binded

1 --> Available and Binded

Fig. 3. Initial Allocation Matrix for considered example

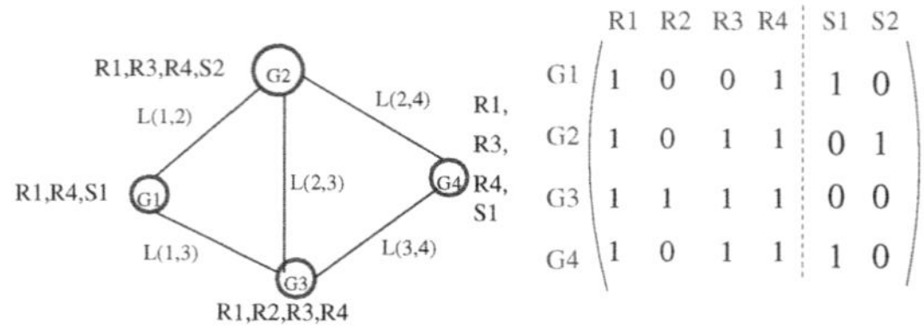

Fig. 4. Initial Resource Allocation for considered example

Initially we take an assumption for resource allocation that all possible free resources allocated. This approach helps the search procedure to search backward.

7.2 Generate All Possible MRST's(Minimum Resource Spanning Tree) of Each Service

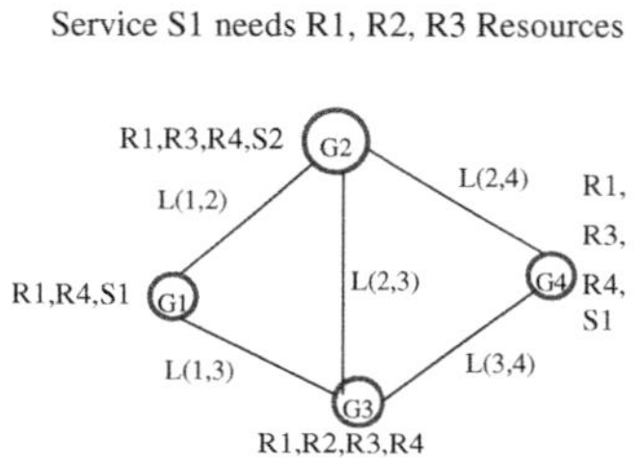

Fig. 5. Initial allocation for generating MRST's for S_1

Table 4. MRST's generated for S_1

MRST's generated for S_1	
MRST1 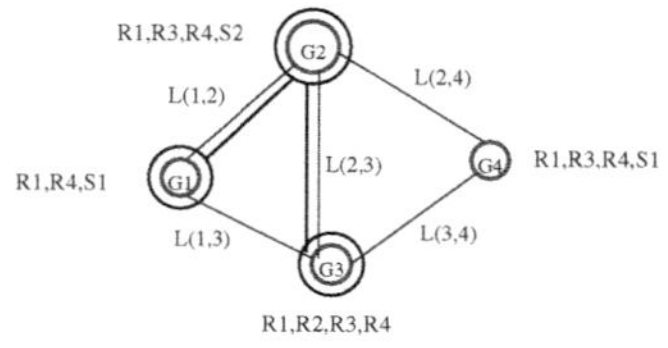	MRST2 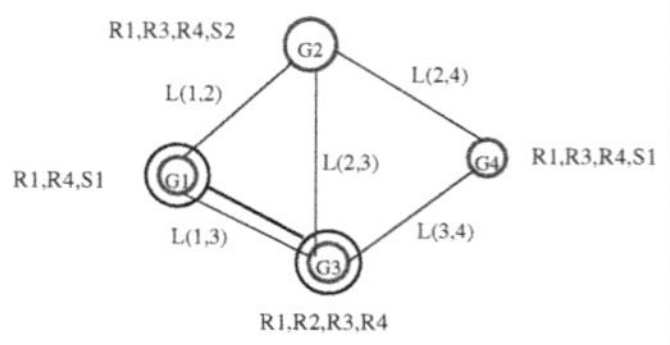
MRST3 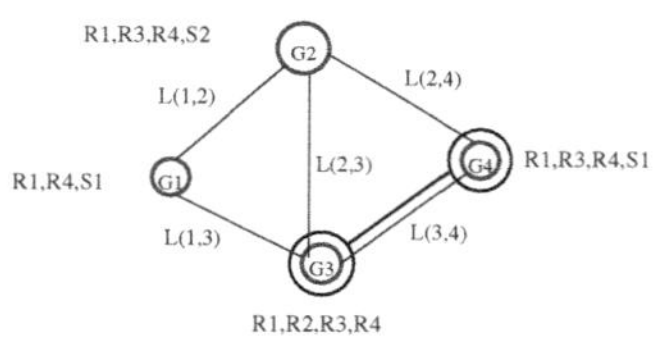	MRST4 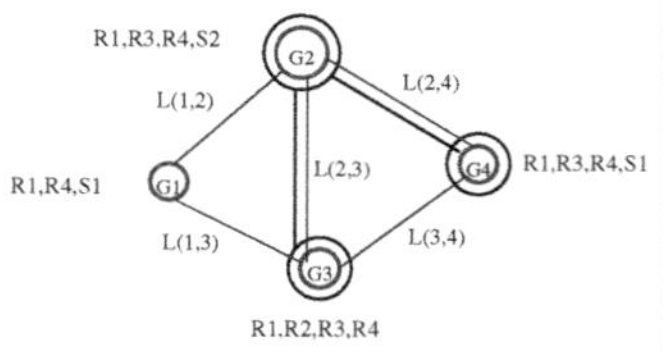

7.3 Compute Reliability of MRST's of a Service in a Grid and Overall Reliability of All Services

- Communication Links.
- Root Node.
- Donor Nodes.

Reliability of Communication Links : Let the time for which the link L(i,j) is used for communication is represented as $\tau(i,j)$, this time is also referred as survival time of link. For values of D(i,j), S(i,j) and λ refer to table. For MRST-4 the $\tau(i,j)$ for its two links are as follows :

$$\tau_{(2,4)} = \frac{D(2,4)}{S(2,4)} = \frac{400}{50} = 8$$
$$\tau_{(2,3)} = \frac{D(2,3)}{S(2,3)} = \frac{400}{40} = 10$$

Let the reliability of link L(i,j) be $R_{L(i,j)}$ and computed as follows :

$$R_{L(2,4)} = e^{(-\lambda_{(2,4)})(\tau_{(2,4)})} = e^{(-.004)(8)} = .9685$$
$$R_{L(2,3)} = e^{(-\lambda_{(2,3)})(\tau_{(2,3)})} = e^{(-.003)(10)} = .9704$$

The reliability of all links is denoted by α and computed as product of reliability $R_{L(i,j)}$ for all links in MRST-4.

$$\beta = \prod (R_{L(i,j)}) = .9685 \times .9704 = .9398$$

Reliability of Donor Nodes : Let the time for which the non-root(donor) node i is busy in communication is represented as τ_i, this time is also referred as survival time of non-root node. For MRST-4 the τ_i for its two donor nodes are as follows :

$$\tau_2 = \tau_{(2,4)} + \tau_{(2,3)} = 8 + 10 = 18$$
$$\tau_3 = \tau_{(2,3)} = 10$$

Let the reliability of non-root(donor) node i be R_i and computed as follows :

$$R_2 = e^{(-\lambda_2)(\tau_2)} = e^{(-.002)(18)} = .9646$$
$$R_3 = e^{(-\lambda_3)(\tau_3)} = e^{(-.003)(10)} = .9704$$

The reliability of all non-root(donor) nodes of MRST-4 is denoted by β and computed as product of reliability R_i for all non-root nodes in MRST-4.

$$\zeta = \prod (R_i) = .9646 \times .9704 = .9360$$

Reliability of Root Nodes: The root node is responsible to communicate with other nodes to pull the deficient resources and execute the task in hand. Let the time for which the root node is busy in communication and execution of task is represented as τ_{root}, this time is also referred as survival time of root node. For MRST-4 and service S_1 the τ_{root} is computed as follows:

$$\tau_{root} = \tau_4 = \text{Execution Time of } S_i + \tau_{(2,4)} = 30 + 8 = 38$$

Let the reliability of root node be α and computed as follows :

$$\alpha = e^{(-\lambda_{root})(\tau_{root})} = e^{(-\lambda_4)(\tau_4)} = e^{(-.004)(38)} = .8589$$

Reliability of MRST: Let reliability of MRST-4 be R_{MRST} and computed by using equation 3.16 as follows :

$$R_{MRST} = \alpha \times \beta \times \zeta = .9398 \times .9360 \times .8589$$

Similarly the reliability of each of MRST capable to execute service S_1 shown in table above is calculated and summarized in table below.

Table 5. Reliability of all MRST's of service S_1

MRST i	Reliability of $MRST_i$
R_{MRST_1}	0.8869
R_{MRST_2}	0.8607
R_{MRST_3}	0.7972
R_{MRST_4}	0.7558

Table 6. Working Times of MRST-1 and MRST-2 of service S_1

MRST i	Elements of MRST								
	G_1	G_2	G_3	G_4	L(1,2)	L(1,3)	L(2,3)	L(2,4)	L(3,4)
MRST-1(T_1)	40.00	20.00	10.00	0.00	10.00	0.00	10.00	0.00	0.00
MRST-2(T_2)	50.00	0.00	20.00	0.00	0.00	20.00	0.00	0.00	0.00

Table 7. Working Times of MRST-1 and MRST-2 of service S_1 which would fail

MRST i	Elements of MRST								
	G_1	G_2	G_3	G_4	L(1,2)	L(1,3)	L(2,3)	L(2,4)	L(3,4)
MRST-3(T_3)	0.00	0.00	8.89	38.89	0.00	0.00	0.00	0.00	8.89
$T_3 < T_1$	40.00	20.00	10.00	0.00	10.00	0.00	10.00	0.00	0.00
$T_3 < T_2$	50.00	0.00	20.00	0.00	0.00	20.00	0.00	0.00	0.00

Table 8. Calculating Reliability of MRST-1

$CEV_3(m)$	$CEV_3(1)$	$CEV_3(2)$	$CEV_3(3)$	$CEV_3(4)$	$CEV_3(5)$
Element	G_1	G_2	G_3	L(1,2)	l(2,3)
T_{b_1}	0.00	0.00	8.89	0.00	0.00
T_{b_2}	40.00	20.00	10.00	10.00	10.00
R(m)$=e^{-\lambda(T_{b_2}-T_{b_1})}$	.9607	.9607	.9967	.9900	.9704

Table 9. Calculating Reliability of MRST-2

$CEV_3(m)$	$CEV_3(1)$	$CEV_3(2)$	$CEV_3(3)$
Element	G_1	G_3	L(1,3)
T_{b_1}	40.00	10.00	0.00
T_{b_2}	50.00	20.00	20.00
R(m)$=e^{-\lambda(T_{b_2}-T_{b_1})}$	.9900	.9704	.9607

Probability that MRST-1 succeeds is given by:

$$P(E_1) = \prod R(m) = .9607 \times .9607 \times .9967 \times .9900 \times .9704 = .8837$$

Probability that MRST-2 succeeds is given by:

$$P(E_2) = \prod R(m) = .9900 \times .9704 \times .9607 = .9229$$

Evaluation of $Pr[\overline{E_1} \wedge \overline{E_2} \mid E_3]$ is explained by simple simplification illustrated bellow. Events E_1, E_2 and E_3 are assumed to be mutually exclusive.

$Pr[\overline{E_1} \wedge \overline{E_2} \mid E_3]$
$= \frac{Pr[\overline{E_1} \wedge \overline{E_2}] \times Pr[E_3]}{Pr[E_3]}$ *as* E_3 *is mutually exclusive with other events*
$= Pr[\overline{E_1} \wedge \overline{E_2}]$
$= Pr[\overline{E_1}] \times Pr[\overline{E_2}]$ *as* E_1 *&* E_2 *are mutually exclusive*
$= (1 - Pr[E_1]) \times (1 - Pr[E_2])$
$= 1 - (Pr[E_1] + Pr[E_2] - Pr[E_1]Pr[E_2])$
$= 1 - Pr[E_1 \cup E_2]$

Reliability of Service S_1 is computed using table 7.10 using equation 3.19 which is $GSR = Pr[E_1] + Pr[E_2]Pr[\overline{E_1}|E_2] + Pr[E_3]Pr[\overline{E_1} \wedge \overline{E_2}|E_3] + Pr[E_4]$ $Pr[\overline{E_1} \wedge \overline{E_2} \wedge \overline{E_3}|E_4]$
$= 0.8869 + .8607 \times .0769 + .7972 \times .0087 + .7558 \times .0001$
$= .9600$

After calculating the working times for S_1 and S_2 commbined above procedure is again repeated to compute OGSR.

Table 10. Reliability of all MRST's of service S_1 and their Conditional Probabilities

MRST i	**Reliability of** $MRST_i$	Conditional Probability for i^{th} MRST to succeed
1	0.8869	——
2	0.8607	0.0769
3	0.7972	0.0087
4	0.7558	0.0001

Table 11. Working Times of MRST's of service S_1

MRST i	Elements of MRST								
	G_1	G_2	G_3	G_4	L(1,2)	L(1,3)	L(2,3)	L(2,4)	L(3,4)
MRST-1(T_1)	40.00	20.00	10.00	0.00	10.00	0.00	10.00	0.00	0.00
MRST-2(T_2)	50.00	0.00	20.00	0.00	0.00	20.00	0.00	0.00	0.00
MRST-3(T_3)	0.00	0.00	8.89	38.89	0.00	0.00	0.00	0.00	8.89
MRST-4(T_4)	0.00	18.00	10.00	38.00	0.00	0.00	10.00	8.00	0.00

Table 12. Working Times of MRST's of service S_2

MRST i	Elements of MRST								
	G_1	G_2	G_3	G_4	L(1,2)	L(1,3)	L(2,3)	L(2,4)	L(3,4)
MRST-1(T_1)	0.00	50.00	0.00	0.00	0.00	0.00	0.00	0.00	0.00

Table 13. Working Times of MRST's of services S_1 and S_2 combined

MRST i	Elements of MRST								
	G_1	G_2	G_3	G_4	L(1,2)	L(1,3)	L(2,3)	L(2,4)	L(3,4)
MRST-1(T_1)	40.00	70.00	10.00	0.00	10.00	0.00	10.00	0.00	0.00
MRST-2(T_2)	50.00	50.00	20.00	0.00	0.00	20.00	0.00	0.00	0.00
MRST-3(T_3)	0.00	50.00	8.89	38.89	0.00	0.00	0.00	0.00	8.89
MRST-4(T_4)	0.00	68.00	10.00	38.00	0.00	0.00	10.00	8.00	0.00

7.4 Generate Possible Resource Allocation Matrices Using 2-Way Split Backward Search Algorithm and Compute OGSR for Each Allocation

7.5 Use Trust Computations to Find Out the Minimal Allocation with Maximal Reliability

Calculation of trust is shown below:

1. Direct Trust(X)=$\frac{Minimum\ number\ of\ free\ resources\ available(MFA)}{total\ number\ of\ free\ resources(TF)} = \frac{4}{8} = 0.5$

2. X=1-X=0.5

3. $TrustValue(TV) = \delta_1[X_i] + \delta_2[Rp(OGSR_i)] \quad \delta_1 + \delta_2 = 1, \delta_1 > 0, \delta_1 > 0$

$TrustValue(TV) = 0.5 \times (X) + 0.5 \times (maximum\ OGSR\ of\ i^{th}\ iteration)$ $where\ \delta_1 = 0.5, \delta_2 = 0.5$

$TrustValue(TV) = 0.5 \times 0.5 + 0.5 \times 0.8936 = .6968$

4. $TV_k = \alpha[TV_k] + (1-\alpha)[TV_{k-1}] \quad 0 \leq \alpha \leq 1$

$TV_k = 0.5 \times [TV_k] + 0.5 \times [TV_{k-1}]$ *where* $\alpha = 0.5$

$TV_k = 0.5 \times .6968 + 0.5 \times .6343 = .6656$

5. As k^{th} trust value $> k-1^{th}$ trust value the resource allocation of kth trust value is minimal with maximal reliability.

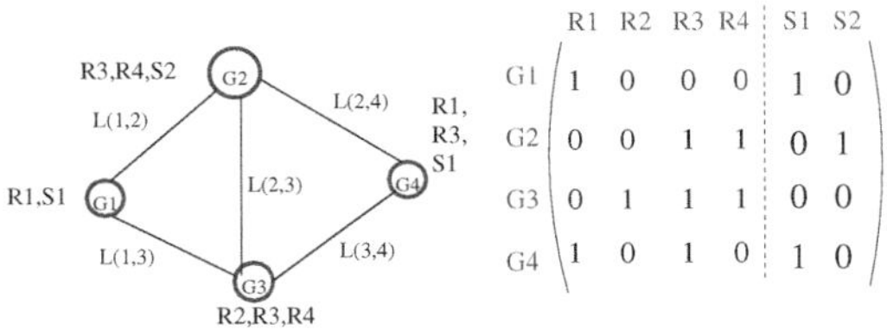

Fig. 6. Minimal Resource Allocation for considered example

8 Advantages

The proposed reliability and trust computations recommender in grid computing system provides many advantages those make it acquitted to be deployed for many applications. The following are some of its advantages:

- Resource Manager Ingredient
- Congestion Control
- Adaptive System
- Cost Benefit

9 Future Work

To the best of our knowledge the work presented is a first attempt to address the problem of resource allocation according to the probability of successful execution. There is enough possibility for further improvement to this work. Multiple Copies of Resources, Availability Factor for Grid Elements, Upgrade to Realtime System are some of the areas of future work.

10 Conclusion

The key factor for the success of any system is its reliability to serve as expected. Whenever the case that a system can allocate resources in multiple schemes then the performance of the system fully depends upon how intelligent it is to make the best choice to pick the best scheme. The scheme which is most probable to get successfully executed is the apt decision.In context of resource allocation in grid computing system, the recommender model is capable to make the apt selection of resource allocation scheme when a resource can be allocated in multiple ways on the grid.

References

1. Carter, R.L., Louis, D.S., Andert, J.: Resource allocation in a distributed computing environment. In: Proceedings of 17th DASC Digital Avionics Systems Conference, October 31-November 7, pp. 1:C32/1–C32/8 (1998)
2. Chakrabarti, A.: Grid Computing Security. Springer, Heidelberg (2007)
3. Dai, Y., Xie, M., Poh, K.: Reliability analysis of grid computing. In: IEEE Pacific Rim International Symposium on Dependable Computing (PRDC 2002), pp. 97–104 (2002)
4. Foster, I.: The anatomy of the grid: Enabling scalable virtual organizations. In: Proceedings First IEEE/ACM International Symposium on Cluster Computing and Grid, May 15-18, pp. 6–7 (2001)
5. Foster, I., Kesselman, C.: The Grid 2: Blueprint for a NewComputing Infrastructure. Morgan Kaufmann, San Francisco (2003)
6. Krishna, G.J., Wankar, R., Rao, C.R.: Finding minimal resource allocation in grid with reliability and trust computations using 2-way split backward search. In: International Conference on Communication, Computing & Security (ICCCS 2011), February 13. ACM Proceedings, pp. 188–193 (2011) ISBN:978-1-4503-0464-1
7. Lai, W.W.K., Ng, K.-w., Lyu, M.R.: Integrating trust in grid computing systems. In: Jin, H., Pan, Y., Xiao, N., Sun, J. (eds.) GCC 2004. LNCS, vol. 3251, pp. 887–890. Springer, Heidelberg (2004)
8. Lin, M.S., Chen, D.J.: Distributed program reliability analysis. In: Proceedings of the Third Workshop on Future Trends of Distributed Computing Systems, April 14-16, pp. 395–401 (1992)
9. Lyu, M.R.: Handbook of Software Reliability Engineering. McGraw-Hill, New York (1996)
10. Russell, S., Norvig, P.: Artificial Intelligence, 2nd edn. Pearson Education, London (2008)
11. Ryabinin, I.: Reliability of Engineering System Principles and Analysis. Mir Publishers (1976)
12. Trivedi, K.S.: Probability and Statistics with Reliability, Queuing, and Computer Science Applications. John Wiley and Sons, Chichester (2001)
13. Xie, M.: Software Reliability Modeling. World Scientific Publishing Company, Singapore (1991)
14. Xiong, K., Perros, H.: Trust–based resource allocation in web services. In: IEEE International Conference on Web Services (ICWS 2006), September 18-22, pp. 663–672 (2006)

Virtualization Techniques: A Methodical Review of XEN and KVM

A. Binu and G. Santhosh Kumar

Department of Computer Science, Cochin University of Science and Technology, Cochin, India
binu_a@rajagiritech.ac.in, san@cusat.ac.in

Abstract. Over the past few years, researchers have been propelled for a Utility Computing Model. Cloud computing allows delivering resource on demand by means of virtualization. Virtualization has been around from the period of Mainframe computing. The proposal of using a computer system to emulate another computer system was early realized as useful for testing and increased resource utilization purposes. As with several computer technologies, IBM initiated the way with their VM system. In the last decennary, VMware's virtual machine monitor has been quite successful. In recent times, open-source hypervisor's like Xen and KVM added virtualization to the open source world, initially with a variant named para-virtualization and later using hardware assisted full virtualization. This paper surveys two main virtualization technologies: Xen and KVM. Also system and network performance evaluation tests are conducted to analyze scalability and performance of the virtualized environment.

Keywords: Virtual Machine Monitors, Hypervisors, Paravirtualization, Fullvirtualization, XEN, KVM.

1 Introduction

A virtual machine (VM) is an abstract entity between hardware components and the end-user. A "real physical machine", sometimes depicted as "bare metal," such as memory, CPU, motherboard, and network interface. The real machine operating system accesses hardware parts by making calls through a low-level program called the BIOS (basic input/output system). Virtual machines are reposed on top of the real machine core parts. Abstraction entity called hypervisors or VMMs (virtual machine monitors) make calls from the virtual machine to the real machine. Hypervisors available today, use the real machine hardware parts, but allows different virtual machine operating systems and configurations. For example, a host system might run on SuSE Linux, and guest virtual machines might run Windows 2003 and Solaris 10.

2 Virtualization Approaches and Implementations

2.1 Overview

Virtualization technology is the base of cloud computing. An efficient, flexible, trusted VMM is a basic requirement. So far, better and better solutions are available

A. Abraham et al. (Eds.): ACC 2011, Part I, CCIS 190, pp. 399–410, 2011.

in CPU and memory virtualization. The performance of virtual machine is almost same as the native system, and intricacy is also improved. Two main virtualization techniques were reviewed in this paper; Xen and KVM. Current approaches to virtualization can be classified into: full virtualization, paravirtualization, and software emulation. Each of them has its own pros and cons. Full virtualization works well but it is hard to put into practice. Paravirtualization is more efficient after lots of optimizations, but the Guest OS should be modified. It is not complicated to implement software emulation, but its performance is poor.

Figure 1 illustrates three approaches to virtualization. The shaded parts should be involved in VMM implementation. Following paragraph introduces three different virtualization approaches.

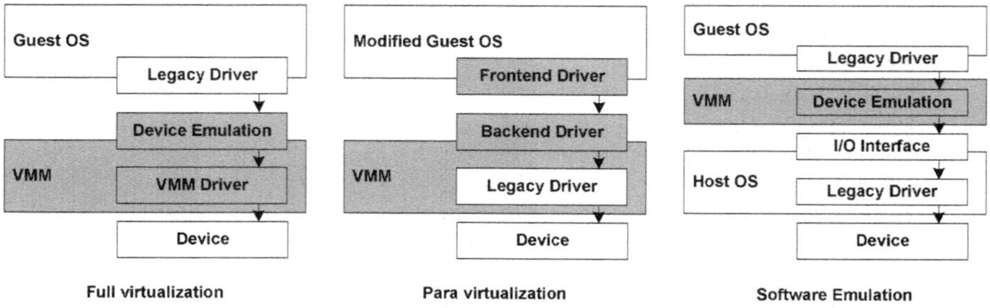

Fig. 1. Three approaches to virtualization

Full Virtualization: In this model, developed by VMware, the virtual machine executes on the CPU , instead of emulated processor. When privilege instructions are identified the CPU will place a trap that could be managed by the hypervisor and emulated. But x86 instructions like pushf/popf do not trap. To manage these instructions a method called Binary Translation was introduced. In this technique the hypervisor glances over the virtual machine memory and taps these system calls before they are carried out and dynamically modifies the code in memory. The kernel of the operating system is incognizant of the change and works normally. This mixture of trap-and-execute and binary translation permits any x86 operating systems to run unmodified on the hypervisor. Even though it has intricacy in implementation, it resulted in significant performance advantages compared to full emulating the CPU.

Para Virtualization: Paravirtualization uses split drivers to handle I/O requests. A backend driver is installed in a privileged VM (Driver Domain) to access physical device. And it provides special virtual interfaces to other VMs for I/O accesses. A frontend driver is installed in Guest OS. The driver handles Guest's I/O requests and passes them to backend driver, which will interpret the I/O requests and map them to physical devices. Physical device drivers in Driver Domain will drive the devices to handle the requests.

Software Emulation: Software emulation is often used in host based VMM. Host based VMM is a normal application and it can't totally control hardware, so I/O requests should be handled by Host OS. I/O requests raised in Guest OS will be intercepted by VMM, and passed to an application in Host OS, which handles I/O requests via system call to Host OS. The main overhead in this approach is context switch, including switch between Guest OS and VMM, switch between kernel space (VMM) and user space (emulation application), and switch between emulation application and Host OS kernel.

Before evaluation, a brief overview of two virtualization technologies: Xen, and KVM is provided. Xen is the most accepted paravirtualization implementation in use today. Because of the paravirtualization, guests exist as independent operating systems. The guests typically exhibit minimal performance overhead, approximating near-native performance. Resource management exists primarily in the form of memory allocation, and CPU allocation. Xen file storage can exist as either a single file on the host file system (file backed storage), or in the form of partitions or logical volumes.

Kernel-based Virtual Machine (KVM) is one of the most recent generations of open source virtualization method. KVM is ported as a kernel module that ensures the Linux kernel act as a bare metal hypervisor. KVM was developed after the introduction of hardware assisted virtualization. So it did not have to employ features that were offered by hardware. The KVM hypervisor needs Intel VT-X or AMD-V based CPUs and leverages those aspects to virtualize the CPU. By using hardware support, KVM was able to devise an optimized hypervisor without demanding the supporting legacy hardware or alterations to the guest operating system.

2.2 XEN: Architecture

While the software emulation and full-virtualization approaches concentrated on how to address a privileged instruction, a different method was taken by the Xen project. Instead of managing a privileged instruction, the paravirtualization modifies the guest operating system and substitute all the privileged instructions with direct system calls into the hypervisor. In this method, the modified guest operating system knows that it is running on top of a hypervisor and can collaborate with the hypervisor for enhanced scheduling and I/O, avoiding the necessity to emulate hardware devices.

The Xen Hypervisor is consisted of two components – the Xen hypervisor, responsible for core hypervisor activities such as CPU scheduling, memory management, power management and slotting of VM's. The Xen hypervisor loads a unique, privileged virtual machine named Domain0 or dom0. This domain0 virtual machine has direct permission to access hardware and provides interfaces for virtual machines to use device drivers and I/O management. Each virtual machine, identified as an unprivileged domain or domU, consists of a modified Linux kernel that communicates with Xen hypervisor which runs on top hardware and serves as an interface between the hardware and the VMs. CPU and main memory access are managed directly by the Xen hypervisor but I/O is managed by domain0. The Linux kernel uses "front end" drivers for network and disk I/O. Requests for I/O are forwarded to the "back end" drivers in domain 0 which negotiates the I/O. The overall Xen architecture is illustrated in figure 2.

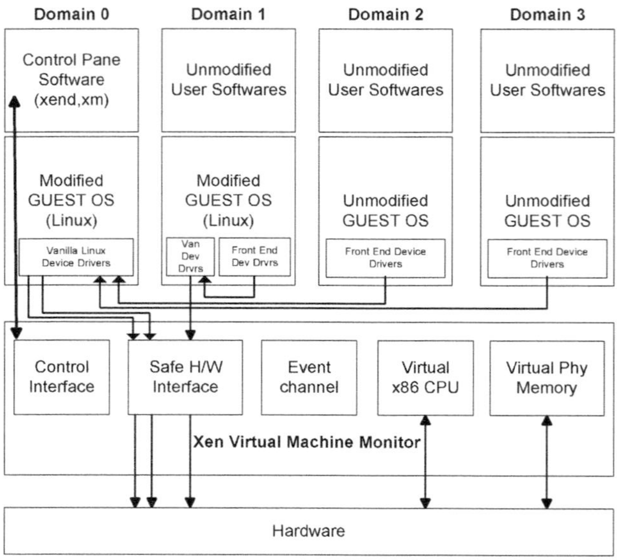

Fig. 2. Architecture of machine running Xen hypervisor [1]

2.2.1 CPU Scheduling

Xen make use of Borrowed Virtual Time (BVT) scheduling algorithm [2] for domain scheduling. This particular algorithm assures low-latency dispatch of a domain when an event is happened. Quick dispatch is particularly important to reduce the effect of virtualization on OS subsystems to run in a timely fashion. BVT by means of virtual-time warping ensures low-latency dispatch. Xen guest OSes uses the concept of real time, virtual time and wall-clock time [1]. Real time is calculated in nanoseconds, from machine boot and is maintained to the precision of the processor's cycle counter. A domain's virtual time only advances while domain is executing to make sure accurate allocation of its time slice between application processes. Wall-clock time is set as an offset to be added to the current real time. This ensures wall-clock time to be adjusted without bearing on the forward progress of real time.

2.2.2 Memory Management

The initial memory allocation for each domain is conditioned at the time of its existence; memory is thus zoned between domains, providing secure isolation. Xen domains use a balloon driver [1], which corrects a domain's memory access by passing memory pages to and fro between Xen hypervisor and domains page allocator. The balloon driver does adaption by using currently available OS memory-management routines, thus minimizes the Linux modifying effort. On the other hand, paravirtualization can be utilized to broaden the features of the balloon driver; such as, the out-of-memory management mechanism in the guest OS can be altered to automatically ease memory pressure by calling for additional memory from Xen. Majority of operating systems assume that memory consists of a few large contiguous blocks. Because Xen does not guarantee to collect contiguous regions of memory, guest OSes will usually craft for themselves the delusion of closest physical memory, even though their inherent allocation of hardware memory is thin. Xen hypervisor uses efficient hardware-to-physical mapping by putting up a shared translation array that is accessible directly by all domains, changes to this array are validated by Xen to make sure that the appropriate guest OS owns the applicable hardware page frames.

2.2.3 Device I/O

Instead of imitating the hardware devices, as is normally done in fully-virtualized environments, Xen make uses a set of simple and uncomplicated device abstractions. This ensures an interface that is both efficient and satisfies requirements for protection and isolation. I/O data is transmitted to and from each domain via Xen, by means of shared-memory asynchronous buffer descriptor rings. These offer a high-performance communication mechanism for transferring buffer information, while ensuring Xen to expeditiously perform validation checks.

2.2.4 Storage

In Xen, only Domain0 has direct access to physical disks. All other domains access storage through the abstraction of virtual block devices (VBDs) [1], which are created and configured by administration software running within Domain0. Allowing Domain0 to handle the VBDs keeps the mechanisms within Xen very simple. A VBD consists of a list of blocks with corresponding access control information and ownership, and is permitted to access via the I/O ring mechanism. A typical guest OS disk scheduling algorithm will rearrange calls for disk access prior to queuing them on the ring in an effort to decrease response time, and to apply differentiated service. A VBD thus looks to the guest OS to some extent like a SCSI disk. Xen daemons batches of requests from competing domains in round-robin fashion; these are then forwarded to a standard elevator scheduler prior to reaching the disk hardware.

2.2.5 Security

Xen assures a high level of security via a mixture of features like Guest separation, privileged access rights, tiny code base and operating system isolation. Guest OS isolation safeguards every DomainU guest with no way to access each other's memory map and networking connections. Privileged access ensures only Domain0 is given the permission to communicate with the hardware via the hypervisor. The Xen hypervisor has a tiny code base which limits the areas for attack. In Xen, the hypervisor is separated from Domain0 and DomainU. So, Xen hypervisor cannot be used as a base to attack other systems.

2.3 KVM: Architecture

Kernel-based Virtual Machine (KVM) project is one of the latest stages of open source virtualization. KVM is developed as a loadable Linux kernel module. The KVM needs Intel VT-X or AMD-V based CPUs. In KVM architecture, virtual machine is devised as normal Linux process, schedule by the Linux scheduler. Here each virtual machine appears as a standard Linux process. This ensures KVM to make use all the advantages of the Linux kernel. Device emulation is managed by a modified version of QEMU that offers emulated BIOS, I/O bus, network interface and disk controllers etc.

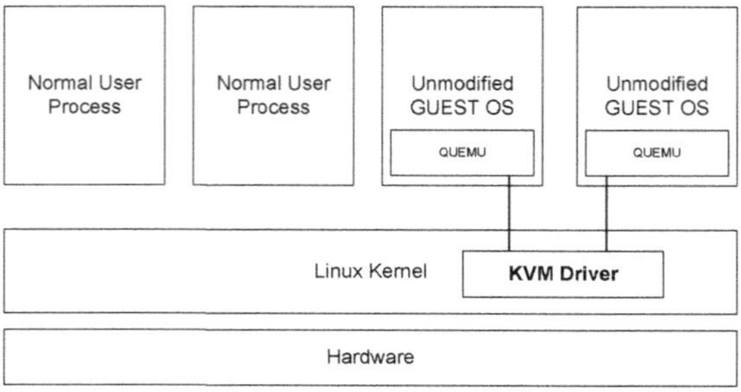

Fig. 3. KVM Architecture [17]

2.3.1 CPU Scheduling

In the KVM model, each virtual machine is considered as Linux process. It is handled and scheduled by the standard Linux kernel. The Linux kernel uses a new advanced process scheduler knows as the completely fair scheduler (CFS) [16] to offer advanced process scheduling. The CFS scheduler modified to include CGroups (control groups) resource manager to allow processes to share the system resources. CGroups allows assured resources to a virtual machine and also permits the virtual machine to utilize more resources if available.

2.3.2 Memory Management

KVM uses the solid memory management services of Linux. The memory of a VM is kept similar to memory for other Linux processes and can be interchanged, backed by large pages for improved performance, shared by a disk file. Memory page sharing is implemented using a kernel feature named as Kernel Same-page Merging (KSM) [17]. KSM examines the memory of each virtual machine and those have got same memory pages, KSM unifies these into a single shared page between the virtual machines, storing only a sole copy. If a virtual machine tries to modify this shared page it will be given its own copy. With KSM more virtual machines can be implemented on each host, cutting down hardware costs and bettering server utilization.

2.3.3 Device I/O

KVM supports crossbreed virtualization where paravirtualized drivers are used in the guest OS to permit virtual machines to exploit an optimized I/O interface, instead of high performance I/O operations of emulated devices. The KVM hypervisor utilizes the VirtIO [15] standard, which is a hypervisor independent device interface for improved guest interoperability.

2.3.4 Storage

KVM is capable to employ all kinds of storage supported by Linux to keep virtual machine images. KVM in addition allows virtual machine images on shared file systems such as the Global File System (GFS2) to permit virtual machine images to be shared among multiple hosts or shared using logical volumes. The standard disk format for KVM is QCOW2[19] which lets in support multiple levels of snapshots.

2.3.5 Security

Since a virtual machine is derived as a Linux process it inherits the standard Linux security model to offer separation and resource controls. Security-Enhanced Linux [20] ensures resource separation and restriction for processes running in the Linux kernel. The sVirt [21] project builds on Security-Enhanced Linux ensures that a virtual machines resources cannot be accessed by any other VM's and this can be extended by the super user to characterize fine grained permissions. Security-Enhanced Linux and sVirt put up an infrastructure that ensures a high level of security and separation.

2.4 Qualitative Comparison

An ideal Virtual machine monitor runs the guest at native speed. Different VMMs face different trade-offs in their attempts to approach this idea. Following tables briefly describes results of the survey. Todd Deshane et.al, compared the performance of KVM and Xen against base linux. Their results are depicted in the following table.

Table 1. Overall performance of Xen, and KVM compared to base linux [13]

Performance	Xen	KVM
CPU	0.999	0.993
Disk Write	0.855	0.934
Disk Read	0.852	0.994

Table 2. Comparison of implementation details of Xen and KVM

	Xen	KVM
Type of Virtualization	Para – Virtualization	Full – virtualization
CPU Scheduling	Borrowed virtual time algorithm	Completely fair scheduler
Memory Management	Balloon driver	Kernel Same Page Merging
I/O operation	Buffer Descriptor Rings	VirtIO
Disk Access	Virtual Block Device	QCOW2
Network	Buffer Descriptor Rings	VirtIO

Table 3. Comparison of general features of Xen and KVM

	Xen	KVM
Type of Hypervisor	Standalone thin hypervisor	Linux kernel as hypervisor
De-privileging	Yes	No
Multiprocessor Guests	Yes	No
Live Migration	Yes	Yes
Hypervisor Complexity - Installation and Management	High	Low
Virtual Machine Complexity – Installation and Management	Low	Low
Security	High	High

In summary, full virtualization and para virtualization VMMs suffer different overheads. While para virtualization used in Xen requires precautious engineering to make sure efficient execution of guest kernel code, full virtualization used in KVM delivers nearly native speed for anything that avoids execution of system exit instruction, but levies a higher cost for the remaining exits.

3 Xen Implementation and Performance Evaluation

3.1 Xen Implementation

Xen installation is conducted in system with Intel i7 processor and 4GB DDR2 RAM. Debian 5.0 (lenny) was used as the primary operating system and Xen3.4.2 as the hypervisor for enabling virtualization. Xen offers good quality performance when virtualizing Linux distributions because of paravirtualization. The Xen version used can also virtualize unmodified guest operating systems on processors that extend virtualization support. In Xen setup, the hypervisor runs directly on top of hardware (bare-metal). The primary guest operating system (dom0) runs above Xen and has full access rights to the hardware. Additional guests (domU) also execute on top of the hypervisor, but with restricted access to the hardware.

Converting an existing Debian 5.0 to a Xen dom0 requires installation of Xen hypervisor. Here, Debian system needs a kernel modification to support Xen hypervisor. There are two main choices for dom0 kernel. The standard Xen kernel or a dom0 pv-ops kernel. The pv-ops kernel can run under the Xen hypervisor. The pv-ops kernel is likely to be incorporated in the standard Linux kernel soon for Xen support. But, the pv-ops kernel will not support binary graphics drivers supplied by Nvidia. Standard Xen kernel was used, since the test machine has an Nvidia graphics card. The standard Xen kernel has to be forward ported using patches for Gentoo Linux.

3.2 Performance Evaluation of Xen Implementation

The results of performance analysis of Xen installation is presented here. A base x86, Xen modified Debian5.0 based machine was used for benchmarking. Xen Hypervisor tests were performed on Intel(R) Core(TM) i7 CPU 930 @ 2.80GHz processor with gigabit Ethernet, 4 GB RAM, and an 1000 GB 7200 RPM SATA hard disk. Virtual Machine test were performed on a single Virtual CPU of configuration, Intel(R) Core(TM) i7 CPU 930 @ 2.80GHz with Ethernet, 128 MB RAM, 256 MB Swap Memory and 1GB of virtual hard disk.

Each system was tested for network performance using Netperf[22], and system performance using UnixBench[23]. These tests served as micro benchmarks, and proved useful in analyzing the scalability and performance of the distributed benchmarks.

3.2.1 Network Performance

Using the Netperf [22] network benchmark tool, the network throughput of different communication strategy was tested and compared it against the native results using fixed message size. All tests were performed multiple times.

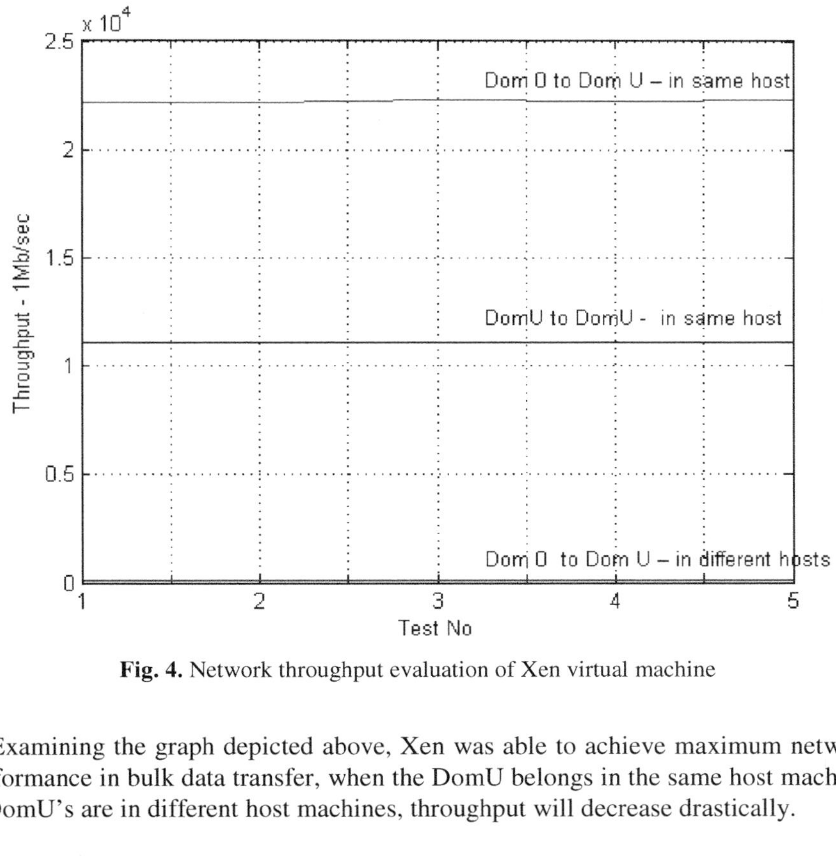

Fig. 4. Network throughput evaluation of Xen virtual machine

Examining the graph depicted above, Xen was able to achieve maximum network performance in bulk data transfer, when the DomU belongs in the same host machine. If DomU's are in different host machines, throughput will decrease drastically.

3.2.2 System Performance

The system performance of physical machine which hosts hypervisor and virtual machine was tested. The test was performed using UnixBench[23], which is a tool designed to assess, the performance of system when running a single task, the performance of system when running multiple tasks, and the gain from system's implementation of parallel processing. Benchmark used for physical machine was, 8 cores of Intel Core i7CPU and 1 parallel process and for virtual machine was 1 core of Intel Core i7CPU and 1 parallel process.

Examining the table, Xen virtual machine out performs a standalone physical machine in terms of systems performance, due to the high overhead of hypervisor running on it.

Table 4. System Performance evaluation of Xen virtual machine and hypervisor

Test	Baseline	Virtual Machine		Physical Machine - Hypervisor	
		Score	Index	Score	Index
Dhrystone 2 using register variables	116700.0	14746538.6	1263.6	14949106.8	1281.0
Double-Precision Whetstone	55.0	2882.6	524.1	2883.7	524.3
Execl Throughput	43.0	3162.3	735.4	2379.5	553.4
File Copy 1024 bufsize 2000 maxblocks	3960.0	725162.4	1831.2	346322.2	874.6
File Copy 256 bufsize 500 maxblocks	1655.0	189847.3	1147.1	89153.0	538.7
File Copy 4096 bufsize 8000 maxblocks	5800.0	935488.1	1612.9	993252.3	1712.5
Pipe Throughput	12440.0	1187283.6	954.4	461744.2	371.2
Pipe-based Context Switching	4000.0	173809.8	434.5	113899.7	284.7
Process Creation	126.0	6679.3	530.1	5223.4	414.6
Shell Scripts (1 concurrent)	42.4	5770.8	1361.0	6308.8	1487.9
Shell Scripts (8 concurrent)	6.0	793.0	1321.6	1561.3	2602.2
System Call Overhead	15000.0	1232328.3	821.6	1169804.5	779.9
System Benchmarks Index Score:			**949.4**		**764.2**

3.2.3 Real World Tests

The mock tests above depict a clear picture about the performance of Xen. But to examine these data correlate to real world application performance an application test was conducted using lamp[24]. The lamp is a bundled package which consist apache web server, mysql database and filezilla FTP server [24]. We hosted our application in two types of operating system which is supported by Xen : Modified OS and Unmodified OS and evaluated the performance.

Table 5. Evaluation of Real world application tests conducted on Xen virtual machines

Test	Xen modified Guest Operating System	Unmodified Guest Operating System
Webpage load time – with standard html tags	0 sec	0 sec
Webpage load time – with "create table" sql query	0.0048 sec	0.0117 sec
FTP – Average Upload time (685 MB of data)	0.58 sec	1.01min
FTP – Average Upload speed (685 MB of data)	11.8 MB/s	10.7MB/s
FTP – Average Download time (685 MB of data)	0.58 sec	1.15min
FTP – Average Download speed (685 MB of data)	11.8 MB/s	8.5MB/s

Looking at the table, Xen virtual machine was able to achieve the maximum performance, when VM operating system is modified for bypassing the hypervisor.

4 Discussion

The qualitative comparison of Xen and KVM presented over here is focusing on CPU scheduling, memory management, device I/O, storage, and security. The most striking difference between the two systems was in CPU scheduling. KVM had substantial problems with handling system trap instruction. KVM has better CPU performance than Xen, but Xen's CPU performance were also quite good.

During the performance evaluation tests using Xen, Network performance is fair, showing some strange asymmetric behavior, but it is acceptable. System performance seems to be the most interesting aspect, providing the VM better performance, particularly when it is compared with a machine which hosts Xen hypervisor.

The overall qualitative and quantitative performance results were mixed, with Xen outperforming KVM on CPU scheduling and KVM outperforming Xen on I/O-intensive operation.

5 Conclusion

Virtualization can be utilized for a plenty of application. Since CPU manufacturer introduced facilities to build VMMs more efficiently, those can be run on popular and widespread x86 architecture. KVM is an open source virtualization solution that extends the CPU's virtualization facilities to operate VMs by means of full virtualization. It allows running various unmodified operating systems in several isolated virtual machines on top of a host. KVM is designed as a loadable kernel module, to turn Linux box into a VMM. Since the developers did not wish to reinvent the wheel, KVM depends on the mechanisms of the Linux kernel to schedule computing power and benefits from the out of the box driver support. But the memory management has been extended to be capable to manage assigned address space of a VM. Also the virtIO device model supported by KVM greatly enhances the I/O performance.

Xen is an open source virtualization solution that uses para virtualization to operate VMs. It allows running various modified operating systems in several isolated virtual machines running on top of a thin hypervisor. Xen uses Borrowed Virtual Time algorithm to schedule CPU. In Xen, the modified guest operating system is aware about its underlying hypervisor and can work together with the hypervisor for enhanced scheduling and I/O, getting rid of the need to emulate hardware resources.

During the performance evaluation tests Xen proved great stability and reliability: it never crashed and integrated seamlessly into existing system. The benchmark tests conducted showed that the system performance by the virtual machine is comparable to the physical machine and in some cases it is even better. Network performance is also fair and has shown good throughput. Real world test using FTP and HTTP also proved the scalability of the virtual machine. To summarize, Xen hypervisor seems to be a good solution, particularly when using the para-virtualized approach.

References

1. Barham, P., Dragovic, B., Fraser, K., Hand, S., Harris, T., Ho, A., Neugebauery, R., Pratt, I., Warfeld, A.: Xen and the Art of Virtualization. In: SOSP 2003, Bolton Landing, New York, USA (2003)
2. Duda, K.J., Cheriton, D.R.: Borrowed-Virtual-Time (BVT) scheduling: supporting latency-sensitive threads in a general-purpose scheduler. In: Proceedings of the 17th ACM SIGOPS Symposium on Operating Systems Principles, USA, ACM Operating Systems Review, vol. 33(5) (December 1999)

3. Adams, K., Agesen, O.: A Comparison of Software and Hardware Techniques for x86 Virtualization. In: ASPLOS 2006, San Jose, California, USA, October 21-25 (2006)
4. Wang, J., Niphadkar, S., Stavrou, A., Ghosh, A.K.: A Virtualization Architecture for In-depth Kernel Isolation. In: Proceedings of the 43rd Hawaii International Conference on System Sciences (2010)
5. Uhlig, R., Neiger, G., Rodgers, D., Santoni, A.L., Martins, F.C.M., Anderson, A.V., Bennett, S.M., Kägi, A., Leung, F.H., Smith, L.: Intel Virtualization Technology. IEEE Computer Society, Los Alamitos (2005)
6. Microsoft Corp., Microsoft Virtual Server 2005 Technical Overview (2004), http://download.microsoft.com/download/5/5/3/55321426-cb43-4672-9123-74ca3af6911d/VS2005TechWP.doc
7. LeVasseur, J., Uhlig, V., Yang, Y., Chapman, M., Chubb, P., Leslie, B., Heiser, G.: Pre-virtualization: soft layering for virtual machines
8. Sukaridhoto, S., et al.: A Comparative Study of Open Source Softwares for Virtualization with Streaming Server Applications. In: The 13th IEEE International Symposium on Consumer Electronics (ISCE 2009) (2009)
9. Smith, J.E., Nair, R.: The Architecture of Virtual Machines. IEEE Computer Society, Los Alamitos (2005)
10. Rosenblum, M., Garfinkel, T.: Virtual Machine Monitors: Current Technology and Future Trends. IEEE Computer Society, Los Alamitos (2005)
11. Kivity, A., Kamay, Y., Laor, D., Lublin, U., Liguori, A.: kvm: the Linux Virtual Machine Monitor. In: Proceedings of the Linux Symposium, Canada (2007)
12. Deshane, T., et al.: Quantitative Comparison of Xen and KVM. Xen Summit, Boston, June 23-24 (2008)
13. Hirt, T.: KVM - The kernel-based virtual machine (2010)
14. Russell, R.: virtio: Towards a De-Facto Standard For Virtual I/O Devices
15. Kumar, A.: Multiprocessing with the Completely Fair Scheduler - Introducing the CFS for Linux (January 2008)
16. White paper on KVM – KERNEL BASED VIRTUAL MACHINE, Redhat (2009)
17. White paper on Best practices for KVM, IBM (2010)
18. Ribot, F.Z.: QLOOP - Linux driver to mount QCOW2 virtual disks, June 23 (2010)
19. White paper on First Steps with Security-Enhanced Linux (SELinux), IBM (2009)
20. Morris, J.: sVirt: Hardening Linux Virtualization with Mandatory Access Control, Linux.conf.au (2009)
21. http://www.netperf.org/netperf/ (accessed on February 10, 2010)
22. http://code.google.com/p/byte-unixbench/ (accessed on February 10, 2010)
23. http://www.apachefriends.org/en/xampp-linux.html (accessed on February 10, 2010)
24. http://www.gentoo.org/ (accessed on February 17, 2010)

An Optimal Workflow Based Scheduling and Resource Allocation in Cloud

P.Varalakshmi, Aravindh Ramaswamy, Aswath Balasubramanian, and Palaniappan Vijaykumar

Department of Information Technology, Anna University Chennai, India
varanip@gmail.com, aravindhramu@gmail.com, aswath78@gmail.com, vijaypalani6@gmail.com

Abstract. The objective of Optimal Workflow based Scheduling (OWS) algorithm is to find a solution that meets the user-preferred Quality of Service (QoS) parameters. The work presented focuses on scheduling cloud workflows. First, the Resource discovery algorithm, indexes all the resources and this helps in locating the free resources. Second, the scheduling algorithm that takes user specified QoS parameters (execution time, reliability, monetary cost etc.) as key factor is used for scheduling workflows. Using a special metric called the QoS heuristic, the sub-task cluster is assigned to its optimal resource. Third, in case resources are not available for allocating to a task, compaction is performed. By this a significant improvement in CPU utilization is achieved.

Keywords: Cloud Computing, Workflows, scheduling, QoS, Resource monitoring.

1 Introduction

Cloud computing is a web-based processing, where software, infrastructure or platforms are offered as a service to the users over the internet. Users are provided total abstraction from the actual processing that takes place "in the cloud". Cloud Computing involves provisioning of dynamical and scalable virtualized resources. Scheduling refers to the allocation of resources to activities over time so that input demands are met in a timely and cost-effective manner.

In the cloud environment the user submitted jobs may be sequential, parallel or a combination of both. Workflow is basically a flow of control between the tasks. A workflow job consists of set of tasks to execute which may be independent or dependent on each other. Workflow scheduling involves challenges like:

- Heterogeneity of the resources.
- Different users compete for resources in the cloud environment.
- Inter dependency between tasks introduces high communication cost as data needs to be transferred from one resource to another.

Also there are several QoS parameters that have to be considered in a Cloud Computing System such as cost, time, security, reliability etc., which are vital in the performance of the Cloud Application.

A. Abraham et al. (Eds.): ACC 2011, Part I, CCIS 190, pp. 411–420, 2011.

2 Related Work

Workflow based scheduling has always been a core research area and hence there are a plethora of papers in the past decade. Since scheduling requires information about the resources beforehand, resource monitoring/discovery plays a vital prerequisite for scheduling.

[1] Deals with scheduling multiple applications made of collections of independent and identical tasks on a heterogeneous master-worker platform. The objective is to minimize the maximum stretch i.e. the maximum ratio between the actual time an application has spent in the system and the time this application would have spent if executed alone. [2] Proposes a real time duplication based algorithm (RT-DBA) for scheduling precedence-related periodic tasks with hard deadlines on networks of workstations (NOWs). The authors have utilized selective subtask duplication that enables some tasks to have earlier start times, which enables additional tasks (and, hence, task sets) to finish before their deadlines, thereby increasing the schedulability of a real-time application.[3] shows a Task scheduling algorithm based on the hybrid combination of FCFS, Priority Scheduling and Backfilling strategies for use in Grids. The simulation results show that CPU Utilization and system throughput are increased to a significant extent.

[4] Proposes an evolution-based dynamic scheduling algorithm in grid computing environments. The proposed algorithm uses the genetic algorithm as search technique to find an efficient schedule in grid computing and adapts to variable number of computing nodes which has different computational capabilities. [5] Introduces a multiple QoS Constrained Scheduling Strategy of Multiple Workflows for Cloud Computing. [6] Discusses an optimized algorithm for task scheduling based on Activity-cost based costing in cloud computing environment. Activity-based costing is a way of measuring both the cost of the objects and the performances of activities and it can measure the cost more accurate than traditional ones in cloud computing. [7] Proposes tree architecture for resource discovery. All resources and user queries are transformed into a bitmap index representation. Each leaf node in the tree will store the information about its local resources. Each Index Server (IS) will store the information about its local resources and the information about its children nodes.

[8] Focuses on the implementation of an efficient Two-level Scheduler for Cloud Computing Environment. It presents the implementation of efficient Quality of Service (QoS) based meta-scheduler and backfill strategy based light weight virtual machine scheduler for dispatching jobs. [9] Proposes a framework for scheduling and supporting virtual resource management using CARE Resource Broker (CRB).

In this paper, we propose the Optimal Workflow based Scheduling (OWS) algorithm for scheduling scientific workflows in cloud. The Algorithm involves 2 phases. First, the Resource discovery algorithm, indexes all the resources. Each resource sends its information to its immediate parent node (resources are organized in a hierarchical manner). This way root node always maintains index of all the resources and hence it is easier to poll the root node to request for any information regarding the resources. Thus this reduces flooding of information. Second, the scheduling algorithm takes user specified QoS parameter (execution time, reliability, monetary cost etc.) as key factor for scheduling task-based clusters to the resources. With this algorithm, a significant improvement in CPU utilization is achieved compared to the conventional FCFS and backfilling algorithms by reducing the slowdown rates and the waiting times. This is achieved due to cluster compaction by which we accumulate the free spaces in all the resources to obtain a virtual disk to execute the job so the jobs need not wait much for the resource.

3 Resource Monitoring

In Cloud Computing, the resource pools change dynamically and virtualizing these resources for satisfying user's request and scheduling the user's job are performed effectively based on this resource information only. Hence resource monitoring is an initial step for scheduling in cloud computing environment.

This section discusses the proposed monitoring tree-based architecture for monitoring cloud resources as shown in Figure 1.

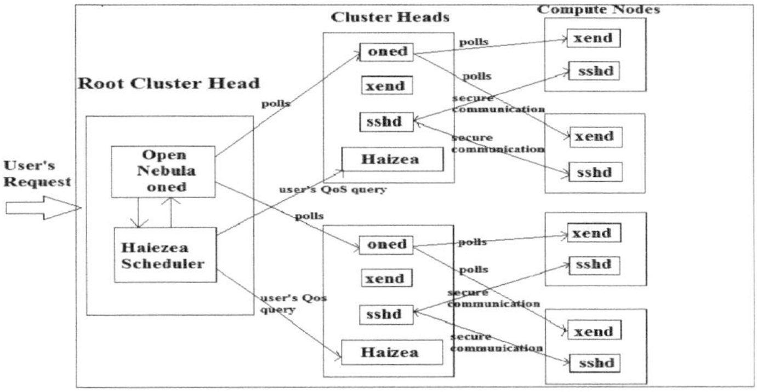

Fig. 1. Proposed tree-based resource monitoring architecture

Our Resource discovery algorithm, indexes all the resources. Each resource sends its information to its immediate parent node (resources are organized in a hierarchical manner). This way root node always maintains index of all the resources and hence it is easier to poll the root to request for any information regarding the resources. Thus a query from a user will be received by the root node. The root node checks whether there is matching resource among its cluster nodes. Then root node forwards its request to only the corresponding cluster head. This way we prevent information flooding.

The hierarchy consists of the three kinds of nodes- the root node, the cluster head and the compute node. The root node maintains the index of all the updated compute nodes. In other words, the leaves of the tree maintain all the "actual" resources that perform the necessary computation or execution of the jobs. The cluster head serves as an intermediate node performing the functionalities of both the root node and the compute node. The nodes require specific daemons to be run in them. The root node runs the Open Nebula daemon (oned[10]) and the Scheduler daemon. The Cluster head runs the oned, xend (xen[12]-daemon) for providing virtualization and the sshd (ssh-daemon) for establishing secure connection. The compute nodes run the sshd and the xend. Once the monitoring information has been obtained, the next step is to segregate the resources according to the various QoS (cost, time and reliability) requirements.

The calculation of these parameters is specified as follows:

1) Cost Preference (CP): This preference indicate the purpose of choosing resource instances of the lowest cost for the user. Hence it considers the user profitability into account. Cost Preference of jth resource in the ith resource pool (CP_{ij}) is given by Equation 1 as:

$$CP_{ij} = \frac{CR_j}{maxcost_i - mincost_i + 1} \quad (1)$$

where $maxcost_i$ is the maximum resource usage cost in the ith resource pool.
$mincost_i$ is the minimum resource usage cost in the ith resource pool.
CR_j is the usage cost of the jth resource in the ith resource pool.

2) Speed Preference (SP): This preference indicate the purpose of choosing resource instances that give the least execution time for the user's job. Speed Preference of jth resource in the ith resource pool (SP_{ij}) is given by Equation 2 as:

$$SP_{ij} = \frac{TR_j}{maxtime_i - mintime_i + 1} \quad (2)$$

where $maxtime_i$ is time taken by slowest resource in the ith resource pool.
$mintime_i$ is time taken by fastest resource in the ith resource pool.
TR_j is time taken for executing job on the jth resource in the ith resource pool.

3) Reliability Preference (RP): This preference indicates the jobs to go to resource instances with higher reliability. Reliability Preference of jth resource in the ith resource pool (RP_{ij}) is given by Equation 3 as:

$$RP_{ij} = \frac{RR_j}{maxreliability_i - minreliability_i + 1} \quad (3)$$

where $maxreliability_i$ is the maximum reliability measure in the ith resource pool.
$minreliability_i$ is the minimum reliability measure in the ith resource pool.
RR_j is the reliability measure of the jth resource in the ith resource pool.

Reliability measure is measured on a scale from 0 to 1 based on the level of reliability that a resource possesses like dual-core, external disk, log file etc.

4) Overall Performance(OP): An average of all the above heuristics of jth resource in the ith resource pool (OP_{ij}) is given by Equation 4 as:

$$OP_{ij} = \frac{CP_{ij} + SP_{ij} + RP_{ij}}{3} \quad (4)$$

where CP_{ij} is the Cost Preference of jth resource in the ith resource pool.
SP_{ij} is the Speed Preference of jth resource in the ith resource pool.
RP_{ij} is the Reliability Preference of jth resource in the ith resource pool.

In all the above equations we are normalizing the metrics between 0 and 1.Because in haizea[11] each resource is associated with priority that helps the scheduler in resource allocation. In case, if there is only one resource in resource cluster then denominator becomes 0. To avoid this we added 1 in denominator. Based on the user-specified QoS parameter, the corresponding metric is calculated.

4 Workflow Based Scheduling Strategy

Most of the cloud jobs are in the form of workflows. For scheduling such workflows, we propose an Optimal Workflow-based Scheduling strategy (OWS). The proposed scheduling architecture is shown in Figure 2.

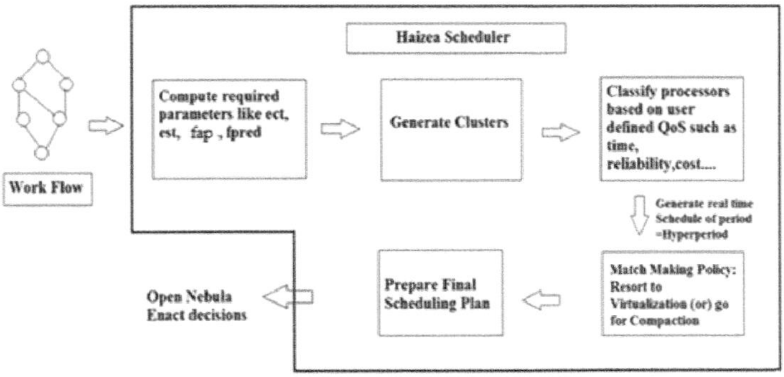

Fig. 2. Architecture for the proposed workflow scheduling strategy

The flow of the OWS algorithm is depicted in the Fig 2. The input for the algorithm is a set of workflows and the output for the algorithm is the schedule that the Open Nebula[10] can enact. Open Nebula accepts the incoming workflows and sends to the Haizea scheduler[11]. Haizea computes required parameters like the earliest completion time (ect), earliest start time(est), favorite processor (FAP) and favorite predecessor (fpred). Based on these parameters, the sub-task clusters are generated from the workflow. Then from the monitoring information, resources are segregated based on the user-desired QoS parameter viz., time, cost or reliability. Then finally, Haizea[11] prepares the decision plan. But since it cannot enact the decision plan on its own, it sends the plan to the open nebula[10] to enact the decision plan.

OWS scheduling algorithm takes user specified QoS parameter as key factors. Based on various data and control dependencies among several sub-tasks, clusters are generated from this job. Then the match making process is carried. In order to ensure fairness, we decrement Processor Fairness Value (PFV) associated with each resource so that further tasks are not attracted towards the same powerful resource. Using the QoS heuristics (that takes care of the various user-specified QoS parameters) we assign the sub-task cluster to its optimal resource. In case resources are not available for allocating to a task, we go for compaction.

The Optimal Workflow-based Scheduling Algorithm for a set of T independent tasks is as shown in Figure 3.

Input:

Processor Set AP: Each processor is assigned PFV which is set to max.

Predecessor set: set of predecessors (parents) of the current subtask.

Successor set: set of successors (children) of the current subtask.

Output:

Real-time schedule of period=hyper period

BEGIN:

1) Obtain the period values of all the tasks $t_i \in T$ and calculate hyper period.

2) Calculate earliest start time, favorite processor, earliest completion time, favorite predecessor for all sub-tasks.

3) Perform cluster generation.

4) While (task list in T not empty)

{

If (processor already assigned)

{

Reduce the PFV value by one

And allocate the sub-task to the processor with the next highest PFV

}

5) Else Schedule the task on to the processor with required processing power and highest PFV.

6) If resources are not available perform cluster compaction.

}

END

Fig. 3. Algorithm for scheduling workflows

The second step in the Fig. 3 is to compute the necessary metrics required for the clustering algorithm. They are as follows:

1) Earliest start time of entry subtask (EST) is initialized as 0.

2) Favorite processor of a subtask in the DAG (FAP): FAP is the processor that gives minimum value of summation of the EST and execution time of a subtask on that processor.

3) Earliest start time of a subtask in the DAG(EST): Earliest start time of a subtask is the maximum value in (the summation of ECT of the predecessor of subtask) and (summation of ECT of predecessor of subtask and communication delay (if both nodes not in same processor))

4) Earliest completion time of a subtask in the DAG (ECT): Earliest completion time of a subtask is the value of summation of EST of that subtask and execution time of that subtask in its favorite processor.

5) Favorite predecessor of a subtask in the DAG (FPRED): Favorite predecessor of a subtask is a subtask in the predecessor list of the given subtask that makes it to wait the longest.

The algorithm for Clustering is in Figure 4.

```
Input        DAG set of predecessor tasks, set of successor tasks and a queue contains all the subtasks in the
             graph arranged in increasing order of their execution time.

Output       Set of task clusters.

Begin:
FQ = first element of queue
current_processor = Favorite processor (FAP) of FQ;
while (NOT all tasks assigned)
{
        FPFQ=Favorite predecessor (fpred) of FQ;
        if FQ has more number of immediate predecessor
        {
        If(difference between the earliest start time of FQ and earliest completion time of FPFQ is less then the
communication delay between the two)
                        assign FQ and FPFQ to same proc
        else if (FPFQ has already been assigned)
                        FPFQ = predecessor of FQ that has least run time in current_processor;
        }
        assign FPFQ to current_processor
        FQ=FPFQ;
        if (FQ is the entry node)
        {
                assign FQ to current_processor
                FQ = next unassigned element in queue;
                Current_processor = next available FAP of FQ;
        }
}
End
```

Fig. 4. Algorithm for Clustering Subtasks

The clustering algorithm is invoked to form clusters of sub-tasks within the job that are independent of each other. Once the clusters are formed, they then represent the leases for the haizea[11] scheduler.

The algorithm for Cluster Compaction is shown in Figure 5.

```
Input

Available number of processors: AP

Critical number of processors: CNP (i.e. number of processors required to execute the given task)

Load: cumulative task lists of all the processors

Sum of execution time of all the subtasks: Cumulative periods (CP)

Set of task clusters

While (AP is less than CNP)

{

        calculate cumulative periods(CP) for each cluster;

        sort available processors in ascending order of CP.

        Merge the task lists of first and the last processor

        decrement CNP;

}
```

Fig. 5. Cluster Compaction Algorithm

In case enough resources are not available to a job, then compaction is performed, i.e., all the empty spaces are accumulated together to create a virtual disk(s) and then the remaining jobs are executed here. Thus the clusters are arranged in ascending order of CP which is defined as sum of the execution times of all the subtasks assigned to processor. This process is carried out till we achieve the required number of free processors.

5 Implementation

The implementation environment used is Open Nebula[10], the open-source toolkit for creating Cloud Environment. We used Haizea[11], an Open Source VM Scheduler as a substitute for the scheduling daemon (mm_sched) of Open Nebula. When a user wants to request computational resources from Haizea[11], he does so in the form of a lease. The subtask-clusters are generated as a part of the pre-processing work and are mapped to leases as the requirements of task-clusters and leases are similar. For this experiment, we considered a hierarchy of nodes as explained in Fig.1.

The main performance metrics considered here is CPU Utilization and waiting time.

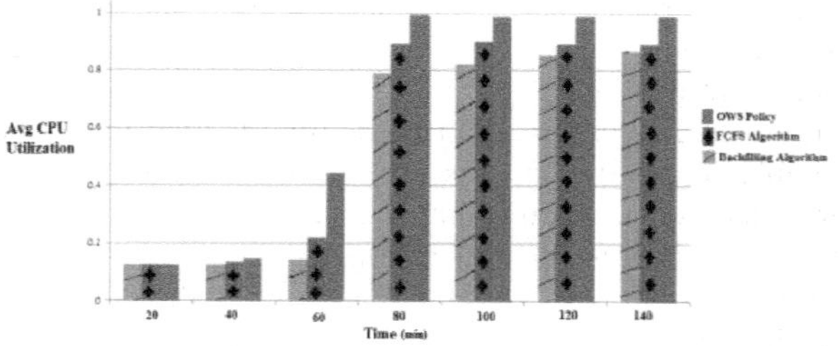

Fig. 6. Comparison of average CPU Utilization

Figure 6 shows the comparison of average CPU utilization (amount of CPU usage for executing the jobs) for OWS algorithm, Backfilling and FCFS algorithms. It is clearly evident from the figure 6 that the CPU Utilization is steadily high for OWS algorithm in comparison with the conventional FCFS and Backfilling algorithms. This is due to cluster compaction by which we accumulate the free spaces in all the resources to obtain a virtual disk to execute the job so the jobs need not wait much for the resource.

The Next performance metric considered here is Waiting time

Figure 7 shows comparison of waiting time (time taken by the jobs in the waiting queue before it is assigned to its resource). The graph clearly shows the drastic increase of waiting times for FCFS and Backfilling due to the starvation problems. In OWS, the starvation is minimized, because whenever a job is allocated to a processor, it has to wait for its next turn. This is done by decrementing the PFV. So, this reduces the affinity of the jobs to a single powerful processor in turn engages all the processors thereby reducing the waiting time.

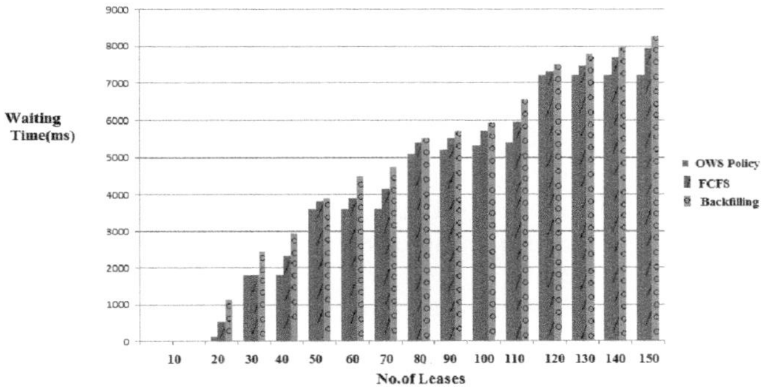

Fig. 7. Comparison of Waiting Time

6 Conclusion and Future Work

In this paper, we propose OWS algorithm for scheduling workflows in a cloud environment. The Resource discovery algorithm, indexes all the resources and hence it is easier to poll the root to request for any information regarding the resources. Thus this reduces flooding of information. The scheduling algorithm finds a solution that meets all user preferred QoS constraints. With this algorithm, a significant improvement in CPU utilization is achieved compared to the conventional FCFS and backfilling algorithms. This is achieved due to cluster compaction by which we accumulate the free spaces in all the resources to obtain a virtual disk to execute the job so the jobs need not wait much for the resource.

In future, trustworthiness of the cloud users and service providers can be considered as another QoS parameter and implemented as a trusted workflow scheduling mechanism in the cloud.

References

1. Benoit, A., Marchal, L., Pineau, J.-F., Robert, Y., Vivien, F.: Scheduling Concurrent Bag-of-Tasks Applications on Heterogeneous Platforms. IEEE Transactions on Computers 59 (2010)
2. Auluck, A.: Enhancing the Schedulability of Real-Time Heterogeneous Networks of Workstations(NOWs). IEEE Transactions on Parallel and Distributed Systems 20 (2009)
3. Jiang, H., Ni, T.: PB-FCFS–A Task Scheduling Algorithm Based on FCFS and Backfilling Strategy for Grid Computing. In: IEEE International Conference (2009)
4. Yu, K.-M., Chen, C.-K.: An Evolution-based Dynamic Scheduling Algorithm in Grid Computing Environment. In: IEEE Conference (2008)
5. Xu, M., Cui, L., Wang, H., Bi, Y.: A Multiple QoS Constrained Scheduling Strategy of Multiple Workflows for Cloud Computing. In: IEEE International Symposium on Parallel and Distributed Processing with Applications (2009)
6. Cao, Q., Wei, Z.-B., Gong, W.-M.: An Optimized Algorithm for Task Scheduling Based On Activity Based Costing in Cloud Computing.In:International Conference on eSciences (2009)

7. Chang, R.-S., Hu, M.-S.: A resource discovery tree using bitmap for grids. In: Future Generation Computer Systems, vol. 26, pp. 29–37 (2010)
8. Sadhasivam, S., Jayarani, R., Nagaveni, N., Vasanth Ram, R.: Design and Implementation of an efficient Two-level Scheduler for Cloud Computing Environment. In: International Conference on Advances in Recent Technologies in Communication and Computing (2009)
9. Somasundaram, T.S., et al.: CARE Resource Broker: A Framework for scheduling and supporting virtual resource management. In: Future Generation Computer Systems, vol. 26, pp. 337–347 (2010)
10. OpenNebula, http://opennebula.org/documentation:archives:rel2.0
11. Haizea, http://haizea.cs.uchicago.edu/
12. Xen, http://www.xen.org/

Energy Efficient Time Synchronization Protocol for Wireless Sensor Networks

Gopal Chand Gautam and T.P. Sharma

Department of Computer Science & Engineering
National Institute of Technology Hamirpur, HP, India
tipugautam@gmail.com, teek@nitham.ac.in

Abstract. In last few years, the Wireless Sensor Network (WSN) have been an important research area because its use has been tremendously increased in different fields such as military, environment, medical, home monitoring and disaster management etc. In such applications, time synchronization is an important problem. To identifying the correct event time, these nodes need to be synchronized with the global time. The energy conservation is one of the important issues in WSNs which helps to prolong the lifetime of the network. In this paper, we present a energy efficient Time Synchronization algorithm in which each layer of the WSN can be synchronized with base station simply by multicasting the synchronization messages The simulation results shows that this algorithm reduce the energy consumption as compare to RBS and TPSN.

Keywords: wireless sensor network, time synchronization, clustered based synchronization, EETS.

1 Introduction

Wireless Sensor Networks [1] (WSNs) comprises various low cost, tiny motes which are provided with one or more sensors to monitor the ambient conditions such as temperature, sound, motion, pressure, vibration and pollutants at different locations [2] and the sensor nodes process the information and uses a transceiver to communicate the data to other nodes in the network. Wireless Sensor Networks forms the network without any infrastructure [3], it is a special type of adhoc network where the wireless nodes work collectively to form a network. These devices are designed in such a way that they can work well in a harsh environmental and geographical conditions i.e. where difficult to go or live.

In Sensors networks, while performing the data fusion time synchronization is very important feature. The main purpose of time synchronization is to make a common time scale in the network which is very important requirement for many applications. The limited energy resources is the pit-fall of the Wireless Sensor Networks, therefore to conserve the energy, the power consumption of the nodes must be reduced. To reduce the consumption the nodes must turn their transceiver on and off at appropriate time, an accurate timing is required between the nodes. Traditional synchronization protocols i.e. Network Time Protocol [4] (NTP) are not suitable for the wireless networks because these protocols are not energy efficient and also very difficult to implement in wireless network.

A. Abraham et al. (Eds.): ACC 2011, Part I, CCIS 190, pp. 421–430, 2011.

In wireless sensor networks lots of research work has been executed to design synchronization algorithms such as Reference Broadcast Synchronization [5] (RBS), Post facto synchronization, Romer synchronization [6], TPSN [7] and Lightweight Fault-tolerant Time synchronization [8].

In this paper, we propose an Energy Efficient Time Synchronization algorithm for Wireless Sensor Networks where the synchronization is performed after the formation of clusters. The base station initiates the synchronization process after formation of the cluster. In first phase, all Cluster Heads (CHs) of level-1 synchronized and then the cluster heads of level-2 and so on. This process remains continue until all the nodes in the network synchronized. Energy analysis for the proposed algorithm defined for two levels of clusters. The performance of algorithm analyzed and performs the simulation. The simulation results shows that our algorithm is energy efficient (i.e consume less energy) and better synchronization accuracy than RBS and TPSN.

The various sections of this paper are organized as follows: The related work in section 2. Section 3 discuss clustered based wireless sensor network. Section 4 contains the energy efficient time synchronization algorithm and energy analysis. Section 5 contains the simulation and finally we conclude in section 6.

2 Related Work

Time synchronization used in the wireless sensor networks to synchronize the clock of all the nodes in the network. Keeping in view the various parameters such as accuracy, scalability, energy efficiency and fault tolerance the time synchronization protocols designed.

2.1 Existing Synchronization Protocols

In Reference Broadcast Synchronization Protocol [5] (RBS) if two receivers are placed within the listening distance of the same sender then they will receive the message approximately at the same time. RBS uses intermediate node to synchronize the local time of two nodes. The intermediate node transmits a "reference packet" to the two nodes. The two nodes record their time and exchange this recorded time to find the difference.

This synchronization protocol proposed by Romer [6] to facilitate synchronization in ad-hoc communication network. Here the mobile computing devices communicate with each other's when they enter each other's communication range. This is obtained via a bi-directional communication link. Romer also suggested that two nodes which do not enter each other's communication range can communicate via store and forward technique. Here an intermediate node receives the sender's message, stores it for a while and transmits it to intended receiver when they enters each other's communication range.

TPSN [7] algorithm works in two steps. In the first step, it establish a hierarchical structure in the network and then performed pair wise Synchronization along the edges of this structure to establish a global timescale throughout the network. Finally, all nodes in the network synchronize their clocks to a reference node.

In FTSP [8], local clocks of the nodes are synchronized. It uses single radio message time stamp to synchronize the multiple receivers. This scheme provides multi-hop synchronization. Here, the root node maintains the global time and all other node synchronize to the root node.

Lightweight and Energy Efficient Time Synchronization (LEETS) Protocols [9] for WSNs has two phases: initial time synchronization and time synchronization maintaining. In Initial time synchronization phase, all the switched on nodes in the network synchronize to the root node. Here the root node is equipped with the GPS. In time synchronization maintaining phase each node in the network uses a slot timer to count slots and maintain node time. Here to maintain the long time synchronization, tracking is needed periodically.

Li-Ming He [10] defines a time synchronization protocol based on spanning tree. A spanning tree of all the nodes in a network is created, and then a spanning tree divided into multiple sub-trees and the sub-tree synchronization process further divided into three phases. In first phase, the father node broadcasts clock-estimating message to all the child nodes. In second phase, father node receives a reply message from the child node and then the father node uses the two-way message exchange method [11] to estimate the clock offset between the father node and the child node. In final phase, a clock-adjusting message which contains the clock offset estimated is broadcasted by father node to all the child nodes. To achieve synchronization all the child nodes use the clock offset and the receiving time recorded in first phase to synchronize with the father node.

3 Clustered Based WSNs Model

In wireless sensor network applications clustering is used for various purposes like data fusion, routing and optimizing energy consumption. A sensor network can be made scalable by gathering the sensor nodes into clusters. Every cluster has a cluster head (CH). In clustered based hierarchical wireless sensor network CHs can be used to process and send the information while the sensor nodes are used to sense the data. The advantage of using the clustering for time synchronization is that CH can prolong the battery life of the individual sensors and also the network lifetime. CH can reduce the rate of energy consumption by scheduling activities in the cluster. Clustering reduce the communication overhead for synchronization. There are various routing protocols for forming the clusters, but in this paper we are using the already existing Low-Energy Adaptive Clustering Hierarchy (LEACH) protocol [12].

In LEACH protocol, initially the node becomes a cluster head with a probability p and broadcast its decision. The nodes choose their cluster head based on the least communication energy to reach the cluster head. The role of the CH keeps on rotating among the nodes of the cluster to enhance the network life time. A node becomes a cluster head for the current rotation round if the number is less than the following threshold:

$$T(n) = \begin{cases} \dfrac{p}{1 - p \times \left(r \bmod \dfrac{1}{p}\right)} & if\ n \in G \\ 0 & otherwise \end{cases}$$

Where the *p* is desired percentage of cluster head nodes, *r* is the current round number and *G* is the set of nodes that have not been cluster head in the last 1/*p* rounds.

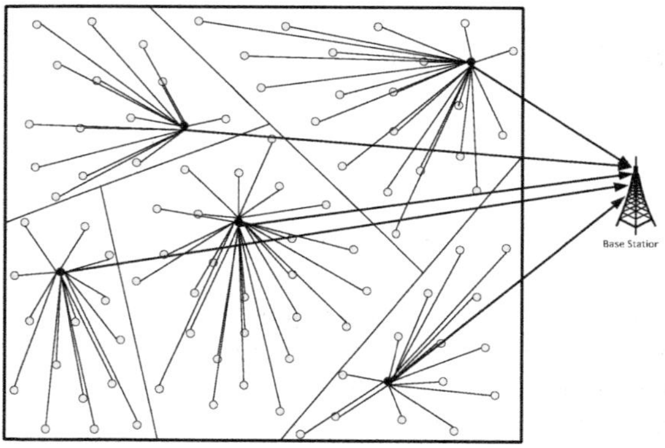

Fig. 1. Cluster formation in LEACH

4 System Model

In wireless sensor network synchronization is necessary because the sensor nodes have a different local clock time. The nodes may provide different time in their clocks because

- The node might have been started at different time.
- The quartz crystal of each node might be running on different frequency.
- The frequency of the clock can change variably over a period of time.

4.1 Assumption of Proposed Algorithm

Some of the assumptions made in energy efficient time synchronization algorithm for wireless sensor network are as following:-

- The network is composed by N sensor nodes deployed in square filed and form cluster hierarchical topology.
- The base station (i.e. Root Node R_n) is located outside the sensing field.
- The base station is equipped with GPS for global time.
- R_n is pre-determined at level-0. Each CH knows their CH ID and level.

- Cluster head (CH) of level-1 can directly communicate (one hop communication) with R_n and delay is constant.
- The cluster head nodes are aware of its members and can directly communicate with them and the CHs are aware of their parent CHs.
- Every CH is synchronizing with its parent CH and finally every cluster head node is synchronized with base station. Each sensor node is synchronized with its CH.
- Communication within the square area is not subjected to multipath fading. The communication channel is symmetric.
- Nodes are left unattended after deployment. Therefore, battery re-charge is not possible.
- The root node (R_n) is well aware of CH_{L1} (CHs of level-1) and their CH IDs.

Algorithm Procedure: In Fig. 4, R_n multicast message M_1 to all CH_{L1} which contain the time t_1. Only the CHs of level-1 receive this message as in the Fig. 4 CH_{L1} nodes receive the message M_1, but CH with ID = 1 responds back by sending message M_2 that contains t_1 the timestamp of R_n, t_2 receiving timestamp of CH and t_3 timestamp of acknowledgement packet. After receiving message M_2, R_n computes delay (d). After the delay computation R_n multicast message M_3 to all CH_{L1} that contains global time t and delay d. When CH_{L1} receives (t, d) then each CHs calculate their offset to set the local clock with global clock. All CHs of level-2 and sensor nodes follow the same process. But their respective CHs become R_n. This new approach drastically reduces the number of message exchange between the nodes to synchronize the sensor network.

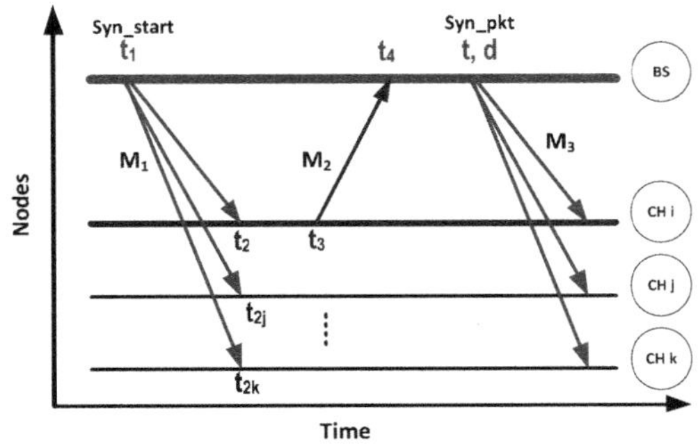

Fig. 2. Message Delay Estimation

The purpose of this algorithm is to set the logical clock of the CHs and cluster nodes with global time. The delay (d) and offset δ can be defined as

$$d = ((t2 - t1) + t3 - t4))/2$$
$$\delta = t + d - LocalTime$$

Where t is global time, d is the delay which will be constant for single hop communication. δ is the time deviation of the two nodes (i.e offset) and LocalTime is CHs/nodes local time.

4.2 Proposed Algorithm

```
Base Station:

1.  Rn multicast (Syn_start, t1);    //* Here the multicast group will be RN and CH of level-1 *//
2.  if receive (Syn_ack, t1, t2, t3) then  // * t1 is RN send time, t2 is the CH packet receive time
         Record (t1, t2, t3, t4);              and t3 is CH packet send time) *//
         Calculate (d);
3.  Rn multicast (Syn_Pkt, t, d);    //* t is Global time, d is propagation delay *//

Cluster head level-1:

4.  i=1 to k1;
5.  if (node = CHL1 ) then                    //* CHL1 is level-1 cluster head *//
       receive (Syn_start, t1);
6.  if (CHID = = i) then        //* One CH will be selected to reply as per their IDS *//
       send (Syn_ack, t1, t2, t3) to Rn;
7.  Wait reply;
8.  if CHL1 receives (Syn_Pkt, t, d) then
        Calculate (δ);                        //* δ is offset*//
        Synchronize;                   //* Correct offset and drift *//
9.  i++;
10. Now for any other CHs lower Cluster level each of the parent CH at level-1
    takes over the role of Rn;
11. Repeat step from 1 to 10;

SNs within a Cluster:

12. j=1 to n;
13. if (node = = SN) then                     //* SN is the sensor node *//
       SN receive (Syn_start, t1)             //* SN will receive Syn_start from PCH *//
14. if (SNID = = j) then
       send (Syn_ack, t1, t2, t3) to PCH;     //* PCH is Parent cluster head *//
15. Wait reply from PCH;
16. if SN receives (Syn_Pkt, t, d) then
       Calculate δ;
       Synchronize SN;
17.    j++;
```

Fig. 3. Energy Efficient Time Synchronization Algorithm

4.3 Energy Analysis

To calculate the energy consumption we use the energy model given in [12] for the transmission and reception of an *l*-bit message from a distance of d. To achieve an acceptable signal-to-noise ratio (SNR) in transmitting *l* bit message over a distance *d*, the energy cost of transmission (ETx) and reception (ERx) are given by:

$$E_{Tx}(l,d) = \begin{cases} l * E_{elec} + l * \varepsilon_{fs} * d^2 & if\ d \le d_0 \\ l * E_{elec} + l * \varepsilon_{mp} * d^4 & if\ d \ge d_0 \end{cases}$$

In the proposed energy efficient time synchronization algorithm we are considering two level network where

- Total number of nodes = N
- Total Number of cluster heads = k
- *Number of CHs at Level-1* = k_1
- *Number of CHs at Level-2* = K_2
- Number of sensor nodes = $N - k$
- *Sensor Area* = $M*M$ *Sq.m.*

The Base Station is at Level-0, there is no energy constraint at base station. The energy consumed in receiving and transmitting l-bit message at Level-1 is given by the equation (1) and (2) respectively. The total energy consumed at Level-1 is given by the equation (3).

$$E_{Rx,CL1} = 3k_1 l E_{elect} \tag{1}$$

$$E_{Tx,CL1} = lE_{elect} + l\varepsilon_{mp} d^4{}_{toBS} + 2k_1\left[lE_{elect} + l\varepsilon_{fs}\frac{M^2}{\pi k_2}\right] \tag{2}$$

$$E_{Total,CL1} = 3k_1 lE_{elect} + lE_{elect} + l\varepsilon_{mp} d^4{}_{toBS} + 2k_1\left[lE_{elect} + l\varepsilon_{fs}\frac{M^2}{\pi k_2}\right] \tag{3}$$

The energy consumed in receiving and transmitting l-bit message at Level-2 with k_2 CHs is given by the equation (4) and (5) respectively. The total energy consumed at Level-2 is given by the equation (6).

$$E_{Rx,CL2} = 3(k_2)lE_{elect} \tag{4}$$

$$E_{Tx,CL2} = k_1\left[lE_{elect} + l\varepsilon_{fs}\frac{M^2}{\pi k_1}\right] + 2(k_2)\left[lE_{elect} + l\varepsilon_{fs}\frac{M^2}{\pi(N-k)}\right] \tag{5}$$

$$E_{Total,CL2} = 3(k_2)lE_{elect} + k_1\left[lE_{elect} + l\varepsilon_{fs}\frac{M^2}{\pi k_1}\right] + 2(k_2)\left[lE_{elect} + l\varepsilon_{fs}\frac{M^2}{\pi(N-k)}\right] \tag{6}$$

The energy consumed in receiving and transmitting l-bit message by N-k sensor nodes is given by the equation (7) and (8) respectively. The total energy consumed by N-k sensor nodes is given by the equation (9).

$$E_{Rx,SN} = 2(N - k)lE_{elect} \tag{7}$$

$$E_{Tx,SN} = (k_2)\left[lE_{elect} + l\varepsilon_{fs} \frac{M^2}{\pi(k_2)} \right] \tag{8}$$

$$E_{Total,SN} = 2(N-k)lE_{elect} + (k_2)\left[lE_{elect} + l\varepsilon_{fs} \frac{M^2}{\pi(k_2)} \right] \tag{9}$$

The total energy consumed in synchronizing all the nodes is given by the following equation (10).

$$E_{Total} = (2N+4k+1)lE_{elect} + 2\left(\frac{2k_2}{N-k} + 2 + \frac{2k_1}{k_2} \right) l\varepsilon_{fs} \frac{M^2}{\pi} + l\varepsilon_{mp} d^4{}_{toBS} \tag{10}$$

We can standardize this equation for level-Z (Z > 2)as following

$$E_{Total,Z} = (2N+4k+1)lE_{elect} + Z\left(\frac{k_2}{N-k} + 1 + \sum_{i=2}^{Z} \frac{k_{i-1}}{k_i} \right) l\varepsilon_{fs} \frac{M^2}{\pi} + l\varepsilon_{mp} d^4{}_{toBS}$$

We can standardize this equation for level-Z (Z > 2)as following

5 Simulation and Analysis

This section compares the performance of proposed algorithm with Reference Broadcast Synchronization (RBS) and Time Synchronization Protocol for Sensor Network (TPSN) synchronization protocols. The performance evaluation includes two parts: message exchange and energy consumption. Simulation is performed using ns-2 [13], a discrete event network simulator. We have compared the performances of Energy Efficient Time Synchronization (EETS) with Reference Broadcast Synchronization (RBS) and Time Synchronization Protocol for Sensor Network (TPSN) synchronization protocols. The basic parameters used are listed in Table-1.

Table 1. Simulation Parameters

Parameter	**Value**
Number of nodes	50
Network grid	100×100 m
Base station position	50×175 m
εfs	10 pJ/bit/m^2
εmp	0.0013 pJ/bit/m^4
Eelec	50 nJ/bit
Size of data packet	500 bits
Initial energy of normal nodes	1 J

Fig. 4 below illustrates the comparison of EETS with RBS and TPSN in terms of message exchange. It is clear that EETS uses very less messages as compare to other two schemes. If the large number of messages sent by the nodes, then more energy is consumed.

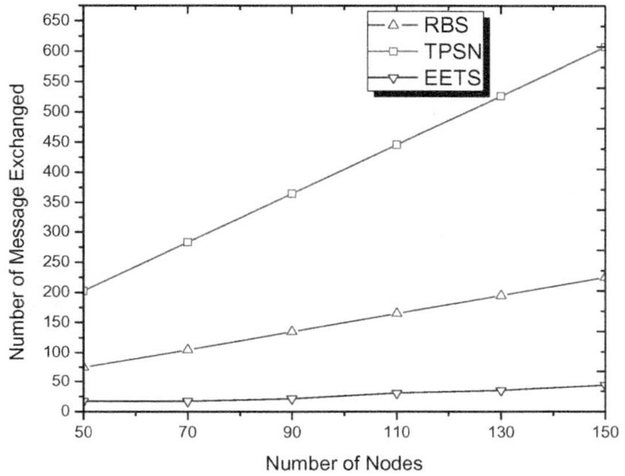

Fig. 4. Message Comparison

Fig. 5 illustrates the performance comparison of EETS with RBS and TPSN in terms of energy consumption. Energy consumption of EETS is less than RBS and TPSN protocols in all cases thus it is energy-efficient. The reason is clear that due to clustering the sensor nodes within the cluster have not to transmit for long distances and message exchange is also very less as compare to the RBS and TPSN.

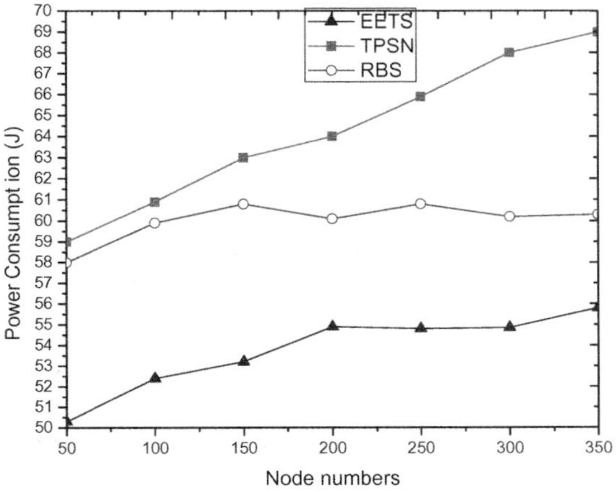

Fig. 5. Power Consumption

6 Conclusion

Time synchronization is critical in the wireless sensor network because nodes have limited energy whereas the various communications consumes energy. The proper usage of energy will prolong the life of the wireless sensor network. In this paper, we have proposed an algorithm based on cluster layer topology to synchronize the logical clocks of the wireless sensor networks which is different from those algorithms that use pair-wise message exchange to synchronize the nodes. The energy model analyze energy consumption while synchronizing the cluster heads and sensor nodes of the WSNs. Theoretical analysis and simulation show that the proposed algorithm is able to save the energy consumption, reduce synchronization time and improve its accuracy.

References

1. Akyildiz, I.F., Su, W., Sankara subramaniam, Y., Cayirci, E.: Wireless Sensor Networks: A Survey. Computer Networks 38(4), 393–422 (2002)
2. Haenselmann, T.: Sensor Networks. Wireless Sensor Network textbook (2006)
3. Sivrikaya, F., Yener, B.: Time Synchronization in Sensor Networks: A Survey. IEEE Network 18(4), 45–50 (2004)
4. Mills, D.: Network Time Protocol (Version 3) Specification, Implementation and Analysis, Technical Report, University of Delaware (1992)
5. Elson, J., Girod, L., Estrin, D.: Fine-grained network time synchronization using reference broadcasts. In: Proceedings of Fifth Symposium on Operating Systems Design and Implementation (OSDI 2002), vol. 36, pp. 147–163 (2002)
6. Romer, K.: Time synchronization in adhoc networks. In: Proceedings of ACM Symposium on Mobile Ad Hoc Networking and Computing (MobiHoc 2001), pp. 173–182 (2001)
7. Ganeriwal, S., Kumar, R., Srivastava, M.: Timing-Sync protocol for sensor networks. In: Proceedings of First International Conference on Embedded Networked Sensor Systems, Los Angeles, California (2003)
8. Seareesavetrat, S., Pornavalai, C., Varakulsiripunth, R.: A light-weight fault-tolerant time synchronization for wireless sensor networks. In: 8th International Conference on ITS Telecommunications, pp. 182–186 (2008)
9. Xu, M., Zhao, M., Li, S.: Lightweight and energy efficient time synchronization for sensor network. In: International Conference on Wireless Communications, Networking and Mobile Computing, vol. 2, pp. 947–950 (2005)
10. He, L.-M.: Time Synchronization Based on Spanning Tree for Wireless Sensor Network. In: IEEE Wireless 4th International Conference on Communication, Networking and Mobile Computing, WiCOM 2008 (2008)
11. Mills, D.L.: Internet Time Synchronization: The Network Time Protocol. IEEE Transaction Communication 39(10), 1482–1493 (1991)
12. Heinzelman, W., Chandrakasan, A., Balakrishnan, H.: Energy-efficient Communication Protocol for Wireless Sensor Networks. In: Proceeding of the Hawaii International Conference on System Sciences, Hawaii, pp. 1–10 (2000)
13. VINT Project. The ucb/lbnl/vint network simulator-ns, `http://www.isi.edu/nsnam/ns`

Elastic VM for Cloud Resources Provisioning Optimization

Wesam Dawoud, Ibrahim Takouna, and Christoph Meinel

Hasso Plattner Institute,
Potsdam University,
Potsdam, Germany
firstname.lastname@hpi.uni-potsdam.de

Abstract. Rapid growth of E-Business and frequent changes in websites contents as well as customers' interest make it difficult to predict workload surge. To maintain a good quality of service (QoS), system administrators must provision enough resources to cope with workload fluctuations considering that resources over-provisioning reduces business profits while under-provisioning degrades performance. In this paper, we present elastic system architecture for dynamic resources management and applications optimization in virtualized environment. In our architecture, we have implemented three controllers for CPU, Memory, and Application. These controllers run in parallel to guarantee efficient resources allocation and optimize application performance on co-hosted VMs dynamically. We evaluated our architecture with extensive experiments and several setups; the results show that considering online optimization of application, with dynamic CPU and Memory allocation, can reduce service level objectives (SLOs) violation and maintain application performance...

Keywords: virtualization, consolidation, elasticity, application performance, automatic provisioning, optimization, cloud computing.

1 Introduction

Later advance in virtualization technology software, e.g. Xen [2] and VMware [16], enabled cloud computing environment to deliver agile, scalable, elastic, and low cost infrastructures, however, current implementation of elasticity in "Infrastructure as a Service" cloud model considers Virtual Machine (VM) as a scalability unit. In this paper, we developed an automated dynamic resources provisioning architecture to optimized resources provisioning in consolidated virtualized environments (e.g., Cloud computing). Unlike current implementation of elasticity in cloud infrastructure, we replaced the VM (as a coarse-grain scalability unit) with fine-grain resources units (i.e. %CPU as a share, Memory as MB). Our Elastic VM is scaled dynamically in-place to cope with workload fluctuations, furthermore, the hosted application is also tuned after each scaling to maintain predetermined (SLOs). As a use case we implemented our approach

A. Abraham et al. (Eds.): ACC 2011, Part I, CCIS 190, pp. 431–445, 2011.

into Xen environment and used Apache web server as an application, our SLO in this paper is to keep the response time of the web requests less than a specified threshold. Nevertheless, our architecture could be extended for any application that has tunable parameters such as Database applications. The key contributions of this work are as follow: First, we have studied Apache application performance under different configuration and different CPU and Memory allocation values. Second, we have developed a dynamic application optimization controller for Apache application to maintain the desired performance. Third, we built CPU and Memory controllers based on [6]. Fourth, we built elastic system architecture that join CPU, Memory, and application optimization controllers for elastic consolidated virtualized environments. Finally, the elastic system architecture has been evaluated with extensive experiments on several synthetic workload and experimental setups, experiments also have included real workload demand requests. Our results show that elastic system architecture can guarantee the best performance for application in terms of throughput and response time. The rest of the paper is organized as follow. Section 2 study the systems and concepts that drive our research. In section 3 we describe our elastic system architecture. Section 4 provides literature review for related work. In section 5, we describe our experimental setup and analyze results.

2 Overview

In this section, we give an overview of systems and concepts that drive our research; we will start with a detailed study of Apache server, then will discuss the complexity of enforcing SLOs into consolidated environments (e.g. clouds), and finally will explain concerns that accompany using feedback control systems in computing systems.

2.1 Apache Server

Apache [1], is structured as a pool of workers processes that handle HTTP requests. Currently, Apache supports two kinds of modules, workers and prefork modules. In our experiments we use Apache with prefork module to handle dynamic requests (e.g., php pages). In prefork mode, requests enter the TCP Accept Queue where they wait for a worker. A worker processes a single request to completion before accepting a new request. Number of worker processes is limited by *MaxClients* parameter.

Figure 1 displays the result of experiments in which Apache is configured with different settings of Memory, traffic rate, and *MaxClients*. By monitoring the throughput, we notice that, there is a value of *MaxClients*, (e.g. 75), which gives the highest throughput (450 req/sec) for specific Memory settings (512MB). Before this value there is no enough workers to handle requests, and after this value, performance regrades because of one of the following problems: CPU spend much time switching between many process or Memory is full so paging to harddisk consumes most of CPU time. Our heuristic Apache controller job is to find this optimum value dynamically.

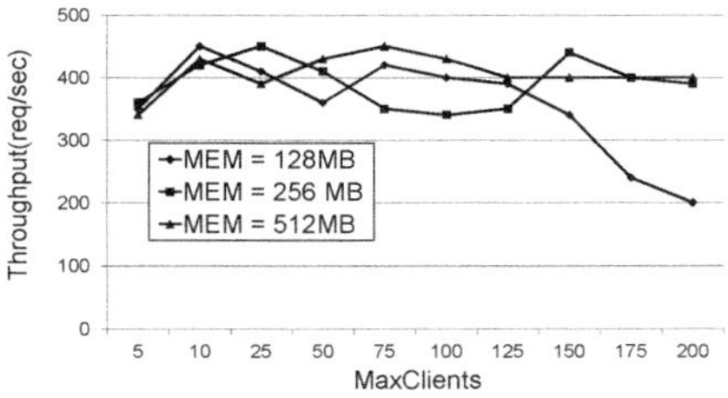

Fig. 1. Throughput vs. MaxClients under different hardware settings

2.2 SLOs Enforcement Complexity

Service-level agreement (or SLA) is a contract between a service provider and its customers. SLA consists of one or more service-level objectives (SLOs). An example of an SLO is: "The homepage should be loaded completely in no longer than 2 seconds". As seen, SLO consists of three parts: QoS metric (e.g., response time), the bound (e.g., 2 seconds), and a relational operator (e.g., no longer than). The violation of these objectives usually associated with penalties to the provider. The challenge is to map QoS metrics into low level resources (e.g. CPU and memory) dynamically.

2.3 Feedback Control of Computing Systems

Controllers are designed mainly for three purposes [5]: First, output regulation to be equal or near to the reference input; for example, maintaining Memory utilization always around 90%. Second, disturbance rejection which means if the CPU is regulated to be 70% utilized, then this must not affected by any other running applications like backup or virus scanning. Third, optimization which can be translated in our system as finding the best value of *MaxClients* that optimize Apache server performance. In terms of the feedback controllers, SLO enforcement often becomes a regulation problem where SLO metric is the measured output, and SLO bound is the reference input. The choice of control objective typically depends on the application. Indeed, with multiuse target systems, the same target system may have multiple controllers with different SLOs, unfortunately, identifying Input-output models for computing systems is not commonly used [19] because of the absence of the first-principle models. As a replacement, many research [18], [13], [6] [17] considered the black-box approach where the relation between the input and output is inferred by experiments. According to [19], to build a feedback controller able to adjust input-output of black-box's model you have to deal with many challenges: First, The controller may not converge to equilibrium, if the system does not have a monotonic relationship between a single input and a single output. Second, without an estimate of the sensitivity of the outputs with respect to the inputs, the controller may become too aggressive (or even unstable) or too slow. Third, the controller can't adapt to different operating regions in the input-output relationship, for example

[19] shows that the mean response time is controllable using CPU allocation only when the CPU consumption is close to the allocated capacity and uncontrollable when the CPU allocation is more than enough. Here the notion of "uncontrollable" refers to the condition where the output is insensitive to changes in the input.

3 Elastic VM Architecture

Our architecture has main component "QoS controller" which communicates with many other modules implemented into the Virtual Machine Manager (VMM) and VMs levels as the following:

- Resources monitor module dynamically measures the resources consumption and updates the QoS controller with new measurements. The module depends on *xentop* tool to get CPU consumption of each VM.
- CPU scheduler is implemented to dynamically change the CPU allocation of the VMs according to determined values by QoS controller, this module depends on Xen credit scheduler as an actuator for setting the CPU shares for VMs. The credit scheduler has a non-work-conserving-mode which enables determining a limited portion of the CPU capacity for each VM. The credit scheduler prevents an overloaded VM from consuming the whole CPU capacity of the VMM and degrading the other VMs performance.
- Memory manger is implemented with help of balloon driver in Xen. This allows online changing of the VMs Memory. The driver doesn't allow VM to exceed the determined variable *maxmem* at the domain creating time, so to have a wide range of the Memory size, we gave the variable *maxmem* an initial high value i.e. 500MB in all user domains configuration files then use the *mem-set* command to change the Memory size into the value determined by the controller.
- Performance monitor also keeps the controller up to date with performance metrics, i.e. the average response time and the throughput. The performance

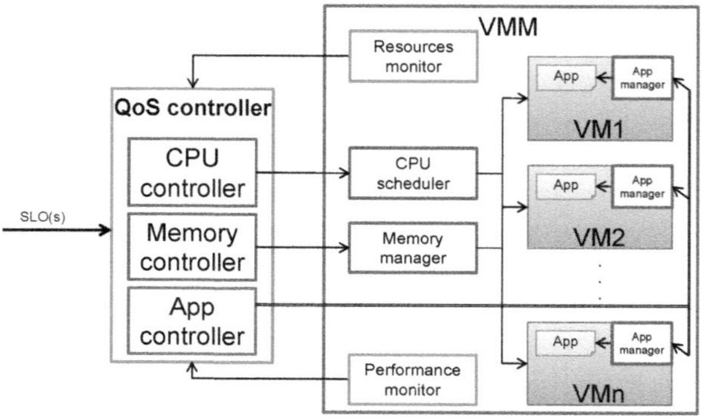

Fig. 2. Elastic VM architecture

monitor is implemented on network device of the VMM, so it can monitor both the incoming and outgoing traffic.
- Application manager (App manager) is implemented into VM level, its job is to get new *MaxClients* value from the Application controller (App controller), to update the Apache configuration file, and then to reload Apache gracefully.

On the left side of figure 2 is the QoS controller; the controller has (SLOs) as inputs and proposed CPU capacity, proposed Memory allocation, and proposed *MaxClients* as outputs. In our approach the main SLO is to keep average response time of Apache web server into specific value regardless of the workload fluctuations, for this purpose we implemented three controllers to run in parallel, these controllers are as the following:

CPU controller: Which is a nested loop controller developed in [20]. The inner controller (CPU utilization controller) is an adaptive-gain integral (I) controller was designed in [17]:

$$a_{cpu}(k+1) = a_{cpu}(k) - K_1(k)(u_{cpu}^{ref} - u_{cpu}(k)), \quad (1)$$

Where

$$K_1(k) = \alpha.c_{cpu}(k)/r_{cpu}^{ref} \quad (2)$$

The controller is designed to predict the next CPU allocation $a_{cpu}(k+1)$ depending on last CPU allocation $a_{cpu}(k)$ and consumption $c_{cpu}(k)$, where the last CPU utilization $u_{cpu}(k) = c_{cpu}(k)/a_{cpu}(k)$. The parameter α is the constant gain which determine the aggressiveness of the controller. In our experiments, we set β=1.5 to allow the controller aggressively allocate more CPU when the system is overloaded, and slowly decrease CPU allocation in the under loaded regions. The disadvantage of this controller is that, it implies determining the reference utilization u_{cpu}^{ref} that will maintain the determined SLO (i.e. response time), whoever, this is not practical because, as seen in figure 3, the response time does not only depend on CPU utilization, but also on the request rate, which changes frequently. So, it is more realistic to have u_{cpu}^{ref} value automatically driven by the application's QoS goals rather than being chosen manually for each application.

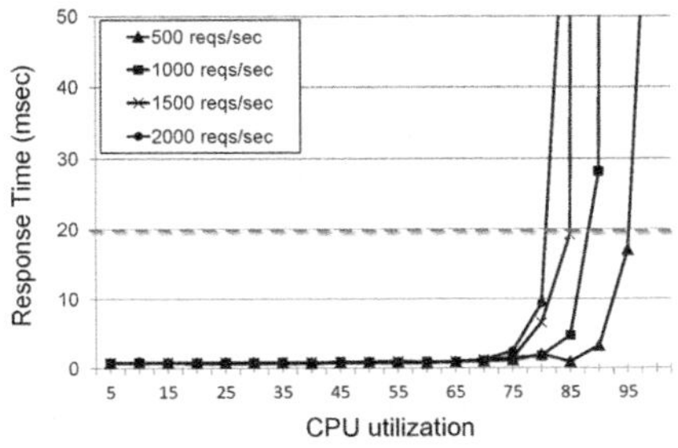

Fig. 3. Mean response time vs. CPU utilization under different request rates

For this goal, another outer loop controller (RT controller) is designed [20] to adjust the u_{cpu}^{ref} value dynamically to ensure that the QoS metric, response time (RT), is around the desired value, this outer loop controller can be interpreted into the following equation:

$$u_{cpu}^{ref}(i+1) = u_{cpu}^{ref}(i) + \beta(RT_{cpu}^{ref} - RT_{cpu}(i))/RT_{cpu}^{ref} \quad (3)$$

Where $u_{cpu}^{ref}(i+1)$ is the desired CPU utilization, $RT_{cpu}(i)$ is the measured response time, and RT_{cpu}^{ref} is the desired response time determined by SLO. The outer controller (RT controller) ensures that the value fed to the CPU controller is always within an acceptable CPU utilization interval $[U_{min}, U_{max}]$.

In our experiments, we set β=1.5, the CPU allocation is limited to the interval [10, 80], and the CPU utilization is also limited to the interval [10, 80]. The desired response time (RT) in all our experiments is 20 milliseconds.

Memory controller: In our experiments we noticed that increasing the number of Apache processes can increase the throughput, but at some level, the performance is degraded drastically when the Apache processes consumed the whole available Memory, at this point, system starts to swap the Memory contents into the hard-disk, this behavior add more workload to the CPU which typically already overloaded by the big number of the processes. To keep the system away from bottlenecks, we implemented the Memory controller designed in [6] to keep the CPU controller run in an operating region away from the CPU contention:

$$a_{mem}(i+1) = a_{mem}(i) + K_2(i)(u_{mem}^{ref} - u_{mem}(i)) \quad (4)$$

Where

$$K_2(i) = \lambda . u_{mem}(i)/u_{mem}^{ref} \quad (5)$$

The controller aggressively allocates more Memory when the previously allocated Memory is close to saturation (i.e. more than 90%), and slowly decreases Memory allocation in the under-load region. Along our experiments, we set u_{mem}^{ref}=90%, λ=1, and the limits of the controller to be [64, 512], where the 64 is the minimum allowed Memory allocated size, and the 512 is the maximum allowed allocated Memory size.

Application controller: after extensive of experiments and monitoring Apache behavior, we found that there was a specific value of *MaxClients* which gives the best throughput and the minimum response time as seen in figure 1, finding the optimum value of *MaxClients* was examined by former research e.g. [8], unfortunately, these optimization methods are not applicable to our case for many reasons: First, we have a dynamic resources, so it will be difficult to dynamically determine the new optimum *MaxClients* value for each new resources allocation. Second, we don't have the chance to run an active optimization using our generated traffic, since it may influence the real service performance. Third, the optimum value is affected by traffic type and CPU utilization.

In the light of the mentioned problems, we designed our heuristic Apache controller to find the best *MaxClients* value passively (depending on the real traffic). The Apache controller monitors four measured values to determine the best *MaxClients*: response time, throughput, CPU utilization, and number of running Apache processes. The controller saves the best record of these values. The best record is calculated by finding the record which satisfies the QoS response time metric and gives the highest throughput with less CPU utilization. With each new measurement of monitored values, Apache compares the current record with the best record, if it is better; the current record will be saved as the best record. While it is running, if the Apache noticed a violation of QoS metrics (response time in our case) it tries to predict the problem by the following rules:

Rule1: Apache processes starving problem: Apache processes starving problem occurs when Apache server runs big number of processes, as a result, CPU spends most of the time switching between these processes while giving small slot of the time to each process, such behavior causes requests to spend longer time in application queue, which end up with high response time and many timed-out requests. To eliminate this problem, the Apache controller reloads the Apache server with the last best record, this reload is supposed to reduce the number of running processes, reduce CPU utilization, and consequently reduce response time.

Rule2: Resources competition problem: The competition on resources is predicted by Apache controller as response time increases, number of running apache processes reaches *MaxClients* value, and at the same time CPU utilization decreases (i.e. less than 90%). The reason behind the low utilization in competition case is that, CPU controller, according to the high response time, suggests allocating more CPU, while the fair share which gives each co-located VM on the same core the same capacity of the CPU (e.g., 50% in case of two VMs) prevents the VM from exceeding this limit. As seen above, with both rules, the proposed Apache controller will not only look for the optimum *MaxClients* value, but also will eliminate performance bottlenecks by keeping a history of the last best running configurations.

4 Related Work

Dynamic provisioning of resources - allocation and de-allocation of the resources to cope with workload - had much interest especially after the widely usage of consolidation environments such as virtualized datacenters and cloud. Significant prior research have been sought to map the (SLOs) such as QoS requirements into low level resources requirements such as CPU, Memory, and I/O requirements. All the studied approaches considered the mean response time (MRT) as their SLO and accordingly developed the suitable controllers for resources management e.g. [4], [17], [15] and [6]. To this end, previous related works can be divided into three main folds: dynamic resources provisioning using controllers, resources management using migration of VM feature and multi-instances provisioning, and application optimization.

Research in [4], [17] and [15] considered only CPU controllers to automate the dynamic resources provisioning, while [6] designed parallel CPU and Memory controllers to be sure that consolidated applications can have access to sufficient CPU and Memory resources, with the help of Memory controller [6] keeps the whole system away from the high levels of utilization that can drastically degrade the performance [12]; nevertheless, applications optimization with dynamic resources provisioning is the common missing issue. Unlike aforementioned works, [15] has developed a multi-tier dynamic provisioning system; it presents novel provisioning technique based on combination of predictive and reactive mechanisms. The application behavior and workload characteristics are analyzed off-line depending on history monitoring, but the provisioning is completely automated. The provisioning of the resources in web server tier is implemented by running more VMs instances. In some productive environments such as Amazon Elastic Load Balancing, the quality of service metrics (e.g., request count and request latency) is watched by Amazon Cloudwatch. Amazon scalability mechanism depends on initiating a VM instance as a load balancer routing the traffic into many similar VMs instances, this approach have many limitations: First, it is limited to specific application like web servers and not applicable to the other applications like Databases. Second, it depends on a VM as a load balancer, which can be a single point of failure. Third, it admits VM as a scaling unit.

Several researches have leveraged VMs migration mechanism for coping with dynamic workload fluctuation as well as providing scalability and load balancing models, for example, [7] and [18] propose migration to handle dynamic workload changes and resource overloads in production systems to avoid application performance degradation. But, migrating VM consumes I/O and CPU and network resources which might contribute at performance degradation of other VMs, furthermore, using migration with applications that have long-running in-memory state or frequently updated data such as database and messaging applications might take too long time causing service level violations during migration. Additionally, security restrictions might increase overhead during migration process [11].

Towards application optimization, [8] have implemented three controllers to optimize the configuration parameters of the Apache web server (i.e. MaxClients) online, the Newton's method optimizer which is inconsistent with the highly variable data, the Fuzzy controller which is more robust but converges slowly, and finally, the heuristic controller which works well under specific circumstances and requires former knowledge of bottleneck resources. [3] developed an agent-based solution to automate system tuning, the agents do both controller design and feedback control, however, slow converges of the system (i.e., 10 minutes for MaxClients), makes it unsuitable for sudden workload changes.

5 Experimental Setup

Our experiment conducted on a testbed of two physical machines (Client and Server) connected by 1 Gbps Ethernet. Server machine has Intel Quad Core i7 Processor, 2.8 GHz and 8GB of Memory, it runs Xen 3.3 with kernel 2.6.26-2-xen-686 as hypervisor. On the hypervisor are hosted VMs with Linux Ubuntu

2.6.24-19. These VMs run Apache 2.0 as a web server in prefork mode. For workload generation, *httperf* tool [10] is installed on client machine. In the following experiments we deal with three VMs setup: First, Static VM, which is a virtual machine initialized with 512MB of RAM and limited to 50% of the CPU capacity. Second, Elastic VM with CPU/Memory controllers, it is a VM controlled with the CPU and Memory controllers seen in equations 1 to 5, the CPU limits of this machine is 80% of CPU capacity, and the Memory is 512MB of RAM. Third, Elastic VM with Apache, it has the same setup of first VM except that it is equipped with our Apache controller in addition to CPU and Memory controllers. In all our experiments, SLO is to keep response time threshold (RT threshold) less than 20 milliseconds.

5.1 Experimental Setup 1

In this experiment, we would like to study our Elastic VM ability to cope with traffic change to maintain the specified SLO. To express the improvements, we ran the same experiment onto a Static VM with similar but static resources. As a basis of our experiments; we used dynamic web pages requests, in each request, the web server executes a public key encryption operation to consume a certain amount of CPU time. The step traffic initiated with the help of *autobensh* tool [14], it started with 20 sessions, each session contains 10 connections. The number of sessions increases by 10 with each load step. The total number of connections for each step is 5000, and the timeout for the request is 5 seconds. Throughput result from the generated web traffic is seen in figure 4(b).

Each step of the graphs in figure 4(b) represents the throughput of a specific traffic rate, for example, in period between 0 to 210 seconds; both VMs respond to 200 req/sec successfully without any requests loss or time-out, in this period of time, both VMs were able to consume the required CPU capacity that copes with coming requests. In first period, we notice in figure 4(a) how the Elastic VM started a slow release of over-allocation CPU from the highest starting allocation (i.e. 80%) to the predicted suitable value. This behavior of Elastic VM, allocating resources aggressively then converging slowly to the optimum allocation, enabled it to respond to the whole traffic rates successfully. In the other hand, the static allocation of CPU, enabled the Static VM to respond successfully until second 780, afterwards, the Static VM's CPU is saturated, which caused requests to wait longer in the TCP accept queue, and consequently increased response time, this results in a continues period of SLO violation as seen in figure 4(c). Furthermore, some of the queued requests timed out before being served, the percentage of timed-out requests with the corresponding traffic rate is illustrated in table 1. The table started at 900 req/sec because there was no significant timed-out traffic before this rate. If compared to the Elastic VM for the same high traffic rate (i.e. 800 to 1200 req/sec), figures 4(a) to 4(c) show how the Elastic VM was able to borrow more resources dynamically, serve more requests, maintain a low response time, and prevent SLO violation.

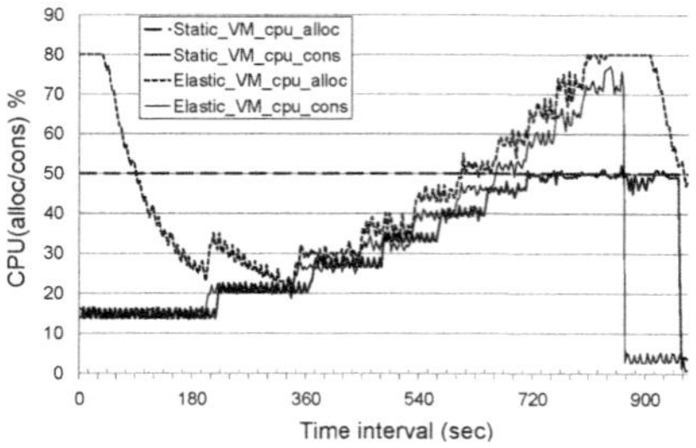

(a) CPU consumption

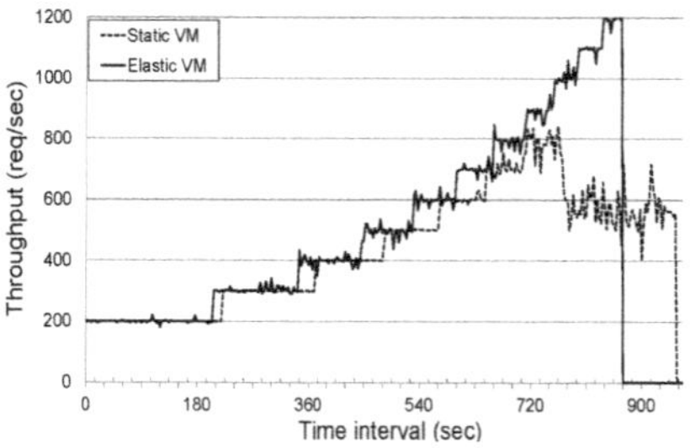

(b) Throughput

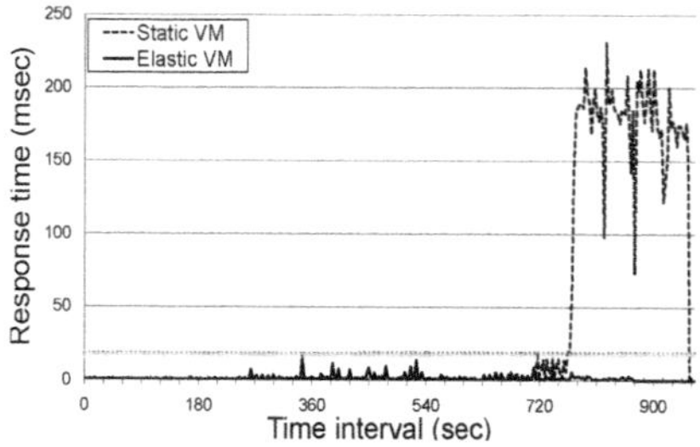

(c) Response time

Fig. 4. Static VM vs. Elastic VM response to step traffic

Table 1. The timeout started after the Static VM received 900 req/sec

Requests rate(req/sec)	Static VM (timeout %)
900	7.232
1000	15.328
1100	18.258
1200	27.772

5.2 Experimental Setup 2

In the previous experiment, we studied the ideal case where the host was able to satisfy the Elastic VM's need for more resources to cope with the increase of incoming requests. In this experiment, we study the competition on the CPU between two Elastic VMs. Unlike experiments that have been done by [6], where each VM's virtual CPU has been pinned into a different physical core, we pinned the virtual CPUs of two Elastic VMs into same physical core to raise the competition level. For the following experiment, the step-traffic has been run two times simultaneously onto both Elastic VMs, one time without Apache controller and another time with Apache controller, to clarify the benefits of Apache controller usage. The first part of the experiment, illustrated in figures 5(a) to 5(c). Figure 5(b), shows that Elastic VMs were not able to cope with the traffic rate higher than 800 req/sec while the host committed only 50% of the CPU power

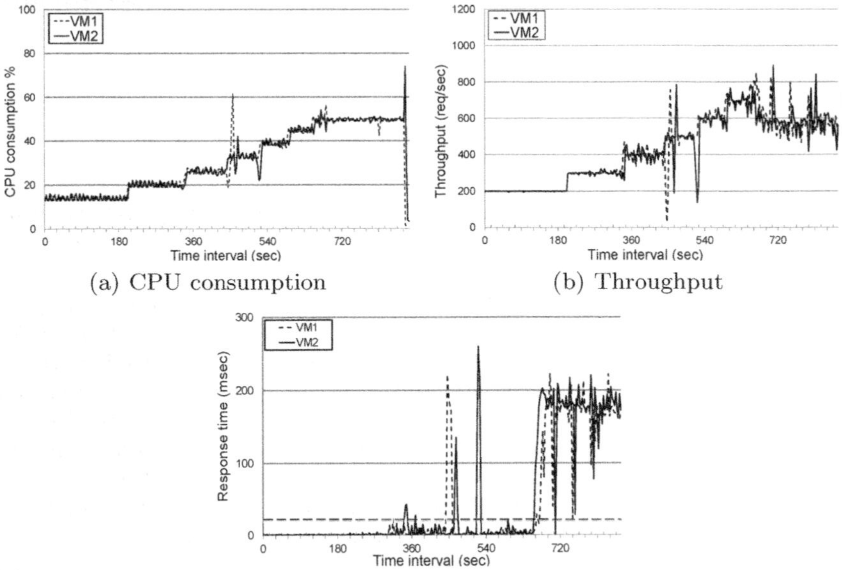

(a) CPU consumption (b) Throughput

(c) Response time

Fig. 5. Two Elastic VMs (without) Apache controller responding to step traffic

for each VM starting from second #660 as seen in figure 5(a). The reason behind this fair sharing is Xen credit scheduler, during this experiment, we setup the scheduler with the same share for running VMs. According to competition on CPU, many requests are queued for a long time causing high response time and continues violation of SLO, as seen in figure 5(c), moreover, many other requests are timed-out before being served as seen in second and third columns of table 2. From the above experiments, we can conclude that Elastic VM can improve the performance if the host has more resource to redistribute, but in case of competition on resources, under the fair scheduling, Elastic VM (without) Apache controller merely behaves as a Static VM. The previous experiment is repeated on two Elastic VMs (with) Apache controller, figure 6(a) shows that in spite of the limited CPU capacity (50%) available to each VM, starting from second #660, the Apache controller do two improvements, first, the moment of the Apache reload is a good chance for the other Apache server to have more processing power and serve more requests as seen in figure 6(a), second, after the reload, the Apache servers are tuned with a new *MaxClients* value, if this value achieved better performance, the Apache controller will keep it, otherwise it will continue looking for more optimum value.

5.3 Experimental Setup 3

In the following experiment, we test our system against more real world demand traces traffic. For this purpose, we generate the same traffic described in [8].

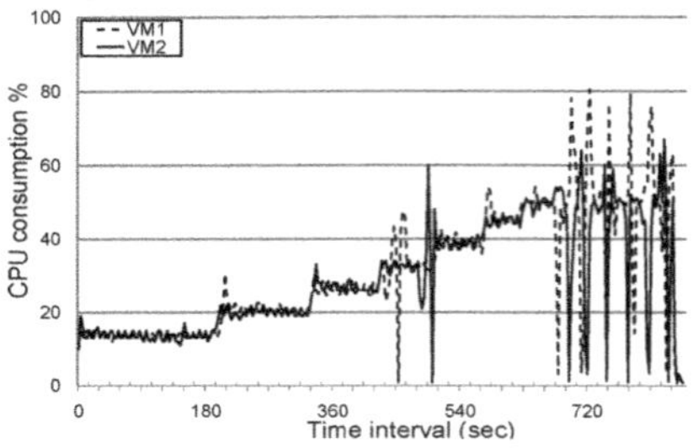

(a) CPU consumption

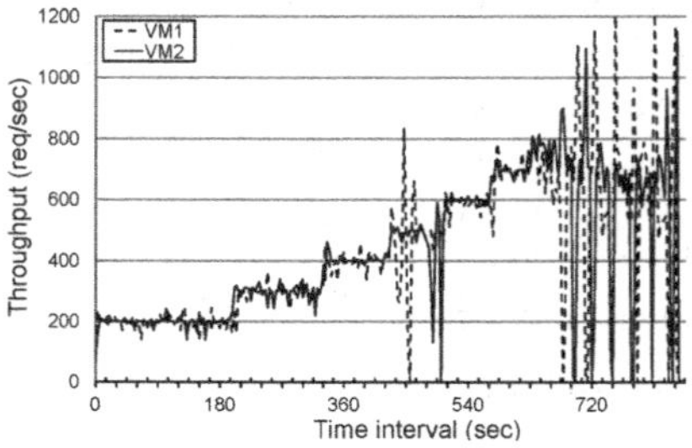

(b) Throughput

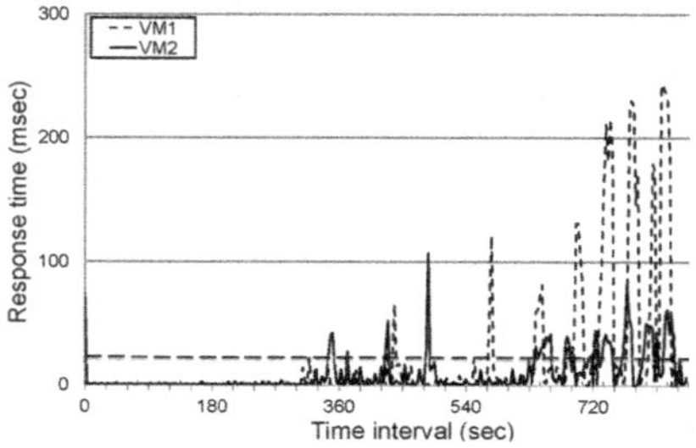

(c) Response time

Fig. 6. Two Elastic VMs (with) Apache controller responding to step web traffic

The parameters of the generated workload are described in table 3 according to "WAGON" [9] benchmark, however, the session rate is selected to have uniform distribution, this enabled us to run the same traffic one time (without) Apache controller, and another time (with) Apache controller, to investigate Apache controller behavior under real workload. For both parts of the experiment, we used the same Elastic VMs described in section 3. First part of this experiment has been started by directing simultaneous instances of the generated traffic to the co-located Elastic VMs. Both Elastic VMs in this part of the experiment are running (without) Apache controller for 15 minutes. As seen in figure 7(a), there is a competition on the CPU power from the first run of the experiment until the 60th second, as a result, the percentage of timed-out requests for VM1 and VM2 were 12.7% and 15.5%, while the percentage of SLO violations are 18.6% and 17.5% as seen in first and second columns of table 3. Along the remaining run of the experiment, there was no competition on the CPU, and Elastic VM1 was able to consume more than 50% of the CPU power in periods from 120 to 180, and from 300 to 360 to keep the response time within the determined value.

In the second part of this experiment, Apache controller has been run in parallel to CPU and Memory controllers. As seen in figure 8(a), the competition on CPU at the beginning of the experiment triggered Apache server tuning in both machines, as a result, Apache server at VM1 is reloaded one time at second #5 with *MaxClients*=160, and another time at second #30 with *MaxClients*=170, while Apache server at VM2 is reloaded at second #30 with *MaxClients*=160.

Table 2. Two Elastic VMs (without) Apache controller vs. two Elastic VMs (with) Apache controller responding to step traffic

	VM1	VM2	VM1	VM2
(req/sec)	Timeout requests(without)		Timeout requests(with)	
800	4.0%	0%	0%	0.2%
900	13.3%	23.8%	8.8%	8.2%
1000	20.5%	23.2%	16.52%	17.0%
1100	25.0%	35.0%	21.0%	22.0%
1200	31.0%	37.0%	26.2%	27.8%
	SLO violation(without)		SLO violation(with)	
	23.9%	26.4%	14.7%	16.8%

Table 3. Workload parameters

Parameter name	Distribution	Parameters
SessionLength	LogNormal	Mean=8, sigma =3
BurstLength	Gaussian	Mean=7, sigma=3
ThinkTime	LogNormal	Mean=30, sigma=30

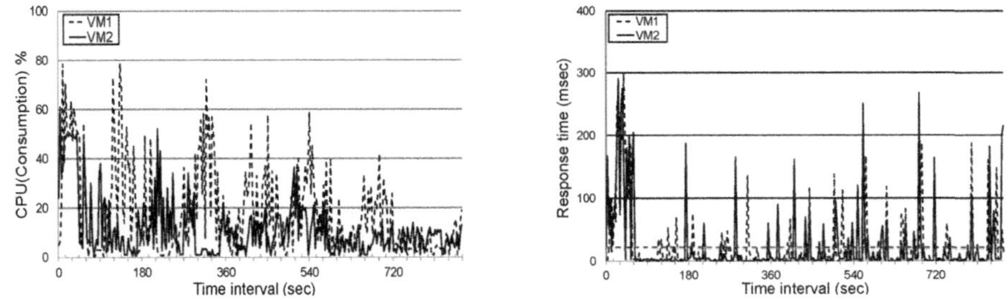

(a) CPU consumption (b) Response time

Fig. 7. Two Elastic VMs (without) Apache controller responding to more realistic traffic

The benefit of application tuning is illustrated in figure 8(b), instead of continues violation of SLO seen in figure 7(b) starting from the beginning of the experiment until second #60, SLO violation is limited to second #30 with the help of Apache controller. The timeout traffic and SLO violation of the complete run of the second part of the experiment is illustrated in third and fourth columns of table 4. First and second columns of table 4 show a small reduction in the percentage of the timed-out requests, but a significant reduction in percentage of SLO violation in case of Apache controller usage.

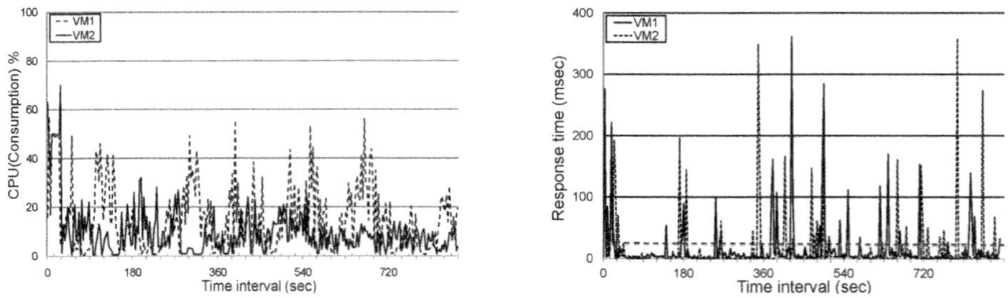

(a) CPU consumption (b) Response time

Fig. 8. Two Elastic VMs (with) Apache controller responding to more realistic traffic

Table 4. Two Elastic VMs (without) Apache controller vs. two Elastic VMs (with) Apache controller responding to more realistic generated traffic

VM1	VM2	VM1	VM2
Timeout requests(without)		Timeout requests(with)	
12.7%	15.5%	11.5%	13.8%
SLO violations(without)		SLO violations(with)	
18.6%	17.5%	13.3%	13.1%

The above results prove that running our Apache controller, in parallel to CPU/Memory controllers, reduces SLO violation and improves application performance for both synthesized and more real generated traffic.

6 Conclusions and Future Work

In this paper, we have presented an implementation for elastic system architecture for optimizing resources consumption in consolidated environments. Our system includes three controllers CPU, Memory, and Application running in parallel to preserve the intended SLO. We have evaluated our system in a real Xen based virtualized environment; the experiments show that using Application controller maintains the performance and mitigates SLO violation and the timeout requests.

Our immediate future work will include analyzing more applications such as database and their optimization feasibility in such dynamic resources allocation environment. The analysis will consider analytical models such as queuing analysis. We will also extend our work to be integrated with other resource management schemes like "VM migration" and "running multiple instances" while considering both performance and security as priorities.

References

1. Apache: The Apache Software Foundation, http://www.apache.org/
2. Barham, P., Dragovic, B., Fraser, K., Hand, S., Harris, T., Ho, A., Neugebauer, R., Pratt, I., Warfield, A.: Xen and the art of virtualization, vol. 37, p. 164. ACM Press, New York (2003)
3. Chess, Y.D., Hellerstein, J.L., Parekh, S., Bigus, J.P.: Managing Web server performance with AutoTune agents. IBM Systems Journal 42(1), 136–149 (2003)
4. Gandhi, N., Tilbury, D.M., Diao, Y., Hellerstein, J., Parekh, S.: MIMO control of an Apache web server: modeling and controller design. In: Proceedings of the 2002 American Control Conference (IEEE Cat. No.CH37301), pp. 4922–4927. American Automatic Control Council (2002)
5. Hellerstein, J.L., Diao, Y., Parekh, S., Tilbury, D.M.: Feedback Control of Computing Systems. John Wiley & Sons, Chichester (2004)
6. Heo, J., Zhu, X., Padala, P., Wang, Z.: Memory Overbooking and Dynamic Control of Xen Virtual Machines in Consolidated Environments. In: Proceedings of IFIPIEEE Symposium on Integrated Management IM 2009 Miniconference, pp. 630–637. IEEE, Los Alamitos (2009)
7. Khanna, G., Beaty, K., Kar, G., Kochut, A.: Application Performance Management in Virtualized Server Environments. In: 2006 IEEE/IFIP Network Operations and Management Symposium NOMS 2006, pp. 373–381. IEEE, Los Alamitos (2006)
8. Liu, X., Sha, L., Diao, Y., Froehlich, S., Hellerstein, J.L., Parekh, S.: Online Response Time Optimization of Apache Web Server (2003)
9. Liu, Z.: Traffic model and performance evaluation of Web servers. Performance Evaluation 46(2-3), 77–100 (2001)
10. Mosberger, D., Jin, T.: httperf - A Tool for Measuring Web Server Performance. In: First Workshop on Internet Server Performance, pp. 59–67 (1998)
11. Oberheide, J., Cooke, E., Jahanian, F.: Empirical exploitation of live virtual machine migration. In: Proc. of BlackHat DC Convention (2008)
12. Bovet, D.P., Cesati, M.: Understanding the Linux Kernel, 3rd edn. O'Reilly Media, Sebastopol (2005)
13. Padala, P., Hou, K.-Y., Shin, K.G., Zhu, X., Uysal, M., Wang, Z., Singhal, S., Merchant, A.: Automated control of multiple virtualized resources. In: European Conference on Computer Systems, pp. 13–26 (2009)
14. Midgley, J.T.J.: Autobench (2008), http://www.xenoclast.org/autobench/
15. Urgaonkar, B., Shenoy, P., Chandra, A., Goyal, P., Wood, T.: Agile dynamic provisioning of multi-tier Internet applications. ACM Transactions on Autonomous and Adaptive Systems (TAAS) 3(1) (2008)
16. VMWare, http://www.vmware.com/
17. Wang, Z., Zhu, X., Singhal, S., Packard, H.: Utilization and slo-based control for dynamic sizing of resource partitions (2005)
18. Wood, T., Shenoy, P., Venkataramani, A., Yousif, M.: Abstract Black-box and Gray-box Strategies for Virtual Machine Migration (2007)
19. Zhu, X., Uysal, M., Wang, Z., Singhal, S., Merchant, A., Padala, P., Shin, K.: What does control theory bring to systems research?. SIGOPS Oper. Syst. Rev. 43(1), 62–69 (2009)
20. Zhu, X., Wang, Z., Singhal, S.: Utility-Driven Workload Management using Nested Control Design. In: 2006 American Control Conference, pp. 6033–6038 (2006)

Employing Bloom Filters for Enforcing Integrity of Outsourced Databases in Cloud Environments

T. Aditya[1], P.K. Baruah[1], and R. Mukkamala[2]

[1] Department of Mathematics and Computer Science,
Sri Sathya Sai Institute of Higher Learning, Prashanti Nilayam, A.P., India
adityatelidevara@gmail.com, baruahpk@sssihl.edu.in

[2] Department of Computer Science Old Dominion University,
Norfolk, Virginia, USA
mukka@cs.odu.edu

Abstract. With the ever increasing growth of cloud computing and the resulting outsourcing of data, concerns of data integrity, security, and privacy are also on the rise. Among these, evidence of data integrity, i.e., being tamper-evident and current, seem to be of immediate concern. While several integrity techniques currently exist, most result in significant overhead at the database owner site. For clients with large databases, these are not viable solutions. In this paper, we propose a computationally efficient alternative—database integrity with Bloom filters. We focus both on the *tamper-evidence* and *freshness* properties of the database as well as *completeness* of query results. We propose two schemes for integrity enforcement—first using aggregates signatures and second using authenticated data structures. We provide detailed analysis and experimental results to prove their efficiency and correctness. The results are compared with the traditional security hash functions such as SHA-1 and are shown to be computationally efficient. We have also implemented the schemes on multiprocessor systems which show further reduction in the execution time. Our results clearly demonstrate the feasibility and efficacy of employing Bloom filters to enforce integrity for outsourced databases in cloud environments.

Keywords: bloom filter, data integrity, hashing, parallel processing, outsourced databases, aggregated signatures, authenticated data structures.

1 Introduction

Data integrity has been an essential requirement of many systems in both data communication and data storage. For example, parity checking, error detection codes, and error-correction codes have long been employed in data communication [1]. CRC or Cyclic Redundancy Check is one such code used as a checksum in communication protocols [2]. Memory-style parity as well as hashes have been used in main memory technologies to ensure integrity [3]. Similarly, systems such as RAID have proposed several ways to store the parity corresponding to each

A. Abraham et al. (Eds.): ACC 2011, Part I, CCIS 190, pp. 446–460, 2011.

disk block to detect/correct any integrity violations [4]. However, in each of these cases, the threat model consisted of accidental corruption of data rather than intentional tampering [1,2,3,4].

Today, with the availability of higher network bandwidths, cloud computing seems to be the fastest emerging technology in the IT industry [5]. In addition to several private clouds, companies such as Google, Microsoft, and Amazon offer these services to the public at low cost. The rate at which data is being collected by data owners (e.g., NASA) is also growing [6]. This has resulted in increasing data and process outsourcing to the clouds. However, a database owner who intends to outsource its database has several concerns regarding data integrity, security, and privacy. In terms of data integrity and freshness the concerns of the owner are:

1. How can the cloud server assure that the database has not been tampered with(tamper-evident)?
2. How can the server ensure that all the relevant results for a database query are returned and nothing is omitted (completeness)?
3. How can the cloud server guarantee that all update transactions (e.g., insertions, deletions, updates) sent to it have been carried out?
4. In case a database relation has been found to be tampered with or found to be out-of-date, can the owner recover it?
5. In case, the database owner is different from the database user, how can the database user be assured that the provided query results have not been tampered with, complete, and current?

Several techniques have been proposed in literature to address these issues. In this paper, we focus mainly on issues 1-3. In particular, we focus on integrity at tuple-level in each database relation.

In this paper, we propose two novel methods for enforcing database integrity, both employ Bloom filters, a space-efficient probabilistic data structure that is used to test whether an element is a member of a set [11]. Bloom filters are in use in several systems such as Googles Bigtable [12], high-speed traffic measurement [13], data aggregation in wireless sensor networks [14], network forensics for IPTraceback [15], and P2P security [16]. Here, we use Bloom filters to replace the individual hashes of each tuple and also the aggregated hashes to ensure integrity. Structure of Bloom filter also easily lends itself to parallel implementation using shared memory programming [17]. In fact, we show that parallel Bloom filters further reduce the execution time at the client during the integrity verification of query results.

The paper is organized as follows. In section 2, we briefly summarize the current work in data integrity. Section 3 describes the proposed methods. in section 4, we summarize results from our analysis and simulation experiments. Finally, section 5 concludes the paper with the contributions of this paper and our plans for future extensions to the work.

2 Related Work

The existing work in integrity of outsourced databases can be broadly classified into three types: (i) Methods which use *Aggregated signatures*; (ii) Methods using *Authenticated Data Structures*; and (iii) Methods that are based on inserting *dummy/fake tuples* into the relations of a database. Here we will not discuss methods of type (iii) because even with 20% of the tuples being fake, there is a probability of 0.5 that the server can successfully delete up to 10 tuples [18] and go undetected.

Mykletun et al [19] proposed a method which uses aggregated RSA signatures to verify the integrity of relational databases supporting only select type of queries. In this method, the owner initially computes the hash of every tuple by concatenating all the attributes as a string, encrypts the hash using his private key and stores this encrypted hash as one more attribute in the relation. The owner then outsources the data. So whenever any client requests a query, the server has to compute the result as well as some verification tokens for the client to verify the result. Sending all the encrypted hashes of each tuple in the result will do the job, but that requires lots of computation at the client. The client has to decrypt each hash, which involves a costly exponentiation operation. Instead, the server computes the query result and computes the aggregated signature for it by multiplying the encrypted hashes for all the tuples in the result. This is called *Condensed-RSA*. So the client has to decrypt only the aggregated signature and multiply each locally computed hash. This is advantageous as multiplication is a cheaper operation than exponentiation.

Tampering in any of the tuple will result in a mismatch of the aggregated signature computed locally and the one sent by the server thereby proving correctness. But the server can omit some of the tuples in the result and also exclude them in the calculation of the aggregated signature which compromises completeness. So an improvement to this was proposed in [20] where the hash inserted in each tuple is the hash of the string formed by concatenating the previous tuples and the current tuple. Here it is assumed that the queries involve only select operation on a particular attribute and the tuples are arranged in the ascending order with respect to that attribute. With this mechanism, if the server omits any tuple in the result, it will corrupt the hash of the next tuple which in turn corrupt the aggregated signature.

The above mentioned methods belong to the first type which use aggregated signatures. But the disadvantage with these methods is that they initially require signing of a large number of tuples. So the set up cost is very high. Several methods addressed this problem by using authenticated data structures [7,20,21]. This category also supports only select type of queries and the tuples are assumed to be arranged in the ascending order with respect to the attribute used in the select query. The authenticated data structure is a tree where each leaf nodes represent the hashes of their corresponding tuples. The hashes at the parents nodes are obtained by taking a hash of the contents of its children. The tree is built this way till the root. The structure of these trees can vary from a binary tree (called Merkle tree)[7] to more complicated B^+-trees and MB-trees [20]. The root hash is then authenticated by the data owner's private key. The difference between Merkle tree, B^+-tree and MB-tree is that Merkle tree is a binary tree where each leaf node corresponds to the hash of a single tuple while in other trees, just as their name suggests, each leaf nodes contains a set of hashes of b consecutive tuples in a relation.

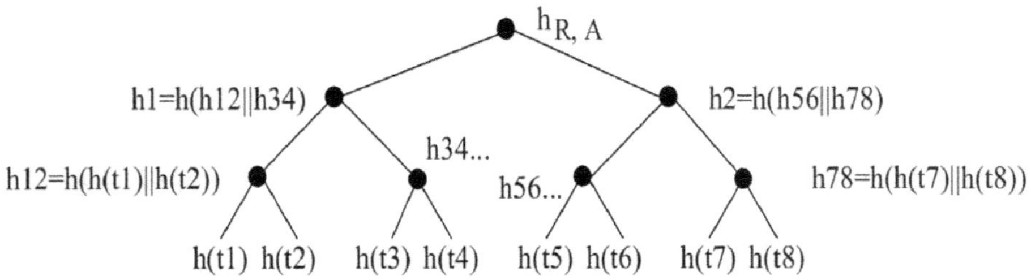

Fig. 1. Computation of the root hash using Merkle hash tree on a sorted relation with tuples $t_1, t_2, ..., t_8$ given in [7]

Fig. 1 illustrates the construction a verification object (VO) for a Merkle hash tree. Along with the hashes of the tuples in the query result, VO contains hashes of those nodes using which the root hash can be recomputed for verification. For example, if the result consists of tuples t_3, t_4, t_5, and t_6, then the VO to recompute the root node will also consist of h_{12} and h_{78}. The process is similar for other trees.

3 Database Integrity with Bloom Filters

A Bloom filter [11] is a vector of m bits, all set to zero initially. It has a set of k hash functions, each of which can take any key as input and return an index $(0..m-1)$ into the vector as output. Two operations are defined on this data structure: (i) Inserting a character string such as a tuple of a database relation. This is implemented by computing k hash values of the character string and setting to 1 the corresponding bits in the vector; (ii) Querying for a string. This is implemented by computing k hash values on the string and checking if the corresponding bits are 1 in the m-bit vector. Due to the many-to-one nature of the hash functions, there is a chance of getting a false positive. However, with appropriate sizes for Bloom filters, we empirically show that the percentage of false positives is negligibly low in the proposed methods.

In this work, we propose two methods which use Bloom filters for maintaining integrity of the outsourced Database. The first method belongs to the class of integrity schemes that use *Aggregated Signatures*. The second method belongs to the class that use *Authenticated Data Structures*. We use a 32-bit Bloom filter for the first method and a 160-bit(size of SHA-1) Bloom filter for the second method. The methods are explained in detail below.

Table 1. Notations used in this paper

Symbol	Description
D	Database with one more relations (tables)
R	Relation (table) in a database
A_i	The ith attribute in a relation. $R(A_1, A_2, .., A_n)$ represents a relation with n attributes
r_i	The ith tuple (record) in a relation (table)
a_i	Value of ith attribute in a relation
h	Hash function (generally SHA-1)
bf	Bloom filter
ebf	Encrypted Bloom filter
$ASig_S$	Aggregated Signature computed by server
$ASig_C$	Aggregated Signature computed by client
$\|\|$	Concatenation operation
$\vee$	Bitwise OR operation
Q	Query
R_Q	Result of query Q
S	Server to which the database is outsourced
O	Owner of the database
C	Client who can query the database at the server
$T_m(x), T_{OR}(x)$	Time to multiply and compute OR of two vectors of length x, respectively
$T_h(x), T_{bf}(x)$	Time to compute hash and Bloom filter, respectively, on input of length x

3.1 Aggregated Signatures with Bloom Filter

This scheme, like most others in literature, assumes static databases with range queries on a single attribute. The table underlying a relation is assumed to be sorted in the ascending order of that single attribute. Both assumptions are in accordance with other work in the literature [18,19,20]. This method assures tamper-evident property for a relation and the completeness property for query results. Since it only handles static databases, the freshness guarantee does not arise [19,20]. We now describe the scheme in terms of the steps taken by the data owner to store a database, for a server to execute a range query, and for a client to verify the query results. We discuss each of these steps with an example. Consider a relation $R_i(A_1, A_2, .., A_n)$ with n attributes and p tuples.

Step 1: Data owner outsources the database to a cloud server
For each relation in the database, the data owner performs the following procedure.

(i) Computes Bloom filter for each tuple (record) r_i, bf_i.
(ii) Computes the modified Bloom filter by bit-wise ORing bf_i with bf_{i-1}. In other words, mbf_i=($bf_{i-1} \vee bf_i$). For the very first tuple, a special initial Bloom filter (IBF) such as the initialization vector (IV) used in most cryptographic schemes could be used. Alternately, a dummy tuple could be added as tuple zero with $mbf_0 = bf_0$. As discussed later, including previous tuple's Bloom filter in the current one helps to guarantee completeness of a query.
(iii) Encrypts mbf_i using owner's private key forming $embf_i$. This is added as an additional attribute in the ith tuple.
(iv) The relation is now outsourced to the server. The data owner keeps *no information* locally.

The primary computation cost involved here is the cost of computing bf_i for each tuple and hence is proportional to the size of the database being outsourced. At each step, we only need to compute bf_i, since bf_{i-1} from the previous tuple is already available. These are simply bit-wise ORed. This is quite inexpensive compared to other methods that use hash values and compute the new hash as $hash(hash(r_{i-1})||hash(r_i))$. In other words, first compute the hash of individual tuple, then perform a second hash with concatenated hashes. The resulting efficiency is shown in section 4.1.

Step 2: Server receives a query either from the data owner or from a client
On receiving a query, the server executes the following procedure.

(i) Server executes the range query resulting in a range of tuples from a relation.
(ii) For the selected range of tuples, server computes the product of the *embf* attribute. This is referred to as the *aggregated signature* for the query. In other words, it computes $ASig_S = \prod embf_i$.
(iii) Server sends the selected tuples and the aggregated signature to the requester. In addition to these, for verification purpose, it also sends two tuples that are just outside the range: one that is adjacent to the lower bound and another one adjacent to the upper bound. For example, if the range consists of tuples in the age range of 30-45, with tuples both of age 30 and 45 selected, the special tuples could be one with age 29 (for example) which is adjacent to the first one with age 30, and the one with age 47 (for example) which is adjacent to the one with age 45 in the underlying table of the relation. The two additional tuples, as shown later, are needed to verify if the tuples have been tampered with as well as to know if all tuples have been sent.

The computation cost involved here is the cost of multiplying all the bf_is and is the same as that for other methods.

Step 3: Query requester (data owner or a third-party client) receives the query results and verifies
In this step, the entity that sent the query validates the results following the below procedure.

(i) Requester recomputes mbf_i for each of the received tuples. For the very first tuple in the range, it uses the one of the two additional tuples received to compute its mbf.
(ii) It determines the product of all the mbf_i resulting in $pmbf = \prod mbf_i$.
(iii) It decrypts the $Asig_S$ sent by the server using the public key of the owner. If the requester is the data owner, there is no problem since it knows both the keys. Otherwise, there should a mechanism for distributing the public key of the owner securely to all its clients. This process is beyond the scope of this paper and here. We assume that the owner has a way of distributing its public key to its clients.

(iv) It now checks for tampering. If $pmbf = decrypt(Asigs_S)$, then there is no tampering. This works due to the homomorphic property of the encryption [22]. Else, there is some tampering or damage.

As in step 1, in this step we save computation time when calculating the individual hashes. Another added advantage here is that the aggregated signature is computed by multiplying 32-bit Bloom filters rather than 160-bit SHA-1 hashes, which brings down the computation overhead at the client drastically. The results are shown in section 4 which also discuss the accuracy of this method. If there are p tuples in R_Q and the average length of each tuple is l, then the total cost of verification is given by the equation

$$Ver\_Cost_{bf} = p * (T_{bf}(l) + T_{OR}(32) + T_m(32)) \quad (1)$$

while in the methods which use SHA-1, the cost is given by

$$Ver\_Cost_h = p * (T_h(2 * l) + T_m(160)) \quad (2)$$

So the computational advantage of the proposed method is obvious.

3.2 Authenticated Data Structures Using Bloom Filters

This method uses authenticated data structures. As before, it supports range queries on a single attribute. Unlike the first method, this method supports dynamic databases. As shown later, it meets freshness, tamper-evident, and completeness criteria. The proposed use of Bloom filters in this method is an improvement over any of the methods which used authenticated data structures [7,20,21]. But for simplicity, in this paper, we will use Merkle hash trees. However, the method, the procedures, and the conclusions are valid for other data structures such as B^+-trees and MB-trees.

Here, for a given relation, the leaf nodes of the corresponding Merkle tree are 160-bit Bloom filters of the corresponding tuples in the relation. It is assumed that all the leaf nodes are arranged in the ascending order with respect to the attribute used in the select statement of the query. To keep the false positive rates of the Bloom filters under acceptance threshold, we define MAX_BF_LEVELS as the number of levels in the tree till which we treat the 160-bit vector as a Bloom filter. After this level, the 160-bit vector will be treated as a SHA-1 hash value. We describe the method in the following steps.

Step 1: Data owner outsources the database to the server
For each relation in the database, the data owner executes the following procedure.

(i) For each tuple in the relation, a Bloom filter bf_i is computed. Unlike the previous aggregated signature method, there is no need to further compute a modified Bloom filter. Further, it does not insert the computed Bloom filter as an attribute in the tuple.

(ii) A tree similar to the Merkle tree is now built for the relation. The tree starts with the individual tuple Bloom filters as the leaf nodes.
(iii) The nodes at levels on top of the leaf nodes are built by bitwise-ORing of the child nodes. This is similar to inserting multiple strings into a single Bloom filter.
(iv) Step (iii) is repeated until a chosen MAX_BF_LEVELS is reached. This is due to the special characteristics of the Bloom filter where false positive rates would increase as the number of strings inserted into a single Bloom filter increases. Thus, we limit this type of node generation only until the false positive rate is below an acceptable threshold.
(v) Above the MAX_BF_LEVELS, the nodes are created by hashing techniques suggested in literature [19] where a parent node is created by hashing the concatenation of the child nodes hashes. This is repeated until the root node is created.
(vi) Finally, the owner encrypts the root value with its private key (or a special secret key). It either stores it locally or publishes it at well-known directories.
(vii) The data owner outsources the relation and the authenticated tree to the server for storing.

The computational cost for this step consists of calculating the Bloom filter for every tuple and building the authenticated tree.

Step 2: Server receives a query either from the data owner or by a third-party client
When a range query is received by the server, it performs the following procedure.

(i) Server executes the query resulting in a range of tuples from a single relation.
(ii) For this range of tuples, it selects that part of the authenticated tree that is required to derive the root node of the authenticated tree assuming that the leaf nodes corresponding to the selected tuples are already available. For example, in Fig. 1, if tuples t3-t6 have been selected in the range, then the portion of the tree that will be selected is h12 and h78. With t3-t6, the requester can compute h34 and h56. With h34 and h12, it can compute h1; using h56 and h78, requester can compute h2. From h1 and h2, it can compute the root. The selected portion of the tree is referred to as the verification object or VO. In this example, VO consists of $\{h12, h78\}$.
(iii) To verify completeness, as in the previous method, the server sends two additional tuples outside the range: one that is adjacent to the lower bound and another one adjacent to the upper bound. Server send the selected tuples in the range, the verification object, and the two additional tuples to the requester.

Step 3: Query requester (data owner or a third-party client) receives and verifies the results

The query requester now verifies the results using the following procedure.

(i) For the tuples in the range, it computes the Bloom filters.
(ii) Using the individual tuple Bloom filters, it builds part of the authenticated tree.
(iii) It completes the tree using the verification object received.
(iv) Finally, it computes the root node. If it is the data owner, it can directly decrypt the published value(or locally stored value) of the root and check if it matches with what was computed . If it is a third-party client, as discussed earlier, we assume that the server has a mechanism to distribute the keys to its clients for decryption of the root. Otherwise, the client will request the data owner for decrypted root value and then verifies with the locally computed value. A match indicates no tampering while a mismatch indicates a problem. Similarly, using the two additional tuples sent, and the fact that the roots matched, it can verify completeness of the query results.

Step 4: Data owner updates a relation
Since this method handles dynamic databases, it is possible for a data owner to later modify a relation by addition, deletion, or update of tuples. For this, it follows the following procedure.

(i) The data owner obtains the authenticated tree from the server.
(ii) For additions, for each added tuple, it computes a Bloom filter and inserts it into the corresponding position at the leaf level in the authenticated tree.
(iii) For each deleted tree, it removes the corresponding leaf from the leaf level of the authenticated tree.
(iv) In case the attribute for which this method is designed is updated, then the old leaf node needs to be deleted and a new recomputed Bloom filter with the modified value needs to be inserted at the right position in the authenticated tree.
(v) It now rebuilds the authenticated tree, encrypts and publishes the new root. It sends the rebuilt authenticated tree along with the update operations to the server.

For all the levels below the MAX_BF_LEVELS, time taken for computing the 160-bit vector at each parent is $T_{OR}(160)$ while other methods in the same category require a cost of $T_h(320)$. Obviously, the cost of bit-wise ORing is much chapter than the expensive operation of hash operations in SHA-1. This efficiency is reflected in the results presented in the next section.

4 Results

In order to determine the efficacy of the proposed two methods for integrity of outsourced databases, we have conducted several experiments. In addition, we have also analyzed the methods for their computational and storage efficiency. The results are summarized below for each method.

4.1 Results for Aggregated Signatures Using Bloom Filters

A. Space requirements at the client
Compared to the secure hashes in use today, Bloom filters require much less space. For example, SHA-1 produces a 20-byte message digest, SHA-2 produces either 32-byte or 64-byte secure hashes, and MD5 produces a 16-byte hash value [22]. On the other hand, the Bloom filters that we consider for this method use 4-byte filters which are far smaller than the secure hashes.

B. Number of hash functions and accuracy of 32-bit Bloom filter
Let us now look at measuring the efficacy or accuracy of a Bloom filter. For a correct operation, if a server tampers with the data, the Bloom filter of the corrupted data should not match with the original Bloom filter (when verified by the data owner or other clients). If a tampered tuple's Bloom filter matches with the computed hash, then we refer to it as a false positive. So the accuracy of the Bloom filter can be measured by the number of false positives obtained for various corrupted blocks. Since the Bloom filter uses a set of hash functions internally, the false positive rate of a Bloom filter is dependent on the uniqueness of each hash function as well as the number of hash functions. While too few hash functions are inadequate to capture the data, too many hash functions over capture it and there is a danger of setting too many bits in the Bloom filter.

We tried to find the optimal number of hash functions by varying the number of hash functions used in the Bloom filter and each time testing its accuracy using a billion tuples. Figure 2(a) shows these results. For example, it may be noticed that with 6 or 8 hash functions for a Bloom filter, the accuracy is as high as 99.9999% or almost 100%. We use 12 hash functions with 32-bit Bloom filters throughout the experiments discussed in this paper for this method.

C. Computational overhead at the client
As discussed in section 3.1, during the verification phase, the time taken to compute the Bloom filter for every tuple (with average tuple length of l bits) is $T_{bf}(l) + T_{OR}(32)$ while the time taken to compute a hash for every tuple is $T_h(2 * l)$. we have measured the time time taken to compute the individual hashes as well as Bloom filters. Figure 2(b) shows that the Computation time is less by using Bloom filters when compared to SHA-1. For example, for a relation with 5000 tuples, SHA-1 takes 180 milliseconds while the proposed method using Bloom filter takes only 100 milliseconds.

Equations 1 and 2 in section 3.1 give mathematical representation of the time taken to compute the aggregated signature using Bloom filters and hashes respectively. We measured the time taken to compute the aggregated signatures using both the methods for various number of tuples. In Figure 2(c) the upper curve represents the time taken by SHA-1 and the lower curve represents the time taken by Bloom filter. It clearly shows a drastic reduction in computation overhead at the client when using Bloom filters. With 10,000 tuples in a relation, SHA-1 takes approximately 11 milliseconds while our method takes only 3 milliseconds.

D. Parallel Implementation
When high data throughput is required by client applications, it is important that the integrity technique does not become a bottleneck in providing such service. For this reason, we started looking into ways to parallelize the hash function evaluation inside Bloom filters. Bloom filter internally uses a set of independent hash functions. So one trivial way to improve the execution time is to allocate different hash functions to different threads when computing the Bloom filter for a single tuple. We have used dual core and quad core systems using Open MP [17] as the computation platform. Fig. 2(d) and 2(e) summarize the results for Bloom filter of 32-bit size with 12 hash functions using dual core (2 *2 GHz) and quad core (4 * 2.83 GHz) Intel processors using 10^6 tuples. Here, the X-axis shows the number of threads and the Y-axis indicates the execution time for computing hashes for all one million tuples. Since it is dual core, the performance improvement beyond 2 threads is insignificant. Similarly, in the quad core, performance improvement beyond 4 threads is insignificant. Fig. 3(f) summarizes the executions times. The 32-bit Bloom filter with Quadcore has the smallest execution time.

4.2 Results for Authenticated Data Structures Using Bloom Filters

Here, we summarize the results for the proposed authenticated data structure method with Bloom filters.

A. Computational Overhead at the Client
We used 160-bit Bloom filters with a set of 12 hash functions. Fig. 3a shows the time required to compute the Bloom filters of individual tuples compared to that of SHA-1. Since it uses 12 hash functions internally, when given the input of the same length, the computation time for Bloom filter is more than that of SHA-1. Since the hash functions used in the Bloom filter are simple hash function with just an index into the array as output, the difference is not 12 times that of SHA-1. Unlike SHA-1, Bloom filter can lend itself easily to parallel implementation. We can see in Fig. 3(a) that the parallel implementations of Bloom filter on Core2duo and Quadcore systems makes the computation time lesser than that of SHA-1. For example, while SHA-1 takes about 49 seconds, for the same tuples Bloom filter with Quadcore takes only 25 seconds.

B. Computation Overhead for Building the Authenticated Data Structure
For all Nodes in the levels below MAX_BF_LEVELS, the time taken to compute the 160-bit vector is $T_{OR}(160)$ which is very small compared to $T_h(320)$. So the total time taken to build the tree is inversely proportional to MAX_BF_LEVELS. We have measured the time taken to build the tree for 65,536 tuples (2^{16}) by varying the number of MAX_BF_LEVELS. Fig. 3(b) shows this result. If we consider the total time taken to calculated the hashes and then build the tree of 65,536 tuples, SHA1 takes 0.8 seconds while using parallel Bloom filter(on quadcore) and a MAX_BF_LEVELS of 5 it takes only 0.28 seconds.

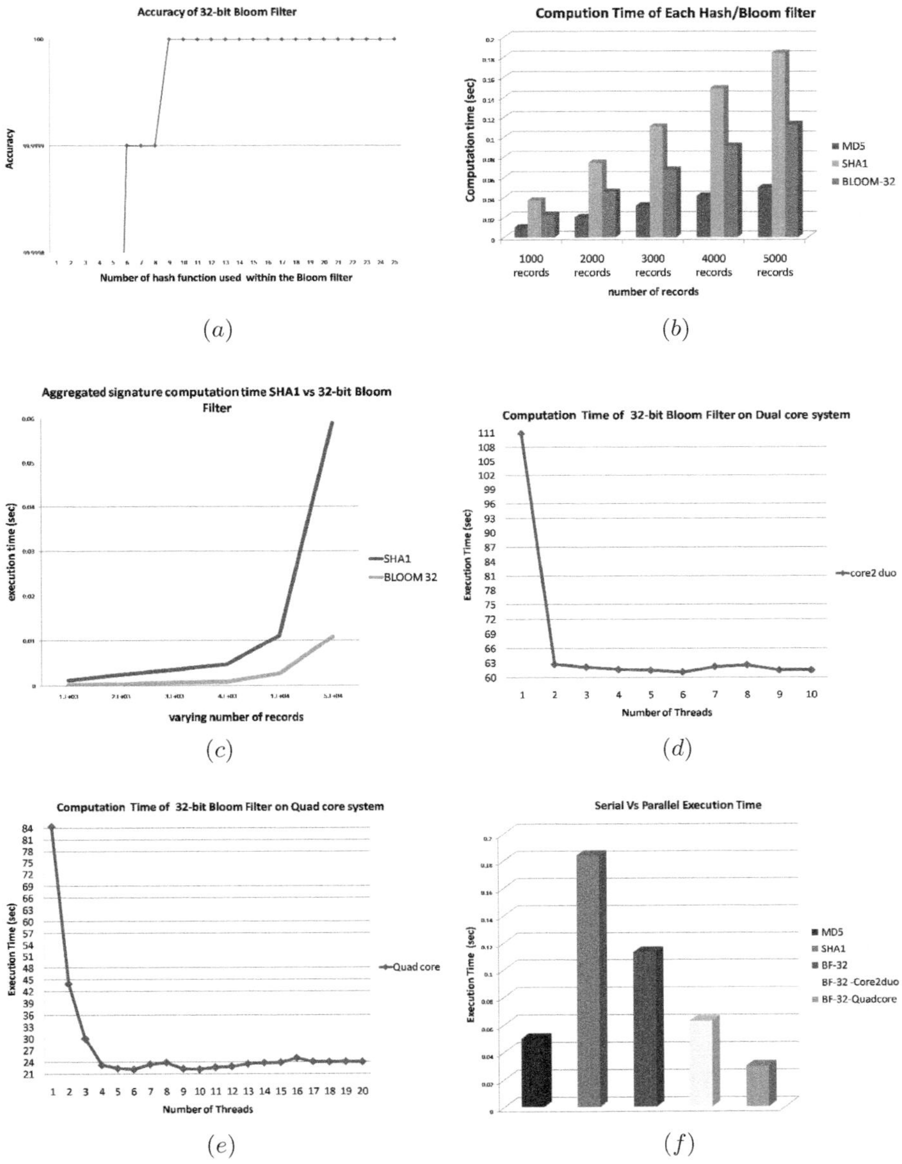

Fig. 2. (a)Number of hash functions and and Accuracy of a 32-bit Bloom filter (b)Time taken to compute SHA-1 hash and Bloom filter (c) Time taken by the client to compute the aggregated signature using SHA-1 hashes and Bloom filters for varying number of tuples (d)Computation time with varying number of threads on a Dual core (2*2GHz) Intel processor (32-bit BF with 12-hashes, 1 Million tuples) (e)Computation time with varying number of threads on a Quad core (4*2.83 GHz) Intel processor (32-bit BF with 12-hashes, 1 Million tuples) (f) Computation time of Serial and Parallel implementations of Bloom filter using 5000 tuples

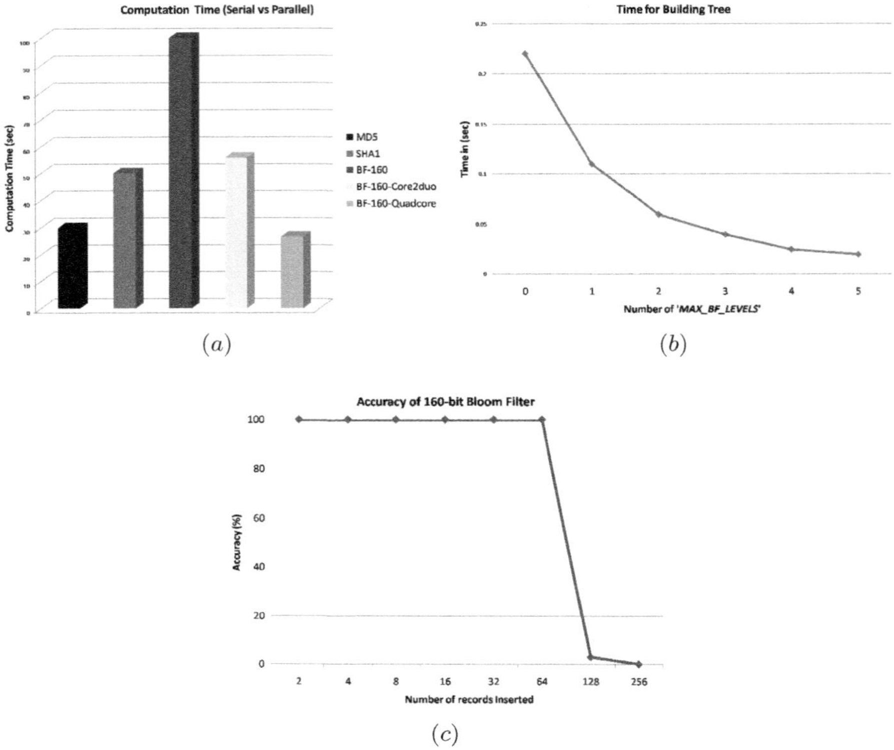

Fig. 3. (a)Computation time of SHA-1, Serial and Parallel implementations of Bloom filter using 5000 tuples (b)Computation time building a tree of 65,356 tuples with varying number of MAX_BF_LEVELS (c)Accuracy of the 160-bit Bloom filter(12 hash functions) with varying number of inserted tuples

C. Optimal Value of MAX_BF_LEVELS

It is very clear from the above results that larger the value of MAX_BF_LEVELS, more is the reduction in computation time. Taking a bit-wise OR of the two 160-bit vectors at level is equivalent to inserting to messages into the same Bloom filter (as discussed in section 3). For example, at level 2 this is equivalent to inserting 4 tuples into the same Bloom filter. Accordingly, at level x, the number of insertions is 2^x. Since higher number of insertions into the same Bloom filters has the risk of increasing its false positive rate, we attempted to find an optimal value for MAX_BF_LEVELS. Thus, we calculated the accuracy of the 160-bit Bloom filter for 1 million tuples by varying the number of insertions into the Bloom filter. Fig. 3(c) shows that the accuracy is very high until 64 insertions (for 160-bit Bloom filter) and falls to low values after this. We chose the optimal value for MAX_BF_LEVELS as 6 ($2^6 = 64$).

From these results, it is clear that the proposed methods are superior to existing methods and are much more amenable for parallization and hence better performance under multicore systems.

5 Conclusion and Future Work

In this paper, we have investigated the feasibility and efficacy of employing Bloom filters for integrity assurance of outsourced databases in cloud environments. Here, we discussed some of the existing methods for data integrity and explained their large computational demands on the data owner and clients. Our methods of employing Bloom filters greatly reduce this overhead.

In the first method, we used Bloom filters for computing the aggregated signatures which greatly reduced the time required for multiplying the hashes to compute the aggregated signature. In the second method, we employed Bloom filters for building authenticated data structures to ensure Integrity. This reduced time taken to build the authenticated tree by a large magnitude. In order to further reduce the computational overhead due to multiple but independent hash function evaluations inside Bloom filters, we have implemented these schemes on dual core and quad core systems using OpenMP shared memory platform. The experiments clearly show the advantage of using multiprocessor systems for these applications. These are especially relevant in high-throughput environments.

In future, we plan to extend our work in three directions. First, we plan to investigate better ways to parallelize and minimize the execution times for Bloom filters in multicore systems. Second, we plan to improve on the methods to further reduce computational overhead. Third, we plan to work towards more complex queries.

References

1. Tanebaum, A.S., Wetherall, D.J.: Computer Networks, 5th edn. Pearson Higher Education, London (2011)
2. Peng, J., Zhou, Y., Yang, Y.: Cyclic redundancy code checking based on small lookup table. In: IEEE Intl. Conf. on Communication Technology and Applications, pp. 596–599 (2010)
3. Gassend, B., Suh, G.E., Clarke, D., van Dijk, M., Devdas, S.: Caches and Merkle trees for efficient memory integrity verification. In: 9th Intl. Symp. High Performnace Computer Architecture (February 2003)
4. Silberschatz, A., Galvin, P.B., Gane, G.: Operating System Concepts, 8th edn. Wiley, Chichester (2009)
5. Gagliardi, R., Marcantoni, F., Polzonetti, A., Re, B., Tapanelli, P.: Cloud computing for network business ecosystem. In: IEEE Intl. Conf. Industrial Engineering and Engineering Managament (IEEM), pp. 862–868 (December 2010)
6. Gurman, J.B.: How many terabytes was that? Archiving and serving solar space data without losing your shirt. Bulletin of the American Astronomical Society 31, 955 (1999)
7. Devanbu, P., Gertz, M., Martel, C., Stubblebine, S.: Authentic data publication over the internet. Journal of Computer Security 11(3), 291–314 (2003)

8. Li, F., Hadjieleftheriou, M., Kollios, G., Reyzin, L.: Dynamic authenticated index structures for outsourced databases. In: Proceedings of ACM SIGMOD International Conference on Management of Data, pp. 121–132 (2006)
9. Yun, A., Shi, C., Kim, Y.: On protecting integrity and confidentiality of cryptographic file system for outsourced storage. In: CCSW 2009 (November 2009)
10. Goodrich, M.T., Papamanthou, C., Tamassia, R., Triandopoulos, N.: Athos: Efficient authentication of outsourced file systems. In: Wu, T.-C., Lei, C.-L., Rijmen, V., Lee, D.-T. (eds.) ISC 2008. LNCS, vol. 5222, pp. 80–96. Springer, Heidelberg (2008)
11. Bloom, B.H.: Space/time trade-offs in hash coding with allowable errors. CACM 13(7), 422–426 (1970)
12. Chang, F., Dean, J., Ghemawat, S., Hseih, W.C., Wallach, D.A., Burrows, M., Chandra, T., Fikes, A., Gruber, R.: Bigtable: A distributed data storage system for structured data. In: Proc. 7th Symp. Operating Systems Design and Implementation (OSDI 2006), pp. 205–218 (2006)
13. Kumar, A., Xu, J., Li, L., Wang, J.: Space-code Bloom filters for efficient traffic flow measurement. IEEE J. Selected Areas in Communication 24(12), 2327–2339 (2006)
14. Li, Z., Gong, G.: On data aggregation with secure Bloom filter in wireless sensor networks. Technical Report, Dept. of Electrical and Computer Engineering, Univ. Waterloo, Canada
15. Telidevara, A., Chandrasekaran, V., Srinivasan, A., Mukkamala, R., Gampa, S.: Similarity coefficient generators for network forensics. In: Proc. IEEE WIFS (2010)
16. Jian-ming, F., Ying, X., Hui-jun, X., Wei, W.: Strategy optimization for P2P security using Bloom filter. In: Intl. Conf. Multimedia Information Networking and Security, MINES 2009, pp. 403–406 (2009)
17. Quinn, M.J.: Parallel Programming in C with MP and OpenMP. McGraw-Hill, New York (2004)
18. Xie, M., Wang, H., Yin, J., Meng, X.: Integrity Auditing of Outsourced Data. In: VLDB (2007)
19. Mykletun, E., Narasimha, M., Tsudik, G.: Authentication and integrity in outsourced databases. In: NDSS. The Internet Society, San Diego (2004)
20. Li, F., Hadjieleftheriou, M., Kollios, G., Reyzin, L.: Dynamic authenticated index structures for outsourced databases. In: SIGMOD Conference, pp. 121–132. ACM, New York (2006)
21. Goodrich, M.T., Tamassia, R., Triandopoulos, N.: Super-efficient verification of dynamic outsourced databases. In: RSA Conference, CRYPTO Track (2008)
22. Rivest, R., Adleman, L., Dertouzos, M.: On data banks and privacy homomorphism. In: Foundations of Secure Computation, pp. 169–170 (1978)

Parallel Implementation of Part of Speech Tagging for Text Mining Using Grid Computing

Naveen Kumar, Saumesh Kumar, and Padam Kumar

Department of Electronics and Computer Engineering,
Indian Institute of Techology Roorkee, Roorkee, India
{navinpec,saumkpec,padamfec}@iitr.ernet.in,
navincse2005@gmail.com

Abstract. There is an urgent need to develop new text mining solutions to tackle exponential growth in text data. Problem sizes are increasing day by day by due to the addition of new text documents. Grid aware text mining is one of the solutions for knowledge extraction from such large volume of text. Part of speech (POS) tagging is an important preprocessing task in text mining. But tagging algorithms working on a very large document collection take very long time on conventional computers to produce results. In this paper we present a framework for parallel implementation of part of speech tagging for text mining using grid computing. Globus Toolkit, which is a middleware for scientific and data intensive grid applications, is used for developing this framework in grid environment. Experimental results show that this model significantly reduces the part of speech tagging time for text mining. This model can be integrated into grid-based text mining tool, helping to improve the overall performance of the text mining process.

Keywords: Part of Speech tagging, Grid computing, Text mining, Globus Toolkit.

1 Introduction

Due to the continuous growth in the volume of available electronic data, automatic knowledge discovery techniques become necessary in order to manipulate huge amounts of data. Huge amounts of numerical data and countless pages of text are produced every day, in the academic or enterprise fields, documenting projects, actions or ideas. All the knowledge expressed in structured or unstructured form represents the most important property of an institution, either competitive advantage for companies or the availability of concepts and ideas for the academia. Text mining aims at extracting implicit knowledge from a collection of texts and documents [1]. The enormous amount of information stored in unstructured texts cannot simply be processed by computers which typically handle text as simple sequences of character strings. Text mining is a relatively new practice derived from Information Retrieval (IR) [2, 3] and Natural Language Processing (NLP) [4]. The strict definition of text mining includes only the methods capable of discovering new information that is not

A. Abraham et al. (Eds.): ACC 2011, Part I, CCIS 190, pp. 461–470, 2011.

obvious or easy to find out in a document collection, i.e. reports, historical documents, e-mails, spreadsheets, research papers and others.

Nowadays, when the information overload is a big problem, knowledge discovery algorithms applied on very large text document collections can help to solve numerous problems and as text is still a premier source of information on the web, the role of text mining is crucial. Although text mining applications are data independent, handling of large text data is an issue when full text data is considered due to the problem sizes in consideration. Each of the steps in the text mining pipeline adds further information to the initial raw text and data size increases as processing progresses. Text mining algorithms working on a very large document collection take very long time on a conventional computer to get results.

Motivation of this work is to use the Grid computational capabilities to solve text mining tasks. This work is the first step towards creating a general text mining framework to enable large scale text mining. The aim is to create a suite of text mining applications based on state-of-the-art text mining approaches that exploit a number of Grid architectures in order to process and handle terabytes of text in reasonable time.

The initial work focuses on the development of framework for parallel POS tagging using Grid environment. The framework developed is portable as it is based on the grid environment, which includes heterogeneous systems. However, scaling to a larger number of processors, data and work distribution will be an issue and more sophisticated load distribution models will need to be investigated. Due to the unstructured nature of the data available, this will become a major issue. In this work, we are laying the foundations towards a parallel text mining framework which should enable processing enormous amount of text in acceptable time. The paper presents and discusses the associated challenges.

The remainder of this paper is organized as follows: Section 2 gives an overview of part of speech tagging, grid computing and Globus toolkit. Section 3 focuses on system design of the framework. In section 4 we provide implementation details and the execution environment for POS tagging. Section 5 describes the experimental setup and results. And finally, section 6 concludes the work and discusses future possibilities.

2 Background

2.1 Part of Speech Tagging

Part of Speech tagging is one of the pre-processing tasks of text mining. In corpus linguistics, part-of-speech(POS) tagging, also called grammatical tagging or word-category disambiguation, is the process of marking up the words in a text (corpus) as corresponding to a particular part of speech, based on both its definition, as well as its context —i.e. relationship with adjacent and related words in a phrase, sentence, or paragraph [20]. A simplified form of this is commonly taught to school-age children, in the identification of words as nouns, verbs, adjectives, adverbs, etc. Part-of-speech tagging is harder than just having a list of words and their parts of speech, because some words can represent more than one part of speech at different times, and because some parts of speech are complex or unspoken. It is not rare in natural languages (as opposed to many artificial languages), that a large percentage of word-forms are ambiguous. For example, "dogs", which is usually thought of as just a plural noun, can also be a verb, e.g., "The sailor dogs the hatch." In order to carry out noise free information extraction, the very basic step is POS tagging which must be performed with high precision. The precision of POS tagging not only directly affects the performance of pattern based approaches but also influences the accuracy of parsing, which in general uses the POS tags on the words as a part of the input.

For documents like newspaper articles, research papers etc., there are many publically available tools for part of speech tagging. Each tool is specifically trained on a particular kind of text. POS tagger trained on newspaper articles will not necessarily work well on biomedical documents because the characteristics of biomedical text are considerably different from those of newspaper articles [7, 8].

All these years, work has been done on improving the accuracy of part of speech tagger, but still so far, little attention has been devoted to make it handle large amount of data efficiently. Due to the large quantity of documents and computationally intensive nature of POS tagging task, preprocessing takes too much time in text mining. In order to reduce the time spent in pre-processing we distribute the POS tagging on a grid environment.

2.2 Grid Computing and Globus Toolkit

A grid is a geographically distributed computation infrastructure composed of a set of heterogeneous machines, often with separate policies for security and resource use, which users can access via a single interface. Grids therefore, provide a common resource access technology and operational services across widely distributed virtual organizations composed of institutions or individuals that share resources. Today grids can be used as effective infrastructures for distributed high-performance computing and data processing.

In this work we use the Globus Toolkit 4 (GT4) [9], which is a widely used middleware in scientific and data-intensive grid applications, and is becoming a standard for implementing grid systems. The toolkit addresses security, information discovery, resource and data management, communication, fault-detection, and portability issues in the grid environment.

The Globus Toolkit provides a number of components for performing data management. Data management tools (GridFTP, RFT, RLS) are concerned with the location, transfer, and management of distributed data [10]. GridFTP protocol provides a secure way to transfer data in a grid. RFT (Reliable File Transfer) is a Web Services Resource Framework (WSRF) [11] compliant web service for managing multiple data transfers. The Replica Location Service (RLS) [12] maintains and provides access to mapping information from logical names for data items onto target names. These target names may represent physical locations of data items, or an entry in the RLS may map to another level of logical naming for the data item. The RLS is intended to be one of a set of services for providing data replication management in grids. In addition to these components, the LIGO Data Replicator (LDR) [13, 14] will be used. LDR is a collection of some components provided by the Globus project with some extra logic to pull the components together. This minimum collection of components is necessary for fast, efficient, robust, and secure replication of data. The Globus components included are: GridFTP, Globus Replica Location Service (RLS) and a metadata service developed by the LDR team, based on a prototype Globus Metadata Catalog Service (MCS) [15] for organizing useful information about the data files pertaining to when and where the data should be replicated.

3 System Design

Steps in the text mining pipeline add further information to the initial raw text and data sizes increase as processing proceeds throughout the whole process. The data generated after every step is either saved to disk to be used in the future or passed to the next step for further processing. Our framework focuses only on the data parallel approaches since task parallel approaches in this area do not provide the desired speed-up [17]. Dynamic work distribution approaches, master/slave models (particularly task farming approaches) would appear to be ideally suited for use on supercomputing and grid resources by employing data parallel approaches to process unbalanced data sets (the length and structure of the sentences is not known before processing starts) [18, 19]. Furthermore, the I/O requirements of each stage and I/O usage will need to be balanced in order to achieve the optimum outcome. Therefore, in this work we are applying a master slave approach to parallelize part of speech tagging process.

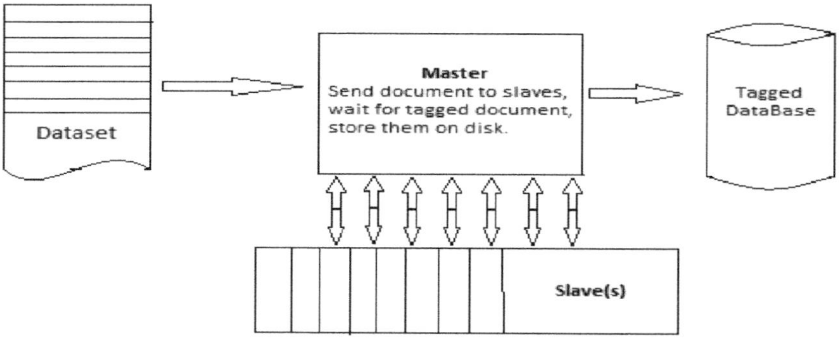

Fig. 1. Master Slave approach to parallelize POS tagging process

Fig. 2 shows the framework for parallel part of speech tagging on a grid model. The grid user log into the grid by means of a Portal accessible from the user's workstation and submit jobs to it. The grid user owns a grid certificate, which provides user the grid credentials [16] to log into the grid and submit jobs to it, which is done by means of a Portal, accessible from the user's workstation. The user can access his documents or public documents that are stored in the grid. He submits to the Portal information about the documents that will be tagged to the Portal (1). The Portal uses the LDR queries to find out whether there is a local copy of the documents, and if not RLS tells the Portal where the documents are in the grid (2). Then the LDR system then generates a request to copy the documents to the local storage system and registers the new copy in the local RLS server. The grid nodes receive from the Portal, the phases to run the tagging task (3), and using the RFT service it copies the replicas of the documents from the storage to the grid nodes (4). When the tagging task is concluded, the Portal collects all sets of documents from each node and returns the result of the tagging to the user, who stores the documents in his grid account area.

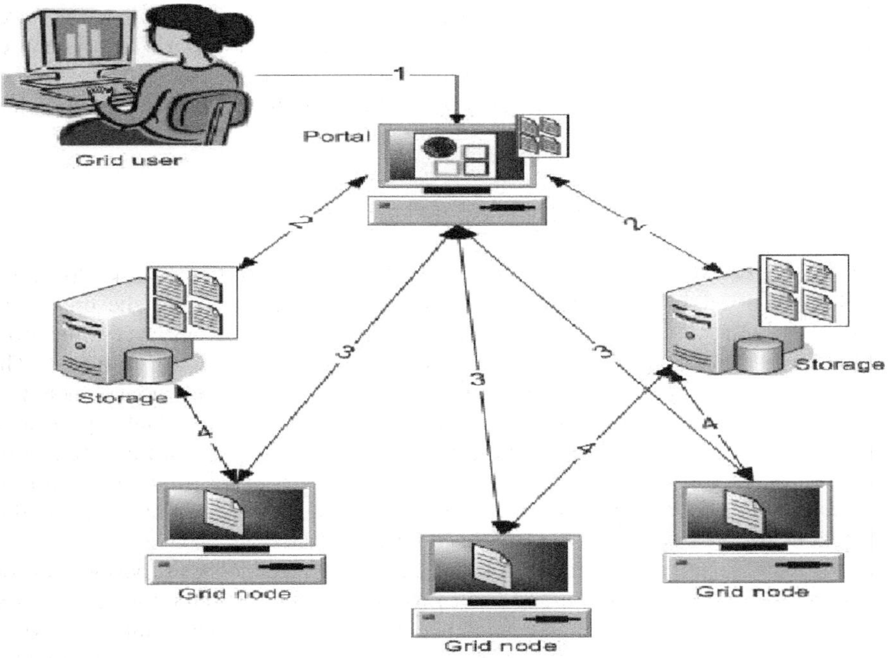

Fig. 2. Framework for parallel implementation of part of speech tagging

Above framework is implemented in grid environment using various web services, which communicate with each other. Following are the web services:

a. Advertise Service

The system proposed is dynamic rather than static where nodes can enter and leave the grid environment as they please. When a new node joins the grid, it registers itself to the broker by providing information about itself to broker like number of processing cores, memory, disk space etc. Broker maintains index of all the active nodes in grid. This service is deployed on each grid client node.

b. Broker Service

This service is deployed on broker machine. Broker node maintains information about all active nodes in grid. When user submits job on portal, broker gives him the information about all the resources present in the grid. Accordingly job of tagging will be distributed across all the grid client nodes. Broker service provides operations for informing user node about resources in grid.

c. Tagger Service

This service is deployed on each grid client node. This is the service which actually does the part of speech tagging. A part of whole dataset is tagged by each client node. Tagging operation is done by some already available POS tagger which will be specific for the dataset.

d. File Transfer Service

The File Transfer service is a stateless service with a single operation (transfer) responsible for sending a file to the specified client node when a user submit job on the portal. And for sending tagged file back to the storage node.

4 Implementation

The first stage of this process involves tokenizing the text by splitting it into a sequence of single word units and punctuations. This includes splitting of hyphenation, parentheses, quotations and contractions, which can otherwise cause errors with POS tagging algorithms. In order to ensure high accuracy the tagging software used, is trained on annotated texts from the same domain as the target documents. With this process being in the early stages of the whole text mining chain any errors at this stage may grow cumulatively and hence it is important to have a POS tagger that is highly accurate.

In this work GENIA tagger is used. The GENIA tagger analyzes English sentences and outputs the base forms, part-of-speech tags, chunk tags, and named entity tags. The tagger is specifically tuned for biomedical text. The GENIA tagger is trained not only on the GENIA corpus and the PennBioIE corpus [1], so the tagger works well on various types of biomedical documents. For information extraction from biomedical documents, this tagger might be a useful preprocessing tool. Medline abstracts are used as datasets. Detail of datasets is given in Table 1.

Table 1. Details of Dataset

Dataset	Lines	Words	Characters
Dataset1	9642050	192938020	1317747750
Dataset2	129559448	1766364087	12220578650

The parallel implementation of the POS tagger works as follows. Abstracts are cleaned and prepared initially and stored as an ASCII text file. Then a rule-based sentence splitter is then applied on this data to separate the sentences. Each sentence is written to a new line and a new line is inserted between each abstract to detect the end of abstracts. This process is not computationally expensive and is completed in less than a minute for a hundred thousand abstracts. Therefore, in order to retain interoperability and portability of the tools we have not integrated this into the parallel POS tagger implementation.

Once the data is cleaned and prepared, the master node reads the cleaned and split abstracts, packs them into groups of sentences (i.e. as entire abstract). Then it asks broker node for the details of active slave nodes and accordingly sends them to the slave nodes. The master continues to read and distribute the data until it reaches to the end of the abstracts.

Each slave node loads the probabilistic models that are obtained by training the application on annotated data. Then slave nodes wait for data from the master node. When the slave node receives the abstract, it splits the abstract into sentences to process on the sentences as the GENIA tagger works only per sentence. Once the processing of the abstract is completed, the POS tagged abstract is then sent back to the master node. The slave process continues processing the next abstract without waiting for the completion of the send process.

5 Results and Discussion

To test this framework a small test grid is made. A heterogeneous grid environment is created by using nodes with different hardware and software configuration. These results are generated by scaling the system up to 8 processing cores.

Table 2. Results when sentences are sent to each tagging nodes

No. of processing core	Time taken for tagging Dataset1(in minutes)	Time taken for tagging Dataset2(in minutes)
1	48	117
2	39	81
4	30	54
6	19	39
8	10	27

Table 2 and Fig. 3 shows that our application scaled linearly for up to 8 processing cores. It can be concluded from the figure that, the application scaled both when the number of processors are increased as well as when the problem size is increased. For example, ten thousand abstracts takes around 48 minutes if processed using a single processing core whereas it will take around 10 minutes on 8 processing cores when the parallel implementation of GENIA tagger is used. This indicates good scaling due to the data independent nature of the application itself. But our objective was to bring the preprocessing time in figures of second; this kind of speedup can be achieved by scaling the current system to hundred of processing cores.

Processing could be parallelized at the sentence level, which would make it easy to distribute the tasks. However, experimental results (Table 2 and Table 3) showed when small amounts of data is sent too frequently (i.e. master distributed the data

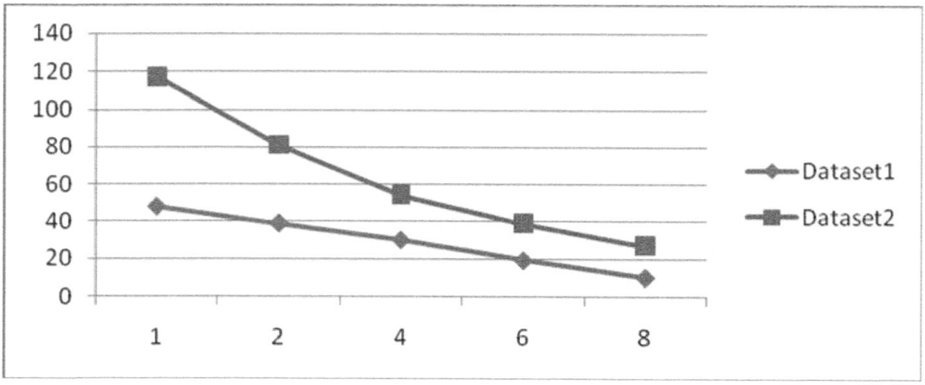

Fig. 3. Scaling of parallel GENIA tagger (X-axis: No. of processing cores, Y-axis: processing time in minutes), when sentences are sent to tagging nodes

sentence on a sentence basis) performance was poorer compared to sending larger chunks of data (i.e. abstracts) in terms of overall processing time. This is due to poor utilization bandwidth and due to lower latency achieved by establishing communication every time between sender and receiver. Table 3 shows that some entries have processing time larger than when sentences are sent. This happens because GENIA tagger works per sentence only not on whole paragraph (like abstracts). So tagging node has to read each abstract sentence by sentence and then tag. This factor is more dominant when numbers of processing core are less. As we can see in Table 3, when we increase the numbers of processing core and send abstracts not sentences to tagging nodes, overall processing time decreases.

Table 3. Results when whole abstracts are sent to each tagging nodes

No. of processing core	Time taken for tagging Dataset1(in minutes)	Time taken for tagging Dataset2(in minutes)
1	48	117
2	37	83
4	31	54
6	18	31
8	7	21

The time taken to process a specific abstract is not known until processing starts as it depends not only on the number and length of the sentences but also on the structure of the sentence. On the other hand, when the problem size is increased by ten fold from around 10 thousand abstracts to 1 million abstracts, it can be seen from the results that time taken to process increased by 10 fold. Although the size of the text datasets depends on the length of abstracts we can consider in this case that on average number of abstracts has a certain number of words and sentences.

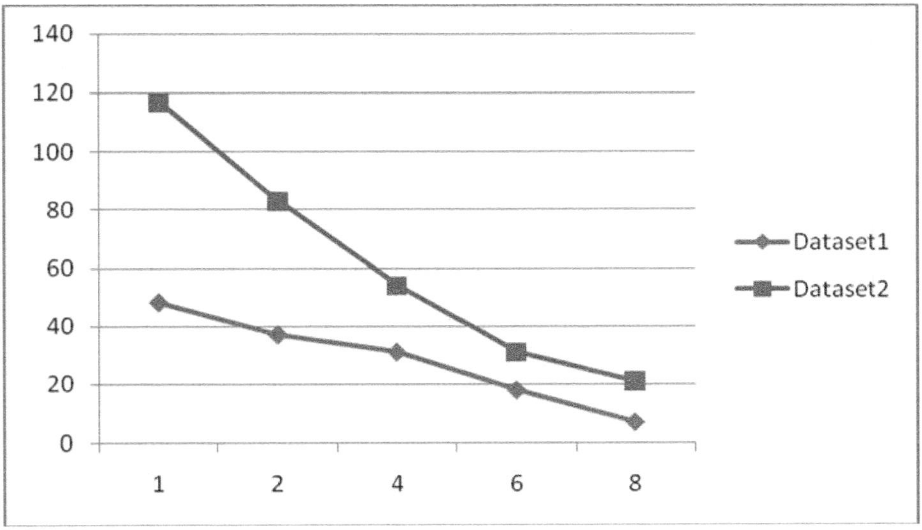

Fig. 4. Scaling of parallel GENIA tagger (X-axis: No. of processing cores, Y-axis: processing time in minutes), when abstracts are sent to tagging nodes

Fig. 3 and Fig. 4 show the speedup gained when the resources are increased. It shows that as the number of processors is increased processing time has been reduced correspondingly. Therefore, one can say that application scales linearly. This was an expected result given the data independent nature of the text mining applications, the size of the dataset and the limited number of processors used. However, the aim of our work is to be able to process problem and data sizes which are almost a thousand times larger than the examples given above. Hence the application is needed to scale up to thousands of processors in order to be able to process the given terabytes of dataset in reasonable time. Furthermore, one of the bottlenecks would be to maintain and handle the data due to the data sizes. Disk and network I/O would be an issue as well as the network of the supercomputing machine.

6 Conclusion and Future Works

In this paper we presented a framework for parallel implementation of part of speech tagging for text mining. This model focuses on reducing the part of speech tagging task processing time, using a grid environment to distribute the documents to speed up the tagging task within a group of documents. The next step is to scale this model to hundreds of nodes and integrate it to a text mining system through a grid service using the Globus Toolkit middleware in the Grid environment.

Acknowledgement

We wish to thank for useful comments and suggestions from faculty members of our institute. This research is supported by Research Scholar Lab, Institute Computer Center of Indian Institute of Technology-Roorkee. We wish to thank our colleagues at IIT-Roorkee.

References

1. Lopes, M.C., Costa, M.C.A., Ebecken, N.F.F.: Text Mining. In: Rezende, S.O. (ed.) Intelligent Systems: Foundations and Applications (in Portuguese). Editora Manole Ltda (2002)
2. Salton, G., McGill, M.J.: Introduction to Modern Information Retrieval. McGraw-Hill Book Company, New York (1983)
3. Baeza-Yates, R., Ribeiro-Neto, B.: Modern Information Retrieval. ACM Press Books, New York (1999)
4. Kao, A., Poteet, S.R.: Natural Language Processing and Text Mining. Springer, Heidelberg (2007)
5. Hearst, M.A.: Untangling text data mining. In: Proceedings of the 37th Annual Meeting on Computational Linguistics, pp. 3–10. Association for Computational Linguistics (1999)
6. Konchady, M.: Text Mining Application Programming. Charles River Media, Hingham (2006)
7. Kudo, S., Bies, A., Libeman, M., Mandel, M., McDonald, R., Palmar, R., Schein, A., Ungar, L.: Integrated annotation for biomedical information extraction. In: Proceedings of HLT/NAACL 2004 (2004)
8. Tateisi, Y., Tsujii, J.: Part-of-speech annotation of biology research abstracts. In: Proceedings of 4th International Conference on Language Resource and Evaluation (LREC 2004), pp. 1267–1270 (2004)
9. The Globus Toolkit, `http://www.globus.org/toolkit/`
10. GT4 Data Management, `http://www.globus.org/toolkit/docs/4.0/data/`
11. The WS-Resource Framework, `http://www.globus.org/wsrf/`
12. Replica Location Service, `http://www.globus.org/toolkit/data/rls/`
13. LIGO Scientific Collaboration Research Group: Ligo Data Replicator, `http://www.lsc-group.phys.uwm.edu/LDR/`
14. Chervenak, A., Schuler, R., Kesselman, C., Koranda, S., Moe, B.: Wide area data replication for scientific collaborations. In: Proceedings of 6th IEEE/ACM International Workshop on Grid Computing, Grid 2005 (November 2005)
15. Metadata Catalog Service, `http://www.globus.org/grid_software/data/mcs.php`
16. GT 4.0: Security: Pre-Web Services Authentication and Authorization, `http://www.globus.org/toolkit/docs/4.0/security/prewsaa/`
17. Ninomiya, T., Torisawa, K., Tsujii, J.: An Agent-based Parallel HPSG Parser for Shared-memory Parallel Machines. Journal of Natural Language Processing 8, Ref number 1, 21–48 (2001) ISSN 1340761
18. Qin, X.: Performance Comparisons of Load Balancing Algorithms for I/O-Intensive Workloads on Clusters, July 2006. Journal of Network and Computer Applications (July 2006)
19. Gonzalez-Velez, H.: Self-adaptive skeletal task farm for computational grids. Parallel Computing 32(7-8), 479–490 (2006)
20. Part-of-Speech tagging, `http://en.wikipedia.org/wiki/Part-of-speech_tagging`

SLA with Dual Party Beneficiality in Distributed Cloud

P. Varalakshmi, K.H. Priya, J. Pradeepa, and V. Perumal

Department of Information Technology, Madras Institute of Technology,
Anna University, Chennai, Tamil Nadu, India
{varanip,priyakh.26,j.pradeepa.mit,perumalv18}@gmail.com

Abstract. Service Level Agreement paves the way to maintain a cordial and a conflict free relationship between the service provider and the service customer. This is done by negotiating with the respected parties and finally agreeing upon an agreement. This agreement called as Service Level Agreement (SLA). The proposed solution deals with negotiation process and SLA formation, grouping of leases as classes and scheduling the lease execution making use of High Aggregate Penalty Class (HAPC) algorithm. With the proposed system, the consumer's QoS parameters like waiting time is reduced, and the system parameters - makespan is improved. Also the provider is able to get the payment in installments on time.

1 Introduction

Though cloud computing was initially considered by many as the offshoot of grid computing, it has now captured the imagination of many and has overtaken its predecessor by leaps and bounds. A cloud is basically a cluster of nodes which provides services to the users. The users specify their needs as lease requests. In each lease request they mention their requirements for memory, CPU, duration, number of virtual machines, etc. Based on these requirements, the head node of the cloud must allocate an appropriate computing node having the required resources on time. To do this, the head node must have knowledge of the resource availability in each computing node present in its cloud. So the head node must monitor the computing nodes regularly. The lease is allotted to the under loaded computing node in that cloud by the head node. This is load balancing in a cloud.

SLA is an agreement between the service provider and the service customer, which contains the service level objectives that must be met by the service provider and the service customer. Any violation of the service level objectives specified in SLA leads to a penalty. The service provider must consider these objectives of the application lease while providing the service. Similarly the customer must be ready to pay the amount on time. Else he must pay the penalty caused.

2 Related Work

Basically cloud services are of three types - Infrastucture as a Service (IaaS), Software as a Service (SaaS) and Platform as a Service (PaaS). SLA exists for each of

A. Abraham et al. (Eds.): ACC 2011, Part I, CCIS 190, pp. 471–479, 2011.

them and the SLA metrics considered for each type of service differs, as discussed in [9]. In our paper, we consider the memory required, CPU speed, number of machines, waiting time, deadline, operating system and software required as SLA measures. In [2], a QoS-aware cloud architecture is proposed containing a Service Manager and a VEE (Virtual Execution Environment) Manager.

A solution concentrating on the minimization of the penalty is proposed in [1]. If the required percentile of requests has response time less than the response time threshold, then no penalty is charged for the deviating requests as the percentile condition is satisfied. gi-FIFO scheduling algorithm is utilized and it is compared with FIFO and Weighted Round Robin (WRR) scheduling policies. This paper considers the penalty minimization for the customers. But our proposed work tries to benefit both the users and the providers by using High Aggregate Penalty Class (HAPC) algorithm.

In cloud computing a layered approach for SLA violation propagation is described in [4]. This paper also explains the knowledge database realization with case based reasoning and finally the architecture for propagation of SLA violation threats. In our paper, the SLA violation is detected by the intermediate agent. A mechanism to automate resource manager which optimizes a global utility function is necessary. A solution for the above is proposed in [10]. A novel communication model based on queuing networks for scalability is proposed in [3]. A bilateral and multilateral negotiation can take place by a two stage process as proposed in [7]. In our paper, for the purpose of negotiation, we introduce the concept of intermediate agent (third party) which in turn improves the reliability for both the parties.

In [5], a solution for SLA enabled CARE resource broker is proposed in Grid Computing. Deviation based resource scheduling is performed. We perform class based scheduling where the lease with highest penalty is the first to get executed, in order to reduce the penalty of entities involved. In [6], they proposed a multi-criteria adaptation service selection broker that provides the possibility to select the best service among the available candidates. A solution for resource allocation and SLA determination for large data processing services over cloud taking into account the network parameters, is proposed in [8]. A solution providing Service Level Agreements for Security (Sec-SLA) is proposed in [11].

3 The Proposed Framework

In order to improve the performance of multiple nodes in a cloud, the head node monitors the computing nodes and allots the accepted leases to the computing nodes based on the lease requirements and the load of the computing nodes. A lease is accepted by the head node through the Intermediate Agent after signing the SLA.

3.1 Cloud Computing Architecture

The block diagram of the cloud computing environment we have setup is shown in Fig 1. Each cloud consists of one head node and the associated compute nodes. The head node monitors the compute nodes in its cluster and stores the status information of each one of them.

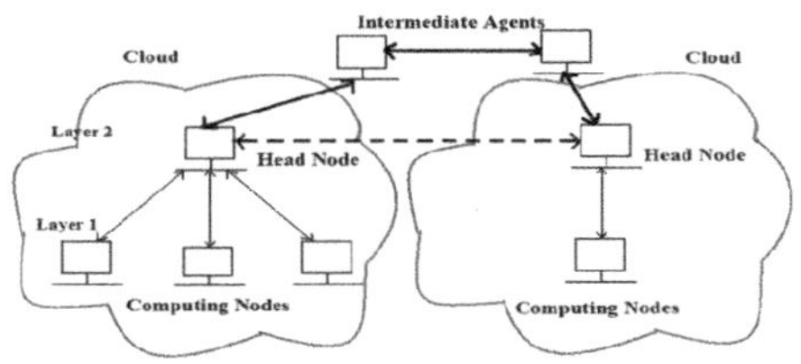

Fig. 1. Block Diagram for Cloud Computing

4 Working Principle of the Architecture

The proposed working principle of our architecture with negotiation, SLA formation and scheduling of leases using High Aggregate Penalty Class (HAPC) algorithm in cloud environment is discussed in this section.

4.1 Lease Request Generation

Each user requests certain services that are to be provided by the service provider. The user specifies his/her requirements in this service request and submits it to the service provider. This service request is termed as the lease request. We have considered the following parameters as a part of the lease request:

- **Amount of memory required** (*mem_req*): This parameter denotes the maximum amount of memory required by the user lease to get serviced, in Kb (kilobytes).
- **CPU speed necessary for the lease** (*cpu_req*): This parameter denotes the CPU speed that is required by the user lease to get serviced, in MHz.
- **Number of machines needed** (*nom*): This parameter denotes the number of machines (virtual machines) required to execute the user lease.
- **Maximum waiting time** (*wt_max*): Waiting time denotes the amount of time that the user should wait after sending the lease request and before getting the acceptance of the lease request, in seconds.
- **Deadline**: Deadline denotes the last date within which the lease should be serviced completely.
- **Operating System used**: The platform required to run the service requested by the user is an important parameter to be checked.
- **Software required:** This parameter denotes the list of software required by the user lease for getting serviced.

The lease request is written in XML format. A sample of this XML file is shown in Fig.2. In the XML file, we have denoted the deadline of the lease making use of the duration period starting from the arrival time, denoted in days.

A weight is assigned to the requested parameters to denote the importance given by the user for each of them. The weight is assigned for memory (*mem_wt*), CPU speed (*cpu_wt*) and waiting time (*w_wt*). The weight must range between 0 and 1 in decimals. The sum of all these weights should be equal to 1. A penalty is also

Fig. 2. Lease request sample

assigned to these parameters. The penalty for memory required (*mem_pty*), CPU speed (*cpu_pty*), waiting time (*wt_pty*) are given as part of lease request. If any one or more of these parameters are not satisfied by the cloud provider after negotiation and SLA formation, then the penalty has to be paid by the cloud provider to the user based on the violation.

4.2 Negotiation

Our proposed solution has an assumption that an intermediate agent is present for each cloud. The main aim of the intermediate agent is to help in the negotiation between the user and the cloud provider before the SLA formation. It is also used to find violations of the agreement, when and how much penalty has to be paid by which party.

The user sends the lease request to the intermediate agent. The intermediate agent receives the request and stores it for comparison with the cloud resources. It receives the monitoring information of computing nodes from the head node. The head node also sends the list of available software and the operating systems present in each computing node. Then the intermediate agent will check if the parameters specified in the lease request are satisfied by anyone of the computing nodes in that cloud.. If these parameters are satisfied, then the intermediate agent intimates the end of negotiation to both the head node and the user node.

If any of these parameters are not satisfied by any of the computing nodes in that cloud, then the agent intimates the user specifies the maximum resource available in that cloud. If the user is ready to accept the available resource, he can change the parameters in the lease request and send it once again to the intermediate agent. Else the intermediate agent will migrate the user lease request to the intermediate agent of the neighboring cloud. This migration is intimated to the user. Then the intermediate agent of that cloud will perform the negotiation between the head node of that cloud and the user node as specified above. So there is a **decentralized communication** between the intermediate agents of the neighboring clouds. Thus the negotiation between the head node and the user is successfully completed.

4.3 SLA Formation

The next step after negotiation is the SLA formation. The SLA formed will contain the Service Level Objectives. This contains the parameters from the user lease request and the parameters specified by the cloud provider. We have considered payment by the user per day as the parameter specified by the cloud provider, denoted as *pay_req*. As cloud services are provided based on "pay as you use", the user must pay for the amount of resources he used. The cloud specifies the way in which the amount should be paid. If the user does not pay the specified amount within the deadline, then the user is charged for the delay. This penalty *pay_pty* is intimated by the intermediate agent to the user. The intermediate agent is responsible for checking the violation of this objective by the user. Even the *pay_pty* parameter has a weight associated with it, which is *pay_wt*. Since we have considered pay_pty as the only parameter from the cloud provider, its weight is one in our consideration. The *pay_req* is calculated by dividing the total amount to be paid by the user, by the total duration he needs the resources for usage.

The cloud provider has to pay the penalty when it does not satisfy any of the parameters specified by the user in the SLA. The intermediate agent is responsible for finding the violation of these parameters too. The penalty for memory required (*mem_pty*), CPU speed (*cpu_pty*), waiting time (*wt_pty*) are given as part of SLA which are into consideration when they are violated by the cloud provider.

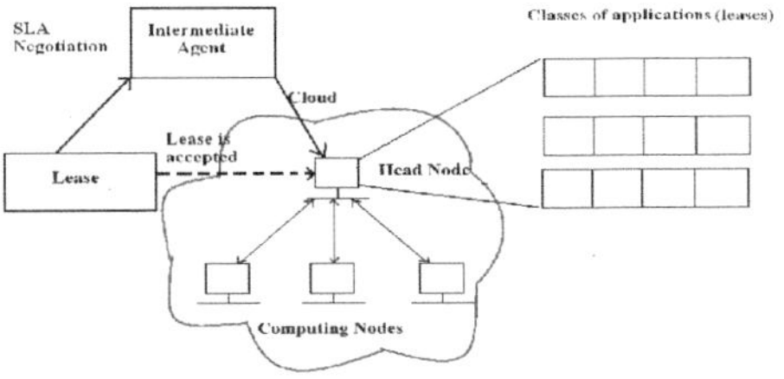

Fig. 3. Negotiation, SLA formation and HAPC algorithm Architecture

4.4 High Aggregate Penalty Class (HAPC) Algorithm

The accepted leases are classified into classes based on the aggregate score (*aggr_score*) of each lease, the aggregate penalty (*aggr_pty*) of each lease and the aggregate penalty of each class (*c_pty*).

The aggregate penalty (*aggr_pty*) of each lease is the addition of the penalties listed by the user in the SLA and the penalty for payment. The aggregate score (*aggr_score*) is calculated by using Eq (1). It is used to classify the leases into classes. Each class has a range of aggregate scores, as shown in Fig3. We have considered 5 classes and we have scaled down the aggregate score to a scale of 1 to 10. In our experiment, the range of first class is 0 to 2, second class is 2 to 4, third class is 4 to 6, fourth class is 6 to 8 and fifth class is 8 to 10. These classes denote the queues of leases waiting to be serviced, at the head node.

$$aggr\_score = (mem\_req \times mem\_wt) + (cpu\_req \times cpu\_wt) + (wt\_max \times w\_wt) + (pay\_req \times pay\_wt) \quad (1)$$

The aggregate penalty of all the leases in each class is added to get the class penalty (*c_pty*). The class having the highest *c_pty* is chosen and the lease having the highest *aggr_pty* in that class is chosen. In this way, we are concentrating on minimizing the penalty paid by both the cloud provider and the user. Since the *aggr_pty* concentrates on the penalty for CPU speed, memory and the waiting time of each lease, the penalty paid by the cloud provider is minimized and the user satisfaction is improved. Since the *aggr_pty* considers the penalty for user payment, it minimizes the penalty paid by the user and the cloud provider satisfaction is improved. Let this lease be l_i. This is High Aggregate Penalty Class (HAPC) algorithm.

The head node checks for the number of machines, the operating system specified and the software required by the lease l_i. The computing nodes satisfying the above conditions are chosen and the head node selects an under loaded node from these chosen computing nodes, which has free memory greater than or equal to mem_req_i and CPU speed greater than or equal to cpu_req_i of the selected lease l_i. The execution of lease l_i is started in that computing node. The time interval between the acceptance of the lease by the head node and the allocation of the lease to the computing node is the waiting time, w_i. If this waiting time w_i is not lesser than wt_max_i, then the cloud provider has to pay the wt_pty_i penalty as agreed in the SLA. If the necessary cpu_spd_i is not provided, the spd_pty_i has to be paid by the cloud provider. Similarly, mem_pty_i penalty is paid by the cloud provider if mem_req_i memory is not allocated.

5 Simulated Scenarios

Xen is used for creating a virtualized environment. On top of Xen, Open Nebula is installed to setup the cloud environment and make it as the head node of cluster. The head node monitors all the computing nodes in that cloud making use of the monitoring algorithm deployed in Open Nebula. We have integrated Haizea with Open Nebula for scheduling the leases to the appropriate computing nodes thereby balancing the load among the computing nodes.

We have created two clouds and each cloud has a head node. One cloud has 3 computing nodes and another cloud has 1 computing node, as shown in Fig.4. H1 and H2 denote the head nodes. 1, 2, 3 and 4 denote the computing nodes. A1 and A2 are the intermediate agents for cloud 1 and cloud 2. The head nodes H1 and H2 are interlinked via the intermediate agents A1 and A2.

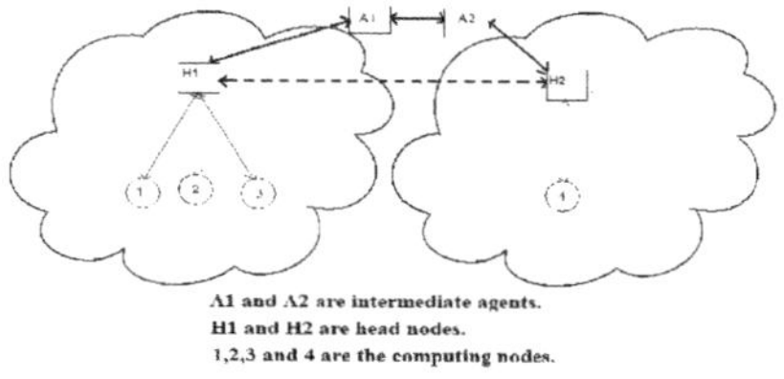

Fig. 4. Cloud setup created

The user leases arrive at dynamic intervals as the leases are based on the requirements of the users. The XML file containing the user lease request is transferred to the intermediate agent. The head node stores the monitored values in a text file and sends it to the intermediate agent. Then the intermediate agent compares the parameter values and negotiates between the head node and the user. The head node specifies the total amount to be paid and the amount to be paid in installments.

Once the negotiation is over, an SLA is formed and the intermediate agent sends a copy of this SLA to the user and the head node. Table 1 shows the value of the computing node based on which the leases are allocated to them. The load of each computing node refers to the maximum number of virtual machines that can be created in it based on the memory and processing speed availability.

Each lease is assigned to the computing node as a virtual machine. So the load of a computing node refers to the maximum number of leases that can be executed in that node. The proposed solution is tested with 4 clusters and each cluster comprised of 2-4 nodes, as shown in Fig.5. 500 leases are tested for the simulation and it can be extended to any number of leases.

Table 1. Computing nodes Information

cloud_id	node_id	Load	Speed(MHz)	free_mem(Gb)	tot_mem(Gb)
1	1	1.1	1000	750	1000
2	2	0.8	2000	500	2000

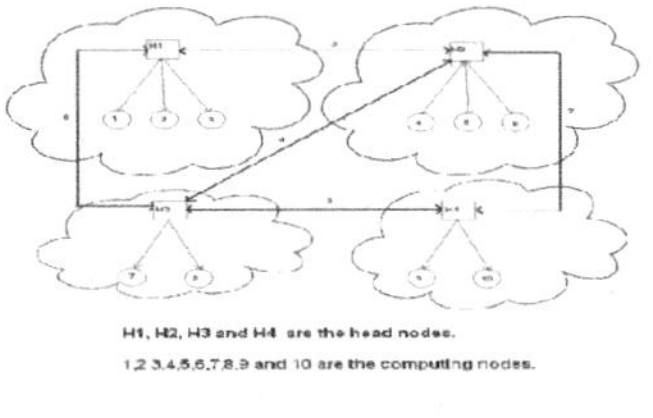

Fig. 5. Cloud architecture considered for the proposed system

6 Performance Analysis

6.1 Waiting Time, Memory and CPU Speed Violation

The performance of the proposed HAPC algorithm is better compared to gi-FIFO algorithm. The proposed HAPC algorithm with negotiation and SLA formation is compared with the same cloud architecture without having negotiation and SLA formation. The penalty caused by both the scenarios is compared and shown in Fig.7 and Fig.8 for violation of memory required and CPU speed required by the user.

6.2 Cloud Provider Income and Makespan

If the payment is done regularly by the customer, the cloud provider will get a uniform income. The penalty is paid by the user if he has not paid the required amount on each day. So the provider is able to get the amount in installments and not the whole amount in the end of usage. In the existing algorithm [1], such a penalty is not considered. The makespan is the time taken to complete all the leases for each node. Fig.9 compares the makespan for using gi-FIFO algorithm and HAPC algorithm.

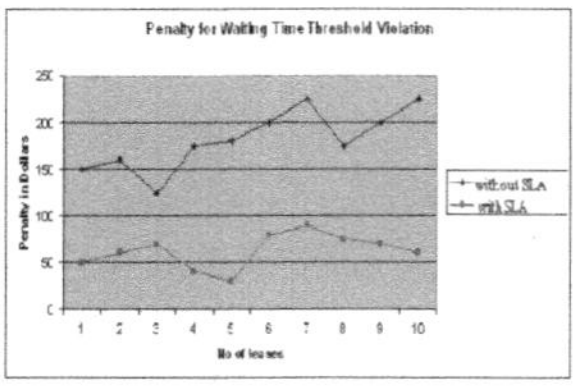

Fig. 6. Comparing penalty for waiting time threshold violation with and without SLA formation

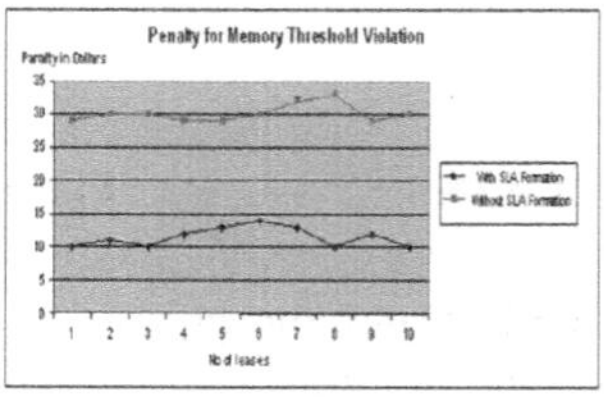

Fig. 7. Comparing penalty for memory violation with and without SLA Formation

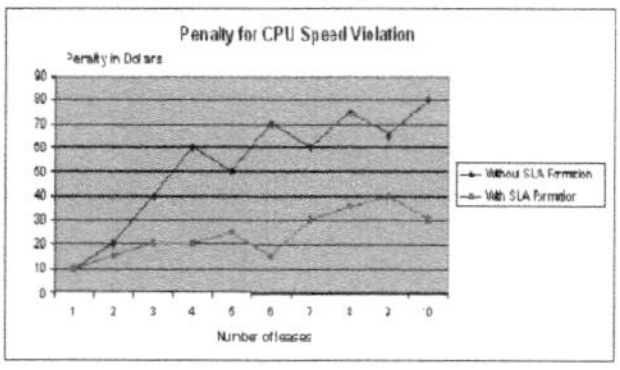

Fig. 8. Comparing penalty for CPU speed violation with and without SLA Formation

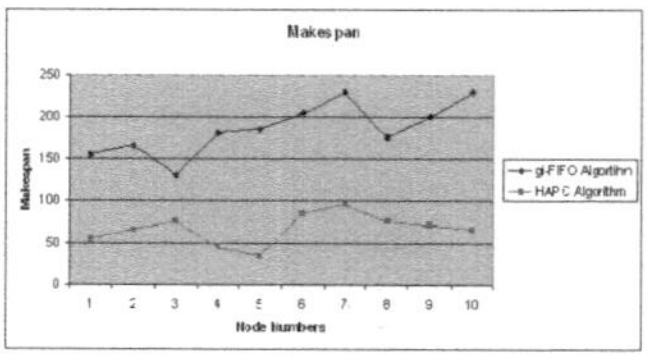

Fig. 9. Comparing the makespan of gi-FIFO and HAPC algorithms

7 Conclusion

Since the leases are accepted after the SLA formation between the head node and the user, the penalty paid by both is reduced. The intermediate agent helps in the negotiation and violation detection between the cloud provider and the user. Though negotiation and SLA formation reduces the penalty paid by the parties and increases the satisfaction of both the parties, there is tolerable time overhead. Making use of HAPC algorithm and classes in each compute node, the leases are effectively scheduled and executed. In future, this can be further expanded by considering other factors like network utilization as the SLA parameters and reducing the time overhead involved in negotiation and SLA formation.

References

[1] Boloor, K., Chirkova, R., Salo, T., Viniotis, Y.: Heuristic-based request scheduling subject to a percentile response time SLA in a distributed cloud. In: GLOBECOM 2010, 2010 IEEE Global Telecommunications Conference, December 6-10, pp. 1–6 (2010)

[2] Fudzee, M.F.M., Abawajy, J.H.: QoS-based adaptation service selection broker. In: Future Generation Computer Systems, vol. 27(3), pp. 256–264 (March 2011)

[3] Emeakaroha, V.C., Brandic, I., Maurer, M., Dustdar, S.: Low Level Metrics to High Level SLAs - LoM2HiS Framework: Bridging the Gap Between Monitored Metrics and SLA Parameters in Cloud Environments. In: 2010 International Conference on High Performance Computing and Simulation (HPCS), June 28-July 2, pp. 48–54 (2010)

[4] Brandic, I., Emeakaroha, V.C., Acs, S., Kertesz, A., Kecskemeti, G.: LAYSI: A Layered Approach for SLA-Violation Propagation in Self-manageable Cloud Infrastructures. In: 2010 IEEE 34th Annual Computer Software and Applications Conference Workshops (COMPSACW), July 19-23, pp. 365–370 (2010)

[5] Balakrishnan, P., Somasundaram, T.S.: SLA Enabled CARE Resource Broker. Springer Journal 27(3), 265–279 (2011)

[6] de Chaves, S.A., Westphall, C.B., Lamin, F.: SLA Perspective in Security Management for Cloud Computing. In: 2010 Sixth International Conference on Networking and Services (ICNS), March 7-13, pp. 212–217 (2010)

[7] Hudert, S., Ludwig, H., Wirtz, G.: Negotiating SLAs-An Approach for a Generic Negotiation Framework for WS-Agreement. Journal of Grid Computing 7(2), 225–246

[8] Hima Prasad, K., Faruquie, T.A., Venkata Subramaniam, L., Mohania, M., Venkatachaliah, G.: Resource Allocation and SLA Determination for Large Data Processing Services Over Cloud. In: 2010 IEEE International Conference on Services Computing (SCC), July 5-10, pp. 522–529 (2010)

[9] Alhamad, M., Dillon, T., Chang, E.: Conceptual SLA Framework for Cloud Computing. In: 2010 4th IEEE International Conference on Digital Ecosystems and Technologies (DEST), April 13-16, pp. 606–610 (2010)

[10] Van, H.N., Tran, F.D., Menaud, J.-M.: SLA-aware Virtual Resource Management for Cloud Infrastructures. In: Ninth IEEE International Conference on Computer and Information Technology, CIT 2009, October 11-14, vol. 1, pp. 357–362 (2009)

[11] Ferretti, S., Ghini, V., Panzieri, F., Pellegrini, M., Turrini, E.: QoS–aware Clouds. In: 2010 IEEE 3rd International Conference on Cloud Computing (CLOUD), July 5-10, pp. 321–328 (2010)

Privacy Preserving Keyword Search over Encrypted Cloud Data

S. Ananthi[1], M. Sadish Sendil[2], and S. Karthik[3]

[1] II ME – CSE
aananthi_s@yahoo.com
[2] Professor, [3]Professor & Head, Department of CSE
SNS College of Technology, Coimbatore, Tamilnadu, India

Abstract. Cloud computing enables the organizations to outsource their data by providing a service model called infrastructure as a service (IaaS). In a public cloud the infrastructure is owned and managed by a cloud service provider and is located in the provider's control. To protect the privacy of sensitive data, documents have to be encrypted before outsourcing. When the number of encrypted documents increases exponentially, the search service and retrieval becomes critical. The process of retrieving the files containing the queried keyword further incurs unnecessary network traffic, which is absolutely undesirable in pay-as-you-use cloud paradigm. In this paper, a search scheme that provides both privacy protection and rank-ordered search capability with less overhead has been proposed. Search indexes and documents are first encrypted by the data owner and then stored onto the cloud server. Retrieval results on an encrypted data and security analysis under different attack models show that data privacy can be preserved while retaining very good retrieval performance.

Keywords: Iaas, Inverted index, COA, KCA, Ranking table.

1 Introduction

Using cloud storage, users can remotely store their data and make use of the on-demand high quality applications and services from a shared pool of configurable computing resources. This brings relief of the burden for storage management, universal data access and avoidance of capital expenditure on hardware and software. By storing user data in the cloud, the data owners can be relieved from the burden of data storage and maintenance. It also brings new and challenging security threats. The sensitive data should be encrypted before outsourcing to protect data privacy against solicited access by untrustworthy service providers and malicious intruders. When the amount of outsourced data files increase, data encryption makes effective data utilization a very challenging task. To share the outsourced data with other users, the owner might want to only retrieve specific data files. One of the efficient way is to selectively retrieve files through keyword based search instead of retrieving all the encrypted files which is impractical due to the huge amount of bandwidth cost in "pay-as-you-use" cloud scale system.

A. Abraham et al. (Eds.): ACC 2011, Part I, CCIS 190, pp. 480–487, 2011.

The goal of information retrieval over an encrypted data is to provide efficient and accurate search over encrypted documents without decrypting them first. The content based retrieval over encrypted data will play an important role to manage the data effectively and securely. To meet the effective data retrieval, the cloud server has to perform result relevant search that allows query and relevant ranking, instead of returning undifferentiated results.

2 Related Work

Many searchable encryption schemes have been developed. Song et.al. [1] proposed a searchable encryption in which each word of a document is encrypted independently. Goh [2] proposed a scheme to build an index of keywords for each document with pseudorandomising functions used as hash functions. This security model is insufficient as it cannot resist certain attacks. Chang [3] and Curtmola [4] both proposed a single encrypted hash table index method for the entire file collection to achieve more efficient search. The index table entry consists of the trapdoor of a keyword and an encrypted set of file identifiers which identifies data files contain the keyword. The existing schemes support only single keyword search. Public key based encryption scheme was proposed by Boneh et.al. [5] which allows anyone with public key can write to the data stored on the server but only authorized users with private key can search. Public key cryptographic schemes are computationally very expensive and are not suitable for cloud computing.

Conjunctive keyword search [6] returns only the documents in which all the keywords that are to be searched appear and incur large overhead for bilinear map and secret sharing. On the other hand disjunctive keyword search returns every document that contains a subset of the specific keyword. Predicate encryption [7] supports both conjunctive and disjunctive search. Inner product queries [8] only predicate whether two vectors are orthogonal or not. Since it is uncapable of comparing concealed inner products, it is not qualified for performing ranked search over encrypted data with single keyword search. Swaminathan et al. [9] proposed a framework for rank-ordered search over encrypted text documents using term frequency table with an index, so that documents can be returned in the order of their relevance to the query term. When the document collection is constantly changing, the secure index information should also be updated.

The technique proposed in this paper enable efficient search directly in the encrypted domain, without multiple rounds of communications between the user and the server. By analyzing the requirements of secure search scenarios, a secure indexing scheme that makes use of inverted indexes of keywords is proposed. This scheme achieves efficient data retrieval and is scalable for large files. We jointly exploit cryptography and search techniques to ensure that the encrypted search indexes can preserve the search capability. Our experiments on an encrypted data documents show that data confidentiality can be preserved while retaining good retrieval performance.

The paper is organized as follows: Section 3 outline the system model for secure keyword search scenario. Section 4 presents the proposed secure indexing scheme. Section 5 provides the search framework and Section 6 provides security analysis of the scheme under different attack models. Section 7 summarizes experimental results on search over encrypted cloud data and. Conclusion is drawn in Section 8.

3 System Model

The data owner has a collection of documents D that he wants to outsource on the cloud server in an encrypted form. To enable the secure search process, the data owner generates an encrypted inverted index I according to each keyword of files and stores both the document collection and an encrypted inverted index to the cloud server. The data owner authorizes the user to search for a keyword of interest. To search the file collection for a given keyword w, an authorized user generates and submits a search request in an encrypted form to prevent the exposure of information to the data center and other intruders by creating a trapdoor T_w of the keyword w to the cloud server. The data users can obtain permission from the data owner to perform a search process without revealing the keywords. Once the search request T_w is received, the cloud server is responsible to search an inverted index I and return the corresponding set of files to the user. To improve document retrieval accuracy, search result should be ranked by cloud server according to some ranking criteria. The encrypted inverted index may be updated to include or exclude documents when they are created or deleted respectively.

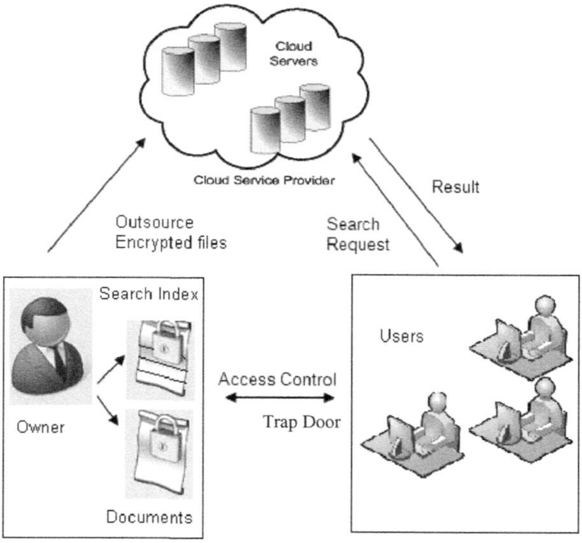

Fig. 1. Architecture of the query over encrypted cloud data

4 Secure Inverted Index Scheme

An inverted index is a data structure storing words or numbers in a document along with its location. The purpose of an inverted index is to improve the time of full text searches. An inverted index contains an index of keywords which stores a distinct list of terms found in the collection and, for each term, a posting list, a list of documents that contain the keyword [10].An inverted index improves search efficiency which is necessary for very large text files.

As shown in Fig. 2, an inverted index consists of a distinct terms and a posting list which stores the IDs of the documents that contain that term. In addition to an ID, each posting list element gives the number of occurrences of that term in the document (its term frequency), which is not considered here as it is not suitable for the documents that will be updated frequently.

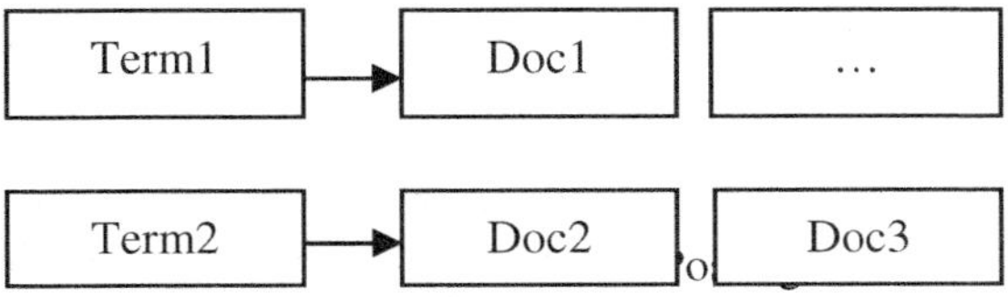

Fig. 2. Structure of an Inverted Index

5 Framework

The data owner employs traditional symmetric encryption with search capabilities to encrypt and then outsource data. The indexing and querying involves the following algorithms:

Table 1. Notations

S.No.	Notation	Meaning
1	D	Document collection
2	d_i	Document id number of the ith document in D
3	w	Unique word contained in the document set
4	w′	subset of w
5	d_j	Document id number of the jth document collected during search process
6	R	Ranking table that contains fields for frequency of term r, term id w′ and document id d_j

Keygen(k): This algorithm takes a security parameter (password) and produce the symmetric key, SK.

BuildIndex(SK, D): The data owner builds an Inverted Index from the list of documents ($D(w_i)$). On every unique word w_i contained in the document set, the following process is performed [11].

1. Create a dictionary structure S
2. For each document id d_i ($1 \leq i \leq N$)
   a. Read d_i, insert it into S as index terms w_i
   b. For each index term $w_i \in d_i$
      i. Search S for w_i
      ii. If w_i is not in S, insert it

Once an inverted index is constructed, the plaintext document and an Inverted index are encrypted using a standard block cipher and the symmetric key SK. The encrypted document and the encrypted index can then be outsourced to the cloud server independently.

Trapdoor(SK, w′): The trapdoor hides the search term from the server. w′ is the subset of w, representing the keywords in a search request, A trapdoor T_w' is generated from the keywords of interest in w. When a user wants to query the server, the query is split into individual terms and then encrypted using a symmetric key provided by the data owner to the user.

Search(I , T_w'): When the user wants to perform a search for keyword w′ with the help of trapdoor T_w' and an inverted index I, the cloud server will perform the following:

1. An inverted index is checked to see if w′ is a member.
2. If w′ is matched with the content of an inverted index, the document is added to the set of documents d_j to be searched for the keyword.

Rank(d_i): Ranked keyword search over encrypted data is used to achieve economies of scale for Cloud Computing. Let R be the ranking table which contains r as a frequency of term w′ in document d_i with the corresponding term and document id . To compute the ranking, the algorithm is as follows:

1. Initialize R
2. For each document id d_i
    a. If w′ is in d_j insert into R as r, w′ and d_j
    b. For each w′ in d_j
        i. Search R for w′ and d_j
        ii. If w′ and d_j are in R, increment r

Sort documents in descending ranked order
Display the top ranked d_j to the user

The server returns the relevant document with higher ranking satisfies the user query. The user can then decrypt the returned document.

6 Security Analysis

As discussed in Section 3, in order to ensure data confidentiality, documents are encrypted by cryptographic ciphers before storing on the server. Built on top of established cryptographic primitives, it can be assumed computationally difficult for the server to decrypt the documents without knowing the secret key. Security analysis focuses on the information the server can learn from the encrypted inverted index) and the security of the indexing scheme under different attack models.

Ciphertext Only Attack (COA): In this model, cloud server has access to the encrypted inverted indexes but does not know anything more. As described in Section 4, the encrypted inverted index contains randomly permuted word IDs so that the server cannot tell which keywords are present in each document. Since each document contains outputs of cryptographically strong trapdoor functions, it is also computationally difficult for the server to infer the original information. As our encrypted indexes allow for similarity comparison in order to enable rank-ordered retrieval, one possible attack from the server is to compare all keywords and obtain their similarity information. The similarity information can also be learned by the server during retrieval because keywords similar to the query will eventually be returned to the user. However, given that both the query and data are encrypted, the similarity information alone does not help the server to infer document content [12].

Known Ciphertext Attack (KCA): In this model, cloud server is supposed to only know encrypted dataset and Inverted index, both of which are outsourced from data owner. The search scheme provides privacy guarantee on search pattern but it will incur trapdoor privacy leakage once cloud server is requested by users to execute two or more times of searches. By analyzing similarity scores obtained during search, cloud server has a chance to deduce a valid trapdoor which violates trapdoor privacy goal. This problem can be fixed through inserting dummy keyword. During the search process some of the dummy keywords are selected in every query. Therefore, similarity scores of documents will not be exactly accurate. To evaluate the purity of the k documents retrieved by the user, we define a measure as precision $P_k = k'/k$ where k' is number of real top-k documents that are returned by cloud server [13].

7 Result

In order to test the system, the dataset had to be chosen. The system could then be used to encrypt and search over this dataset in order to quantitatively evaluate the implementation. Choosing a suitable dataset is important. Properties such as the size on disk should be reasonable, capable of being stored in less than a few gigabytes of space in order to keep testing times down, causing the search scheme implementation to be thoroughly tested and also the number of individual documents should be considered. This number should be fairly large in order to mimic a real world situation. The number of documents will also depend on the size of each individual document.

The set of Request For Comments (RFCs) that contains a large number of technical terms, a lot of which are unique to the document was chosen to evaluate the system. It provides a wide range of possible queries due to its technical content and contains a large number of separate documents.

The experiments were conducted on a machine with an Intel Core2 Duo CPU running at 2.33GHz, 7200rpm disk drive, 2GB of RAM and Linux Server as an Operating system. The number of documents in dataset determines the number of distinct keywords. Standard information retrieval techniques can be used to significantly reduce the number of distinct keywords, such as case folding, stemming, and stop words. The system is configured to use the AES cipher to encrypt the document contents and the indices.

Fig. 3 shows that the time of building an encrypted inverted index is almost linear with the number of documents in dataset. Since the process of building inverted index is an one-time operation before data outsourcing, the time required for this process is not a negligible overhead for data owner. The time to generate a trapdoor is greatly affected by the number of documents in dataset.

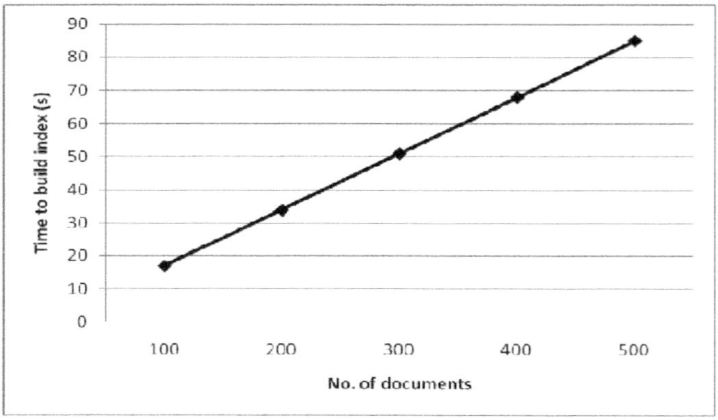

Fig. 3. Time of building searchable index

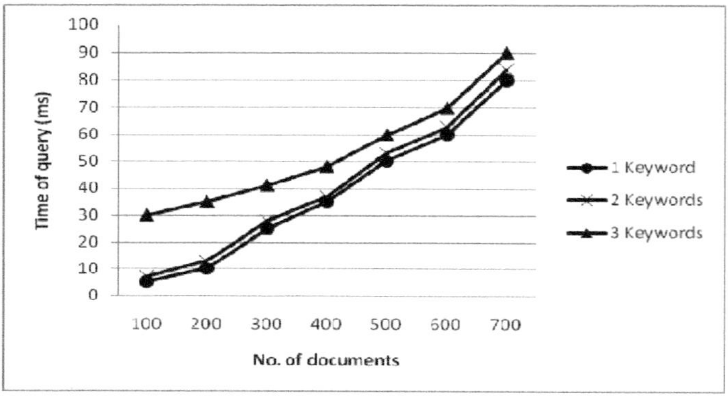

Fig. 4. Runtime overhead of query

Query execution in cloud server consists of computing and ranking similarity scores for all documents in the dataset. Fig. 4 shows the query time is dominated by the number of documents in dataset, and the number of keywords in the query has very slight impact on it like the trapdoor generation.

While the computation and communication cost in the query procedure is linear with the number of query keywords, our proposed scheme enjoy the constant overhead in the query which makes it more practical in the cloud paradigm.

8 Conclusion

In this paper, a search scheme that provides both privacy protection and rank-ordered search capability with less overhead has been proposed. Retrieval results on an encrypted data and security analysis under different attack models show that data privacy can be preserved while retaining very good retrieval performance. Future work will further improve the efficiency and security of search and retrieval. And also focus on other important security issues include protecting communication links and combating traffic analysis.

References

1. Song, D., Wagner, D., Perrig, A.: Practical techniques for searches on encrypted data. In: Proc. of S&P (2000)
2. Goh, E.J.: Secure indexes. Cryptology ePrint Archive (2003), http://eprint.iacr.org/2003/216
3. Chang, Y.-C., Mitzenmacher, M.: Privacy preserving keyword searches on remote encrypted data. In: Ioannidis, J., Keromytis, A.D., Yung, M. (eds.) ACNS 2005. LNCS, vol. 3531, pp. 442–455. Springer, Heidelberg (2005)
4. Curtmola, R., Garay, J.A., Kamara, S., Ostrovsky, R.: Searchable symmetric encryption: improved definitions and efficient constructions. In: Proc. of ACM CCS (2006)
5. Boneh, D., Di Crescenzo, G., Ostrovsky, R., Persiano, G.: Public key encryption with keyword search. In: Cachin, C., Camenisch, J.L. (eds.) EUROCRYPT 2004. LNCS, vol. 3027, pp. 506–522. Springer, Heidelberg (2004)
6. Golle, P., Staddon, J., Waters, B.: Secure conjunctive keyword search over encrypted data. In: Jakobsson, M., Yung, M., Zhou, J. (eds.) ACNS 2004. LNCS, vol. 3089, pp. 31–45. Springer, Heidelberg (2004)
7. Katz, J., Sahai, A., Waters, B.: Predicate encryption supporting disjunctions, polynomial equations, and inner products. In: Smart, N.P. (ed.) EUROCRYPT 2008. LNCS, vol. 4965, pp. 146–162. Springer, Heidelberg (2008)
8. Lewko, A., Okamoto, T., Sahai, A., Takashima, K., Waters, B.: Fully secure functional encryption: Attribute-based encryption and (Hierarchical) inner product encryption. In: Gilbert, H. (ed.) EUROCRYPT 2010. LNCS, vol. 6110, pp. 62–91. Springer, Heidelberg (2010)
9. Swaminathan, A., et al.: Confidentiality preserving rank-ordered search. In: ACM Workshop on Storage, Security, and Survivability, pp. 7–12 (2001)
10. http://lbd-ri.googlecode.com/files/inverted_index.pdf
11. http://www.slidefinder.net/I/Indexing_Tolerant_Dictionaries_Make_Class/6657298
12. Lu, W., Swaminathan, A., Varna, A.L., Wu, M.: Enabling Search over Encrypted Multimedia Databases. Media Forensics and Security (2009)
13. Cao, N., Wang, C., Li, M., Ren, K., Lou, W.: Privacy-Preserving Multi-keyword Ranked Search over Encrypted Cloud Data. In: IEEE INFOCOM 2011, Shanghai, China (2011)

Preventing Insider Attacks in the Cloud*

Sudharsan Sundararajan[1], Hari Narayanan[1], Vipin Pavithran[1], Kaladhar Vorungati[2], and Krishnashree Achuthan[1]

[1] Center for Cyber Security, Amrita Vishwa Vidyapeetham University, Amritapuri, Kollam, 690 525 India
{krishnashree,sudharsan,hari,vipinp}@am.amrita.edu
[2] NetApp, Sunnyvale, CA - 94089
kaladhar.voruganti@netapp.com

Abstract. Cloud computing is becoming popular due to its ability to provide dynamic scalability and elasticity of resources at affordable cost. In spite of these advantages key concerns that prevent large scale adoption of cloud computing today are related to security and privacy of customer's data in the cloud. The main security concerns of clients are loss of direct control of their data and being forced to trust a third party provider with confidential information. Among security threats in the cloud, insider threats pose a serious risk to clients. This paper presents a new access control mechanism that can mitigate security threats in the cloud including those caused by insiders, such as malicious system administrators. The problem is challenging because the cloud provider's system administrators have elevated privileges for performing genuine system maintenance and administration tasks. We describe an access control mechanism that generates immutable security policies for a client, propagates and enforces them at the provider's infrastructure.

Keywords: Insider Threats, Cloud Computing, Security, Security Policy, Access Control, Hypervisor instrumentation.

1 Introduction

Cloud computing represents the next evolutionary phase in computing. Cloud computing combines a set of existing and new techniques from research areas such as Service-Oriented Architectures (SOA) and virtualization. It is a computing paradigm in which various resources such as computing, software, infrastructure, storage etc are provided as paid services over the Internet. Some of the cloud vendors are Amazon's EC2 and S3 [1], Google App Engine [2], and Microsoft Azure [3] who provide users with elastic and scalable resources in the pay-as-you-use fashion at relatively low prices. As compared to building its own infrastructures, a company is able to cut down on expenditure significantly by migrating computation, storage and hosting onto the cloud. Although this provides savings in terms of finance and manpower

* This work is supported by the Department of Information Technology (DIT), Government of India. The contents of this paper do not necessarily reflect the position or the policies of the Indian Government.

A. Abraham et al. (Eds.): ACC 2011, Part I, CCIS 190, pp. 488–500, 2011.

along with it come new security risks. The primary security concern is the loss of direct control over potentially business sensitive and confidential data. This is a big security risk as the cloud providers are outside the trusted domain of users.

Though there has been research on making cloud computing more secure, very little has been done with specific focus on insider attacks in a cloud environment. Insider attacks are on the rise [4] and the Verizon 2010 data breach report indicates that there is a 26% increase in the data breaches by malicious insiders [5] accounting to a total of 48% of data breaches being carried out by insiders. The cloud security alliance report [6] lists malicious insiders as the number three threat in cloud computing. So even though the cloud provider may be trusted a cloud administrator could potentially be a rogue.

In this paper we describe a mechanism for

1. Creation of an access control policy file based on the inputs from the client and the provider.
2. Secure propagation of the user policies across the nodes and datacenters of the provider on which client data or virtual machines are hosted.
3. Policy enforcement at the nodes and datacenters on which client data or virtual machines are hosted.

The key challenge in evolving a policy enforcement mechanism for the cloud is in preventing a system administrator of the provider from performing malicious actions. This is because the administrator may need to perform legitimate actions like taking back-up of the client data, migrating virtual machines of users to different nodes for load balancing. To the best of our knowledge currently there are no standard policies and/or policy enforcements available or defined for the cloud. The problem in other words is how do we distinguish the malicious actions from legitimate actions and prevent the former while permitting the latter.

The rest of the paper is organized as follows. Section 2 discusses related work in the area of cloud security. Section 3 presents the proposed architecture of our access control mechanism. Section 4 describes the different protocols we propose to enforce access control. Finally the paper concludes in Section 5.

2 Related Work

The cloud security alliance document [6] outlines the different kinds of threats in the area of cloud computing. G Atienese et.al [7] discusses a mechanism to detect compromise of data integrity in public cloud storage. R Curtmola et.al [8] introduce ways to use challenge response protocol using unique identification mechanism to detect a cloud provider storing lesser number of copies than what is agreed with the client. In [9] A Juels et.al describe a mechanism based on sentinel records to generate proof of retrievability of data stored in a cloud storage to detect deletions or modification of part of client data. T. Ristenpart et.al [10] show that it is possible to map the internal structure of a cloud provider network and identify where a particular target VM is likely to reside. They show that this information can be used to instantiate new VMs until one is placed co-resident with a target VM of a client and how such placement can then be used to mount cross-VM side-channel attacks to extract information from the target VM. R Sailer et.al describe sHype[13] an operating system independent hypervisor security architecture and its application to control information flow between operating systems sharing a single hardware platform.

Z Wang and X Jiang discuss HyperSafe [14], a lightweight approach to provide lifetime control flow integrity for commodity Type-I or bare metal hypervisors. Work done by Nuno Santos et.al [11] proposes a solution where an External Trusted Entity is used to ensure that clients run on trusted machines alone, both in case of launching and migration of VMs. As in [11] we adopt the use of a dedicated Trusted Entity to enforce the trust policy on machines running VM instances but the role of this is extended to setup a secure trusted Policy enforcement Entity. T.Gartfinkel et.al have designed and discussed a trusted computing platform Terra [12], where the user can run a computation securely on a virtual machine, without any chance of intervention by the owner of the physical host. In this work we do not guarantee a secure trusted platform but we evaluate the underlying platform to determine whether it is trusted to host the VMs and enforce access control policies.

In [15] Dirk Kuhlmann et.al propose a mechanism based on Trusted Computing to secure VMs and implement user defined policies on them. Ahmed. M Azab et.al discuss a hypervisor based integrity measurement system HIMA[16], which provides both static and runtime integrity of guest OSes, providing integrity to applications running on the VMs. S Berger et.al [17] have implemented a Trusted Virtual Datacenter for providing strong isolation and integrity guarantee. Reiner Sailer et.al describe their integrity measurement architecture in [18] which extends the TCG trust concepts to dynamic executable content from the BIOS all the way up into the application layer.

3 Architecture

The generic architecture of an Infrastructure-as-a-Service (IaaS) cloud computing model as described in Eucalyptus [20], an open source cloud computing platform is shown in Figure 1 [21].

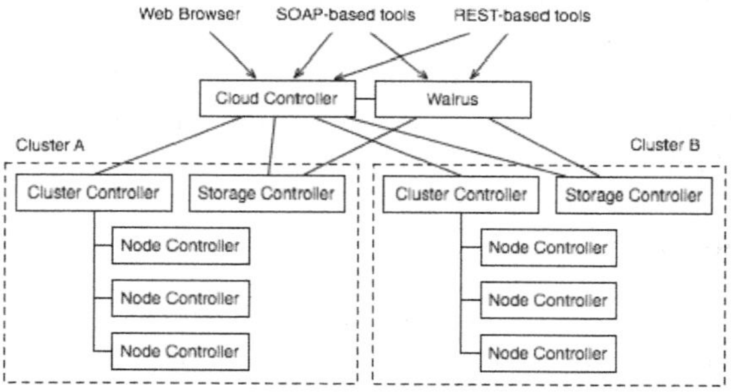

Fig. 1. Eucalyptus Software Architecture

Here we briefly describe the different components of the Eucalyptus architecture

- Node Controller controls the execution, inspection and terminating of VM instances on the host where it runs.

- Cluster Controller gathers information about and schedules VM execution on specific node controllers, as well as manages virtual instance network.
- Storage Controller (Walrus) is a put/get storage service that implements Amazon's S3 interface, providing a mechanism for storing and accessing virtual machine images and user data.
- Cloud Controller is the entry-point into the cloud for users and administrators. It queries node managers for information about resources, makes high level scheduling decisions, and implements them by making requests to cluster controllers.

Figure 2 shows the different components of our proposed architecture used to implement the access control mechanism. The three major steps involved in designing a secure architecture for preventing cyber attacks in cloud computing include defining a policy, propagation of this policy via a secure policy propagation module and enforcing it through a policy enforcement module.. All the modules that are shown in the Figure 2 need to run on a platform which guarantees to the client that none of these modules can be compromised by the cloud provider or by any malicious attacker. We

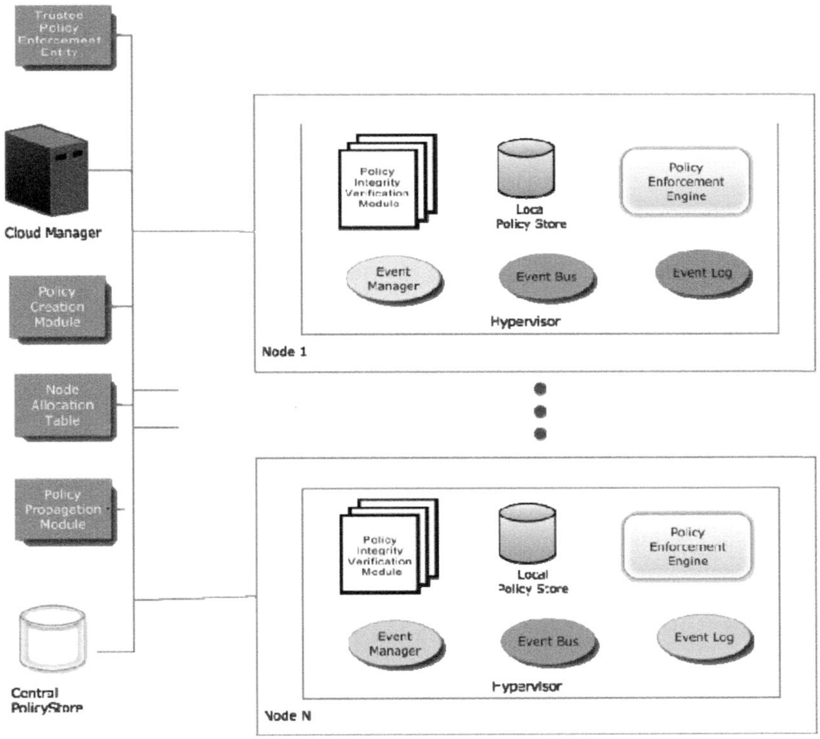

Fig. 2. System Architecture

call this platform as a trusted platform. The proposed policy enforcement mechanism architecture operates at two levels of granularity, one at the level of the data-center wherein the global policies apply (e.g. the nodes on which the client VM instances can be launched nodes to which administrator access is allowed etc.) and at the local level of the node where the instrumented Hypervisor enforces the policies as to what rights a client has on the node and what administrator actions are allowed on the node.

3.1 Cloud Manager

The Cloud manager module in the data center is akin to the cloud controller in the Eucalyptus architecture. This controls the access to the different nodes in the data center and also handles all the requests from the users and administrator to launch/migrate VM instances on the nodes. This module is the interface between the users, system administrators and the nodes for setting up any sessions on the nodes. This module has the following sub-modules

Session Interface: This interface module allows users to launch VM instances or execute administration commands on the nodes. It also forwards all the commands entered by the user to the Command Interface.

Command Interface: This module interprets the user commands and passes the commands to the underlying control layers.

Event Bus: This module records any events that happen on the system (hardware, software events) that are caused by the execution of the commands from the command interface.

Event Manager: This module gets input from the Event bus whenever any event that requires policy enforcement happens on the Event Bus. The Event Manager will examine the events that are logged in the Event Bus and form a Request for access that is sent to a policy enforcement module. Based on the response (allow / deny) it receives from the policy enforcement module the event manager will trigger an event in the Event Bus which will launch the session if the policy allows the request or it will log the denied access in the event log file. This log file is stored periodically in a secure store and can be used for auditing the events.

Secure Log Store: This is a secure storage of the logs of all the events recorded by the Event Bus module. This is processed later for the audit reports of client and administrator activities.

3.2 Trusted Policy Enforcement Entity (TPEE)

TPEE module is responsible for responding to requests from the Cloud Manager and to enforce user policies and for propagation of policies in the cloud. It consists of:

Policy Enforcement Module: This module is responsible for selecting and activating the corresponding policy file for a user/client from the secure Central Policy Store. Additionally it checks the integrity of the policy file by verifying the hash of the file periodically and informing the client in case of any anomaly. The module evaluates the request from the Event Manager and checks if the policy allows the requested action and sends a corresponding response back to the Event Manager. Further the module also informs the Policy Propagation Module about the launch or migration of a VM instance on a node and the corresponding client credentials.

Policy Propagation Module: This module is responsible for propagation of the specific user policy file to the node on which the user/client VM instance will be hosted. The module gets the information from the Policy Enforcement Module about the client credentials and the node on which his VM will be hosted and this will propagate the policy to the particular node so the node can store the policy in its local store and have the policy file of the user before his VM can be hosted on the node.

3.3 Node Allocation Table

This is a secure table which is used to implement a policy where a user can request that his VM should not be co-located with any other VM instances and he is ready to bear the cost of reserving the hardware for exclusive use. An entry in this table indicates that the user has reserved the particular node for his VM instances alone. The table is created, owned and maintained by the policy enforcement entity. This is a dynamic table and when a user releases a node reserved by him for exclusive use, the node entry is removed from this table and similarly when any user requests a node to be reserved for launching his VM instances alone, a new entry is made in this table against the user name. In order to prevent any tampering of this table by the cloud administrator, the access to the table is strictly restricted to the policy enforcement entity.

3.4 Policy Creation Module

This module is responsible for creating and registering the client policy when he sets up an account with the cloud service provider. The policy is derived from the Service Level Agreement (SLA) between the client and the provider and the inputs from the client based on his security level requirements.

3.5 Policy Stores

There is a Central Policy store which centralizes storage for all the client policies and also contains a hash which is securely stored. The policy of every client is propagated to the individual nodes from this central policy store. Additionally there is a Local Policy store present at every node. For every user who has launched a VM instance on a node this will store user policies. Only those users who have launched or are about to launch a VM instance on a node will have their user policy in the local policy store. Policies of other users will not be stored.

3.6 Policy Integrity Verification Module

This module ensures the integrity of the policy files in the local store of the node by verifying the hash of the file periodically against the original hash in the central policy store and informing the client in case of any anomaly. The verification will be triggered if there is any write access to the policy file in the local policy store. Thus it ensures the immutability of the policy file.

3.7 Policy Enforcement Engine

This is the instrumented entity in the hypervisor that enforces the access control policies on the VM instances running on the particular node.

4 Access Control Protocols

The protocols involved in building trusted channels between a client and the trusted nodes in the cloud service provider infrastructure and as well as the cloud system administrator and the infrastructure are shown in Figure 3. The trusted channels are necessary for the establishing security and trust between the client and the provider. They can also be used for auditing administrator activities of the cloud service provider. In the paragraphs below we describe a mechanism for enforcing Access Control Policies using a Trusted Entity.

4.1 Establishing Mutual Trust

The architecture discussed in this paper is based on the existence of a Trusted Policy Enforcement Entity (TPEE), which can be located either at the cloud service provider premises or can be hosted at a secure external infrastructure agreeable to both the service provider and the clients. The TPEE will have access to a database containing public keys of all the Trusted Nodes (TNode) that are present at the Provider's infrastructure. At the time of boot up of any node the TPEE and the TNode use Public Key Infrastructure (PKI), making use of a public – private key pair for secure communication, to exchange their authentication information and thereby establish their identity and mutual trust. The architecture banks on the concept of Trusted Computing that makes use of a set of hardware and software techniques used to construct a Trusted Platform. The Trusted Platform Module (TPM), a chip, that serves as the root of trust is a very integral module. This chip contains an Endorsement Key that uniquely identifies the TPM and some cryptographic functions that cannot be modified. The manufacturers of TPM sign the corresponding public key to guarantee the correctness of the chip and the validity of the key. All the nodes that validate the element of Trust in our protocol make use of the Trusted Computing Base (TCB) created using the TPM of each node.

The TPEE has both its hardware and the software application, that evaluates the clients and administrator credentials and enforces the Access Control Policy, validated using the TCB. The TPEE and the TNodes establish mutual authentication and verification of trust by exchanging their trust credentials. Our architecture follows a similar setup as followed by Nuno Santos et.al in [11] with the exception that the nodes and the TPEE will execute the mutual trust establishment protocol just once at the point where the node is booted or added as a Trusted Node to the cloud infrastructure. From then on the credentials of the node are stored in a secure Key-Value store

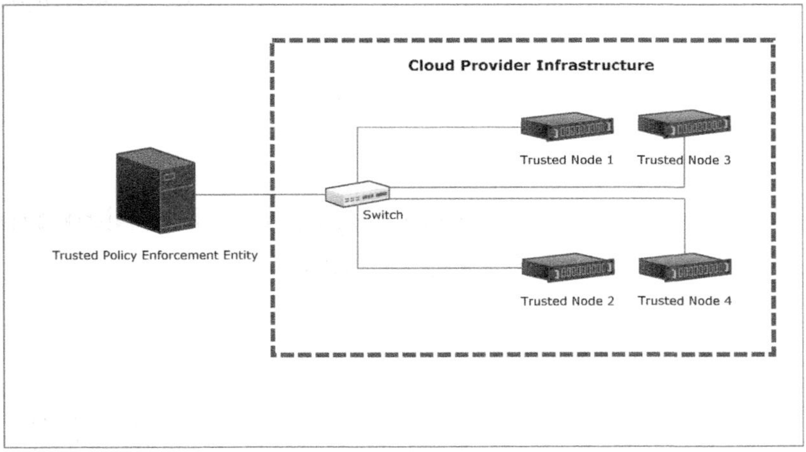

Fig. 3. Establishing Mutual Trust

accessible to the TPEE. This establishment of mutual trust between the TPEE and the TNodes is the first step of the proposed secure access mechanism.

4.2 Policy Creation

The Policy Creation mechanism utilizes the Access Control Policies of the client and the cloud service provider and some policies in the SLA (Service Level Agreement) to generate a policy file of the client. The Policy Creation mechanism of our design is shown in Figure 4 and is described as follows.

1. The client creates an account with the provider.
2. The provider and the client create a policy file agreed upon by both.
3. A hash of the policy file is generated and stored by the Provider in a Trusted Key-Value Store and the client will store the hash in a secure local storage for future reference.
4. The policy file is then signed by both the provider and the client respectively.
5. The signed policy file is then stored in the Trusted Key-Value Store along with the corresponding hash of the policy file.

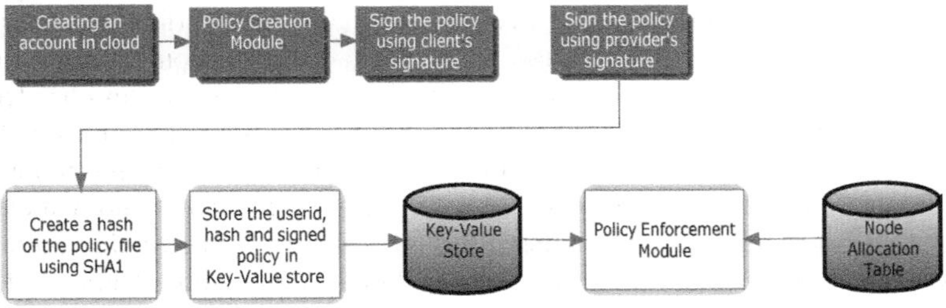

Fig. 4. Policy Creation

The trusted store uses the client user name as the key and the values stored are the policy file and its corresponding hash value. The policy files stored in the Key-Value store are accessible only to the Trusted Policy Enforcement Entity.

When a client signs up for a cloud account, he is given the flexibility to choose the machine configuration (memory, processor configurations, storage size), network specifications (bandwidth requirements) and geographical location (region) of where he wants his data and virtual machine instances to be located. The client can also specify preferences like whether he allows co-location of other clients i.e. other clients sharing the same physical hardware. A sample policy XML file is shown in Figure 5 below.

policy.xml

```
<cloud-policy>
    <account-name> Fedex </account-name>
    <location>
        <region> North America </region>
          <centers>
              <country> US </country>
              <state> CA </state>
              <site> San Jose D1</site>
          </centers>
        </region>
    </location>
    <instance-type>Medium</instance-type>
    <zone>ANY</zone>
    <max-instances>1000</max-instances>
    <co-location>Deny<co-location>
</cloud-policy>
```

Fig. 5. Sample Policy Definition XML File

4.3 Policy Propagation

When a user creates a new account with the cloud provider the process also creates a policy for the particular user as discussed in the policy creation module. The cloud provider has multiple data centers across multiple regions. The question arises how to securely propagate the policy. The policy could be stored in a central policy store. We go with the approach of distributing the policy file across data centers as a central policy store will lead to a single point of failure. Also potentially a DDoS attack on a central policy store will slow down or even bring down the entire cloud [19].

Initially when a user creates an account the policy is stored in a policy database associated with the data center. Next time the user logs in and wants to perform an action, for example, launch a new VM instance first the Event Manager needs to determine if this is allowed as per the user policy and does this as described in the Policy Enforcement work flow. If the policy allows the launch of a VM on a particular node the Policy Enforcement module sends the user-id and the node-id to the Policy Propagation module which is a part of the Policy Manager. The Policy Propagation module then picks the appropriate policy from the Policy Store and makes a copy of it to the node on which the VM instance of the user will be launched. In this way as shown in

Figure 6 below, the policy is propagated to the appropriate nodes in case of VM launch and a similar mechanism is followed for the VM migration and other events as well.

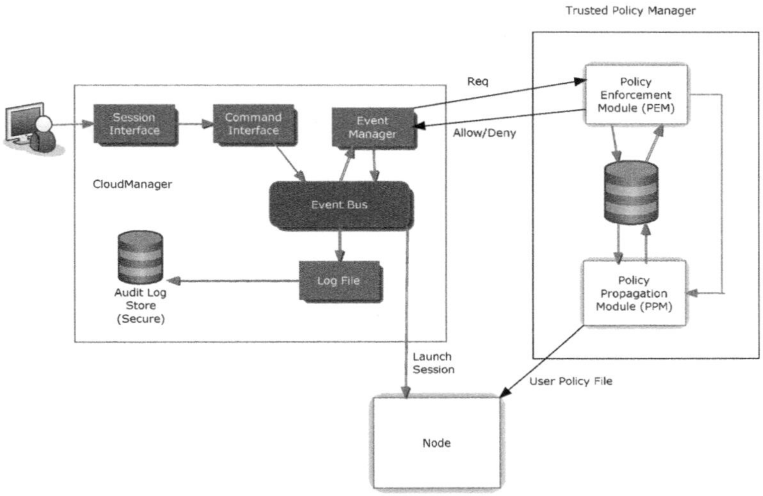

Fig. 6. Policy Propagation

4.4 Policy Enforcement

The policy enforcement mechanism in the present design uses Mandatory Access Control (MAC). A set of security attributes is associated with every subject (user or cloud administrator). An object (VM instances, Nodes) and a set of rules that takes these attributes determine whether the operation is allowed or not. A rule will contain subject, object, action (parameters) and action to be invoked on Denial. The action to be invoked on denial is specified in the policy so that the Policy Enforcement Entity can take evasive action and prevent a malicious administrator or user from causing extensive damage to the data in the cloud. Depending upon the severity of the policy violation the action associated with denial of permission will vary from logging to the secure log file and notifying the user to locking the malicious user account to prevent further damage the data in the cloud. The high level architecture of the policy enforcement is shown in Figure 7.

4.5 Illustration

To illustrate the working of our Access Control Mechanism we describe some typical user scenarios below.

A user launching a VM instance

The policy file corresponding to the user will have entries of the list of nodes the user has agreed for his VM instances to be hosted on. The command interface interprets the VM launch command and executes it, which causes a VM launch event in the

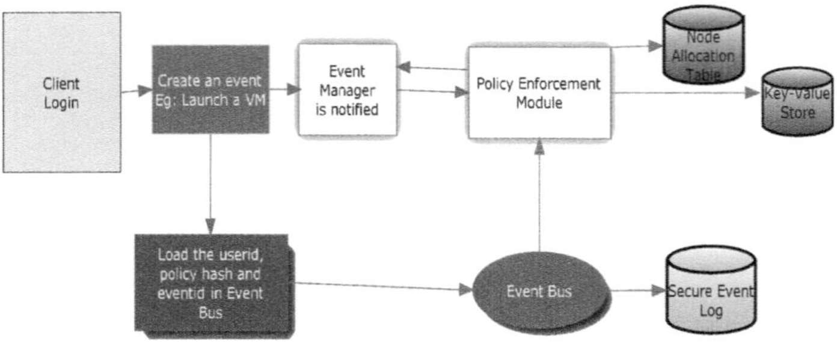

Fig. 7. Policy Enforcement

Event Bus. The Event Bus Module notifies the Event Manager causing it to check the events in the Event Bus. The Event Manager then notifies the Trusted Policy Enforcement Entity (TPEE) with the request to launch a VM instance of that user on the node. The TPEE uses the user id to lookup the corresponding policy file from the Key-Value Store and check if the user is allowed to launch his VM on that node. If allowed by the policy, it intimates the Event Manager that the command can be executed. This causes the Event Manager to invoke a corresponding event in the Event Bus which will launch the VM instance on the node.

A system administrator trying migration of a client VM to an unauthorized node As mentioned in the above scenario, the command interface interprets and executes the system administrator's command, which will cause a VM migration event on the Event Bus. This is passed via the Event Manager to the TPEE. The TPEE looks up the VM instance and has the associated user id for that instance. Using this user id it looks up the policy file corresponding to that client and checks if the migration to the node is allowed. Since the node does not figure in the list of trusted nodes of the client the TPEE signals a Denial of execution to the Event Manager. The Event manager triggers a command denied event in the event bus and provides the command and the details of the administrator who executed the command. This event is logged in the secure log file and can be used later for auditing for malicious activities.

5 Conclusions

In this paper we have presented the architecture for a new security mechanism which will be able to detect malicious operations performed by a rogue administrator in addition to enforcing the access control rules in the cloud. We plan to instrument the XEN hypervisor in order to implement our architecture. We foresee that the major challenge will be to distinguish between the legitimate operations and the malicious operations. Our architecture allows user policies to be constructed from the Service Level Agreement (SLA) proposed by the user and agreed by the provider. We have also described a mechanism to securely store and propagate the policies on the fly in the case of VM migration to other nodes or data centers.

Our goal is to make the architecture as lightweight as possible so that it provides least overhead in the system operations and these will be analyzed for its impact on performance and cost.

References

1. Amazon Web Services (AWS), http://aws.amazon.com
2. Google App Engine, http://code.google.com/appengine/
3. Microsoft Azure, http://www.microsoft.com/azure/
4. Malicious insider attacks to rise, http://news.bbc.co.uk/2/hi/7875904.stm
5. 2010 DataBreach Investigations Report, http://www.verizonbusiness.com/resources/reports/rp_2010-data-breach-report_en_xg.pdf
6. Top Threats to Cloud computing by Cloud Security Alliance (2010), http://www.cloudsecurityalliance.org/topthreats/csathreats.v1.0.pdf
7. Ateniese, G., Burns, R., Curtmola, R., Herring, J., Kissner, L., Peterson, Z., Song, D.: Provable Data Possession at Un-trusted Stores. In: Proc. of ACM CCS 2007 (2007); Full version: Cryptology ePrint Archive. Report 2007/202
8. Curtmola, R., Khan, O., Burns, R., Ateniese, G.: MR-PDP: Multiple-Replica Provable Data Possession. In: Proceedings The 28th International Conference on Distributed Computing Systems, pp. 411–420 (2008)
9. Juels, A., Bowers, K.D., Oprea, A.: Proofs of Retrievability: Theory and Implementation. In: Proceedings of the 2009 ACM Workshop on Cloud Computing Security, pp. 43–54. ACM, New York (2009)
10. Ristenpart, T., Tromer, E., Shacham, S., Savage, S.: Hey, You, Get Off of My Cloud: Exploring Information Leakage in Third-Party Compute Clouds. In: Proceedings of the 16th ACM Conference on Computer and Communications Security, pp. 199–212. ACM, New York (2009)
11. Sailer, R., Zhang, X., Jaeger, T., van Doorn, L.: Design and Implementation of a TCG-Based Integrity Measurement Architecture. In: Proceedings of the 13th conference on USENIX Security Symposium. Usenix Association, Berkeley (2004)
12. Garfinkel, T., Pfaff, B., Chow, J., Rosenblum, M., Boneh, D.: Terra: A Virtual Machine-Based Platform for Trusted Computing. In: Proceedings of the Nineteenth ACM Symposium on Operating Systems Principles, pp. 193–206. ACM, New York (2009)
13. Sailer, R., Valdez, E., Jaeger, T., Perez, R., van Doorn, L., Griffin, J.L., Berger, S.: sHype: Secure Hypervisor Approach to Trusted Virtualized System, IBM Research Report, New York (2005)
14. Wang, Z., Jiang, X.: HyperSafe - A Lightweight Approach to Provide Lifetime Hypervisor Control-Flow Integrity. In: IEEE Symposium on Security and Privacy, pp. 380–395 (2010)
15. Kuhlmann, D., Landfermann, R., Ramasamy, H., Schunter, M., Ramunno, G., Vernizzi, D.: An Open Trusted Computing Architecture — Secure Virtual Machines Enabling User - Defined Policy Enforcement, IBM Research Report, New York (2006)
16. Azab, A.M., Ning, P., Sezer, E.C., Zhang, X.: HIMA: A Hypervisor-Based Integrity Measurement Agent. In: Proceedings of the 2009 Annual Computer Security Applications Conference, pp. 461–470. IEEE Computer Society, Washington, DC (2009)
17. Berger, S., Caceres, R., Goldman, K., Pendarakis, D., Perez, R., Rao, J.R., Rom, E., Sailer, R., Schildhauer, W., Srinivasan, D., Tal, S., Valdez, E.: Security for the Cloud Infrastructure: Trusted Virtual Data Center Implementation. IBM Journal of Research and Development 4, 6:1–6:12 (2009)

18. Sailer, R., Zhang, X., Jaeger, T., van Doorn, L.: Design and Implementation of a TCG-Based Integrity Measurement Architecture. In: Proceedings of the 13th conference on USENIX Security Symposium. Usenix Association, Berkeley (2004)
19. DDoS Attack Rains Down on Amazon cloud, http://www.theregister.co.uk/2009/10/05/amazon_bitbucket_outage/
20. Nurmi, D., Wolski, R., Grzegorczyk, C., Obertelli, G., Soman, S., Youseff, L., Zagorodnov, D.: Eucalyptus opensource cloud-computing system. In: CCA 2008: Cloud Computing and Its Applications (2008)
21. http://upload.wikimedia.org/wikipedia/commons/2/2f/Eucalyptus_cloud_architecture-1.6.png

C2C (Cloud-to-Cloud): An Ecosystem of Cloud Service Providers for Dynamic Resource Provisioning

Ankur Gupta, Lohit Kapoor, and Manisha Wattal

Model Institute of Engineering and Technology, Jammu, India
ankurgupta@mietjammu.in, lohit_kapoor@yahoo.com,
wattalmanisha@gmail.com

Abstract. Cloud Computing has caught the fancy of the research community, big technology companies, application developers and consumers with its promise of on-demand computing and an intuitive service delivery model. While large corporations like Google have invested in creating their million-server warehouses to cater to the tremendous expected demand for cloud resources, smaller service providers may not have enough resources to cater to the "elasticity" inherent in the cloud model. The ability to dynamically provision resources in the face of a volatile resource requests is one of the key performance indicators for cloud service providers and remains a challenge. It is always theoretically possible that the resource requirement exceeds the physically available resources, especially when flash-crowd scenarios are factored in. Catering to peak expected resource requirements by provisioning surplus resources is not a cost-effective strategy especially for smaller cloud service providers. This paper proposes the C2C framework or the Cloud-to-Cloud network of cloud service providers; a shared ecosystem of pooled compute resources. Resource requests which cannot be provisioned from within the dedicated resources of the service provider can be met from the shared pool of C2C resources in a seamless manner. Simulation shows that the proposed framework effectively meets volatile resource requirements, allowing cloud service providers to scale effectively.

Keywords: cloud-to-cloud (c2c), dynamic resource provisioning, cloud service provider eco-system.

1 Introduction

Cloud computing is a model for enabling convenient, on demand network access to a shared pool of configurable computing resources (e.g., networks, servers, storage, applications, and services) that can be provisioned and released with minimal management effort or service provider interaction [1]. Ensuring dynamic resource provisioning forms the very basis of cloud computing which is "elastic" by nature. However, predicting dynamic resource requirements for cloud service providers including peak usage scenarios is not trivial to say the least. While virtualization has helped drive the utilization levels of cloud datacenters by logically partitioning a physical server into many virtual machines or server instances, creating virtual

A. Abraham et al. (Eds.): ACC 2011, Part I, CCIS 190, pp. 501–510, 2011.

machines on a physical server beyond a limit reduces performance and increases resource management overheads. Thus, provisioning more physical resources seems to be the only feasible solution to cater to increased demand for cloud resources. Moreover, to meet the QoS (Quality-of-Service) agreements, cloud service providers need to create redundancy in computing, storage and network paths to ensure 24x7 uptime and access to cloud resources, which requires heavy financial inputs. Thus, the current cloud computing landscape excludes the smaller cloud service providers who may not want to tie up their capital in creating large datacenters.

This paper proposes the creation of a peer-to-peer based market ecosystem of cloud service providers which facilitates resource sharing across cloud service providers. Such a model allows the smaller service providers to pool their resources to provide greater elasticity and ensure that they are able to cater to volatile resource requests. Simulation results show that the proposed framework is entirely feasible, with acceptable performance in meeting dynamic resource requests and leads to fewer service denials. The proposed framework opens up exciting possibilities in the areas of inter-cloud resource provisioning and economic models.

The rest of the paper is organized as follows: section 2 presents the background and related work. The system model is discussed in detail in section 3, while section 4 presents the experimental results obtained from simulation. Finally section 5 concludes the paper and presents some directions for future work.

2 Background and Related Work

One of the promises of cloud computing is the perception of infinite resources it provides to the service users, able to scale up and down as the resource demand varies. However, resources are finite and to meet peak resource demands cloud service providers need to provision a much higher level of physical resources than required. Thus, the problem of under and over-provisioning of resources persists for cloud service providers and ensuring elasticity with rapid scaling to meet surge computing is a challenge [2]. This challenge is exacerbated for small and medium cloud service providers who may not be able to create their million server warehouses to cater to peak resource demands. It is intuitive to assume that such a cloud service provider needs to fulfill its resource requirement from an external source, most likely from another cloud service provider. The concept of "Intercloud" [3] or a cloud of clouds is receiving attention of the research community, which in theory addresses this very challenge. An architecture for the enhancing cloud computing to enable cross-federated interactions is proposed in [4], while a detailed set of protocols describing the blueprint for the Intercloud is presented in [5]. Buyya et.al [6] discuss the scalability and load coordinating aspects in sourcing compute resources from geographically distributed data-centers. Other schemes have also been proposed in literature, which do not rely on other clouds to meet their resource requirements. In [7] the authors present a forecasting model to predict resource requirements so that resources can be provisioned in advance, while a dynamic resource provisioning model specifically for media streaming applications in the cloud is discussed in [8]. However, these schemes still require individual cloud service providers to invest in creating physical resources which can meet dynamic and volatile requirements. Thus, the intercloud model looks the most promising solution to address the infinite elasticity issue in cloud computing.

However, for the intercloud model to succeed requires that all cloud service providers agree to a common set of protocols and standards to enable interactions across cloud service providers. Currently, each cloud offering (Amazon EC2 [9], Google AppEngine [10], Microsoft Azure [11] etc.) has its own way on how cloud clients/applications/users interact with the cloud and at what level services are provided (ranging from servers to services). The Cloud Computing Interoperability Forum (CCIF) [12] has been formed with this very purpose. It is in the process of defining the standards that will make the intercloud interactions a reality. However, the success of such initiatives is purely driven by market realities and usually a few competing standards promoted by the big players in the market co-exist.

This research papers proposes a cloud-to-cloud model, based on creating a marketplace for compute resources. The unique contributions of this paper are a simplified architecture based on a peer-to-peer organization allowing easy sharing of resources. Also, the proposed model does not require cloud service providers to migrate to a common standard for interoperability. It just requires the representative edge servers belonging to cloud service providers to participate in a P2P network for sharing resource availability information. Thus the model is extremely flexible and caters effectively to volatile resource requirements.

3 System Model

Each Cloud Service Provider (CSP) provides services through its datacenter which houses physical servers. The unit of resource acquisition in the cloud is a Virtual Machine (VM) with many VM instances being instantiated on a physical server to cater to resource demand from end-users. This instantiation is typically done by the Hypervisor, which is a part of the cloud operating system and controls the virtualization aspects of cloud computing. Different cloud service providers have different implementations of the Hypervisor, which is one reason why implementing an interoperability strategy for different clouds is such a challenge. Making all cloud service providers to agree on a set of standard protocols and virtualization strategies is not trivial, although many initiatives are directed in this direction [4].

Each CSP has a datacenter with a dedicated edge server, which is responsible for participating in a P2P network comprising edge servers belonging to other CSPs. The edge server is responsible for sending out Resource Requests (RR) and responding to RRs issued by other edge servers. Each RR issued in the P2P network of edge servers includes the physical servers required. This is done because VM instances of one cloud service provider cannot be used as is by another. Thus, physical servers are acquired and the Hypervisor of the acquiring cloud service provider then instantiates the VMs as required on those physical servers. Obviously, this incurs some overheads, which are discussed in the results section.

3.1 Sequence of Operations

1. Nomination/selection of edge peer at the CSP level and specification of the CSP policy for resource contribution to the C2C. This includes the maximum percentage of

physical servers to be contributed to the C2C and the costing mechanism for the resources. A CSP may specify that upto 20% of its total resources (servers) can be shared and the cost of the resources can vary as per the demand scenario. For instance during peak utilization hours the cost of the resources may be higher than at other times. Thus, the quantum of shared resources and their associated cost varies as per the local demand scenario of a CSP. The resource sharing policy is not made public within the C2C. A CSP merely responds to resource requests from other CSPs within the C2C with the resources and their cost.

2. An individual edge peer discovers and links up with other peers within the C2C as in a normal P2P network. A P2P middleware for instance one based on JXTA [13] provides all the peer services for discovering and communicating with other peers.

3. An optimization is performed at the time when edge peers link to other edge peers in the C2C network. To begin with the strategy creates a cluster of "physically close" nodes in the overlay topology, with new edge servers being placed adjacent to edge servers which are physically close to them in the underlying network. Random Landmarking [14] for static networks and mobile adhoc networks is a well-known approach utilized to construct such P2P networks. Before a node joins the overlay it collects information regarding its physical neighborhood (against some landmark nodes) and uses this information to assign itself an overlay ID. This results in physically close nodes being clustered close together in the overlay network. On an average random landmarking ensures an overlay to physical hop distance ratio of 1:1.6 for networks upto 10,000 peers. This approach ensures that the communication overheads between edge peers are minimized.

4. As resource requests are received by a CSP, it determines whether it can meet the resource requests from its locally available pool of resources. When the resource utilization levels cross a certain threshold (say 95%), it sends out a Resource Request (RR) via the edge server within the C2C explicitly stating the resources required (number of physical servers).

5. The query is propagated one hop at a time within the C2C network, starting from its neighboring edge server, which is also physically closer to it. Query propagation is controlled by specifying a hop count. Alternately, a TTL (time-to-live) parameter can also be specified, so that responses are received in a deterministic manner.

6. The edge server receiving the RR query checks whether it has surplus resources to share. If the resources requested are less than its available resources (kept aside for sharing), it sends back a positive response to the edge server which had initiated the request along with the associated cost (usually expressed in $/hour per server). It then propagates the query further if the current hop count is less than the specified hop count for the RR query.

7. The edge server continues to receive responses from other edge servers till the hop count is exhausted. It then evaluates all the responses and chooses the one which best

meets its resource requirements. The best response shall be the one with the lowest overall cost i.e. the cost of the server and the communication cost i.e. from the edge server which is physically closest to it and has the lowest communication latency. Once an edge server is selected (based on its response), a confirmation is sent to it to seal the deal.

8. The edge server on receiving the confirmation, sends the IP and MAC addresses for the servers which are assigned to the requesting edge server.

9. The Hypervisor layer at the requesting edge server then proceeds to install the VM instances on the acquired servers making them ready to receive service requests from its customers. The service requests are routed seamlessly to the acquired resources without the end-customer knowing about it.

All operations are summed up schematically in Figure 1, which depicts the process of resource acquisition.

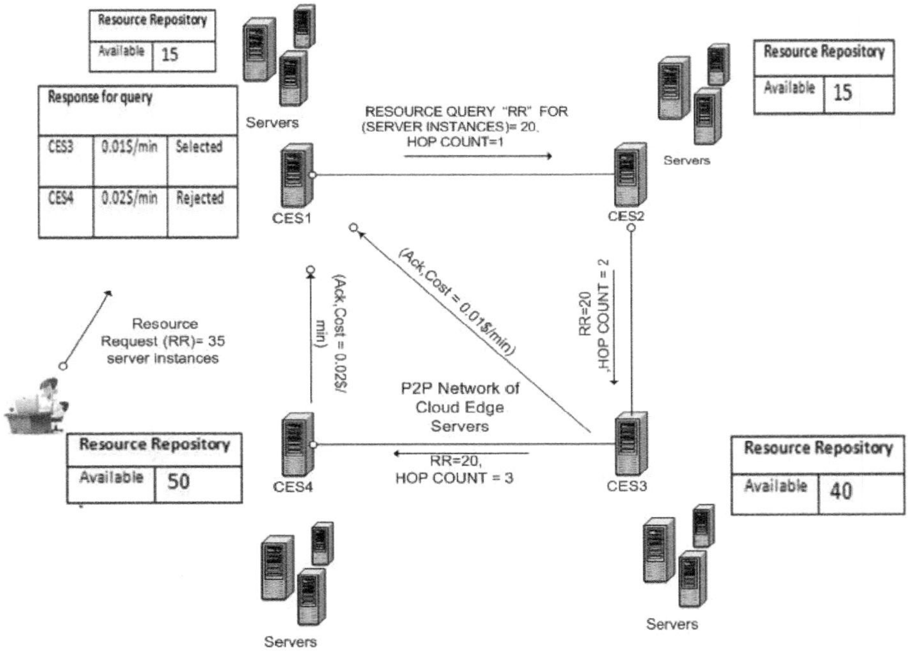

Fig. 1. Schematic of the C2C Framework

CSP_1 sends out a RR query for 20 servers, which is processed by CSP_2 which does not have the requested resources at its disposal. Hence, it propagates the query further, which is processed by CSP_3 and CSP_4. Both CSP_3 and CSP_4 have the required resources and respond back with their quotes. CSP_1 evaluates the responses and finally selects CSP_3 based on its lower cost.The pseudocode for the CSP selection process is provided below:

```
SendRRQuery ()
    //propagates the query containing the specified
    number of servers required within the C2C network
    query= new query();
    query.add(this); // Adds self to enable responses
    to be directed to it
    query.add(numServersRequired); // Adds required
    servers
    query. add(maxHops); // Adds maximum number of hops
    required
    sendQuery(query) ; // Sends "query" to neighbor
    edge server
```

```
ProcessQuery (query) // implemented at each edge server
//if maximum number of hops specified in the query is
exceeded drop it
    query.numHops++; //increment the hop count for the
    current query
    IF (query.numHops > query.maxHops)
        dropQuery (query);
    END IF
    //if this edge server meets the selection criteria
    i.e. if available Resource are greater than the
    resources requested, send response to the CES which
    initiated the query.
    IF(thisCES.getAvailableresources()>=query.
    numInstanceRequired)
        sendResponse (sourceCES,thisCES,cost)
        propogateQuery(Query) //in any case, even if
        requirements not met
    END IF
```

```
ProcessQueryResponse(response)//will receive only
positive responses
    list =response.Addtolist ();// Adds the responses
    to its list
    wait(time); //wait for all responses to come in
    list.ranklist ();// Ranks all the responses from
    the list on the basis of overall cost
    selectedEdgeServer = selectTopRank(list); //select
    the top ranked one
    sendConfirmation (selectedEdgeServer); //seal the
    deal
    intimateHyperVisor (selectedEdgeServer); //tell
    Hypervisor to take over
```

4 Experimental Results

To evaluate the effectiveness of the proposed scheme, we have implemented a custom simulator. CloudSim [15] was also considered for this purpose, but it provides support only for federated cloud model i.e. datacenters belonging to the same cloud service provider, with a provision for virtual machine migration between datacenters in case of failures.

The following parameters were considered during simulation:

- Number of cloud service providers: 50
- Number of physical servers per datacenter: 100~300
- Maximum Virtual Machines per server: 5
- Resource request quantum: 10~50 vm per request
- Resource request frequency: 2~5 per minute
- Duration of resource usage: 30~60 minutes
- Flash-crowd scenario frequency: once every 3 hours
- Flash-crowd scenario duration: 10 minutes
- Flash-crowd resource request frequency: 15~20 per minute

Figure 3 depicts the average resource requests failure rate comparison between C2C and the individual cloud service provider model. As can be seen there are hardly any resource request failures on an average over a 24 hour period for C2C. During flash-crowd scenarios (once every three hours) the resource request failure rates spike in case of the individual model, while they remain relatively stable for the C2C model showing a marginal increase. Thus, the C2C model is capable of handling volatile resource requests providing enhanced elasticity to the cloud computing model. The resource request failures for the C2C model occur due to the assumption made that only one CSP can service one resource request.

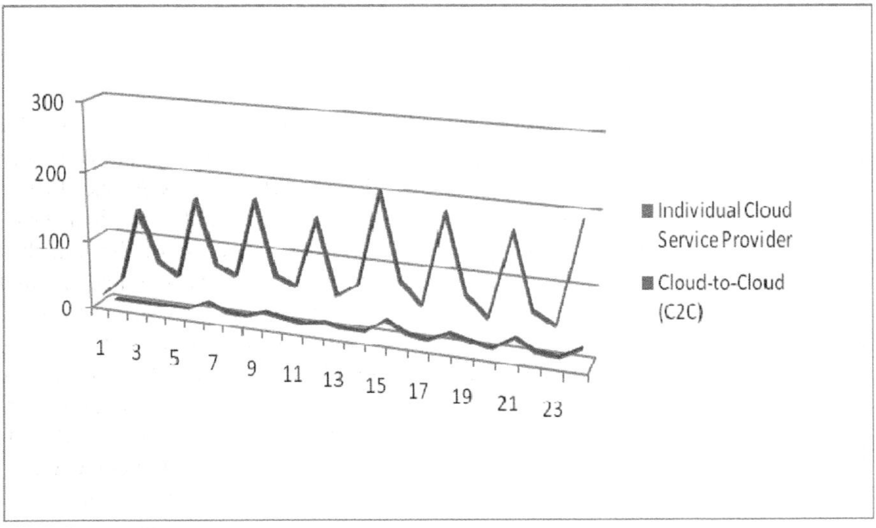

Fig. 3. Average resource request failures: C2C vs. Individual CSP Model

Figure 4 depicts the communication overheads (in milliseconds) for the resource acquisition scheme in the C2C model as a function of number of cloud service providers. The overhead measurement includes the time taken by one cloud service provider to issue a Resource Request, receive multiple Resource Responses, decide on the best request-response match and communicate the decision to the selected cloud service provider. The C2C network is organized in a random unstructured manner. As can be seen the communication overheads increase linearly with the increase in number of cloud service providers.

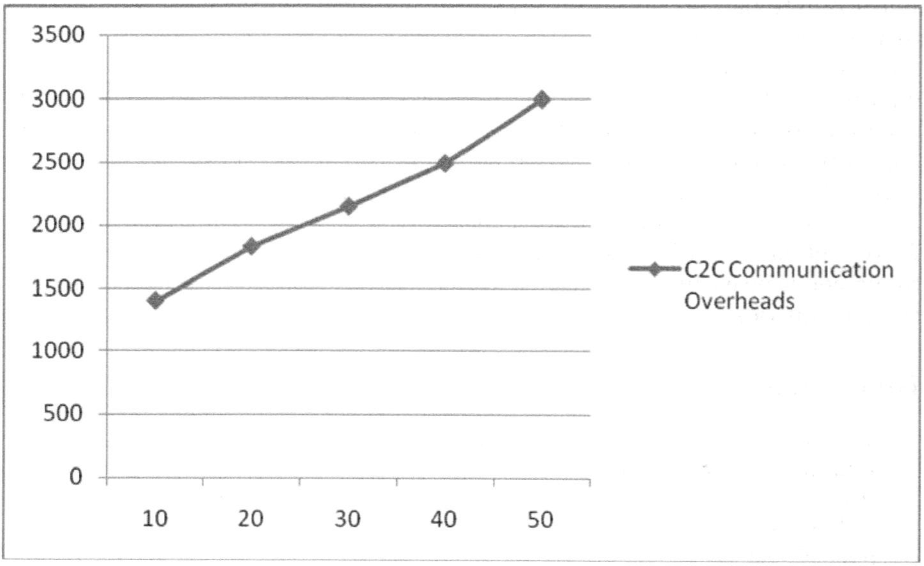

Fig. 4. Communication overheads in milliseconds for the C2C framework as the number of CSPs increase

4.1 Assumptions

a. Since, the proposed model caters to small to medium cloud service providers, we consider only one datacenter per cloud service provider, although it can be easily extended to include multiple datacenters.

b. For simplicity, we assume that the physical servers in datacenters are of similar configuration and have the capability of running the same number of VM instances.

c. The resource requests are in terms of VM instances, although cloud users consume services ranging from Infrastructure-as-a-Service (in terms of physical server instances) to Software-as-a-Service (higher order applications and services). We assume that the "Broker" will translate such requests into VM instances required to provide those services.

d. For simplicity, we assume that a single RR can be provisioned from only one CSP and not broken up and serviced by resource contributions from multiple CSPs.

5 Conclusions and Future Work

This paper presents a viable strategy for the creation of an ecosystem of cloud service providers to more effectively meet volatile resource requirements. Early simulation results establish the effectiveness of the proposed scheme. Future work shall involve extending the CloudSim simulator to accurately model the proposed framework and getting comprehensive measurements on various aspects of the C2C model. The simplifying assumptions made such as requiring resource acquisitions to be atomic operations shall also be dropped, allowing one resource request to be partially serviced by another cloud service provider. Other assumptions like assigning one datacenter to a cloud service provider shall also be relaxed. This shall introduce further complexities into the model requiring end-of-day settlements with multiple CSPs. However, it can also potentially improve the success ratio of resource requests further. A detailed economic model shall also be formulated as part of this work. Going forward security considerations shall also become relevant and the introduction of a trusted-third party for establishing credentials and providing authentication needs to be explored.

References

1. Mell, P., Grance, T.: NIST working definition of Cloud Computing - v15 (July 2009), http://csrc.nist.gov/groups/SNS/cloud-computing/cloud-def-v15.doc
2. Armbrust, M., Fox, A., Griffith, R., Joseph, A.D., Katz, R.H., Konwinski, A., Lee, G., Patterson, D.A., Rabkin, A., Stoica, I., Zaharia, M.: Above the Clouds: A Berkeley View of Cloud Computing. University of California, Berkeley, Technical Report, http://www.eecs.berkeley.edu/Pubs/TechRpts/2009/EECS-2009-28.pdf
3. Wikipedia definition of the Intercloud, http://en.wikipedia.org/wiki/Intercloud (accessed March 03, 2011)
4. Celesti, A., Tusa, F., Villari, M., Puliafito, A.: How to Enhance Cloud Architectures to Enable Cross-Federation. In: IEEE 3rd International Conference on Cloud Computing, pp. 337–345 (2010)
5. Bernstein, D., Ludvigson, E., Sankar, K., Diamond, S., Morrow, M.: Blueprint for the Intercloud - Protocols and Formats for Cloud Computing Interoperability, pp. 328–336. IEEE Computer Society, Los Alamitos
6. Buyya, R., Ranjan, R., Calheiros, R.: InterCloud: Scaling of Applications across multiple Cloud Computing Environments. In: Proceedings of the 10th International Conference on Algorithms and Architectures for Parallel Processing (2010)
7. Andrzejak, A., Kondo, D., Anderson, D.P.: Ensuring collective availability in volatile resource pools via forecasting. In: 19th IFIP/IEEE Distributed System: Operations and Management (September 2008)

8. Vijayakumar, S., Zhu, Q., Agrawal, G.: Dynamic Resource Provisioning for Data Streaming Applications in a Cloud Environment. In: 2010 IEEE Second International Conference on Cloud Computing Technology and Science, pp. 441–444 (2010)
9. Amazon Elastic Cloud Compute (EC2), http://aws.amazon.com/ec2 (accessed March 01, 2011)
10. Google AppEngine, http://code.google.com/appengine (accessed March 01, 2011)
11. Microsoft Azure, http://microsoft.com/windowsazure/ (accessed March 01, 2011)
12. Cloud Computing Interoperability Forum, http://www.cloudforum.org/ (accessed March 06, 2011)
13. Juxtapose (JXTA) Home Page, http://java.net/projects/jxta/ (accessed March 07, 2011)
14. Winter, R., Zahn, T., Schiller, J.: Random Landmarking in Mobile, Topology-Aware Peer-To-Peer Networks. In: IEEE Workshop on Future Trends of Distributed Computing Systems, pp. 319–324 (2004)
15. Calheiros, R.N., Ranjan, R., Beloglazov, A., De Rose, C.A.F., Buyya, R.: CloudSim: A Toolkit for Modeling and Simulation of Cloud Computing Environments and Evaluation of Resource Provisioning Algorithms. Software: Practice and Experience 41(1), 23–50 (2011) ISSN: 0038-0644

Modeling Cloud SaaS with SOA and MDA

Ritu Sharma[1], Manu Sood[1], and Divya Sharma[2]

[1] Himachal Pradesh University, Summer Hill, Shimla 5, Himachal Pradesh, India
[2] National Informatics Centre, New Delhi, India
rituchetan@gmail.com, soodm_67@yahoo.com, divya.sharma@nic.in

Abstract. Cloud computing, a more recent computing paradigm, has evolved from a variety of legacy technologies that include Service oriented Architecture (SOA) and Web services besides several others. The software services in a cloud must be developed based on the service-oriented approach, in order to derive their full potential and benefits. Since, SOA inherently nurtures interoperability; it will enhance the integration and interaction among the cloud software services. Also, leveraging the Model Driven Architecture (MDA) approach to develop individual cloud software services will result in services that are more robust, flexible and agile in the wake of ever changing technologies. This paper is an attempt by the authors to lay emphasis on the convergence of Cloud computing, SOA and MDA in development of optimum business solutions.

Keywords: Cloud computing, Cloud SaaS, Service Oriented Architecture (SOA), Model-Driven Architecture (MDA), Computation Independent Model (CIM), Platform Independent Model (PIM), Platform Specific Model (PSM), Interoperability.

1 Introduction

Recent years have witnessed rapid transitions in the field of Information and Communication technology (ICT). Service Oriented Architecture (SOA), a recent software development approach, has evolved from distributed systems; the distributed systems have evolved from the client-server systems, which in turn have evolved from the mainframe systems. In addition, the specification of functionality in software design and code has abstracted to higher levels – from modules, to objects, to components and now the services. The SOA paradigm is based on 'separation of concerns' whereby the automation logic required to solve a large problem is decomposed into several smaller related pieces, each addressing a specific concern of the problem. A more recent computing approach is cloud computing which has evolved from SOA and Web services, besides several other legacy technologies. Cloud computing attempts to optimize the utilization of hardware and software resources distributed in a network, by sharing them among multiple users. The resources are acquired and released in response to the fluctuating demands of the user. Yet another software development approach is the Model Driven Architecture (MDA) wherein the models drive the process of software development.

A. Abraham et al. (Eds.): ACC 2011, Part I, CCIS 190, pp. 511–518, 2011.

The platform-independent model specifies the business functionality of the system independent of the specific technology used for its implementation. The transformation among the models at different levels is carried out using automated transformation tools. Instead of considering these approaches in isolation, integrating all three together while developing the automated enterprise solutions will result in software systems that are more agile, flexible, portable, interoperable and robust.

In this paper, the authors attempt to emphasize on the significance of Service-oriented Architecture (SOA) and Model Driven Architecture (MDA) in the development of cloud software services. Sections 2, 3 and 4 briefly discuss the basic concepts of Cloud computing, Model Driven Architecture and Service Oriented Architecture, respectively. The authors illustrate their approach in Section 5 and 6 with the help of an example. Section 5 illustrates the interoperability among cloud SaaS in the light of SOA whereas Section 6 discusses the significance of MDA in the development of cloud SaaS. Section 7 draws the conclusion of the paper and the future work undertaken by the authors.

2 Cloud Computing

Cloud computing is a promising computing paradigm wherein shared pool of configurable computing resources such as processors, networks, servers, storage, applications, operating systems, software development environments, databases etc. are provided as services, remotely over a network on-demand, on a pay-per-use or subscription basis. The services can be accessed by the customers through a simple interface such as a browser, running on a thin client or even a mobile phone. Based on the nature of resources provided as services, the cloud service models are broadly categorized into cloud SaaS (Software-as-a-Service), cloud PaaS (Platform-as-a-Service) and cloud IaaS (Infrastructure-as-a-Service) [1, 2].

The Cloud computing technology has evolved from a range of legacy technologies and concepts such as distributed computing, grid computing, cluster computing, utility computing, virtualization, Software-as-a-Service (SaaS), Web services and Service Oriented Architecture (SOA) to mention a few [3, 4].

3 Model Driven Architecture (MDA)

Model Driven Architecture (MDA) is an open, vendor-neutral approach [5] to enterprise application development wherein the software development process is driven by the activity of modeling the software system. The models are the prime artifacts and are formal in nature. They are specified at three levels of abstraction – Computation Independent Model (CIM), Platform Independent Model (PIM) and Platform Specific Model (PSM), to represent the various aspects of the system. The CIM or the domain model is software independent and aims at bridging the gap between the domain experts and system experts. The PIM specifies the structure, behavior and functionality of the system independent of the platform that would be used for its implementation. The PSM describes the system with respect to the specific platform on which it would finally be implemented. The three primary goals of MDA are interoperability, reusability and portability through architectural separation of concerns [6].

Automated transformation tools are used to transform higher-level, platform-independent business models into lower-level platform-specific models and finally to implementation code. The models are defined using formal, well-defined modeling language so that they can be interpreted by a computer [7]. The MDA approach to software development benefits the stakeholders by enhancing the productivity, improving software quality, preserving the Return on Investment, reducing the development cost and reducing the time to market.

4 Service Oriented Architecture (SOA)

Service Oriented Architecture (SOA) represents an architectural style in which the automation logic is decomposed into smaller, distinct units of logic, called services. Individually, these units may be distributed, yet they are autonomous and isolated from each other. These services communicate with each other by exchanging messages through well-defined interfaces. Figure 1 depicts a model of an SOA with its services and interfaces.

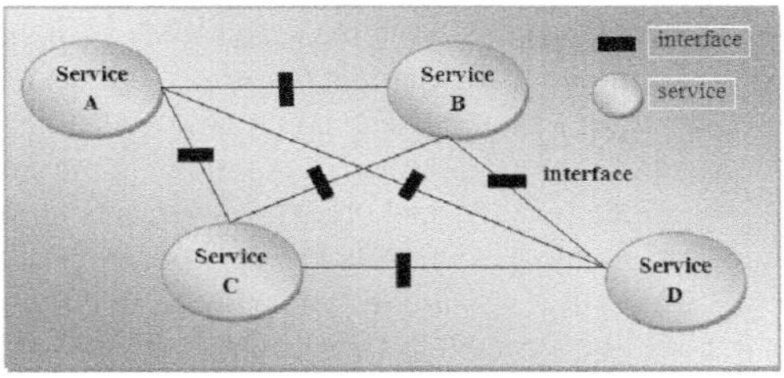

Fig. 1. SOA – Services and Interfaces

The services in SOA are governed by a set of key principles that include – loose-coupling, autonomy, abstraction, reusability, compos ability, statelessness, discoverability and adherence to a service contract [8]. These principles enable the services to evolve independently. SOA results in the creation of business solutions that consist of inherently interoperable services. An XML-based, vendor-neutral communications framework established by web services-driven SOA enables cross-platform integration and intrinsic interoperability among the services. The standards comprising this framework are – Web Service Description Language (WSDL), Simple Object Access Protocol (SOAP) and Universal Description, Discovery, and Integration (UDDI). WSDL is an XML-based standard for service description. A service description specifies the name of the service, the data to be provided to the service and the data that would be returned by the service. SOAP provides XML-compliant communications format required by the services. The service description registry and discovery is realized through UDDI.

A service-oriented software design approach may follow a top-down or a bottom-up approach. The top-down approach is an "analysis-first" approach which is closely tied to or derived from organization's existing business logic. This approach requires an overall business model of the organization to be created prior to modeling services for individual business processes. The bottom-up approach encourages the creation of individual services to fulfill application-centric requirements which are then integrated to achieve the overall business logic [8].

5 Cloud SaaS, SOA and Interoperability

US NIST (National Institute of Standards and Technology) defines Cloud Software-as-a-Service (SaaS) as a capability provided to the consumer to use the provider's applications running on a cloud infrastructure. The applications are accessible from various client devices through a thin client interface such as a web browser. The consumer does not manage or control the underlying cloud infrastructure including network, servers, operating systems, storage, or even individual application capabilities, with the possible exception of limited user-specific application configuration settings [9]. The applications in the cloud may be as simple as a time zone converter performing a single discrete function, or as complex as a holiday packaging system performing a set of related business functions.

As mentioned earlier, SOA and Web services are the technologies, besides several others, from which cloud computing has evolved. The cloud should not be looked at as a new architecture but instead as another option of storing and running services within SOA [10]. In addition to developing a cloud based on service-oriented architecture, the individual software applications deployed therein may themselves be service-oriented.

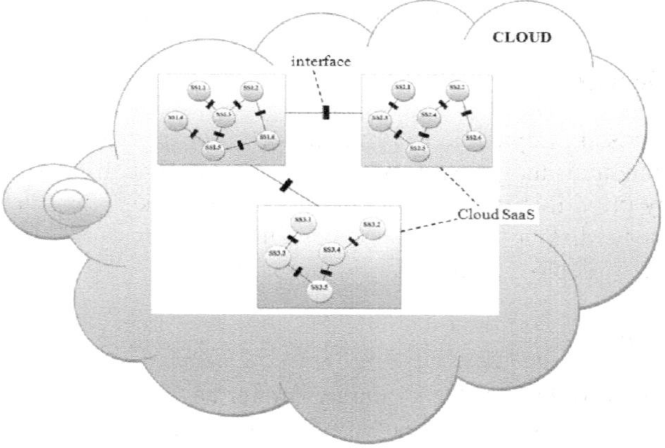

Fig. 2. Software Services in a cloud interact through interfaces

A cloud may host a variety of software applications as cloud services which fulfill the business requirements of its varied customers. Based on the requirements of the customers (or service consumers) these software services in the cloud may need to interact with each other. This interaction is accomplished through formal, standardized interfaces defined using WSDL. A cloud with cloud software services interacting through interfaces is depicted in Figure 2.

As SOA promotes intrinsic interoperability [8], the SOA-based cloud architecture would have cloud software services that are inherently interoperable. The XML-based vendor-neutral communications framework, comprising of WSDL, SOAP and UDDI for defining, publishing, and using the services, would ensure interoperability among the various cloud services running on different software platforms and hardware architectures. An important aspect of SOA is the separation of the service interface (the what) from its implementation (the how) [11]. As a result, a client (which may be another service) need not be concerned with the implementation details of the service in order to use it. The service implementation performs the necessary processing. A change in the implementation of the service does not prevent the client from communicating with the service, so long as the interface remains the same.

We illustrate this with the help of an example. We identify two services – an Online Hotel Reservation system (OHRS) and Cab-On-Hire system (COHS) – in the cloud. A fictitious business enterprise, ABC hotel, subscribes to OHRS application in order to provide online services to its clients (customer and hotel personnel) through its website ABCHotel.com. The services (functionalities) enable the clients to book accommodation, cancel a booking, check availability status, generate reports etc. XYZ Cabs is another fictitious business enterprise which subscribes to COHS application, to provide online services to its clients through its website XYZCabs.com. The COHS allows its clients (online customers and its staff) to book a cab and cancel a booking. The ABC Hotel also hires the cabs for its in-house customers from XYZ Cabs. In order to fulfill the additional functional requirements the two cloud services must be able to interact with each other. For example, the ABC Hotel requires determining the total number of its customers hiring the cabs on a specific day. In an SOA-based cloud this interaction is enabled through an XML-based communication framework that uses SOAP messages, as depicted in Figure 3 [12].

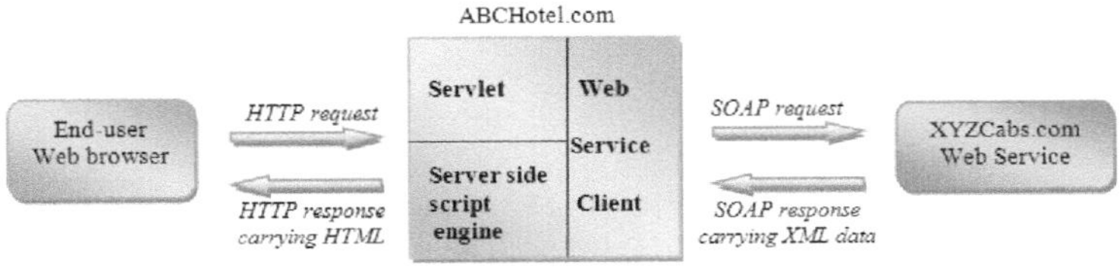

Fig. 3. XML-based Interaction between the cloud SaaS

The hotel administrator submits a request, from one of the ABCHotel.com web pages, to XYZCabs.com to determine the number of its customers availing the cab service on a particular day. The HTTP request generated is routed via a controlling servlet on the ABCHotel.com web server, which determines that it needs to retrieve the information (raw data) from XYZ Cabs. The servlet obtains this data by using a web service client implemented by ABCHotel.com developers. This client uses the web service interface published by XYZCabs.com to invoke a method on its server that returns the required information. The method invocation is performed by creating an XML message that contains the method name and any required parameters and then sending it to XYZCabs.com's server using the SOAP protocol. The value(s) returned by the method call are then wrapped in another XML message and sent back to the ABCHotel.com's web client, which extracts the information that it needs and uses a server-side script engine to render it as HTML. The HTML is then returned to the client's browser. The advantage of using XML instead of HTML is that only raw data is required to be transferred which does not include presentation markups, thereby reducing network traffic. Also, the code required to make a request is much simpler than that required to extract data from an HTML page.

6 Cloud SaaS and Model Driven Architecture (MDA)

As is evident, the technologies are constantly evolving. The technology evolution has serious ramifications in B2B context as it is more difficult to control the impact of change when external partners are involved. Rather then directly developing the cloud software services using available technologies, modeling them at a higher level of abstraction will decouple them from the undesired effects of technology change and enhance their longevity. An MDA based development of cloud SaaS (application) will enable defining these services in a technology-independent manner and will play a significant role in improving the quality of cloud software services, making them more robust, flexible and agile [13]. Encapsulating business logic in a manner that is independent of the technical mechanisms will formally capture the essence of the applications; and will also make it possible to reuse them in a variety of contexts [14]. Web service is a fundamental technology underlying the cloud computing paradigm; and is evolving too. Based on MDA approach, a formal, semantically rich platform-independent model of the Web service capturing the information and functionality provided by it, may be defined which may then be used to generate the artifacts that support the service over some other set of technologies.

We illustrate this with the help of the example illustrated in the previous section. In order to meet the business requirements the OHRS and the COHS cloud SaaS must be able to interact with each other. For example the ABC Hotel utilizing the OHRS service requires determining the total number of its customers who availed the cabs from XYZ Cabs on a specific day. The application uses a business service for the purpose. In the context of enterprise architecture, a business service may be represented as a Web service, a Web page, a fat-client application screen, or an API [15].

Figure 4 depicts a business service model for the Hotel_Cab Service that includes a method (operation) to determine the total number of customers availing the cabs. The OCL (Object Constraint Language) is used to express the invariants, the pre-conditions and post-conditions for the operation.

Figure 5 depicts the PSM targeted on WSDL for the business service under consideration. The business service example is expanded to include the declaration of the output parameter – total_customers. The transformation rule involves mapping the input parameters to WSDL input messages and the output parameters to WSDL output messages. The lower part of Figure 5 represents a formal model of WSDL itself. WSDL defines port types, which in turn own operations. Operation definitions reference message definitions, with some messages playing the role of inputs and some playing the role of outputs for the operation [15].

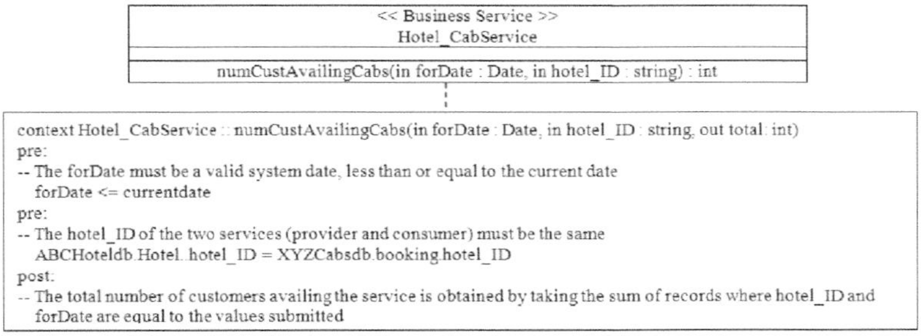

Fig. 4. A PIM of business service

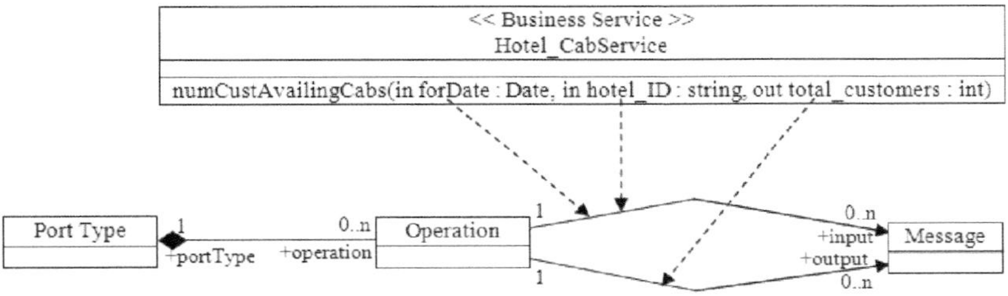

Fig. 5. Business service mapped to WSDL (PSM)

7 Conclusion and Future Work

Cloud computing is fast emerging as a computing paradigm where the computations would be performed using third-party hardware and software resources. In the wake of constantly changing technologies, the authors in this paper stress on the need to leverage the MDA approach in the development of cloud SaaS. Besides, SOA-based cloud architecture will ensure improved integration and inherent interoperability among the software services in the cloud. Thus, the developers as well as the service consumers would be able to harvest the benefits of cloud computing, MDA and SOA.

At present, the authors are developing a transformation tool based on the transformation rules defined for business service. An SOA-based approach for developing the illustrated cloud application is also underway. The efforts are being made to ensure interoperability among the SOA-based cloud services.

References

[1] Aymerich, F.M., Fenu, G., Surcis, S.: An Approach to a Cloud Computing Network. In: First International Conference on the Applications of Digital Information and Web Technologies, pp. 113–118 (2008) ISBN: 978-1-4244-2623-2, doi:10.1109/ICADIWT.2008.4664329

[2] Foster, I., Zhao, Y., Raicu, I., Lu, S.: Cloud Computing and Grid Computing 360-Degree Compared. In: IEEE Grid Computing Environments Workshop, pp. 1–10 (November 2008)

[3] Rimal, B.P., Choi, E., Lumb, I.: A Taxonomy and Survey of Cloud Computing systems. In: Fifth International Joint Conference on INC, IMS and IDC, pp. 44–51 (2009)

[4] Maggiani, R.: Cloud computing is changing how we communicate. In: IEEE International Professional Communication Conference, pp. 1–4 (2009)

[5] OMG Model Driven Architecture, `http://www.omg.org/mda/`

[6] Miller, J., Mukerji, J.: MDA Guide Version 1.0.1, `http://www.omg.org/docs/omg/03-06-01.pdf`

[7] Kleppe, A., Warmer, J., Bast, W.: MDA Explained: The Model Driven ArchitectureTM: Practice and Promise. Addison-Wesley Longman Publishing Co., Inc., Amsterdam (2003)

[8] Erl, T.: Service Oriented Architecture: Concepts, Technology and Design. Pearson Education, Inc., London (2005)

[9] Mell, P., Grance, T.: The NIST Definition of Cloud Computing. Version 15, 10-7-09, `http://thecloudtutorial.com/nistcloudcomputingdefinition.html`

[10] Cloud Computing and SOA Convergence in Your Enterprise, `http://searchsoa.techtarget.com/generic/0,295582,sid26_gci1375000_mem1,00.html`

[11] Mahmoud, Q.H.: Service-Oriented Architecture (SOA) and Web Services: The Road to Enterprise Application Integration (EAI). Oracle Technology Network (April 2005)

[12] Topley, K.: Java Web Services in a Nutshell. O'Reilly & Associates Inc., Sebastopol (2003)

[13] Sharma, R., Sood, M.: Cloud SaaS and Model Driven Architecture. In: International Conference on Advanced Computing and Communication Technologies (RGES), pp. 18-22 (2011) ISBN: 978-981-08-7932-7

[14] Frankel, D., Parodi, J.: Using MDA to develop Web Services. IONA Technologies PLC, 2 edn. (April 2002)

[15] Frankel, D.S.: Model Driven Architecture: Applying MDA to Enterprise Computing. Wiley Publishing Inc., Chichester (2003)

Optimized Subcarrier Power Allocation in OFDM Underlay Cognitive Radio System

Dibyajnan Basak[1], Seba Maity[2], and Santi P. Maity[1]

[1] Department of Information Technology, Bengal Engineering & Science University, Shibpur, P.O. Botanic Garden, Howrah, India, 711 103

[2] Department of EI & ECE, College of Engineering & Management, Kolaghat, P.O. KTPP Township, India, 711 171

dibyajnan@gmail.com, seba_cemk@yahoo.co.in, santipmaity@it.becs.ac.in

Abstract. This paper develops an optimized subcarrier power allocation mechanism for orthogonal frequency division multiplexing (OFDM) based cognitive radio (CR) system. It is reported in the literature that both classical i.e. uniform power loading scheme and water filling method that allocates power based on the channel gain developed for OFDM system, are not effective for cognitive radio network (CRN) as the schemes introduce large interference to primary user (PU). To this aim, the present work proposes a simple, computationally efficient yet effective power loading scheme that maximizes the transmission capacity of CR while keeping the interference introduced to the PU and the total power below acceptable limits. To meet the objective, proposed power allocation to subcarriers not only consider channel gains but also the relative distances between CR subcarriers and PU band. Numerical results show that the relative gain on CR capacity is ~ 1.7 times compared to the existing hybrid and suboptimal OFDM power allocation schemes when interference introduced to PU is set at 3×10^{-6} (in watt).

1 Introduction

Radio frequency spectrum scarcity is becoming nowadays a serious issue due to the high demand for spectrum resources inspired by the increasing number of wireless users and data intensive applications such as interactive and multimedia services. However, government regulatory agencies, such as the Federal Communications Commission (FCC) bodies, on recent measurement on spectrum utilization, have shown that most of the time large portions about 15 to 85% of certain licensed frequency bands assigned to primary users (PU) remain empty. To remedy this, new regulations would allow for devices which are able to sense and adapt to their spectral environment, such as cognitive radios (CR), to become secondary users (SU). To this aim, cognitive radio network (CRN) has recently been emerged as one of the prime techniques for exploiting the increasingly flexible licensing of wireless spectrum [1].

Spectrum sensing, dynamic spectrum access, spectrum management, spectrum utilization with cooperative relay concept etc. are the couple of primary

A. Abraham et al. (Eds.): ACC 2011, Part I, CCIS 190, pp. 519–528, 2011.

issues in cognitive radio research [2]. Spectrum sensing has been identified as a key enabling to detect a spectrum hole by reliably detecting PU's signal. Spectrum utilization can then be improved by making a SU (CR) to access a spectrum hole unoccupied by PU at the right location and the right time. Dynamic spectrum access (DSA) is the concept of unlicensed users "borrowing" spectrum from license holders [2].

Two popular network architectures, namely centralized and distributed approach have been emerged for spectrum sharing. In a centralized spectrum sharing approach, a centralized server collects information from a collaborating group of SUs, which learn about the PU transmission characteristics, along with PU cooperation (if possible) and manages a database for the spectrum access and availability information [2]. On the other hand, in a distributed spectrum sharing approach, each node is responsible for its own spectrum allocation and access based on PU's transmission in its vicinity. In other words, SUs can sense and share the local spectrum access information among themselves without enforcing PU's contribution [3]. A hybrid approach is also developed in which the centralized controller only knows about the distribution of the instantaneous channel gains of the CR [4]. Each distributed controller for each CR knows the channel gains (instantaneous) and interference threshold for each user. Results showed that orthogonal frequency division multiplexing (OFDM) based hybrid power allocation performs very close to the case of centralized power allocation with the knowledge of distribution about channel gains, but requires less overhead as centralized controller does not need the information of the instantaneous channel gains [4].

Concurrent cognitive and non-cognitive transmission is possible through spectrum sharing if the interference generated by the CR users is below a certain acceptable threshold at the PU's intended receiver. There are three types of spectrum-sharing techniques, namely, interweave, underlay, and overlay [2]; each one offers benefits along with different challenges. Underlay scheme assumes the knowledge of channel gains between the secondary and primary user to be available so that the secondary user can adapt itself to the channel changes in order to meet the primary interference requirements. In such situation, the OFDM is perhaps one of the most promising candidates because of its natural adaptive ability to utilize different portions of the spectrum. A subcarrier of orthogonal frequency division multiple access (OFDMA) that is in deep fading and not suitable for one user, may have a good gain for another user. In general, since fast Fourier transform (FFT) and its inverse are used for OFDM based system implementation, various parameters such as FFT size, filters, windows, modulation, coding rate, cyclic prefix size, transmit power, subcarrier allocation, bit loading etc. may be made use for overall performance improvement [4]. Among all these, adaptive resource allocation in terms of subcarrier, bit and power to users according to their channel conditions become the most appealing for effectively improving the spectrum utilization [5],[6]. Two popular classes of resource allocation problems, namely, margin adaptive (MA) (to minimize transmit power under data rate constraints) and rate adaptive (RA) (to maximize data rate subject to power constraints) are studied and reported in literature for conventional wireless network as well as in CRNs.

This work develops optimized subcarrier power allocation for OFDM based CRN to maximize data transmission rate of CR under the constraint of interference threshold to the primary user as well as transmit power. Therefore a simple power loading policy is proposed that not only considers fading gain of the radio channel but also the spectral distance of the respective subcarriers from the PU. Simulation results show the strength of the proposed scheme for improved data transmission rate of CR compared to the existing works while simultaneously meeting the constraints of interference and transmit power.

The rest of the paper is organized as follows: Section 2 makes the review of the related works, limitations and scope of the present work. Section 3 describes proposed power allocation algorithm. Section 4 presents performance evaluation along with discussion. Finally, the paper is concluded in Section 5 along with the scope of future work.

2 Review of Related Works, Limitation and Scope of the Present Work

In this section, we present a brief literature review related to recently published OFDM based power loading in CRN system. The objective of this review section is to discuss the merits and limitations of some related works and scope of the present work.

2.1 Review of Related Works

Power loading algorithm across different OFDM subcarriers is proposed in [7] for multiuser CR system. First a suboptimal subcarrier allocation scheme is proposed followed by optimal power loading algorithm that maximizes the capacity of CR users while maintaining the interference threshold to PU and transmit power below certain prescribed values. In [8], Lagrangian dual function is used to allocate power in each subcarrier by considering the received interference as a fairness metric. Subcarrier, bit and power allocation technique for CRN based on integer linear programming has been considered in [9]. In [10] user scheduling and MA based resource allocation have been proposed for a multiple input multiple output (MIMO)-OFDMA based uplink CRN. The aim is to admit as many SUs as possible in various subcarriers while ensuring no interference is leaked to PUs. In [11], binary power allocation for CRN with centralized and distributed system is proposed for sum rate maximization. In [12], the combined use of distributed power allocation and scheduling policy for OFDM in the context of parallel multi-access fading channels is presented where each user‘s actions depend only on knowledge of its own channel gains.

The review of conventional OFDM-based wireless communication system reveals the fact that water filling maximizes the overall transmission capacity. Water filling policy in the frequency domain suggests that more power should be allocated to the subcarriers that have relatively better channel quality, while less power should be allocated to those with poor channel quality [3,5,6]. However, due to the implementation complexity of water filling policy, uniform power loading was proposed later on. However, in CRN where primary and secondary users exist side by side with each one experiences interference due to other, use of the classical loading algorithm e.g. uniform power to all subcarriers lead to higher mutual interference in the PU band [7,8,9,10]. In other words, the throughput of CR is limited by the interference caused to the PUs. This in other words suggest that power profile would depend not only on channel gains but also on interference caused to primary user. Moreover, power loading based centralized OFDM systems largely suffer from overhead, delay, and/or large computational complexity [4].

2.2 Scope of the Work

The notable facts emerged from the above review works are as follows

(1)OFDM based power loading scheme is promising to maximize transmission rate of CR user provided interference constraint to the PU is well maintained.
(2)The amount of interference introduced to the primary users band by a CR's subcarrier depends on the power allocated in that subcarrier as well as spectral distance between that particular subcarrier and PU band. To take into account these two aspects in power profile, uniform power over the subband i.e over bandwidth of the subcarrier but relatively smaller in magnitude nearer to PU is desirable, which in turn suggests an approximate stair-case like power profile as shown in Fig. 1(a) below.
(3)A computationally simple yet effective mathematical form of power profile is desirable so that it is suitable for fast-fading environment as well as for large number of subcarriers in CR bands.

On summarization, the design problem is that given an interference threshold prescribed by the PU transmit power remains within a certain value, a simple analytical form of power profile for CR subcarriers need to be developed which under certain approximation may be like as shown in Fig. 1(a). In other words, design problem is how much power should be transmitted from each CR user's subcarrier so that the transmission rate of the CR user is maximized under certain interference constraint to PU.

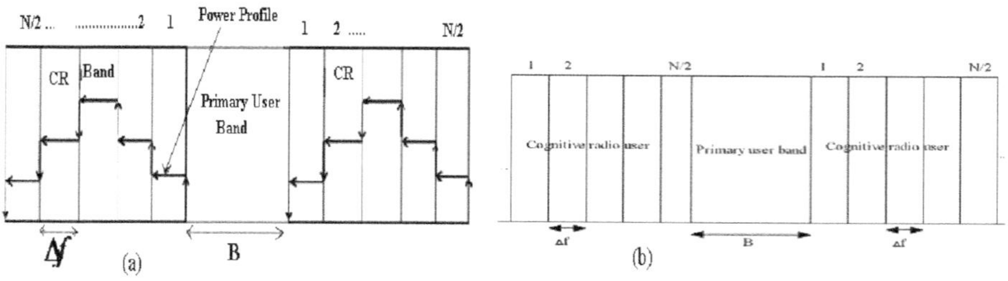

Fig. 1. (a)Approximate power profile, (b) coexistence of PU and CR side by side

3 Proposed Power Allocation Algorithm

This section would develop the mathematical form of power profile for CR's subcarriers. Prior to that we would briefly describe the system model.

3.1 System Model

It is assumed that frequency band B which has been occupied by PU is known, and the available frequency band for CR user is located on both sides of the primary user i.e we consider the side-by-side CR access model as shown in Fig. 1(a). The available bandwidth for CR transmission is divided into N subcarriers, N/2 subcarriers on each side, and each with a bandwidth of Δf. Further, it is assumed that the CR user does not have any knowledge of the PUs' data transmission method i.e. whether it is also OFDM or not. If the PU also uses OFDM modulation and the SU has knowledge of it, their transmission could be made orthogonal. However, in practice the PU might not be using OFDM, even if it is, it would be very difficult for the CR user to know the required parameters of the PU in order to maintain orthogonality.

The model presented here is a generalized picture of co-existence of both types of users according to a spectrum pooling strategy. In other words, the interference introduced into a PU's band is dominated by the adjacent SUs' transmission. Interference from the distant SUs decays as distance increases. However, the co-existence of PU and SU, would introduce two types of interference in the system.

(a) One is introduced by the PU into the CR user's band.
(b) Other is the interference introduced by the SU (CR) to PU band.

3.2 Interference Introduced by the Secondary User's Signal

The power density spectrum of the i-th subcarrier in the CR user's band can be written as

$$\phi_i = P_i T_s \left(\frac{Sin\ \pi f T_s}{\pi f T_s} \right)^2 \tag{1}$$

where P_i is the transmitted power assigned to the i-th subcarrier in the CR user band and T_s is the symbol duration. The interference introduced by the i-th subcarrier of CR to the PU's band is the integration of the power density spectrum of the i-th subcarrier across the PU's band, and can be written as

$$I_i(d_i, P_i) = {h^i}_{sp}{}^2 P_i T_s \int_{d-B/2}^{d+B/2} \left(\frac{Sin\ \pi f T_s}{\pi f T_s} \right)^2 df = P_i * k_i \tag{2}$$

where $k_i = {h^i}_{sp}{}^2 T_s \int_{d-B/2}^{d+B/2} (\frac{Sin\ \pi f T_s}{\pi f T_s})^2 df$.

Here d_i represents the spectral distance between the i-th subcarrier of the CR user's band and the PU's band, $I_i(d_i, P_i)$ represents the interference introduced by the i-th subcarrier of CR for a transmit power P_i to the PU's band, h^i_{sp}

represents channel gain for i-th subcarrier of CR to PU. We assume that both PU and CR users are located in a same device. In such co-located scenario which indicates that primary receiver can estimate the channel gain h^i_{sp} and reports it to CR transmitter.

3.3 Interference Introduced by the Primary User's Signal

The power density spectrum of the PU signal after M-point fast Fourier transform (FFT) processing can be expressed by the following expected value of the periodogram.

$$E[I_N < W >] = \frac{1}{2\pi.M}\int_{-\pi}^{\pi}\phi_{PU}(e^{jw})\left(\frac{Sin(w-\varphi)M/2}{Sin(w-\varphi)/2}\right)d\varphi \qquad (3)$$

where W represents the frequency normalized to the sampling frequency and $\phi_{PU}\left(e^{jw}\right)$ is the power density spectrum of the PU signal.

$$J(d_i, P_{PU}) = {h^i}_{ps}^{\ 2}\int_{d-\Delta f/2}^{d+\Delta f/2} E\{I_N(W)\}dw \qquad (4)$$

Assume that there are L number of PUs, and also assume that J^i_n is the interference introduced by the n-th PU to the i-th subcarrier of a CR under consideration at a distance d_i. If J^i_n is treated as a random variable, for large value of L, $\mathbf{J}_i = \sum_{n=1}^{L} J^i_n$ is considered to be random variable (RV) with Gaussian distribution (according to central limit theorem). Henceforth, we denote this interference $\mathbf{J}_i$ introduced by a group of PUs to the i-th subcarrier of a CR under consideration as additive white Gaussian noise (AWGN)-like signal filtered by elliptical filter with certain amplitude [4].

The transmit power is adjusted in each subcarrier of CR user. The transmission rate of i-th subcarrier, R_i, for the transmit power P_i is given by Shannon's capacity formula

$$R_i = \Delta f \log_2\left(1 + \frac{{h^i}_{ss}^{\ 2} * P_i}{\sigma^2 + \mathbf{J}_i}\right) \qquad (5)$$

where h^i_{ss} is the channel gain between i-th subcarrier of CR transmitter and CR receiver. Here again it is assumed that channel gain h^i_{ss} is perfectly known to CR transmitter.

3.4 Problem Formulation

Our objective is to maximize the total transmission rate of CR user while keeping the interference introduced to the PU below a certain threshold. Expressing mathematically the data transmission rate as

$$C = \max_{p_i}\sum_{i=1}^{N}\Delta f \log_2\left(1 + \frac{{h^i}_{ss}^{\ 2} * P_i}{\sigma^2 + \mathbf{J}_\mathrm{i}}\right) \qquad (6)$$

subject to $\sum_{i=1}^{N} I_i(d_i, p_i) \leq I_{th}$, $p_i \geq 0, \forall i$. The symbol 'C' denotes the transmission capacity of the CR user, N denotes the total number of OFDM subcarriers, I_{th} denotes the interference threshold to the PU band. We like to apply Lagrangian to solve this optimization problem and the simplified form of cost function is

$$L(P_i, \lambda) = \sum_{i=1}^{N} \Delta f \log_2 \left(1 + \frac{{h^i}_{ss}{}^2 * P_i}{\sigma^2 + \mathbf{J}_i}\right) - \lambda\Big(\sum_{i=1}^{N} I_i - I_{th}\Big) \tag{7}$$

λ is called as Lagrange multiplier. Differentiating this equation with respect to P_i we get,

$$\frac{\partial L}{\partial P_i} = \frac{1}{\left(1 + \frac{{h^i}_{ss}{}^2 * P_i}{\sigma^2 + \mathbf{J}_i}\right)} * \left(\frac{{h^i}_{ss}{}^2}{\sigma^2 + \mathbf{J}_i}\right) - \lambda \frac{\partial I_i}{\partial P_i} \tag{8}$$

From Eq. (8) by making $\frac{\partial L(P_i, \lambda)}{\partial P_i} = 0$ and substituting $\frac{\partial I_i}{\partial P_i}$ by k_i(see Eq. 2), we get

$$\frac{{h^i}_{ss}{}^2}{(\sigma^2 + \mathbf{J}_i + {h^i}_{ss}{}^2 + P_i)} = \lambda . k_i \tag{9}$$

Now the value of λ can be calculated from the following relation $\sum_{i=1}^{N} I_i(d_i, P_i) = I_{th}$ and $I_i = P_i * k_i$
i.e

$$P_i * k_i = \frac{1}{\lambda} - \sum_{i=1}^{N} \frac{\sigma^2 + \mathbf{J}_i}{{h^i}_{ss}{}^2} * k_i \tag{10}$$

We now find the value of λ as

$$\lambda = \frac{N}{I_{th} + \sum_{i=1}^{N} \left(\frac{(\sigma^2 + \mathbf{J}_i) * k_i}{{h^i}_{ss}{}^2}\right)} \tag{11}$$

Substitution of the value of λ in Eq.(10) would allow to find P_i value. Under certain approximation, if we ignore the second term in Eq.(10), we can follow that power is inversely proportional to the term k_i which depends on the spectral distance of the i-th subcarrier of CR user from the PU band as well as channel gains, satisfying an approximate nature of power profile shown in Fig.1(a).

4 Performance Evaluation and Discussion

This section describes the performance of the proposed OFDM based power allocation in CR system. Maximum possible data transmission rate for different values of interference threshold to PU and power budget are reported along with comparative results for the two recently reported works, namely hybrid OFDM based power allocation [4] and joint subcarrier and power adaptation in OFDMA based CRN system [7]. To run simulations we have considered the following

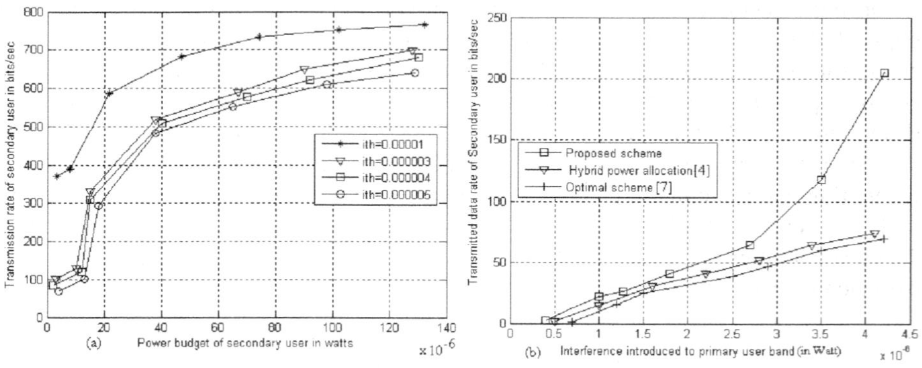

Fig. 2. (a) Transmission capacity of SU versus power budget at different values of I_{th} (b) Performance comparison of CR transmission capacity versus interference introduced to PU

parameter sets, symbol duration T_s to be 4μ second, Δf is taken as 0.5 MHZ, we assume there are two PU and two SU (CR) bands. We assume bandwidth B of first PU to be 1 MHZ and the second PU band to be 2 MHZ. The channel gain h^i_{ss},h^i_{sp} and h^i_{ps} is assumed to be Rayleigh fading with an average channel power gain -10dB. Different realizations for channel fading would result different sets of fading gains, hence, an average transmission capacity for CR obtained over 10000 independent run is reported here. Further we assume there are ten subcarriers for secondary user, five on each side of the primary user band. Noise variance σ^2 is taken as 10^{-5}. Interference from primary user to secondary user (Denoted by J) is assumed to be additive white Gaussian noise and power of the output noise filter is kept at 8 mW.

Fig. 2(a) shows power budget of CR versus data transmission capacity for different interference threshold (I_{th}) values to PU. As expected, with the increase of I_{th} values, data transmission capacity of CR increases. Numerical results show that for an increase in I_{th} value ~ 0.000002, an improvement of 0.4 times in data transmission rate is achieved, while for an improvement of 20 times in I_{th} value, an improvement in data transmission capacity of $\sim$ 25 to 15 times is achieved. Moreover, even at lower power budget, capacity for CR is significantly high making this algorithm quiet efficient for CRN system in power limited channel. Fig. 2(b) shows the comparative performance results for maximum possible data transmission rate of CR with interference introduced to PU. Numerical values show that for a given interference threshold to PU, the proposed scheme always offers the best data transmission capacity, while subcarrier and power adaptation method [7] shows the worst performance. Relatively inferior performance of [7] is possibly due to suboptimal subcarrier allocation which is preceded for the optimal power allocation and also does not take into account the distance measure. Numerical values in the graph also show that CR data transmission capacity is significantly improved at high values of interference introduced to PU compared to the other works [4], [7], while performance of later two follow

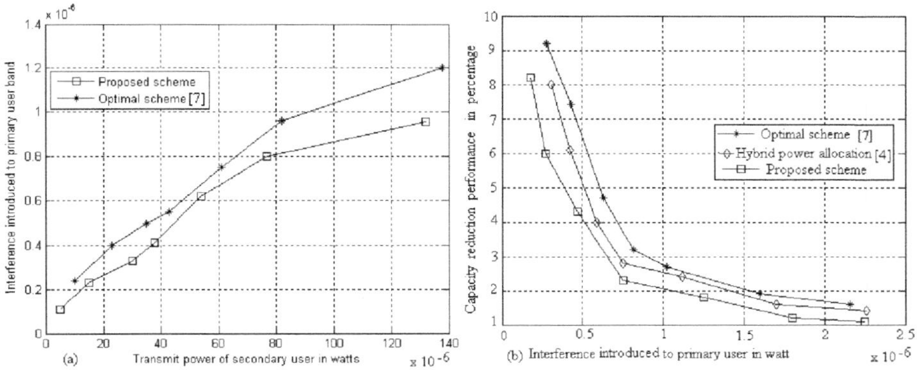

Fig. 3. Performance comparison of interference introduced to PU versus (a) transmit power budget, (b)% reduction in capacity

almost closely. It is clear from the graph that at interference introduced to PU set to 3×10^{-6}, almost 1.7 times improvement in CR capacity is possible to achieve compared to the other two methods [4],[7].

Fig.3(a) shows transmit power budget versus interference introduced to the PU. Graphical presentation shows the trend that even with the increase of transmit power for the CR, interference introduced to PU is significantly lower compared to Bansal et al [4] method, which in turn indicates that proposed power loading mechanism increases CR capacity while always keeping the interference threshold to a specified limit. The combination of Fig.2(a) and 3(a) would help to determine for the given interference threshold what particular value for power budget to be set so that target capacity can be achieved. Finally, the difference in maximum achievable transmission rate expressed in terms of percentage reduction as a function of interference introduced to PU is shown in Fig. 3(b). This is accomplished by taking the difference between the capacity achieved in this work and the capacity obtained by allocating mean equal power to all subcarriers but without considering any interference to PU, and then converting this reduction (as difference is negative) in term of percentage, calculated for different values of interference to PU. It is seen that falling rate for the present method is much higher and difference in capacity value is low (which means the capacity for the proposed method quickly i.e. at even low interference value and closely follows the capacity for the equal power) indicating that system performance increases and continues with the increase of value of interference to PU. Here also comparison shows the best performance for the proposed one, compared to the other two [4],[7].

5 Conclusions and Scope of Future Works

In this paper, we propose an optimum subcarrier power allocation for OFDM based underlay CR system that meets the interference to PU within a certain limit. The power profile calculation is computationally simple and not only depends on channel gain but also distance of CR subcarriers to PU band. Simulation results show the improved data transmission capacity of CR for the proposed method compared to OFDM based hybrid power allocation as well as joint subcarrier and power adaption methods at lower value of interference threshold. Future work would extend this concept for power allocation in relay based cognitive system for further improvement in both PU and SU capacity considering OFDM transmission.

References

1. Haykin, S.: Cognitive Radio: Brain-Empowered Wireless Communications. IEEE Journal on Selected Areas in Communications 23, 201–220 (2005)
2. Goldsmith, A., Syed, A.J., Maric, I., Srinivasa, S.: Breaking Spectrum Gridlock With Cognitive Radios:An Information Theoretic Perspective. Proc. of the IEEE 97, 894–914 (2009)
3. Wang, P., Zhong, X., Xiao, L., Zhou, S., Wang, J.: A eneral Power Allocation Algorithm for OFDM-Based Cognitive Radio Systems. In: Proc. IEEE Int. Conf. on Commun., Dresden, Germany (2009)
4. Malik, S., Banerjee, A.: On hybrid power allocation scheme for OFDM based cognitive radios. In: First UK-India Int. Workshop on Cognitive Wireless System (UKIWCWS 2009), Indian Institute of Technology, Delhi, India, December 11-12 (2009)
5. Mao, Z., Wang, X.: Efficient optimal and subop-timal radio resource allocation in OFDMA system. IEEE Trans. Wireless Commun. 7, 440–445 (2008)
6. Zhang, Y.J., Letaief, K.B.: An efficient resource-allocation scheme for spatial multiuser access in MIMO/OFDM systems. IEEE Trans. Commun. 13, 38–47 (2006)
7. Bansal, G., Hassan, Z., Hossain, J., Bhargava, V.K.: Subcarrier and power adaptation for multiuser OFDM-based cognitive radio systems. In: Proc. National Conf. on Comm., Indian Institute of Technology, Chennai, India, January 29-31, pp. 1–5 (2010)
8. Attar, A., Holland, O., Nakhai, M.R., Aghvami, A.H.: Inteference-limited resource allocation for cognitive radio in orthogonal frequency division mul- tiplexing networks. IET J. Commun. 2, 806–814 (2008)
9. Rahulamathavan, Y., Cumanan, K., Musavian, L., Lambotharan, S.: Optimal subcarrier and bit allocation techniques for cognitive radio networks using integer linear programming. In: Proc. IEEE Statistical Signal Proc. Workshop, Cardiff, UK (2009)
10. Rahulamathavan, Y., Cumanan, K., Krishna, R., Lambotharan, S.: Adaptive subcarrier and bit allocation techniques for MIMO-OFDMA based uplink cognitive radio networks. In: First UK-India Int. Workshop on Cognitive Wireless System (UKIWCWS 2009), Indian Institute of Technology, Delhi, India, December 11-12 (2009)
11. Zayen, B., Haddad, M., Hayar, A., Oien, G.E.: Binary ower allocation for congnitive radio networks with centralized and distributed user selection strategy. Physical Communication 1, 183–193 (2008)
12. Qin, X., Berry, R.A.: Distributed power allocation and scheduling for parallel channel wireless netwoks. Wireless Sensor Networks 14, 601–613 (2008)

Multimedia Traffic Transmission over Cognitive Radio Networks Using Multiple Description Coding

Abdelaali Chaoub[1], Elhassane Ibn Elhaj[2], and Jamal El Abbadi[1]

[1] Electronic and Communication Laboratory, Mohammadia School of Engineers, Rabat, Morocco
chaoub.abdelaali@gmail.com,
elabbadi@emi.ac.ma

[2] Department of Telecommunications, National Institute of Posts and Telecommunications, Rabat, Morocco
ibnelhaj@inpt.ac.ma

Abstract. In this paper, we propose a solution to multimedia transmission problem over Cognitive Radio networks in lossy environments. For Cognitive Radio networks where the spectrum is owned by Primary Users having Poissonian traffic, Secondary Users are allowed to use these spectral resources for some delay constrained multimedia applications. The service provider produces layered stream based on a progressive source coder like SPIHT. We use a specific packetization framework for Multiple Description Coding derived from the Priority Encoding Transmission to cope with both primary traffic interruptions and subchannels fading. An efficient exhaustive algorithm that implements an Unequal Loss Protection mechanism will be introduced to maximize the received PSNR as a function of our transmission model parameters. Numerical simulations for image transmission case show that the proposed scheme can protect the important layers from packet losses to a meaningful degree and improves the perceived image quality even when packet losses increase.

Keywords: Cognitive Radio network; multimedia traffic transmission; Poissonian traffic; SPIHT; Multiple Description Coding; Priority Encoding Transmission.

1 Introduction

Mobile and multimedia communication services have experienced a great evolution over the last decades. Increasing demand for the frequency spectrum resource makes the radio spectrum more precious. On the other hand, actual observations of the spectrum occupancy taken on some bands reveal the low and discontinuous usage of the licensed spectrum in time and space [1] [2], hence the emergence of the Cognitive Radio (CR) [3] as a new paradigm to find strategies for enhancing and sustaining the growth of multimedia and wireless networks with limited spectrum.

A. Abraham et al. (Eds.): ACC 2011, Part I, CCIS 190, pp. 529–543, 2011.

This spectral coexistence concept has been proposed in the objective of enabling devices to occupy the spectrum that has been left vacant by licensed users. Therefore, every telecommunication system will be divided into two networks: a primary network called Primary Users (PUs), which owns the spectrum license and has full rights on it, and a secondary network called Secondary Users (SUs), which is allowed to use the primary network's bandwidth in case of PU absence. While using a certain band of spectrum, the secondary user must avoid disturbing and interfering with the corresponding primary user, the SU must free the spectrum in case of PU reclaim and needs to restructure his communication link. Consequently, SU link maintenance becomes a necessity.

The frequency bands are incessantly sensed and from that sensing-derived informations, Secondary User Links (SULs) can be formed from a composition of multiple subchannels (SCs) that are currently not used by licensed users (Fig. 1). The SUL maintenance mechanism deals with two main crucial aspects. The first one is to minimize the effect of PU arrival on the established SU link by adopting a suitable link structure. In this article we propose to make use of the Spectrum Pooling Concept [4], subchannels selected to create a SUL should be scattered over multiple PU frequencies. The major advantages of this principle are twofold: 1) it limits performance degradation due to the interference caused by primary user reappearance, and 2) it reduces the number of jammed subchannels once the primary user appears during the lifetime of a Secondary User Path. The second one is to remedy the problem of packets loss due to PU interruptions, for this purpose we modelize the lost packets as erasures and we make use of erasure correcting codes. There are two approaches to do it: channel coding approach and source coding approach. The channel coding is used to compensate for the loss due to PU appearance and source coding is used to recover the content up to a certain quality depending on the number of packets received. In this contribution, we propose to exploit the Joint Source Channel Coding (JSCC) approach that combines the benefits of both methods already mentioned.

More precisely, in this work we adopt a Multiple Description Source Coding method which is among the most appropriate JSCC ways to communicate multimedia content over a lossy packets network.

Furthermore, there exist little research efforts on the problem of secondary traffic transmission over Cognitive Radio networks using Multiple Description Coding (MDC). In [5], Kushwaha, Xing, Chandramouli and Subbalakshmi have studied the coding aspect over CR networks, a brief summary of Spectrum pooling concept has been introduced [4]. Then, different coding types have been presented and their applications on the secondary use have been analyzed and discussed. Principally, the paper has given an overview of the MDC as source coding well suited for use in CR networks. For simulation results, the paper has adopted the LT codes to combat the secondary use losses under the CR architecture model defined in [6]. This study was an attempt to give a general analyze of MDC applications on CR networks and no numerical results have been presented for this specific coding scheme. In [7], Husheng has investigated the use of MDC in cognitive radio systems to overcome the losses caused by the primary

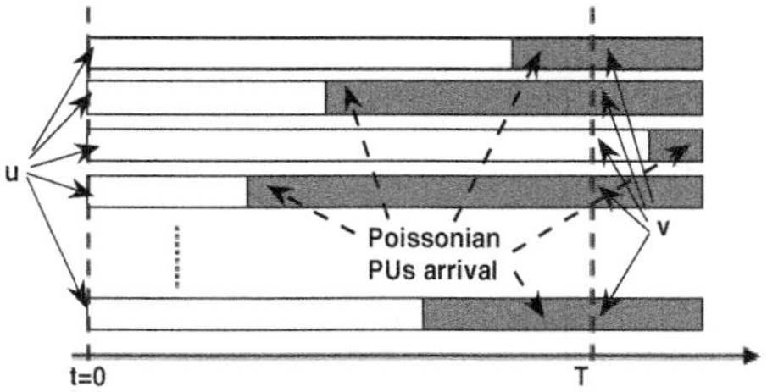

Fig. 1. Subchannel access model

traffic arrival on the secondary applications that are delay sensitive and distortion tolerable. Using a Gaussian source, he has proposed an algorithm to transform the selection of rates and distortions problem into an optimization problem for the expected utility. The primary users occupancy over each frequency channel was modeled as a Markov chain. Numerical results have been presented for real time image coding. However, this contribution has not considered the noise and fading aspect of networks and consequently there is an additional packets lost average due to lossy environment which degrades considerably the performance of the selected SUL. The study explores only the applications with traffic that fits well with the markovian process and there are other CR applications where the Markov chain is not applicable. Moreover, this study has considered only the Gaussian sources and need to be generalized to more sources types.

In previous work [8], we have done some contribution on the problem of image transmission over lossy networks using progressive source codes associated to fountain codes where the stream delivery is reinforced by the use of Unequal Error Protection (ULP) based on the block duplication technique. Currently, our work is addressing the multimedia traffic transmission problem through distributed CR networks in lossy environments. So, we have treated this problem in [9] by using fountain codes under different subchannel selection policies in a fading environment with the assumption that the primary traffic arrival follows a Poisson process. Herein, we consider the same primary applications that have a traffic which is dynamic and have less correlation [10] (Fig. 1). We depict the network topology that provides the infrastructure for the multimedia communication in a secondary use scenario. Particularly, we focus on multimedia applications that are delay constrained with some tolerable quality degradation, which means that the transmission has to respect a given delay with some distortion. Multiple description coding is used as a source coding to cope with packet losses caused by both Poissonian primary traffic interruptions and subchannels noise and fading (Fig. 2). Some descriptions may be lost in the network, nevertheless, the use of MDC enables reconstituting the multimedia data with some achieved distortion. The source stream is progressively encoded using a progressive compression scheme like SPIHT, this mechanism generates a base layer and several enhancement layers, the base layer is indispensable for the media stream to be decoded and enhancement layers are applied to improve stream quality. A specific source coding structure is used here making use of the Priority Encoding

Transmission (PET) packetization technique of Albanese et al. [11]. The proposed technique assigns different amounts of Forward Error Correction (FEC) to different descriptions according to their importance (Fig. 2). Those amounts of FEC are calculated based on a given algorithm that we will introduce here. Our algorithm finds exhaustively a good compromise between the packet corruptions pattern and the PSNR of the received image. The used FEC can be Reed Solomon (RS) codes [12] or any error correcting codes like Fountain codes [13]. The use of the MDC associated to the specific packetization scheme enables recovering the multimedia data content up to a certain quality commensurate to the number of received descriptions and provides reliability in various secondary applications. The novel idea of making use of this specific JSCC scheme in CR networks kills two birds with one stone: first, the use of progressive source coding with multiple descriptions protects the original stream against the resulting PU arrival erasures. Secondly, the Unequal Loss Protection ensured by the progressive FEC amounts make the transmission robust against unreliable subchannels and enables heavy protection to the base layers.

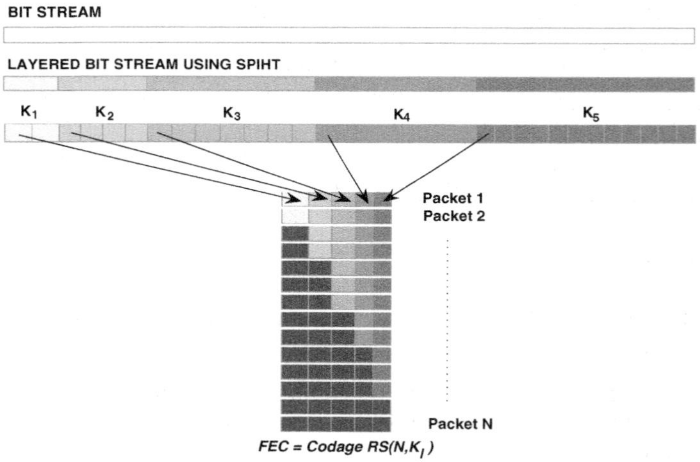

Fig. 2. Multiple Description Coding framework based Priority Encoding Transmission

The remainder of this work is organized as follows: Section 2 gives a brief summary about the Spectrum Pooling Concept. In Section 3 we compute the analytic expression of the successful transmission probability of a given description on the chosen SUL. We evaluate the losses due to subchannels characteristics and we adapt the Priority Encoding Transmission framework to our CR network model. We will introduce an exhaustive algorithm to maximize the received PSNR depending on the MDC coding scheme settings. In Section 4 we present the numerical results for a real image transmission and we show the resulting gains in terms of the achieved PSNR. Then we compare our introduced MDC scheme to the one introduced in [7], and finally Section 5 draws our conclusions.

2 System Descriptions

Here we introduce some concepts that will be used in our study.

2.1 Spectrum Pooling Concept

The Spectrum Pooling Concept [4] basically consists of selecting several spectral ranges from the primary frequency bands to constitute a common pool. The so called COgnitive Radio for Virtual Unlicensed Spectrum (CORVUS) [14] is based on this approach. The whole frequency spectrum covered by the system is divided into N_{sc} subchannels each of bandwidth $W = B/N_{\mathrm{sc}}$ where the total available system bandwidth is B. The dashed frequency bands in Fig. 3 indicate that de PU is currently active, consequently this frequency band can not be used by any secondary user. The gradient grey color in Fig. 3 shows the vacant subchannels that are selected to construct a Secondary User Link.

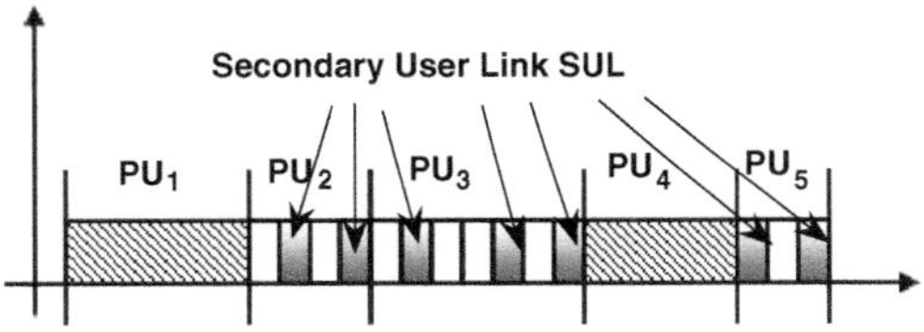

Fig. 3. Spectrum Pooling Concept

3 Proposed Work

In this section, we introduce a robust way to communicate an image over a lossy packets network such as CR networks by the use of a progressive encoding system (Fig. 2) which allows transmitting the coded image as a sequence of descriptions over CR networks. The use of progressive amounts of FEC guarantees a high protection level to the most important data i.e. the base layer of the stream.

3.1 General Analysis

On a distributed Cognitive Radio network, we consider a Secondary User providing access to multimedia information (image, audio, video,...) directly available to a given population of many Secondary Users.

In our study, we pay special attention to the real time image transmission. There is a deadline for all codewords, denoted by T_{image}. Only packets entirely received before the deadline can be used for the reconstruction of the image.

In our system model, time is slotted into frames of length T. We use the frame structure as shown in Fig. 4. At the start of every frame T, a SUL is set up by selecting a set of S subchannels from different PU bands of the spectrum pool. Let T_{sens} denotes the Secondary User Link setup time ($T_{\mathrm{sens}} \approx T_{\mathrm{setup}}$).

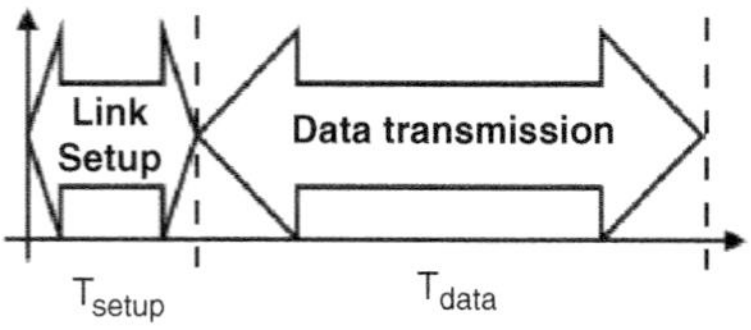

Fig. 4. Time frame structure

Then the SU starts transmitting his packets over this link during T_{data}. We have $T = T_{\text{sens}} + T_{\text{data}}$.

We make the following assumption: $T = T_{\text{data}}$, because T_{sens} is so small as to be negligible compared to T_{data}. For simplicity of analysis and without loss of generality, we suppose also that the image time duration T_{image} and the time frame T are equal: $T \approx T_{\text{image}}$.

The primary traffic on the selected bands is considered dynamic. Hence, the PU arrival process on every subchannel $s \in \{1, \cdots, S\}$ is modeled as a Poisson process with arrival rate λ_s and interarrival time τ_s, S is the set of available subchannels (Fig. 1).

Let u and v be two active SUs. Sophisticated signal processing and coding techniques remains the cornerstone of a successful transmission $u \rightarrow v$.

3.2 Formalizing the Transmission Problem

To guarantee a successful transmission of the multimedia content through the available subchannels over the CR network, we have to battle on two major challenges: First, CR networks are subject to PUs interferences and fading across subchannels. Secondly, multimedia applications have to respect the heterogeneity in terms of available clients bandwidth and delay constraints. That is, the use of MDC is very suitable for that kind of traffic. The Multiple Description Source Coding associated to an appropriate progressive compression scheme allows us to generate multiple levels of quality and alleviate the packet losses for delay constrained applications.

Over the last years, many contributions have been made on the problem of Multiple Description Coding and several MDC techniques have been introduced. Among the most practical approaches, we find the technique introduced in [12] which is based on the Priority Encoding Transmission (PET) method of Albanese et al. [11]. The idea is borrowed here and the derived PET mechanism transforms a scalable source bit stream into a robust multiple description stream (Fig. 2). Progressive forward error correction (FEC) channel code is applied to the source layers ordered in a descending order according to their importance (Fig. 2) to provide graceful quality degradation as packet losses increase. The proposed approach deals with primary traffic interferences and adapts easily to subchannels erasures. The given mechanism is capable of providing protection from the effects of packet loss irrespective of the loss model of the SUL. This packetization scheme has the property that all packets are equally important;

only the number of packets received determines the reconstructed image quality. That is, no special coordination is needed between the several subchannels.

The Multiple Description encoded message is divided into L descriptions and consists of N packets. Stream 1 is the first stream (most important data), and stream L is the last stream (least important data).

The question of how much FEC amount to assign to each layer is of great interest and will be addressed in the following paragraph.

3.3 Priority Encoding Transmission Framework for CR Networks

From the initial message, we first form a scalable bit stream by applying the progressive compression scheme SPIHT [15] on the image. We partition the bit stream source into L fragments $(R_l)_{1\leq l\leq L}$ indexed in order of decreasing importance; we use the fact that the most important data are emitted first in a progressive source coder. Each layer R_l is blocked into K_l source blocks each of length M_l bytes, and the l'th source block is expanded into channel codewords of length N using the minimum distance separable Reed Solomon code $RS(N, K_l)$ as a forward error correction. We add FEC to each message fragment to protect it against packet losses caused by both primary traffic interruptions and subchannels characteristics such that the sub stream R_l and the FEC form a description D_l. RS codes have the ability to decode the transmitted description D_l using any set of K_l received packets. We have a total of L descriptions $(D_l)_{1\leq l\leq L}$ and each description D_l has a RS rate of K_l/N. In the rest of this paper, our goal is to adapt the proposed coding scheme to our CR network model.

Let *FEC* be an L-tuple whose entries are the length of FEC assigned to each stream i.e. $FEC = (FEC_1, FEC_2, \cdots, FEC_{\mathrm{L}})$, where FEC_l is the Forward Error Correction (FEC) amount assigned to the description l where $l \in \{1, \cdots, L\}$. We state that $N > FEC_1 \geq FEC_2 \geq \cdots \geq FEC_{\mathrm{L}}$.

In this study, the primary metric that we investigate is the Peak Signal-to-Noise Ratio (PSNR) of the received image. The PSNR represents an efficient distortion measure to quantify the perceived quality of the reconstructed image.

The expected PSNR of the received image is the sum of different PSNR amounts corresponding to the received descriptions each weighted by the probability of receiving its corresponding description, it is given by:

$$PSNR\left((D_l)_{1\leq l\leq L}\right) = \sum_{l=1}^{L} P(D_l)PSNR(D_l) \ . \tag{1}$$

Where $P(D_l)$ is the probability of successfully decoding the description D_l at the receiver and the quantity $PSNR(D_l)$ is the additional PSNR amount gained when the receiver decodes the l'th description given that *l-1* descriptions have already been successfully decoded.

In our scenario, there are mainly two events that affect the traffic distribution on the selected SUL and consequently we must achieve two goals simultaneously: 1) cope with packet losses caused by the frequent primary user arrival, and 2) remedy to packet erasures due to subchannels fading and noise.

So, the description D_l can be decoded at the receiver if: on one hand, the number of PET encoded packets needed to recover the original description D_l could be successfully transmitted over the S subchannels and, on the other hand at most FEC_l packets get lost du to subchannels fading and noise.

Let N_{PU} be the number of packets received across the subchannels S constituting the SUL prone to Poissonian primary traffic reclaims (Fig. 1) and let N_{SC} be the number of packets corrupted as a result of subchannels fading and noise over the set of S subchannels. We recall that the minimum number of PET encoded packets needed to reconstruct the layer l at the receiver is $N - FEC_l$. Then,

$$P(D_l) = Prob\left(\{N_{\mathrm{PU}} \geq N - FEC_l\} \text{ and } \{N_{\mathrm{SC}} \leq FEC_l\}\right) . \tag{2}$$

Therefore, the total expected PSNR depends on the MD coding scheme applied to the original stream. That is, the multimedia transmission problem over CR networks could be transformed to a challenging optimization problem. We seek the FEC vector which maximizes the expected PSNR of the received message.

To completely define the probability $P(D_l)$ we should define both random variables N_{PU} and N_{SC}. We introduce both probabilities $P_{\mathrm{PU}}(n)$ and $P_{\mathrm{SC}}(n)$ as:

$$P_{\mathrm{PU}}(n) = Prob\left(N_{\mathrm{PU}} \geq n\right) . \tag{3}$$

And

$$P_{\mathrm{SC}}(n) = Prob\left(N_{\mathrm{SC}} \leq n\right) . \tag{4}$$

3.4 An Analytical Expression for $P_{\mathrm{PU}}(n)$

First we compute $P_{\mathrm{PU}}(n)$, N_{PU} is given by:

$$N_{\mathrm{PU}} = \sum_{s=1}^{S} N_{\mathrm{PU}}^{s} . \tag{5}$$

Where N_{PU}^{s} denotes the number of packets transmitted over the subchannel s with $s \in \{1, \cdots, S\}$ (Fig. 1).

Let each SC has a loss probability π_s and channel capacity R_s. We suppose that the channel capacity is the same for all the SCs, we note R_0 this capacity.

The random variable N_{PU}^{s} is proportional to the available time on the s'th subchannel (white color in Fig. 1) denoted by a random variable T_{PU}^{s}.

Primary user traffic is modeled as a Poisson process then T_{PU}^{s} is given by:

$$T_{\mathrm{PU}}^{s} = \begin{cases} \tau_s, & \text{if } \tau_s \leq T \\ T, & \text{if } \tau_s > T \end{cases} . \tag{6}$$

Where $\tau_s \sim \exp \lambda_s$. Hence,

$$N_{\mathrm{PU}}^{s} = \frac{(1-\pi_s) \times R_0 \times T_{\mathrm{PU}}^{s}}{T} . \tag{7}$$

In fact, we have entirely defined the random variables $(N_{\mathrm{PU}}^{s})_{s\in\{1,\cdots,S\}}$, consequently using (3), (5), (6) and (7) we can compute $P_{\mathrm{PU}}(n)$. We use the property that the PDF of a sum of Random Variables is computed as the convolution of the individual PDFs of those variables:

$$PDF(N_{\mathrm{PU}}) = \bigotimes_{s=1}^{S} PDF(N_{\mathrm{PU}}^{s}) \ . \tag{8}$$

3.5 An Analytical Expression for $P_{\mathrm{SC}}(n)$

We have:

$$N_{\mathrm{SC}} = \sum_{s=1}^{S} N_{\mathrm{SC}}^{s} \ . \tag{9}$$

Where N_{SC}^{s} denotes the number of lost packets due to subchannel fading and noise on the path s where $s \in \{1, \cdots, S\}$.

The losses caused by subchannels characteristics affect the number of packets that can be transmitted over the subchannel before the primary user arrival given by N_{PU}^{s}. Hence, if we assume an independent loss process, the probability density function (pdf) of N_{SC}^{s} can be expressed as:

$$p_{\mathrm{SC}}^{s}(n) = Prob(N_{\mathrm{SC}}^{s} = n) = \binom{N_{\mathrm{PU}}^{s}}{n} \times \pi_s^{n} \times (1-\pi_s)^{(N_{\mathrm{PU}}^{s}-n)} \ . \tag{10}$$

Where N_{PU}^{s} is defined in expression (7).

The pdf of N_{SC} is the convolution of S binomial density functions, it can be written as:

$$p_{\mathrm{SC}}(n) = Prob(N_{\mathrm{SC}} = n) = Prob\left(\sum_{s=1}^{S} N_{\mathrm{SC}}^{s} = n\right) = \bigotimes_{s=1}^{S} p_{\mathrm{SC}}^{s} \ . \tag{11}$$

The corresponding cumulative density function $P_{\mathrm{SC}}(n)$ represents the probability that at most n packets are lost. It is simply given by:

$$P_{\mathrm{SC}}(n) = \sum_{i=0}^{n} p_{\mathrm{SC}}(i) \ . \tag{12}$$

3.6 PSNR Maximization Problem

We have now characterized the packet losses distribution, namely N_{PU} and N_{SC}, relevant to our problem. From the given formulas in (1), (2), (8) and (12) we conclude that the reliability of the transmitted progressively-coded image with multiple description coding is depending on the parameters setting of the adopted packet loss protection mechanism. Therefore, we render the PSNR maximization problem tractable by adjusting the *FEC* values of the given MDC scheme applied on the image.

Herein, we develop a procedure to find an optimal *FEC* assignment:

1. Define:
   $G = \{FEC = (FEC_1, FEC_2, \cdots, FEC_{\mathrm{L}}) / N > FEC_1 \geq \cdots \geq FEC_{\mathrm{L}}\}$
   Enumerate all the $FEC \in G$ possibilities . Let $PSNR_{\max}$ be the maximum achieved PSNR for the received image, $PSNR_{\max}$ is initially set to 0.
2. For given *FEC*, evaluate the probabilities $(P(D_l))_{1 \leq l \leq L}$ and the gained PSNR amounts $(PSNR(D_l))_{1 \leq l \leq L}$ and then evaluate the average PSNR: $PSNR\left((D_l)_{1 \leq l \leq L}\right)$.
3. Set $PSNR_{\max} = \max\left(PSNR_{\max}, PSNR\left((D_l)_{1 \leq l \leq L}\right)\right)$.
4. Iterate the procedure for all the vectors *FEC* belonging to the group *G*.

There are some developed algorithms that reach a better tradeoff between the achieved image quality measures like PSNR and the packets loss model, the algorithm introduced in [16] is applicable to our field of research with some stated assumptions[1], we will use it for the numerical simulations.

4 Numerical Results

In this section, we present some numerical results to reinforce the theoretical aspect previously addressed and to outline the achieved gains when using Multiple Description Coding in Cognitive Radio networks.

4.1 General Simulations

For these experiments, we used the standard 512×512 gray Lenna image (Fig. 7) compressed with SPIHT using a bit rate of $r = 0.2$bit/pixel for data and FEC bytes. We consider an ATM transmission. ATM Packets consist of 48 bytes where 1 byte is reserved for sequence number. Therefore, we need a total of $N = 127$ packets. The image needs to be transmitted over a Cognitive Radio network with a common pool of $S = 7$ subchannels and in a maximum delay of $T_{\mathrm{image}} = 10$s.

For numerical simulations, we consider the following set of parameters: $\lambda = [0.3\ 0.2\ 0.1\ 0.3\ 0.36\ 0.4\ 0.6]$ and $\pi = [0.01\ 0.013\ 0.012\ 0.02\ 0.05\ 0.025\ 0.06]$ Subchannel capacity $R_0 = 1000$ Packets.

The PSNR of the received image is computed as the following:
$PSNR = 10 \times \log\left(\frac{PEAK^2}{MSE}\right)$ where $MSE = \frac{1}{XY} \sum_{x=1}^{X} \sum_{y=1}^{Y} |I'(x,y) - I(x,y)|$
I: Original image, I': Received image, $X \times Y$: Image dimensions and $PEAK$: Image peak.

Figure 5 illustrates the probability of successful transmission over Cognitive Radio network shared by several SUs plotted against the number of subchannels S for different packets number. Thus, for a fixed value of S and while decreasing

[1] In [16], the number of message fragments is equal to the number of bytes in each packet and each description has only one byte of each of the N packets.

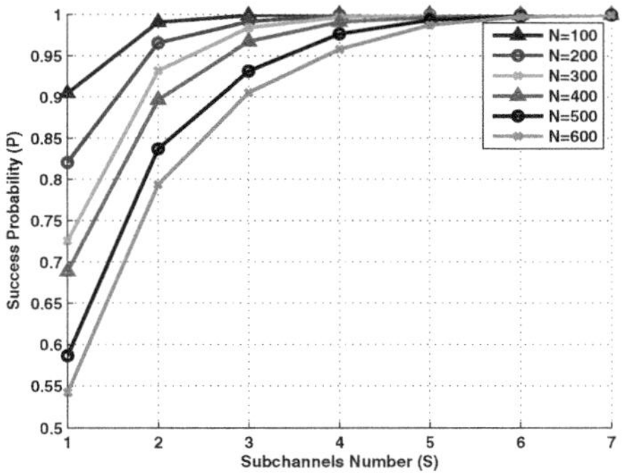

Fig. 5. Transmission Success Probability Versus Packets number N

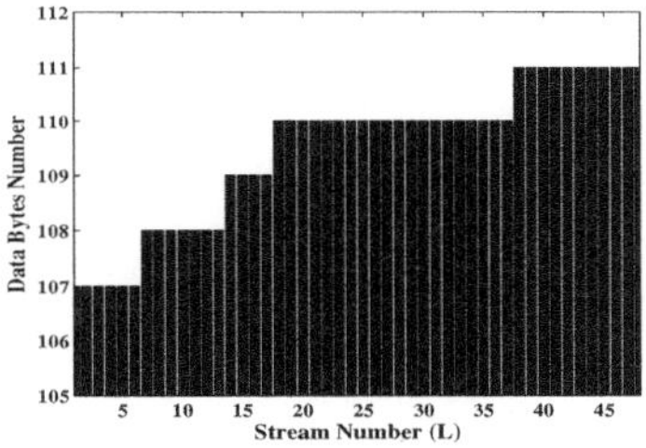

Fig. 6. Data bytes number for each stream (Lenna image)

the number of the transmitted packets, the proposed network model provides better results in terms of successful transmission probability. This is due to the fact that when the SU is decreasing the traffic transmission on his assigned subchannels, data packets are more likely to be correctly received for a fixed S value. It is also interesting to note that only transmitting base layers improves the successful transmission probability on the selected SUL for a fixed number of Cognitive Radio resources and permits the service continuity in case of a lossy SUL. The given result justifies the use of MDC in Cognitive Radio networks. We should state that there is a value of S ($S = 3$) which maximizes the probability of successful transmission. Adding other SCs to the Secondary User Link over this value doesnt give any amelioration in terms of successful transmission probability. Hence, for all the following numerical result, S has been fixed to 3.

In Fig. 6, the FEC amounts are given for each description to maximize the received image PSNR subject to primary interruptions λ and subchannels losses process π. The quantities $(P(D_l))_{1\leq l\leq L}$ are derived from the graph in Fig. 5 and $(PSNR(D_l))_{1\leq l\leq L}$ are given by the SPIHT compression scheme. Base layers are heavily protected and enhancement ones are less protected which implements an ULP for the Lenna image.

Figure 7 represents the reconstructed Lenna images depending on the number of successfully received descriptions. That is, the perceived visual of the received image is acceptable despite of the presence of primary traffic interruptions and

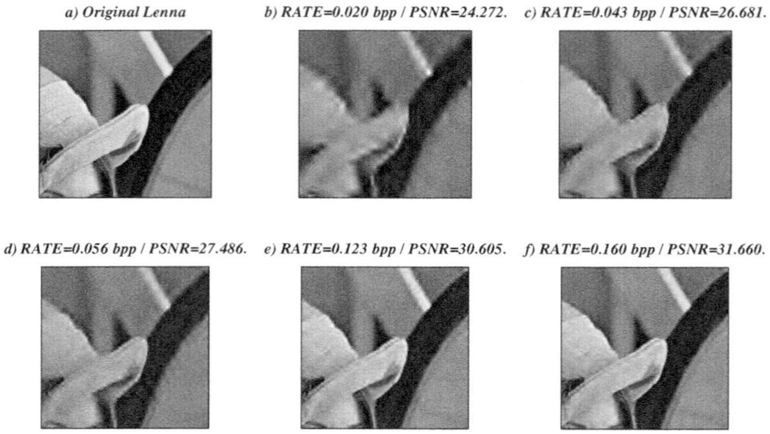

Fig. 7. a) The original 512×512 Lenna image transmitted on Cognitive Radio networks. The reconstructed Lenna using b) 1 received Description. c) 2 received Descriptions. d) 3 received Descriptions. e) 4 received Descriptions. f) All received Descriptions.

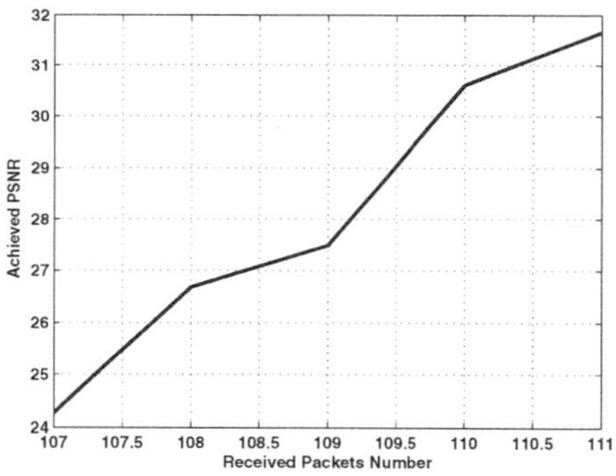

Fig. 8. Achieved PSNR in terms of the number of received descriptions

fading subchannels losses. In extreme conditions (only one description received), the proposed MDC scheme still exhibit acceptable perceived image quality.

Figure 8 depicts the impact of the number of received descriptions on the obtained PSNR in CR networks. The given results show that the achieved quality remains acceptable in case of packets corruptions increase. Depending on the received packets number and not witch packets received, the multimedia consumer can always reconstruct the transmitted image up to a certain good quality.

4.2 Comparison with Previous Works

We assume the same conditions of the numerical simulations defined in [7]. We consider a transmission rate $R_0 = 10$Mbps of and a deadline of $T_{\text{image}} = 40$ms. Using 16QAM as channel symbol, the deadline is of $100k$ channel symbol periods.

In [7], the primary traffic is modeled as a Markov Chain, so that in 40ms there are 100000 chances that the channel will become occupied. In the Poissonian case, if a certain type of event occurs on average of J times per period T, to analyze the number of events occurring in this period we choose as model a Poisson distribution with parameter $\lambda = J \times T$. Therefore, we take $\lambda_1 = \lambda_2 = 4000$. We consider both single and two-channel cases $S = 1$ and $S = 2$. We consider always the grey Lenna image, we note that it has the same size as the grey Barbara image used in [7].

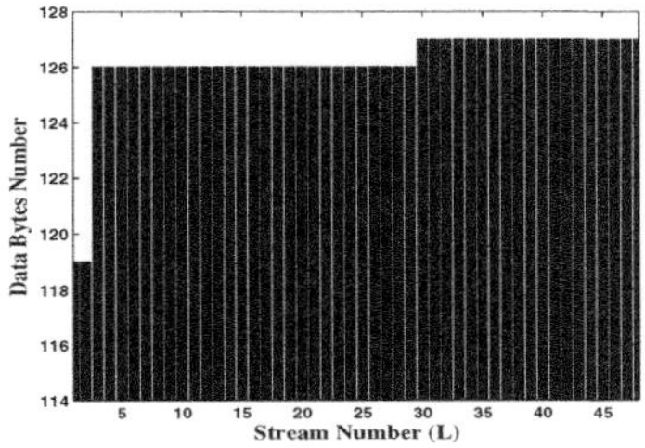

Fig. 9. Data bytes number for each stream (Lenna image)

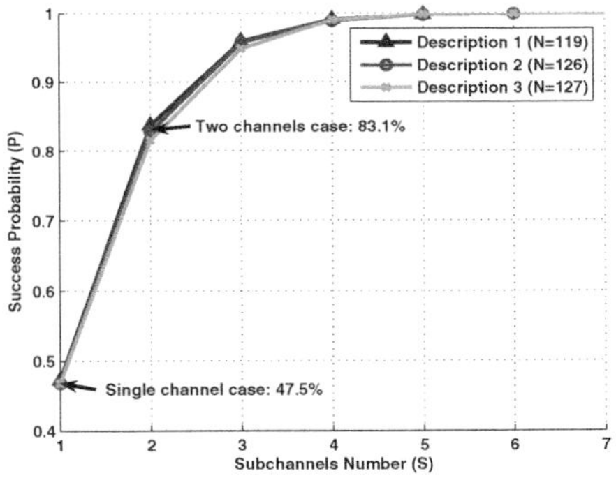

Fig. 10. Transmission Success Probability Versus received descriptions number

In [7], and when using one subchannel we receive the both descriptions just only in 28.5% of time. Generally (in 71.5% of time) we receive only one description. Using two subchannels, in 57.7% of time the both descriptions are received and only one in 36.4% of time. In other words, if we loss just a few number of packets from the second description, the whole description get useless. In our introduced scheme, in Fig. 9 we give different FEC amount that permits to reach a good compromise between the achieved PSNR and packet corruption average. Fig. 10 illustrates the transmission success probability comparison for different values of received descriptions. Using the plotted graph and for $N = 127$, we state that for $S = 2$ the Success Probability attains 0.825 and reaches 0.476 for $S = 1$. Therefore, we summarize that where using two subchannels, 82.5% (versus 57.7% in [7]) of time we are able to receive all the descriptions versus

47.6% (versus 28.5% in [7]) of time in single channel case, which is obviously more efficient than the proposed scheme in [7].

5 Conclusion

In this paper, we consider distributed multimedia traffic transmission over lossy CR networks. That is, we have exploited a progressive compression scheme using a specific Multiple Description Source Coding technique which is based on the Priority Encoding Transmission framework. Our introduced mechanism allows generating multiple levels of quality using multiple layers simultaneously with a network delivery protection model that allows us to deliver subsets of layers to a given population of receivers over unreliable Secondary User Links. Finally, we have supported our theoretical analyses by practical simulations for a real image transmission in a secondary use. The obtained results let us confirm the effectiveness of our multimedia transmission model in Cognitive Radio systems.

References

1. Shared Spectrum Compagny. Spectrum occupancy measurement, `http://www.sharedspectrum.com/measurements/`
2. NTIA, U.S. frequency allocations, `http://www.ntia.doc.gov/osmhome/allochrt.pdf`
3. Mitola III, J.: Cognitive Radio: An Integrated Agent Architecture for Software Defined Radio. Ph.D Thesis, KTH Royal Institute of Technology (2000)
4. Weiss, T., Jondral, F.: Spectrum Pooling: An Innovative Strategy for the Enhancement of Spectrum Efficiency. IEEE Communications Magazine 42, 8–14 (2004)
5. Kushwaha, H., Xing, Y., Chandramouli, R., Subbalakshmi, K.P.: Erasure Tolerant Coding for Cognitive Radios. In: Mahmoud, Q.H. (ed.) Cognitive Networks: Towards Self-Aware Networks. Wiley, Chichester (2007)
6. Willkomm, D., Gross, J., Wolisz, A.: Reliable link maintenance in cognitive radio systems. In: First IEEE International Symposium on New Frontiers in Dynamic Spectrum Access Networks, Baltimore, pp. 371–378 (2005)
7. Li, H.: Multiple description source coding for cognitive radio systems. In: 2010 Proceedings of the Fifth International Conference on Cognitive Radio Oriented Wireless Networks & Communications (CROWNCOM), Cannes, pp. 1–5 (2010)
8. Chaoub, A., Ibn Elhaj, E., El Abbadi, J.: Unequal protected fountain code for progressive image source coding using block duplication. In: 7th JFMMA & TELECOM 2011. IEEE Press, Tangier (2011)
9. Chaoub, A., Ibn Elhaj, E., El Abbadi, J.: Multimedia traffic transmission over TDMA shared Cognitive Radio networks with Poissonian Primary traffic. In: International Conference on Multimedia Computing and Systems. IEEE Press, Ouarzazat (2011)
10. Kushwaha, H., Xing, Y., Chandramouli, R., Heffes, H.: Reliable multimedia transmission over cognitive radio networks using fountain codes. Proceedings of the IEEE 96, 155–165 (2008)
11. Albanese, A., Blömer, J., Edmonds, J., Luby, M., Sudan, M.: Priority encoding transmission. IEEE Transactions on Information Theory 42, 1737–1744 (1996)

12. Mohr, A.E., Riskin, E.A., Ladner, R.: Generalized multiple description coding through unequal loss protection. In: IEEE International Conference on Image Processing, Kobe, pp. 411–415 (1999)
13. MacKay, D.J.C.: Fountain codes. IEE Proceedings Communications 152, 1062–1068 (2005)
14. Broderson, R.W., Wolisz, A., Cabric, D., Mishra, S.M., Willkomm Foster, D.: Corvus: A cognitive radio approach for usage of virtual unlicensed spectrum. Technical report, Univ. California Berkeley (2004)
15. Said, A., Pearlman, W.A.: A new, fast, and efficient image codec based on set partitioning in hierarchical trees. IEEE Transactions on Circuits and Systems for Video Technology 6, 243–250 (1996)
16. Mohr, A.E., Riskin, E.A., Ladner, R.: Unequal loss protection: graceful degradation of image quality over packet erasure channels through forward error correction. IEEE Journal on Selected Areas in Communications 18, 819–828 (2000)

Digital Image Evidence Detection Based on Skin Tone Filtering Technique

Digambar Povar, Divya S. Vidyadharan, and K.L. Thomas

Center for Development of Advanced Computing, Trivandrum, Kerala, India
Ministry of Communications and Information Technology, Govt. of India
{paward,divyasv,thomaskl}@cdactvm.in

Abstract. Distribution of child pornography material is one of the most disturbing cyber crimes. Cyber crime is a form of crime where the Internet or computer is used as a medium to commit the crime. With the growth of the Internet and the ease of file sharing in these days, child pornography has grown to become a worldwide issue. Most of the tools available today retrieve all the files and folders from the digital evidence file. The investigator has to search through all these files to identify relevant picture files pertaining to the child grooming case. To make an investigator's job easier, we evolved methods to retrieve only picture files from the whole digital media or digital evidence file. Also, we suggest an optimal method to find skin component in a given picture file using skin tone detection technique.

Keywords: Cybercrime, child pornography, skin tone detection, file system, slack space and data carving.

1 Introduction

Proliferation of Internet has increased exponentially in recent years leading to easy access of any kind of data anytime. This is very useful in different scenarios like expanding the horizon of knowledge, for getting updates about current financial, political status of a nation, etc. But at the same time this Internet access has led to put dark shadows over normal social life. It is very difficult to prevent antisocial people from using the Internet as an easily available mechanism for defacing people. Some people use Internet as a method to take revenge on people to whom they bear a grudge. They may use some specialized tools to modify pornographic pictures and add the face of innocent people in order to black mail them. Adolescent people become addicted to pornographic pictures. This is a major social issue where a nations budding population becomes attracted to such anti social activities and become vulnerable to sexual exploitation. This condition is very severe when the culprits try to establish a favorable relationship with children and take advantage of them. So it is a very difficult task for governments, organizations and parents to control the access of obscene contents by children. According to Indian Information Technology Act 2000, publishing obscene information is a cyber crime under section 67. Cyber crime encompasses a broad range of potentially illegal activities and child pornography is one of them.

A. Abraham et al. (Eds.): ACC 2011, Part I, CCIS 190, pp. 544–551, 2011.

Computer is a device used for many applications and hence support various file types to perform the task. Assuming storage media of computer is of terabytes size, which is common today, can store large number of files that may not be related to digital evidence pertaining to pornography cases. Hence there is a need for an optimal method that can retrieve all picture files based on the file signatures from whole digital media or image. Also, an optimal method is required to find skin-tone percentage in a retrieved picture file to minimize the analysis process. We use file system information to retrieve undeleted files and data carving methods to retrieve deleted files where file system exists for digital media. For a digital media that does not support file system, we use data carving methods to retrieve files, but it is a time consuming process.

2 Retrieving Picture Files from Digital Media

2.1 Introduction to File Systems

File systems organize storage media into set of basic allocation units known as clusters or blocks. Different storage management features like storage allocation, reallocation are implemented through a set of data structures. Each file will have its own data structures; the sophisticated nature of the data structures determines the features available within the file system. In this paper, we will explain two commonly used file systems, FAT and NTFS.

In FAT file system, the important data structures used are File Allocation Table (FAT) and the Root Directory [6]. The FAT contains the allocation status of all the clusters within the partition [11]. Root Directory contains a set of records. Each record contains information regarding a file or folder within the partition. Using these two data structures and the information from the boot sector of the partition, all the files and folders within the partition can be retrieved without accessing the operating system.

The New Technology File System (NTFS) has a lot of in-house data structures to support security, fast retrieval of small files, indexing, etc. The main data structure used by this file system is Master File Table. This is a collection of equal sized records. Each record contains information related to a file or folder within the NTFS partition. The information related to the time when a file is created/modified etc is stored in Standard Information attribute, the file name is stored in Filename attribute, and the data is stored in Data attribute and so on. The data attribute will contain either the data in the case of small files or cluster chain in the case of large files. So if the content of a file is only a few bytes, it is stored in the MFT record itself. In the case of large file, the cluster chain is stored.

2.2 Retrieval of Undeleted Files

With the help of the data structures of the file system, we can retrieve normal file and even deleted files from some file systems. FAT file system stores file information in the Root Directory. Root directory contains filename, time stamp information and the starting cluster of a file [9]. The next cluster information is stored in File Allocation Table. To get the next cluster, read the FAT entry for the current cluster. If the entry value is EOF marker, then the file has only one cluster. Otherwise the FAT entry will contain the next cluster information. So by reading the cluster chain from FAT entries we can retrieve entire contents of a file. This is the case of normal undeleted file. Retrieval of deleted files is not completely possible in FAT through the Root Directory and FAT entries. Because whenever a file is deleted its FAT entries are reset to zeroes. So we can get only the first cluster from the Root Directory. So if the first cluster is not overwritten then the deleted file can be retrieved partially. Since the file header is available it can be confirmed whether this is a picture file or not.

In NTFS, the MFT is the main data structure that contains all the information required to retrieve files. The first record of MFT gives details about the layout of MFT, the total size of MFT and whether a particular record is currently in-use or not. The Bitmap attribute in the first record indicates the status of an MFT record. The attribute contains a sequence of bits where each bit represents the allocation status of an MFT record. If a bit is set to 1 then the corresponding MFT record is in-use. It means that the record represents a normal undeleted file. If the bit is zero then the record is not used currently and it may contain information about a file that has been deleted.

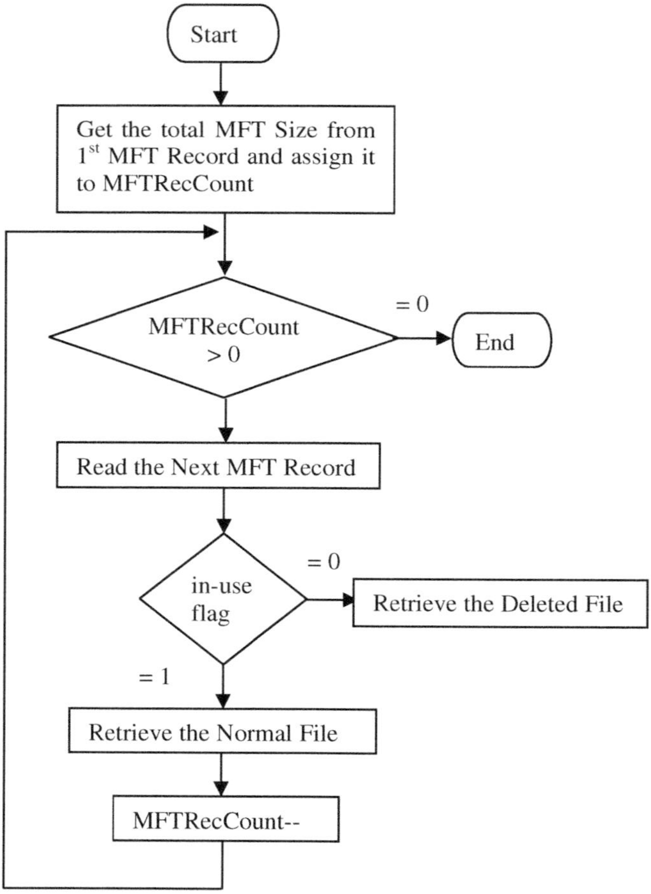

Fig. 1. Flow chart for retrieving deleted and undeleted files in NTFS

For retrieving all the files within an NTFS file system, we have to scan every record in MFT. Each record begins with an MFT header that contains a flag, the 'in-use flag' that indicates whether the current record is in use, representing a normal file or not in-use representing a deleted file [4]. The flow chart depicted in Fig. 1 shows the retrieval of deleted and undeleted files in NTFS.

On analyzing the contents of MFT Record, different attributes including filename, time stamp information and file contents can be recovered. But it is required to read the file header to check whether the retrieved file is an image file. It can be made sure that the file the analyst is looking for is an image file only after checking the file signature in the file header. Because any one can manipulate the original type of the file by changing the file extension. In such a case file is called as signature mis-match file. In the MFT record, the file contents are kept within the MFT record if the file is small and fits within the MFT record. So the contents of small image files can be read directly from the record itself [5]. On the other hand if the file is too large, then, only cluster chain information is stored in the DATA attribute. So, it is required to read the clusters to get the file contents. On checking the header portion the analyst will be able to confirm the file type. All picture files will have unique header signature, so it is easy to identify the picture file from different file types. Unique file headers and footers of different picture files that are supported by this tool are shown Table 1 in hexadecimal [2].

Table 1. Header, footer signatures

File Name	Header signature	Footer signature
bmp	424D	--
gif	47494638	003B
jpeg	FFD8	FFD9
png	89504E470D0A1A0A	49454E44
psd	38425053	--
tiff	4D4D,4949,492049	--

2.3 Retrieval of Deleted Files

A deleted file may be available in areas like lost clusters, unallocated clusters and slack space of the disk or digital media [2]. To retrieve a deleted picture from these areas, we use one or more of the file carving methods proposed by Simson Garfinkel and Joachim Metz [10]. Identifying and recovering files based on analysis of file formats is known as file carving [2]. To carve a file from digital media, a search is performed to locate the file header and continued till file footer (end of the file) is reached. The data between these two points will be extracted and analyzed to validate the file. This method of file retrieval is used when supported file system in the digital media is FAT. The approach that minimizes the search time of carving files is already explained in the paper titled "Forensic Data Carving" [2]. This method of file retrieval also supports carving files that are embedded into other files such as picture files embedded into documents and thumbs.db containing picture thumbnails. To perform this operation we use Boyer-Moore string search algorithm [7].

3 Skin Tone Filtering

Forensic image retrieval techniques deal with the important problem of retrieving different picture files having digital evidence value from a digital media and to identify the skin component in retrieved files. Skin color detection is one of the preliminary steps involved in methods like gesture recognition, hand tracking, video indexing, region of interest, face detection, etc. In any skin color detection method we have to devise a classifier to differentiate skin pixels and non-skin pixels [12]. A color space is a specification of a coordinate system and subspace within a system where each color is represented by a single point. Various color spaces are used for processing digital images [13].

The skin tone-filtering algorithm explained in this paper is applied to only picture files carved from the digital evidence and hence minimizes the filtering space.

3.1 RGB Skin Detection Technique

RGB is a color space originated from CRT display applications, when it was convenient to describe color as a combination of three colored rays (red, green and blue). It is one of the most commonly used color spaces, with a lot of research activities being based on it [3]. Therefore, skin color is classified by heuristic rules that take into account two different conditions: uniform daylight and flash or lateral illumination. The chosen skin cluster for RGB is [3]:

(R,G,B) is classified as skin if:
$R > 95$ and $G > 40$ and $B > 20$
$\max\{R,G,B\} - \min\{R,G,B\} > 15$
$|R-G| > 15$ and $R > G$ and $R > B$, ______________________first RGB filter.

In case of flashlight or daylight lateral illumination:

(R,G,B) is classified as skin if:
$| R-G | \leq 15$, $B<R$, $B<G$, ____________________________ second RGB filter.
where $R,G,B = [0 .. 255]$.

We have studied different skin tone detection techniques like HSV (Hue, Saturation and Value), HSI (Hue, Saturation and Intensity), HSL (Hue, Saturation and Lightness), YCrCb, etc. According to our analysis RGB skin detection is accurate to Indian conditions and the algorithm for the same is described below.

3.2 Algorithm to Detect Skin Tone in a Given Picture File

Step1: Read a pixel in the input image and apply first RGB filter thresholds.
Step2: If the pixel detected by the RGB filter is a skin then go to step1.
Step3: In order to ensure that missed detections do not cause any evidence to be neglected due to flashlight or daylight lateral illumination, second RGB filter is applied.

Step4: For each pixel for which first RGB thresholds are not satisfied but second RGB thresholds hold true, mark the pixel as skin pixel.
Step5: Repeat steps 1 to 4.
Step6: Compute the percentage of skin pixels in a given picture
Step7: If computed percentage of pixels is greater than or equal to 60, then selected picture is set as skin contained picture otherwise non-skin picture.

Activity diagram or flowchart of the algorithm explained is given in Fig 2. We assume a picture that contains 60 percent or more skin tone as pornographic in nature. It is very clear that pictures containing 60% or more of skin tone area could be pornographic. Sometimes this can lead to mis-matches, for example when the picture contains only faces of people and this region counts to 60% or more of the total area.

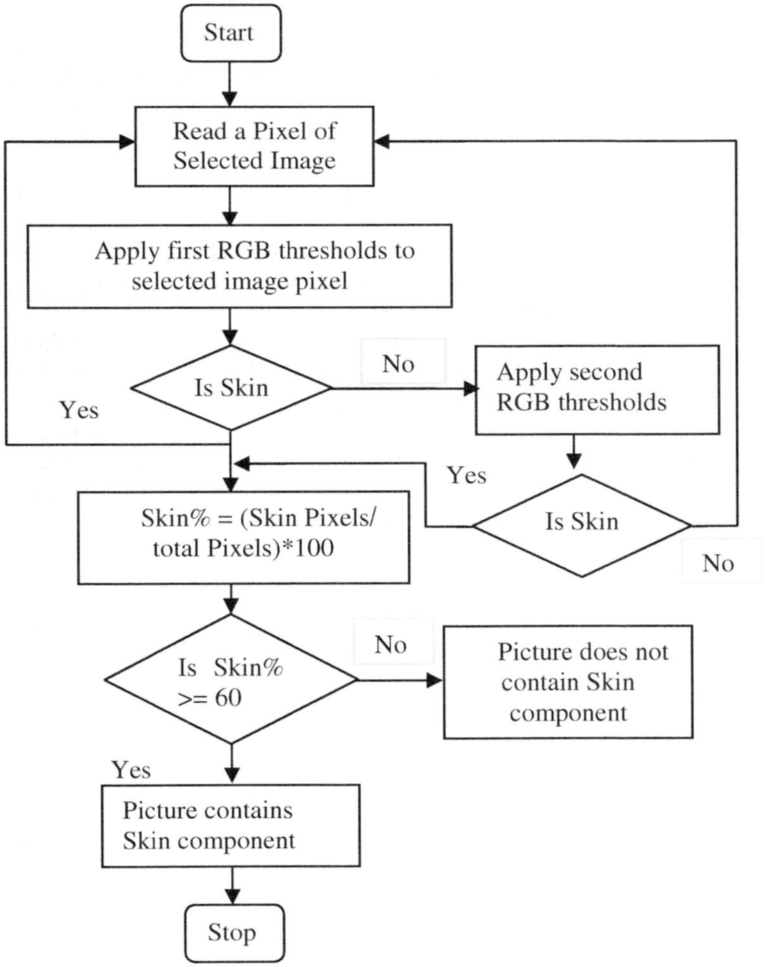

Fig. 2. Flow chart for skin tone detection algorithm

4 Results

The method for forensic image recovery was applied on a number of digital images of varying sizes to retrieve different picture files. The method "RGB skin filter" was used to find the skin component in retrieved picture files. The statistics of our analysis using the tool is given in table 2. Also, as an example, a jpeg picture with skin tone component is depicted in Fig. 3. The digital images for testing were obtained from external disks (USB or Hard disk) containing different picture files. Picture files contained in the disks were down loaded from web as well as taken using digital cameras.

Table 2. Results

Test case/ Digital image size	No: of picture files containing skin component (10-100%)	Accuracy of skin component identification (%)
Test1: 1GB	289	97.6
Test2: 2GB	573	96.0
Test3: 4GB	1396	98.3
Test4: 8GB	3178	95.7
Test5: 16GB	8612	97.8
Average accuracy of skin component identification (%) = 97.08		

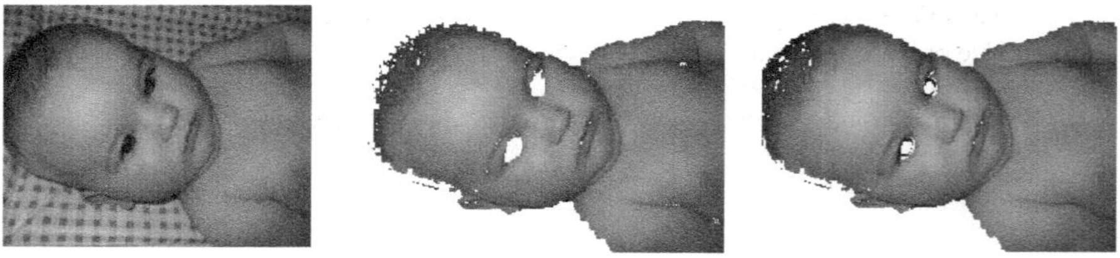

Fig. 3. a)Original image b) Using RGB filter (97% accuracy) c) Using other filters (93% accuracy)

5 Conclusion

In recent times, child grooming is growing at the pace of Moore's law. Investigating such a case is difficult due to size of the digital media also growing proportionally. Our sincere effort to develop this windows based tool, "Forensic Image Recovery with skin tone filtering technique" for analyzing pornographical picture files would benefit the Law Enforcement Agency in minimizing the overall analysis process.Presently we are providing facility to retrieve picture files like bmp, gif, jpeg, png, psd and tiff. This tool can be used to retrieve picture files from digital media that does or does not support a file system. In future, the tool can be made compatible for other operating systems.

Acknowledgement

The presented work "Forensic Image Recovery based on skin tone filtering technique" is a part of Resource Center for Cyber Forensics initiative, funded by Department of Information Technology (DIT), Ministry of Communications and Information Technology (MCIT), Govt. of India. The goal of this initiative is to establish C-DAC, Trivandrum as one of the center of excellence for research and development in Cyber Forensics technology. We would like to thank Shri. Rajan T. Joseph, Director General, Shri. Muralidharan. V, Assoc. Director, Shri. Ramani. B, Assoc. Director, Shri. Balan C, Dy. Director, C-DAC, Trivandrum, India, for providing constructive comments and help in improving the contents of this paper.

References

1. Duan, L., Cui, G., Gao, W., Zhang, H.: Adult image detection method base-on skin color model and support vector machine. In: Asian Conference on Computer Vision, Melbourne, Australia, pp. 797–800 (2002)
2. Povar, D., Bhadran, V.K.: Forensic data carving. In: Baggili, I. (ed.) ICDF2C 2010. Lecture Notes of the Institute for Computer Sciences, Social Informatics and Telecommunications Engineering, vol. 53, pp. 137–148. Springer, Heidelberg (2011)
3. Peer, P., Solina, F.: An automatic human face detection method. In: Proc. 4th Computer Vision Winter Workshop (CVWW), Rastenfeld, Austria, pp. 122–130 (1999)
4. Carrier, B.: File System Forensic Analysis. Addison Wesley Professional, Reading (2005)
5. http://www.ntfs.com
6. http://www.pcguide.com/ref/hdd/file/ntfs/arch_MFT.htm
7. Boyer, R.S., Moore, J.S.: A Fast String Searching Algorithm. Communications of the Association for Computing Machinery 20(10), 762–772 (1977)
8. http://www.jpeg.org
9. http://www.pctechguide.com/31HardDisk_File_systems.htm
10. http://www.forensicswiki.org
11. http://www.pcguide.com/ref/hdd/file/fat.htm
12. Mahmouod, T.K.: A New Fast Skin Color Detection Technique. World Academy of Science, Engineering and Technology 43 (2008)
13. Ap-apid, R.: An Algorithm for Nudity Detection. In: Proceedings of The 5th Philippine Computing Science Congress (2005)

BlackBerry Forensics: An Agent Based Approach for Database Acquisition

Satheesh Kumar Sasidharan and K.L. Thomas

Resource Centre for Cyber Forensics (RCCF)
Centre for Development of Advanced Computing (CDAC)
Thiruvananthapuram
{satheeshks,thomaskl}@cdactvm.in

Abstract. Digital forensics is a field of prime concern, as the cyber crimes are becoming dominant in the modern world. Gadgets like mobile phones and smart phones are very commonplace in today's society with powerful features. Criminals started using handheld devices for committing crimes as it is easy to handle and always portable. BlackBerry is a widely used smart phone because of its unique features. As the usage is very high, the evidentiary value of this device assumes greater importance in the litigation process. The very common methodology applied in BlackBerry forensics is the **IPD** file generation using Blackberry Desktop Manager. The methodology explained in this paper uses a different approach. Here forensic image of the BlackBerry handheld is generated using a software agent, which is injected on the device before acquisition. The tool also analyzes the forensic image and shows phone contents in different file viewers.

Keywords: BlackBerry, cell phone forensics, smart phone, hashing.

1 Introduction

Cyber crimes using mobile phones and other handheld devices are increasing day by day. Also the process of cyber forensics, which addresses such crimes, is in a paradigm shift from storage devices to handheld devices. Cyber forensics is basically the application of scientific methods for collecting, acquiring and analyzing evidence from digital sources such as hard disks, CDs, pen drives etc under forensically sound conditions. The classical computer forensics mainly looks into the computer and related storage devices. The procedures and tools, which are used in the classical computer forensics, cannot be applied to handheld devices. The reason is handheld devices use embedded systems and are totally different from hard disks and other storage devices. To address such devices a branch of computer forensics called small-scale digital device forensics (SSDDF) was evolved. SSDDF deals with the forensics acquisition and analysis of Personal Digital Assistants (PDAs), Cell Phones, Embedded Chip devices, Gaming devices and Audio/Video devices. Separate tools and procedures are used to forensically analyze each category of these devices. In cell

A. Abraham et al. (Eds.): ACC 2011, Part I, CCIS 190, pp. 552–561, 2011.

phone forensics the acquisition of phone memory requires specific forensics tools based on the type of operating system used in the device. The acquisition software, which is developed for windows mobile, will not work with BlackBerry or Symbian or any other type of mobile phones. That means separate imaging modules are required to address each type of mobile phones or smart phones. Here this paper discusses the acquisition and analysis of BlackBerry mobile phones. Many software as well as hardware tools are available for acquisition and analysis of BlackBerry phones. Most of these tools employ the widely used IPD [13] file generation method or its variant.

In this paper, we suggest an agent-based approach to acquire the evidence from Blackberry handheld device. Here the device is connected to a desktop computer and an agent, which is a **.cod** file, is temporarily injected into the device. After acquisition, this .cod file is removed from the device. This paper describes details of the method applied and the result obtained.

2 Digital Evidential Principles

Digital evidence has some unique features when compared to the normal physical evidence. It is intangible in nature, easily tampered and highly volatile also. Since all type of evidence has to be accepted by the court of law, digital evidence also needs to be produced in an acceptable manner to the court. The conventional forensics methods, when we apply, cannot ensure the authenticity and completeness of the evidence. So digital evidence needs to be identified and collected in a forensically sound manner and this imposes following principles that ensure the integrity of data. The Association of Chief Police Officers (ACPO) Good Practice Guide for Computer based Electronic Evidence [16] suggests four principles when dealing with digital evidence. They are:

1) No actions performed by investigators or their agents should change data contained on digital devices or storage media.
2) In exceptional cases, individuals accessing original data must be competent to do so and be able to explain their actions.
3) An audit trail or other record of all applied processes must be created and preserved for an independent third party review.
4) The person in charge of the investigation has overall responsibility for ensuring the above-mentioned procedures and principles are followed.

The first principle states that no action performed should change the data contained in digital devices. This is however not possible with mobile phones or smart phone since the phone has to be kept switched on in order to acquire data from it. Switching on the phone or connecting the phone to a computer will very likely change some data, even without explicitly doing so. This means that in the best case, data must be modified as little as possible [3]. Since BlackBerry is a hand held device, forensics procedures and processes must be applied with respect to these evidential principles.

2.1 BlackBerry Device

BlackBerry is a mobile device developed by Canadian company Research In Motion (RIM). Initially this device was mainly used for the push e-mail service. But today BlackBerry is a powerful messaging phone with number of messaging features including auto-text, auto-correct, text prediction, push Facebook, Twitter and Myspace notifications, push Ebay notifications, push instant BlackBerry messenger etc. BlackBerry also functions like a personal digital assistant and a smart phone with address book, calendar, memo pad, tasks, Bluetooth, SMS, MMS, etc.

The operating system in BlackBerry is a proprietary one and the company RIM has not disclosed its internal structure and other details yet. So it's really a challenging task to forensically acquire and analyze such a device as the necessary and sufficient information are unavailable. BlackBerry stores data in databases. The table 1 below shows important databases associated with BlackBerry smart phones. Since these data are stored as databases, during forensics analysis, we need to acquire such databases first and then interpret the data properly. The BlackBerry provides Desktop Manager software, which is normally used to synchronize the device with desktop PC. It also helps to perform a back up of these databases, creating an IPD file.

Table 1. Important databases associated with BlackBerry smart phones

Address Book	Calendar Options	Memos	Recipient Cache
Address Book Options	Categories	Message List Options	Ribbon Bar Positions
Alarm Options	Content Store	Messages	RMS Databases
Attachment Data	Custom Words Collection	Options	Service Book
Attachment Options	Default Service Selector	Phone Call Logs	SMS Messages
AutoText	Email Filters	Phone Hotlist	Tasks
Browser Bookmarks	Email Settings	Phone Options	TLS Options
Browser Data Cache	Firewall Options	Policy	Trusted Key Store
Browser Folders	Folders	Profiles	Random Pool
Browser Options	Handheld Agent	Profiles Options	WTLS Options
Browser Push Options	Handheld Key Store	Purged Messages	WLAN Profiles
Browser URLs	Key Store Options	Quick Contacts	WordToGoPrefs
Calendar	Memo Pad Options	WAP Push Messages	Voice Activated Dialing Options

2.2 IPD File Generation

The easiest way to analyze a BlackBerry phone is to generate an **.ipd** file using BlackBerry desktop software. The desktop software is freely downloadable from the blackberry website. Here this software supports to generate a database back up which will be an exact copy of the databases present in the device. The ipd file is generated with a default filename format *Backup-(date).ipd*. Here date corresponds to the created date of ipd file. As the ipd file has a proprietary structure, the normal file viewers cannot show the content of ipd files. So separate file viewers are used to display databases content present in the ipd file. ABC Amber BlackBerry Converter [11] is one of such software. The ipd file can also be loaded in a BlackBerry emulator so that the emulator functions like the real device with all databases exactly as present in the device. Here in the proposed approach, we are not creating any ipd file. Instead logically acquiring BlackBerry device using an external agent application.

3 The Proposed Approach

In this approach, the BlackBerry Desktop Manager is not used for creating the *ipd* file or any other backup file. The proposed approach is an agent based one. An acquisition agent, which is a small programme, is uploaded to the BlackBerry device for accessing and reading the database present in the device. This agent is also capable of exchanging data between the device and desktop PC. This approach uses Client-Server architecture with the agent acting as the server. The client side programme running on the desktop PC receives the data sent by server programme and stores database as an image file. This approach is depicted in the Fig.1 given below. The image created is a forensic image of databases such as Address book, notepad, calls logs, files, folders, etc present in the device. The image file is created in a specific format other than the ipd, so that it can be easily decoded through analysis software instead of using ABC Amber BlackBerry or its kind. We have also developed an analysis module, which will decode all the data present in the image file in separate file viewers.

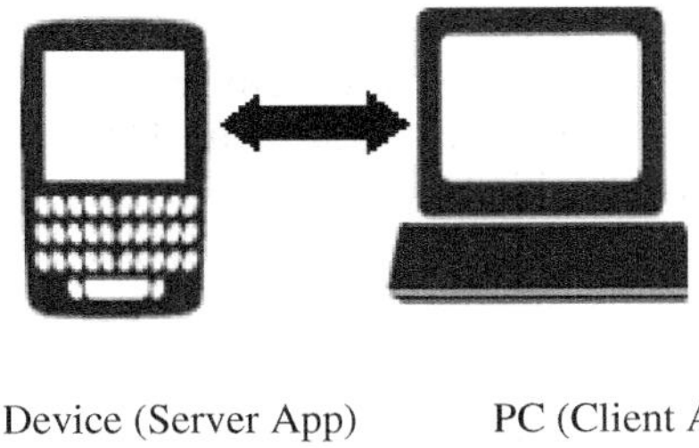

Fig. 1. Client-Server approach

3.1 Agent File Accessing BlackBerry Data

BlackBerry uses its own operating system and proprietary file system structure for its functioning and data storage. We cannot access the databases present in BlackBerry device directly from PC, without using BlackBerry desktop software. In this case, an application installed on the device can only access the databases present in it. So, we need to inject an external application into the device even though it contradicts the ACPO good forensic practice. Here we are making changes as little as possible in accordance with the Brian Carrier [3] principles. The .cod file is developed in BlackBerry Java Development Environment (JDE). The JDE provides different application programming interfaces (API) to access and read data from different database files present in BlackBerry. We identified the data, which have more forensic value and could access and read such data without modifying it. The .cod file that we developed in the JDE environment has been named as **BlackBerryImager.cod.** The name represents itself as an imaging application for Blackberry device.

3.2 Uploading Agent to Blackberry Device

For proper working of this software tool, the java based agent (.cod) file needs to uploaded on the blackberry device before acquisition starts. We make use of the *javaloader.exe* to upload ***.cod*** file into the device under acquisition. *Javaloader.exe* is part of the BlackBerry JDE software development package. This executable file is used for low-level debugging and application loading on to the BlackBerry device. It is a command line application that runs from Windows command prompt. We uploaded the file to BlackBerry device using the command *javaloader -usb load BlackBerryImager.cod*

3.3 Agent Based Acquisition

BlackBerry phone acquisition is carried out using a Client-Server approach. We have developed a client application, which we can install on the PC. Similarly a server application was developed which is to be copied on the BlackBerry Phone. First we need to connect the Blackberry device to the PC using USB cable and then through the client application, we are copying the .cod file to the desktop of the blackberry device using the javaloader. Now the server application is to be initiated manually from the blackberry device. In the client side, there are different options for acquisition is present. Depending up on the options the user select, the server is initiated to access and read the databases from BlackBerry device. Also at the same time, the server programme sends databases to the client side. The communication is established through the USB port so that the data can be sent to the PC. The connection from desktop computer to a BlackBerry device is implemented through *IChannelEvents* interface using *BBDevMgr.exe* file. Once the connection is established data transfer can be easily carried out. We create an image file at the PC side, which is nothing but the content of the BlackBerry databases. Some of the APIs, which we used, require digital signature from BlackBerry authority for accessing the databases. So APIs were signed from the BlackBerry signing authority and we used the signed BlackBerryImager.cod file for acquisition. Fig.2 given below illustrates the agent-based acquisition process.

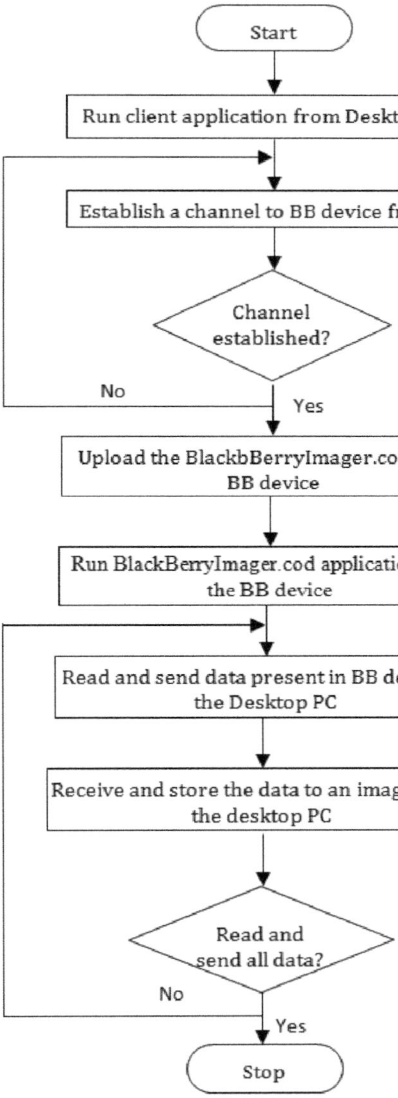

Fig. 2. Agent-based acquisition process

3.4 Authentication of Evidence

Authentication of evidence is a major step in digital forensics process. Taking the hash value of the digital evidence does this. The commonly used hash algorithms are MD5 and SHA1. Our imaging tool not only acquires the data, but also takes the MD5 hash value of each and every file present in the device. Like hard disks and pen drives, we cannot prove the authenticity of the evidence of mobile phones or smart phones using a singe media hash value. This is because we need to switch on and connect such devices to the PC each time before acquisition where we cannot avoid the internal changes happening during the so-called cold booting. So it is a practice in hand held device forensics that to take hash values of each and every file present in the device than depending on a single media (device) hash. Changes to the files other than the system files will occur only if it is accessed manually. So a change in hash value of the files (strongly) indicates that it is manually accessed or modified. A change in media hash value does not mean that the device data is purposefully manipulated.

4 BlackBerry Acquisition and Analysis Tool

We have developed a complete forensics tool called BAAT for acquisition as well as analysis of BlackBerry phones. This software tool contains two modules; one is for agent based acquisition and the other is for analysis. The acquisition part includes many features like case data collection where we can input the investigator details, the case details, place and nature of crime etc. Also there is an option to select databases for acquisition where we can include necessary or exclude unnecessary databases. During the acquisition process, only the selected databases will be acquired from the Blackberry device. After acquisition the tool will generate an html based report with the device details and database details. The report also includes hash values of databases present in the device.

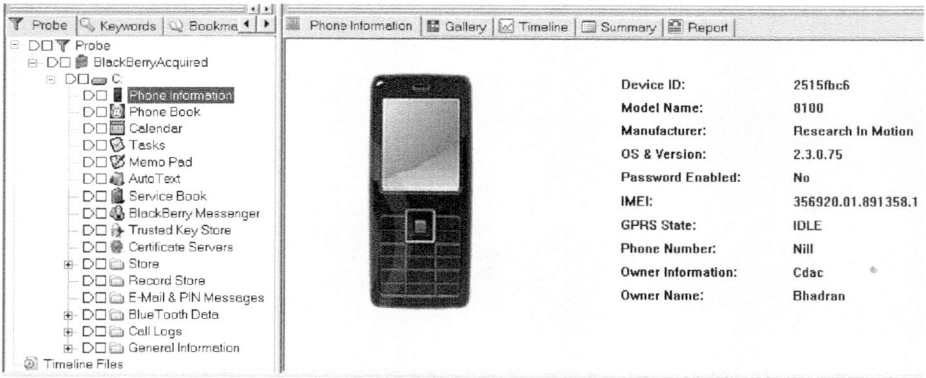

Fig. 3. Blackberry Phone Information

Usually, the IPD file, after creating, is loaded on third party software like ABC Amber BlackBerry to see the contents. The IPD file structure is used to develop such file viewers. Since have created the image file in a specific format, we decoded the image file and displayed all the databases such as Call logs, Phonebook, Picture files, in separate file viewers. The analysis part shows the folders in a tree view. When you click on the tree view it will expand to the sub folders and the files under the folders are displayed in a table view. In addition to hex view and text view of data, there is a gallery viewer where we can display all the pictures piles. Also facilities for searching, bookmaking etc are also given in the analyzer module. The important feature of this tool is that it will generate a report of the analysis done with details of the device such as IMEI number, device id, operating system version etc. Also another feature we have given in the tool, which helps the user to add important files or databases in the report for verification by the court. Fig.3 given below shows the phone information acquired from a blackberry phone which includes the Device ID, Model Name, Manufacturer, OS version, IMEI number etc.

The Fig.4 shows Phone Book (Contacts) details acquired from a blackberry phone. Here it displays Name, Mobile phone number, Home phone number, Office phone number, Email address etc.

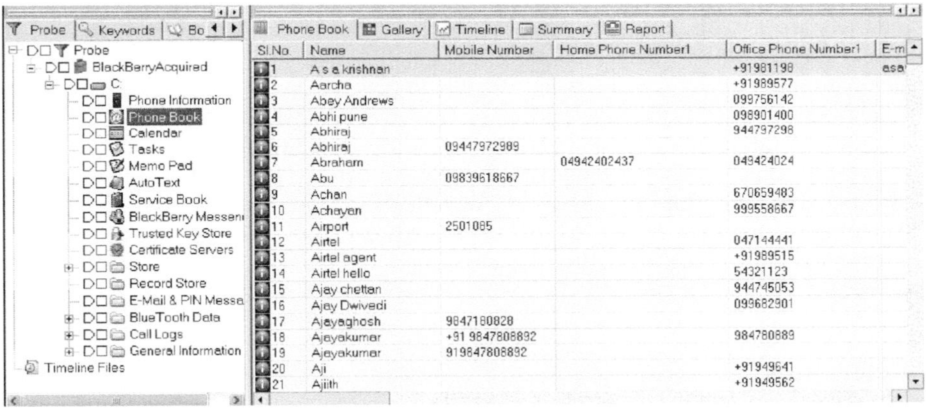

Fig. 4. Phone Book entries

4.1 Advantages of the Tool

We tested this tool with BlackBerry pearl 8100 and 8230 devices. Using this tool, we could successfully acquire Phone Information, Calendar, Phonebook, Tasks, Memo Pad, Auto Text, Service Book, BlackBerry Messenger, Trusted Key Store, Certification Servers, Record Store, E-mail and PIN Messages, Bluetooth Info, Bluetooth Log, Call Logs, RAM Info, Radio Info, Display Details, Coverage, Clipboard Info, Backlight Info, Audio Info and Code modules. In addition to this we could logically read and copy all the files and folders present in the BlackBerry device, which is called the Content Store. One of the major advantages of our tool is that it can read the Phone information, which includes the IMEI number, Device ID and OS version, which are important in a court of law. The IMEI number is unique to every device. When we give a forensic report to a court, it should be complete in every aspect. Since there are number of BlackBerry phones and a single media hash value cannot assure the credibility of evidence, we have to use other features also to prove device identity and evidence authenticity. The major tools in the market do not support such features. Another thing is that since we used the BlackBerry JDE APIs for the development of server program, we could directly read and parse whatever data the API supported to access. This is another advantage of using agent-based approach. The databases like Bluetooth log information, BlackBerry messenger, etc are not parsed in many of the major tools in the market. Also after the acquisition, we remove the external agent from the BlackBerry device. Effort has been taken to make the agent program as small as possible, so as to limit the changes that makes in the device as minimum as possible. Change, which is unavoidable, in the device to a certain extent is acceptable in mobile phone forensics process, as per the NIST standards.

5 Conclusion

Forensic analysis of BlackBerry device is a challenging area as its structure and other internals are not disclosed by the RIM. Most of the research done is based on the BlackBerry Desktop Manger creating an .ipd file. We imaged the device with an agent installed on the device where we could acquire some additional information, which are not provided by the ipd file, or any other forensics tools in the market. We also developed an analysis module, which directly interpret the image created by the imaging module. Whatever data we acquired, we could parse it, as the databases are directly accessed from the device. But we could not read and parse the SMS databases as the present version of the BlackBerry JDE does not supports API to access SMS databases from the device, which we left as the future work of this research.

References

1. Jansen, W., Ayers, R.: Guidelines on cell phone forensics, National Institute of Standards and Technology, Special Publication 800-101 (2007)
2. Ayers, R., Jansen, W., Cilleros, N., Daniellou, R.: Cell phone forensic tools: An overview and analysis. Technical Report NISTIR 7250, National Institute of Standards and Technology (2005)
3. Carrier, B.: Defining Digital Forensic Examination and Analysis Tools. In: Digital Forensics Research Workshop II (August 2002)
4. Mellars, B.: Forensic Examination of Mobile Phones. Digital Investigation. The International Journal of Digital Forensics & Incident Response 1(4), 266–272 (2004)
5. Punja, C.S.: BlackBerry Forensics, Mobile Forensics World Conference, Chicago: Calgary Police Service, Technological Crimes Team (2009)
6. Kessler, G.: Cell Phone Analysis: Technology, Tools, and Processes. Mobile Forensics World. Purdue University, Chicago (2010)
7. Mislan, R.P., Casey, E., Kessler, G.C.: The Growing Need for On-Scene Triage of Mobile Devices. Digital Investigation 6(3-4), 112–124 (2010)
8. Punja, S., Mislan, R.: Mobile Device Analysis. Small Scale Digital Device Forensics Journal 2(1), 2–4 (2008)
9. McCarthy, P.: Forensic analysis of mobile phones. Master's thesis, University of South Australia (2005)
10. ABC Amber BlackBerry Converter from `http://abc-amber-blackberry-converter.en.softonic.com/`

11. Ayers, R., Dankar, A., Mislan, R.: Hashing Techniques for Mobile Device Forensics. Small Scale Digital Device Forensics Journal, 1–6 (2009)
12. Research In Motion. (n.d.). BlackBerry Device Software Version 5.0, retrieved from http://us.blackberry.com/apps-software/devices/
13. Harrington, M. (n.d.). IPD Files Demystified, retrieved from http://mobileforensics.wordpress.com/category/black-berry/
14. Napieralski, B. (n.d.). How to Easily Process a BlackBerry Device, retrieved from http://www.mfi-training.com/forum
15. BlackBerry Database details from, RIM KB Doc ID KB03974, http://www.blackberry.com
16. ACPO Good Practice Guide for Computer based Electronic Evidence, retrieved from http://cryptome.org/acpo-guide.htm

Scattered Feature Space for Malware Analysis

P. Vinod, V. Laxmi, and M.S. Gaur

Department of Computer Engineering
Malaviya National Institute of Technology, Jaipur, India
{vinodp,vlaxmi,gaurms}@mnit.ac.in

Abstract. Malware prevention methods are gaining attention amongst researchers due to proliferation of new variants. Malware detection methods can be basically categorized as *static* and *dynamic*. In this paper, we investigate the use of features like Portable Executable (PE) headers and body (mnemonic n–gram, instruction opcodes) for classifying the executables as malware or benign. The features are preprocessed using *Scatter Criterion* to reduce the processing overheads incurred during training and testing phase by reducing the dimensionality of the feature space. The results of our experimental study show that the proposed methods can detect packed and obfuscated variants of malware as well as classify malware and benign executables. Through our proposed work we also highlight that the PE Header fields are less obfuscated in comparison with the raw data present in body of executables. Thus, evolutionary possibilities are more pronounced in malware code or Hex dump other than PE Header Fields.

1 Introduction

The term Malware refers to viruses, worms, Trojans, adware, botnets, spyware etc. Malware exploits vulnerabilities of Internet, open network ports, operating system, devices etc. for infecting machine and for its propagation. Most of the antivirus vendors use signatures of malware for malware detection. A signature is a unique byte/string pattern that acts as finger print for identifying malicious codes. The main limitation of signature based detection method are (a) lack of semantic knowledge of the program (b) human expertise required to prepare the signature or (c) instability towards obfuscation techniques (d) frequent updation of signature repository, thereby increasing the size of database (signature database). Thus, all the above mentioned facts related to signature based techniques must be complimented with *non–signature* methods.

Our research targets Portable Executable (PE) file formats of malware and benign samples. The motivation for PE samples was obtained by examining the frequency of the samples (in PE format) submitted to Virus Total [18] website. This site provides assistance for scanning suspicious files and DLLs using various malware scanners. We extract mnemonic n–gram ($n = 4$), instruction opcodes, PE header fields from malware (packed, unpacked, obfuscated) and benign executables. The features are preprocessed using *Scatter Criterion* to remove redundant features. The samples are trained and tested using classifiers supported by WEKA [17]. Our experimental results demonstrate that the proposed method using *non–signature* based approach is capable of (a) classifying malware and benign samples (b) detecting packed and obfuscated malware.

A. Abraham et al. (Eds.): ACC 2011, Part I, CCIS 190, pp. 562–571, 2011.

This paper is structured as follows: In Section 2, we review prior work in the area of malware analysis and detection. In Section 3, we briefly outline our proposed approach. Section 4 and Section 5 introduce executable features and preprocessing using *Scatter Criterion*. Evaluation metrics are discussed in Section 6. Experimental setup and discussion of the results are explained in Section 7 and Section 8. Finally concluding remarks and directions for future work is covered in Section 9.

2 Related Work

Yuvul *et al* [20] proposed an Early Detection and Response system for synthesizing web traffic. The traffic is monitored using machine learning methods to extract suspicious (variants) or unseen malicious samples. Two types of features are extracted from each sample (a) 5–grams binary representation (b) Portable Executable Header data. Tzu–Yen Wang [15] proposed a novel method for detecting unseen malware in Portable Executable (PE) format. Static analysis is performed to extract PE header entries and the classifier (Support Vector Machine) is trained using reduced features. The proposed model detects viruses and worms with considerable accuracy but the detection accuracy for Trojans and backdoors requires improvement. Ronny Merkel [12] *et al* proposed a statistical detection model for detecting malware executables. PE header features (23 attributes) are extracted and the quality of each feature is estimated. A hypothesis based statistical model is generated, which is evaluated with the classification algorithms supported by WEKA [17].

Kephart *et al* [5] proposed a signature based method which examines the source code of computer viruses and estimates the probability of instructions appearing in legitimate programs. The authors in [1] proposed a *"phylogeny"* model, used in areas of bioinformatics. The feature extraction technique proposed is n-gram and fixed permutation is applied on the code to generate new sequences, called n-perms. A detection method using data mining methods is proposed in [14]. It is a heuristics based technique to detect unknown computer viruses using *decision trees* and *Naïve Bayesian* network algorithm. Non–signature based method using Self-organizing maps (SOMs) was proposed in [3] by Seon Yoo *et al.* The infected files project a high density area in SOM for malware samples. Malicious code detection using text categorization and imbalance problem is proposed by authors in [8].

The authors in [4] extract n–grams from the benign and malicious executables and use *k-nearest neighbour algorithm* to identify the unseen instances. Henchiri *et al* [2] present a method based on generic features applicable to different families of viruses. The classification accuracies of different classifiers are evaluated with the proposed classifier. The developed classifier reports higher detection rate. In their proposed work[6], the authors extract the byte code features, relevant n–grams and evaluate on various inductive methods. The authors [7] proposed a method to identify file types using 1-gram analysis of binary contents. Their work gives an insight into the distribution of the general pattern predominant over files that can be used to predict security violations over files. A non–signature based method using byte level file content is proposed in [16]. This method computes diverse features in block–wise manner over the byte level content of the file. The authors in [21] proposed a method using text categorization for malware analysis. The experimental studies show that the proposed method has potential for automated malware detection and analysis. The authors in [13] proposed a new method for detecting variants of malware making use of Opcode–sequences. This approach is based on the frequency of appearance of opcodes. The relevant opcodes are mined and assigned with certain weights.

3 Proposed Method for Malware Analysis

In our proposed method we collected malware samples from VX Heavens [19] and some of the samples are created using virus construction kits NGVCK (Next Generation Virus Kit) and VCL (Virus Creation Lab) [19]. The benign samples constitute executables from fresh installation of Windows XP operating system (`System32 folder`), `CYGWIN` utility, games, media players, browsers etc. From each executable, features (mnemonic n–gram, instruction opcode, PE Header entries) are extracted. Each category of feature is refined using feature reduction method such as *Scatter Criterion*. Reduction of feature size is important as it reduces the processing overhead of classifiers during the training and testing phase. Classifiers are trained using the feature vector table (of a part of data set) constructed by considering each category of feature (mnemonic 4–gram, instruction opcode, PE Header information). Classification model is tested using unknown samples not considered during training. Figure 1 depicts the proposed method used for identifying malware samples.

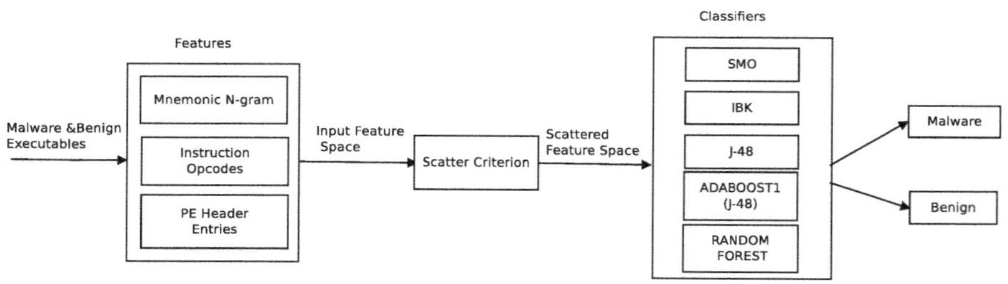

Fig. 1. Proposed Method for Malware Analysis and Detection. Scattered feature space is a subset of input space and each feature vector consists of only prominent features.

4 Portable Executable Features

Features are meaningful information or patterns occurring in the data set. In our proposed method, we have considered three different type of features (a) mnemonic 4–gram (b) principal instruction opcodes (c) PE Header entries. Brief explanation of these features is given below.

- **Mnemonic n–gram:** n–grams are overlapping sub–strings collected in sliding window fashion. Basically, they are sequences of length n. We have extracted mnemonic

4–gram from assembly code of malware and benign programs, motivated by our previous work [10].

- **Principal Instruction Opcodes:** Prominent instruction opcodes of malware and benign samples are extracted by methods proposed in [11]. The instruction opcodes are extracted by (a) Identification of valid PE samples (b) Identification and Extraction of executable sections and (c) Extraction of instruction opcode from raw data existing in the executable sections.
- **PE Header Entries:** Portable Executable (PE) is a file format supported by Microsoft Windows operating system [9]. Some of the PE header entries like *MajorOperatingSystemVersion*, *MinorOperatingSystemVersion*, *SizeOfImage*, *SizeOfHeaders*, *Characteristics* etc. can be used as features.

5 Feature Processing

All attributes extracted from a sample might not carry useful information. Irrelevant attributes must be eliminated to avoid training and testing overheads. In our proposed method, we have used *Scatter Criterion* for feature reduction. *Scatter criterion* selects a feature based on the ratio of the *mixture* scatter and *within* class scatter. The mixture scatter is the sum of *within* and *between–class* scatter. High value of this ratio indicates prominence of the feature for classification. The *within-class* scatter for any feature f is computed as

$$S_{w,f} = \sum_{i=0}^{C} P_i S_{if}$$

where, S_{if} is the variance for a class C_i (malware or benign) and P_i is the prior probability for a class C_i. The variance S_{if} can be computed as follows:

$$S_{if} = \frac{1}{N} \sum_{j=1}^{N} (F_{jif} - \overline{F_{if}})^2$$

and $P_i = \frac{1}{C}$

Between class scatter, S_{bf}, is the variance of class center with respect to a global center. It can be computed as:

$$S_{mf} = \sum_{i=1}^{N} P_i (\overline{F_{if}} - \overline{F_f})^2$$

$$MixtureScatter = S_{w,f} + S_{bf}$$

Scatter Criterion for f_{th} feature is thus,

$$H_f = \frac{S_{mf}}{S_{w,f}}$$

A large value of H_f, for a feature f, indicates that the feature is more discriminant for classification purpose.

6 Evaluation Metrics

True positive (TP) are the number of malicious samples classified as malware, whereas, True negative (TN) are total benign samples classified as benign. The performance of a classifier can be measured by primarily checking the *TPR* and *TNR* values which are also known as *sensitivity* and *specificity* respectively [23].

- **True Positive Rate (TPR):** Is the ratio of actual positives correctly classified as positives, defined as $TPR = TP/(TP+FN)$.
- **False Positive Rate (FPR):** The proportion of benign samples incorrectly classified as malicious. This is also called *false alarm rate* or *fall out*, defined as $FPR = FP/(FP+TN)$.
- **True Negative Rate (TNR):** The proportion of benign samples correctly identified as benign, defined as $TNR = TN/(TN+FP)$.
- **False Negative Rate (FNR):** The proportion of cases in which a test produces negative outcome for a malicious sample, defined as $FNR = FN/(FN+TP)$.

In case of a good protection system, high values of *TPR* and *TNR*, along with low *FPR* and *FNR* are desired. This would ascertain capability of malware scanners to correctly distinguish samples as malware or benign.

7 Experimental Setup

The experiments were performed on an Intel Pentium Core 2 Duo 2.19 GHz processor with 2GB RAM with Microsoft Windows XP SP2 installed on the machines. Dataset consisting of 4384 executables in PE format is collected. This dataset contains 2781 malware downloaded from VX Heaven [19]. We obtained 1603 benign programs some were obtained from **System32** folder of fresh installation of Windows XP operating system, and some from **Cygwin** utility, games, Internet Browsers, media players and other sources. The training set consisted of 2679 samples (malware = 1594 and benign = 1085). Two Test sets were created (a) Test set1 consisting of 693 obfuscated malware 518 benign samples(b) Test set2 consisting of 494 packed malware and 518 benign samples. The test set was kept separate and none of these samples are included in training. The experiments were performed using *SMO*, *IBK*, *AdaBoost1* (with J-48 as base classifier), *J-48* and *Random Forest* algorithms implemented in WEKA [17]. The results were evaluated using the evaluation metrics defined in Section 6. The experiments were performed on three category of features (a) *mnemonic n–gram* (b) *Instruction Opcodes* and (c) *PE Header Entries*. We retrieved 50 *mnemonic n–gram* of 250 mnemonics, 37 *Instruction Opcode* of 193 opcodes and 35 *PE Header Entries* features of 48 entries after applying *Scatter Criterion*.

Table 2, Table 3 and Table 4 show the outcome of classification using both test sets viz. Test set1 and Test set2.

Table 1. Top 10 Prominent features extracted using Scatter Criterion

Mnemonic 4–gram	Instruction Opcode	PE Header Fields
cmpjzmovlea	0x0F84	.data
cmpjnbmovmov	0x0F85	.text
movmovjmpcmp	0x33C0	Characteristics
movjmpmovcmp	0x50	SizeOfRawData[.data]
pushmovsubmov	0x51	SizeOfRawData[.text]
movmovmovadd	0x53	.reloc
movmovmovpop	0x55	.idata
movcmpjzcmp	0x56	SizeOfRawData[.reloc]
movmovmovcmp	0x57	Subsystem
submovmovmov	0x59	SizeOfRawData[.bss]

Table 2. Classification results of 4–gram feature vector

Classifiers	Test Set1				Test Set2			
	TPR	FNR	TNR	FPR	TPR	FNR	TNR	FPR
SMO	0.960	0.040	0.613	0.387	0.976	0.024	0.613	0.387
IBK	**0.947**	**0.053**	**0.862**	**0.138**	**0.968**	**0.032**	**0.862**	**0.138**
AdaBoost1	0.924	0.076	0.837	0.163	0.950	0.050	0.837	0.163
J–48	0.933	0.067	0.831	0.169	0.962	0.038	0.831	0.169
Random Forest	**0.944**	**0.056**	**0.837**	**0.163**	**0.960**	**0.040**	**0.837**	**0.163**

Table 3. Classification results of prominent Instruction Opcodes as feature vector.

Classifiers	Test Set1				Test Set2			
	TPR	FNR	TNR	FPR	TPR	FNR	TNR	FPR
SMO	0.961	0.038	0.239	0.76	0.981	0.018	0.252	0.747
IBK	0.924	0.075	0.891	0.108	0.963	0.036	0.85	0.149
AdaBoost1	0.922	0.077	0.894	0.101	0.956	0.043	0.854	0.145
J–48	0.927	0.072	0.893	0.106	0.953	0.046	0.833	0.166
Random Forest	**0.938**	**0.061**	**0.891**	**0.108**	**0.976**	**0.023**	**0.84**	**0.159**

Table 4. Classification results of prominent PE Header Entries as feature vector.

Classifiers	Test Set1				Test Set2			
	TPR	FNR	TNR	FPR	TPR	FNR	TNR	FPR
SMO	0.870	0.129	0.888	0.111	0.9534	0.046	0.888	0.111
IBK	0.602	0.399	0.776	0.223	0.9736	0.026	0.776	0.223
J–48	0.837	0.163	0.832	0.167	0.9271	0.072	0.832	0.167
AdaBoost1	0.863	0.137	0.899	0.103	0.945	0.054	0.899	0.103
Random Forest	**0.969**	**0.0303**	**0.901**	**0.0984**	**0.981**	**0.018**	**0.901**	**0.0984**

8 Results and Analysis

The experiments were performed on malware and benign samples (both in PE format) and results were evaluated using evaluation metrics. From each malware sample three different features like *mnemonic n–gram*, *instruction opcodes*, and *PE Header Entries* was extracted and feature space was reduced using *Scatter Criterion* to obtain prominent features.

8.1 Classification Results

The experimental results demonstrate that the non–signature based method discussed above can also be used to classify executables as malware and benign. The experimental results also illustrate that the proposed method of malware analysis can also distinguish packed and clean malware samples.

If we observe the classification results tabulated in Table 2 to Table 4 we can find that the performance of *Random Forest* classifier is better than other classifiers. *Random Forest* is an ensemble of many trees where each tree votes for a class. The classifier collects the maximum votes for all trees in the forest for classifying instances. The main reason for the better performance of this classifier is due to *bagging* and *boosting* properties [22].

We can contemplate that better classification accuracies may be obtained only with *PE Header Entries*. This may be because malware variants used in study had little obfuscation in header fields but mnemonic/opcodes may have changed because of obfuscation. The tabulated results also explains that the evolutionary possibilities are more when features are extracted using body information compared to the header fields. Inclusion of header field information may improve malware detection probability.

8.2 Effect of Feature Vector Lengths (PE Header)

Figure 2 depicts the values of TPR and FPR plotted for different feature lengths extracted using *Scatter Criteria*. We can observe that when feature length is 35 (PE Header Information), better values of TPR and FPR are obtained compared to other feature lengths. The figure also shows that initial classification is also possible with feature length of 5 PE Header Entries, where the values of TPR and FPR are 81.2% and 76.06% respectively. This indicates the effectiveness of *Scatter Criteria* for better classification of executables (malware & benign), even with small feature vector length (i.e. 5 prominent PE Header Fields).

8.3 Prominent PE Header Entries

To verify whether prominent features extracted using *Scatter Criteria* are capable of differentiating malware, benign and packed malware executables, we computed the percentage of appearance of these features in respective samples. Using *Scatter Criterion*, we extracted prominent 35 features having high scatter ratio from PE samples (malware and benign). Top two prominent features are `.data` and `.text`. Least prominent features for classification are `AddressOfEntryPoint` and `LoaderFlag`, as they have minimum value of scatter ratio.

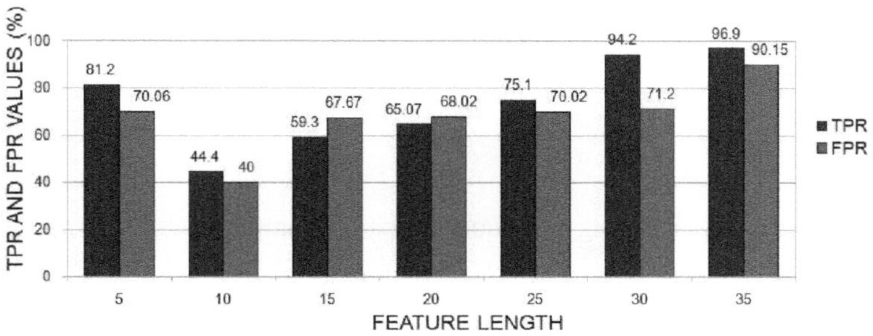

Fig. 2. Effect of feature vector length on TPR and FPR values (in %)

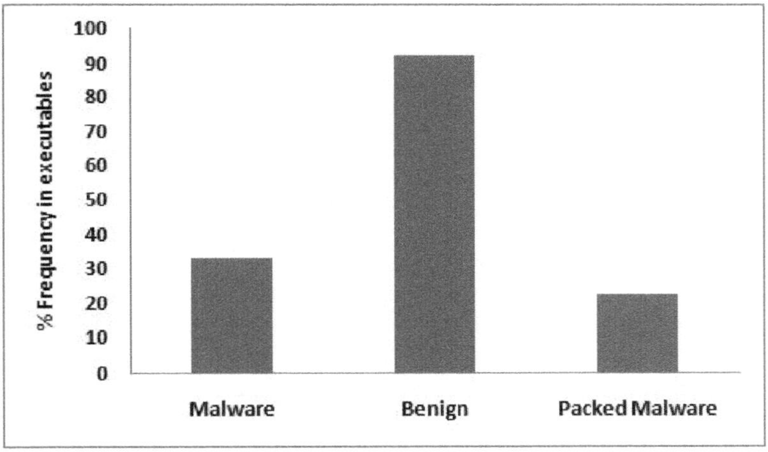

Fig. 3. Frequency of occurrence of most predominant feature in various categories of executables

Figure 3 depicts the percentage of malware (packed/clean) and benign samples consisting of `.data` section. From Figure 3, we can observe that malware (packed/clean) executables can be easily classified from benign samples. This can be easily visualized by a high difference in the average frequency of instances consisting of `.data` attribute for both malware and benign executables. Like wise, we can notice from the same figure that clean malware and packed malware samples can also be differentiated even though the difference is less as compared to malware versus benign sample. Results highlight that features with high scatter ratio play a vital role in accurate classification.

8.4 Performance of Classifiers

Performance of decision tree classifiers (*J48* and *AdaBoost1* with J-48 as base classifier) is not better in comparison to *Random Forest*. Some of the reasons may be (a) attributes are correlated (b) partial overlap of classes (c) works on the principal of local decision, i.e. if one of the decision fails, error propagates to all other trees (d) improper scaling of all decision factors to common units. The results highlight that the initial analysis of malware and benign samples can be performed using PE header fields.

9 Conclusions

Malicious software is emerging as a major threat for computer systems. The number of new malware variants is increasing at an alarming rate because of complex obfuscation techniques employed by malware authors. The signature based detection techniques fail to scale in detection of malicious software. In order to address the problem faced using signature based method, we have proposed *non–signature* based techniques for malware analysis. The features are extracted considering the body information (*mnemonic–*4gram, *instruction opcodes*) collected from assembly code, Hex dump and PE Header entries. We have tested features extracted from *mnemonic* and *instruction opcodes* that are likely to undergo obfuscation. Less obfuscation is likely on PE Header fields compared to raw data collected from assembly code or Hex dump of the malicious executable. Results shows that better classification is obtained using *Random Forest* classifier using header entries as feature. This classifiers also performs better in respect of low false alarms. The proposed method is capable of identifying malware (packed, obfuscated) and benign samples. The experimental results show that the current classification model based on header can classify executables but malware authors can evade detection by changing header information. To understand the infection mechanism and propagation mode of the suspicious samples, detailed analysis of assembly code or Hex dump would play a major role. In future, the effect of classification accuracies by combining these features (mnemonic *n*–gram, APIs, instruction opcode, PE Header fields) will all be investigated.

Acknowledgement

The authors are grateful to the Ministry of Communication and Information Technology, Government of India, for supporting and funding this project.

References

1. Enamul, K.M., Andrew, W., Arun, L.: Malware Phylogeny Generation using Permutations of code. Journal in Computer Virology (1-2), 13–23 (2005)
2. Henchiri, O., Japkowicz, N.: A Feature Selection and Evaluation Scheme for Computer Virus Detection. In: Proceedings of the Sixth International Conference on Data Mining (IEEE) (ICDM 2006), pp. 891–895. IEEE Computer Society, Los Alamitos (2006)
3. Yoo, I.S., Ultes-Nitsche, U.: Towards Establishing a Unknown Virus Detection Technique using SOM. Journal in Computer Virology 2(3), 163–186 (2006)
4. Kephart, J.O., Arnold, B.: N-grams-Based File Signatures For Malware Detection, pp. 178–184 (1994)
5. Kephart, J.O., Arnold, B.: A Feature Selection and Evaluation of Computer Virus Signatures. In: Proceeding of the 4th Virus Bulletin International Conference, pp. 178–184 (1994)

6. Kolter, J.Z., Maloof, M.A.: Learning to Detect Malicious Executables in the Wild. In: Proceedings of the tenth ACM SIGKDD International Conference on Knowledge Discovery and Data mining (KDD 2004), pp. 470–478 (2004)
7. Li, W.J., Wang, K., Stolfo, S.J., Herzog, B.: Fileprints:Identifying File types by n-gram analysis. In: Proceedings of the Sixth Annual IEEE SMC 4th Virus Bulletin International Conference, pp. 64–71 (2005)
8. Moskovitch, R., Stopel, D., Feher, C., Nissim, N., Japkowicz, N., Elovici, Y.: Unknown Malcode Detection and the Imbalance Problem. Journal in Computer Virology 5(4), 295–308 (2009)
9. Microsoft Portable Executable and Common Object File Format Specification `www.osdever.net/documents/PECOFF.pdf`
10. Vinod, P., Laxmi, V., Gaur, M.S.: Mnemonics as Predictor for Malware Analysis. In: Proceedings of IEEE International Conference on Advances in Communication, Network, and Computing (CNC 2011), pp. 366–368 (2011)
11. Vinod, P., Laxmi, V., Gaur, M.S., Chauhan, G.: Malware Analysis using Non-Signature based Method. In: Proceedings of IEEE International Conference on Network Communication and Computer (ICNCC 2011), New Delhi, India, March 21-23 (to appear, 2011)
12. Merkel, R., Hoppe, T., Kraetzer, C., Dittmann, J.: Statistical detection of malicious PE-executables for fast offline analysis. In: De Decker, B., Schaumüller-Bichl, I. (eds.) CMS 2010. LNCS, vol. 6109, pp. 93–105. Springer, Heidelberg (2010)
13. Santos, I., Brezo, F., Nieves, J., Penya, Y.K., Sanz, B., Laorden, C., Bringas, P.G.: Idea: Opcode-sequence-based malware detection. In: Massacci, F., Wallach, D., Zannone, N. (eds.) ESSoS 2010. LNCS, vol. 5965, pp. 35–43. Springer, Heidelberg (2010)
14. Schultz, M.G., Eskin, E., Zadok, E., Stolfo, S.J.: Data Mining Methods for Detection of New Malicious Executables. Proceedings of the IEEE Symposium on Security and Privacy (2001)
15. Tzu-Yen, W., Chin-Hsiung, W., Chu-Cheng, H.: Detecting Unknown Malicious Executables Using Portable Executable Headers. In: Proceedings of the 2009 Fifth International Joint Conference on INC, IMS and IDC (NCM 2009), pp. 278–284 (2009)
16. Tabish, S.M., Shafiq, M.Z., Farooq, M.: Malware Detection using Statistical Analysis of byte-level file content. In: Proceedings of the ACM SIGKDD Workshop on CyberSecurity and Intelligence Informatics (CSI-KDD), pp. 23–31 (2009)
17. University of Waikato. Open Source Machine Learning Software WEKA, `http://www.cs.waikato.ac.nz/ml/weka/`
18. Virus Total, `http://www.virustotal.com/stats.html`
19. VX Heavens, `http://vx.netlux.org/lib`
20. Yuval, E., Asaf, S., Robert, M., Gil, T., Chanan, G.: Applying Machine Learning Techniques for Detection of Malicious Code in Network Traffic. In: Proceedings of the 30th Annual German Conference on Advances in Artificial Intelligence (KI 2007), pp. 44–50 (2007)
21. Walenstein, A., Venable, M., Hayes, M., Thompson, C., Lakhotia, A.:Exploiting Similarity between Variants to Ddefeat Malware: Vilo Method for Comparing and Searching Binary Programs. In: Proceedings of BlackHat DC, `https://blackhat.com/presentations/bh-dc-07/Walenstein/Paper/bh-dc-07-walenstein-W%P.pdf`
22. Witten, I.H., Frank, E.: Data Mining: Practical Machine Learning Tools and Techniques with Java Implementations. Morgan Kaufmann, San Francisco (1999)
23. Fawcett, T.: An Introduction to ROC Analysis. Pattern Recognition Letter 27(8), 861–874 (2006)

Multilevel Policy Based Security in Distributed Database

Neera Batra and Manpreet Singh

Department of Computer Engineering, M. M. Engineering College,
M. M. University, Mullana
batraneera1@gmail.com, dr.manpreet.singh.in@gmail.com

Abstract. Addressing security demands under fixed budgets and tight time constraints are becoming extremely challenging, time consuming and resource intensive. Moreover, securing the distributed database in compliance with several security guidelines makes the system more complex. Mission critical systems, military, government and financial institutions have been under tremendous pressure to secure their databases. Such requirements mandate that each system passes a strict security scan before it is deemed suitable to go into operational mode. This paper presents a framework that embeds security capabilities into distributed database by replicating different predefined security policies at different sites using multilevel secure database management system.

Keywords: Policy based security, Replication, Multilevel secure database, Covert channel, Distributed database.

1 Introduction

A distributed database is a collection of databases which are distributed and stored on multiple computers within a network [9]. Distributed database system functions include distributed query management, distributed transaction processing, distributed metadata management and enforcing security and integrity across the multiple nodes. Database security is the system, processes, and procedures that protect a database from unintended activity. Unintended activity can be categorized as authenticated misuse, malicious attacks or inadvertent mistakes made by authorized individuals or processes. But the most important issues in security are authentication, identification [14] and enforcing appropriate access controls [8]. Databases provide many layers and types of information security, typically specified in the data dictionary, including access control, auditing, authentication and encryption. Access control [15] is a system which enables an authority to control access to areas and resources in a given physical facility or computer-based information system. An access control system, within the field of physical security, is generally seen as the second layer in the security. Authentication [4] is the act of establishing or confirming something (or someone) as authentic, that is, that claims made by or about the subject are true. All organizations, ranging from commercial organizations to social organizations, in a variety of domains such as healthcare and homeland

A. Abraham et al. (Eds.): ACC 2011, Part I, CCIS 190, pp. 572–580, 2011.

protection, may suffer heavy losses from both financial and human points of view as a consequence of unauthorized data observation [11]. In cryptography, encryption [5] is the process of transforming information (referred to as plaintext) using an algorithm (called cipher) to make it unreadable to anyone except those possessing special knowledge, usually referred to as a key Integrity. Some of the most important security requirements for database management systems are: Multi-Level Access Control, Confidentiality [11], Reliability, Integrity and Recovery. Thus, a complete solution to data security must meet the following three requirements: 1) secrecy or confidentiality refers to the protection of data against unauthorized disclosure, 2) integrity refers to the prevention of unauthorized and improper data modification [1], and 3) availability [10] refers to the prevention and recovery from hardware and software errors and from malicious data access denials making the database system unavailable. A DBMS fulfilling these mandatory requirements becomes capable of providing security at different levels. But in order to provide concurrent access of replicated data to multiple users at different locations, multilevel security mainly on distributed environment becomes a major issue.

Multilevel secure database systems have a set of requirements that are beyond those of conventional database systems. A number of conceptual models exist that specify access rules for transactions in secure database systems. One important model is the Bell La Padula model. In this model, a security level is assigned to transactions and data [6]. A security level for transaction represents its clearance level and for data, the security level represents the classification level [9]. Transactions are forbidden from reading data at higher security level, and from writing data to a lower security level. Thus, by delaying low security level transactions in a predetermined manner, high security level information can be indirectly transferred to the lower security level. This is called a covert channel. A covert channel is any component or feature of a system that is misused to encode or represent information for unauthorized transmission, without violating the stated access control policy. Covert channels are paths not normally meant for information flow. In multilevel secure databases, a low security level transaction can be delayed or aborted by a high security level transaction due to shared data access.

Security Policy: A computer security policy consists of a clearly defined and precise set of rules, for determining authorization as a basis for making access control decisions. A security policy captures the security requirements of an establishment or describes the steps that have to be taken to achieve the desired level of security. A security policy is typically stated in terms of subjects and objects, Given the desired subject and object, there must be a set of rules that are used by the system to determine whether a given subject can be given access to a specific object.

In this paper, we focus mainly on the confidentiality requirement and we discuss access control policies to provide high-assurance confidentiality because however, access control deals with controlling accesses to the data, the discussion in this paper is also relevant to the access control aspect of integrity, that is, enforcing that no unauthorized modifications to data occur.

2 Proposed Model

The proposed model consists of MLS [16] database that is distributed [2] in a replicated manner over N sites connected by a network. As shown in Figure 1, at each site when the user request is received, the first job a secure server does is to authenticate the user.

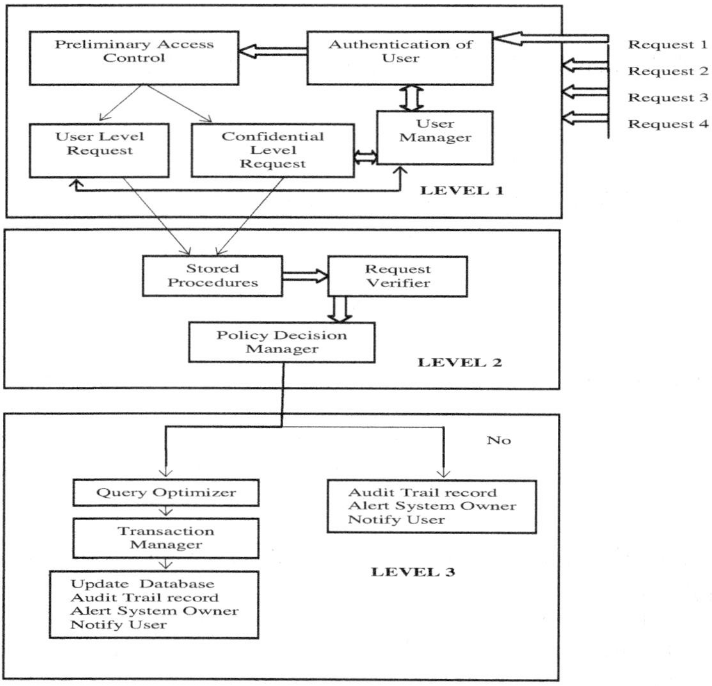

Fig. 1. System Model

The authentication is performed based on factors user name, password or IP address. Once user is authenticated successfully, the user's request, IP address, and digital credentials are forwarded to the preliminary access control system which can be achieved with a firewall system filtering the traffic based on user's request. For example, a user can check for the balance available in his account in the local databases. He doesn't have the permission to access the similar information located in the remote databases. The preliminary access control is a valid way to improve the system efficiency because the user's disallowed requests are terminated at an early stage. If the user's request is allowed by the preliminary access control, the user's request is forwarded to the security manager. The different request levels proposed are user level request ($SL(Du)$) and confidential level request which is further divided in to secret level request ($SL(Ds)$) and top secret level request ($SL(Dt)$) . If the user is permitted access to the user level, the query is limited with the user level transaction ($SL(Q)\langle SL(D_u)$) otherwise the query is rolled back to confidential level security. At level second, the request $SL(Q)$ goes through a process of verification before it can be processed. This step is carried out by database stored procedures that have built-in logic for checking the request against the policies .If the request complies with the set policies that govern its scope of applicability, the request is forwarded to query optimizer.

The query optimizer further divides the request or query $SL(Q)$ into various levels for distributed access and creates a new optimized query according to the data distribution. The transaction Manager pools the query in the transaction queue and allows the transaction to be executed .The lock signal is sent to the entire distributed database sites. The transaction is allowed to update the data only when it passes all the clearance from all security levels otherwise it rolls back the transaction. When there is no objection from other sites, audit trail, database system tables/views are updated to reflect the change and an audit trail is recorded otherwise the request is rejected and the system owner is alerted, the user notified and an audit trail is recorded. Thus the proposed model felicitates to access data only after passing thru multiple security levels.

In this paper, use of policies is applied for access control to different users depending upon privileges given to them. The system owner is allowed to create database configuration-specific policies. These policies control and decide which changes are allowed and which ones are not.

The framework gives the system owners the ability to institute a composite password where each part of the password is owned by a different member of the system owners team for added security. The purpose of using policies is to enforce system owner requirements and constraints onto a system. Policies are implemented into a database system for the purpose of making the database perform specific actions in response to attempts to alter its state or its configuration settings. Therefore the creation and enforcement of policies require the establishment of rules that invoke certain actions to be performed under certain conditions.

2.1 Consistency Controlled System

To implement concurrency, each transaction in this security model, must obtain a read lock before reading a data item and a write lock before writing a data item. A transaction can only read at its own level or low level but can write at its own level only [3]. This is sufficient to prove that security is not violated through data access. The access permissions in the proposed model are shown in Table 1. Let $L(T_t)$ denotes the top security level transaction, $L(T_s)$ the security level and $L(T_u)$ as user level transaction i.e. $L(T_u) < L(T_s) < L(T_t)$. whereas $L(Z_t)$ denotes the data item Z as the top security level data item, $L(Y_s)$ the security level data item and $L(X_u)$ as user level data item i.e. $L(X_u) < L(Y_s) < L(Z_t)$.

Table 1. Access Permission

Data Item / Transaction	$L(X_u)$	$L(Y_s)$	$L(Z_t)$
$L(T_t)$	$r[x]$	$r[y]$	$r[z]$, $w[z]$
$L(T_s)$	$r[x]$	$r[y]$, $w[y]$	-
$L(T_u)$	$r[x]$	-	-

The execution of a distributed transaction T is divided into sub-transactions T_i, where $\sum_{i=1}^{n} T_i$ A sub-transaction Ti is sent to the node N I where the data is available and executed under local security. If a sub-transaction fails, then the parent transaction is rolled–back and restarts after some delay to avoid repeated restart. The transaction manager determines at which node, data item requested by a transaction are located. If the data is available in the parent node Ni, it is accessed in the same node Ni, otherwise if there is no local copy and multiple copies exist at more than one node, then one copy is randomly selected and other copies of the same data are locked.

In case of data replication, it implements a read-one and write-all policy for read requests. For a write request, it consults all nodes that hold a copy of the desired data item. Each node contains information about data distribution and replication. A transaction can't request additional locks once it has issued an unlock action. It holds onto all its locks (read or write) until it completes. A top secret security level transaction must release its read lock on a low data item when a low security level transaction requests a write lock on the same data item and the aborted top secret security level transaction is restarted after some delay. Thus multiple transactions are performed simultaneously with minimum cost.

2.2 Policy Integration

As mentioned earlier, our framework is built on the notion that all policies must be an integral part of the database that they are meant to defend in a fashion that makes them directly associated with its very existence. Hosting them in an external application or database or even in another database instance on the same server as the target database, introduces the risk of isolating the policies from the target database and therefore, creating an opportunity for accessing and compromising the database without any lines of defense. In our framework, the policies are fed into physical database tables where they are stored and managed by the system owner. These tables are owned by the database itself and are not accessible to applications, application servers, or even power users.

In this paper, we apply the use of policies to implement autonomic capabilities into a database. We allow the system owner to create database configuration-specific policies that decide the actual run-time behavior of the database. These policies control and decide which changes are allowed and which ones are not. This is based on the database being aware of its operational state being able to defend itself against input from various environmental sources such as users, malicious code, or external software systems.

To support policy-based framework, three types of policies are enumerated that can be embed into an Oracle 10g database to demonstrate the effectiveness of the approach. While policy of type one (Top secret policy) is intended to govern the areas of enforcement of configuration security, policies of type two and three govern fine–grained access control (secret level) and user action verification(user level) respectively. The system owner can write as many policies as needed to govern database security. The policies are concise, targeted and simple which makes this approach effective, scalable, flexible and extensible.

2.3 Policy Implementation

This section presents some implementation scenarios where the policy-based framework is utilized to autonomically enforce security configuration in databases thus enabling them to self-protect. To demonstrate the usability of the proposed framework we consider a policy for enforcing the password life time security.

TYPE 1 (Top Security Level Policy) Example

The role of this policy is to verify and control the actions of privileged users such as database administrators and power users. The validation process is performed as a response to the users input as shown below. The DBA calls a stored procedure specific for changing the life time of a password and chooses the values of the parameters he/she intends to change. These values are then verified according to the policy that governs their applicability. The policy specifies a maximum lifetime for passwords. When the specified amount of time passes and the password expires, the user or DBA must change the password otherwise access to an account is denied until a new password is supplied. For example, the following statements create and assign a profile to user john, and the PASSWORD_LIFE_TIME clause specifies that john can use the same password for 50 days before it expires.

```
CREATE PROFILE prof LIMIT
FAILED_LOGIN_ATTEMPTS 4
PASSWORD_LOCK_TIME 30
PASSWORD_LIFE_TIME 50; ALTER USER john PROFILE prof;
```

The permissible number of failed login attempts and the amount of time for which accounts remain locked are specified as four and 30 days respectively. When a particular user exceeds a designated number of failed login attempts, the server automatically locks that user account. The account will unlock automatically after the passage of 30 days. After a user successfully logs into an account, the unsuccessful login attempt count for the user, if it exists, is reset to 0.

TYPE 2 (Security Level Policy) Example

Fine-grained access control is based on dynamically modified statements.To change any option of a user's security domain, DBA uses the ALTER USER system privilege. DBA are normally the only users that have this system privilege, as it allows a modification of any user's security domain. This privilege includes the ability to set table space quotas for a user on any table space in the database, even if the user performing the modification does not have a quota for a specified table space. Changing a user's security settings affects the user's future sessions, not current sessions. The following statement alters the security settings for user John:

```
ALTER USER John
IDENTIFIED EXTERNALLY
DEFAULT TABLESPACE data_ts
TEMPORARY TABLESPACE temp_ts
QUOTA 100M ON data_ts
QUOTA 0 ON test_ts
PROFILE clerk;
```

The ALTER USER statement here changes John's security settings as follows: Authentication is changed to use John's operating system account. His default and temporary table spaces are explicitly set. He is given a 100M quota for the data_ts table space. His quota on the test_ts is revoked. He is assigned the clerk profile.

TYPE 3 (User Level Policy) Example

In an example of this type of policy, a policy is created which does not expose salaries of employees outside the sales department.

```
SELECT ENAME, JOB, SAL, COMM from emp , dept WHERE d.deptno = e.deptno
AND d.dname="Sales";
```

It is important to note that the stored procedures do not allow the user to input values into variables. Instead, the procedures present the user with a set of values to select from. This is important because it removes any possibility of the users injecting variations to the expected input.

3 Comparisons with Other Related Approaches

This paper is concerned with the application of policies to securing a database by embedding the policies in the database itself and enabling these policies to block every attempt to compromise the state of the database. Oliver Jorns et al.[13] proposed another security architecture that not only incorporated easy to compute and flexible transaction pseudonyms for security and privacy assurance, but also allowed the implementation of different kinds of location based services.

A different approach to securing the database was presented by Sang H. Son through the offering of timeliness support using partial security policies [8]. It violates security in order to uphold a timeliness requirement and works on the basis of partial security policies. Moreover, it works in a non-replicated environment.

Leon Pan[7] also worked on providing security in distributed database using preliminary and fine access control policies but in a non replicated manner and policies are stored and executed at a different server, it introduces risk of isolating the policies from the target database and can create opportunity for accessing and compromising the database without any lines of defense. In our approach, the policies are fed into physical database tables where they are stored and managed by the system owner. These tables are owned by the database itself and are not accessible to applications, application servers, or even power users.

In [12], an OWL-DL ontology is created that expresses the modeling abstractions of RBAC. This ontology is attached to domain ontology and explains the tasks that are performed by the security administrator and by the DL classifier. The background knowledge is used to make the access decisions which are available as Semantic Web ontologies. The model has established a secure infrastructure to register, propagate, request and verify user attributes. This functionality is offered by network services that support single sign-on across domains and trusted user directories. Again, conversion techniques are required if the native format is different, while our approach is more flexible and easy to handle. Moreover, the implementation of the security enforcement mechanism is embedded in the database itself and inseparable part of the system making it enable for self-protection, self-healing and self-configuring.

4 Conclusion

This paper presented an advanced approach to implement security capabilities into distributed database in order to secure systems at multilevel while maintaining consistency of the system as well. Security is a serious concern while accessing data.

In this paper, use of policies is applied for access control to different users depending upon privileges given to them. Policies implemented at different security levels ensure the integrity, availability and correctness of data replicated at multiple nodes. This model can be applied for any distributed environment such as corporate, financial organization etc.

References

1. Bonatti, P.A., Kraus, S., Subrahmanian, V.S.: Foundations of Secure Deductive Databases. IEEE Transactions on Knowledge and Data Engineering 7(3), 406–422 (1995)
2. Zubi, Z.S.: On Distributed Database Security Aspect. In: International Conference on Multimedia Computing and Systems, pp. 231–235. IEEE, Los Alamitos (2009)
3. Kaur, N., Singh, R., Sarje, A.K., Misra, M.: Performance Evaluation of Secure Concurrency Control Algorithm for Multilevel Secure Distributed Database systems. In: ITCC 2005, vol. 01, pp. 249–254. IEEE, Los Alamitos (2005)

4. Wang, H., Dang, D., Min, S.: The Analysis of the Security Strategy of Embedded Mobile Database, pp. 476–478. IEEE, Los Alamitos (2010)
5. Lin, M.: Static Security Optimization for Real-Time Systems. IEEE Transactions on Industrial Informatics 5(1), 22–37 (2009)
6. Veluchandhar, J.: A backup mechanism with concurrency control for multilevel secure distributed database systems, pp. 57–62. IEEE, Los Alamitos (2008)
7. Pan, L.: A unified network security and fine-grained database access control model, pp. 265–269. IEEE, Los Alamitos (2009)
8. Son, S.H., Chaney, C., Thomlinson, N.P.: Partial security policies to support timeliness in secure real-time databases. In: Proceedings of the IEEE Symposium on Security and Privacy, pp. 136–147 (1998)
9. Thuraisingham, B.: Multilevel Security Issues in Distributed Database Management Systems II. Journal of Computers and Security 10(9), 727–747 (1991)
10. Ghorbanzadeh, P., Shaddeli, A., Malekzadeh, R., Jahanbakhsh, Z.: A Survey of Mobile Database Security Threats and Solutions for It. In: ICIS 2010, pp. 676–682 (2010)
11. Bertino, E., Sandhu, R.: Database Security—Concepts, Approaches, and Challenges. IEEE Transactions on Dependable and Secure Computing 2(1), 2–18 (2005)
12. Cirio, L., Cruz, I.F., Tamassia, R.: A role and attribute based access control system using semantic web technologies. In: Chung, S., Herrero, P. (eds.) OTM-WS 2007, Part II. LNCS, vol. 4806, pp. 1256–1266. Springer, Heidelberg (2007)
13. Jorns, O., Quirchmayr, G., Jung, O.: A Privacy Enhancing mechanism based on Pseudonyms for Identity Protection in Location-Based Services. In: Brankovic, L., Steketee, C. (eds.) Proc. Fifth Australasian Information Security Workshop (Privacy Enhancing Technologies) (AISW 2007), Ballarat, Australia. CRPIT, vol. 68, pp. 133–142 (2007)
14. Thuraisingham, B., Ford, W.: Security Constraint Processing in a multilevel Secure Distributed Database Management System. IEEE Transactions on Knowledge and Data Engineering 1(2), 274–293 (1995)
15. Tadano, K., Kawato, M., Machida, F., Maeno, Y.: Resource Information Cache Update Control for Scalable Access Control Management Systems. In: IEEE 3rd International Conference on Cloud Computing, pp. 538–539 (2010)
16. Ray, I., Mancini, L.V., Jajodia, S., Bertino, E.: ASEP: A Secure and Flexible Commit Protocol for MLS Distributed Database Systems. IEEE Transactions on Knowledge and Data Engineering 12(6), 880–899 (2000)

Mining Indirect Positive and Negative Association Rules

B. Ramasubbareddy[1], A. Govardhan[2], and A. Ramamohanreddy[3]

[1] Associate.Professor, Jyothishmathi Institute of Technology and Science, Karimnagar, India
rsreddyphd@gmail.com
[2] Professor & Principal, JNTUH college of Engineering, Karimnagar, India
govardhan_cse@yahoo.co.in
[3] Professor, S.V.U. College of Engineering, S.V. University, Tirupati, India
ramamohansvu@yahoo.com

Abstract. Indirect association is a new kind of infrequent pattern, which provides a new way for interpreting the value of infrequent patterns and can effectively reduce the number of uninteresting infrequent patterns. The concept of indirect association is to "indirectly" connect two rarely co-occurred items via a frequent itemset called mediator, and if appropriately utilized it can help to identify real interesting "infrequent itempairs" from databases. Indirect association rule is said to be positive (Negative) if mediator set contains presence (presence or absence) of items. Existing indirect association mining methods mine positive mediator sets. To the best of our knowledge, no research work has been conducted on mining indirect negative associations. In this paper, we propose an approach for mining indirect negative associations. The proposed method can discover all positive and negative indirect association between itemsets.

Keywords: Data mining; positive and negative association rules; indirect association.

1 Introduction

Association rule mining is a data mining task that discovers associations among items in a transactional database. Association rules have been extensively studied in the literature for their usefulness in many application domains such as recommender systems, diagnosis decisions support, telecommunication, intrusion detection, etc. Efficient discovery of such rules has been a major focus in the data mining research. From the celebrated *Apriori* algorithm [1] there have been a remarkable number of variants and improvements of association rule mining algorithms [2]. A typical example of association rule mining application is the market basket analysis. In this example, the behavior of the customers is studied with reference to buying different products in a shopping store. The discovery of interesting patterns in this collection of data can lead to important marketing and management strategic decisions. For instance, if a customer buys bread, what are chances that customer buys milk as well?. Depending on some measure to represent the said chances of such an association, marketing personnel can develop better planning of the shelf space in the store or can

A. Abraham et al. (Eds.): ACC 2011, Part I, CCIS 190, pp. 581–591, 2011.

base their discount strategies on such associations/correlations found in the data. All the traditional association rule mining algorithms were developed to find positive associations between items.

A new class of patterns called indirect associations has been proposed and its utilities have been examined in various application domains [8]. Consider a pair of items X and Y that are rarely present together in the same transaction. If both items are highly dependent on the presence of another itemset M, then the pair (X, Y) is said to be indirectly associated via M. There are many advantages in mining indirect associations in large data sets. For example, an indirect association between a pair of words in text documents can be used to classify query results into categories [8]. For instance, the words *coal* and *data* can be indirectly associated via *mining*. If only the word *mining* is used in a query, documents in both *mining* domains are returned. Discovery of the indirect association between *coal* and *data* enables us to classify the retrieved documents into *coal mining* and *data mining*. There are also potential applications of indirect associations in many other real-world domains, such as competitive product analysis and stock market analysis [8]. For market basket data, this method can be used to perform competitive analysis. For example, x and y may represent products of competing products, such as Reebok and Nike. Suppose Reebok marketers are interested in expanding their current market share by attracting Nike customers through direct marketing campaigns. However, instead of promoting to every Nike customers, such a campaign can be more effective, in-terms of cost-benefit and lift analysis by selecting a smaller target group whose buying behavior resemble that of Reebok customers. Indirect association provides an approach to characterize the group by identifying the set of items that are often bought by both group of customers.

In the text domain, indirect association often corresponds synonyms, antonyms or words that are used in the different contexts of another word. As an example, the words *coal* and *data* can be indirectly associated via *mining*. If a user queries on the word *mining*, the collection of documents returned often contains a mixture of both mining contexts. However, with indirect association, one can potentially identify explicitly the different ways in which queried word appears in the corpus of text documents. Similarly, for stock market data, indirect association can help to identify the different set of events influencing the movement of stock price.

This paper is structured as follows: the next section contains preliminaries about Indirect Association Rules, In Section3 existing strategies for mining indirect association rules are reviewed. The proposed algorithm is presented in Section 4 for finding all valid indirect association rules for pairs of multiple itemsets. Section 5 contains conclusions and future work.

2 Basic Concepts and Terminology

Let $I = \{i_1, i_2, . . . , i_m\}$ be a set of m items. A subset $X \subseteq I$ is called an itemset. A k-itemset is an itemset that contains k items. Let $D = \{T_1, T_2, . . . , T_n\}$ be a set of n transactions, called a transaction database, where each transaction T_j, $j = 1, 2, . . . , n$, is a set of items such that $T_j \subseteq I$. Each transaction is associated with a unique identifier, called its TID. A transaction T contains an itemset X if and only if $X \subseteq T$.

The support of an itemset X is the percentage of transactions in D containing X. An itemset X in a transaction database D is called "frequent itemset" if its support is at least a user-specified minimum support threshold viz., minsup. Accordingly, an infrequent itemset is an itemset that is not a frequent itemset.

2.1 Negative Association Rules

An association rule is an implication of the form $X \Rightarrow Y$, where $X \subset I$, $Y \subset I$, and $X \cap Y = \emptyset$. Here, X is called the antecedent and Y is called the consequent of the rule. The confidence of an association rule $X \Rightarrow Y$ is the conditional probability that a transaction contains Y, given that it contains X. The support of rule $X \Rightarrow Y$ is defined as: $sup(X \Rightarrow Y) = sup(X \cup Y)$. Negative association was first pointed out by Brin et al. in [6]. Since then, many techniques for mining negative associations have been developed [7, 8, 9]. In the case of negative associations we are interested in finding itemsets that have a very low probability of occurring together. That is, a negative association between two itemsets X and Y, denoted as $X \Rightarrow \rceil Y$ or $Y \Rightarrow \rceil X$, means that X and Y appear very rarely in the same transaction. Mining negative association rules is computational intractable with a naive approach because billions of negative associations may be found in a large database while almost all of them are extremely uninteresting. This problem was addressed in [7] by combining previously discovered positive associations with domain knowledge to constrain the search space such that fewer but more interesting negative rules are mined. A general framework for mining both positive and negative association rules of interest was presented in [9], in which no domain knowledge was required and the negative association rules were given in more concrete expressions to indicate actual relationships between different itemsets. However, although the sets of the positive and negative itemsets of interest in the database were minimized in this framework, the search space for negative itemsets of interest was still huge. Another problem was that it tended to produce too many negative association rules, thus the practical application of this framework remained uncertain. An innovative approach has proposed in [22]. In this generating positive and negative association rules consists of four steps: (1) Generate all positive frequent itemsets L (P1) (ii) for all itemsets I in L(P1), generate negative frequent itemsets of the form $\neg$ (I1 I2) (iii) Generate all negative frequent itemsets $\neg$ I1 $\neg$ I2 (iv) Generate all negative frequent itemsets I1 $\neg$ I2 and (v) Generate all valid positive and negative association rules. Authors generated negative rules without adding additional interesting measure(s) to Support-Confidence frame work.ï

2.2 Indirect Association

Indirect association is a new kind of infrequent pattern, which provides a new way for interpreting the value of infrequent patterns and can effectively reduce the number of uninteresting infrequent patterns. The concept of indirect association is to "indirectly" connect two rarely co-occurred items via a frequent itemset called mediator, and if appropriately utilized it can help to identify real interesting "infrequent itempairs" from databases. Indirect association is closely related to negative association, they are both dealing with itemsets that do not have sufficiently high support. Indirect associations provide an effective way to detect interesting negative associations by discovering only "infrequent itempairs that are highly expected to be frequent" without using negative items or domain knowledge.

Definition (Indirect Association). A pair of itemsets X and Y is indirectly associated via a mediator M, if the following conditions hold:

1. sup(X, Y) < t_s (Itepair Support Condition)
2. There exists a non-empty set M such that

(a) sup(X ∪ M) $\geq t_f$, sup(Y ∪ M) $\geq t_f$; (Mediator Support Condition)
(b) dep(X , M) $\geq t_d$, dep(Y, M) $\geq t_d$, where dep(P, Q) is a measure of the dependence between itemsets P and Q. (Mediator Dependence Condition)

The thresholds above are called itemset pair support threshold (t_s), mediator support threshold (t_f), and mediator dependence threshold (t_d), respectively. In practice, it is reasonably to set $t_f \geq t_s$

Condition 1 is needed because an indirect relationship between two items is significant only if both items rarely occur together in the same transaction. Otherwise, it makes more sense to characterize the pair in terms of their direct association.

Condition 2(a) can be used to guarantee that the statistical significance of the mediator setIn particular, for market basket data, the support of an itemset affects the amount of revenue generated and justifies the feasibility of a marketing decision. Moreover, support has a nice downward closure property which allows us to prune the combinatorial search space of the problem.Condition 2(b) ensures that only items that are highly dependent on the presence of x and y will be used to form the mediator set.

Over the years, many measures have been proposed to quantify the degree of dependence between attributes of a dataset. From statistics, the Chi-Square test is often used for this purpose. However, the drawback of this approach is that it does not measure the strength of dependencies between items [18]. Furthermore, the Chi-Square statistic depends on the number of transactions in the database. As a result, other statistical measures of association are often used, including Pearson's Φ coefficient, Goodman and Krushkal's λ, Yule's Q and Y coefficients, etc [15].

Interest factor is another measure that has been used quite extensively to quantify the strength of dependency among items [10,11,12].

Definition: Given a pair of itemsets, say X and Y, its' IS measure can be computed using the following equation:

$$IS(X,Y) = \frac{P(X,Y)}{P(X)P(Y)} \tag{1}$$

Where P denotes the probability that the given itemset appears in a transaction

2.3 Indirect Negative Association

Indirect association rule is said to be Indirect Negative Association Rule if mediator set used to generate it, contains both presence and absence of items. Thus, for a given indirect itemset pair X, Y and mediator itemset M (=X^1Y^1) where X^1 and Y^1 may be positive and/or negative itemsets. If both X^1 and Y^1 are positive then (X, Y/M) is said to be an indirect positive association rule otherwise it is said to be an indirect negative association rule.

3 Related Work in Indirect Association Rule Mining

It is observed that automated document translation systems tend to produce lexicon translation tables that are full of indirectly-associated words [14]. A lexicon translation table encodes the probability that two words from different languages being semantically equivalent to another. The presence of indirect association can pollute the resulting tables, thereby reducing the overall precision of the system. An iterative strategy was proposed in [14] to clean up existing translation tables by finding only the most probable translations for a given word.

The notion of internal and external measures of similarity between attributes of a database relation was introduced in [13]. Internal similarity between two attributes x and y is a measure whose value depends only on the values of x and y columns. Conversely, external measure takes into account data from other columns (called the probe attributes). Their notion of probe attributes is similar to mediators for indirect association in [13]. However, their sole purpose of using probe attributes is to perform attribute clustering.

An approach is proposed in [21] for mining indirect association rules among itemsets and is modified here for finding indirect negative association rules. In [3,4,5], the authors have proposed series of techniques for finding negative association rules. These proposals are also act as basis for the proposed algorithm in this paper.

Indirect association is closely related to the notion of negative association rules [16]. In both cases, we are dealing with itemsets that do not have sufficiently high support. A negative association rule discovers the set of items a customer will not likely to buy given that he/she bought a certain set of other items. Typically, the number of negative association rules can be prohibitively large and the majority of them are not interesting to a data analyst. The use of domain knowledge, in the form of item taxonomy, was proposed in [16] to decide what constitutes an interesting negative association rule. The intuition here is that items belonging to the same parent node in taxonomy are expected to have similar types of associations with other items. If the observed support is significantly smaller than its expected value, then there is a negative association exists between the items. Again, unlike indirect association, these types of regularities do not specifically look for mediating elements.

Another related area is the study of functional dependencies in relational databases. Functional dependencies are relationships that exist between attributes of a relation. However, the emphasis of functional dependencies is to find dependent and independent attributes for applications such as semantic query optimization [17] and reverse engineering [17].

In [20], IAM algorithm proceeds in four phases: an initialization phase, a pruning phase, a bridge itemset calculation phase, and a ranking phase. The purpose of the initialization phase is to allocate the memory needed. The second phase is a process of pruning for the purpose of minimizing the search space of problem. The threshold value of pruning is min-sup(s). The third phase, the Bridge Itemset Calculation Phase, is the most important for this algorithm. The last phase, a ranking phase, is mainly to finish the ranking operation according to' the closeness value in the linked vector C for the purpose of providing decision makers the most useful indirect association rules

An efficient algorithm, called HI-mine, based on a new data structure, called HI-struct, for mining the complete set of indirect associations between items[19]. Experimental results show that HI-mine's performance is significantly better than that of the previously developed algorithm for mining indirect associations on both synthetic and real world data sets over practical ranges of support specifications.

4 Algorithm

In literature, a little work was done on generating indirect positive associations between pair of items only. In this paper, we propose a new method which generates indirect positive and negative associations between pair of itemsets. This method contains three algorithms. Algorithm1 finds set of all frequent itemsets and set of all Valid Candidates (VC). An itemset V is said to be Valid candidate if sup (V) $\leq t_s$ and all subsets of V are frequent. Algorithm 2 finds set of all indirect positive association rules between pairs of itemsets. Though Algorithms 1 and 2 were presented in [21], they are stated in this paper for self-containment. In this paper, proposed Algorithm 3 finds set of all indirect negative associations between pair of itemsets in which mediator set is of the form $\rceil X^1 \rceil Y^1$. In addition, Algorithm 4 finds set of all indirect negative associations between pair of itemsets in which mediator set is of the form $(\rceil X^1)\ Y^1$.

Algorithm 1: Finding Positive Frequent(P), and ValidCandidates (VC)
Input: TDB- Transactional Database, m_s, t_s
Output: P- Positive Frequent itemsets, VC- ValidCandidates,
Method:

```
Find P1, the set all frequent 1-itemsets
for(K=2;Pk-1 != Φ ; K++)
{       CK = PK-1 ⋈ PK-1
      // Pruning infrequent itemsets
        for each c ∈ CK   {
      if any sub-set of c is not a member of PK-1 then  CK = CK−{ c}
                          }
      // find positive frequent itemsets Pk and Valid  Candidates (VC) in CK
for each c in CK  {
          if support(c )≥ ms then Pk = Pk U { c }
          if support(c )≤ ts then VC= VC U { c }
                  }
      P= P U PK
}
return P,VC
```

Algorithm 2: Mining Indirect Positive Association

```
Input: P, VC, t_f, t_d, IAR= Ø
Output: Indirect Positive Association Rules
Method:
for each l (= X U Y) ∈ VC {
 for each I ∈ P {
   if ( support(X U I ) ≥ t_f && support ( Y U I )≥ t_f )
if ( dependency( X U I ) ≥ t_d && dependency ( Y U I )≥ t_d )
   IAR= IAR  U (X,Y/I )
                    }            }
return IAR
```

Algorithm 3: Mining Indirect Negative Association

```
Input: L_1- frequent 1-itemset, m_s-minsup, VC, t_f,t_d,IAR= Ø
Output: Indirect Negative Association Rules
Method:
C_2 = {]{i_1}]{i_2}|i_1, i_2 ε L_1, i_1 ≠ i_2}
for (k = 2;C_k ≠ Ø; k ++)
{ for all I = ]X]Y  ∈ C_k
 { if supp(I) ≥ m_s
     { for each  l (= X U Y) ∈ VC
{ if ( support(X U I ) ≥ t_f && support ( Y U I )≥ t_f )
if ( dependency( X U I ) ≥ t_d && dependency ( Y U I )≥ t_d
 IAR= IAR  U (X,Y/I )
                 }
          }
       else
       {      for all I  ∉ XY do
   Cand =check candidates(I, i)  // i, is one the items of DB, is not a member of I
                C_k+1 = C_k+1 U Cand
   // S the set of positive itemsets whose supports are known
if Cand  ≠ Ø, XY {i} ∉ S and (∄I^1 ⊆  XY {i})(supp(I^1) = 0) then
                S_k+1 = S_k+1 U { XY {i }}
          }
     }
compute support of itemsets in S_k+1
S = S U S_k+1
}
return IAR;
```

Algorithm 4: Mining Indirect Negative Association

Input: L_1- frequent 1-itemset, m_s-minsup,
VC- ValidCandidates, t_f- mediator Support, t_d- mediator dependency, IAR= Ø
Output: Indirect Negative Association Rules
Method:

```
C1,1 = {¬{i1}{i2}|i1, i2 ∈ L1, i1 ≠ i2}
   for {k = 1;Ck,1≠ Ø; k ++}
   { for {p = 1;Ck,p ≠ Ø; p++}  // Ck,p- k length negative and p length positive
     { for all I ∈ Ck,p
        {  if supp(I) ≥ ms
      { for each l (= X U Y) ∈ VC
   { if ( support(X U I ) ≥ tf && support ( Y U I )≥ tf
   if ( dependency( X U I ) ≥ td && dependency ( Y U I )≥ td
                         IAR= IAR  U (X,Y/I )
                   }
              }
          }
      for all joinable I1, I2 ∈ Lk,p do
         {      X = I1.negative, Y = I1.positiveUI2.positive
            I = ¬XY
if (∄X¹ ⊂ X)(supp(¬X¹Y ) ≥ ms) and  (∄Y¹ ⊂ Y )(supp(¬XY¹ ) < ms) then
      insert I into Ck,p+1
 if (XY ∉ S and ∄I¹ ⊂ XY, supp(I¹ ) = 0 then  Sk,p+1 = Sk,p+1 U { XY }
          }
     compute support of itemsets in Sk,p+1
     S = S ∪ Sk,p+1
       }
       for all X ∈ Lk+1, i ∈ L1 do
 if (∄X¹ ⊂ X)(¬X¹{i} ∈ L then  Ck+1,1 = Ck+1,1  ∪¬X{i}
}
return IAR;
```

5 Experimental Results and Performance Evaluation

To evaluate the performance of proposed algorithm experiments are performed on two synthetic transactional databases containing 5400 and 12000 transactions each and implemented on java platform. We concentrate on mediator support(t_f) which is a support of itemset and mediator and mediator dependency(t_d) which is estimated by "Eq. (1)".

Data set consisting of 5400 transactions with mediator support as 0.2,0.25,0.3,0.35; mediator dependence as 0.4,0.45,0.5,0.55 and the total number of rules generated as 205,20,63,31 and 13 respectively. Figure 1 shows the graph showing the mediator support and mediator dependency vs. total number of rules

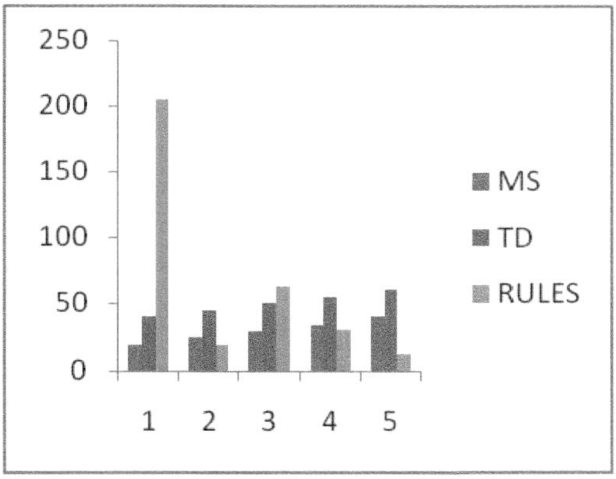

Fig. 1. graph showing the mediator support and mediator dependency vs. total number of rules for 5400 transactions

Figure 2 is generated by considering 12000 transactions with mediator support as 0.2,0.25,0.3,0.35,0.4 mediator dependence as 0.4,0.45,0.5,0.55,0.6 and the total number of rules generated 35,31,7,7 and 6 respectively

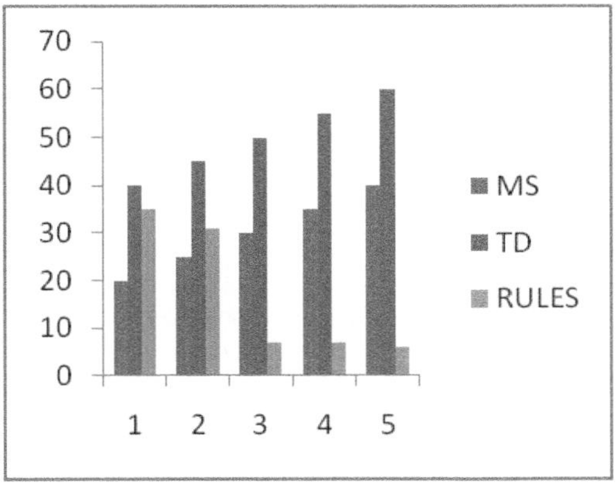

Fig. 2. graph showing the mediator support and mediator dependency vs. total number of rules for 5400 transactions

6 Conclusion and Future Work

Currently, available indirect association mining algorithms mine indirect positive associations between itempairs [8] and later we have extended to itemsets [21]. Further, in this paper, we propose an algorithm to discover all indirect positive and negative associations between itemsets. In indirect association mining for itempairs, algorithms require two join operations. To overcome this disadvantage we have proposed a new algorithm to mine indirect associations between itempairs and itemsets. This algorithm features, performing only one join operation and generating indirect positive and negative associations for pair of items and itemsets. In future we propose to elaborate this work by conducting experiments on large databases to test the scalability. Threshold selection is another issue that needs further investigation.

References

1. Agarwal, R., Aggarwal, C., Prasad, V.V.V.: Depth first generation of long patterns. In: Proceedings of ACM-SIGKDD International Conference on Knowledge Discovery and Data Mining (2000)
2. Agarwal, R., Aggarwal, C., Prasad, V.V.V.: A tree projection algorithm for generation of frequent itemsets. Journal of Parallel and Distributed Computing (Special Issue on High Performance Data Mining) (2000)
3. Ramasubbareddy, B., Govardhan, A., Ramamohanreddy, A.: Mining Positive and Negative Association Rules. In: IEEE ICSE 2010, Hefeai, China (August 2010)
4. Ramasubbareddy, B., Govardhan, A., Ramamohanreddy, A.: Adaptive approaches in mining negative association rules. In: Intl. Conference on ITFRWP 2009, India (December 2009)
5. Ramasubbareddy, B., Govardhan, A., Ramamohanreddy, A.: An Approach for Mining Positive and Negative Association Rules. In: Second International Joint Journal Conference in Computer, Electronics and Electrical, CEE 2010 (2010)
6. Brin, S., Motwani, R., Ullman, J., Tsur, S.: Dynamic itemset counting and implication rules for market basket data. In: Proceedings of the International ACM SIGMOD Conference, Tucson, Arizona, USA, pp. 255–264 (May 1997)
7. Savasere, A., Omiecinski, E., Navathe, S.: Mining for strong negative associations in a large database of customer transactions. In: Proceedings of the 14th International Conference on Data Engineering, Orlando, Florida, pp. 494–502 (February 1998)
8. Tan, P., Kumar, V., Srivastava, J.: Indirect association: mining higher order dependencies in data. In: Proceedings of the 4th European Conference on Principles and Practice of Knowledge Discovery in Databases, Lyon, France, pp. 632–637 (2000)
9. Wu, X., Zhang, C., Zhang, S.: Mining both positive and negative association rules. In: Proceedings of the 19th International Conference on Machine Learning (ICML 2002), Sydney, Australia, pp. 658–665 (July 2002)
10. Brin, S., Motwani, R., Silverstein, C.: Beyond market baskets: Generalizing association rules to correlations. In: Proc. ACM SIGMOD Intl.Conf.Management of Data, Tuscon, AZ, pp. 265–276 (1997)
11. Brijs, T., Swinnen, G., Vanhoof, K., Wets, G.: Using association rules for product assortment decisions: A case study. In: Proc.of the fifth ACM SIGKDD Conf on Knowledge Discovery and Data Mining, San Diego, Calif., pp. 254–260 (August 1999)
12. Cooley, R., Clifton, C.: Topcat: Data mining for topic identification in a text corpus. In: Procedings of the 3rd European Conference of Principles and Practice of Knowledge Discovery in Databases (1999)
13. Das, G., Mannila, H., Ronkainen, P.: Similarity of attributes by external probes. In: Proc. Of the Fourth ACM SIGKDD Intl Conf on Knowledge Discovery and Data Mining, New York, NY, pp. 23–29 (1998)
14. Melamed, D.: Automatic construction of clean broad-coverage translation lexicons. In: 2nd Conference of the Association for Machine Translation in the Americas, ATMA 1996 (1996)

15. Reynolds, H.T.: The Analysis of Cross-Classifications. Macmillan Publishing Co., New York (1997)
16. Savasere, A., Omiecinski, E., Navathe, S.: Mining for strong negative associations in a large database of customer transactions. In: Proceedings of the 14th International Conference on Data Engineering, Orlando, Florida, pp. 494–502 (February 1998)
17. Tari, Z., Bukhres, O., Stokes, J., Hammoudi, S.: The reengineering of relational databases based on key and data correlations. In: Sspaccapietra, S., Maryanski, F. (eds.) Searching for Semantics: Data Mining, Reverse Engineering, Etc. Chapman and Hall, Boca Raton (1993)
18. Winkler, R., Hays, W.: Statistics: Probabilty, Inference and Decision, 2nd edn. Holt, Rinehart & Winston, New York (1975)
19. Wan, Q., An, A.: An Efficient Approach to Mining Indirect Associations, pp. 1–26. Kluwer Academic Publishers, Boston
20. Li, L., Xu, F., Wang, H., She, C., Fan, Z.: IAM: An Algorithm of Indirect Association Mining. In: Proceedings of the 2004 International Conference on Intelligent Mechatronics and Automation Chengdu, China (August 2004)
21. Ramasubbareddy, B., Govardhan, A., Ramamohanreddy, A.: Mining Indirect Association between Itemsets. In: Proceedings of Intl Conference on Advances in Information Technology and Mobile Communication, AIM 2011, Nagapur, Maharastra, India. LNCS. Springer, Heidelberg (2011)
22. Cornelis, C., Yan, P., Zhang, X., Chen, G.: Mining Positive and Negative Association Rules from Large Databases. In: IEEE Conference (2006)

Application of FOP and AOP Methodologies in Concert for Developing Insurance Software Using Eclipse-Based Open Source Environment

Amita Sharma[1] and S.S. Sarangdevot[2]

[1] Tulsi Shree, B-16, Kanta Khaturia Colony, Bikaner-334003, India
amita214@rediffmail.com
[2] Director, Deptt. of Computer Science & I.T., J.R.N. Rajasthan Vidyapeeth (Deemed) University, Udaipur-313001, India
drsssarangdevat@yahoo.com

Abstract. Feature-Oriented Programming (FOP) and Aspect-Oriented Programming (AOP) are complementary methodologies that can be combined to overcome their individual limitations. In the present study, usefulness of this approach has been investigated in developing Insurance Software: TG_LifeInsurancesoft, using Eclipse-FeatureIDE-AJDT open source environment with Feature composition framework and enhanced tool chain: FeatureHouse. It is observed that integration of AOP concepts into stepwise refinement method of FOP enhances its capability of expressing and handling homogeneous as well as advanced dynamic crosscutting, thus reducing code redundancy, complexity, development time, maintainability and cost of the software system. The study concludes that combination of FOP and AOP methodologies using Eclipse-FeatureIDE-AJDT environment offers a powerful support for modular design and implementation of comprehensible, reusable, consistent, maintainable and cost effective insurance software system with user selected features.

Keywords: Feature-Oriented Programming, Aspect-Oriented Programming, Feature Model, Software Product Lines, Collaboration-based design, Stepwise development, Separation of Concerns, Crosscutting, Eclipse-FeatureIDE-AJDT Environment, FeatureHouse, Insurance Software.

1 Introduction

Feature-Oriented Programming (FOP) [1, 2, 3, 4] is a programming paradigm that allows decomposition of a program into its constituent features and thus extends the principle of separation of concerns [5, 6] to features. A feature [7, 8] is a logically cohesive piece of functionality or end-user characteristic or requirement that is relevant to a stakeholder. It is used to express the commonalities and variabilities of the domain specific programs and software systems [9]. FOP aims at the modularity of features and models a program as sets of user selected features that in aggregate represent the final product.

A. Abraham et al. (Eds.): ACC 2011, Part I, CCIS 190, pp. 592–606, 2011.

One of the strengths of FOP is its ability to produce many similar but functionally different programs simply by selecting the desired features. With the same set of features, a developer can generate several different software systems that share common features and differ in other features. Features refine other features incrementally. This stepwise refinement [10] leads to a layered stack of features. This helps in constructing well-structured software that can be tailored to the specific needs of the user and the application scenario.

AHEAD (Algebraic Hierarchical Equations for Application Design) [11, 12] is an architectural model for FOP. It is a basis for large-scale compositional programming [3]. It extends the concept of FOP to all software artifacts. However, command line operation is its big limitation. FeatureIDE [13, 14] is an Eclipse-based IDE that supports evolution of program families following architecture model. It provides tools for the feature-oriented design and implementation process.

FeatureHouse [15] is a descendent of AHEAD program generator. It provides facilities for feature composition based on a language independent model of software artifacts. It also provides an automatic plug-in mechanism for the integration of new artifact languages. It relies on a general model of the structure of software artifacts, called feature structure tree (FST), which represents the essential modular structure of a software artifact and abstracts from language-specific details. FeatureHouse can be used with the Eclipse-based open source visual development environment FeatureIDE.

Designing software using FOP provides significant advantages. However some issues emerge which reveal shortcomings of FOP approach and require further consideration. It is observed that lack of crosscutting modularity, scalability and feature interactions are the main drawbacks of FOP. During software evolution several modifications and extensions are made to fit the unanticipated requirements. These crosscut many existing implementation units in numerous ways and cause code scattering [16] and tangling [17], thereby increasing the complexity and impairing software quality. This highlights the need for the improvement in the approach so that efficient software can be evolved to suit the tailor made requirements of the user.

Aspect-Oriented Programming (AOP) [18, 19, 20] focuses on the separation and modularization of crosscutting concerns [21]. Invented by Kiczales [18], AOP defines a new program construct – **'aspect'** [8, 22], which is a software entity that implements crosscutting functionality in a modular way and provides most promising solution for elimination of code scattering and tangling. This reduces software complexity and improves quality. AspectJ [23, 24] is the most popular general purpose AOP extension to Java. It adds to Java a few new constructs: pointcuts, advice, intertype declarations and aspects. AspectJ Development Tools (AJDT) [25, 26] provides most popular and commercially successful Eclipse-based IDE support for AspectJ implementations with a rich set of features like Aspect Visualizer, Outline View, Editor Support and Debugger. Thus Eclipse-AJDT [27, 28] provides the most useful environment for AOP implementations.

However, in many cases aspects of AOP are not adequate to implement features stand alone. This is because features are mostly implemented by collaborations, and AOP technique is not very suitable to express and encapsulate collaborations. Another drawback is that aspect cannot be bounded to a certain scope. Also AOP technique does not support incremental software development process.

It is very interesting to note that AOP is complementary towards FOP systems [29, 30, 8]. If an architecture based on features is needed, AOP can add valuable capabilities which make up for FOP shortcomings [31,32]. The close integration of aspects and features holds several advantages. This approach improves the crosscutting modularity and enhances the ability to integrate structural independent features. Thus through their symbiosis, both FOP and AOP approaches profit from their individual strengths and overcome their individual limitations.

FOP and AOP integration approach has not so far been investigated in detail, in the evolution of business software. This motivated the authors to undertake this study to investigate the usefulness of this approach in developing Insurance Software: TG_LifeInsurancesoft for a representative life insurance system.

In summary, we make the following contributions:

- Systematic development of 'Feature Model' for the new domain of insurance.
- Identification of its important crosscutting concerns.
- Examining the feasibility and usefulness of FOP and AOP in concert approach for insurance software evolution.
- Testing the usefulness of Eclipse-FeatureIDE-AJDT environment and FeatureHouse tool chain for design and implementation of software.

The rest of the paper is organized as follows: Section 2 presents the overview of the representative Insurance System. Section 3 explains software requirements. Section 4 focuses on the design and implementation of the system using symbiosis of FOP and AOP approach. Section 5 discusses the observations regarding the impact of using this approach on various quality factors of the designed software. Section 6 provides the concluding remarks.

2 Insurance System

Insurance can be defined as a contract between two parties, where one promises the other to indemnify or make good any financial loss suffered by the later (the insured) in consideration for an amount received by way of 'premium' [33]. Man's desire for reduction of his uncertainty gave rise to the institution of insurance [34]. It is a form of risk management primarily used to hedge against the risk of contingent loss [35]. In addition, insurance provides economic and social benefit in the society i.e. prevention of losses, reduction in anxiousness, fear and increasing employment [36].

A life insurance policy is aimed to protect the income of the family's breadwinners. It allows saving of money for future needs in a tax efficient manner [37]. In the present scenario, the life insurance industry faces a dynamic global business environment. Radical changes have been taking place due to internationalization of activities, new risks, and innovative ideas on customer services [38].

This study focuses on modeling the life insurance system. Policies are taken by the customers, who pay for their insurance in accordance with some payment schedule. This model facilitates the recording of customer details, policy details, type of insurance plans, claim made against policy and loan on policy.

The functionalities of the system are - adding new customer and new policy, updating policy and customer information, recording claims, recording loans, keeping track on policy, customer, claim and loan database etc. The system classifies the insurance plans and furnishes relevant information about various plans. It also allows the user to select the plan according to his/her requirements.

The claims have been classified into three categories:

(1) *Policy maturity claim*: When the policy matures, customer asks for the claim.
(2) *Policy surrender claim*: When customer intends to surrender the policy.
(3) *Death claim*: When customer is no more in the world.

Whenever the customer takes a policy, the company issues a policy bond. The policy bond is the valid document which states that the customer and insurance company are bound with the insurance contract. It describes the rules of contract which both have to follow. It is a valuable document, because whenever customer requests for claim or loan on policy, he has to submit this bond to the insurance company.

On claim request or loan request, insurance company checks the policy status and policy duration. The policy status defines the position of policy - active or inactive (Whether the premium has been paid regularly or there are due premiums). Whenever due premiums are more than 5 (in case of yearly payment) or more than 10 (in case of half yearly payment /premium mode) the policy status is set inactive. The policy duration is determined by the number of years, premium has been paid by the customer.

The system is extensible and flexible. New services or functionalities can be added to or removed from the system with changing needs and requirements.

3 Software Requirements

The insurance system requires a software product with multi features that can be added or removed incrementally on demand. It should also modularize and implement the crosscutting requirements. Object-Oriented Programming (OOP) methodology has been found to be inadequate for this work. Designing insurance software using Feature-Oriented Programming makes software evolution faster and new features can be added as increments on existing software. In this way, a line of similar products with varying features is developed for the insurance domain. The software product meeting the user's requirements can be generated by simply selecting the suitable features. However, some crosscutting concerns of the system are not properly handled by FOP and for their implementation AOP methodology is required.

First step in the software evolution is to identify the system requirements and to depict them as **Use-Case Diagram** (Figure 1). This diagram explains the requirements from user's perspective. The software should include the end-user visible features. The product also demands a high degree of customizability, reusability, and evolvability.

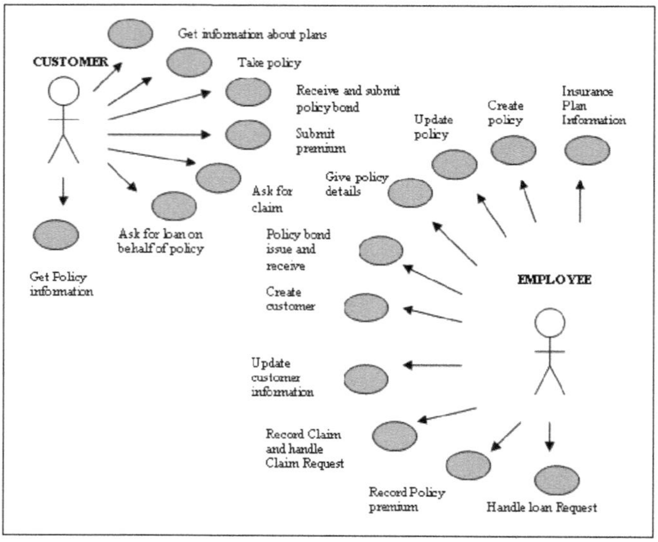

Fig. 1. Use Case Diagram of Insurance System

4 Design and Implementation

The TG_LifeInsurancesoft has been developed using symbiosis of FOP and AOP methodologies. It is user friendly and menu driven. The core program and functionality has been developed using FeatureHouse through FeatureIDE tool suite on Eclipse development platform. This was straightforward FOP development. In the first phase, the domain was analyzed to identify the features and their relationships and to represent them graphically, the Feature Model was developed. Next, features were implemented as feature modules. To produce a specific program, core features are selected from the feature model. Based on core feature selection FOP system is generated. The crosscutting concerns are implemented as aspects in AspectJ, using AOP methodology through Eclipse plug-in: AJDT, thus producing the final product.

4.1 Feature Model

FOP methodology modularizes software into feature modules which represent features. Features encapsulate user requirements in software modules. From the study and analysis of the system and problem domain, mandatory features and optional features are identified.

Figure 2 shows the feature model diagram for this system. The diagram clearly defines the mandatory features with filled balloons and optional features with empty balloons. TG_LifeInsurance is the root feature which has two mandatory features: Insurance Plan and Insurance Operations and one optional feature: Extra Services. Insurance Plan feature classifies the policy plans and has one mandatory: General and two optional features: Children Policy (which covers plans for children) and Female Policy. Female Policy is abstract feature which covers insurance plans for females. General feature describes the plans for all. It has two mandatory features: WholeLifePlan and ShortDurationPlan. WholeLifePlan is insurance policy for longer durations i.e. policy that matures nearly 60-70 years of policy holder's age or after his death. ShortDurationPlan generally covers insurance plan for short periods, for investment or tax saving or for good returns. This feature has two mandatory features: PlanWithNoreturn and PlanWithreturn and Three optional features: ShareBasedPlan, PlanforInvestment and PensionPlan.

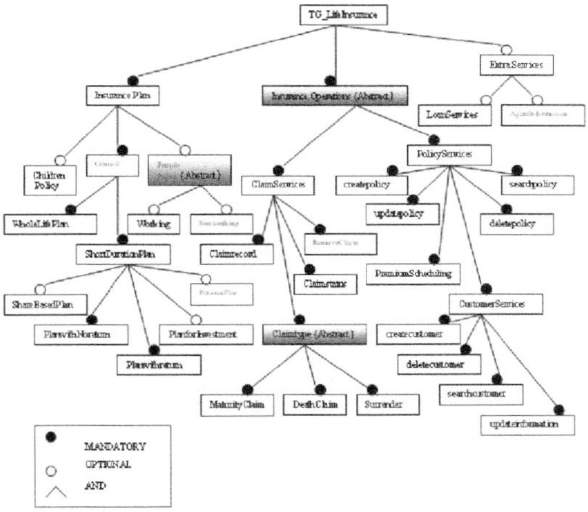

Fig. 2. Feature Model Diagram for Insurance System

Insurance Operations is abstract feature which covers insurances operations. It has two mandatory features: PolicyServices and ClaimServices which include all the policy and claim services and their information. In PolicyServices there are six features and all are mandatory. One of the features is CustomerServices which handles customer information and services. ClaimServices has four mandatory features and one of them is abstract feature: Claimtype. The Claimtype classifies claims into three categories: MaturityClaim, DeathClaim and Surrender. Extra Services feature has two optional features: LoanServices and AgentInformation.

Mandatory features are compulsory features of the system whereas the optional features can be included or excluded as per requirements. With the selection and exclusion of features, software provides different facilities in different configurations. Organization may choose the best configuration for meeting the system requirements.

4.2 Feature Implementation

The basic classes of this software include Policy, PolicyOper, PolicyPlan, PolicyClaim, Schedule, Customer, InsDatabase, InsDatabasePolicyplan, ServiceClass, ServiceforLoan, Welcomeform, Parentform, Scheduleform, Serviceform etc. Initially in FeatureIDE, the feature diagram for the system with model.m file is created..

Feature diagram is tree structure where each node represents the particular feature. FeatureIDE provides facility to edit these features. As soon as Feature diagram is created, feature folder reflects the related features in the form of separate folders. Here in each folder classes are coded. These are java files. In the next stage some classes are refined to add new features in the software and some new classes are also created. Welcomeform is the main interface class in this software.

The classes refined with features are:

(1) Interface Classes: Parentform and Serviceform are interface classes which are refined with InsurancePlan, InsuranceOperations and ExtraServices features. At every level of Feature Model tree, new feature is coded in these classes. A few new interface classes like Policyinfoform, Query_Customerform, PolicyPlanform etc are also coded.

(2) Intermediate classes: Policy, PolicyOper, PolicyPlan, PolicyClaim, Service, ServiceForLoan, Customer, Schedule etc are intermediate classes that control the system functionality. Policy, PolicyOpe, PolicyClaim, Customer, Scheduler classes are refined in InsuranceOperations by including features like the policy working, customer services, scheduling policy services and claim services. PolicyClaim is further refined in claimtype feature and new classes like PolicyDeathClaim, PolicySurrender, PolicyMaturityClaim are created. PolicyPlan and PolicyOper are refined in InsurancePan features to add different insurance plan information. PolicyCategory, PolicyPlanWomen etc. classes, are created under this feature. ServiceForLoan and Service classes are refined in ExtraServices feature.

(3) Database classes: InsDatabase, InsDatabasePolicyPlan etc are classes for database controlling which are refined in different features.

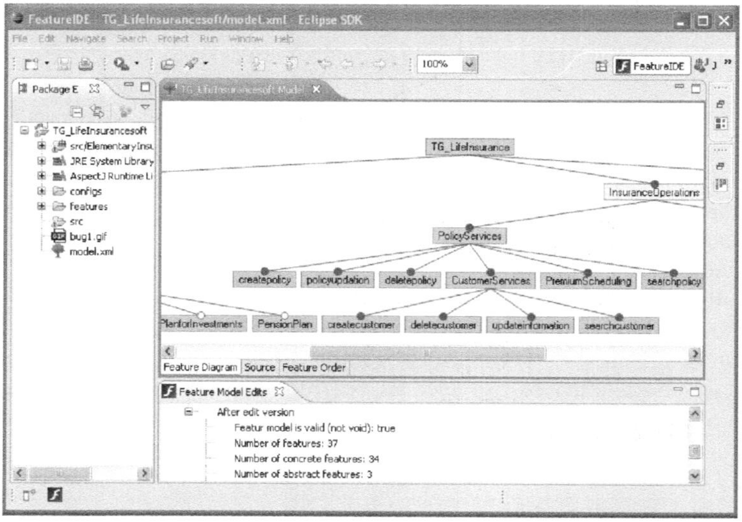

Fig. 3. Feature Diagram view, Feature Model view and Package Explorer view of TG_LifeInsurancesoft

As coding phase is over, user can select the required features and configure software accordingly. In FeatureIDE, the software is executed by forming an equaton file in configs folder. Equation represents the set of features selected in the software.There can be more than one equation file composed with different feature selections. These equation files run independently, one at a time by setting run configuration.

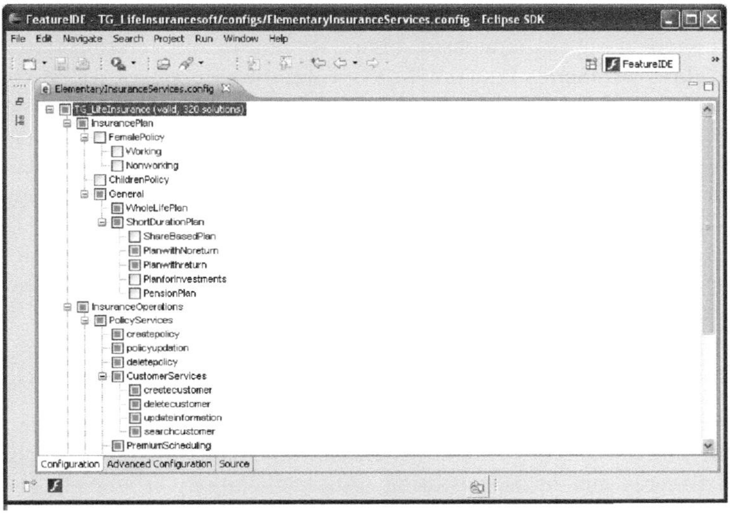

Fig. 4. Configuration view of ElementaryInsuranceServices Equation of TG_LifeInsurancesoft

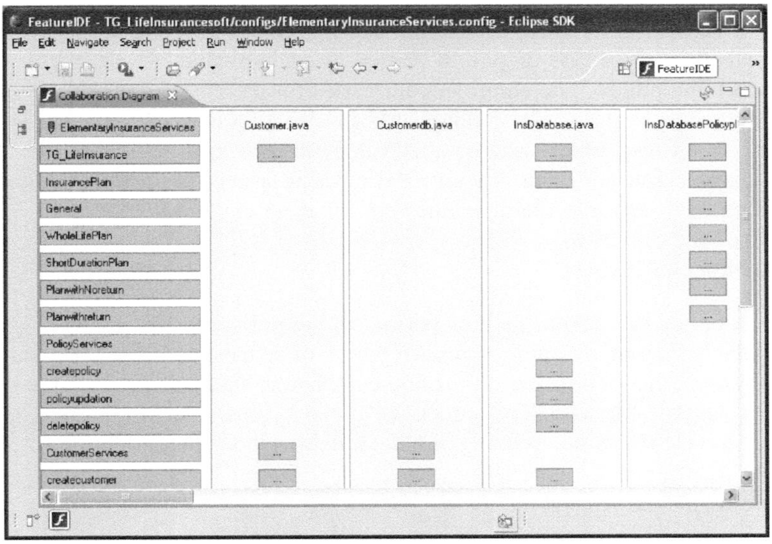

Fig. 5. Collaboration Diagram view of ElementaryInsuranceServices equation of TG_LifeInsurancesoft

In this study, FeatureIDE provided good tool support for editing, building and debugging FOP part of the program on Eclipse platform. Feature Model Editor and Feature Diagram are fascinating tools, which make development of the software more real and understandable. Figure 3 shows the Feature Model Editor with Package Explorer View of TG_LifeInsurancesoft. Another important view is the Configuration Editor View. This editor helps the user to select or deselect the required features for the system. It also specifies the valid and invalid combinations of the features. Thus only the correct design is simulated. Figure 4 shows Configuration Editor View of ElementaryInsuranceSeries Equation of TG_LifeInsurancesoft.

Collaboration diagram is an important tool which shows all the features and classes in a particular equation. The vertical side shows all the features and upper horizontal side shows all the classes. This diagram describes how classes are included or refined in different features. Figure 5 shows the Collaboration diagram for the ElementaryInsuranceSeries equation of TG_LifeInsurancesoft.

The various navigational views of FeatureIDE ease the software development and help in understanding the system behavior. With their help, software design can be easily modified and updated.

4.3 Identification of Crosscutting Concerns and Aspects

It is observed that there are ten crosscutting concerns in the system, which may cause code scattering and tangling, thereby increasing the complexity of the system. They can be best represented as aspects using AOP methodology. These aspects are coded in AspectJ through AJDT plug-in of Eclipse platform

Policyvalue Aspect

Whenever the customer requests for claim or loan on policy, the insurance company has to calculate the value of policy known as paidupvalue. It is the current value acquired by the policy. The claim amount varies for different categories of claim but the paidupvalue is the same. Paidupvalue is also required for calculation of loan amount. So, instead of calculating this value in each calamt function of different categories of claim and loan amount, **Policyvalue** aspect is created. This aspect is invoked on the function getpaidupvalue () of PolicyOper class.

Checklockperiod Aspect

There is a policy rule about 'locking period' of the policy. Locking period is the time before which customer cannot surrender policy or request for loan on policy. In the present system, the locking period is of 5 years, before that customer cannot surrender policy or request for loan. On request of claim or loan, locking period is always checked; and for the same invoking of **Checklockperiod** aspect is required.

Checkpolicyperiod Aspect

Policy period is the duration of policy being active. Policy status informs whether the customer is paying regular premiums or not i.e. whether the policy is live or elapsed. As stated earlier if due premium number is more than 5 (when mode is yearly) or 10 (when mode is half yearly) policy is elapsed. During the claim or loan request, policy status is always checked. If policy is elapsed, no loan can be issued. In case of claim, due premium amount and extra charges will be subtracted from the total amount of policy. This work is better handled by this aspect.

Checkpolicybond Aspect

Whenever the customer requests for claim or loan, he has to submit the policy bond to the company. Before giving the claim amount or loan amount, it is always checked whether the customer has submitted the policy bond to the company or not. This concern is again crosscutting to the claim and loan classes and requires the invocation of **Checkpolicybond** aspect.

ReportNullentry Aspect

This Insurance system has several interfaces (forms) for user interactions with text boxes where user has to input certain values. The text box value should never be null. This crosscutting concern is taken care by ReportNullentry aspect.

UpdateNotification Aspect

Whenever the policy values in the system database are updated, the customer should be notified. This crosscutting concern requires **UpdateNotification** aspect.

Policybonuscheck Aspect

Every year company adds bonus to the policy value and whenever the claim amount is calculated, the pending bonus is added to the policy value. This concern automatically checks the bonus and if not added, it adds it to the policy value.

Logging Aspect

Policy and claim details are recorded and maintained in separate log files. The file records the modifications on policy which is done by **Logging** aspect.

Servicetracing Aspect

The tracing of policy methods is handled by Servicetracing aspect. This displays the flow of execution which helps in understanding the system.

Validplancheck Aspect

Whenever a policy is updated and claim request is handled. The policy plan is checked whether the policy modification and claim request is valid in respect of plan or not. This job is neatly done by **Validplancheck** aspect.

4.4 Implementation of Aspects

Each crosscutting concern is modeled as aspect using join point model of AspectJ with well defined join points, pointcuts and advice. Aspects are woven in the core program by aspect weaver to produce the final system. This is done by AspectJ compiler through AJDT. AJDT provides good AOP tool support. The most important are Outline View, Cross References View, Aspect Visualizer and Debugger. Figure 6 shows the Outline, Cross References, and Advice View for Policybonuscheck aspect.

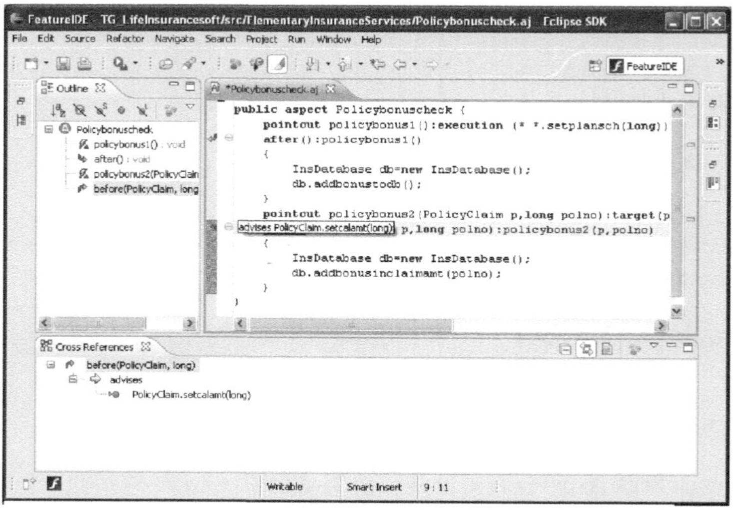

Fig. 6. Outline view, Cross References view and Advice view of TG_LifeInsurancesoft

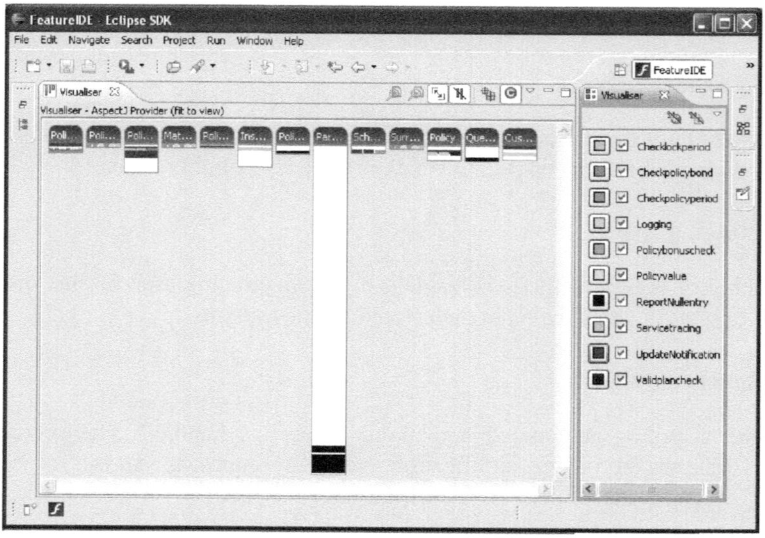

Fig. 7. Aspect Visualiser view of TG_LifeInsurancesoft

Aspect Visualizer is the most powerful tool of AJDT. This tool helps in understanding the impact of aspects on the entire software system. Figure 7 shows the screen shot of Aspect Visualizer which represent the classes and aspects within the application as bars and the places where aspects affect the code as stripes on the bars. The full flow of the program can be viewed in the debugger window provided by AJDT. In this way correct implementation of the aspects can be checked.

For verification and validation, the software was tested by entering different data sets and the resulting output was examined. It was noticed that all the functionalities of the system worked correctly. This indicated the 'Correctness' of the application software. The software met all the desired specifications and needs.

5 Discussion

This investigation has been made to study the usefulness of combination of FOP and AOP methodologies in developing real world insurance application software. Impact of using this approach on various quality factors of the software has been examined. Observations made in the study are presented in this section.

Benefits of incorporating FOP and AOP together are fairly obvious. AOP is able to enhance FOP in providing mechanism to deal with homogeneous as well as dynamic crosscutting concerns. This eliminates code scattering and tangling. In this way concerns are cleanly separated and modularity is enhanced. This also eliminates code redundancy and reduces complexity.

Feature classification via Feature Model increases the comprehensibility and understandability. Features can be easily added, removed and modified. This clearly reflects the flexible nature of features which makes software highly adaptive to changing requirements.

Features can refine other features incrementally. Thus FOP designed software supports reusability. From a single Feature model, different versions of the software can be produced by selecting or deselecting the set of features. This is called 'Software Product Line' (SPL). This supports development of a product family and reduces software design cost and time considerably. Reduction of maintainability cost and software evolution time, are also observed. Software can be tailored to the specific needs of the user and the application scenario.

Eclipse-FeatureIDE-AJDT provides the most advanced and comprehensive IDE environment that represents a proven, reliable, open source technology, on which consistent commercial products can be quickly designed, developed and deployed using the selected approach. Several views and editors of this environment make the work of the programmer easier, less error prone and reliable. This facilitates easier system evolution and reduced development time and cost. With the use of FeatureHouse tool chain, software artifacts written in different languages are easily composed in the model. Using aspect-enhanced FOP, the power of aspect is controlled. Thus FOP and AOP are complementary to each other and their integration overcomes their individual shortcomings.

6 Conclusion

In this study, a user friendly and menu driven application software TG-LifeInsurancesoft, for the selected Insurance system has been designed and implemented using FOP and AOP methodologies in concert, using Eclipse-FeatureIDE environment and FeatureHouse tool chain.

It is observed that FOP and AOP are complementary methodologies and their combination overcomes their individual limitations. Integration of AOP concepts into stepwise refinement method of FOP enhances its capability of expressing and handling homogeneous as well as advanced dynamic crosscutting. Using aspect-enhanced FOP, the power of aspect is controlled.

Use of this approach increased several software quality factors such as modularity, understandability, readability, maintainability, extendibility, reusability, flexibility, adaptability and ease of evolution. Reduction in development time and costing were also observed.

There is overall improvement in the quality and performance of the software. Several innovative visual and navigational features of Eclipse-FeatureIDE-AJDT environment made the development work of the software easy and reliable.

Successful implementation of the application concludes that combination of FOP and AOP methodologies using Eclipse-FeatureIDE environment offers a powerful support for modular design and implementation of comprehensible, reusable, consistent, maintainable and cost effective insurance software system with user selected features.

Acknowledgments. The authors thank Prof. Divya Prabha Nagar, Vice Chancellor, J.R.N. Rajasthan Vidyapeeth (Deemed) University Udaipur, for encouragement and providing necessary research facilities.

References

1. Prehofer, C.: Feature-Oriented Programming: Back to the Future (Keynote). In: Apel, S., et al. (eds.) FOSD 2010, Eindhoven, The Netherlands, vol. 1 (2010)
2. Gunther, S., Sunkle, S.: Feature-Oriented Programming with Ruby. In: Apel, S., et al. (eds.) FOSD 2009, Denver, Colorado, USA (11-18 2009)
3. Apel, S., Lengauer, C., Möller, B., Kästner, C.: An algebra for features and feature composition. In: Bevilacqua, V., Roşu, G. (eds.) AMAST 2008. LNCS, vol. 5140, pp. 36–50. Springer, Heidelberg (2008)
4. Sharma, A., Sarangdevot, S.S.: Investigating the Application of Feature-Oriented Programming in the Development of DirectToHome Service Customer-Information Software Using Eclipse-FeatureIDE Environment. Int'l J. of Knowledge and Research in Management and E-Commerce 1(1), 11–15 (2011)
5. Dijkstra, E.W.: On the role of scientific thought. EWD 447, Nuenen, The Netherlands (1974)
6. Hursch, W., Lopes, C.V.: Separation of Concerns. Technical Report NU-CCS-5-03 (1995)
7. Batory, D.: Feature models, grammars, and propositional formulas. In: Obbink, H., Pohl, K. (eds.) SPLC 2005. LNCS, vol. 3714, pp. 7–20. Springer, Heidelberg (2005)

8. Apel, S.: The Role of Features and Aspects in Software Development. Ph.D. dissertation, School of Computer Science, University of Magdeberg (2007)
9. Apel, S., Leich, T., Saake, G.: Aspectual Feature Modules. IEEE Trans. On Software Engineering 34(2), 162–180 (2008)
10. Batory, D., Sarvela, J.N., Rauschmayer, A.: Scaling Step-Wise Refinement. IEEE Trans. On Software Engineering 30(6), 355–371 (2004)
11. Batory, D.: Feature-Oriented Programming and the AHEAD Tool Suite. In: Proc. ICSE 2004 (2004)
12. Batory, D.: A Tutorial on Feature-Oriented Programming and the AHEAD Tool Suite (ATS), Revised (2004)
13. Leich, T., Apel, S., Marnitz, L.: Tool Support for Feature-Oriented Software Development – FeatureIDE: An Eclipse-Based Approach. In: OOPSLA Workshop on eclipse technology eXchange (ETX), San Diego, USA (2005)
14. Kastner, C., et al.: FeatureIDE: A Tool Framework for Feature-Oriented Software Development. In: Proc. ICSE 2009, Vancouver, Canada, May 16-24 (2009)
15. Apel, S., Kastner, C., Lengauer, C.: FeatureHouse: Language-Independent, Automated Software Composition. In: Proc. ICSE 2009, pp. 221–231. IEEE Computer Society, Washington DC, USA (2009)
16. Sommerville, I.: Software Engineering, 8th edn. Pearson Education Limited, London (2009)
17. Gradecki, J.: Mastering AspectJ. Wiley Publishing Inc., Chichester (2003)
18. Kiczales, G., et al.: Aspect-Oriented Programming. In: Aksit, M., Auletta, V. (eds.) ECOOP 1997. LNCS, vol. 1241, pp. 220–242. Springer, Heidelberg (1997)
19. Elrad, T., Filman, R.E., Bader, A.: Aspect-Oriented Programming. Communications of the ACM 44(10), 29–32 (2001)
20. Sharma, A., Sarangdevot, S.S.: Investigating the Application of AOP Methodology in Development of Financial Accounting Software Using Eclipse-AJDT Environment. In: Proc. ICM2ST 2010. AIP Conference Proc, vol. 1324, pp. 224–228 (2010)
21. Kaur, A., Johari, K.: Identification of Crosscutting Concerns: A Survey. Int'l J. of Computer Science and Technology 1(3), 166–172 (2009)
22. Elrad, T., et al.: Discussing Aspects of AOP. Communications of the ACM 44(10), 33–38 (2001)
23. Kiczales, G., et al.: Getting Started with AspectJ. Communications of the ACM 44(10), 59–65 (2001)
24. Kiczales, G., Hilsdale, E., Hugunin, J., Kersten, M., Palm, J., Griswold, W.G.: An Overview of AspectJ. In: Lee, S.H. (ed.) ECOOP 2001. LNCS, vol. 2072, pp. 327–353. Springer, Heidelberg (2001)
25. Colyer, A., Clements, A., Harley, G., Webster, M.: Eclipse AspectJ: Aspect-Oriented Programming with AspectJ and the AspectJ Development Tools. Addison-Wesley Professional, Reading (2004)
26. AJDT: Frequently Asked Questions, `http://www.eclipse.org/ajdt/faq.php`
27. Sharma, A., Sarangdevot, S.S.: Eclipse-AJDT Environment: A Diamond from Open Source Technology. In: Proc. ICNGC2S 2010. IETAN Conference Proceedings, vol. 0123, pp. 120–125 (2010)
28. Sharma, A., Sarangdevot, S.S.: Event Management System: Design and Implementation Using AOP Methodology in Eclipse-AJDT Environment. Int'l J. of Engineering Science and Technology 3(1), 139–149 (2011)
29. Apel, S., Batory, D.: When to Use Features and Aspects? In: Proc. Int'l Conf. Generative Programming and Component Engineering, pp. 59–68 (2006)

30. Apel, S., Leich, T., Saake, G.: Aspectual Mixin Layers: Aspects and Features in Concert. In: Proc. Int'l Conf. Software Engineering, pp. 122–132 (2006)
31. Apel, S., Leich, T., Rosenmuller, M., Saake, G.: FeatureC++: On the Symbiosis of Feature-Oriented and Aspect-Oriented Programming. In: Proc. Int'l Conf. Generative Programming and Component Engineering, pp. 125–140 (2005)
32. Wang, J.-h., Bai, C.-z.: Software Evolution with Feature-Oriented and Aspect-Oriented Programming. In: Proc. ICICIC 2008. IEEE Computer Society, Los Alamitos (2008)
33. Principles and Practice of Life Insurance. Committee on Insurance and Pension, The Institute of Chartered Accountants of India, New Delhi (2008)
34. Mellon, J.J.: Are Non – Insured Pension Plans Engaged in the Business of Insurance? The Journal of Insurance 30(4), 505–516 (1963)
35. Sinha, T.: The Indian Insurance Industry: Challenge and Prospects. Swiss Reinsurance Company, Swiss Reinsurance Company, Hong Kong (2005)
36. Ahmed, N., et al.: Determinants of Performance: A Case of Life Insurance Sector of Pakistan. Int'l Research J. of Finance and Economics 61, 123–128 (2011)
37. Kumar, J.: Life Insurance Industry – Past, Present and the Future. Bimaquest VIII(1), 41–55 (2008)
38. Murthy, T.N., et al.: Emerging Trends in Indian Insurance Market. The IUP Journal of Risk and Insurance (July-October 2009)

Revisiting B-Trees

Kushal Gore, Pankaj Doke, and Sanjay Kimbahune

Tata Consultancy Services Limited, TCS Innovation Labs, Mumbai, India
{kushal.gore,pankaj.doke,sanjay.kimbahune}@tcs.com

Abstract In this paper we calculate value of k (minimum number of keys that need to be present in a page of B-Tree) for the hardware properties of most common desktops. Prior to that we provide an easy to understand introduction to B-Trees since they are used in all popular software constructs and systems. We believe that a good conceptual understanding of B-Trees along with an appreciation for the mathematical rigor would always be helpful to a software person. Given their ubiquity in almost all the systems we are exposed to, for example, databases, mobile phones, server software, networking equipment, it is critical that software professional have a good understanding of them. In this paper, we refer to the original papers of B-Trees and elucidate the various terms and concepts with appropriate examples.

Keywords: B-Trees, multi-way search trees, data structures, random access files, dynamic index maintenance.

1 Introduction

In today's world large amount of digital data (image, voice, video etc.) gets generated on classical personal computers as well as on modern computing and multimedia devices such as mobile phones, digital cameras. This data needs to be organized in such a way that its retrieval at any time later in the future is faster. Various data structures [4][5] are used for this purpose. (Does one know what data structures are used to store data on memory card? Does one know what data structures are used for storing a simple address book on the cell phone?) B-Trees are data structures used to organize and maintain very huge amount of data on secondary memory (like hard disks, memory cards). B-Trees were introduced in 1969 by R. Bayer and E. McCreight in their classical paper [1]. In 1969 E.F. Codd also developed Relational database model which was a revolutionary model based on the mathematical theories of relations, relational algebra and predicate logic. During the 1970s it turned out that B-Trees and relational database systems are complementary [2]; therefore, most of the relational database systems are developed using B-Trees today. Various variants of this data structure have been developed, for example simple prefix B-Trees as described in [3].

To understand the concept of B-Trees we will try to provide lucid introduction to the B-Trees, but at the same time we will use terms and notations used in the original paper [1]. Due to lack of space we will not explain the retrieval, insertion and deletion algorithms for B-Trees in this paper but one can refer to [1],[7] to know the details and explanation of these algorithms. Time complexities of these algorithms depend on

A. Abraham et al. (Eds.): ACC 2011, Part I, CCIS 190, pp. 607–618, 2011.

the height of the B-Tree. Author of [1] has given upper and lower bounds on the height. We would explain how these values can be computed. The height depends on the parameter k (Minimum number of keys that a page in B-Tree must hold). The value of k depends upon some hardware properties (average disk seek time, transfer rate, etc.) of computing machines. We revisit the formula given in [1] for choosing optimum value of k . Using this formula we compute value of k for hardware properties of most common desktop used in year 2010.

2 Literature Survey

In [7] author has described basics of B-Trees. The paper has described the methods for insertion, deletion presented in [1]. It also has described few variations of the B-tree, like B+-tree, B*-Trees. It has reviewed the problems of maintaining a B-tree in a multiple user environment. It has also presented. IBM's general purpose file access method which is based on the B-Tree. Although this paper gives a good understanding of B-Trees it is not devoted wholly for B-Trees.

In [8] authors have explained B-Tees and its variants B*Trees, B+ Trees, and B*+Trees. The paper has presented a new method for finding the approximate operation costs and storage utilization in a B-tree and its variants.

3 Our Contribution

Our contribution to this paper is in terms of calculating value of k for the hardware properties of most common desktops using the formula given in [1] and comprehending the original papers and explaining it in simple terms to the audience. This paper is organized as follows.

In the subsection 3.1 we start with definition of a B-Tree and present its examples. In subsection 3.2 we explain how the author of [1] has arrived at upper and lower bounds on the height of a B-Tree, mentioned in [1]. In subsection 3.5 we have explained how the time complexity of retrieval, insertion, deletion algorithms for B-Trees depends on height of the tree and ultimately on the value of k . In the section 5 of observations we have described in detail how we have computed the value for k for the hardware properties of most common desktops of year 2010.

3.1 B-Tree Definition and Examples

B-Trees were designed to organize (organization refers to retrieval, insertion and deletion of keys) and maintain large scale *index* for a random access file. Index is collection of *index elements*. These index elements are fixed sized pairs (x, α) of data items placed one after another. Here x is a key and α is the information associated with x . This information α could either be a pointer storing address of the data (which could be raw data like a video file or a huge text file) or actual data itself. Generally α holds the address of the data (because we have restriction that index elements should be of fixed size.) instead of storing the actual data.

Large index can't be stored in main memory (RAM) at one time [6]. Thus it is kept on a backup store (secondary memory like hard disk, memory card).

Pages are blocks of information transferred between main memory and backup store (Not to be confused with memory paging). The index is organized in pages of fixed size; each page could hold up to $2k$ number of keys (k is a natural number that generally depends on hardware properties; it is chosen such that the performance of retrieval algorithm becomes optimal. Refer to section 3.5 and observations section to know more about choice of the number k). These pages are nodes of a tree called *B-tree*, as shown in Fig.1.

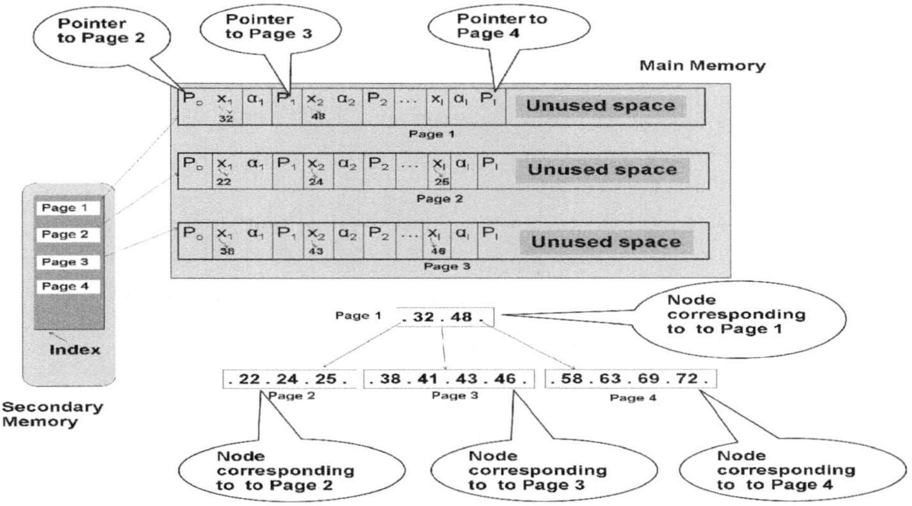

Fig. 1. Relation between Pages in an Index and Nodes of the B-Tree corresponding to the index

In Fig.1, there is an index stored in secondary memory consisting of 4 pages namely Page 1, Page 2, Page 3, and Page 4. A B-Tree corresponding to this index consists of 4 nodes where each node corresponds to a page in the index. These nodes reside on main memory. Index is collection of pages and each page can be visualized as an array of triplets as shown in the Fig.1. Consider organization of Page 1 in the main memory. P_0 is a pointer to the Page 2. (It means P_0 stores address of Page 2) Similarly P_1 is pointer to the Page 3 and P_2 is pointer to the Page 4. Key $x_1 = 32$ and α_1 is information associated with the key x_1. Key $x_2 = 48$ and α_2 is information associated with the key x_2. How the keys are organized in pages of B-Tree is described in detail in the section 3.3.

From the above discussion we could relate it to the definition from the original paper.

Definition of B-Tree

This is the definition of a B-Tree from the paper [1].

"A directed tree denoted by $T(k,h)$ for $k>0$, $h \geq 0$ is a B-tree if $h=0$ OR

Each path from the root to any leaf has length h, h is called height of the tree, that is, h = number of nodes in path.

Each node except the root has at least $k+1$ children. The root is leaf or has at least two children.

Each node has at most $2k+1$ children."

Examples of a B-Tree

Consider an index consisting of the index elements (x_i, α_i) where keys $x_i \in$ {22, 24, 25, 32, 38, 41, 43, 46, 48, 58, 63, 69, 72}. If we chose value of k as 2 and if we insert these keys in an empty tree[1] in the order 24, 25, 38, 41, 32, 22, 69, 72, 48, 43, 46, 58, 63; we will get the tree in Fig.2

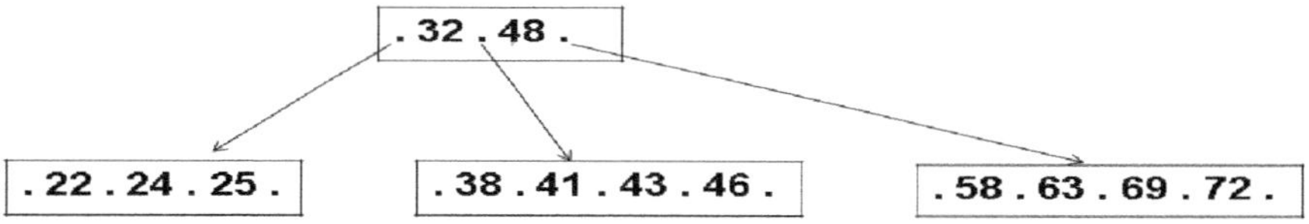

Fig. 2. Example of a B-Tree with k=2, h =1

Consider an index consisting of the index elements (x_i, α_i) where keys $x_i \in$ {22, 24, 25, 32, 38, 41, 43, 46, 48, 52, 58, 60, 63, 66, 69, 72, 78, 80, 84, 88, 92, 96, 98}.

Tree in Fig.3 is obtained by inserting keys in an empty tree in following sequence: 24, 25, 38, 41, 32, 22, 69, 72, 48, 43, 46, 58, 63, 28, 80, 84, 88, 92, 96, 98, 78, 80, 66, 52, 60. It can also be obtained from a Tree in Fig.2 by inserting in it the keys in following sequence 28, 80, 84, 88, 92, 96, 98, 78, 66, 52, 60. One can refer to the Insertion algorithm presented in [1].

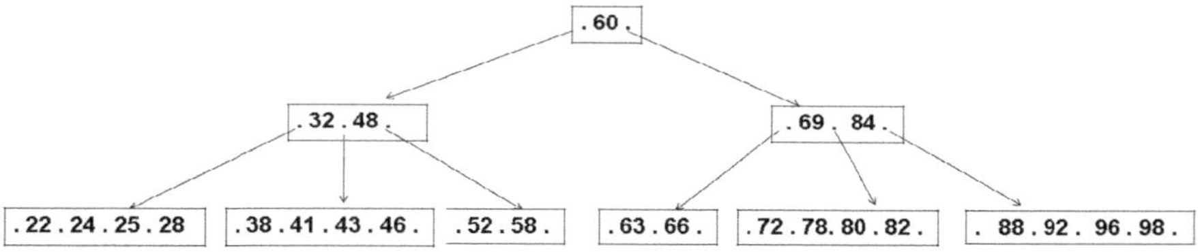

Fig. 3. Example of a B-Tree with k=2, h =3

[1] Empty tree is a tree with zero number of pages/nodes.

A B-Tree propagates if a node is split into two nodes and it contracts (shrinks) if two siblings are merged or *catenated* into a single node. The splitting and catenation processes are initiated at the leaves and propagate toward the root. If the root node splits, a new root is created and this is the only point at which the height of the B-Tree increases. We notice that, a B-Tree depends upon two parameters k and h, where k is the page size which depends on some hardware properties (like average disk seek time, transfer rate, etc.) of the computing machine used; k is the height which depends on the value k.

3.2 Upper and Lower Bounds on Height of a B-Tree

If we study algorithms for retrieval insertion and deletion presented in [1], we observe that number of operations[2] required for retrieval, insertion and deletion of a key from the index depend upon the height of the B-Tree corresponding to the index. Therefore it is necessary to know the upper and lower limits on the height of the tree for given value of k. These bounds are given in [1]. We will now present some computations to explain how these values are found.

Let $N_{\min}$, $N_{\max}$ be minimum and maximum number of nodes and $I_{\min}$, $I_{\max}$ be minimum and maximum number of keys present in a B-Tree $T(k,h)$.

Calculation of $N_{\min}$

In this case root will have single key, hence it can have at the most two children. Every node apart from root should have at least k number of keys. Hence they will have $k+1$ children each. This indicates that at any level we will have certain number of nodes. The exact figure can be found from the table 1.

Table 1. Minimum number of nodes in the tree at any level

Level	Minimum number of nodes at level	Maximum number of nodes at level
1	1	1
2	2	$(2k+1)$
3	$2(k+1)$	$(2k+1)\times(2k+1) = (2k+1)^2$
4	$2(k+1)\times(k+1) = 2(k+1)^2$	$(2k+1)^2\times(2k+1) = (2k+1)^3$
.	.	.
h	$2(k+1)^{h-2}$	$(2k+1)^{h-1}$

[2] Operation – fetching of a page from secondary memory or writing a page to secondary memory.

Hence total number of nodes in the tree is summation of all the entities in the second column of the table 1.

$$N_{\min} = 1 + 2 + 2(k+1) + 2(k+1)^2 + \dots\dots\dots\dots + 2(k+1)^{h-2}$$

$$= 1 + 2((k+1)^0 + (k+1)^1 + (k+1)^2 + +(k+1)^{h-2})$$

$$= 1 + 2 * \sum_{i=0}^{h-2} (k+1)^i$$

$$= 1 + \frac{2}{k}((k+1)^{h-1} - 1) \qquad (1)$$

The last term is calculated using the formula for summation of n terms in geometric series.

Calculation o f $I_{\min}$

Minimum number of keys present in the tree $I_{\min}$ can be calculated as,

$$I_{\min} = 1*1 + \mathrm{k}* \frac{2}{k}((k+1)^{h-1} - 1)$$

$$I_{\min} + 1 = 2(k+1)^{h-1}$$

$$\left(\frac{I_{\min} + 1}{2}\right) = (k+1)^{h-1} \qquad (2)$$

Calculation of $N_{\max}$

In this case every node (including root) will have maximum allowed i.e. $2k$ number of keys. Hence total number of nodes in the tree is summation of all the entities in the third column of Table 1.

$$N_{\max} = \sum_{i=0}^{h-1} (2k+1)^i = \frac{1}{2k}((2k+1)^h - 1) \qquad (3)$$

Calculation of $I_{\max}$

Maximum number of keys present in the tree $I_{\max}$ can be calculated as,

$$I_{\max} = 2\mathrm{k}* \frac{1}{2k}((2k+1)^h - 1)$$

$$\therefore I_{\max} + 1 = (2k+1)^h \qquad (4)$$

Taking $\log_{2k+1}$ on both sides of (4) we get

$$\log_{2k+1}(I_{\max} + 1) = \log_{2k+1}(2k+1)^h$$

$$\therefore \log_{2k+1}(I_{\max} + 1) = h$$

Similarly,

Taking $\log_{k+1}$ on both sides of (2) we get

$$\log_{k+1}\left(\frac{I_{\min}+1}{2}\right)=\log_{k+1}(k+1)^{h-1}$$

$$\therefore \log_{k+1}\left(\frac{I_{\min}+1}{2}\right)=h-1$$

$$\therefore 1+\log_{k+1}\left(\frac{I_{\min}+1}{2}\right)=h$$

Bounds on the Height

In the last subsection we have found two values of h, one for minimum number of keys and one for maximum number of keys. These are the upper and lower limits for the height.

$$\log_{2k+1}(I+1)\leq h\leq 1+\log_{k+1}(\frac{I+1}{2}) \text{ for } I\geq 1 \tag{5}$$

$h=0$ for $I=0$.

Here I is number of keys in the B-Tree. Observe that h depends on value k only. Larger the k lower will be the value of h.

3.3 Organization of the Page

Each page in an index (stored in secondary memory) corresponds to a node of a B-Tree as shown in Fig.1. A page contains at least k and at the most $2k$ number of keys. Root page (page corresponding to root node of the tree) can hold minimum 1 and maximum up to $2k$ keys. If a page P is not a leaf and has l number of keys then P has $l+1$ children.

In each page, keys are sequential in increasing order say $x_{1,}x_2,\ldots,x_{l;}$ where

$k\leq l\leq 2k$ For non root pages and

$1\leq l\leq 2k$ For the root page.

Further P contains l+1 pointer $P_{o,}P_1,P_2,\ldots,P_l$ to the children of P. If P is leaf page this pointers are undefined. Logically a page can be visualized as shown in Fig.4.

P_o	x_1	α_1	P_1	x_2	α_2	P_2	...	x_l	α_l	P_l	Unused space

Fig. 4. Organization of a page

α_i is information associated with the key x_i. The triplet (x_i,α_i,P_i) or omitting information associated with α_i, the pair (x_i,P_i) is called as the *entry*.

Let $P(P_i)$ be the page pointed by P_i. Let $K(P_i)$ be the set of all keys in the maximal sub-tree whose root is P_i, (A sub-tree T_P with root P is said to be maximal sub-tree if T'_P is any other sub-tree with root P then T'_P is contained in T_P), then keys are arrange in such a way that following conditions always hold.

$$y < x_1 \text{ if } y \in K(P_0) \tag{6}$$

$$x_i \leq y < x_{i+1} \text{ if } y \in K(P_i) \tag{7}$$

$$x_l \leq y \text{ if } y \in K(P_l) \tag{8}$$

These conditions suggest that all keys less than x_1 can be traced by traversing the maximal sub-tree with root is $P(P_0)$. All the keys less than x_{i+1} but greater than or equal to x_i can be traced by traversing the maximal sub-tree with root $P(P_i)$. Similarly all keys greater than or equal to x_l can be traced by traversing the maximal sub-tree with root $P(P_l)$.

Trees in Fig.2 and Fig.3 are examples of B-Trees in $T(2,2)$ and $T(2,3)$ respectively. They satisfy all the 3 conditions mentioned above.

3.4 Time Complexity of the Algorithms

Let $f_{\min}$ and $f_{\max}$ be minimum and maximum number of pages fetched from the secondary memory and $w_{\min}$ and $w_{\max}$ be minimum and maximum number of pages written on secondary memory. By comprehending algorithms given in [1] for retrieval, insertion and deletion of key y from an Index, we observe that,

Worst case operations required for retrieval is

$f_{\max} = h$

Worst case operations required for insertion is

$f_{\max} = 3h - 2$ (In case of overflow)

$w_{\max} = 2h + 1$

Worst case operations required for deletion is

$f_{\max} = 2h - 1$

$w_{\max} = h + 1$

Here, h is the height of the B-Tree $T(k, h)$ corresponding to the index.

Notice that all these operations depend linearly on height of the tree. Hence these algorithms are of $O(h)$.

From inequality (5) we could see that,

For $I \geq 1$,

$$h \leq 1 + \log_{k+1}(\frac{I+1}{2})$$

$$\therefore h \leq 1 + \log_{k+1}(\frac{I+1}{2}) \leq \log_{k+1}(I) \leq \log_k(I)$$

It shows that retrieval, insertion and deletion algorithms are of $O(\log_k(I))$.

3.5 Choosing Optimum Value for *k*

In the last subsection we have seen that retrieval, insertion and deletion algorithms depend on the parameter k, hence we should choose the value of k such that their performance is as high as possible. Now we will revisit the formula given in [1] for calculating the optimum value of k.

In [1], it is mentioned that the time taken for writing or fetching a single page can be expressed in the form:

$$\alpha + \beta(2k+1) + \gamma \ln(\upsilon k + 1)$$

Where,

α is fixed time spent per page, (e.g., average disc seek time plus fixed CPU overhead, etc.)

β is time to transfer single page entry.

γ is constant for the logarithmic part of the time(e.g., for a binary search)

υ is factor for average page occupancy, $1 \leq \upsilon \leq 2$

We have seen that number of pages fetched, written during these operations is proportional to h, we could take it as δh. Then the total time T spent per operation can be approximated by,

$$T \approx \delta h(\alpha + \beta(2k+1) + \gamma \ln(\upsilon k + 1))$$

Approximating h by $\log_{\upsilon k+1}(I+1)$ we get,

$$T \approx \delta \log_{\upsilon k+1}(I+1)(\alpha + \beta(2k+1) + \gamma \ln(\upsilon k + 1))$$

Minimum value of T is obtained if k is chosen such that,

$$\frac{\alpha}{\beta} = \frac{2}{\upsilon}((\upsilon k+1)\ln(\upsilon k+1) - (2k+1)) = f(k,\upsilon) \quad (9)$$

We need to choose k such that $f(k,\upsilon) \approx \frac{\alpha}{\beta}$.

To obtain a near optimal page size for the test examples given in paper [1] it is assumed that α = 50 ms and $\beta = 90\mu s$. It was been observed that an acceptable choice should be $64 < k < 128$.

4 Observations

Now we compute the value of k for typical hardware properties of most common desktop in year 2010. To calculate k we will need values of α and β.

We assume that average disk seek time for most common desktop to be 9 milliseconds [9]. We can take this as value of α. We can take data transfer rate of a typical 7200 rpm desktop hard drive approximately equal to 1030 Mbits/second which is equal to 128.75 MB/second [9].

We have value of β for year 1969. Using this value we will first calculate *entry size* of the each entry of the page for year 1969. Then using this value of *entry size* we will calculate value of β for current hardware properties of most common desktop.

Calculation of Entry Size

In [1] author has used value of β (= time to transfer single page entry) as 90 microseconds. According to a table given in [2], the transfer rate for year 1969 was considered as 150 KB/second. That is 150 KB data gets transferred in 1 second. Hence amount of data transferred in 90 microseconds is

$$90*10^{-6}*150*10^{3}=13500*10^{-3}=13.5\text{ Bytes}$$

Therefore the entry size would have been considered as 13.5 Bytes in 1969 while writing the paper [1].

Calculation of β

To compute the value of β for current hardware properties of a most common desktop in year 2010, we will consider entry size as 13.5 Bytes as obtained above. As discussed at the beginning of the section we have taken data transfer rate equal to 128.75 MB/second.

It shows that 128.75 MB data gets transferred in 1 second. Therefore β (= Time required to transfer single entry of page) is

$$\beta=\frac{(\text{size of single entry})}{128.75}=\frac{13.5}{128.75*10^{6}}=0.1049*10^{-6}\text{ sec}=0.1049\mu s$$

Therefore value of β would turn out to be 0.1049 microseconds.

As mentioned at the beginning of the section we have taken value of α as 9 milliseconds. Now we also have found the value of $\beta=0.1049$ microseconds. Hence,

$$\frac{\alpha}{\beta}=\frac{9*10^{-3}}{0.1049*10^{-6}}\approx 85833$$

Equation (9) says that, we will have to find value of k such that,

$$f(k,v)\approx\frac{\alpha}{\beta}=\frac{\left(\begin{array}{c}\text{fixed time spent per page, (e.g., average disc}\\ \text{seek time plus fixed CPU overhead, etc.)}\end{array}\right)}{\text{time to transfer single page entry}}=85833$$

Using the right hand side of the equation (9) we have computed value of $f(k,v)$ for different values of k and v. These values are presented in Table 2. By observing

Table 2. Values of $f(k, \upsilon)$ for different values of k and υ

K	f(k, 1)	f(k, 1.5)	f(k, 2.0)
5000	65188.96739	75905.14756	82112.61507
5050	65941.20496	76764.59168	83034.15741
5100	66694.43245	77625.02578	83956.68977
5150	67448.64015	78486.44016	84880.20244
5190	68052.70567	79176.27106	85619.712
5200	68203.81856	79348.8253	85804.6859
5210	68354.9699	79521.41799	85989.69827
5250	68959.95833	80212.17187	86730.13083
5300	69717.05032	81076.47072	87656.52805
5350	70475.08554	81941.71286	88583.8686
5400	71234.05518	82807.88947	89512.14366
5450	71993.95058	83674.99191	90441.34457
5500	72754.76326	84543.01168	91371.46284
5550	73516.48488	85411.94045	92302.49013
5560	73668.93756	85585.83456	92488.80394
5570	73821.4262	85759.76463	92675.15373
5580	73973.95073	85933.73061	92861.53942
5600	74279.10725	86281.77002	93234.41825
5650	75042.62233	87152.49235	94167.23916
5700	75807.02222	88024.09955	95100.94496
5750	76572.29917	88896.58384	96035.52789
5800	77338.44553	89769.93762	96970.98031
5850	78105.45383	90644.15337	97907.29475
5900	78873.31669	91519.22374	98844.46382
5950	79642.02688	92395.14148	99782.48029
6000	80411.57727	93271.89947	100721.337
6050	81181.96086	94149.49071	101661.027
6100	81953.17078	95027.90831	102601.5434
6150	82725.20024	95907.14551	103542.8795
6200	83498.04259	96787.19564	104485.0284
6250	84271.69126	97668.05214	105427.9838
6300	85046.13982	98549.70856	106371.7391
6350	85821.38191	99432.15856	107316.288
6360	85976.525	99608.74324	107505.2925

these entries we could see that if k is chosen such that $5190 < k < 6360$ then the value of $f(k, v)$ is approximately equals to 85833.

5 Conclusion

We have made an attempt to provide an easy to understand introduction to B-Trees. We have explained how the bounds on the height of the B-Tree are computed. We have shown that how the value of k can be calculated for the hardware properties of most common desktop in year 2010.

Acknowledgments. We thank Ananth Krishnan (CTO, TCSL), Arun Pande (Chief Scientist & Head TCS Innovation Labs, Mumbai), the developers at TCS Innovation Labs, Thane, Arijit De, Hiten Panchal, Lajish VL, Bhushan Jagyasi and Della Sajan for their invaluable support, feedback and efforts.

References

1. Bayer, R., McCreight, E.: Organization and maintenance of large ordered indices. Acta Informatica 1(3), 173–189 (1972)
2. Bayer, R.: B-Trees and Databases, Past and Future, Software Pioneers. Springer, Heidelberg (2002)
3. Bayer, R., Unterauer, G.: Prefix B-Trees. ACM Transactions on Databa'se Systems 2(1), 11–26 (1977)
4. Foster, C.C.: Information retrieval: information storage and retrieval using AVL trees. In: Proceedings of the 20th National Conference, Cleveland, Ohio, United States, August 24-26, pp. 192–205 (1965)
5. Knott, G.D.: A Balanced Tree Storage and Retrieval Algorithm. In: Proceedings of the 1971 International ACM SIGIR Conference on Information Storage and Retrieval (1971)
6. Ammann, A., Hanrahan, M., Krishnamurthy, R.: Design of a memory resident DBMS. In: Proc. IEEE Spring Computer Conference, pp. 54–57 (1985)
7. Comer, D.: The Ubiquitous B-Tree. ACM Computing Surverys 11(2), 121–137 (1979)
8. Chu, J., Knott, G.: An analysis of B-trees and their variants. Information Systems 14(5), 359–370 (1989)
9. Hard disk drive information on Wikipedia, `http://en.wikipedia.org/wiki/Hard_disk_drive`

Multi-density Clustering Algorithm for Anomaly Detection Using KDD'99 Dataset

Santosh Kumar, Sumit Kumar, and Sukumar Nandi

Department of Computer Science and Engineering
Indian Institute of Technology Guwahati
Guwahati, India
{santosh.kr,sumit.kr,sukumar}@iitg.ernet.in

Abstract. Anomaly detection is currently an important and active research problem in many fields and involved in numerous application. Handle huge amount of data or traffic over the network is most challenge full task in area of Intrusion Detection System to identify the intrusion by analyzing network traffic. So we have required the some efficient technique for analyze the anomaly from network traffic which have good detection rate with less false alarm and it should be also time efficient. Motivation by above, in this paper we present a Multi-density Clustering Algorithm for anomaly detection (MCAD) over huge network traffic (Offline statistical traffic). In this approach we have improved the Birch Clustering [1] index problem with ADWICE (Anomaly detection with fast Incremental Clustering) [2] model using grid index. We have used the Intra cluster distance parameter property which can improve the quality of cluster in respect of outliers by the average intra cluster distance reduction. So in this approach rather than threshold concept at insertion of data point in the cluster we have used the cluster quality indices for insert a data point in the cluster and checked it is being optimized or not. The method is verified by experimental of proposed approach on KDD'99 [3] data set which is standard off line data set. Experimental results illustrate better false alarm detection rate and time efficiency by using proposed MCAD approach.

Keywords: Anomaly Detection, k-mean clustering, ADWICE model of clustering, BIRCH model of clustering, MCAD clustering.

1 Introduction

A network intrusion attack can be any use of network that compromises its stability or the security information that is stored on computers connected to it. A very wide range of activity falls under this definition, including attempts to destabilize the network as a whole, gain unauthorized access to file or privilege, or simply mishandling and misuse of software. Intrusion detection is the process of identifying and responding the malicious activity targeted at computing and networking resources. Intrusion detection systems are software or hardware product that monitor and analyze network. In particular Network based intrusion detection system called row data packets from the network and carefully analyze for abnormal or anomaly packets thereby detecting

A. Abraham et al. (Eds.): ACC 2011, Part I, CCIS 190, pp. 619–630, 2011.

security violations. Unlike host based IDS [4], network based IDS [5] protects a group of system by generalizing the security concept to a network.

In anomaly detection models the behavior of the system with a profile and any deviation from the known pattern is considered as intrusion. There are mainly three types of Anomaly detection techniques according the data labels, namely as Supervised anomaly detection [6], Unsupervised anomaly detection [6] and Semi-supervised anomaly detection [6]. In supervised anomaly detection training data set are labeled as normal and abnormal or we can build a model with both type of data set. A classifier model in which only normal data set used for the training is called Semi-supervised anomaly detection. While in Unsupervised anomaly detection the training data instances are not labeled so it is less complex. In unsupervised assumption is made that normal data are larger in comparison of abnormal or anomaly data.

Anomaly detection still faces many challenges, where one of the most important is the relatively high false alarm. Recently many data mining techniques used for the anomaly detection, some of them are: Machine learning based [7], decision tree based [8], self-organizing map based, K-mean clustering based [9], Birch clustering based, fuzzy c-Mean clustering [10] and finite automata based etc. We have proposed a Multi-density clustering based approach for anomaly detection, which is an improvement of ADWICE model of Birch clustering. In this approach we have used an average intra cluster distance in which rather than threshold concept at insertion of data point cluster we have used the cluster quality indices for insert the data point into the cluster and check the optimality for same. For experiment of proposed model we have used the KDD'99 standard data set for training and testing data.

2 Literature Survey

In this part we have to explain some basic knowledge of clustering to make obvious sense of problem statement and description of aim of the paper. Literature survey follows as:

2.1 Clustering

A process of grouping a set of physical or abstract objects into classes of similar objects is called clustering and a cluster is a collection of data objects that are similar to one another within the same cluster and are dissimilar to the objects in other clusters. Given two objects, represented as normalized feature vectors with continuous roughly linear variables, the similarities can be computed by considering the geometrical distance between the two vectors. A common distance measure is the well known Euclidian distance [1]. There are various types of clustering as:

2.1.1 k-Mean Clustering [9]

K-mean is partitioning clustering. It divides the data points into k clusters. In this clustering randomly choose k data instance from data points and make them initial cluster center after that assign the points nearest of the cluster center the replace each center with mean f the points around the cluster center. Repeat above process until there is no further updating of cluster center. The advantages of K-mean clustering are its scalability and its time complexity $O(nkt)$. Where n denotes the number of points, While k is number of partitions and t is a number of iterations. The disadvantages of K-mean clustering are, it is not able to find non convex cluster and defining number k cluster before clustering and obtaining k is NP hard.

2.1.2 BIRCH (Balanced Iterative Reducing and Clustering Using Hierarchies) Cluster [1]

It is designed for large amount of numerical data by integration of hierarchical clustering and other iterative clustering. It overcomes the two problem of hierarchical clustering by making it scalable and making it able to undo what was previously done. BIRCH store a compact summarization in from of clustering feature and thus reduce the problem of clustering the original data points into one of clustering the set of summaries, which is much smaller than the original dataset. Clustering decisions in BIRCH are made without scanning all data points or all currently existing clusters and thus it is said to be incremental. There is a Database oriented constraint in BIRCH that the amount of memory available is limited where as dataset can be arbitrary large mean that memory available can be 20% of the database. The advantages of BIRCH clustering's fast enough due to no I/O operations are needed. In this clustering we don't have to work on entire data points rather than we have to work on sub clusters and more accurate because more outlier can be eliminated. The time complexity of BIRCH clustering is $O(n)$. The disadvantages of this clustering's, this clustering is not suitable for multi-density cluster. It keeps same threshold for the entire sub cluster for insertion of points whether cluster are small and dense or sparse and big.

3 Problem Definition and Proposed Algorithm

Kalle Burbeck and Simin Nadjm-Tehrani presents an ADWICE model [2] which used the first phase of the existing BIRCH clustering framework to implement fast, scalable and adaptive pure anomaly detection. In this model ADWICE they used BIRCH clustering in which only cluster feature of the data points of clusters are stored and it used grid index to detect the anomaly. It works on the concept of pure anomaly detection based system in which it form cluster of normal packets while training a model. According to this model we had to work on cluster features rather than data points. The distance between data point and a cluster is calculated from Euclidean distance between data point and the centroid of the cluster and the distance between two clusters can be calculated from the Euclidean distance between the centroids. Each cluster of the leaf node can absorb new data point if Euclidean distance between data point and centroid is less than threshold requirement.

There are three basic principle of ADWICE model for learning or adapting.

a) If no cluster is close enough to absorb the data point then data point vector v_i is inserted into the model as a new cluster. If there does not exist a leaf subspace in which the new cluster fits, the new leaf is created. However, there is no need of any additional update of the tree, since higher up nodes do not contain any summary of data below.

b) When the closet cluster absorbs to v_i, its centroid is updated accordingly. This may cause the cluster to move in space. A cluster may potentially move outside its current subspace. In this case, the cluster is removed from its current leaf and inserted into a new tree from the root, since the path all the way up to the root may have changed. It the cluster was the only one in the original leaf, the leaf itself is removed to keep unused subspace without any leaf representations.

c) If cluster is removed or forgotten the index is only changed if the leaf is now empty in which case the leaf of the removed cluster will also removed.

As ADWICE model uses BIRCH clustering for cluster the data and BIRCH cluster itself unable to hold multi-density cluster as it use distance based measures to determine that whether to include data point in the cluster or not. At the same time it use same threshold for forming all cluster whether the cluster is sparse and big cluster or the cluster is small and dense. The BIRCH cluster uses same threshold while insertion of a point and then during merging of cluster it increment same threshold so lots of points which should not be included in the cluster are being included.

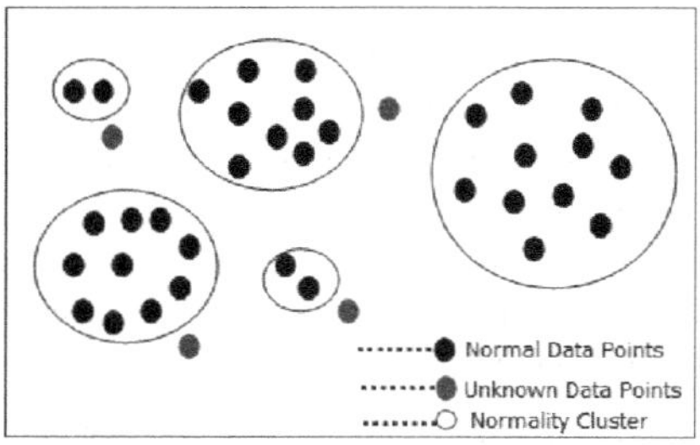

Fig. 1. ADWICE model for anomaly

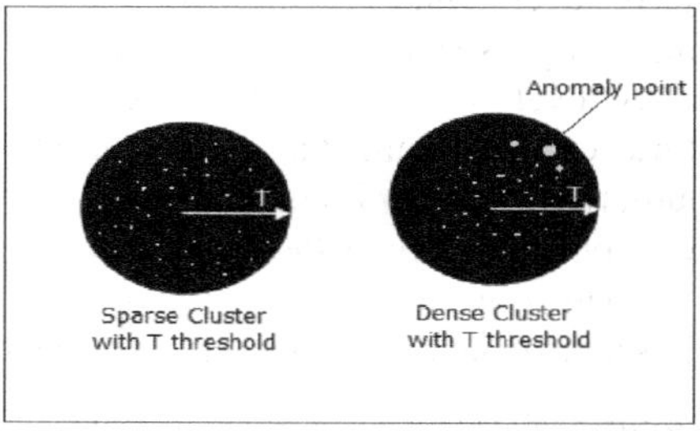

Fig. 2. ADWICE model thresholds

We got motivation form above disadvantages of ADWICE model consequently we are proposing a Multi-density Clustering Anomaly Detection (MCAD) algorithm for pure anomaly detection to reduced the diameter of dense and small cluster and keeps the advantages of BIRCH cluster. Our algorithm remains linear using summarization technique of cluster. According to Ying zhao and George Karypsis in Hierarchical Clustering Algorithms for Document Datasets [12], the average intra-cluster distance is the parameter which can be used to make the quality cluster. We have used the property of cluster quality improvement in which the cluster quality will improve however the average intra cluster distance reduces. So we have used cluster quality indices to insert a point in the cluster rather than threshold concept of insertion point in the cluster and checked whether it is being optimized or not. The proposed training and testing as followed.

3.1 Training Steps for Proposed Anomaly Detection Algorithm

INPUT: NC Number of clusters, Training data packets, $\alpha - constant$ which is a multiple of cluster quality indices ratio of intra-cluster distance and inter-cluster distance used while merging step.

OUTPUT: Trained model with NC number of clusters.

- **Step1:** insert (data packets m)
- **Step2:** Descend cluster feature (CF) tree if average intra-cluster distance reduces or have minimum change
- **Step3:** if m optimizes leaf node average intra-cluster distance
- **Step4:** then add cluster feature (CF) packet to the leaf node
- **Step5:** else
- **Step6:** if $(leafnode \prec BranchingFactor)$
- **Step7:** add it next to leaf where it reduces AID minimum.
- **Step8:** update the CF tree up to parent node
- **Step9:** else
- **Step10:** split (leaf node, m)
- **Step11:** repeat step 1-10 till number of node equals to N
- **Step12:** rebuild tree
- **Step13:** traverse from left to right
- **Step14:** merge the cluster represented by node if average intra-cluster distance doesn't increases by $\alpha - constant$
- **Step15:**if $\left(size_{initial} (\bmod el) = size_{final} (\bmod el)\right)$
- **Step16:** increase $\alpha - constant$ repeat step 12-15.
- **Step17:** else repeat step 1-10.

Details of some above steps are given here as follows:

Step1: Insertion: For inserting m points into cluster feature tree we are looking for cluster indices quality which means that cluster becomes better quality if average intra-cluster distance decreases. So if point's m optimizes the average intra-cluster distance then it should be included in the cluster.

Step2: Identify the appropriate leaf: Starting from the root node we recursively descend the CF tree where it optimizes the average intra-cluster distance or if it does not reduces the average intra-cluster distance the we will looked for child node to which it have done minimum changes in average intra-cluster distance after merging so it will avoid the condition that if points are equal distance to the two cluster where it to be proceed.

Step3: Modifying the leaf and path: Reaching at the leaf node, find out the leaf entry which is being optimized and update the CF tree. If none of the leaf node is being optimized then we will add it besides the leaf entry to which it is nearest and if the number of leaf entry are lesser than branching factor of tree then it is nearest otherwise we had to split the nodes and modify up to the parent node and check out for

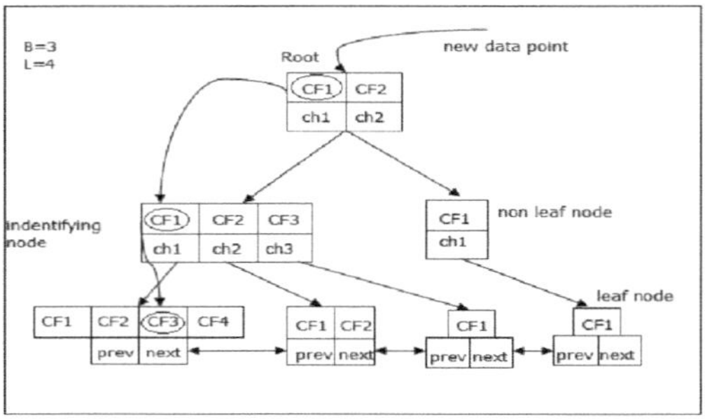

Fig. 3. Optimization of node in case of threshold and intra clustering distance

them also if the number of entry exceed branching factor than splitting occur at parent node also. Splitting occurs by taking the two farthest node of cluster and merging other node according to their closeness so after insertion of point we had to modify up to parent node of cluster summary, fig.4 shows the splitting of leaf node.

Step4: Rebuilding the tree: When the number of nodes representing each cluster reaches at maximum number of cluster then we had to rebuild the tree. For rebuilding the tree when we have single point as a cluster representative, then we cannot directly merge the closest point as though they are inter-relatively closer but rather than that point can be far apart into the overall scenario. So that for merge firstly we have required threshold parameter when we have only a single point for merging. This threshold is calculated by the calculating of average distance of the closest node center and to search closed node we had to check next node and previous node. After putting this threshold we assured that at least few points merged in to the cluster. Fig.5 shows the splitting of parent node and modified up to parent node.

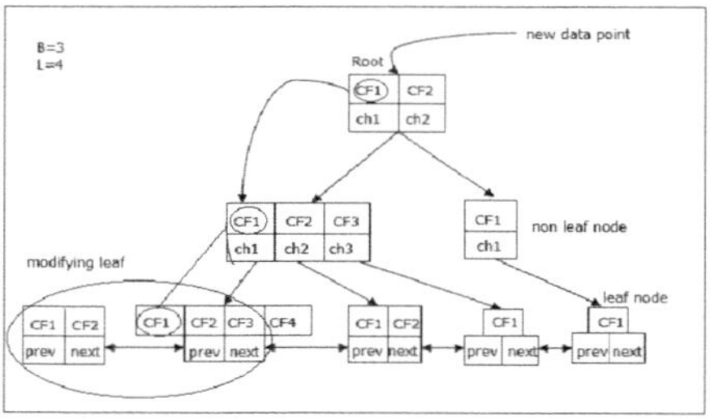

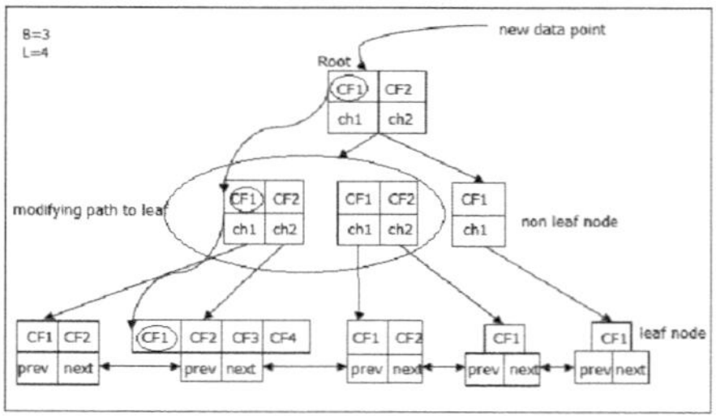

Fig. 4. Splitting of leaf node

Fig. 5. Splitting of parent node

Step5: Identifying the proper child while descending from root node: In ADWICE model while descending from root node we have come across the problem where, the root node has equal distance from two child cluster. This problem we have solved in our proposed algorithm by using a condition that the point will goes to that cluster where it will increase lesser intra cluster distance, fig.7 shows the same condition where the point "m" has equal distance from cluster1 (left cluster) and cluster2.

According to ADWICE model the points goes to cluster2 (which is a error in ADWICE model) and according to our proposed MACD algorithm it will goes to cluster1.

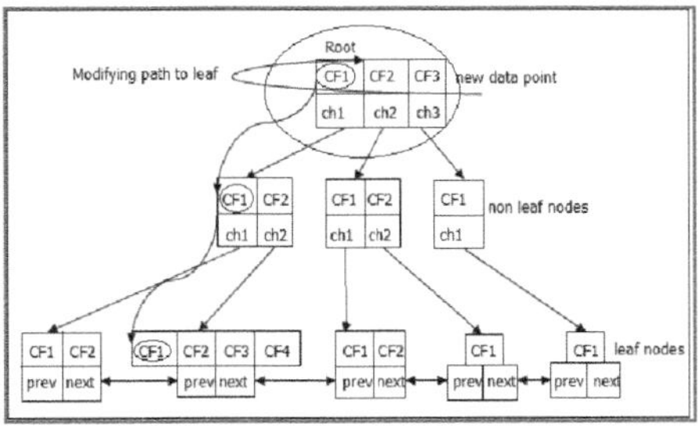

Fig. 6. Modification up to parent node

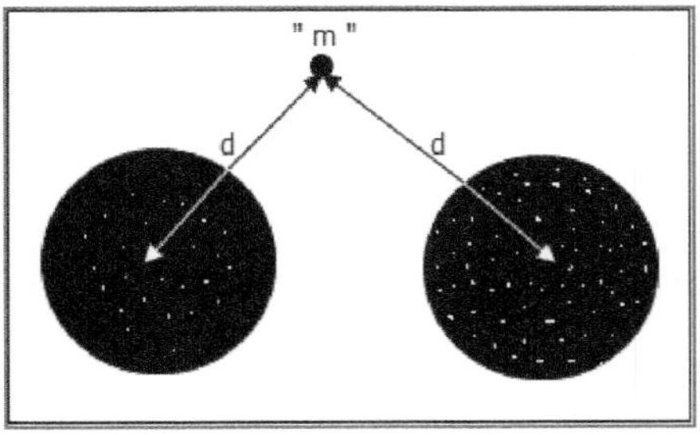

Fig. 7. Point m same distance from cluster 1 and 2

Step6: α(Avg. intra cluster distance)$_{\text{initial}}$ >(Avg. intra cluster distance)$_{\text{final}}$: In ADWICE model if the cluster is far from denser and smaller cluster although it is within the range of threshold then it will not be merged when it has same threshold for all merging cluster whether it is bigger cluster or it is smaller cluster. For solving the problem we have used a condition where α(Avg. intra cluster distance) $_{\text{initial}}$ > (Avg. intra cluster distance) $_{\text{final}}$ used for cluster merging (not for direct merging). In this condition closest cluster merging if clusters are inter-relatively closer but and in overall scenario if they are far apart of it then they will not be merged. Figure8 shows C2 cluster is closer to C3 cluster but it will not merged to any cluster and if we increases the intra-cluster distance between cluster C2 and cluster C3 to a large ratio then it resulting as decreasing the cluster quality.

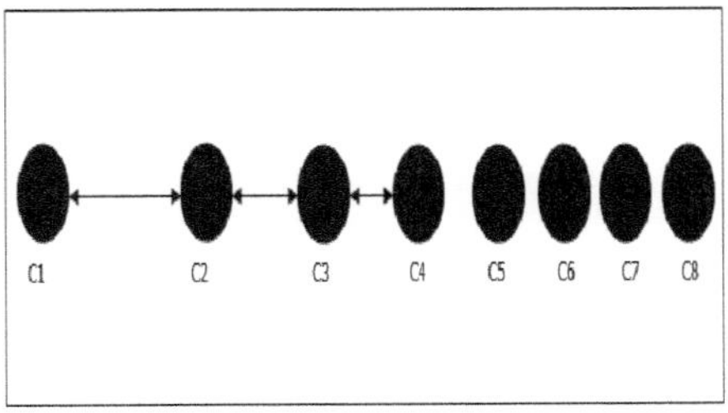

Fig. 8. Intracluster distance comparison

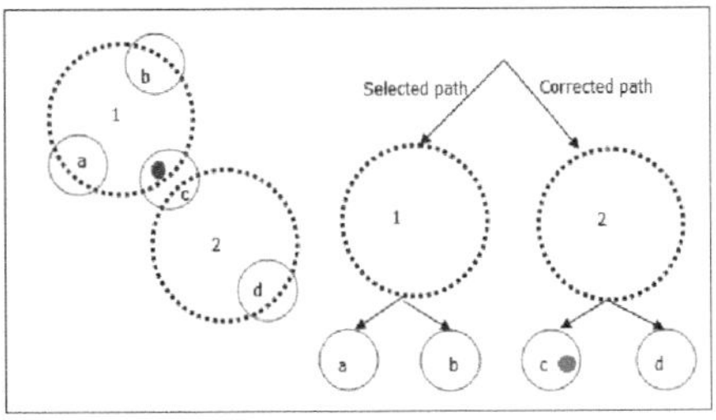

Fig. 9. Indexing of testing point in MCAD

Step7: Solving the Grid indexing problem of BIRCH and ADWICE model: BIRCH and ADWICE both model of clustering have used grid indexes for indexing the testing data points which suffers from high computational complexity and time complexity. The proposed model is based on intra clustering and inters clustering distance of each data point. So the proposed model doesn't suffer from complexity problem. Figure 9 shows that the point should goes to node2 but it goes to node1 at left.

3.2 Proposed Testing Algorithm for Anomaly Detection

After build a training model for anomaly detection, we have to test this training algorithm by following testing algorithm for anomaly detection algorithm. In the testing algorithm we have started the testing a point from the root node, if the testing point reduced the average intra cluster distance of parent node then we go ahead further for testing. If testing point does not optimizes any of the descendent node then it declared as anomaly point and if optimizes the leaf node then it declared as normal point. The algorithm shows the important steps of the testing algorithm.

Input: Clusters construct by training model.
Output: Decision on testing data points as anomaly or normal.

- **Step1:** Insert testing data
- **Step2:** Descend CF tree if the average intra cluster distance reduces or have a minimum change
- **Step3:** if a testing data point m optimizes the leaf node by reducing the average intra cluster distance then testing data point is normal.
- **Step4:** else if distance from center radius of cluster is greater than the average intra cluster distance then the testing data point is attack.

4 Experiment and Results

In order to estimate the performance of MCAD algorithm in anomaly detection, the algorithm is tested based on the KDD'99 data set [3] and compared with the traditional ADWICE and BIRCH algorithms for intrusion detection.

4.1 Experimental Data

KDD'99 data set have 5,000,000 records altogether including mainly four intrusion sorts: Dos, R2L, U2R and Probe. Each intrusion sorts contains some different small sorts. This is to large number of initial data of training and testing set for processing into the proposed training and model. So we have chosen the 30% of total training and testing data set of KDD'99 data.

The training set consists of 97500 normal records and the testing set contains the 20500 records including 19447 normal records and 1025 abnormal records. The percentage of anomaly records in testing data is 5% which is far less than the normal data set. Table 1 shows the experimental abnormal data used for testing model.

Each record in the KDD'99 data set is a network linked record. Each link consists of 41 features containing 3 symbolic variables and the others which are numerical variables.

Table 1. Abnormal testing data set distribution

Dos	R2L	U2R	Probe
Neptune (220)	Phf (40)	Buffover (9)	Portsweep(95)
Smurf (146)	Multihop (70)		Ipsweep (40)
Teardrop (80)	Warezmaster (95)		Satan (200)
	Root-kit (30)		

There are different measurement standards for the different features. In order not to affect the clustering result, the attribute values of data need to be process. The processing includes two steps. Firstly, the method in accordance with the protocol layer division is adopted to realize transforming the symbolic variable to the numerical value. When the TCP, UDP and ICMP in the protocol attribute, they should be separately set as 1, 2 and 3. Then all numerical variables are standardized and normalized to the number of [0, 1]. The standard deviation transform is as follows

$$x_{ik}^{'} = \frac{x_{ik} - x_k^{-}}{S_k} \tag{1}$$

Where $x_{ik}^{'}$ is the kth attribute value of the ith record in the 30% data set of KDD'99. The sample typical value x_k^{-} and the standard deviation s_k are given as follows

$$x_k^{-} = \frac{1}{n}\sum_{i=1}^{n} x_{ik} \tag{2}$$

$$S_k = \left(\frac{1}{n-1} \sum_{i=1}^{n} \left(x_{ik}^{'} - x_k^{-} \right)^2 \right)^{1/2} \tag{3}$$

4.2 Determination of Number of Cluster and Branching Factor

The number of clusters N is to be decided by the experiment. If we set N to be the number of training data presents, then it will be the case in which all cluster contains the unique data points and a model in which if testing normal data is different from the training normal data set, hence results as a large number of false positive. So the number of clusters N should be lesser than the number of training data points. If the number of clusters N set to be one then there will be only one cluster representing the training data set which results as low detection rate of anomaly. So we can conclude that the number of clusters depends on the distribution of data. We have experimented with N=9000 to 13000 clusters. At 12500 we got the better detection rate and comparably lesser false positive rate. Similarly the branching factor also increases the training and testing time. The parameter branching factor equal to the number of data points would make the tree flat completely and make the algorithm linear as opposed to algorithmic in time. We have chosen the branching factor as 18. Figure 10 shows the importance of number of clusters required for anomaly detection.

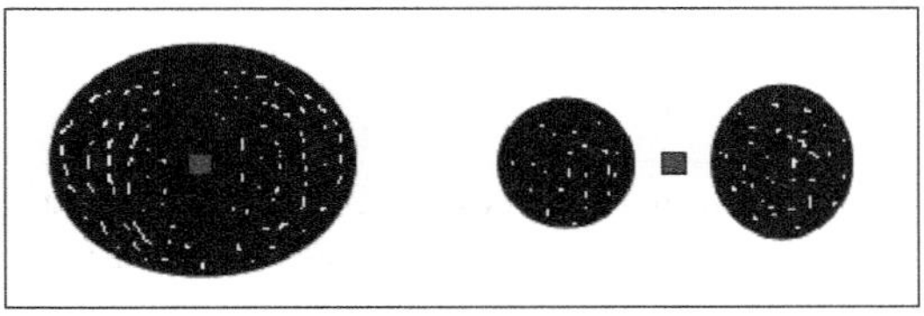

Fig. 10. Importance of numbers of clusters of Intrusion detection

4.3 Results

The proposed MCAD algorithm is realized by programming with java on PC (4 GB memory, Pentium 2.5 GHz CPU and Ubuntu10.4 operating system). The clustering MCAD algorithm is firstly trained with the training data set. Then the intrusion detection performance is evaluated in the testing data set. The detection rate and the false alarm rate adopted to interpret the performance of the algorithm. The detection rate denotes the percentage of the correctly detection intrusion number in all the recorded intrusion number in the testing data set. False alarm rate denotes the percentage of the number of normal data which is wrongly detected in all the normal number in a test set. Table 2 shows the detection rate of proposed algorithm with branching factor 18 along the number of clusters used in experiment.

Table 2. Attack and normal Detection rate of proposed algorithm using branching factor =18

Number of Clusters	Dos	Prob	U2R	R2L	Normal
9050	98.8	96.0	55.0	48.0	97.9
10000	98.9	96.2	61.2	52.1	97.4
11000	99.0	96.4	65.0	59.6	96.8
12000	99.2	97.0	72.8	69.2	95.2
13000	99.4	97.4	80.2	79.5	94.1

4.4 Comparison of Results with Other Clustering Algorithms

First we compare proposed MCAD algorithm space and time requirement with other clustering algorithms such as BIRCH, ADWICE and DBSCAN. Our algorithm gets less training space and training time among all the algorithms. Table 3 shows the results.

Table 3. Results of various cluster algorithms

	Various Clustering			
	MCAD	BRICH	ADWICE	DBSCAN
Training Space (k)	3298	5124	4425	13312
Training Time (ms)	4124	12923	5546	21478
Detection Time(ms)	264	947	341	1392

After comparison of time space and training time of our algorithm with other clustering algorithms we have compared the performance of our MCAD algorithm. Table 4 has shown the results of performance comparisons of various clustering algorithm.

Table 4. Performance comparison of proposed Clustering Algorithm

Attack	MCAD	BRICH	ADWICE	DBSCAN
Dos	99.2	97.8	98.3	96.3
Probe	97.0	95.5	96.0	93.8
U2R	72.8	81.2	81.1	56.2
R2L	69.2	70.1	70.8	46.2

5 Conclusion

In this paper we have proposed a novel clustering algorithm for anomaly detection. The algorithm achieved improved detection rate over some important clustering algorithm for anomaly detection. Results and Experimental part validate the proposed algorithm on KDD'99 Intrusion detection data set. We have also solved the BIRCH model indexing problem by including the cluster quality average intra cluster distance in our proposed algorithm which results as a conclusion that multi density clustering algorithm provide the better cluster as it make compact and small clusters.

References

1. Zhang, T., Ramakrishnan, R., Livny, M.: Birch: an efficient data clustering method for very large databases. In: SIGMOD Record 1996 ACM SIGMOD International Conference on Management of Data, pp. 103–114 (1996)
2. Burbeck, K., Nadjm-Tehrani, S.: ADWICE – anomaly detection with real-time incremental clustering. In: Park, C.-s., Chee, S. (eds.) ICISC 2004. LNCS, vol. 3506, pp. 407–424. Springer, Heidelberg (2005)
3. Mahoney, M.V., Chan, P.K.: An analysis of the KDD,99 darpa/lincoln laboratory evaluation data for network anomaly detection. In: Proceedings of 6th International Symposium on Recent Advances in Intrusion Detection, pp. 220–237 (2003)
4. Mukhrjee, B., Levitt, N.: Network Intrusion Detection. IEEE Networks 24, 26–29 (2005)
5. Han, H., Lu, X.L., Lu, J., Bo, C.: Data mining aided signature discovery in network-based intrusion detection system. ACM SIGOPS Operating System Review 36, 7–13 (2002)
6. Hilas, C.S., Mastorocostas, P.A.: An application of supervised and Unsupervised learning approaches to telecommunications fraud detection. ACM Journal of Knowledge-Based systems 21, 721–726 (2008)
7. Kumar, S., Nandi, S., Biswas, S.: Research and application of one-class small hypersphere Support Vector Machine for Network anomaly detection. In: The Third International Conference on Communication System and Networks (COMSNETS), pp. 1–4 (2011)
8. Yasami, Y., Mozaffari, S.P.: A novel unsupervised classification approach for network anomaly detection by k-means clustering and ID3 decision tree learning method. ACM Jounal of Supercomputing 53, 231–245 (2010)
9. Kanungo, T., Mount, D.M., Netanyahu, N.S.: An efficient k-Mean clustering Algorithm: Analysis and Implement. ACM/IEEE Transactions on Pattern Analysis and Machine Intelligence 24, 881–892 (2002)
10. Hilal Inan, Z., Kuntalp, M.: A study on fuzzy C-mean clustering-based systems in automatic spike detection. ACM Journal of Computers in Biology and Medicine 37, 1160–1166 (2007)
11. Ester, M., Kriegel, H.-P., Sander, J.: A Desnsity-Based Algorithm for Discovering Clusters in Large Spatial Databased with Noise. In: Proceeding on 2nd International Conference on Knowledge Discovery and Data Mining, pp. 226–231 (1996)
12. Zhao, Y., Karypis, G.: Criterion functions for document clustering, Experiments and Analysis. Technical report, 1–130 (2002)

Appendix

Intra and Inter-cluster distance: There is large difference between Intra-cluster and Inter-cluster distance. Inter-cluster distance measured by within-cluster sum of squares. Its measures cluster "compactness".
For one cluster r:

$$D_r = \sum_i \sum_j \|x_i - x_j\|^2$$

$$= 2n_r \sum_i \|x_i - x^-\|^2$$

For all k clusters:

$$W_k = \sum_{r=1}^{k} \frac{1}{2n_r} D_r$$

Clustering Features, Radius and Centroid of clusters: Clustering features (CF) includes the number of data points in a cluster (N), linear sum of data points (LS) and square sum of data points in a cluster (SS).

$$CF = \langle N, LS, SS \rangle$$

The centroid of a cluster given by:

$$X_0 = \int_{i=1}^{n} X_i$$

The radius of cluster given by:

$$R = \sum_{i=0}^{n} \left[(X_i - X_0)^2 / n \right]$$

where i=1 to n

α **Value:** α represents the central value of cluster, can be calculated as

$$\alpha = \frac{1}{N} \sum_{i=1}^{r} X_i$$

LLAC: Lazy Learning in Associative Classification

S.P. Syed Ibrahim[1], K.R. Chandran[2], and R.V. Nataraj[3]

[1] Assistant Professor, Department of Computer Science and Engineering,
PSG College of Technology, Coimbatore, India
sps_phd@yahoo.co.in
[2] Professor of IT & Head, Computer and Information Sciences,
PSG College of Technology, Coimbatore, India
chandran_k_r@yahoo.co.in
[3] Assistant Professor (Sl. Gr), Department of Information Technology,
PSG College of Technology, Coimbatore, India
rv.nataraj@gmail.com

Abstract. Associative classification method applies association rule mining technique in classification and achieves higher classification accuracy. However, it is a known fact that associative classification typically yields a large number of rules, from which a set of high quality rules are chosen to construct an efficient classifier. Hence, generating, ranking and selecting a small subset of high-quality rules without jeopardizing the classification accuracy is of prime importance but a challenging task indeed. This paper proposes lazy learning associative classification method, which delays processing of the data until a new sample needs to be classified. This proposed method is useful for applications where the training dataset needs to be frequently updated. Experimental results show that the proposed method outperforms the CBA method.

Keywords: Classification, data mining.

1 Introduction

Classification and association rule mining are two of the very important tasks addressed in the data mining literature. Association rule mining searches items in the dataset globally for all rules that satisfy minimum support and minimum confidence thresholds. It uses unsupervised learning where no class attribute is involved in finding the association rule. On the other hand, classification uses supervised learning where class attribute is involved to compute classifier. Associative classification method aims to amalgamate classification and association rule mining techniques in order to build a model known as associative classifier [11]. This classifier is used to predict the new unknown class object.

Associative classifier is constructed in two separate phases. In the first phase, association rule mining is applied to discover class association rules. The important element in controlling the number of rules generated in associative rule mining is the support threshold. If the support value is high then number of rules generated is very less, but many high confidence rules may get eliminated. On the other hand, if support

A. Abraham et al. (Eds.): ACC 2011, Part I, CCIS 190, pp. 631–638, 2011.

value is set to minimum, then huge numbers of rules are generated. So in the next phase some rules are pruned using the techniques like database coverage [11], chi – square testing [10] and Lazy pruning [2] [4] to choose the optimal rule set. This method is suitable for static dataset but construction of classifier for dynamic dataset is very costly with regards to processing time.

Merschmann et., al [12] [13] proposed Lazy learning method based on Probabilistic Analysis of Patterns to classify dataset, which delays processing of data until a new sample needs to be classified. This motivates us to propose a new associative classification method (Lazy Learning Associative Classification) that does not build a generalized classifier from training data for classification of new samples. Instead this proposed method computes support and confidence value for each given sample of dataset with respect to each class. Then from this knowledge, class value is assigned to the sample. So this proposed method is very useful for dynamic databases.

The rest of the paper is organized as follows: Section 2 deals with the pros and cons of the existing systems in the associative classification. Section 3 gives a brief introduction about the proposed method. The proposed Lazy Learning algorithm and the various components and parameters of the algorithm and a short example is also explained for the sake of concept comprehension in section 4 followed by the experimental results and conclusion in section 5 and section 6.

2 Related Works

Recently, methods based on association rule mining and classifications have been proposed to address the associative classification problem [6] [7] [10] [11] [14] [16] [19]. The Class based on association rule mining (CBA) [11] was the first Associative Classification method that used the Apriori algorithm [1] for rule generation. The CBA-Rule Generation algorithm generates all the frequent ruleitems by making multiple passes over the data. In the first pass, it counts the support of individual ruleitem and discovers the frequent items. From this set of frequent ruleitems, it produces the class association rules.

Even after pruning the infrequent items, a huge number of association rules are generated in CBA method. Experimental results reported in Baralis et.al. [4] Showed that CBA method which follows apriori association rule mining algorithm generates more than 80,000 rules for some datasets that leads to memory exceptions and other severe problems, such as overfitting [2]. If all the rules are used in the classifier then the accuracy of the classifier would be high but the process of classification will be slow and time-consuming. So several rule pruning techniques are proposed to choose an optimal rule set.

To apply rule pruning, generated rules are ranked based on several parameters and interestingness measures such as confidence, support, lexicographical order of items etc. In CBA method, the rules are arranged based on their confidence value. If two rules have the same value for the confidence measure then the rules are sorted based on their support. If both confident and support values are same for two rules then sorting is done based on rule length. Even after considering confidence, support, and cardinality and if some rules have the same values for all three parameters then the rules are sorted based on its lexicographic order in Lazy pruning [13] method.

After rule ranking, CBA method uses database coverage method to prune some rules to construct an optimal rule set. Database coverage chooses the highest ranked rule and checks it against the training data set. Even if it covers at least one training data element then it will be considered for the construction of the classifier. This process is repeated until all the sorted rules or training objects are covered. The bottleneck of Apriori generation is the task of finding frequent itemsets from all possible candidate itemsets at each level. In case of large datasets or lower support measures, the potential number of candidate ruleitems at each level can be enormous and hence these algorithms may consume considerable CPU time and storage [17].

Li et al., [10] proposed the classification based on multiple association rules (CMAR) algorithm that uses the FP-growth approach [9] to find frequent itemsets and stores the classification rules in a prefix tree data structure, know as a CR-tree. Given a new data object, CMAR collects the subset of rules matching the new object from the set of rules for classification. If all the rules have a common class, then CMAR simply assigns that class to the test object else CMAR first groups the rules according to class labels. Then, for each group of class the strength is measured by adopting a *weighted* $\chi 2$ measure to determine the final class membership of the object.

Baralis et. al., [2] [3] [4] proposed lazy pruning approach for rule pruning where a rule is pruned only if it misclassifies the data. The entire ruleset is segregated into three sets namely, useful rules, harmful rules and spare rules. A rule which classifies atleast one data item correctly is said to be a useful rule and that which misclassifies a data item is a harmful rule and the leftovers are the spare rules which are not pruned but used when needed. Lazy pruning strategy works well for small dataset but in the case of large datasets there exist constraints in memory space and ruleset quality.

Evolutionary based associative classification method [14] is proposed recently. This approach takes subset of rules randomly to construct the classifier. Richness of the ruleset is improved over the generation.

In [16] statistical based rule ranking method is proposed. Here after generating the rules using associative classification rule generation algorithm, rules are ranked based on statistical measure.

Guoqing Chen et.al [7] proposed a new approach based on information gain where more informative attribute are chosen for rule generation. An informative attribute centred rule generation produces a compact ruleset.

The traditional associative classification methods constructs generalized model to classify the new data sample but introduction of Lazy Learning Associative Classification may eliminate the use generalized model.

3 Lazy Learning Associative Classification (LLAC)

Traditional associative classifier construction consists of two phases. The first phase includes the extraction of complete set of associative classification rules from the training dataset. This is followed by rule ranking, rule pruning techniques, to construct a generalization model from a training dataset. Then it classifies new samples directly by using the learned model. However these rule extraction, rule ranking and rule pruning are time consuming process. Therefore this paper proposes Lazy associative classification method which does not build a generalized model rather, it predicts

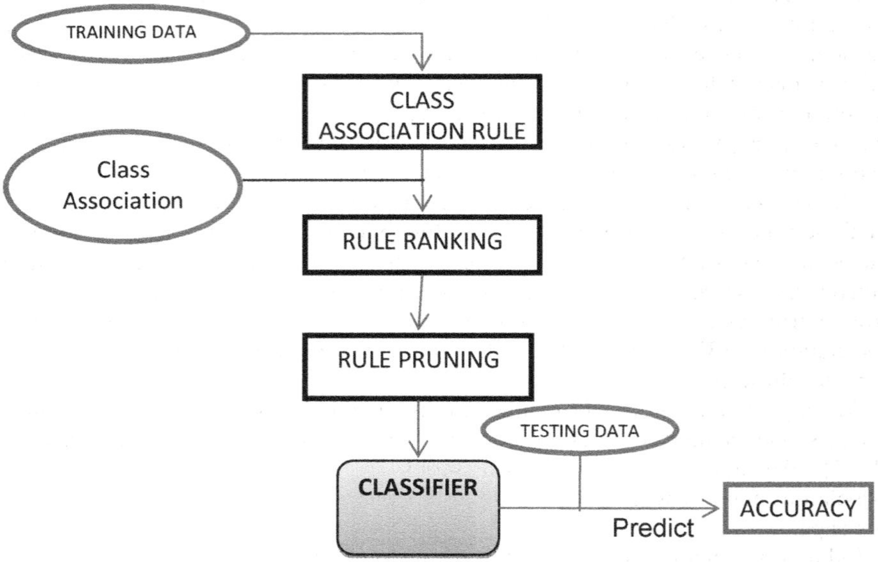

Fig. 1. Traditional Associative Classification

the class for the test sample directly from the training dataset. This method is very much useful where the dataset needs to be updated frequently.

4 Problem Definition

Let database D is a set of instances where each instance is represented by < a_1, a_2 ...a_m , C>, where a_1, a_2 ...a_m, are attributes and C are class value. A class association rule X → C holds in D with confidence c, if c% of cases in D that contain X are labeled with class C. The rule X →C has support s in D if s% of the cases in D contain X and are labeled with class C.

The task is to predict the class label for new data instance. Lazy learning algorithm takes testing dataset as input and calculates the support and confidence for each combination of class values. Then Class labels are assigned based on high probability of support and confidence extracted from training dataset.

This subsection presents the lazy learning associative classification algorithm.

LAZY LEARNING ASSOCIATIVE CLASSIFICATION ALGORITHM

Input: **Training dataset and testing set**

Output: **Class predicted by the dynamic associative classifier.**

Step 1: Find the total number of transaction in the training dataset.
Step 2: Find the number of classes in the training dataset.

Step 3: Get the testing data as input where class labels needs to be predicted.
Step 4: Compute support and confidence for various combination of input dataset using training dataset.
Step 5: Assign high score to the highest support and confidence pair.
Step 6: predict the class based on the score.

Table 1. Training Dataset

Outlook	**Temp**	**humidity**	**Windy**	**Play**
Sunny	Hot	High	False	No
Sunny	Hot	High	True	No
Overcast	Hot	High	False	Yes
Rainy	Mild	High	False	Yes
Rainy	Cool	Normal	True	No
Overcast	Cool	Normal	True	Yes
Sunny	Mild	High	False	No
Sunny	Cool	Normal	False	Yes
Rainy	Mild	Normal	False	Yes
Sunny	Mild	Normal	True	Yes
Overcast	Mild	High	True	Yes
Overcast	Hot	Normal	False	Yes
Rainy	Mild	High	True	No

Table 2. Testing Dataset

Rainy	Cool	Normal	False	?

Table 3. Sample Computation

ItemSet	**Support**	**Class**	**Confidence**
Rainy, Cool	1	Yes	0
		No	100
Raily, Normal	2	Yes	50
		No	50
Rainy, False	2	Yes	100
		No	0
Cool, Normal	3	Yes	66
		No	33
Cool, False	1	Yes	100
		No	0
Normal, False	3	Yes	100
		No	0
Rainy, Cool, Normal	1	Yes	0
		No	100

Table 3. (*continued*)

Rainy, Cool, False	0	Yes	0
		No	0
Rainy, Normal, True	1	Yes	100
		No	0

Highest value of confidence is assigned as 1.

For Yes Class : 2*1 + 3*1 +1*1 + 3*1 + 1*1 = 10
For No Class : 1*1+1*1 = 2

So **yes** class is assigned as class value for the new data tuple.

5 Experimental Results

The computational experiments are designed extensively to evaluate the accuracy of the proposed LLAC method with the existing system. The experiments are performed on a 1.6 GHz Centrino core 2 CPU with 2.49 Gbytes of main memory, running Windows XP. The working of the LLAC algorithm against CBA is tested on datasets from UCI Machine Learning Repository [5]. A brief description about the main characteristics of datasets is presented in Table 4. Continuous attributes have been discretized using WEKA [18] software.

Table 4. UCI Datasets Characteristics

Dataset	Transactions	Classes	Number of Attributes	Number of Attributes after attribute selection
Anneal	998	6	39	11
Breast-w*	699	2	10	-
Dematology	366	6	35	20
Flare*	1389	9	13	-
Glass*	214	7	10	-
Hepatitis	155	2	20	10
Ionosphere	351	2	35	14
Iris*	150	3	5	-
Mushroom	8124	2	23	5
Nursery*	12960	5	9	-
PageBlocks	5473	5	11	7
TicTacToe	958	2	10	6
Wine	178	3	14	12

*- Attribute reduction method is not applied.

The proposed LLAC is compared with CBA [11] by taking accuracy as a metric. Accuracy can be defined ability of the classifier to correctly classify unlabeled data. It is the ratio of the number of correctly classified data over the total number of given data.

Accuracy is computed using Holdout approach [10] where 90% of the data is randomly selected from the dataset and used as training dataset. The remaining data is used as the testing dataset. The support threshold is set to 1% in both LLAC and CBA. The experimental results are shown in the Table 5. It is evident from the Table 5.2 that the proposed LLAC method achieves higher accuracy than the traditional CBA method.

However, LLAC has high computation cost depending on number of attributes. In order to make LLAC work feasible for any size of dataset, it is necessary to preprocess the dataset to reduce the number of attributes. Here, correlation based feature selection is applied to reduce the number of attribute, which not only reduce the computation cost but also improves the accuracy.

Table 5. Accuracy Comparison

Dataset	**CBA**	**LLAC**	**LLAC with Attribute reduction**
Anneal	80.18	77.42	77.77
Breast-w	93.7	**97.14**	-
Dematology	47.54	**48.64**	**48.64**
Flare	84.58	**85.61**	-
Glass	57.94	57.94	-
Hepatitis	44.16	**56.25**	**68.75**
Ionosphere	82.29	**90.90**	**92.04**
Iris	96.0	96.0	96
Mushroom	46.65	**55.71**	**97.90**
Nursery	74.17	71.45	-
PageBlocks	91.08	**91.24**	**91.78**
TicTacToe	77.24	66.17	69.62
Wine	92.44	79.77	**94.44**
Average	74.45	**74.94**	**81.88**

6 Conclusion

The main objective of this paper is to introduce a new associative classification method. Unlike the other traditional method, the proposed Lazy learning Associative Classification classifies the new sample data without constructing the classifier but this lazy approach results in high CPU utilization time and cost. It is interesting to further enhance this proposed method to reduce the CPU time and cost by reducing number of attributes. The experiments are done on several datasets which validates the proposed method. The experimental results show that the proposed LLAC method outperformed the CBA method in most cases.

References

[1] Agrawal, R., Srikant, R.: Fast algorithms for mining association rule. In: Proceedings of the 20th International Conference on Very Large Data Bases, pp. 487–499 (1994)
[2] Baralis, E., Torino, P.: A lazy approach to pruning classification rules. In: Proceedings of the 2002 IEEE International Conference on Data Mining (ICDM 2002), Maebashi City, Japan, pp. 35–42 (2002)
[3] Baralis, E., Chiusano, S., Graza, P.: On support thresholds in associative classification. In: Proceedings of the 2004 ACM Symposium on Applied Computing, pp. 553–558. ACM Press, Nicosia (2004)
[4] Baralis, E., Chiusano, S., Garza, P.: A Lazy Approach to Associative Classification. IEEE Transactions on Knowledge and Data Engineering 20(2), 156–171 (2008)
[5] Blake, C.L., Merz, C.J.: UCI Repository of machine learning databases (1998)
[6] Dong, G., Zhang, X., Wong, L., Li, J.: CAEP: Classification by Aggregating Emerging Patterns. In: Proc. Second Int'l Conf. Discovery Science (December 2009)
[7] Chen, G., Liu, H., Yu, L., Wei, Q., Zhang, X.: 'A new approach to classification based on association rule mining'. Science Direct, Decision Support Systems 42, 674–689 (2006)
[8] Han, J., Pei, J., Yin, Y.: Mining frequent patterns without candidate generation. In: Proceedings of the 2000 ACM SIGMOD International Conference on Management of Data, pp. 1–12. ACM Press, Dallas (2000)
[9] Han, J., Kamber, M.: Data Mining: Concepts and Techniques. Morgan Kaufmann Publishers, New York (2001)
[10] Li, W., Han, J., Pei, J.: CMAR: Accurate and Efficient Classification Based on Multiple Class-Association Rules. In: Proc. IEEE Int'l Conf. Data Mining, ICDM 2001 (November 2001)
[11] Liu, B., Hsu, W., Ma, Y.: Integrating Classification and Association Rule Mining. In: Proceedings of the Fourth International Conference on Knowledge Discovery and Data Mining, pp. 80–86 (1998)
[12] Merschmann, L., Plastino, A.: HiSP-GC: A Classification Method Based on Probabilistic Analysis of Patterns. Journal of Information and Data Management 1(3), 423–438 (2010)
[13] Merschmann, L., Plastino, A.: A lazy data mining approach for protein classification. IEEE Transactions on Nanobioscience 6(1), 36–42 (2007)
[14] Syed Ibrahim, S.P., Chandran, K.R., Jabez Christopher, J.: An Evolutionary Approach for Ruleset Selection in a Class Based Associative Classifier. European Journal of Scientific Research 50(3), 422–429 (2011) ISSN 1450-216X
[15] Syed Ibrahim, S.P., Chandran, K.R., Jabez Christopher, J.: A Comparison Of Associative Classifiers. In: The Conference On Research Issues In Engineering And Technology (Computer Science And Engineering Stream), Organized by PSG College of Technology, Coimbatore, India, April 28 (2011)
[16] Syed Ibrahim, S.P., Chandran, K.R., Muniasamy, R.: Efficient Rule Ranking And Rule Pruning In Associative Classification. In: The Conference On Research Issues In Engineering And Technology (Computer Science And Engineering Stream), Organized by PSG College of Technology, Coimbatore, India, April 28 (2011)
[17] Abdeljaber, T.F.: A review of associative classification mining. Knowledge Engineering Review 22(1), 37–65 (2007)
[18] `http://www.cs.waikato.ac.nz/ml/weka`
[19] Yin, X., Han, J.: CPAR: Classification Based on Predictive Association Rules. In: Proc. Third SIAM Int'l Conf. Data Mining (SDM 2003) (May 2003)

Association Rule Mining Using Genetic Algorithm: The Role of Estimation Parameters

K. Indira[1] and S. Kanmani[2]

[1] Research Scholar, Department of Computer Science,
Pondicherry Engineering College, Puducherry, India
induharini@gmail.com
[2] Professor, Department of Information Technology,
Pondicherry Engineering College, Puducherry, India
kanmani@pec.eu

Abstract. Genetic Algorithms (GA) have emerged as practical, robust optimization and search methods to generate accurate and reliable Association Rules. The performance of GA for mining association rules greatly depends on the GA parameters namely population size, crossover rate, mutation rate, fitness function adopted and selection method. The objective of this paper is to compare the performance of the Genetic algorithm for association rule mining by varying these parameters. The algorithm when tested on three datasets namely Lenses, Iris and Haberman indicates that the accuracy depends mainly on the fitness function which is the key parameter of GA. The population size is affected by the size of the dataset under study. The crossover probability brings changes in convergence rate with minimal changes in accuracy. The size of the dataset and relationship between its attributes also plays a role in achieving the optimum accuracy.

Keywords: Association rules, Genetic Algorithm, Population size, Crossover rate, Fitness function.

1 Introduction

Data mining, also referred as knowledge discovery in database, means a process of nontrivial extraction of implicit, previously unknown and potentially useful information (such as knowledge rules, constraints, regularities) from data in database. Data mining combines theory and technology of several domains which include artificial intelligence, machine learning, statistics, neural network and so on. Association rule mining is a major area in data mining that discovers the relations between different attributes by analyzing and disposing data in the database.

Many algorithms for generating association rules were developed over time. Some of the well known algorithms are Apriori, Eclat and FP-Growth tree. Many existing algorithms traverse the database many times so the I/O overhead and computational complexity becomes very high and cannot meet the requirements of large-scale database mining. Genetic algorithm is an algorithm which based on the biological theory of evolution and molecular genetics of the global random search, the algorithm has a

A. Abraham et al. (Eds.): ACC 2011, Part I, CCIS 190, pp. 639–648, 2011.

strong randomness, robust and implicit parallelism and can quickly and effectively search for global optimization, in an effective way to deal with large-scale data sets. At present, genetic algorithm-based data mining methods have yielded some progress, and based on genetic algorithms classification system has also yielded some results.

This paper analyses the mining of Association Rules by applying Genetic Algorithms. There have been several attempts for mining association rules using Genetic Algorithm. Robert Cattral et al. [1] describe the evolution of hierarchy of rule using genetic algorithm with chromosomes of varying length and macro mutations. The initial population is seeded rather than random selection. Manish Saggar et al. [2] proposes an algorithm with binary encoding and the fitness function was generated based on confusion matrix. The individuals are represented using the Michigan's Approach. Roulette Wheel selection is done by first normalizing the values of all candidates.

Genetic algorithm based on the concept of strength of implication of rules was presented by Zhou et al. [3]. The properties of independence and correlation of descriptions in rules are taken up for fitness calculation. Genxiang et al. [4] introduced dynamic immune evolution, and biometric mechanism in Engineering immune computing namely immune recognition, immune memory and immune regulation to GA for mining association rules.

Gonzales. E et al. [5] introduced the Genetic Relation Algorithm (GRA) based on evaluating the distances between rules. The distance is calculated using both matching criteria namely complete match and partial match. Genetic algorithm easily leads to premature convergence or takes too much time to converge during evolution process. Hong Lei et al. [6] propose GA where the fitness function is based on predictive accuracy, comprehensibility and interestingness factor. The selection method is based on elitist recombination.

In Haiying Ma et al. [7] the encoding of data is done with gene string structure where the complexity concepts are mapped to form linear symbols. The fitness function is the measure of the overall performance of the process rather than that of individual rules when the bit strings were interpreted as a complex process. Adaptive exchange probability (Pc) and mutation probability (Pm) are adopted in this paper. Hong Guo et al. [8] adopt the method of adaptive mutation rate to avoid excessive variation causing non-convergence, or into a local optimal solution. A sort of individual-based selection method is applied to the evolution in genetic algorithm, in order to prevent the high-fitness individuals converging early by the rapid growth of the number of individual.

As the parameters of the genetic algorithm and the fitness function are found to be the major area of interest in the above studies, this paper tries to explore on the effects of the genetic parameters and the controlling variables of fitness function on three different datasets.

A brief introduction about Association Rule Mining and GA is given in Section 2, followed by methodology in section 3, which describes the basic implementation details of Association Rule Mining with GA. In section 4 the parameters that decides on efficiency of the algorithm is presented. Section 5 presents the experimental results followed by conclusion in the last section.

2 Association Rules and Genetic Algorithms

2.1 Association Rules

Association rule is a popular and well researched method for discovering interesting relations between variables in large databases. It studies the frequency of items occurring together in transactional databases, and based on a threshold called support, identifies the frequent item sets. Another threshold, confidence, which is the conditional probability that an item appears in a transaction when another item appears, is used to pinpoint association rules.

The discovered association rules are of the form: P→Q [s, c], where P and Q are conjunctions of attribute value-pairs, and s (for support) is the probability that P and Q appear together in a transaction and c (for confidence) is the conditional probability that Q appears in a transaction when P is present.

2.2 Genetic Algorithm

A Genetic Algorithm (GA) is a procedure used to find approximate solutions to search problems through the application of the principles of evolutionary biology. Genetic algorithms use biologically inspired techniques such as genetic inheritance, natural selection, mutation, and sexual reproduction (recombination, or crossover).

Genetic algorithms are typically implemented using computer simulations in which an optimization problem is specified. For this problem, members of a space of candidate solutions, called individuals, are represented using abstract representations called chromosomes. The GA consists of an iterative process that evolves a working set of individuals called a population towards an objective function, or fitness function. Traditionally, solutions are represented using fixed length strings especially binary strings, but alternative encodings have also been developed.

3 Methodology

The evolutionary process of GA is a highly simplified and stylized simulation of the biological version. It starts from a population of individuals randomly generated according to some probability distribution, usually uniform and updates this population in steps called generations. In each generation, multiple individuals are randomly selected from the current population based on application of fitness, crossover, and modified through mutation to form a new population.

A. **[Start]** Generate random population of n chromosomes.
B. **[Fitness]** Evaluate the fitness $f(x)$ of each chromosome x in the population.
C. **[New population]** Create a new population by repeating the following steps until the new population is complete.
   i. **[Selection]** Select two parent chromosomes from a population according to their fitness.
   ii. **[Crossover]** With a crossover probability alter the parents to form a new offspring.

iii. **[Mutation]** With a mutation probability mutate new offspring at each locus.

iv. **[Accepting]** Place new offspring in a new population

D. **[Replace]** Use newly generated population for a further run of the algorithm

E. **[Test]** If the end condition is satisfied, **stop**, and return the best solution in current population

F. **[Loop]** Go to step **B**

4 Parameters in Genetic Algorithm

The GA parameters are the key components enabling the system to achieve good enough solution for possible terminating conditions.

4.1 Encoding

Encoding is the process of representing individual solutions. The most common way of encoding is binary encoding. Here each chromosome encodes a binary string where each bit in the string represents some characteristics of the solution. Other encoding schemes are octal, hexadecimal, permutation value and tree encoding.

4.2 Population

Population refers to the number of chromosomes taken up for optimization. A chromosome is the raw genetic information that the GA deals with. If there are too few chromosomes, GA has few possibilities to perform crossover and only a small part of search space is explored. On the other hand, if there are too many chromosomes, GA slows down. The initial population generation and population size are the two aspects of population. The initial population is either selected randomly from the data or selected with prior knowledge on the data.

The population size is calculated by

$$\boldsymbol{popsiz} = \boldsymbol{order} \left\lfloor \frac{l}{k} + \mathbf{2}^{k} \right\rfloor \tag{1}$$

Where l = number of chromosomes in data and k is the average size of the schema of interest. If uniform crossover is adopted we can most likely get with population size at least twice as small as the number of instances in the dataset.

4.3 Selection

During each successive generation, a proportion of the existing population is selected to breed a new generation. Individuals are selected through a fitness-based process, where fitter solutions as measured by a fitness function are typically more likely to be selected. The Tournament, Roulette Wheel, Random, Rank and Boltzmann selection are the commonly used selection methods. Elitism and stochastic universal sampling significantly improves the GA's performance.

4.4 Fitness Function

A fitness function is a particular type of objective function that prescribes the optimality of a chromosome in a genetic algorithm, so that the particular chromosome may be ranked against all the other chromosomes [9, 10]. An ideal fitness function correlates closely with the algorithm's goal, and yet may be computed quickly. Speed of execution is very important, as a typical genetic algorithm must be iterated many times in order to produce an usable result for a non-trivial problem.

This paper adopts minimum support and minimum confidence for filtering rules. Then correlative degree is confirmed in rules which satisfy minimum support-degree and minimum confidence-degree. After support-degree and confidence-degree are synthetically taken into account, fit degree function is defined as follows.

$$\boldsymbol{Fitness}\ (X) = R_S.\frac{Supp(X)}{Supp_{min}} + R_C.\frac{Conf(X)}{Conf_{min}} \tag{2}$$

In the above formula, $R_s + R_c = 1$ ($R_s \geq 0$, $R_c \geq 0$) and $Supp_{min}$, $Conf_{min}$ are respective values of minimum support and minimum confidence. By all appearances if the $Supp_{min}$ and $Conf_{min}$ are set to higher values, then the value of fitness function is also found to be high.

4.5 Crossover Operator

Crossover entails choosing two individuals to swap segments of their code, producing artificial "offspring" that are combinations of their parents. This process is intended to simulate the analogous process of recombination that occurs to chromosomes during sexual reproduction. Common forms of crossover include single-point crossover, in which a point of exchange is set at a random location in the two individual genomes, where one individual contributes all its code till the point of crossover, the second individual contributes all its code after the point of crossover to produce an offspring, and uniform crossover, in which the value at any given location in the offspring's genome is either the value of one parent's genome at that location or the value of the other parent's genome at that location, chosen with 50/50 probability[8].

4.6 Mutation Operator

Partial gene values of individuals are adjusted by using mutation operation [5]. This part of the genetic algorithm, require great care, here there are two probabilities, one usually called as P_m, this probability will be used to judge whether mutation has to be done or not, when the candidate fulfills this criterion it will be fed to another probability, the locus probability that is on which point of the candidate the mutation has to be done.

4.7 Number of Generations

The generational process of mining association rules by Genetic algorithm is repeated until a termination condition has been reached. Common terminating conditions are:

A solution is found that satisfies minimum criteria.

- Fixed number of generations reached.
- Allocated budget (computation time/money) reached.
- The highest ranking solution's fitness is reaching or has reached a plateau such that successive iterations no longer produce better results.
- Manual inspection.
- Combinations of the above.

5 Experimental Studies

The objective of this study is to compare the accuracy achieved in datasets by varying the GA Parameters. The encoding of chromosome is binary encoding with fixed length. As the crossover is performed on attribute level the mutation rate is set to zero so as to retain the original attribute values. The selection method used is tournament selection. The fitness function adopted is as given in equation (1).

Three datasets namely Lenses, Haberman survival and Iris Data Set from UCI Machine Learning Repository have been taken up for experimentation. Lenses dataset has 4 attributes with 24 instances. Haberman's Survival data Set has 3 attributes and 306 instances and Iris dataset has 5 attributes and 150 instances. The Algorithm is implemented using MATLAB R2008a simulation package. The flow of the system is as shown in flowchart below.

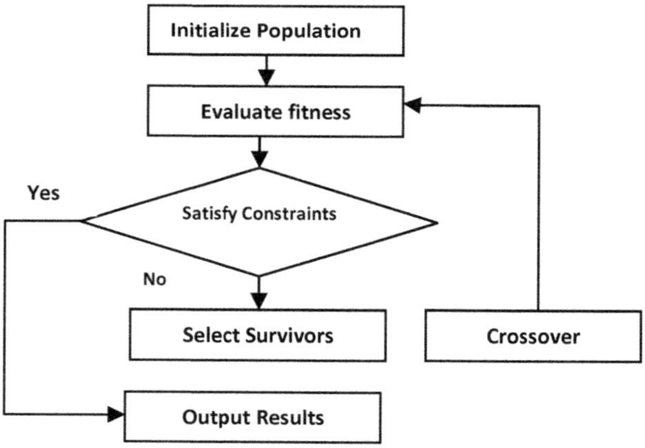

Fig. 1. Flow chart of the GA

The default values set for the GA parameters are given in Table 1.

The accuracy and the convergence rate by controlling the GA parameters are recorded in the table 2. Accuracy is the count of dataset matching between the original dataset and resulting population divided by the number of instances in dataset. The convergence rate is the generation at which the fitness value becomes fixed. The population size is varied for the three dataset, from the size of the dataset to one and half times the dataset size while keeping the other parameters fixed.

Table 1. Default GA Parameters

Parameter	Value
Population Size	Instances * 1.5
Crossover Rate	0.5
Mutation Rate	0.0
Selection Method	Tournament Selection
Minimum Support	0.2
Minimum Confidence	0.8

Table 2. Comparison based on variation in population Size

	No. of Instances		No. of Instances * 1.25		No. of Instances *1.5	
	Accuracy %	No. of Generations	Accuracy %	No. of Generations	Accuracy %	No. of Generations
Lenses	75	7	82	12	95	17
Haberman	71	114	68	88	64	70
Iris	77	88	87	53	82	45

It could be seen from Table 2 that for the Lenses dataset whose size is small, an optimal accuracy is achieved, when the population size is one and half times the size of the dataset whereas for the larger dataset, Haberman the accuracy is maximum when the population size is equivalent to dataset size. For the Iris dataset of moderate size the population has to be set to 1.25 times the size of the dataset to achieve optimum result.

As the fitness function is considered to be the crucial factor for the GA, variations are introduced in the fitness function while other parameters remain unchanged. In Table 3 the minimum confidence and support values are altered when others are at default values and the results are recorded.

From the Table 3 it is clear that the variation in minimum support and confidence brings greater changes in accuracy. When the values of minimum support and confidence are set to minimum, the accuracy if found to be low regardless of the size of the dataset. The same is noted when both the values are set to maximum. Optimum accuracy is achieved when a tradeoff value between minimum confidence and minimum support is set.

Table 3. Comparison based on variation in Minimum Support and Confidence

	Minimum Support & Minimum Confidence							
	Sup = 0.4 & con =0.4		Sup =0.9 & con =0.9		Sup = 0.9 & con = 0.2		Sup = 0.2 & con = 0.9	
	Accuracy %	No. of Gen.	Accuracy %	No. of Gen.	Accuracy %	No. of Gen.	Accuracy %	No. of Gen.
Lenses	22	20	49	11	70	21	95	18
Haberman	45	68	58	83	71	90	62	75
Iris	40	28	59	37	78	48	87	55

When the parameters R_s and R_c are altered in the fitness function, minimum alterations in accuracy are noted and hence their impact is not taken up for analysis.

In Table 4 the crossover probability is altered when other GA parameters are set to default values and the results observed are recorded.

Table 4. Comparison based on variation in Crossover Probability

	Cross Over					
	Pc = .25		Pc = .5		Pc = .75	
	Accuracy %	No. of Generations	Accuracy %	No. of Generations	Accuracy %	No. of Generations
Lenses	95	8	95	16	95	13
Haberman	69	77	71	83	70	80
Iris	84	45	86	51	87	55

From the Table 4 it is evident that the accuracy achieved is almost same for all the three datasets whatever the crossover probability adopted. The effect of the crossover probability on convergence rate is noticeable, the data size and population size being set also alters the convergence rate.

The results observed are compared for the three datasets as shown in figures 2 and 3.

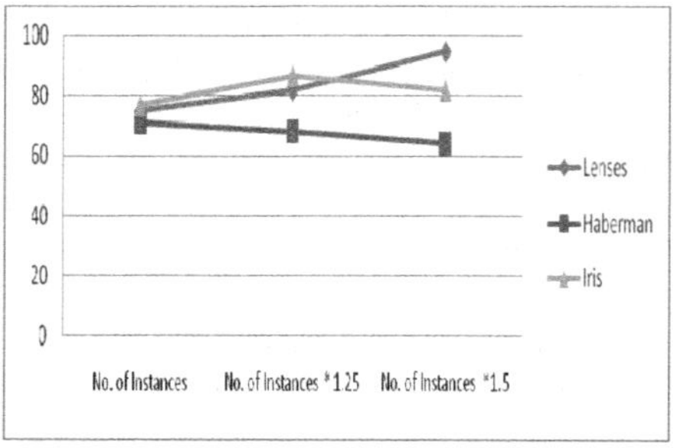

Fig. 2. Population Size Vs Accuracy

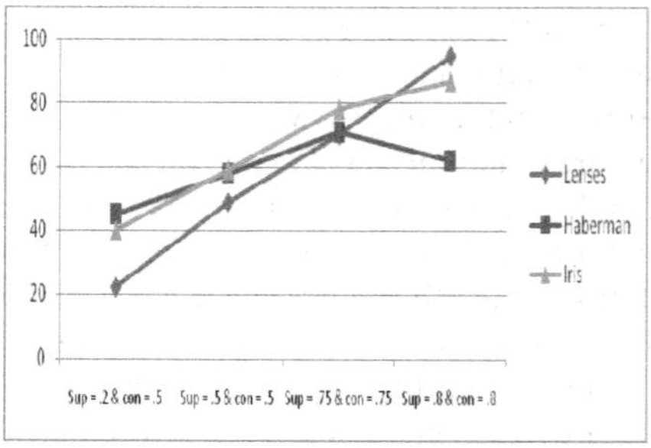

Fig. 3. Minimum Support and Confidence Vs Accuracy

The values of the GA parameters set for the three datasets when maximum efficiency is achieved is shown in Table 5.

Table 5. Comparison of the optimum value of Parameters for maximum Accuracy achieved

Dataset	No. of Instances	No. of attributes	Minimum Support	Minimum confidence	Crossover rate	Accuracy in %
Lenses	24	4	0.2	0.9	0.25	95
Haberman	306	3	0.9	0.2	0.5	71
Iris	150	5	0.2	0.9	0.75	87

It is observed from the experimental analysis that the choice of optimum population size for better accuracy depends upon the number of instances in dataset. If dataset size is larger, then the population size same as the number of instances in dataset is found to produce better accuracy.

Setting up values for minimum support and confidence depends on the dataset and their relationship between attributes. Tradeoff between minimum confidence and minimum support has to be scored to attain optimum results. Cross over rate affects the convergence rate of the system mainly and has minimum effect on the accuracy of the system.

6 Conclusion

Genetic Algorithms have been used to solve difficult optimization problems in a number of fields and have proved to produce optimum results in mining Association rules. When Genetic algorithm is used for mining association rules the GA parameters decides the efficiency of the system. Minimum support, minimum confidence and population size are the key parameters deciding the accuracy of the system. The setting of the population size is based on the size of the problem under study, whereas the minimum confidence and minimum support to be set depends upon the problem under study. The optimum value of crossover rate leads to earlier convergence while playing minimum role in achieving better accuracy. The setting of optimum value of the GA parameters varies from data to data and the fitness function plays a major role in optimizing the results. The size of the dataset and relationship between attributes in data contributes to the setting up of the parameters. The efficiency of the methodology could be further explored on more datasets with varying attribute sizes.

References

1. Cattral, R., Oppacher, F., Deugo, D.: Rule Acquisition with a Genetic Algorithm. In: Proceedings of the 1999 Congress on Evolutionary Computation, CEC 1999 (1999)
2. Saggar, M., Agrawal, A.K., Lad, A.: Optimization of Association Rule Mining. In: IEEE International Conference on Systems, Man and Cybernetics, vol. 4, pp. 3725–3729 (2004)
3. Zhou, J., Li, S.-y., Mei, H.-y., Liu, H.-x.: A Method for Finding Implicating Rules Based on the Genetic Algorithm. In: Third International Conference on Natural Computation,, vol. 3, pp. 400–405 (2007)
4. Zhang, H. Chen. : Immune Optimization Based Genetic Algorithm for Incremental Association Rules Mining. In : International Conference on Artificial Intelligence and Computational Intelligence, AICI '09, Volume: 4, Page(s): 341 – 345, 2009.
5. Gonzales, E., Mabu, S., Taboada, K., Shimada, K., Hirasawa, K.: Mining Multi-class Datasets using Genetic Relation Algorithm for Rule Reduction. In: IEEE Congress on Evolutionary Computation, CEC 2009, pp. 3249–3255 (2009)
6. Shi, X.-J., Lei, H.: Genetic Algorithm-Based Approach for Classification Rule Discovery. In: International Conference on Information Management, Innovation Management and Industrial Engineering, ICIII 2008, vol. 1, pp. 175–178 (2008)
7. Ma, H., Li, X.: Application of Data Mining in Preventing Credit Card Fraud. In: International Conference on Management and Service Science, MASS 2009, pp. 1–6 (2009)

8. Guo, H., Zhou, Y.: An Algorithm for Mining Association Rules Based on Improved Genetic Algorithm and its Application. In: 3rd International Conference on Genetic and Evolutionary Computing, WGEC 2009, pp. 117–120 (2009)
9. Tang, H., Lu, J.: Hybrid Algorithm Combined Genetic Algorithm with Information Entropy for Data Mining. In: 2nd IEEE Conference on Industrial Electronics and Applications, pp. 753–757 (2007)
10. Dou, W., Hu, J., Hirasawa, K., Wu, G.: Quick Response Data Mining Model using Genetic Algorithm. In: SICE Annual Conference, pp. 1214–1219 (2008)

UDSCA: Uniform Distribution Based Spatial Clustering Algorithm

Animesh Tripathy[1], Sumit Kumar Maji[1], and Prashanta Kumar Patra[2]

[1] KIIT University, Bhubaneswar, India
[2] CET, Bhubaneswar, India

Abstract. Detection of clusters in Spatial Databases is a major task for knowledge discovery. Density based clustering algorithms plays a major role in this domain. DBSCAN algorithm effectively manages to detect clusters of any arbitrary shape with noise, but it fails to detect local clusters. DDSC and LDBSCAN does manages to detect local clusters effectively, but the number of input parameters are high. In this paper we have proposed a new density based clustering algorithm which introduces a concept called *Cluster Constant*. It basically represent the uniformity of distribution of points in a cluster. The proposed algorithm has minimized the input to be provided by the user down to one parameter (Minpts) and has made the other parameter (Eps) adaptive. Further we have also used some heuristics in order to improve the running time of the algorithm. Experiment results shows that the proposed algorithm detects local clusters of any arbitrary shape very effectively and also improves the running time of the algorithm.

Keywords: Data Mining, Clustering, Spatial Database.

1 Introduction

Spatial database contains huge amount of spatial featured data [8]. Hence to extract knowledge from these huge database we need a better method for organization of these data. Clustering based framework has widely been used for the organization of spatial data. The law of geography says that, ***"everything is related to everything, but the nearby things are more related than distant things"***. For example: economies of nearby region tend to be more similar. Hence it would be natural to use clustering to group the spatial objects because of their inherent similarity with the nearby spatial objects. Many clustering based framework exist for grouping data. For spatial objects, density based methods provide effective frameworks. It groups the objects based on similar density region. When density based clustering methods are used in spatial databases, following requirements are needed to be fulfilled [11]:

1. Minimizing the number of input parameter as these parameter values are very difficult to gather in advance.
2. Should be able to detect cluster of any arbitrary shape.

A. Abraham et al. (Eds.): ACC 2011, Part I, CCIS 190, pp. 649–660, 2011.

3. Good runtime complexity, because the algorithm operates on a database whose size is large.

In this paper, a new density based clustering algorithm is proposed which introduces a new concept, "*Cluster Constant*", which basically represents the uniformity of distribution in a cluster. The algorithm requires only one input parameter (Minpts) and has made the other parameter (Eps) adaptive. We have also used a heuristic in order to improve the running time of the algorithm. The paper is organized as follows. In section 2, the related work is briefly discussed. The basic definitions which are used in this algorithm are presented in section 3. In section 4, the algorithm called UDSCA is explained. In section 5, implementation results are shown. In the end, a conclusion is given along with some directions for future works.

2 Related Works

DBSCAN [1] algorithm is the base of the all density based clustering algorithms. The algorithm grows regions with sufficiently high density into clusters and discovers clusters of any arbitrary shape in spatial databases with noise. It defines a cluster as a maximal set of density-connected points. It requires two inputs from user, i.e. Eps and Minpts, based on which it detects clusters. It can identify noise effectively, but it cannot identify local clusters if present very close to other clusters. Therefore, the clusters which it detects has wide variation in its local density.

OPTICS [9] is an extension of DBSCAN algorithm which generates an order in which the objects needed to be processed. It then uses core-distance and reachability-distance in order to assign the each object a cluster membership. This order is generated through the reachability-distance and put in an ordered file. This ordered file is then used for assigning the cluster ID to each object. OPTICS also uses Eps parameter that plays an important role. By changing the Eps value, different structure of cluster is detected.

IDBSCAN [3] is an improvement of DBSCAN algorithm in terms of execution time. DBSCAN algorithm spends its major time for each object's region query. So, instead of expanding every object inside the region of core objects, IDBSCAN proposed the expansion of only those objects which are at the boundary of the cluster. This is because the expansion of boundary objects would cover the objects which would have been covered by the objects, situated inside the region of core object, if they had been expanded. But it suffers from the limitations, similar to that of the DBSCAN.

LD-BSCA [7] is an improvement of DBSCAN algorithm in terms of reduction of number of input parameter and execution time. It requires only Eps as an input parameter. During the expansion of cluster, it considers density of only those objects which has not been assigned a cluster ID. Hence the neighborhood query is not performed for the Eps-neighborhood objects of core object. In this way, it removes the neighborhood query of many objects and hence achieves an improvement over execution time. But the limitations are same as that of the DBSCAN.

LDBSCAN [6] is another algorithm which can detect different density based cluster. It uses the concept of LOF [5] which represent the degree of outlierness and hence indicates whether the object is a core object or not. It then uses LRD [5] in order to assign an object, to its corresponding cluster during the cluster expansion.

In [4] DDSC is proposed, which can identify cluster of different shape, size and density. It detects the change in density as the change in the number of objects inside a region. If the change in the density of region of an object is significant, then it indicates that the region query is entering into different density cluster and hence the cluster assignment proceeds with different cluster identification.

DENCLUE [2] is an algorithm which generalizes many clustering algorithm (DBSCAN, k-means, Hierarchical). It uses the concept of gradient in order to find the object which is density-attractor. All the objects which are density attracted to density-attractor are assigned to same cluster identity as that of density attractor.

LOF [5] is another density based algorithm that assigns a degree of oulierness to each objects. Instead of assigning a cluster ID, it assign how much outlier a point is in comparison to its surrounding region. It uses LRD to measure the local density of the objects. Through LRD, the LOF of each object is calculated which measures the outlierness of the object.

P-DBSCAN [10] is the parallel version of DBSCAN algorithm. Here the dataset is distributed into several computer nodes. Each computer nodes carries out clustering separately on the sub-dataset. The local clusters are aggregated to produce the final result. The algorithm is an improvement over DBSCAN algorithm in terms of execution time, as the dataset is clustered in parallel.

2.1 Benefits and Limitations

Table 1 shows the benefits and limitations of some algorithms which are surveyed in this paper.

Table 1. Comparisons of the algorithms

Algorithm	Benefits	Limitations
DBSCAN	Detects arbitrary shape clusters with noise	Cannot detect local clusters of different density
OPTICS	Produces different cluster structures	It is order dependent
LDBSCAN	Detects clusters of different density	Too many input parameters
DDSC	Detects clusters of different density	Too many input parameters

3 Basic Notions of UDSCA

3.1 Problems in Existing Approaches

DBSCAN algorithm does manage to find cluster effectively with noise, but it cannot identify local clusters which is present inside a cluster. The value of Eps largely responsible for this problem. Hence the Eps value needs to be adaptive in order to remove this problem. DDSC and LDBSCAN algorithm does manages to find local clusters which are present, but the number of parameters that are needed to be optimized has also increased in case of these two algorithms. Larger the number of input more will the be user involvement and hence less accurate will be the cluster result. So there is a need to reduce the number of input parameter.

There exist two problems that can be identified from above discussion. First is to make the Eps value adaptive and second is to reduce the number of input parameter. The algorithm which is proposed here, does manages to solve these two problems.

3.2 Formal Definition of LRD (Local Reachability Density)

In order to find the local density of objects there needs to be a better metric. The LRD of object fulfill that requirement. LRD of an object represents its local-density. A detail explanation of LRD can be obtained from [5]. The formal definition of LRD will be presented shortly in the following which requires the explanation of following concepts:

Definition 1 *(Minpts-Distance of object p)*: For any positive integer Minpts, the Minpts-distance of object p, denoted as Minpts-distance(p), is defined as the distance d(p,o) between p and an object o ∈D, such that

1. for at least Minpts objects o' D
   {p} it holds that d(p,o') ≤ d(p,o), and
2. for at most Minpts-1 objects o' D|{p} it holds that d(p,o') < d(p,o).

Definition 2 *(Minpts-Distance neighborhood of an object p)*: Given the Minpts-distance of object p, *the Minpts-Distance neighborhood of an object p* contains every object whose distance from p is not greater than *Minpts-distance*, i.e. $N_{Minpts-distance(p)}$=$\{q \in D|\{p\}|d(p,q) \leq$ *Minpts-distance(p)*$\}$. These objects are called Minpts-nearest neighbors of p.

Definition 3 *(Reachability distance of an object p)*: Let Minpts be a natural number. The *reachability distance of an object p*, with respect to an object o is defined as $Reach - dist_{Minpts}(p,o)$=*max(Minpts-distance(o), d(p,o))*.

Definition 4 *(LRD of an object p)*: The LRD of p is defined as

$$LRD_{Minpts(p)} = 1/\left(\frac{\sum_{o \in N_{Minpts}(p)} reach-dist_{Minpts}(p,o)}{|N_{Minpts}(p)|}\right)$$

The LRD of an object is inverse of average *reachabilty-distance* based on the Minpts-nearest neighbors of p. If the Minpts-neighbors of object p are very close to object p then it will have very low average reachability-distance, thus will have a high LRD, which will indicate a high density.

Density Based Notion of Cluster

Definition 5 *(Core point)*: A point p is a core w.r.t. LRD if

$$1.2 * LRD_p \geq LRD_o \tag{1}$$

where LRD_o is the LRD of previous core object which is already been processed. Initially, the first core object which is selected is the object whose LRD is highest. Subsequent core object is selected based on equation 1.

Definition 6 *(Noise)*: A point p is treated as noise if $1.2 * LRD_p \leq LRD_o$, where LRDo is the LRD of previous core object which is already been processed or if the Eps-neighborhood query overlaps with clustered points.

Definition 7 *(Directly density reachable)*: A point p is *directly density reachable* to point q w.r.t. Eps if p $\in N_{Eps}(q)$, where Eps is the radius of the circular region.

Definition 8 *(Density reachable)*: A point p is *density reachable* from point q w.r.t. Eps if there is chain of points $p_1, p_2, ..., p_n, p_1 = q$ and $p_n = p$ such that p_{i+1} is directly density reachable from p_i.

Definition 9 *(Density connected)*: A point p is *density connected* to a point q from o if there is a point o such that both p and q are density reachable from o.

Definition 10 *(Cluster)*: Let D be a database of points. A cluster C w.r.t. Minpts is a non-empty subset of D satisfying following conditions:

1. For all p, p is density reachable from o w.r.t. Minpts, then p $\in$ C. (Maximality)
2. for all p,q C, p is density connected to q by o w.r.t Minpts. (Connectivity)

4 UDSCA

4.1 Proposed Approach of Making Eps Adaptive

For a given Mints value, the points which are inside the cluster will have high LRD value than the points which belongs to the edge of cluster. Hence, the LRD value will give the position of the point within a cluster.

In this approach, the cluster expansion process starts from inside the cluster and proceeds towards the edge. As we move towards the edge, if the Eps values remains same then, its Eps-neighborhood query might include points of another cluster which is present in its close proximity. This problem is removed by reducing the Eps value as we move towards the edge of cluster. So, by the time the objects which is present at the edge of cluster is expanded, its Eps will become so small that it will not include objects of another cluster present in its close proximity.

So, it can be said that as we move towards the edge of a cluster, Eps value is reduced, or it can be said that as we move towards the edge of cluster the LRD value reduces and accordingly the Eps value is reduced i.e.

$$LRD \propto Eps \tag{2}$$

$$LRD = K^{*}Eps \tag{3}$$

From equation 3, this K is called "Cluster Constant" and is used as guide for calculating the Eps value of a point during the cluster expansion i.e.

$$Eps = \frac{LRD}{K} \tag{4}$$

For the first core-object of a cluster its Eps value is equal to its Minpts-nearest neighbor distance. Having got the LRD value of that object, the value of K is calculated. Now, this K is used for calculating the Eps values of the objects during the cluster expansion as shown in equation 4. In this way, the Eps value is made adaptive.

4.2 Heuristic for Improving the Running Time of the Algorithm

During the expansion of a cluster, every point which is present in the Eps-neighborhood are expanded. From [3] it can be seen that, it is not necessary to expand each and every point present in the Eps-neighborhood. Instead, the points which are present at the boundary of cluster are expanded, which will cover the points, which would have been covered if the points which are present inside the region of cluster are expanded.

4.3 The Algorithm

To find a cluster, the algorithm selects a point which has the highest LRD value. This point is treated as core point and it yields a cluster. It then assigns the same cluster ID to all the points which are density reachable to the core point according to definition 8. This process is repeated until there is no more points left which is density reachable to the core point; in that case the algorithm selects another core-point according to definition 5.

The following shows the pseudo code of *UDSCA*:

UDSCA(Set-Of-Points, Minpts)
Initialize the database by calculating LRD and Eps (Minpts-nearest neighbor distance) of each object.
Sort the objects in descending order of LRD.

```
clusterID = 0;
FOR i FROM 1 TO Set-Of-Points.size DO
      Point = Set-Of-Points.get(i);
      IF the Point is not processed
          lrd = Point.getLRD();
          IF the Point is core-point
              eps = Point.getEPS();
              const = lrd/eps;
              IF Set-Of-Points.regionQuery(Point,eps) does not overlap with
                  other clusters
                  clusterID = clusterID+1;
                  ExpandCluster (Set-Of-Points, Point, clusterID, eps, const)
              ELSE
                  Set-Of-Points.changeclusterID (Point, noise);
                  Point.processed = true;
          ELSE
              Set-Of-Points.changeclusterID (Point, noise);
              Point.processed = true;
          END IF
      END IF
END FOR
END UDSCA
```

The Set-Of-Points is the entire database and Minpts is provided by the user. The algorithm starts with the calculation of LRD of each point. The points are given the Eps value which is equal to the Minpts-nearest neighbor distance. The points are then sorted in descending order of LRD values. Initially all the points are unclassified and unprocessed. Set-Of-Points.get(i) returns the ith element of Set-Of-Points. If that point is a core point then, its Eps is found through Point.getEPS() method. Then its *Cluster Constant* is calculated which used for calculation of Eps of points during cluster expansion.

```
ExpandCluster (Set-Of-Points, Point, clusterID, eps, const)
tempseeds = Set-Of-Points.regionQuery(Point, eps);
Set-Of-Points.changeclusterID(tempseeds, clusterID);
Put points in the seeds from tempseeds according to the heuristic-
of section 4.2
WHILE seeds <> Empty
      curentP = seeds.first();
      lrd = current.getLRD();
      eps = lrd/const;
      temp-seeds = Set-Of-Points.regionQuery(currentP, eps);
      Set-Of-Points.changeclusterID(temp-seeds, clusterID);
      Delete the points from the seeds which are also member
      of temp-seeds
      Put points in seeds from temp-seeds according to the heuristic-
      of section 4.2
```

seeds.delete(currentP);
END WHILE
END ExpandCluster

ExpandCluster procedure is called during the expansion of cluster once a cluster is identified. The procedure Set-Of-Points.regionQuery(Point, eps) returns the Eps-neighborhood of Point in Set-Of-Points. These points are assigned the same cluster ID as that of Point. After this, the heuristic is used as shown in section 4.2, in order the select points which are present at the boundary of Eps-region. These points are used as seeds for further expansion of cluster.

4.4 Parameter Minpts

Our main objective here is to initiate the cluster expansion process from the inside of a cluster and proceeds towards the edge of cluster. In order to satisfy this requirement we need have high LRD valued points from inside of cluster. For a given cluster, if the Minpts value is low(10-25), then its points will have high LRD value at the edge of cluster. But, if the Minpts value is increased(35-50), we will get more high LRD values at the inside of cluster. Hence high Minpts value is recommended in order to begin cluster expansion process inside the cluster.

5 Performance Evaluation

5.1 Complexity Analysis

For a database of size n, the runtime complexity of region query is $O(n)$, if no indexing is used. If indexing such as R-tree is used, then the complexity is $O(log_m n)$, where m is the depth of tree. In order to calculate LRD of each object, the object needs to perform a region query, this would take a runtime complexity of $O(log_m n)$. Hence for entire database, this would be $O(nlog_m n)$. During the cluster identification and expansion process, each object needs to perform a region query, hence its complexity would be $O(log_m n)$. Hence for entire database the complexity would be $O(nlog_m n)$. Hence the resultant complexity of the algorithm is $O(nlog_m n)$. But because of the heuristic, the running time of the algorithm reduces significantly as will be shown in the later section.

5.2 Experimental Evaluation

Here we have evaluated the performance of UDSCA. The algorithm is implemented in Matlab R2009b software tool. The implementation is done on a system with 2.0GHz CPU and 1GB RAM. The Chameleon datasets (http://glaros.dtc.umn.edu/gkhome/cluto/cluto/download)- t4.8k.dat, t5.8k.dat and t8.8k.dat and a user generated dataset(data1) is used in order to test the performance of the algorithm.

Figure 1 and 2 shows the result of the algorithm on the Chameleon dataset. Points with same colors indicates that, those points are assigned the same cluster

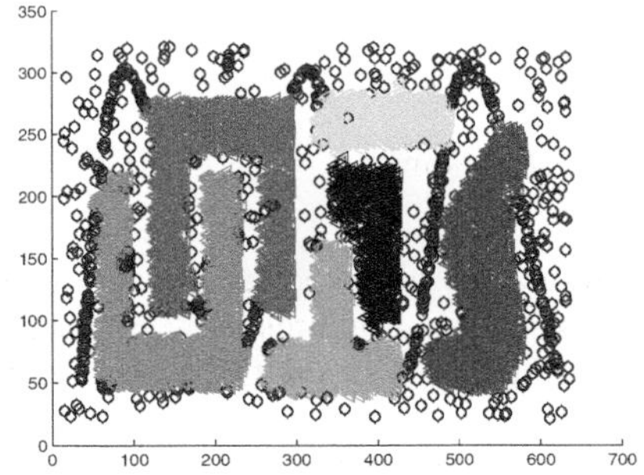

Fig. 1. Cluster result on Chameleon dataset t4.8k.dat(Minpts = 40)

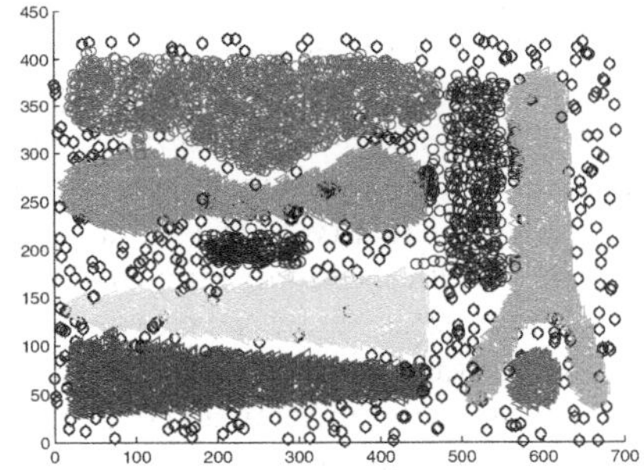

Fig. 2. Cluster result on Chameleon dataset t8.8k (Minpts = 40)

ID. The points that are noise are shown in circles with brown color. Figure 3 also shows the effectiveness of the algorithm in detecting clusters. The results prove that the proposed algorithm is capable of detecting clusters of different shapes, sizes with local clusters present in its close proximity. Table 2 shows the comparison of the running time of the algorithm with and without the heuristic as explained in section 4.2. The results prove that the heuristic greatly improves the running time of the algorithm. Figure 4 and 5 shows the comparison of DDSC and LDBSCAN against UDSCA. The results shows that the proposed algorithm (UDSCA) is better capable of detecting arbitrary shape clusters of different density than DDSC and LDBSCAN.

Figure 6(a) shows the problem which exist in DBSCAN algorithm when there is presence of a local cluster. This problem exist because the Eps value remains constant as a result of which most of the dataset is assigned the same cluster ID. The UDSCA algorithm solves this problem by having an adaptive Eps, whose result is shown in Fig. 6(b). This solution is also achieved through a single parameter (Minpts). Hence the proposed algorithm solves the problem of DBSCAN as seen from the results of Fig. 6.

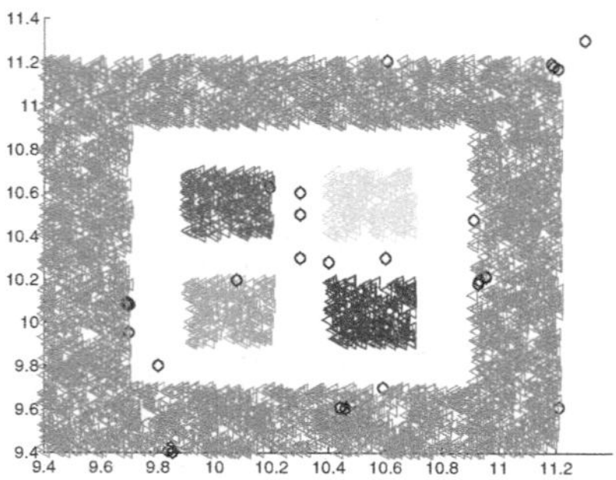

Fig. 3. Cluster result on Data1 dataset(Minpts=50)

Table 2. Comparison of algorithm with and without the heurisic

Dataset	With heuristic running time(sec)	Without heuristic running time(sec)
t4.8k	132.86	365.55
t5.8k	70.24	327.33
t8.8k	120.063	345.50
data1	30.27	140.50

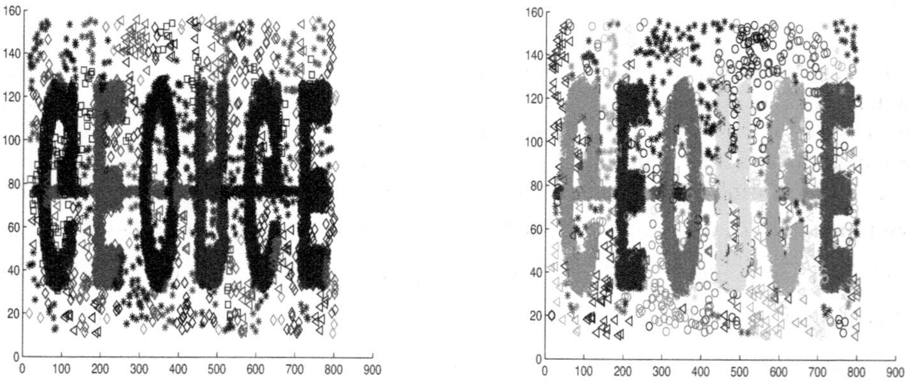

(a) (b)

Fig. 4. (a)DDSC, (b)LDBSCAN

5.3 Limitations of UDSCA

Following are some of the limitations of UDSCA:

1. For this algorithm to perform better, each cluster must contain at least Minpts-number of objects in its Eps-neighborhood.
2. The running time of the algorithm is O(nlog$_m$n).

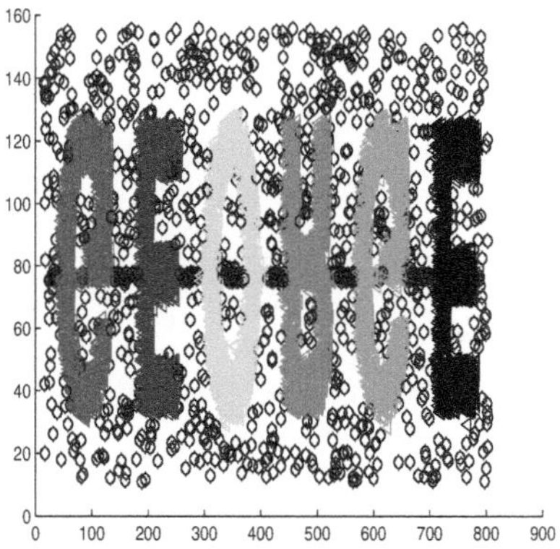

Fig. 5. UDSCA

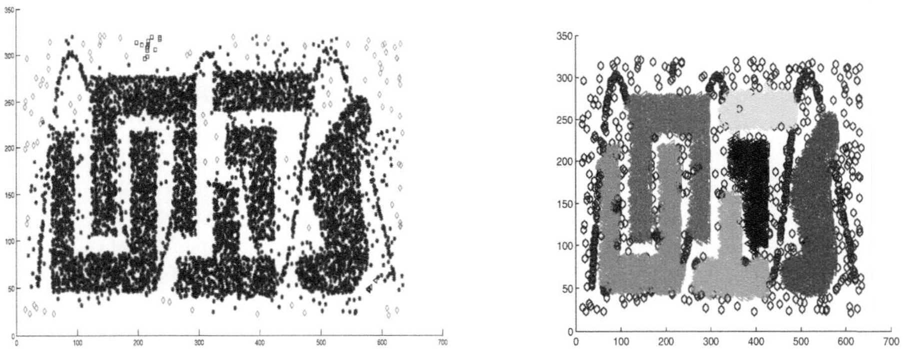

(a) (b)

Fig. 6. (a)DBSCAN, (b)UDSCA

6 Conclusion

For identification of groups in spatial databases density based clustering algorithms are logical choice. But the task become very time consuming because of the huge size of database. Also the problem of detecting clusters become difficult when there are local clusters present. The algorithm which is proposed here is capable of detecting clusters of any arbitrary shape, size with local clusters present in its close proximity, which requires lesser number of input parameters. We have also used a heuristic in order to improve the running time of the algorithm which is very useful for large datasets. The evaluation of the algorithm is performed on Chameleon datasets and user generated datasets. The results of these experiments prove that the proposed algorithm is an improvement over DBSCAN, DDSC and LDBSCAN. There should be a method for calculation of optimum Minpts value for a cluster. Also, further research can be done in order to make the Minpts adaptive.

References

1. Ester, M., Kriegel, H.P., Snader, J., Xu, X.: A density Based Algorithm for Discovering clusters in Large Spatial Databases with Noise. In: Proc. 2nd Int. Conf. on Knowledge Discovery and Data Mining, OR, pp. 226–231. AAAI Press, Menlo Park (1996)
2. Hinneburg, A., Hinneburg, E., Keim, D.A.: An Efficient Approach to Clustering in Large Multimedia Databases with Noise, pp. 58–65. AAAI Press, Menlo Park (1998)
3. Borah, B., Bhattacharyya, D.K.: An Improved Sampling-Based DBSCAN for Large Spatial Databases. In: Int. Conf. on Intelligent Sensing, pp. 92–96 (2004)
4. Borah, B., Bhattacharyya, D.K.: DDSC:A Density Differentiated Spatial Clustering Technique. Journal of Computers 3(2), 72–79 (2008)
5. Breunig, M.M., Kriegel, H.-P., Ng, R.T., Sander, J.: LOF: Identifying Density-Based Local Outliers. In: Proceedings of the 2000 ACM SIGMOD International Conference on Management of Data, vol. 29, pp. 93–104. ACM, New York (2000)
6. Duan, L., Xu, L., Guo, F., Lee, J., Yan, B.: A local-density based spatial clustering algorithm with noise. Inf. Syst. 32, 978–986 (2007)
7. Wei, G., Wu, H.: LD-BSCA:A Local Density Based Spatial Clustering Algoithm. In: IEEE Symposium on Computational Intelligence and Data Mining, pp. 291–298. IEEE Computer Scoiety, Los Alamitos (2009)
8. Gueting, R.H.: An introduction to spatial database system. The VLDB Journal 3(4), 357–399 (1994)
9. Ankerst, M., Breunig, M.M., Kriegel, H.P., Sander, J.: OPTICS:Ordering Points to Identify the Clustering Sructure. In: Proc. of ACM SIGMOD Int. Conf. on Management of Data, Philadelphia, P.A., pp. 49–60. ACM, New York (1999)
10. Chen, M., Gao, X., Li, H.: Parallel DBSCAN with Priority R-tree. In: 2nd IEEE International Conference on Information Management and Engineering, pp. 508–511. IEEE, Los Alamitos (2010)
11. Xu, X., Ester, M., Kriegel, H.-P., Sander, J.: A distribution Based Clustering Algorithm for Mining in Large Spatial Databases. In: 14th Int. Conf. on Data Engineering, pp. 324–331 (1998)

A Classification Model for Customer Segmentation

Chithra Ramaraju[1] and Nickolas Savarimuthu[2]

[1] Research Scholar, [2] Associate Professor
Department of Computer Applications,
National Institute of Technology, Tiruchirappalli-620015
chithra_viswanathan@yahoo.co.in, nickolas@nitt.edu

Abstract. Customer management is one of the important aspects in retail business. It is vital for the retailers to adopt different methodologies by which high valued customers can be identified, in order to perform suitable target marketing effectively. In this paper, a novel model is proposed for classifying retail customers into different categories based on purchasing behavior of customers. A class label for each transaction is determined based upon customer profit value (CPV), and a classifier model is build for predicting different categories of customers. The classifier model is constructed using SPSS tool for market basket data. Finally, the classifier model is verified with test data set, and used for predicting customer category. The extracted information is helpful for planning customer retention and providing personalized customer services by understanding their needs, preferences and behavior.

Keywords: Data mining, Classification, Prediction, customer value.

1 Introduction

Customer relationship management (CRM) has become inevitable business strategies in the new millennium. Customer segmentation is a CRM concept based on core marketing idea. CRM can be viewed as 'Managerial efforts to manage business interactions with customers by combining business processes and technologies that seek to understand a company's customers [1]. Now business organizations are realizing the importance of CRM, and its two main objectives are 1. Customer retention through customer satisfaction. 2. Customer development through customer insight.

Present day retail shops are accumulating, millions of sales transactions, and customer information in their day-to-day business, which are stored in the databases. These databases are hidden with valuable information and can be directly applied for making intelligent business decision. The main goal of retailers is to provide best customer services by knowing their needs and preferences and it is essential for retailer to predict and find out most profitable customers who account for the major portion of their future profits.

Retailers recognized that valuable, non trivial useful information can be extracted from voluminous retail data, which helps decision makers to take vital decision for business operations. Customer purchasing behavior is considered significant, based on past sales transactions. Customer segmentation is one of the fundamental tasks, which

A. Abraham et al. (Eds.): ACC 2011, Part I, CCIS 190, pp. 661–670, 2011.

has been more widely used to identifying right customers, knowing their needs and offering right services at the right time are the main goals of retailers which lead retail organization to employ and plan a clear strategy for treating different types of customers. When evaluating customer profitability, marketers often use 80/20 rule (80% of the profits are produced by top 20% of profitable customers and 80% of the costs are spent on top 20% of unprofitable customers) [2][3]. So many companies are interested in measuring customer value, by which most profitable customers are identified and retained by building retention strategies [3][4][5].

KDD (Knowledge Discovery from Database) is the nontrivial process of extracting valid, novel, potentially useful, and ultimately understandable patterns from database. Data mining is one of the processes in the KDD process which includes several knowledge discovery methods, such as frequent pattern mining, association rule mining, sequential pattern mining, classification and clustering. These data mining techniques are used to assess the value of customers, understand and predict their behavior. The extracted information can then be used to identify trends and associations, form a prediction or classification model, refine an existing model, or provide a summary of the database being mined. Business intelligence has emerged as one of the most popular applications in the past four decades, which can help in extracting more valuable information.

The objective of this study is

1. To compute CPV value
2. To determine class label for each customer (high, medium and low profitable customers) based upon CPV value.
3. To construct classifier model in order to predict customer category.
4. To plan customer retention strategy and provide personalized customer services by understanding each customer category, their needs, preferences and behavior.

The rest of the paper is organized as follows: Section 2 presents related work and section 3 provides terms and definitions for customer profit value calculation. Section 4 presents a conceptual framework and experimental results. Section 5 discusses on conclusion and future scope in this work.

2 Related Works

2.1 Customer Value

Analyzing customers in groups is one of the most fundamental issues in Marketing. Customer segmentation is the process of dividing the customer details into distinct and internally homogeneous groups in order to develop different marketing strategies tailored to their characteristics. There are different segmentation types based on the specific criteria or attributes used for segmentation.

Frederick F. R [6] proposed customer lifecycle value model, which was most popular and recognized by many scholars. The theory and idea proposed by Kotler [7] customer lifecycle value, which is the current value of all profits the customers contributes to companies during the whole lifetime. Customer value has been widely used and studied under the name of LTV (Life Time Value), CLV (Customer Lifetime Value), CE (Customer Equity) and Customer Profitability. The LTV is the sum of the revenues gained from company's customers over the lifetime of transactions after deducting the total cost of servicing customers. The long-term value (CLV) of a customer "represents the present value of the expected benefits (e.g., gross margin) less the burdens (e.g., direct costs of servicing and communicating) from customers" (Dwyer et al [8]). Current value and potential value are used to segment the customers of insurance company in [5]. Lot of research is done for calculating customer value. Hwang et al [9] used three attributes, namely current value, potential value, and customer loyalty to consider the customer defection in Telecommunication Company. A frame work for analyzing customer value and segmenting customer based on their value and building strategies according to customer segment are illustrated with case study in [10]. A three dimensional customer classification model and customer potential contribution value estimate model in stock market is put forward by [11]. Customer value in retail industry is defined as the profit that customers' purchase brings to the companies [12].

Many researchers used the basic model for calculating LTV where

$$\mathrm{LTV} = \sum_{i=1}^{n} \frac{(R_i - C_i)}{(1 + d)^{i-.5}} \tag{1}$$

where i is the period of cash flow from customer transactions, R_i is the profit from the customer at period i. C_i is the total cost spent in generating the profit R_i in period i, and n is the total number of years customers having relationship with an organization. The discount value d, given in the denominator, transforms the net profit value into current value. In the proposed work, profit of the customer (R_i) is defined as customer profit contribution value (CPV). The calculation of CPV is similar to the transaction utility computation of high utility pattern mining [13].

2.2 High Utility Pattern Mining

The methodology used for calculating customer profit value contribution (CPV), is the same as used for calculating transaction utility, in high utility pattern mining. In recent years, the problem of high utility pattern mining has become one of the most important research areas in data mining. The goal of high utility pattern mining process is to find all itemsets that give utility value greater or equal to the user specified threshold. A high utility pattern mining model was defined by Yao, Hamilton and Butz [13]. Two types of utilities for attributes are generalized as transaction utility and external utility. The transaction utility of an item i_p in a transaction T_q is defined according to the numerical quantity x_p stored in the transaction, which is transaction dependent. This model allows users to express their preference or expectations regarding each attributes of the transactional database, in the form of weight or external utility value. The external utility of an item i_p is a numerical value y_p, defined by the user. It is transaction independent and reflects importance (usually profit) of the item. External utilities are stored in a profit table. Utility function f is the product of internal and external utility: $x_p \times y_p$.

3 Basic Terms and Definitions

Let I = $\{i_1, i_2, i_3 \ldots i_m\}$ be a set of items. Let TDB= $\{T_1, T_2, T_3 \ldots T_n\}$ be a set of transactions in transactional database, and each transaction is associated with a unique identifier called its TID. Every transaction T of TDB contains customer details and set of purchased items such that purchased items of $T \subseteq I$. Let X be an itemset, a transaction T is said to contain X if and only if $X \subseteq T$. The item $i_p \in I$ in transaction Tq is denoted by p (i_p, Tq), is the number of item i_p purchased in transaction Tq called purchased quantity of item i_p. For example, p (a, T_1) = 10, p (b, T_1) = 1, and p (d, T_1) = 5, in Table 1 (a).

The external utility of item $i_p \in$ I, pr (i_p), is the value associated with item i_p in the profit table called profit per unit. This value reflects the importance of an item, which is independent of transactions. For example, in Table I (b), the profit per unit of item a, pr (a), is 5. The sample database in Table 1 (a) contains only five items named as 'a', 'b', 'c', 'd' and 'e'. The customer T_1, purchases items a, b, d and, e and corresponding quantities are 10, 1, 5 and 6.

Definition 1: The **profit value** of an item i_p in transaction Tq, is the quantity measure denoted by PV (i_p, T_q), where

$$PV(i_p, T_q) = p(i_p, T_q) * pr(i_p) \tag{2}$$

For example profit of a in T_1, PV (a, T_1) = 10×5=50.

Definition 2: The **profit value** of transaction Tq, or **Customer profit value contribution** (CPV) denoted as transaction utility (tu) of Tq, is the sum of the total profit value of all items in Tq and it is defined

$$\text{CPV or } PV(T_q) = \sum_{i_p \varepsilon T_q} PV(i_p, T_q) \tag{3}$$

For example, $PV(T_1)=PV(a,T_1)+PV(b,T_1)+PV(c,T_1)+PV(d,T_1)=50+6+2+45+12=113$. The profit value column of Table 1 (a) gives the transaction utility or customer profit value of each transaction.

Sales transactions of retail store for certain period (for example one year) is assumed for calculating CPV. During that period, some customers may frequently visit the shop (n number of visits). In this case, CPV is the sum of profit of each transaction performed by the customer during the period t. The parameters like retention rate, discount rate may be considered for future expansion.

$$CPV = \sum_{t=0}^{n} PV(Tq) \tag{4}$$

Table 1 (a). Transactional Database

Customer Demographic Details							Purchase Details							
Tid	Candid	value	P- method	sex	House own	income	age	a	b	c	d	e	Profit or CPV	Class Label
T1	39808	42.71	CQ	M	N	27000	46	10	1	0	5	6	113	High
T2	67362	25.35	CS	F	N	30000	28	4	5	0	7	1	115	High
T3	10872	20.61	CS	M	N	13200	36	0	1	13	0	2	23	Low
T4	26748	23.68	CA	F	N	12200	26	6	5	0	0	10	80	Medium
T5	91609	18.81	CA	M	Y	11000	24	7	1	0	4	3	83	Medium

Table 1 (b). Profit Table

Item	a	b	c	d	e
Profit	5	6	1	9	2

4 A Conceptual Framework for Customer Category Prediction Model

A conceptual framework for building classification model is shown in Fig 2, with three phases. Phase I, collects and prepares data for customer segmentation. In Phase II, customer profit value contribution is calculated and class label is determined. Once the class label is determined, classification can be performed on customer demographic details to build classifier model, using which customer can be categorized. In Phase III, each customer segment is analyzed, marketing strategy is planned to provide personalized service. Finally classifier model is used for predicting new customer category and their potential profit contribution.

4.1 Dataset Description

The dataset used for this study is called market basket data, captured from Alpha miner open source data mining tool. This dataset consists of eleven (11) items collected from a retail store with one thousand (1,000) past sales transaction data with demographic details of customer. For simplicity, only five items are shown in the sample database in Table 1 (a) named as 'a', 'b', 'c', 'd', and 'e'. Each transaction contains, items purchased by a customer along with customers demographic details. The demographic details contain 'Card id', 'Card value' (as rated by the retailer), 'p-method' (payment method by cheque /cash/card expressed in (CQ) /(CS) /(CA).), 'sex' (Male/Female expressed in M/F), 'home own' (yes/no), 'income' and 'age'. Tid is a transaction identifier.

The details of the dataset are meant for frequent pattern mining, and do not provide profit values or purchase quantity of each item in the transaction. For each item, purchased quantity is assigned with random numbers generated between 1 to 9. Profit

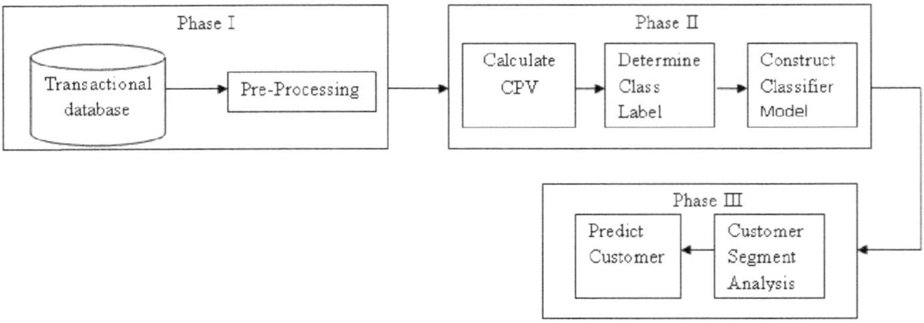

Fig. 1. Conceptual Framework for customer segmentation

values of each items is taken randomly between 1 to 50. After preprocessing, only 926 transactions are obtained due to the removal of noisy and missing values.

4.2 Determination of Class Label

CPV is the profit value contributed by each customer while performing the transaction for certain period t, and is calculated using equation (3). This derived attribute, namely, profit is then used to determine the class label of each customer. The class label for each transaction can be computed by two different methods. In the first method namely naïve method, the sales transactions are sorted in the descending order of CPV value. In this case, customers are segmented by dividing its percentile. For example, in order to have three classes, the first 33 percentile of transaction are assigned with class label 'high profit' and next 33 percentile of transactions are assigned with class label 'medium profit' and the remaining transactions are assigned with a class label 'low profit' as shown in Fig 2. The drawback of this method is that, the profit value range for all these classes may not be uniform.

The second method determines class label for each transaction by dividing the attribute (CPV) into desired number of ranges. In this example, the number of class label N is 3 and **max** and **min** are the maximum and minimum customer CPV values. The width interval is given by, W = (max – min)/N. The maximum and minimum transaction values are 115, and 23 respectively for the given data set and the width interval W is 31.

The range for each partition is computed using width value W, which is given in Table 2. After determining range for each class label, a new attribute (class label) is appended to every transaction of the transactional database. Class label is determined based upon the CPV value. The transactions whose profit values range from 23 to 53 is assigned with class label 'low profit'. For example, in Table 1(a), transaction T3 is assigned with class label 'low profit'. 'Medium profit' class label is assigned to transactions, whose profit values lies between 54 to 84. Transactions T4 and T5 are assigned with class label 'medium profit'. The 'high profit' class label is assigned to transactions with transaction profit values between 85 to 115. Transactions T1 and T2 are assigned with label 'high profit'.

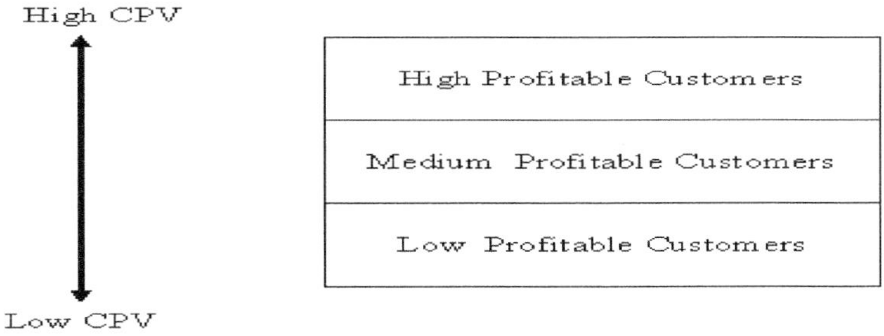

Fig. 2. Customer segmentation based on CPV

4.3 Constructing Classifier Model

The CPV value in retail store mostly depends on customer demographic details. Once, class label is determined using second method for each customer transaction, classification is performed to derive the relationship between demographic details and class labels. Classification model provide better understanding of the data at large. Many classification algorithms have been proposed in data mining, such as decision trees, naïve Bayesian classifiers, k-nearest neighborhood classifier, case based reasoning, and rough set and fuzzy set approaches. One of the popularly used algorithms from statistics is decision tree induction, which constructs decision trees in a top-down recursive divide-and-conquer manner. Decision tree is a well known method of predictive modeling, since the model provides interpretable rules and logic statements which enable more intelligent decision making. Each node in a decision tree represents attribute in a training sample to be classified, and each branch represents a value that the node can assume. The algorithm uses any one of the numerous measures such as information gain [14], gini index [15] to find best splitting attribute criteria that will best separate the samples into individual classes and allows tree to grow further. The algorithm uses the same process recursively to form a decision tree for the samples at each partition.

Decision tree classifier model is built, to predict customer class category. CHAID modeling from SPSS Clementine data mining tool with 10 fold cross validation technique is used in this work. After determining class label for each transaction, the dataset is imported to SPSS. In the database, class label is set as target variable, and gender, own house, income and age are treated as predictor variables. Out of this predictor variable, only two attributes namely income and gender are influencing target variable. The resulting decision tree is given in Fig 3.

There are three leaves in the decision tree; the rule of the decision tree is explained as follows from left to right.

(1) If (Income <= 18100 , gender ='M') Then the probability of customer is medium profitable, is 50.8%.
(2) If (Income <= 18100 , gender ='F') Then the probability of customer is low profitable, is 72.8%.
(3) If (Income >18100) Then the probability of customer is low profitable is 75.3%.

Table 2. Profit Value Range for Class Labels

Class Label	Width		Range (CPV values)
	Lower	Upper	
Low profit	L1=Min	U1=L1+(W-1)	23-53
Medium profit	L2=U1+1	U2=L2+(W-1)	54 -84
High profit	L3=U2+1	U3=Max	85-115

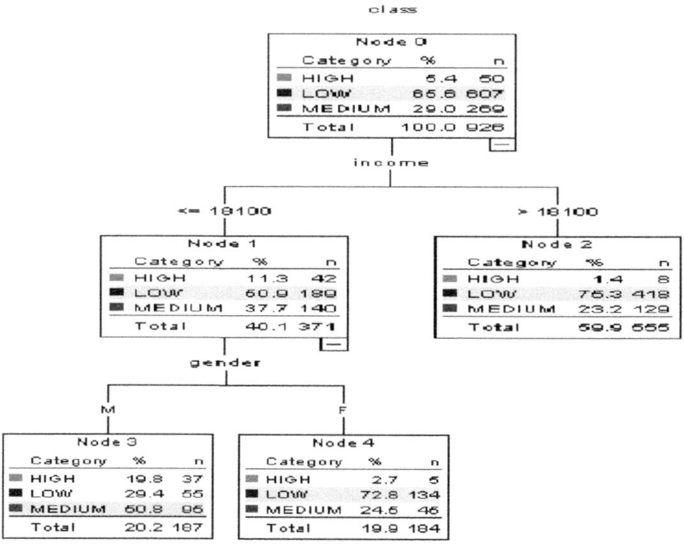

Fig. 3. Decision Tree Model

Analysis of result:

1. From this decision tree, it is concluded that 19.8% (out of 187) of customers are high profitable customers whose income <=18100 and gender =male. These are the customers who account for major profit contribution to the business. Marketing people may recommend a suitable marketing strategy to this group to increase overall profit of an organization. Only 50.8% (out of 187) of customers are medium profitable, whose income <=18100 and gender =male. The same rule account for 29.4% of low profitable customers.
2. From the second leaf node, 72.8% (out of 184) customers low profitable, whose income <=18100 and gender =female. The same rule account for 24.5% (out of 184) of customers as medium profitable.

3. From the last leaf node, it is concluded that 75.3% (out of 555) of customers are low profitable whose income > 18100. The same condition account for 23.2% of medium profitable customers.

5 Conclusion

The approach for customer segmentation according to their profit contribution to retail industry is presented in this paper. Initially for each customer, the class label is determined based upon the profit value contributed by the customer. Classifier model is built, for estimating each customer potential profit contribution. The synthetic market basket data is used empirically to validate the proposed approach. Results indicate that the maximum classifier accuracy is 75.3%. After identifying highly profitable customer, promotional strategies can be proposed to target the specific group of customers, which will earn more profit to the seller.

The proposed work can further be extended using real dataset, which consist of both customer demographic profiles as well as purchase details, to improve the prediction accuracy. In future study, soft computing techniques could be considered for determining class label instead of discrete profit value range. Aiming new marketing strategy for handling of customers personalized needs and preferences will be examined in more detail. For each category of customers, frequent significant itemsets can be derived to promote cross selling products.

References

1. Kim, J., Suh, E., Hwang, H.: A model for evaluating the effectiveness of CRM using the balanced scorecard. Journal of Interactive Marketing 17(2), 5–19 (2003)
2. Duboff, R.S.: Marketing to maximize profitability. The Journal of Business Strategy 13(6), 10–13 (1992)
3. Gloy, B.A., Akridge, J.T., Preckel, P.V.: Customer lifetime value: An application in the rural petroleum market. Agribusiness 13(3), 335–347 (1997)
4. Rosset, S., Neumann, E., Eick, U., Vatnik, N., Idan, Y.: Customer lifetime value modeling and its use for customer retention planning. In: Proceedings of ACM SIGKDD International Conference on Knowledge Discovery and Data Mining, pp. 332–340 (2002)
5. Verhoef, P.C., Donkers, B.: Predicting customer potential value an application in the insurance industry. Decision Support Systems 32, 189–19 (2001)
6. Fredrick, F.R.: The loyalty effect: The hidden force behind growth, profits and lasting value. Harvard Business School Press, Boston (1996)
7. Kotler, P., Armstrong, G.: Principles of Marketing, 7th edn. Prentice Hill, Englewood Cliff (1996)
8. Dwyer, F.R.: Customer lifetime valuation to support marketing decision making. Journal Interactive Marketing 11(4), 6–13 (1997)
9. Hwang, H., Jung, T., Suh, E.: An LTV model and customer segmentation based on customer value: a case study on the wireless telecommunication industry. Expert Systems with Applications 26, 181–188 (2004)

10. Kim, S., Jung, T., Suh, E., Hwang, H.: Customer segmentation and strategy development based on customer lifetime value: A case study. Expert Systems with Applications 31, 101–107 (2006)
11. Lao, G., Zhang, Z.: A three-dimensional customer classification model based on knowledge discovery and empirical study. In: Chang, K.C.-C., Wang, W., Chen, L., Ellis, C.A., Hsu, C.-H., Tsoi, A.C., Wang, H. (eds.) APWeb/WAIM 2007. LNCS, vol. 4537, pp. 510–515. Springer, Heidelberg (2007)
12. Jiaying, Q., Suh, H.: Assessing modeling and decision making of customer value, Beijing University of Posts and Telecommunication Press (2005)
13. Yao, H., Hamilton, H.J., Butz, C.J.: A Foundational approach to mining Itemset Utilities From Databases. In: Third SIAM International Conference on Data Mining, pp. 482–486 (2004)
14. Hunt, E.B., Marin, J., Stone, P.J.: Experiments in induction. Academic Press, New York (1966)
15. Breiman, L., Friedman, J., Olshen, L., Stone, J.: Classification and Regression trees. Wadsworth Statistics/Probability series. CRC Press, Boca Raton (1984)

A Rough Set Based Approach for Ranking Decision Rules

M.K. Sabu [1] and G. Raju[2]

[1] School of Computer Sciences, Mahatma Gandhi University, Kottayam, Kerala, India
sabu.mes@rediffmail.com
[2] Department of Information Technology, Kannur University, Kerala, India
kurupgraju@rediffmail.com

Abstract. In this paper we propose a new method for ranking decision rules generated from an information system. This process will reduce the overhead incurred in selecting appropriate rules for classification and hence speed up the decision making process. The algorithm proposed for rule ranking is based on discernibility matrix in Rough Set Theory. In this approach, rules generated from the given dataset using Apriori algorithm are considered as conditional attributes to construct a new decision table. From this decision table, degree of significance of each rule is calculated and rules are ranked according to this degree of significance. The algorithm is explained with the help of a test dataset. Further it is applied on a Learning Disability (LD) dataset consisting of signs and symptoms causing learning disability, which is collected from a local clinic handling learning disability in school aged children. The experiments on these datasets show that the new method is efficient and effective for ranking decision rules.

Keywords: Rough Set Theory, Discernibility matrix, Association rule mining, Learning disability.

1 Introduction

Rough Set Theory (RST) is a mathematical tool to deal with imperfect knowledge. In RST, the uncertainty is managed by considering the granularity structure of the data. If we have exactly the same information in two objects then we say that they are indiscernible (similar), which means we cannot distinguish them with known knowledge [1]. These granules or group of similar objects are the basic building blocks for handling uncertainty. The Rough Set approach provides efficient algorithms for finding out hidden patterns in data, minimal sets of data (data reduction), evaluating significance of data and generating sets of decision rules from data [1]. In RST, all computations are performed directly on datasets. It requires no additional parameters to operate such as a probability distribution in statistics, a grade of membership from fuzzy set theory etc., other than the supplied data [9]. One advantage of RST is that it provides a well understood formal model which is very helpful in generating several kinds of information such as relevant features or association rules using minimal model assumptions [2]. The discernibility matrix in RST is useful for representing the knowledge regarding the discrimination between

A. Abraham et al. (Eds.): ACC 2011, Part I, CCIS 190, pp. 671–682, 2011.

various objects of an information system. The discernibility matrix constructed from a new decision table with decision rules generated from the original decision table as conditional attributes is useful for exploring the significance of various decision rules [3]. This approach provides a new way for ranking decision rules automatically.

Rule mining is a process to search relationships among data items in a given dataset for future predictions [4]. Association rule algorithms can be used to extract rules from decision tables. A challenging problem in rule generation is that an extensive number of rules are extracted by these rule mining algorithms over large datasets, and it is infeasible for human beings to select important, useful and interesting rules manually [3]. Li and Cercone proposed a Rule Importance Measure [3] to measure the quality of extracted rules and they suggested a ranking based on this measure. But this measure is defined based on various reducts generated from a dataset and generating all the reducts of a dataset is NP hard. In Apriori rule generation algorithm, Support and Confidence [4] are used as interestingness measures to select interesting association rules. Generally a rule is considered interesting, if the rule has higher support and higher confidence than the predefined minimum support and confidence for rule generation [4]. These two measures evaluate rules based on the statistical significance of the rule. Hence these two measures are objective measures and are commonly used in the situation when the interest of the application is to find the significance of item-item relation or association between different items [5]. But this is not the case when we consider the decision rules from a dataset because each rule has its own relative importance and it is always domain dependent. Objective measures usually do not consider any knowledge or pre-defined opinions from the domain of the data. Hence such objective measures are insufficient to evaluate whether a rule is important for a certain domain [5]. If this information is taken into consideration while defining a measure it becomes a subjective measure. In this work, to evaluate the quality of a rule we introduce a measure known as degree of significance. It bring together the statistical properties of the data as well as domain related information such as discrimination information.

In this paper, we propose a new algorithm for ranking decision rules generated from a dataset for the purpose of facilitating the knowledge understanding process. Rules are ranked based on the degree of significance of each rule. For ranking decision rules generated from the original decision table, a new decision table is constructed by considering each derived rule as condition attribute [2]. The decision attribute of the original decision table is taken as the decision attribute for the newly constructed decision table. The conditional attributes of the newly constructed decision table are then ranked by employing an attribute ranking method developed by using the idea of discernibility matrix [6] defined in RST. Since the conditional attributes are rules, this will produce a ranking for various rules generated from the given dataset. This ranking is mainly based on the degree of significance of each rule generated from the original dataset. Degree of significance gives a measure of how important a rule is. If the significance degree is higher, more objects can be distinguished using that rule and the power of classification is higher. By this ranking, significant rules of the dataset can be identified and unimportant rules can be ignored from the large number of rules generated by the data mining system.

This paper is structured as follows. In Section 2, we review the idea of rule induction followed by the method of ranking of conditional attributes of a decision table based on the discernibility matrix of rough set theory in Section 3. Section 4 presents the concept of degree of significance, a measure used in this work to evaluate the significance of a generated rule. In Section 5, the proposed algorithm used to rank the rules generated by the data mining system is described. In Section 6, the proposed method is demonstrated with the help of datasets and the results are listed. Finally, in Section 7, we conclude this paper.

2 Rule Induction

Rule induction is one of the most important techniques of machine learning. Since regularities hidden in data are frequently expressed in terms of rules, rule induction is important in data mining also [7]. Decision rules are the most common approach for developing expressive and human readable representations of knowledge. A decision rule is an implication of the form

($attribute_1$, $value_1$) & ($attribute_2$, $value_2$) & ... & ($attribute_n$, $value_n$) $\rightarrow$ (decision_attribute, value)

Real life problem domains usually lack generic and systematic expert rules for mapping collected feature patterns onto underlying classes. Data from which rules induced are usually presented in a decision table. A decision table is usually defined as an information system $I = (U, A \cup \{d\})$, where U is the finite set of objects called the Universe and $d \notin A$. The elements of A are called conditional attributes and d is called the decision attribute. Conditional attributes are independent variables and the decision is the dependent variable. Attribute values in a real world application dataset are often both symbolic and real-valued. It is better to convert all real-valued attributes into symbolic attributes before or during the rule induction. The process of converting numerical attributes to symbolic attributes is called discretization. Also, in a dataset used for rule induction, data values may be affected by errors. Such errors may be corrected before applying the rule induction process. To extract rules from a decision table, a commonly used data mining tool, Apriori association rule algorithm can be used [4]. The main problem with association rule algorithm is that too many rules are generated. So it is very difficult to analyze these rules and discover interesting and important rules.

3 Ranking of Conditional Attributes of a Decision Table

Ranking of attributes according to their relative significance in extracting knowledge is an important issue in data analysis and decision making. The process is also helpful for attribute reduction. The key idea of this attribute ranking process is borrowed from attribute reduction based on discernibility matrix in RST [8]. For this purpose the actual definition of discernibility matrix is slightly modified. This modification is mainly done by capturing the discrimination information involved in various object pairs. The advantage of this method is that this will work not only with dataset consisting of discrete attributes, but also with continuous attribute values. In order to handle continuous attribute values, the basic definition of discernibility matrix is modified using a distance function such as absolute distance [8].

In RST, the discernibility matrix is a symmetric |U| × |U| matrix, which can represent the discrimination information involved in all the conditional attributes of the given information system. Its entries C_{ij} can be defined as

$$C_{ij} = \begin{cases} a \in A : a(x_i) \neq a(x_j) & if \quad d(x_i) \neq d(x_j) \\ \phi \quad otherwise \end{cases} \tag{1}$$

To perform attribute ranking, a modified discernibility matrix of size m×n is defined, where m is the number of object pairs (x, y) such that d(x) ≠ d(y) and n is the number of conditional attributes. The entries d_{ij} of the new matrix is defined as

$$d_{ij} = \begin{cases} 1, & a_j(x) \neq a_j(y) \\ 0, & otherwise \end{cases} \tag{2}$$

where (x, y) represents the ith object pair O_i in which d(x) ≠d(y) and j represents the index of the conditional attribute. The column sum of this matrix gives the significance (frequency) of each conditional attribute. This significance value is proportional to the discrimination power of the attribute. Hence these values play an important role in the ranking of the conditional attributes. This will provide a method to select the significant attributes automatically.

The discernibility matrix obtained from a sample decision table shown in Table 1 is given in Table 2. In Table 1, u_1, u_2, u_3 and u_4 represent the objects, a_1, a_2, and a_3 represent the condition attributes and d represents the decision attribute.

Table 1. A sample decision table

U	a_1	a_2	a_3	d
u_1	True	True	Very_high	1
u_2	False	True	Normal	0
u_3	False	False	High	0
u_4	False	True	Very_high	1

Table 2. The modified discernibility matrix of Table1

Object pairs	a_1	a_2	a_3
(1, 2)	1	0	1
(1, 3)	1	1	1
(2, 4)	0	0	1
(3, 4)	0	1	1

A ‘1’ entry in the discernibility matrix indicates that the corresponding conditional attribute can discriminate the objects in the pair separately. After completing the matrix with the discernibility information, the significance (frequency) of each attribute can be computed by summing the corresponding column. The larger the sum is, more example pairs the attribute can discriminate, that is, the power of discrimination of that attribute is high. For example, according to Table 2, the significance of a_3 is 4; the significance of both a_1 and a_2 is 2. Hence a_3 is more significant compared to a_1 or a_2, for discriminating various objects of the decision table.

For the purpose of ranking various decision rules given by a data mining system, a new decision table is constructed by considering the derived rules as attributes and then applying the above method on this newly constructed decision table. The significance of induced rules can then be computed separately and rules are ranked based on this frequency value. This will automatically extract important rules representing the whole knowledge base and eliminate unimportant ones from the large number of extracted rules.

4 Degree of Significance of a Rule

Evaluating the significance of a rule is very important in data mining, because the selection of appropriate rules for decision making from large number of generated rules is a very difficult task. Numerous methods are available to measure rule interestingness and rule quality. Li and Cercone proposed a Rule Importance Measure [3] to measure the quality of extracted rules. . This measure is formulated by considering various reducts generated from a dataset. But generating all the reducts of the dataset is NP hard. In Apriori Association Rule algorithm, to assess the quality of a rule the measures used are ‘support’ and ‘confidence’ proposed by Agrawal [10]. The support of a rule measures how often the antecedent and the consequent of a rule appear together in the transaction. The confidence of a rule gives a ratio of the number of transactions that the antecedent and the consequent appear together to the number of transactions the antecedent appears [5]. The confidence of a rule measures how often the antecedent and consequent exist together given that the antecedent appears in the transaction [4]. The minimum values of support and confidence are predetermined to generate the association rules. These two measures evaluate rules based on the statistical significance of the rule and are defined to measure the quality of the data itself without any predefined opinions. Hence these two measures are objective measures [5]. Support and confidence are used in the situation when the interest of the application is to find associations between different items. Generally, a rule is considered interesting if the rule has higher support and higher confidence than the pre-defined minimum support and confidence for the rule generation. Also these measures do not consider any knowledge from the domain of the data. Hence such objective measures are insufficient to evaluate whether a rule is important for a certain domain. So to measure the quality of a rule, it is important to consider domain experts opinions towards the particular application. If this is the case, the measure becomes a subjective measure. Subjective measures that use real human evaluations are the optimal measure to evaluate rules. But they are sometimes infeasible and expensive because they may require humans to look large number of rules [5]. In this work rules are ranked based on the rule evaluation measure, degree of significance, that can bring both domain related knowledge (such as discrimination information) and objective measures. Degree of significance is actually a normalized value of the discrimination frequency of each rule. The normalization is done by dividing each frequency value with total number of object pairs available in the modified discernibility matrix. Formally, the degree of significance is defined as follows:

If f_i represent the frequency with which the ith rule R_i can discriminate various object pairs (x, y) with d(x)≠d(y) and C represent the total number of object combinations (x, y) satisfying the condition d(x)≠d(y), then the degree of significance of the ith rule, $\delta_i = f_i / C$, where i =1, 2, 3,…,n.

5 Proposed Work

Consider a decision table T={U, A, d}, where U is a finite set of objects $\{x_1, x_2, \ldots, x_n\}$, A is a finite set of conditional attributes and d is a finite set of decision attributes. Here we consider a decision table with only one decision attribute. From the given decision table T, a set of decision rules R is generated, where R= $\{R_1, R_2, \ldots, R_m\}$. For the purpose of ranking rules, a new decision table D is constructed. The rows of this new table represents the objects of the original table and columns represents the rules $R_1, R_2, \ldots, R_m$ and the given decision attribute. The entries of the n×m+1 matrix D represent the information obtained as a result of applying each rule to various objects of the decision table. If both the antecedent and consequent of the rule $Rule_j$ appear together in an object (record) x_i of the decision table, then rule R_j can be applied on object x_i or in other words object x_i follows rule R_j [3]. By applying this technique, the different entries D[i, j] of this new decision table are defined as

$$D[i\,j] = \begin{cases} 1, & \textit{if object } x_i \textit{ follows rule } R_j \\ 0, & \textit{otherwise} \end{cases} \tag{3}$$

where i=1, 2,…, n; j=1, 2, …, m. The entry D[i, m+1] represent the same decision attribute value of the ith object in the original decision table.

5.1 Rules Ranking Algorithm

In the Rules Ranking Algorithm, the new decision table constructed with rules as attributes is given as input and rules arranged as per their significance in the domain is obtained as output.

Algorithm: Rules Ranking

Step 1: Input the decision table.

Step 2: Sort the rows of the decision table in ascending order of the decision attribute values.

Step 3: Generate a Boolean matrix C from the decision table obtained in step 2 using expression 2.

Step 4: Find the sum of each column of the matrix C.

Step 5: Calculate degree of significance by dividing each value with the total number of rows of C.

Step 6: Select various attributes from the decision table D and arrange according to the descending order of their degree of significance calculated in step 5.

Step 7: Display the sorted attributes. Since the attributes are rules, this will produce a ranking for the rules which represents the desired output.

The algorithm will produce all the rules generated from the original dataset but arranged in an order and the order is determined by considering the relative importance of various rules in the knowledge domain. By setting a suitable threshold value for degree of significance important rules can be selected automatically from among the large number of rules generated by conventional rule generation algorithms.

6 Experiments

We apply this methodology on two sample datasets. The first dataset, an artificial car dataset [3], designed to explain the procedure in detail. The second dataset is an actual dataset consisting of the signs and symptoms of the LEARNING DISABILITIES in school aged children. It is collected from a local clinic handling learning disabilities in school students. This dataset is helpful for physicians handling learning disabilities to determine the existence of learning disability in a suspected child.

A Car Dataset

To study the working of the algorithm, we first consider an artificial dataset about cars [5] as shown in Table 3. It is used to decide the mileage of different cars. This dataset contains 14 records, 8 condition attributes and a decision attribute. There is no inconsistent or incomplete data existing in the dataset.

Table 3. Artificial Car Data Set

make_model	cyl	door	displace	compress	power	trans	weight	mileage
USA	6	2	medium	high	high	auto	medium	medium
USA	6	4	medium	medium	medium	manual	medium	medium
USA	4	2	small	high	medium	auto	medium	medium
USA	4	2	medium	medium	medium	manual	medium	medium
USA	4	2	medium	medium	high	manual	medium	medium
USA	6	4	medium	medium	high	auto	medium	medium
USA	4	2	medium	medium	high	auto	medium	medium
USA	4	2	medium	high	medium	manual	light	high
Japan	4	2	small	high	low	manual	light	high
Japan	4	2	medium	medium	medium	manual	medium	high
Japan	4	2	small	high	high	manual	medium	high
Japan	4	2	small	medium	low	manual	medium	high
Japan	4	2	small	high	medium	manual	medium	high
USA	4	2	small	high	medium	manual	medium	high

To generate rules, we used apriori association rule algorithm. Rules with only decision attribute mileage on the consequent part are generated; and subsumed rules are removed. There are 19 rules generated by apriori algorithm with support =1%, confidence =100%, as shown in Table 4.

Table 4. Rules Generated from the Car Dataset

No	Rules
R_1	(Make_model, USA)&(displace, medium)&(weight, medium) → (mileage, medium)
R_2	(Make_model, USA)&(compress, medium) → (mileage, medium)
R_3	(Make_model, USA)&(power, high)→ (mileage, medium)
R_4	(cyl, 6) → (mileage, medium)
R_5	(door, 4) → (mileage, medium)
R_6	(displace, medium)&(compress, high)&(weight, medium) → (mileage, medium)
R_7	(displace, medium)&(power, high) → (mileage, medium)
R_8	(compress,medium)&(power, high) → (mileage, medium)
R_9	(trans, auto) → (mileage, medium)
R_{10}	(make_model, Japan) → (mileage, high)
R_{11}	(cyl, 4)&(displace, medium)&(compress, high) → (mileage, high)
R_{12}	(cyl, 4)&(compress, high)&(power, high) → (mileage, high)
R_{13}	(displace, small)&(compress, medium) → (mileage, high)
R_{14}	(displace, small)&(power, high)→ (mileage, high)
R_{15}	(displace, small)&(trans, manual) → (mileage, high)
R_{16}	(displace, medium)&(compress, high)&(power, medium) → (mileage, high)
R_{17}	(compress, high)&(trans, manual) → (mileage, high)
R_{18}	(power, low) → (mileage, high)
R_{19}	(weight, light) → (mileage, high)

Table 5. New Decision Table for Car Dataset

R_1	R_2	R_3	R_4	R_5	R_6	R_7	R_8	R_9	R_{10}	R_{11}	R_{12}	R_{13}	R_{14}	R_{15}	R_{16}	R_{17}	R_{18}	R_{19}	Mile age
1	0	1	1	0	1	1	0	1	0	0	0	0	0	0	0	0	0	0	0
1	1	0	1	1	0	0	0	0	0	0	0	0	0	0	0	0	0	0	0
0	0	0	0	0	0	0	0	1	0	0	0	0	0	0	0	0	0	0	0
1	1	0	0	0	0	0	0	0	0	0	0	0	0	0	0	0	0	0	0
1	1	1	0	0	0	1	1	0	0	0	0	0	0	0	0	0	0	0	0
1	1	1	1	1	0	1	1	1	0	0	0	0	0	0	0	0	0	0	0
1	1	1	0	0	0	1	1	1	0	0	0	0	0	0	0	0	0	0	0
0	0	0	0	0	0	0	0	0	0	1	1	0	0	0	1	1	0	1	1
0	0	0	0	0	0	0	0	0	1	0	0	0	0	1	0	1	1	1	1
0	0	0	0	0	0	0	0	0	1	0	0	0	0	0	0	0	0	0	1
0	0	0	0	0	0	0	0	0	1	0	1	0	1	1	0	1	0	0	1
0	0	0	0	0	0	0	0	0	1	0	0	1	0	1	0	0	1	0	1
0	0	0	0	0	0	0	0	0	1	0	0	0	0	1	0	1	0	0	1
0	0	0	0	0	0	0	0	0	0	0	0	0	0	1	0	1	0	0	1

A new decision table A with 14 rows and 20 columns is constructed by using the 19 rules as condition attributes and original decision on the mileage as the decision attribute [3]. The content of the matrix A is formed by considering the information regarding whether a particular rule can be applied to different records of the original table. For example, rule R_1 (make_model, USA) & (displace, medium) & (weight, medium) → (mileage, medium) can be applied to the first record, because both the antecedent (make_model, USA) & (displace, medium) & (weight, medium) and the consequent (mileage, medium) appear together in the rule. Therefore, we assign A[1, 1]=1. Also, we can apply R_1, to second record as well. Hence, A[2, 1]=1. However R_1 cannot be applied to the third record, because the value for 'displace' is 'small' instead of 'medium'. Therefore, A[3,1]=0. In this way we can fill all the entries of the matrix A. For the car dataset, the newly constructed decision table is given in Table 5.

In this table the decision attribute value mileage medium is set to 0 and mileage high is set to 1. There is no inconsistency in this new decision table. This new decision table A is the input for the proposed rules ranking algorithm given in section 5. The algorithm will output all the rules generated from the dataset but in descending order of their degree of significance. In other words, the rules are ranked according to the classification power of each rule. The ranked rules are given in Table 6. In Table 6, along with the rules, the degree of significance is also given.

Table 6. Rules Ranked as per their Degree of Significance

Rule No.	Rank	Rules	Degree of Significance
R_1	1	(Make_model, USA)&(displace, medium)&(weight, medium) → (mileage, medium)	0.8571
R_2	2	(Make_model, USA)&(compress, medium) → (mileage, medium)	0.7143
R_{10}	3	(make_model, Japan) → (mileage, high)	0.7143
R_{15}	4	(displace, small)&(trans, manual) → (mileage, high)	0.7143
R_{17}	5	(compress, high)&(trans, manual) → (mileage, high)	0.7143
R_3	6	(Make_model, USA)&(power, high)→ (mileage, medium)	0.5714
R_7	7	(displace, medium)&(power, high) → (mileage, medium)	0.5714
R_9	8	(trans, auto) → (mileage, medium)	0.5714
R_4	9	(cyl, 6) → (mileage, medium)	0.4286
R_8	10	(compress,medium)&(power, high) → (mileage, medium)	0.4286
R_5	11	(door, 4) → (mileage, medium)	0.2857
R_{12}	12	(cyl, 4)&(compress, high)&(power, high) → (mileage, high)	0.2857
R_{18}	13	(power, low) → (mileage, high)	0.2857
R_{19}	14	(weight, light) → (mileage, high)	0.2857
R_{11}	15	(cyl, 4)&(displace, medium)&(compress, high) → (mileage, high)	0.1423
R_{16}	16	(displace, medium)&(compress, high)&(power, medium) → (mileage, high)	0.1423
R_6	17	(displace, medium)&(compress, high)&(weight, medium) → (mileage, medium)	0.1423
R_{13}	18	(displace, small)&(compress, medium) → (mileage, high)	0.1423
R_{14}	19	(displace, small)&(power, high)→ (mileage, high)	0.1423

In Table 6, the rule R_1 is ranked first, because its degree of significance is calculated as 42/49 (=0.8571) and all other rules have degree of significance less than this value. This is because, the frequency with which the rule can discriminate various object pairs (x, y) with $d(x) \neq d(y)$ is 42 and the total number of object pairs satisfying the same condition is 49. The next rule in ranking is R_2 with degree of significance 0.7143. There are three more rules with the same degree of significance as R_2. They are R_{10}, R_{15} and R_{17}. In this way rules can be ranked. By properly selecting a threshold value for degree of significance, we can automatically select the required number of significant rules. The ranking given in Table 6 is mainly based on the classification power of each rule. Also this ranking is subjective to the problem domain because it is mainly based on the knowledge available in the dataset. With this method the problem of selecting important, useful and interesting rules from large number of rules extracted by the data mining system can be solved to a great extend.

B Experiment on the Learning Disability Dataset

To test the algorithm, we use a dataset consisting of the signs and symptoms of the LEARNING DISBILITIES in school aged children. Learning disabilities affect children both academically and socially. Learning disabilities affect about 10% of all children enrolled in schools and hence it becomes a serious social problem. Learning disabilities can cause a child to have trouble in learning and using certain skills such as reading, writing, listening, speaking etc. With the right help at the right time, children with learning disabilities can learn successfully. This dataset is collected from a local clinic providing assistance for handling learning disability in school aged children. We select this dataset for our experiment with a view to provide tools for researchers and physicians handling Learning disability to analyze the data collected from various LD patients and to facilitate the decision making process.

Table 7. Learning Disability Dataset

DR	DS	DH	DWE	DBA	DHA	DA	ED	DM	LM	DSS	DNS	DLL	DLS	STL	RG	LD
t	t	f	f	f	f	f	f	f	f	f	f	f	f	f	f	t
t	t	f	t	f	t	f	t	t	t	t	f	t	f	t	f	t
t	t	f	t	f	t	f	t	t	t	t	f	t	f	t	f	t
t	t	f	f	f	f	t	t	t	t	f	f	f	f	f	f	t
f	f	f	t	t	f	f	f	f	f	f	f	f	f	f	f	f
f	f	f	f	f	f	t	t	t	f	f	f	f	f	f	f	f
t	t	t	t	t	f	t	t	t	t	f	f	f	f	t	f	t
f	f	f	f	f	f	f	f	f	t	f	f	t	f	t	f	f
t	t	f	t	f	f	f	f	f	f	f	f	t	f	f	f	t
t	t	f	t	f	t	t	t	t	t	t	f	t	t	t	f	t
t	t	f	t	f	t	t	t	t	t	t	f	f	f	t	f	t
f	f	f	t	f	f	t	f	f	f	f	f	f	f	f	f	f
t	t	f	t	f	t	f	t	f	t	t	f	t	f	t	f	t
f	f	f	f	f	t	f	t	f	f	f	f	f	f	f	f	f
t	t	f	t	f	f	f	t	f	f	t	t	t	f	t	f	t

Table 8. Key and its Abbreviations

Key	Abbreviations	Key	Abbreviations
DR	Difficulty with Reading	LM	Lack of Motivation
DS	Difficulty with Spelling	DSS	Difficulty with Study Skills
DH	Difficulty with Handwriting	DNS	Does Not like School
DWE	Difficulty with Written Expression	DLL	Difficulty in Learning a Language
DBA	Difficulty with Basic Arithmetic skills	DLS	Difficulty in Learning a Subject
DHA	Difficulty with Higher Arithmetic skills	STL	Is Slow To Learn
DA	Difficulty with Attention	RG	Repeated a Grade
ED	Easily Distracted	LD	Learning Disability
DM	Difficulty with Memory		

Table 9. First 10 Rules Generated by the Predictive Apriori Algorithm

Rule No.	Rules
1	DR=true DWE=true RG=false ==> LD=true
2	DS=true DWE=true RG=false ==> LD=true
3	DR=true STL=true RG=false ==> LD=true
4	DS=true STL=true RG=false ==> LD=true
5	DWE=true STL=true RG=false ==> LD=true
6	DWE=true DLL=true ==> LD=true
7	DR=true ED=true RG=false ==> LD=true
8	DS=false DSS=false ==> LD=false
9	DR=true DH=false DWE=true ==> LD=true
10	DR=true LM=True DNS=false RG=false ==> LD=true

Table 10. Ranked Rules for LD Dataset

Rank	Rule No.	Rule	Degree of significance
1	100	DS=true DA=false DM=false DSS=true ==> LD=true	1
2	97	DWE=true LM=true RG=false ==> LD=true	0.9907
3	64	DS=true DWE=true DM=false ==> LD=true	0.8965
4	65	DWE=true DSS=true ==> LD=true	0.8965
5	54	DS=true DH=false DLL=true ==> LD=true	0.8832
6	56	DR=true STL=true ==> LD=true	0.8832
7	61	DS=true DA=true RG=false ==> LD=true	0.8657
8	70	DR=true DBA=true ==> LD=true	0.6963
9	66	DR=true DNS=false DLL=true ==> LD=true	0.6674
10	18	DR=true DLL=true STL=true ==> LD=true	0.6598
11	17	DWE=true DSS=true RG=false ==> LD=true	0.657
12	92	DS=true DH=false DA=true ==> LD=true	0.6402
13	57	DS=true STL=true ==> LD=true	0.6168
14	58	DWE=true STL=true ==> LD=true	0.6168
15	59	DS=false DWE=false ==> LD=false	0.6146

The dataset contains 249 student records with 16 conditional attributes as signs and symptoms of LD and the existence of LD in a child as decision attribute. Various signs and symptoms collected includes the information regarding the child has any difficulty with reading(DR), any difficulty with spelling(DS), any difficulty with handwriting(DH) and so on. There are no missing values in the dataset. Table 7 gives a portion of the dataset used for the experiment. In this table, t represents the attribute value true and f represents the attribute value false. Table 8 gives key used for representing the symptoms and its abbreviations. There is no inconsistency exist in the dataset. For generating rules, Predictive Apriori algorithm from Weka machine learning tool kit is used. For the experiment, first 100 rules with decision attribute LD on the consequent part are considered. The rule set derived from apriori algorithm is given in Table 9. A new decision table $A_{249\times100}$ is constructed by considering these 100 rules as condition attributes and the original decision attribute as the decision attribute. After removing the inconsistent data records, the table is processed by using the proposed algorithm. The resulting ranked rules with respective degree of significance is given in Table 10.

From the ranked rule set, by specifying a pre-defined size for the number of rules to be selected or by specifying a pre-defined threshold value for degree of significance, we can extract the required number of significant rules from the dataset.

7 Conclusion

This paper gives a novel and computationally efficient method of ranking decision rules generated by a data mining system. In this approach, rules are ranked by defining a new rule evaluation measure, degree of significance, which is purely a rough set based rule evaluation measure derived using the discrimination information involved in various object pairs. Using this method, domain related knowledge can be incorporated into rule evaluations for identifying useful and interesting rules along with the conventional statistical measures. Through the application of this technique in a learning discernibility data set consisting of the signs and symptoms of Learning Disability in school aged children, we show how the proposed method can be adapted and utilized to an actual system for extracting important rules automatically for effective decision making.

References

1. Pawlak, Z.: Rough sets and intelligent data analysis. Information Sciences 147, 1–12 (2002)
2. Jensen, R., Shen, Q.: New approaches to Fuzzy–Rough Feature Selection. IEEE Transactions on Fuzzy Systems 17(4) (August 2009)
3. Li, J., Cercone, N.: Discovering and Ranking Important Rules. In: KDM Workshop, Waterloo, Canada, October 30-31 (2006)
4. Han, J., Kamber, M.: Data Mining: Concepts and Techniques. Morgan Kaufmann, Elsevier (2006)
5. Li, J.: Rough Set Based Rule Evaluations and their Applications. Ph.D thesis from Internet (2007)
6. Pawlak, Z.: Theoretical Aspects of Reasoning about Data. Kluwer Academic Publishers, Dordrecht (1991)
7. Maimon, O., Rokach, L.: The Data Mining and Knowledge Discovery Handbook. Springer, Heidelberg (2005)
8. Tan, S., Wang, Y., Cheng, X.: An Efficient Feature Ranking Measure text Categorization. In: Proceedings of the ACM symposium on Applied Computing, New York (2008)
9. Grzymala-Busse, J.W.: Rough Set Theory with Applications to Data Mining from Internet
10. Agrawal, R., Srikant, R.: Fast algorithms for mining association rules. In: Bocca, J.B., Jarke, M., Zaniolo, C. (eds.) Proc. 20th Int. Conf. Very Large Data Bases, VLDB, pp. 487–499. Morgan Kaufmann, San Francisco (1994)

A Kernel Based Feature Selection Method Used in the Diagnosis of Wisconsin Breast Cancer Dataset

P. Jaganathan, IEEE member[1], N. Rajkumar[2], and R. Nagalakshmi[3]

[1] Professor and Head, [2]Associate Professor, [3] Student
Dept. of Computer Applications, PSNA College of Engineering and Technology, Dindigul, Tamilnadu, India
jaganathodc@yahoo.com, {rknpsna,naga.dharsika}@gmail.com

Abstract. In this paper, a novel feature selection method called kernel F-score is applied for Breast cancer diagnosis. In this method, feature selection for removing the irrelevant/redundant features is achieved in high dimensional spaces than the original spaces. Basically, the datasets in the input space are moved to high dimensional kernel spaces for clear separation of nonlinearity through kernel functions. Then the F-score values for all the features in the kernel space are computed and mean kernel F-score value is set as the threshold for selection or rejection of features. The features lesser than the threshold are removed from feature space. The features above and equal to the threshold are selected for classification and used in the classification of benign and malignant cases using Support Vector Machines (SVM). The results obtained from Wisconsin Breast Cancer Dataset (WBCD) have been satisfied as it produced efficient results than F-score. So, we conclude kernel F-score with SVM for WBCD is promising than F-score with SVM.

Keywords: Feature Selection, Kernel F-score Support Vector Machines, RBF kernel.

1 Introduction

Feature selection process is a technique in data mining widely used in classification tasks. The presence or absence of a feature in any case determines the performance of the classifier in terms of time and cost [2]. Eventhough we have filter and wrapper methods for feature selection, these methods individually produce only fair results when the features are non linear. So it becomes very difficult to select them in the low dimensional space. Therefore kernels are used for nonlinear features separation. Here in this case, features have to be transferred to highdimensional space, where they are comfortably separated.

In order to map the features to high dimensional space Kernel methods are introduced. Kernels select the most discriminative and informative features for classification and data analysis [3]. There are several kernel methods like Kernel Principle Component Analysis (KPCA) has been proposed to obtain non-linear

A. Abraham et al. (Eds.): ACC 2011, Part I, CCIS 190, pp. 683–690, 2011.

principal components [9]. Here in our work we have used radial basis function kernel for mapping and kernel F-score for Wisconsin breast cancer dataset classification.

2 Related Work and Literature Survey

Support vector machine is an effective statistical method used in medical diagnosis for pattern recognition machine learning and datamining (cortes and vapnik 1995). In the literature, there are some works related to breast cancer diagnosis. Among these, Mehmet Faith Akay has proposed a feature selection method with F-score and support vector machines reaching a classification accuracy of 99.51% [7]. Polat et al obtained classification accuracy of 98.53%. With neuro and fuzzy techniques nauck et al produced 95.06% of classification. Goodman et al produced three different results with three different methods such as Optimized-LVQ , Big LVQ, AIRS and accuracies 96.70%,96.80%,97.20% respectively[4].

This research work is supported by All India Council for Technical education, New Delhi under Research Promotion scheme. Ref No. 8023/BDR/RID/RPS/17/08/9

Abonyi and Szeifert (2003) using Supervised fuzzy clustering techniques produced a classification accuracy of 95.57%. logarithmic simulated annealing and perceptron algorithm applied by Albrecht obtained 98.80%. Hamilton et al. (1996) using RIAC method obtained 95.00% classification accuracy[5].with LDA technique Ster and Dobnikar (1996) produced a classification accuracy of 96.80%. Pena-Reyes and Sipper (1999) obtained classification accuracy of 97.36% using Fuzzy-GAI method. Setiono (2000) using Neuro-rule 2a technique obtained classification accuracy of 98.10% . With AR and NN Murat karabatak & M.Cevdet Ince produced classification accuracy of 97.40%[8]. T.S.Subashini et al obtained 97.33% classification accuracy using RBFNN and SVM techniques[10]. Polat et al .have proposed a method called Kernel F-score feature selection (KFFS) used as pre-processing step in the classification of medical datasets[6].

3 Feature Selection

The main idea of feature selection is to select an optimal subset of input variables by removing features with little or no predictive information. There are many feature selection methods. In general it contains two methods which are filter and wrapper methods. The filter methods are independent of learning algorithms where as wrapper methods are dependent on learning algorithms. The F-score method and computation of kernel F-score values are described below.

3.1 F-Score

F-score is a simple method which measures the discrimination of two sets of real numbers. Given training vectors x k , k=1,2,....,m, if the number of positive and negative instances are n + and n – respectively, then the F-score of the ith feature is defined as

$$F_i = \frac{(\bar{x}_i^{(+)} - \bar{x}_i)^2 + (\bar{x}_i^{(-)} - \bar{x}_i)^2}{\frac{1}{n_+ - 1}\sum_{k=1}^{n_+}(x_{k,i}^{(+)} - \bar{x}_i^{(+)})^2 + \frac{1}{n_- - 1}\sum_{k=1}^{n_-}(x_{k,i}^{(-)} - \bar{x}_i^{(-)})^2} \tag{1}$$

Where are the average of the ith feature of the whole, positive, and negative datasets, respectively; is the ith feature of the kth positive instance, and is the ith feature of the kth negative instance. The numerator denotes the discrimination between the positive and negative sets, and the denominator indicates the one within each of the two sets. The larger the F-score is, the more likely this feature is more discriminative Chen and Lin, 2003[3].The flowchart in Fig1. shows the how the classification accuracy for breast cancer is determined. It demonstrates the computation of kernel F-score values which helps in discriminating the relevant and irrelevant features. Firstly the Kernel Fscore of each feature is calculated and the mean f-score value is determined. The features which are above the mean f-score are selected for classification. With the selected features is passed to SVM classifier with tenfold cross validations. The outcome of this procedure has produces efficient results.

4 Support Vector Machines

Support vector machine is a technique for learning in pattern classification and non-linear regression , pioneered by Cortes and Vapnik in 1995, Boser, Guyon, Vapnik in 1992 and modified by Vapnik in 1999[11]. The main idea of a support vector machine is to construct a hyper plane as the decision surface such that there exists maximum margin between any two different categories. Consider a set of training vectors belonging to two linearly separable classes,

$$(x_i, y_i), x_i \epsilon R^n, y_i \epsilon \{+1, -1\}, i = 1,2, \dots n. \tag{2}$$

where x_i is a n-dimensional input vector and y_i is a label that determines the class of x_i. A separating hyper plane is determined by an orthogonal vector w and a bias b, which identifies the points that satisfy

$$w.x_i + b = 0 \tag{3}$$

The parameters w and b are constrained by

$$\min /w.x_i + b/ \geq 1. \tag{4}$$

A hyper plane in canonical form must satisfy the following constraints,

$$y_i.(w.x_i + b) \geq 1, i = 1,2, \dots n. \tag{5}$$

The hyper plane that optimally separates the data is the one that minimizes

$$\phi(w) = \frac{1}{2}(w.w). \tag{6}$$

Relaxing the constraints of (4) by introducing slack variables £$_I$ >=0, i=1,2,…,n, becomes

$$y_i.(w.x_i + b) \geq 1 - \xi_i, i = 1,2, \dots n. \tag{7}$$

In this case the optimization problem becomes

$$\Phi(w, \xi) = \frac{1}{2}(w.w) + C\sum_{i=1}^{n} \xi_i \tag{8}$$

with a user defined positive finite constant C. The solution for (7), under the constraints of (6), could be obtained in the saddle point of Lagrangian function

$$L(w, b, \alpha, \xi, \gamma) - \frac{1}{2}(w.w) + C\sum_{i=1}^{n} \xi_i - \sum_{i=1}^{n} \alpha_i |\gamma_i (w.x_i + b) - 1$$

$$+\xi_i| - \sum_{i=1}^{n} \gamma_i \xi_i, \tag{9}$$

where a_i >=0, £$_I$ >=0, i=1,2,..,n are the Lagrange multipliers. The Lagrangian function has to be minimized with respect to w,b, and £$_I$. Classical Lagrangian duality enables primal problem(8), to be transformed into its dual problem, which is easier to solve. The dual problem is given by

$$\max_{\alpha} \quad [\sum_{i=1}^{n} \alpha_i - \frac{1}{2}\sum_{ij=1}^{n} \alpha_i \alpha_j \gamma_i \gamma_j K(x_i, x_j)] \tag{10}$$

with constraints

$$\sum_{i=1}^{n} \alpha_i, \gamma_i = 0, \quad 0 \leq \alpha_i \leq C, \qquad i = 1,2, \dots, n. \tag{11}$$

This is a quadratic optimization problem that exists a unique solution. As per K T theorem of optimization theory , the optimal solution satisfies

$$\alpha_i[\gamma_i(w.x_i + b) - 1] = 0, i = 1,2, \dots n. \tag{12}$$

has non-zero Lagrange multipliers if and only if the points x_i satisfy

$$\gamma_i(w.x + b) = 1. \tag{13}$$

These points are termed SV. The hyperplane is determined by the SV, which is a small subset of the training vectors. Hence if α_i^* is the non –zero optimal solution, the classifier function can be expressed as

$$f(x) = \operatorname{sgn}\left\{\sum_{ij=1}^{n} \alpha_i^* \gamma_i (x_i . x) + b^*\right\} \tag{14}$$

Where b* is the solution of (14) for any non-zero α_i^* .

By defining a non-linear boundary, the SVM constructs an optimal hyperplane in this higher dimensional space. usually non-linear mapping is defined as

$$\phi(.): R^n \to R^n. \tag{15}$$

In this case, optimal function becomes (15) with the constraints

$$\max_{\alpha} \, [\sum_{i=1}^{n} \alpha_i - \frac{1}{2} \sum_{ij=1}^{n} \alpha_i \alpha_j \gamma_i \gamma_j K(x_i, x_j)], \tag{16}$$

Where $K(x_i\ x_j) = \{\varphi(x_i).\varphi(x_j)\}$ is the kernel function performing the non-linear mapping into feature space. The kernel function may be any of the symmetric functions that satisfy the Mercel conditions (Courant &Hilbert, 1953). The most commonly used functions are the Radial Basis Function (RBF): $K(x_i, x_j) = \exp\{-\gamma| x_i - x_j|^2\}$ and the polynomial Function $K(x_i, x_j) = (x_i x_j + 1)^q$, q = 1,2,....,

5 Experimental Observations

Wisconsin Breast cancer dataset:
This database is taken from the UCI machine learning repository for our experiments. It is collected by Dr.William H. Wolberg(1989-91) at the University of Wisconsin-Madison Hospitals.There are 699 records in this database. Each record in the database has nine attributes. The aim of the dataset is to classify the presence or absence of breast cancer given the results of various medical tests carried out on a patient. This database includes 9 attributes. These features are (1) Clump thickness,(2) Uniformity of cell size, (3)Uniformity of cell shape, (4) Marginal adhesion, (5) single epithelial cell cell size, (6) Bare nuclei, (7) Bland chromatin, (8) Normal nucleoli, (9) Mitosis. The nine attributes are represented as an integer value between 1 -10 and detailed in Table 1. In this database, Two hundred and forty one records (65.5%) are malignant and four hundred and fifty eight records (34.5%) are benign[1].In order to evaluate the efficiency of the method, performance measures like sensitivity, specificity, ROC curves, positive predictive value, negative predictive value were considered. The measures were compiled by the following units.

Classification accuracy (%) = TP + TN / TP + FP + FN + TN,

Sensitivity (%) = TP/ TP + FN * 100,

Specificity (%) = TN/ FP + TN * 100,

ROC Curve provides trade-off between sensitivity and specificity.

6 Results and Discussion

In this paper, a new feature selection method called kernel F-score is applied for Wisconsin breast cancer dataset diagnosis. The selected features by applying kernel F-score have been used in the classification of benign and malignant cases using support vector machines. Table 1 shows the obtained reduced number of features before and after applying kernel mapping. we have used two different feature selection methods i) F-Score feature selection without kernel mapping and ii) Kernel F-Score feature selection.Table2 shows the performance of the classifiers with two feature selection methods. Sensitivity, Specificity, Classification accuracy and AUC has been presented. Table3 shows the performance comparison of various training-test partitions with two different methods. 95.70% for 50-50% training-test partition, 95.35% for 60-40% training-test partition, 95.23% for 70-30% training-test partition, 96.41% for 80-20% training-test partition for F-Score with SVM. 96.56% for 50-50% training-test partition, 96.07% for 60-40% training-test partition, 95.71% for 70-30% training-test partition, 96.42% for 80-20% training-test partition for Kernel F-Score with SVM. Fig2 describes ROC curve for kernel F-score with SVM. The results here depicts that our new method Kernel F-Score with Support vector machines for diagnosis of breast cancer produces far better result than F-score combined with Support vector machines.

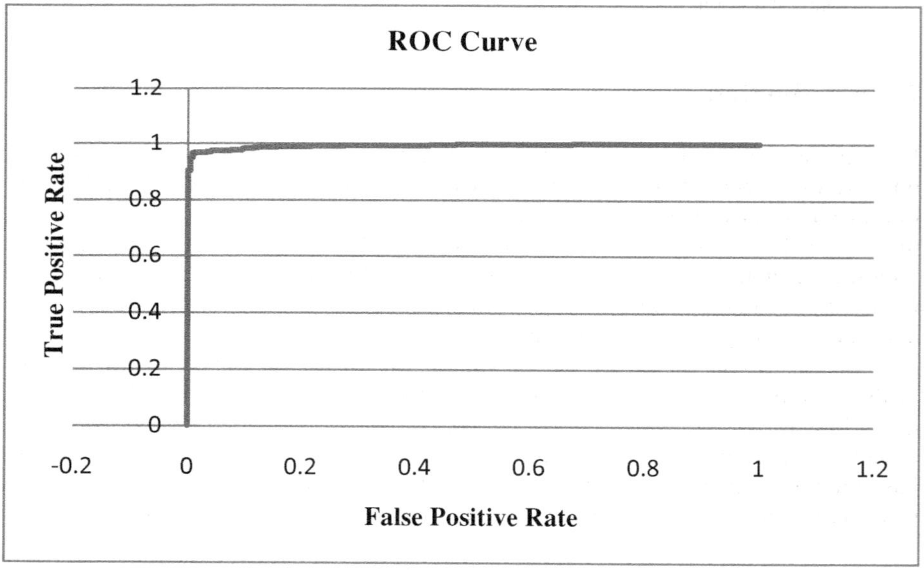

Fig. 2. Area under ROC Curve graph from kernel F-score with SVM

Table 1. The obtained features from kernel mapping

Method	The number of original features in input space	The number of features in kernel space	The number of reduced features with feature selection
F-Score	9	Nil	4
Kernel F-score	9	699	315

Table 2. Performance of the classifier with different methods using Ten-Fold cross validation

Method	Classification accuracy	Sensitivity	Specificity	AUC
F-Score + SVM	95.56	0.97	0.95	0.94
Kernel F-score + SVM	96.99	0.97	0.96	0.97

Table 3. Performance comparison of various training – test partitions with different methods

Method	50-50% training – test partition	60-40% training – test partition	70-30% training – test partition	80-20% training – test partition
F-Score + SVM	95.70	95.35	95.23	96.41
Kernel F-score + SVM	96.56	96.07	95.71	96.42

7 Conclusion

Feature selection is the best technique for obtaining improved classification accuracies in machine learning and pattern recognition. The main idea of feature selection is to select an optimal subset of input variables by removing features with little or no predictive information. In this article kernel F-score feature selection method has been applied for Wisconsin breast cancer dataset diagnosis. In this study, Kernel F-score combined with support vector machine produced better results than F-score method without kernel mapping. The performance measure criteria are classification accuracy, sensitivity–specificity values, and Area under ROC curve values (AUC).The AUC values obtained from F-score and Kernel F-Score with SVM on the classification of Wisconsin breast cancer dataset is found to be 0.94–0.97, respectively. In this way, a new feature selection method is applied on the classification of WBCD datasets. In future, this method can be applied to other medical datasets which can be used to improve the accuracies in medical diagnosis.

References

[1] Blake, C.L., Merz, C.J.: UCI repository of machine learning database. University of California, Irvine (1998), http://www.ics.uci.edu/mlearn/MLRepository.html

[2] Cao, B., Shen, D., Sun, J.-T., Yang, Q., Chen, Z.: Feature selection in a kernel space. In: International Conference on Machine Learning (ICML), Oregon, USA, June 20-24, pp. 121–128 (2007)

[3] Chen, Y.-W., Lin, C.-J.: Combining SVMs with various feature selection strategies, NIPS 2003 feature selection challenge, 1–10 (2003)

[4] Goodman, D.E., Boggess, L., Watkins, A.: Artificial immune system classification of multiple-class problems. In: Proceedings of the Artificial Neural Networks in Engineering, pp. 179–183

[5] Hamilton, H.J., Shan, N., Cercone, N.: RIAC: A rule induction algorithm based on approximate classification. Technical Report CS 96-06, University of Regina (1996)

[6] Polat, K., Güneş, S.: A new feature selection method on classification of medical datasets: Kernel F-score feature selection. Expert Systems with Applications 36(7), 10367–10373 (2009)

[7] Akay, M.F.: Support vector machines combined with feature selection for breast cancer diagnosis. Expert Systems with Applications 36(2), Part 2, 3240–3247 (2009)

[8] Karabatak, M., Cevdet Ince, M.: Expert Systems with Applications 36(2), Part 2, 3465–3469 (2009)

[9] Scholkopf, B., Smola, A.J.: Learning with Kernels. The MIT Press, Cambridge (2002)

[10] Subashini, T.S., Ramalingam, V., Palanivel, S.: Expert Systems with Applications 36(3), Part 1, 5284–5290 (2009)

[11] Vapnik, V.: The Nature of Statistical Learning Theory. Springer, New York (1995), http://www.emeraldinsight.com

Comparative Study on Data Warehouse Evolution Techniques

Garima Thakur and Anjana Gosain

Guru Gobind Singh Indraprastha University
Delhi, India
thakur_garima_27@yahoo.co.in, anjana_gosain@hotmail.com

Abstract. Data warehouse integrates data from various heterogeneous information sources under a unified structure to facilitate reporting & analysis done by the organizations to provide strategic information to the decision support systems. These information sources are autonomous in nature and they frequently change their data owing to transactions being carried out within the organization and may change their schema due to evolving requirements. The existing requirements are updated and some new requirements are added in order to cope up with the latest business scenarios. In fact, data warehouse never ceases to evolve. Thus, appropriate techniques should be devised in order to handle the evolving data and schema changes so that the DW can be stored in its most updated version with all types of modifications being incorporated accurately to reflect the correct form of data subject to analysis. This paper provides a comprehensive comparison of various approaches, techniques and tools being developed by various researchers in order to resolve these issues. We have examined four techniques that address the DW evolution namely schema evolution, schema versioning, temporal warehousing and view maintenance and presented a brief tabular comparison of the explored methodologies based on various parameters.

Keywords: Data warehouse evolution, schema evolution, schema versions, view maintenance, materialized views, temporal warehouse, bi-temporal warehouse.

1 Introduction

A data warehouse is a central repository of an organization's electronically stored data. It is a subject-oriented, integrated, time-variant and non-volatile collection of data in support of management's decision making process [18].

Data from various sub-systems of an organization is accumulated and stored under a unified format in order to maximize user access and analysis. Information sources which are integrated in the DW are autonomous and they may change or evolve in terms of their data and structure consequently, DW must also evolve to be preserved in the most current state. Possible reasons for the evolution of the data warehouse are given as under:

A. Abraham et al. (Eds.): ACC 2011, Part I, CCIS 190, pp. 691–703, 2011.

1. Ambiguous or insufficient requirements during the developmental phase [6].
2. Change in the requirements during the operational phase of the Data Warehouse which results in the structural evolution of the data warehouse [23].
3. Reorganization of the data warehouse schema during the operational phase of the data warehouse as a result of different design solutions that are decided upon [2].
4. New user or business requirements arise or new versions need to be created [23].
5. Periodical revisions are made in order to eliminate the errors & redundancies [6] [2].
6. The data warehouse must be adapted to any changes which occur in the underlying data sources [23].

Such changes result in the evolution of the DW to reflect the modified data, which is needed for good decision-making. Data Warehouse systems exhibit very little flexibility in context of modifications to the organizational data. Yet, they need to evolve over time. In fact, data warehouse design is a continuous process, i.e. the data warehouse must evolve in reaction to the above mentioned reasons **[18]**.

The goal of this paper is to present a survey of efforts done by various researchers in context of DW evolution and related issues along with the devised techniques to deal with them.

The paper is organized as follows. In section 2, we discuss the existing approaches for data warehouse evolution. Section 3 presents a comparative analysis of the related works in a tabular manner based on certain parameters. Lastly, we draw the conclusion in section 4.

2 State of the Art

In literature, different approaches have been proposed to deal with DW evolution namely schema evolution [3, 4, 5, 7, 8, 13, 14, 19], schema versioning [2, 6, 17, 21, 22, 23, 24, 29], view maintenance [25, 26, 27, 28] and temporal warehousing [9, 10, 11, 12, 20].

2.1 Schema Evolution

In schema versioning techniques, previous schema and its corresponding data are replaced by a fresh schema and its new data. This may lead to loss of information and inability of applications using the old schema to utilize the new database. This renders the approach unsuitable in most real-world scenarios [4, 5].

When carrying out an evolution process, there are mainly two problems that should be well though-out: the semantics of changes, i.e., their effects on the schema, and the change propagation, which refers to the proliferation of the schema changes to the existent instances [4, 5]. Schema evolution has been comprehensively addressed in the history and a range of techniques has been proposed to implement the changes in the most reliable way feasible to avoid interference in the operation of the data warehouse [7].

In [20] author has focused on DW design and DW evolution. They proposed a set of schema transformation primitives. In this work they have addressed the problem of source schema evolution. In addition, a set of instance conversion functions have been defined to convert instances from one version of the DW to another.

In [14] the author describes how a general object oriented model for schema versioning and evolution can be formed; how the semantics of schema change operations can be defined; how attractive reasoning tasks can be developed, based on an encoding in Description Logics. However, this approach has not thoroughly addressed the so-called *change propagation* problem, which concerns the effects of schema changes on the data instances.

In [7], authors have presented a conceptual temporal multidimensional model. They have redefined the fact and dimension tables with valid times and added the notions of multi-version fact table and mapping relationships. To support modifications in the structure of a temporal multidimensional Schema, they have produced four basic operators: *Insert*, *Exclude*, *Associate* and *Reclassify*. They also support the use of two main categories of metadata: - metadata related to the versions of members and metadata related to the evolution of the members. This model still suffers from the fact that a structure version is composed of the set of the temporal dimensions validated for that version.

[3] Describes a *Warehouse Evolution System (WHES)* prototype that demonstrates a data warehouse evolution model based on dimensions and cubes and its associated Multi-dimensional data definition language. The authors have proposed 16 operators to change multidimensional schemas. WHES implements a set of translation rules to provide one-to-one mapping between multidimensional schema and relational model. It also defines a set of propagation rules that modify the relational model whenever a change occurs in corresponding multidimensional model. A limitation of this approach is that historical data is lost.

In [13] authors have described how a data integration toolkit, AutoMed, can be used to handle issues of schema evolution process in heterogeneous environments. They have also discussed how AutoMed metadata can be used to express the schemas and the cleansing, transformation and integration processes.

In [8] a tool named PRISM has been highlighted that effectively reduces the cost of evolving the schema of a data warehouse. The PRISM framework handles the issue of evolving the schema of a data warehouse by completely automating the management of data migration, query, and views adaptation upon structural schema changes. The authors have developed a language of Schema Modification Operators (SMO) to express schema evolution histories. The system offers an SQL-inspired, operational language of Schema Modification Operators (SMO) to concisely represent the desired schema changes.

2.2 Schema Versioning

In schema versioning techniques, the old schema and its corresponding data are preserved (and continue to be used by existing applications), but a new version of the schema is created, which incorporates the desired changes [16].

The two most used versioning methods are described [7]:

- **Revisions (Sequential):** consist of making each new version a modification of the most recent one. At the end, the versions form sequentially a single linked list called a revision chain. Each version in the chain represents an evolution of the previous one. Each version is associated with only one ancestor (i.e. one-to-one relationship).

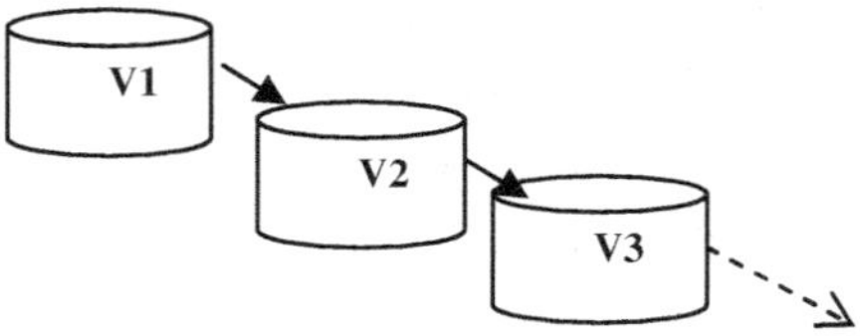

Fig. 1. Sequential versioning

Version V1is initial DW version. A new version V2 is created from V1. V3 created from V2 and so versions keep on evolving in a linear fashion.

- **Variants (Parallel):** mean changing the relationships for revision from one-to-one to many-to one, so that many versions may have the same relationship with a common "ancestor".

A variant does not replace another, as a revision does, but is instead an alternative to the current version [7].

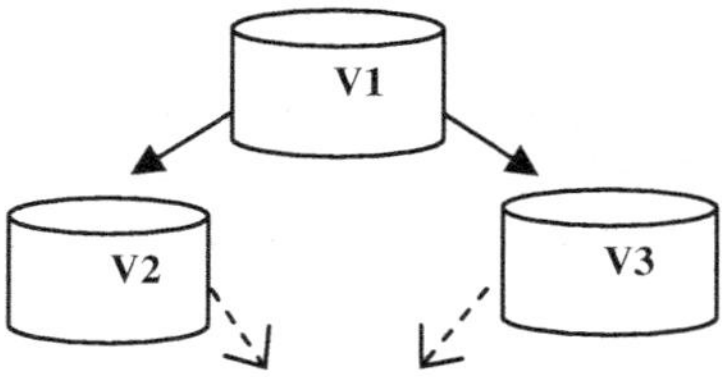

Fig. 2. Parallel versioning

Version V1 is initial DW version that evolves into versions V2 and V3 in a parallel fashion. They both are variants of the same version V1. We distinguish these two kinds of DW versions: *real versions and alternative versions.* A *real version* reflects changes in the real world. Real versions are created in order to keep up with the changes in a real-world business environment. Real versions are organized in a linear fashion along the time axis where intervals depict their valid time. The main purpose of maintaining *alternative ver*sions is to support the what-if analysis purposes. An alternative version is created from a real version or from an alternative one. Several alternative versions may be created from the same parent version [21]. Maintaining real and alternative versions of the whole data warehouse allows us on the one hand, to run queries that span multiple versions and compare various factors computed in those versions, and on the other hand, to create and manage alternative virtual business scenarios required for the what-if analysis [1].

Figure 3 schematically shows real versions and alternative versions. *R1* is a base real version of a DW that will act as an origin for creating further versions. Based on *R1*, a new real version *R2* is created. Similarly, *R3* is derived from *R2*. *A1.1* is an alternative DW version derived from *R1*, whereas *A2.1* and *A2.2* form the alternative versions derived from *R2* that can be used for simulation purposes. Note that real versions are linearly ordered, whereas alternative versions branch out [21].

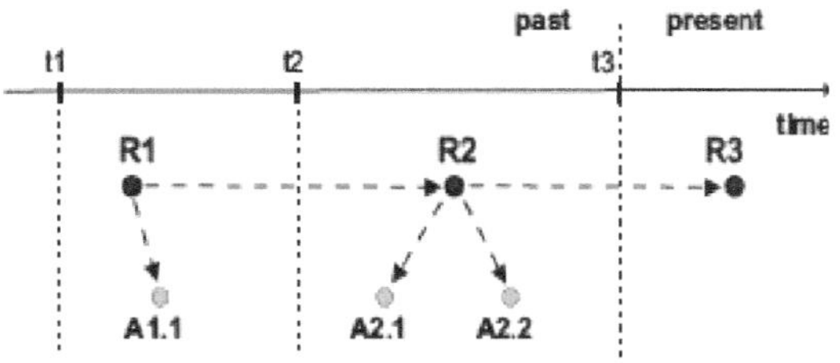

Fig. 3. Real and Alternate versions [21]

In [6] authors have presented a concept of an ongoing implementation of a multi-version data warehouse that is capable of handling changes in the structure of its schema as well as simulating alternative business scenarios by means of modeling alternative DW versions. But this model has a drawback that time overhead for processing queries spanning multiple versions increases as the number of versions increases.

In [21] a DW capable of managing its multiple versions will further be called a *multi-version data warehouse* (MVDW). Also the authors have employed an approach to querying a multi-version DW where their result sets are annotated with information about metadata. An extension to traditional SQL language has been proposed with additional functionality of querying multiple versions, comparing and combining the results into a common result set. Though, metadata is supported by this work but, no schema is augmented with useful information. Also partial querying and result combining consumes a lot of time.

In [24] authors have proposed to use a bi-temporal schema version model of a historical medical DW (which has been taken as a case study) for the storage, management and visualization of current and historical data in a medical environment. They have also described some primitives along with the integrity rules to execute them for handling the evolution.

In [2] authors have presented a model of a multi-version data warehouse, along with a set of operators with their formal semantics that support a DW evolution. They distinguish two groups of operators that modify the structure of a data warehouse. A major drawback is that all operators deal with a particular version of a data warehouse no cross-versioning is allowed. Hence, cross-version querying also not supported.

In [17] the authors have proposed an approach to schema versioning in DWs and formulating cross-version queries, i.e., queries that cover data across numerous schema versions. First, they introduced a representation of DW schemata as graphs of simple functional dependencies. Then, they define algebra of schema graph modification operations in order to create new schema versions. They have also discussed how augmented schemata can be introduced to speed up the cross-version querying process. One drawback is that no alternate versions are created.

In [23] the authors have discussed about how to maintain different versions of a warehouse based on bi-temporal pertinence with same valid time but different transaction times. Also they have generated 16 operators for handling the evolution in multi-dimensional schemas. But it does not support metadata and data transformation.

In [22] authors have described about how to deal with the problem of 'what-if' analysis when data warehouse source schema/data tend to evolve. They have abstracted queries, software modules, ETL workflows, SQL queries with functions in the form of a graph annotated with policies as graph elements. Then are able to detect which all parts of the graph are affected and also suggest ways to tackle those modifications. However, graphs can become quite complex in some cases and exact methods to handle different versions have not been expressed apart from 'what-if' scenarios.

A multi-version schema and data cube model has been proposed in [29] in order to handle dynamically evolving schema implementations. The authors have also addressed the optimization of maintenance and query processing by defining an evaluation function. The optimization in terms of data migration has not been addressed in the paper. They have not focused much on storage space as a constraint. Also, no schema augmentation and metadata is presented in the research.

2.3 View Maintenance

The information stored at the warehouse is in the form of derived views of data from the sources. These views are referred to as *materialized views*. Materialized views can enhance the query execution process to a greater extent. Any query which can be rewritten to use a materialized view reduces the time, effort & cost significantly. In fact, materialized views are regarded as one of the primary means for managing performance in a data warehouse [25]. The prime focus is to:

(1) Select the most appropriate materialized views to be stored in the DW:
The selected materialized views must be closely-related to the queries. We cannot materialize all the views due to some limitations like- space, cost & time. Thus, *view selection* problem can be defined as a way to identify a set of views to be materialized so that the query response time and maintenance cost is minimum.

(2) Perform necessary tasks for view maintenance:

We have three view maintenance tasks as described in [26]:

VIEW MAINTENACE- Aims at maintaining the view scope under the source data updates. A maintenance query is issued based on the update done in the source data in order to calculate the delta change on the view.

VIEW SYNCHRONIZATION- Aims to evolve the view definition when the schema of the base relation is changed. It supports both equivalent & non-equivalent view rewritings.

VIEW ADAPTABILITY- Aims at adapting a view in case the rewritten view definition is not equivalent to the original one in order to make it consistent with the new view definition.

An EVE (Evolvable View Environment) has been developed in [27] to handle view synchronization in dynamic environments. A view definition language, *E-SQL*, has also been developed along with some replacement strategies for affected view components. Though they have addressed issues to handle evolution in very large distributed environments but, they have restricted their research to schema changes only. They have not focused on data or instance changes. In addition, they have not discussed about cost and quality constraints as well.

In [26] authors have discussed about algebra based incremental maintenance of views by schema restructuring. They have proposed a *SchemaSQL* framework to handle data updates and schema changes in order to be applied to the views. They have also developed a prototype Schema SQL view maintainer & query processor. Algebra based process can be easily adapted to several query languages but, this can be time consuming.

In [25] authors have designed a framework for called *DyDa*, for view maintenance in order to handle both concurrent schema and data changes in distributed or dynamic environments. They have identified three types of anomalies and also proposed some algorithms to tackle them. The framework can handle concurrent changes but cannot handle mixed changes in a single process. In addition, the cost incurred increases for data updates.

Authors in [28] have developed a graph based approach to handle view selection problem in data cubes to minimize the query response time by taking an example of TPC-D benchmark database. The approach is quite simple and based heuristics. But the limitations are that the algorithm cannot be applied on the whole data cube (in case of multi-dimensional model) rather it is applicable to a lattice only.

2.4 Temporal Warehousing

Temporal data warehouses are an extension of traditional DW systems with an added dimension of *TIME*. The dimension *Time* ensures to keep a track of the changes in the transaction data [19].

Considering only one schema version, valid at any time here are a number versions based on temporal nature of data:

TRANSACTION TIME SCHEMA VERSIONING:
If transaction time schema versioning is supported all the successive versions of the schema time stamped with its corresponding transaction time. Most researchers consider only this kind of schema versioning, but it is more limited because the

modifications concern only the current schema version. In this case the meta-schema is managed as transaction time tables [15].

VALID TIME SCHEMA VERSIONING:
In this type, each schema version is time stamped with its corresponding valid time. A new schema version is declared active as soon as its validity is approached. The problem here is that more than one schema version may be affected by a single change, because all schema versions totally or partially overlapped by the validity of the change are affected. The meta-schema is managed as valid time tables, whose rows correspond to schema versions [15].

BI-TEMPORAL SCHEMA VERSIONING:
In this type, each schema version is time stamped with both transaction and valid time. The transaction time tells when the modification was proposed and the valid time tells the period when the schema version is valid. A schema change can only concern the current and the overlapped bi-temporal schema versions. Bi-temporal database is adopted to model the schema versioning mechanism; all temporal labels must include the following attributes: initial transaction time (tTimei), final transaction time (tTimef), initial valid time (vTimei) and final valid time (vTimef) [19].

In [19] authors have presented a bi-temporal extension to COMET model. They have focused on both the valid and transaction timestamps on both schema and instance level. It allows representing changes of transaction data and structure data. Version can be mapped by applying transformation functions. However, no comprehensive metadata or schema augmentation is provided in this work.

In [10] the authors have proposed a temporal data warehouse architecture COMET metamodel which extends multidimensional data warehouses to incorporate all changes of schema and structure of data warehouses. The improvement lies in the temporal attribution of *all* elements of a data warehouse. This then forms the basis for OLAP tools for querying data spanning several structural versions and analysis of data according to new and old versions. But a major drawback is that only valid timestamp is considered no transaction time is considered.

In [11] authors have proposed a temporal data warehouse architecture to represent changes in structural data and permit accurate analysis of data over periods with changing master data. They have presented a series of typical business cases involving change in structural data or master data. They have time stamped the master data to make data warehouse more useful in dynamic situations along with two architectural variants namely, direct approach and indirect approach. The limitation of the work is that only valid timestamp is considered. Also, this approach may fail on some real-world cases.

In [12] authors have discussed about CoSM, comet structure manager that handles data warehouse structures based on Comet model. It allows uploading, downloading and managing different structure versions of schema and instancing level data and changes as well. It also supports the maintenance of these cubes, i.e., to update their structure, to keep track of the valid time of different structure versions of the cubes, to store information about who modified which parts of a cube and so forth [12]. These versions can be compared but no mapping/data migration is allowed. No metadata support addressed.

In [9] authors have discussed about a DWT tool for the maintenance of data warehouses based on COMET model. DWT allows keeping track of changes made in the dimension-structure of multidimensional cubes. DWT allows uploading and downloading data warehouses in different customized notations and also finds out difference between two versions in the form of edit scripts. It offers three ways for identifying differences between two subsequent versions: a semiautomatic structure comparison, change-log application, and manual change identification. Each version is tagged with its valid timestamp. A drawback is that no mapping and metadata provided.

3 Comparison of Research Works

We have analyzed various research works in context of data warehouse evolution and its related issues. A brief tabular comparison has been provided below.

Table 2. Comparison of work by different authors in tabular manner

Features / Authors	*Approach*	*Types of changes handled*	*Proposed work*	*Query Language Supports*	*Timestamp*	*Meta Data supported*	*Versions*	*Schema Augmentation*	*Data Migration*	*Tool support / implementation*
Lee, Nica & Elke (2002) [27]	View synchronization in dynamic environment	Schema changes	EVE framework + replacement strategies + Algorithms	E-SQL view definition language	✗	Meta Knowledge base	Not addressed	Replacement strategies	Through MKB	JAVA + JDBC + MS-Access
Eder, Koncilia & Morzy (2002) [10]	Temporal data + Schema evolution	Schema + dimension data + structural changes	COMET MODEL	Multiple periods in time + Different dimensions (SQL based)	Based on valid timestamps	✗	Based on timestamps + Structural changes	✗	Through Transformation Functions	Basis for OLAP tools
Eder, Koncilia & Kogler (2002) [11]	Temporal DW in business cases & their solutions	Schema + instance	Temporal DWs + Transformation functions	Query includes time to specify base version	✓	✗	Based on timestamps + Changes in master data	✗	Transformation Function mapping between different structures	JAVA + Oracle 8.1i + C++
Franconi, Grandi & Mandreoli (2002) [14]	Schema versioning in general Object-Oriented data model	Schema changes + Data changes	Object oriented model with encoding in DL + semantics of changes + Reasoning tasks	Schema translation + Multi-Schema (SQL based)	For objects of same data pool (OID + timestamp)	✗	Based on OIDs + Timestamp	✓	Not handled	Not addressed
Body, Miquel, Bedard & Tchounikine (2003) [7]	Temporal multi-dimensional model	Dimensions + hierarchy levels + members	Evolution operators + Multi-version fact tables	Implicit hierarchies (SQL SERVER) + Parent-child relationship	Based on multi-version fact tables	✓	Based on valid time	✗	Through mapping relationships + Confidence factor	SQL Server + OLE DB + ProClarity 4.0

Table 2. *(continued)*

Koncilia (2003) **[19]**	Schema evolution + Bi-temporal versions	Master data changes + Transaction data changes	Extension to COMET meta-model	Query Includes two Timestamps (SQL based)	Valid + transaction timestamps	✗	Based on timestamps + Structural changes	✗	Through Transformation Functions mapping.	OLAP tools
Koncilia & Eder (2003) **[12]**	Maintenance of temporal data warehouse model COMET	Schema + Dimension structure changes	CoSM interface between temporal & non-temporal data	Query supports Valid time	Based on valid time stamp of dimension data	✗	Structure versions created based on differences	✗	Comparison of structures possible but no mapping allowed	Microsoft Visual C++ + OLAP server + API
Benitez, Collet, Adiba (2004) **[3]**	Schema evolution of multi-dimensional model.	Cube + Dimensions changes	WHES approach	Extension to SQL: Multi-dimensional DDL	✗	✗	No version, history is not preserved	✗	Translation rules + Propagation rules	RDBMS + Java Beans + XML data
Fan & Poulovassilis (2004) **[13]**	Schema evolution in materialized integration scenarios (heterogeneous environments)	Source schema + Warehouse schema + Derived data marts	Evolvable Integration framework by means of integration toolkit	IQL : a comprehension based functional query language	✗	Supports schemas, cleansing, transformat-ions and Integration	AutoMed transforma-tions & Transformation pathways	✗	Through transformation on primitives	AutoMed: Data integration toolkit
Morzy & Wrembel (2004) **[21]**	Querying multiple versions of a DW	Schema + Dimension structure	Multi-version DW + Query Language interface (GUI, parser, executor & visualizer)	Extension to SQL: query multiple versions, compare and merge results	Based on valid lifetime of a version	Query results annotated with meta data in Oracle 9i	Real + Alternate based on valid lifetime	✗	Homogeneous/ heterogeneous structures for integrating results of partial queries	JAVA & Oracle PL/SQL
Koeller & Rundenstein er (2004) **[26]**	Incremental maintenance of Schema–restructuring views	Data + Schema changes	Algebra based incremental maintenance + SchemaSQL prototypes	Schema SQL queries	✗	SchemaSQL metadata	Not addressed	✓	Algebra based view query mapped to sequence of changes	JAVA + Oracle 8 (JDBC)
Golfarelli, Lechtenborger, Rizzi & Vossen (2005) **[17]**	Schema Versioning in multi-dimensional model	Elementary graph modifications and changes	FD based schema graphs + graph operators	Cross-version queries + aggregation	✗	Schema graphs managed as large data repository	Only current version no viable alternate versions	✓	Based on valid events and instances of hierarchies	Dictionary of fact & dimension instances

Table 2. *(continued)*

Encinas & Adiba (2005) [24]	Schema versions of medical DW.	Cubes + Dimensions + hierarchies	Bi-temporal schema versioning model + Primitives + Integrity rules + Evolution manager	SQL Based queries	Valid + transaction	Meta-schema + Historical repositories	Unique Current version & many historical versions	✗	By means of Correspondence tables	ADELEM: tool to aid logistics in medical decisions
Eder, Konciliа& Wiggisser (2006) [9]	Maintenance of temporal DW based on COMET	OLAP cube changes both dimensions and structural	DWT tool: interface between temporal & non-temporal data	Not addressed	Valid time + transaction (in case of bi-temporal)	✗	Through structural changes that are tagged and member classes	✗	Very little through transformation functions like in COMET	JAVA 1.4 + Oracle 9i
Bebel, Krolikowski & Wrembel (2006) [2]	Based on schema and data versioning	Schema change + Dimension instance change	Formal multi-version DW model (MVDW) + Evolution operators	Multi-version + What-if analysis	Store historical data from different time periods	✓	schema version + set of data versions	✗	Conversion to enable transformations between adjacent versions	Not addressed
Chen, Zhang & Elke (2006) [25]	View maintenance In dynamic environments	Source schema & data updates	DyDa Framework + Maintenance Anomalies + Algorithms	SQL based maintenance & compensation queries	✗	✗	No versions, views adapted or synchronized or maintained	✗	Not addressed	JAVA & Oracle 8i
Janet, Ramirez & Guerrero (2006) [23]	Based on schema versioning	Dimension + Cube Schema	Bi-temporal evolution model + 16 operators	SQL-like Query language	Valid time + transaction	✗	Based on valid + multiple Transaction time	✗	Not addressed	Not addressed
Papastefanatos, Vassiliadis, Simitsis & Vassiliou (2007) [22]	What-if analysis for changes in schema/ Structures	Schema changes in sources	Graph modeling technique where queries are represented as graphs annotated with policies	SQL queries Enriched with functions	✗	Annotated graph stored as a repository	✗	In the form of policies attached with graph to handle changes	Mapping between source & target graphs in case of evolution through match operator.	Hecataeus: A What-If Analysis Tool for Schema Evolution
Dhote & Ali (2007) [28]	Graph based approach for View selection problem	Data cube changes	AND/OR DAG to minimize the query response time	SQL based	✗	Not addressed	✗	✗	Not addressed	✗
Curino, Moon & Zoniolo (2009) [8]	Schema evolution + Temporal versions	Schema changes + View changes + Query re-writing	Schema modification operators + Information Systems archival	SQL-inspired, language + Temporal queries + historical queries	Time-stamping subsequent version	✓	Based on time stamped transaction-time databases	✓	Schema mapping + query re-writing capabilities	PRISM: to develop methods & tools for schema evolution
Sahpaski, Velinov, Jakimovski & Kon-Popovska (2009) [29]	Multi-version DW & Optimization of DW design + Vertical view fragmentation	Changes in query + Schema changes	Multi-version schema & data cube Model + Evaluation function to handle optimization problem through experimentation	SQL based	✗	Not addressed	Both schema and instance	✗	Not addressed	Java Genetic Algorithm Framework (JGAP) + Java Grid Framework for Genetic Algorithm (JGFGA)

4 Conclusion

In this paper we have presented an analysis of different approaches being proposed by various researchers to deal with data warehouse evolution namely, schema evolution, versioning, view maintenance and temporal warehousing. We have compared these techniques on various parameters. Several tools like-DWT, CoSM, AutoMed, etc. that have been designed primarily to handle the DW evolution have also been discussed in this paper. As future work, so far, we have concentrated only on the conceptual level and skipped the impacts of evolution on DW requirement and physical design phase. An investigation of the impacts of Evolution process on both these levels seems worth further attention.

References

1. Bebel, B., Eder, J., Koncilia, C., Morzy, T., Wrembel, R.: Creation and Management of Versions in Multiversion data warehouse. In: Proc. ACM SAC, pp. 717–723 (2004)
2. B¸ebel, B., Krolikowski, Z., Wrembel, R.: Formal Approach to Modeling Data Warehouse. Bulletin of the Polish Academy of Sciences 54, 1 (2006)
3. Benitez-Guerrero, E., Collet, C., Adiba, M.: The WHES Approach to Data Warehouse Evolution. e-Gnosis [online], vol. 2, Art (2004)
4. Blaschka, M.: FIESTA: A Framework for Schema Evolution in Multidimensional Databases. PhD thesis, Technische Universitat Munchen, Germany (2000)
5. Blaschka, M., Sapia, C., Höfling, G.: On Schema Evolution in Multidimensional Databases. In: Proc. of DaWaK (2000)
6. Body, M., Miquel, M., Bedard, Y., Tchounikine, A.: Multidimensional and Multiversion Structure for OLAP applications. In: Proc. of the 5th ACM Intl. Workshop DOLAP, pp. 1–6 (2002)
7. Body, M., Miquel, M., Bedard, Y., Tchounikine, A.: Handling Evolutions in Multidimensional Structures. In: Int. Conf. on Data Engineering (2003)
8. Curino, C., Moon, H., Zaniolo, C.: Automating Database Schema Evolution in Information System Upgrades. In: HotSWUp (2009)
9. Eder, J., Koncilia, C., Wiggisser, K.: Maintaining Temporal Warehouse Models. In: Proc. of CONFENIS, vol. 205, pp. 21–30 (2006)
10. Eder, J., Koncilia, C., Morzy, T.: The COMET metamodel for temporal data warehouses. In: Pidduck, A.B., Mylopoulos, J., Woo, C.C., Ozsu, M.T. (eds.) CAiSE 2002. LNCS, vol. 2348, pp. 83–99. Springer, Heidelberg (2002)
11. Eder, J., Koncilia, C., Kogler, H.: Temporal Data Warehousing: Business Cases and Solutions. In: Proc. of the 4th International Conference on Enterprise Information Systems, vol. 1, pp. 81–88 (2002)
12. Eder, J., Koncilia, C.: CoSM: A Maintenance Tool for Data Warehouse Structures. In: Proc. of International Conference on Conceptual Modeling, vol. 24 (2003)
13. Fan, H., Poulovassilis, A.: Schema evolution in data warehousing environments – A schema transformation-based approach. In: Atzeni, P., Chu, W., Lu, H., Zhou, S., Ling, T.-W. (eds.) ER 2004. LNCS, vol. 3288, pp. 639–653. Springer, Heidelberg (2004)
14. Franconi, E., Grandi, F., Mandreoli, F.: Schema Evolution and Versioning: A Logical and Computational Characterization (2002)

15. Galante, R., Silva Roma, A., Edelweiss, A., Saraiva, C.: Dynamic Schema Evolution Management Using Version in Temporal Object-oriented Databases. Springer, Heidelberg (2002)
16. Golfarelli, M., Lechtenbörger, J., Rizzi, S., Vossen, G.: Schema versioning in data warehouses. In: Wang, S., Tanaka, K., Zhou, S., Ling, T.-W., Guan, J., Yang, D.-q., Grandi, F., Mangina, E.E., Song, I.-Y., Mayr, H.C. (eds.) ER Workshops 2004. LNCS, vol. 3289, pp. 415–428. Springer, Heidelberg (2004)
17. Golfarelli, M., Lechtenbörger, J., Rizzi, S., Vossen, G.: Schema Versioning in Data Warehouses: Enabling Cross-version Querying via Schema Augmentation. In: Data & Knowledge Engineering (2005)
18. Inmon, W.: Building the Data Warehouse, p. 23 (1991)
19. Koncilia, C.: A Bi-temporal Data Warehouse Model. Thesis, University of Klagenfurt, Dep. of Informatics-Systems (2001)
20. Marotta, A.: Data Warehouse Design and Maintenance through Schema Transformations. Master thesis, Universidad de la República Uruguay (2000)
21. Morzy, T., Wrembel, R.: On Querying Versions of Multiversion Data Warehouse. In: Proc. of the 7th ACM Intl. Workshop DOLAP, pp. 92–101 (2004)
22. Papastefanatos, G., Vassiliadis, P., Simitsis, A., Vassiliou, Y.: What-if Analysis for Data Warehouse Evolution (2007)
23. Janet, E., Ramirez, R., Guerrero, E.: A Model and Language for Bi-temporal Schema Versioning in Data Warehouses. In: Proc. of 15th International Conference on Computing (2006)
24. Encinas, M., Adiba, M.: Exploiting Bi-temporal Schema Versions for Managing an Historical Medical DW: A Case Study. In: Proc of 6th International Conference on Computer Science (2005)
25. Chen, S., Zhang, X., Rundensteiner, E.: A Compensation Based Approach for View Maintenance in Distributed Environments. IEEE Transactions and Data Engineering 18 (2006)
26. Koeller, A., Rundensteiner, A.: Incremental Maintenance of Schema–restructuring View in SchemaSQL. IEEE Transactions and Data Engineering 16 (2004)
27. Lee, A., Nica, A., Rundensteiner, A.: The EVE Approach View Synchronization in Dynamic Distributed Environments. IEEE Transactions and Data Engineering 14 (2002)
28. Dhote, C., Ali, M.: Materialized View Selection in Data Warehouse. In: International Conference on Information Technology (2007)
29. Sahpaski, D., Vellnov, G., Jakimovski, B., Kon-Popovska, M.: Dynamic Evolution and Improvement of Data Warehouse Design. In: Balkan Conference in Informatics (2009)

An Adaptive Framework for Clustering Data Streams

Chandrika[1] and K.R. Ananda Kumar[2]

[1] Dept. of Computer Science and Engineering, MCE, Hassan, India
jc@mcehassan.ac.in
[2] Dept. of Computer Science and Engineering, SJBIT, Bangalore, India
kra_megha_tn@hotmail.com

Abstract. In recent years, advances in hardware technology have facilitated the ability to collect data continuously. Simple transactions of everyday life such as using a credit card, a phone or browsing the web lead to automated data storage thus generating massive streams of data. These streams consist of millions or billions of updates and must be processed to extract the useful information to enable timely strategic decisions. Mining data streams have many inherent challenges among which the most important challenges are adapting to available resources and assuring quality of the output result. The purpose of this paper is to use a novel framework that accounts for both quality awareness and resource adaptation for clustering data streams.

Keywords: Data streams, Methodical quality, temporal quality, resource adaptation, Algorithm granularity, adaptation factors, Data stream Clustering.

1 Introduction

At present a growing number of applications generate massive streams of data that need intelligent data processing and online analysis. This rapid generation of continuous streams of information has challenged the storage, computation and communication capabilities in computing systems [1]. Mining data streams is concerned with extracting knowledge structures represented in models and patterns in non stopping streams of information [2]. In the data stream model, some or all of the input data that are to be operated on are not available for random access from disk or memory, but rather arrive as one or more *continuous data streams*. Data streams differ from the conventional stored relation model in several ways [4]: Data elements in the stream arrive online. The system has no control over the order in which data elements arrive to be processed, either within a data stream or across data streams. Data streams are potentially unbounded in size.

The imminent need for turning stream data into useful information and knowledge augments the development of systems, algorithms and frameworks that addresses streaming challenges. Data stream mining is a stimulating field of study that has raised challenges and research issues to be addressed by the database and data mining community [2] [3].

Due to the unique characteristics of data streams, like their potentially infinite nature and the vast amount of data they are carrying, data stream mining requires a

A. Abraham et al. (Eds.): ACC 2011, Part I, CCIS 190, pp. 704–711, 2011.

different kind of processing than mining on databases and data warehouses. Efficient resource consumption is one of the major objectives when designing stream mining algorithms. Rather than storing the incoming data and processing it offline like in traditional data mining, data stream mining is much more constrained in terms of available resources. Most data stream algorithms provide approximate results, often by using a summarization of the stream called synopsis and determining precise error bounds. Thus, a notion of output quality is immediately associated with this process. A framework that assesses the output quality and the current status of resources and adapts the algorithm's resource consumption accordingly is therefore used. With our framework, available resources are utilized in an optimal way at any point in time. The concepts presented are applied to the task of data stream clustering.

Rest of the paper is organized as follows. Section two reviews the basic concept of resource adaptation and quality awareness. Section three describes a framework that accounts for both of these factors. Section four outlines the requirements on the algorithm to use this framework for data stream clustering. Section five concludes with directions for future work.

2 Related Work

2.1 Data Stream Mining Quality

Quality is an important aspect of mining results, as it indicates how accurate and reliable the mining results are. A set of quality measures can be used to assess the quality of stream mining algorithms. The various quality measures in the context of data stream mining and their classification is discussed in detail in [10]. They have introduced Methodical quality Q_M and temporal quality Q_T. Methodical quality is specific to investigated problem and algorithm whereas temporal quality is identical to all problems. The classification of quality measures that are used in the context of data stream mining is as indicated by the diagram Fig. 1 Q_M represents classes of measures that are always specific to the investigated problem and the applied algorithm(s). For example, in the context of clustering these measures may indicate sum of square of distances between every point and the cluster centre, measure for the problem of frequent itemset mining is the error rate which defines the maximal

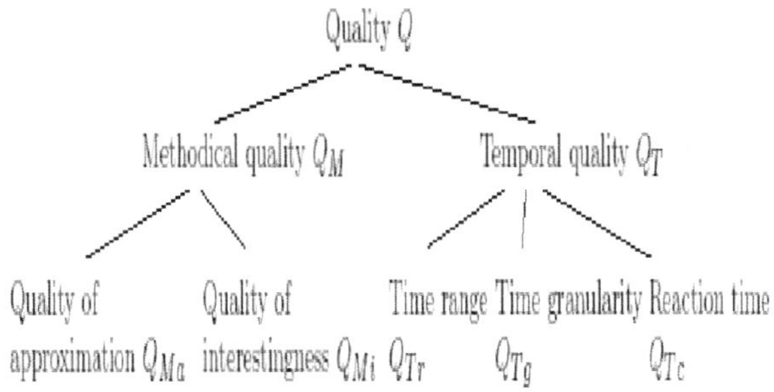

Fig 1. Classification of Quality Measures

deviation of the observed frequency to the actual frequency of an itemset. For several specific mining applications, special interestingness measures (QMi) have been proposed. In the context of frequent itemsets the support is one such interestingness measure.

QTr describes how far we can look back into the history of the processed data stream and QTg how exactly we can do this, which means which time granularity we can provide. QTc corresponds to one of the main challenges of stream mining: the actual time necessary to register changes in the stream.

Recent work in the area of data stream mining addresses quality as an important factor. The quality issue is addressed by Marcel Karnstedt et.al [9]. They argue that Quality-of-Service (QoS) requirements are mandatory when creating stream processing systems applicable to a wide and general range of data stream applications. They discuss QoS requirements and QoS-driven stream mining techniques as building blocks of the proposed framework quality-aware stream processing systems. Sven Schmidt et. al.[8] focus on applications monitoring analog sensor data and having QOS constraints attached to the queries. They have proposed the generic data stream model QDM comprising of structural as well as operational entities. Operators exhibit a functional description as well as a nonfunctional specification to exactly specify the requirements for the execution environment.

2.2 Resource Adaptation

Adaptive algorithms do not use more resources than the available resources, thus avoiding running out of resources during processing. Thus, one of the goals of adaptive algorithm is to provide the best performance possible in the given environment. For most existing stream mining algorithms their input parameters are fixed for the entire runtime of the algorithm. This has two effects in a dynamic environment:

1. at some point in time the algorithm can run out of resources during processing, because the given input parameters require more CPU-time and/or more memory than is available.
2. the algorithm uses less than the available resources, thus yielding mining results with lower quality than would have been possible with an optimal utilization of the available resources.

Increasing the resource requirement of a stream mining algorithm aimlessly is a waste. But as a better approximation can be achieved in the mining results using more resources, the increased resource requirements are beneficial for improving the quality of the mining results. An algorithm's resource requirements are tightly bound to the values of its input parameters. The goal of resource adaptivity is therefore to set these values automatically and dynamically based on the current resource availability and properties of the data stream. A challenge in this context is to find optimal parameter values for any given setting. Data adaptation techniques to catch up with the high-speed data stream and at the same time to achieve the optimum accuracy according to the available resources have to be designed. The resource adaptation issue has been addressed recently by many researchers. Gaber et al. [5][6] propose a generic model for resource adaptive data stream mining. The model uses algorithm granularity (AG) settings to adapt an algorithm's resource consumption to the amount of available resources. The AG model aims at prolonging the lifetime of a running stream mining algorithm in critical situations of low availability of resources. AG has been classified into three classes, AIG, AOG, and APG. Algorithm input granularity (AIG) adapts the input streaming data to the mining algorithm. Algorithm output granularity (AOG) changes the size of the algorithm's output, for example, the number of clusters returned for a user query. Finally, algorithm processing granularity (APG) can adapt the algorithm parameters. These three classes represent all existing interfaces that are available to adapt resource requirements in data stream mining. Based on the concept of AOG light weight algorithms are designed for clustering, Classification and frequent item counting [7]. All these algorithms do not take quality parameters while adjusting the granularity. The changes in the AG settings are not quality-aware. That means the algorithm changes according to the availability of computational resources. This may lead to accuracy loss and/or extra use of computational resources, because in some cases, we can gain the same accuracy using lesser resources.

3 A Generic Framework

In the context of stream mining we have to process the stream data while adhering to limited resources available. Thus, we propose resource awareness in conjunction with quality awareness as one of the main requirements – and challenges in parallel. In a data stream mining application several resources are constrained and thus have to be carefully allotted in order to keep up with the pace of the data stream and answer queries in a timely manner. The constrained resources in a data stream mining application are memory, CPU cycles, bandwidth and battery power. There are three aspects of stream mining algorithm that affects the resource usage they are:

Stream rate - One can change the amount of data to be processed by reducing the volume of the data stream using methods like sampling and load shedding

Input parameters- Most stream mining algorithms have input parameters that influence how well their output approximates the actual mining result. Consequently, these input parameters are one of the main aspects that determine the resource requirements of a stream mining algorithm.

Query to retrieve mining results - The query time interval specifies which portion of the stream should be considered when the mining result is computed, e.g., clusters of all stream elements that arrived within the last five hours. The more of the data stored in the synopsis needs to be accessed in order to answer a query, the more CPU cycles will be required.

These three aspects are identified as algorithm granularity setting by Gaber et. al[7]. There is an upper bound and lower bound on the usage of these constrained resources. The quality parameters discussed in section 2.1 also have a lower bound and upper bound. The desired quality has a strong influence on the workload of the stream mining algorithm as well as on the size of the synopsis it maintains. In general, the higher the quality should be, the more resources the algorithm requires. Conversely, the quality is influenced by all changes that are done in order to influence an algorithm's resource requirements. The three aspects mentioned above that influence an algorithm's resource requirements also impact the quality. For example, a poor sampling scheme is likely to reduce the quality because many significant stream elements are discarded. As described above, input parameters of stream mining algorithms have a strong impact on the quality as well, because they determine how thoroughly the stream is mined and how detailed the characteristics of the stream are stored in the synopsis.

Adaptation factors - There are a lot of variables present in data stream mining. Besides variables that are stream specific, such as the stream rate and properties of the items in the data stream, many variables are algorithm specific, like input and query parameters of a stream mining algorithm. The variables in data stream mining are not independent of each other. In most cases, a change of one variable's value causes other variables to change as well. For example, if the number clusters in clustering algorithm is changed, the number of required CPU cycles, the main memory requirements, and the methodical quality QM of the clustering algorithm change as well. This example illustrates that parameters are tuning knobs for the data stream mining process, as they influence resource requirements and quality. In our framework, the parameters P are selected as adaptation factors, i.e., parameters that are automatically adjusted in order to adapt an algorithm's resource requirements and quality to the resource and quality constraints at any point in time. Parameters that are not chosen as adaptation factors remain constant throughout the lifetime of the stream mining process. Because of this, we only denote adaptation factors as parameters throughout the rest of this paper. That is, the set P of parameters only contains the variables that can be automatically adjusted. With parameter adaptation the goal of data stream mining process can be stated as:

Mine the data stream continuously with the maximum possible quality at every point in time, such that each quality measure Q is within its constraints. The input parameters that determine the quality are subject to dynamic resource constraints, so they have to be chosen such that the requirements for each resource are within its constraints.

With this background the framework for mining data streams accounting quality and resource requirements can be indicated diagrammatically as shown in fig. 2:

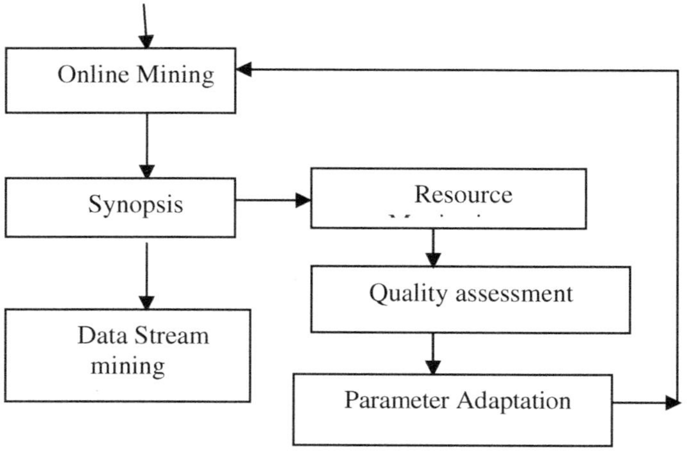

Fig 2. Generic Framework

The online mining of input data stream results in summary structure called synopsis. All the stream data mining tasks like querying, frequent pattern mining, clustering and classification will further refer to the synopsis structure. According to our proposed framework at regular intervals of time the resource usage will be monitored by resource monitoring component. Based on the outcome of resource usage the adaptation parameters are set so that there is no compromise on the quality. Then the new parameters are set in the stream mining algorithm and the stream analysis continues until next time resource monitoring component is activated.

3.2 Description of the Framework

Let R indicate set of all constrained resources. Rmax denotes maximum limit on resource usage, Rmin indicates that at least a certain amount of that resource has to be used by the stream mining algorithm. Let Q denote set of all quality measures. Like resources quality measures have upper and lower bounds let Qmax denotes maximum limit on quality, Qmin denote minimum limit on quality. Let P denote set of parameters of stream mining algorithm that influences resource requirements and quality factors. Examples of such parameters are sampling rate, number of output objects etc. The framework uses the following functions:

Resource_check: This function decides whether resource utilization should be increased decreased or maintained. It is used in resource monitoring layer of the proposed framework.

Resource_measure: This function determines the resource usage at the given instance of time. It is used in resource monitoring layer of the proposed framework.

Quality_check: Used to calculate the current measure of quality parameters. It is used in quality assessment layer of the proposed framework.

Adapt_parameters: Used to give new value for the adaptation parameters. It is used in Parameter adaptation layer of the proposed framework.

Quality_adaptation: These will adjust the adaptation parameters value based on the quality measures. It is used in Parameter adaptation layer of the proposed framework.

The generic framework works according to the following steps

Step 1: Resource monitoring component is activated with Rmax and P.

Step 2: Resource_check function is called to decide whether resource utilization should be increased decreased or maintained. If adaptation is needed go to step 3 else continue online mining.

Step 3: Give new values for adaptation parameters using adapt_parameters functions.

Step 4: Find the current level of quality parameters using Quality_check.

Step 5: New parameters computed in step3 will be adjusted based on quality requirements using Quality_adaptation function.

Step 6: Set new values for mining algorithm parameters and continue online mining.

The proposed framework is a generic one and it can be adapted to any data stream mining task. In the next section we will use it for data stream clustering.

4 Using the Framework for Data Stream Clustering

Data stream clustering involves partitioning the data set into subsets (clusters) such that members of the same cluster are similar and members of distinct clusters are dissimilar [11]. Given an integer k and a collection N of n points in a metric space, find k centroids (cluster centers) in the metric space so that each point in N is assigned to the cluster defined by the median point nearest to it. The quality of the clustering is measured by the sum of squared distances (SSQ) of data points to their assigned medians. The goal is to find a set of k medians which minimize the SSQ measure. There are many algorithms for clustering data streams among which clustream [12] is the algorithm which we have considered. The quality factors and resource adaptation concept is applied to clustream algorithm. The clustream algorithm uses microclusters which are temporal extensions of cluster feature vector. Microclusters are stored at snapshots in time that follow pyramidal pattern.

The primary resource of concern is the amount of memory needed. A proportion between q (the number of microclusters) and k (the number of end-clusters) has an impact on quality. The adaptation factors influencing the amount of memory are:

- k: number of end-clusters
- W: width of dynamic pyramidal time frame.

The q/k proportion and the average width w of the pyramidal time frame have to be computed in the quality check function to achieve good quality of clusters. According to the framework used first we need to monitor the ratio of amount of memory used to maximal amount of memory available. Depending on the value of the ratio, width of pyramidal timeframe can be increased or decreased or can remain unchanged. The resource check function involves the calculation of the ratio as indicated by the following formula :

r = (actual_memory_usage) / (maximal_memory).

The adapt_parameter function will adjust the width of pyramidal timeframe as shown below:

The width of the pyramidal time frame has to be increased by one if $r<0.85$.

The width of the pyramidal time frame is unchanged if r lies in the range 0.85 to 1.

The width of the pyramidal time frame is reduced, as long as f is above 1 (too much of memory consumption). The clustering algorithm continues to work with the new value for w. In this manner the algorithm adapts itself to the amount of available memory.

5 Conclusion and Future Work

Mining data streams stresses our computational resources with regard to processing power, memory requirements, energy and communication. In order to ensure the continuity and consistency of a data stream mining process, adaptation to available resources is required. Although adaptation is crucial for the success of the data mining process, its effect on the quality is of concern. Thus, in this paper we propose a data stream clustering approach where both resource adaptation and quality awareness is included. In future we plan to implement the functions proposed in the framework and also extend this concept to other stream mining tasks like frequent itemset mining.

References

1. Dong, G., Han, J., Lakshmanan, L.V.S., Pei, J., Wang, H., Yu, P.S.: Online mining of changes from datastreams: Research problems and preliminary results. In: ACM SIGMOD (2003)
2. Gaber, M.M., Zaslavsky, A., Krishnaswamy, S.: Mining Data Streams: A Review. SIGMOD Record 34(2) (2005)
3. Jiang, N., Gruenwald, L.: Research Issues in Data Stream Association Rule Mining. Sigmod Record 35(1) (March 2006)
4. Babcock, B., Babu, S., Datar, M., Motwani, R., Widom, J.: Models and issues in data stream systems. In: Proceedings of Symposium on Principles of Database Systems, pp. 1–16. ACM Press, New York (2002)
5. Gaber, M.M., Krishnaswamy, S., Zaslavsky, A.: Cost-Efficient Mining Techniques for Data Streams. Australian Computer Society, Inc. (2004)
6. Gaber, M.M., Krishnaswamy, S., Zaslavsky, A.: Resource-aware Mining of Data Streams. Journal of Universal Computer Science 11(8), 1440–1453 (2005)
7. Gaber, M.M.: Foundations of adaptive data stream mining for mobile and embedded applications. In: Proceedings of the CIBEC 2008. IEEE, Los Alamitos (2008)
8. Schmidt, S., Schlegel, B., Lehner, W.: QDM: A Generic QoS-aware Data Model for Real-Time Data Stream Processing. In: Proceedings of second International Conference on Digital Telecommunications (ICDT 2007). IEEE, Los Alamitos (2007) 0-7695-2910-0/07
9. Karnstedt, M., Sattler, K.-U., Habich, D., Lehner, W.: Quality of service driven data stream mining. In: Seventh IEEE International Conference on Data mining (2007)
10. Franke, C., Hartung, M., Karnstedt, M., Sattler, K.: Quality-Aware Mining of Data Streams. In: Information Quality (ICIQ), pp. 300–315 (2005)
11. O'Callaghan, L., Mishra, N., Meyersonz, A., Guha, S., Motwani, R.: Streaming-Data Algorithms For High-Quality Clustering. In: Proceedings of the 18th International Conference on Data Engineering (2002)
12. Aggarwal, C.C., Han, J., Wang, J., Yu, P.S.: A Framework for Clustering Evolving Data Streams. In: Proceedings of VLDB, Berlin, Germany, pp. 81–92 (2003)

Author Index

Abbadi, Imad M. IV-406, IV-557
Abbas, Ash Mohammad II-307
Abraham, Anuj III-503
Abraham, John T. III-168
Abraham, Siby I-328
Achuthan, Krishnashree I-488, II-337
AdiSrikanth, III-570
Aditya, T. I-446
Adusumalli, Sri Krishna IV-572
Agarwal, Vikas II-595
Aghila, G. II-327, IV-98
Agrawal, P.K. IV-244
Agrawal, Rohit II-162
Agrawal, Shaishav III-452
Agushinta R., Dewi II-130, II-138, II-146
Ahmed, Imran II-317
Ahn, Do-Seob II-595
Aishwarya, Nandakumar II-490, II-498, III-269
Akhtar, Zahid II-604
Al-Sadi, Azzat A. II-535
Alam, Md. Mahabubul III-349
Alam Kotwal, Mohammed Rokibul II-154
Ananthi, S. I-480
Andres, Frederic IV-79
Anisha, K.K. III-315
Anita, E.A. Mary I-111
Anju, S.S. II-490, II-498, III-269
Annappa, B. IV-396
Anto, P. Babu III-406
Anusiya, M. IV-155
Aradhya, V.N. Manjunath III-289, III-297
Arifuzzaman, Md. III-349
Asif Naeem, M. II-30
Asokan, Shimmi IV-63
Athira, B. II-80
Awais, Muhammad II-374
Awasthi, Lalit Kr III-609
Azeem, Mukhtar II-525
Azeez, A.A. Arifa IV-145
Babu, Korra Sathya II-1
Babu, K. Suresh II-636
Babu, L.D. Dhinesh I-223
Babu, M. Rajasekhara I-182
Baburaj, E. I-172
Badache, N. IV-593
Bagan, K. Bhoopathy IV-524
Bajwa, Imran Sarwar II-30
Bakshi, Sambit III-178
Balasubramanian, Aswath I-411
Banati, Hema II-273
Banerjee, Indrajit III-68
Banerjee, Joydeep III-82
Banerjee, Pradipta K. II-480
Banerjee, Usha II-648
Bansal, Roli III-259
Banu, R.S.D. Wahida II-545
Baruah, P.K. I-446
Basak, Dibyajnan I-519
Basil Morris, Peter Joseph II-577
Baskaran, R. II-234, IV-269
Bastos, Carlos Alberto Malcher IV-195
Batra, Neera I-572
Bedi, Punam II-273, III-259
Bedi, R.K. II-397
Behl, Abhishek II-273
Bhadoria, P.B.S. IV-211
Bhardwaj, Ved Prakash II-568
Bharti, Brijendra K. IV-358
Bhat, Veena H. III-522
Bhattacharyya, Abhijan I-242
Bhosale, Arvind IV-512
Bhuvanagiri, Kiran Kumar IV-293
Bhuvaneswary, A. II-327
Biji, C.L. IV-300
Binu, A. I-399
Biswas, G.P. II-628
Biswas, Subir III-54
Biswas, Suparna II-417
Biswas, Sushanta II-612, II-620
Biswash, Sanjay Kumar I-11
Boddu, Bhaskara Rao II-296
Borah, Samarjeet III-35

Borkar, Meenal A. IV-25
Boutekkouk, Fateh II-40

Chaganty, Aparna IV-19
Chaitanya, N. Sandeep IV-70
Chakraborty, Suchetana II-585
Chakravorty, Debaditya III-35
Challa, Rama Krishna IV-608
Chanak, Prasenjit III-68
Chand, Narottam III-122, III-609
Chandra, Deka Ganesh II-210
Chandra, Jayanta K. II-480
Chandran, K.R. I-631
Chandrika, I-704
Chanijani, S.S. Mozaffari III-289
Chaoub, Abdelaali I-529
Chaudhary, Ankit III-488
Chauhan, Durg Singh I-21
Chawhan, Chandan III-35
Chawla, Suneeta II-430
Chia, Tsorng-Lin III-334
Chintapalli, Venkatarami Reddy IV-455
Chitrakala, S. III-415
Chittineni, Suresh III-543
Choudhary, Surendra Singh I-54
Chouhan, Madhu I-119
Chowdhury, Chandreyee I-129
Chowdhury, Roy Saikat II-577

Dadhich, Reena I-54
Dahiya, Ratna III-157
Dandapat, S. IV-165
Das, Madhabananda IV-113
Das, Satya Ranjan II-172
Das, Subhalaxmi IV-549
Datta, Asit K. II-480
Dawoud, Wesam I-431
Deb, Debasish II-577
Dedavath, Saritha I-34
Deepa, S.N. III-503
Dehalwar, Vasudev I-153
Dehuri, Satchidananda IV-113
Desai, Sharmishta II-397
Devakumari, D. II-358
Devani, Mahesh I-213
Dhanya, P.M. IV-126
Dhar, Pawan K. I-284
Dharanyadevi, P. II-234
Dhavachelvan, P. II-234
Dhivya, M. II-99
Dilna, K.T. III-185
Dimililer, Kamil III-357
Diwakar, Shyam II-337
Doke, Pankaj I-607, II-430
Dongardive, Jyotshna I-328
Donoso, Yezid II-386
Doraipandian, Manivannan III-111
Dorizzi, Bernadette III-20
Durga Bhavani, S. III-1
Dutta, Paramartha I-83
Dutta, Ratna IV-223

El Abbadi, Jamal I-529
El-Alfy, El Sayed M. II-535
Elhaj, Elhassane Ibn I-529
Elizabeth, Indu I-302
Elumalai, Ezhilarasi I-1

Ferreira, Ana Elisa IV-195
Ferri, Fernando IV-79

Gadia, Shashi II-191
Gaiti, Dominique II-471
Ganeshan, Kathiravelu IV-501
Garcia, Andrés III-664
Garcia, Anilton Salles IV-195
Gaur, Manoj Singh I-44, I-162, I-562, II-183, II-452, III-478, III-644
Gaur, Vibha II-284
Gautam, Gopal Chand I-421
Geetha, V. II-48
Geevar, C.Z. III-460
Ghosh, Pradipta III-82
Ghosh, Saswati II-620
Giluka, Mukesh Kumar I-153
Gindi, Sanjyot IV-349
Gireesh Kumar, T. II-506
Giuliani, Alessandro I-284
Godavarthi, Dinesh III-543
Gómez-Skarmeta, Antonio Fernando III-664
Gondane, Sneha G. II-99
Gopakumar, G. I-320
Gopalan, Kaliappan IV-463
Gore, Kushal I-607
Gosain, Anjana I-691
Gosalia, Jenish IV-378
Govardhan, A. I-581
Govindan, Geetha I-294
Govindarajan, Karthik I-192

Grifoni, Patrizia IV-79
Grover, Jyoti III-644
Gualotuña, Tatiana IV-481
Guerroumi, M. IV-593
Gunaraj, G. I-192
Gunjan, Reena III-478
Gupta, Ankur I-501
Gupta, B.B. IV-244
Gupta, Deepika II-183
Gupta, J.P. I-260
Gupta, Juhi IV-205
Gupta, Priya IV-512

Habib, Sami J. II-349
Hafizul Islam, SK II-628
Harivinod, N. III-396
Harmya, P. II-490, II-498, III-269
Harshith, C. II-506
Hassan, Foyzul II-154, III-349
Hati, Sumanta III-580
Hazarika, Shyamanta M. II-109, II-119
Hazra, Sayantan III-601
Hemamalini, M. IV-175
Hivarkar, Umesh N. IV-358
Hsieh, Chaur-Heh III-334
Huang, Chin-Pan III-334
Huang, Ping S. III-334

Ibrahim, S.P. Syed I-631
Indira, K. I-639
Isaac, Elizabeth IV-145

Jaganathan, P. I-683
Jagdale, B.N. II-397
Jain, Jitendra III-326
Jain, Kavindra R. III-239
Jain, Kavita I-328
Jalal, Anand Singh II-516, IV-329
Jameson, Justy II-693
Janani, S. IV-175
Jaya, IV-233
Jayakumar, S.K.V. II-234
Jayaprakash, R. II-656
Jena, Sanjay Kumar II-1
Jia, Lulu IV-421
Jiménez, Gustavo II-386
Jisha, G. IV-1, IV-137
Joseph, Shijo M. III-406
Juluru, Tarun Kumar I-34, III-590

Kacholiya, Anil IV-205
Kahlon, K.S. II-58
Kakoty, Nayan M. II-119
Kakulapati, Vijayalaxmi IV-284
Kalaivaani, P.T. III-143
Kale, Sandeep II-604
Kanade, Sanjay Ganesh III-20
Kanavalli, Anita I-141
Kancharla, Tarun IV-349, IV-368
Kanitkar, Aditya R. IV-358
Kanivadhana, P. IV-155
Kankacharla, Anitha Sheela I-34, III-590
Kanmani, S. I-639, II-69
Kannan, A. II-19
Kannan, Rajkumar IV-79
Kapoor, Lohit I-501
Karamoy, Jennifer Sabrina Karla II-138
Karande, Vishal M. IV-386
Karmakar, Sushanta II-585
Karthi, R. III-552
Karthik, S. I-480
Karunanithi, D. IV-284
Karunanithi, Priya III-624
Karuppanan, Komathy III-425, III-615, III-624, III-634
Katiyar, Vivek III-122
Kaur, Rajbir I-44, I-162
Kaushal, Sakshi IV-445
Kavalcioğlu, Cemal III-357
Kayarvizhy, N. II-69
Keromytis, Angelos D. III-44
Khajaria, Krishna II-9
Khalid, M. I-182
Khan, Majid Iqbal II-471, II-525
Khan, Srabani II-620
Khan Jehad, Abdur Rahman III-349
Khanna, Rajesh III-205
Khattak, Zubair Ahmad IV-250
Khilar, P.M. I-119
Kim, Pansoo II-595
Kimbahune, Sanjay I-607, II-430
Kiran, N. Chandra I-141
Kishore, J.K. II-460
Ko, Ryan K.L. IV-432
Kolikipogu, Ramakrishna IV-284
Kopparapu, Sunil Kumar II-317, IV-293
Koschnicke, Sven I-371
Kothari, Nikhil I-213

Krishna, Gutha Jaya I-382
Krishna, P. Venkata I-182
Krishna, S. III-522
Krishnan, Saranya D. IV-63
Krishnan, Suraj III-374
Kopparapu, Sunil Kumar III-230
Kulkarni, Nandakishore J. III-570
Kumar, Chiranjeev I-11
Kumar, C. Sasi II-162
Kumar, G.H. III-289
Kumar, G. Ravi IV-70
Kumar, G. Santhosh I-399
Kumar, Ishan IV-205
Kumar, K.R. Ananda I-704
Kumar, K. Vinod IV-19
Kumar, Manish I-44
Kumar, Manoj II-9
Kumar, Naveen I-461
Kumar, Padam I-461
Kumar, Ravindra II-307
Kumar, Santosh I-619
Kumar, Santhosh G. III-93
Kumar, Saumesh I-461
Kumar, Sumit I-619
Kumaraswamy, Rajeev IV-339
Kumari, M. Sharmila III-396
Kumari, V. Valli IV-572
Kumar Pandey, Vinod III-230
Kumar Sarma, Kandarpa III-512
Kurakula, Sudheer IV-165
Kussmaul, Clifton III-533

Lachiri, Zied IV-318
Lal, Chhagan II-452
Latif, Md. Abdul II-154
Laxmi, V. II-183, II-452
Laxmi, Vijay I-44, I-162, I-562, III-478, III-644
Lee, Bu Sung IV-432
Li, Tiantian IV-421
Limachia, Mitesh I-213
Lincoln Z.S., Ricky II-130
Linganagouda, K. III-444
Lingeshwaraa, C. II-19
Liu, Chenglian IV-534
Lobiyal, D.K. III-132, III-654
Londhe, Priyadarshini IV-512
López, Elsa Macías IV-481

Madheswari, A. Neela II-545
Madhusudhan, Mishra III-365
Mahalakshmi, T. I-310
Mahalingam, P.R. III-562, IV-137
Maheshwari, Saurabh III-478
Maiti, Santa II-172
Maity, G.K. III-249
Maity, Santi P. I-519, III-249, III-580
Maity, Seba I-519
Majhi, Banshidhar III-178
Majhi, Bansidhar IV-549
Maji, Sumit Kumar I-649
Malay, Nath III-365
Malaya, Dutta Borah II-210
Malik, Jyoti III-157
Mallya, Anita I-302
Manan, Jamalul-lail Ab IV-250
Mandava, Ajay K. I-351
Mannava, Vishnuvardhan I-250
Manomathi, M. III-415
Maralappanavar, Meena S. III-444
Marcillo, Diego IV-481
Marimuthu, Paulvanna N. II-349
Mary, S. Roselin IV-9
Masera, Guido II-374
Mastan, J. Mohamedmoideen Kader IV-524
Mehrotra, Hunny III-178
Meinel, Christoph I-431
Mendiratta, Varun II-273
Menta, Sudhanshu III-205
Mishra, A. IV-244
Mishra, Ashok II-223
Mishra, Dheerendra IV-223
Mishra, Shivendu II-407
Misra, Rajiv I-101
Missaoui, Ibrahim IV-318
Mitra, Abhijit III-512, III-601
Mitra, Swarup Kumar III-82
Mittal, Puneet II-58
Modi, Chintan K. III-239
Mohammadi, M. III-289
Mohandas, Neethu IV-187
Mohandas, Radhesh II-685, III-10
Mohanty, Sujata IV-549
Mol, P.M. Ameera III-193
Moodgal, Darshan II-162
Moragón, Antonio III-664
More, Seema I-361
Moussaoui, S. IV-593
Mubarak, T. Mohamed III-102
Mukhopadhyay, Sourav IV-223

Mukkamala, R. I-446
Muniraj, N.J.R. I-270, III-168
Murthy, G. Rama IV-19

Nadarajan, R. II-366
Nadkarni, Tanusha S. II-685
Nag, Amitava II-612, II-620
Nagalakshmi, R. I-683
Nagaradjane, Prabagarane III-374
Nair, Achuthsankar S. I-284, I-294, I-302, I-320
Nair, Bipin II-337
Nair, Madhu S. III-193, III-276
Nair, Smita IV-368
Nair, Vrinda V. I-302
Namboodiri, Saritha I-284
Namritha, R. III-634
Nandi, Sukumar I-619
Narayanan, Hari I-488
Nasiruddin, Mohammad II-154
Naskar, Mrinal Kanti III-82
Nataraj, R.V. I-631
Naveen, K. Venkat III-570, III-615
Naveena, C. III-297
Nazir, Arfan II-525
Neelamegam, P. III-111
Neogy, Sarmistha I-129, II-417
Nigam, Apurv II-430
Nimi, P.U. IV-46
Niranjan, S.K. III-297
Nirmala, M. I-223
Nirmala, S.R. III-365
Nitin, I-21, II-568, IV-25
Noopa, Jagadeesh II-490, II-498, III-269
Nurul Huda, Mohammad II-154, III-349

Oh, Deock-Gil II-595
Okab, Mustapha II-40
Oliya, Mohammad I-232
Olsen, Rasmus L. IV-37

Padmanabhan, Jayashree I-1, IV-541
Padmavathi, B. IV-70
Pai, P.S. Sreejith IV-339
Pai, Radhika M. II-460
Paily, Roy IV-165
Pais, Alwyn R. II-685, IV-386
Pais, Alwyn Roshan III-10
Pal, Arindarjit I-83
Palaniappan, Ramaswamy IV-378
Palaty, Abel IV-56
Pandey, Kumar Sambhav IV-56
Panicker, Asha IV-300
Panneerselvam, S. I-223
Pappas, Vasilis III-44
Parasuram, Harilal II-337
Parmar, Rohit R. III-239
Parthasarathy, Magesh Kannan I-192
Parvathy, B. I-204
PatilKulkarni, Sudarshan III-342
Patnaik, L.M. I-141, II-636, III-522
Patra, Prashanta Kumar I-649
Pattanshetti, M.K. IV-244
Paul, Anu II-201
Paul, Richu III-213
Paul, Varghese II-201
Paulsen, Niklas I-371
Pavithran, Vipin I-488
Pearson, Siani IV-432
Perumal, V. I-471
Petrovska-Delacrétaz, Dijana III-20
Phani, G. Lakshmi IV-19
Ponpandiyan, Vigneswaran IV-541
Poornalatha, G. II-243
Povar, Digambar I-544
Prabha, S. Lakshmi I-192
Prabhu, Lekhesh V. IV-339
Pradeep, A.N.S. III-543
Pradeepa, J. I-471
Prajapati, Nitesh Kumar III-644
Prakasam, Kumaresh IV-541
Pramod, K. III-444
Prasad, Ramjee IV-37
Prasath, Rajendra II-555
Prasanna, S.R. Mahadeva III-326
Prasanth Kumar, M. Lakshmi I-11
Pratheepraj, E. III-503
Priya, K.H. I-471
Priyadharshini, M. IV-269
Priyadharshini, V. IV-175
Pung, Hung Keng I-232

Qadeer, Mohammed Abdul II-442

Radhamani, A.S. I-172
Rafsanjani, Marjan Kuchaki IV-534
Raghavendra, Prakash S. II-243
Raghuvanshi, Rahul I-153
Rahaman, Hafizur III-68

Raheja, J.L. III-488
Raheja, Shekhar III-488
Rahiman, M. Abdul III-304
Rahman, Md. Mostafizur II-154
Rai, Anjani Kumar II-407
Rai, Anuj Kumar III-111
Rai, Mahendra K. III-469
Raja, K.B. II-636
Rajapackiyam, Ezhilarasie III-111
Rajasekhar, Ch. I-78
Rajasree, M.S. III-304
Rajendran, C. III-552
Rajesh, R. III-497
Rajeswari, A. III-143
Rajimol, A. II-253
Rajkumar, K.K. III-435
Rajkumar, N. I-683
Raju, C.K. II-223, IV-211
Raju, G. I-671, II-253, III-435
Ramachandram, S. IV-70
Ramamohanreddy, A. I-581
Ramaraju, Chithra I-661
Ramasubbareddy, B. I-581
Ramaswamy, Aravindh I-411
Ramesh, Sunanda I-1
Ramesh, T. I-250
Rameshkumar, K. III-552
Rana, Sanjeev I-91
Rani, Prathuri Jhansi III-1
Rao, Appa III-102
Rao, Avani I-213
rao, D. Srinivasa I-78
Rao, Prasanth G. III-522
Rastogi, Ravi I-21
Rathi, Manisha I-260
Rathore, Wilson Naik II-676
Razi, Muhammad II-146
Reddy, B. Vivekavardhana IV-309
Reddy, G. Ram Mohana IV-473
Reddy, P.V.G.D. Prasad III-543
Reddy, Sateesh II-460
Regentova, Emma E. I-351
Reji, J. III-276
Revathy, P. IV-284
Revett, Kenneth IV-378
Roberta, Kezia Velda II-146
Rodrigues, Paul IV-9, IV-269
Rokibul Alam Kotwal, Mohammed III-349
Roopalakshmi, R. IV-473
Roy, J.N. III-249
Roy, Rahul IV-113

Sabu, M.K. I-671
Saha, Aritra III-35
Sahaya, Nuniek Nur II-138
Sahoo, Manmath Narayan I-119
Sahoo, Soyuj Kumar III-326
Saikia, Adity II-109, II-119
Sainarayanan, G. III-157
Sajeev, J. I-310
Sajitha, M. III-102
Saljooghinejad, Hamed II-676
Samad, Sumi A. III-93
Samanta, Debasis II-172
Sambyal, Rakesh IV-608
Samerendra, Dandapat III-365
Samraj, Andrews IV-378
Samuel, Philip II-80, IV-1
Sandhya, S. II-88
Santa, José III-664
Santhi, K. III-221
SanthoshKumar, G. II-263
Santhoshkumar, S. I-223
Saralaya, Vikram II-460
Sarangdevot, S.S. I-592
Saraswathi, S. IV-155, IV-175
Sardana, Anjali IV-233
Saritha, S. II-263
Sarkar, D. II-612, II-620
Sarkar, Partha Pratim II-612, II-620
Sarma, Monalisa II-172
Saruladha, K. II-327
Sasho, Ai I-340
Sasidharan, Satheesh Kumar I-552
Satapathy, Chandra Suresh III-543
Sathisha, N. II-636
Sathishkumar, G.A. IV-524
Sathiya, S. IV-155
Sathu, Hira IV-491, IV-501
Satria, Denny II-138
Sattar, Syed Abdul III-102
Savarimuthu, Nickolas I-661
Sayeesh, K. Venkat IV-19
Schatz, Florian I-371
Schimmler, Manfred I-371
Sebastian, Bhavya I-302
Sehgal, Priti III-259
Selvan, A. Muthamizh III-497

Selvathi, D. IV-300
Sen, Jaydip IV-580
Sendil, M. Sadish I-480
Senthilkumar, Radha II-19
Senthilkumar, T.D. III-185
Shah, Mohib A. IV-491, IV-501
Shahram, Latifi I-351
Shajan, P.X. III-168
Sharma, Amita I-592
Sharma, Dhirendra Kumar I-11
Sharma, Divya I-511
Sharma, H. Meena I-162
Sharma, Neeraj Kumar II-284
Sharma, Ritu I-511
Sharma, Sattvik II-506
Sharma, Sugam II-191
Sharma, Surbhi III-205
Sharma, T.P. I-421
Shekar, B.H. III-396
Shenoy, P. Deepa I-141, III-522
Shenoy, S.K. III-93
Sherly, K.K. II-693
Shringar Raw, Ram III-654
Shukla, Shailendra I-101
Shyam, D. II-99
Sikdar, Biplab Kumar III-68
Singal, Kunal III-488
Singh, Anurag III-609
Singh, Ashwani II-374
Singh, Jai Prakash IV-89
Singh, Jyoti Prakash I-83, II-612, II-620
Singh, Manpreet I-91, I-572
Singh, Puneet III-570
Singh, Rahul I-340
Singh, Sanjay II-460
Singh, Satwinder II-58
Singh, Vijander I-54
Singh, Vrijendra II-516, IV-329
Singh, Preety II-183
Sinha, Adwitiya III-132
Sivakumar, N. II-88
Skandha, S. Shiva IV-70
Smith, Patrick II-191
Sojan Lal, P. III-460
Song, Jie IV-421
Soni, Surender III-122
Sood, Manu I-511
Soumya, H.D. I-361
Sreenath, N. II-48
Sreenu, G. IV-126
Sreevathsan, R. II-506
Srikanth, M.V.V.N.S. II-506
Srinivasan, Avinash IV-260
Srinivasan, Madhan Kumar IV-269
Srivastava, Praveen Ranjan III-570
Srivastava, Shweta I-260
Starke, Christoph I-371
Suaib, Mohammad IV-56
Suárez-Sarmiento, Alvaro IV-481
Subramaniam, Tamil Selvan Raman IV-541
Suchithra, K. IV-339
Sudarsan, Dhanya IV-137
Sudhansh, A.S.D.P. IV-165
Sujana, N. I-361
Sukumar, Abhinaya I-1
Sulaiman, Suziah IV-250
Sundararajan, Sudharsan I-488
Swaminathan, A. II-648
Swaminathan, Shriram III-374
Swamy, Y.S. Kumara IV-309

Tahir, Muhammad II-471
Takouna, Ibrahim I-431
Thakur, Garima I-691
Thampi, Sabu M. I-64, IV-126, IV-145, IV-187
Thangavel, K. II-358
Thilagu, M. II-366
Thiyagarajan, P. IV-98
Thomas, Diya I-64
Thomas, K.L. I-544, I-552
Thomas, Likewin IV-396
Thomas, Lincy III-425
Thomas, Lisha III-221
Thukral, Anjali II-273
Tim, U.S. II-191
Tiwary, U.S. III-452, III-469
Tobgay, Sonam IV-37
Tolba, Zakaria II-40
Tripathi, Pramod Narayan II-407
Tripathi, Rajeev I-11
Tripathy, Animesh I-649
Tripti, C. IV-46
Tyagi, Neeraj I-11
Tyagi, Vipin II-568

Uma, V. II-656
Umber, Ashfa II-30
Unnikrishnan, C. III-562

Usha, N. IV-309
Utomo, Bima Shakti Ramadhan II-138

Vanaja, M. I-78
Varalakshmi, P. I-411, I-471
Varghese, Elizabeth B. III-383
Varshney, Abhishek II-442
Vasanthi, S. III-213
Vatsavayi, Valli Kumari II-296
Venkatachalapathy, V.S.K. II-234
Venkatesan, V. Prasanna IV-98
Venugopal, K.R. I-141, II-636, III-522
Verma, Amandeep IV-445
Verma, Chandra I-284
Verma, Gyanendra K. III-452, III-469
Verma, Rohit I-21
Vidya, M. I-361
Vidyadharan, Divya S. I-544
Vijay, K. I-78
Vijaykumar, Palaniappan I-411
VijayLakshmi, H.C. III-342
Vinod, P. I-562
Vipeesh, P. I-270
Vishnani, Kalpa III-10
Vivekanandan, K. II-88
Vorungati, Kaladhar I-488
Vykopal, Jan II-666

Wadhai, V.M. II-397
Wankar, Rajeev I-382
Wattal, Manisha I-501
William, II-130
Wilscy, M. III-315, III-383
Wirjono, Adityo Ashari II-130
Wisudawati, Lulu Mawaddah II-146
Wu, Jie IV-260

Xavier, Agnes I-328

Yadav, Gaurav Kumar IV-368
Yu, Fan III-54
Yuvaraj, V. III-503

Zaeri, Naser II-349
Zheng, Liyun IV-534
Zhu, Shenhaochen I-340
Zhu, Zhiliang IV-421

GPSR Compliance

The European Union's (EU) General Product Safety Regulation (GPSR) is a set of rules that requires consumer products to be safe and our obligations to ensure this.

If you have any concerns about our products, you can contact us on ProductSafety@springernature.com

In case Publisher is established outside the EU, the EU authorized representative is:

Springer Nature Customer Service Center GmbH
Europaplatz 3
69115 Heidelberg, Germany

Batch number: 10838023

Printed by Printforce, the Netherlands